to Carmarthen 225
to Carmarthen 224
to Tlandilo
to Carmarthen
ByeWays Kidwelly
to Carmarthen
Vanvr R.
20
29
to Llantaron
8
to Llantaron

240
to Tenby   to Carmarthen
239
to New Inn Marras   to Handagwin
237   to Treselan Park
to Pertogan   to Andrura House
236
to Tenby   Egloys Kemen
235
to the Sea   to Carmarthen
to Llanmelon   234
233   St. Cleer
to the Sea   to Carmarthen
232   to Tlantogh
Tlansadurne
to Broadway   231   Laugharn
Ferry
230   Carmarthen
229   to Moohu
228   Llinbrea
Llanstuffan
213   Torva R.   227
ByeWay
212 to Tlangan   226
to Pencoyd

to Kowlton   Haverford West
254   Pranghurst
Dungledy
253
252
251
250
Mid County Hou.
Picton Castle   249
to Wiston   248
Clethy R.
Canaston   247
to the Wood   Llanhaddo
246   to Cardigan
to Templeton   Robeston
245
to Grove   to Narbarth
244
to Templeton
243
242
Llangwdo
241   to Llampiter
to Pembroke
to Wiston

St. Davids
to Cardi
269
268
Nine Wells
267   to Whitchurch
266
265
264   to Brandon
to the Cliffs
263
Grickhonell   262
261
to Knolton
to Faire Castle   260   Roche
to Simpson
259   to Camaras
to Rogerson   to Keason
258
Keason Bri.
to Dunson   to Pelkam
257
256   Pelkam Bri.
to Llanston
255

St. Brides Bay

CAARMAARTHEENSH.   CAARMAARTHEENSH.   PEMBROOKESH.   PEMBROOKE

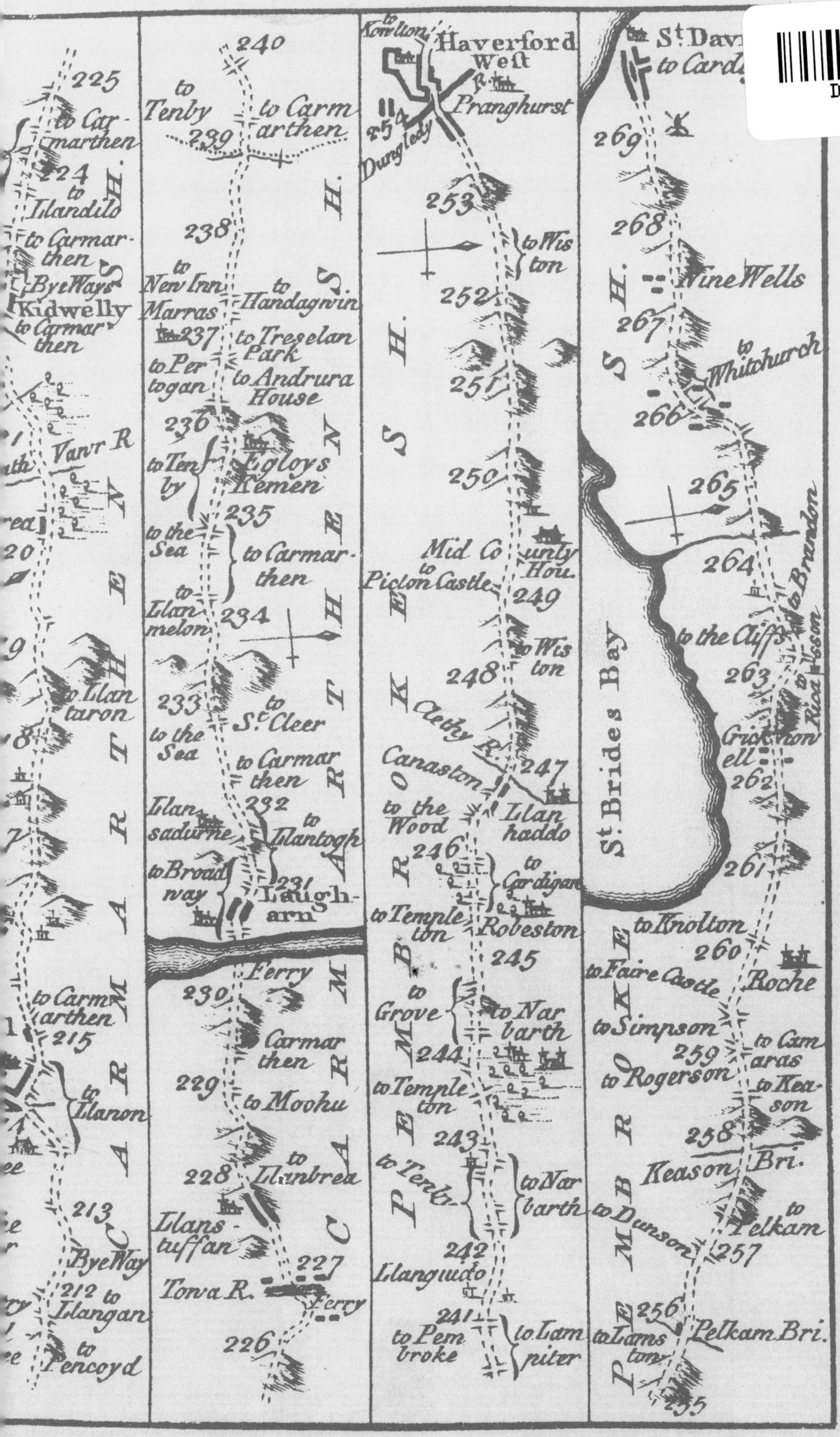

AA TOURING GUIDE TO WALES

Ever charming, ever new,
When will the landskip tire the view!
The fountain's fall, the river's flow,
The woody vallies warm and low;
The windy summit, wild and high,
Roughly rushing on the sky!
The pleasant seat, the ruin'd tow'r,
The naked rock, the shady bow'r;
The town and village, dome and farm,
Each give each a double charm . . .

from Grongar Hill by John Dyer 1701–1757

Contents

Produced by the Publications Division of the
Automobile Association

Editor Russell Beach
Art Editor Michael Preedy MSIA

Assistant editor Michael Cady
Assistant designer Robert Johnson

Feature writers:
Alan Reeve-Jones, Charles Quant,
Cynric Mytton-Davies FJI, Guy Adams, John Eilian OBE,
Lindsay Evans, Martin Boddy, Phillip Llewelin

Day Drives compiled by the Publications
Research Unit of the Automobile Association

Gazetteer compiled by the Publications Research Unit
of the Automobile Association, Cynric Mytton-Davies FJI,
George Campbell-Williams, Tony Lloyd

Artists:
Anderson Dykes Organization, Bernard Baker,
Chris Woolmer, Don Cordery, Fleet Design,
Outline Art Services, Robert Geary MSIA, Vic Bates

Picture researchers: Diana Phillips, Angela Murphy

Extract from *Grongar Hill* from *A Book of Wales*,
published by Collins

Day Drives, Town Plans, Leisure Maps, and Special
Feature maps by the Cartographic Services Unit of
the Automobile Association

Topographical models by Fairey Surveys Ltd

Touring Atlas © Copyright by Geographia Ltd

Maps in this book are based upon the
Ordnance Survey maps, with the sanction of the
Controller of Her Majesty's Stationery Office
Crown Copyright Reserved

Phototypeset by Petty and Sons Ltd, Leeds

Colour separations by Mullis Morgan Ltd, London

Printed and bound by Purnell and Sons Ltd,
Paulton, Bristol

Foreword
By His Royal Highness The Prince of Wales

Following the publication of their mammoth *Touring Guide to England* the Automobile Association have once again rushed into print with this splendid Welsh sequel. It is obvious that an immense amount of hard work has gone into the production of this Guide – I often wondered what those indispensable gentlemen in mustard-coloured uniforms did when they gave up saluting members of the Automobile Association, now I know!

It is one of those curious ironies that the majority of people who can travel tend to be tourists in other people's countries rather than their own. And yet there is an unlimited store of fascinating places to explore all over this country – particularly in Wales. This Guide helps to emphasize the richness of the Welsh heritage: the contrasts within its historical experiences and the effects of those contrasts upon the Welsh countryside. Far too often one misses things of beauty and historical interest through lack of observation or lack of knowledge of what is comprised in the environment. If you want to find out and explore, then this Guide will be of enormous assistance. However, I feel somewhat guilty in these days of energy conservation and astronomic petrol costs, in advocating motorized tourism throughout my principality. Perhaps it would be better to acquire a four-seater bicycle and pedal the family through Wales – you will be amazed how much more you see and feel of the countryside . . .

This Guide, I am sure, will prove essential to tourists of any nationality and will leave them with a far deeper appreciation and knowledge of Wales than would otherwise have been possible. If they follow the day drives so carefully laid out in this book they will either become expert navigators or hopelessly and inextricably lost – but lost in the most beautiful and spectacular scenery until found by one of those excellent gentlemen in a yellow van!

Charles.

Magical Refuge

Modern West Wales offers the wildness of primeval nature, the black wealth of oil, and one of the richest historical heritages in Britain.

Savagely contorted cliffs at Cemaes Head are reminders of the violent geological distortions which formed much of the West Wales landscape.

*One-time Pembrokeshire was known in Welsh as *Gwlad yr Hud* – The Land of Enchantment – a description which can be extended to embrace the whole of West Wales. It fits the region as neatly as any tailor-made glove. Here, within two or three hours of the heavily-populated valleys and ports of Gwent and Glamorgan, and within increasingly easy reach of the great cities of England, are more than enough contrasts, scenic splendour, recreational opportunities, wildlife, legends, and history to revive, stimulate, and satisfy the most jaded of tourists. Even those who think they know the area well can constantly discover new sources of wonder and delight.

Here, as in few other places, the time-honoured cliché about variety being the spice of life takes on a fresh significance. There is a wealth of raw material to delight the archaeologist, the student of architecture, and the sandcastle builder; the geologist, botanist, ornithologist, artist, and photographer; the sunbather, fisherman, ship-spotter, and surf-rider; the deckchair lounger and the dedicated long-distance walker; the historian, the sub-aqua enthusiast, and those who seek nothing more specialized than views that will remain forever etched upon the mind's eye. Here too it is possible to create what is perhaps the next best thing to a time machine. In the space of a day, or even a couple of hours, the visitor can walk over some of the oldest rocks on our planet, leap through the aeons to a prehistoric burial chamber, find links with the Age of Saints, explore a medieval stronghold, examine relics of the Industrial Revolution, and then drive past the science-fiction landscape of an oil refinery.

Geography of the west

Like the rest of the country – with the notable exception of Anglesey – West Wales is a region of hills and mountains, although none of them approach the height or stark grandeur of the peaks found in Snowdonia and elsewhere. Most of the hills are of modest size and gently rounded, but there are so many of them that every journey tends to be a series of constantly changing views. It is only in the east, where old Carmarthenshire runs into one-time Breconshire, that the land begins to heave itself up and stand out boldly against the sky. This great whale-back of lonely upland is known as the Black Mountain – not to be confused with the Black Mountains of old Monmouthshire – and in the area of old Carmarthenshire it reaches

2,460ft. A few hundred yards away, just over the county boundary, the steepest slope of the mountain rises to 2,632ft above sea level and is every bit as impressive as the nearby Brecon Beacons. Elsewhere few of the hills are much more than 1,000ft high, and the summit of Mynydd Prescelly in one-time Pembrokeshire is only 1,760ft – modest indeed by Welsh standards. Until the coast is reached it is difficult to appreciate that the land as a whole is some 200ft above the sea and ends in mile after mile of splendid cliffs punctuated by scores of lovely bays sheltered by lofty headlands. The massive grinding action of Ice-Age glaciers helped to smooth the landscape, but the bulk of the work must have been done many millions of years earlier, when much of West Wales lay beneath the waves of a primeval sea.

The unquiet earth

In many places there is clear evidence that the sea regained a little ground when the last of the glaciers melted in comparatively recent times, little more than 10,000 years ago. The remains of ancient forests are revealed when the tide goes right out at Newgale and Amroth, and bones of prehistoric land animals have been found among peaty deposits in Whitesand Bay, near St David's. The rising sea also helped to create harbours in areas that had previously been valleys; Milford Haven, deep enough to take supertankers, is the most obvious example, but there are many smaller ones such as Solva. The melting glaciers formed a series of lakes, but many rivers that flowed from them found their obvious routes to the sea blocked by lingering masses of ice. The Gwaun, for instance, now joins the sea at Fishguard, but originally ran through the valley between Cwm-yr-Eglwys and Pwllgwaelod; although it is now firmly linked to the mainland, the headland immediately north of the valley is still known as Dinas Island.

The inland areas reveal little of their geological mysteries to the layman – although the great crag at Carreg Cennen is a notable exception in the hills near Llandeilo – but fascinating and in places extremely beautiful rock formations are displayed for all to see along the coasts. The cliffs near the coastguard lookout station on St Ann's Head, for instance, have been twisted into enormous curves by pressures exerted deep down in the Earth's crust at times when the landscape was undergoing major changes. Spectacular evidence of folding can also be seen in the high cliffs near Cemaes Head, at the northern end of the Pembrokeshire coast's long-distance footpath. The rocks of West Wales range from areas of Pre-Cambrian, which are at least 4,000 million years old, to relics of the

*The old counties of Pembrokeshire, Carmarthenshire, and Cardiganshire now form the new county of Dyfed (see map on page 146).

Ice Age. The latter includes many erratics – stones transported far from their original sites by the moving ice. Boulders carried from Scotland and North Wales now rest in and near Bosherston, for example, while rocks from the Isle of Man can be found elsewhere. The geology of the area is extremely complex – even greatly simplified maps make it look like the confused remains of a many-decked sandwich – and this complexity is easily appreciated by travelling along the southern coast of old Pembrokeshire. Between Linney Head and Stackpole Head there are formidable cliffs of carboniferous limestone that jut out into the sea like vast, pale-grey tables. This is one of the most magnificent stretches of coast imaginable.

There are places where the limestone ramparts seem to go on forever, but a few miles east at Manorbier they give way to a band of old red sandstone that can be traced back across the county to the Angle peninsula, St Ann's Head, and the lonely little island of Skokholm. Continuing eastwards towards Tenby, the sandstone gives way once again to limestone and a pocket of millstone grit around Lydstep Haven. Between Tenby and Amroth are the coal measures that run inland to cross the head of Milford Haven and once supported a number of flourishing mines. On the eastern border of old Carmarthenshire, along the fringe of the great coalfields of South Wales, miners used to call millstone grit the 'Farewell Rock' because they knew to their cost that it marked the end of the coal seam. Outcrops of slate can also be found in many parts of the region. At Abereiddi Bay the quarrymen blasted a deep lagoon from the cliffs, and the beach of clean but dark-grey sand is a remarkable sight. Here too the complicated structure of the land is vividly illustrated; the next little harbour, Porthgain, was noted not for slate but for its exceptionally hard granite. To the north the cliffs around New Quay are formed of very thin layers of brittle, friable rock formed under the sea 400-million years ago, during the Silurian period. Some of these layers have been almost literally tied into knots by earth movements. Others are stacked neatly on top of each other and could almost have been built by a very neat and industrious giant using a spirit level.

The majestic coast in its many moods and the multiplicity of inland hills are dominant features of West Wales, but the region is also carved by the valleys of two major rivers. The Teifi and Tywi rise within 3m of each other, but follow very different routes to the sea. The Teifi's birthplace is an area riddled with old lead mines, and the infant river is heavily polluted at first. It then passes through the wilderness of Tregaron Bog and emerges clean and fresh to water such pleasant little market towns as Newcastle Emlyn before wriggling through the hills to reach the sea beyond Cardigan, or Aberteifi as it is known in Welsh. The stretch around

Pentre Ifan burial chamber is a superb example of bronze-age building situated near Newport.

Cilgerran, where there are old slate quarries and a splendid cliff-top castle on the brink of the gorge, is particularly dramatic. The Twyi races southwards through breathtaking scenery, but enters a long, broad valley near Llandovery and then begins to curl its lazy way towards Carmarthen in a series of broad meanders. The lush green pastures that line its banks are among the most productive dairylands in Britain. Below Carmarthen the hills close in again before the sea is reached, and there the waters of the Tywi mingle with those of the Taf and Gwendraeth at the corner of a broad bay where vast areas of sandbanks and saltings are revealed at low tide.

Prehistoric cultures

All these geographical details have remained basically unchanged, apart from the finishing touches given by the last stages of the final Ice Age, since man first appeared on the scene. The exact date cannot be pin-pointed with any degree of accuracy, but the cave-dwellers of the old stone age are known to have made their homes in the one-time counties of Pembrokeshire and Carmarthenshire between 20,000 and 10,000BC. Coastal caverns provided them with shelters and the areas around Tenby and Laugharne have produced several notable finds in the shapes of stone implements, bones, and other relics. About 3,000 years BC these primitive hunters were gradually replaced by the neolithic men who spread slowly westwards from such centres as Wiltshire. They were farmers and, above all, great builders who have left us many striking reminders of their skill and ingenuity. Pembrokeshire is exceptionally rich in relics of this fascinating age, and the maps are speckled with sites of burial chambers.

Bronze-age men also prepared great tombs for their dead, and many of these were built on or close to the ancient trackways that were the motorways of prehistory. Several of these routes, such as The Ridgeway of Carmarthenshire and southern Pembrokeshire, and the so-called Flemings' Way over the Prescelly range, can still be traced and in some cases are now followed by modern roads. None of these peoples seem to have needed elaborate defences, and it is likely that their settlements were protected by nothing more substantial than fences of pointed stakes. However, as the bronze age gave way to the iron age c550BC, man began to feel the need for greater security. The Celtic newcomers built hilltop forts in many parts of Britain, but in West Wales the many headlands and promontories offered even more suitable sites. With the sea protecting three sides of the settlement, which may only have been used as a refuge in times of trouble, banks of earth or stones could be built across the narrow neck

linking it to the main body of the land. The remains of these strongholds can be seen all along the coast, but one of the best-preserved is on the rocky tip of St David's Head, where a path passes through the tumbled stones of 'Warriors' Dyke'.

New blood

The land around the base of Carn Llidi is also criss-crossed with lines of stones that mark the edges of fields used by iron-age farmers. Many have become submerged beneath centuries of tangled undergrowth, but others, kept in a good state of repair, are still in use after more than 2,000 years. Similar field patterns can still be seen on Skomer Island. The seaways and valleys that flank and carve the land had provided convenient routes for generations of newcomers, friendly and otherwise, before the arrival of the Romans. This new wave of highly-organized, well-equipped and technically very advanced invaders had established themselves in South Wales before the end of the 1stcAD; the walls at Caerwent and the great amphitheatre at Caerleon are their finest legacies. Marching steadily westwards, probably supported by a fleet on the Bristol Channel, the legions eventually reached *Moridunum*, the modern Carmarthen, and there established the most westerly base in the whole of Britain. The main local tribe, the *Demetae*, seem to have been friendly because no evidence of any military settlements has ever been found in Pembrokeshire. The alien but highly sophisticated culture imported from far-off Italy soon began to disintegrate and the people returned to their old ways. However, this period also witnessed a remarkable revival in Celtic art that was to flourish for several centuries and is beautifully illustrated by the tall, richly carved crosses that still stand at Nevern and Carew.

This was also the Age of Saints. St Teilo, for one, was born in Pembrokeshire and the centre of his area of influence became known as Llandeilo – Teilo's Church – over the old county boundary in Carmarthenshire. St Justinian, a friend of St David, lived on Ramsey Island during the 6thc at a time when, according to legend, it was joined to the mainland by a narrow neck of rocks. The saint, tired of having his devotions disturbed by a constant stream of visitors, eventually prayed that the rocks would tumble into the sea, leaving him to contemplate in peace. His prayer was answered, and all that remains of the land-bridge is a wicked reef known as The Bitches. St Justinian was eventually killed by raiders, but swam to the mainland clutching his own severed head in one hand. A chapel dedicated to the martyr stands on the shore by the slipway from which visitors depart for trips around Ramsey. The 16th-c building stands on the site of a much older shrine. A number of churches are dedicated to St Brynach, a missionary who sailed to Milford Haven from Ireland and who seems to have been a forerunner of St Francis of Assisi, for he had a magical way with animals.

Tiny St Govan's chapel crouches in a ravine where the saint is said to have hidden from pagan raiders.

Several legends surround the little-known figure of St Govan, who is sometimes said to have been one of King Arthur's knights before setting his sword aside and becoming a hermit. A tiny chapel only 20ft long and 12ft wide stands in a rocky chasm washed by the sea near Bosherston, and is said to mark the site of the saint's original refuge. According to one story, St Govan sheltered in the ravine while being chased by pagan enemies; the rocks obligingly closed over him, opening again when the danger had passed. Another tale tells of a pirate who was so enchanted by the sound of the chapel bell that he landed and stole it, only to have his ship wrecked by a sudden storm. The saint was promptly compensated by finding a miraculous stone which, when struck, gave off a note exactly the same as that of the stolen bell. There are also strong links with St Patrick. He may have been born in South Wales and is supposed to have sailed to Ireland from Whitesand Bay, where a stone set in the turf marks the site of an old chapel. As an old man Patrick is said to have met St Non and prophesied that her child would become a great preacher of the faith. Some time later, on the cliffs near what is now St David's, Non gave birth during a great storm. The boy became St David, the patron saint of Wales, and the well that sprung up at his birthplace can still be seen. Many stories are told about St David, and one of the most famous recalls the stormy synod held at Llanddewi Brefi, a village in the Teifi valley. It was a very well attended meeting and, it seems, a very badly-chaired one. Nobody could make himself heard above the general hubbub until David persuaded the ground beneath his feet to rise up into a little hill from which he had no difficulty in commanding the attention of the throng. The village church was built on the hill and has a striking modern statue of the saint, as well as a fine collection of Celtic carved stones that certainly indicate the long religious history of the site.

Legends of Merlin and King Arthur are another feature of West Wales. Merlin is said to have been born in old Carmarthenshire, and there is still a curious link with the wizard in the county town. It takes the shape of a very old oak, only wizened fragments of which remain, carefully supported by concrete and iron props. These precautions are taken because, it is said;

> When Merlin's Oak shall tumble down,
> Then shall fall Carmarthen town.

Wales as a nation

Despite its galaxy of wizards, heroes and saints, West Wales was constantly plagued by marauders from Ireland

By 1148 Welsh archers were marching with the often-victorious Norman army.

and Scandinavia, but the Viking raids did not become really severe until towards the end of the 8thc. Skomer, Skokholm, Gateholm, Grassholm, and several other places have names with obvious Norse roots. The ravages of the Vikings might have continued unchecked had it not been for the emergence in the 9thc of one of the greatest of all Welsh leaders. Anglesey was the centre of power of Rhodri Mawr – Rhoderick the Great – and his army eventually crushed the Norsemen in a decisive battle. Rhodri also achieved the near-impossible by uniting Wales for the first time by a series of diplomatic marriages.

Rhodri's grandson, Hywel Dda – Howell the Good – continued the great work, but after his death the country once more became a squabbling-ground for princes and chieftains. By that time, however, the basic political and social regions of Wales had been defined and West Wales was known as Dyfed. In 1974, when the reorganization of local government took place, the ancient name was revived and given to the authority that now embraces Cardiganshire, Pembrokeshire, and Carmarthenshire.

England, in sharp contrast, had been more or less united for many years. There were times when the Welsh rose up under charismatic leaders. In the 12thc for instance the powerful Lord Rhys ap Gruffydd and his warrior sons raised armies against the Normans and harried them to such an extent that Henry II was eventually forced to acknowledge the independence of the kingdom of Deheubarth. At this time the area covered the whole of West Wales and was ruled from Dynevor, near Llandeilo. Lord Rhys is also remembered as the probable founder of Carreg Cennen Castle, the organizer of the first great Welsh eisteddfod at Cardigan in 1177, and the founder of the once-great abbey of Strata Florida, in a lovely secluded valley amidst the mountains near Tregaron.

Age of castles

In general, however, the Norman invasion was a success. It started before the end of the 11thc and brought many new and enduring features to West Wales; towns and great castles built of stone were both previously unknown and are the Normans' most obvious memorials. Having established themselves in an area, the invaders first constructed bases of the motte-and-bailey type; these were mounds topped with a wooden tower and surrounded by earthworks protected by stout fences. They were soon replaced by more substantial strongholds, remains of which can be seen at such places as Pembroke, Kidwelly, Laugharne, Llanstephan, Carew, Cilgerran, Newport, Haverfordwest, Roch, and Tenby. The latter also retains its ancient town walls. Like the castles built by Edward I in North Wales, these fortresses stand by the sea that

provided them with a lifeline when the land was roamed by enemies. The castles of the Welsh were generally inland, where they could command passes and valleys.

Carreg Cennen, perched on its limestone cliff with views southwards over the slopes of the Black Mountain, shows that the more powerful Welsh princes could raise sufficient funds and manpower to play the Normans at their own game. Most of the very substantial ruins date from the end of the 13th and the start of the 14thc, and clearly demonstrate the new developments that were introduced at about that time to counteract the ever-increasing efficiency of siege engines and techniques. In 1462, during the Wars of the Roses, the Yorkists decided to make it useless for military purposes. They engaged 500 men to do the work and the bill came to £28 5s 6d. West Wales had been a staging post along the way to Ireland since prehistoric times. This tradition was maintained by the Normans, for Pembroke became their base for operations beyond St George's Channel. It was from Pembroke in 1148 that the first invasion fleet sailed westwards, with Welsh archers among the Norman cavalry and infantry.

Little England

The Normans left another legacy that is quickly appreciated by the visitor. Thanks to their influence an invisible line was drawn across West Wales from Newgale in the north-west to Laugharne in the south-east. Below this line the people spoke, and still speak, English; those born north of the line tend to use Welsh as their mother tongue. This long-lasting division has resulted in southern Pembrokeshire being dubbed 'Little England beyond Wales', but the differences are linguistic rather than racial. The 13thc witnessed a major but short-lived revival in the contorted fortunes of Welsh nationalism. A great leader arose in the shape of Llywelyn ap Iorwerth, who eventually held sway over most of the country and earned himself the title of Llywelyn the Great. He was a statesman as well as a soldier, and like Rhodri Mawr 400 years earlier appreciated the value of forging family links with potential enemies; he married King John of England's daughter. Llywelyn died in 1240, but following the death of his son Dafydd his mantle was assumed by Llywelyn ap Gruffydd, the ill-fated Prince of Wales who is more frequently remembered as Llywelyn the Last. He met his death on an enemy lance during a minor skirmish in Mid Wales in 1282, and with him died the last real hope of Welsh independence. Edward I encircled the north with his ring of castles, and Norman rule took an even firmer hold on the rest of the country. Welsh bowmen were soon marching under the leadership of English kings, winning great victories in France with their deadly longbows and clothyard arrows that could pass through the leg of an armoured knight, through his horse, and right through the other leg. But at the start of the 15thc a new hero arose – the Owain Glyndwr immortalized by Shakespeare – and

The last invading force to set foot on
British soil landed near Fishguard in 1797 – and was
scattered by the appearance of a few women in traditional red shawls.

for almost ten years it seemed as if the old dream of a free Wales would be realized at last. Despite many initial successes the uprising petered out, and by 1410 its leader had vanished from the pages of history.

Forging a nation

Even the most patriotic and optimistic of Welshmen must have assumed that all hopes of national greatness had vanished with the demise of Glyndwr, but the spirit of the people was soon to be uplifted yet again. It was from Wales that the Tudor dynasty came, and the founder of that dynasty, Henry VII, was born in Pembroke Castle in 1457. The family's roots were in North Wales, on the island of Anglesey, and the Tudors had been prominent in Welsh affairs for at least 200 years before the Wars of the Roses ended with Henry's coronation. Henry Tudor had a complicated and tortuous claim to the throne, but his path was cleared by the many deaths of the Wars of the Roses. When his grandfather was executed young Henry was promptly taken away to the safety of France, where he lived in exile for fourteen years. In 1485 Henry and his followers landed at Mill Bay near Dale, at the western end of Milford Haven. His march to victory at Bosworth Field has been likened to Napoleon's return from Elba for the Hundred Days.

Henry's triumph at Bosworth brought a fresh sense of purpose to Wales as a whole and West Wales in particular, for the new king fully appreciated the support given by his countrymen and realized that without it his cause would have been doomed to failure. Henry's son Henry VIII finally sealed the union between Wales and England, and also drew-up a definite border to replace the hazy line that had existed since the days when William the Conqueror gave his barons a free hand to carve their own little empires all along the Welsh Marches. The Tudors brought peace, honour, and a new sense of pride to Wales, because the old urge for total independence lost much of its drive with a Welsh-rooted dynasty firmly established on the throne in London. The land prospered quietly for almost 200 years, until the start of the first civil war. Many Welshmen had cheerfully accepted the Stuarts who took over from the Tudors and were even happy to pay the notorious Ship Money tax levied by Charles I if it would be used to protect the principality's ever-vulnerable coastline. When the smouldering powder keg of discontent finally ignited, large areas of Wales, including Carmarthen, supported the royalist cause. Haverfordwest, Tenby, and Pembroke were among the fortress-towns that threw in their lots with parliament. Pembroke was exceptionally important because then, as always in the past, it was a key point on the way to Ireland.

In the second civil war, however, Pembroke switched sides and supported the crown. Cromwell himself marched across Wales to organize the siege, and it lasted for 48 days before John Poyer, Mayor of Pembroke and the garrison's commander, was forced to surrender. He was taken to London and put to death at Covent Garden. When Charles was executed in 1649, Thomas Wogan, MP for the Cardiganshire boroughs, was among those who signed his death warrant; he fled the country when the monarchy was restored in 1660. The return of Charles II drew down the curtain on West Wales' long history of bloodshed. Other parts of Britain had also suffered throughout the centuries of strife, but Pembroke's vital strategic role had made this part of the country particularly important. There must have been times when the tramp of marching feet and the clash of swords seemed as unending as the ebb and flow of the tides. There was, however, to be one more notable incident and it came during the Napoleonic Wars when the nation steeled itself for an invasion that never came. But that is not strictly true. Bonaparte's army never crossed the English Channel, but a force did land at Carregwastad Point near Fishguard in 1797.

The last invasion

Commanded by William Tate, an Irish-American soldier of fortune, the 1,200 troops were mainly convicts and deserters who had undertaken the expedition in the hope of gaining free pardons and plenty of booty. Their original destination was Bristol, where they hoped to foment a revolution, but strong winds drove the little fleet northwards and Tate decided to attack Pembrokeshire instead, no doubt hoping that the Welsh would revive their old hatred for the English and flock to his banner. They ransacked farms, became hopelessly drunk, deserted in dribs and drabs, then surrendered on Goodwick Sands. Tradition steadfastly maintains that the decision to surrender came when the invaders saw what appeared to be a regiment of redcoats marching to join the Pembroke Yeomanry under Lord Cawdor. The newcomers were actually local women wearing the traditional red shawls of Wales. 'Fishguard' is the only battle honour ever won by a regiment on British soil. The last invasion may have been little more than a bizarre joke, but it once again emphasized the vulnerability and military importance of West Wales. The region became an important and heavily-defended base for operations in the North Atlantic during the two world wars, when warships lurked in the harbours, Sunderland and Catalina flying boats roared up and down Milford Haven, and hydrophone stations – remains of which can still be seen – were established on St David's Head to listen for U-boats prowling in the Irish Sea.

Pembroke Dock was bombed, Milford Haven was strafed, and hundreds of sorties were flown from airfields that sprang up all along the coast. It was to the sandy beaches between Saundersfoot and Pendine that 100,000 troops were transported in 1943 to take part in the most important and spectacular dress rehearsal ever staged; the rehearsal for the D-Day landings in Normandy, a year later. The soldiers splashed ashore from their landing crafts under the eyes of three men who had met at the Wiseman's Bridge Inn – Prime Minister Winston Churchill, General Dwight Eisenhower, and Field Marshal Bernard Montgomery.

Threat and fortune

The sea has been a mixed blessing to West Wales. It often provided an uncomfortably convenient approach route for hostile forces, but it was also the region's main commercial link with the outside world from prehistoric times right up to the 19thc. The men of West Wales were trading with Ireland for gold and copper many centuries before the birth of Christ, and one of the most remarkable series of voyages ever made started from Pembrokeshire. Turn the clock back 3,500 years to the bronze age, and travel to the Prescelly range in the north of the county. There, on the bleak moorland, primitive men are laboriously wresting no fewer than 80 bluestone monoliths, weighing up to four tons each, from a lonely, windswept quarry. This is remarkable enough in itself, but the quarrying operation seems modest when it is realized that the stones are destined for the second phase of the unique monument at Stonehenge, far away on Salisbury Plain in Wiltshire, one of the cradles of British civilization. Even the straightest of lines – conveniently ignoring hills, valleys, rivers, and estuaries – shows the two points to be 150m apart. Transporting the great stones would pose formidable problems even today. For all their skill the sailors of West Wales did not embark on any of the great voyages of discovery that opened up the world at the end of the Middle Ages. One reason, no doubt, is that the region had no wealthy cities such as Bristol to encourage and finance expeditions. Even now the largest population in the region – that of Llanelli – is well under 30,000, while that of Milford Haven is less than 15,000 and the old-established town of Haverfordwest has 10,000. Only 13,000 people live in Carmarthen, where there has been a thriving community since Roman times. The remains of what is sometimes claimed to be a Roman breakwater still stand in the little cove of Porth-clais, near St David's, but most of the relics of the old sea-trading days date from the 18thc. Sturdy quays and wharves are obvious enough, but look for the squat kilns where lime was unloaded from coasters and burned to provide mortar for buildings and fertilizer to combat the peaty, acidic soil. A fine row of kilns, huddled together like a Lilliputian fortress, stands beside the little river at Solva. There are many others all along the coast from New Quay to old Carmarthenshire.

At Porthgain, the outlet for the granite quarries mentioned earlier, the gaunt remains of the crushing plant tower stand above the snug harbour while white-painted cairns, now used as landmarks by weekend sailors and lobster fishermen, crown the headlands flanking the mouth of the rocky inlet. The last tall-masted trader sailed away from here as recently as 1932, and its yellowing photograph hangs in the bar of the local pub. Iron mooring rings, almost eaten away by rust, are set into the rocks at St Bride's Haven. At Haverfordwest, at the upper tidal limit of the Western Cleddau, warehouses and the handsome old Custom House are reminders that this was once one of the busiest ports in Wales; the mayor still bears the additional title of Admiral of the Port.

Maritime towns

Cardigan was a bustling centre for sea-borne trade when Cardiff and Swansea were insignificant villages, and this ancient town on the estuary of the beautiful River Teifi still had almost 300 ships on its register as late as the middle of the 19thc. The Romans sailed in and out of Carmarthen, pitting their craft against the notorious Cefn Sidan sands that do their best to block the way to the open sea. Derelict storehouses overlook the beaches at such places as Newport and Abercastell. Records reveal that sleepy little Laugharne had 90 houses and a few ships in the 16thc, trading with Bristol, Dublin, and Rochelle; at that time it also had a reputation as the haunt of pirates who preyed on vessels in the Bristol Channel, or the Severn Sea as it was then known. The harbour at Aberaeron, flanked by delightful Regency buildings, was developed at the start of the 19thc and flourished for several decades, while nearby New Quay has a particularly well-documented history that vividly illustrates the importance of the sea to small coastal towns in years gone by.

The first official mention of New Quay, now one of the most popular holiday resorts on Cardigan Bay, appears in an Admiralty report on ports and harbours published in 1748. Half a century later, like so many other places along the coasts of Wales, it had high hopes of becoming a major ferry-port for Ireland, but nothing came of the proposal. Despite the setback New Quay began to develop rapidly at

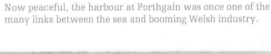

Now peaceful, the harbour at Porthgain was once one of the many links between the sea and booming Welsh industry.

11

Coracles built to a basic design which is some 2,000 years old can still be seen on the Tywi and Teifi rivers.

the start of the 19thc and shipbuilding is believed to have commenced in 1820, when the brig 'Friendship' was launched. This ship now appears on the town's insignia, together with three silver herrings that indicate New Quay's long-established fishing interests. A harbour company was formed in 1833 and, two years later, the New Quay Harbour Act was passed by parliament and the stone pier was built. Some 40 years of considerable prosperity followed. In the 1860's there were about 300 shipwrights working in the town, while half a dozen smithies echoed to the clangour of men beating out anchors, stanchions, and other fittings. Most of the shipbuilders' hardwood was obtained locally, but softwoods came from Canada and a ship was regularly employed on the long run across the North Atlantic. The boom was short-lived, however, for the advent of iron-built steamships and the coming of the railways crippled the colourful coastal trade. By the 1920's, when road transport provided additional competition, it had died out completely in New Quay and its days were short-numbered elsewhere. The old harbour dues displayed at New Quay are delightful reminders. They reveal, for instance, that it cost five shillings to land a billiard table or barrel organ, four pence for every calf, sheep, pig, or fox – the latter presumably imported for the benefit of local sportsmen who had decimated the local population – two shillings for every hundredweight of feathers, and one shilling and sixpence for a marble tombstone.

New Quay is sheltered from prevailing south-westerly winds by a lofty headland and was an ideal centre for shipbuilding and trade, but there were many others, such as Landshipping Quay, that are much less obvious. Now a lonely, muddy creek on the upper reaches of Milford Haven, Landshipping was a bustling place when coasters called regularly to load coal and culm – a slow-burning mixture of coal dust and clay – from the local mines. Eight small ships were built here in the early 1800's.

Black wealth
The last of the Pembrokeshire coal mines did not close until 1947, but although the workings were of considerable importance and produced high-grade anthracite they could never match the output of those on the border between Carmarthenshire and Glamorgan. The development of those rich coalfields in the east of the region saw Burry Port develop from a fishing village to an important harbour town in a few short years during the middle of the 19thc. Neighbouring Llanelli also grew rapidly, waxing prosperous on its exports of coal and tinplate. In later years this thriving industrial town became one of the great centres of Welsh rugby.

The Industrial Revolution flourished in the valleys beyond Burry Port and Llanelli, and even essentially rural Pembrokeshire played its part in making Britain the workshop of the world. There were more than 30 woollen mills operating in the county at the start of the present century; three are still in business and two of them, at Tregwynt and Wallis, are open to visitors. Haverfordwest was a great centre for paper-making, but the gems of the county's industrial archaeology are to be found around Stepaside, near Saundersfoot, where there were thriving coal mines and ironworks, a network of tramways, and even a small canal. Saundersfoot itself is now a busy holiday resort. To the north, in the dramatic gorge carved by the Teifi between Llechryd, Cilgerran, and Cardigan, there were several slate quarries and a busy tin works. The old towpath beside the river, crumbling quays tangled with undergrowth, and the remains of another canal running roughly parallel to the river, are evocative links with the not-too-distant past. When Giraldus Cambrensis – Gerald the Welshman – the much-travelled priest and chronicler visited Cilgerran in the 12thc he recorded: 'The Teifi has another singular peculiarity, being the only river in Wales or England which has beavers; in Scotland they are said to be found in one river, but are very scarce.' Like the quarries the beavers have vanished, but this remains one of the few rivers where primitive coracles are still used by fishermen seeking salmon and sewin, the Welsh name for sea-trout. Although the materials have changed, coracles are still built to a basic design that has been used for more than 2,000 years. They are perhaps the most colourful of all the region's links with the past and can be seen on the Tywi as well as the Teifi.

Towns such as Llanelli and Burry Port continue to manufacture a wide variety of goods that are sold throughout the world, but West Wales' greatest hope for long-term riches is concentrated on Milford Haven, the great harbour that has played such an important role in the life of the region for so many years. The natural assets of this very extensive drowned valley, initially formed by earth-shaking movements some 280 million years ago, have been appreciated for centuries. It is many years since traders nosed upstream to Haverfordwest, but deep-keeled yachts still cluster in the estuary at such places as Lawrenny, 15m from the open sea, where the water is 30ft deep even at low tide. The most welcome accolade came from none other than Nelson, the greatest of Britain's seafaring heroes, who hailed the waterway as the second finest natural harbour in the world after Trincomalee in Ceylon, when he visited the new town of Milford Haven in 1802.

The Haven is a drowned valley which provides superb deep-water facilities for heavy craft.

Milford, as it was then known, had been founded a few years earlier on land owned by Sir William Hamilton, whose wife Emma became Nelson's mistress. Its gridiron pattern of streets and solidly handsome, unpretentious buildings are typical products of the Regency period's admirable aptitude for town planning that can be admired on a much smaller scale at Aberaeron. There are fine views over the haven, for the oldest part of the town stands on a slope so steep that many buildings have two or three side doors all leading out on to the same street, but at different levels. Hamilton Terrace, the main block of buildings on the sea front, stands on a cliff high above the docks but its rooftops are below the level of the doorsteps in Charles Street, less than 100yds on up the hill. Features such as these combine to create a town with plenty of character, and it is virtually impossible to think of another place in Britain quite like it. Charles Greville, Hamilton's nephew, was given the task of organizing the new town and its harbour. Greville found the basis of his population by somehow organizing a remarkable and almost certainly unique reversal of the trans-Atlantic immigration pattern. At a time when thousands of settlers from the British Isles were bravely, hopefully setting out for the New World, he arranged for a colony of Quaker whalers from Nantucket, on the north-eastern coast of the USA, to settle in Milford. Their trade flourished until the introduction of gas meant that whale oil was no longer needed to light the streets of Britain's cities and big towns.

Town of ill fortune

This was the first of many setbacks, and for more than a century and a half Milford's fortunes followed a frustrating series of ups and downs. Greville's harbour had been designed with the Royal Navy very much in mind, but in 1814 the Admiralty decided to switch its shipbuilding operations to the equally new town of Pembroke Dock, on the far side of the haven. More than 250 ships were built there between 1816 and 1922; they included three royal yachts and the biggest wooden ships ever made, the battleships 'Lord Clyde' and 'Lord Warden', which weighed 7,750 tons and 7,940 tons respectively and were launched in 1866 and 1867. Pembroke Dock's most remarkable relic, HMS 'Warrior', Britain's first ironclad warship, has been a derelict hulk for many years but there are hopes that this historic vessel will be rescued and restored before it is too late. Drab and battered though she is, 'Warrior' is the most important link in the chain that joins the wooden walls of Nelson's navy to the dreadnoughts and the highly sophisticated warships of today. The loss of the naval dockyard was a bitter blow to Milford Haven, and it increased the town's reliance on its ferry traffic with Ireland until disaster struck again. Isambard Kingdom Brunel chose Neyland (confusingly

known as Milford Haven until 1859, and as New Milford until 1906) as the terminus for the South Wales Railway and the packet-boats left Milford for ever. Brunel's prodigious talents are recalled at Neyland by a terrace named after his immense and ill-fated 'Great Eastern', a frequent visitor to special berthing facilities in the haven.

Chauvinistic Milfordians probably gained some measure of sour satisfaction in 1906, when the new harbour at Fishguard was completed and assumed responsibility for the Irish trade, leaving Neyland with its memories. Milford Haven, meanwhile, had become one of the five greatest fishing ports in Britain and for many years the sight of the fleet of trawlers and drifters entering and leaving the docks was a memorable one. Blocks of ice slithered down the runway from the ice factory to the fish market, where all was noise and excitement as the catch was displayed, sold and packed off into the waiting trains. Almost inevitably, in view of the town's past experiences, the fishing business declined after the second world war and Milford seemed once again to be living up to its reputation as the town that never quite made the grade.

What price oil?

Then came a dramatic change of fortune that seems to have put an end to all those long years of dashed hopes and bitter frustrations. In the 1950's the size of oiltankers began to increase at an unprecedented rate; the 90,000-ton giants of today became tomorrow's minnows, just as the 250,000-ton VLCC's – the oil trade's abbreviation for Very Large Crude Carriers – have been left far behind by the 360,000-ton and 500,000-ton monsters launched in the 1960's and early 70's. Even the 250,000-tonners cost well over £1,000 an hour to operate, and it soon became obvious that a new deepwater terminal on the western coast of Britain would reduce costs and also cut down the risks of an accident happening in the crowded waters of the English Channel.

The haven was an obvious choice and its development was pioneered by Esso, who built their £20,000,000 refinery to the west of Milford Haven town between 1958 and 1960, when it was officially opened by the Duke of Edinburgh. Some 19m of pre-stressed concrete piles were driven into the seabed to support the jetty, almost three-quarters of a mile long, that runs out to the channel used by 250,000-ton VLCC's that have sailed non-stop from the Persian Gulf in 28 days. More than 6,000,000 tons of crude oil are processed every year, but the refinery, which has expanded considerably since it was opened, can be operated by less than a dozen skilled technicians. Gulf,

Giant supertankers entering and leaving the Haven have added a new dimension to the seascapes of West Wales.

Texaco, and others soon followed in Esso's footsteps, completely changing the appearance of the haven in less than a decade and transforming it into the second largest oil port in Europe after Rotterdam. The coming of the oil men has also given a new lease of life to some of the forts, most of them built in the 19thc, that stud the shores of the haven and its small islands. Some have been incorporated in the refineries and terminals. Another at Dale is a field-studies centre, and the one on Thorn Island, where a 100-strong garrison once tended a battery of nine big guns, has been converted for use as a hotel. Some of the forts had more than 30 guns, and the most expensive one of the lot – on Stack Rock close to the Esso jetty – cost almost £100,000 to build, a very considerable sum by the monetary standards of the 1850's. There were plans to protect the forts from landward attacks by building another ring of strongholds a few miles inland. Only one was completed, Fort Scoveston, and its derelict remains form the apex of a roughly equilateral triangle based on Neyland and the nearby Gulf refinery. Other plans suggested extending the fortified line along the southern coast, but there again only one was built, at Tenby. It stands on a rocky little island which is joined to the mainland at low tide, and is now home to a small zoo.

A law for industry . . .

Despite the efforts of the oil companies, the refineries stand out from the rolling Pembrokeshire plateau like so many of the proverbial sore thumbs, while the 700ft-high chimney at Pembroke's new power station can be seen with the naked eye from as far away as the western tip of the Gower Peninsula. The prospect of rich deposits of oil being found and exploited beneath the bed of the Irish Sea is also a cause of great concern to conservationists. Whatever problems may lie ahead, however, the coast has been mercifully free of major oil spillages, although the prospect of another Torrey Canyon disaster cannot be completely banished from any realistic mind.

One of the main fears is that the offshore oil boom, if it ever materializes, will, 'in the interests of the national economy', allow industrial developments of one sort or another to encroach upon the Pembrokeshire Coast national park. This ranks with Britain's greatest and most priceless assets. The park came into being in 1952, under the auspices of the National Parks and Access to the Countryside Act passed three years earlier, but in less than a decade its supposedly sacrosanct borders on Milford Haven had been overlapped by Esso on the north shore, and the British Petroleum depot on the southern one. The latter is an unloading, storage, and pumping terminal

that sends its crude oil by pipeline to the refinery at Llandarcy, near Swansea. The park's designated area has since been invaded again, by the building of the huge Amoco refinery between Sandy Haven and Milford Haven town. These and other developments, including the Pembroke power station, represent more than £200 million of capital investment packed into an area of some 20 square miles, much of which comprises salt water. The immense refineries and tank farms may have done nothing to enhance Milford Haven's natural beauty, but few would deny that the sight of the great tankers slipping cautiously to and from their berths has given an exciting new dimension to the seascapes. The tankers can be seen at their best from St Ann's Head, where they pick up a pilot for the slow, infinitely careful last stage of their 12,000m, non-stop voyages from Kuwait, Bahrein and the other oil ports of the Middle East.

Rich wilderness

Vast though the oil installations may be, as yet they affect only a small, compact area of the 225sqm national park. A delightful feature of the inland area is the Forestry Commission nature trail in Minwear Wood, close to the old mill at Blackpool that now houses an interesting agricultural museum.

The park's emblem, a razorbill, is entirely appropriate. The area has the richest variety of seabirds found anywhere in Wales or England. They are exceptionally abundant on the offshore islands such as Skokholm, where Britain's first bird observatory was founded by the naturalist and author R M Lockley in 1933. Skokholm is now a reserve of major importance run by the West Wales Naturalists' Trust, and its feathered inhabitants include about 1,000 pairs of storm petrels. Known to generations of sailors as Mother Carey's Chickens, these graceful little birds spend much of their lives soaring over the open seas, coming ashore only to breed or when driven in by severe weather. The neighbouring island of Skomer, reached during the holiday months by a regular boat that runs across Jack Sound from Martin's Haven, a rocky bay west of Marloes, was farmed until the start of this century but is now a national nature reserve. Its 722 acres provide a home for many small mammals, including the unique Skomer vole, and countless birds that include guillemots, razorbills, puffins, several varieties of gull, shags, cormorants, fulmar petrels, and oyster-catchers. The puffins are particularly delightful, but the island's most fascinating creatures are the Manx shearwaters. These big, powerful birds, black above and white underneath, live in burrows like the puffins but return to them only at night, screaming and wailing after a day spent out over the open sea. At least 100,000 pairs breed on Skomer and another 35,000 pairs live on Skokholm, making this the greatest concentration of Manx shearwaters anywhere in the world.

Grassholm is a lonely, waterless, 22-acre speck of land out beyond Skomer, which is very difficult to reach and forms a reserve run by the Royal Society for the Protection of Birds. It has the second largest colony of gannets in Britain and one of the largest in the world. More than 15,000 pairs nest on the island, and when the chicks hatch in mid-summer the population increases to over 60,000. The natural isolation of the islands, plus the protection extended to them in recent years, has enabled them to remain outstanding refuges for seabirds; but thousands more birds can be seen along the mainland coast. Eligug Stacks, on the south coast of one-time Pembrokeshire, is perhaps the finest of these relatively easy to reach sites; immense numbers of guillemots and razorbills nest on the rocks and the adjacent cliffs. Near by the sheltered lily pools of Bosherston provide a delightful change of scenery and attract such birds as kingfishers, herons, moorhens, swans, tufted ducks, and a few Slavonian grebes.

To the east, beyond the boundaries of the national park, the estuarine saltings at the mouths of the Taf, Tywi, and Gwendraeth rivers are the homes of many wildfowl and waders. It was here that Dylan Thomas meant when he wrote of 'the heron-priested shore' in his richly evocative *Poem in October*. Here, too, 'the hawk on fire hangs still' at sunset over the gentle swell of St John's Hill, that gave its name to another of the poet's finest works. The coast of old Cardiganshire is also well blessed with birds – particularly the stretch near New Quay Head – and the rocky shores and islands of West Wales as a whole are breeding grounds for the grey seal. About 400 pups are believed to be born along the coasts of Pembrokeshire alone each year, and Ramsey Island is the main breeding ground.

Last refuge

Inland, vivid kingfishers may be seen darting hither and thither on some of the rivers, while the uplands are the haunts of curlews, snipe, ravens, buzzards, kestrels, sparrowhawks, ring ouzels – often called mountain blackbirds because of their sweet songs – and many others. A drive northwards from Llandovery through spectacular wooded mountains to the huge new Llyn Brianne Reservoir may be rewarded with a glimpse of the rarest of all birds in West Wales and one of the rarest in Britain – the kite. Easily recognized by its deeply-forked tail, the kite resembles a buzzard but is longer, sleeker, and has a distinctive pale patch on the underside of each wing. This was once a very common bird; visitors to London in Tudor times commented on how many could be seen scavenging in the streets of the city. Their numbers gradually dwindled, however, and by 1905 it was thought that only five kites were still alive in the whole of Britain. Only seven pairs were located in 1928, but the total population of these handsome birds of prey is believed to have increased to about 80 since then. The magnificent mountain wilderness of central Wales is their only breeding ground in Britain.

Legends and tempests

Between Rhandirmwyn and Llyn Brianne the road passes a craggy hill where trees and bushes shroud the entrance to Twm Shon Catti's cave. The cave itself is nothing special, although the surrounding countryside is superb, but tradition pinpoints it as a hiding place used by one of the most colourful characters in Welsh folk-history. Twm Shon Catti's real name was Thomas Jones, and he was born near Tregaron in Mid Wales during the 16thc. He was a bard, a great practical joker, and a highwayman with

The wildernesses of West and South Wales are the last strongholds of the red kite.

more than a hint of Robin Hood in his character. Like the adventures of the uncrowned king of Sherwood Forest, Twm's exploits were given plenty of additional colouring as the years went by and received a tremendous final gloss when *The Adventures and Vagaries of Twm Shon Catti* were published in 1828. The true nature of the man has probably been lost, but he has romped down through the centuries as perhaps the most notable rogue-hero of the Welsh people.

In his much-quoted *Wild Wales* the 19th-c author, linguist, traveller, and lover of good ale George Borrow relates how a native of Tregaron described Twm as a clever thief who eventually became Mayor of Brecon; 'Oh,' he explained, 'Twm Shon Catti was very different from other thieves; funny fellow, and so good natured that everybody loved him – so that they made him magistrate.' Borrow was also told how Twm once called at an ironmonger's shop in Llandovery, selected a large iron porridge pot, held it up to the light and declared there was a hole in it. 'Nonsense' said the shopkeeper, so Twm suggested he put his head right into the pot to see the defect for himself. Twm then pulled the vessel down over the man's eyes, helped himself to a selection of goods, and departed with the words; 'Friend, I suppose you now see that there is a hole in the pot, otherwise how could you have got your head inside?'

The mountains once roamed by Twm form part of the hilly wilderness that has been aptly described as the great desert of central Wales. There are few roads and the human population is heavily outnumbered by sheep. It was to Dolaucothi, on the southern edge of the area, that the Romans came in search of gold during the 1st c AD. Iron-age men had probably picked away at the rocks

15

The scanty remains of Talley Abbey are picturesquely set in beautiful surroundings.

before then, but the advanced Roman technology quickly modernized the workings by building an extensive system of aqueducts, sluices, and reservoirs – substantial traces of which can be clearly seen to this day on what is now National Trust land. These remains are easily the most remarkable of their type and age in Britain, and have the added attraction of being in an outstandingly beautiful setting on wooded slopes and broad fields between the rivers Cothi and Annell.

On the edge of the site, beside the road opposite Ogofau Lodge, stands an ancient stone pitted with smooth hollows. According to legend these impressions were made by the shoulders of five saints – Gwynne, Gwynno, Gwynoro, Cilynen, and Ceitho – who clustered round the stone for shelter when caught in a blizzard one winter night. The tale may be fanciful, but the name of the nearby village, Pumsaint, is Welsh for Five Saints. The gold mines, which were worked until just before the start of the second world war, should not be missed, and the ruined abbey at nearby Talley is also well worth a visit. The remains are scanty, although they include a ruined tower almost 100ft high, but the surrounding countryside is most attractive. Like Strata Florida, Talley was founded by the powerful Lord Rhys in the 12thc.

Lampeter, in the Teifi valley to the north-west of Pumsaint, stands on the imaginary boundary between West and Mid Wales and a population of just over 2,000 makes it the biggest place for many miles around. It stands at the meeting place of several principal class roads, but traffic is rarely anything but light and this ancient market town – its earliest known charter was granted in 1284 – has retained more of its character than others on busier roads.

Western produce
Every Tuesday the streets of Lampeter bustle with activity, when farmers and their families come down from the hills and along the Teifi valley to buy and sell livestock and other produce, keeping up a tradition that is at least 700-years old. Cardiganshire has long been known for the quality of its livestock, including horses and ponies, and also for its dairy goods. The building of the turnpike road that is now the A40 opened up the route eastwards in the early 19thc, when Cardiganshire and Carmarthenshire became two of the well-stocked larders that supplied the booming new industrial towns of South Wales. 'Cardy carts' left the farms on Monday, jogged and creaked their way in little convoys to Brecon, then continued to the markets of such towns as Merthyr Tydfil and Pontypool before returning home at the end of the week.

Pembrokeshire is also noted for its sheep and cattle, while its mild climate, influenced by the relatively warm waters of the benign Gulf Stream, has made it an important area for early potatoes. The county's most unusual harvest comes from the shores of St Bride's Bay where the seaweed *Porphyra umbilicus* is gathered and made into the great Welsh delicacy known as laver bread. Popular throughout West Wales, the Gower, and the region around Swansea, it is traditionally eaten with bacon or ham. The Gulf Stream plays an important part in the climate of West Wales, because so much of the region is so close to the sea. The overall effect is mild and equable – although winters can be bitterly cold on the hills – and both frost and snow are virtually unknown on the coast.

Sun and storm
The area of old Pembrokeshire is particularly fortunate because no part of the county is more than 10m from tidal waters as the crow flies. Dale, at the mouth of Milford Haven, is claimed to be the sunniest place in Wales and the region's overall sunshine record is a good one. From the beginning of June to the end of August the coast averages 6.4 hours of sunshine a day. By way of comparison, Torquay has 7.2 hours, Brighton 7.3 hours, Skegness 5.9 hours, Prestwick 5.3 hours and Blackpool 6.2 hours. The coast is, however, wide open to the full fury of the Atlantic. Wind speeds in excess of 130mph were recorded on the Dale Peninsula in the winter of 1954, but even storms have a wild attraction, and the coast off St David's looks magnificent when long lines of foam crash against the flanks of Ramsey Island and surge over the rocks known as the Bishop and Clerks. The combination of on-shore winds, reefs, and cliffs made this a murderous coast in the days of sail, and the first lighthouses were built to warn mariners in the 18thc. One was on St Ann's Head and the other, almost 19m out to sea, stood on The Smalls reef. Its successor is still in use and is the most remote of all the manned lights maintained by Trinity House. The terrible isolation of The Smalls was underlined in the winter of 1800 to 1801. Two keepers were on duty, but one of them died. His companion, unable to attract attention to his plight and unwilling to throw the corpse to the fishes, made a coffin from the panels of the living room and lashed it to the outside of the tower until help came, three months later.

At Cwm-yr-eglwys, the lovely little bay between Newport and Fishguard, the ruined church of St Brynach bears silent witness to the fury of the elements. On the night of 25 October 1859 it was smashed down by a hurricane that claimed 114 ships along the coasts of Wales in the space of a few hours. Its most famous victim was the treasure-laden clipper 'Royal Charter', nearing the end of its long voyage from Australia to Liverpool, which sunk with the loss of more than 400 lives within a stone's throw of the Anglesey cliffs.

J G Parry Thomas was killed on Pendine Sands while trying
to break the land-speed record in his car 'Babs'.

A place to relax

Lesser winds blowing in from the west and south-west
have made Pembrokeshire an increasingly lively centre for
surfing. Whitesand Bay and the long stretch of shingle-
backed sand at Newgale are the most popular beaches for
this fascinating and often dramatic sport. The coasts have
also become great favourites with amateur sailors, and the
sight of bright-sailed boats scudding through the water off
such centres as Dale contrasts delightfully with views of
the great oil tankers. The rocky areas, with their deep,
clear water and many old wrecks, attract plenty of
sub-aqua enthusiasts who can often be seen putting out to
sea from a score of tiny bays.

All these comparatively new activities help to explain the
rapid increase in the popularity of West Wales as a prime
holiday area. Great though the influx of visitors has been,
the coasts of West Wales have retained much of their
magic and untamed splendour. All but the most popular
beaches still seem miraculously uncrowded to anyone
accustomed to the resorts of England, while visitors who
enjoy plenty of company can always head for such
popular seaside towns as New Quay, Tenby, and
Saundersfoot. One of the busiest of the villages is Pendine,
where Sir Malcolm Campbell and the Welshman J G Parry
Thomas broke and re-broke the world's land speed record
on the immense beach in the 1920's. Parry Thomas, a
great driver and one of the most talented engineers of his
time, was killed on the beach in 1927 while trying to beat
Campbell's record of 174.88mph.

The coasts and inland areas of southern Cardiganshire
and Carmarthenshire are criss-crossed with footpaths and
bridleways, many of them following routes pioneered by
prehistoric travellers or the Romans, and Pembrokeshire
has its superb long-distance footpath. Starting near
St Dogmaels, with its ruined abbey, the path follows the
magnificent coastline down to Neyland, crosses Milford
Haven and then, after a detour inland to avoid the military
training area at Castlemartin, continues all the way to
Amroth on the old Carmarthenshire border. The total
distance is 168m, and the complete walk takes about two
weeks. Linger over every view, explore every place of
interest along the way, and the time can easily be
extended to something more like two years. Unlike many
of the other long-distance paths in Britain, this one is
broken by many roads and lanes leading down to the
shore. It has opened up a scenic wonderland previously
denied to the public, and offers the opportunity to enjoy
an almost endless variety of short walks if the prospect
of tackling the entire route seems too formidable. Many of
the headlands have subsidiary paths cutting across their

necks and are therefore ideal for relatively short strolls.
Dinas Island lies between Newport Bay and Fishguard Bay
and is a fine example, but there are many others.

Journey through enchantment

There are also abundant opportunities for those who
prefer to explore solely by car. Pembrokeshire,
Carmarthenshire, and Cardiganshire – taking the county
as a whole – have just over 5,000m of road between
them, and almost half of that mileage is accounted for by
unclassified by-ways. The area roughly bordered by
Aberaeron, Cardigan, Narberth, and Carmarthen is laced
with lanes that twist and turn, climb and descend between
rolling pastures, lonely farms, and snug valleys sheltered
by slopes green with trees. Despite the tangled skein of
roads, this is a part of the country where villages of more
than 100 people ranks as cities, and it is possible to
travel for miles without seeing another vehicle. It is easy
to get lost, but that is all part of the fun. Progress is slow,
but no stranger in a tearing hurry would consider taking
the cross-country route from, say, Cynwyl Elfed to
Crymmych in the first place.

Visitors prepared to wander off the beaten tracks and
pause to chat with the locals are likely to be delighted,
particularly if the conversation happens to be conducted
over a glass or three of ale. The average West Walian is
a warm-hearted raconteur, bubbling over with vivid
phrases – and this is a corner of Britain where hilariously
unlikely happenings seem commonplace and lose nothing
in the telling.

Much of West Wales has a whimsical and somehow other-
worldly atmosphere that is clearly reflected in the
characters of many of its people. This very real yet
intangible quality was captured best of all, perhaps, by
Dylan Thomas. Although he was born in Swansea, the
rumbustious bard spent much of his life in West Wales.
His superlative poem *Fern Hill* was inspired by childhood
visits to his uncle's farm near Llanstephan, and for many
years he lived in Laugharne, the old sea-town that more
than any other epitomizes to this day the delightful,
unconventional and essentially fun-loving spirit of the
region as a whole.

The Changing Valleys

The South Wales of today rises from the ashes and tips of industrial exploitation to a future of enlightened restoration

To a great number of people who have never visited the country, Wales is South Wales; an image of stricken landscape and lurid cumulus; an inheritance of pit disasters, long streets, hillside chapels, and hymns in the minor key. Such pictures die a hard death, but they are not unreal or accidental – no more than the reality that gave rise to them was accidental. It is simply that they are a large part of what constitutes the character of South Wales, the most thoroughly exploited, densely populated, intensely urbanized, and irrepressibly optimistic region in the principality. South Wales is 'modern' Wales, since it owes so many of its present features to the industrial development of the last two centuries. The process which started towards the end of the 18thc with the smelting of copper at Neath and Swansea gained momentum soon afterwards with the development of iron works at Hirwaun, Merthyr, and Dowlais. It reached alarming speed in the middle of the last century, when the rich coal seams of the valleys were struck, converting a peaceful, wild, and green countryside into dark and ferocious furrows of harzardous human habitation stretching for miles and with little to distinguish one valley from another.

Much of South Wales today is a pathetically scarred and pitted casualty of this intense warfare between nature and the generals of industry and capitalism. Nature lost. Some 50 years ago an attempt was made to hide the deep incisions and the mounds of decay. Afforestation proved successful, and great areas were transformed into scenes of reassuring vitality. And yet, side by side with this effort to save the face of the countryside, the industrial process continued elsewhere. The works of Hirwaun, Dowlais, and Merthyr, having lit the night skies with their furnaces, were forsaken; the valleys, plundered and sacked, were exhausted; the exploiters now looked to the coast. Copper, iron, and coal had passed their glory; it was now the turn of oil, steel, and chemicals.

The scene today is grimly fascinating: mile after mile of gigantic buildings, their bland exteriors betraying none of the secrets of their machines and machinations, a concentric fortification of cooling towers and water towers here and a mass of pipes, jets, and stacks there, filling the low sky with a multicoloured mixture of waste. The view from Stormy Down, on the road between Bridgend and

Two aspects of the South Wales landscape – brash young industry and ancient Margam Abbey.

Port Talbot, presents not only a panorama of this post-war growth, but the sharp contrast that characterizes so many parts of South Wales, when the green of unspoiled land is suddenly sacrificed to insidious speculation. A few miles to the west the estates of Margam Castle and Abbey, with their background of wooded mountain, give way to a plethora of productivity. The Abbey Steelworks, the Baglan Bay Chemical Plant, and the National Oil Refineries are all seen in their satanic strength from the 5m stretch of A48(M), probably the best viewing platform in the country. For the motorist it is at its most impressive at night, when the ever-burning flames of waste-gas products look like gigantic cigarette lighters. Their effect on inhabitants for miles around is nothing like so fanciful; the constant flaring has produced a generation of anguished insomniacs, and the industrial complex as a whole has produced an uncanny accuracy in local weather forecasting.

Captives of industry

Development has brought about many changes in the social and religious pattern of the lives of the inhabitants. New housing estates as well as the ribbon development of the earlier part of the century accommodate a high proportion, but a large number travel to work by car from Swansea and the Swansea Valley. The closures in the 50's of the steel and tinplate works forced men, who had spent their entire lives working in front of furnaces and in the strip mills, to find alternative employment in an environment and culture that was akin to that which they knew. The great new works near Port Talbot and Felindre, and the 1956 tinplate plant near Swansea provided the solution.

Steel has been made at Port Talbot since 1903, but it can no longer be described as representative of a steel town. The traditional gear of the steel-worker has disappeared: the flannel shirt, the towel around the neck, the thick leather belt, the tin foodbox, and the white enamel tea-can. Development here, as at Llanwern near Newport, has perhaps been too great; individuality and identity are rapidly disappearing, although the rugby teams of Newport and Port Talbot – Aberafan – provide a focal point of considerable pride and social interest. The Afan Lido and the quick car ride to Porthcawl have taken precedence over chapel, and the Severn Bridge now provides easy access to the lions of Longleat and other attractions that have not yet penetrated South Wales. And yet, in 1966 when Port Talbot was host to the Royal Welsh National Eisteddfod – which is held during the first week of August every year and alternates between north and south – the former character of the town was restored.

With the affluence of the Margam steelworker, Port Talbot showed all the symptoms of becoming a boom town a decade ago. Clubs flourished, steak bars encouraged new and more adventurous eating habits, alcohol was no longer synonymous with beer, and a gambling casino offered a monkey-jacketed kingdom of hushed temptation. But this last venture into the unknown was itself suddenly too much of a gamble. The first indications of short time and furnace closure enlivened the bitter memories of the older generation and caused the young to concentrate more on essentials. Prosperity and poverty were often perilously close to each other, as experience of the 20's and 30's had shown all too nastily. Disquieting rumours of the fate of the iron and steel plant at Ebbw Vale were a reminder that industrial history could repeat itself.

The wreckage of wealth
By the end of the 70's the rundown of the steel industry at Ebbw Vale will result in 7,000 acres of derelict land. A major programme for the treatment of this area has already been examined by the Welsh Office Task Force, and the promise of a reclamation scheme of this magnitude is a reflection of the brisk response and enlightened attitude of the Welsh Office. The Special Environmental Assistance Scheme, or Operation Eyesore, enabling local authorities to make minor improvements thereby offering further employment, was introduced in 1972. Between them there is now a fair certainty that never again will the landscape of industrial South Wales be allowed to degenerate into a nightmare of martian devastation, such as the Lower Swansea Valley, a scene that has appalled and fascinated generations of natives as well as strangers coming into the town on the London train. The deserted industrial buildings, the forsaken railway tracks, the copper slag tips, and the yellow-brown canal have shocked the senses and blunted reasoning powers.
The American and French wars of the 18thc created a

Industry turned the Swansea Valley into an alien wasteland, a barren desert where the only things that moved were men and machines.

market of enormous size for copper. Swansea, with its easily accessible coal seams and its eminently navigable river, had become a mad inferno. Nearly all the copper works in Britain were to be found here, making the town the largest copper-smelting region in the world. Place names like Landore – an anglicization of Glandŵr, 'waters edge' or 'river bank', and Hafod, 'summer dwelling-place' become acridly inappropriate in an area where the copper smoke had such a disastrous effect that: '. . . cattle that feed upon the grass . . . are affected with a great thickening of the knee joints and their teeth suffer so that they must be frequently removed from such localities to preserve them,' and where 80 years later in 1890 the foul conditions of smoke, tastes and smells inspired:

> It came to pass in days of yore
> The Devil chanced upon Landore,
> Quoth he, 'By all this fume and stink
> I can't be far from home I think.'

The best view of the lower valley is from the Llansamlet to Swansea road. On the hillside, looking like the ruins of a pair of gate towers belonging to a 13th-c fortification, are the remains of a block of flats built in 1750 by a Swansea copper master Robert Morris. His philanthropic instincts were not as strong as his business acumen, but were nevertheless commendable. The purpose of the building was to house 40 of his copper and coal workers in the healthy atmosphere of the elevated ground above Landore. Copper was followed by zinc and tinplate, and by the end of the 19thc the Lower Valley was a thriving metallurgical centre of considerable importance. In 1902 the future employment of the valley was guaranteed by the Mond Nickel Works at Clydach, the largest of its kind in the world. This also caused further devastation.

Decline and repair
By the 50's of this century the works that had once thrived could no longer compete with modern techniques of production, and gradually the large lugubrious buildings became the echoing naves of industrial cathedrals. Engine houses, at their best as gothic and proportionate as the finest chapel architecture, became the paradisiac dens of schoolboys; the monastery-like skeletons of foundries became not-so-secret meeting-places. And all around the sulphur heaps, the slag tips, and mounds of rubbish created a new range of mountains. The valley was a slum; something was needed. In the early 60's the Lower Swansea Valley Project was put into operation. General clearance and attempts at revegetation were to be the first attempts in an arduous campaign to obliterate the aftermath of the industrialization of a Norman borough.

19

Welsh industrial communities were close in more senses than one. These terraces are typical of the cramped conditions in which the workers lived.

The expansion that took place in Swansea through copper smelting happened in Merthyr Tydfil through iron, but it happened at an alarmingly rapid rate. By 1801 Merthyr, as it is now generally called, was the largest town in Wales. The area which Daniel Defoe had visited in 1723 and had found to be 'a most agreeable vale opening to the south, with a pleasant river running through it called the Taaff', had become completely transformed by four iron works – Dowlais, Penydarren, Plymouth, and Cyfarthfa – placed near to each other to exploit the natural resources of the area to the full. Guest, Homfray, Bacon, and Crawshay came from various parts of England and between them made Merthyr the most important iron and steel manufacturing town in the world. They also made vast personal fortunes.

In 1860 Merthyr was still the largest town in Wales, with its population of 70,000 mostly living in communities centred on the four main iron works. Its prosperity continued for another 60 years, regardless of the emergence of Cardiff as an urban leviathan and the continued expansion of Swansea. At the end of the first world war the demand for iron and steel suddenly dropped, the economy was fractured, and the 20's brought a crippling depression to the area. Merthyr had become synonymous with martyrdom, and the adjoining hillside community of Dowlais with despair. By the mid-30's it had been declared a Special Area. Today light industry has taken the place of the old, salvage work has been carried out on a ruthless scale, and ironically enough one or two town buildings of architectural interest and representing the very few contributions made to the community by the Iron Masters have been demolished; an instance of civic vandalism rather than a gesture of retaliation.

Desert makers
Benjamin Malkin's description of Merthyr Tydfil should be compared with his observations on the Rhondda Valley, a place which has been charged with associations of the industrial revolution, squalor, and pit disasters for over a century, but which at the beginning of the last century was a pastoral scene where the river: 'fertilizes the valley with its pure transparent stream, rolling over loose stones. . . . Hereabouts, and for some miles to come, there is a degree of luxuriance in the valley, infinitely beyond what my entrance on this district led me to expect. The contrast of the meadows, rich and verdant, with mountains the most wild and romantic, surrounding them on every side, is in the highest degree picturesque.' All that was to change as dramatically as Merthyr changed. The coal industry, which up until 1830 had served the needs of the iron works, now began to exist in its own right.

Other valleys yielded their riches, among them Ogmore and Neath; railways were strained to their limit, and the Marquis of Bute, the biggest of the coal owners, had to build dock after dock at Cardiff – which only a few years previously had been a small market town. Near by a contestant called David Davies opened another dock, thereby converting the peaceful village of Barry into a mammoth terminal. Coal export from the two places made the Bristol Channel the busiest stretch of water in the world. The Pierhead Building in Butetown ('Tiger Bay'), the Coal Exchange at Mount Stuart Square in Cardiff, and the Barry Port Building give some indication of the prestige of the trade. Nothing so grand can be seen in the valleys themselves. Tunnels of identical houses still face each other under the constant frown of a mountain or the threat of a landslide; a solitary row of houses on the hillside looks like a train of derailed coaches. The pine end of the Miners' Library and Institute dominates one view of the village, and the entrance front of the Baptist chapel another. A long row of holes in the dark hillside reminds everybody of the Depression and the strike-ridden years, when miners found their only source of fuel by digging away at the coal outcrops. The band room is still there, but there is no band.

People of the south
The new areas of dense employment and habitation were almost entirely Welsh speaking. Immigrant workers from rural Wales brought with them the oral traditions, the folk songs, and the crafts of their native counties. In the towns and later in the coal valleys, this rich heritage was a vital force in the formation of a new community and a new society; it was also a panacea for the emotional and spiritual ills which result so easily from relentless labour. South Wales in the 19thc created the first Welsh towns, for the most ancient 'towns' in Wales, having been subject to castle administration, were by tradition English. Never until the first half of the last century had so many Welsh people gathered together in a community to pursue their employment as in Merthyr Tydfil. The intensely Welsh spirit of this town found its most effective expression in Nonconformity. From then on the two forces were to have an incalculable influence on the inhabitants of Merthyr and on a vast majority of people in the industrial south. If workmen were able to find new impetus and strength of their Welsh roots as human beings, their situation as employees was completely different. The new society was a breeding ground of discontent, animosity, and revolt.

Another major upheaval in industrial South Wales took place in 1839. This involved the Chartist movement, which fought a hard and often bitter fight for political reform and better social conditions. A demonstration by 5,000 Chartists was held outside the Westgate Hotel, Newport, in November of that year. The incident heralded the first working-class movement in Wales and, indeed, England. As recently as 1910 troops had to be called out to quell the riots of discontented and disillusioned South Wales workers. A disaster of a different nature happened in the coal field in 1913. This was to symbolize the almost inhuman predicament of coalworkers, not only in South Wales but everywhere. At the Universal, Senghennydd, near Caerphilly on 14 October, 439 men perished 2,000ft underground. Half a century later, in the safety and familiar surroundings of their school, a generation of children under eleven years of age were smothered suddenly by an onrush of slurry from the enormous tip of coal waste that had surmounted the village of Aberfan for decades. The news shocked man's mind to a fresh awareness of the horrors of the coalfield; an entire world listened hour-by-hour as the awful fight against masonry and debris proceeded and hope dwindled. Of all the tragedies of South Wales, this seemed the worst.

For all their squalor and sordidness, the south and south-east valleys could do nothing to stifle the natural resilience and ironic humour of the inhabitants. The hard conditions of their existence provided a suitably durable whetstone for their determination and energy. The Welsh proverb roughly translated as 'it takes iron to sharpen iron' might have been a fitting motto for the iron and steel workers and colliers whose fight was as often against the management as their own personal circumstances. The 'them and us' society of the valleys underlined a great deal of the natural conviviality and sociability between immigrants from rural Wales, and helped to forge a warm, closely-knit, and interdependent community which has characterized the area for generations. This has only recently shown the slightest suggestion of change.
In the gregarious nature of the families lay their main defence against a multitude of problems. It produced a facility for repartee, sharpened a mordant wit, encouraged a 'gift of the gab', and engendered a classless society.

The long street
In the 'long street' the great relief from the predictable terrace house was the chapel. If this is a mere visual or architectural distraction for us as visitors today, it was far more than that for the inhabitants during the last 100 years. The building itself, whether a quirky interpretation of the gothic or an inhibited representation of the

neo-classical, meant little to the people of the valley. It was what it stood for that mattered. The chapels were galleried auditoria where the pitch pine worked wonders with the vocal chords and encouraged sounds which could disturb the soul with their clarity and sonority. Trapped human beings were released; the transfer from their subterranean enslavement to the joy of God's eternal paradise was deftly achieved, and Monday-morning early was not to be contemplated. And there was more than hymns, with their allusions to pastures green and sacred portals, wretched sinners or pathetic mortals, relevant or inappropriate, according to mood and circumstance. Great works of the masters were the test pieces of a great choral tradition, and the chapels were the arenas where they were given the honour due to them.

Hell and harmony
Boy choristers of ten years of age would have sung the treble or alto runs of *O Thou that Tellest Good Tidings to Zion* from *The Messiah* or *Lift Thine Eyes* from *Elijah* with an almost professional ease that in no way detracted from their personal enjoyment of the experience. On Monday morning they too would be down the pit or in the rolling mills. Such a world was that of young Joseph Parry from Merthyr Tydfil, working in the colliery at the age of ten and in the iron works two years later, whose body and spirit were alive with the great love of music which had been fostered by Rosser Beynon, the conductor at Soar Independent Chapel. Beynon had started work at the age of eight. He now held regular classes where youngsters were taught to read music, interpret the great oratorios, and learn the new hymn tunes that were appearing in such profusion.

At the age of thirteen Parry went to Pennsylvania with his parents. He worked in the iron mills and studied harmony and composition whenever he had the opportunity, with the result that his great promise won the attention of the Welsh public through his entries in the competitions of the National Eisteddfod. A fund was established to enable him to study at the Royal Academy of Music. He returned only briefly before taking up a music post in Wales, the first of a number which led eventually to the lectureship he held at Cardiff University until his death in 1903. A man of immense energy and enthusiasm, a prodigious worker in all aspects of musical life, and a prolific

Aberfan's memorial to the death of its children is a sharp reminder of conditions in many of the southern valleys.

21

composer producing oratorios in the great tradition with such titles as *Emmanuel* and *Saul*, Joseph Parry was the foremost composer of his day and of the first part of this century. The sound of his name even now commands hushed reverence in chapel circles. Although his oratorios are never sung, and despite the fact that his opera *Blodwen* – which was performed over 500 times in the first fifteen years of its life – is now rarely presented, his hymn tunes are sung with great fervour. This is particularly so in the *Cymanfa Ganu*, an annual singing festival held by representatives of most denominations up and down the valleys and in some rural areas, either on Good Friday or Easter Monday. When this characteristically Welsh institution came into being in the middle of the last century, it was considerably aided by the introduction of a new method of musical notation called tonic sol-fa, in which notes were identified by letters. One of the distinctions between a choir in a rural or working class area and a middle class or professional town choir was that most of the former read sol-fa, while all the latter read 'staff'. Nowadays the complexity and intricacy of modern music have ruled out the possibility of sol-fa completely.

But the voices are still there. Tonic sol-fa or not, the Welshman has an instinctive grasp of harmony and will improvise with ease and satisfaction around a hymn or song that is not part of his inherited repertoire. Now that cars are plentiful, the last bus up the valley on Saturday nights no longer rings with hymns about Christian militancy and songs about Myfanwy, but pubs and clubs still resound with fervent pleas for forgiveness in the minor key. And where can Welsh voices be heard to better advantage than at a rugby international in Cardiff Arms, so near the city centre that the entire community rocks with the glorious blast? This is no mere shouting. A high percentage of the spectators belong to male-voice choirs and mixed choral unions, and singing here demands the same scrupulous care for tone and diction as the chief choral competition at the National Eisteddfod. The first British singer to be knighted for two generations comes from a South Wales valley. Born in the same street as Sir Geraint Evans, Stuart Burrows was one of the world's finest Mozart tenors.

A will to learn
It was not only the love and practise of choral music that was engendered in the chapel during the last century. In a country where opportunities for formal education were sparse and haphazard, workers and their families found that the only provision for literacy was through the Sunday schools which had been established in Wales at the end of the 18thc. The curriculum was based squarely on the Bible and religious themes, and was taught through the medium of Welsh. Although an enormous proportion of the population learned to read, the number of those who could write was by no means as high. Nevertheless, the influence that these schools exerted was immense, and discussion groups which very often resulted from them became the nearest thing to a learning academy that the working men of that period could ever experience. Here, as in certain chapel societies, the sound of words, the thrill of argument, the passion for understanding and the heady rush of rhetoric produced a fiery oratory which the social and industrial landscape along the valleys gave a lacerating edge. This explains the intimate connection between religion and politics in South Wales. It is little wonder that when the Education Act of 1870 introduced compulsory schooling up to the age of thirteen, many Welsh people saw this as their one escape route. If England has been described as a nation of shopkeepers, Wales was to become a nation of preachers and teachers from then for at least three quarters of a century. Both offered an immediate prominence and security in a society blighted with servitude and misfortune.

A new awareness
It was a society that still had no true national identity. It had no institutions that reflected and encouraged a life that was not subservient to an English autocracy which governed, among other establishments, the Church, and which in turn determined the individual's prospects of a university education. In a country which did not have its own university, Welsh Nonconformists were forced to study for degrees in the University of Scotland. The foundation of a University College of Wales at Aberystwyth in 1872, and further university colleges at Cardiff and Bangor in the 1880's, led to a Royal Charter of 1893 and the formation of a federal University of Wales. This had its own authority to award degrees. By 1920 a college at Swansea had been added. Today the Welsh School of Medicine and the Institute of Science and Technology at Cardiff, together with the 1822 Anglican foundation of St David's College Lampeter, are all constituents of the University of Wales. In the wake of the new university came scores of grammar schools in South Wales, and the start of a tradition which was tough and virile in a country where, until comparatively recently and for political as well as economic reasons, the English public school system was completely alien.

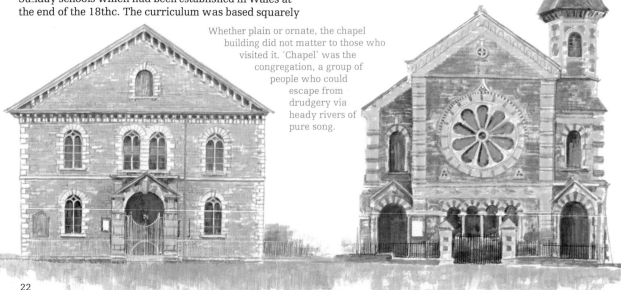

Whether plain or ornate, the chapel building did not matter to those who visited it. 'Chapel' was the congregation, a group of people who could escape from drudgery via heady rivers of pure song.

'Mrs Cocks' was once a common feature of Welsh markets, but the cockle beds are fast being depleted and the industry is on the decline.

The output of the grammar schools of the South Wales valleys is a fascinating sociological phenomenon which has yet to be explored dispassionately. Glib and dismissive though it may seem to attribute their extraordinary success rate to the overpowering urge of its pupils to get away from their early environment, there is nevertheless more than an element of accuracy in such a contention. But parents were great pushers too. Whatever the delights of the great world may offer, origins are still vital and roots have always been a strong source of bizarre comfort and identity. The National Library of Wales at Aberystwyth was opened in 1916 as a result of Glamorgan and Monmouthshire miners having agreed to a levy of a shilling a head on their wages towards a building fund – a spirit of generosity, sacrifice, and national pride similar to that which helped to establish the University College of Wales.

New idealism
Gradually a building programme was being fulfilled which would show the world the result of the Welsh fervour and ferment, painfully grown and strengthened with each decade of the preceding century. It illustrated a new idealism that had been expressed in song as far back as 1856, when Evan James and his son James from Pontypridd composed the tune for *Hen Wlad fy Nhadau – The Land of my Fathers*. This was sung at concerts, eisteddfodau, and other large gatherings, and gradually won for itself the status of a national anthem. In 1930, at Ynysangharad Park in their native town, a monument to father and son was unveiled. This was another visible proof of the growing awareness of Wales.

The National Museum houses geological, botanical, and zoological galleries; a Department of Archaeology, which is also responsible for the Legionary Museum at Caerleon outside Newport; an industrial section, which shows the development of the Welsh iron, steel, tinplate, and coal industries; and a Department of Art containing fine paintings by Richard Wilson, Augustus John, Ceri Richards, and works by English and European artists of Welsh places and scenery. Thanks to the Gwendoline Davies Bequest the museum possesses one of the best collections in Britain of the French Impressionists, including the famous *La Parisienne* by Renoir. In the turmoil of the Industrial Revolution South Wales managed to produce extraordinary examples of Fine Art, including the delicate porcelains of Nantgarw and Swansea, and the Pontypool 'japan ware' – a special treatment given to tin before being fashioned in a variety of shapes for luxurious display as well as functional use. The museum displays a good cross-section of examples of all three. Elsewhere is Rodin's bronze group, entitled *The Kiss*.

Marble is a splendid setting in the City Hall for the series of sculptures of Welsh heroes presented by the first Lord Rhondda, D A Thomas the coal owner. This was a fitting gift from a man who had been closely involved with the making of modern Wales and who had profited greatly from the enterprise. Not all beneficiaries were so liberal or so civic-minded. One exception was Richard Glynn Vivian, a Swansea copper manufacturer and a relative of Hussey Vivian, the first Lord Swansea. In 1905 he offered the town corporation £10,000 to build a gallery which he intended to endow with his own collection of paintings and porcelain. By 1911 the building had been completed, and it is today one of the most enjoyable and attractive art galleries in the country. Exhibits include a marvellous collection of Swansea porcelain and a wide range of fine paintings, including a number by Evan Walters, a local artist of coal-mining background who died in the 1950's. Walters found inspiration in the faces of the colliers and in members of his own family, but perhaps the most striking work is his portrait of a *Penclawdd Cockle Woman* – a rotund, rubicund, and jolly creature who typifies that garrulous and lovable breed of stall-holder in Swansea Market, and who still ventures up the valley as far as Morriston.

Great institutions
Years ago, 'Mrs Cocks' – the same name applied to any and all of them – would walk along the main road with all the grace of a caryatid, balancing on her head a large wooden tub full of cockles from the Burry Estuary in North Gower. She could be sure of finding ready buyers in each house every Saturday morning. Nowadays the orange plastic bucket and bowl have replaced the tubs, but the cockles still taste as good. The future of this industry is a matter of concern to the Penclawdd families, who have for the last few years found their livelihood seriously threatened by oyster catchers who swoop down by the hundreds and feast themselves in the cockle beds. Very soon the sight of carts, ponies, and small dark figures bent double over their work way out in the glistening sands of the estuary will be seen only in family photographs and film archives. The cocklewoman also sells laverbread, a great speciality of the area. This green-black sludge is made of seaweed treated in a way known only by the few, and is delicious when fried in oatmeal and eaten with ham and eggs – a rare delicacy, in spite of its appearance. Swansea market in many ways is Swansea; a huge glass-covered, celery-scented exchange of the world's inconsequentialities, where buying a couple of chops can be an experience and where a 'lady' butcher

Workers from Swansea found relief in the beautiful surroundings of Mumbles Head.

sells her "am, steek, and poke' with a refined reverence for her goods. It is an institution. 'Ralph the Books' is also an institution, but not because it was a favourite haunt of Dylan Thomas – that is why it was a favourite haunt of his. Ralph and Winnie exist in their own right. An effervescent host and an exclamatory hostess in a world of bargains, frayed encyclopaedias, 'finds', wilting pelicans, and rare talk ranging from a polite enquiry about out-of-print paperbacks to a diatribe about recent major surgical experiences in the new hospital.

The Royal Institution is a royal institution, 'the museum that should be in a museum' as Dylan Thomas described it. One of the finest neo-classical buildings in Swansea, this stands in an area where uprooted railway tracks, demolished arches, shunting grounds, a filled-in dock, and a row of crumbling early 19th-c houses give it an ironic grandeur and make the visitor wonder how a corporation could have made such a mess of their post-war rebuilding.

Swansea nostalgia

For many acquainted with the area the sight of the truncated front of a red Mumbles Railway coach, now kept behind the Institution, will produce the most poignant recollections of the electric train that used to ply between Stamison and Mumbles pier. It ran in close proximity to the road, and for part of the way to the main Shrewsbury line along the lovely bow of Swansea bay, stopping at names like Brynmill, Blackpill, Norton, Oystermouth, and Southend. If Richard Trevithick's steam-driven locomotive drawing a load of ten tons and 70 people from Penydarren to Quaker's Yard in 1804 was the first of its kind in the world, the Mumbles Railway could claim the distinction of being the oldest passenger railway in the world. In 1807 horses drew carriages along its tracks from Swansea to Oystermouth. Steam and an extension as far as Mumbles followed, and in 1929 it became electric. Successive generations of inhabitants used it daily; day visitors revelled in the sway of its double-decker coaches and the views from the windows; holiday-makers had rarely seen anything to compare with it, for there were few electric trains in Britain that offered that combination of coach and rail. In 1960 the South Wales Transport Company decided to dispense with this pleasurable service; the trains were destroyed and the rails were uprooted, leaving only memories, the odd photograph, and a badly-congested road between Swansea and Mumbles. In the early days of the Mumbles Railway Swansea was

becoming a popular watering place. There were a few houses on the hillside overlooking the bay, a regency villa here and there between the town and Oystermouth would have drawn the attention of a water colourist, and a shrimpman would have inspired another. Writer and poet Walter Savage Landor compared the bay to the Bay of Naples. Today the similarity is even more striking; they are both heavily polluted. And yet, if the eastern side of the bay is damned, the western side still offers a great deal of holiday pleasure. Oystermouth is a thriving shopping centre and Southend a lively haunt of yachts, motor boats, and water skiers. Beyond Mumbles Head and its lighthouse are the two small coves of Bracelet and Limeslade, and beyond them again but approached from Oystermouth is the popular and comparatively 'developed' Langland Bay. Also here are the ample sands of Caswell, with a freshwater stream cutting it in two. This is the Gower, a different world from the industrial Swansea Valley. For decades the copper, coal, steel, and tinplate communities found their relief and release in the free air of the coast and in the golden arcs of its beaches. Their steamer still calls at Mumbles pier on its way to North Devon. Trade is not what it was in the days of the old paddle steamers, when 'Combe' was more accessible and convenient for carless people than a number of the more far-flung bays of Gower, and the service that used to operate between Cardiff and Weston-super-Mare has disappeared completely. For the older generation 'Combe' will be synonymous with rushing to catch the one o'clock train to St Thomas' station in the heart of dockland – where pubs with names like Cuba Inn were agog with turban and fez – and with crossing the Bristol Channel in a state of masochistic suspense, often confirming the old sailors' adage that it was one of the worst currents in the world.

Norman legacy

If the Swansea Valley is still very Welsh – in spirit, if not altogether in language – Gower is still very English. It always has been. The south-western part of the peninsula is particularly so, for this was the Gower Anglicana of the Norman Marcher Lordship, as opposed to the Gower Wallicana in the north-eastern section. This explains why some of the villages of the peninsula – Reynoldston in particular – are so 'English' in shape and atmosphere. They are a legacy of the Norman settlements and have developed very little in modern times. In the Gower Wallicana the Welsh-speaking inhabitants did not live in such closely-knit and organized communities, but in isolated farmsteads. The social change that swamped this area came during the end of the last century and the beginning of this one. The result was the typically 'Welsh village – long, unplanned, and industrial.

Cowbridge is a town which personifies the 'Englishness' of the Glamorgan Vale.

The Gower lies west of Swansea Bay. East is the Vale of Glamorgan, a mixture of indigenous and extraneous influences. The south of the vale has been relatively untouched by frenzied expansion and survives as another example of the development and growth of Norman settlements. The names Flemingston, Boverton, and Beaupre are indications of their non-Welsh ancestry. The busy A48 between Cardiff and Swansea cuts through the northern part of the vale – though it is not a vale at all in any strict geographical sense, but a particularly fertile lowland area – affording glimpses of a number of villages and their thatched cottages. It was perhaps no mere coincidence that a French passenger coming in to land at Rhoose airport remarked that the vale looked like 'a little Normandy'. The English ethos and atmosphere of the vale had been further intensified during the last half century by the influx of professional classes and wealthy businessmen, who have found it within convenient travelling distance of the greatly expanding city of Cardiff. The trend has increased in the last decade, leaving a number of villages untouched but causing uncharacteristic bungaloid growths in other areas.

Churches in the vale

The Englishness of the vale is seen in its most concentrated form in the small walled town of Cowbridge, often called the capital of the vale, a pleasing country community which has regained most of its former leisurely and untroubled atmosphere since it was by-passed. Although a Vale of Glamorgan Hunt involves very many of the people who would be part of the Cowbridge Show organization, hunting in South Wales is not confined to the 'set' with whom one normally associates the sport. Llandeilo Farmers – which hunts in Gower and along the northern edges of the Swansea Valley – is not typical, nor indeed is the Banwen Miners' Hunt in the Vale of Neath and along the southern Breconshire plateau, once the hunting preserve of the Welsh Princes. That they exist at all is a reflection of the Welshman's attitude to sport rather than an observance of any social mores. Rugby in England is a middle-class sport overlaid with public-school tradition; in Wales it is a great leveller and as classless as the Welsh Nonconformist chapel – works managers tended to occupy a corner place in the Big Seat, it is true, but deacons were democratically elected!

One of the glories of the vale is the wealth of its old churches, a sure indication of Englishry and Englishness even though they owe their foundations to Celtic Saints.

The Welshman who was to make one of the greatest impressions on modern Wales was born in the vale in 1747. Although his entire adult life was devoted to the pursuit of literature – often in a most unorthodox way – Edward Williams or Iolo Morgannwg (Iolo of Glamorgan) learned to read by watching his father sculpting names on grave stones. He became a stonemason himself, but found increasing interest and pleasure in study, and eventually spent a great deal of his time and energy forging manuscripts and writing poetry in the guise and style of a number of Welsh medieval writers. He caused some demanding and expert detective work from eminent literary scholars earlier this century. His greatest claim to distinction, however, is that he was responsible for introducing the *Gorsedd* ceremony into the National Eisteddfod, for he supposedly resurrected and gave prominence to the ancient rites of the Druidic Circle. The idea gained great popularity and has played an important part in the proceedings of the festival ever since.

The vale was an active academy of the early Celtic saints, and although there are few remains of original foundations or any substantial visible relics of the formation of the Celtic Church, there is an unmistakable feel and atmosphere of a tradition as strong as any evidence which art or architecture could provide. Here again, as in southern Gower, the idea of a communal entity prior to the 19thc is of great social as well as architectural interest. This is an observation that only comes about because of the close proximity between the industrial scene on the one hand and the rural and country-town community on the other. Both southern Gower and the southern part of the Vale of Glamorgan are south of the coal field. Beyond the coal field, to the north of the great divide of the Brecon Beacons, is another world which owes little, if anything, to the Industrial Revolution.

Geographical boundaries

On the western extremity is the Llwchwr (Loughor in English) estuary, which divides the north coast of the Gower and the long ribbon development which extends from Bynea to Burry Port. The southern frame consists of the Bristol Channel, which gradually eases itself into the mouth of the Severn. Between the Brecon Beacons and the coastal plain are a number of almost parallel valleys running southwards, as if a monstrous primeval being had torn away at the terrain with its rapacious claws and

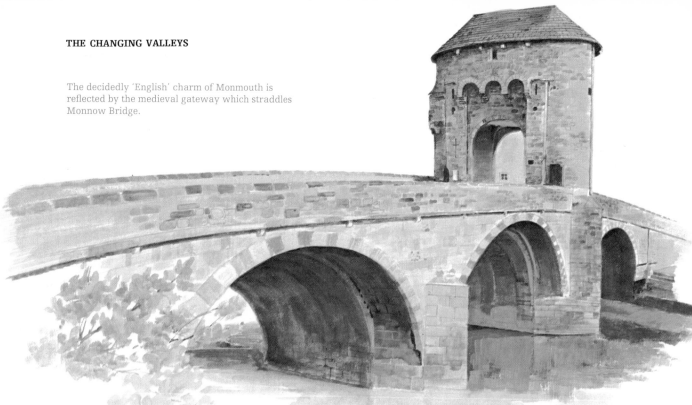

The decidedly 'English' charm of Monmouth is
reflected by the medieval gateway which straddles
Monnow Bridge.

dug out deep, narrow gorges. This is what is recognized
as the 'modern' Wales, for most of the families living there
can claim only 120-years standing at most. North of the
Beacons and east of Abergavenny are scenes of
outstanding natural beauty, and a pace of life that has
been quickened by the time of the next television
programme rather than anything more drastic. On coming
into South Wales from the Midlands the visitor climbs
from Abergavenny to Brynmawr to start the long parade
along the Heads of the Valleys, an emotive name and a
sight that sums up the social and economic history of
South Wales in under 50m. The change of scenery at
Brynmawr is as dramatic as any change of scenery can
be in South Wales. Farm, moorland, industry, and Italian
cafés all come together in a bizarre, disorganized mass.
West is the solid floor of the Neath Valley, where the
Wordsworthian cataract at Pontneddfechan and the
remoteness of Ystradfellte are strange, unknown qualities.
But the Neath Valley itself is a recent success story, a
beautiful vale which has almost been revived to its former
state of pride. Chepstow has become even more charming
and infinitely less neurotic now that enormous lorries do
not trundle down the hill, and Newport – the border town
in so many respects – has once more asserted itself. Near
to Bristol and much nearer to London than it used to be,
the town has started to take a new and intense pride in
its present, past, and future. When Newport played the
schizoid game of wondering if it were either in Wales or in
England, there was never any question as to which
country a rugby player wished to represent. Being only
12m from Cardiff has had a great deal to do with it, and
certainly guaranteed the highest standards in both teams.
Both Cardiff and Newport spectators have had their
money's worth for generations. Welsh in few things but in
its attitude towards rugby, Newport was an anomaly.

The tradition continues in Monmouth, farther north-east
and completely un-Welsh. A Roman encampment, a town
built around a Norman castle on the border in an area
unaffected by the Industrial Revolution, Monmouth
developed into an English market of considerable charm.
Brecon, the birthplace of the actress Sarah Siddons, is
almost exclusively English-speaking. The curator of the

museum is a staunch Welsh speaker, and one or two
shopkeepers seem to be naturally and unpretentiously
dedicated to the Welsh books and prints in stock. The
cathedral, together with St Mary's Church in Swansea,
governs the diocese of Swansea and Brecon. Like the
diocese of Newport, this was formed after the
establishment of the independent Church in Wales in the
1920's, but in attitude it is no more Welsh than the
atmosphere of Llandaff Cathedral, just outside Cardiff.
The latter was a casualty of wartime bombing, but was
restored in the 50's and is an unforgettably splendid
shrine for Epstein's aluminium figure of Christ in Majesty.

Welsh country houses
The stranger to South Wales will see in the region's
prehistoric and Roman remains, its vast network of ruined
castles, its cathedrals and churches, its farmsteads,
undisturbed villages, and market towns, the history
of the whole of Wales up until the 19thc. If one were
discussing the parallel development of an English
community, one aspect which would demand attention
would be the growth of great country houses and the vast
estates which supported them. These have governed the
social and political pattern of the country throughout the
ages, and through the work of European and British
artists, architects, and craftsmen have become inhabited
galleries of some of the finest works of art. What, then,
of South Wales, and indeed of Wales? Was the social
structure here so different that the phenomenon did not
exist, or is it that such houses do exist but are not open to
the public? There is a historical reason why there are no
great palaces or stately homes of the stature and splendour
of Hatfield and Burghley, or Wilton and Badminton, in
Wales – or indeed, houses on a far less grand scale. Since
the reign of Henry VIII and his Act of Union of 1536 the
Welsh squirearchy and gentry have realized that their
prestige, if not their wealth, would depend less and less
on the Welsh social framework and more on London.
Opportunities in politics, the law, and commerce depended
not only on the English language, but on living as near to
the capital as possible. This was the beginning of a
strange social erosion which was to affect not only the
domestic architecture of the Welsh aristocracy and gentry,
but which was ultimately to have a fateful influence on
the Welsh language.

Beaupre Castle is one of the few Welsh houses that can be termed a 'stately home'.

Many manor houses were left empty, or were tenanted and eventually became farmhouses while their owners made fortunes in London. No grand house was built by this new Tudor class to parade the wealth acquired by fresh opportunities, as was the case with the Trevor houses of Trevalyn and Plas Teg in North Wales. The family of Allt-yr-Ynys, ancestors of the great Elizabethan statesmen who built Hatfield and Burghley, never returned; Lord Pembroke, the builder of Wilton House, had ancestral roots deep in the soil of South Wales – the same roots as the Earl of Worcester, who abandoned the magnificent Raglan Castle so brutally reduced after the civil war, built himself Badminton, and established the dukedom of Beaufort. Other families kept a London house as well as the Welsh home. One of exceptional interest is Fonmon Castle in the Vale of Glamorgan, which like the two North Wales castles of Powis and Chirk, and the West Wales Picton Castle, has been continually inhabited since the 13thc.

A number of manor houses in South Wales have been restored during this century. Many of the larger 17th- and 18th-c houses have become publicly owned, and some of the cumbersome structures built with industrial wealth have been either institutionalized or demolished. Those which are open to the public, or whose grounds and gardens may be visited, are noted here since they reflect – even in their present state – a great deal of the conditions and circumstances which prevailed at the time of their construction, or the social changes, upheavals, and uncertainties which brought about their transformation.

A time to build

Raglan Castle is a ruin in the care of the Department of the Environment, a most evocative example of the transformation of castle into country mansion. A large part of the pleasure of the visit is to look for as much surviving evidence of the domestic appurtenances and decorative detail as possible. Enough of the fabric of Weobley Castle remains to give a very clear indication of the accommodation of a large private house which was defensible. In a way the term 'castle' is a misnomer, as there was not enough space to keep a garrison here. The building is in fact a fortified house of the late 13thc, with many later additions. Again, by strict definition Old Beaupre Castle near Cowbridge is a misnomer, since it is a ruined medieval manor house which was rebuilt during the reign of Elizabeth and which has one of the most ambitious and aesthetically pleasing porches of any house in Wales. A three-storey building, it is adorned with a pair

of columns to the height of the frieze, and incorporates three Orders: Doric on the ground floor, flanking the four-centred Tudor arch; Ionic on the first, both sides of an elaborate shield of arms of the family and ancestors of Richard Bassett, who was responsible for the addition; and Corinthian on the second, giving further enrichment to the eight-light mullion and transom window which occupies most of the floor. The elevation is surmounted by a scrolled pediment of involved classical motifs, which give the structure a wonderfully slender grace and dominates the courtyard. Although the outer gate was built fourteen years previously, it embodies a number of the decorative features which were to be given greater attention in the porch. The Welsh motto which it bears, *'Gwell Angau na Chywilydd'* – 'Better death than dishonour', was adopted by the Welch Regiment.

A similar courtyard reminiscent of an Oxbridge college quadrangle can be seen at Tretower Court near Crickhowell, or Crughywel. A medieval house associated with the Vaughan family, of whom the metaphysical poet Henry Vaughan was a member, this is the best preserved building of its type and period in South Wales. Basically it is a 14th- and 15th-c house, but additions were made up until the first quarter of the 17thc. Towards the end of the 18thc it became a farm, but earlier this century it came into the care of the local historical society, who entrusted it to the Ministry of Public Buildings and Works. Restoration work has now revealed the dignity of the Great Hall with its handsome oriel window, the service quarters, the retiring rooms, and the gatehouse. A wall-walk along the curtain suggests a certain consideration for military defence, even at a time when increasing wealth and attention could be given to the more peaceful pursuit of leisure and comfort. In its state of completeness Tretower is probably the only domestic building in Wales which can compare with the magnificent and much larger and earlier fortified manor house of Stokesay Castle in Shropshire.

A fine 16th-c country house open to the public is Llanvihangel Court in the village of Llanvihangel Crucorney, 5m outside Abergavenny on the Hereford road. Originally a medieval hall-type house, it underwent considerable renovation in the mid 16thc and displays excellent plaster work and panelling contemporary with the alterations. The interior of the house was redesigned after the Restoration, but unlike a number of houses of its size and type it did not fall victim to 19th-c 'improvements', and remains as a very evocative example of a manor house which was aggrandized as a result of Elizabethan expansion and security. Another 16th-c hall-type house is St Fagans Castle, so called because it is sited within the curtain walls of the original fortification – the scene of the last battle of the civil war in Wales. It is a handsome symmetrical house of the traditional E-type plan, and relies little on any form of adornment. Its gables are a distinctive feature. It was given to the National Museum of Wales by the Earl of Plymouth in 1947 to house the Welsh Folk Museum, a unique institution in Britain. The interior is furnished with donations and bequests, and contains a wealth of traditional Welsh furniture and domestic appliances, as well as the more sophisticated and refined examples of 18th-c cabinet work. Each piece is seen to its full advantage. The rooms are arranged according to function and period, thereby creating very rich and colourful tableaux of historical progress.

The vast grounds of the museum itself are dotted with a comprehensive selection of re-erected buildings from all over Wales, including a cruck barn, a woollen mill, a 16th-c half-timbered farmhouse, a 17th-c stone-built farmhouse, an early 19th-c tollgate house, a cockpit, and a Unitarian chapel. Between them these structures offer a very vivid and often moving reconstruction of traditional Welsh rural and pastoral life, a lifestyle which would have existed in Cardiff itself as recently as the turn of the 19thc. With its formal gardens, its balustraded terraces, its clipped yews, and its woodland, St Fagans retains the atmosphere of a historic country house, while its grounds offer a microcosm of most other aspects of Welsh life. Many 16th-c country houses have lost all semblance of their original social position. An interesting anomaly for more than one reason is the case of Llancaiach Fawr. Peace and expansion during the Tudor period had made for a settled society, and considerable mansions were built even in upland districts. What is interesting about Llancaiach is not that it followed the tradition of becoming a farm, but that it has survived as a farm and house of some consequence although now situated in the heart of industrial South Wales and the middle of the Glamorgan coalfield – within yards of a miners' housing estate. The finest 17th-c country house in South Wales is Tredegar Park, where twin red-brick lodges and rapidly decaying steep roofs are now under constant threat from juggernauts coming off the Cardiff to Newport road to join the M4. A red-brick house with mullioned windows and swags, it has some distinguished panelling and plaster work and an imposing staircase, all of which have been in danger during the last few years.

Institutions such as schools, hospitals, conference centres, and colleges have saved a number of large houses in South Wales from demolition or oblivion. In one or two cases their chief interest is that they belonged to famous people who were perhaps not Welsh, but who were such notable personalities or people of such rare gifts that their impact was tremendous. Such a person was Adelina Patti the Victorian opera singer, who lived in Craig-y-nos Castle in the upper reaches of the Swansea Valley. In Craig-y-Nos she built her own opera house, complete with prompt box and a proscenium arch, which reflected all the extravagant taste of 19th-c opera house interiors. If she was the Queen of Song, she was also the Queen of the Swansea Valley. The house now serves as a hospital, but a decade ago Madame Patti's miniature opera house (about 150 seats) was used by the Neath Operatic Society, and since then for a fortnight every June they perform grand opera here, with well-known singers in the principal rôles.

A new aristocracy
St Donat's Castle in the Vale of Glamorgan is now the home of Atlantic College, the international sixth-form school, and is occasionally open in the summer months. It was refurbished in the 30's by Randolph Hearst, the American newspaper magnate, on whom it was said Orson Welles based his film character Citizen Kane. Here he permanently entertained his friend the actress Marion Davies, and for some time the place was the centre of a rich and important international set. The original castle was founded by William Stradling, one of the twelve Norman knights who conquered Glamorgan, but a later building on the same site changed hands several times and at the turn of the century it was owned for a time by the Williams family of Aberpergwm in the Neath Valley. The expansion of his collieries had become so great that his own house and comforts became all but engulfed by industry. Other coal-owners in South Wales made no such mistake, but built their mansions far enough away from the less acceptable aspects of their wealth. In 1893 John Cory built Dyffryn House about 5m outside Cardiff off the Cowbridge road, and this is now used for residential courses. On an infinitely grander and more ambitious scale is Cardiff Castle, built by the third Marquis of Bute, who was also responsible for commissioning the architect William Burgess to restore 13th-c Castell Coch or Red Castle. Situated north of Cardiff on the Caerphilly road, this structure is now an extravagant Victorian interpretation of a medieval fortification. Copper manufacturers also built their houses the right end of town. Two houses owned by the Vivian family, later Lord Swansea, are Clyne Castle in Blackpill on the Mumbles road and Singleton Abbey. Both are owned by the University College of Swansea. Although neither is open to the public, they

The Welsh National Folk Museum at St Fagans displays all aspects of the country's vernacular culture – including complete historical buildings re-erected in the grounds.

Music – in particular choral music – is a way of life in South Wales.

are surrounded by fine gardens which are seen at their best in May and June, when the azaleas and rhododendrons are in their prime. The Iron Masters, on the other hand, built their grand residences as near to the fiery furnace as possible. This phenomenon was practised not only in Merthyr and Hirwaun, but also in the Swansea Valley. When William Crawshay employed Richard Lugar to design his house, he followed the fashion for turrets and battlements. The result, Cyfarthfa Castle, is worthy of the name and today houses a museum of local and industrial history.

One of the most impressive 'castles' in South Wales has been unoccupied since the end of the second world war. Margam Castle was designed by Thomas Hopper, the same architect as for Penrhyn Castle, and started in 1827. The house and the deer park in which it stands were bought in 1973 by Glamorgan County Council – as it then was – at a cost of £455,000 and with an eye to making it a country park. This body's successor, the West Glamorgan County Council, hopes that plans will have been completed for an official opening in 1975, although there is no certainty that the mansion itself or the beautiful 18th-c orangery built on the site of a former house will not be demolished. The cost of restoration is monumentally high. Belonging to none of the above categories is the stately 19th-c pile of Pennoyre, a large country house in the classical style near Brecon. Now a country club and golfing centre, its external features have so far escaped the 'improvements' carried out with such enthusiasm indoors. It is some consolation that it will take a mammoth building programme to obliterate the view from this house.

A Place for the arts
When the secretary of a small South Wales choir wrote to the nearest prison a few years ago to discover if its inmates would appreciate an evening of choral music, the reply was that there was a waiting list of three years. The story is true and reveals an essential part of the South Walian's temperament: he prefers performing to being a member of an audience, and he would rather play than be a spectator. Known for such a long time as a country of amateurs, Wales has nevertheless been changing its status in the field of the arts and entertainment during the last ten years. Previously all those singers, instrumentalists, actors, and comedians either went to try their luck in London or led a dual life at home, becoming contorted and tortured by the pull of daily employment one side and rigorous evening rehearsals or performances the other.

Cardiff these days is playing an increasingly important part in the life and prospects of a new breed of entertainer – the Welsh-speaking professional. Such a status was impossible until recently, for in a country of few theatres those that managed to survive served only an English-speaking audience. The lot of the Welsh entertainer was a poor one. The expansion of radio and television has changed all that, and opportunities for musicians, actors, scriptwriters, and funny-men are opening up week by week with the growing market for variety and light entertainment, discos, schools programmes, children's programmes, chat-shows, arts features, and straight plays. Young solo singers, groups, comedians, and comperes have enlivened a scene that until the mid-60's was careful, if not mannered, and diplomatic if not downright stodgy. Many young performers are committed to the Welsh cause, and active in the fight for the survival of the language, arranging and appearing in a number of charitable or social shows each week and often sparking off highly-successful sessions of a completely spontaneous nature. Few of them have ambitions to perform outside Wales, unless to Welsh people in English cities, or at the occasional festival in one of the other countries. Their identity is in their Welshness, and their political motivation is often as strong as their artistic dedication. They are from all over Wales, they wear trendy gear, some of them have smart cars, and they have all helped to make Wales a direct contemporary of England.

Stage and small screen
The television drama studios of Cardiff, with rare exceptions, produce Welsh-speaking plays. The English output comes from London in the case of the BBC, and from Bristol in the case of HTV. In both studios, by some strange set of coincidences, the camera men, floor crew, vision and sound mixers, and most of the people concerned with the production, except the director and his secretary, are non-Welsh speaking. It seems particularly unjust that they never have a chance of seeing and understanding something which involves so much of their energy.

Because *Theatr Cymru* – the Welsh-speaking section of the Welsh Drama Company – is based in Bangor, a number of actors have recently formed an experimental company in Cardiff. Calling themselves *Theatr yr Ymylon,* 'Fringe Theatre', they are without a home, and their aims for the future are understandably greater than their achievements. But they are a lively and hardworking group, and their determination to establish a secure company which will act not only in Cardiff but in Welsh rural areas is a commendable attempt to improve the standard of performances still so often seen and uncritically accepted by audiences. The lot of the monoglot English actor in Wales is not such a happy one. There is

The flourishing Welsh National Opera Company have been fully operational since 1968.

insufficient work to keep him employed in radio and television, unless he is used as a presenter or anchor-man. The only professional theatre outside Cardiff is the Grand – Swansea's civic theatre – with its own repertory for only part of the year. Pantomime and summer touring companies take up the rest of the time. The Sherman, Cardiff's newest theatre, so far has had limited opportunity to show what its policy for a resident company is going to be, but ideally it should provide work for a nucleus of Welsh actors who could be seen in plays by Welsh-born as well as English and European dramatists. So far, one of the most dramatic nations in Europe has had no drama. The St David's Trust was set up more years ago than most people care to remember with a view to establishing a Welsh National Theatre in Cardiff; a stage which could occasionally lure back to Wales the famous Welsh names in the English theatre and film world who have had little if any opportunity to act on a stage in their native country for years. In the meantime, of course, both Richard Baker and Stanley Baker have become directors of HTV. The theatre would also be a training ground for young Welsh actors in both languages. Such an institution might at last give new writers, as well as those who have concentrated their energies on other literary forms and on the mass media, the incentive to devote some of their time to working in a permanent professional theatre.

The Prince of Wales Theatre once staged some of the finest London productions; now it is a continuous flickering exhibition of Scandinavian celluloid and other similar attractions. Only the New Theatre is left to remind people of the days of the large provincial theatres which attracted some of the most distinguished names in the entertainment world. The future of this solitary survivor was in the balance a few years ago, but threats of demolition have been quietened since it has become Cardiff's civic theatre. It seems likely to remain the nearest thing to a home – until Cardiff or Wales can produce the obvious alternative – for the Welsh National Opera Company is now affiliated to the Welsh Drama Company.

Musicians and writers
The Welsh National has been fully professional since 1968 and has been supported since 1970 by its own orchestra, the Welsh Philharmonia, which performs in various concerts and festivals when opera schedules permit. With

the BBC Welsh Orchestra becoming the BBC Welsh Symphony Orchestra in August 1974, and celebrating the new status with a performance at the Henry Wood Promenade Concert, Wales now has two orchestras. Both are based in Cardiff and both are without a suitable concert hall in which to be heard to full advantage. Until now the concert studio of Broadcasting House has been used for both recorded and live broadcasts, with invited audiences, and regular mid-day concerts have been broadcast from the City Hall. But the capital city still has no accommodation worthy of resident musicians or touring orchestras from England and Europe, nor indeed a centre which could show that South Wales is an area which has a regard for the arts in all their live and varied forms. This drawback has not impeded the very healthy growth of two major music festivals: that at Llandaff Cathedral every June, and the more recently formed Cardiff Festival of 20th-c Music, which makes use of a range of accommodation according to the demands of the programme. In the same way, the Vale of Glamorgan Festival, only 15m or so from Cardiff, takes advantage of the settings of historic churches and country-house drawing rooms to enhance the nature and period of the music presented.

The lack of suitably appointed accommodation is not confined to Cardiff, for there is no real concert hall in the whole of South Wales. The Swansea Festival of Music, one of the first to be instituted after the second world war, is housed for the most part in the Brangwyn Hall – a multi-purpose, coffin-shaped temple to Frank Brangwyn's murals and civic pride. The alternative throughout the area is either the 1930's cinema or the school hall, both so inadequate that it is always a source of amazement that the crushed morale of orchestras is not seen more often.

Artists other than performers can, and usually have to, function most of the time on their own. The fact that there are few publishing houses in Cardiff and no literary agents means that the writers who live in the capital live there through personal choice or by accident, rather than through professional necessity. If there are few 'English' professional writers in Wales, there are far fewer if any able to earn a living through writing in Welsh. However, through the mass media and substantial support from the Welsh Art's Council, this is becoming more and more a possibility. The new Art's Council Bookshop 'Gallery' reflects the growing status of the Welsh novelist and poet in a non-eisteddfodic environment. In the past neither live drama nor live music would have survived in any professional capacity in Wales without generous backing from the Art's Council; now a similar attitude of largesse is being shown towards writers. Bursaries, travel scholarships, and awards have given writers in both languages a prestige, an independence, and a self-respect. In the case of the writer in Welsh, whose sole source of remuneration (apart, of course, from the mass media) was the eisteddfod prizes (often a gesture rather than a financial reality), these schemes have been particularly important. Dial-a-poem, lectures to schools, and poetry recitals to literary clubs have all helped to break down the image of the Welsh poet as a druidical figure intoning from the carved oak of his bardic chair.

Growth of the arts in Wales, the reclamation of industrial wastelands, and an enlightened appreciation of Welsh culture are encouraging signs of a virile and healthy society which reflects a growing national consciousness. This reveals itself as much in the Welsh craftshops as in the Welsh Language Society.

A Quieter Splendour

Largely without the spectacular, often violent features of the north and south, Mid Wales is nevertheless just as unique in its own, gentler fashion

The Breiddens, a gateway to Mid Wales

To define Mid Wales as a geographical entity is not easy, since differing viewpoints tend to include one area and exclude another. But for present purposes it can be taken, based broadly on the old counties, as comprising all Montgomeryshire and Radnorshire, Cardiganshire down as far as the Aberaeron to Lampeter road, and Breconshire north of the River Irfon. Since there is no major characteristic that dominates the area, such as the Snowdonia massif of the north or the mining valleys of the south, Mid Wales reveals itself as a land of vignettes, each with an individuality of its own. Some of these merge with those adjoining, while others contrast with their neighbouring areas.

The Breidden gateway

The Breiddens can be seen long before the visitor gets anywhere near Wales, a long scallop-edged series of whalebacks tailing away from the triple peaks of the Golfa, the Breidden, and Middletown Hill towards the English border, which lies only just behind them. Opposite is the Long Mountain, a single long ridge with a Roman road running along its crest, reached by three approach roads from three different sides with the picturesque names of the Heldre, Pentre, and Stubb. On the Breidden there were prehistoric settlements and a hill fort, and the monument to Admiral Rodney set up by the gentlemen of Shropshire and Montgomeryshire is still standing after two renovations. It is a landmark visible for miles around. The twin Golfa Hill also has a monument on it, though less imposing, which was erected a few years ago to a gypsy queen's son who wanted his ashes scattered on a hill overlooking the Severn valley and Llansantffraid. The queen herself has an elaborate tombstone surmounted by a freestanding angel figure in the village churchyard. On the scarp face of the Breidden is a vast quarry which has left a bare rock wall hundreds of feet in height from top to base. At the foot are the quarry buildings, and a little way away is the Post Office radio station at Criggion. Its multitudes of aerials, some of them anchored to the hill by steel hawsers suspended from soaring pylons, form a web of wires above the meadows.

This stretch of the Border from the northern boundary of the county at Llanymynech to Welshpool and Newtown is the Vale of Powys, a pastoral countryside with the Severn meandering quietly through lush meadows, heavily embanked against floods. This is an anglicized area of Wales, with English the normal speech of the people and houses very similar to those across the Border – some red-brick, others half-timbered. The Vale of Powys is a tangle of narrow, winding lanes and small roads which link diminutive villages and hamlets, but this strip of lowland pasture is no more than 10m wide. It contains another entry from England, less spectacular than the Breidden Gateway but with an interesting historical association. Right on the Border between Alberbury and Coedway is an oak tree known as the Prince's Oak, with a plate set into the bank below it recording that here George IV as Prince of Wales set foot in his Principality for the first time.

Just across the river from Buttington was the important monastery of Strata Marcella, of which nothing now remains except the site in a meadow alongside the Welshpool to Oswestry road. The Shropshire Union Canal sweeps in from under the Rhallt to accompany this highway for 2m to Pool Quay. In the whole of Mid Wales there are only three sets of permanent traffic lights, and they are all situated in the Vale of Powys. One is at Llandrinio Bridge between the Prince's Oak and Four Crosses; a second is at the Cross in the centre of Welshpool; and the third is at Brynderwen Bridge, which spans the Severn between Welshpool and Newtown. The lowland country comes to an abrupt end at Llanymynech, just above where the Vyrnwy joins the Severn as it changes its northward course to turn east into the English Midlands. This is an international village, with the Anglo-Welsh frontier actually running through the houses of the main street. Behind the village is the great wall of Llanymynech Rocks, and within the hill of which they form the edge is a cave system which the Romans mined for copper and lead. Roman coins have been found here, and there is a legend that music can sometimes be heard in the caves – spirit music of a fiddler who once lost his way while trying to find a supposed exit to nearby Carreghofa Hall.

Mountains and moors

Westward from Llanymynech is the valley of the Cain, beyond which the fooothills of the Berwyns begin to climb towards the long crescent of rock which marks the summit of the range. The most northerly town of the County of Powys is Llanfyllin, which stands on the Cain and boasts a broad highway joined by dark, narrow streets. On the approach to Llanfyllin from the east is a pretty cottage set on the bank at the roadside. This is Rock Cottage, which was the home of one of the most incorrigible thieves to be encountered anywhere. He was known as the Dartmoor Shepherd, and his speciality was robbing the offertory boxes of churches. He spent 50 of his 80 years in jail, was a jail-bird at 21, and was given his last sentence at the age of 76.

Magnificent Lake Vyrnwy is set among mountains clothed with dark pines – a veritable Welsh Black Forest.

The neighbouring village of Bwlchycibau has a motor-racing association; Parry Thomas, who was killed when his racing car 'Babs' burst into flames on Pendine sands, spent his boyhood at the vicarage while his father was vicar of the parish. 'Babs' was recently disinterred from the sands where it had been buried after the tragedy. West of Llanfyllin is the village of Llanfihangel yng Ngwynfa, with Dolanog 3m farther on along the road to Llanfair Caereinion. Both these villages are associated with Anne Griffiths, the Welsh hymn writer who died young and is still greatly revered in Welsh Nonconformist circles. Also in this sector of the county is Meifod, which is associated with the Prince of Powys who held their court at nearby Mathrafal – of which only a mound now remains.

On the other side of Broniarth Hill, between Meifod and Guilsfield, is a little district known as Europa Plain. It is claimed that if a visitor's vision could reach far enough he could see the Urals from here. Beyond Llanfyllin the country becomes more mountainous, and behind Llanrhaeadr ym Mochnant – which is half in Powys and half in Clwyd – is the famous waterfall Pistyll Rhaeadr, one of the Seven Wonders of Wales. Westward towards the most northerly corner of Powys is a land of high bare mountains with scree on their sides and quarries at their feet. Here is Llangynog, a compact, low-profile village at the foot of an immense mountain, threaded with a road which vanishes at a turn to climb over the crest of the watershed and then descend to the Dee Valley and Bala 12m away. A small side road from Llangynog runs up a lonely valley which ends in a waterfall at an unclimbable dalehead. This is Cwm Pennant, with the headwaters of the River Tanat; two thirds of the way up this valley is Pennant Melangell, with a tiny church dedicated to St Monacella who traditionally saved a hare from Prince Brochwel Ysgythrog's hounds and was granted land here for a religious foundation. Still up in this northernmost sector of Powys is Lake Vyrnwy, 5m long and set deep in heavily-forested mountains – dark pine woods which spread for miles in all directions along the mountainsides and valleys like Welsh Black Forest. Two small roads lead off from the northern end of the lake to climb over this tail of the Berwyns. One runs to Bala, the other has a precipitous descent which frightens some people into turning back and leads to Dinas Mawddwy. Both pass through fine scenery.

Wilderness byways

South of Lake Vyrnwy is the Dyfnant Forest, and below that across the Welshpool-Dolgellau road are empty moorlands which extend all the way to the Caersws-Machynlleth road. Between these two highways are desolate tracts of bog and coarse grass, inhabited only by sheep and buzzards. Scattered over this countryside are small lakes that are the haunt of gulls and the fishing grounds of anglers. There is Llyn Hir, the Long Lake; Llyn y Tarw, the Bull Lake; Llyn y Bugail, the Shepherd's Lake; and others. Some are being slowly dried up by encroaching reeds and rushes, others remain clear. Some have islands in them that are the nesting places of gulls which fly up and wheel round in screaming multitudes if anyone approaches. A new road has recently been constructed across these moorlands from Llanerfyl on the Welshpool-Dolgellau road to Talerddig on the Newtown-Machynlleth road. There was once a rough track here, a kind of bridle way which probably developed centuries ago from a sheep track which formed along the hard ground amid the bogland. A few years ago the track was converted into a properly metalled tarmac road suitable for cars. Driving along it the visitor wonders when he will come to the end, but the moorland views are superb, with never a building or even a tree to be seen for miles. So far the area has remained largely undiscovered. The River Gam flows across this moorland country through the Nant yr Eira, or Snow Pass, to join the Banwy at Llangadfan after collecting tributary streams along the way.

Ruins and rivers

Occasionally near the edges of these moors one may find the ruins of a cottage, once long ago the home of a shepherd or small sheep farmer, a stone house of the Welsh long-house type with barn and byre under the same roof as the living quarters, often interconnected internally. Some of these houses have 'gone down' so long ago that only the outlines of the foundations remain, or sometimes a fragment of wall with part of a window opening. The men and women who lived in these houses seldom went farther than their market town, and to go as far afield as Shrewsbury was an adventure.

East of the moors is, again, the Vale of Powys – this time its upper end between Welshpool and Newtown. Four tributary rivers join the Severn along this reach, the Bechan and the Rhiw on the western side, the Mule and the Camlad on the east. The Bechan wanders through a gentle countryside; the Mule descends through a richly-wooded dingle; the Rhiw has two sources, a fine gorge at the jaws of the valley, and pretty falls at Berriew; the Camlad is the only river to flow from England into Wales. This countryside is a maze of lanes linking scattered villages and hamlets, with Berriew as the midway point of the upper Vale of Powys; Leighton, under the protecting flank of Long Mountain; Forden and Kingswood, two villages virtually joined into one by the ancient Offa's Dyke. South is Montgomery, original capital of the one-time county of Montgomery.

The edge of England

Below Montgomery Wales makes a drive into England, with the Church Stoke peninsula pushing out 5m into Salop. The driver entering Wales from the Craven Arms road drives into the Principality at Snead, only to pass back into England again on leaving Church Stoke, and then re-entering Wales just after leaving the Blue Bell Inn on both the Newtown and Montgomery roads. To strangers this repeated change from country to country, coming into Wales and then finding themselves coming into it again when they thought they were already there, can be quite confusing until they consult a map. West of Church Stoke, between the villages of Sarn and Kerry, the Kerry Hills rise on the left in a long line against the sky. Kerry sheep take their name from these hills, not from the Irish county. The range comprises forest and moorland and has a small prehistoric stone circle near the Anchor Inn, but this is difficult to find because the stones are low to the ground. There is an anemometer close by which gives a rough indication of where to look for the circle. Approached from the road the stones are to the right and above a set of revolving wind-cups. The Kerry Pole, recently renewed, marks the summit of the ridge where two tracks cross, one running north from the Anchor and the other east from the Cider House on the Dolfor-Knighton road.

A signpost at the Anchor points the way to the Cantlin Stone. To find this the visitor should follow the signposted road to a T-junction, and then turn right and continue to woodlands and a fork. Take the right-hand arm of the fork and in about half a mile reach a grass break in the woodlands on the right, with a gate into a field. The stone lies beyond the gate and commemorates the death of W Cantlin, a pedlar who had a lonely round in this district and died – probably of a heart attack – right on the border between two parishes. When his body was found a dispute arose as to which was responsible for burying him – Betws-y-Crwyn or Mainstone. Betws finally agreed to take the responsibility and nothing more was thought of the matter for nearly two centuries. But in 1875, when the Clun Forest Enclosure Act was passed, this action on the part of Betws was held to be proof that where Cantlin died was within their boundaries. As a consequence Betws was awarded several hundred more acres of land than it had up till then possessed. No one knows who set up the stone at the place of Cantlin's death. The inscription on it is very roughly cut, as though done by an amateur, and reads 'W C died here, buried 1691 RIP Betws'. Alongside the memorial stone is a stone cross carved with a motif of entwined serpents, eggs, and seeds. This was set up in 1858 by Beriah Botfield, a botanist and bibliographer who was MP for Ludlow.

Turning back from the Cantlin Stone, the road ultimately dwindles to a rough track and finally to a grass bridle way that ends by the Cider House farm on the road running from Dolfor along the Teme Valley. Some years ago, when workmen were driving stakes to re-fence this stretch of green road, they found their spades striking hard material only a little way below the surface. This proved to be the metalling of an early road, which the straightness of $5\frac{1}{2}$m of this trackway would suggest to be of Roman origin. The road has never been properly investigated, nor the underlying pavement excavated; it would seem to be something worth doing. Close to the road's end and the Cider House is the Kerry watershed, where three rivers all rise within a few hundred yards of each other, each flowing in a different direction. The Teme flows south-east through a deep defile in the hills to start its long journey to the Severn just below Worcester; the Ithon takes a southerly course to the Wye below Newbridge; the Mule has a short northward run of some 12m to Abermule, the lowest reach through a pretty dingle. A narrow strip of pastoral country accompanies the Teme on its uppermost reach from near the source to Knighton, and along it are four interesting villages – Felindre or the Mill Village, Beguildy which means the Shepherd's House, Lloyney, and Knucklas. Opposite Lloyney, on the English bank, the hamlet of Llanfair Waterdine has a church with a barrel organ, strange writing carved on the communion rails, and a gypsy gravestone in the garth with an inscription in Romany. All the countryside within a great half-circle on the English side of the Teme up to the Bishops Castle-Knighton road is full of Welsh names; these are the Clun Lands, part of the Clun Forest which once belonged to Wales.

Pioneer trains

At Knucklas, the last of the four upper Teme villages, the Teme widens out from a stream into a river. Some 2m lower down it meets its first town, Knighton. Here it turns eastward into England, but 7m farther south over the watershed between Teme and Lugg is Presteigne, the old county town of one-time Radnor. At a point where the road begins to descend the other side of the ridge is an obelisk standing in a field on the right. This is a commemorative monument to Sir Richard Green-Price's achievement in bringing the railway to Radnorshire last century; the line is one of the only two still working in Mid Wales.

Picturesque Beguildy is typical of many little Mid Wales villages.

Lovely Nant-y-Groes was once the home of John Dee, court astrologer to Queen Elizabeth I.

Presteigne is almost in England; it could hardly be any closer, and is the most easterly not only of the Mid Wales towns but of all the towns in Wales between Overton in the north and Chepstow in the south. The bridge over the River Lugg links Wales and England in what is surely the prettiest corner of the town. The cottages on the far side are actually in England but still belong to Presteigne, which also has a wealth of beautiful Georgian houses. The driver can pass right through the town from end to end or side to side quicker than he could drive from Trafalgar Square to Piccadilly Circus, yet he could spend more time exploring its attractions than he would need for St Paul's Cathedral.

The wild forest of Radnor

Between Knighton and Presteigne is Offa's Dyke, which cuts off the easternmost sector of Mid Wales from the remainder of the Principality. What was constructed originally to keep the Welsh at home has now been designated from end to end as a long distance footpath. But even the area west of the dyke is not free of geographical barriers, for behind it rises the vast green dome of Radnor Forest with Domen Ddu, the Black Mound, rising to 2,135ft. This is a forest in the original sense of the word – a wild domain, not necessarily wooded but with heavily wooded areas, especially on the northern side. There is also a grey stone tower, marked on the maps as an observatory, which was set up not for observing the stars but as a look-out post for forest fires. Curiously ridged strips running down the southern slopes of the Forest are known as Riggles, and near the top is a small tarn and a spring which is known as the Shepherd's Well.

The forest is encircled by roads along which are a string of villages and hamlets. At the northern tip is Bleddfa, where the last wolf in Radnorshire was caught. A little farther on at a cross roads is the splendid stone mansion Monaughty, where the Abbot of Strata Florida went to live after the dissolution of his monastery. South from this cross roads, on the way to Whitton, a line of twelve Wellingtonia cedars border the road and are matched by another twelve at the roadside between Norton and Presteigne. These were planted as a family memento to mark the birth of a Green-Price heir. Fields below the road were the site of a fierce battle fought in 1402 between the English forces under Edmund Mortimer, and Owain Glyndwr's Welsh army – with victory for the Welsh. Fragments of weapons and armour dug up on the site are now housed in the little church that stands on the bank opposite. Close by the church is Nant-y-Groes, a lovely old house associated with John Dee – the Court Astrologer to Queen Elizabeth I and a brilliant mathematician. Midway

along a straight line across the Forest from Beggars Bush to Bleddfa and accessible by a series of narrow lanes, is Cascob – a church without a village; without even a hamlet.

Christian magic

This church is a stone building with a half-timbered tower, and contains a Deed of Exorcism and a Gnostic talisman. Lonely and tucked away at the head of one of the small valleys, it is not easy to find but is a delight to discover. New Radnor, south of the forest, was the local seat of government which succeeded Old Radnor back in the reign of King Harold, long before the county of Radnor was created. Today both are no more than villages, and Old Radnor scarcely that. It lies off the forest circle $3\frac{1}{2}$m away, and its only feature of interest is a church which has the oldest organ casing in Britain and a tower which was once a military strong point. A little way down the road to Dolyhir and Burlingjobb there are caves in the hillside, but these are difficult to find, harder to enter, and harder still to penetrate. At New Radnor the chief feature of interest is the Lewis memorial, which looks like a miniature Albert Memorial. There are also the remains of the castle and traces of former town walls. Between here and Llanfihangel Nant Melan, at the southern tip of the forest, a pretty dingle runs up into the massif for about half a mile to end at a high and wooded waterfall with the evocative name of Water-break-its-neck. This is an easy walk and the fall is well worth finding. There is verge space for car parking just a few yards away on the other side of the road.

Along both sides of the road which borders the western edge of Radnor Forest are a number of interesting features. A good starting point for a walk over the forest lies just half a mile up the road from Llanfihangel Rhydithon on the corner of the Dolau road. A path leads past The Riggles and the Shepherd's Well, almost to the summit of Domen Ddu, then down the Harley Dingle past the Three Riggles to within half a mile of New Radnor. In the opposite direction from Llanfihangel Rhydithon school is Penybont Common, which is really the western extremity of the forest, with Penybont village at the end of it. This was once an important coaching stop; later it became the agricultural market for Llandrindod Wells, the surprise town of Mid Wales where exotic architecture and red brick replaces grey stone. It stands on the lowest reach of the Ithon, just 4m from its outflow into the Wye and 15m from its source in the Kerry Hills.

Spa town and ecclesiastical capital of Wales,
Llandrindod Wells is also the chief town in the
new county of Powys.

Country of the Ithon

This river cuts a valley directly north and south, neatly
dividing into two almost equal parts the whole countryside
between the English border and the River Wye. Most of
the area is rough, mountainous land, except for a pastoral
strip along each bank. The moorlands fall away gently on
the English side, but in the west they form a steep
escarpment above the Severn between Newtown and
Llanidloes – and again above the Wye between Llangurig
and Rhayader. High up at the Ithon source a line of
immense tumuli cuts across the northern skyline, forming
an unmistakable landmark for a vast distance on all sides.
One of the mounds is such an almost-perfect pyramid that
it is amazing that it has never been excavated. On the
other side of the valley are the Dugwm Rocks, a
tremendous cleft in the earth with a frightening drop into
the valley of the little Mochdre Brook, which flows
northward into the Severn above Newtown. The chasm is
something like the Twymyn Gorge at Dylife, and although
access is by foot only the half-mile walk is easy.

This side of the Ithon is a land of wells. Close to the
Dugwm Rocks are the Seven Wells, seven springs emerging
from the ground close to each other; farther south beyond
the compact, almost rectangular hamlet of Llaithddu is
David's Well – which has no connection with the patron
saint of Wales; and beyond that again the New Well,
which seeps up in the middle of a boggy field and is
practically unidentifiable. Once there was a tremendous
well cult all over Mid Wales, with gatherings about the
springs accompanied by sports and the drinking of their
waters sweetened with sugar, usually on Trinity Sunday.
Many of these wells and springs had curative properties.
Some were good for eye complaints, others for rheumatic
conditions, and others again for internal ills. Others were
credited with magic properties and developed into wishing
wells. It was customary at certain times to dress them
with pieces of rag hung on the surrounding bushes. A more
curious custom was that of throwing pins into them.

The eastern side of the Ithon Valley was a land with a
thriving population which remained stable through the
days of the Princes. There are the ruins of castles here –
Dinboeth, Castell-y-Blaidd, Castell Cwm Aran, the Gaer,
and Cwm-Cefn-y-Gaer, with Cefnllys lower down and
many earthwork strong points. At Llynwynt, on the hills
above Llanbadarn Fynydd, a farmhouse now stands where
Dafydd Fychan had his palace and kept court with
minstrels, bards, a host of retainers, and a continuous
flow of guests. Now there is not even an echo of that
pulsing life left on these empty hills. The Ithon valley is
also a land of tumuli, prehistoric camps, castle mounds,
giants graves, standing stones, stone circles, and
earthworks – all of which testify to an ancient civilization
that has long vanished with no other trace of its existence
save these tantalizing relics.

Edge of a continent

Remains of the great Cistercian abbey of Cwm Hir, the
Long Valley, lie in the Ithon lands in the deeply-cut valley
of the tributary Clywedog Brook. Despite its name this
stream has no connections with the river and lake of the
same name behind Llanidloes. On the hillside above the
Hall is Fowler's Cave, named after a local squire of whom
it was said:

> *Radnorshire, poor Radnorshire*
> *With never a squire with four hundred a year,*
> *Saving Squire Fowler of Abbey Cwm Hir.*

Nothing seems to be known about this vast, deep cavern
in the rock of the mountainside except that it may have
been a shepherd's shelter or a look-out post. Access is easy
via a path which zig-zags all the way up to it. There are
several villages along the Ithon itself: Llanbadarn Fynydd,
which lies largely behind the church and below the road,
so can be passed without the traveller knowing of its
existence; Llananno, with a roadside church and buildings
scattered about the Castle Vale; Llandewi Ystradenny,
with a hall containing some fine old panelling; Penybont,
with a racecourse and a stock market; and Howey, with
its local joke about non-existent docks which equate with
Wigan Pier. Between Howey and Llanelwedd are the
Carneddau Rocks, a long line of escarpment like a great
cliff overlooking the road on its eastern side. Millions of
years ago this was the western edge of Europe, with the
Atlantic coming right to the foot of the cliffs – as marine
fossils found here testify.

The spa town of Llandrindod Wells is the capital of the
Ithon Valley, and the town stretches between the tops of
two meander loops of the river. It is both the ecclesiastical
capital of Wales, where the archbishops are elected and
the governing body of the Church in Wales holds its
meetings, and the capital of the new county of Powys,
which comprises the old counties of Montgomery, Radnor,
and most of Breconshire.

Waters of the Wye

Behind the Carneddau Rocks at Llanelwedd the old county
of Radnor spreads south and east within the great bend
of the Wye, right across to the English border which here
runs up from Hay to Huntington and the Stanner Rocks
beside Old Radnor. This vast diamond-shaped tract of
land is filled with mountains and great hills almost to its
extreme southerly tip, and has a sharp escarpment
along its north-western edge where the River Edw cuts
across a corner and flows into the Wye some 4m below
Builth. Behind this escarpment is a terrain of moorland
and peat bogs, dotted here and there with tiny tarns.
These are also called mawn pools, *mawn* being an old
name for peat, and there is a larger lake called Llan
Bwch-llyn. This is wild, empty countryside where a
walker can wander all day and see no one but an
occasional shepherd.

The whole of the Edw Valley is lovely, and a narrow road
which in parts is attractively wooded follows beside the
river. In places there are verges of short turf which make
delightful picnic places. The road rises and falls; the
valley closes in and opens out; there are glades; glimpses
of water through trees; and little bridges. There are four
hamlets in this valley, Aberedw at its lower end;
Llanbadarn-y-garreg; Rhulen standing a little way off the
river; and Cregrina. At the head of a tributary stream
called the Glas Brook is Glascwm, which clings to a small
central green like an English village. The road makes a
hairpin bend through the village, so the driver can
approach high above it along a ledge of the mountainside,
drop down into it, and return to the starting point along the
valley floor. In the Edw valley there is a chain of tiny
churches, each one unusual and interesting, with Rhulen
probably the most fascinating of all – a tiny, almost
windowless building washed dazzlingly white and with a
west wall leaning alarmingly backwards.

Behind Aberedw is a curious escarpment formed of
impacted slabs of rock locked together like giant stone
walling. These are the Aberedw Rocks. Trees and shrubs
sprout from the stone, and the onlooker can be deceived
into thinking that there are caves here. But this is not so –
what look like caves are merely the deep interstices
between the rock slabs. There is, however, one cave in
this area – the big single cavern where Llywelyn the Last
sheltered before his assassination at Cilmery. Although
marked on the Ordnance Survey maps is not easy to find.
The visitor has to go through Aberedw village, take a
right fork in the road, and at the top turn along a rough
track on the right and look for the cave in a field on the
left. From Glascwm the roads leading from the Edw Valley
converge to continue to Gladestry, with a fork turning

*Mysterious Craig Pwll Ddu is so isolated that many
of the local people have never seen it.*

south to Newchurch. Just half a mile down this fork is
Dreavour farm, where in 1912 a plane made a forced
landing on one of the fields. It was piloted by Corbett
Wilson, who was having a race with another plane
piloted by Leslie Allen for the honour of being the first to
fly from England to Ireland. Wilson had to wait three days
to get his plane repaired, and then made the crossing, but
Allen's plane was never seen again after it had passed
over Holyhead. The present owner of Dreavour has
boyhood memories of the plane's landing and sightseers
coming from miles around to see it. A couple of miles
south of Dreavour is a curious patch of countryside called
Rhos-goch, or Red Moor, which has been described as
200 acres of quaking bogland. There is a legend that in
time past this bog swallowed up a mighty city 'the largest
between Radnorshire and London', and another tells of a
dreadful battle fought here with carnage so terrible that
the River Bach Howey ran red with blood. What is far
better established is that this is a haunt of rare birds and
plants, including the royal fern Osmunda.

Pool of mystery

There are famous features in this district which find a
place in every guide book and volume of Welsh legends,
but which few people ever see. These are Craig Pwll Du –
the Crag of the Black Pool – and the Fairies Oven; indeed it
is not advisable for anyone to try and reach them without a
guide, and even thus accompanied it is a difficult expedition.
If somebody should believe he can get there unaided
he will find the descent of the gorge almost impossible, so
steep and wooded are the sides. And even if he should
manage to reach the valley floor and the waters of the
Bach Howey, he will find his way both up and downstream
impeded by vegetation and patches of sucking mud. But
finding a guide is far from easy, for most people in the area
will say 'Yes, we've heard of Craig Pwll Du but we've
never been there'. The legend attaching to this place is
that a Welsh prince who lived in a castle near by in the
13thc used to throw his prisoners off the crag into the
pool below, and that he ultimately suffered the same fate
himself after being shot with an arrow by Owain Yscrain.
There is, in fact, the mound of an ancient prehistoric
camp near by, so the legend may go back much further
than the 13thc and have been given a new interpretation
following the savagery of this local prince, who earned
himself the nickname of the Pwll Du Butcher. When the
right spot is reached the visitor will find a narrow gorge
with sheer rock sides and a waterfall upstream. Close by

are a number of holes which have been called Fairies Ovens and were gouged out by the rushing waters; downstream there are more waterfalls. The sight from the pool is ample reward for the difficult climb down and the equally difficult climb up which has to follow. It is small wonder that even few of the local inhabitants have been to see it. About 1m upstream from where the Bach Howey flows into the Wye a new bridge has been built across that river, a wide modern structure of pleasant appearance – but the bridge that it replaced was a treasure worth preserving. This was only a single-width suspension bridge with a wooden slat floor which rumbled heavily as cars passed across it, and carried only a limited weight. But its piers were of ornamental iron joined by Tudor arches, and it had latticework sides. It really was a delight to the eye. Happily it has a twin, the bridge over the Wye at Llanstephan 2m downstream, and many people are hoping that this one will be allowed to remain.

The twin of this fascinating little bridge at Llanstephan once spanned the Wye some 2m farther upstream, but has been replaced by a modern structure.

Gentle isolation
Below the Bach Howey the country is less wild, though there are still pockets of deep and lonely isolation – notably in the region of the Begwns, where there is a church described as the loneliest in Wales. Llandewi Fach is a church without a village or hamlet, but only the Cwm Farm near by, yet between twelve and 20 people still attend the services here on Sundays, and until a few years ago some of them still came on horseback. There is not even a footpath to it, let alone a road. Access is by foot along the edge of a field, and the entrance to the churchyard is through a five-barred farm gate. Its earliest gravestone can be seen beside the door and is dated 1676, but burials were still taking place there in the 1960's.

The southern tip of old Radnorshire ends at the great bend in the Wye where it changes direction from a southward to a northward flow and meanders in a series of gigantic right-angle bends over a broad valley floor. Along this Radnorshire shore is a string of villages – Boughrood, Glasbury, Llowes, Clyro, and Rhydspence – and behind them stretching back to the Llandeilo Graban-Painscastle-Newchurch road is another network of small roads linking farms and hamlets. Behind Glasbury is Maes yr Onnen, a Congregational chapel dating back to 1697 but utterly unlike the usual austere Nonconformist chapels both outside and in. The floor of the valley along this reach is wide and flat, forming a pastoral strip between the high Radnorshire uplands and the Black Mountains of Breconshire. There are main roads on each side of the river, and at one time there was a railway.

Valley of spas
At Builth the Wye is joined by its tributary the Irfon, a river which has its source high in the Cambrian massif which forms the backbone of Wales, running straight down its centre from north to south. The river runs south until it reaches Llanwrtyd, when it makes an abrupt turn

eastward towards Builth and the Wye. This is a valley of spas. Builth itself had two sources, the Park Wells and Glannau Wells; then there are the wells at Llangammarch and the two springs at Llanwrtyd, the Dolecoed and Victoria Wells; and Garth too had a medicinal spring, though this never developed into a watering place as the others did. Along the Irfon's south bank runs the high scarp of the Mynydd Epynt, with one road climbing it from Garth to Upper Chapel. On the north bank rise the foothills of the Cambrian massif, scored deeply with the valleys and dingles of innumerable small waters. On this west-east reach the Irfon meanders in a series of great arched loops, crossing and recrossing between the Epynt and the main road, which is accompanied by the Central Wales railway line between Garth and Cilmery. Beulah, $2\frac{1}{2}$m north of Llangammarch, has given its name to a breed of speckle-faced sheep. From here north of the road to Newbridge the country opens out to wild moorlands stretching to the Elan river and lakes.

These moors rise to as much as 2,000ft and contain the Seven Stones, various monoliths, and a multitude of cairns Right at the northern tip is the Corngafallt, a high wooded hill with a road right round it, and on the other side is Elan village – a delightful grey-stone garden city built by Birmingham Corporation for the employees working on the Elan Valley estates and reservoirs. The village has its own church and school, a playing field, riverside lawns and gardens, and a lovely ornamental suspension bridge over the Elan on the entrance road. North-westward from here the mountain ranges climb higher and higher towards and beyond the Claerwen lake. But until the shoreside road is made up across the bogs to link with the Teifi Pools the only Mid Wales crossing of the central massif is by the road from Llanwrtyd Wells, up the Irfon Valley, and past old Llanwrtyd. Above old Llanwrtyd the valley scenery becomes more magnificent with each mile, and beyond Abergwesyn is the Camddwr Blaidiadd – literally the crooked water of the wolves – a deep narrow gorge where the river in its downward course has cut a way through the rocks. Now the Irfon is left behind and the road crosses the headwaters of the Tywi, climbing by a series of sharp zig-zags called the Devil's Staircase to the roof of the Cambrian range, where it runs for mile after mile over the empty treeless wilderness with never a house, barn, or any kind of building to be seen until it begins to drop down into Tregaron.

The spectacular falls, gorges, and bridges at Devil's Bridge comprise one of the foremost scenic attractions in Mid Wales.

Around the little mountain

Tregaron is the eastern gateway to old mid Cardigan, a vast quadrilateral of country with Aberystwyth, Cwm Ystwyth, Lampeter, and Aberaeron as its corner points. Right at the centre of this oblong is the Mynydd Bach or Little Mountain, which is not empty and desolate like the Cambrian spine but just a high upland containing villages and patterned with lanes. At the summit is a chalybeate spring called Ffynnon Drevi and the small lake of Llyn Eiddwen. The scarp side is on the west, beyond which is a wide pastoral band of country stretching out to the coastal highway; a countryside of small villages and farms with an air of prosperity about it; good agricultural country. But the most interesting area of Mid Cardigan is the vast Tregaron Bog, the largest expanse of its kind in all Wales and England. It is known as the Red Bog from the red grass heads in the summer and autumn, though at times it is white with the snowy flecks of bog cotton. It contains rare plants which include the bog rosemary, unusual butterflies like the marsh fritillaries, and also the scarlet tiger moth. The bog is a nature reserve, and permission to explore off the paths has to be obtained from the Nature Conservancy at Plas Gogerddan, Aberystwyth. Wild life on the moors of this part of Dyfed is rich and varied, with peregrine falcons, merlins, and golden plovers among the species to be seen. Very occasionally red kites may be observed. This is one of the latter's last refuges in Britain, and it is a heavily-protected bird today. Up at the top north-west corner of this area are two villages with London names, Chancery and New Cross. The first got its name from the observation of a judge on its position in a valley bottom into which one has to descend from every direction. He said it was 'like Chancery – easy to get into but difficult to get out of'.

The origin of New Cross probably derives from its position at a road intersection. It is, however, notable as the burial place of a husband and wife who were both literary celebrities in their own right earlier this century. They are Caradoc Evans and Countess Barcynska, who also wrote under the name of Oliver Sandys. Caradoc scandalized the Welsh with such novels as *Taffy* and *My People*, and was always a picturesque and controversial figure. The countess, who was beautiful and had tremendous charm, wrote a prolific number of light romantic novels which gave pleasure to millions of readers. The ruins of Strata Florida Abbey are in this quadrilateral, and behind it the Teifi Pools, a series of pretty tarns lying in the depressions of the moors. They were opened up by the Cardiganshire Water Authority and are now much visited. In Mid Cardigan also are the wooded valleys of the Aeron and Wyre and the impressive gorges of the Ystwyth and Rheidol. Between the heads of these two valleys there is a stone arch across the old coach road, set up by Thomas Johnes of Hafod in 1810 to commemorate the Golden Jubilee of King George III.

Hafod in its prime must have been a fantastic house. It was a treasure house of books and *objects d'art*, and the resort of the most famous and learned people of the day. Fire destroyed the mansion and most of the valuables, and Johnes the owner never properly recovered from this and the subsequent untimely death of his daughter. The bridges and gorges at Devil's Bridge are among the most spectacular features of this region, while down in the Rheidol Valley is a hydro-electric plant which has been so beautifully landscaped that it merges naturally into its surroundings without spoiling the view.

Salt in the air

Some 12m to the West of Devil's Bridge is Aberystwyth, the capital of Cardigan Bay and central point of the Mid Wales coastline, which runs from the head of the Dyfi estuary at Garreg down to Aberaeron. The northernmost section is entirely taken up with Cors Fochno, another area of bogland similar to that at Tregaron, except that here the sea invades the platforms of green tussocks with channels like narrow silver ribbons winding in and out among them, and at low tide leaves soft brown bands like Lilliputian roads. There is a tiny village standing in the middle of the bog, Llancynfelin, which grew up on what is virtually an island standing above the tide level. But this is not at once apparent since it is situated right alongside the causeway road which links Tre'r Ddol with Ynyslas. The bog extends right up to the coastal road, which at Ynyslas turns south to Borth and neatly cuts off the Twyni Peninsula. This projects northward into the Dyfi estuary, a promontory of dunes fringed by vast acres of golden sands and served by a single road which fades out where the sands begin. There is a long wall on the north side of Borth, a necessary protection against the encroachments of the sea, and the beach here is striped with wooded breakwaters as far as the cliffs at the lower end of the village. From this point it is cliffs and rocks all the way to Aberystwyth, but the low-tide 5m walk is pleasant and enjoyable. Two coves eat into the cliffs along this part of the coast – Wallog and Clarach. At Wallog the submerged reef of rocks known as the Sarn Cynfelin runs out into the bay. Legend links this reef with

Cantref Gwaelog, the Submerged Hundred farther up the coast. Clarach has become a 'caravan city', with caravan estates on both sides of the small river which reaches the sea here. Between Clarach and Aberystwyth a deep cavern penetrates Constitution Hill and forms a favourite picnic place – especially in bad weather. From the top of the coastal belt at Ynyslas the road crosses the Cors Fochno to Tre'r Ddol, a village which suddenly became famous when Elma Williams founded her Valley of Animals near by. A little farther along the main road to Machynlleth a right turn leads up the Artists Valley, a pretty dingle in the hillside. By Glandyfi station the road briefly meets the river, then the two part company again until near Derwenlas, once the port of Machynlleth and the centre of a small shipbuilding industry which spread along this bank of the river.

Mountain forest

North from Machynlleth runs the Afon Dulas, and an interesting feature of this district are the fences formed of upright slabs of slate set side by side and sometimes bound together with wire. Fences of this type run for miles here. A railway once ran up this valley, but like so many others it was closed down. There is a preservation society railway museum at Lower Corris. All this north-western corner of the old county of Montgomery, occupying the north bank of the Dyfi, is mountainous and thickly wooded, chiefly comprising the Dyfi Forest. This is almost entirely devoid of roads except for those constructed by the Forestry Commission, and is without villages too – only Aberllefenni forming a tiny community in the midst of the woodlands, and Llanwrin on the river bank. This is probably and least known and least visited of any part of the county of Powys.

Along the south bank of the Dyfi runs the main road through Cemmaes and Cwmllinau to Mallwyd, where a right fork leads to Welshpool, while Dolgellau lies ahead. At Cemmaes Lloyd George was once involved in an attempt to cite him in a divorce case, but this failed. The story is well known locally. Just out of the actual Dyfi Valley but on a tributary stream called the Carrog is the village of Aberhosan, which became famous in the 1950's with the discovery of a set of diaries kept by a carpenter in rough note books and illustrated with his own sketches. These give a vivid insight into the daily life of a village craftsman. From Aberhosan and the other villages in this district east and south of Machynlleth the land climbs sharply, with

Curious fences fashioned from upright slabs are a common feature of the slate-producing regions.

its slopes scored by wooded gorges carved out by streams and small rivers plunging down to the Dyfi. There are no roads across this terrain, which culminates in the fivefold summit of Plynlimon, but there is a well-surfaced mountain road cutting across the corner of it. This leads from Machynlleth through Forge to Dylife, a dead village consisting of nothing but an inn which has recently been enlarged and contemporized. But once 1,000 miners lived here and worked in the mines round about, and the outlines of their terraces of houses can still be seen. Until quite recently there was a local church, but that too has gone the way of the houses. Dylife today is like a huge patch of scorched earth, a great circus of sterile brown ground with only the scarlet flash of a letter box on a post striking a note of life amid the desolation.

A few yards farther on along the road is the head of the Twymyn Gorge, a frightening chasm plunging down to the stream at the bottom in a dizzying precipice. The road passes within feet of this sheer drop, but the view down the valley is superlative. Within minutes the wild country is left behind and open country spreads ahead as the Llanbrynmair-Llanidloes road is approached. A right turn here leads to Staylittle, snug in its dip in the road, with a scrap of history lying forlorn on the mountainside where a Quaker graveyard still exists with nothing to indicate it except the name plate on the gate – which can't be seen from the road. The old road goes straight on to Van and Llanidloes, while a new road leads to the Clywedog lake, with its high dam observation terrace, and scenic routes through the surrounding countryside. Part of the scenic drive leads up the Severn Valley to the river's headwaters, beyond which are the bare Plynlimon mountainsides. Here the river has its source, very close to that of the Wye, nearly 2,500ft up on the country boundary between Powys and Dyfed. A signposted path from Eisteddfa Gurig on the Llangurig-Aberystwyth road leads to the summit of Plynlimon. Behind the mountain on its western side are several tarns and reservoirs, including the recently created Nant-y-Moch, or Pig Valley Lake, which is another showpiece and tourist attraction.

The pious tramp

Through Ponterwyd the River Rheidol runs in its southward flow from the Plynlimon slopes to drop into its deep gorge at Devil's Bridge and turn west to the sea; at Devil's Bridge is the start of the long lonely road through Cwm Ystwyth to the great lakes of old Radnorshire. The road starts beside the Hafod Arms Hotel, and about half a mile along it is a quarry in a shoulder of the hill on the right. Here in the 1950's a tramp with a strong sense of piety made a little shrine by painting a crucifix on the rock face

with a word or two beside it. It is still there, though now somewhat faded. This shrine is one of several created by this tramp along his regular round, the most elaborate being the one in a quarry just across Machynlleth bridge on the Aberdyfi road. He was an Irishman named Paddy, who was well known all over the district for his honesty and piety. When he died he was given a municipal funeral at Machynlleth, and the Bard Idris ap Harri, the Llanbrynmair monumental mason, gave him an inscribed gravestone. The shrines naturally became known as Paddy Shrines. This 26m coach road over the mountains takes the traveller through Cwm Ystwyth, with its derelict mines and wild scenery, across to the headwaters of the Elan and down into Rhayader. This is the capital of the Radnorshire lake district, a cosy little town where four main streets meet at a low grey clock tower, and old inns exude an air of that now-vanished Wales — farmers in black broadcloth riding cobs or driving in traps to the market and chattering away in Welsh. Despite modern shops and motor cars Rhayader is redolent of yesterday.

Radnorshire's lakes

There are five lakes in the Radnorshire group, all artificially constructed but so beautifully contrived and landscaped that they look entirely natural, as though they had always been there. They were created by Birmingham Corporation as reservoirs for supplying fresh water to the city. The first four were opened by King Edward VII in 1904; the Claerwen was not added until 1952, when it was opened by Queen Elizabeth II. A turn off the coach road at Pont ar Elan allows a zig-zag descent to the lakes, but better views can be enjoyed if the motorist continues to Rhayader and starts from there, driving up the valley to the top lakehead and back to Pont ar Elan. Just before the first lake is Elan village, far down on the left, and a series of filters can be seen on the right up above the road. Neither of these features are noticed unless they are particularly looked for. When the dams were being constructed a railway was laid down for the transportation of men, plant, and materials. At the first dam a branch line was taken across the other side, and the stone face still carries brackets which took the track across it. It is possible to follow the course of the railway all the way, for the track bed still remains along the side of the road up to the lakes and alongside them close to the shore. Near the top of the second lake, Garreg Ddu, a stream comes down the mountainside. A view to the left reveals the track bed of the railway and the remains of a bridge which carried it over the stream — complete with a section of the old rails still in place.

Farther on and nearer the lakehead the railway continues straight ahead up what is now a climbing road on the right, while the main road crosses to the other side of the valley. The climbing road follows the railway track through a cutting which had to be blasted out of the solid rock beside Pen-y-Garreg lake. It is possible to go right up to the end of the line by Craig Goch dam, where a slope down into the water reveals that this was where the waste material from the construction work was disposed of. On the way up to the railhead is a small wooden building at the lakeside. What is particularly striking about this is the cross over its door. It was originally a 'tommy shop' for the workers, but was swept away in a flood and carried down river. When it was recovered the owner presented it to the Birmingham Corporation to be used as a church, since there was nowhere for the workers to worship on Sundays. The seats, altar, and pulpit are still there and can be seen through the windows. The bridge where the road crosses the valley is interesting, for careful examination will reveal numbers painted on the stonework. These were put there by an employee of the Corporation who undertook to widen the bridge, since it had proved incapable of carrying the volume of summer traffic in recent years. He drew a plan of the side of the bridge, imitating exactly the shape of each stone in it, and gave the drawn shapes numbers corresponding with those he had painted on the actual stonework. He then dismantled the bridge side, and after the carriageway had been widened replaced each stone in its original position according to the plan. One or two had become broken in the dismantling process, so he cut and chipped new stone to the precise shape of the broken pieces. It was a fantastic job, and that employee surely deserves a commemorative plate on the bridge to record the story of his achievement.

Moorland mirror

Above the dam, in the middle of Pen-y-Garreg lake, is a wooded island which adds to the appeal of the landscape but allows no public access. The top lake, called Craig Goch, is the least interesting because it is the most featureless — just a sheet of water surrounded by treeless moorland. There are plans to increase its size and depth considerably, which will make it one of the largest lakes in Britain and radically alter the appearance of the countryside. It will also necessitate the construction of a new road higher up, since the present one will be inundated. One dam in this lake system was never completed – the Dol-y-Mynach dam near the head of Caban Coch. The foundations were laid and are plain to see, but the super-structure was never added.

Pen-y-Garreg dam was one of the first steps towards the now considerable Elan Valley water-supply scheme for Birmingham.

Above Dol-y-Mynach the road continues to the Claerwen lake. At a fork the lower branch goes to the foot of the dam, and the upper to the lake itself, which is impressive rather than pretty. Only half of the lake can be seen from the dam. A series of gulfs on its northern side run up ravines formed by streams that come down from the heights. These slopes are vast peat bogs which spread as far as the eye can see. There are only two houses on the Claerwen slopes, Nant-y-Beddau above the head of the third gulf, a grey house where the peat fire burns in the sitting room all the year round and is never allowed to go out, and the Claerwen Farm at the lakehead – both of them lonely and isolated. A rough road along the north shore follows up and down the gulfs, and beyond the lake deteriorates into a rough track across the mountains to the Teifi Pools. A few years ago the former Cardiganshire County Council proposed to Radnorshire that this road should be made up, but the Radnorshire County Council turned down the suggestion on the grounds of cost. Now there are different councils, Powys and Dyfed, but still two. So whether the project will ever materialize is anyone's guess, but such a road would certainly be a big tourist attraction. There are two scraps of literary history preserved among these lakes in the sites of two famous houses submerged in Caban Coch – Cwm Elan, which was the subject of Francis Brett Young's novel *The House under the Water*, and Nant Gwillt, where Shelley and Harriet Westbrook stayed after their marriage.

Great rivers
The River Elan between the Caban Coch lake and its outflow into the Wye, opposite the Cerriggwynion quarries, used to constitute the old county boundary between Breconshire and Radnorshire. Above the confluence the Wye became an exclusively Radnorshire river. Some 3m east of the confluence there is another lake, unconnected with the Elan valley series, a small natural water named Llyn Gwyn – the White Lake. This has a curious earthwork at one end, rather like a small amphitheatre, with a miniature harbour near by. Divers have brought up fragments of ancient timber from the bed of this lake, but so far no one has solved any of its mysteries. The reach of the Wye between Rhayader and Llangurig is one of the most breathtakingly beautiful of any on its course, particularly the 3m up to Marteg where the high and magnificent countryside towers above it, in turn golden with gorse, purple with heather, and bronze with autumn bracken. The most impressive views of this can be enjoyed by the traveller coming downstream towards the high bulk of Gamallt. At Marteg, which was never at any time anything more than a railway halt with one or two houses and takes its name from the River Marteg, there is a cave at the roadside which is unfortunately too much used as a repository for picnic litter. Opposite there is a slope down to an old ford which is still in existence and

One of the most attractive reaches of the Wye is between Rhayader and Llangurig, where the river weaves between splendid hills which change colour from season to season.

can be clearly distinguished, although now superseded by a picturesque little footbridge. This was the crossing point of the Wye on the old monks' road between Abbey Cwm Hir and Strata Florida. Some sections of this still exist as modern road, and others just as faint tracks across the bogland and rough pasture. A pleasant diversion here is to turn up the small road beside the cave and drive up the Marteg Valley to St Harmon, a lovely run which starts with open mountain and later negotiates country lanes.

Back to the border
The main road from Marteg continues to Llangurig, which has a historic church and two hotels but little else. From here a route runs 5m north-east over the watershed between the Wye and Severn to Llanidloes. It is also possible to reach Llanidloes by direct road from St Harmon, but a turn-off at Pantydwr by the Mid Wales Inn leads to Bwlch-y-Sarnau. Just where the road crosses the Marteg by a little white bridge there is a pool in the river which is used for total immersion baptisms by some of the Nonconformist sects. A narrow meadow at the waterside accommodates the congregations – which are surprisingly large – and on the occasions of baptisms the road is lined with cars. The visitor to Llanidloes has the first impression that this is a grey town, but on investigation it reveals itself as a town of many colours interspersed amid the grey. The next village down the Severn is Llandinam, where the Davies family – most generous benefactors to Montgomeryshire – has its seat. At the bridge is a statue of David Davies, who founded the family fortunes early last century building railways, roads, bridges, and docks. Beyond Llandinam is Caersws, actually on the confluence of three rivers – the Severn, Cerist, and Trannon.

Other villages in this district are Tregynon and Bettws Cedewain, both on the River Bechan. Tregynon once had a temperance pub, and the house is still called The Temperance. Bettws church has a rare pre-Reformation brass and a barrel organ. All these villages centre upon Newtown, the next large town on the Severn after Llanidloes, a lively, thriving centre made up of such varied architecture that no two blocks are identical. Unlike Newtown, where the streets weave in and out of each other, at Welshpool the traveller has to keep coming back to the cross; there is almost no cross-sector communication except by the four main streets. Welshpool is only 5m from the Breidden Gateway.

41

The Roof of Wales

North Wales – a land of savage landscapes and fertile vales, a refuge of princes and the cradle of our Royal Tudor line

If Chester is chosen as the approach to North Wales the visitor can survey the hills as the Romans did from the walk along the top of their own superlative wall. He will see how suddenly North Wales begins; the plains of England just come to an end and the mysterious hills show their brows in a long low ridge stretching from north to south. Along those slopes King Offa of Mercia built his famous dyke c784 as a defence against Welsh claims and raids. This wall of earth, with a ditch on the Welsh side, must have been an impressive piece of work, for much of it may be seen to this day. King Harold decreed that any Briton (Welshman) found with a weapon on the east side of it should have his right hand cut off. Earlier the penalty was death. Zestful walkers these days make it a test of stamina to trek the whole 168m length from the mouth of the Dee to the mouth of the Wye. A very well-preserved section survives in the park of Chirk Castle.

Among the mountains ahead the life of an older Britain lingers on, and though no tartans are worn in Wales the clans are not far below the surface. Not so much perhaps in South Wales, which is now industrialized and full of newcomers, but certainly in the mosaic of glens in North and Mid Wales. In the north the river Conwy divides two ancient principalities, and a string of castles carries echoes of a 1,000 years of strife. The strains of the *March of the Men of Harlech* are there still, but so also are *The Bells of Aberdyfi* and the spirit of romance. Above all, the old language that was spoken throughout Britain before English is here in all its lilt as a tool of daily life. In 1969 Caernarfon, almost at the foot of Snowdon itself, welcomed Prince Charles with banners and fanfares, and there his mother invested him with his badges of office as Prince of Wales and future king.

Often the rains will sweep through the hills and there will be the sound of many waters. But there will also be glimmering skies and limpid lights, so that from hilltops near the north coast the watcher will sense that he is somewhere at the centre of the British Isles. He may see with his own eyes the mountains of the Isle of Man, Sca Fell or Helvellyn in Cumbria, and the Irish Mountains of Mourne where they sweep down to the sea. Snowdon and her lesser peaks are bunched in a radius of 25m, with the sea always near. This makes them dramatic and full of surprises. They are also a wall against the weather, for

King Offa of Mercia built his famous dyke *c*784 as a boundary defence. It is now the basis for a 168m footpath from the Dee to the Wye.

they take the brunt of the snows, leaving to those who live in the peninsula – the long arm that tapers away towards Ireland – the comfort of a balmy winter.

Along the Dee

The quietly flowing Dee links Chester with Wales. Almost as the traveller leaves the city he is over the border. The river bends south before it swerves west towards its source, and he could pause in the Welsh strip of plain before reaching the hills. There's the lovely Gresford church with its peal of twelve bells; Holt church among the strawberry fields; Chirk with its castle still lived in; Bangor Isycoed with its racecourse and its memory of slaughtered monks; Ruabon balancing Monsanto chemicals with Wynnstay Park; or Telford's great aqueduct. Wrexham is the largest town in North Wales. Its most prized possession is its large parish church, which has strong connections with Yale University, one of the top universities of the USA. This is because the churchyard contains the tomb of Elihu Yale, regarded as the main founder of the university.

North Wales is all hills, but they are cut into a few neat parcels by the leading rivers and their valleys. These are the Clwyd, the Conwy, the Dee, the Vyrnwy, and flowing into the western sea, the Mawddach. All the stretches between these main rivers have captivating mountain roads. The easiest and shortest cut to the Vale of Clwyd from the Chester approach is by way of Mold and over the Clwydian Range, but the A55 can be taken to enter the vale at St Asaph. All the roads are impressive. The name Clwyd is the same as Clyde, and in 1974 it became the name of the merged shires of Denbigh and Flint. The Clwydian Range, an area of outstanding natural beauty, looks deceptively near from St John's Beacon observation point in Liverpool. In any event it is hardly an hour's drive away. Hawarden, with its residential library and connections with the Gladstone family, Flint Castle, Holywell where the Catholic pilgrims go – all are accessible by the industrial estuary road.

The International Eisteddfod at Llangollen is more than an expression of the arts – it is a step towards world-wide understanding and mutual respect.

A tragic piece of history happened at Flint Castle when King Richard II was captured after being inveigled from the shelter and security of Conwy Castle. He was treacherously lured from safety and made prisoner. It was in Flint Castle too that Edward II (born in Caernarfon, first Prince of Wales under the new dispensation) met his favourite Piers Gaveston on his recall from exile in Ireland as Lord Lieutenant. The castle is the earliest and most eastern of the chain of magnificent structures which Edward I erected or re-built along the coast of North Wales: Flint, Rhuddlan, Conwy, Beaumaris, Caernarfon, Criccieth, and Harlech.

Vale of plenty

The Vale of Clwyd is dotted with the most prosperous homesteads in Wales, and is a plentiful place where the cornfields, villages, and churches still 'afford us the most pleasant prospect imaginable' as they did to William Camden in 1695. The dairy produce of the vale largely supplies the industrial population of towns such as Wrexham, Ruabon, Shotton, Flint, Brymbo, and Buckley. Ruthin Castle and Denbigh Castle dominate the vale. A dispute with Lord Grey of Ruthin over a common called Croesau sparked off the revolt of Owain Glyndwr. This arch-burner and destroyer made himself, by guerrilla warfare, master of Wales for sixteen years from 1400 and called himself Prince of Wales. His own home was over the hills in the valley of the Dee.

Along the vale at its foot the road runs through St Asaph, which has the smallest cathedral in England and Wales, to Rhuddlan and its castle, and Rhyl. On the land side Denbigh Castle guards the way to inner North Wales. The high ground on which the castle stands marks the beginning of the plateau-land that extends from the Vale of Clwyd to the Conwy Valley. Southwards lie the Denbigh Moors, crossed by the A543 on its way to join the A5. Westward flow the farm lands, and there the old roads meander, up and down. between hedges of broom or edges of foxglove in season through Llansannan,

Llangernyw and Llanfair Talhaearn. The names and places are Welsh poetry which punctuate the ways either to the Conwy Valley or the A55 coastal road.

World of Song

Entering North Wales by the A5 along the Valley of the Dee the first place of real note that the visitor comes to is Llangollen – a difficult name to pronounce with those two sets of *lls* but, however they manage it, it is a name often on the lips of the peoples of many lands. This small market town in its beautiful glen has been a European Common Market of music since the end of the 1939–1945 war. Strangely inspired, it burst out to organize an international festival of song and dance on the lines of the old, purely Welsh competitive gathering, the eisteddfod, and it is as the Llangollen International Music Eisteddfod that this is known throughout the world. How did it happen? Was it a beam of light after the gloom of war – the hopelessness of nations and then the unconquerable spirit of man? Europe and many parts of the world lay in ruins, and the governments and peoples of all lands were on the brink of economic and moral bankruptcy. The drama began when a young man, cycling along a country lane in the spring of 1945, stopped to listen to a milkboy singing a hymn as he swung his can. The thought came to Harold Tudor: 'could we gather the world into Wales to sing?' Fired by the thought he pleaded in many quarters, but in vain. He then went to a Llangollen musician, W S Gwynn Williams, who was already a figure in the world of folk music. The response was warm. Before long the new town council and all the people were involved in this idea for promoting international understanding through music.

The Llangollen Eisteddfod is held in July, a month ahead of the National Eisteddfod of Wales, so that the two main holiday months of the summer season are marked by these two notable events. The 'national', where the official language is Welsh, also lasts a week and is held alternately in North Wales and South Wales. This eisteddfod becomes something of a 'gathering of the clans' from all over Wales. In the Middle Ages the eisteddfod was an affair of the bards under the protection of the ruling prince, and was centred on poetry and the harp. Since the 19thc it has become a popular local competitive

43

Snowdon was part of a powerful land where princes and outlaws alike could seek refuge among easily-defensible mountains.

festival of the arts, a small one being held in almost every rural village for at least an evening or two. They were, and are, often held by a church or school, a whole scheme of them being held by the *Urdd* (or Order) of Welsh Youth. Some eisteddfodau used to be on a county basis, others are 'semi-national', as the prouder ones in South Wales call themselves. They are also held in towns in England where there are Welsh people in sufficient numbers. On Tyneside the English themselves hold a large eisteddfod every year.

The Welsh Rhine

The Conwy River is the Rhine of North Wales and the line which the Princes of Gwynedd had to hold. Here the defenders held all the advantages – in front of them a broad river and behind them the wild mountains of which they claimed they were the masters. This line could be held even now; the crossing at Conwy still holds up the traffic, miles of it sometimes, in spite of a new bridge. The Conwy river may be a poorer thing than the Rhine, but the castle is indisputably finer than anything the Rhine can show. The reign of Edward I was a brilliant period of military architecture. Some of the most powerful castles of any age or country were then built in Britain. Conwy Castle stands alone on a high rock on the shore of the estuary. It follows the contour of the rock and is long and relatively narrow. It was started in 1283 while castles were also being built at Caernarfon, Criccieth, and Harlech. It is said that the workmen employed on building Conwy Castle were brought from Rutland, which produced the best masons in England.

The traditional Welsh castle used to be on the east bank at Deganwy. From here long ago – as long before Edward I as we are after him – Prince Maelgwn ruled over half of Britain from Carlisle to the Isle of Wight. He had a small fleet of fighting ships where the yachts and dinghies are now. Prince Llywelyn destroyed this castle in 1260, presumably to prevent its use by the enemy. Edward I made Conwy a fine place. Even today the mile-long town wall is almost complete, and with its 21 towers is almost a castle in itself. The king himself was besieged in the castle in January 1295, and only the arrival of a provision ship in time saved the garrison from starvation. But there is a happier legend. Queen Eleanor is said to have planted the first sweet peas in Britain in the little terrace that

overlooks the river. It could be that King Edward and Queen Eleanor had a sentimental affection for this spot. When they were here first the queen was bearing the child (after 30 years of marriage) who was to become Edward II, the only one of their four sons to survive them. They spent Christmas at Conwy in 1284 and 1290. The king also seems to have made the castle his base during some of his campaigns against the Welsh.

Apart from the fascinating position of the castle – and it can be imagined new and gleaming white – it appears to have been a homely place as well as impregnable. The magnificent dining hall is built on a curve and the roof was formerly sustained by eight stone arches. It was lit by nine early-English windows, and at the east end is a chapel. The castle, though decayed, was garrisoned for King Charles in the civil wars by the warlike John Williams, a local boy who had become Archbishop of York. When General Mytton took the castle it was defended by Irish soldiers, and so great was the resentment felt against these auxiliaries that he had them all tied back to back and flung into the river to drown. Charles II granted the castle to the Earl of Conwy, who stripped the lead from the roof and carried the timbers away to convert them to his own use. But for this, what a residence it would have made for the Princes of Wales!

Strong refuge

The Conwy Valley is not only the Rhine of North Wales, but also the beginning of the Snowdonia national park. As one draws near from Colwyn Bay on the coastal A55 the breathcatching, jagged heap of Snowdonia looms ahead. This is it; the strong land of Gwynedd which was independent for a time even when England ruled Aquitaine and Gascony. In 1974 it became Gwynedd again, a single county after being three shires for centuries. Strangely enough, as the diocese of Bangor, the old province had been preserved as a unit of administration from medieval times without a break. Leaving Conwy and its frontier valley for the moment and taking the coast road to Bangor, everything now becomes more precipitous and wild. The A55 begins to pick its way along the rims of mountains that wash their feet in the sea, and the country does not open out until the A55 has been left at Bangor and the A487 approaches Caernarfon.

The Llanberis Pass to Caernarfon is narrow and tricky, but unfailingly dramatic.

As for the A5, the last stages before Bangor descend through the Nant Ffrancon Pass, then past Ogwen Lake and the peak of Tryfan, where the tenderfoot climbers go, and by towering slate quarries – all this after the ascent from the cosiness of Betws-y-coed through the eerie cross-ways of Capel Curig. Those who venture up Tryfan can run into trouble, but at RAF Valley (Anglesey) there is a helicopter mountain rescue team. Nant Ffrancon Pass held a lake in geological aeons past. There are many who believe that it should become a lake once more, that the barren place demands it. From the parting of the ways at Capel Curig the traveller can aim for Caernarfon either from Bangor (A5) or via the shorter A4086 through the Pass of Llanberis. By the latter he will come to the highest rib of Snowdon that can be reached by road. Before the top of the pass is the Pen-y-Gwryd Hotel, where the mountaineers come. Climbers know it as PYG, and this is how the Pyg track to the summit of Snowdon got its name. The signatures of the team that trained here for the Himalayas may be seen on the ceiling of the Everest room.

Mountain passes

The Llanberis Pass to Caernarfon is smaller and narrower than the Nant Ffrancon. It is more rocky and tricky but it is dramatic. As the vale opens out there are twin lakes, Padarn and Peris, one of which was used in the Empire Games. Now the second hydro-electric pumped storage scheme in North Wales is being built here. This is an impressive, beautiful pass, with Snowdon in its many moods towering at its head. A modern Welsh poet wrote a chromatic poem for the National Eisteddfod in which he saw his native Snowdonia in three colours – black, white, and red. This is what Prince Charles wrote about the park: 'Our countryside is a most precious heritage, and because it is vulnerable, must be looked after and used with great care. Although this part of North Wales is in the form of a national park, it is in fact the home of farmers and other people whose families have lived here for many years. It is their home and should be respected as such. 'People living in a town would not appreciate it if someone came to exercise an assumed right to trample through

their garden and leave their lawn strewn with plastic bags, tins, and paper. This is, nevertheless, what happens in the countryside. Gates are frequently left open, the animals stray and are sometimes injured or killed. Fields may appear to be God's gift to snobbish dumpers, but they are part of someone's farm and as much 'home' as the actual house. By thoughtful consideration for others we can prolong the outstanding beauty of the park, the pure enjoyment it gives the visitor, and the unspoilt environment of the resident. Please remember that.'

Magnificent Snowdon

There is not much doubt that the prince's words are being heeded, and that the uses of land can go hand in hand with recreation to make this splendid area a park of international standing. As yet the Snowdonia national park is a largely unspoilt region of mountains and coast. Its future is being planned with care so that the excitement that the landscape arouses in its visitors will never be lost. Farmers, foresters, and water authorities between them are the real landscape artists of the national park. Some hill farmers in unfrequented areas wish to remain off the tourist map. One claimed that his valley had been quiet for centuries and that he only wanted to get on with his work in peace. He and others like him felt that visitors who need their kind of countryside are better pleased to make their discoveries unaided. It's an old and established life that one meets among these mountains. Old Welsh literature presents Snowdonia as being heavily forested, full of wild beasts – the deer, the boar, and even the wolf. Little by little the forests were cut down either to create more grazing land or to supply timber for wars. Sheep were allowed to graze in deciduous woodlands which resulted in many of these dying away. Now the Forestry Commission is replacing the native trees with conifers. It has its reasons. The hill lands will not yield paying crops of hardwood but they are well suited for softwoods. Many people are upset by the effect this has on the landscape. They maintain that conifers are an intrusion which affects the wild life. The solution in the national park may be smaller stands of conifers with hardwoods planted around them. The value of the Snowdonia national park to the naturalist is clear – there are no less than sixteen national nature reserves within its boundaries, ranging from mountain reserves to those of seashore and estuary.

Famous Bodnant Gardens offer the visitor cascades of plants and flowers sweeping over mellow terraces, walls, and bridges.

As for the weather in Snowdonia, a lot of abuse of Welsh weather stems from a failure to appreciate the fact that the west gets it first. To arrive in Snowdonia in the rain, the park's information officer says, is often just bad timing. 'Set off in the wet, arrive in the dry' is a handy ready-reckoner. Those who strike a bad week, when all they have come for is to sit on a beach and picnic on the moors, are unlucky. If it has been raining heavily for two days or more, think of those happy mortals who fly rod and line in the swollen rivers and lakes and who have been praying for such a fine run. Or see the waterfalls in all their power and thrust roaring into their black pools. Go on a circuit of the churches, castles, or ancient monuments; travel every mile of the narrow-gauge railways; tour the great power-stations or the woollen mills. The vintage months for seeing Snowdonia are undoubtedly May and June. The wettest month of the year is August, when most visitors arrive – perhaps another reason for the unfavourable image of Welsh weather. It is hardly fair to judge a region's climate by its extremes, but people active in some pursuit can be surprised how much good weather there is.

Conwy, elbowing as it does into both Snowdonia and the valley with Llandudno only a stone's throw away, calls a halt to everybody. It has been called the most interesting old town in Wales, and it is certainly an arresting centre for enjoyment of both past and present in the North. Two roads run up the wooded and pastoral vale of Conwy, one on each side of the river, and both reach the A5 at opposite ends of Betws-y-coed. The westerly one goes through the aluminium-making village of Dolgarrog, which some years ago was swept by a dam-burst, then through the one-time spa of Trefriw, from where a pretty mountain road winds up to two high lakes. The road on the east side of the river faces the first mountains of Snowdonia, passes the world-famed Bodnant Gardens, and goes through Llanrwst – a small town once famous for its harps and harpists. The 17th-c architect Inigo Jones came from this district. Near by is some of the most fertile land in North Wales, famous for fattening bullocks and pasturing dairy cows.

Woodland chapel
Betws-y-coed lives up to its name, which means 'the chapel of the woods'. The word *betws* is really the English 'bead-house' or oratory. It is many centuries since the particular holy place was there that gave Betws-y-coed its name, but the old church could be on its site and the woods are certainly flourishing. Some have compared these gorges to the Black Forest – new plantations of conifers give it that air. David Cox the artist made it famous, and one traveller has written that 'the surrounding district contains more beauty spots to the square mile than almost any other region in the United Kingdom.' From Corwen to Betws-y-coed it is a country of wind-swept hill farms, quick to catch the snow when it comes. As Betws is approached the trees begin and the road snakes and drops to the saucer below. Betws now commands the roads – it's either the A5 still for the Nant Ffrancon ravine, Bangor, and Holyhead, or a left turn at Capel Curig for Pen-y-gwryd and the Llanberis Pass to Caernarfon – unless at Pen-y-gwryd the fair Nant Gwynant Pass under Snowdon's south face is chosen as a route down to the softer hills and the western shores.

Softer landscapes
The softer uplands of old Merioneth could have also been reached by turning left at Corwen on the A5 for Bala and the lakes (Bala and Tryweryn). At the farthest corner of Bala lake rise the majestic Arans, the most beautiful of Welsh mountains and next to Snowdon's peaks the highest. Not so long ago Bala town was one of the most important intellectual centres of Wales. From its colleges Nonconformist Wales received an unbroken supply of earnest and eloquent preachers, and from here Sunday schools were organized.

Tryweryn river used to meander through the ill-drained glacier clay of an upland valley north of Bala. It provided bottom land of sufficient quality to meet the needs of fifteen hill-farms served by the hamlet of Capel Celyn, with its chapel, post office, and four cottages. It formed a completely Welsh-speaking community observing its traditional way of life, with Bala as the nearest market town. Liverpool Corporation, needing more water, found at Capel Celyn a bar across the valley made of hard volcanic rock on which a dam could be safely built. The clay of the valley was ideal for excavating and building into a dam. The beautiful new Llyn Celyn was the eventual result. Generous compensation was won for the

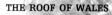

Pistyll Rhaeadr waterfall plunges
230ft from the top of a sheer
cliff into a deep basin.

inhabitants of Capel Celyn; a new road with a viewpoint
layby was built at the corporation's expense around one
shore of the lake, and the roads were improved. Because
the valley was in the national park a landscape consultant
was appointed, so that people could enjoy the beauty of
the area all the more. As for the Dee, here it is a mere
mountain torrent winding down the slopes of Garneddwen,
which forms the watershed between the Dee and the
tributaries of the Mawddach near Bala. Right on the
watershed stands a farmhouse. A raindrop falling on one
side of the roof runs to Liverpool Bay, a raindrop falling on
the other joins the Mawddach and runs into Cardigan Bay.

Land of precipices
The route now plunges into the valley of this river and its
tributaries, a land of rocky precipices, forest-clad hills,
and torrents. This valley runs to Barmouth and is grander
than the valley of the Dee. In some respects the view from
Barmouth bridge is like the view of the Aran and its
companions over the waters of Bala Lake, but it is more
varied. The first ring of hills is more wooded, and there
are more mountain peaks beyond. Above all there is a
wealth of colour with which no scene in Wales can vie.
To the south the high, rugged offshoots of Cader Idris
seem to jut out into the sea. To the north the coast of
Ardudwy, with its legends of Celt and Roman, terminates
in the castle of Harlech perched on its rock. Round the
bay, in a beautiful curve, the promontory of Lleyn ends in
the ridge of Garn Fadryn and Bardsey Island. The bay was
once a rich plain according to tradition, and many a Welsh
poet has told the story of its inundation. In a drunken
revel Seithenyn neglected the flood-gates, and the sea
came over the land.

The bleak but bracing stretch of A5 between Corwen and
Betws-y-coed has many side-roads that lead to remoter
places, such as south-west to Bala or northwards over the
hills to the Vale of Clwyd. There is another romantic way
to the same vale from Llangollen, past ruined Valle
Crucis Abbey and over the great sweep of the Horseshoe
Pass to Nant-y-Ffrith and Ruthin. Of the less frequented
border roads the most notable are those through the
valleys of the Vyrnwy river and the Ceiriog – the latter
from Chirk (B4500) and the former by turning from
the A490 from Welshpool or branching from the A483
south of Oswestry. Lake Vyrnwy is Liverpool's high
reservoir. The road approaches the lake via 1 in 9
gradients and climbs to 1,104ft before an awkward
descent. The lake is the largest in Wales and was formed
by blocking the River Vyrnwy with a masonry dam 160ft
high and 1,200ft long.

Roads from the border in this direction can either go
through or around Llanfyllin. This is a picturesque little
market town noted for the sweet tone of its church bells.

It is from Llanfyllin that one can best get to the most
remarkable waterfall in Wales, the 230ft Pistyll Rhaeadr
which drops over a sheer cliff, through a natural arch,
and into a deep basin. The attractive road from Lake
Vyrnwy to Bala Lake (the largest natural lake in Wales),
is rough and steep but one of the grandest mountain
ways. River Dee rises south west of Bala Lake. Indeed, the
name Bala means an outlet. A species of whitefish called
the gwyniad is found only here, and there is a road right
round the lake shores.

Power in plenty
The amount of water that tumbles over North-West Wales
and runs into the sea is beyond comprehension, but its
power is known. Since men first lived in these parts it has
been used to work on farms and to drive mills. Now a lake
and a dam are being used to provide instant power for the
National Grid. The Ffestiniog power station is the first
pumped storage scheme in Britain, and employs a method
which calls for two reservoirs at very different heights.
At Ffestiniog a high glacier lake called Stwlan has been
enlarged and dammed. A thousand feet below a river was
dammed to form a lower reservoir. During the day the
water stored in Llyn Stwlan is utilized by the turbines in
the power station below to generate power, and the water
then discharges into the lower reservoir. At off-peak
periods that water is pumped back to Llyn Stwlan, using
the surplus power provided by stations in other parts
of the country which would otherwise have been shut
down. The advantage of this method is the speed at which
the plant can operate. Electricity cannot be stored on a
large scale, but the same results can indirectly be
achieved by pumped storage.

Telford's graceful bridge over the Menai Strait
echoes the strength and beauty of mountains which
dip their feet into the sea.

This power station is probably the largest building to have been built of local stone in north Wales since the castles of Harlech and Criccieth. Ffestiniog was probably also the first of the Generating Board's power stations which involved detailed discussions on amenity, and the first to include the appointment of a consultant from outside. The pipe-lines from the upper to the lower lake have been buried, and the completed work stands as a monument to the success of attention to landscaped beauty. Now a similar scheme is being built in the fastnesses of Snowdon at Dinorwic, near Llanberis, on the very ground of what was for many years the largest slate quarry in the world. Dinorwic will be able to supply more than 1,500,000 kilowatts to the National Grid. The Central Electricity Generating Board believes that this station too will be a great attraction to visitors, and that with its machinery out of sight below ground it will be a notable example of man's ability to preserve beauty as well as meet material needs. It will be the only underground power station in England and Wales. The board plans to include a car and coach park, plus a well-equipped centre with exhibits, films, and refreshments. Minibuses will take visitors through a tunnel to the turbine hall two-thirds of a mile inside the old quarry. From a gallery they will be able to watch the operation of the largest power scheme of its kind in Europe. As the comparatively small pumped storage scheme at Ffestiniog has about 40,000 visitors a year, Dinorwic, with its special features, should draw many more.

Pride in preservation
But power in North-West Wales has not been limited to water. Recent years have seen the building of two nuclear power stations, one at Trawsfynydd within the park and one at Wylfa on the rocky north coast of Anglesey. These are the new castles of Gwynedd – and how small in comparison are those of Edward I. Yet how even the Trawsfynydd 'castle' is dwarfed by these remote, wild hills – and of course every effort has been made, in designing the station, to intrude as little as possible into the surrounding scenery. A stranger may easily pass the station without noticing it. Its lay-out is compact, and this in itself reduced the levelling and excavating work. Nevertheless, the contract involved nearly 3,823 cubic metres of excavation, much of it rock which had to be

blasted for the laying of the foundations. Trawsfynydd was the first nuclear station to be built inland, and the first to use a lake for obtaining cooling water. Fishing is fostered, and the character of the wild landscape has been carried right up to the structure. To build a station in such a place was a feat. Most of the equipment came by road, but some of the larger loads were shipped to Porthmadog and thence by road to the site some miles away. This meant strengthening the quay at Porthmadog harbour and dredging the approaches to it, as well as improving the road between the harbour and the site. For building the Anglesey station much material was brought by sea to Holyhead.

The stately straits
It could be argued that the central feature of North Wales is not Snowdon but the Menai Straits. The majestic straits, their 14m of water flowing between sloping fields and parklands, somehow embrace and summarize the whole of Snowdonia – they reflect it; they take it all in. Even Telford's suspension bridge echoes it with the gracious contours of its chains. On the A5 over in Anglesey, before the village with the long name, there is a spot where one can stay to survey the stately scene – the long run of Snowdonia against a hem of water. Along the shores of the strait are little towns full of history and charm – Bangor, Beaumaris, Port Dinorwic, and Caernarfon. Rural villages and ancient churches lie near. It has so happened that one of the most beautiful stretches of waterway in the British Isles holds two world-famous feats of engineering, both crossing the straits at their sweetest spot – the suspension road bridge and the rebuilt Britannia railway bridge, the latter by Robert Stephenson.

With the sea at both ends, the straits ranging in width from 200yds to a couple of miles, and with tricky tides, currents, and sand-banks to cope with as well as the swirling Swellies, these waters call for good sailing. Skill is put to the test in a Regatta Fortnight every August. Before Telford built his bridge and laid down this end of the A5 with such vision of the future, this section of the journey to Holyhead was terrifying for travellers. They had to cross the 'league-long sands of Lavan' at low tide from Aber to the ferry for Beaumaris. In foggy weather a bell was tolled in Aber church to guide them. It was

In 1969 Caernarfon Castle was the scene of the
Prince of Wales' Investiture – pageantry the like of
which had not been seen since the coronation of Elizabeth II.

also hair-raising farther back at Penmaenmawr. The old
road was cut on the cliff face and there was nothing to
keep the traveller from falling over the edge. Also the
track, especially after storms, grew dangerously narrow,
or might easily disappear as one passed over it. The Earl
of Clarendon, on his way to Ireland, had to have his coach
dismantled and carried round by the sands at low tide.
It is no wonder that at one end there was an inn called
'Live in Hope', and at the other the 'Rest and be Thankful'.
The road from Penmaenmawr through the dramatic little
Sychnant Pass was at one time the main road.

Seat of learning

It is strange that a small North Wales town should have
the French name of Beaumaris, but no doubt it came from
the king of the castle, Edward I. On the other side of the
water at Bangor there was a time when the cathedral,
Bangor Vawr, stood alone in its hollow with only a fishing
village on the Straits. Students travel long distances to
this little city these days. They find a university college
renowned for its forestry, agriculture, and electronics, and
lively in the arts as well; also teachers' training colleges
of high quality. They find that here they can live and learn
in idyllic surroundings where life still has the more
leisurely beat of other days.

After the Britannia bridge the straits make a graceful curve,
and it is here that the Marquis of Anglesey, historian and
author, has his imposing 18th-c residence, Plas Newydd.
In the grounds is a fine new building which used to be the
headquarters of the famous mercantile marine training
ship HMS 'Conway'. The ship, an old 'heart of oak', used
to be anchored close by, but in being towed away for
repair it came to grief in the Swellies and drifted ashore.
Later it caught fire and was destroyed. Around this bend
in the Straits are old Port Dinorwic and its new marina.
Here the Straits open out like a loch towards Caernarfon
Bay. Caernarfon is the natural historic centre of the
most Welsh-speaking part of Britain, and it is the heart of
Snowdonia. What this means can be properly understood
only by those who know something of the history. Around
Snowdon are fastnesses to which the hard-pressed princes
of Gwynedd could retract before overwhelming odds. It
was an impregnable stronghold. The foe could not
penetrate into it and could only hope to starve into
surrender those who took refuge there.

Trumpets for the prince

'It looks as though a great flourish of trumpets had just
died over it,' wrote H V Morton about Caernarfon Castle.
Could these words, or this conception, have inspired the
arrangements for the Investiture of Charles as Prince of
Wales on 1 July 1969? The trumpeters were certainly
there, and in this amazing castle a piece of real history
was enacted. For weeks the Household Cavalry had been
rehearsing. It was a dream which Shakespeare might
have visualized, a pageant of history and of kings
among peers, ambassadors, and commoners assembled.
The Queen put Lord Snowdon, as Constable of the castle
(his father lived a couple of miles away), in charge of
designing the whole Investiture ceremony. He grasped the
job with enthusiasm, realizing that it was to be the most
spectacular piece of pageantry the world had seen since
the Coronation of the queen in 1953. As far as Lord
Snowdon was concerned there was no argument what it
was all about – it was a big show for a big audience – in
colour. 'Caernarfon Castle,' he told the Press before the
event, 'is visited by 300,000 people a year, so I saw it as
my responsibility to make it something really worth while.
We *have* this great piece of medieval architecture as a set,
so why clutter it up – why hide it? It means about five
hours performance on television for an audience of 500
million people. We are spending £55,000 on the castle.
On those terms alone it must be good value.' Now why
should this be done in Caernarfon Castle? According to
tradition which goes back several hundred years.
Edward I promised to give the Welsh a prince without a
blemish on his honour, one who was Welsh by birth and
one who could not speak a word of English (or French, the
language then spoken by the court).

He escorted his Queen Eleanor to Caernarfon, where
she gave birth to a son who was christened Edward.
Taking his baby in his arms, the king offered him to the
Welsh chiefs. 'Here is the prince who is to rule you,' he
said. 'He has been born in your country, his character is
unimpeachable, and he can speak neither English nor
French. His first words shall be in Welsh, if it pleases you.
This is how it came to pass that the Prince of Wales, if
there is one, always becomes the king of England, and it
is why the Welsh people have a special care for the Royal

49

Devastated Parys Mountain stands as a symbol to greed which overwhelmed any finer feelings for natural beauty.

Family. The baby of the story was born on 25 April 1284. At the age of sixteen his father formally created him Prince of Wales and Earl of Chester at the Parliament of Lincoln in 1301. He was thus the first to be invested with the chaplet, ring, and verge (rod), and the sword was girded on for the Earldom of Chester. Some princes were invested in their cradles, others at Westminster. It was Lloyd George who caused the Investiture of 1911 to be held at Caernarfon Castle – that of another Edward, who was to become King Edward VIII. It seems to have established a tradition. In 1969 Caernarfon Castle once again resounded to the ringing phrases of the investiture ceremony and cheering of the Welsh people, this time for Prince Charles.

World in miniature

Anglesey, which gave England the Tudor kings, might be described as the platform isle. Here the whole Snowdon Range from east to west can be viewed, the line expanding as one moves farther north. All winter the mountains are capped with snow. As the traveller continues north he seems to retreat from the mountain air; in about 8m the sea takes over. The island is a world in miniature. Holyhead Mountain is 719ft high, and there are other 'mountains' of 500ft or so. Brooks are called rivers, meres and tarns are called lakes, trees are wispy and wind-bent except in the hollow of the straits. Anglesey looks flat from Snowdonia and the foothills but is, in fact, wavy, the waves running parallel with the Menai Straits. If the straits are busy with the small craft, the north coast of Anglesey is on the highway of commerce. Can there be another spot on our coasts which can offer such close views of big ships? And now the largest of oil-tankers are to berth and unload here (at Amlwch) because this coast happens to have the deepest sea in the approaches to Merseyside. Here also is the Wylfa nuclear power station.

Up to now a good balance has been kept between farming and new industry in Anglesey. People care for the island's charm and defend it, and it may be said that Anglesey has been much more scarred by older industries than by the new. Farming still reveals the ancient pattern, and the island remains a place of high winds and of golden sunsets across the Irish Sea, of wide beaches rich in coloured pebbles, of bird sanctuaries and of relics of a civilization existing 3,000 years ago. It is a place of joy for the botanist as well. Here each of the rock formations has developed its own kind of scenery. It has a number of reed-lined fresh-water lakes or *llyns*, again rich in bird and plant life and often covered with water-lilies. The name Anglesey came into use in the 9thc when Egbert, king of the West Saxons, invaded Wales with a powerful army and wreaked havoc. He crossed into Mona at Llanfaes, near Beaumaris, and took possession after 'sore conflicte' with the Britons. The island was later recovered by the king of the Isle of Man.

Sunken treasure

The north coast is a coast of rocks, coves, and caves; of inlets and promontories; of sea-birds and steep lagoons; of footpaths along cliffs wild with heather and gorse and alpine flowers, all under a wide sky. At night the lighthouse on the Skerries reef to the west, 'the leading light of a great sea route', sends round its double flash. A few miles away lie Holyhead and the boats to Dublin. Irish coins even circulate and pass in Anglesey. This coast forms the north rim of an island of history and mystery. The rock underfoot is pre-Cambrian, the oldest to be found in Britain. Behind are cromlechs – unearthed burial chambers of 2000BC and earlier; hill forts almost as old; churches that link with the Christianity of 1,400 to 1,600 years ago; castles; remains of some 48 windmills; traces of the golden wreck of the 'Royal Charter' – the most famous of the last century, described by Charles Dickens in *The Uncommercial Traveller*; and the relic of what was once the leading copper mine in the world – Parys Mountain, still full of brimstone if not fire, and looking like a mountain of the moon.

The wheel of industry in Anglesey has come full circle. The copper mining went down in the last century because of the competition of copper from Spain produced by the Rio Tinto company. Now Rio Tinto has come to Anglesey with an aluminium smelter at Holyhead. Ruskin described Holyhead Mountain as 'that mighty granite rock beyond the moors of Anglesey, splendid in

its heathery crest and its foot planted in the deep sea'. At South Stack there is a savage precipice and a lighthouse which is so far below that it does not seem high. In fact it is 150ft tall and stands on a rock 75ft above the water – a gaunt place resounding with the might and the fury of the sea. Down the face of the cliff is a long flight of steps, and at the bottom a little suspension bridge crosses a chasm to the lighthouse. To the north the face of the rock is smoother; the cliffs are sheer, but in a light-pointed fashion that makes one think of magnificent gothic architecture; caverns at the base help the illusion.

Avian moot

Parliament House Cave is the name given to a large cavern near North Stack. This is because of the great concourse of nesting seabirds making a disagreeable gobbling noise, as if in some mighty debate concerning their civil polity, the better regulation of their fishing, or some other affair of the moment. It has been observed by some wit that the cormorants represent the bishops, the peregrine falcons the lords, the razorbills the commons, and the gulls the people. On the South Stack are the remains of a large group of round stone-age dwellings known as the huts of the *Goidels* (early Irish). These abound on Holy Island, are made of stone, and measure some 15 or 20ft across. The early inhabitants had no vessels to resist fire and boiled their water in tanks by throwing heated stones into them. At a later period metal was worked in the huts. Clearly men must have lived here for thousands of years. Trearddur Bay is an appealing holiday place on Holy Island, and the sands of Rhoscolyn are reached by a series of lanes that twist and turn.

Telford's road was the last in the island to be made free of tolls. The old post road is still there, running its delightful course inland. Now to Anglesey's royal traditions. They centre first on the now rather remote hamlet and district of Aberffraw in the south-west of the island. Here in the year 870 Rhodri (Rhoderic) the Great built a palace, but in 966 it was razed to the ground. Nevertheless it remained the capital of Gwynedd, and the princes took the title 'brenin (king of) Aberffraw'. One of Rhodri's descendants was Prince Llywelyn the Great, who married Joan, daughter of King John. They too had a palace at Aberffraw, as well as one over the straits from Beaumaris at Aber. Joan's sarcophagus stands in the porch of Beaumaris church. It has been said that many of the stones and some

of the timber used in building Caernarfon Castle were brought from Aberffraw. Be that as it may, nobody can say with any certainty today where the Aberffraw palaces even stood. There is no trace, but a prophecy said to be Merlin's stated: 'There shall a king come to England from a princely race, with his noble descent from Anglesey.'

Foundation of a dynasty

The love that grew between Katherine de Valois, daughter of the King of France and widow of King Henry V, and Owain Tudor, an esquire of Penmynydd in Anglesey, gave us the Royal House of Tudor. It is one of the enigmas of history how this love and marriage were kept a secret. King Hal and his sweet Kate, after their marriage at Troyes and coronation at Westminster, had only two years together. 'Katherine the Fair' was 21 when she crossed the Channel from Meaux in France with the body of Henry V. Owain Tudor was among the Welshmen who followed King Henry to the French wars. He had fought at Agincourt, and there is a tradition that he was made a Squire of the Bodyguard for his bravery at Alençon. He is described as 'a goodly gentylman and a beautiful person, garniged with many godly gifts both of nature and grace.' After the war he was given a position at Court as Clerk of the Wardrobe. It was his duty to guard the queen's jewels, to discuss new clothes with her, and to buy the materials for her gowns. She bore him three sons in secret. The first was Edmund of Hadham, the second Jasper of Hatfield, the third Owain of Westminster. It is not known exactly when they were married – the date has been given as 1428 – but there must have been suspicions because in the reign of Henry VI a law was passed forbidding the marriage of a queen-dowager without the consent of the king.

In 1436 Katherine gave birth to a daughter, who was called Margaret and who died a few days after birth. Katherine was then only 35, her husband 51. At this point things ceased to run smoothly. Katherine either went or was sent to the abbey of Bermondsey, and her three Welsh sons were taken from her by order of the Council. Owain

The Pass of Aberglaslyn is so narrow that there is barely room for the highway and river.

was arrested and imprisoned at Newgate. Katherine died and was buried with pomp in the Chapel of Our Lady at Westminster Abbey. Shortly after her death Owain escaped from prison and was at large in Daventry. Young King Henry summoned him to Court but he refused. Instead he took sanctuary at Westminster. Later he appeared suddenly before the Privy Council and defended himself with such spirit that Henry VI (his own stepson) set him free. He retired to North Wales, but his enemy the Duke of Gloucester pursued him. He was recaptured and again flung into Newgate. He broke out a second time and again fled to Wales. But in the rejoicings which followed the birth of an heir to the throne he was summoned to London and given an annuity out of the Privy Purse. His son Edmund Tudor was created Earl of Richmond, and his son Jasper became Earl of Pembroke. The third son Owain of Westminster became a monk. The gallant Owain himself received no title, but was made 'keeper of our parks in Denbigh'.

Return of a king
It was through the influence of the King that Edmund Tudor was married to the learned Margaret Beaufort, daughter of the Duke of Somerset and heiress of John of Gaunt. She gave birth to a son at Pembroke Castle in 1456. The boy, grandson of Owain Tudor and Katherine, escaped to Brittany during the reign of Richard III but in 1485, the time being ripe, he landed at Milford Haven, collected Welsh supporters as he marched through Wales to England, defeated Richard III at Bosworth, and was crowned king as Henry VII. The bards of Wales had long spoken of a young prince beyond the seas who would restore the throne to a son of the true British line. Amongst the banners that Henry VII offered up at St Paul's Cathedral as a thanksgiving for his victory at Bosworth was the Red Dragon of Cadwaladr, and at his Coronation he was attired in a doublet of green and white, the colours of Wales. The prophecy of the bards had come true – a Briton, a Welshman of royal descent, had re-conquered the realm. Henry VII was regarded in Wales as a Welsh king; the way he had obtained his crown satisfied Welsh pride. He showed himself at all times ready to play the part assigned to him by his fellow-

countryman. Welshmen received promotion at Court and in Wales itself. Ever since the Welsh as a whole have been fervent royalists, and Owain Tudor led a royalist army against the Yorkists at the age of 76. He was defeated at Mortimer's Cross, fell into the hands of Yorkists, and was beheaded in Hereford market-place. There is a story that a mad woman combed his hair. After the death of Henry VII the body, or mummy, of Queen Katherine was exhumed. It was 'most marvellously preserved' and was not reburied. It lay about Westminster Abbey and became one of the sights of London for at least 300 years. In the reign of Charles II poor Katherine was shown to the curious for twopence. It was not until 1716, in the reign of George III, that her bones were decently interred in the Westminster vaults.

West to the sea
What is now left of North Wales is the descent from Snowdon to the sunset. The tangled heart of Snowdonia breaks out to the western sea in two ways, either through the tumultuous slate quarries of Blaenau Ffestiniog or into the soft green basins of the Glaslyn valley. Both lead to a group of charming little estuary communities – Porthmadog, Penrhyndeudraeth, and Harlech. The River Glaslyn, or blue lake, descends from a group of lakes at the bottom of a huge cwm surrounded by precipices on the eastern side of Snowdon. It flows down Nant Gwynant to the picturesque village of Beddgelert, which is associated with Wordsworth, Froude, Kingsley, and many Welsh men of letters. The scene of Kingsley's *Two Years Ago* is laid mainly at Beddgelert. The film *The Inn of the Sixth Happiness* was set in this area because it is so like some parts of China. There was once a monastery here, said to have been the oldest in North Wales except the one on Bardsey Island. The Glaslyn River is here joined by the Colwyn, and their combined waters enter the famous Pass of Aberglaslyn. This is a deep-cut gorge, a rent in the body of the mountains so narrow at the bottom that there is barely room for the highway and the river, which rushes down its rough channel in a wild, foaming, roaring torrent. Pine and heather-clad cliffs rise in precipices for 700 or 800ft on each side. For a while the river runs through rocky walls and wooded banks, then it flows in a silent and wider stream through the vale of Tremadog and empties its waters into Cardigan Bay at the town of Porthmadog.

Abersoch lies on sheltered Cardigan Bay and is considered by some to be second only to Cowes for yachting.

Shipping used to come up the estuary almost to the Aberglaslyn before a 1m-long embankment called the Cob was built across the river mouth. This reclaimed some 7,000 acres and was the achievement of Mr William Madocks MP. His name is sometimes confused with that of Madog, a young prince who is said to have sailed from here with thirteen ships in the 12thc and discovered America long before Columbus. But he never returned. Southey's poem *Madoc* is founded on this story, as well as T Gwynn Jones's Welsh ode, *Madog*. Tremadog was also built by Madocks, who had hopes of its becoming a big town. The rise of neighbouring Porthmadog unfortunately dwarfed its growth.

This is a countryside crammed with the Welsh story, old and new. At Porthmadog there is a low timbered building where David Lloyd George started his career in law and, a short way down the street, the office where he practised as a solicitor. But he made his home a few miles to the west at Criccieth, and there he died. He did not wish to be buried at Westminster Abbey, but wanted to be laid to rest beneath the stone where he had so often gazed at the rushing river Dwyfor. The ground at Llanystumdwy, the village where he was brought up by his cobbler uncle, was specially consecrated. The architect who designed Portmeirion, Mr Clough Williams-Ellis, designed the tomb and it was built with the weathered stone of an old barn. The grave and its woodland surroundings are in the keeping of the village trustees. There too is the Lloyd George Museum, with the illuminated Deeds of Freedom, the caskets of gold and silver, and other mementoes presented to him as tokens of gratitude for his great services to the nation. The collection has been given to the village by Frances, Countess Lloyd George of Dwyfor.

Brave knight
'It's quiet down here' is the Criccieth motto. It gets the shelter of Snowdonia but escapes its rainfall, and is a small seaside town of great appeal. The old castle, on a mound running out to sea, divides the foreshore into two charming sandy beaches. A valiant man known as Sir Howel of the Battleaxe lived in the castle during the reign of Edward III. He had fought with distinction at the battle of Poitiers, using a poleaxe as a weapon, and so brave was he that the Black Prince knighted him on the field. The prince further ordered that a mess of meat, prepared at the Royal expense, should be offered every day before the axe. This meat, after being shown to Sir Howel,

was distributed among the poor of Criccieth. The custom was kept on until the reign of Queen Elizabeth I. There are high and low roads to the 'Land's End' of the Lleyn Peninsula, which reaches out like a lesser Cornwall towards its last lonely stepping-stone across the sound – the once sacred Bardsey. The high is from Caernarfon, hugging the north coast. The low may be said to start at Criccieth and follows the southern shores. The name Lleyn is said to be same as Lein in Leinster across the water. Thus do place-names preserve the memory of ancient movements of peoples.

Fair winds and sails
The beach at Pwllheli is almost a mile from the old town, which lies at the foot of a low range. Up to the beginning of this century it had streets paved with cobbles. Abersoch is 8m on, and is now the most eminent place on this bend of Cardigan Bay. Sheltered and mild, yet with constant breezes, it has become a great place for yachting – second only to Cowes, some say. Yachts and dinghies are heeled over on the dried-out sides of the creek and on the hill beyond, and many yachts stand supported by their sheerlegs, hauled up for the season. Tucked under the rocky headland is the little harbour, full of brightly-painted sailing dinghies and other small craft. Farther out in the roads between the harbour and St Tudwal's Islands the larger yachts ride at anchor. The sea temperature between Pwllheli and Abersoch is remarkably high. The Abersoch yacht fleet is one of the largest on the North Wales coast, and the August regatta has been held for 80 years, attracting yachtsmen from far afield. Abersoch is the headquarters of the South Caernarfonshire Yacht Club. As for the golf course, it can be played on within an hour of the heaviest shower ceasing. Behind Abersoch are country lanes winding through moorland and among the farms, and Abersoch itself is a genuine village where the Welsh language thrives. The coast is full of surprising beaches and coves, and a car can reach any point in the peninsula from Abersoch in 45 minutes.

The long, melodious line of the Snowdon Range as seen from Anglesey breaks into a triad at its western end before it falls into the sea. These three prongs are called The Rivals, but this is only a rough rendering of the group's

Welsh name *Yr Eifl* – the fork. They are prominent for miles around, and the highest point is over 1,840ft. Granite is quarried above Trefor, a village which huddles between the mountain and the mackerel. A cloud cap on the Rivals is a sign of bad weather, and the view from the top is the crowning point of all the coast scenery of Wales to many people. It commands the entire coastline from Llandudno's Great Orme to old Pembrokeshire, and it is from here that one realizes the majesty of Snowdon as it towers in its central position above all its attendant peaks. On the sea side there is a series of precipices, in some places 600ft in height. The grandeur of the scenery is seen to its full effect only from the sea.

On the 1,591ft east peak is Tre'r Ceiri, pronounced Trayr Kiry, an early village of a 100 hut-circles enclosed by a great rampant. It is the most complete of these old hill strongholds in North Wales, and could be the finest example in existence. It was probably built by the Goidels in the late bronze age and occupied during the iron age and Roman era – and perhaps even later. The settlement covers an area of about five acres and comprises several groups of huts. The inner wall has two gateways, one on the west, the other on the south, and a sally port in the north. On the inner side of the wall is a step or walk which enabled the defenders to stand behind a stone parapet, and the gateways are strongly defended by outworks. There are similar but much smaller settlements on other hills in the vicinity. At the foot of the Rivals runs the Pilgrim Way to Bardsey.

The Pilgrim Way takes a hilly route through Llithfaen, Nefyn, and Llangwnnadl to Aberdaron, with ancient little churches punctuating the trek. In those days there was a chain of resting places, each with its sanctuary, its attendant priest, and its holy well. In this way such places as Llanaelhaearn, Nefyn, and Tudweiliog in the north, and Abererch, Llanbedrog, and Llanengan in the south originated. At Aberdaron the Pilgrim Way meets the low road from Pwllheli and beyond. It is the last place – an old, grey, picturesque fishing village which stands on a sandy nook guarded by sharp rocks and rugged cliffs. The old church had the privilege of sanctuary, and the hospice here was the last shelter of the Bardsey pilgrims when they huddled waiting to cross to the Holy Isle.

The Iona of Wales

Bardsey Island, the Iona of Wales, rises out of the sea 3m south-west of Braich-y-Pwll. At times wind and tide and a deep fierce current make the passage between island and mainland one of great danger, and often it is impossible to reach or leave the island for weeks together. The Welsh name of the island, *Ynys Enlli*, could mean the Island of the Great Current. Bardsey is about 2m in length, 5m round, and rises on its north-eastern face in cliffs 600ft high. From a very early period it was the resort of holy men, and it is reputed that 20,000 saints are buried here. A church historian wrote: 'For many centuries the island was to Welshmen what Westminster Abbey is to Englishmen – the holy place of burial of all that were bravest and best in the land. It was known at one time as "the Rome of Britain", and the Welsh bards called it the land of Indulgences, Absolution, and Pardon, the road to heaven, and the gate to Paradise. So great was the holiness of the place considered that three pilgrimages to *Enlli* were regarded as equal to one pilgrimage to Rome.' In the early part of the 20thc the number of the inhabitants had increased from the four families of the 18thc to more than 100 people. An island community of such importance, cut off from the outside world as they so often were, needed some ruling hand. The landlord, Lord Newborough, appointed one of their number to be King of Bardsey, and his office with its regalia was continued until about 1920, when the number of inhabitants had dwindled. All it has today is a lighthouse.

At one time three pilgrimages to the holy island of Bardsey were considered equal to one pilgrimage to Rome.

Somewhere in a Crystal Cave . . .

The qualities of light and substance which man terms beautiful are those he seeks when artificial pleasures lose their sheen. The sand and the sea become his new companions, euphonic streams the voice of freedom, and mountains cloaked in wind and rain the sentinels that guard his brief escape. Deep down it is the story of us all. For the bulk of the year we bow to our captors, the architects of our forced environment; but while the gate is open, and so until the curfew rings us back, the need for change, the need for what we call a holiday, has roots far deeper than we know. It is not enough that the journey should lead towards sunny beaches, good hotels, and the taking of daily trips along a beaten track to the places custom has favoured. The true lodestone is the scenery, the overall shape of countryside which had its beginnings at the turbulent start of the world. We are walkers of the wind, whose savouring of mountains, cool lakes, and the wonders of the shore may stem from memories long dormant in the human mind. We collect silences and reminders of silence. Our birthright is the ground we tread, and our dream the fabled crock of gold which lies at the rainbow's end.

What we are looking for may well be a kind of nostalgia, an instinctive harking back to surroundings no city can provide. The land formation of Wales, as different from England's as granite is from clay, is a natural hunting-ground for the seeker after solitude, but to see no more than the surface attraction, and ignore the bones to which the flesh is added, is to see the paint without the canvas, the picture without the frame. One does not have to be a geologist to appreciate the grandeurs of landscape, but a little knowledge instilled at the start brings a whole new dimension to everyone's enjoyment of the holiday. Why is a mountain? How is a valley? When are the pebbles of the beach? It is surprisingly exciting to find out.

In a sense there are two Wales', the ancient and the old. The north and west, as far south as St David's in Pembrokeshire, is in the order of pre-Cambrian, Cambrian, and Ordovician, merging with Silurian in the central region; and in the south and east the primordial rocks are broadly overlaid by the younger sedimentary layers of the Devonian

and Carboniferous ages. All belong to the vast Palaeozoic era, the formative dawn of stone. These are very rough divisions, for any expert will tell you that constant attack by tide and wind, ice and rain, inexorably wears down the heights, builds fresh deposits on existing strata, and over the years creates succeeding barriers of solidifying gravel and sand which in turn give way to the relentless laws of mutation.

A visitor to Anglesey may or may not know that the ground he stands on is the eroded outcrop of some of the earliest living rock in existence, the pre-Cambrian, perhaps five hundred million years old. If he chips away a sliver of this proterozoic material he will hold in his hand a fraction of the earth's original, an authentic piece of unrecorded and unrecordable history. Igneous rock, as the name suggests, is fire-made. It burst through the planet's five-million-year-old crust in a welter of volcanic eruption, forced by gigantic pressures from the seething magma beneath. This magma was,

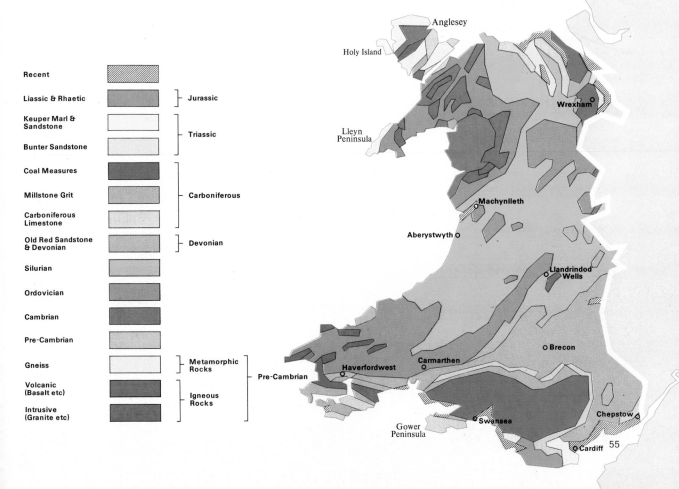

Legend	
Recent	
Liassic & Rhaetic	Jurassic
Keuper Marl & Sandstone	Triassic
Bunter Sandstone	Triassic
Coal Measures	Carboniferous
Millstone Grit	Carboniferous
Carboniferous Limestone	Carboniferous
Old Red Sandstone & Devonian	Devonian
Silurian	
Ordovician	
Cambrian	
Pre-Cambrian	
Gneiss	Metamorphic Rocks
Volcanic (Basalt etc)	Igneous Rocks
Intrusive (Granite etc)	Igneous Rocks

and is today, a zone of molten rock and dissolved gases in pockets measurably some 18 to 50m down. On reaching the atmosphere the magma loses most of its gas and becomes lava, solidifying or crystallizing into ridges of almost impenetrable matter. In geological parlance, igneous rocks which have solidified below the surface from magma are called intrusive; those that have solidified on the surface from lava or volcanic deposit are referred to as extrusive. The other two major classes are sedimentary rocks, made up of worn particles carried by water, wind, or glaciers and deposited in layers elsewhere and metamorphic rocks, like slate, gneiss, marble, and quartzite, which are igneous or sedimentary rocks altered by heat and pressure into a different physical form.

The holder of the rock fragment from Anglesey, if he feels sensations of awe in contemplating his find, may consider that every meteorite that falls from the sky is composed of the same materials, largely iron and nickel, in the same proportions and of the same densities as those coming up from the earth. Indeed, we already know more about outer space than we do about the interior of our own planet, the core of which is probably solid iron surrounded by molten iron, incomputably massive, its 4,000m of radial distance as remote from exploration as the stars. Between the two, in conditions undisturbed by mathematical calculation, and leaving technicalities aside, there is for the

amateur lapidary a little world of semi-precious stones for the finding, children of the parent rock in bright gems flashed with irridescent colour, crystals and mineral specimens which will later respond magnificently to polishing and display. The quest is not a difficult one. The successful 'rockhound', as the name implies, must be something of a detective – observant, patient, and at least knowledgeable enough to recognize the likelier terrain at a glance. This does not take long to learn.

It is true that diamonds, sapphires, gold, and giant-size semi-precious crystals have at one time or another been discovered in Wales, and that almost every known geological formation, rare mineral, and precious gem is still somewhere there to be found. But this does not mean that the amateur collector may confidently expect to come home in a car laden with valuable pickings. Nature is too good at camouflage. Even so, one day's outing on the right Welsh beaches will almost certainly yield amethyst, cairngorm, citrine, agate, cornelian, amber, and jet – all of quality enough to be interesting – and a spoil heap near a disused mine in an igneous region must as assuredly provide the collector with fragments of quartz, topaz, tourmaline, and the commoner felspars. These fine-sounding names will have no special meaning for the beginner whose time is limited, therefore he should perhaps look first for colour and sparkle in his specimens and leave identification to the museums, rock-shops, or lapidary

clubs he takes them to later on. Some of his better finds will be in the neighbourhood of the igneous rocks already mentioned, variously definable as coarse-grained granite with its characteristic crystals in white, grey, pink, and yellowish brown; gabbro, dark green, grey or black; syenite, darker than granite, and of a grey or reddish hue. Others will be on the foreshores, the rounded harvest of nature's largesse in the grip of the restless tides.

A car will provide transport to the selected locality and leisurely walking may soon reveal a likely pitch to reconnoitre, but fingers and thumbs are poorly equipped to deal with adamantine stone. Even on shingle beaches and spoil heaps, where collection is easier, it is wise to be armed with a knife, a file, and at least one special tool designed for extracting crystals. On a mountain outcrop it is essential. The most serviceable of all aids to rockhounding is a small geological hammer with a flat edge opposite the head, called a chisel-head hammer; and another, almost equally useful, is the pick-head hammer with a pointed tip to the rear of the block. Both kinds are obtainable from rock-shops. Next in order of importance comes a rucksack, and after that a reliable compass and a large-scale map of the area selected for exploration. With these packed away in the back of the car, and one or two commonsense extras like strong boots, warm clothing, and a thermos flask added for comfort, the search is ready to begin.

The M5 and M6 motorways skirt the eastern borders of Wales and provide easy access to two main routes converging on Bangor, the only springboard for the Anglesey landmass. These are the A5 from Shrewsbury and the A55 out of Chester. In contrast with the rest of

Gwynedd – the new collective name for the counties of Caernarfonshire, Merioneth, and part of Denbighshire – Anglesey has no mountains but is crossed by parallel lines of low hills, only nine of which exceed 500ft. It is a place of wide horizons and glorious panoramic views of the Snowdon range; full of lakes and marshlands; surrounded by sandy bays, quiet havens, and islets. The rocks are for the most part pre-Cambrian but there are also a few Ordovician areas, some Silurian, a ridge of old red sandstone, and scattered deposits of Carboniferous limestone and pillow lavas which were formed when volcanic eruptions occurred underwater or as a result of boiling lava flowing into the sea. Pillow lava, recognized by its spectacular pillow-like grouping, is a characteristic of the whole of the south-west coast of Anglesey and is a known repository for many kinds of chalcedony.

It should be explained here that chalcedony is a general title for minute quartz crystals compacted with hydrated silica in a variety of ways. Cornelian is a yellowish-red or reddish chalcedony. Bloodstone, or heliotrope, is speckled

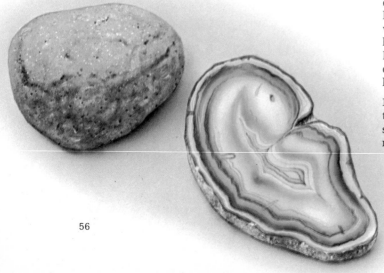

Agate is a particularly attractive form of chalcedony.

56

Rough jasper pebbles can be polished to reveal rich varigations formed by mineral impurities in the opaque quartz.

Spoil heaps of many Welsh mines yield specimens of bright green malachite.

with red. Jaspers are an opaque quartz, heavily impregnated with impurities, and according to their nature coloured brown, red or yellow. In ribbon-jasper the colours run in stripes. There is a bright green chalcedony called plasma, sometimes flecked with white spots. Chert is a flinty rock and flint itself an opaque dull-coloured chalcedony which emits showers of sparks when rubbed in the dark. Its capacity for doing this if struck by steel is common knowledge, but the other phenomenon, known as triboluminescence, is not. Possibly the most sought-after chalcedony is agate, at once attractive to look at because of its peculiar banded structure. The stones are usually irregular in shape, although often almond, as they conform to the shape of the cavity in which the mineral substance was formed and vary considerably in thickness and in colour. These semi-precious gems weather out of the surrounding rock and are most often found on beaches and in appropriate mountain streams. The predominant colours in the banding are white, black, yellow, and blue. Still on the south-west coast, but part of Holy Island in the extreme west, are the sandy windswept beaches of Rhoscolyn and Trearddur Bay, almost totally pre-Cambrian and remarkable for generous scatterings of greenish serpentine pebbles, glossy surfaced, silky to the touch, and so named because their frequently mottled appearance is suggestive of a serpent's skin. The rock varies greatly in appearance and colour-character. It is an alteration product due to the decomposition of olivine and other silicates, and the most highly-prized pieces are always some shade of green. Besides its value to the collector, serpentine in its fibrous form, chrysolite, provides much of the asbestos in commerce. Pebbles of serpentine come from the three main rocks that compose the island: mica schist, flaky and of a shimmering lustre; Holyhead quartzite; and a very hard grit material. It should be pointed out that exposed fragments of serpentine are dingy at first and will need polishing to reveal the colours in their true splendour.

Also on Holy Island and to the west of Holyhead is the miniature Holyhead Mountain, which rises to only 719ft above sea level but a platform for the best of all views of the Caernarfonshire range from Carneddau to the end of Lleyn. On a good day the island air is so remarkably clear and crisp that the superb length of the range, even from 20m away, appears almost close at hand. The quartz schists of Holyhead Mountain, running down to formidable and ancient cliffs on the west side and over to the contorted ruggedness of the South Stack rocks, gives evidence of enormous pressures once active in the crust of the earth. Coarse-grained sparkling granite crystals in

white, grey, pink, and yellowish brown may be found in the vast caves below the cliffs, but the caverns of this stormy coast can be very dangerous and great care must be taken. Back on Anglesey and north on the A5025 is Parys Mountain, the largest copper working in Europe two centuries ago. Today it lies derelict and empty, its summit hollowed out, and the skeletal rocks of its sides and terraces tinged with pink and sometimes a coppery green. The spoil heaps in the area, although worked through by many generations of collectors, may still yield specimens coloured by ochre and umber, as well as the occasional piece of malachite. The north coast, especially Cemaes Bay and Cemlyn Bay, has storm-produced shingle ridges which offer sporadic finds of a purple jasper. This chalcedonic silica is a mixture of quartz and opal and more generally occurs in red or brown.

Anglesey in its entirety is an admirable practising ground for the discriminating amateur lapidary. Geologists call it the Mona Complex, from the Roman name for the island, because so much of the native rock has been crushed, folded, and sheared into intricate patterns that the primordial outcrops emerge quite differently from anywhere else in Britain. The limestone cliffs contain considerable quantities of chert, a compact crypto-crystalling silica similar to flint, and the granite metamorphosed into gneiss yields mineral crystals of quartz, felspar, and mica arranged in scintillating bands or streaks. All of this adds up to a splendid opportunity for the not too experienced rockhound to prepare for the more challenging excursions into noviciate geology which await him in other parts of the principality.

Caernarfonshire, Merioneth, and parts of Denbighshire, the remainder of the county of Gwynedd, are the tall dark giants of Wales, with heads in the clouds and feet immovably entrenched in the plutonic underworld of the lands their mountains straddle. Although not as old as the oldest parts of Anglesey, the massive formations of the Snowdon range rank amongst the most ancient in Europe. Snowdon at 3,560ft and Glyder Fawr at 3,279ft are of Ordovician and in part Cambrian origin. Penmaenmawr Mountain on the north Caernarfonshire coast is a solid block of igneous rock called diorite, a very hard blue-green stone used extensively for ballast and road metal. Farther towards the south-west, sweeping alongside the Menai Strait, the range merges with the colossal pre-Cambrian Lleyn Peninsula which once was joined to Anglesey.

57

This article is concerned directly with the mineralogical aspects of the terrain, but it may as well be admitted that in first arriving in Snowdonia proper, conveniently reached by turning off the A5 at Capel Curig, the visual impact of its sheer magnificence will make the commendable exercise of gem-collecting seem paltry by comparison, and an ounce of rock-crystal a niggardly reward for perhaps three hours of climbing. But the feeling will soon wear off. The summit of Snowdon itself and its sprinkling of discoverable treasures is a not unreasonable walk from where cars can be left at Pen-y-pass on the A4086. Be sure, however, to choose only the months of May, June, and July for the attempt to the top. Away from the tourist track at other times of the year the treacherous weather conditions which suddenly develop at high altitudes create a hazard too great to be risked. A better rummaging field would be around the spoil heaps near the dilapidated copper mines a thousand feet lower down, at the side of the lakes Llyn Teyrn and the mile-long Llyn Llydaw. A short way away the copper content of the rocks has turned the waters of Lake Glaslyn into an extraordinarily beautiful and permanent peacock blue. The main finds, in addition to extractions of variegated rock crystal, will be malachite, bright green and banded with a silky lustre on the edges; amethyst, a purple or violet quartz; and azurite, a fine blue copper ore often located with malachite. Snowdonia national park, comprising 845sqm, imposes no restrictions in the way of permits. It is yours to chip bits off whenever you please.

Llanberis, at the northern end of the narrow-gauge Snowdon railway, was the centre of a slate-quarrying industry which has scarred and depleted the sombre black mountain dominating its famous pass. Slates generally, although composed of white mica, green chlorite, and quartz together with smaller quantities of other minerals, make poor collectors' items because of their quality of cleavage and the diminution of banded colour in the composition. Just the same, pyrites or 'fool's gold' is also sometimes present. From the rockhound's point of view the same limitations apply to Blaenau Ffestiniog, over the border in old Merioneth, a grey and desolate little town in total contrast with the lush slopes of Capel Curig a few miles due north. Much more interesting are the mineral springs at Trefriw, near Llanrwst in the Vale of Conwy. These are rich in chalybeate, or sulphate of iron, and are allegedly good for alleviating the symptoms of anaemia. At Black Rock, near Criccieth on the Lleyn Peninsula, the medium-textured dolerite produces quartz and felspar, but most

promising of all are the west-coast deposits of Trevor granite, a beautiful stone outstandingly suited to polishing. The predominant rock in this section is pre-Cambrian schist, highly laminated, flaky, greyish-green in colour, and pleasantly lustrous when newly broken.

Where Caernarfonshire's mountains soften into the gentler curves of Denbighshire it denotes a complete change in the geological structure of the country. The Cambrian and Ordovician rocks have given way to those of the Silurian period, the third-born layer in the Palaeozoic era, perhaps 200-million years younger than its neighbours. Younger still are the Carboniferous rocks east of Llangollen, running into coal measures at Ruabon and Wrexham. Coal is simply peat, the spongy brown debris of decayed plant life, buried by later deposits, compressed, materially affected by slow chemical action, and converted with the passage of time into lignite. Lignite, or brown coal, later becomes humic coal, recognizable in series from house or coking coals through to bituminous coals and finally to steam coals, or anthracite. In each progression of the series the carbon content increases, as does to some extent the calorific value. It is calculated that in seams of one foot thickness or more to a depth of 4000 feet, the proved resources of coal in Great Britain amount to 120,000,000,000 tons. Wales is no mean purveyor of this, perhaps still the most valuable substance on earth. It may be that in and around the spoil heaps adjacent to these collieries and at St Asaph and Abergele the collector will find small crystalline cubes of iron pyrites, the 'fool's gold' already mentioned. It is a very common sulphide mineral readily distinguished from its royal counterpart by its more brassy hue and by the fact that it is only scratched by good quality steel.

As well as being coal-producing Denbighshire is also a limestoned area and therefore riddled with subterranean caves due to the action of slightly acidic water moving down joints and bedding planes. An eerie feature of most limestone caves is the formation of stalactites hanging from the roofs and stalagmites rising from the floor. These are gradually shaped by the evaporation of lime-charged water into pale and rather sinister-looking cones, many of which show pigmentation from traces of iron and copper. There are caves just north of Denbigh at Plas Heaton, but as with other showplace labyrinths the taking of specimens is forbidden. Rockhounds should also note that some of the national nature reserves in North Wales require the obtaining of a permit before visiting for any purpose. These may be requested from The Nature Conservancy, Penrhos Road, Bangor, Caernarfonshire. They apply to the following places: Anglesey: southern end – dunes and rocky coast at Newborough and Llanddwyn. Caernarfonshire: 3m south of Conwy – scenic woodland slopes at Coed Gorswen; 7m south of Conwy – steep woodlands at Coed Dolgarrog; near Capel Curig – rocks and vegetation at Cwm Glas, Crafnant. Merioneth: near Ffestiniog – scenic area at Coed Cymerau; south of Harlech – shore and dunes at Morfa Dyffryn; 3m south of Dolgellau – enclosed woods near Cader Idris Mountain.

Semi-precious amethyst is a purple or violet form of quartz.

About a hundred years ago the industrialized coal-bearing regions centred on Gresford and Wrexham experienced a sudden bonanza in lead and iron. At about the same time the nearby town of Minera produced such quantities of silver, lead, and zinc from the native limestone that it came to be called the El Dorado of Wales. Prosperity on this scale has long since departed from the district, but the spoil heaps from its mines and quarries must even today be infinitely explorable. Apart from the mineral bonus from the limestone belt, the main finds in Denbighshire will probably be malachite, chalcedon, deep blue or purple fluorite, rock crystal, and agate.

It must be said at once that even the most resourceful and diligent searcher is unlikely to find gold anywhere in Wales. The formerly profitable mine at Llanelltyd on the A470 near Dolgellau in old Merioneth was indeed specially re-opened to obtain sufficient of the precious metal to make the wedding ring for Queen Elizabeth II, but the auriferous quartz veins of the Cambrian granite there are now exhausted and the spoil heaps have been so meticulously sifted that nothing but rubble remains. It is nevertheless in the waste rubble of the screes that one or two other finds can be made. Merioneth is not a very productive county for the gem-collector until he finds accumulations of boulder clay, quartz, and felspar again at the start of the Lleyn Peninsula. There is evidence of manganese ore at Barmouth and of lead and copper spoil material scattered in the grassy verges bordering the derelict mines at Tywyn. A better territory for screening, and one which offers a welcome return to bewildering views of countryside, is from high up the 2,927ft slopes of Cader Idris, or Aran Fawddy, even more towering at 2,970ft. These huge mountains have volcanic ashbeds 2,000ft thick. The choice of Gwynedd as a combination name for the greater part of the counties of Anglesey, Caernarfonshire, and Merioneth is not, as might be supposed, a bureaucratic invention. Gwynedd, now covering a million and a quarter acres, was one of four Welsh kingdoms in the Dark Ages, the other three being Dyfed, Gwent, and Powys. To these have been added Clwyd and Mid, South, and West Glamorgan. The borders do not conform exactly with the delimitations of the old counties, in that some of the new boundary lines take in areas previously identified with the old; but in order to avoid too much confusion both styles continue to be used.

Powys encompasses the old counties of Montgomeryshire, Radnorshire, and most of Breconshire. North Powys is quickly reached from the English Midlands by the A5 and A458, through wonderful scenery based on Cambrian and Silurian rocks, softer and more rounded than those of the north-western counties. At Newtown and

Machynlleth in Montgomeryshire, the lead, silver, and zinc workings – as so often happened in Wales – long ago fell into ruin; and again it is around the spoil heaps that occasional specimens of agate and malachite can be discovered. Radnorshire's peaty acid moorlands largely overtop layers of old red sandstone, in turn folded over the Silurian base. Where the igneous prominences occur, at such places as Gilwern Hill, Llandegle Rocks, Old Radnor Hill, and Worsell Wood, all near Llandrindod Wells, there are chances of finding agate. The best mineral feature of the area is the extrusion of chalybeate, saline, and sulphurous waters at Llandrindod Wells itself. For more than two centuries the taking of the spring waters has been recommended as a specific remedy for gout, but recent medical advances have brought the practice into decline. Where Denbighshire and Merioneth extend into Flintshire, to complete the new county of Clwyd, there is a wide arc of carboniferous limestone also producing medicinal springs, the most famous of which is at Holywell – the 'Lourdes of Wales', as it is called – on the A55 from Chester. Its source is Halkyn Mountain, 3m inland, a tall limestone ridge from which Flint derived much of its prosperity in the days of mining for lead ore. The Lead Brook, rushing from Northop (on the A55) down to the estuary, is a stream marking 2,000 years of association with the lead-smelting industry. The spoil heaps of the old mine workings hereabouts are satisfyingly filled with mineral waste, particularly green malachite and white, green, and yellow fluorite. As they have minute amounts of manganese in their makeup many fluorite specimens are fluorescent, and in certain conditions glow with an intense violet light. The lead and zinc mines at Talargoch are still operational and so may well have excellent cast-out material. Needless to say, it is sensible to request permission before rummaging begins. This is seldom refused, and as the idea of probing their gigantic rubbish heaps for scrap is sometimes regarded by miners as an eccentric occupation, the courtesy of asking is often wryly met with quite kind advice on where to do the searching.

Wild peaty uplands of the north, with their grey shale and rolling acres of grass, are very like those of Radnorshire and barren of even the most commonplace gem material. However, in Radnorshire there is a profusion of medicinal springs set in a countryside necklaced with lakes and reservoirs down towards the Wye and the

The semi-precious cairngorm is yet another form of quartz – this time a clear, smoky-brown crystal.

Wales has many derelict lead and silver mines which can yield good specimens of galena.

59

Beautiful aquamarine is a rare, blue variety of beryl, closely related to emerald.

billowing escarpment of the Black Mountains. Llanwrtyd Wells, 800ft above sea level, has sulphur and chalybeate; Llangammarch Wells, at about 600ft, has waters containing chlorides of calcium, sodium, barium and magnesium; Builth Wells collects chalybeates, sulphurs, and salines from the Llandeilo Flags. This is the only region of Breconshire where rocks other than sedimentary can be found. An igneous outcrop, often with pillow lava formations, extends for several miles north-east from Llanwrtyd Wells and it is these volcanic rocks that account for the mineral content of the springs.

The Brecon Beacons with Fforest Fawr, flanked on the north by the A40, are compounded principally of old-red sandstone and end abruptly where glaciation halted its southwards march. Felspar, mica, garnet, magnetite, and other minerals are mixed with the quartz of this sedimentary rock, but in such tiny particles that it is pointless to collect them. Far better to turn from amateur lapidary to try geology for a while and examine the astounding caves eroded out of the underlying limestone. There is one at Dan-yr-Ogof, on the Tawe River, which is illuminated and open to the public for part of the way in. Beyond the barrier drawn across for safety there are endless passages, stalactite caves, and subterranean lakes which have never been satisfactorily explored. Farther downstream the vast cavern of Ogof Ffynnon Ddu runs into a nocturnal maze extending for several miles, and at Fan Fraith there is the 50ft Pant Mawr pot-hole, with a stream cutting through into nothingness. Above all this are 30m of treeless hills and mountains affording views comparable with the best the adjacent Cambrians can offer. This is a complicated and difficult country for the itinerant motorist, but at Mynydd Illtyd, 5m south-west of Brecon, the very experienced staff of the Mountain Centre will give detailed information on where to go, what to see, and how to get back without incident.

As with the North Wales nature reserves, permits are sometimes needed in the south. These may be had from the Nature Conservancy, Plas Goggerddan, Aberystwyth, Cardiganshire. The following is a list applying to geological features: Brecon: 5m north of Llanwrtyd Wells – moors at Nant Irfon; 6m south-west of Brecon – sandstone cliff at Craig Cerrig Gleisiad; 2m south-west of Crickhowell – limestone caves at Craig y Cilau; 3m north of Merthyr Tydfil – woodlands on limestone at Penmoelallt. Monmouth: north of Chepstow – woodland on limestone at Blackcliff. Cardigan: north-east of Aberystwyth – peat bog at Cors Fochno; 10m east of Aberystwyth – forest reserve at Coed Rheidol; 12m south-east of Aberystwyth – peat bog at Cors Tregaron. Glamorgan: west end of Gower –

shore and dunes at Whitford; 3m east of Port Eynon – dunes, marshes, and pools at Oxwich, Pembroke: 14m west of Haverfordwest – offshore island of Skomer.

Monmouthshire, now the new county of Gwent, is well served by the A40 and the A465. Its two extremes of rock formation take in the spectacular Carboniferous limestone ravine at Chepstow, and in the north-west the long valleys overtopping the immense South Wales coalfield. The greatest altitude here is that of the nearly 2,000ft Sugar Loaf, an outlier of the Black Mountains. The new counties of South Glamorgan and West Glamorgan, centred respectively on Cardiff and Swansea, are almost exclusively lands of coal and iron ore and so are of little value to the lapidary. The ugly waste tips of the Rhondda and Rhymney valleys consist mainly of prodigious quantities of wet slack from mines delved into alternate layers of coaly and ferruginous material laid down in the Mesozoic and Tertiary Ages. Semi-precious stones and metals are very rarely present. Towards the west the coal measures continue from Kidwelly to Llanelli and north-west to Ammanford, the principal coalfield of the Swansea region, and south to Tenby, where the highest-grade Welsh anthracites are mined. All of these are in Dyfed, the new county of which Carmarthenshire, Pembrokeshire, and Cardiganshire are constituent parts and mark a return westwards to igneous regions not dissimilar from those abutting on the Lleyn massif. Carmarthenshire is made up of Ordovician slates, sandstones, and grits, with the familiar Silurian layers superimposing. Lead ore was once worked near Carmarthen itself, and farther north, approaching the Cardigan border on the A482, there is a large National Trust property which also owns the second of Wales's gold mines, the Dolaucothi Caves near Pumsaint on the River Cothi. It is no longer economical to work the remnant of the meagre lode left by the Romans and the Normans, but the site is open to the public and there is nothing to deter hopeful amateur prospectors from fossicking in the local rubble – except an assurance that this has been tried many times before. By way of compensation it might be mentioned that for practical purposes gold is one of the most useless substances on earth.

The A484 winds up from old Carmarthenshire into one-time Cardiganshire and joins the A487 coast road with its miles of sanded and pebbly beaches on the west side, and it is here throughout its length that the beachcombing rockhound has some of his best chances of making a haul. From Aberporth northwards the probability of picking up agate and jasper is certain, so much so that polishing these gems for sale, especially at Aberystwyth, has become a flourishing local craft. The most valued find is aquamarine, a rare blue variety of beryl which is closely related to emerald. The major part of the rock inland is Ordovician and Silurian sandstones and grits, with flags, shales and lavas building up to 2,468ft Plynlimon Mountain above the sea. The high country abounds with gorges, cataracts and falls, less publicized than the well-known ones of Snowdonia perhaps but quite as splendid to look at and having the extra merit of isolating the gem-collector from other groups of enthusiasts. Pembrokeshire is composed of three distinct kinds of rock, igneous, sandstone, and limestone, all of which provide quantities of semi-precious stones in excess of other sorts. The pebbly beaches of Amroth and Milford Haven, the limestone cliffs at Tenby, the sands and cliffs at Saundersfoot, Fishguard, and Goodwick could in fact be second only to Anglesey in the choice of ideal rockhounding conditions. There are no towering mountains to climb, the weather is usually mild, and the gem yield is consistently above average. The main finds are jasper, sphene, apatite, and agate. Sphene, lustrous and fiery, is an accessory mineral in acid igneous rocks and is particularly abundant in contact-altered rocks rich in lime, such as are found here. Apatite, a phosphate of calcium with fluorine and chlorine, also a limestone product, is less common and softer but very attractive for uses as a gemstone where hardness is not a required quality. The crystals are usually green, but can be blue, brick red, yellow, or colourless.

Inland from Fishguard and off the A478 are the Prescelly Mountains, the sources of the half-ton blocks of bluestone which nearly 4,000 years ago were somehow transported to Stonehenge in Wiltshire to form its inner ring of monoliths. At St Ann's Head, west of Milford Haven, the dark cliffs show where at last the coal measures reach the sea, and out in the bay are the bleak volcanic Smalls – the westernmost fragment of Wales. In some sense this puts a full stop to the amateur geologist's odyssey, leaving him with a background wealth of adventure for holidays to come.

Rose quartz, malachite, jasper, amethyst, serpentine, and the rest of the treasure trove of the beaches and rocks may comfortably be turned into baroque jewellery at home. All that is needed to start with is a machine called a tumbler, abrasive powder, epoxy resin, a selection of fittings, and a book of simple instructions. The whole lot should not cost more than £10. The tumbler is a small revolving plastic drum worked by an electric motor plugged into the household mains. Stones are loaded into the container with an abrasive material and set in motion. The tumbler then does what the sea itself has been doing since the beginning, churning and rolling pebbles of all shapes and sizes until they are worn smooth; but with this difference, that the tumbler refines and speeds up the process to bring out the intrinsic lustre of the gems. Extractions of rock crystal, after cutting down to size, are treated in the same way. But remember that all that glisters is not amethyst; it is easy to mistake a smoothed-out bit of broken glass or pottery for the real thing. There are several booklets now on sale which will help to determine the hardness of specimens by carefully nicking the surface with a sharp knife. It also saves time and

trouble to bear in mind that seaside pebbles which take rather long to dry may be porous, perhaps because they are of sandstone, and will crumble away under treatment. And note too that, 'full many a gem of purest ray serene' may at first have a dull exterior and should not be rejected because of this. The keen eye will soon detect what lies beneath after a little judicious scraping of the stained and weathered skin. No semi-precious stone can show at its best until it has been polished in a machine.

When the tumbler has done its work, and the container of mixed specimens has turned into a miniature Aladdin's cave, the next stage is to grade the finished samples for conversion into ornamental jewellery for rings, brooches, necklaces, bracelets, pendants, cufflinks, earrings, or perhaps with larger crystals as a fixed and glowing reminder on the sittingroom mantelpiece of a happy and successful holiday. The special fittings are obtainable from any rock-shop, as are the tumblers and their accessories in addition to the full range of rockhounding equipment. Rock-shops by nature of the goods they sell are delightful places to call in on, and the people who run them are always willing to give advice. It is, after all, in their own interests to do so. Among those to be found in the telephone directory are Gemrocks Ltd, London; the Fidra Stone Shop, Brighton; The Rocks, Gems, and Crafts Centre, Chaddesden, Derby; Solent Lapidary, Southsea; Norgems, Sandbach, Cheshire; Ammonite Ltd, Cowbridge, Glamorgan; Hillside Gems, Sutton Coldfield, Warwickshire; Rough & Tumble Ltd, North Shields, Northumberland; Glenjoy Lapidary Supplies, Wakefield, Yorkshire; Portbeag Pebblecraft, Oban, Scotland; and the' Worldwide Mineralogical Co, Great Shelford, Cambridge. A great many more are located in other towns throughout the country.

There is such fascination in the geological structure of Wales that the holidaymaker who has taken up lapidary as a hobby will never again see only the beautiful but superficial panorama of trees and lakes, of sun and sand and the coming of evening. Beaches demand a closer scrutiny; waste heaps of forgotten mines beckon from the fields; and picture-postcard mountains, immutable as time, condone the theft from spur and scree of all for which they stand. Scientific jargon adds nothing to the quest, but a new eye seeing leaves the memory enriched, the tales of the holiday grander in the telling, and the rucksack heavy with spoil. A rockhound is a born explorer with curiosity in his veins, insatiable of perfection as an artist. With luck he will also have luck.

When perfectly clear and un-tinted by any other mineral, quartz is simply and descriptively known as rock crystal.

Great Little Trains

The Earl crossing a viaduct on the Welshpool and Llanfair line.

The narrow-gauge railways have become as great an attraction in North Wales as Snowdon and the famous castles. Their impact on the tourist scene has been tremendous, although they would have little variety or interest to the general public without the superb scenery through which they run. Nine railways are described here. Eight of them are associated with the Joint Marketing Panel set up by the Wales Tourist Board, who ensure that the lines do not compete with each other but are seen as individual attractions to be visited in turn. These are the Festiniog, Talyllyn, Vale of Rheidol, Llanberis Lake, Welshpool and Llanfair, Snowdon Mountain, Fairbourne, and Bala Lake Railways. The odd one is the Welsh Highland Railway, now closed and with the track lifted but in the process of restoration.

Figures give an idea of the popularity of the railways. Approximately three-quarters of a million people travel on the lines each year. Some lines are running to full capacity, while others are not yet fully restored and are operating limited services. In 1973 the Festiniog carried over 200,000 people, the Talyllyn about 90,000, the Vale of Rheidol about 70,000, the Fairbourne 50,000, and the Welshpool and Llanfair some 20,000. In addition to the train journeys visitors are interested in the large selection of guide books and railwayana available, including models, records, and magazines. The railways' value to the Welsh economy is demonstrated by the assistance given by the Wales Tourist Board to suitable railway restoration projects.

The creation and development of narrow-gauge railways in Wales was brought about by the mining of slate. Found sporadically from Machynlleth to Bangor, this material had been quarried on a limited scale since Roman times and exploited commercially since the 16thc. In spite of increasing demand in the late 18th and 19thc, transportation was generally by packhorse to a waiting barge or ship. Richard Pennant, the owner of the Penrhyn Quarry at Bethesda, was the first to consider railway transportation and built the first narrow-gauge railway to a gauge of 2ft in 1801 from Bethesda to Port Penrhyn

at Bangor. A neighbouring quarry owner Robert Assheton-Smith followed suit in 1824 by building a horse-drawn tramway from his quarry at Dinorwic – opposite Llanberis – to Port Dinorwic on the Menai Straits. This was replaced in 1848 by a new route constructed to 4ft gauge and known as the Padarn Railway, the first line to use steam locomotives.

In 1836 a third line was opened up. This was the 2ft-gauge gravity-worked Festiniog Railway running from the huge quarries at Blaenau Ffestiniog to Porthmadog. The next line to be constructed was the 2ft 3in-gauge Corris Railway in 1859, connecting the quarries at Corris with the River Dyfi at Machynlleth. Following decades saw the peak of the slate industry and a spate of new lines and revolutionary ideas. In 1863 came the 2ft-gauge horse-drawn Croesor Tramway, running from Croesor slate quarry down to Porthmadog. While insignificant in itself, in later years this formed part of the important Welsh Highland Light Railway. This year also saw the introduction of steam traction on the Festiniog Railway, the first time steam had been tried on such a narrow gauge anywhere in the world. Two years later the Festiniog was the first narrow-gauge railway to introduce passenger trains. This event was followed in the next year by the opening of the steam-operated Talyllyn, a 2ft 3in-gauge line carrying slate and passengers from the Abergynolwyn quarries down to Tywyn.

The 1870's saw the birth of another horse line – the 2ft 4in-gauge Glyn Valley Tramway near Chirk, and the opening of another steam-worked passenger and slate line – the North Wales Narrow Gauge Railway. This 2ft-gauge line was opened in sections from Dinas to Rhyd-Ddu below Snowdon. Like the Croesor it created little impact at first but later formed part of the Welsh Highland. Meanwhile the Festiniog had been showing the world how successful a narrow-gauge line could be, and demonstrating the hauling power of its Fairlie locomotives. It scored another first in 1872 with the introduction of bogie coaches. Other railways were going over to steam traction by this time; the Dinorwic quarry introduced steam engines on its 2ft-gauge gallery system in 1870, the Penrhyn Railway in 1876, and the Corris in 1879. Further developments occurred in 1883 when a passenger service started on the Corris Railway, and in 1888 when the Glyn Valley was rebuilt as a steam-operated passenger and goods line. The Padarn and Penrhyn railways did not operate a public passenger service, but provided workmens' trains.

By this time there were seven lines conveying slate, and four of these also carried public passengers. From this time there was no more expansion from the slate industry, and the story becomes one of decline, death, and rebirth. However, by the turn of the century other factors were emerging which were to bring about a new series of lines. Tourism grew steadily during the 19thc and led to the construction of an 800mm (2ft 7½in)-gauge rack railway from Llanberis almost to the top of Snowdon, which was fully opened in 1897. Another passenger line of unusual construction was the Great Orme 3ft 6in-gauge cable railway which ran from Llandudno almost to the Great Orme summit. This opened in 1903.

Transportation of lead ore was a major reason for the construction of the 2ft-gauge Vale of Rheidol Railway in 1902, but it was more than coincidence that it terminated at the beauty spot of Devil's Bridge, some 12m from Aberystywyth. Away to the east at Welshpool general agricultural freight and passengers were conveyed between Welshpool and Llanfair Caereinion on a 2ft 6in-gauge railway opened in 1903. As tourism grew so did the flexibility and competition of road transport for passengers. Slate was on the decline, and together with other local industries was affected by the economic troubles during and after the first world war. The North Wales Narrow Gauge Railway withdrew its passenger service in 1916, and the Vale of Rheidol suffered neglect under its new owners the Cambrian Railway. The Festiniog was also in trouble. One bright spark in that year, was the Fairbourne Railway, a tramway of the 1860's which was converted into a 15in-gauge line to carry tourists. The 1920's saw the birth of the Welsh Highland Light Railway, linking the North Wales Narrow Gauge with the Croesor and Festiniog Railways. At the same time the Vale of Rheidol withdrew their freight facilities.

Tourists were not attracted to the through services between Dinas and Blaenau Ffestiniog, and the Festiniog's involvement with the Welsh Highland brought no benefit at all. The take-over of the Vale of Rheidol and Welshpool and Llanfair by the Great Western Railway in 1923

A volunteer labour force working on the loop of the Festiniog. The locomotive illustrated is pilot engine Prince.

ensured their existence for some years, but by 1931 the Welshpool and Llanfair had lost its passenger service. In that year the Corris was taken over by the GWR, who promptly withdrew that passenger service as well. In 1931 the Vale of Rheidol lost its winter passenger service and was reduced to a summer-only tourist line. The Festiniog had lost its winter service in 1930, but still carried summer passengers and freight. Even further decay set in during the 1930's, with only the GWR-run Vale of Rheidol being in a sound condition. Passenger services on the Festiniog just about survived until the start of the second world war, when the Fairbourne closed for the duration of hostilities. The Welsh Highland ran its last passenger trains in 1936 and the final goods and slate service in 1937. On the Glyn Valley line passenger services were withdrawn in 1933 and the line closed on withdrawal of freight facilities in 1935.

Several lines continued to run slate trains during the war – the Penrhyn, Padarn, Festiniog, Talyllyn, and Corris. Passenger lines vanished with the exception of the tourist-orientated Snowdon and Great Orme, but in 1945 the Vale of Rheidol was re-opened. In the following year the Festiniog dropped out, and 1946 saw the re-opening of the Fairbourne. There seemed to be a spark of hope for the Corris when it passed to British Rail, but then flooding so damaged the Dyfi bridge that it was not considered worth repairing and the line was closed. The railway was dismantled before the end of the year, and in 1950 it was the turn of the run-down Talyllyn Railway to go under. In this year only seven lines remained in use. Welshpool and Llanfair lost its freight service in 1956 and closed down; not long after it was the turn of the two original lines – the Padarn Railway in 1961 and the Penrhyn in 1962. Thus of all the lines that existed in North Wales only the Great Orme, Snowdon, Vale of Rheidol, and Fairbourne survived without incurring financial collapse.

However, the preservation movement has resulted in the re-opening of the Festiniog, Talyllyn, and Welshpool and Llanfair for tourist traffic, and may yet see the re-opening of part of the Welsh Highland. In addition two new lines have been created – the Llanberis Lake Railway on the site of the former Padarn in 1971, and the Bala Lake Railway on the route of former standard-gauge line in 1972. An idea of the interest and affection which the British have for their railways is revealed by the fact that three of the lines, ie the Festiniog, Talyllyn, and Welshpool and Llanfair, would have disappeared forever without the intervention of preservation societies in the 1950's. Members, often in large numbers, travel from all parts of the country to do voluntary work on their railways at week-ends and during their summer holidays. Properly supervised by former employees and ex or current British

Rail staff in their spare time, unskilled enthusiasts come to learn all aspects of railway operation and maintenance. Work could range from the digging of drainage ditches to cleaning locomotives, running sales-stands, or acting as firemen, guards, signalmen, and running the trains themselves. The standards are very high, for each line is inspected by officers from the Department of the Environment and has to satisfy stringent safety regulations.

What makes a railway narrow gauge? This term applies to any line between 3ft 6in and 1ft 6in wide. Any lines above 3ft 6in are known as sub-standard gauge while a line below 1ft 6in is a miniature railway. At 15in-gauge the Fairbourne is really a true miniature railway, but for the purposes of this article it can be considered as narrow gauge. Standard gauge, as used by British Rail, is 4ft 8½in. Different gauges found in North Wales are 2ft 6in for the Welshpool and Llanfair, 2ft 3in for the Talyllyn, and 2ft for the Festiniog, Bala Lake, Llanberis Lake, and Vale of Rheidol. The odd one out is the Snowdon Mountain Railway, which uses the continental width of 800mm (2ft 7½in). Most if not all the lines in North Wales have had to be constructed by Act of Parliament, and it is at that stage that the gauge for the particular railway is determined. The most common gauge, 60cm, is known in Britain as 1ft 11½in, but for the sake of convenience this is generally referred to as 2ft. This gauge has been used for centuries on plateways and tramways because it is the largest on which loaded wagons could be pushed by one man.

Because many of the lines have the same gauges a certain amount of interchange of locomotives and rolling stock is possible. For example the Festiniog loaned one of its locomotives to the Vale of Rheidol before and after the first world war. The transfer of rolling stock is more difficult to record, because it is far easier to re-gauge carriages and wagons than locomotives. Two former Glyn Valley Tramway coaches of 2ft 4½in-gauge are now running on the 2ft 3in-gauge Talyllyn, which also owns carriages from the old 2ft-gauge Penrhyn Railway. It also has a very fine bogie coach of the correct gauge from the Corris. Most of the locomotives are steam driven, and in recent years two companies have decided to convert these engines from coal to oil-firing. This will obviously disappoint the purists but the advantages are obvious. Oil is a cleaner fuel to handle, and properly controlled with the improvements and experience now available it produces a very clean exhaust. This in turn means cleaner locomotives, rolling stock – and cleaner passengers. It considerably improves the steaming of engines on long and severe gradients, with an adjustable or constant fire available where necessary. It also shortens the preparation time – an oil-fired engine can raise steam in about half an hour, whereas a coal-fired one takes two hours. The shed staff do not have to rake out fire- and smoke-boxes, and engine crews benefit – particularly on the Snowdon Mountain Railway, where the fireman has to move as much as 7cwt of coal on each journey to the summit! Finally, an oil fire considerably reduces the risk of lineside fires started by sparks, a major consideration for railways which pass through extensive Forestry Commission or private plantations.

Oil as a basic fuel was considerably cheaper than coal at the time when evaluation was carried out on the Festiniog and Snowdon railways after 1970, but this is now a debateable point. Just as the cost of oil has risen

astronomically, the price of coal has also substantially increased. Furthermore, since the elimination of steam locomotives on British Rail the availability of suitable locomotive coal has decreased. The two railways which have converted engines to oil firing are probably the largest companies financially; the Snowdon is concerned primarily with getting passengers to the mountain's summit by the most effective means, and the Festiniog the largest of the narrow-gauge lines – must operate frequent services over its 9¾m in the most efficient manner. There is no room for sentiment here. Heartfelt enthusiasm is left to those who run the Talyllyn and Welshpool and Llanfair, railway societies whose members not only wish to preserve the genuine unmodified character of the original railways, but also enjoy learning the skills and craft of coal-fired locomotive operation. Locomotives thus converted so far are No. 3 Wyddfa and No. 8 Eryri on the Snowdon Railway, and Mountaineer, Linda, Blanche, and Merddin Emrys on the Festiniog. Both companies say that all other engines will be converted as and when time permits.

Old disc signal on the Festiniog.

Station buildings are usually simple structures of stone, slate, or corrugated iron, and the platforms of cinders or gravel are usually only a few inches above the ground. Some railways such as the Festiniog have substantial buildings, and some have repair facilities housed in good accommodation – such as Boston Lodge Works on the Festiniog; Gilfach-Ddu on the Llanberis Lake; Tywyn Pendre on the Talyllyn; in Aberystwyth on the Vale of Rheidol. Nearly all the railways have a variety of bridges, tunnels, and other engineering works. The Vale of Rheidol includes a seven-span viaduct over the Afon Rheidol; several stone-built viaducts carry the Festiniog, which also crosses the Cob Causeway and once had a 730-yd tunnel; the construction of Snowdon's line presented engineering problems previously unknown in Great Britain; the Welshpool and Llanfair line has two viaducts.

In addition to the railways themselves there are several small museums worth visiting. The Festiniog has a small one at its Harbour station, and one at Lower Corris relates to the former Corris Railway. The most comprehensive is the Narrow Gauge Railway Museum at the Talyllyn Railway's headquarters of Tywyn Wharf Station, and this displays the finest collection of narrow-gauge relics in Britain. Exhibits include eight engines from Britain, Ireland, and France, plus a large and varied display of nameplates, station signs, and other small items of narrow-gauge railway operation. Another museum is to be found in Penrhyn Castle, where items from the Penrhyn Railway and the Padarn Railway are exhibited. Those interested in the slate industry can now do more than merely survey with awe the vast disused workings at Dinorwic, Nantlle, and Blaenau Ffestiniog – destined for years to remain as memorials to the industry and the tough breed of men who had to work on them. In 1972 the Llechwedd Slate Caverns at Blaenau Ffestiniog were opened to the public as a permanent exhibition of the workings of a slate mine. A battery-driven electric railway conveys passengers through ½m of tunnels, past galleries and vast caverns containing demonstration models. More recently opened in the same area and also situated off the A470 Betws-y-coed road is the Gloddfa Ganol Ffestiniog Mountain Tourist Centre. This is a surface quarry combining a museum, trails, viewpoints, and underground workings. It even gives the visitor a chance to try slate-splitting for himself. The interesting North Wales Quarrying Museum at Gilfach Ddu is part of the National Museum of Wales.

Bala Lake Railway

In 1965 the British Railways line from Barmouth Junction, through Dolgellau to Llangollen and Ruabon, was closed to all traffic. All of the trackbed in the area of Gwynedd that used to form the county of Merionethshire was later sold to the County Council, including a section which ran alongside the very attractive Bala Lake – or Llyn Tegid. The great scenic attraction of this piece of track led to the suggestion that it should be converted for use as a narrow-gauge railway, to be used as a tourism facility. As a result a company was formed to re-open part of the Llanuwchllyn to Bala Junction section along the shores of the lake. The gauge was to be 2ft, and altogether 5m of trackbed ending at the north extremity of the lake were leased. The intention is to finally extend the line to reach the town of Bala, and subject to approval a new section of line will be constructed to enter the town from the south.

The company achieved two 'firsts' in the course of its opening on 14 August 1972. Its proper name Rheilffordd Llyn Tegid is the first of any railway company in Wales to have been registered entirely in the Welsh language; it is also the first narrow-gauge railway to have been constructed on the trackbed of a closed British Rail line. Starting from the original station at Llanuwchllyn, the line commenced operations along a $1\frac{1}{4}$m track with a small Ruston industrial diesel locomotive and two open-sided, toast-rack coaches. By 15 September a further $\frac{3}{4}$m of track had been opened to traffic, bringing the railway as far as Llangower village about halfway along the lake's shore. This is the present terminus and includes a proper station and a locomotive run-round loop.

In 1973 a bogie diesel locomotive took over the passenger service, and two new, fully-enclosed passenger coaches were acquired. It was also in that year that the steam locomotive Helen Katrina arrived, a well-tank built in Germany during the year 1948. This has a boiler-pressure of 140lbs per sq in and weighs 8 tons. A saddle-tank steam locomotive with a boiler pressure of 120lbs and a weight of 4 tons was delivered in the summer of 1974. Both are in blue livery. It is hoped that the first stage of the section from Llangower to Bala will be in operation during 1975. Passenger figures for 1973 were 23,000.

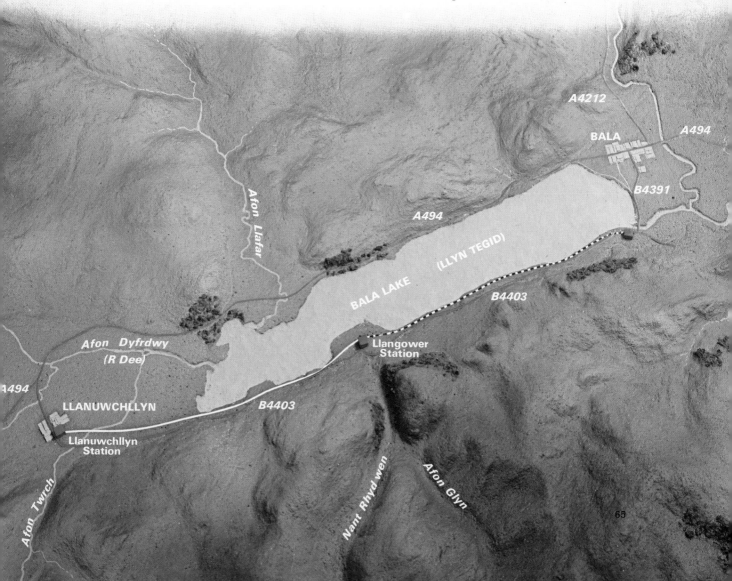

The Festiniog Railway

The oldest, most historical, and most scenic of the Welsh narrow-gauge railways still in operation, the Festiniog is justifiably the most famous. It was originally built to carry slate from the great quarries that ringed Blaenau Ffestiniog. At first the slate was taken by packhorse to barges waiting on the Afon Dwyryd, but the use of a tramway to build the famous Cob across the Glaslyn Estuary to Porthmadog in the 19thc led to several railway schemes. The idea was to run a line from the quarries to the Cob and the new harbour at Porthmadog, but it was not until 1832 that a Bill for such a construction reached parliament. James Spooner engineered the railway to a design which allowed a continuous falling gradient from the quarries to the

port, meaning that loaded slate wagons could be gravity worked and would carry horses to haul the empty wagons back up. The line was built to a 2ft gauge and completed in 1836. By 1860 traffic had increased to such a level that steam locomotion had to be considered – previously unheard of on such a narrow gauge. In 1863 George England of New Cross in London supplied four small tank engines. Until this time only standard-gauge railways were permitted to carry passengers, but after due Board of Trade inspection permission was granted for this in 1865.
As the railway entered its most prosperous and famous period, around the 1870's, more locomotives and better rolling stock were introduced; but by the

1880's competition in the form of the LNWR from Llandudno Junction and the GWR from Bala began to appear. The slate market hit its final peak in 1897, by which time the Festiniog had been robbed of much of its traffic by standard-gauge lines and the fact that the harbour could not take larger ships. After world war one, when the financial troubles were at their worst, money was put into a connection with the ill-fated Welsh Highland Railway. Equipment and services deteriorated; winter services were dropped in 1930 and the railway declined further in 1934 after a brief burst of energy. Passenger services ceased at the start of world war two, and the line closed completely in 1946. The line and stock entered a swift phase of decay and dereliction until 1951, when a group of enthusiasts founded the successful Festiniog Railway Society. Alan Pegler, former owner of the famous Flying Scotsman, saved the Festiniog by buying the controlling interest and using the considerable voluntary aid of the society to get the line going again.

The take over occurred in 1954. July 1955 saw the first short section between Porthmadog and Boston Lodge opened; in 1956 the line had re-opened to Minffordd, and by 1958 a further 4m to Tan-y-Bwlch had been rescued. In 1968 the present terminus at Ddaullt was reached. Legal battles resulted in the track from here having to use the western shore of the Llyn Stwlan lower storage reservoir to rejoin the old route at the end of a flooded section, and current works include the construction

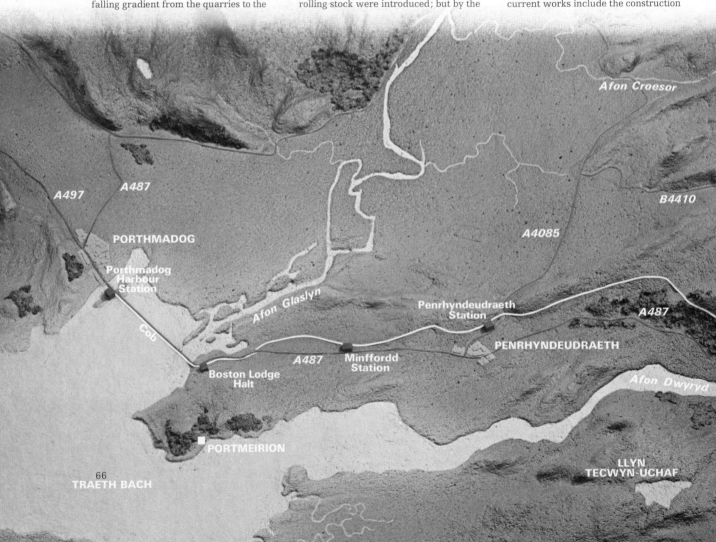

of a unique spiral and a new tunnel from the present terminus at Dduallt. By 1978 the track should be completed to the new Blaenau terminus. This incredible success story is due to the efforts of volunteers, and the unprecedented figure of 407,558 passenger journeys which was achieved in 1973.

The line starts from Porthmadog Harbour Station, where there are company offices plus a refreshment and souvenir shop, and runs for 9¾m over fascinating engineering works and through beautiful countryside. Features of the ride include the ¾m Cob, distant mountains, and views which include Harlech Castle and Snowdon. The famous Boston Lodge works where locomotives and rolling stock are repaired, rebuilt, or newly constructed is passed before the line runs beneath the main road. The railway continues through varied countryside and then curves sharply to pass through Tyler's Cutting and along the wooded slopes of a tributary valley. After a curving run the line comes into Tan-y-Bwlch, 7½m from the start and the second largest station on the railway. There is road access here. The remainder of the journey is along high valley sides, and finally up to the 600ft Dduallt terminus, the present end of the line. The old route to Blaenau is still clearly visible in places beyond Tanygrisiau.

The railway's selection of motive power is wide and interesting, and all engines have been converted to burn oil. Two of the original saddle tanks, Prince and Princess, still survive. The former is

awaiting rebuilding and the latter is on display at Blaenau Ffestiniog, also awaiting attention. Both have been considerably modified and bear no resemblance to their original condition. Welsh Pony is a larger engine built to the same basic design in 1869, and is also stored in Boston Lodge. The largest locomotive in use is Merddin Emrys, one of two remaining engines designed by Robert Fairlie and built at Boston Lodge. Each is really two engines in one, incorporating the articulated principle of pivoted driving bogies, and the two boilers share one common firebox. The aforenamed engine dates from 1879, and the other – called the Earl of Merioneth – was built in 1885 and is being completely rebuilt. Linda and Blanche are two engines from the former Penrhyn Railway and were built by the Hunslet Engine Co in 1893. Once conventional saddle tanks, these were converted by the Festiniog and equipped with tenders. A regular passenger engine is the American tank Mountaineer, which was built in 1917 for war service in France and used on a light railway in that country until purchased in the 1960's. The most unusual engine which will run on the line is a Beyer-Peacock unit built for a Tasmanian railway in 1909. It is a Garrett type, a variation of the articulated principle, and was obtained from the manufacturer's works in Manchester in 1966.

Passenger stock comprises 22 bogie coaches and seven four-wheeled coaches, split into three main types: four-wheeled, compartmented, and corridor. Of the original 19th-c four-wheeled stock, coaches 3, 4, 5, and 6 have survived. Some of the original, crude coaches were known as bug-boxes, but in 1872 the Festiniog introduced the first bogie coaches to run on a narrow-gauge railway. Since then much of the surviving stock has been carefully restored, and that which has been scrapped replaced by modern vehicles. About 100 of the original 1,000 slate wagons survive, and over 180 wagons are in current use – mostly on ballast and permanent way trains. Normal passenger services are worked with three train sets, all of which include a first-class observation car and a buffet. All passenger doors are locked before the trains leave the stations, due to the tight clearances through tunnels, bridges, and cuttings. The fine variety of signals includes upper-quadrant and somersault semaphores, a rare disc-type signal of early origins, and modern colour-light signals.

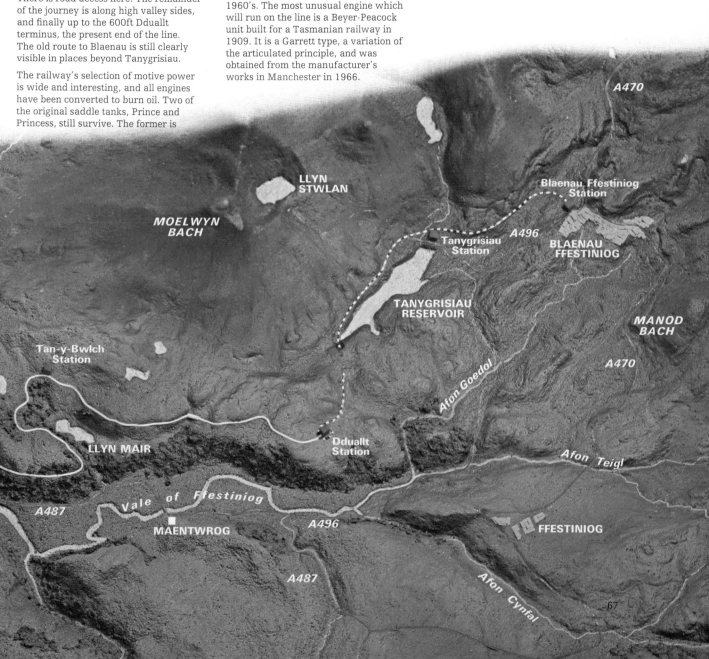

67

The Talyllyn Railway

The Talyllyn is considered the birthplace of railway preservation. It also has the distinction of having continuously run a public service since its opening in 1866. Like many other narrow-gauge railways its origins were connected with the extractive industry – in this case slate. For years the finished slate from a quarry at Bryn Eglwys, south of Abergynolwyn, was transported by packhorse to the nearest port – Aberdyfi. When the McConnel brothers gained possession of the quarry they realized the need for a steam-operated railway and engaged James Spooner of Porthmadog to survey a route down the Fathew Valley to the standard-gauge track at Tywyn. The line was designed from the start to carry passengers and was passed for operation in December 1866. The unusual 2ft 3in gauge was probably chosen for compatibility with the quarry.

The railway had a mundane existence until fairly late in this century. Although most of the passengers were quarrymen a small but expanding number of tourists also used the line, and by 1883 horse buses were employed to convey them from the terminus at Abergynolwyn to the Corris Railway – another 2ft 3in-gauge slate line that ran to Machynlleth.

In 1911 both line and quarry passed to Sir Henry Haydn-Jones MP, but no changes were made and the railway continued much as before. A decline in the fortunes of the quarry led to closure in 1947, leaving the Talyllyn entirely dependent on passenger traffic. Sir Henry kept the line running in the summer, although it made a loss every year. He died in 1950 and it is remarkable that the line outlasted him as no money had been spent on it for many years. Only one engine was operational; the 19th-c rolling stock was worn out; grass grew between rotten sleepers, and breakdowns and derailments were frequent. The only thing that stopped the line being lifted was a group of enthusiasts who formed the Talyllyn Railway Preservation Society. Through the generous co-operation of the executors they acquired control by creating a limited shareholding company. They managed to keep the service going without a break by taking over before the 1951 season, and since then an incredible amount of volunteer work – both physical and financial – has built the society and company into what they are today.

The line from Tywyn Wharf Station to the present terminus of Abergynolwyn is 6½m long and climbs 200ft on fairly easy gradients through the Fathew Valley. It starts from a slate wharf adjacent to the main line a short distance from the Tywyn British Rail station, and has a narrow-gauge railway museum which exhibits no less than eight locomotives and a large collection of smaller items. Passing immediately beneath the main road the line skirts the southern side of Tywyn to reach Pendre

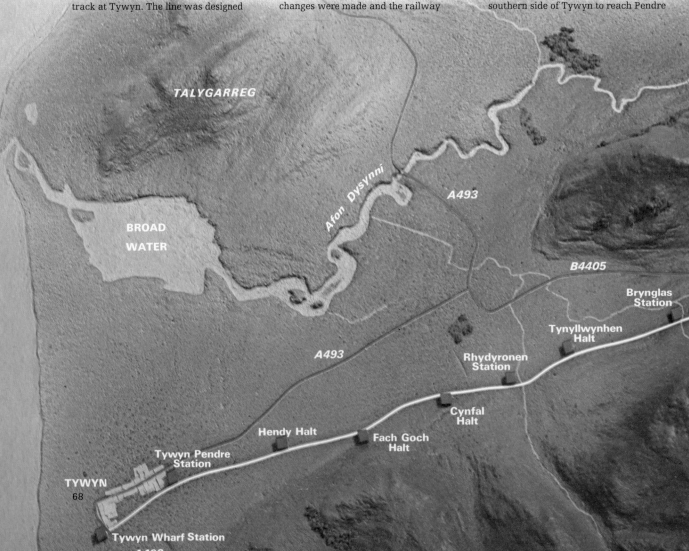

station, site of the railway's sheds and workshops which have been considerably modernized since 1950. After a gated level crossing the line starts a long climb to Rhydyronen, the oldest intermediate station (1867). The next station, situated at the halfway point in both height and distance, is Brynglas. This serves the hamlet of Pandy and the attractive 17th-c farmhouse of Dolau-gwyn, which can be seen across the valley. After running along the valley bottom the line enters woodland which is broken by the Nant Dolgoch, tumbling through a rocky gorge and hurling itself over the Dolgoch Falls. The railway is carried over the river by the three-arched, 51ft-high Dolgoch viaduct before entering Dolgoch itself, some 5m from Tywyn. This is the most photographed of all stations; its picturesque combination of shrubs, slate building, and water column make it irresistible.

Following a wooded ledge the line then passes Quarry Siding Halt, where the quarry which supplies ballast for the railway is situated. The valley narrows and the hills become steeper as the train approaches Abergynolwyn, the present terminus. The station is situated about ¾m short of the village and is preceded by a belt of woodland. A new building with a booking office and refreshment facilities was erected here in 1969. Originally the line continued for another mile and passed high above this quarry

village to reach the lower end of the Nant Gwernol Valley and the inclines to the Bryn Eglwys quarry. This section never carried passengers, but a scheme which has been under way for several years will extend the line for ¾m to a new terminus at Nant Gwernol. The project is being conducted entirely by supervised volunteer labour and is expected to cost about £17,000. A strange aspect of the system is that it does not go to Talyllyn, nor was it ever intended to; there is no reason why the name should appear in the title.

The two original locomotives and four of the original carriages are still in use. Number 1 Talyllyn is a saddle tank, and number 2 Dolgoch is a well tank. Both were built by Fletcher Jennings and Co of Whitehaven, and both needed complete rebuilding. The urgent need for replacement motive power was satisfied by the dismantling of the nearby Corris Railway, which was closed in 1948. The two locomotives that were acquired were number 3 Sir Haydn, built by Hughes Engine Co of Loughborough in 1878, and number 4 Edward Thomas, built by Kerr Stuart of Stoke-on-Trent in 1921. A fifth engine was the number 6 Douglas, built by Andrew Barclay of Kilmarnock in 1918 and used by the RAF until 1945. Engine number 7, Irish Pete, is a modern 3ft-gauge unit offered to

the railway in 1969 by the Irish Turf Board as the basis for building a completely new locomotive. This is not yet running (at time of publication). Locomotive livery is dark brunswick green with yellow lining. Rolling stock comprises nine enclosed bogie carriages and twelve mixed four-wheeled carriages; the latter include four of the original stock dating from 1866. Some of the vehicles originated from other lines, and most of the stock has been converted, restored, built, or rebuilt by the Talyllyn in recent years. Passenger livery is mainly red with green lining, although some vehicles from other lines are exceptions. The only original wagon of the 120 that used to run on the line is preserved in the museum at Tywyn Wharf, and the current complement in use for permanent way work numbers about 45.

All stations are on the north side of the line, and because of limited clearance under certain bridges the doors and windows on the south sides of the carriages are all locked. The trains have no continuous brakes, but a brake van is marshalled at the Tywyn end of every train. The line recorded 184,574 passenger journeys in 1973, and its popularity does not seem to be waning.

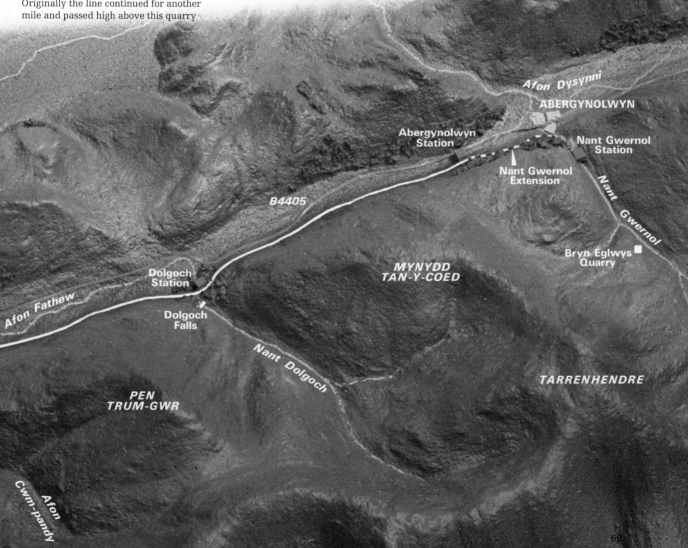

The Vale of Rheidol Railway

This 12m line from Aberystwyth to Devil's Bridge is the only narrow-gauge line owned by British Rail, and the only one on which they operate steam locomotives. The town of Aberystwyth had developed into an established holiday resort by the 19thc, and inland near the head of the Rheidol Valley the Devil's Bridge beauty spot was also receiving its fair share of attention. Several large lead mines were functioning in the Rheidol and Ystwyth valleys. A railway to Aberystwyth was considered desirable for the development of tourism and the mining industry, and in the mid 1890's a 2ft narrow-gauge scheme was promoted. In 1897 the Vale of Rheidol Light Railway Co was incorporated to build a main line from Aberystwyth to Devil's Bridge, with a branch to Aberystwyth Harbour.

In spite of initial enthusiasm for the scheme, capital was hard to raise and the contracting firm of Pethick Bros was not appointed until 1901. The railway was completed in July 1902 and opened for goods traffic in August. Passenger trains ran from December, stopping at Llanbadarn, Capel Bangor, Nantyronen, Aberffrwd, and Devil's Bridge. Halts were added at Glanrafon and Rhiwfron soon afterwards, and both passenger and goods traffic exceeded all expectations. The Rheidol mine conveyed its ore to Rhiwfron by aerial ropeway, and the others delivered to the Devil's Bridge Station. By 1912 traffic was so heavy that an engine (Palmerston) had to be borrowed from the Festiniog Railway. At the height of the Vale of Rheidol's prosperity it was sold to the Cambrian Railway, but with the declaration of the

first world war the lead mines declined and the Cambrian lost interest. A tourism revival after the war led to Palmerston being borrowed for a second time.

Full recovery might never have been made without the takeover by the Great Western in the grouping of 1922. Fully aware of the tourist potential, the company built two new locomotives and four new bogie observation coaches in 1923, and extended the Aberystwyth end of the line to a new terminus alongside the mainline station in 1925. Mineral and general goods traffic never revived and the service to the harbour was withdrawn in 1924. Passenger services were depleted by the growing popularity of the motor car, and after winter services were withdrawn in 1931 the line became totally dependent on tourism. In 1938 the Great Western replaced original passenger rolling stock with specially-designed coaches, but the start of the second world war prevented further development. The line closed at the end of the summer of 1939, but the track and stock were maintained and the railway re-opened in 1945. Although services were thin they remained reasonably consistent, but the nationalization of 1948 made the line part of British Railways Western Region and by 1954 there was a serious threat of closure due to low passenger figures. A big effort in 1955 included the re-introduction of Sunday services among other incentives, and the year showed a record passenger total. A new

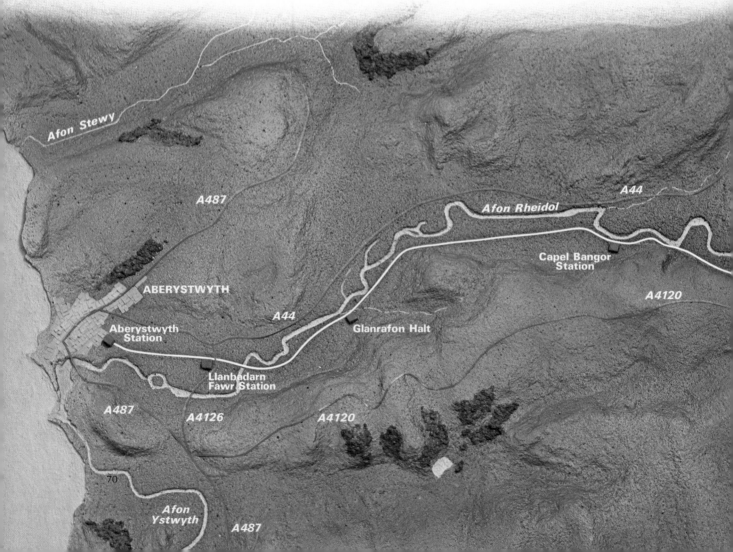

look was given to the trains in 1956, when the chocolate and cream of the Great Western livery re-appeared on the coaches.

The increase in passengers continued through 1957, then in 1963 the railways in Aberystwyth and North Wales were transferred to the London Midland Region. During the winter of 1966 the Aberystwyth end of the railway was realigned to follow the main line from Llanbadarn Fawr and enter redundant platforms at the main station. The large engine shed was converted into a combined locomotive and carriage shed for the narrow-gauge railway. The rise in prosperity continued, and in 1972 the line carried some 75,000 passengers. The elimination of all British Rail steam locomotives in 1968 – apart from on this line – ensured world-wide fame for the three Vale of Rheidol locomotives.

A journey on the railway starts at sea level from Aberystwyth and proceeds east along the wide Rheidol Valley. The National Library of Wales is passed on the left before Llanbadarn Fawr, and shortly after this station the line crosses the Afon Rheidol by a low, seven-span timber-built viaduct. Glanrafon Halt is passed 2½m from Aberystwyth; after Capel Bangor, some 4½m from the start, the gradient steepens amongst mixed woodlands and the line passes along a succession of low embankments and shallow rock cuttings. From Nantyronen to Aberffrwd the gradients steepen in a series of steps, and the locomotives stop to take water at the last-mentioned place – 7½m from the start and at an altitude of 200ft in the Rheidol Forest. The next 4½m to Devil's Bridge is along a ledge cut into the rock to give a constant gradient, affording spectacular views over the almost sheer drop into the Rheidol Valley. Numerous sharp curves also allow fine views, and a path from the 400ft Rheidol Falls Halt leads to attractive waterfalls. The climb continues to Rhiwfron, another conditional halt some 11m from the start and set at 580ft – loading point for the old Rheidol mine. Spoil tips can be seen on the far side of the valley, and a steep path leads down to a hydro-electricity complex on the Rheidol. One more mile brings the line through a deep rock cutting and into the Devil's Bridge terminus, at a height of 680ft. The famous three bridges, Mynach Falls, and splendid views down the Rheidol Valley are near by.

The three locomotives operated by the line have a distinctive, boxed-in appearance due to their long side tanks. Their respective names and numbers are: 7 Llywelyn; 8 Owain Glyndwr; 9 Prince of Wales. Three engines were obtained at the opening of the line in 1902, two being tanks from Davies and Metcalfe of Manchester, numbered and named 1 Edward VII and 2 Prince of Wales respectively. In 1923 the Great Western constructed two similar, though slightly heavier and more powerful locomotives, and numbered them 7 and 8. This had no connection with the original numbering of the locomotives. To add to the confusion the original engines 1 and 2 were renumbered 1212 and 1213. In 1932 number 1212 was withdrawn and sent to Swindon; soon after number 1213 followed for an overhaul and emerged rebuilt to conform with the others in major respects. It lost its name 'Prince of Wales', and was renumbered 9 in 1949. A naming programme of 1956 saw its old title restored and new names for the other two. All three display typically Great-Western brass-ringed chimneys and similar 'family' features.

The rolling stock comprises sixteen bogie coaches, seven open and the rest – from 1938 – closed. All have been designed for maximum vision, and the livery has finally stabilized as Rail Blue to conform with British Rail policy. All trains are operated under the staff and ticket system.

The Llanberis Lake Railway

This is one of the most recent of the narrow-gauge lines to be established in Wales, and owes its existence to the once famous Dinorwic Slate Quarries. The locomotives belonged to one of the quarry's two railway systems, and the trackbed belonged to the other. The quarries themselves are now closed, but their remains lie on the southern slopes of Elidir Fach, opposite Llanberis. Faces were worked from nearly 20 different galleries up the mountainside, reaching an altitude of 2,200ft. The railway system was laid to a gauge of 2ft and begun in 1800. It remained horse drawn until a vertical-boilered steam engine was introduced in 1870, but this was not a success and was later replaced by a specially-designed locomotive from the Hunslet Engine Co of Leeds. This proved the start of a very successful arrangement; all but one of the 22 engines eventually working on the galleries came from the same company. Basically all the Hunslet engines were of the same design – 7-ton saddle tanks with a very short wheel base. They were delivered at irregular intervals between 1870 and 1932. Few of the engines had cabs because of the numerous overhead obstacles, and the standard livery was bright red. All the engines were named, mostly after members of the Assheton Smith family and race horses owned by them. This family owned the quarries, and of the 21 engines nineteen have been preserved. Three were bought by the Llanberis Lake Railway, and a fourth which now runs on the railway was purchased by a preservation group and returned to Llanberis.

The second quarry rail system was the 4ft-gauge Padarn, which carried finished slate from the processing points to the docks at Port Dinorwic. During the 18thc the slate was taken by boat and packhorse to Caernarfon, the nearest port. This line was built in 1824 and the traffic to the Menai Straits was horse drawn. By the late 1840's it was abandoned in favour of a new route which ran at a lower level, along the shores of the lake for about 2m. An interesting feature is the retaining wall along which the trackbed was laid. Steam-operated from the start, its two unusual original engines had tenders and were named Jenny Lind and Fire Queen. The former was withdrawn in 1882 and the latter followed the same fate in 1886. Fortunately one of these engines was placed in a small shed which was later bricked up, and remained untouched until 1969 when it was rescued and put on display at Penrhyn Castle.

In 1882 the first of three new tank engines arrived from Hunslets, and were used to haul flat-wagon slate trains which carried the 2ft-gauge wagons from the galleries. For many years there were

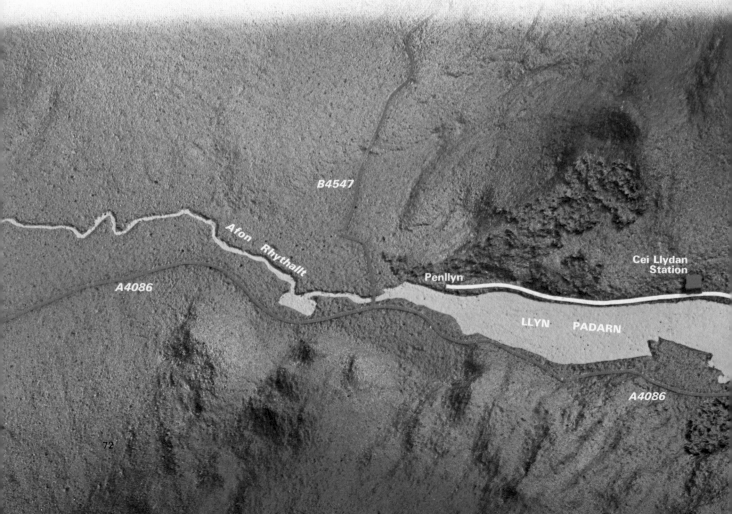

no workmen's trains, so the men bought hand or foot-operated rail cars called Velocipedes. A proper train service started in 1895 and survived until November of 1947. The railway continued to carry slate until road haulage took over completely in 1961, at a time when the preservation movement was in its infancy, and the entire line was sold for scrap. Track lifting was complete by early 1963, the locomotives were cut up, and all but one vehicle was burnt. This lone survivor was a special yellow-painted carriage used for conveying the quarry owner and visiting officials – as well as the wages. The Yellow Carriage recently joined Fire Queen at Penrhyn Castle. Three small, open passenger trucks that served a similar purpose on the 2ft gauge track are preserved at Gilfach Ddu. Engineering facilities were provided at Gilfach Ddu works, a beautifully designed granite building of 1870, and the Head Office was at Port Dinorwic.

The final part of the story concerns the run-down and closure of the quarry and the creation of the Llanberis Lake Railway. In spite of a revival during world war two there was a steady decline in the demand for slate. By 1961 this had brought about the closure of the Padarn Railway, and although extensive modernization was tried it seemed that nothing could save the situation. By 1964 only three engines were in use, two of which were withdrawn in 1967, leaving only Holy War as the last slate-quarry engine working in North Wales. This went in November of the same year. The financial situation worsened, and in

July of 1969 the world's largest slate quarry closed down. From here the picture is one of preservation and rebirth. The County Council placed a preservation order on the Gilfach Ddu works with the intention of establishing a museum, and in 1972 the National Museum of Wales opened it as the North Wales Quarrying Museum. The auction of equipment which included the last three steam engines took place in a blaze of publicity at one of the slate mills in 1969.

The idea of a railway along Llyn Padarn occurred to many people after the closure of the Padarn line in 1961, and a scheme to use the trackbed in conjunction with the closed British Railways Llanberis branch was put forward. The quarry company decided against the project, and a later scheme was forstalled by the closure. A Mr Lowry Porter, initiator of the second scheme, hurriedly formed the Llanberis Lake Railway Society before the auction, and the council secured the future of the project by taking over the derelict trackbed and allowing the use of facilities at Gilfach Ddu. The Llanberis Lake Railway Company was formed, track was laid, and a Ruston diesel and the Hunslet Dolbadarn were restored for the official opening in July 1971. Dolbadarn had been given a cab, and the line ran for about 1m along the lake shore to Cei Llydan. Red Damsel was renamed Elidir and joined Dolbadarn at the end of the 1972 season. Also during this year the line was extended to the Penllyn

terminus near the far end of the lake. A trip on the line starts from the original terminus at Gilfach Ddu, passes beneath the Vivian Arch, then follows a lakeside shelf below the extensive Allt Wen Woods. The route is interspersed with embankments and cuttings, and affords views which include Dinorwic village before the end of the line at Penllyn. Passengers cannot leave the train here. The return journey allows splendid views down the lake towards the Llanberis Pass, with the bonus of a magnificent view of Snowdon.

Rolling stock comprises open and semi-enclosed bogie coaches in green livery, with doors on the landward side only. Motive power is supplied by four Hunslet steam locomotives, a German engine, and four small diesel engines used mainly for permanent-way and shunting work. The names, numbers, and dates of engines are: number 1 Elidir, built 1889 and withdrawn 1957 as Red Damsel, then purchased 1969; number 2 Wild Aster, built 1904, withdrawn 1961, bought 1969; number 3 Dolbadarn, built 1922, ceased working 1967, re-acquired 1969; un-numbered Maid Marian, dated 1903, withdrawn 1964, bought by a group of enthusiasts and brought to the Llanberis Lake Railway in 1971; un-numbered Cyclops, a German well tank built 1937 and currently undergoing restoration.

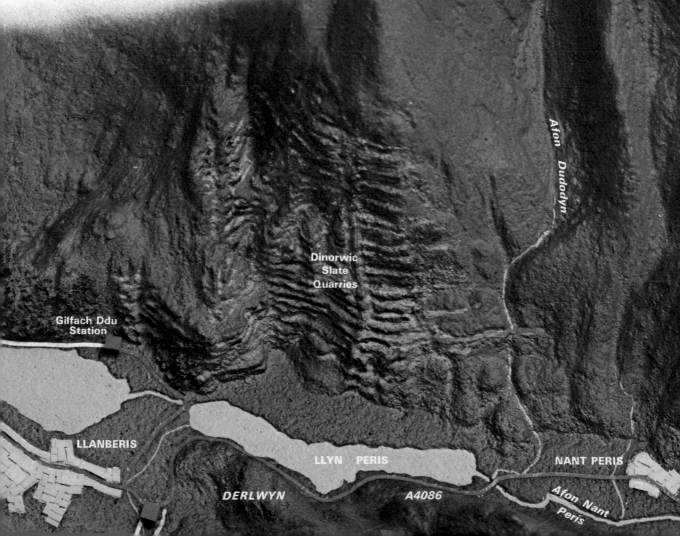

Afon Dudodyn

Dinorwic Slate Quarries

Gilfach Ddu Station

LLANBERIS

LLYN PERIS

NANT PERIS

DERLWYN A4086

Afon Nant Peris

The Welshpool and Llanfair Light Railway

Laid to a gauge of 2ft 6in in the rural border area of Montgomery – now part of Powys, this is the only narrow-gauge railway built to carry general goods traffic in Wales. It continued to do so until its closure in 1956. The line was re-opened by a railway preservation group and is noted for its interesting variety of imported motive power and rolling stock. The standard-gauge railway reached Welshpool in 1860, and plans were discussed to push on to the small market town of Llanfair Caereinion – shortened to Llanfair for convenience. Nothing happened until 1895 when parliament debated the Light Railway Act, legislation designed to open and improve rural areas with the aid of government money. This permitted the construction of rural lines to standard or narrow gauge, subject to certain weight and speed restrictions, but with many of the usual provisos lifted. Llanfair Council favoured such a railway but found difficulty in choosing a route.

In 1896 the Welshpool Council were given an estimate for the development of the shorter of two possible difficult routes, and in December of the same year the townspeople voted in favour. The Light Railway's Act settled the wrangling over the route by deciding on a narrow-gauge line from Welshpool. An Order authorizing construction was issued in 1899, and it was decided that the line would be operated by the Cambrian Railway. Work was completed in 1903 at twice the original estimate of £25,000. Good's traffic started in March, and passenger traffic began in April of the same year. As trains ran 'mixed' the traffic never required more than one engine in use. Freight comprised coal, building materials, lime, cattle food, flour, etc to Llanfair and timber, sheep, and cattle to Welshpool. The Cambrian and Welshpool and Llanfair Railways became part of the Great Western in 1922, whose policy with unremunerative branch lines was to run a bus service in direct competition. This happened with the Welshpool and Llanfair, with the result that the passenger service was dropped in 1931. Freight services continued beyond nationalization in 1948, when the Great Western became the Western Region of British Railways; soon after came rumours of closure. The line survived until 1956, with the volume of goods traffic remaining constant right up to the end.

Happily this was not the end of the railway. A society was formed and later became The Welshpool and Llanfair Light Railway Preservation Co in 1960; in 1962 a Light Railway Order was passed bearing the new name and a 21-year lease was granted. This excluded the first mile of line which ran through the town of Welshpool. In 1973 the company was able to purchase the line outright; they opened headquarters at Llanfair and gradually restored sections of line as funds permitted. In 1963 the section from

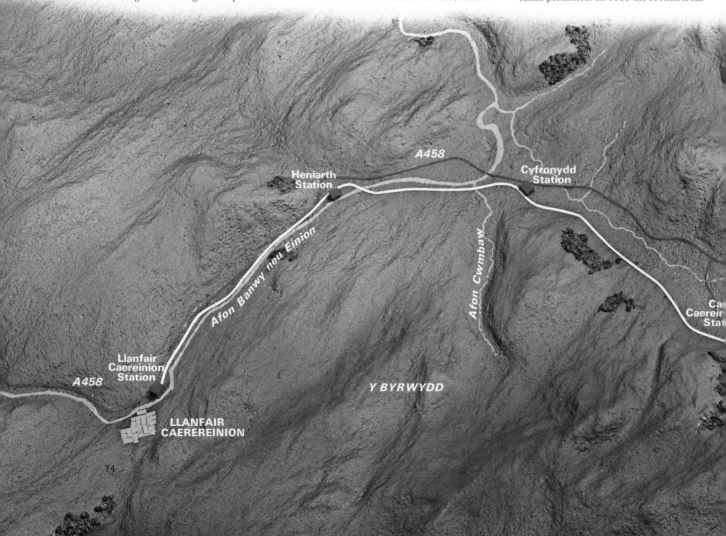

Llanfair to Castle Caereinion was opened by the Earl of Powys; the section to Sylfaen was re-opened by the Mayor of Welshpool in 1972 after complete rebuilding; the final section to the terminus in Welshpool will be ready in the near future.

The journey starts from Llanfair station, at an altitude of 450ft on the north side of the River Banwy, and follows gentle downhill gradients alongside the river before stopping at the only water tank on the railway. The first station at Heniarth is passed after $1\frac{3}{8}$m and thence the line curves south east to cross the river by a three-span girder viaduct at the start of a fierce, $2\frac{1}{4}$m incline. In 1964 flood damage to this structure nearly caused disaster to the entire project, but funds from a national appeal and the aid of the Royal Engineers put the matter to rights. Attractive views are afforded of the river before the line continues along a tributary valley and crosses the Afon Cwmbaw by the six-arch, stone-built Brynelin Viaduct – the largest engineering work on the railway. Cyfronydd Station is passed $2\frac{1}{4}$m from Llanfair, Castle Caereinion after $4\frac{1}{2}$m, then after reaching a summit of 578ft the line descends steeply to Sylfaen. From here the line is still intact to Welshpool. A further short climb leads to the 603ft main summit, then the line reaches Golfa Station at the top of the famous Golfa Incline, some $6\frac{1}{4}$m from the start. The incline has a mile of track at a gradient of 1 in 30 – equal to the steepest on any British Rail passenger line. High on a bank above Sylfaen Brook the line

curves repeatedly on the descent to the future terminus at Raven Square Halt, 8m from Llanfair and at an altitude of 309ft. The remaining section to the original Welshpool terminus, now lifted, was the most interesting and can still be traced between the houses to the old terminus near the mainline station.

Motive power is supplied by a varied and interesting range of engines which include the two original 20-ton tanks acquired from Beyer Peacock of Manchester in 1902. Numbered and named 1 The Earl and 2 Countess, these contrast with engines acquired from other railways. The appearance of both was altered completely during overhaul at Swindon works during 1929 and 1930, mainly by the inclusion of copper and brass-ornamented components. The Great Western renumbered them 822 and 823 in 1922, but the present numbers are the originals. The fact that the Great Western sent the locomotives to Swindon for overhaul in 1947 probably saved the line – British Rail would probably have closed the line had the engines become unusable, but the Welshpool and Llanfair survived until 1956 and the preservation society was able to rebuild from an existing railway. Other locomotives include number 6 Monarch, a four-cylinder unit which is the heaviest on the line, built by Bagnalls of Stafford in 1953 and donated to the railway in 1966; number 10, Sir

Drefaldwyn, a German designed tank of 1944 which was brought from Austria in 1969, is the only German military engine to come to Britain; number 12 Joan, a 20-ton tank built by Kerr Stuart in 1927 and acquired in 1971 after sugar-plantation working in the West Indies; number 8 Dougal, an Andrew Barclay engine of very cut-down appearance and with no cab, from Provan Gasworks in Glasgow.

The company had to buy new rolling stock because the original bogie passenger coaches were broken up, and five coaches were acquired from an Admiralty line in Kent. A distinctive feature of the stock are the coaches obtained from the Continent, generously donated by the 760mm-gauge Zillertalbahn in Austria during 1968. Other coaches are being obtained. Original freight stock comprised 60 assorted wagons, of which a representative collection can be seen at Llanfair, and some modern stock has been purchased for permanent-way work. Signalling is by the staff and ticket system, with passing loops and block posts at Cyfronydd and Castle Caereinion. Passenger journeys totalled 42,007 in 1973 – a continued increase on the figures of previous years.

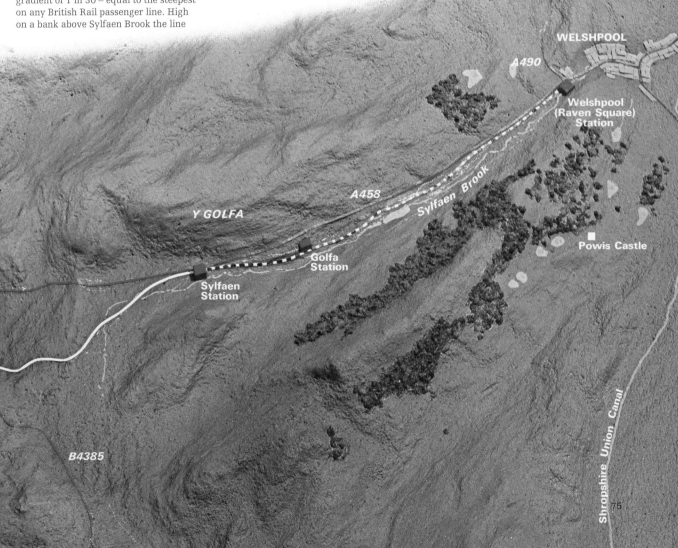

The Snowdon Mountain Railway

This should be considered apart from all other narrow-gauge lines in North Wales. It is the only rack railway in Britain and terminates within 70ft of the highest summit in England and Wales. Of 19th-c origin, the line opened at a time when Snowdon was becoming an established tourist attraction and was virtually guaranteed of success from the start. After the LNWR branch from Caernarfon to Llanberis opened there were demands for a railway up the relatively easy north slope of the mountain, to save the long and arduous walk to the summit. It was pointed out that the lower terminus – Llanberis – would profit greatly from

such a scheme, and the opening of mountain railways in the USA and Switzerland proved that the idea was feasible. Unfortunately the owner of the land, among others, considered that a railway would mar the scenic attraction of the mountain and a deadlock situation persisted for some years. Supporters of the scheme looked for alternative ways to the summit, and the answer was finally provided by the North Wales Narrow-Gauge Railway – later part of the Welsh Highland. This solution presented a threat to Llanberis by taking tourist trade away from the town, and the awkward landowner

eventually capitulated and became chairman of the Snowdon Mountain Tramroad and Hotels Co Ltd of 1893. Consulting engineers went to Switzerland to study various forms of rack system and decided on the Abt method. Electrification was vetoed because of the high cost and uncertain environment, and steam locomotives were chosen. Swiss engines were suggested, and an order was placed with the Swiss Locomotive Co for five engines. The Swiss 800mm gauge (2ft 7½in) was accepted for convenience.

Construction started in December of 1894 and was completed some two years later in 1896. Because the railway was built on private land its construction did not require an Act of Parliament, but the Board of Trade was still invited to inspect the work. The line was opened to the public on Easter Monday of 1896, a day of disaster. Locomotive number 1 Ladas became derailed while returning from the summit and plunged over a precipice. The train was not coupled to the engine for safety reasons and came to a full stop in a matter of yards, and the only fatality was one of the passengers who panicked and jumped from the carriage. Ladas was wrecked, and the company has been without a number 1 ever since. Closure of the line and subsequent investigation revealed that frost action had caused slight subsidence, and after rack girders and grippers had been incorporated the line re-opened a year later. It has operated safely ever since. Early wooden buildings constructed by the railway at the summit of Snowdon

were replaced by the present hotel in 1936. In 1920 the name of the company was changed to the Snowdon Mountain Railway Ltd, and three more locomotives and three coaches were bought in 1922 and 1923. Llanberis station is situated at an altitude of 353ft, and trains take about one hour to travel the $4\frac{5}{8}$m line with a maximum speed of 5mph in both directions. Ascending trains take longer than those descending, because they have to stop for water at one or more of the intermediate stations. Each train comprises a locomotive running chimney first, pushing a single bogie coach up the gradient, and the service only operates during daylight in summer. Trains are controlled by the telephone and ticket system, with the line divided into four blocks by the stations. It is allowable for two trains to enter the same section during a busy period, provided that a time interval of five minutes is maintained between each. The easiest gradient is the 1 in 50 at Llanberis, and there is no level track on the entire route. Features of the route include the locomotive shed at Llanberis, the long Afon Hwrch Viaduct, the short Upper Viaduct near the Ceunant Mawr Waterfall, various other engineering works, and spectacular mountain views. Halfway Station is reached about $2\frac{1}{2}$m from the start. Situated at 1,600ft, this is an important crossing place and watering point where the engine's regulator valve is opened fully to tackle the 1 in 6 gradients ahead. Clogwyn Station is situated adjacent to the precipice over which the unfortunate Ladas was lost,

some $3\frac{1}{2}$m from Llanberis and at an altitude of 2,550ft. Mountains, the Isle of Anglesey, and the Menai Straits can be seen from here. The remaining journey to the summit takes in views of 1,000ft precipices, rugged rock scenery, forests, lakes, and valleys. In the course of the journey the engine is fed no less than 6cwt of coal. Although the summit is often shrouded with mist, Clogwyn is usually clear and forms a superb viewpoint.

The construction of this remarkable line presented problems previously unknown in Britain. The nature of the rack system meant that the line had to be laid from the lower end forward, and the work had to wait for the completion of the two viaducts. The pointwork at the stations is very complicated because both the running rails and the rack sections have to move when the point is operated. The possibility of the track sliding downhill has been forestalled by pinning it to the mountainside with steel girders. With only 150 men employed, the entire line was constructed at an average rate of 120yds per day — sometimes in very poor conditions of rain and bitter cold.

Rolling stock comprises seven totally-enclosed bogie carriages and several freight wagons. The latter are used on the workmen's train employed to carry water and supplies up to the hotel. As a safety precaution the doors of the carriages are locked from the outside, and the conductor can operate an automatic friction brake from his

compartment at the front end of the coach. The distinctive engines are all tanks with unusual sloping boilers specially designed for operation on the severe gradients. Numbered 2 to 8, the locomotives are Enid, Wyddfa, Snowdon, Moel Siabod, Padarn, Aylwin, and Eryri. The original locomotives were numbered 1 to 5 and are of a different design to those obtained between 1922 and 1923. Being rack locomotives, the drive is to the rack pinions on the driving axles and the wheels on these are used only to carry the weight of the engine. The cylinders and motion are mounted above the wheels and face the opposite direction to normal. Drive is transmitted to the coupling rods by means of large rocker arms, which give an unusual appearance when the engines are in motion. Numbers 7 and 8 have large water tanks and can make the round trip without replenishment, and numbers 3 and 8 were converted to burn oil in 1972. As well as providing motive power, the engines also act in a braking capacity. On the descent the cylinders become air compressors which control the piston, and therefore locomotive speed. The locomotives are able to negotiate the steep inclines due to the Abt system, staggered, toothed rails in which pinions on the engine's driving axles engage and push the unit forward.

The Fairbourne Railway

Unlike other narrow-gauge railways in Wales the Fairbourne was not built to transport slate or minerals to a harbour for export. It was intended first to carry materials for the construction of a railway bridge, and later to facilitate the building of a holiday resort on Cardigan Bay. The line is situated west of the Barmouth railway bridge, which spans the beautiful Mawddach Estuary, and runs for 2m up the Morfa Henddol, a spit of sand dunes extending into the estuary opposite Barmouth from the southern shore at Fairbourne. The course of the line is from the shed, workshop, and terminus near the British Rail station at Fairbourne, north west to the shore at Beach Halt, thence north through Golf Club Halt with a golf course to the right. After passing a sea wall on the left the track turns north east through sand dunes to reach the northern terminus of Barmouth ferry. This is situated on Penrhyn Point, only 400yds across the estuary from Barmouth. The lofty volcanic crags of Cader Idris can be seen to the right after the train has passed the golf course, and the attractive resort of Barmouth lies ahead and to the left, overshadowed by the cliffs and crags of 870ft Garn Gorllwyn. Also to the right is the ½m-long Barmouth railway bridge, built by the Cambrian Railway in 1867. Although this restricts the magnificent view up the Mawddach Estuary, the bridge is a very impressive feature in its own right.

Having always been a public-service line and tourist attraction, this railway is unique in that its history is not punctuated by the financial crisis and eventual downfall of its *raison d'etre*. The narrow-gauge lines built to serve the slate and mining industries gradually fell into disuse as their industries declined, but the Fairbourne was and still is the fastest means of travel – in conjunction with the ferry – between Fairbourne and Barmouth.

The line started life as a 2ft-gauge tramway for the sole purpose of carrying stone etc for the construction of Barmouth bridge. At that time the Barmouth shore was inaccessible by road. Soon after the completion of the bridge had allowed the Cambrian Railway to reach Barmouth, the potential of the locality as a holiday resort was realized and development took place. Fairbourne, at the southern end of a very fine 2m-long stretch of beach, came into existence and the tramway was again employed for the transportation of building materials. In 1890 a brickworks with a connection to the tramway was built near Fairbourne Station – a further reason for its continued survival.

Until 1916 the tramway was horse drawn, and because the braking system was rather primitive and the gauge was

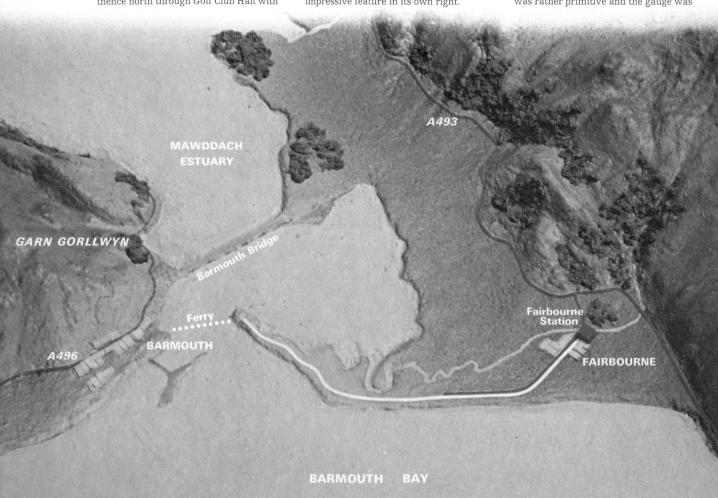

so narrow the horses pulled to one side rather than from directly in front of the cars. Several open-sided passenger carriages were introduced for the benefit of summer visitors. The first decades of this century saw the development of a great interest in steam-operated miniature railways – those with a gauge of less than 2ft – for use in pleasure grounds and private estates. A company known as Narrow-Gauge Railways Ltd was formed, and in 1916 leased the Fairbourne line in association with the firm of Bassett Lowke, the famous model and miniature-locomotive builders. The lease holders first converted the line's gauge from 2ft to 15in, then introduced steam locomotives to replace the horse power and built facilities which included a proper station, signal box, locomotive shed, and several halts. The effect of this was to turn the old tramway into a proper, tourist-orientated miniature railway. In order to further reflect the new position the name was changed to the Fairbourne Miniature Railway.

In 1924 it was taken over by the Fairbourne Estate and Development Company, who ran the line until its first-ever closure in 1940. Gradual decay and damage caused by the weather and the use of the beach by army amphibious vehicles made it unlikely that the line

would be re-opened after world war two. Fortunately, three industrialists from the Midlands took an interest in the railway during 1946 and purchased what remained of the line. Sections of the track and the old locomotives were renewed or restored, and new rolling stock was delivered. In 1947 the terminus was brought closer to the ferry by a realignment of the north end, and in 1956 a completely new terminus – with covered accommodation for rolling stock – was built at Fairbourne. A static refreshment car which is believed to be the first of its kind on such a small gauge in Britain was introduced in 1953. This is taken to Barmouth ferry in the morning and brought back each night. By 1958 it was felt that the many improvements made the term 'miniature' misleading, so a new crest was designed and the name was changed to Fairbourne Railway Ltd.

The line has prospered ever since its re-opening and is still very popular with summer visitors. It rightly takes its place among the 'Great Little Trains of Wales'. Rolling stock mainly comprises open and enclosed coaches in green livery, and some of the stock is in the form of three-coach articulated sets. There are four steam locomotives and two petrol

engines. The steam-driven units are: Count Louis, an Atlantic built by Bassett Lowke in 1924; Ernest W Twining, a free-lance Pacific built by a West Midlands company in 1949; Sian, built by the same company in 1963; and Katie, which dates from 1950 and was also built by the West Midlands firm. Obtained in 1925, Count Louis was built for Count Louis Zborowski, who was killed in 1924. The Count owned a miniature railway near Canterbury and was associated with Captain Howey in the planning of the famous Romney, Hythe, and Dymchurch narrow-gauge line. Sian was introduced in 1963 and designed specifically for the conditions on the Fairbourne. These conditions include the major hazard of wind-blown sand, requiring all frames, moving parts, etc to be cleaned continuously. In 1965 a similar but earlier engine – Katie – was purchased from an estate in Anglesey and brought into operation. Both Sian and Katie, although to a freelance design, have Great Western features and are painted green. The livery of Count Louis is also green, and Ernest W Twining (illustrated opposite) is resplendent in blue.

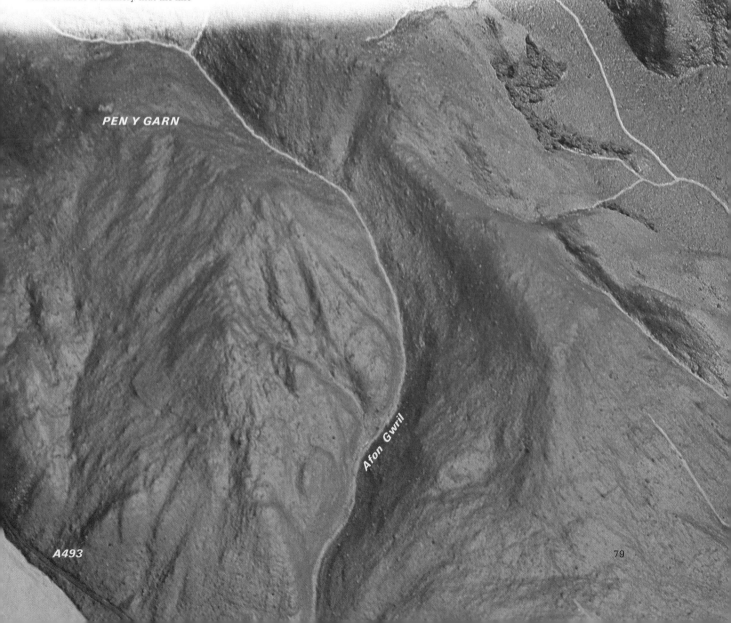

PEN Y GARN

Afon Gwril

The Welsh Highland Light Railway

The Welsh Highland Railway Society was formed in 1961 to restore as much of the line as possible, and in 1964 it was incorporated as a limited company known as the Welsh Highland Light Railway (1964) Ltd. Since then negotiations with the Official Receiver and local authorities have taken place to lease as much trackbed as possible. The site of exchange sidings to the east of Porthmadog station has been purchased for the development of a new southern terminus, which will include locomotive and carriage sheds and a workshop. The first stage of the re-opening will include some 900yds of track. While efforts to restore the route have been under way a considerable quantity of stock, including a bogie coach from East Germany, has been obtained.

Locomotives waiting to run on the new track include four small diesels, an Andrew Barclay tank named Gertrude, and a Hunslet tank known as Russell. The history of the Welsh Highland is the story of a line opened too late to have any real chance of survival; started in 1923, it had a brief life of fourteen years and was constantly dogged by financial difficulties. In 1863 the 1ft 11½in-gauge, horse-operated Croesor Tramway was opened to Porthmadog, running south west from the Croesor slate quarries. Following the success of the passenger-carrying Festiniog, the North Wales Narrow Gauge Railways Co (NWNGR) was incorporated in 1872 with powers to build a line from the C & PR through Beddgelert to Betws-y-coed. It also had permission to construct a second line

from Dinas, on the LNWR line south of Caernarfon, to a point west of Snowdon at Rhyd-ddu in the Cwellyn Valley. The first scheme was later abandoned but the second was opened for goods and passengers from 1877 reaching Rhyd-ddu in 1881. Even at this time there were financial difficulties, and an Official Receiver was appointed in 1878. In 1879 the C & PR became the Porthmadog, Croesor and Beddgelert Tram Railway, with powers to construct a 4m line up to Beddgelert. This did not reach fruition either, and by 1882 a Receiver was in charge of the company. Nothing further happened until several schemes to join the two railways were proposed early this century. In 1901 the Porthmadog, Beddgelert and South Snowdon Railway Co (PB & SSR) was formed with powers to build the branch to Beddgelert. In 1906 an Order gave the new company permission to construct a further line from Beddgelert to Rhyd-ddu, but once again nothing was done. The Croesor line remained horse drawn until well into this century, and the passenger services on the NWNGR were withdrawn in October of 1916.

During and after the first world war local authorities expressed an interest in completion of the link. This led to the incorporation of the Welsh Highland Railway (Light Railway) Co (WHLR) in 1922, taking over the NWNGR, the PB & SSR, and any rights of construction between Caernarfon and Porthmadog. Some capital came from the councils involved, and construction started in March of the same year with the

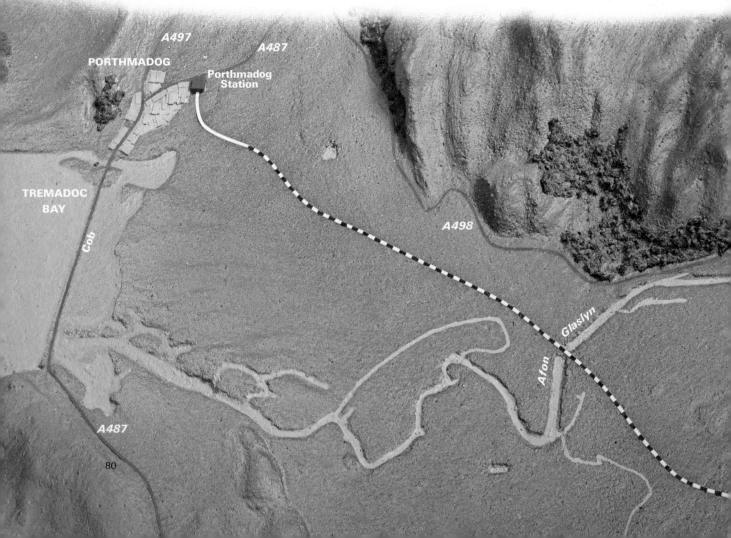

A497
A487
PORTHMADOG
Porthmadog Station
TREMADOC BAY
Cob
A498
A487
Afon Glaslyn

reconditioning of the Dinas Junction to Rhyd-ddu section and improvement of the Croesor line. The entire WHLR line from Dinas to Porthmadog was opened in June of 1923. Porthmadog New Station was built immediately south of its level crossing with the GW Cambrian coast line, and the WHLR then continued south to cross the High Street and reach the slate wharves. A connection was provided to the Festiniog in 1923 via Britannia Bridge. Through-working was introduced, often in connection with the LMS and GW lines, to improve tourist traffic. Many of the Festiniog trains ran through to the Welsh Highland station and by-passed their own terminus at the harbour. Russell and Moel Tryfan were two Welsh Highland engines which were modified at the Boston Lodge works to run on the Festiniog line, but an unfortunate miscalculation caused Russell to become stuck in the 730yd Moelwyn tunnel on its first run.

In company with its predecessors the Welsh Highland soon developed financial troubles; the slate industry was entering its decline and the passenger service was infrequent and unattractive. By March 1927 the Official Receiver was once again in control, and economies had to be made. The service was split at Porthmadog, with a shuttle service running from New Station to the harbour to avoid the GW crossing fee, and the Festiniog went back to using its own station. By 1931 there was a passenger

service on three weekdays during summer months only, with goods trains running on the other days. November of 1933 saw the suggestion of complete closure, but the Porthmadog Council recommended retention of the southern section in view of expected quarrying developments. The Festiniog, LMS, and GW railways were approached regarding a take over, and in 1934 the Welsh Highland became leased to the only company that had expressed an interest – the Festiniog. The latter carried out permanent-way repairs, repainted locomotives, stock, and some stations, and generally made a real effort to improve the line. First four and later six trains per day were provided, but with a change at Beddgelert for the through journey to Dinas. Passenger traffic ceased in 1936, and the goods traffic ceased in June of the following year. In 1941 the Ministry of Supply requisitioned the line for scrap or re-use, including two locomotives, eight passenger carriages, 104 wagons, 1,200 tons of good rail, and thousands of sleepers. Demolition began in August of 1941, and an auction of locomotives and rolling stock took place at Dinas in June of 1942. In spite of these disasters all but one of the bridges, the tunnels, and the trackbed are as sound today as they were in the 1930's. A winding-up order was made in February of 1944 and the remains of the line are still in the hands of the Official Receiver.

Of the original locomotives only Russell has survived. The tank Moel Tryfan was in Boston Lodge for repairs when the line closed, and remained there as a unique survival until the early 1950's; then it was cut up. The through services of 1923 required more motive power and a Government-surplus Baldwin tank (USA) was bought. Built in 1917 for war service in Europe, this was cut up for scrap after the auction of 1942. Russell was more fortunate in that it was bought for work elsewhere, offered back to the Welsh Highland by the Birmingham Locomotive Club, and restored for re-introduction to its old line.

A restored Welsh Highland will be able to take passengers through some of the most scenic areas in Wales if it is once more in operation, and will be a great asset to enthusiast and sightseer alike. Membership of the society has increased to over 700, and although the problems to be faced are greater than most of the other narrow-gauge lines the same over-riding enthusiasm is present. With this type of support the Welsh Highland may once more run through the Pass of Aberglaslyn to Beddgelert.

The Gentle Revolution

Change is the very essence of life. Progress and evolution are life and change; imperceptible perhaps in the short term and span of our experience, yet set against the time-scale of nature even evolution is revolution. It would be unreasonable to expect that the countryside of Wales could be excluded from the effects of evolutionary change, especially when man the creator and despoiler supreme dominates the landscape and adds his work to nature. Today international engineers push the frontiers of their empires as far as the uplands of Trawsfynydd or Cwm Rheidol. But change is not only expressed in stone, steel, and spruce forests; people also change. People are part of their countryside, and the people of Wales are changing. Industry in Wales is also changing, going out into the countryside instead of sticking to the towns – on the insistence of the Welsh people themselves. The holiday industry is changing, no longer confined to inland spas and coastal resorts. The caravan, the B&B sign, the pony-trekking centre, and even the second home are seeing to that. In terms of physical space the countryside is losing steadily to the town by hundreds of acres every year for housing, factories, roads – all the paraphernalia of urbanization – change indeed.

Yet in one vital respect the countryside is the gainer. Amid the black alps of the South Wales valleys, where coal spilled its filth for generations, the countryside is clawing back vital space from the dereliction of centuries. Goaded by the horror of Aberfan, today's engineers are restoring the valleys to the green beauty they must once have been. In 1973 Prince Charles, Chairman of the Prince of Wales' Committee concerned with the conservation of town and country, visited Gilfach Goch – the valley immortalized in *How Green was my Valley* – and saw the start of restoration work. As chairman of the European Conservation Year Committee for Wales he told the 1970 conference that if in the process of compromising between such things as mechanization of agriculture, tourism, water conservation, and other modern developments on the one hand, and the unspoilt nature of the countryside on the other, we managed to destroy social patterns and part of the culture of rural Wales, we would not be witnessing progress. That was why ECY 1970 grew into the Prince of Wales' Committee in 1971, and the prince's inaugural message stated 'One of the aims of this committee is to prove to every Welshman that it is a feasible proposition to do something constructive for the community's benefit, rather than merely indulge in armchair criticism'.

Bwlch Oerddws Pass shows the contrasts that exist in the Welsh countryside – pine-clothed slopes, fertile valley floors, and bare hillsides.

The people of Wales are not only sharing in the work pioneered by Prince Charles and the committee, but are pushing governments, councils, industries, organizations, and voluntary bodies to ensure that the countryside – and townscapes – of Wales are changing for the better. The visitor to Wales, or the Welshman moving about in his own country, will see ample evidence of beneficial change.

Past experience suggests that nine out of ten visitors come by road – not just because of the comparative scarcity of railway routes in Wales, many of which have been closed for lack of custom in the past, but because the car or coach offers the best method of reaching the choice corners of the deep countryside. For the motorist who is prepared to leave his car by the roadside and take to the footpaths for even a short distance, there are the iron- and bronze-age trackways, trading and raiding ways of two thousand and more years ago, together with such more recent warlike constructions such as Offa's Dyke along the old English-Welsh border. Change may have come dramatically to the modern communications system, but the unchanging is never far away.

Reverting for a moment to the role of the railways, it is encouraging to note the revival of one form of rail transport – the narrow-gauge railways of Wales. After the 1939–45 war, the majority of lines which used to carry slate from the mountains to the coastal ports fizzled out – yet within a few years the nostalgic interest in steam that is now hitting England had developed in Wales and restored not one, but six steam-operated lines.

A changing need

No part of the countryside of Wales could have felt the effect of change as much as agriculture, and the pace has quickened beyond all measure in recent years. The total land area of Wales is just over five million acres, of which over four million are in agricultural use. Some 1.8 million acres are grassland and 700,000 acres are under crops. The rest is rough grazing. The main emphasis in the hill areas is on rearing sheep and cattle, while the lowlands favour dairying. Barley, oats, and mixed corn are grown mainly for livestock feed, but potatoes are an important cash crop in the mild areas of old Pembrokeshire. The difference in the countryside is the result of profound change. Machinery is taking the place of the labour which

Highest point in the Brecon Beacons national park, Pen-y-fan is a fine example of the Wales which has remained aloof from industrial devastation.

drifts to the towns and better-paid industry. One farmer runs three farms full-time instead of one or two part-time. He sells the vacant cottages to second-home owners, or modernizes and lets them to visitors. He may raise ready cash by selling poor top land to the Forestry Commission or private forest groups. So the labour-intensive hedges of yesterday are brutalized by machine instead of being carefully tended by hand – or grubbed out altogether and replaced by post and wire. New stone walls or well-repaired walls are a thing of the past. Nobody can afford the time, even if anybody remembers the infinite skill of the old builders. Careless walkers clamber over them and complete the destruction. Farm, let alone field boundaries are obliterated in the interest of mechanized agriculture. Application of fertilizers and weedkillers by helicopter and fixed-wing aircraft has pushed the limits of controlled grazing farther up the mountainsides than was ever dreamt of a generation ago.

The Welsh language, the 2,000-year-old medium of the hill farmer and the country community, was in danger of disappearing even from the most isolated areas despite frantic efforts by enthusiasts, councils, committees, and even the government to put back the clock. Yet the visitor can still walk down many a village street and hear nothing but Welsh spoken, though until recently every sign in sight was in English. The Welsh speaker now wears his language like a red badge of pride, not just in the changing countryside, but in many urban communities as well. Let it not be thought that farming and farming people are the only features of the countryside of Wales, either in the past or today. Even centuries ago countryside life was remarkably diversified. Every village had its complement of rural craftsmen, and many of the old crafts and skills are being revived for the benefit of today's tourist.

Even so, nothing could have saved the sad communities whose *raison d'être* has ceased, and Wales has the unenviable distinction of possessing many totally deserted villages. Places like the Dylife lead-mining village, where only the waste tips plus the graves of long-dead miners in a churchyard remain, and even the church has been removed stone by stone. The slate-quarrying village on the slopes of Moel Siabod in Gwynedd has been so long-deserted that even the Ordnance Survey has taken away its name. These changes can never be reversed. But tourism has come to take the place of rural industries in the rural economy. Visitors have not as yet come in such vast numbers or concentrations that they destroy what they come to enjoy. Yet Wales is proving so popular that over-use of the countryside could pose a challenge which even its open spaces might fail to assimilate.

Tourism in Wales today can cater for almost any conceivable taste or demand. For the historian or archeologist there are ancient remains galore, from medieval castles to bronze-age burial mounds which are actually being excavated every year. Exquisite leaf-shaped arrow and spear heads of worked flint are turned up under the noses of the visitor. For the energetic there is golf, fishing, climbing, pony trekking, boating in all its forms, or just walking the timeless hills out of sight of any other soul. Most of the sea coast of Wales is still untouched by industry or commerce, with glorious beaches, noble cliffs, and sweet green hinterland. Apart from a few estuaries – and nobody in their right mind bathes in estuaries anywhere – the bathing is safe. Inland waters are plentiful and accessible. Upland streams are a fascination of wild life. All this is within two hours' drive for ten million people, and four hours for 30 million.

Perhaps the fastest-growing sector of public interest in the countryside is directed, not to provision for some specific sport or activity, but to the enjoyment of the countryside as such. Wales is supremely well placed to provide just that, for three of the ten national parks are in Wales. One could say that apart from the inevitable changes in agriculture, life in the national park areas has changed least of all in Wales, and where change has come it has been best controlled. The Government, local authorities, Countryside Commission, and best of all, the people of the area, are now wide awake to the challenge of change, and determined to keep the best and reject the worst. They may not always succeed, but they are trying.

National parks in Wales are the main foci of interest in conservation and enjoyment of unspoilt countryside, but a growing role is also played by the smaller country parks, Forestry Commission centres, picnic sites, nature reserves, designated areas of outstanding natural beauty, and other officially recognized sites open to the public. Wales is particularly rich in them all, both in numbers and variety. The Forestry Commission and the old Nature Conservancy, now the Nature Conservancy Council, are in the lead in the development of new interests, and today's visitor or traveller is heavily in their debt. Nature reserves cover mountain and moorland, bog and shore, dry and wet sites. Picnic sites are found on publicly- and privately-owned land. Nature trails owe their inception to civic and private enterprise. Sites of special scientific interest usually cover

A marked increase in the red squirrel population is a welcome result of coniferous afforestation.

notable but localized points of rarity, which need protecting from over-use or despoliation, but are available to the serious enquirer in search of anything from the breeding ground of seals, birds, or butterflies, to the toehold which some plant surviving from the Ice Age manages to maintain on an exposed mountainside. Promising progress for the future stems from the fact that substantial grants are forthcoming from the Countryside Commission for local authority and private individuals to develop country parks in particular, and many interesting schemes are coming forward. They represent concentrated facilities at strategic pressure points, usually near to main or popular routes.

New enlightenment
The fastest learner of all the countryside interests is the Forestry Commission, whose image is changing more quickly than its activities are changing the countryside. In the last 50 years the commission has developed from an agency to replant the war-ravaged forests after 1918, to a lively multi-purpose organization well aware of modern trends. State forests in the early days richly earned the accusation of regimented conifers and corduroy woodlands. Mono-species planting in geometric blocks carved up the hills into jagged patterns. Relics of the old broad-leaved species were swiftly ring-barked and left to die. Pollen in the bogs tells the archeologist that Wales was probably blanketed with Scots pine thousands of years ago, and much of the uplands was densely wooded with birch and alder even a few centuries ago – until the sheep and the charcoal burner obliterated the trees. But at no time can historical forests have been as bare and forbidding as the worst of the Commission's efforts. Fortunately they learnt fast. Mixed plantings are a routine. Selective felling is ameliorating the excesses of the past. Forest rides have opened up inaccessible areas to visitors, and given hill farming manageable communications. The commission's picnic sites and visitor centres are superb. As the commission so often emphasises, a massive influx of car-borne visitors can be better absorbed and hidden within a wooded landscape than in bare open country. Even sizeable caravan camps for touring vans are to be found in commission woodlands. Small pools double duty as amenity features and fire precautions. Schools, youth clubs, and groups of naturalists are encouraged to use the woodlands and their wild life for study and observation. Hundreds of miles of tracks are open for walkers, provided that they leave their cars on the outskirts of the forest.

Productive refuge
Forestry itself as an industry is changing fast. Much of the production from the conifer plantations now goes away as young pulp logs from early thinnings, leaving the selected poles to grow on to saw-timber size. Yet despite the concentration on commercial conifers, there is a growing interest in fine hardwoods, broad-leaved species of high amenity value. Forest margins are often planted to some depth with hardwoods and ornamentals. Landscape consultants are regularly employed when new planting is taking place. The industry's impact on the landscape has changed beyond all recognition. In one respect only has the forest remained a refuge for the old ways. Occasionally – just occasionally – the visitor may see a horse working its way between the standing trees, hauling out a bundle of raw timber.

As the natural cover and the agricultural character of Wales changes, so does the wildlife population. Unobtrusively perhaps, but profoundly. This does not necessarily mean that wild life is in aggregate less, but perhaps that some species now find existence harder, and move out or die out, while conditions become easier for others which flourish and extend their habitat. One welcome result of conifer-planting in some areas is that the red squirrel seems able to get away from 90 years of persecution by its grey cousin. The red has already almost disappeared from south-west Wales, but foresters in Mid and North Wales report continuing numbers of reds in the big new forests there, particularly those with vari-planted fringes. Certainly the long-tailed tit and the firecrest seem to flourish among the conifers, and circuses of long-tailed little acrobats can often be seen moving through spruce or larch, talking busily as they forage.

Mid Wales alone is now the last refuge for the whole of the UK of the red kite, that one-time common predator which even lived, bred, and foraged among the streets of London. A very few years ago the kite was down to half-a-dozen pairs, harried by gamekeepers and farmers for no good reason at all, and its nests plundered by egg-collectors. This nucleus of birds had hung on, incredibly, but it was the effort of the Royal Society for the Protection of Birds that made the crucial difference.

Another hawk under close protection and which is slowly growing in numbers is the peregrine falcon, which favours cliff sites in the western areas of old Pembroke and Cardigan for its nests. It almost disappeared in the 1950's when pesticides accumulated in its system after it had eaten small creatures which fed on insects or herbage that had been sprayed, and egg-collectors nearly finished the breed off. But again the RSPB came to the rescue, and today there are perhaps a dozen breeding pairs in Wales. A ground hunter which spends almost as much time in the trees as the birds, and is slowly increasing in Wales, is the pine marten. They too have found refuge in the conifer forests, hunting small birds or mice and voles on the ground. It is about the size of a cat, red to dark brown on the back, and creamy on the throat.

The otter, that fascinating denizen of Welsh rivers and streams, is under severe pressure from hunts. A growing campaign is being mounted to ban or severely restrict otter hunting. Whether it will ever succeed is open to question. Even today the visitor is very lucky to see an otter in some deep pool, or glissading from a muddy bank into the water, giving vent to its irrepressible sense of fun. But there is hope for legislation to help the otter to survive, for at long last it has helped the badger. The Women's Institute tried year after year to stir parliament to action, but it was not till 1973 that an Act went through banning badger-baiting and its allied activities. Today the badger is even on the increase, and most rough country in Wales, particularly where there is scrubland cover, has a population of badgers earning their living by keeping down mice, voles, and rabbits.

Appalling though the effects of myxomatosis were, the disease made a profound difference to the countryside in decimating the rabbit population. This not only increased farm crop yields but meant that for the first time for centuries natural regeneration of old woodland and scrub returned. Seedling trees are no longer bitten off. Varied species of flower have a chance to get on top of the enveloping coarser grasses and plants. They may not survive the selective spray in farm pastures, but at last highway surveyors are appreciating the effect of varied roadside verges and holding their mulching machines in check. Natural herbaceous borders beside many roads are coming back, thanks to the environmental movement – and the disappearing rabbit. In the world of conservation, wildlife, and endangered species, some change at least is to the good.

Freedom on foot

There is one change affecting Wales that has nothing to do with the land of Wales, its farms, forests, wildlife, industries – or even its people. It is a change in the public attitude to Wales. Maybe it affects England as well, but the impact is more striking in Wales because of the small scale of the Principality. It is the welcome readiness by people of all ages to get out of their cars or other transport and walk. Fortunately Wales is supremely well equipped to cater for the walker, whether as a potterer from the carpark, or the family out for the day, the rambling club out for the weekend, or the ambitious individual making a month of it. There are the long-distance footpaths of Offa's Dyke and the Pembrokeshire Coast; the old iron-age trackways; the mule and packhorse routes; the drovers' roads along which little black Welsh cattle were driven to the fattening pastures of England; and for the patient searcher the routes of long-gone narrow-gauge railways which took quarry stone from the hills to the valleys. All are there to be found, walked, and enjoyed, and because most of them have been the routes that people used for generations or even centuries, there are few which do not possess inns, old hotels, or farms with bed-and-breakfast accommodation. Unless the traveller prefers the rugged accommodation of a tent and sleeping bag, Wales can usually find him a place to rest his head for the night after a fair day's walk.

Preserving the balance

In one place the visitor to Wales may find change is more than he can tolerate, depending on his attitude to life and progress. Driving to the shores of Milford Haven, or walking the Pembrokeshire Coast Path, he will look down on the superb deep-water anchorage where Nelson moored his battle fleet when he was calling on Lady Hamilton. It is a very different spectacle today. The Haven is now occupied by some of the world's biggest tankers, easing their way in or discharging oil for the five big refineries clustered round its shores. This is change beyond all imagining a generation ago. For better or worse? Beauty and ugliness are in the eye of the beholder. Certainly the installations fit into the landscape as well as any such monsters anywhere, all credit to the architects

Stackpole Quay is just one of the many isolated and picturesque places waiting to be discovered along the Pembrokeshire Coast Path.

and builders. It is to be hoped that if and when Celtic Sea oil comes ashore in West Wales the science developed for the refineries will have become even more effective. In Wales generally the coming of industry on such a scale has been earnestly studied with a view to easing its impact. Wales has so much to regret in its heritage of past industry, not least the lost lives of Aberfan. Few people will tolerate future despoliation for selfish exploitation. Modern industry in Wales has learnt the lesson of the past and some remarkably seemly buildings have gone up, even in national park areas or on the coast. Architects are proving that industrial change need not necessarily mean the creation of concrete deserts.

The Council for Small Industries in Rural Areas – successor to the old Rural Industries Bureau – is adept at finding new and contemporary uses for old buildings in the countryside. Chapels in particular are getting a new lease of life as weavers' workshops and small factories, just as the communities whose spiritual needs they used to serve now benefit from the extra income of light industry. The essentially country market town of Newtown in Mid Wales is taking on a pioneering job in proving that a growth point policy is possible to rejuvenate the countryside by selected drafts of industry and population. It may be significant that this area of Wales possesses a pattern of lakes which could well become the Welsh Lakeland, creating an industry in their own right by widening and extending the tourist season in an area little touched so far, and taking Newtown as its focal point.

Repairing the damage
Because so much is being done to make modern industry acceptable in the landscape, it does mean that industrial ugliness is disappearing. There are still some 13,000 acres of derelict land in Wales. Six thousand acres have been treated already and the pace is quickening despite the financial stringency of the times. The cost has been £14m, with an additional £4m worth of Operation Eyesore work. Statistics prove little. It is the visual result that has most impact. To see this the visitor should visit some of the once-bleak valleys of South Wales, where the coal waste was heaped mountain-high above the valley communities. One such mountain overwhelmed Aberfan, its school, houses, mothers, fathers, and children. Formation of the Derelict Land Unit in the Welsh Office flowed from that tragedy. Today, with DLU guidance, the site of that disaster is greening over, and other Welsh valleys are changing also beyond recognition.

Even more spectacular is the work of restoring land after open-cast coal mining. Monster draglines which take out rock, coal, and shale down to 200ft at 30 tons at a bite are producing coal for power stations and industry from the hills between the valleys, and as fast as the coal is won from the ground the land is replaced and restored.

In North Wales the attack is opening up on the wastelands of the slate industry, derelict sterile mountains looming over Bethesda, Llanberis, Blaenau Ffestiniog, Nantlle, and other slate-mining communities. Ways are being evolved to spread, redistribute, and reduce even these intimidating, man-made deserts of rock. Always the theme is that if man changed the land for the worse in days of limited power, surely he can change it now for the better with unlimited machines at his command.

Future threats
Yet the threat of change is still there, and by a sad paradox it endangers those very areas of Wales which have most to lose if change is not controlled. Only a few years ago an international mining company showed interest in the copper deposits near Dolgellau, and a bevy of smaller companies began exploring the Snowdon area itself for copper, manganese, lead, silver, and other unspecified minerals – including even gold. What they had found so interesting was the Harlech Dome, a vast area of extremely old rocks of volcanic origins which had been superficially mined at intervals during the last century and the early part of this. Gold for many royal wedding rings and other regalia came from near Barmouth, for instance. Open-cast methods can now literally move mountains, and get at the minerals deep within their core. In the end, it all came to nothing, for the main company established that at the level of then-current prices it would not be an economic proposition. The other companies presumably lost interest. But the minerals are still there, and methods may improve. Prices may rise and make such unviable ores economic. The exquisite countryside overlaying the ancient volcanoes of the Harlech Dome could still see violent, unseemly change. For that matter many other areas of countryside are under more immediate threat. Granite, limestone, shale, slate, sand, and clay are common minerals in many parts of Wales, and increasingly valuable. All quarries cannot be closed or restricted. The life of the countryside as well as that of the town depends on bricks, cement, roadstone, and other products stemming from the quarries. Fortunately,

It is difficult to imagine that the rolling farmlands on the left were once part of ugly open-cast coal workings. This illustration shows actual restoration work conducted at the Royal Arms Site near Merthyr Tydfil.

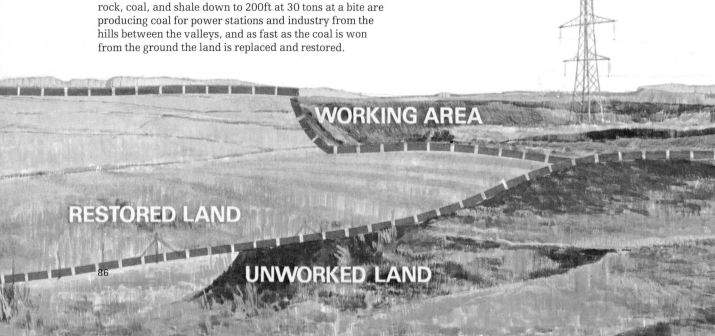

WORKING AREA

RESTORED LAND

UNWORKED LAND

environmentally sensitive quarrying is not difficult. It merely calls for some forethought. Already the tourist is finding that even quarrying areas of Wales are worth a visit, for he may catch a glimpse of industry restoring its own image as well as its handiwork.

The expanding lakes

The Lake District of England is world famous. Wales has many more lakes, of equal loveliness, which are only now gaining in popularity and public appreciation. Most of them are a natural heritage from the Ice Age, which piled up moraines and dammed upland valleys. Towards the end of the last century the thirst of the cities of England and Wales began to outstrip local resources, and engineers turned their attention to the uplands of Wales, where high rainfalls in the wet seasons produce a vast run-off that normally goes straight into the rivers and the sea. Pipelines were drawn across country to cities as far distant as Liverpool, Birmingham, and Birkenhead from reservoirs in Wales. The process was extended this century, and more dams were built. The principle of river regulation was evolved, with the rivers themselves serving as pipelines to the distant urban areas, and dams on their headwaters detaining rainfall in wet weather and releasing it in times of drought to permit augmentation of dry weather flow.

The result of this major industry has been a profound change in the whole geography of Wales. Particularly important has been the river regulation development, for it is no longer necessary to restrict public access to the new dams. Their water goes downstream to the domestic tap via a river anyway, and has to be subjected to major purification. A spot more pollution by picnickers at source makes no difference. Indeed the water undertakings themselves, conscious of mounting criticism of their valley-flooding – however poor the valley land and beneficial the lake upon the total environment – are encouraging public access, and making provision for it. Amenity features have been built into the construction of the latest reservoirs such as Celyn in North Wales, Clywedog in Mid Wales, and Llandegfedd in South Wales. Sailing, boating – but usually not water ski-ing, fishing for coarse and game fish, bird watching, and many other forms of outdoor activity are encouraged and provided for.

These commitments have been taken over and honoured by the Welsh National Water Development Authority, the governing body of the water supply industry in Wales following the latest government reorganization. Perhaps the most imaginative project in planning a reservoir is the master plan for the Brenig Reservoir in North Wales, where landscape architects were in on the conception

of the man-made lake as a centre for all manner of activities right from the start. Bronze-age burial mounds and hut-village sites are being excavated, and will probably form part of an archeological trail round the perimeter of the lake. All this means that the local population derives more than casual benefit from these massive engineering works. The best of them will represent substantial economic spin-off. In time even the old 'closed' reservoirs now feeding the cities by pipeline will be converted to a river-regulating role and discharge their water down the rivers, so that the lakesides and general environment can be thrown open to the public.

Considerably more controversial than the water supply lakes are the hydro-electric installations in Wales. One more was started in 1974, and still more may ultimately be built. Early hydro electricity was generated at Maentwrog in North Wales, using the waters of an artificially dammed valley at Trawsfynydd. That lake now serves a dual purpose, for its waters are also used to cool the reactors of the nuclear power station on the lakeside. Overflow still goes downhill to the power station near the sea, but it is a pigmy beside some of the giants which have since been built. In the early 1960's two further hydro-electric stages were built, which made substantial additions to the artificial lakes of Mid Wales. On the River Rheidol, near Aberystwyth, an orthodox station harnessed the water from the Nant-y-Moch and Dinas Reservoirs. The first 'pumped storage' station was built at Tanygrisiau, near Blaenau Ffestiniog, creating two more reservoirs. Amenity considerations were carefully observed in each case, and on the Rheidol in particular very special attention was paid to the naturalizing of all artificial features. Both stations annually attract tens of thousands of visitors.

Design for leisure

This did not save the Central Electricity Generating Board from opprobrium by the conservation and amenity interests when a further proposal was published to create an even bigger pumped storage station near Llanberis at the foot of Snowdon, utilizing the water of two dams with a 1,650ft difference in height. Major concessions were extracted from the CEGB, and when the scheme comes into operation in the 1980's it will undoubtedly provide a tourist attraction quite unique in the British Isles, with

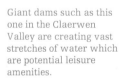

Giant dams such as this one in the Claerwen Valley are creating vast stretches of water which are potential leisure amenities.

87

access to the cathedral-like underground cavern housing the generators and other spectacular features. All this amounts to quite shattering changes in the countryside of Wales, even the countryside hitherto considered inviolate and immutable by any human agency. But man is beginning to match the forces which in prehistory reared up Snowdon itself, and success in preserving or even improving the public enjoyability of mountainous Wales in the process of creating public utilities will be a formidable precedent for extracting major amenity concessions from the engineers.

Water in a very different form, for very different purposes, moves tranquilly across Wales in two very old, very lovely, and until recently sadly-neglected canals. The Brecon Canal and the Montgomery Canal were built about the start of the 19thc, while Napoleon was still on the rampage, and for many years served their areas by transporting coal, limestone, corn, and other products. But as with other canals the railways killed them off or allowed them to die, which amounted to the same thing in the end. Now however, the Brecon has been restored by volunteers and is enjoyed by barge and boat people from a very wide area. The Montgomery is due for an even more exciting role. The Prince of Wales' Committee and the Variety Club of Great Britain are raising £250,000 to restore a key section of 7m to the north of Welshpool, and to put on it a specially built barge to carry handicapped and crippled children for holiday and day cruises, and for general public use.

New attitudes

Engineers are on the lookout for ways of restoring the countryside's old beauty by the ingenious use of old industrial wastes. One such scheme near Ruabon in North Wales is transforming a dead valley full of poisonous and offensive wastes into a park for the public. Even in the voluntary field, modest but significant schemes can be undertaken by determined and public spirited people, like the group of North Walians who decided to commemorate the Investiture of Prince Charles by a project on the top of a 1,800ft-high mountain. On Moel Fammau, a peak on the borders of old Denbighshire and

Flintshire, the Jubilee Tower erected to mark the 50-year reign of George III had lain as a collapsed ruin for nearly a century, covering an acre of the mountaintop with fallen stones. The volunteers cleared the debris, rebuilt the stump of the tower, installed a public viewing point and plane tables indicating the main features round the horizon, and increased the attractiveness of a mountain which had always been a mecca for visitors – despite its old decrepitude. The new local authority of Clwyd has backed them up by buying several hundred acres of the mountain and nearby valleys to create a country park in public ownership, adding even further to the public importance of the site.

And so to work . . .

And so change goes on. Some is for the better, and it can truthfully be said that more is for the better as the public conscience is aroused and public sensitivity to the quality of the Welsh countryside is sharpened. Occasionally it is necessary to admit that change has come and left Wales worse off. It is not possible, for instance, for Wales to absorb many more caravans than the 70,000 or so reputed to be stationed in the Principality, without suffering even more irreparable damage than already. One day the public may revolt against the cruder manifestations of caravan-mania, and break up the vast fleets of them which now almost obliterate some of the finest stretches of coastal and inland landscape. Not all the debris of the Industrial Revolution, let alone of more recent industrial eras, has been cleared. People are still too ready to live with ugliness. People need to change, as well as the landscape they live in, provided that change can be beneficial. There is so much to do which will bring out the best in Wales, apart from getting rid of the worst. Her legends – rich, rare, and unique, founded in millenia of history, language, and individualistic culture – are a world all of their own for the visitor to discover and enjoy. Tourism is still too superficial.

The visitor always comes back to Wales. It may not be quite the same Wales the next time, and every time thereafter, but what matter? For Wales is changing. The countryside, its people, life, animals, birds, scenery – everything that is Wales is changing. The sensitive traveller, making himself a part of the land he visits, can contribute his small part to the process, take a little of Wales away with him in his memories, and leave something of himself behind.

Afforestation is a fundamental change which has benefited the rare pine marten. Careful use of water and other resources by enlightened people will help preserve the evolving Welsh countryside, conserve and encourage its wildlife, and create valuable amenity areas. Although industry needs the earth's wealth, it has been proved that there is no need to permanently disfigure the land to get it.

Rare and Ancient Skills

The ancient village crafts of Wales have pulled through a long slump and are now on the verge of revival – mainly for the benefit of tourism. Originally the work of the local craftsman, *eg* the potter, the wheelwright, the weaver, and the coracle maker, was essential if communities isolated by deep valleys and bleak mountains were to maintain their self sufficiency. The advent of the industrial revolution heralded a re-distribution of population, with people being sucked from these tiny communities to swell the working ranks of the growing industrial conurbations; the village craftsman became obsolete as a result. Welsh workers could buy all their requirements from their company shop, and skilled craftwork declined almost to the point of extinction. Then, during the mid 1960's, a sudden tourist demand for 'things Welsh' created new possibilities for trades that had almost died under the heel of industry. Wales was at first slow to respond, but cheap labour areas of Hong Kong and Taiwan were not. They flooded the Welsh market with thousands of examples of 'Welsh' crafts. But if the cheap Asian imitations of Welsh Craft had most of the souvenir market to themselves in the early and middle 60's, the 1970's are seeing a very different and rapidly changing situation. The home Welsh craft industry began its fight back towards the end of the last decade.

Craft industries often arise from the availability of suitable local material. Illustrated is a craftsman making clock cases from Welsh slate.

Strength to strength

At first it was only the few traditional craftsmen who had continued with the arts handed down through generations of their family, but this small band is now being joined by a growing army of men and women who are seeking a rewarding existence through craft revival. By 1972 the craft business was an industry in its own right, and this brought advantages not only to those employed in it, but also to the customers. One of the ancient industries which has benefitted greatly from the craft boom is Welsh textiles. These had all but faded away by the 1960's, and their comeback has been quite remarkable. One firm, Welsh Textiles Ltd, was founded in 1968 to supply both the upholstery trade and craft shops. Within two years of its launch it had doubled the size of its factory and was supplying nearly 300 shops throughout Britain. The main problem facing the newly-born small craft business is one of cash. Most industries need a steady flow of money all the year round to enable them to expand, and the craft industry in Wales is still based on a comparatively short and intensive selling season, backed by a long production period. The craftsmen say that the demand for their work is there, and if there was government aid production could be increased – providing Wales with many badly needed jobs. In the forefront of the fight to put the Welsh craft industry on its feet is the Welsh Crafts Trade Association. This was formed in October 1972 by four Welsh craftsmen. It now has 150 members employing well over 1,200 people. Within three months of its formation the association had organized the first highly successful Welsh Trade Fair at Aberystwyth, now an annual event held in the first week of January.

Mr Roger Crossley, then secretary of the Trade Association, said the competition from foreign goods had been one of the main instigators of the exhibition. 'It was decided the best positive action to launch the new association would be to promote a trade fair of Welsh products, produced for the Welsh crafts, gift, and tourist outlets, where trade buyers could see what is available within their own country before placing orders outside Wales.'

A great escape

The new craftsmen of Wales come from all over Britain and from very different backgrounds. Some are people wishing to escape from the rat-race which has trapped those who yearn to create rather than compete in the production line of big business. Wales is also an area where the old industries of coal, iron, and steel are contracting, and the new industries have not yet taken their place. This has caused many young people to feel they have a limited future in their own land, and massive redundancy has also thrown thousands out of work. This disillusionment with Welsh industry has led a small number of daring men and women to attempt to make a satisfying, if initially sparse, living from the Welsh craft industry. The craft industry also provides pocket money for housewives and pensioners who work part time at home. A shop was opened at the end of 1973 in Cardiff which is almost totally supplied with craft goods made in this fashion. Mrs Teleri Gray, one of the three partners in Gwerin Welsh Crafts, in Albany Road, says that only about two per cent of the items they sell have been bought outside Wales.

The rapid growth of the Welsh craft industry has also to some extent been fired by fervent nationalism which is at present sweeping Wales. The trend which has demonstrated itself so forcibly in politics and in the activities of *Cymdeithos yr Iaith Gymraeg*, the Welsh Language Society, has filtered down to a pride in all of Wales's heritage, not least its crafts. A thoroughbred Welshman is a member of the oldest race of British people. Evidence has been found of human life in Wales 8,000 years before Christ, but the first civilized peoples to settle in Wales did not arrive until between 2,000 and

Modern silversmiths are perpetuating a skill which has existed at least since the Romans mined the precious metal in the Welsh hills.

3,000 years before the Christian era. They originated from the Mediterranean area, and brought with them the more developed crafts of that area. They were an agricultural people and were looking for pastures and fields to sow their corn, but also with them came their knowledge and organization. Their way of life was sophisticated enough for an axe factory to be set up at Graig Lwyd, Penmaenmawr. Later colonizers from central and eastern Europe were skilled in bronze and gold work, and better tools enabled them to cultivate areas which before had only been useful as pasture land. As the years passed these skills were gradually moulded and merged to form crafts which had distinctive local Welsh styles. To these were added still others, imported from the continent by the rich warlords. In the last few hundred years before Christ, Celts from the middle Rhine and Upper Danube began to arrive with a knowledge of iron work. Much of this was directed towards producing superior weapons with which to conquer, but there were also tools and implements.

New influences
Settlements were often in the form of hill forts with earthen walls, reinforced with timber and stones. These insular communities had to be self sufficient in most things, and crafts and arts became peculiar to one village or area. Such isolated settlements along the coast of Wales and in the hills and plains presented the Roman conquerors with considerable problems when they first invaded Britain. But gradually much of Wales was Romanized, and the Welsh people were exposed to advanced civilization with its works of art and sophisticated tools. Skills brought by the Romans, however, gradually disappeared after they left. Civilization gradually receded and production from metal mining fell severely. The deterioration was particularly acute inland. The coastal

areas still remained exposed to outside influences, and in these is evidence that craft work was brought by traders from Ireland, Gaul, and even as far away as the Mediterranean. Such items of often highly-decorative silverware and glassware were copied by local Welsh craftsmen.

Around the 6thc AD Christian missionaries started to arrive from Gaul. A monastery was set up in Llantwit Major in old Glamorgan, and another in old Pembrokeshire. The main contribution from the monks was their learning, but they also brought with them superior crafts and art. About this time too the Welsh language was beginning to emerge from the primitive British, giving Wales a strong national identity. This was enhanced by war-like aggression from the east and on the western seaboard of Wales, which tended to isolate the country from Europe. Cut off as they were from the rest of civilization the Welsh could not help but begin to develop a separate culture, which included very individual Welsh crafts. The Welsh have clung to this national identity throughout history. Even when the Normans conquered England they achieved only partial success in Wales, although it was due to them that the title of 'king' in Wales finally died.

Weaving and mining
Evidence of the Welsh way of life around the 11thc is thin, but contemporary chroniclers told of the small fishing coracles which still survive on a few rivers in Wales today. Even at this time the Welsh hills were famous for their sheep, and one early historian says these animals provided virtually all of the meat diet of many Welshmen, while the wool was used for their clothes. In most parts of Wales at this time the spinning and weaving of wool was limited to farming households and the domestic staff of the local landowners. But in a large part of eastern Wales the weaving industry was more organized due to an Act during Elizabeth's reign, which gave the Shrewsbury Drapers' Company the selling rights of Welsh cloth. This company held its monopoly to the mid 18thc, encouraging Welsh weaving by giving the industry a protected market.

During the 17thc mining for lead, gold, silver, copper, and coal also became more organized. Welsh craftsmen produced beautiful works of art which were exported to many parts of Europe. By the 18thc, however, the importance of iron was out-weighing all others. The demand for weapons during the wars with the French further boosted the iron industry, and an influx of Englishmen seeking their fortunes began one of the bitterest periods of exploitation the Welsh have known – and one from which Wales is still recovering. Iron was the father of industrialization in much of Wales, and it is worth noting that the differing geographical regions of Wales had a definite bearing on the wide range of crafts. The highlands produced little as there was no cultivation or cattle grazing. There were only the shepherds who wiled away the long hours by producing individual items of woodwork. On the lowland slopes, which form the largest proportion of land, there was mixed farming. Cattle were on the fertile land and sheep elsewhere. This produced a demand for farming implements and thus a need for blacksmiths. The timber growing on the slopes provided raw material for woodland industries. The river valleys, however, produced the greatest abundance of craftsmen. The valleys were fertile and well wooded, providing ample raw materials. Around the coast of Wales the fishing industry dominated the demand for craftwork. This was mainly centred on the making of nets and wicker baskets for lobster pots. In Anglesey rushes

Coracle making is one of the few truly ancient skills which has survived virtually unchanged.

Rushes and grasses were once used to make ropes, nets, and large mats designed to cover haystacks and barn roofs. Nowadays the industry concentrates on domestic items.

were also used for making mats and ropes. In later years the need for water power to drive the new industries was an important factor in deciding the situation of such things as woolmills.

The ancient coracle

A coracle is a bowl shaped river boat which was in existance centuries before the Romans came to Britain. It is highly manoeuverable in the hands of a skilled boatman, and its essential design has remained the same throughout history. Varying in weight from only 20 to 30lbs, it can be carried with ease and is basically a willow frame covered in calico soaked in boiled linseed oil and pitch. Coracles were used for fishing on most rivers in Wales at one time or another, and are still used in the west. The size of each coracle varies considerably because they are custom-made for owners whose height and weight must be taken into account. The Teifi is usually from 5ft to 6ft in length with a maximum of 40in across the prow and 34in across the seat. The coracle has largely died out in Wales, and the Teifi is one of the few rivers where it is still seen. Fly fishing and sheep dipping are the two main uses for the vessel now, and it is particularly efficient in the latter task as it can be manoeuvered very easily among the sheep. Salmon netting from two craft is so productive that it is no longer encouraged.

The earliest coracles had their frames covered with hide tied with leather thongs, but for many hundreds of years up to the present day this covering has been of calico which is stretched tight across the framework and bound into the gunwale. When a craftsman is building a coracle he first selects suitable willows – usually about seven to ten years old and cut in autumn or winter when there is no sap in the branches. Willow grows wild along many of the Welsh rivers. Each rod from the willow is split into two; these are then laid lengthways and crossways and alternatively woven. The shaped lathes are put in a tub of boiling water until they can be bent to the contours of the coracle. The longer lathes are arranged about 5in apart and the nine shorter lathes woven at right angles to them. Heavy weights or stones are placed at the intersection of the lathes, and then the sides are bent upwards. Now hazel

saplings are woven to form the upper rim of the coracle. The willow lathes are then inserted into the hazel gunwale and nailed into place.

The final structure looks much like a basket, and except for a two-handled draw knife, spokeshave, and hammer, hardly any tools have been necessary. To complete the framework a piece of flanking cut to the right size is put into the gunwale, and finally the leather carrying strap is added and fixed firmly to the seat. Five yards of calico are needed for the covering. The material is firmly stretched over the frame and tacked, then it is soaked again and again with coats of boiling linseed and pitch until the coracle is waterproof. The paddle consists of a shaft with a bulb-like top for manoeuvering, and a parallel blade. The length varies for each type of coracle.

Mat making

The art of rush plaiting stretches back through history. In earlier days rushes were used for mats which were made to cover haystacks and barn roofs. Ropes and fishermen's nets were also made from rushes. The marran grass of Anglesey provided a very useful raw material, and plaiting in this part of Wales has become famous. Two-year-old reed was cut in the summer with a reaping hook. Each family had their own traditional plot, and the grass was carefully cut to ensure that it would continue to grow. It was harvested while green and left in a dry, sheltered position to ripen. The reed was then gathered into bundles and stacked together with roots at the bottom, and again left for a few weeks.

Any green stalks were then discarded, and two bundles were tied together for further ripening. After more sorting the sheaves were put into water to soften. The women usually gathered their own reeds, and if they had any spare they would sell them to the older women in the village who were unable to harvest their own. The plaiting of the mats is all done by the right hand, with the left hand supporting the work and renewing the bunches of reed as the strand gets thin. The craftsman of Newborough also produced grass ropes which were used for packing pottery, polished furniture, and barbed wire for transportation. Despite the work of the Newborough

Many Welsh woollen mills still use 19th-c machinery because this is well suited to their size and output.

Besom brooms can be made from seareed, heather, or birch twigs, and are still very much in demand..

Mat Makers Association the demand for rush mats declined, and the industry had largely disappeared by the last quarter of the 20thc.

Welsh woollens

The Welsh woollen-cloth industry is based on a very ancient craft going back many centuries. Although the process is now conducted mostly by machines, it is fundamentally the same method that has been used throughout history. Many of the first factories were run by water power, and hence some of the woollen mills still surviving are situated next to fast flowing streams. Some of these works flourished in Wales until the first part of the 20thc. The mills were usually established through generations of one family who had produced a certain style and tradition with distinctive weaves. Some of the mills were very small and combined with farming, so that labourers had to be able to turn their hands to weaving during the winter months. There are still about 25 woollen mills operating in Wales, and members of the Welsh Weavers Association mark their products with a Welsh wool mark sign. It is advisable to check for this when buying anything which purports to be a Welsh woollen.

Raw wool has to go through many processes before it can be woven and first has to be sorted into different qualities and grades, which are used for various purposes. The finest wool goes for making good-quality clothes, while the coarsest goes for carpeting. The wool is then washed to remove dirt and grease. After washing the wool is dyed by boiling, traditionally in a copper boiler. The dyed wool has then to be disentangled, a process which is aided by a machine known as the 'willy'. This loosens the matted fibres and can also be used to mix two different colours together, such as black and white to make the grey

material for flannel. The wool is then carded, originally by women and children with a teasil or with combs and cards. Since 1850 condenser carder has been used to cut out the piecing process and allow the wool to be spun immediately.

After carding the wool must be spun to increase the strength and decrease the thickness. Welsh mills still use machines that date back to the 19thc because these are well suited to the size and output of the mills. The weaving of cloth continued to be a handcraft until the mid 19thc. After the cloth has been woven it has to undergo fulling to give more body by pushing the threads closer together. When the fulling process is completed the woven cloth is dried.

The versatile besom

A besom is the traditional broom associated with witches, and besoms have been made in Wales since at least Saxon times. They can still be bought in many areas and are available in three basic types: heather, rush, and birch. The rush besoms were made in Valley, Rhosneigr, and Abreffraw out of seareed. The seareed was cut during August with a scythe, usually by the besom maker himself, and left to dry in the open. There are no special tools involved in the making of besoms as the maker usually bought the wood for the broomstick and the cord to tie the reeds. They are easy to make, and one man could make dozens a day. The besom maker tied a bunch of reeds around the bottom of the broomstick, with about 2ft remaining uncovered as a handle. He then bent the reeds downward to give a double thickness and bound them together. This type of besom was confined to Anglesey, and was usually sold directly to the customer or the ironmonger. Their main use was for light work like dusting, but as they were cheap to replace they were often used for whitewashing.

The Welsh hills have always had an abundant supply of heather, which is of little economic value but provided farm labourers living in the highland areas with a plentiful reserve of raw material for heather besom making. A bunch of heather would be pressed together and tied with strips of split willow, then the broomstick would be inserted. There is still a market today for birch besoms, which are made in many parts of Wales and are used by gardeners, road sweepers for sweeping leaves, and also in the modern steel industry for sweeping away impurities from newly-made steel plates. Some tools are required for the making of birch besoms, including pliers, an axe, and a billhook.

From basic clay

The pottery industry in Wales began near the basic raw materials needed for the craft. These were clay for the pottery itself, and coal for fuel. Small studio potteries can easily buy in their raw materials, and so their locations are not so tied. Throughout Wales there are many small potteries, and the art of the potter is still very basic. The choice and preparation of the clay is very important, so it is uneconomical for the small studio potter to prepare his own. The clay is dug in the autumn before the heavy rains and then exposed to the weather. The heaps of clay are broken up at intervals to allow the atmosphere to penetrate, and special spades made out of a single piece of willow and shod with metal sheeting are then used to dig out the material. This then goes through a pug-mill, where it is churned up and comes out as a fairly hard block. The potter can then break off small pieces and wedge or press them to remove the air holes. The clay is now shaped into a ball and thrown on a wheel, which is based on a very old design and can be operated by the foot or by electricity. Many potters in Wales prefer the slower revolving foot-operated wheel to shape larger pots, as earlier electric wheels were not able to go slowly enough. The wheel is quite heavy so as to maintain a steady rotation and balance.

The potter sits on a projecting seat and throws the ball of clay on to the wheel with moderate force. The clay is centred, moulded into a cone, and flattened before being shaped into the finished article with the fingers and thumb. The potter dips his hands in water at frequent intervals during the process to keep them moist. When the article is finished it is removed from the wheel with a wire. It is dried, either artificially or in the sun, and then put back on the wheel to be trimmed. After this it is ready for the first firing; care has to be taken because the item could explode in the kiln if any moisture has been left in it.

The firing of pottery requires skilful judgement, and the kilns today are usually heated by electricity as opposed to the solid fuel which was previously used. Some kinds of ceramics are still fired by solid fuel. The pottery is placed in trays of coarse clay known as saggers, and is carefully placed in the kilns. It is heated to a very high temperature and then allowed to cool before it is removed. Unglazed pottery requires only one firing. A glazed pot is either painted or immersed in glaze, and replaced in the kiln very carefully so that no two pots touch each other. At the sides of the kiln are loose bricks which can be removed so that the potter can see what is happening. He places clay cones near these windows, and when these begin to bend he knows it is time to reduce the heat. Another method of pottery also exists for the more irregular shapes, where the potter uses a plaster of Paris mould which can be used many times to produce the same object.

A way with wood

Wooden implements have been used in country households for centuries, and for a great number of different purposes. Wood was the material from which much of the household equipment which is now made from plastic, tin, glass, and pottery was originally fashioned. One of the most essential items in the household was the spoon. It

The 17th- to 19th-c vogue for lovespoons turned simple spoon making into a demanding test of the woodcarver's art.

had many uses, and in Wales a wooden spoon is still used in some homes for eating that typically Welsh dish 'Cawl'. This is a highly-seasoned Welsh soup which comprises bacon, leeks, and vegetables. The art of spoon carving still survives in many parts of Wales. Sycamore is one of the most popular woods used for this, and is traditionally felled in winter to ensure a pale lustrious wood. Working solely by eye and with hand tools, the spoon carver can produce a perfectly shaped spoon in fifteen minutes. The sycamore ends are chopped into sections of about 12in long. These are then cut into the approximate shape of a spoon with a small axe, and the bowl is hollowed with a knife. The handle of the spoon is shaped with a spokeshave and the rough edges which remain are finished with a short-bladed knife. If a larger spoon or ladle is needed the sycamore is cut into larger sections. The same process is carried out as with the ordinary spoon, except in the case of the ladle where the bowl of the spoon has to be deeper.

From the 17thc to the end of the 19thc highly-decorated lovespoons became a common feature of rural life. They were carved out of a single piece of wood and included elaborate designs which often sported slotted handles, chainlinks, patterns, and initials. They were then presented by their makers to their sweethearts as a token of affection, and the more ornate the spoon the more passionately the man who carved it was meant to be in love. It is not certain how this custom began, but it was taken very seriously and some of the spoons were superb works of art. These unique souvenirs can be bought at some workshops and craft shops, and a fine collection of them can be seen in the Brecknock County Museum. Wood turning was also very widespread in Wales, and there are still several workshops where the products of the woodcraftsman can be bought.

One of the most well known types of lathes used by wood craftsmen is the pole lathe. This is worked by a foot treadle

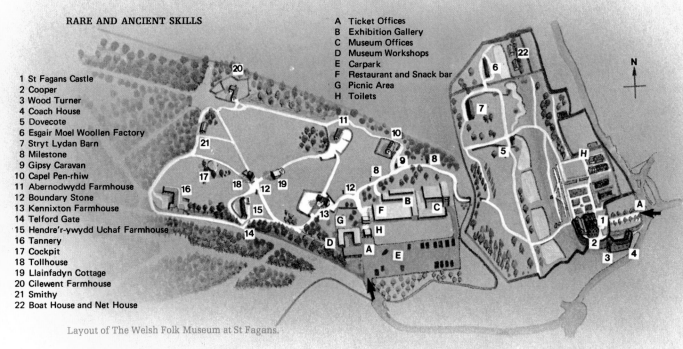

A Ticket Offices
B Exhibition Gallery
C Museum Offices
D Museum Workshops
E Carpark
F Restaurant and Snack bar
G Picnic Area
H Toilets

1 St Fagans Castle
2 Cooper
3 Wood Turner
4 Coach House
5 Dovecote
6 Esgair Moel Woollen Factory
7 Stryt Lydan Barn
8 Milestone
9 Gipsy Caravan
10 Capel Pen-rhiw
11 Abernodwydd Farmhouse
12 Boundary Stone
13 Kennixton Farmhouse
14 Telford Gate
15 Hendre'r-ywydd Uchaf Farmhouse
16 Tannery
17 Cockpit
18 Tollhouse
19 Llainfadyn Cottage
20 Cilewent Farmhouse
21 Smithy
22 Boat House and Net House

Layout of The Welsh Folk Museum at St Fagans.

which bends a pole and turns the chuck; the pole springs back again as soon as the foot is removed. In the making of a bowl, the outside is shaped first and then the inside is roughly gouged out. When the final shape of the bowl is almost complete the craftsman takes a smaller chisel and works on the inside until it is smooth. Finally the wood is polished with beeswax.

Clogs and clogging

This craft has all but disappeared from the rural areas of Wales. Clogs were worn by both rich and poor in the middle ages, and in Wales they are known as country clogs because they were heavier than the Lancashire clogs. Clogs were common in the mines, factories, and on the land, but by the beginning of the 20thc demand for them declined because of the stigma of poverty. They were made of alder, birch, beech, or sycamore – depending on their purpose. Many of the makers preferred to stick to one or two types of wood, and as alder was common in Wales it was one of the most popular. It is coarse grained and soft, making it easy to shape and comfortable to wear. Some people also believed that alder contained medicinal qualities and was good for the feet, but it was not suitable to wear in damp places as it absorbed water. There were traditionally two types of clogger. There was the one who made shoes for his village to individual requirements, and the man who rough-shaped the clog soles and sold them to the factories of Lancashire, where leather uppers were added.

For the individual clogs measurements from each customer were taken and then transferred to a paper pattern. The clogger roughly shaped the block with a stock knife and then used a convex-bladed knife to shape the surface. A channel was cut for fitting the leather uppers, which were tacked in place with stiffeners at the heels. The leather was then left for hours to mould itself into shape, and was finally nailed to the sole with a welting over the join. It was finished with a clasp for fastening, a metal cap at the toe, and irons underneath the sole. Again alder wood was mainly used, which was harvested in spring and summer and left for nine months to season. Cloggers worked in gangs during the cutting season and lived in temporary shelters to enable them to move easily. After a tree was felled the first job was to cut it into logs of four sizes to fit men, women, adolescents, and children. The block was then cut into the rough shape of a clog. This craft required a considerable amount of strength and was

a skill which had to be learnt at a young age. At the end of the day the clogger put the clog blocks into cubical stacks so that the air could circulate through them. They were then ready to be transported to the factory.

Living history

The Welsh Folk Museum near Cardiff is different to the traditional museum. St Fagans is not a place of dark corners and linoleum floors, but it is alive and allows the visitor to recapture the rural atmosphere of ancient Wales. It is in three basic sections: St Fagans castle, with its gardens and house; the actual museum section in a new building; and buildings and houses from several parts of Wales which have been dismantled and rebuilt in the grounds of the museum. The castle, its gardens, and grounds were given to the National Museum of Wales in 1946 as a centre for a folk museum by Lord Plymouth. This initially totalled only 18 acres, which would not have been enough to create an adequate display, so Lord Plymouth agreed to the transfer of 80 acres of St Fagans park right next to the gardens. The museum attempts to capture the essential spirit of the country, and by a variety of methods to illustrate the evolution of the society of Wales over a period of several hundred years. St Fagans is not just a place for the visitor; only a fraction of its wealth is on display, and much is kept solely for the eyes of the serious student or researcher, including an extensive library dealing with the history of Wales.

The houses in the open section have the furniture and furnishings of their period, with carts, ploughs, and other implements in the barns, sheds, and other outbuildings. While visiting St Fagans it is well worth seeing the woodturner and the cooper at work. Both produce goods which can be bought by the public. The woodturner, as well as working on a modern electrical lathe, also uses the traditional pole lathe. The cooper is one of the last people practising this craft in Wales. St Fagans new building, which also houses the administrative block, includes the agricultural gallery and the gallery of material culture. Both of these are a little more in the vein of the traditional museum, but the former in particular is recognized as the avant-garde in museum design and layout. The gallery is sub-divided into various sections dealing with different aspects of the farmer's work. In the gallery of material culture are objects illustrating different aspects of domestic, social, and cultural life in Wales. This is a fascinating section and should not be missed.

Day Drives

Key to Day Drives

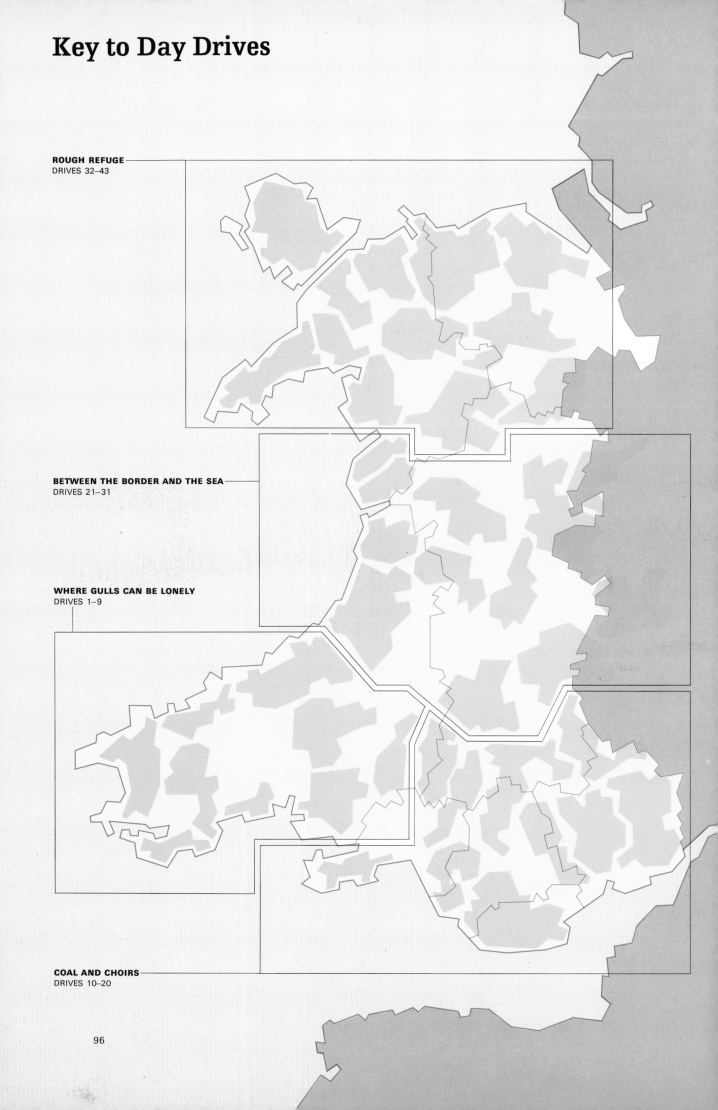

ROUGH REFUGE
DRIVES 32–43

BETWEEN THE BORDER AND THE SEA
DRIVES 21–31

WHERE GULLS CAN BE LONELY
DRIVES 1–9

COAL AND CHOIRS
DRIVES 10–20

Land of Princes

The old saying about good things coming in small packages certainly applies to Wales, the history-steeped land of Celtic legends, great castles, choirs, mountains, moorland, tree-clad valleys, rushing rivers teeming with fish, and long stretches of coast that rate highly among the most spectacular in the whole of Europe. It is just under 200m from Holyhead to Cardiff, and less than 150 from Fishguard to the English border at Chepstow, but there are almost 20,000m of roads in the principality – only about 6,000 less than the total for the whole of Scotland – and these two factors combine to make a country that is ideal for the motorist to explore.

In the space of a single day it is possible, for instance, to sample the candy-floss delights of Rhyl, Colwyn Bay, or one of the other popular seaside resorts in North Wales, admire the majestic, saw-toothed mountains – Snowdon's summit is less than 10m from salt water as the seagull flies – and then cross the Menai Strait to the contrast of Anglesey, which is less rugged than most of southern England.

Another day could embrace the rolling, wood-dappled landscape of the area which once comprised eastern Montgomeryshire, the windswept wilderness of Plynlimon, and then the trim, Victorian-and-Edwardian elegance of Aberystwyth, on the long, curving shore of Cardigan Bay.

Yet another might involve travelling from Cardiff or Swansea to the lofty grandeur of the Brecon Beacons; then westwards through the lush dairy pastures near Carmarthen to the breathtaking splendours of the untamed Pembrokeshire coast, where cliffs and beaches are washed by seas that roll unchecked from North America.

A sudden change of personal mood can generally be catered for by the shortest of drives. Within a few minutes of the centre of a bustling old market town the driver can be nosing through lanes flanked by high, grassy banks bright with foxgloves and wild roses; or climbing a pass between vertical cliffs speckled with climbers; or on a lonely beach where the music of restless waves mingles with the cries of seabirds and the whisper of a gentle breeze conspiring with the nodding marram grass.

Use the main roads by all means; but no visit to Wales is really complete unless the by-ways have been explored, or the car has been left in favour of a more personal form of travel over untracked countryside. Like Britain as a whole, Wales has rather more than its fair share of richly-assorted wonders. Many have retained that touch of magic by being those critical few miles off the A-class roads.

Carreg Cennen, one of the most dramatic castles in the country, perches on a sheer cliff down a narrow lane near Llandeilo and is missed by countless visitors every year as they hurry to and from the coast. Castell-y-Bere, within a few miles of Tywyn, was the last stronghold of the Welsh princes and its evocative ruins sleep beside a little road that soon peters out at the foot of Cader Idris. Pistyll Rhaeadr, the highest waterfall in Wales or England, cascades down a sheer cliff at a dead-end in the heart of the Berwyns.

Park by the wayside near the village of Llanaelhaearn, on the lovely Lleyn peninsula, the 'Land's End of North Wales', and walk up to the superb remains of Tre'r Ceiri – The Giants' Town – a great iron-age encampment with immense views that can embrace Ireland, the Isle of Man, Snowdonia, and the whole sweep of Cardigan Bay. Another walk, from the car park near Ystradfellte in the Brecon Beacons national park, leads to Scwd-yr-Eira, where a naturally-carved footpath runs right behind the foaming curtain of a fairy-tale waterfall.

Thread a way through the tangle of lanes between St David's and Fishguard, visiting a series of lovely little bays and fascinating reminders of the days when this magnificent coast throbbed to the pulse of commerce and little ships were the only real links with the outside world.

Cross old Monmouthshire's Gospel Pass and there, in the heart of the Honddu Valley, and clasped in a fold of the Black Mountains, are the ruins of Llanthony Priory; on the same road, north of the priory, the view over the Wye valley may include the sight of an intrepid birdman hang-gliding from Hay Bluff. Near Porthmadog, where trains puff and clatter along the oldest narrow-gauge railway still operating anywhere in the world, lies Portmeirion, an Italianate dream-come-true of a village created by Sir Clough Williams-Ellis since the 1920's.

Between Chepstow and Newport, the shortest of detours from the busy A48 leads to Caerwent, an easily-missed village with a huge section of wall that pays silent tribute to the craftsmanship of its Roman builders. Visit the parish church at Montgomery, where in the southern transept stands the marvellous canopied tomb of two local notables, with their children kneeling in prayer beside them.

Follow the Forestry Commission nature trail to the summit of Moel Fammau, between Ruthin and Mold, and find the remains of an Egyptian-style tower built to commemorate George III's golden jubilee. Pendine, on the old Carmarthenshire coast, has memories of Sir Malcolm Campbell and J G Parry Thomas, great racing drivers who broke the world's land speed record on the seemingly endless beach.

Walk and drive around Moelfre, on the north-east coast of Anglesey. Within a mile of the little fishing village, famous for the valour of its lifeboat crews, discover Din Lligwy – the remains of a village 2,000 years old – and the huge prehistoric Lligwy burial chamber. Right on the rocky coast is a memorial to the 459 people who died one terrible night in 1859, when hurricane-force winds wrecked the treasure-laden 'Royal Charter'.

cont

97

Gold mines worked by Romans delve into the wooded hillsides at Pumsaint, south of Lampeter. Also in this part of Wales are the fork-tailed kites, among the rarest birds of prey in Britain. A tiny chapel dedicated to St Govan huddles in a wave-lashed, boulder-strewn chasm on the coast near Tenby, close to the tranquil lily pools of Bosherston. At Clywedog the recently-restored remains of an old lead mine stand at the foot of an immense dam, providing a delightful contrast between old and new technologies . . . The list is almost endless, and sights such as these are so personal that it is easy to find completely new ones of your own in the course of a holiday, a weekend, or even a single day out.

The steady growth of car ownership in general and the motorway network in particular has brought the *Wild Wales* of George Borrow – the much-travelled 19th-c writer, linguist and quaffer of ale – within easy reach of most of Britain. Traffic has inevitably increased, particularly on the main roads to the coast, and the number of vehicles passing through Betws-y-Coed on an average August day is more than 50 per cent higher than it was in 1965.

In recent years, however, Wales has made a tremendous and praiseworthy effort to cater for its motorized guests. Smoothly-surfaced car parks have been built up and down the country by local councils, the National Trust, the Forestry Commission, and those responsible for the Snowdonia, Brecon Beacons, and Pembrokeshire Coast national parks. A lot of these facilities are in out-of-the-way beauty spots, and many of them have toilets and pleasant, grassy areas set aside specially for picnics. The opening of long-distance footpaths, one along the old Pembrokeshire coast and the other following the line of Offa's Dyke, has enabled many people to enjoy hitherto inaccessible countryside.

Despite the overall increase in traffic, it is still remarkably easy to find roads on which other cars are heavily outnumbered by sheep, buzzards, and the occasional fox. These lonely by-ways, many of them first stamped out by the feet of prehistoric man, twist and climb over a crumpled landscape that changes with every corner.

At first some of these uncannily quiet roads can seem just a little eerie to the city-dweller accustomed to endless traffic jams; but the faint question mark – 'Should I really be here?' is soon replaced by a deliciously heady sensation of new-found freedom. The out-of-season visitor will soon realise that its native population is indeed tiny and its roads, with very few exceptions, virtually devoid of traffic. There are other benefits too. In late spring and early summer exotic cascades of rhododendrons shroud the roads. In autumn the countryside glows with gold, brown, and orange as trees and bracken prepare for winter. Even winter itself can be quite astonishingly beautiful; the frosty air is crystal clear, snow makes the mountain peaks sparkle against the blue sky, and footsteps leave Man-Friday impressions on deserted beaches.

At times such as these the spine-tingling feeling of enchantment that delighted George Borrow and countless other visitors in the past can be recaptured. Granted a fragment of luck the visitor can delve back even deeper and savour the Wales chronicled by Giraldus Cambrensis – Gerald the Welshman – a priest who travelled throughout the land in the 12thc, preaching the Third Crusade in scores of little towns and villages.

A century later the power of the proud Welsh princes was finally crushed by Edward I, one of the greatest of England's medieval warrior kings. Determined to hold his new domain in an iron grip, Edward encircled the mountainous north with a ring of great castles, from beside the chocolate swirls of the Dee estuary to Aberystwyth. There are many memorable sights in Wales, but few can match the first glimpse of Harlech Castle, standing high on its massive fist of rock; or Caernarfon, where Edward presented his first-born son to the people of Wales and, more than 600 years later, Prince Charles was invested as Prince of Wales.

The English built their castles on the coast where they could be supplied from the sea, but Welsh fortresses tended to guard routes into the interior; Criccieth is one of few

exceptions. Castell-y-Bere and Carreg Cennen have already been mentioned; others include Dolbadarn, beside the deep, blue lake at the foot of the majestic Pass of Llanberis, and Dolwyddelan, set on a crag between Betws-y-Coed and Blaenau Ffestiniog – traditionally the birthplace of Llewelyn the Great in 1173.

There are plenty of fine castles elsewhere in Wales. Pembroke and Chepstow are famous, but Llanstephan, Kidwelly, and Manorbier should not be missed, while the quaint old heart of Tenby is still encased by its medieval walls, like Conwy in the north.

Wales has relatively few of the stately homes that are a feature of England, but their quality tends to compensate for the lack of sheer numbers. Penrhyn Castle for instance is a medieval-style Victorian extravaganza built with the fortunes accumulated from the vast slate quarries at Bethesda, in nearby Snowdonia. At Bodnant, in the Vale of Conwy, the house itself is not open to the public, but the gardens are rightly hailed as being among the most splendid in Britain and have rare plants and trees from all over the world. Powis Castle, on the outskirts of Welshpool, is still inhabited – unlike the great strongholds built by Edward I – and the deer that roam its spacious parkland are overlooked by the tallest tree in the United Kingdom, a noble Douglas fir almost 200ft high.

The oldest of the Welsh castles date back more than 800 years, but even they seem little more than brash newcomers when compared with the prehistoric camps and burial chambers that cover the map from Anglesey to the Bristol Channel. Many are tucked away down quiet country lanes, but most are signposted; others, such as the great stone rampart on St David's Head, can only be visited on foot. Can it be possible that a drive over Prescelly's lonely, windswept hills, in old Pembrokeshire follows the footsteps of men who, incredibly, carved great bluestone monoliths from the ancient rocks and transported them all the way to Stonehenge some 4,500 years ago?

These peoples were followed, many centuries later, by the Romans, but the eventual departure of the legions heralded the arrival of the Dark Ages. In Wales, however, this period is generally called the Age of Saints, for the mountains, the western coasts, and the little islands provided some measure of safety for many holy men, including St David, in those troubled times. Drive from Haverfordwest towards St David's – Britain's smallest city with a population of less than 2,000 – full of the expectation that the towers and pinnacles of the cathedral will stand up like a great ship above the undulating land ahead. They do not. It is not until the village-city is actually penetrated that the visitor catches the first glimpse of the cathedral, for it was built in a valley to escape the merciless eyes of the Norsemen who so often ravaged the shores of Wales.

The longships of today are the super-tankers that bring their cargoes of oil to Milford Haven and the newly-established deepwater terminal off Amlwch, on the northern coast of Anglesey. Almost a quarter of a mile long and displacing more than 250,000 tons, these immense ships – known in the trade as VLCC's, for Very Large Crude Carriers – can be watched feeling their way into Milford Haven from St Ann's Head, where the road ends at a grassy parking area with superb views.

Oil has brought a new air of ultra-modern commercial life to some of the wilder corners of Wales, but for many centuries the story has been one of humble, hard-working folk, many of whom – such as the charismatic David Lloyd George – struggled to achieve greatness in the wide world beyond the mountains. This age-old, grassroots aspect of Welsh life can still be sensed in many of the country's homely, tight-knit, and sturdily self-sufficient little towns and villages. It is brought together in the Welsh Folk Museum near Cardiff.

This unique enterprise was started in 1946 when the Earl of Plymouth offered St Fagans Castle and its grounds to the National Museum of Wales. Here, in a village setting, are buildings and bye-gones rescued from every corner of the land – a 16th-c barn from Flintshire, a wool factory from Breconshire, a 200-year-old Caernarfonshire cottage, a Carmarthenshire chapel, several farmhouses, and many others.

The museum underlines a fact that is quickly appreciated by the visitor to Wales; this is a country that had no really big towns until the advent of the Industrial Revolution and the start of large-scale mining in the southern valleys. The population of Cardiff was only 2,000 at the start of the 19thc; it is now almost 300,000. Elsewhere, a mere 11,000 residents makes Aberystwyth an urban giant in Mid Wales, where the whole of one-time Radnorshire has a population of only 18,000. The whole of old Montgomeryshire has fewer people than Shrewsbury. It comes as no surprise to learn that the number of traffic lights in Mid Wales can be counted on the fingers of one hand.

Like the land itself, the character of the people varies considerably from place to place. The combination of a small, thinly-spread population and a formidably rugged interior meant there was little communication between the various parts of Wales in the days when horsepower consisted of precisely that. Distinct sub-cultures developed and even today subtle differences can be detected between, for example, natives of Caernarfon, Llandrindod Wells, and Swansea. Even the Welsh they speak is different and, if they come from opposite ends of the principality, even the most fervent Welsh-language advocates sometimes have to resort to English to understand each other.

Many of the tongue-tangling placenames seem to consist of letters picked at random from an alphabetical lucky dip, but this can give a sense of being in a foreign, slightly mysterious land without all the bother of crossing the English Channel. The average Welshman is only too pleased to explain the rudiments of pronunciation, which certainly helps when asking for directions. Most people will quickly learn the meaning of such familiar fragments as 'llan' and 'aber'. Llanymynech, for example, is pronounced Lan-ur-mun-uk and means The Church of the Monks. Aberaeron is the name of that delightful little Regency town at the Mouth of the Aeron.

It is worth remembering that Swansea-born Dylan Thomas, the greatest of modern Welsh poets,

spoke only English. Even he might have had difficulty asking the way to Llanfairpwllgwyngyllgogerychwyrndrobwllllantysiliogogogoch! The following single-day drives have been specially selected to guide the motorist through the scenic and historical splendour of Wales.

DAY DRIVE SYMBOLS

AA Viewpoint	
Abbey	
Airport	
Battle Site	1750
Boating Centre	
Bridge	
Castle	
Church	
Crags	
Drive Route	A458
Heights in Feet	1236
Hill Fort	
Houses Open to the Public	
Industrial Building	
Inn	
Lighthouse	
Marshland	
Motorway	M4 2
Motorway Service Station	S
Other Roads	B4594
Places off main route	Clydach
Places of Interest	Caves
Places on Route	Crynant
Racecourse	
Rivers and Lakes	R Ure
Sandy Beaches	
Station	
Tower	
TV or Radio Mast	
Waterfall	
Windmill	
Woodland	

Where Gulls can be Lonely

Geological upheavals and waves eternally rolling in from the North Atlantic have combined to carve a scenic wonderland from the coasts of south-west Wales. There are broad bays and beautiful little inlets hidden away at the end of narrow lanes; long beaches pounded by surf and mile after mile of some of the most majestic cliffs in Europe; excellent deepwater harbours and broad, meandering estuaries where, in the words of Dylan Thomas, 'gulls go to be lonely'.

Nearly all of the old Pembrokeshire coast is a national park, and its long-distance footpath has opened up cliffs and coves that were previously denied to the public. The sea is speckled with islands where seals and seabirds breed in profusion, and boat trips run to most of these sanctuaries. Caldy Island, where the monks make perfume from flowers and herbs, lies off the picture-postcard resort of Tenby and is a particularly fascinating place to visit.

Other places that should not be missed include St David's Cathedral, the nearby ruined Bishop's Palace, and the fact-packed countryside unit that overlooks the sea at Broad Haven.

The coasts have many reminders of the not-so-distant days, when sturdy little sailing ships were the main trading links with the outside world. Today, the picturesque old schooners and brigs have been replaced by 250,000-ton supertankers that can often be seen edging towards their berths in Milford Haven, hailed by Nelson as the second finest natural harbour in the world.

The region's turbulent past is clearly recalled by names that are a legacy of Viking raids and also by a wealth of castles; those at Carreg Cennen, Kidwelly, Cilgerran, Llanstephan, and Pembroke – birthplace of Henry VII – are outstanding. This part of Wales also has the distinction of witnessing the last invasion of Britain.

A memorial on the headland near Fishguard recalls the landing of 1,200 French troops in 1797.

Pembrokeshire's coast is so superb that it is easy to overlook the shores of one-time Carmarthenshire. Here too are long stretches of sand, and the huge beach at Pendine was used for successful attacks on the world's land-speed record in the 1920's. Nearby Laugharne was for many years the home of Dylan Thomas, and this quaint little town with its ivy-covered castle evokes rich memories of the poet's masterpiece, *Under Milk Wood.*

Inland the hilly countryside is criss-crossed with lanes, and old Carmarthenshire has more miles of roads than any of the one-time county areas in Wales – apart from old Glamorgan. There are many surprises. A nature trail explores the Roman gold mines at Dolaucothi, near Pumsaint. Quarries worked by the builders of Stonehenge scar the Prescelly Hills. Coracles, relics of the dawn of history, skim over the rivers at Carmarthen, Cenarth, and Cilgerran.

The land around Carmarthen is noted for its rich dairy pastures. North of Llandovery, one of several old market towns in the lush valley of the Tywi, a road runs through breathtaking scenery to the huge Llyn Brianne Reservoir. This is the only part of Britain where fork-tailed kites can still be seen, wheeling and hovering in search of their prey.

South-west Wales has many well-preserved prehistoric monuments, such as the massive Pentre Ifan burial chamber, and dozens of headlands have clear traces of ancient fortifications. Delightful period-piece artillery forts can be seen, but not visited, at Milford Haven.

This remote corner of Wales was a refuge for holy men in the Age of Saints that followed the withdrawal of the Roman legions, and the great crosses at Nevern and Carew are remarkable tributes to the Celtic craftsmen who carved their intricate patterns shortly after the dawn of Christianity.

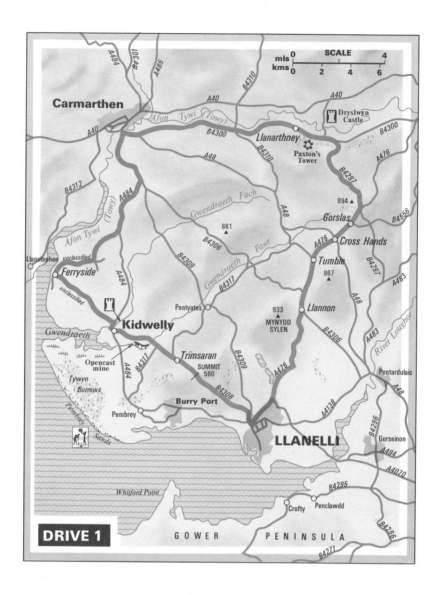

DRIVE 1

Through the Tywi Valley

From Llanelli

Drive 1   46 miles

Starting at the industrial centre of *Llanelli*, this route runs along the coast to *Kidwelly's* famous castle and on to the pleasant market town of *Carmarthen*. Turning E the road follows the Afon Tywi river before climbing through woodland for views over the Loughor estuary. From Llanelli follow the A484 towards Carmarthen, looking out for an early right turn on to the B4309, signposted Cynheidre and *Pontyates*. In ½m turn left on to the B4308, signposted Trimsaran. The road gradually rises through woodlands to reach the top of the Mynydd Pemy-bre ridge.

On the descent through the built-up village of Trimsaran there are extensive views over the coast and the converging estuaries of the Taf, Tywi, and Gwendraeth Fawr. An open-cast mine lies to the left before the drive enters Kidwelly, a town, which is well-known for its 12th-c castle. At the main road turn right on to the A484, and in ¼m turn left on to an unclassified road signposted *Ferryside*. As this road rises it affords good backward

views across to the Gower. *Llanstephan* and the ruined 11th- to 13th-c castle can be seen across the Tywi estuary on the descent to Ferryside. Turn right into the straggling village and follow an attractively wooded stretch of road. In 2m meet crossroads and turn left, then 2m farther turn left on to the A484 Carmarthen road. Continue through open countryside with views of Carmarthen and the Tywi Valley.

At the edge of Carmarthen go straight ahead for the town centre, then on entering a roundabout take the third exit on to the A48 *Swansea* road. In ¾m turn left on to the B4300, signposted Llandeilo, and follow the road on the S side of the Tywi Valley, with glimpses of the river in places.

Beyond Llanarthney there are views across the river to ruined 13th-c Dryslwyn Castle; high above the road on the right is *Paxton's Tower*, a folly built in 1811 to the memory of Nelson. Ahead are good views along the valley. Turn right on to the B4297 Maesybont road, then follow a winding

climb through woodlands with extensive views S across the valley to the hills beyond. The descent allows panoramic views over an industrial area. Continue downhill and turn right on to the A476, passing through the mining villages of *Gorslas* and Cross Hands before climbing a 1 in 7 hill to Tumble. On the way to *Llannon* the road undulates through more pleasantly wooded hill country before reaching the final descent into Llanelli. This 1 in 8 hill affords panoramic views over the Loughor estuary to the high ground of the Gower peninsula.

Placenames in *italic* type are worth stopping at; each is listed and described in the main gazetteer section of the book   101

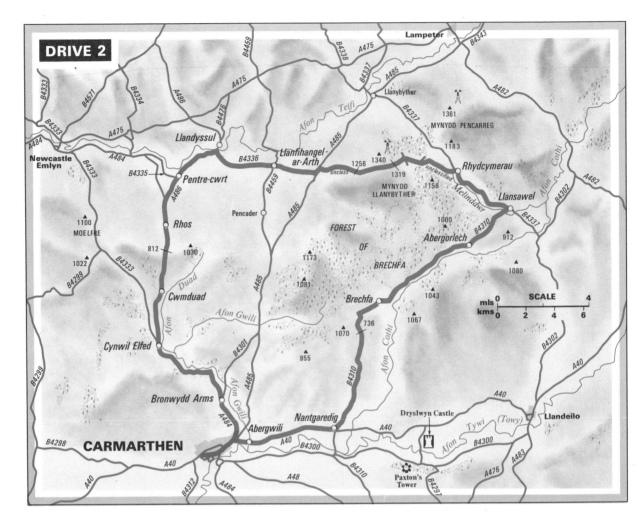

Woodland Roads

From Carmarthen

Drive 2   52 miles

From the market town of *Carmarthen*, on
the Afon Tywi, this route heads into wooded
river valleys and gradually climbs through
moorland to a 1,300ft summit which affords
superb all-round views. The leisurely return
ride leads to more wooded slopes beside the
clear waters of the Afon Cothi.
Leave Carmarthen by the A40 *Llandeilo*
road, and in 1m bear left on to the A484,
signposted *Newcastle Emlyn*. Beyond
Bronwydd Arms the drive follows the deep
wooded gorge of the Afon Gwili for several
miles. Before Cynwl Elfed the road leaves
the valley, but later continues through
another prettily wooded stretch to
Cwmduad, where three valleys meet. The
long easy climb out of the valley to *Rhos*
gives plenty of opportunities to admire the
view. In 1m, as the road falls, turn right on
to the A486 *Llandyssul* road. This 1 in 10
descent allows views of the Teifi Valley
before the drive approaches the river itself
after Pentre-cwrt.

At Llandyssul turn right on to the B4336
Llanybyther road and climb out of the valley
to Llanfihangel-ar-Arth. In 2m meet the
A485 and turn left then immediately right on
to an unsignposted and unclassified road.
Follow a long climb on to moorland; the

summit of over 1,300ft is topped by radio
masts and affords magnificent all-round
views. A long descent follows through
pleasant woodland which forms part of the
extensive *Forest of Brechfa*. Continue over
crossroads and at the next fork bear right.
In 1½m turn right on to the B4337,
signposted Llansawel, and drive into the
hamlet of Rhydcymerau. Continue along
the wooded Melinddwr Valley to the edge of
Llansawel. At the chapel turn sharply right
on to the B4310, signposted
Abergorlech and Brechfa, to join the Afon
Cothi at the pretty village of Abergorlech.
The latter is noted for the unusual decorative
stones found in the river.

The countryside here is very relaxing as the
road continues through the picturesque
wooded slopes of the Cothi Valley to
Brechfa. A steady climb through more
woodlands is followed by a long and
gradual descent through pastoral country
to the Tywi Valley. At the main crossroads
turn right on to the A40 into Nantgaredig,
and continue through the wide Tywi Valley.
Pass through *Abergwili*, the site of the
modern palace of the Bishop of St David's,
and return to Carmarthen.

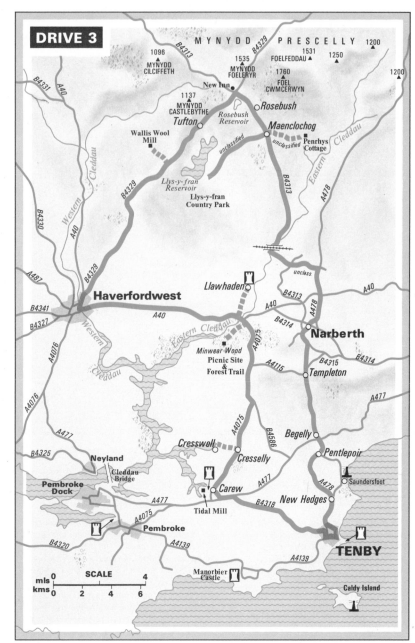

Pembrokeshire's Heartland

From Tenby

Drive 3   68 miles

Starting at *Tenby*, one of the premier resorts of W Wales, this drive takes in the friendly little shopping centre of *Haverfordwest* and the rolling downland of the Prescelly Hills.

Take the A478 *Narberth* road from Tenby, and while still in the town take the B4318 *Pembroke* road. Meet a fork after ½m and turn right. At first the drive follows winding roads which afford occasional views, then it straightens out as it approaches a main road. Turn left here on to the A477, signposted Pembroke. Take the next turning right on to an unclassified road for *Carew*, which boasts a ruined 13th-c castle and a 14th-c church. A magnificent Celtic cross dating from *c*1033 stands near by. Meet a T-junction and turn right on to the A4075 Haverfordwest road, passing through Cressely. Cresswell, with its old quay and inn, lies to the left. As the drive approaches the A40 it passes an unclassified road on the left which leads to Minwear Wood. Features of the latter include a picnic site, forest trail, and delightful views of the Eastern Cleddau. On reaching the A40 turn left. The next turning on the right is an unclassified road which leads to the village of *Llawhaden* and its ruined 13th-c castle. Return to the A40 by the same road and turn right. Continue towards Haverfordwest with the Prescelly range to the right, and descend into the town with good views of its old castle.

Haverfordwest is sited on the Western Cleddau River and was the county town of old Pembrokeshire. The castle is perched on a steep slope high above the river and dates from the 12thc. Leave by the A40 *Fishguard* road and in ¾m turn right on to the B4329 *Cardigan* road. Continue along winding roads through agricultural and woodland country, then follow a long steady climb on to the Prescelly Hills. The drive passes a left turn which leads to Wallis wool mill. Pass *Tufton* and the 1,137ft summit of Mynydd Castlebythe on the left before reaching crossroads by the New Inn, a haunt of the Prescelly shepherds. Here turn right on to the B4313 Narberth road, with glimpses of *Rosebush Reservoir* to the right. Beyond the edge of Rosebush, with its old slate quarry, there are further extensive views as the road gradually falls to *Maenclochog*. The unclassified road to the left leads for 1m to Penrhys Cottage at

Temple Druid, now restored by the county council. At the end of Maenclochog keep forward on to an unclassified road and continue for 3½m to reach *Llys-y-Fran* reservoir and country park. Car park and picnic facilities are available here.

Return to Maenclochog, turn right on to the B4313, and continue the descent to the E Cleddau Valley. Beyond the railway bridge leave the valley and ascend along a winding road which becomes unclassified after meeting crossroads. In 2½m meet crossroads and turn right on to the A478 Tenby road. Cross the A40 and in 1m branch right to enter Narberth, a pleasant market town with remains of a 13th-c castle. Continue with the A478 Tenby road and pass through Templeton, *Begelly*, Pentlepoir, and New Hedges to Tenby.

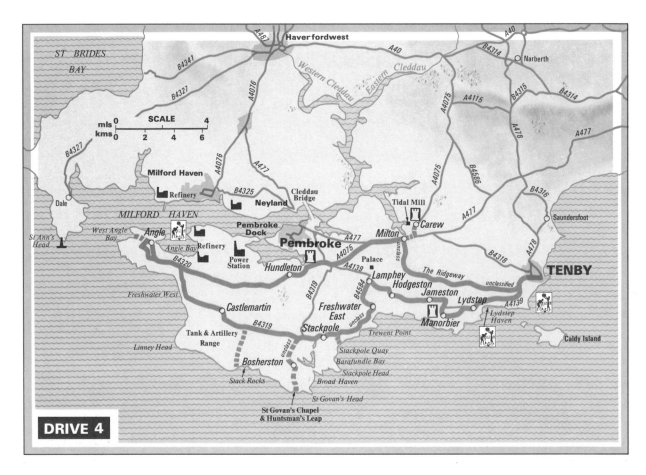

DRIVE 4

Along the Dyfed Coast

From Tenby

Drive 4 48 miles

This popular route leads to some of the most impressive cliff scenery in S Wales. There are fine views of *Caldy Island*, the home of Trappist Cistercian monks who sell perfume made from flowers and herbs. Visitors are welcome, but only men are allowed to visit the monastery. Excursions sail from *Tenby* and *Saundersfoot*. Farther along the route is the pretty seaside village of *Angle*, with its views over *Milford Haven*.

Leave Tenby by the A4319 *Pembroke* road, skirt a military area with glimpses of the coastline, Caldy Island, and the bird sanctuary of St Margaret's Island. At *Lydstep* there is a sandy beach overlooked by magnificent limestone cliffs. Beyond Lydstep Point are the noted caves. In ½m turn left on to the B4585 *Manorbier* road. At Manorbier turn left on the one-way system then keep straight on for the sand and shingle beach, passing one of the most picturesque ruins in Wales – the 13th-c castle. Return to Manorbier and keep left. In ½m rejoin the A4139 and turn left to enter the valley of the Pembroke River. Pass through Jameston and *Hodgeston* before *Lamphey*, then turn left and immediately left again on to the B4584 *Freshwater East* road. For the ruined 13th-c Bishop's Palace turn right and follow the signposts. At Freshwater East there is a pleasant sandy beach overlooked by caravan and camping sites. Turn right on to the

unclassified *Stackpole* road, and continue down a 1 in 5 gradient with occasional glimpses of the sea. The road on the left leads to Stackpole Quay, a lonely harbour sheltered by cliffs. A cliff walk leads from here to sandy Barafundle Bay. Pass through Stackpole, descending (1 in 6) through a short stretch of delightful woodland, then turn left on to the B4319 *Bosherston* road. After ½m an unclassified road on the left leads to Bosherston. Near the church is a path which leads to three lily ponds nestling in woodlands. For impressive cliff scenery bear right beyond the village to St Govan's Chapel. Near here is Huntsman's Leap where, according to legend, a horseman leapt over a narrow ravine only to die of fright. Return to the B4319 and after 1½m a road to the left, which is open when there is no firing at the *Castlemartin* tank range, leads to the impressive Stack Rocks and cliff scenery.

At Castlemartin keep left, signed *Angle* and Freshwater West, to the sand dunes of Freshwater West. Views across to St Ann's Head and *Skokholm Island* can be enjoyed from here. Strong currents and patches of quicksand make the beach unsuitable for bathing or paddling. In 1m turn left on to the B4320 with glimpses ahead of Angle Bay and *Milford Haven*. After 1½m take the unclassified road on the right and continue down to Angle Bay; turn left into the quaint village of Angle. Pass the church, and in ½m

turn left on to the B4320, signposted Pembroke, or go straight on for the delightfully sandy West Angle Bay. After ½m the B4320 turns sharp left and climbs. Fine views to the left are afforded by the higher ground, but extensive oil refineries occupy both sides of the inlet. A 700ft chimney which is part of a power station serves as a local landmark. Continue through Hundleton and descend through a curtain of pretty woodland. The road finally reveals a spectacular view of Pembroke's impressive 12th- to 13th-c castle, birthplace of Henry VII, as the drive enters the town.

Leave Pembroke on the A4139 Tenby road, and at the end of the town turn left on to the A4075, signposted *Carmarthen*. In 2m turn right on to the A477, and ½m beyond *Milton* turn left on to the A4075 for *Carew*. This village is famous for its ruined 13th-c castle, 14th-c church, Celtic cross, and rare tidal mill. Return to Milton and at the crossroads turn left on to an unclassified road signposted Lamphey and Manorbier. After the gradual climb to higher ground turn left at the T-junction on to the Ridgeway, an old hill-road which runs from Tenby to Pembroke. Follow Tenby signposts along this ridge at an altitude which affords all-round panoramic views in places. Finally, descend a 1 in 7 gradient on the return to Tenby.

Around the Black Mountain

From Llandeilo

Drive 5   88 miles

Narrow valleys, wooded gorges and the moorland slopes of the Black Mountain are features of this drive from *Llandeilo*. A mile to the west of this pleasant market town is *Dynevor* Castle, which dates from the 17thc, and its grounds contain the ruins of an even earlier fortress. Compare these with 13th-c *Carreg-Cennan* Castle, which is seen at the end of the drive.

Leave Llandeilo, situated in the Vale of Tywy, by the A40 *Llandovery* road. Follow the river through pleasant hill country, with views across the valley to the Black Mountains, and enter Llandovery. The name of this pleasant town means 'the church amidst the waters', and it lies between the rivers Tywi and Bran. The castle remains date from Norman times. Drive over a level crossing and turn left on to the A483, signposted *Builth Wells*, then in $\frac{1}{4}$m meet a crossroads and turn left on to the unclassified Rhandirmwyn road. Several roads on the left lead to the attractively situated village of *Cilycwm*. The drive now enters spectacular hill country as it follows the valley to Rhandirmwyn. Later the valley narrows and the river tumbles over rocks through a wooded gorge as the drive reaches the car park and viewing area of the huge Llyn Brianne reservoir. A narrow but well-surfaced road with passing places winds for 7m through pine forests high above the water, and affords further magnificent views before it ends at the

reservoir's farthest arm. If this road is taken, return along the same route to Llandovery and turn right then left on to the A40, signposted *Brecon*. Take the next turning right on to the A4069, signposted *Llangadog*, and follow the S side of the Tywi Valley for Llangadog.

Meet a T-junction and turn left, signposted *Brynamman*, to follow the pretty Afon Sawdde Valley to enter another attractively wooded gorge. The river wanders off to the left as the road begins a long, winding ascent on to the moorland slopes of the Black Mountain. There are several hairpin bends, but the views from a height of over 1,600ft are spectacular and well worth the

effort. A car park and viewpoint are provided. On the easier descent there are views over a partly industrial area. At Brynamman turn right for *Gwaun-Cae-Gurwen*, keeping on the A4069, and on the near side of the level-crossing turn right again on to the A474 for *Glanaman*, Garnant, and *Ammanford* – all associated with the old mining industry. At the traffic signals in Ammanford turn right on to the A483, signposted Llandeilo, passing through *Llandybie*. Continue to Ffairfach, meet crossroads, and turn right on to an unclassified road. Turn right again to visit the impressively-situated 13th-c *Carreg-Cennan Castle* before returning to Llandeilo.

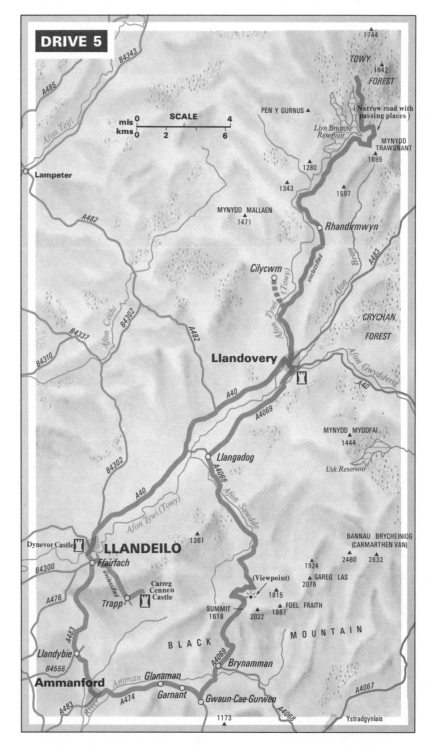

Placenames in *italic* type are worth stopping at; each is listed and described in the main gazetteer section of the book

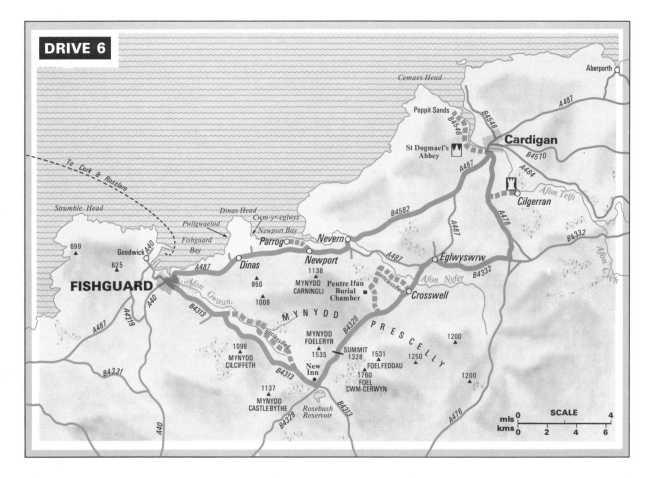

Sand and Seascapes

From Fishguard

Drive 6   43 miles

Set high on wooded slopes overlooking the
fine natural harbour of Fishguard Bay, the
resort of *Fishguard* has given its name to
the major port for Southern Ireland, which
is located below *Goodwick* village. It is an
ideal starting point for taking in the hill and
moorland scenery of the Prescelly Hills, as
a contrast to the sea views at the beginning
of the route.

From Fishguard take the A487
Cardigan road for the attractive Lower Town.
The 1 in 7 descent provides views across the
old harbour before the road crosses the Afon
Gwaun. Rock outcrops to the right on the
approach to *Dinas* are part of the Prescelly
Hills. Side roads to the left lead to the sandy
coves of Pwllgwaelod and Cwm-yr-eglwys.
Continue to *Newport*, on the Afon Nyfer,
below the slopes of 1,138ft Mynydd
Carningli. Sandy beaches can be enjoyed at
Parrog on the S side of the estuary,
and at Newport Sands on the N side.
Meet crossroads 2m beyond Newport and
turn left on to the B4582. Continue through
woodlands and cross the Afon Nyfer into
Nevern. This attractive hamlet is set in a
wooded valley and has a Norman church
with a fine carved cross. Follow the Cardigan
road along mainly high-banked roads,
and in 5m turn left and rejoin the A487.

The descent offers panoramic views of
the Teifi estuary and Cardigan. Formerly a
major port, Cardigan is a pleasant market

town on the River Teifi. Overlooking the
town are the slight remains of a 12th-c
castle, now converted to a private house. On
the approach to the town the B4546 to the
left leads to *St Dogmaels* – where there are
remains of a 12th-c abbey – and Poppit
Sands. Leave Cardigan by following the
A478 *Tenby* road. After 2m a road to the left
leads to *Cilgerran*, where the ruined Norman
to 13th-c castle stands above the Teifi in a
picturesque setting. After 3m turn right on
to the B4332 Eglwyswrw road, which
allows fine views of the Prescelly range on
the left. At Eglwyswrw, an attractive village
with an old inn, meet a T-junction and turn
left on to the A487, signposted Fishguard.
After ¾m turn left again on the B4329
Haverfordwest road for Crosswell. For the
notable ancient monument of *Pentre Ifan*
burial chamber, turn right on to an
unclassified road at Crosswell and follow a
stretch of the wooded Afon Nyfer, then in
1½m turn left. Continue, and then
climb steadily on to moorland and the
1,328ft summit. The national park
viewpoint to the left of the road provides an
opportunity to relax and admire the
scenery before crossing the Prescelly Hills.
Descend to the crossroads at the New Inn
and turn right on to the B4313 Fishguard
road. This high-banked road drops through
the western Prescelly range, with extensive
views above the wooded Gwaun Valley. An
unclassified road to the right, just over 1m

beyond New Inn, leads to a beautifully-
wooded gorge which can be followed
downstream. Approach Fishguard on the
B4313 and climb a 1 in 5 gradient for
views across the harbour. Descend into
Fishguard.

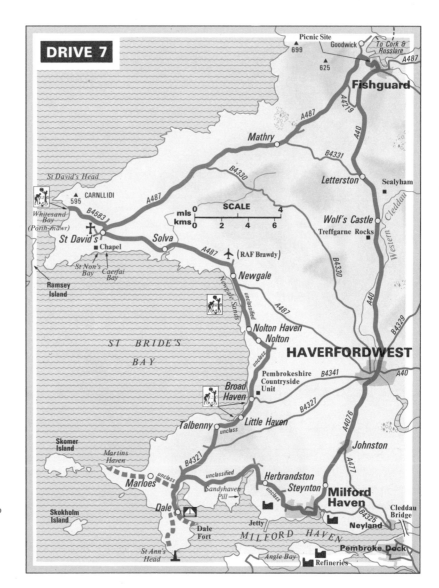

The Smallest City

From Haverfordwest

Drive 7   75 miles

Haverfordwest, on the Western Cleddau River, was the county town of old Pembrokeshire. Within easy reach are picturesque seaside villages, sandy beaches, sheer cliffs, and the tanker port of *Milford Haven*. The route also takes in 12th-c St David's Cathedral. Leave by the A4076 Milford Haven road and pass through *Johnston* and Steynton to Milford Haven. Go forward to the Promenade and turn right, then at the war memorial turn left. The busy Haven is used by fishing boats, cargo ships and giant supertankers. At the end of the town turn left across a bridge, then turn right on to an unclassified road signposted Hubberston and *Dale* to pass a large oil refinery. The jetty built to serve this installation is $\frac{3}{4}$m long and its construction required 19m of concrete piles. On reaching the edge of Herbrandston bear right, signposted Dale, and continue along winding, high-banked roads for 5m.

Turn left on to the B4327. Views of Milford Haven are offered as the road gradually falls to the pleasantly situated, well-sheltered and popular boating centre of Dale. A lane leads to the field centre of Dale Fort on the narrow neck of land reaching out into the bay. Go forward into a one-way street where a left turn leads to St Ann's Head. This rocky headland provides magnificent views of Milford Haven and the incoming and outgoing oil tankers. The lighthouse is open to visitors. Turn right with Haverfordwest signposts and return along the B4327. After 1m a left turn leads to *Marloes* and Martin's Haven. To the N of Marloes are Musselwick Sands, sheltered and uncrowded; S are the Marloes Sands, a long sandy beach overlooking the island bird sanctuary of *Skokholm*. During the summer boats sail from Martin's Haven to *Skomer Island*, a nature reserve inhabited by thousands of sea birds. Continue with the B4327 and after $2\frac{1}{2}$m meet crossroads and

turn left on to an unclassified road signposted Talbenny. The road descends towards the S end of *St Bride's Bay*, with its sandy coves and sheer cliffs, and continues to Little Haven. This is one of the area's most picturesque seaside villages and has a sandy beach at low tide. The road climbs a 1 in 5 gradient and turns sharply left before dipping into *Broad Haven*, which has a good sandy beach flanked by cliffs.

The Pembrokeshire Countryside Unit is here. At the end of the village keep left on to a high-banked unclassified road, signposted *Nolton* and *Newgale*. At Druidston a lane to the left leads to sheer 250ft cliffs, but in summer it is usually difficult to park. Just beyond this turning ($\frac{1}{2}$m) meet crossroads and turn left to follow Nolton signs for Nolton Haven. Grandstand views across St Bride's Bay take in *Ramsey Island* as the road dips and climbs to the long sandy beaches of *Newgale* Sands, which are excellent for bathing and surfing. At the A487 turn left into the village of Newgale. After 3m the road descends a 1 in 8 hill into picturesque *Solva*, a popular boating centre sheltered in a deep river valley. Continue along a winding road through more undulating country to *St David's*, Britain's smallest

city. The magnificent cathedral dates from the 12thc. Leave by the A487 *Fishguard* road, and after $\frac{1}{2}$m turn left on to the B4583, signposted Whitesands. Turn left again for the attractive Whitesand Bay, one of the best surfing beaches in Wales. Swirling currents at the N end of the bay make it dangerous for bathing. Overlooking the bay is the isolated hill of Carnllidi, which rises steeply to 595ft. Return to the A487 and turn left for the 16m run to Fishguard. The road passes through undulating countryside, with rocky outcrops and occasional glimpses of the sea from higher ground. At the A40 Fishguard Harbour lies 1m to the left, but the drive turns right and climbs past a picnic area on the left to Fishguard.

Continue to the town centre and turn right, still on the A40, signposted *Letterston* and Haverfordwest. To the left, 1m beyond Letterston and some distance from the main road, is Sealyham. This village has given its name to the breed of terriers. The road joins the waters of the Western Cleddau at Wolf's Castle where, according to legend, the last wolf in Britain was killed. After a narrow gorge and the prominent Treffgarne Rocks, the drive continues along the E side of the valley for the return to Haverfordwest.

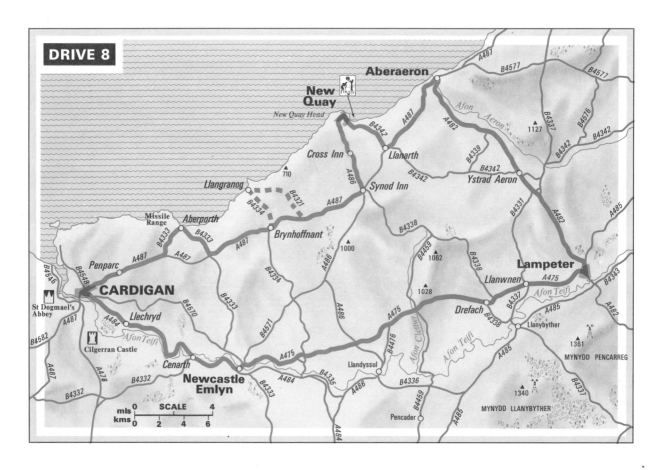

DRIVE 8

Coracles on the Teifi

From Cardigan

Drive 8   73 miles

This route starts from *Cardigan* and wanders through varied countryside, taking in sea views, sandy beaches, wooded river valleys and ancient castles. Near the waterfalls at *Cenarth* there may be fishermen using the Welsh coracle, a portable boat made of tarred canvas on a light wooden frame.

Cardigan, formerly a major port, is a pleasant market town on the River Teifi with slight remains of a 12th-c castle, now a private house. Leave by the A487 *Aberaeron* and *Aberystwyth* road, gradually ascending to high ground beyond Penparc. In 2¼m turn left on to the B4333 *Aberporth* road. Pleasant views of the sea are offered as this road winds down to the pleasant sheltered resort of Aberporth and its sandy beaches. The headland to the W is now a missile-testing range. Continue on the B4333, climbing away from the sea, and after 2¼m turn left on to the A487. For several miles there are good views on both sides as the road keeps to high ground. At Brynhoffnant a detour can be made by following the B4334 for 2½m to the attractive coastal village of *Llangranog*, which lies in a ravine and has a sandy beach. A footpath leads N to a rocky headland and two sheltered sandy coves. Between the village and the headland there are the remains of a prehistoric fort. The main drive can be rejoined by taking the B4321 through Pentgarreg. Continue from Brynhoffnant for 5m and then turn left at Synod Inn on to the A486 *New Quay* road.

Pass through Cross Inn and descend (1 in 8), with good views ahead of the coast, into the popular and picturesque sailing centre of New Quay. To the E of the harbour is a sandy beach, and to the N of the town are the sheer 300ft cliffs of New Quay Head, noisy with sea birds. The clifftop provides a magnificent view across Cardigan Bay.

Leave the town on the B4342, signposted Aberaeron, then continue through wooded countryside. In 3m turn left on to the A487 and pass through *Llanarth*, then enjoy excellent coastal views on the approach to Aberaeron. Situated at the mouth of the Afon Aeron, the town's broad streets and elegant houses present a fine example of Regency planning. The large, sheltered harbour has seen busier days, but is still used by small fishing boats and pleasure craft. For a change to woodland scenery leave by the A482 *Lampeter* road and continue along the pleasant Aeron Valley. The drive leaves the valley beyond Ystrad Aeron, along winding roads which pass through hill country before entering Lampeter in the Teifi Valley. Leave this pleasant market town by the A475 *Newcastle Emlyn* road along the N side of the Teifi Valley. Continue through *Llanwnen* and Drefach, then climb out of the valley and cross moorland to the Clettwr Valley. The next stretch of road has several steep dips and climbs, with a maximum gradient of 1 in 6, and passes through

mainly well-wooded country. It rejoins the Teifi Valley before Newcastle Emlyn, a little market town with traces of a castle dating from Henry VII's time. Leave by the A484 Cardigan road for Cenarth, which is noted for the attractive waterfalls near the old river bridge. The traditional Welsh coracle is still used here. Continue with the valley through *Llechryd* to return to Cardigan.

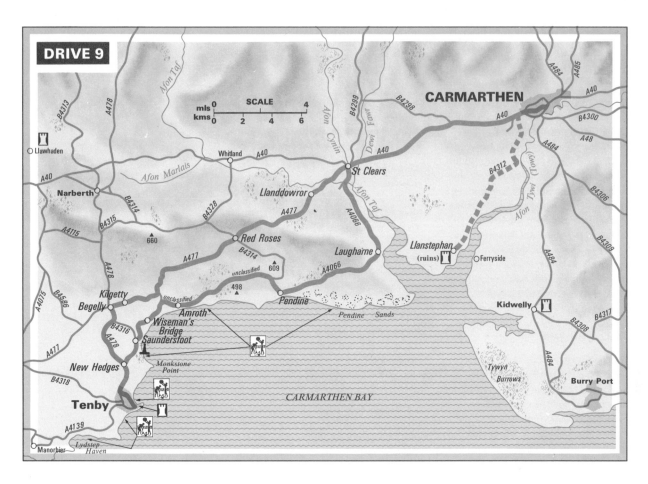

DRIVE 9

CARMARTHEN

Home of a Poet

From Carmarthen

Drive 9

Carmarthen, on the Afon Tywi, was the county and market town of old Carmarthenshire. From here the relaxing drive towards *Tenby* passes through *Laugharne*, the home of Dylan Thomas, and past sandy beaches and a ruined castle. The scenery on the return journey changes to wooded hill country. Leave Carmarthen by the A40 *Haverfordwest* road. After 1m continue with the A40; the B4312 to the left leads to *Llanstephan*, where remains of the 11th- to 13th-c castle occupy an impressive site above the Tywi estuary. At the traffic signals in St Clears turn left on to the A4066 *Pendine* road to Laugharne — pronounced Larne — on the Taf estuary.

The town is famous as the home of poet Dylan Thomas, who is buried in the 15th-c church. Continue on the A4066, passing steep wooded slopes on the right. The dunes and marshy land on the left are part of a Ministry of Defence establishment. Pendine, with its caravan and camping sites, has one of the longest stretches of firm, flat sand in Britain. It was used in the 1920's for attempts on the world land speed record by Sir Malcolm Campbell. The steep 1 in 5 climb from the village gives fine backward views before the route reaches the summit and turns left on to the unclassified *Amroth* road. As the road falls to the sea there are more views across the water to Tenby and *Caldy Island* before the drive

reaches Amroth. The sandy shore here is known for its submerged forest, which is revealed at very low tide. At the end of the village the road climbs away from the sea.

After ½m turn left on the road signposted Tenby, and pass through woodland before dipping to Wiseman's Bridge, a hamlet with a shingle and sand beach flanked by rocks. Churchill, Montgomery, and Eisenhower met here during D-Day rehearsals on the beaches of Carmarthen Bay. Climb through another wooded stretch, and at the summit keep left before taking the 1 in 7 descent to *Saundersfoot*. This popular boating and fishing resort is an attractive place to break the tour, and offers sandy beaches and plenty of amusements. Leave on the B4316, with its 1 in 8 climb, then at the main road turn left on to the A478 for Tenby, the premier resort of SW Wales. Wander through the narrow streets for a while or visit some of the town's many old buildings. Return along the A478, signposted *Narberth*, then in 5m meet the *Begelly* roundabout and take the third exit on to the A477 to pass through *Kilgetty*. From here on the scenery changes to woodland, and beyond Red Roses the road descends gradually through pleasantly-wooded hill country to reach the flatter land around the Taf, Cynin, and Dewi Fawr Rivers before entering Carmarthen.

Placenames in *italic* type are worth stopping at; each is listed and described in the main gazetteer section of the book

Coal and Choirs

Cardiff, Swansea, Newport, Neath, Ebbw Vale, Treorchy, Rhondda; the placenames of south Wales immediately evoke vivid pictures of coal, choirs, and stirring deeds on the rugby field. The Industrial Revolution of the 19thc completely changed the character of the hills and valleys that run southwards from the Brecon Beacons to the Bristol Channel, and coastal villages quickly became major ports. Barry, now a big and lively holiday resort, had a population of 85 in 1880; by 1889 it had increased to 13,000, and the new 74-acre dock was the biggest in the world at that time.

Barry alone exported 11,000,000 tons of coal in 1913 – a record for any port – but many of the mines are now closed and the valleys are becoming treasure-houses of industrial archaeology. Welsh life through the ages is brilliantly portrayed in the national folk museum at St Fagans, on the outskirts of Cardiff.

Cardiff itself, the national capital since 1955, has a basically Norman castle and many other handsome buildings. It is the home of the National Museum of Wales and has all the other social, cultural, and recreational facilities expected of a major city.

Swansea, elevated to city status in 1969, sprawls along the gentle curve of a splendid bay and is an ideal centre for exploring the lovely Gower Peninsula, most of which is designated an area of outstanding natural beauty. Gower's southern coast has high cliffs punctuated by a series of delightful sandy beaches. It ends at Worms Head, a huge, wave-lashed outcrop of rock that can be reached on foot at low tide. The northern shore, in contrast, is as flat as a billiard table; it is famous for cockles which are still gathered by men and women who jog out over the saltings on horse-drawn carts.

Backed by a wilderness of high dunes, the long beach between industrial Port Talbot and the bright lights of Porthcawl is one of the finest in Wales. The old town of Kenfig, a flourishing community in the Middle Ages, sleeps beneath the wind-blown sand that had choked it by the 16thc.

Although the region is thickly populated by Welsh standards, there is plenty of open country within very easy reach of the cities and big towns. To the north lie the 519 sqm of the beautiful Brecon Beacons national park, with its enchanting waterfalls, many caves, and mountains that rise to 2,907ft at the summit of Pen-y-Fan. A feature of the park is the canal that runs between Brecon and Pontypool; this is one of the loveliest inland waterways in Britain, and the stretch near Llangattock is superb.

The splendour of the Brecon Beacons is matched by the grandeur of the Black Mountain that sprawls over the old county boundary into one-time Carmarthenshire. Its high, precipitous eastern face is seen at its best from the minor road to the west of the A4067. Near by are the Dan-yr-Ogof show caves.

Raglan, Chepstow, and Caerphilly have impressive castles – Caerphilly's being the second biggest in Britain. There are very fine relics of the Roman occupation at Caerwent and Caerleon, where an amphitheatre has survived for almost 2,000 years. Another remarkable building is Castell Coch, a romantic castle that seems to have been transplanted from the banks of the Loire or Rhine.

Pontypridd has a famous bridge which was built in 1755, and a great musical reputation. Its native sons include pop singers, opera stars, and the men who wrote *Land of My Fathers,* the Welsh national anthem. This and many other songs fill the air when rugby internationals are played at Cardiff; the city streets are thronged with fans sporting *Cymru am Byth* rosettes and waving banners emblazoned with the red dragon.

Where Arthur Ruled

From Newport

Drive 10   59 miles

From *Newport* follow B4596 and *Caerleon* signposts to cross the M4, and drive alongside the River Usk to Caerleon – the traditional capital of King Arthur. Turn left along a one-way street to pass the site of the fine Roman Fort and Amphitheatre of Isca.

From here follow *Usk* signposts along an unclassified road which traces the edge of the Usk Valley. Reach Usk and turn right on to the A471 to cross the river into the town. A picturesque ruined Norman castle and an interesting old church are of interest. Turn left with the A471 *Abergavenny* road, and continue up the Usk Valley. After 3½m cross the river via the impressive Chain Bridge. After 2¾m turn left on to the A40. The 1,833ft summit ahead is Blorenge. Beyond are the Black Mountains of Gwent, with the 1,955ft conical peak of Sugar Loaf prominent. Enter a roundabout and take the third exit into Abergavenny, a market town and popular touring centre. Leave by following the A40, signposted *Brecon*, then take the A465 Merthyr road. After 1m take the B4246 and follow Blaenavon signposts. In 1¼m bear left and cross the Brecon and Abergavenny Canal before climbing a sharply-winding road. The twisting of the road reveals fine views along the Usk Valley to the 2,000ft Black Mountains.

Approach the 1,500ft summit, near Penffordd-goch Pond. An unclassified road on the right leads to a point below Gilwern Hill which affords views up the Clydach Valley to *Brynmawr*. The main drive continues and turns left on to the unclassified *Llanellen* road to reach the Foxhunter Memorial. This is set into rock beside the Blorenge viewpoint, which gives a grandstand view over E Gwent to the Forest of Dean. Return to the B4246 and turn left for the descent to the edge of Blaenavon. Turn right on to the B4248 Brynmawr road. On the left is the Dragon derelict land reclamation scheme. Later a long descent brings the drive to Brynmawr, a village standing 1,150ft above sea level. Turn left on the one-way road, then turn right with Merthyr signposts and turn left again on to the Beaufort road. Pass through Beaufort and as the road rises turn left on to the A4046 for *Ebbw Vale*. This town is situated at the head of the Ebbw Valley and is famous for its massive steelworks.

In ½m enter a roundabout and take the first exit; at the next roundabout take the third exit, and at the third roundabout take the second exit into Newport road. Pass the steelworks before turning sharp left. Enter *Cwm* and turn right, signposted Newport. Cross the railway bridge and turn left. Farther down into Ebbw Vale the road passes Ocean Colliery, then enters a wooded stretch on the approach to *Aberbeeg*. Ebbw Fach and the road from *Blaina* and *Abertillery* join the valley here. After turning right on to the A467 the road traces a cliff edge in places and passes through *Llanhilleth* to *Crumlin*. Meet crossroads and keep forward.

Near here the valley was once spanned by a 185ft-high railway viaduct, built in 1857 and recently demolished. After a while the drive passes the Celynen collieries on the approach to the *Abercarn*, Crosskeys by-pass. An unclassified road to the left leads to Cwmcarn, the start of a 7m scenic drive through the Ebbw Forest which affords views of the Brecon Beacons and Bristol Channel from a 1,260ft viewpoint. The main drive continues through the edge of Abercarn and Cwmcarn to Pontywaun, where the road from Cwmcarn rejoins the drive. Carry on through Crosskeys and *Risca* and after 2m, on the edge of Rogerstone, go forward for Newport.

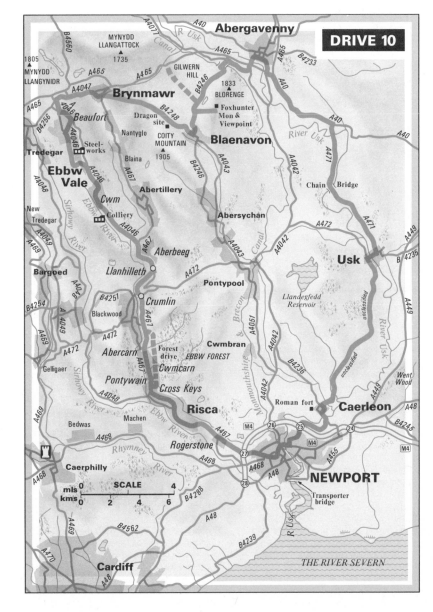

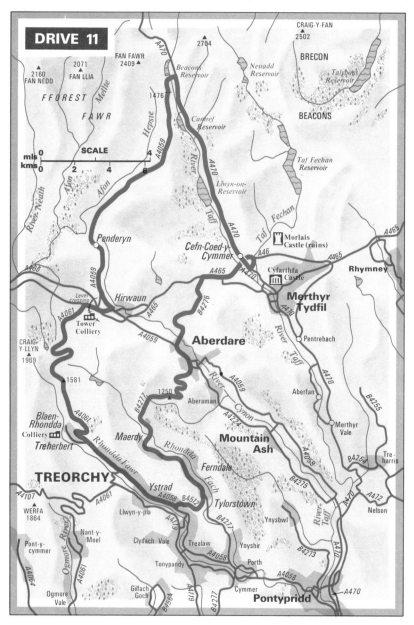

Mines and Mountains

From Treorchy

Drive 11   45 miles

The drive leaves *Treorchy*, junction for the spectacular inter-valley road to *Bridgend*, by the A4061 *Hirwaun* road and passes through the major *Rhondda* town of *Treherbert*. From here a winding ascent of the valley side, high above Blaen-Rhondda Colliery, leads to a summit of nearly 1,600ft. This road is one of the fine inter-valley routes constructed by miners during the depression of the 1930's. Ahead are magnificent views of the Fforest Fawr mountains and the Brecon Beacons. To the left above Llyn Fawr is Craig-y-Llyn. At 1,969ft, this is the highest point in the area that used to comprise Glamorgan. After a long winding descent turn right and pass Tower Colliery, then in ¾m enter a roundabout and take the second exit. Turn immediately right on the A4059 into Hirwaun. Turn left, signposted *Brecon*, and take the gradual ascent through Penderyn to open moorland.

There are good views ahead of a 2,700ft ridge which later screens the Brecon Beacons. Below 2,409ft Fan Fawr the road reaches a summit of 1,476ft. On the right is the thickly-wooded Taff Valley. Descend, and at the T-junction by the Beacons Reservoir spillway turn right on to the A470 Merthyr road. The road follows the valley past the *Cantref* and *Llwyn-on* reservoirs. At *Cefn-Coed-y-Cymmer*, on the outskirts of *Merthyr Tydfil*, cross the A465 'Heads of the Valleys Road', and turn left, signposted *Neath*, then left again on the A465. At the summit of a long climb out of the Taff Valley turn left on to the B4276 *Aberdare* road. After a short run the road falls into the Cynon Valley and affords hill views. At the junction with the A4059 turn left into the light-industrial town of Aberdare. From the town centre, which has an almost rural appearance, follow the *Maerdy*

signposts to join the B4277. A steep, winding climb which is wooded to begin with reveals spectacular views of the town and the surrounding valley before reaching a 1,250ft summit. The road continues across flat moorland and skirts woods and deep valleys, offering views of distant hill-tops. It then drops steeply into the Little Rhondda Valley, with views of Maerdy ahead. At Maerdy turn left, then drive down the valley and through Ferndale. Bear right here and turn left to reach Tylorstown. Turn right on to the B4512 Treorchy road and climb to cross the ridge into the main Rhondda Valley. At the roundabout take the second exit. As the road descends along the valley there are fine views in both directions. At the valley-bottom turn right on the A4058 for the return through Ystrad to Treorchy.

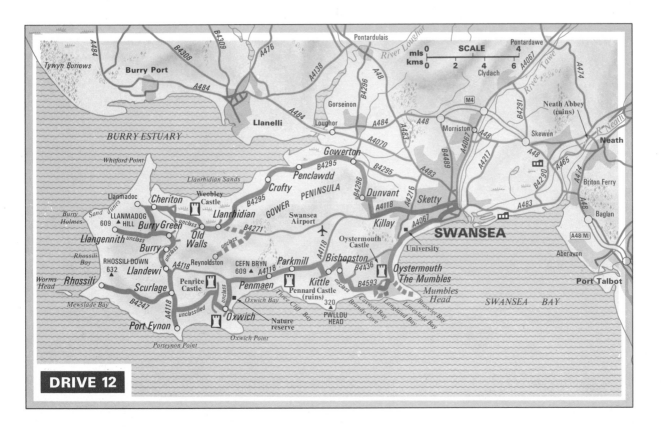

DRIVE 12

The Beautiful Wilderness

From Swansea

Drive 12   55 miles

From *Swansea* follow Mumbles and *Gower* signposts along the A4067. Continue along the sweeping curve of Swansea Bay, pass the university, and in another 1¼m follow the signposts pointing ahead for Mumbles. In 1½m the drive reaches *Oystermouth* and turns right on to the B4593, signposted Langland. For Mumbles Head, Bracelet Bay, and Limeslade Bay go forward on the B4433 signposted Mumbles Pier. The main drive turns left at Oystermouth church, then in ½m meets crossroads and bears right. For picturesque Langland Bay keep forward along an unclassified road, which descends through sharp bends. To rejoin the main drive, turn right at the car park into Brynfield Road and climb away from the bay. After ½m go forward on to the B4593. The main drive continues to Caswell Bay, a popular surfing beach next to the former smugglers' haunt of Brandy Cove.

Continue forward along an unclassified road and ascend inland. In ¾m meet a T-junction and turn left, following the road as it turns right into *Bishopston*. After 1¼m turn left on to the B4436 signposted *Port Eynon*. Pass through Kittle and in ½m turn right. In ¾m turn left on to the A4118, signposted Parkmill and Port Eynon. Beyond Parkmill village and to the left are the ruins of *Pennard Castle*. From Penmaen there are views of *Oxwich* Bay and the 280ft cliffs of Oxwich Point. On the right is the ridge of Cefn Bryn, at 609ft one of the highest points in the Gower. Several tracks lead to the top. In 1¾m, at the gatehouse entrance to 11th-c *Penrice* Castle, turn left

on to the unclassified Oxwich Road and descend through woods to marshland behind the bay. To the right are brief glimpses of Penrice Castle and house. The sand-dunes on the left are part of a 540 acre national nature reserve with herons, mallards and reed warblers. Oxwich is a small scattered village with a good sandy beach. A submerged forest is revealed at low tide. There are tracks to the cliff tops, and across the bay to the left are some memorable cliff views to 320ft Pwlldu Head.

At the crossroads the road straight on leads to the ruined castle, but the main drive takes the right turn along an unsignposted road. In ½m at a T-junction turn right, signposted Port Eynon, and after ¾m meet another T-junction and turn left, following Horton signposts. After 2m go straight across at the crossroads and in ¾m turn left on to the A4118 for the run down to the attractive village of Port Eynon. Return along the A4118 Swansea road and in 1¾m at Scurlage turn left on to the B4247 *Rhossili* road. Rhossili lies in an area designated as one of outstanding natural beauty, high above the golden sands of Rhossili Bay. To the W is the long narrow point of Worms Head, a rocky nature reserve with 250ft limestone cliffs. To the N are fine cliff walks beneath and over Rhossili Down, which at 632ft is the highest point in the Gower. Some way S of Rhossili lies beautiful Mewslade Bay, a small sheltered beach covered at high tide. Return along the B4247, and at Scurlage turn left on to the A4118. After 1m go forward along an

unclassified road, signposted Llandewi and *Burry*. Continue through Burry and at Burry Green turn left for *Llangennith*, sited beneath 609ft *Llanmadoc* Hill. The church tower here is the best example of the local saddle-back type. Return along the Burry Green road and in 1½m turn left for Cheriton. As the road descends there are good views across the Burry estuary.

At the T-junction in Cheriton a left turn leads to Whiteford Sands, a pleasant beach not suitable for bathing. At the junction, however, the route turns right, passing on the left after 2m the ruined 12th- to 14th-c *Weobley* Castle. This fortified manor house is on a grassy hill overlooking *Llanrhidian* Marsh and sands, and affords sweeping views across the estuary. At the village of Old Walls keep left and at the end of Llanrhidian go forward on to the B4295 Gowerton road. For a good viewpoint on Cefn Bryn (3m) turn right here on to the B4271, signposted Swansea. In 1¼m turn sharp right on to the unclassified *Reynoldston* road. The main drive continues on the B4295, following the estuary through Crofty and *Penclawdd* to Gowerton. Go forward over crossroads and then bear right on to the B4296. At Dunvant turn left and ascend into the suburbs of Swansea. In ½m turn right with Swansea signposts, and at Killay keep forward on to the A4118. Continue through Sketty for the city centre.

Placenames in *italic* type are worth stopping at; each is listed and described in the main gazetteer section of the book   113

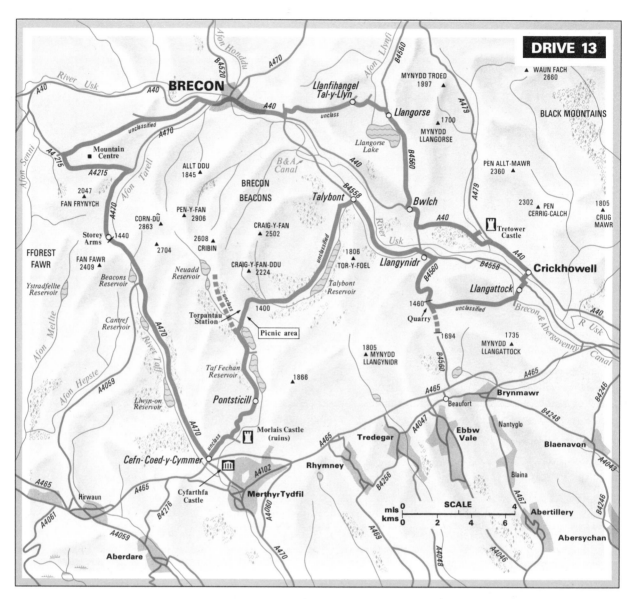

DRIVE 13

Through the Brecon Beacons

From Brecon

Drive 13   63 miles

Leave *Brecon* by following *Llandovery* signposts along the A40 and cross the River Usk. After 1m cross the Afon Tarell and at the roundabout take the second exit. Take the next turning left on to an unclassified road signposted Mountain Centre. A gradual climb to moorland at 1,100ft reveals excellent views (to the left) of the Brecon Beacons, with the summits of 2,906ft Pen-y-Fan and 2,863ft Corn Dû clearly visible.

The route continues forward past the entrance to the Mountain Centre on the left, which contains models and information on the Beacons national park. This is also a recognised picnic site. In 1m meet crossroads and turn left on to the A4215 – no signposts – with 2,047ft Fan Frynych rising straight ahead. After 3m descend to the Tarell Valley and turn right on to the A470, signposted Merthyr. A long, easy ascent with 2,409ft Fan Fawr ahead leads to a summit of 1,440ft. On the left after ½m is the starting point of paths to the main

peaks. The road then begins the descent along the wooded Taff Valley, passing three reservoirs before reaching the edge of Merthyr. Continue to *Cefn-Coed-y-Cymmer* on the outskirts of *Merthyr Tydfil* and turn left on to the unclassified Pontsticill and *Talybont* road. For a detour to the museum at 19th-c *Cyfathfa* Castle continue on the A470 for 1¼m. The main drive passes the gorge of the Taf Fechan on the right, then in 1¼m turns left after passing under a railway bridge. A short detour (½m) can be taken from here to the ruins of 13th-c *Morlais* Castle by turning right after passing under the railway bridge.

The main drive continues through Pontsticill and at the end of the village keep left to follow the shores of the *Taf Fechan Reservoir*. Ahead there are distant views of the lower Brecon Beacon summits. After 2¾m the route turns right, but for the *Neuadd Reservoirs* below the Beacons go straight on. The main route crosses the river before passing a picnic area. On the ascent to a 1,400ft summit, the site of the former Torpantau Station – 1,350ft above sea level – is passed on the left. At the top there are views of 2,224ft Craig-y-

Fan-ddu and 2,502ft Craig-y-Fan to the left before a long steep descent through woodland to the Talybont Valley. With 2,000ft hills on the left and the prominent 1,806ft peak of Tor-y-Foel ahead, the drive follows the 2m long Talybont Reservoir. About 1¼m beyond the reservoir turn right – no signpost – into *Talybont* village.

The road then crosses the restored Brecon and *Abergavenny* Canal, which is open for pleasure craft from Brecon to *Newport*. Turn right on to the B4558 – no signpost – and beyond the village keep forward, signposted *Llangynidr* and *Crickhowell*. The road continues along the lovely wooded Usk Valley, with views of the canal on the right. Beyond the canal bridge at the edge of Llangynidr turn right on to the B4560 Beaufort road. Climb through sharp bends to an altitude of 1,460ft, from where the views across the Usk Valley to the Black Mountain are magnificent. The major hills to be seen from here include 1,700ft Mynydd Llangorse, 2,302ft Pen Cerrig-Calch, 2,360ft Pen Allt-Mawr, 1,805ft Crug Mawr, and the famous 1,955ft Sugar Loaf above Abergavenny. Continue past a quarry and turn left on to an unclassified road

114

Mountain Roads

From Neath

Drive 14   69 miles

Although *Neath* is a large industrial town formerly known for its metal-smelting works, it is only a short ride away from the most attractive countryside that South Wales has to offer.

Follow the B4434 Resolven and Tonna road alongside the River Neath to leave the town. Beyond Tonna the route enters a wooded valley and affords fine views ahead. Enter Melincourt and in ½m pass a footpath to the right which leads to an 80ft waterfall on the Melincourt Brook. Beyond Resolven turn right on to the A465 *Merthyr Tydfil* road, below the slopes of the Rheola Forest. On the right of the valley is the Glencastle Forest. Continue to *Glyn Neath*, with views to the right of craggy Craig-y-Llyn overlooking the Rhigos Forest. Situated at 1,969ft, this is the area's highest point. Pass

the A4109 road on the left before turning left on to the B4242 Pontneddfechan road. Near Pontneddfechan the Afon Mellte joins the Neath and both rivers have attractive waterfalls which are accessible only on foot. At the Dinas Hotel turn left on to the unclassified *Ystradfellte* road and climb along the 800ft ridge between the two rivers. Fine views ahead include the four summits of the Fforest Fawr Mountains. From the left they are 2,150ft Fan Fraith, 2,160ft Fan Nedd, 2,071ft Fan Llia, and 2,409ft Fan Fawr.

After 3½m pass a youth hostel. Below in the Mellte Valley the river disappears for a short distance into the Porth-yr-Ogof Caves. To visit these caves take the next turning right for the car park. At the New Inn in Ystradfellte the main drive bears left with *Sennybridge* signposts and continues to a gated section of road before a long climb across bleak moorland between Fan Nedd and Fan Llia. From the 1,470ft summit there are magnificent views across the Senni Valley, which lies 600ft below. To the left are the distant crags of 2,381ft Fan Gihirych. The steep descent to the valley floor is through unprotected hairpin bends, and great care should be taken. On completing the descent continue forward for 2½m to a T-junction. Turn left – no signpost – on to the *Cray* and

Ystradgynlais road. Another climb to 1,373ft, affords further views before the drive descends to join the A4067 above the *Cray Reservoir*. On the left is Fan Gihirych. In 2m the road dips down alongside a tributary of the Tawe to join the main valley. Pass the Gwyn Arms and continue for ½m to the spectacular Dan-yr-Ogof Caves. In another mile is Craig-y-nos. High above the valley on the left, reached by the Penwyllt road, is a quarry served by the railway line used in the shooting of railway crash scenes in the film *The Young Winston*. Craig-y-nos station was renamed Chieveley for the occasion. At *Pen-y-cae* turn left along an unclassified road, signposted Henrhyd Waterfall, and ascend. In 1m turn left, and in ¾m turn right at a crossroads to enter *Coelbren*. A footpath on the right leads to the cascading waters of the 100ft Henrhyd Waterfalls. Beyond the railway bridge turn left – no signpost – for Onllwyn, passing a colliery and washery on the left.

Meet a T-junction and turn right on the A4109 towards Neath. The road now descends through the pleasantly-wooded Dulais Valley and passes through the former colliery villages of Seven Sisters, Crynant, and Blaenant Colliery. On returning to the Vale of Neath turn right on to the A465 and follow signposts for the return to the town.

Drive 13 continued

signposted Crickhowell. For a detour to views from 1,694ft, continue the ascent on the B4560 for ½m. The main drive continues by descending gradually before recrossing the canal at *Llangattock*. Keep forward to the end of the village and turn left on to the A4077, then turn right to cross the Usk by an attractive old bridge into Crickhowell.

Here there are several Georgian houses and a restored 14th-c church with a shingled spire. Leave by the A40 Brecon road and continue through pleasant valley scenery. After 2¾m the drive passes a right turn which leads to Tretower, with its picturesque manor house and ruined castle. In 2½m the drive climbs to Bwlch, a good Usk Valley viewpoint. Beyond the village, at the war memorial, turn right on to the B4560 *Talgarth* road and continue along high ground below 1,700ft Mynydd Llangorse. To the left is *Llangorse Lake*, the second largest natural lake in Wales. At the end of Llangorse village turn left on to an unclassified road and proceed towards Brecon, shortly passing a road to the lakeside. In 1½m turn left across a bridge and pass through Llanfihangel Tal-y-Llyn. After 2½m, with occasional views of the Brecon Beacons, turn left. In ½m turn right on to the A40 for the return to Brecon alongside the Brecon and Abergavenny Canal.

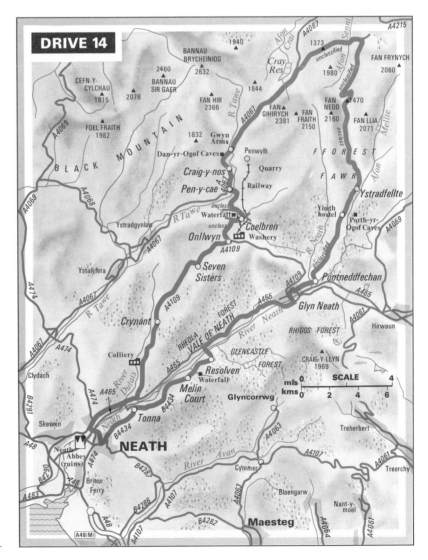

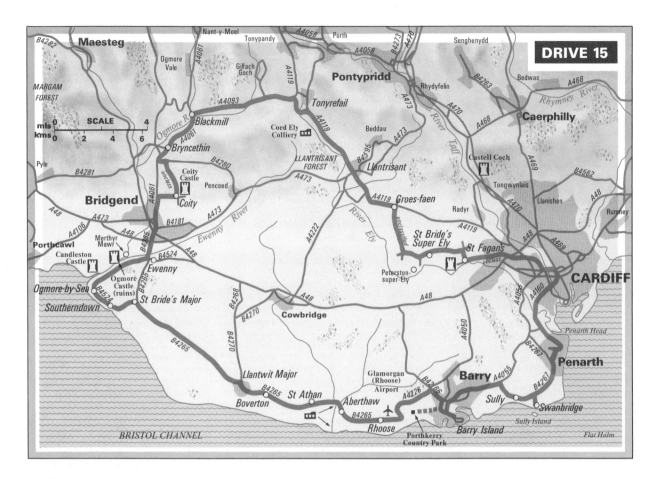

Castles by the Sea

From Cardiff

Drive 15   67 miles

From *Cardiff* this varied route takes in coastal scenery and ruined castles before returning through moorland and river valleys. Leave Cardiff from the castle, following signposts marked the Docks, A470. In ½m enter the one-way system and take the A4160 *Penarth* road. In 3½m enter the pleasant resort and suburb of Penarth. Penarth Head, on the left (no signpost) is a Bristol Channel viewpoint, and Turner House is an art gallery. From the roundabout follow the signposts for *Barry* into unclassified Westbourne Road, and in 1m turn left on to the B4267. In ¾m turn left on to the unclassified Swanbridge road to reach the coast opposite Sully Island. From here there are good views of the islands in the Bristol Channel and of shipping for Cardiff and *Newport* docks.

Return to the B4267 and turn left, passing the edge of Sully. After 1m turn left on the A4055 into Barry. Ascend and at the roundabout and all crossroads keep forward following the signposts for Barry Island. On the descent turn right. In the dock area on the left is a scrapyard from which many ex-British Rail steam locomotives have been salvaged for preservation. Pass the station then bear left and take an early turn left for Barry Island, the town's resort. Sandy beaches and varied holiday entertainments are the resort's main features. Return across the causeway and keep forward, climbing with the A4050 Cardiff road. After ¼m, near

a church, there is an unsignposted road on the left which leads to Porthkerry country park, passing slight ruins of 13th-c Barry Castle on the way. The main drive continues to a roundabout to take the first exit on to the B4266 with *Cowbridge* signposts.

At the next roundabout take the first exit on to the A4226, signposted *Llantwit Major*. In 1¾m meet another roundabout and take the first exit on to the B4265 to pass *Rhoose* Airport. There are panoramic views across the estuary to the Somerset and Exmoor hills as the road continues through Rhoose. Pass through Aberthaw, the edge of *St Athan*, and Boverton. At the picturesque old town of Llantwit Major – or Llanylltyd Fawr – turn right following the signposts for *Bridgend*. For the partly 12th-c town hall turn left here with *St Donat's* signposts. The main drive continues through typical Vale of Glamorgan scenery to *St Bride's Major*. Turn left on to the B4524 *Southerndown* road to pass through the cliff-top resorts of Southerndown and *Ogmore-by-Sea*. Fine coastal scenery includes views over *Porthcawl* before the drive turns inland past the mouth of the Ogmore River, below the dunes of *Merthyrmawr* warren. In 1¼m the ruins of 12th-c Ogmore Castle lie to the left. After 1½m keep forward on the B4265, passing the edge of *Ewenny* where there is a ruined 12th-c priory. In 1m cross the A48 to enter Bridgend, an expanding market and light-industrial town. Follow the A4061 towards Blackmill, and negotiate the extensive one-way system. After 1½m turn right on to an unclassified road signposted *Coity* for 12th- to 16th-c Coity Castle. At Coity turn left on to the

Bryncethin road and pass the castle entrance. The road rises and affords further hill views before descending to join the B4280. Turn right on to the A4061, and under the railway bridge bear right into Bryncethin. From here the Ogmore Valley becomes deeper and more wooded. At Blackmill turn right on to the A4093 Tonyrefail road, shortly climbing the valley of the Little Ogmore River – or Ogwr Fach.

The scenery changes to farm and moorland country before the drive reaches the edge of Tonyrefail. Turn right on to the unclassified Thomastown and *Llantrisant* road, then in 1¼m turn right again on to the A4119 to follow the Ely River. Beyond Coed Ely Colliery the road passes Llantrisant Forest. At Llantrisant roundabout take the second exit, signposted Cardiff. In 2½m meet the Groes-faen crossroads and turn right on to the unclassified Peterston-super-Ely road. After 2¼m meet another crossroads and turn left, signposted St Bride's and Super Ely, and in 1m turn left on to the St Fagan's road. After another 2m reach crossroads and turn right – no signpost – to enter the pleasant village of *St Fagan's* on the Ely. On the right is a restored 16th-c castle and famous Welsh folk museum. Turn left, following the river, and keep forward through Cardiff suburbs for the city centre.

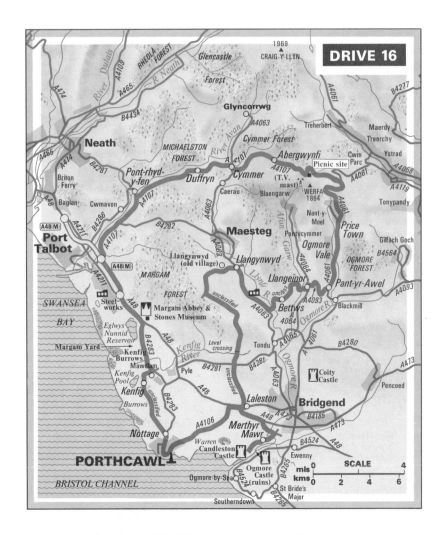

DRIVE 16

Among the Valleys

From Porthcawl

Drive 16   57 miles

From the popular and attractively situated resort of *Porthcawl* follow *Port Talbot* signposts on the B4283. In 1¼m at Nottage turn left on to an unclassified road signposted *Kenfig*, to follow a level route before skirting sand dunes and Kenfig Pool at Kenfig. Ahead are distant views of *Margam* marshalling yard, and the vast Abbey steelworks below the hills of Margam Forest. Pass the edge of Mawdlam and in ½m at a crossroads turn left on to the B4283 Port Talbot road. After 2¼m turn left on to the A48. In ½m on the right is Margam village, where there is a ruined 12th-c Cistercian abbey set in parkland. Further views of the steelworks are offered as the drive approaches Port Talbot, with 700ft hills hanging threateningly over the road.

At the roundabout follow *Swansea* signposts to join the A48(M). After 2m branch left on the A4107 towards Port Talbot, then at the roundabout take the third exit on to the A4107, signposted *Cymmer*. The road now enters the narrow Afan Valley, and the tall spire ahead belongs to Cwmavon church. There are no longer any working colleries in the Afan Valley, but traces of former industry can be seen as far up as Pontrhydyfen, where there is a high road bridge. From here the hillsides are thickly wooded. Climb past the former Duffryn Colliery to Cymmer,

which is perched on a steep hillside. This is the junction for roads to *Maesteg* and Glyncorrwg. Follow the signposts for *Treorchy*, continuing up the valley and past the extensive Cymmer Forest. From Abergwynfi, another former mining village, the road twists and turns as it climbs high above the valley-end, reaching 1,750ft opposite the TV station on the 1,864ft summit of Werfa. A picnic site is situated here.

For the next mile the road descends along a narrow ridge, with occasional impressive views of the surrounding mountains. Beyond a rock cutting turn right on to the A4061 *Bridgend* road. Opposite is a lay-by which overlooks Cwm Parc in the *Rhondda Valley*. The road slips down beneath the crags of Craig Ogwr on the right, with fine views into the valley of the River Ogmore. Skirt the mining town of Nant-y-Moel, and at Price Town roundabout take the second exit and continue through steeply-sloped Ogmore Vale. At Pant-yr-Awel bear right on to the A4093 Llangeinor road. Climb through sharp bends before descending into the Afon Garw Valley at Llangeinor. Turn left on to the A4064, then take the next turning right along an unclassified and unsignposted road.

Ascend through hilly country and at Bettws church, on the right, turn right on to an unsignposted road. Descend and in 1m cross the Llynfi River before turning right on to the A4063 Maesteg road. Continue along

the valley past Llynfi power station, and at Llangynwyd crossroads turn left on to an unclassified road signed Llan. Drive up to the old village and by the church turn left. At the war memorial keep forward on an unsignposted road, then in ½m bear left to make a long gradual climb for good views over the Llynfi Valley. On the edge of a plantation growing at the summit of the climb turn left, then proceed along a 750ft ridge.

Another short climb affords good views towards Port Talbot and across the Vale of Glamorgan. Descend to the Kenfig Valley, and at the main road turn right then left. Continue, passing over a level crossing, and at the edge of Cefn Cribwr cross the B4281. In 2m reach the edge of *Laleston* and turn right on to the A473, signposted Port Talbot. At a roundabout take the second exit if requiring the direct route to Porthcawl.

The main drive, however, takes the first exit on to the A48. In 1¼m turn right on to the unclassified Merthyr Mawr road, later crossing the Ogmore River. After ¼m turn right to cross the river again before reaching the attractive and unusual thatched village of *Merthyr Mawr*. Continue through woodland for 15th-c *Candleston Castle*, situated below the sandhills of Merthyr Mawr warren. Return to the A48 and turn left. In 1¼m meet a roundabout and keep forward. At the next roundabout take the first exit on to the A4106 for the return to Porthcawl.

Placenames in *italic* type are worth stopping at; each is listed and described in the main gazetteer section of the book

Where Rivers Run

From Caerphilly

Drive 17   52 miles

Caerphilly, an expanding light-industrial town near the River Rhymney, is well-known for its magnificent 13th-c castle. It is also the starting point for a tour of three attractive river valleys.

From the castle follow Rudry signposts into unclassified Van Road. Beyond the town this road runs through pleasant wooded country, climbing to over 600ft to give backward views over Caerphilly and the Rhymney Valley. Continue through the edge of Rudry, following Lower Machen signposts, and pass a forest walk on the left.

At Draethen keep forward to cross the river, then in $\frac{1}{4}$m meet crossroads and turn right on to the A468 *Newport* road. Continue to the Newport suburbs of Bassaleg and Rogerstone in the Ebbw Valley. At the railway bridge turn left on to the A4072 *Risca* road, and in $1\frac{3}{4}$m turn left at a T-junction on to the A467. Pass through Pontymister into *Risca*. Immediately beyond the railway bridge bear left on the B4490 towards *Blackwood* and Tredegar, following the Ebbw River into Cross Keys. Meet a T-junction and turn left on to the A4048 Blackwood road to enter partly-wooded Sirhowy Valley. Formerly a mining area, the valley is now being restored through the efforts of the Derelict Land Unit at Nine Mile Point Colliery between Brynawel and Cwmfelinfach.

Continue through Ynysddu and Gelligroes to Pontllanfraith, then turn left on the A472. In $\frac{1}{4}$m meet a roundabout and turn right on to the A4048 Tredegar road, which follows the Sirhowy River through Blackwood and past Markham Colliery. As the drive approaches the former coal and iron town of Tredegar, there are signs of industrialization which provide a contrast to the old town centre. Tredegar stands at over 1,000ft above sea level. Drive to the clock tower and go forward along an unsignposted road. In $\frac{3}{4}$m reach a T-junction and turn left. In 1m enter a roundabout and take the first exit on to the A465, signposted Merthyr, to join the Heads of the Valleys Road. At the next roundabout keep forward, passing the end of the Rhymney Valley. In 2m at the next roundabout take the first

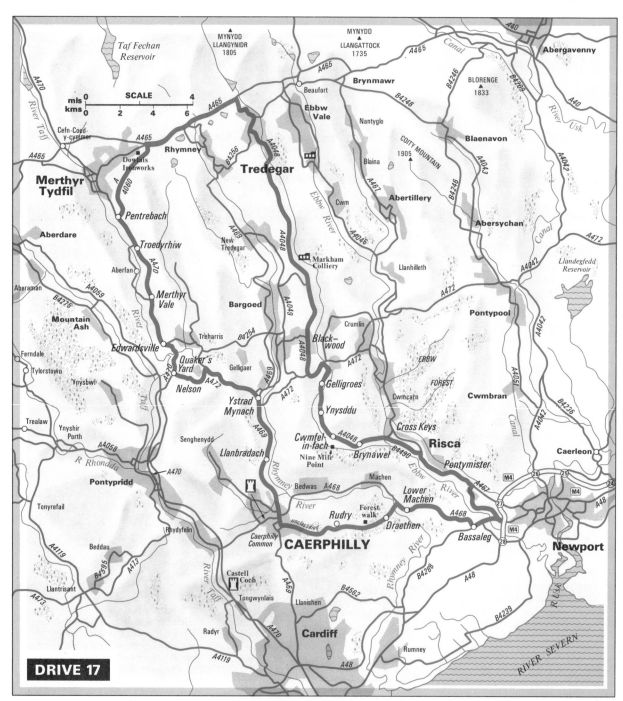

DRIVE 17

Drive 17 continued

exit on to the A4060 *Cardiff* road to avoid the centre of *Merthyr Tydfil.* Continue past slag heaps, gaunt remnants of the once-great ironworks that flourished at Dowlais and now disfigure the country below the road on the right. A long descent with occasional views across the Taff Valley leads to Pentrebach roundabout.

Take the first exit on to the A470 and continue alongside the River Taff through Merthyr Vale and Edwardsville. About 1m beyond *Quaker's Yard* turn left on to the A472 Ystrad Mynach road. At *Nelson* turn sharp right. At Ystrad Mynach turn right on to the A469, signposted Caerphilly, then right again to rejoin the Rhymney Valley. The short run from here is through pleasant, partly-wooded countryside through Llanbradach to Caerphilly.

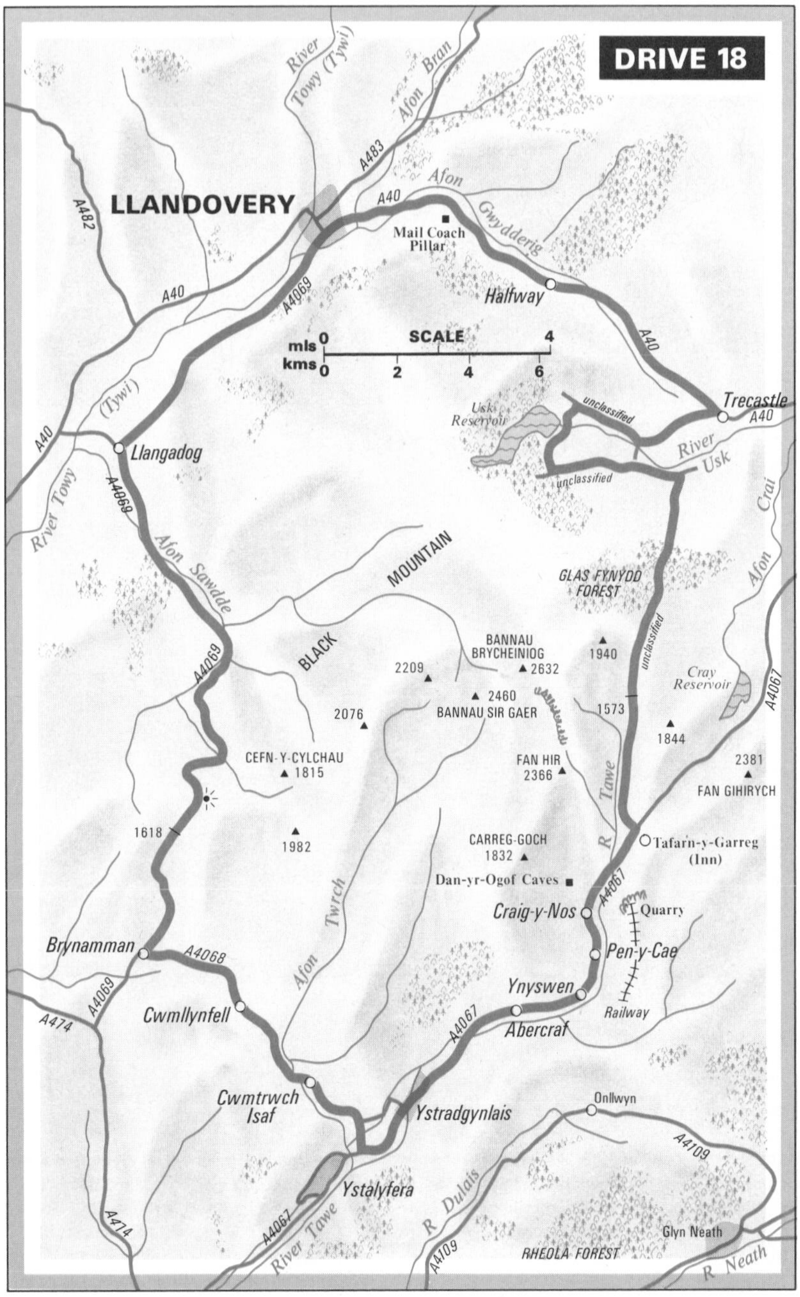

Across the Dyfed Heights

From Llandovery

Drive 18   55 miles

This route leaves the pleasant market town of *Llandovery* along the valley of the Tywi before turning into the Black Mountain for spectacular views. Take the A4069 *Llangadog* road from Llandovery and follow the river valley. Cross a tributary, continue to Llangadog, and turn left with *Brynamman* signposts. Follow the Afon Sawdde to an attractive wooded gorge. Several miles farther the road leaves the river to make a long, winding ascent below 1,815ft Cefn-y-Cylchau, and then crosses the magnificent Dyfed Black Mountain.

From a viewpoint close to the 1,600ft summit of the climb there are superb views over E Dyfed. On the descent the panoramic views change to take in the *Neath* industrial area and the W hills of the *Gower Peninsula.* At Brynamman turn left on to the A4068 *Ystalyfera* road, continuing along a winding, switchback route through Cwmllynfell and Cwmtwrch

Isaf (Upper). In 1m follow *Ystradgynlais* and *Brecon* signposts, and at a T-junction turn left on to the A4067. In 1¼m bear right across a river bridge into Ystradgynlais. Follow the Tawe Valley past Abercraf, Ynyswen and *Pen-y-Cae,* where a road to the right leads to the 100ft Henrhyd Waterfall. At Craig-y-nos there are brief views of the quarry and railway line high up to the right. Beyond the hospital the spectacular Dan-yr-Ogof Caves lie 1m to the left. In another mile, just after the Tafarn-y-Garreg Inn, turn left on to an unclassified, unsignposted road to follow the River Tawe. On the left is a long crag from 2,366ft Fan Hir, leading to the summit of the Black Mountain at 2,632ft Bannau Brycheiniog — better known as Carmarthen Van. Better views of this can be enjoyed farther on. The river and its tumbling rapids accompanies the drive on to open moorland. A gradual climb over a 1,570ft pass leads high above

the Cray Valley and offers fine wide views to the distant Brecon Beacons and the Fforest Fawr mountain range. The road then drops down to enter the Glas Fynydd Forest. In 2½m meet a T-junction and turn left, signposted Usk Reservoir, for a short run along the valley to the reservoir. After 2¾m turn right, entering part of the forest which covers the reservoir's banks. Continue forward past the dam wall and climb to a bridge, then turn right. Keep forward along the valley and after 1½m ascend to high ground. Later the road falls again, and at the edge of *Trecastle* the route turns left on to the A40 for the return to Llandovery. The drive now follows a long wooded descent between 1,000ft hills, alongside the headstreams of the Afon Gwydderig. Pass through the village of Halfway, then after 2½m the Mail Coach Pillar, with its long inscription is seen in a lay-by to the left. This was erected in 1841.

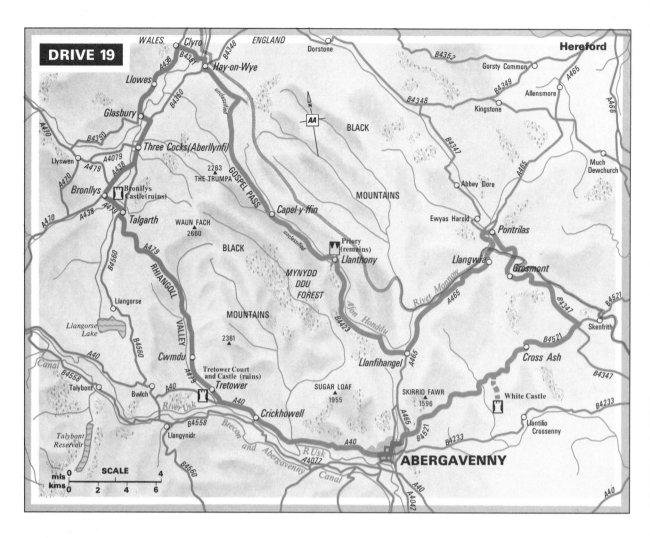

The Marcher Lands

From Abergavenny

Drive 19   72 miles

Situated on the River Usk, *Abergavenny* is one of the most important market towns in the South Wales Marches. From here the route heads into the Black Mountains over the second highest road in Wales.

First follow Hereford signposts, then look for an early right turn on to the B4521 Ross road. Follow a winding road through pleasant countryside, passing 1,596ft Skirrid Fawr on the left. After 6m a by-road to the right may be taken to *White Castle.* Continue through Cross Ash and in 2¾m turn left on to the B4347 towards *Grosmont*, picturesquely situated high above the Monnow Valley.

The road now winds down the hillside and crosses the river to enter the Monnow Valley. At the edge of Pontrilas turn left with Abergavenny signposts and cross the River Dore. Turn left again to join the A465. Re-enter Gwent to follow the Monnow, then pass through Llangwia and continue to *Llanfihangel.* Turn right on to the B4423 with *Llanthony* signposts and enter the Vale of Ewyas. Follow the Honddu River to Llanthony, where there are remains of a 12th-c priory.

Continue forward on an unclassified road and in ¼m, at the Half Moon Hotel, cross a

narrow bridge. The small winding road from here passes *Capel-y-ffin* to climb over the Black Mountains through the narrow Gospel Pass – the second highest road in Wales. There are extensive views on the long descent from the 1,778ft summit. After 5m meet a T-junction and turn right on to the B4350 road into *Hay-on-Wye*, a small market town in Powys. Turn left to join the B4351, signposted Hereford, and cross the Wye. At the edge of *Clyro* turn left on to the A438, signposted *Brecon.* The road then follows the river through *Llowes* to Glasbury. Meet a T-junction and turn right for Three Cocks (*Aberllynfi* in Welsh) and *Bronllys.* Turn left on to the A479, signposted Abergavenny. After ½m the ruins of Bronllys Castle can be seen on the left.

At *Talgarth* turn right across the bridge and then turn left. Ahead is a long, switchback climb through the Black Mountains before the road drops down into the Rhiangoll Valley for Cwmdu and *Tretower.* In 1¼m turn left on to the A40 for *Crickhowell*, a pleasant little market town standing on the River Usk. The *Sugar Loaf* mountain stands out on the left before the drive re-enters Abergavenny.

Guardian of the Wye

From Chepstow

Drive 20   70 miles

The historic fortress town of *Chepstow* is built on limestone cliffs at the lowest crossing-point of the River Wye. Follow *Monmouth* signposts to leave by the B3235, and in ¾m enter a roundabout and take the third exit on to the A466 for *St Arvans*. Turn left on to the B4293, signposted *Trelleck*, and later climb through wooded country to reach Devauden. Continue through Llanishen to Trelleck, an attractive village with an interesting church. In 4½m keep right, then in ¾m meet a T-junction and turn left. Meet a roundabout and turn right, crossing the Monnow Bridge

and passing its unique, fortified 13th-c gatehouse, to enter Monmouth. This old county town contains a number of Tudor and Georgian buildings within a network of old streets. Return across the Monnow Bridge and follow *Abergavenny* signposts. At the next roundabout turn right on to the B4233 with *Llantilio Crossenny* signposts. Proceed to *Rockfield* and bear left for Hendre. After another 2m the road follows the River Trothy, then at the edge of Llantilio Crossenny the drive turns right on to an unclassified road signposted *White Castle*. This by-road leads to the ruined walls

of White Castle, a vantage point with extensive views. Return to the edge of Llantilio Crossenny and turn right to rejoin the B4233 for Llanfapley, where there is a rural crafts museum. Later the road affords more fine views as it descends into Abergavenny. Follow the A40 *Raglan* road and in 1m enter a roundabout and take the second exit to remain on the A40. After 3¾m turn right on to the A471 Usk road and follow the river as it runs down the Usk Valley.

The market town of *Usk* preserves an old church and the ruins of a Norman castle. Turn right and cross the river bridge, then turn left on to an unclassified road. Pass through *Llangybi* to reach *Caerleon*, where notable Roman excavations include a fine amphitheatre. Continue to crossroads and turn left, then in ½m keep forward. The Roman amphitheatre can be reached by turning right here with one-way traffic into the High Street. The main drive re-crosses the Usk, then turns immediately left on to the B4236, signposted Christchurch. Ascend, and on reaching the main road turn left to join the A48. In ½m meet a roundabout and follow Langstone signposts. After 1¼m turn right on to the B4245, signposted Severn Tunnel. Pass through *Llanmartin* for *Magor* and turn left at the Wheatsheaf Inn. In 2¼m skirt Rogiet, then in 1½m turn left into *Caldicot*, where an interesting church and a modernized castle are of interest.

At the next roundabout the second exit leads to the castle and church, but the main drive takes the third exit and after ½m turns left. In another 2m turn right to rejoin the A48. After crossing the M4 motorway, a short detour along the second right turn leads to *Mathern*. Features of this village include Moynes Court and Mathern Palace (not open), both beautifully situated near the interesting 13th-c church. The main drive returns to Chepstow via the A48 and Pwllmeyric.

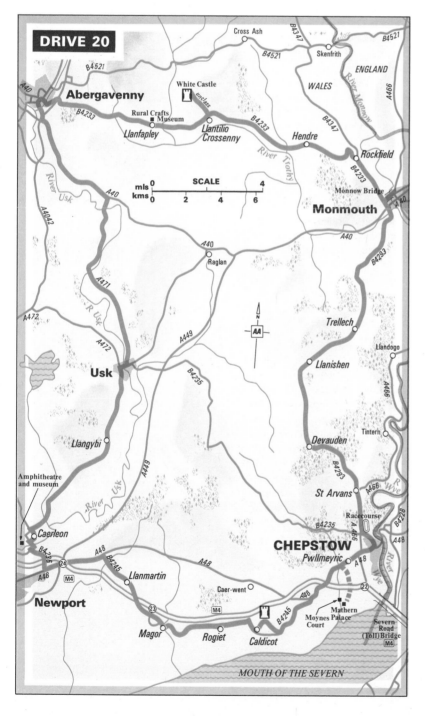

Between the Border and the Sea

Mid-Wales has the greatest variety of scenery in the principality. To the north and south the region is bordered by the great mountain ranges of Cader Idris and the Brecon Beacons, while in between is a rolling sea of wild uplands where animals and birds heavily outnumber the thinly-spread human population.

The countryside along the border with England is particularly delightful, and its past is filled with stirring tales of great battles and sieges, heroic deeds, and acts of dark treachery. Shrewsbury and Ludlow were two of the great Norman strongholds; both have retained their castles and a wealth of black-and-white buildings.

Montgomery, Bishop's Castle, and Clun — one of the 'quietest places under the sun,' according to the poet A E Housman — are notable among the pocket-sized border towns that have lost none of their charm with the passing years. Like Knighton, Kington, and others they are on or near the line of Offa's Dyke, the great earthwork built by the King of Mercia in the 8thc and now followed by a long-distance footpath which runs from Liverpool Bay to the Bristol Channel.

Between the border and the sea are the gently rounded mountains, dappled with huge, man-made lakes at Clywedog, Nant-y-Moch, and the Elan Valley. Car parks and picnic areas make these ideal stopping places, and Clywedog has the added attractions of sailing, a scenic nature trail, and a restored lead mine.

Narrow-gauge railways — rescued and restored by dedicated enthusiasts — are a feature of Wales. This part of the country has four of them; one is just to the west of Welshpool and others are at Fairbourne, Tywyn, and Aberystwyth. The last, the outstandingly beautiful Vale of Rheidol line, runs inland to Devil's Bridge and has the only steam locomotives still used by British Rail. The line was originally conceived as part of an ambitious, ill-fated plan to link Manchester and Milford Haven. Bustling Welshpool has Powis Castle, which stands amidst lovely gardens and parkland and has been inhabited for 600 years.

The entire coastline of mid-Wales forms part of Cardigan Bay — the biggest in the British Isles — and there are very good beaches at Fairbourne, Tywyn, Aberdyfi, and Borth. The coast is steeped in misty legends that tell of Cantref-y-Gwaelod, a rich and fair land protected by great embankments, a nation that flourished until the sea broke through in the 6thc. Great banks of shingle running far out into the bay are said to be the remains of the sea defences, but they are more probably relics of the Ice Age. Songs link the sailing centre of Aberdovey with tales of church bells ringing far beneath the waves.

Aberystwyth, the biggest town on the coast, is the home of the National Library of Wales; its priceless collection of books includes the 12th-c *Black Book of Carmarthen*, the oldest existing manuscript in the Welsh language. To the south is Aberaeron, a little gem of a town built at the start of the 19thc and once famous for the speed and strength of schooners built from local oak.

Mid-Wales has strong and tangible links with two of the greatest figures in the nation's history — Llywelyn ap Gruffydd, last of the native princes, and Owain Glyndwr, immortalised by Shakespeare, who lead a long revolt against the English in the first decade of the 15thc. A memorial near Builth Wells marks the spot where Llywelyn was killed in 1282, and the building where Glyndwr held a parliament still stands in Machynlleth.

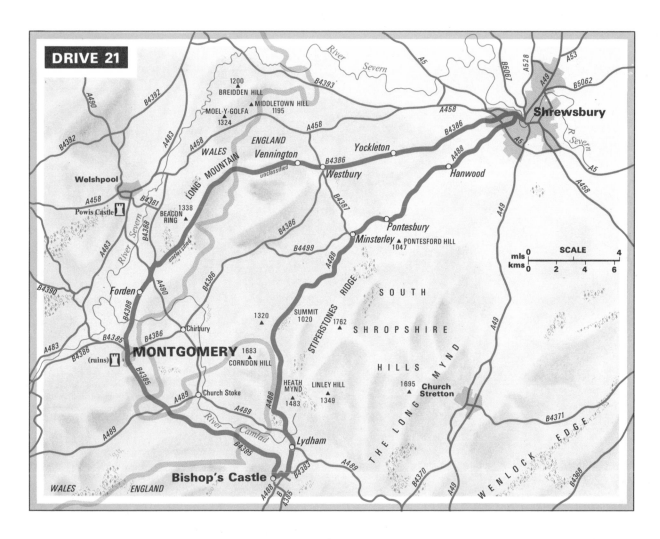

DRIVE 21

1200 BREIDDEN HILL
MIDDLETOWN HILL 1195
MOEL-Y-GOLFA 1324
ENGLAND
WALES
Vennington
Yockleton
B4386
Westbury
Hanwood
LONG MOUNTAIN
Welshpool
A458
Powis Castle
BEACON RING 1338
unclassified
River Severn
B4499
Pontesbury
Minsterley ▲ PONTESFORD HILL 1047
Forden
Chirbury
1320
SUMMIT 1020
STIPERSTONES RIDGE 1762
SOUTH SHROPSHIRE HILLS
MONTGOMERY 1683 CORNDON HILL
HEATH MYND 1483
LINLEY HILL 1349
1695 Church Stretton
Church Stoke
THE LONG MYND
River Camlad
Lydham
WENLOCK EDGE
Bishop's Castle
WALES ENGLAND

Shrewsbury
R Severn

SCALE
mls 0 ... 4
kms 0 2 4 6

The Border Country

From Montgomery

Drive 21   56 miles

Montgomery, 1m from the English border, is a former county town and a historic point to start the journey. Its many Georgian buildings and the attractive square all add to its charm. Dominating the town are the ruins of the Norman castle. Set on a narrow, rocky ridge it makes an excellent viewpoint. Leave by the B4385 *Welshpool* road and at the Cottage Inn turn right on to the B4388, signposted Welshpool. Beyond Forden go forward to join the A490 and in $\frac{1}{4}$m turn right on to the B4388, signposted Leighton. In $\frac{1}{2}$m turn right on to an unclassified, unsignposted road and climb through woodland on to the flat-topped Long Mountain. At the crossroads go forward, following Westbury signposts, and in 1m pass Beacon Ring hill fort. This is the highest point of the drive (1,388ft).

Attractive hill views can be enjoyed to the right as the road continues for several miles at over 1,200ft. Seen briefly on the left before the descent are 1,200ft Breidden Hill, 1,324ft Moel-y-golfa, and 1,195ft Middletown Hill. As the road descends it provides extensive views of the English Shropshire Plain. Pass through Vennington, then bear right for Westbury. At Westbury, turn right towards Shrewsbury, then right

again. Meet a main road and turn left on to the B4386, passing through Yockleton to Shrewsbury. The River Severn is spanned by the English and Welsh bridges here, and many half-timbered houses and inns can be seen in the town. The 12th-c castle has 18th-c alterations by Telford, and half-timbered Rowley's House contains Roman remains from Wroxeter. The Georgian Clive House contains the Regimental Museum of the 1st Queen's Dragoon Guards and the art gallery and museum are housed in a 17th-c building. The riverside Quarry Gardens, the Council House, the Abbey Church, St Mary's Church and St Alkmund's Church are all worth visiting. Whitehall dates from 1582 and the Old Market Hall from 1595. Notable buildings include the Old House in Dogpole, the Unicorn Inn in Wyle Cop, and some fine Georgian houses. Lord Hill's Column stands 134ft high. Charles Darwin was born at The Mount and Admiral Benbow at Benbow House. The remains of the town walls include a 14th-c tower.

Leave Shrewsbury by returning along the A458 Welshpool road, watching for an early turn left on to the A488 to Bishop's Castle. The road crosses part of the extensive Shropshire Plain, and beyond Hanwood 1,047ft Pontesford Hill stands out ahead. At Pontesbury, an old village associated with the writer Mary Webb, go forward on the one-way road for an early left turn for

Minsterley, situated at the foot of the 1,750ft-high S Shropshire Hills. Continue on the A488 below the 1,650ft Stiperstones ridge, later entering thickly-wooded Hope Valley. A gradual, winding climb leads to a 1,020ft summit close to the remains of old mine workings. Ahead on the long descent is 1,683ft Corndon Hill, situated in the Welsh county of Powys. The Welsh/English border follows the main road for several miles with Wales on the right.

On the approach to Lydham the 1,695ft ridge of Long Mynd is visible on the left. Just beyond the village turn right on to the B4384 into Bishop's Castle. Fragmentary remains of a 12th-c castle exist here, and the town hall is of 18th-c origin. The timbered 'House on Crutches' dates from 1573. In $\frac{1}{4}$m the town centre road continues straight ahead, but the drive turns right on to the B4385 Montgomery road. Further views from this road take in the Camlad Valley to Corndon Hill, the 1,483ft Heath Mynd, and several other hills of the S Shropshire range as the drive returns to Montgomery. The River Camlad is unusual in that it is the only English river to flow into Wales.

123

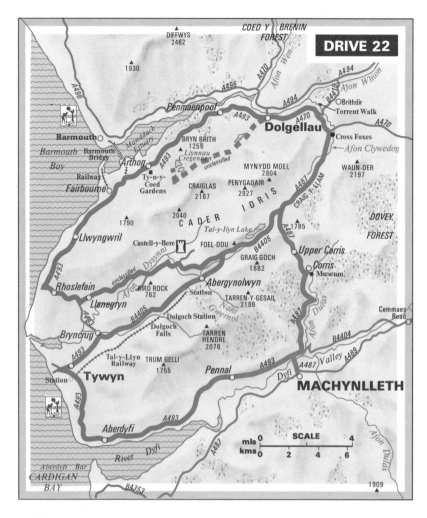

DRIVE 22

Boats and Small Trains

From Machynlleth

Drive 22   73 miles

Machynlleth, a pleasant market town and touring centre in the Dyfi Valley, is dominated by its massive clock-tower. The drive starts here and goes through some of the most picturesque Welsh countryside. Follow the signposts for *Dolgellau* on the A487 and after crossing the River Dyfi turn left on to the A493 *Aberdyfi* road. Follow the valley below high, wooded slopes to *Pennal*, then after another 3m reach the Dyfi estuary. Fine views take in *Borth* and the country towards Aberdyfi, and the estuary is used by dozens of small boats. Aberdyfi is a popular and very attractive resort with a long sandy beach, and the sheltered estuary is ideal for yachting. Continue away from the shore to *Tywyn*, which also boasts fine bathing sands. This place is well-known as the starting point for the narrow-gauge *Tal-y-llyn* Railway to *Abergynolwyn*. There is a museum at the Wharf Station on the left of the road. Turn right into the town centre and continue on the A493 Dolgellau road.

Immediately on entering Bryncrug turn right on to the B4405 Tal-y-llyn road and drive along the Fathew Valley. There are fine views up this steep-sided valley as the route passes Dolgoch Falls, famous for the waterfalls and the picturesque Tal-y-llyn

railway station. At Abergynolwyn, the terminus of the railway, enter the Dysynni Valley and cross the Nant Gwernol tributary. Follow the river below high mountain ridges to its source at the beautiful Tal-y-llyn Lake, situated below the 2,300ft slopes of *Cader Idris*; at 2,927ft this is the second highest Welsh mountain outside the *Snowdon* range. One mile beyond the lake join the A487 Dolgellau road, and make the gradual climb to a 938ft summit below the overhanging cliffs of Craig-y-Llam. Descend to the Cross Foxes Hotel and turn left on to the A470. From the B4416 *Brithdir* road on the right of the A470, a footpath known as the Torrent Walk follows the Afon Clywedog on its descent to the Wnion Valley. The A470 continues a long, winding descent to Dolgellau, the former county town of one-time Merionethshire and an important market centre.

Leave by the A493 Tywyn road to follow the S shore of the highly attractive Mawddach estuary. For a mountain road which gives excellent views, turn left on to an unclassified road signed Cader Idris on leaving Dolgellau. This road climbs easily to Llyn Gwernan, with excellent views to the left of the main Cader Idris summits of 2,927ft Penygadair and 2,804ft Mynydd Moel. From here are the Foxes' Path to the summit and in $\frac{1}{2}$m, at Dyffrydan Farm, the pony track. Continue along this road below 2,167ft Craiglas, and later turn right with

Llynnau Cregennen and Arthog signposts. Climb to the attractive Llynnau Cregennen, where a NT car park and information board are sited. Near by is a marked footpath which leads to the conical summit of 1,256ft Bryn Brith. From here and from near the car park there are magnificent views of the Mawddach estuary. The 1m-long railway bridge at Barmouth is a prominent feature. Return to Dolgellau and turn left on to the main road to rejoin the main drive.

Pass through Penmaenpool, with the 2,462ft peak of Diffwys on the N side of the estuary, and proceed to *Arthog*. The Tyn-y-Coed gardens and waterfall are on the left and *Barmouth* Bridge stands on the right. Continue past the edge of *Fairbourne*, a small resort with a good sandy beach and a 1$\frac{1}{2}$m-long miniature railway. Beyond the village the 750ft-high hills extend to the sea, causing the road and railway to climb high above the shore and allow extensive views across Barmouth and *Tremadog* bays. Pass through *Llwyngwril* and later turn sharply inland. Go through Rhoslefain and after 1$\frac{1}{2}$m turn left on to the unclassified *Llanegryn* road, with its fine views of the Dysynni Valley and surrounding hills. At Llanegryn keep forward across the river bridge and follow the attractive valley. The view ahead is of the massive 762ft Bird Rock. Cross the river and at the foot of the Rock turn left, signposted Abergynolwyn. In 2m turn right. Turn left for the native Welsh castle of Castell-y-Bere, seen 1m distant on a wooded rock.

Follow the River Dysynni for 1m then turn left with Tal-y-llyn signposts, avoiding Abergynolwyn. The drive soon rejoins the B4405, and again passes Tal-y-llyn lake. In 1m turn right on to the A487 Machynlleth road, climbing a low pass with attractive views down the valley to the right. Upper Corris displays extensive remains of former slate quarries before the main valley of the Afon Dulas is joined at *Corris*. In the village, which lies to the left, is the Corris Railway Museum. This is associated with the former narrow-gauge line which ran alongside the main road to Machynlleth. Continue down the winding and thickly-wooded valley to enter the Dovey Valley, and recross the river into Machynlleth.

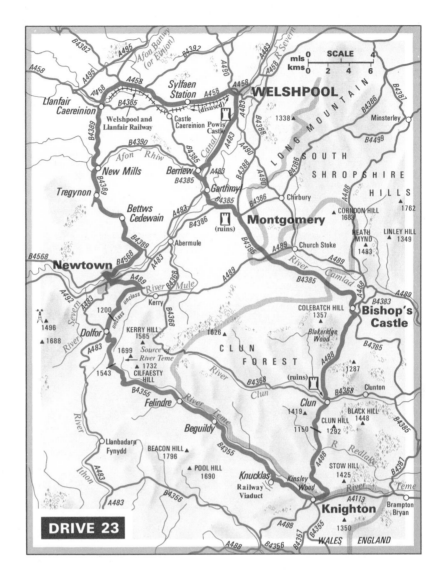

SCALE

DRIVE 23

Around the Severn Valley

From Welshpool

Drive 23   78 miles

Welshpool, an important market town and the gateway to central Wales, is situated in the Severn Valley below 1,330ft Long Mountain. For a ride through picturesque villages leave Welshpool by the A483 *Newtown* road, following the Shropshire Union Canal past *Powis Castle*. The 'Red Castle' is beautifully sited in grounds laid out by 'Capability' Brown. In 4m turn right on to the B4390 for *Berriew*, an attractive village of black-and-white houses. Turn left on to the B4385 to cross the River Rhiw, then turn left again to rejoin the A483 Newtown road. At Garthmyl turn left on to the B4385 for *Montgomery*, crossing the River Severn after a short distance. As the drive enters Montgomery the Norman castle is seen on a cliff-top to the right. In the mainly 13th-c church is the Robbers Grave. Before John Newton Davies was hanged in 1821 he swore that as a testimony to his innocence the grass over his grave would never flourish. Continue on the B4385, signposted Bishop's Castle, with views to the left over the English S Shropshire Hills across the valley of the Camlad, the only river to flow from England into Wales.

The 1,683ft Corndon Hill and 1,483ft Heath Mynd are prominent as the drive approaches Bishop's Castle. Fragmentary remains of a 12th-c castle and the 18th-c town hall are of interest here. The timbered House on Crutches dates from 1573. Turn right into the town then follow Clun signposts. In ½m meet crossroads and turn right on to the A488. This road continues through pleasantly wooded hill country to Clun, a

quiet little town with attractive remains of a Norman castle which is associated with Scott's *Betrothed*. The Court House of 1780 is used as a town hall and contains the Town Trust Museum. Picturesque old almshouses of 1618 and the mainly 12th-c church are worth visiting. Leave by the *Knighton* road, crossing the river, and climb to the 1,154ft summit of Clun Hill. Take the long descent to cross the River Redlake, then climb to 1,020ft. The drive skirts Kinsley Wood on the approach to Knighton in the Teme Valley. At the T-junction in the town centre turn right, then go forward on to the B4355, signposted Newtown. Pass the clock-tower, then in ¼m turn right to follow the River Teme, shortly passing the 75ft-high railway viaduct at *Knucklas*. The road winds through pleasant valley scenery, passing *Beguildy* and *Felindre* before a twisting climb takes the drive on to open moorland. Below the 1,732ft Cilfaesty Hill and to the right lies the source of the River Teme, and the River Ithon rises further to the left.

The winding descent affords fine views, and at *Dolfor* the drive turns right on to the A483 then right again on to a narrow, unclassified and unsignposted road past the church. Keep forward on this road and climb to 1,200ft for magnificent views over

Newtown, the Severn Valley from *Caersws* to Welshpool and the surrounding hills. To the E are the Long Mountain and Breidden Hills, and in the far distance, *Cader Idris* and the Aran and Berwyn mountains – all over 2,700ft in height. After a long descent meet crossroads and turn left on to the A489 for Newtown, an important market centre once famous for the manufacture of woollens. Go forward across the A483 main road on to the B4568 and pass through the town centre. At the roundabout beyond the Severn Bridge take the third exit, signposted *Bettws Cedewain* and Gregynog.

After 2½m turn left on to the B4389 *Llanfair Caereinion* road and follow a pleasant valley to Bettws Cedewain. Some 2m later turn right to enter Tregynon. In 1½m cross the River Rhiw before entering New Mills and turning left. A winding stretch of road climbs away from the river to reach a 980ft summit before the long, steep descent into Llanfair Caereinion. Turn right then bear left to cross the River Einion, then turn right again on to the A458 Welshpool road. In ¼m on the right is the terminus of the restored narrow-gauge Welshpool and Llanfair Railway, operating to Sylfaen. The road to Castle Caereinon is passed on the return to Welshpool.

Placenames in *italic* type are worth stopping at; each is listed and described in the main gazetteer section of the book

Devil's Bridge

From Lampeter

Drive 24   75 miles

From the Teifi Valley market town of *Lampeter* follow the A482 towards *Aberaeron* for a relaxing drive through pleasant hill country. The road joins the waters of the Aeron Valley at the combined villages of Felin Fach and Ystrad Aeron, and continues through attractive wooded scenery to Aberaeron. This is a pleasant resort with elegant Georgian houses. Its large harbour and wide quays are used by a few fishing boats, but it is popular with private craft. Cross the river and in ½m turn right on to the A487 *Aberystwyth* road. For the main street and harbour turn left.

Continue on the A487 and enjoy the coastal scenery as the drive passes through Aberarth, *Llanon*, and *Llanrhystyd*. The road leads past a rocky coastline and opposite Berth-Rhys is Monk's Cave, said to be a secret tunnel to the Strata Florida Abbey. Climb away from the sea, then dip down again to the Ystwyth Valley at Llanfarian. The drive then enters Aberystwyth and crosses the River Rheidol for the town centre. Leave by returning on the A487 Aberaeron road, recrossing the Rheidol Bridge, then in 1¼m continue forward on to the A4120 *Devil's Bridge* road. This road climbs steadily and affords good views down into the Rheidol Valley. Pass through Capel Seion and after 5m climb to 990ft, with fine views into the thickly-wooded valley. Several hundred feet below the road

is the narrow ledge used by the *Vale of Rheidol Railway* on its 700ft climb to Devil's Bridge. On entering Devil's Bridge turn right on to the B4343 *Tregaron* road. For the village centre, the station, and the famous Devil's Bridge keep forward. There are three bridges here spanning the deep Mynach gorge with its famous waterfalls. Continue on the B4343 through pleasant hill country before descending into the thickly-wooded Ystwyth Valley. Cross the river into *Pontrhydygroes* and in ¼m pass the Miners' Arms public house. Bear right on to an unclassified road signposted Trawscoed. Another pleasant drive follows the river through a deep wooded valley to the Tyn-y-Bedw picnic site. Continue and turn left on to the B4340 *Pontrhydfendigaid* road. Beyond Ystrad Meurig the extensive

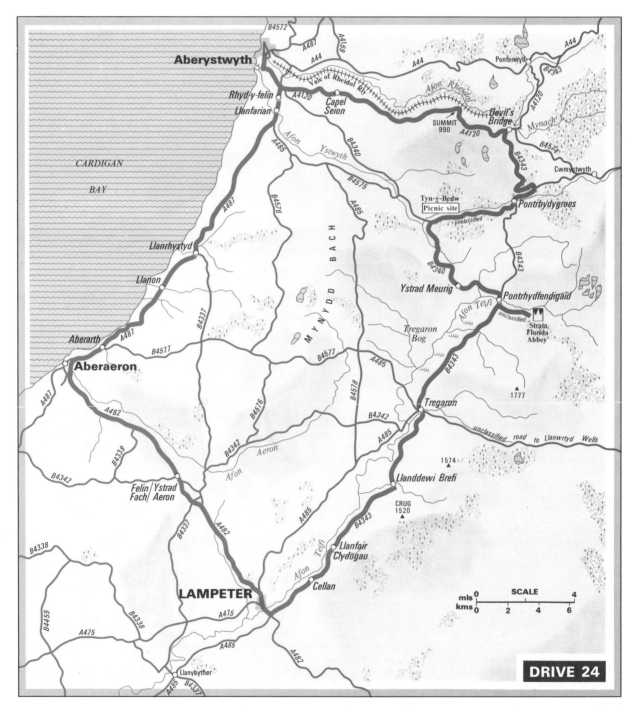

Drive 24 continued

Tregaron Bog stretches to the right. At Pontrhydfendigaid go forward on to the B4343 Tregaron road. After crossing the River Teifi take the next turning left on to the unclassified *Strata Florida* road. In 1m the drive reaches the extensive remains of the 12th-c Cistercian Strata Florida Abbey which preserves a richly-ornamented west doorway.

Return to Pontrhydfendigaid, which means the bridge of the blessed ford, and turn left on to the B4343. Skirt Tregaron Bog, a nature reserve which is over 4m long and is still expanding. At Tregaron, where there is a circular churchyard, turn left with *Llanddewi Brefi* signposts and cross the river. Bear right on to the B4343. The unclassified road ahead leads 20m over the mountains to *Llanwrtyd Wells*. With high ground to the left, the drive follows the Teifi Valley and passes through Llanddewi Brefi, where it turns right with Lampeter, Llanfair Clydogau, and Cellan signposts before turning right again on to the A482 for the return to Lampeter.

By Wooded Banks

From Llandrindod Wells

Drive 25   65 miles

Llandrindod Wells, a well-known and pleasant Victorian spa town, is a convenient starting point for this drive through wooded river valleys overlooked by mountains.

Leave Llandrindod Wells by the A483 *Newtown* road and cross the Ithon before the Cross Gates roundabout. At the roundabout keep forward. The road keeps company with the river on the approach to *Llanddewi* and follows it through a pleasant winding valley past the edge of *Llanbister* to *Llanbadarn Fynydd*. Pass the New Inn, then turn right on to an unclassified road signposted *Dolfor*, gradually climbing to 1,500ft moorland with good all-round views. Later go forward on to the B4355 Newtown road. The higher ground to the right is the source of the River Teme, while the River Ithon rises on the left. A winding descent affords good views and leads to Dolfor, where the drive turns right on to the A483 then right again on to an unsignposted unclassified road past the church. Keep forward on this road and climb to 1,200ft with magnificent views over Newtown, the Severn Valley from *Caersws* to *Welshpool*, and the surrounding hills. To the E are the Long Mountain and Breidden Hills, and in the far distance *Cader Idris* and the Aran and Berwyn mountains — all over 2,700ft.

After a long descent turn left at the crossroads on to the A489 to Newtown. This is an important market town on the Severn, once famous for the manufacture of woollens. Robert Owen, the father of the co-operative movements, is buried in the old churchyard. At the junction with the A483 the drive turns left with Llandrindod Wells signposts, but for the town centre continue forward on to the B4568. After leaving the town the drive takes a long, winding ascent past Dolfor to a 1,150ft summit. In 2½m go forward on to an unclassified road — taking great care on the sharp bend — following

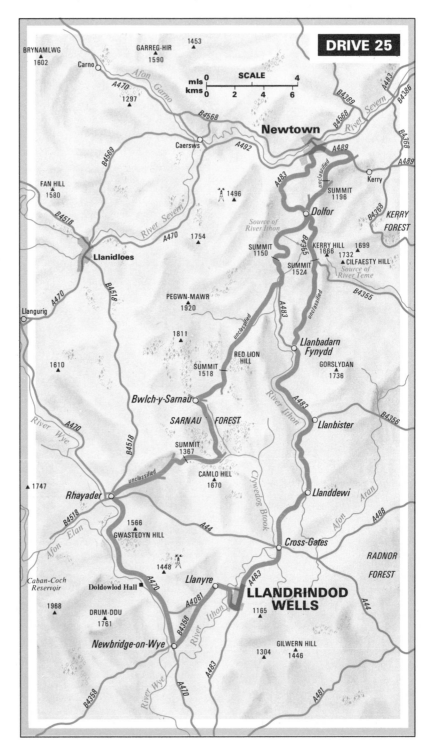

Bwlch-y-Sarnau signposts. This road crosses the River Ithon, then follows tributaries of the river upstream through pleasant country to a 1,500ft level. At this level the road runs near thickly-wooded Red Lion Hill, and other extensive hill views are afforded before the drive bears right to reach the hamlet of Bwlch-y-Sarnau. Continue forward and after a short distance descend along a narrow road to the Clywedog Brook in its pleasant valley. Pass through wooded hills, part of the Sarnau Forest, and at the T-junction turn right towards *Rhayader*. The road again climbs through woodland, this time to 1,370ft. Sweeping views W over Rhayader and the hills surrounding the Elan Valley

reservoirs can be enjoyed from this section. Descend to a T-junction and turn left. In 1m turn right and continue to Rhayader, a small market town popular with pony-trekkers. Go forward on the A470 into the town centre and turn left on to the *Builth* road. Follow the attractive, partly-wooded valley of the River Wye, and after 5m pass Doldowlod Hall (not open) on the right. This was built by Sir James Watt. At *Newbridge-on-Wye*, a good fishing centre near the confluence of the Wye and Ithon, turn left on to the B4358 Llandrindod road. In 2m go forward on to the A4081, and shortly beyond Llanyre cross the River Ithon. Bear right into Llandrindod.

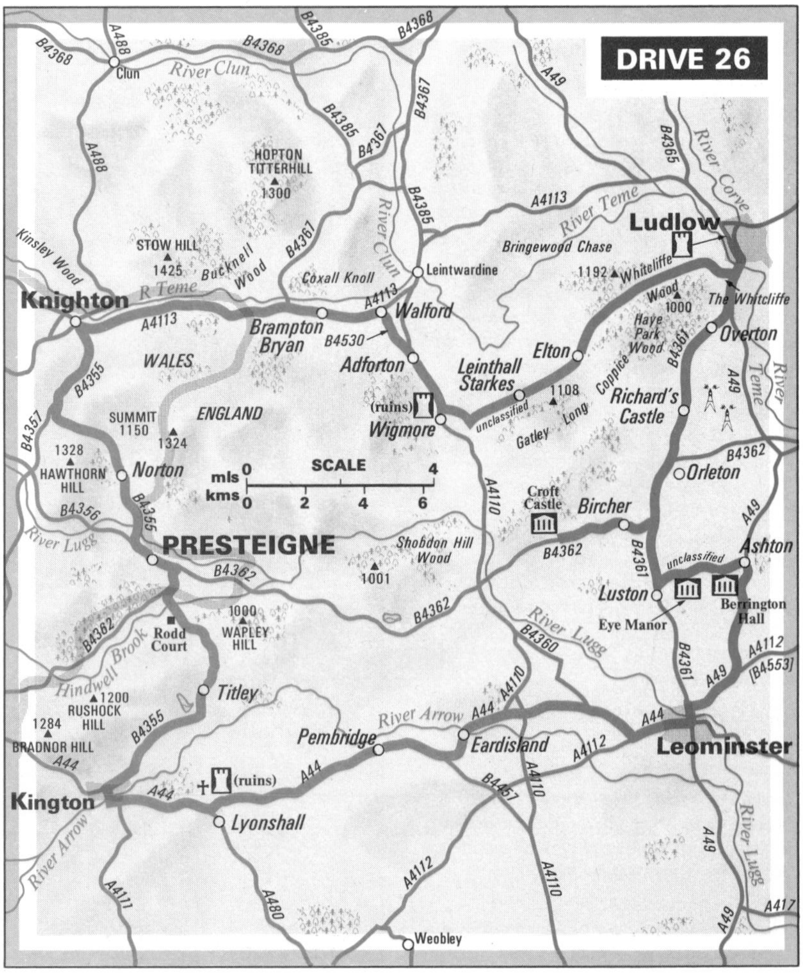

DRIVE 26

Shades of Border History

From Presteigne

Drive 26   63 miles

Presteigne is a historic and attractive old town set on the Welsh bank of the River Lugg. This drive takes picturesque roads through countryside steeped in Border history. Leave by the B4355 *Knighton* road and after a short distance turn right to cross the river. Beyond Norton there is a long climb round the 1,328ft Hawthorn Hill to a summit of 1,150ft. After a long descent to the edge of Knighton the main drive turns right on to the A4113 Ludlow road. For the town centre turn left. The A4113 follows the Teme Valley past 1,425ft Stow Hill and Bucknell Wood, and continues to Brampton Bryan in the one-time county of Herefordshire.

Here there are remains of a 14th-c castle which was the scene of a famous Civil War siege. The church was rebuilt in 1656 and has a good hammer-beam roof. In 1½m at Walford turn right, signposted Hereford A4110, and in 1m turn right on to the A4110. Pass through Adforton with wooded hills on the right and the wide plain of the River Teme on the left. At Wigmore there are remains of a moated 14th-c castle and an abbey, and the timbered hall is of 16th-c date. At Ye Olde Oak public house turn left on to an unclassified road signposted Ludlow. Pass through Leinthall Starkes, below 1,108ft Gately Long Coppice, to Elton. The 18th-c hall here is not open, but the Norman church has the Royal Arms of Elizabeth I and can be visited. Continue to follow Ludlow signposts and take a long attractive climb through woodland with 1,192ft Bringewood Chase on the left.

After the 906ft road summit the drive descends through Whitcliffe Wood and affords a magnificent view of Ludlow from the Whitcliffe. At the main road turn right on to the A49, signposted Leominster. For the town centre turn left. Ludlow is a picturesque town with Georgian and half-timbered houses. The castle is a fine 11th-c structure and the 15th-c church has many interesting features. There is a 14th-c grammar school and Broad Gate is the last surviving town gate. Ludford Bridge across the River Teme is attractive. Ludford House, Lane's Hospital, and Hoyser's almshouses (founded in 1486), are an interesting part of Ludlow's history. The 15th-c Guildhall, the Tolsey, the Reader's House, the Ludlow Museum, and the Butter Cross all add to Ludlow's charm. Old inns include the half-timbered Feathers, the Angel, and the Bull.

In 1m turn right on to the B4361 Presteigne road. Go through *Overton*, Richard's Castle, and the edge of Orleton. In 1m bear right on to the B4362, signposted Presteigne, and then almost immediately bear right into Bircher. In 1m meet crossroads and turn right for the entrance to Croft Castle, a partly 14th-c fortified mansion.

Return on the B4362 towards Orleton and in 1¾m turn right on to the B4361 towards Leominster. At the edge of Luston an unclassified road signposted Ashton turns left to reach Eye Manor, which dates from 1680. Continue, passing in 1½m the entrance to Berrington Hall and its 'Capability' Brown park of 450 acres. Stop at the main road and take care while turning right on to the A49. Pass alongside Berrington Park to Leominster.

Leominster is an old woollen-manufacturing town between the rivers Lugg and Arrow. A special part of its attraction is the many Georgian and black-and-white timbered houses. Grange Hall, the work of the 17th-c master-builder John Abel, was dismantled and re-erected in the recreation ground. The 12th- to 15th-c priory church has a double nave, fine 15th-c windows, and a good example of a ducking stool.

Leave by the A44 *Rhayader* road, and in 5m enter Eardisland on the River Arrow. The many old black-and-white houses here are also an attraction. Notable buildings include the 14th-c and later Staick House and an old dovecote by the bridge. Another village with black-and-white houses is Pembridge, where the 'Clear Brook', the New Inn, and the ancient market hall are of interest. The spacious 14th-c church has an unusual detached timber belfry. At Lyonshall, opposite the junction with the Hereford road, stands the mainly 13th-c church. Near by are the slight remains of a moated 11th-c castle. At Kington turn right on to the B4355 Presteigne road. Pass through Titley before descending to the Hindwell Brook, with 17th-c Rodd Court on the left. Cross the border into the Welsh county of Powys, and shortly turn left into Presteigne.

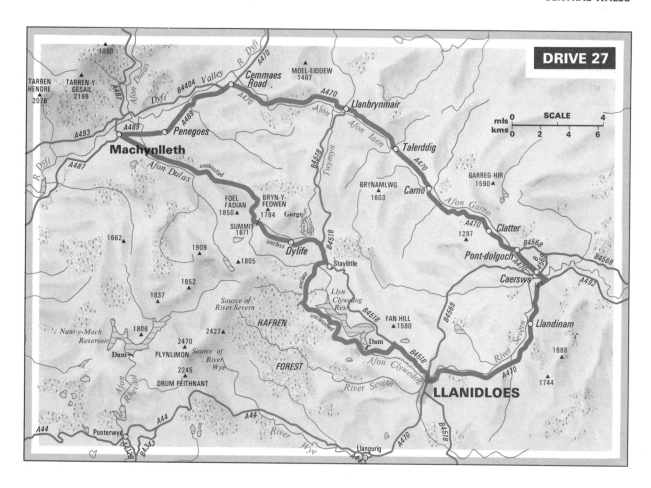

DRIVE 27

SCALE

Over the High Moors

From Llanidloes

Drive 27   56 miles

Llanidloes stands at the junction of the
Clywedog and Upper Severn rivers and is
an attractive market town. From here the
route winds NW into high moorland for
some impressive views.

Leave Llanidloes by the B4518 *Llyn
Clywedog* road and cross the River Severn,
then turn left to follow the Clywedog Valley.
In 2m, with views of the 1,580ft Fan Hill
on the right, turn left on to an unclassified
road. Cross the valley before making the
ascent past the Clywedog Dam. There is a
viewing area to the right, and the dam was
opened in 1968. Its 237ft dam wall is the
highest in Britain. There are further views of
the reservoir before the drive enters the
extensive Hafren Forest. At the T-junction
turn right on to the *Llanbrynmair* road. In
2¼m reach the edge of *Staylittle* and turn
left on to the B4518. In ¾m turn left on to
the unclassified *Machynlleth* road. Take
care as the road is unprotected and after a
short distance passes high above the deep,
V-shaped gorge of the Afon Twymyn on the
right. Continue to the former mine workings
at the remote hamlet of *Dylife*. A long
climb to 1,700ft-high moorland gives wide,
distant mountain views.

On the descent the views are even more
impressive. Beyond a range of 2,000ft
hills above the *Dovey Valley* are the
distant summits of 2,927ft *Cader Idris*,

13m away, and 2,970ft Aran Fawddwy –
16m away and the higher of the two
Aran mountains. This is the highest
Welsh summit outside the *Snowdon* range.
After a long, easy descent keep forward
at all road junctions before dropping more
steeply into the wooded Dulas Valley. Follow
this through to Machynlleth, a pleasant
market town and touring centre which lies
in the Dovey Valley and is dominated by its
massive clock-tower. Leave by the A489
Newtown road and pass through *Penegoes*
before re-entering the Dovey Valley and
following it up to Cemmaes Road. Views up
the valley towards *Mallwyd* can be enjoyed
before the drive turns away on the A470
Newtown road to continue up the Twymyn
Valley – an important road and rail route
between W and Central Wales. At
Llanbrynmair the river turns S and
tributaries join from the N and E. It is up one
of the latter, the Afon Iaen, that the drive
continues. The road climbs through a
wooded gorge to the road and rail summit
at Talerddig, a climb of 700ft from
Machynlleth. Follow the broad Carno
Valley through *Carno*. The curiously named
Aleppo Merchant Inn lies on the right.

Continue through Clatter and Pont-dolgoch
to reach *Caersws* on the River Severn.
Continue on the A470, then in ¾m meet a
T-junction and turn right on to the
Llangurig road. Pass over a level crossing
and follow the River Severn through
Llandinam, the birthplace of David Davies
in 1818. Davies did much to develop railways
and coal-mining in Wales, and his statue
is seen to the right on the way to Llanidloes.

Placenames in *italic* type are worth stopping at; each is listed and described in the main gazetteer section of the book

Between Two Countries

From Builth Wells

Drive 28   64 miles

Builth Wells is a pleasant market town on the River Wye which also serves as an inland spa resort with saline and sulphur wells.

Leave Builth Wells on the A470 *Abergavenny* road, following the tree-lined River Wye between 1,400ft hills. A modern river bridge on the B4567 *Aberedw* and *Painscastle* road can be seen on the left. At *Erwood*, the Erwood Inn is associated with Henry Mayhew and the founding of *Punch* Magazine. There are good views ahead of the Gwent Black Mountains and 2,660ft Waun Fach, the highest point, on the approach to *Llyswen*. Drive ½m beyond the village and turn right to ascend before entering the Llynfi Valley, with the distinctive shape of the 1,997ft Mynydd Troed ahead. At the T-junction turn right on to the A438, and on entering *Bronllys* turn left on to the A470 towards *Talgarth*. In ½m Bronllys Castle, dating from c1200,

can be seen on the left. Continue into Talgarth and turn left on to the A4078 Three Cocks and *Glasbury* road. In 2m turn right on to the A438 Hereford road and drive through Three Cocks – or *Aberllynfi* – to the edge of Glasbury. Here go forward on to the B4350 Hay road, following the Wye Valley to *Hay-on-Wye*. Turn right on to the B4348 Bredwardine road, entering the English county of Hereford and Worcester at Cusop. In 2¼m turn right with Peterchurch signposts and continue along an undulating road with views to the left before passing 1,045ft Merbach Hill. Ahead is the Golden Valley. At the edge of Dorstone bear left, and after a short distance pass a church which displays old glass and a 13th-c tower arch. In ¼m go forward on to an unclassified road signposted Bredwardine, and climb the steep Dorstone Hill to an 824ft summit. Fine views from the steep descent encompass W Hereford and Worcester and the Wye Valley. A road on the left, signposted *Arthur's Stone*, climbs to over 900ft. In ¾m go forward on to the B4352 Hay road, and after a short distance enter Bredwardine.

Turn right at the Red Lion Hotel on to the unclassified Staunton road. Cross the River Wye by an old bridge, then turn left with Letton signposts and follow the wooded banks of the river. In 1½m turn left on to the A438 *Brecon* road into Letton. After 1½m go forward on to the A4111, signposted *Rhayader*, shortly entering Eardisley. This picturesque village has many black-and-white houses and a Norman church with a finely-carved font. There is a long, gradual climb before the descent to Kington, on the River Arrow. Turn left into the town on the A44 and continue to the far side. Pass an old church which contains a good 13th-c chancel. Follow the Cynon Brook between 1,394ft Hergest Ridge and the conical 1,361ft Hanter Hill on the left, and 1,284ft Bradnor Hill on the right. In 2m reach the Welsh border and cross into Powys. The picturesque Stanner Rocks stand out on the right. Beyond *Walton* there are views of the Radnor Forest area on the approach to *New Radnor*. Enter the village and later turn left below the earthworks of a former castle. In ½m, on the right, the deep valley of Harley Dingle cuts

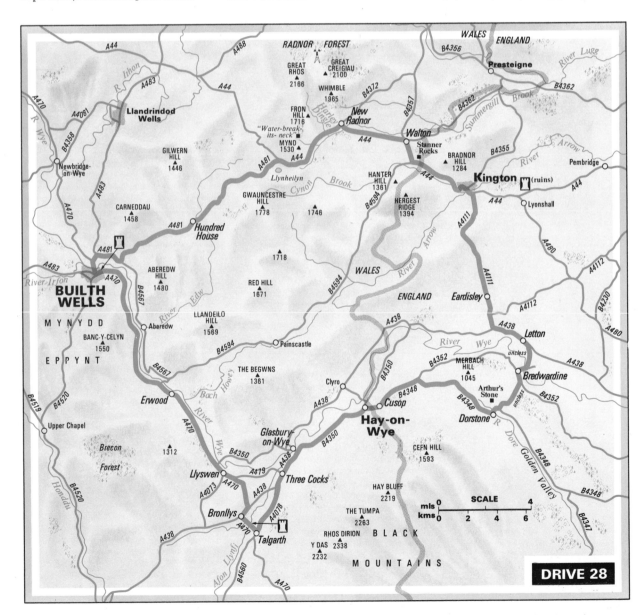

Drive 28 continued

through the Radnor Forest. On the left is 1,916ft Fron Hill with the 2,166ft summit of Great Rhos behind it, and on the right are 2,100ft Great Creigiau and the 1,965ft Whimble. About 1m farther on, below the 1,530ft Mynd, a footpath on the right leads to woodland surrounding the 70ft-high Water Break-its-Neck waterfall. In 2m at the Forest Inn turn left on to the A481 Builth road, passing Llynheilyn on the left. Continue through pleasant hill country, later crossing the River Edw at Hundred House. After 4m rejoin the Wye Valley, passing a quarry before re-entering Builth Wells.

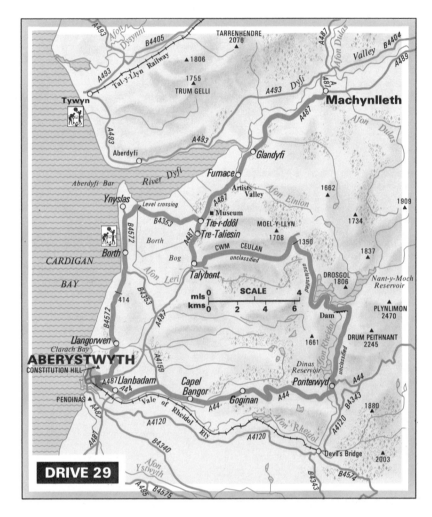

Into the Artist's Valley

From Aberystwyth

Drive 29   58 miles

Situated on the shores of Cardigan Bay at the mouths of the rivers Ystwyth and Rheidol, *Aberystwyth* has developed from a market town and small fishing and commercial port to the most important university and commercial centre in mid Wales. This drive takes in coastal views before heading towards some of Wales' finest scenery.

From Aberystwyth follow the A487, signposted *Machynlleth*, and in 1m, at the top of a climb, turn left on to the B4572 Llangorwen road. In 1m, on the descent, turn sharp right before passing through Llangorwen, signposted *Borth*. From here, a road leads to Clarach Bay with its holiday chalets. The B4572 climbs to 414ft for grandstand views ahead over the marshes and the Dyfi estuary, before a steep descent into the popular holiday resort of Borth, with 3m of safe bathing sands and a submerged forest. Continue on the B4353 to the edge of Ynyslas, then bear right. The road soon crosses the canalized Afon Leri and the railway opposite *Aberdyfi*. There are further extensive views as the drive crosses reclaimed marshland to *Tré-r-ddôl*, where it turns left to rejoin the A487 Machynlleth road. On the right is the Tré-r-ddôl Museum, which houses a small folk museum and art gallery.

The road is well wooded, with views across the estuary before Furnace on the Afon Einion. There are waterfalls here and farther up is the beautiful wooded glen, known as the 'Artists' Valley'. This is reached by an unclassified road. Beyond Furnace after 1½m are the Cymerau Gardens at Glandyfi, on show mid-week afternoons only. Continue through attractive valley scenery to reach Machynlleth, a pleasant market town and touring centre in the Dyfi Valley. Return on the A487 Aberystwyth road through Tré-r-ddôl and Tre-Taliesin, with views across to Borth, to reach *Talybont*. At the White Lion Hotel turn left on to an unclassified road signposted Nant-y-Moch Reservoir and in ½m bear left. There is a long, gradual climb up the side of the attractive Ceulan Valley.

This unfenced road has a steep slope on the left and looks out across the hills to the sea. At the valley end, near the 1,350ft summit, turn right. Ahead are a small forest and distant views of 2,470ft Plynlimon, well-known as the source of the rivers Wye and Severn. After further attractive hill views the drive reaches the shores of the modern *Nant-y-Moch Reservoir*. The road follows the water's edge for several miles, affording different views which are all dominated by Plynlimon rising above the far

side of the reservoir, and the 2,245ft Drum Peithnant to its right. Cross the dam wall and ascend to 1,300ft with pleasant views down the Rheidol Valley. Pass the much smaller Dinas Reservoir on the approach to *Ponterwyd* and here turn left then right on to the A44 Aberystwyth road. There is a further climb to 1,027ft before a long, winding descent with views down the Melindwr Valley through Goginan, to Capel Bangor. The route re-enters the Rheidol Valley here and continues to *Llanbadarn Fawr* and Aberystwyth.

Spas and Peaks

From Brecon

Drive 30   64 miles

Brecon, situated below the famous Brecon Beacons – at 2,900ft the highest mountains in S Wales – is an attractive market town on the River Usk. The route follows river valleys, climbing in places round the moorland range of Mynydd Eppynt.

From Brecon town centre follow the A438, signposted Hereford, and in $\frac{1}{4}$m reach the Bulls Head Hotel and turn left on to the B4520 Upper Chapel road. After a short distance pass the cathedral. Continue through pleasant hill scenery, following the Honddu Valley and later passing Lower Chapel. Beyond Upper Chapel, on the S edge of the Mynydd Eppynt hills, keep forward on the *Builth Wells* road. To avoid Builth Wells bear left here on to the B4519 *Garth* road, crossing an army firing range. Extensive views from the 1,500ft summit of this road take in the Irfon Valley, the 2,000ft hills above the Elan reservoirs, and *Llandrindod Wells* to the NE. On the

B4520 a summit of 1,370ft affords views over the hills before the long descent into Builth Wells. Turn left, joining the A483 *Llandovery* road, and cross the Irfon by an Iron Bridge. Continue along the valley to reach Garth. For the extensive views described on the route avoiding Builth, turn left on to the B4519 Upper Chapel road and in 1m ascend to the summit. At the end of Garth village turn left on to the unclassified *Llangammarch Wells* road. At the edge of Llangammarch Wells turn right with *LLanwrtyd Wells* signposts and cross the Afon Cammarch. In 1m turn left, following the railway into Llanwrtyd Wells, then turn left on to the A483 Llandovery road.

There is a gradual climb through the edge of Crychan Forest to a 950ft summit below the easily-climbed, 1,000ft *Sugar Loaf*, which stands at the head of the Bran Valley. The conical shape of the hill is revealed on the descent to Llandovery. In the town an unclassified road on the right, signposted Rhandirmwyn, leads for 11$\frac{1}{2}$m along the very pleasant *Tywi* Valley. There is spectacular hill scenery as the drive nears the end of the valley and approaches the

recently-completed Llyn Brianne Reservoir and Dam. From the viewing point a narrow road with passing places leads high above the shores for 7m into the Tywi Forest. Situated between the rivers Tywi and Bran, the pleasant market town of Llandovery is well known for its public school and ruined Norman castle. Turn left and follow the A40 towards Brecon to leave the town, shortly joining the deep, wooded valley of the Afon Gwydderig. Make a long, gradual ascent and in 2$\frac{1}{2}$m pass the Mail Coach Pillar, set in a lay-by on the right.

Beyond *Trecastle* join the River Usk for the short distance to *Sennybridge*. Beyond the village turn right on to the A4067 *Swansea* road, and at *Defynnog* bear left on to the A4215 *Merthyr* road. Continue along the Senni Valley, with views ahead of 2,047ft Fan Frynych and other Fforest Fawr hills. After 2$\frac{1}{4}$m turn left at the signpost for the Mountain Centre on to a narrow, unclassified road crossing the 1,100ft Mynydd Illtyd. To the right are sweeping views of the Brecon Beacons, with the main summits of 2,906ft Pen-y-Fan and 2,863ft Corn-Du clearly visible. The Mountain Centre is a Beacons

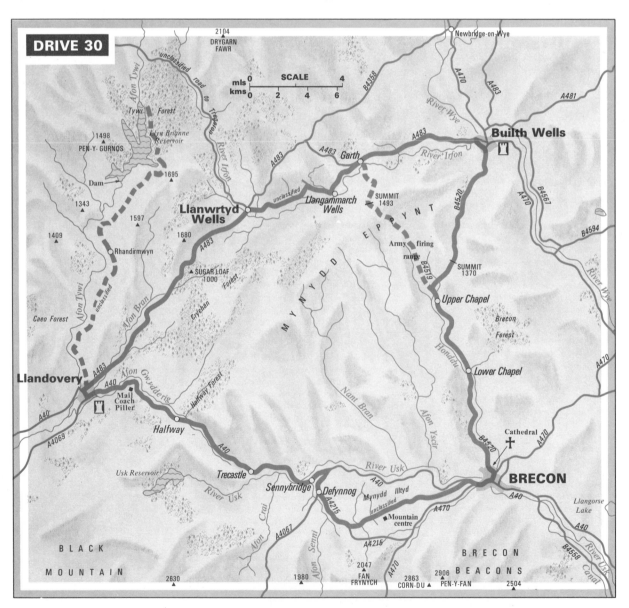

Drive 30 continued

national park information centre, with a
viewing gallery and picnic area. Gradually
descend, with views of the Black
Mountains ahead, and on reaching the A40
turn right for Brecon.

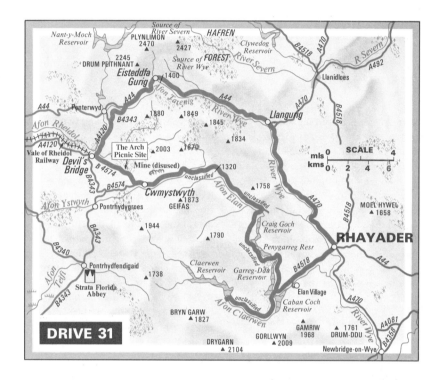

Water, water . . .

From Rhayader

Drive 31   60 miles

Rhayader, in the Upper Wye Valley, is a
popular touring and pony-trekking centre
and an ideal starting point for a pleasant
day's ride. Within easy reach are woodlands,
reservoirs, river valleys with waterfalls,
and mountain views.

Leave by the B4518 Elan Valley road for the
highly-attractive Elan Valley reservoirs.
These were built in 1904 for Birmingham
Corporation. At the edge of Elan village keep
forward on an unsignposted and unclassified
road, and climb to the *Caban Coch* Dam and
Reservoir. Follow the road round to the
Garreg-Ddu viaduct, then turn left to cross
it on the road to the *Claerwen Reservoir*
which was opened in 1952. Continue
through pleasant woodland at first, with the
remains of the Dol-y-Mynach Dam on the
left, then drive along the attractive
Claerwen Valley. Turn right at the AA
telephone box to reach the Claerwen Dam.
Return along the same road to the Garreg-
Ddu viaduct then turn left, following the
wooded shores of Garreg-Ddu Reservoir.
At the end is a short, winding climb which
leads to the *Penygarreg* Dam and Reservoir.
Beyond is the dam of *Craig Goch Reservoir*.
The water stretches out beside the road as
the drive passes through pleasant moorland
before climbing to turn left on to the
Aberystwyth road.

Continue along the wide moorland valley
beside the River Elan to reach the 1,320ft
summit, then make the long descent into the
deep and wild Ystwyth Valley. After 3½m
the road passes the extensive remains of
former lead and silver mines. After
Cwmystwyth the road climbs again to join
the B4574 *Devil's Bridge* road. A tree-lined
climb leads to the Arch picnic site, and is
followed by a long descent with the Rheidol

Valley ahead and the deep Mynach Valley
on the right. The descent continues to
Devil's Bridge, where there are three
bridges spanning the deep Mynach gorge
and spectacular waterfalls cascading
through the rocky chasm. Turn sharp right
on to the A4120 *Ponterwyd* road, crossing
the Devil's Bridge and keeping high above
the Rheidol Valley. After 2¼m turn right on
to the B4343 *Dyffryn Castell* road, climbing
to 1,000ft, high above the main A44 road.
Later take the A44 towards *Llangurig* to
make the long, gradual climb out of the
broad Castell Valley. Eisteddfa Gurig, at the
1,400ft summit, is the starting point of
several footpaths and pony-trails to the
2,470ft summit of Plynlimon, away to the
left. This famous mountain is the source of
the River Wye; the River Severn rises 3m
farther N. On the long descent the road
follows the Afon Tarenig before the River
Wye joins it from the left. There are good
views of the river as the drive approaches
Llangurig, a pretty village attractively
situated at over 900ft. Bear right with
Rhayader signposts on to the A470. This
very pleasant road runs down the Wye
Valley between 1,600ft-high hills to
Rhayader.

Placenames in *italic* type are worth stopping at; each is listed and described in the main gazetteer section of the book   133

Rough Refuge

North Wales is one of the most spectacular touring areas in Europe. Its major attractions include the majestic mountains of Snowdonia – the highest in the United Kingdom outside Scotland – medieval castles that are among the finest of their type in the world, steep and rock-flanked passes of breathtaking splendour, many miles of safe, sandy beaches, and huge cliffs that echo with the cries of countless seabirds.

There are more than enough contrasts to satisfy the most fickle of visitors. Popular resorts with piers, funfairs, bingo halls and 'trips round the bay' punctuate the coast between the Dee and Conwy estuaries, and even these seaside towns have their own clearly-defined characters. Rhyl, for instance, is as bright and breezy as they come. Llandudno, with its splendid crescent of buildings overlooking the promenade, has managed to retain the gay but genteel atmosphere of a late-Victorian or Edwardian watering place. Inland there are the mountains on which man has made very little impression, even though a colourful rack-and-pinion railway carries visitors to the summit of Snowdon. There are still ample opportunities for long walks in settings of untamed grandeur, or more gentle strolls beside lakes and gleaming rivers in deep, sheltered valleys shaded by ancient oaks.

Anglesey, reached by crossing Thomas Telford's noble suspension bridge over the fast-flowing Menai Strait, presents a landscape of low, gently-undulating hills unlike any other part of Wales. But first impressions are deceptive, for some of the coast is as wild and rocky as any in Britain. The cliffs at South Stack are particularly impressive and there are panoramic views from the rocky top of Holyhead Mountain, at 720ft easily the highest point on the island. Anglesey is exceptionally well endowed with prehistoric remains; a Roman wall surrounds Holyhead's parish church; and the castle at Beaumaris should not be missed.

The lovely Lleyn peninsula, with its tangled skein of lanes, its lofty cliffs, and superb beaches has been described by a Welsh poet as the place 'where the spirit finds peace'. Its many bays are bright with boats throughout the summer – Abersoch is one of the most attractive little seaside towns – and divers revel in the deep, clear waters off the northern coast. The road down the peninsula from Caernarfon to Aberdaron follows the route taken by countless pilgrims on their way to the holy island of Bardsey, said to be the last resting place of 20,000 saints.

At Porthmadog the Festiniog narrow-gauge railway is a flourishing link with the days when Welsh slate was transported down from the mountains and shipped all over the world. The great days of the quarries are recalled at Blaenau Ffestiniog, where guided tours explore the old underground workings, and at the fascinating Dinorwic Museum across the lake from Llanberis.

The mountain ranges are carved by memorable valleys speckled with little towns, villages, and isolated farms. The Vale of Clwyd is superb; so is the Vale of Llangollen, where the Dee races over rapids and beneath the great Pontcysyllte aqueduct that is one of the Seven Wonders of the Waterways. Pistyl Rhaeadr waterfall, the highest in Wales and England, is at the head of a valley in the heart of the Berwyns.

On the coast, the Mawddach estuary at the foot of Cader Idris was lavishly praised by John Ruskin, the eminent Victoria art critic. He said there was only one walk in the kingdom more beautiful than that from Dolgellau to Barmouth, and that was the walk from Barmouth to Dolgellau.

The fascinating old city of Chester lies just over the English border and is well worth a visit, while Oswestry's iron-age hillfort is considered to be the second finest in Britain after Maiden Castle in Dorset.

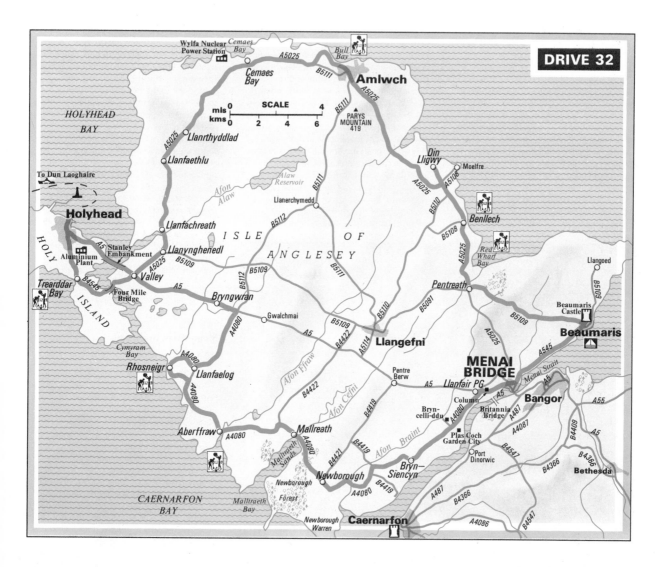

DRIVE 32

Island of Saints

From Menai Bridge

Drive 32   80 miles

This circular route round Anglesey links sandy beaches with craggy cliffs, especially near Holyhead, before returning past Newborough nature reserve and a bronze-age burial site.

Leave *Menai Bridge* by the A545 *Beaumaris* road and drive alongside the Menai Strait to the popular boating centre of Beaumaris. Turn inland on the B5109 Benllech road, crossing rolling countryside to *Pentraeth*, then turn right on to the A5025. Approach *Benllech* with fine views to the right across *Red Wharf Bay*. The large beach here is very inviting, but not safe for swimming on the ebb tides.

Beyond Benllech in 2m take the first exit at a roundabout. A detour can be made here by keeping forward on to an unclassified road for *Din Lligwy*, where there are remains of a 4th-c village. The main drive continues to *Amlwch* with minor roads to the right leading to beaches and cliff scenery. This small resort was once an important port for shipping the copper ore mined at Parys Mountain. On the coast beyond Caemas Bay is the Wylfa nuclear power station. The

rocky coastline here is dotted with picturesque bays popular with seabirds. Continue through pleasant countryside, with more roads on the right leading to the sea, and drive into *Valley*. Meet traffic signals and turn right on to the A5. Cross the Stanley Embankment, which links *Holyhead* on Holy Island with Anglesey, and pass the Anglesey Aluminium Plant.

Holyhead is well-known for its steamer services to Ireland, and is the largest town in Anglesey. Return along the A5, then branch right on to the B4545. Pass *Trearddur Bay* for Valley and turn right at traffic signals on to the A5. Go through Bryngwran and after 1m meet crossroads and turn right on to the A4080 to cross open country with distant views of the *Snowdonia* peaks. At Llanfaelog turn right for the quiet resort of *Rhosneigr*, with its large beach. At the clock tower turn left, and in 1¼m turn right to *Aberffraw* and *Malltraeth*. Skirt the Malltraeth Sands, a popular haven for swans, curlews and many other birds, and pass through Newborough Forest to reach *Newborough*. The extensive Newborough Warren to the right is a national nature reserve covering 1,500 acres, which includes three nature trails. Two miles beyond *Bryn-Siencyn* the drive passes the road leading to *Bryn-Celliddu* on

the left. This is the site of one of the best bronze-age burial chambers in Britain. Pass by Plas Coch Garden City on the right before reaching the outskirts of *Llanfair PG* – full name Llanfairpwllgwyngyllgogerychwyrndro-bwllllantysiliogogogoch. Turn right along the A5, passing the 90ft-high Anglesey Column. There are occasional views of the Britannia tubular railway bridge and the Menai suspension bridge on the return to Menai Bridge.

135

Land of Falling Water

From Betws-y-coed

Drive 33   54 miles

Betws-y-coed is attractively situated in the wooded hills of the Gwydyr Forest, with four rivers converging near by. It is one of the best centres for touring the neighbouring mountains. From the village centre follow the A5 *Llangollen* road, then at Waterloo Bridge – built in 1815 – turn right and immediately right again on to the A470, signposted *Dolgellau*. Pass the entrance to the pretty Fairy Glen and follow a thickly wooded valley to *Dolwyddelan*, and its castle in the Upper Lledr Valley.

The landscape becomes wilder as the road climbs Crimea Pass to its 1,263ft summit, and then descends to pass the Llechwedd Slate Caverns. The latter have been opened to the public, and visitors travel on a miniature railway. From the quarry town of *Blaenau Ffestiniog* the drive returns along the A470 and in ¼m turns left on to the B4414, signposted *Porthmadog*. Pass the entrance to Ffestiniog hydro-electric station – which is open for guided tours – and enjoy excellent views to the S from the Stwlan Dam. In 1¼m turn left on to the A496. On reaching a T-junction turn right on to the A470 for *Ffestiniog*. To the right of the village in the deep valley of the Afon Cynfal is the spectacular 300ft waterfall, Raeadr Cynfal.

The drive turns sharply left with the main road and passes under the railway bridge, then it turns left again on to the B4391, signposted *Bala*. The road climbs on to high open moorland and in 2m passes, on the right, close to the Rhaeadr-y-cwm waterfall and viewpoint. Continue over open moorland, descend to join the A4212, and pass by the *Llyn Celyn* reservoir. Later on the descent turn left on to the B4501, signposted *Cerrigydrudion*. Cross more high ground, then on reaching the A5 turn left, signposted Betws-y-coed. Skirt Cerrigydrudion and continue through *Pentrefoelas*. Beyond here a winding descent takes the drive through the attractively wooded Conwy Valley. On the left, near the junction with the B4406, are the impressive Conwy and Machno waterfalls. Continue with the A5 and turn left over Waterloo Bridge for the return to Betws-y-coed.

Magnificent Snowdon

From Caernarfon

Drive 34   48 miles

The ancient walled city of *Caernarfon* is famous for its magnificent 13th-c castle, scene of the investiture of the present Prince of Wales in 1969. It is a majestic place from which to drive through the Pass of Llanberis to the equally splendid peaks of *Snowdon*. Leave on the A487, signposted *Bangor*, with views across the Menai Strait to Anglesey. Beyond the former slate port of *Port Dinorwic* the road branches off left for Telford's famous Menai Suspension Bridge. Enter a roundabout and join the A5 for the cathedral city of Bangor. Leave the town on the A5 *Betws-y-coed* road, and at the traffic signals at the entrance to *Penrhyn Castle* Estate turn right, then right again on to the B4409, signposted Caernarfon. In 4¼m enter a roundabout and turn left on to the B4547, signposted *Llanberis*. After 2m turn right and enjoy the views as the drive descends to Brynrefail, at the W end of *Llyn Padarn*. A detour can be taken from here by turning right on to the A4086 to Lanrug, then turning left on to an unclassified road to *Bryn Bras* Castle and grounds. The main drive continues by turning left on to the A4086, skirting the shore of Llyn Padarn. Ahead there are fine mountain views along the valley as the road reaches Llanberis, the terminus of the Snowdon Mountain Railway.

To the E of the village lies the 13th-c native Welsh stronghold of *Dolbadarn* Castle. The drive passes *Llyn Peris*, then at Nant Peris begins to ascend the Pass of Llanberis. At the 1,169ft summit is the Pen-y-Pass car park, which is the start of the Miner's Track nature trail and path to Snowdon. On the right is the descent to the *Pen-y-Gwryd* Hotel, lying in a V-shaped hollow known as Nant Cynnyd and situated at the head of the Gwryd Valley. Meet a T-junction and turn right on to the A498, signposted *Beddgelert*, and descend past an excellent viewpoint of the Snowdon Peaks before reaching the waters of *Llyn Gwynant*.

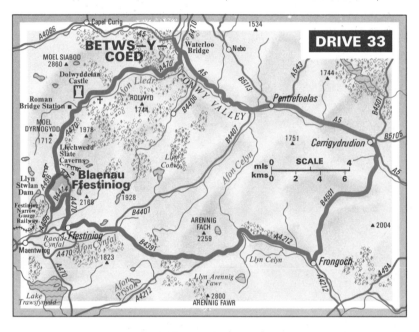

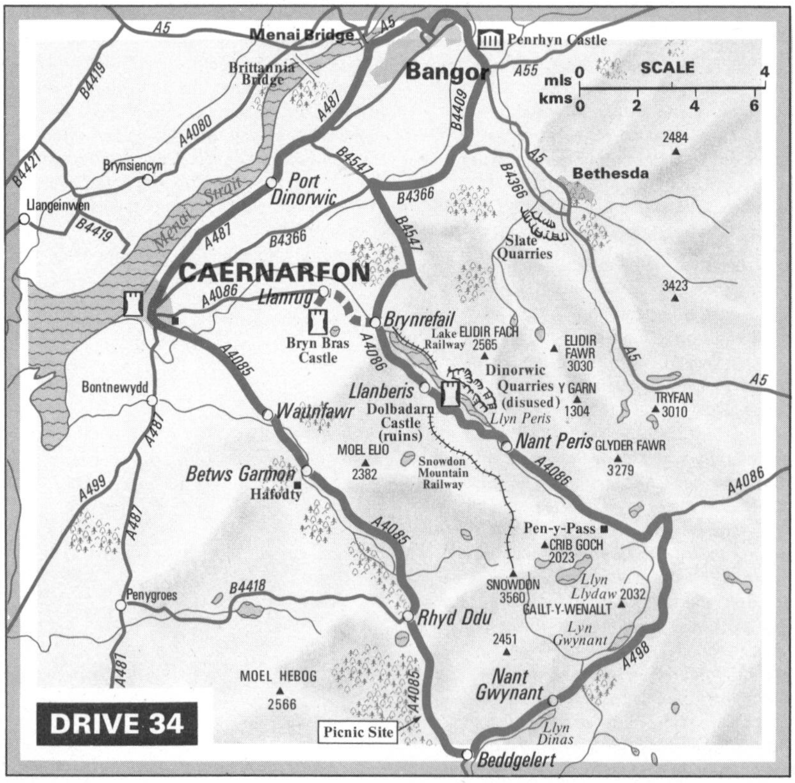

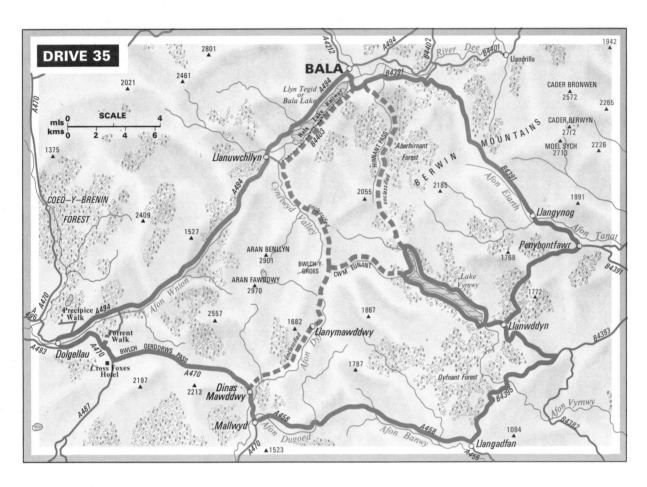

DRIVE 35

Roads Round the Lakes

From Bala

Drive 35   85 miles

The popular inland resort of *Bala* is situated on the Afon Tryweryn in the Dee Valley and lies at the N end of Bala Lake. This is the largest natural lake in Wales, and its Welsh name is Llyn Tegid. Leave on the B4391 *Llangynog* road and skirt the N extremity of the lake. Cross the River Dee and follow its valley for a few miles before climbing steeply on to open moorland across the

Drive 34 continued

In the small hamlet of *Nant Gwyant* is the beginning of the Cwm-y-Llan nature trail. Continue along a narrow valley and skirt the shores of *Llyn Dinas* on the approach to Beddgelert, a pleasant village at the junctions of the Nant Colwyn and Afon Glaslyn. In a field near by is the reputed grave of Llewellyn the Great's dog, Gelert. Keep forward on the A4085 Caernarfon road and gradually climb. The ascent skirts Beddgelert Forest, the site of a Forestry Commission picnic area and a nature trail. From *Rhyd-Ddu* a footpath to the right leads to the summit of Snowdon. Pass by the shore of *Llyn Cwellyn*, and later at *Betws Garmon* pass the road leading to *Hafodty*, with its beautiful gardens and salmon leap. Continue through *Waunfawr* for the return to Caernarfon.

Milltir Gerrig Pass at a height of almost 1,600ft in the Berwyn Mountains. There are fine views of the surrounding heights before the steep descent into the impressive Eirth Valley to Llangynog. Follow the Tanat Valley from here to *Penybontfawr*, then turn right on to the B6396 with *Lake Vyrnwy* signposts. Continue along a narrow, winding road through wooded country to *Llanwddyn*. Turn right on to the B4393 to reach the 4¾m-long Lake Vyrnwy, a reservoir for Liverpool. Turn left across the dam and skirt the wooded S shores of the lake. On the way pass two unclassified mountain roads on the left, the first climbing through the steep Cwm Eunant to Bwlch-y-Groes summit, and the second ascending the spectacular 1,600ft Hirnant Pass to Bala. Return along the N side of the lake to Llanwddyn and follow the *Llanfyllin* road for 4m. Turn right in to the Dyfnant Forest along a winding road and drive to the edge of Llangadfan. Once here turn right on to the A458 *Dolgellau* road. The route then climbs gradually out of the Banwy valley before descending the wooded Dugoed Valley to *Mallwyd*. At the Brigands Inn turn right on to the A470 and follow a short stretch of the Dovey Valley to the edge of *Dinas-Mawddwy*, situated at the junction of the Cerist and the Dyfi in an attractive mountain setting. For an alternative route to Bala over the Bwlch-y-Groes pass see the end of this drive. The route now climbs the

bleak 1,170ft Oerddrws Pass before descending with fine views of the prominent *Cader Idris* mountain range.

Beyond the Cross Foxes Hotel a detour can be made by turning right on to the B4416 *Brithdir* road to visit the spectacular Torrent Walk alongside the Afon Clywedog. The drive continues the long descent to Dolgellau, a market town on the Afon Wnion. Follow the A494 Bala road, passing on the left a road leading to the spectacular Precipice Walk, then climb the wooded Wnion Valley and cross high ground before the descent to *Llanuwchllyn*. This brings the drive to the S end of Bala Lake and the starting point of the Bala Lake Railway. Continue along the NW shore for the return to Bala.

From *Dinas-Mawddwy* an alternative – and 4m shorter – route to Bala, can be taken by turning right on to an unclassified road to Llanymawddwy. Ascend the steep and narrow Bwlch-y-Groes (the Great Pass), then follow the steep sided Dyfi Valley before a stiff 1 in 4 climb to the top of the pass, overlooked by the rocky Aran Peaks. At 1,790ft this is the highest summit in Wales. There are some fine views as the road descends the Cynllwyd Valley and the B4403. The latter road then skirts the SE shore of Bala Lake, and the drive turns left on to the B4391 for Bala.

Placenames in *italic* type are worth stopping at; each is listed and described in the main gazetteer section of the book

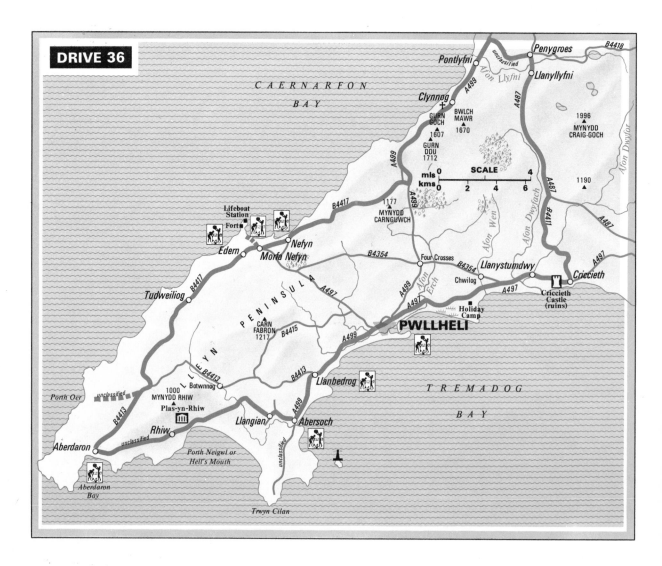

DRIVE 36

The Beautiful Lleyn

From Pwllheli

Drive 36   66 miles

Pwllheli is a small harbour resort with a sandy beach, and a convenient point from which to tour the delightful Lleyn Peninsula. Leave on the A497 *Criccieth* road for *Llanystumdwy*, where Lloyd George is buried.

At the attractive resort of Criccieth there are views towards the *Snowdon* range, especially from the 13th-c castle, which overlooks the sea. Turn left on to the B4411, signposted *Caernarfon*, and on reaching the A487 turn left. There are views of 1,996ft Mynydd Craig-goch to the right and later to the left 1,670ft Bwlch Mawr. On the approach to *Llanllyfni* there are coastal views into Caernarfon Bay. At *Penygroes* turn left on to an unclassified road signposted *Clynnog* and Pwllheli, then in 2m meet a T-junction and turn left on to the A499. Pass through Pontlyfni to Clynnog, with its 15th-c church. There are views of the coast and the bay on the climb through the Rival Mountains before the drive turns right on to the B4417, signposted *Nefyn*. There are excellent views near Llithraen and on the descent to Nefyn, a pleasant resort with a sandy beach. Turn right on to the *Aberdaron*

road for *Morfa Nefyn*, another small resort with a long sheltered beach backed by rocky headlands. An unclassified road on the right can be taken to the rocky peninsula where there is a fort and a lifeboat station. The drive continues on the B4417 passing pleasant countryside through the villages of Edern and *Tudweiliog*. Lanes on the right lead to rocky headlands and sandy coves.

On reaching the B4413 turn right. In $\frac{1}{2}$m a detour can be taken by turning right on to an unclassified road to visit Porth Oer, around which are some curious 'whistling' sands. The main route dips into Aberdaron, a small resort situated in a sheltered bay popular with surfers. Boats run to *Bardsey Island*, the legendary home of Merlin, King Arthur's wizard. Leave on an unclassified road and climb E to Rhiw, then keep forward on the *Abersoch* road. The drive now descends steeply and affords splendid views of Porth Neigwl, or Hell's Mouth, a 4m long sandy beach which is not suitable for bathing. After passing the 16th-c house of *Plas-yn-Rhiw* the tour crosses more level country. At Llangian turn left, and at the top of the ascent turn right and descend

to Abersoch, with its picturesque yachting harbour and fine sands. To the S is the headland of Trwyn Cilan, and offshore to the E are the two small islands of *St Tudwal's*. Follow the A499 Pwllheli road and pass through *Llanbedrog*, which has a sandy beach. Continue through low-lying countryside, then join the A497 for the return to Pwllheli.

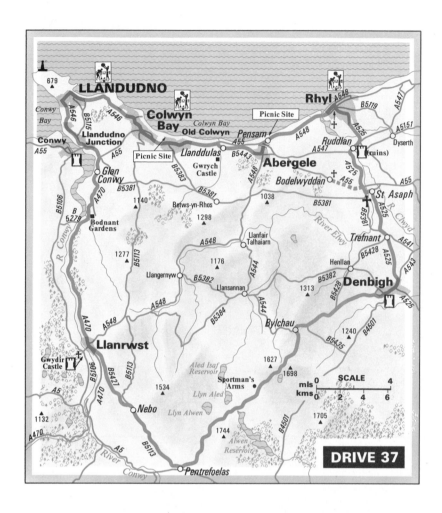

DRIVE 37

Soft Vales, Bleak Moors

From Llandudno

Drive 37   70 miles

The large and popular resort of *Llandudno* lies below 679ft Great Ormes Head. It has a long sandy shore, and at the W end is a statue of the White Rabbit – for it was here that

Lewis Carroll met Alice, the daughter of the Rev Henry Liddell. Follow the A546 with *Conwy* signposts, and in ¾m turn left. Views across the river to Conwy can be enjoyed from beside the Conwy Estuary at *Deganwy*. In 1¼m meet a roundabout and take the first exit on to the A55, signposted *Betws-y-coed*, to enter *Llandudno Junction*. After ¾m take the third exit at another roundabout on to the A470. Pass through Glan Conwy, then in 2m pass the road to *Bodnant Gardens* on the left. The fine house is of 19th-c date. Follow the beautiful Vale of Conwy with views of the river, wooded slopes, and surrounding hills to *Llanrwst*, a popular fishing centre. Continue through the town, then turn left on to the B5427, signposted *Nebo*, to leave the Vale of Conwy. As the road climbs over the hillside there are occasional glimpses of the Conwy Valley far below. On reaching a T-junction turn right on to the B5113, and pass through Nebo where there are mountain views to the right.

Descend into *Pentrefoelas*, where an inscribed pillar called the Levelinus Stone records the burial place of the Welsh champion, Prince Llewelyn. Turn left on to the A5, then in ¼m turn left again on to the A543 *Denbigh* road. The drive crosses the bleak Denbigh Moor to a summit crowned by the lonely Sportsmen's Arms, the highest inn in Wales. Pass through *Bylchau* and descend through pleasant countryside to Denbigh, where the 13th-c castle forms a good viewpoint. Part of

the old town walls, which date from the 13thc, are still standing. The drive then follows the A525 *Rhyl* road, through the wide Vale of Clwyd, with the ridge of the Clwdian Range prominent to the right. Pass through *Trefnant* and keep forward for *St Asaph*, the second smallest city in England and Wales. Follow signposts for Rhyl and in ¾m keep forward at a roundabout. A detour can be made by turning left on to the A55 Conwy road for *Bodelwyddan*, where the 'marble church' has a spire towering to 202ft. The main drive continues to *Rhuddlan* and its castle.

Continue to Rhyl, a popular resort with miles of safe sands. Keep forward to the promenade, then turn left on to the B5118 *Abergele* road. Meet the main road and turn right on to the A548. Follow the coast through a popular holiday area to *Pensarn*, then at the roundabout turn left to the ancient market town of Abergele. Follow the B5443 Conwy road and pass the walls of modern Gwrych Castle. The castle is open and worth a visit. Carry on through Llanddulas, a village nestling in a steep valley, before joining the A55. There are coastal views before the drive enters the modern resort of *Colwyn Bay*. Situated here are the Welsh Mountain Zoo and Botanic Gardens. The Pwllycrochan Woods nature trail begins ½m from the town centre. Continue on the Conwy road, then in ¾m take the second exit at a roundabout on to the A546 to cross Little Ormes Head and return to Llandudno.

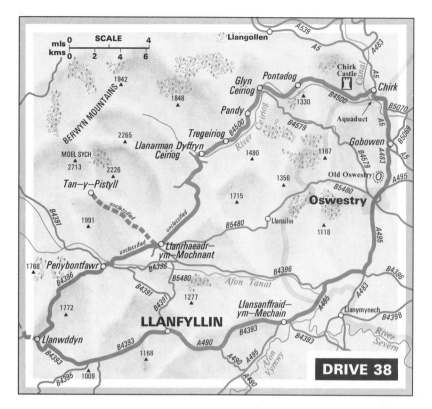

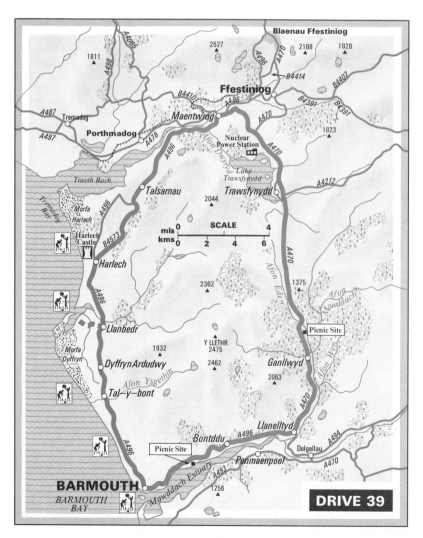

From *Llanfyllin*, a small town set in the wooded hills of the Cain valley, the route begins on the A490 *Welshpool* road and in 2m turns left on to the B4393, signposted Oswestry. The road winds beside the river along the Cain Valley, with its fine hill scenery, to *Llansantffraid-ym-Mechain*. Turn left on to the A495, passing through part of the wider Vyrnwy Valley before entering England.
Follow signposts to the picturesque

Barmouth is a pleasant resort with a sandy beach huddled between the sea and the Rhinog Mountains. The route round the 2,000ft peaks goes through historic Harlech, past Lake Trawsfynydd, and through woodland and moorland. Leave by the A496 *Harlech* road and climb above the coastal plain for fine forward views of *Snowdonia*, and, to the left, the Lleyn Peninsula. Pass through *Tal-y-bont* and *Dyffryn Ardudwy* to *Llanbedr*. Lanes lead off left along the route to sandy beaches.

A detour turns left at Llanbedr on to an unclassified road to visit Shell Island, unique for the rare shells to be found on its beach. It is also a popular haunt for many kinds of birds. The main drive continues and in 2m goes forward with the B4573 into the historic old town of Harlech, dominated by its noble castle. Continue N to rejoin the A496, and approach *Talsarnau* with views of the *Portmeirion* Italianate village to the left of the far side of Traeth Bach inlet. This attractive village has been featured in several television programmes, notably *The Prisoner*. Follow the S bank of the Afon Dwyryd and enter the Vale of Ffestiniog at the delightful village of *Maentwrog*. Beyond the village turn right on to the A487 *Dolgellau* road, gradually climbing to higher ground. In 2m keep forward and join the A470 to pass Lake Trawsfynydd and its nuclear power station. Skirt the village of *Trawsfynydd*, and cross a stretch of bleak moorland before dropping down through the attractive scenery of Coed-y-Brenin Forest.

The road runs alongside the Afon Eden, and near this river's confluence with the Afon Mawddach is the Dolgefeilian picnic site and forest trail. Beyond Ganllwyd a detour can be made by turning left to the *Tyn-y-Groes* forest trail. The main drive continues the descent to *Llanelltyd*, situated at the head of the Mawddach estuary. Branch right on to the A496 and follow the sandy shore of the estuary to *Bontddu*, picturesquely situated beneath steep wooded slopes. Just beyond the village a lay-by can be used for the start of a woodland path leading to the Farchynys Woodlands estuary picnic site. Return to Barmouth by following the widening estuary, with fine mountain views up to *Cader Idris* on the far side.

Drive 38 continued

market town of Oswestry, which for centuries was the scene of warfare between the English and the Welsh. Follow the A483 *Wrexham* road, and in 1m pass the iron-age hill fort of Old Oswestry on the left. At Gobowen turn left on to the A5 *Llangollen* road. After 2m descend into the Ceiriog Valley, where the Chirk Aqueduct carries the Shropshire Union Canal across the river. Cross the river into Wales, climb to the edge of *Chirk*, and turn left on to the B4500, signposted Glyn Ceiriog. In ¼m a road on the right leads to Chirk Castle. Continue along the valley, passing through Pontfadog to *Glyn Ceiriog*.

The drive ascends the narrowing valley and passes through *Pandy* and Tregeiriog on the approach to the foothills of the Berwyn Mountains. Continue to *Llanarmon Dyffryn Ceiriog*, then on meeting crossroads go forward on to an unclassified road signposted Llanrhaeadr. Climb out of the valley along a narrow road. In 1½m turn left for the run down to *Llanrhaeadr-ym-Mochnant* and keep forward through this village. A detour can be made by turning right to Tan-y-Pistyll, where the remarkable Pistyll Rhaeadr waterfall drops 240ft – one of the 'Seven Wonders of Wales'. The main drive continues from Llanrhaeadr across the river bridge and bears right, then climbs before descending the Tenat Valley at *Penybontfawr*. The drive meets a T-junction here and turns right then left on to the B4396, signposted Lake Vyrnwy. Proceed along a winding and narrow road through

wooded country to *Llanwddyn* at the SE end of the lake. From here a 12m circular drive can be made round the 4¾m long Lake Vyrnwy, a reservoir for Liverpool. The main drive continues on the B4393 Llanfyllin road, passing through rolling hill scenery before turning right on to the A490 for the return to Llanfyllin.

Through the Clwydian Hills

From Rhyl

Drive 40   65 miles

Rhyl is a popular seaside resort with an excellent sandy beach and two of the largest fun-fairs in Wales. Leave by the A525 *St Asaph* road, and in 2½m at a roundabout go forward on to the A5151, signposted *Dyserth*. Pass the entrance to *Bodrhyddan Hall* on the left. This mainly 17th-c house is set in fine grounds. From Dyserth continue on the main road, passing through *Trelawnyd* and Lloc, then turn left on to the A55. After 2½m turn left on to the A5026 into Holywell. According to legend a spring with miraculous healing powers rose from the spot where St Winifred was decapitated, and she was brought back to life. The well is one of the traditional 'Seven Wonders of Wales'.

Continue on the A5026 *Flint* road, and in 1½m turn right on to the A548, overlooking the Dee estuary. At Flint a ruined 13th-c castle on the foreshore gives sweeping views across the estuary to the Wirral peninsula. Leave the town by the A5119 *Mold* road, and at *Northop* turn left on to the A55. After 3m the remains of *Ewloe Castle* can be seen on the left. On reaching *Hawarden* it is possible to make a 7m diversion to Chester on the A55. To continue with the main drive follow the A550 *Wrexham* road, then in 2m turn right at a roundabout on to the A5118 Mold road. Later at a T-junction turn right on to the A541 to Mold in the pleasant Alyn Valley.

There is a restored 15th-c church and a Norman Motte here. Follow the A494 *Ruthin* road and pass through *Gwernymynydd* to Loggerheads. At the crossing of the River Alyn there is a short nature trail. The road then climbs to cross the Clwydian Hills, and on the long descent there are fine views across the gentle Vale of Clwyd. Keep forward for the centre of Ruthin, with its narrow streets and interesting buildings. Continue on the A525 *Denbigh* road through the Vale of Clwyd. Beyond Rhewl there are good views of the Clwydian Hills to the right. At the outskirts of Denbigh – the town centre is ¾m to the left – the route turns on to the Rhyl road. After 1m turn right again on to the A543 Mold road. Then after 1½m go forward on to the A541, and after a further 1½m turn left on to the B5429 Rhuallt road. Ascend through *Bodfari* to follow a narrow winding road along the edge of the Clwydian Hills, with fine views to the left.

cont

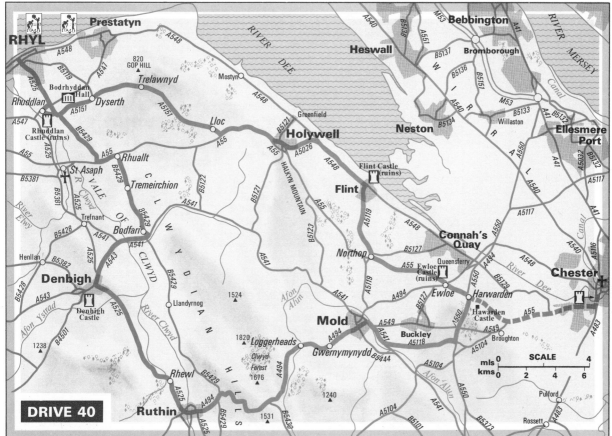

Drive 40 continued

At the edge of Tremeirchion follow
St Asaph signposts and continue to Rhuallt.
At the main road turn left on to the A55,
and in 1m turn right on to the B5429. At the
end of this road turn left on to the A5151,
then turn left again into *Rhuddlan*. The
castle here was started in 1277 for
Edward I. The drive is completed by
following the A525 to Rhyl.

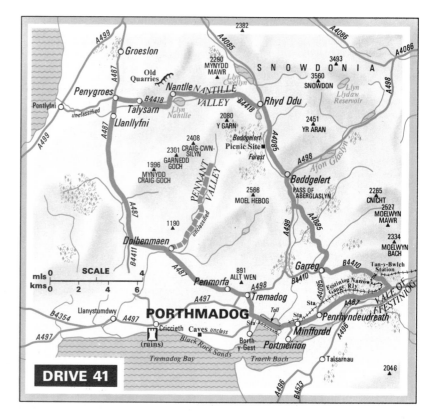

DRIVE 41

Llewellyn's Wales

From Porthmadog

Drive 41   40 miles

Porthmadog was once an important port for
shipping slate from the quarries of
Blaenau Ffestiniog. On the coast near by are
the sandy coves of *Borth-y-Gest* and a
splendid stretch of wide sands at Black
Rock. Follow the A487 *Caernarfon* road to
Tremadog – an attractive planned village
which was the birthplace of Lawrence of
Arabia. Turn left at the square and climb
through Penmorfa before skirting
Dolbenmaen. A detour can be made from
here by turning right on to an unclassified
road to the attractive Pennant Valley. At the
end of the valley is an amphitheatre of
mountains topped by the 2,566ft peak of
Moel Hebog.

The main drive continues with views of
1,996ft Mynydd Craig-goch to the right,
and later 1,670ft Bwlch Mawr to the left.
On the approach to *Llanllyfni* there are views
across to Caernarfon Bay. At *Penygroes*
turn right on to the B4418, signposted
Rhyd-Ddu, and between Talysarn and
Nantlle pass old disused slate quarries. To
the right above the waters of the Llyn
Nantlle rise 2,301ft Garnedd Goch and
2,408ft Craig-cwm-Silyn. Beyond Nantlle
the road becomes narrow and steeper as it
climbs out of the valley, and then winds
down to Rhyd-Ddu. Turn right on to the
A4085, passing on the left a footpath to
Snowdon. Later, on the gradual descent,
skirt Beddgelert Forest, site of a Forestry
Commission picnic area and a nature trail.

Beddgelert is a pleasant village at the
junction of the Nant Colwyn and Afon
Glaslyn. In a field near by is the reputed

grave of Llewellyn the Great's dog, Gelert.
Follow the A498 Porthmadog road into the
beautiful rocky Pass of Aberglaslyn, and
then turn left over Aberglaslyn Bridge on to
the A4085, signposted *Penrhyndeudraeth*.
There are glimpses to the left of 2,265ft
Cnicht, known as the Matterhorn of Wales
because of its conical shape. At Garreg turn
left on to the B4410, signposted Rhyd, and
climb to the edge of high ground for splendid
views of the mountains and the coastal
plain to Porthmadog. On the descent
through thickly wooded country the road
passes Tan-y-Bwlch Station on the
Festiniog Railway. A nature trail begins
from the station. Pass by Llyn Mair, then
descend steeply to a main road where the
drive turns right on to the A487. Pass along
the wooded Vale of Ffestiniog to
Penrhyndeudraeth and then Minffordd. On
the left is the entrance to *Portmeirion*, the
romantic Italian-style village created by Sir
Clough Williams-Ellis. In ¾m pass through
the tollgate at the beginning of the massive
embankment known as The Cob, which
leads to Porthmadog.

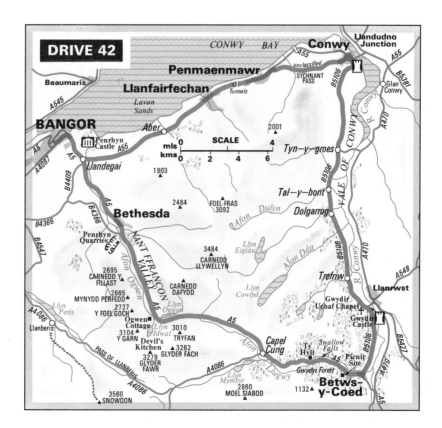

High Passes

From Bangor

Drive 42   52 miles

From the cathedral city of *Bangor*, the home of the University College of North Wales, the route begins by following the coast but later turns up the Vale of Conwy for some beautiful mountain views. Leave on the A5, signposted *Conwy*, to pass the entrance to the wooded parkland of *Penrhyn Castle* and Estate.

Keep forward with the A55 and enjoy the fine views across the Lavan Sands to *Beaumaris* and *Puffin Island* on the way to *Llanfairfechan*. Ahead there are also views across Conwy Bay, to the craggy Great Ormes Head, and *Llandudno*. The road tunnels through a quarry-scarred headland approaching *Penmaenmawr*. Reach the Mountain View Inn and branch right on to an unclassified road signposted Sychnant. Cross the beautiful Sychnant Pass to the harbour town of Conwy and its magnificent castle. Continue on the B5106 *Betws-y-coed* road, passing *Tyn-y-groes* and *Tal-y-bont*. Dolgarrog is noted for its hydro-electric power station which is fed by water coming from *Llyn Cowlyd* and *Llyn Eigiau* mountain lakes. *Trefriw* is the highest navigable point on the River Conwy. The drive continues along the W side of the valley and in 1¾m turns right to pass *Gwydir Castle*, a historic royal residence, and Gwydir Uchaf Chapel – the castle's former private chapel. A fine nature trail known as Lady Mary's Walk starts from above the castle. Continue along the pleasant valley to *Betws-y-coed*, which nestles in the densely wooded hills of the Gwydyr Forest, with four rivers converging near by. Turn

right on to the A5, signposted Bangor, and proceed along the wooded valley of the Afon Llugwy to pass a picnic site and arboretum on the left. In 2m pass the well-known, Swallow Falls on the right, and ¾m farther pass Ty Hyll – the Ugly House – made from blocks of stone held together without cement. The Gwydyr Forest nature trail starts from here. As the drive approaches *Capel Curig* there are views to the left of 2,860ft Moel Siabod. Later there are distant views to the left of the *Snowdon* Range.

The drive continues along the A5, following the Afon Llugwy into another wide valley with *Llyn Ogwen* at its end. To the left is the 3,262ft Glyder Fach with Tryfan, the famous 3,010ft rock peak, overshadowing the lake. Also to the left is the long 3,104ft ridge of Y-Garn, and across the lake to the right is 3,427ft Carnedd Dafydd. Pass Ogwen Cottage, a mountain rescue post which is the start of the Cwm Idwal nature trail. A good path leads from here to Llyn Idwal and the Devil's Kitchen, a deep corrie at the back of Glyder Fawr. The drive continues past a steep waterfall, and descends into the magnificent U-shaped Nant Ffrancon Valley. On the left are the high ridges of 2,727ft Y-Foel Goch, 2,665ft Mynydd Perfedd and 2,695ft Carnedd y Filiast, each separated by deep corries. *Bethesda* boasts the famous *Penrhyn* slate quarries. From here the drive follows the wooded banks of Afon Ogwen to return to Bangor.

143

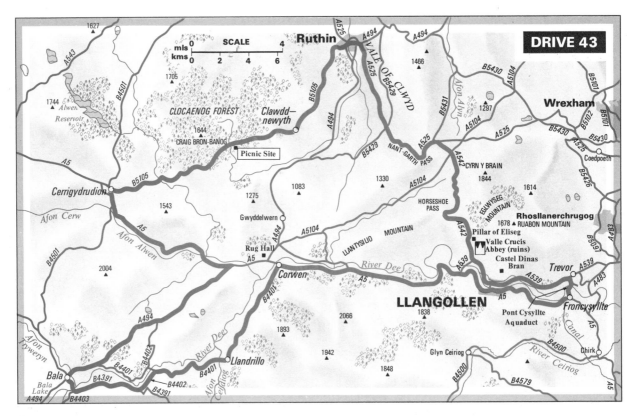

The Vale of Music

From Llangollen

Drive 43   76 miles

Llangollen is a popular tourist centre which is well-known for its annual International Eisteddfod. From here the drive follows the A5 Shrewsbury road through the widening Vale of Llangollen to Froncysyllte. Turn left on to the B5434, signposted *Trevor*, for the short run down into the valley. On the right is Pont Cysyllte. Telford's famous aqueduct of 1804 which carries the Shropshire Union Canal across the Dee. Cross the river, turn right, and climb to the edge of Trevor where the drive turns left on to the A539 to return along the N side of the valley to Llangollen.

Continue on the A542 *Ruthin* road to leave the River Dee Valley and follow the Eglwyseg Valley past ruined *Valle Crucis Abbey* and the Pillar of Eliseg. The ascent of the spectacular 1,367ft Horseshoe Pass on the E flank of Llantysilio Mountain affords magnificent views of the rocky Eglwyseg ridge and 1,844ft Cyrn-y-Brain. On reaching the A525 turn left and descend the wooded Nant-y-Garth Pass, at the S end of the Clwdian Range, into the Vale of Clwyd for Ruthin. Go forward into the town centre and descend across the river bridge, then turn left on to the B5105 with *Cerrigydrudion* signposts. Cross rolling countryside and pass through Clawdd-newydd, then cross the extensive Clocaenog Forest. There is a picnic site to the left, and more fine views as the road passes through open country to Cerrigydrudion. Turn left here on to the Llangollen road, then left again on to the A5.

A long descent is then made through the Alwen Valley. In $7\frac{1}{2}$m meet traffic signals and turn right on to the A494 *Bala* road.

The direct route to Llangollen along the A5 saves 20m, but the drive route passes through pleasant countryside to Bala. The A494 skirts the lake and the main route turns left on to the B4391, signposted *Llangynog*, passing the far N end of Bala Lake. Cross the River Dee and follow the valley, then in $3\frac{1}{4}$m turn left on to the B4402, signposted *Corwen*. In 1m turn right on to the B4401 for *Llandrillo*. The grassy Berwyn Mountains make this a good centre for hill walking. Attractive views of the wooded Dee Valley can be enjoyed before the route joins the A5 to Corwen. Continue with the Llangollen road for the return to Llangollen.

Gazetteer

Key to Town Plans and Gazetteer

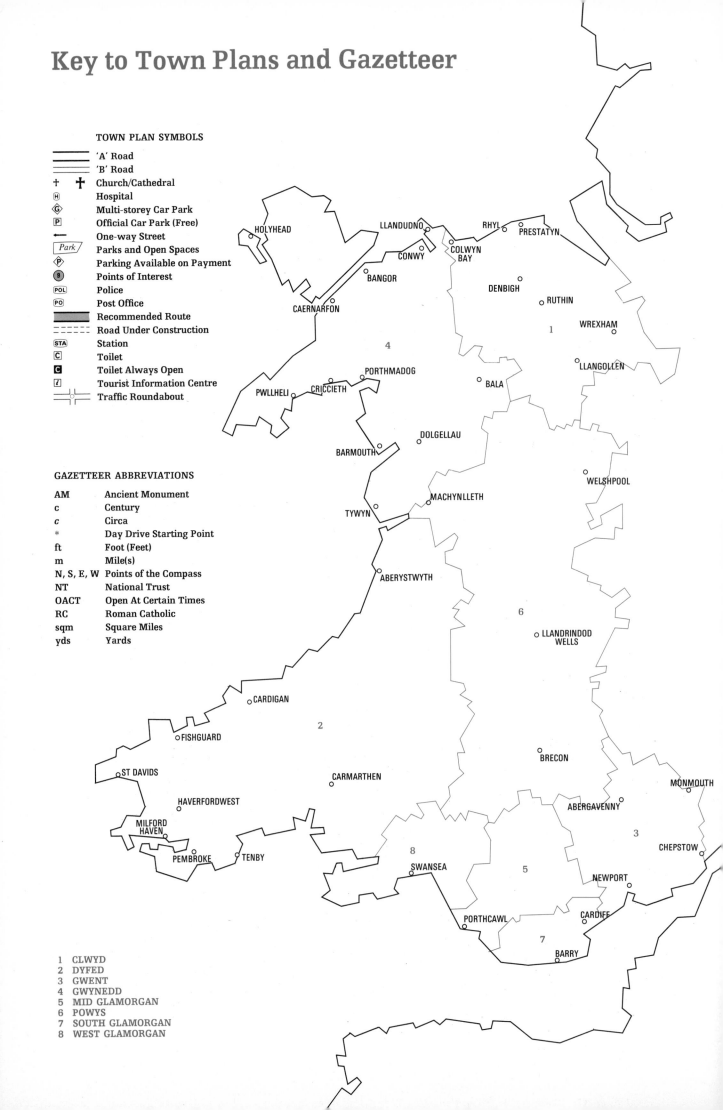

TOWN PLAN SYMBOLS

═══	'A' Road
≡≡≡	'B' Road
+ ✝	Church/Cathedral
Ⓗ	Hospital
◈	Multi-storey Car Park
Ⓟ	Official Car Park (Free)
←	One-way Street
Park	Parks and Open Spaces
Ⓟ	Parking Available on Payment
❾	Points of Interest
POL	Police
PO	Post Office
▬▬▬	Recommended Route
------	Road Under Construction
STA	Station
C	Toilet
C	Toilet Always Open
i	Tourist Information Centre
⊕	Traffic Roundabout

GAZETTEER ABBREVIATIONS

AM	Ancient Monument
c	Century
c	Circa
*	Day Drive Starting Point
ft	Foot (Feet)
m	Mile(s)
N, S, E, W	Points of the Compass
NT	National Trust
OACT	Open At Certain Times
RC	Roman Catholic
sqm	Square Miles
yds	Yards

1 CLWYD
2 DYFED
3 GWENT
4 GWYNEDD
5 MID GLAMORGAN
6 POWYS
7 SOUTH GLAMORGAN
8 WEST GLAMORGAN

ABBEY CWM HIR, Powys 13 SO77

One of the first things the visitor notices in the village of Abbey Cwm Hir is an interesting inn curiously named the Happy Union. The church on the opposite side of the road has an interesting Light of the World window and the stone coffin lid of Abbot Mabli, who died in 1200. Built in 1836, the building suggests a sympathy for the theology of the Oxford Movement. It has an aumbry and an unusual single sedilia.

The remains of the great abbey are the showpiece of this village. They lie among a scatter of elms and sycamores down below the road. Only parts of the walls remain, together with the bases of what must in their time have been truly magnificent columns. It is said that the body of Llywelyn the Last was buried under the high altar. His head was sent to London and exhibited as a sign of Edward's victory. The abbey was founded in 1143 by Cadwallon ap Madog, a cousin of Rhys ap Gruffydd who was the founder of Whitland Abbey. The first monks were brought in from Whitland. Henry III plundered the abbey to avenge the misdirection of some of his soldiers by a friar, but it was the Welsh Owain Glyndwr who destroyed it, believing that the monks were spies for England. At the Dissolution there were only three monks left there. The choir of the abbey was never built, but the nave was the longest in Wales. The whole building was dedicated to the Blessed Virgin Mary and was a Cistercian house.

ABER, Gwynedd 5 SH67

In pre-Menai Bridge days Aber was the starting point for the perilous crossing to Anglesey – one of several crossings of the Menai Straits. The journey was made across the Lavan Sands at low tide and was completed by ferry to Beaumaris. Travellers usually had about three hours to make the crossing safely, and everything depended on their ability to catch the attention of the ferrymen at Beaumaris. Foggy weather added to the dangers, and a bell once used to warn travellers of fog is now preserved at Aber church. A row of poles was also erected to guide travellers in bad weather. The sands are still exposed at low tide and are best seen from the sea front at Llanfairfechan. A mound known as Y Mwd was the site of a castle built at Aber by Llywelyn the Great, and it was from here in 1282 that Llywelyn the Last defied the summons of Edward I to attend the English parliament at Westminster. Aber Falls, a 170ft spectacular, is about an hour's walk up the valley of the Afon Goch.

ABERAERON, Dyfed 12 SN46

A coastal town built mostly during the 19thc in Regency style, Aberaeron has no individual buildings of outstanding merit but has a sense of coherence that is entirely satisfactory. Alban's Square and Mason's Row are especially noteworthy. The harbour, where schooners were once built, is a popular sailing centre. The beach is safe and comprises a mixture of gravel and stone.

ABERANGELL, Gwynedd 10 SH81

This lonely village lies 5m E of Aberdyfi and is set deep in forests on the slopes of the Cwm Celli hills beside the Angell stream. The surrounding wooded area has been opened up by the Forestry Commission, who have introduced new roads and paths.

The spectacular 170ft Aber Falls in the Afon Goch Valley.

ABERAVON, West Glamorgan 24 SS79

One of the newest Welsh seaside resorts, Aberavon has an attractive promenade and 2m of firm sand which may surprise a stranger who thinks of the area as being principally industrial. The town merges with Port Talbot between the Bristol Channel and mountains, and the seafront has become very popular. The municipal Afan Lido is a major sports and entertainment centre.

ABERBEEG, Gwent 22 SO20

Aberbeeg is one of a strip of villages along the valley of the Ebbw Fach, the largest of which is Abertillery. Railway Terrace is said to be built on the line of a Roman road.

ABERCARN, Gwent 26 ST29

This industrial town is set in the lower Ebbw Valley, and farther up the valley on the slopes of the mountains is the Ebbw Forest. The fairly new church has a peal of eight bells, all of which have names – Faith, Peace, Love, Joy, Meekness, Long Suffering, Gentleness, and Goodness.

ABERDARE, Mid Glamorgan 21 SO00

The 13th-c Church of St John is one of the oldest in Glamorgan but has been considerably restored. In 1789 David Williams of nearby Aberaman insisted on being buried standing upright in the churchyard, to be ready for the Day of Judgement. The town is an industrial centre in a valley which still retains much of its natural beauty. Victoria Square has a statue of Caradog (Griffith Rhys Jones), with baton raised. He was conductor of the great choir – the South Wales Choral Union – which won the chief prize at Crystal Palace in 1872 and 1873.

ABERDARON, Gwynedd 8 SH12

This romantic hamlet is clustered around an ancient bridge on what is known as the 'Land's End' of Lleyn Peninsula. Gegin Fawr (Big Kitchen), now a cafe, is reputedly the place where pilgrims to Bardsey Island were fed while waiting for favourable weather to cross the treacherous Bardsey Sound. Aberdaron's church is surprisingly large for the size of the community and is separated from the beach by a granite rampart. It stands on the site of an older church established by St Hywyn in the 5th or 6thc. The present 12th-c church was the scene of a dramatic political incident when Gruffydd, prince of South Wales, sought sanctuary from both the clutches of his

northern counterpart and Henry I of England. The military force sent to capture him was forestalled by the local clergy, who forbade them entry to the church, and Gruffydd escaped under cover of darkness. The church's Norman doorway is an interesting feature. The curious post office is an architectural exercise by Welsh architect Clough Williams-Ellis.

A magnificent horseshoe-shaped beach is enclosed by impressive headlands, and offshore are the two gull islands of Ynys Gwylan Fawr and Ynys Gwylan Fach. Aberdaron was the home of Richard Robert Jones (1780–1843), better known as Dic Aberdaron. His genius for languages – ragged and uncultured though he was – earned him a place among famous Welsh characters. Magnificent cliff scenery and close views of Bardsey Island are afforded from Braich-y-Pwll (NT), which lies 2m NW of Aberdaron. Ffynnon Fair (Our Lady's Well) is uncovered at low tide and takes some finding. Its existence and the remains of a church recall Bardsey pilgrims who embarked at this point. One of the most agreeable spots for a day out along this coastline is Porth Oer, a sheltered sandy bay with excellent facilities. To the E of Aberdaron is Bodwrdda, a stone building with brick-built wings, incorporating parts of a medieval structure. The house is dated 1621 and is noted as one of the first large houses to be built of brick in this county.

ABERDESACH, Gwynedd 4 SH45

A small village on Caernarfon Bay between Pontllyfni and Clynnog-Fawr, Aberdesach has a mainly shingle and rock beach. Small areas of sand are revealed at low tide.

ABERDYFI, Gwynedd 12 SN69

If thou art as true to me,
Just as I am true to thee.
Un, dau, tri, pedwar, pump, chwech,
Say the Bells of Aberdyfi.

This song is still sung by children, but the light opera *Liberty Hall* for which Charles Dibdin wrote it has long been forgotten. Aberdyfi is a genteel resort with a pleasant Edwardian/Victorian feel about it. Being off the well-trodden tourist track it has managed to retain its personality better than most places. For the same reasons of inaccessibility Aberdyfi has remained singularly unscathed by the tribal conflicts between England and Wales.

The *Bells of Aberdyfi* is not an allusion to an existing church but to the legendary bells of a submerged church which, according to folklore, was part of a town lost beneath the sea – the lost land of *Cantref Gwaelod*. There is certainly evidence to support the theory that there was once a fertile plain along this coastline, for just N of Aberdyfi is a causeway running out to sea, and a similar one farther N which is even more apparent at low tide. Yet another lies S of Aberdyfi. They could have been protective embankments, but on the other hand they could be purely natural phenomena caused by the tide.

The resort basks with its head in the sun and its feet in the waters of the Dyfi estuary, and boasts a very agreeable climate. It has good sands, but its original business was not with tourism – rather with seafaring and shipbuilding. At one time it had several shipyards, the last being where Pennelig Terrace now stands. Aberdyfi's last boat was built in 1880. The town was listed as one of the most important ports along the Welsh coast, and during the 16thc was accommodating Continental as well as coastal shipping. The port expanded with the export trade in slates from Corris and Abergynolwyn, and woollen cloth from Dolgellau and Barmouth. Coal, malt, flour, and salt were imported, and towards the end of the 19thc as many as 180 vessels were recorded as standing off waiting to enter harbour.

Today, Aberdyfi's seafaring links are largely kept alive by yachtsmen and the young people of the Outward Bound Sea School, who have their shore base here. Youngsters from all walks of life receive leadership training at the centre. Sailing enthusiasts will be interested to know that the GP14 sailing dinghy, one of the most popular small boats ever designed, was first adopted by the Dyfi Sailing Club as a club boat. The Black Bell, a sail sign of the class, is a twin compliment to Aberdyfi and the Wolverhampton designing firm whose name was Bell. The area abounds with pleasant walking areas, including Cwm Dyffryn, often referred to as Happy Valley. The town does have a church and bells apart from the legendary undersea structure, but it is a modern edifice built because worshippers previously had to journey to neighbouring Tywyn.

ABEREDW, Powys   21 SO04
The Edw flows into the Wye in this place of rocks, water, and wooded slopes. In the rocks above Aberedw is a cave where Llywelyn the Last sheltered shortly before he met his death at the hands of an English soldier in 1282. A railway line, now closed, cuts through the remains of Llywelyn's castle – the stones of which were used as ballast for the tracks. Aberedw's beautiful church has a 15th-c screen, an ancient wooden roof over the nave, and a porch that is decorated with clover-leaf ornamentation.

ABERERCH, Gwynedd   8 SH33
Neat cottages make up this coastal community between Criccieth and Pwllheli, and the whole place has the look of a model village. This impression is enhanced by a secluded setting among lanes which run between flowered

hedgerows. Abererch's main attraction is its wide, lonely beach where fragments of rock known as Cerrig-y-Baredy jut upwards out of the sea and provide a haven for families of seals. The parish church is extraordinarily large for such a small place. It is a restored medieval building containing ancient seats and some 15th-c woodwork.

ABERFAN, Mid Glamorgan   21 SO00
Tragedy struck this mining village, 4m S of Merthyr Tydfil, on 21 October 1966. Part of a big coal-tip slipped down a mountainside, and sludge engulfed terraced houses and a junior school. A total of 116 children and 26 adults died. A memorial to the children can be seen in the cemetery from the main Cardiff to Merthyr road on the other side of the valley. The tip has been levelled and well landscaped to fit in with the 1,500ft mountain.

ABERFFRAW, Gwynedd   4 SH36
Abberffraw is a grey, somnolent Anglesey village which has little to show of its historic past. Between the 7th and 13thc it was the capital of the Kingdom of Gwynedd. Llywelyn the Great (1194–1240) held court here, as did Llywelyn the Last, but no trace remains of the palace. It was probably of wooden construction. Mountainous sand dunes hide the sea, but at high tide the water rushes down towards the village's historic hump-backed bridge. Accessible at low tide on a rocky islet near by is the 7th-c church of St Cwyfan, restored in 1893.

*ABERGAVENNY, Gwent   22 SO31
This busy market town is held to be the gateway to Wales, and is certainly a natural entrance to the Brecon Beacons national park. To the N is 1,950ft Sugar Loaf, an extinct volcano, and NE is Ysgyryd Fawr, upon whose slopes are the remains of a chapel dedicated to St Michael. To the SW is 1,832ft Blorenge, a good viewpoint. The beautiful River Usk flows just to the S of the town and runs roughly parallel to the Monmouthshire and Brecon Canal. The Romans had a fort here called *Gobannium*, and the foundations of this are thought to lie under the castle mound.

The castle was founded by Hameline de Balun early in the 11thc. By 1172 it belonged to William de Braose, from whom it was captured in the same year by the native Welsh chieftain Sytsylt ap Dyferwald. Braose soon regained control, and in 1177 he invited all the local Welsh chieftains to a Christmas dinner. When all the Welshmen were 'at meat' and therefore unarmed and unaware, William had them slaughtered. Strangely enough William de Braose got his just deserts, not from the Welsh – although they tried very hard – but from King John, who took a dislike to him and forced him to go abroad where he died in poverty. William s wife and child starved to death in Windsor Castle. The castle at Abergavenny was captured in 1215 by Llywelyn the Great, extensively damaged during the Glyndwr uprising, and destroyed by parliamentary forces in 1645. The few remains date from the 13th and 14thc and consist of two broken towers, the gateway, and fragments of wall. The interesting town museum is situated in the castle grounds.

Abergavenny's main street contains buildings from many periods. Especially noteworthy are the 19th-c Angel hotel, which was an important coaching inn, and the gothic-revival town hall. The old tower of St John's church can still be seen, although the body of the church has been in use as a masonic hall for 70 years. Prior to this it was the Henry VIII Grammar School. Other interesting buildings in the town include the 16th- to 17th-c King's Arms Inn; the early 19th-c King's Head Inn and adjoining medieval arch; the Old Court, a house dating from 1500 built into the old town walls. St Mary's Church in Monk Street is the town's most important piece of architecture. Originally it was the church of a Benedictine priory founded in 11thc, but today only the tythe barn and prior's house remain of the priory buildings. The church contains many treasures, including 24 choir stalls dating from the late 14thc and a huge wooden figure of the patriarch Jesse in the Lewes chapel. Several fine tombs dating from 13th to 17thc include that of a young knight, perhaps George de Cantelupe, who died in 1273. This is especially interesting in that it is carved from a solid block of wood. Here also is the tomb of Dr David Lewis, who was the first principal of Jesus College in Oxford.

ABERGELE, Clwyd   6 SH97
Abergele is easily overlooked in the headlong rush to the more distant parts of N Wales, but it was one of the first places where sea bathing became popular. Plenty of history is evident both inside and outside the 16th-c church. The screen is pitted with carved initials and dates – the work of schoolboys when the church was used as a school in Tudor times; stone pillars still carry the marks made by archers sharpening their arrow heads; mass graves in the churchyard recall two transport disasters during the last century.

Outside the town is Gwrych Castle, a mock-Norman extravagance which catches the eye with its castellated walls and fairy-tale turrets strung along the wooded hillside. It was built in 1814 for a Mr L B Hesketh. Lord Dundonald was a later resident, and it now serves as a holiday centre offering medieval banquets and jousting knights among its attractions. It was at Gwrych Castle that boxer Randolph Turpin trained for his world championship fight, and it was at Pensarn Beach a few generations earlier that Captain Matthew Webb, of matchbox fame, trained for his channel swim.

ABERGLASLYN, Gwynedd   9 SH54
The picturesquely-wooded pass of Aberglaslyn carries the road from Tremadog Bay to Beddgelert. Awesome scenery moved 18th-c Joseph Cradock to write: 'How shall I express my feelings. The dark tremendous precipices, the rapid river roaring over disjointed rocks, black caverns, and issuing cataracts all serve to make this the noblest specimen of the finely Horrid the eye can behold . . . The Poet has not described, nor the Painter pictured so gloomy a retreat, 'tis the last Approach to the mansion of Pluto through the regions of Despair'

In 1817 Thomas Love Peacock wrote more sympathetically about the majestic scenery and lamented the loss of the 'liquid mirror' through Madocks' draining of the estuary. To the W of the pass is 2,566ft Moel Hebog (Hill of the Hawk), and to the E stand the twin Moelwyns. The Welsh Highland Light Railway once crossed this region.

ABERGORLECH, Dyfed 20 SN53
This small, isolated village stands on the River Cothi. The picturesque, three-arched bridge which spans the river here is of interest.

ABERGWESYN, Powys 13 SN85
This is the last hamlet on the Llanwrtyd side of the sharp spine of Cambrian Mountains, which runs lengthwise down mid Wales and separates the old counties of Brecon and Cardigan. It stands 5m up the Irfon valley from Llanwrtyd – a restored church dedicated to St David, a chapel, and a sprinkle of cottages at a road fork deep in the mountains. A mile higher up the valley the river flows through a narrow rocky gorge known as the Wolf's Leap. The scenery here is wild and grand, and the road accompanying the river climbs a zig-zag called The Devil's Stairway up to the high, empty mountain moors and over to Tregaron. Travelling this road is an exhilarating experience.

ABERGWILI, Dyfed 20 SN42
Above the village is Brynmyrddin – Merlin's Hill – where the enchanter is supposed to have had his retreat from the ups and downs of Arthur's Britain. An early Bishop of St David's, anticipating the transfer of the see to Carmarthen, had a palace constructed at Abergwili. The see was never moved but the palace remains. The present reconstruction replaces the original building, which burnt down in 1903.

ABERGYNOLWYN, Gwynedd 9 SH60
Terminus for travellers on the Talyllyn narrow-gauge railway and starting point for some interesting walks, Abergynolwyn lies at the head of the Dysynni Valley. A substantial village for these parts, it developed as a result of extensive slate quarrying at Bryn Eglwys up the steep valley to the S. Ownership of the quarry passed from the McConnell family to Sir Haydn Jones MP early in the century, along with the Talyllyn Railway which started as a mineral line but developed a passenger service. (see feature starting page 62). Talyllyn, one of the loveliest of Welsh lakes, is 3m W of Abergynolwyn. To the N is Castell-y-Bere and Craig Aderyn, or Bird Rock, a curiously-shaped rock which is the haunt of cormorants and hawks

and is supervised by the West Wales Naturalists' Trust. Keen eyes will also pick out wild goats grazing unconcernedly on precipitous ledges.

ABERLLYNFI, Powys 20 SO13
This village stands on the beautiful River Wye – known for its salmon – and boasts an ancient inn called the Three Cocks.

ABERMULE, Powys 14 SO19
Situated at the confluence of the Rivers Mule and Severn, Abermule is noted for its connection with a terrible railway disaster in 1921. The Aberystwyth to Manchester express collided head-on with a stopping train from Welshpool 1m down the line. Fifteen people died in the crash, including Lord Herbert Vane-Tempest, one of the directors of the Cambrian Railways.

The Severn here is the legendary setting of the suicide of the maiden Sabrina, who drowned herself to escape her stepmother. Her name was taken by both Romans and Welsh for the river itself – the Welsh *Hafren* is a Celtic form of Sabrina. The Brynderwen Bridge which spans the Severn is historic, being the second iron bridge to be built and erected in Britain. This fact is recorded in the ironwork of its sides.
cont overleaf

1   Abergavenny & District Museum
2   Angel Hotel
3   Castle
4   St Mary's Church

5   King's Arms Inn
6   King's Head Inn
7   Old Court
8   Peter Jones (traditional leather work)

9   St John's Church
10 WTB Information Centre

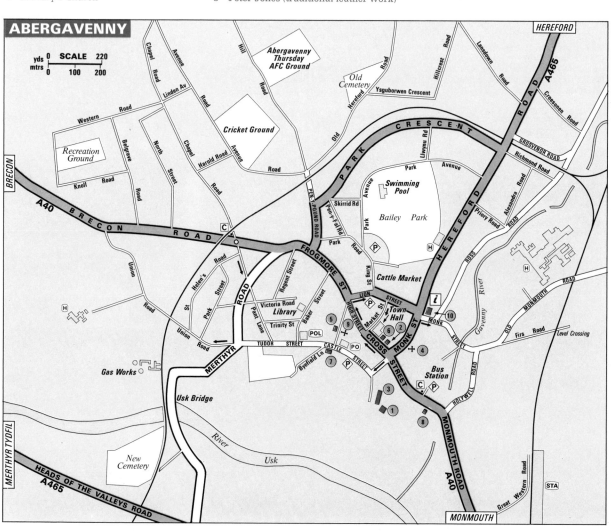

Abermule is a village without a church; its parish church is at Llanmerewig, a tiny hamlet on the hillside 1½m up the Mule Dingle, a very pretty drive which leads out to the Kerry Hills. Close by on the other side of the Severn are the remains of Dolforwyn Castle. A new bridge is being built across the Severn, with a new road which will bypass the village. This is due to open in 1975 and will ease the traffic pressure on the Brynderwen Bridge, which is controlled by traffic lights – one of only three sets permanently installed in mid Wales.

ABERNANT, Dyfed   17 SN32
The countryside around this village 5m NW of Carmarthen is typical of the many quiet areas to be found in Dyfed. Small trout streams and wooded hills lie to the N. The interesting village church was rebuilt in 1706.

ABERPORTH, Dyfed   17 SN25
An experimental rocket station is sited near this large seaside village on Pencribach headland. The excellent bathing beach is a major attraction, and two sandy coves lie W of the A487 between Cardigan and Aberystwyth.

ABERSOCH, Gwynedd   8 SH32
Smart villas, expensive-looking yachts, and plush hotels – Abersoch, situated on the Lleyn Peninsula, wears all these outward signs of an affluent and fashionable resort. It has mushroomed out of all recognition during the past few decades, and its popularity can be attributed largely to its sheltered position and mild climate.

Offshore are the two small grass-covered islands named after St Tudwal, a Breton who set up a cell here in the 6thc after fleeing from fear of persecution after the fall of the Roman Empire. During the

middle ages an Augustinian priory was established here, and after the Reformation a pirate band took control of the islands. Father Hughes led a spartan existence on one of the islands in the 19thc, and more recently there were abortive plans to establish a nudist colony. All that can be seen today are the ruins of a 12th-c chapel and an automatic lighthouse. The islands are privately owned and provide a sanctuary for sea birds, but boat trips can be made around their shores from Abersoch.

The Warren (Traeth Castellmarch) runs parallel with the Abersoch to Llanbedrog road, and is one of the finest beaches on the Lleyn Peninsula. According to legend Castellmarch – a Jacobean manor house N of the road – is the site of a castle of a king called March, who had horse's ears. To keep this awful deformity secret he killed each barber who trimmed his hair.

ABERTHAW, South Glamorgan   25 ST06
Smeaton used limestone from this village, 7m W of Barry, in the building of the Eddystone lighthouse between 1756 and 1759. There was a small port here before the railways came. The church is at Penmark, but an inn and a mission hall in the village are of interest.

ABERTILLERY, Gwent   22 SO20
Situated in the industrial, mountain-flanked valley of the Ebbw Fach this and neighbouring towns saw the growth and decline of the coal trade in the second half of the 19thc. New industries have since come to the area. Chartists held a secret meeting at Nantyglo in 1839, and decided to march on Newport. Nantyglo, which is higher up the valley between Blaina and Brynmawr, was the site of famous ironworks.

*ABERYSTWYTH, Dyfed   12 SN58
Aberystwyth is not just a holiday resort; it is also the seat of local and some national government departments, a university centre, and an important shopping focus. Although there was a prehistoric settlement at Pen Dinas, the hill at the lower end of the town, the rise of Aberystwyth dates from the year 1277. This was when Edmund Crouchback, brother of Edward I, built the castle which the Welsh destroyed five years later – and the king rebuilt two years after that. Owain Glyndwr held it from 1404 to 1408. Cromwell's forces captured and destroyed it in the civil war, and today the ruins have been laid out as gardens which form a viewpoint for sitting and looking out over Cardigan Bay. Charles I established a mint here which was operated by Thomas Bushell, who minted coins from silver obtained from local mines.

Between the castle and the remnant of the pier (the top end of which was burnt out) is the oldest of the university buildings – a splendid edifice of Victorian gothic which was originally intended as a hotel. It was built by the railway pioneer Thomas Savin in 1860, who conceived the idea of popularizing Aberystwyth by giving a week's free holiday to anyone buying a return ticket from London. He intended to accommodate them here. The project collapsed after he had spent £80,000 on it, and the building was bought for £10,000 in 1870 for use as a university college. This is considered one of the most impressive buildings in the town.

Another is the Town Hall at the end of Portland Street, a new structure built in 1961 and opened a year later. It is a white building with a Palladian front to the centre block and two plain Georgian-style wings. It gained a Civic Trust award in 1962. The previous building originated from 1842 and was burnt down in 1957. Seion Church, at the end of Queen's Road, is a modern building with an interesting open cupola containing an eagle and Bible. At the northern end of the graceful crescent-shaped Promenade is Constitution Hill, which can be ascended by funicular railway built in 1895 by Croyden Marks. Marks also constructed the cliff railways at Lynton, Clifton, and Bridgnorth. It was originally hydraulically operated but is now electric. Every possible safety device has been incorporated, including brakes which operate on both cars simultaneously, governors which control the speed of the cars, and cables capable of holding ten times the required load. There is an interesting grave in St Michael's churchyard, quite close to the fence near the Great Darkgate Street entrance. The inscription on the stone, still legible after a century and a quarter, reads 'Stop, Traveller, Stop and

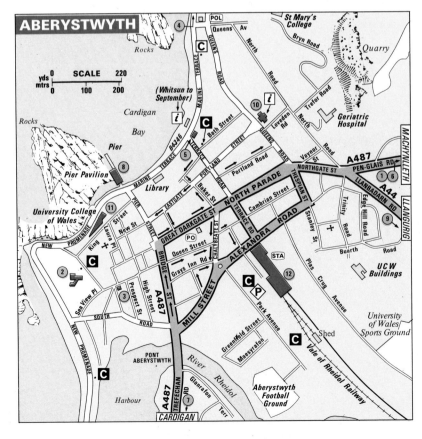

1   Arts Centre
2   Castle
3   Ceredigion Museum
4   Constitution Hill (funicular railway)
5   King's Hall
6   National Library of Wales
7   Pen Dinas Earthworks
8   Pier
9   Recreation Centre
10 Town Hall and WTB Information Centre
11 University College of Wales
12 Vale of Rheidol Railway

read. This stone was erected by those who fully appreciated the integrity and fidelity of David Lewis, alias the Good Old Commodore, who departed this life on the 16th day of February 1850 aged 66 years. He nobly fought on board the 'Conqueror' at the Battle of Trafalgar and for the last 15 years performed zealously the duties of Deputy Harbour Master at this port'.

Aberystwyth is the terminus of two remaining railway lines – the old mid Wales line from Shrewsbury and the narrow-gauge Vale of Rheidol, which runs 12m up the Rheidol valley to Devil's Bridge and is the only narrow-gauge railway owned and operated by British Rail (see page 62). The newest of the university buildings are up on Penglais Hill on the N side of the town, and here too is the National Library of Wales which contains over 5½ million books, manuscripts, and documents of all kinds. Among the treasures housed here are the *Black Book of Carmarthen*, the earliest Welsh manuscript; the *Book of Taliesin*; the *Laws of Hywel Dda*; the earliest complete text of the *Mabinogion*; and a manuscript copy of the *Canterbury Tales*. The foundation stones of the National Library were laid by King George V and Queen Mary in 1911, and it was opened in 1937 by King George VI and Queen Elizabeth, the present Queen Mother. Attached to the agricultural faculty of the university is the Welsh Plant-Breeding Station, where new strains of cereals and grass are developed and seeds produced for export all over the world. Other interesting places include the Art's Centre, King's Hall, Ceredigion Museum, and a Recreation Centre.

ACREFAIR, Clwyd 11 SJ24
Acrefair is an industrial community at the entry to the Vale of Llangollen. The nineteen-arch Pontcysylltau aqueduct carries the Shropshire Union Canal over the River Dee and was built by Telford at the beginning of the 19thc.

ALLTMAWR, Powys 21 SO04
The tiny parish of Alltmawr lies S of Builth Wells in the wooded Wye Valley. The church reflects the size of the community it serves and is only 35ft long. It preserves interesting box pews which date from the 18thc.

ALLT RHYD-Y-GROES, Dyfed 21 SN74
A national nature reserve situated about 9m N of Llandovery, Allt Rhyd-y-Groes covers 153 acres and mainly comprises oakwoods. A permit is required to visit it.

ALWEN RESERVOIR, Clwyd 6 SH95
This reservoir is about 3m long and ¼m wide. It is situated in the moors near Pentrefoelas, and is a good place for trout fishing.

AMBLESTON, Dyfed 16 SN02
Ambleston church has been rebuilt but retains its Norman tower. Its font has been variously used as a cheese-press and pig trough. A field at Scullock West Farm contains a monument to a farmer and his wife inscribed 'By the blessing of God on their joint understanding and thrift they bought this farm and hand it down without encumbrance to their heirs. Endeavour to pull together as they did. Union is strength'.

AMLWCH, Gwynedd 4 SH49
Amlwch port wears a sad, contemplative frown these days, probably dreaming of fortunes made and lost when it dominated the world copper trade. The harbour, literally gouged out of the granite cliffs, was once alive with small ships exporting the precious metal all over the world. Today the harbour is as derelict as Parys Mountain, the source of the copper.

There is evidence to suggest that the Romans discovered copper on Parys Mountain, but the big strike came in 1768 – appropriately enough on St David's Day – after about four years of abortive prospecting. The man Puw, who first struck the rich vein, is said to have been rewarded with a new suit annually. The big name in Amlwch copper was Thomas Williams of Llaniden, often called the Copper King, but in 1778 the Rev Edward Hughes – owner of another part of the mountain and whose son became Lord Dinorben – made another big copper strike. During the height of the boom the mines produced between 60,000 and 80,000 tons, and profits were said to have been £300,000 a year. Some 1,500 men and women were employed and Amlwch dictated the world price of copper.

By 1820 the best days of Amlwch were over. In the following years falling world prices and technical difficulties caused by water seepage into the workings spelled the end of the great days. In 1793, at the passing of the Harbour Act, Amlwch was said to have had a population of 4,977 and 1,025 ale houses. The port's excellent deep harbour could accommodate 30 vessels of up to 200 tons. There was a substantial boat-building industry run by the Treweek family, and there is still evidence of the kilns which were used for smelting copper. The mines had their own currency, and tokens called Amlwch Pennies are still unearthed in gardens in N Wales.

A thriving but unusual industry in Amlwch was tobacco processing, and Amlwch Shag was widely known among pipe smokers. Shipbuilding continued here until the 1930's, but now the harbour is mainly used by pleasure craft and Liverpool pilot boats. Amlwch town is some distance from the port, and Parys Mountain rises 2m inland.

AMMANFORD, Dyfed 20 SN61
Until the late 19thc the Cross Inn at the centre of Ammanford was almost the only building here. The town developed quickly because it is situated on the anthracite coalfield, and although the landscape is dotted with coaltips the surrounding area is not an industrial wasteland. There is a great deal of agricultural land and some beautiful scenery. Rev John Jenkins, later to become Archdruid of Wales, had a school here at the beginning of the 20thc that produced a large number of prominent men. The school building is now the English Congregational chapel. George Borrow stayed at nearby Brynamman in 1854. Good views are afforded from a main road that runs over the Black Mountain to the Tywi Valley.

AMROTH, Dyfed 19 SN10
This seaside village, 6m from Tenby on Carmarthen Bay, is the beginning of the 167m Pembrokeshire Coast long-distance footpath. Remains of a submerged forest appear in the sands at very low tide. Lord Nelson visited Amroth Castle, a late 18th-c house, when he toured S Wales in 1802. Flats and maisonettes have recently been built behind the beach. Marros Sands, 1m E, is a good bass beach. The restored church houses fine monuments, and Colby Lodge – situated high in the valley – was designed by John Nash. An earthwork near Trelissey Farm marks the site of a small Roman army outpost.

ANGLE, Dyfed 18 SM80
Angle is a fishing and lifeboat village in Angle Bay, at the end of the long peninsula on the S side of the Milford Haven. About ½m W at West Angle Bay is a sand beach open to the sea, with a small natural harbour. From the

Constitution Hill funicular railway, Aberystwyth.

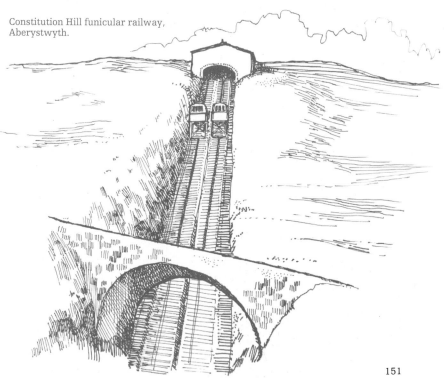

headlands that face the creeks of the haven there are good views of giant tankers moving in to tie up at oil terminals. Rhoscrowther church is dedicated under the Latin name of St Tegfan, known in Somerset as St Decuman. He is said to have sailed across the Bristol Channel to Somerset on a raft. Oil installations have changed Pwllcrochan, near Rhoscrowther, and a power station overlooks the Pwllcrochan Flats – once well known for cockles. The Globe Inn at Angle is a colonial-style building, and The Hall stands in fine gardens (NT).

ARANS, THE, Gwynedd

To the SW of Bala Lake rises a range of mountains as impressive as Cader Idris and some of the Snowdon peaks. This is the Aran group, consisting of extrusive igneous rocks similar to those of the Arennigs and other mountains surrounding the Harlech Dome. They are unusual in having long grassy W slopes rising to a high craggy ridge, overlooking glacier scoured cwms, valleys, and lakes. This boulder-strewn ridge, with rock-faces up to 1,000ft high, reaches two distinct summits. These are 2,901ft Aran Benllyn, and 1m S 2,970ft Aran Fawddwy – the highest mountain in Wales outside the Snowdon area.

Views up to the Aran mountains from their surrounding valleys are not easy to find. The best view of Aran Benllyn and its smooth W slopes is probably from Bala, where the mountain towers over the SW end of Bala Lake. It is possible to see the long precipices of the Aran peaks from Talardd, on the unclassified road from Llanuwchllyn to Dinas Mawddwy, and from the high ground on this road around the 1,790ft-high summit of the pass at Bwlch-y-Groes. There may also be glimpses of Aran Fawddwy from the area of Dinas Mawddwy and Minllyn in the Dyfi Valley. High winds sweep the summit at times, and thunderstorms building up around these mountains create 'an impressive sight as they clear the top of the ridge. The views from the Arans' summits encompass magnificent scenery in all directions.

ARENNIGS, THE, Gwynedd

Situated on the E side of the Migneint area, the Arennig mountains have three distinct summits – 2,259ft Arennig Fach, 2,800ft Arennig Fawr, and 2,461ft Moel Llyfnant. The summit of Arennig Fach gives very good views of Llyn Celyn to the E. The easiest path up to the summit of Arennig Fawr starts from a ruined farmhouse between the bridge and a quarry along an unclassified road off the A4212. On the summit is a cairn and tablet dedicated to eight American airmen whose bomber crashed on the mountain in 1943, and almost the entire Snowdon range can be seen from here.

ARTHOG, Gwynedd 9 SN61

The profusion of hydrangeas in cottage gardens testify to the climate of this region, which lies S of the Mawddach estuary. Tynycoed House is an interesting private residence with a waterfall and woodland walks, but Arthog is best known as one of the gateways to Cader Idris. Travelling along a steep and winding road, the motorist first reaches the twin lakes of Cregennen, where splended views of Cardigan Bay are offered. Cader Idris lies beyond.

ARTHUR'S STONE, West Galmorgan 24 SS49

Estimated to weigh more than 20 tons, this megalithic tomb is situated on the Cefn Bryn ridge to the NE of the Gower village of Reynoldston. Thought to date from c2500BC, the monument comprises a capstone supported on nine smaller stones. A partial split in the capstone is said to have been caused by King Arthur's mystic sword (full OS map reference SS 490 905).

BACHWEN, Gwynedd 8 SH44

Bachwen lies W of Clynnog-fawr between the A499 road and the sea, and is a prehistoric burial chamber of the type known as Portal Dolmen. It comprises a wedge-shaped capstone supported by four widely-spaced uprights. The monument had deteriorated but has been re-erected (OS map reference SH 408 496).

BAGLAN, West Glamorgan 24 SS79

Behind this old village, which today has a great deal of new housing, are the wooded slopes of 1,028ft Mynydd-y-Gaer. An iron-age fort crowns the summit. The modern church is in the decorated style, and alabaster quarried at Penarth near Cardiff was used inside. It is dedicated to St Catherine. The east window has glass by Burne-Jones, and there is a cross slab that may date from the 9thc. Ruins of an old church believed to date from Norman times are in the churchyard. St Baglan settled here in the 6thc. A Roman milestone which stood at the side of the main Swansea road between Baglan and Briton Ferry is now in the Swansea Museum.

*BALA, Gwynedd 10 SH93

Gateway to the wilder, craggier regions of Wales, Bala is in the SE corner of the Snowdonia national park. Here the breathtaking panorama of the mid-Wales mountains begins to unfold – Cader Idris, Arenig Fawr, and the twin Arans. A pretty town with a spacious tree-lined main street, Bala copes cheerfully with motorists who find it a convenient stopping place. Bala's main feature of interest is its lake, the largest natural expanse of water in Wales, running for more than 4m alongside the Dolgellau road. The lake never attains as much as 1m in width; but it is as deep as 150ft in places. Llyn Tegid is its more usual name, but it has featured as 'Pimbermere' in old travel books and 'Penpelmere' in an old charter. It is possible to travel around the lake, and road improvements in recent years have opened up several new vantage points.

In latter years Bala has burgeoned as an important inland sailing centre. Conditions when the prevailing SW winds are funnelled across the lake can provide choppy surfaces and testing sailing. The lake has also been used for long-distance swimming events. Fish in the lake include roach, perch, and trout, but it is unique as being the only home of the gwyniad, a shy fish which is rarely caught on the line and gets its name from the whiteness of its scales. Anyone who thinks the mysterious fish is just an angler's tale can be referred to the White Lion Hotel in Bala, where a fine specimen is displayed. The lake has its share of legends, including that of a drowned city, but the most interesting is that the River Dee flows through it without its waters mingling. This may be a plausible story, because in the middle of the lake a definite current courses through the placid waters.

Bala itself seems to have remained singularly untouched by the feuding which has scarred most Welsh towns. It has no castle, and all it can point out to the visitor is a grassy mound known as Tomen-y-Bala, probably the remnant of a Norman fortification. More recent history records that this grassy mound

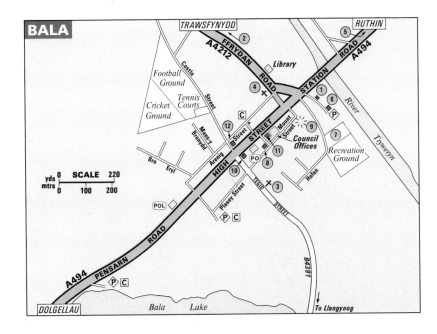

```
BALA        TRAWSFYNYDD                    RUTHIN
                                            5
                       2
              Football         Library
              Ground
         Tennis
   Cricket Courts                    1
   Ground                       6
              12                    9
                    Council
                    Offices
              11                    7
              10         Recreation
                         Ground
   yds 0   SCALE  220
   mtrs 0  100  200

   POL

   A494 PENSARN ROAD
   DOLGELLAU    Bala    Lake    To Llangynog
```

1   Bernard Barnes' Pottery
2   Calvinistic Methodist College
3   Capel Tegid
4   Eglwys Crist (19th-c parish church)
5   Llanfor Church
6   Old Bala Grammar School
7   The Green
8   The Seren Centre (craftwork)
9   Tomen-y-Bala
10 Town Hall (Georgian)
11 WTB Information Centre
12 White Lion Hotel

Entries marked * are the starting point of drives included in the Day Drive section of the book (pages 95 to 144).

was a popular resort with the women knitters of Bala on fine days. The town was famous for its knitted stockings – a cottage industry which has long since disappeared. George III insisted on wearing Bala stockings when he suffered from rheumatism. Bala's more enduring claim to fame, however, is as one of the leading centres of the Nonconformist movement in Wales. In the forefront of this breakaway movement from the established church in the latter half of the 18thc was Thomas Charles. Carmarthen born, he settled in Bala after graduating from Jesus College Oxford and spending a brief curacy in Somerset. His attraction to the new Methodism lost him his next curacy at Llanymawddwy, 14m over the mountains from Bala. Another brief curacy at Llanwddyn, and he broke completely from the state church. His statue stands near Capel Tegid in Tegid Street.

His organizing ability enabled him to set up a chain of Sunday schools, which unlike the English Sunday schools were attended by adults as well as children. This movement fired a latent desire for learning among the Welsh peasantry, and thousands of Welsh bibles were produced and distributed. The epic journey over the mountains made by Mary Jones of Llanfihangel-y-Pennant, aged sixteen, inspired Charles and some friends to found the British and Foreign Bible Society, an organization dedicated 'to providing a bible for all the people of the

world'. 'God's gift to North Wales' was the tribute paid by a colleague when Charles died in 1814.

His pioneering work was carried on, and it was his grandson David Charles who, with Dr Lewis Edwards, founded the Calvinistic Methodist College in the hills above Bala in 1837. Bala was famous at the height of the Methodist revival for its religious assemblies, and crowds of 20,000 are recorded as having attended what the Methodists call a *sasiwn* (session) at Bala Green. Charles' statue stands in front of the Calvinistic Methodist Church, but a more prominent memorial is that of Tom Ellis MP, standing in the main street. Farmer's son Tom Ellis, in a parliamentary career shortened by his death at 40, became Chief Liberal Whip.

Another celebrated figure of Bala is commemorated in a more light-hearted way. At Llanfor, about a mile outside the town, a family vault carries the inscription 'As to my latter end I go to meet my jubilee, I bless the good horse, Bendigo who built this tomb for me'. The vault is the last resting place of Lloyd Price, a somewhat eccentric squire who lived at Rhiwlas. The impressive entrance to this house stands just outside the town on the Llangollen side. Bendigo was a racehorse who romped home in the Cambridgeshire, getting Lloyd Price out of financial difficulties. Lloyd Price initiated sheepdog trials, now a

well-established country attraction. The first-ever event of this nature was held on his estate and became so popular that one was held as a regular event in London's Hyde Park.

Alongside Llyn Tegid are two interesting churches, both dedicated to Celtic saints. At Llangower on the S shore of the lake there is a two-horse bier, a ladder arrangement with shafts at either end, used for carrying a body over difficult mountain terrain. Llanycil is sometimes called the Westminster Abbey of Wales because of the distinguished Welshmen, Thomas Charles among them, who are buried there. A recent tourist attraction at Bala is the little railway which runs from Llangower and along the lakeside to Llanuwchllyn (see feature on page 62).

*BANGOR, Gwynedd   5 SH57

The visitor who comes here expecting to find an elegant university city of dreaming spires is likely to be disappointed, for old Bangor is an undistinguished maze which only redeems itself when the university buildings take over on the outskirts. To anyone brought up on the resplendent cathedrals of England the Cathedral of St Deiniol must be an anti-climax, being squat, rather dark, and heavily-embowered by trees. The cathedral's importance lies in the antiquity of its foundation, being the oldest bishopric in Britain – older even

1 Bible Garden
2 Cathedral

3 Museum of Welsh Antiquities & Art Gallery
4 Pier

5 Town Hall
6 University College

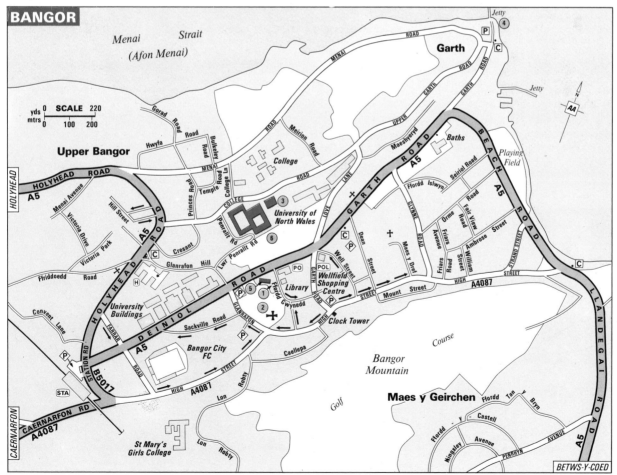

than Canterbury. Deiniol its founder came from the monastery of Bangor Isycoed, near Wrexham, in the year AD550 to form a branch of the brotherhood. Eventually Maelgwyn Gwynedd endowed the community with lands and privileges. St Dyfrig is credited with installing Deiniol as the first Bishop of Bangor 50 years before the arrival in Britain of St Augustine from Rome. The Bangor settlement became a haven of refuge for those monks of Bangor Isycoed who survived the massacre by King Aethelfrith of Northumbria. Bangor prospered for several centuries, but by 1102 the cathedral had fallen into a sad state of disrepair. Owain Glyndwr's forces inflicted a lot of damage in 1402, and rebuilding took place in the 15thc. The cathedral was considerably restored in the 1860's by Gilbert Scott. One of the more interesting phases of Bangor's history was the early 18th-c bishopric of Benjamin Hoadley, whose theology came to be known as the Bangorian Controversy. The 16th-c bishop's palace has been restored as the Town Hall.

Near the cathedral is a unique garden of bible-mentioned flowers. The University College of North Wales, one of the four constituent colleges of the Welsh University, was established at Bangor in 1884 in an old hostelry. In 1902 the corporation contributed land to form the main site of the present college. Bangor established an educational reputation for itself long before this, having had Friars Grammar School since 1557 and Bangor Normal College since 1858. There was also the Bala-Bangor Congregational College and the North Wales Baptist College. St Mary's, a teachers' training college, was moved to Bangor after its previous home in Caernarfon had been destroyed by fire. The busy streets of Bangor dip down to the shores of the Menai Straits and, surprisingly, a pier – a venerable piece of Victoriana which seems to stretch within a pebble's throw of Anglesey's wooded shore. The town's Museum of Welsh Antiquities and Art Gallery are of considerable interest.

BANGOR ISYCOED, Clwyd   *11 SJ34*
An ancient stone bridge, much battered

by present-day juggernauts, is the dominating feature of this picturesque village. Situated on the Dee as it meanders along the Welsh border towards Chester, Bangor Isycoed was once the site of college and monastery of the Celtic Church, with more than 2,400 monks accommodated here. The monastery had flourished for more than three centuries when Aethelfrith, king of Northumbria, ordered the slaughter of the monks at the Battle of Chester in 615. He had interpreted their prayers for his defeat and the triumph of their church as an act of war. The monastery was so thoroughly destroyed that no trace of it now remains. Survivors established a new monastery at Bardsey Island. Bangor Isycoed is the commonly accepted name of this village, but to racegoers it is known as Bangor-on-Dee, one of only two racecourses in Wales; Chepstow is the other. National Hunt racing takes place on several dates at a pleasant course in a loop of the Dee.

BARCLODIAD-Y-GAWRES, Gwynedd   *4 SH37*
This is a megalithic tomb (AM, OACT) on the coast near the hamlet of Trecastell in Llanwyfan parish. A cruciform passage grave, it was raised in neolithic times and has been excavated and restored. The carved stones are among the finest of their kind in Britain. (Full OS map reference SH 329 707).

BARDSEY ISLAND, Gwynedd   *8 SH12*
Best-known of the N Wales off-shore islands, Bardsey is 2m from the tip of the Lleyn Peninsula. The name, like Caldy, Ramsey, and Lundy, is Norse, but the Welsh name *Ynys Enlli* (island in the current) is more descriptive; the island is separated from the mainland by strong currents. Access is limited to bona-fide ornithologists and local people with permits. However, there is nothing apart from bad weather to prevent the curious visitor from cruising around these fascinating and historic shores for a closer inspection. Until well into this century it supported a flourishing community of farming and fishing families. The population in 1911 was 111, but today there are only two

families, plus staff manning a bird observatory which was established in 1954. Bardsey has everything to be expected of an island – a ruined monastery, scattered farmhouses, a mountain with high cliffs, a sheltered harbour, and a lighthouse.

Bardsey was colonized by the early Celts, who built the monastery, and in AD516 St Cadfan is said to have started the building of St Mary's Abbey on the N part of the island. Little remains of these buildings now, much of the material having been cannibalized for building farmsteads during the last century. Bardsey was the last remaining stronghold of the Celtic form of monasticism and remained active until the 12thc. It is often referred to as the Island of 20,000 saints, and it is apparent that numerous pilgrims and holy men ended their days here. Many bones have been dug up in the extensive churchyard, none of them of women or children. Survivors of the massacre of monks at Bangor Isycoed near Wrexham fled here. At one time the island was so celebrated that three pilgrimages to Bardsey were equal to one pilgrimage to Rome. Following the Dissolution of the monasteries in 1538 the island became infamous as a hideout for pirates preying on shipping and terrorizing mainland people.

The next phase in Bardsey's history was *c*1870, when the third Lord Newborough built farmhouses and cottages which enabled the island to be recolonized. In 1874 the earl created a king of Bardsey, crowning an islander named John Williams and swearing him 'to rule justly and righteously'. The last 'king' was Love Pritchard who 'ruled' until 1926. Visiting the National Eisteddfod at Pwllheli in 1925, he was introduced as a visitor from overseas! The tin crown and regalia are preserved at Plas Bodfuan near Pwllheli. The island community disintegrated during the last war, but the lighthouse – a square 99ft tower built in 1821 – is still operating.

*BARMOUTH, Gwynedd   *9 SH61*
Visitors who fall for the quiet charm of Barmouth are in good company, for Wordsworth and Ruskin were equally

1 Barmouth Bridge
2 Dinas Oleu (first NT property)
3 Ferry to Fairbourne Railway

4 Friar's Island
5 Old Lock-up
6 St John's Church

7 Ty Gwyn yn y Bermo (home of Henry VII when Earl of Richmond)
8 WTB Information Centre

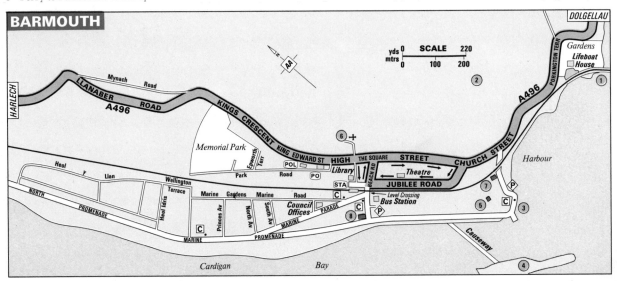

Entries marked * are the starting point of drives included in the Day Drive section of the book (pages 95 to 144).

enchanted. A popular resort offering traditional seaside attractions, Barmouth (Welsh name *Bermo*) squeezes itself between dark cliffs and the sea shore. Its lengthy and spacious promenade is one of the finest frontages along the Welsh coast. Its beach is extensive, but bathers are warned not to be too adventurous because this is the Mawddach estuary and there is a strong tidal race. A dominating feature of Barmouth is its railway bridge, spanning the wide estuary and made almost entirely of wood. A footwalk alongside the bridge gives the resort a unique kind of pier and provides a useful vantage point for admiring the incomparable and tiny Friar's Island.

The quaintness of the town becomes apparent away from the main street, up the steep alleyways, and at Panorama Walk – a well-named beauty spot. Here the NT acquired its first property, a modest four-acres of clifftop handed over by Mrs F Talbot in 1895. Aberamffra is Barmouth's harbour and was once a place of bustling activity, building a large percentage of the vessels used along the Welsh coast before the railways opened up the hinterland. Ty Gwyn yn y Bermo is a historic building on the quayside reputed to have been built for Henry Tudor, Earl of Richmond (later to become Henry VII), when he landed before the campaign that ended with his defeat of Richard III at Bosworth. It is now a coffee bar.

An old lock up for housing disorderly inhabitants and drunken seamen was divided for detaining refractory females, who apparently could be as troublesome as the males. Neither building is signposted; Barmouth is over modest about its monuments. A ferry from the quayside connects with the Fairbourne narrow-gauge railway. The 19th-c St John's Church is very large by Welsh standards.

BARRY and BARRY ISLAND, South Glamorgan *26 ST16*
Holidays and industry are neighbours in this town of 42,000 population, which lies 8m SW of Cardiff. A ½m-wide peninsula has port installations on one side and a holiday resort on the other. Massive docks were built to export coal as it poured out of the Rhondda and other valleys in the 1880's. After the decline of the coal trade in the 1930's the docks switched to cargoes ranging from bananas to oil. Big chemical industries have grown to the E of the town. At New Jerusalem Congregational Church (OACT) in Tynewydd Road are 67 panels of a mural covering 450sq ft, painted by Alan Fairhurst. They depict the development of Christianity from Genesis to the journey of St Paul. The 1,200-seat Barry Memorial Hall offers orchestral concerts, variety shows, and cabaret. Barry Island draws vast crowds in the summer. The S slope of the island has Butlin's Holiday Camp, a

5-acre pleasure park, seafront restaurants, and gardens which flank Whitmore Bay. The bay is sheltered from the sea by Nell's Point and Friar's Point. Beyond Nell's Point is the sandy and secluded Jackson's Bay, which has a large breakwater popular with anglers and yacht-race spectators. At the landward end of the island's causeway is Knap Lido, which has an open-air swimming pool 350ft long and 90ft wide – the largest in Wales; a boating lake; gardens; and the 1m Pebble Beach to the W. Near by is the 225-acre Porthkerry country park, a valley in its natural state. Through this runs an impressive railway viaduct that was built to take coal to the docks. Glamorgan (Rhoose) Airport is on Barry's W boundary.

BASINGWERK ABBEY, Clwydd *7 SJ17*
Situated near Holywell in an industrialized area of the N Wales coast, Basingwerk Abbey (AM) was founded in about 1131 for the Order of Savigny, which was amalgamated with the Cistercians in 1147. Remains of the church, cloisters, refectory, dormitory, and gatehouse are amongst the ruins, now partly obscured by the remains of a soap works.

BATTLE, Powys *21 SO03*
The name of this parish is derived from Battle in Sussex, from where the Benedictine Priory of St John in Brecon – which held the land at one time – had its

1 Cadoxton Church (13thc)
2 Castle Ruins
3 Jenner Park (sports stadium)

4 Knap Lido
5 Memorial Hall
6 New Jerusalem Congregational Church

7 Pleasure Park
8 Porthkerry Country Park
9 Zoological Gardens

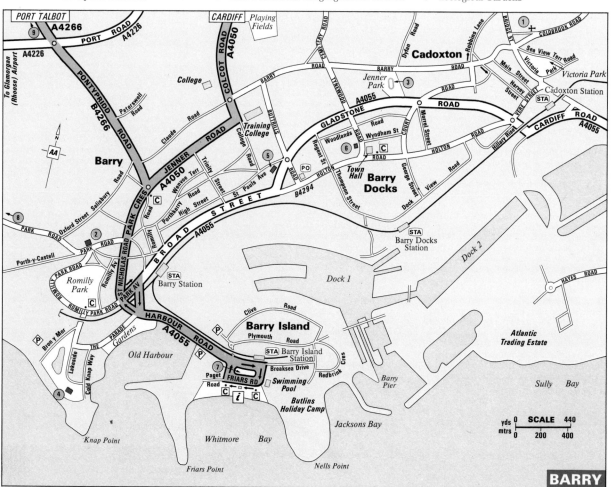

BARRY

foundation. The church in this hill parish was rebuilt in 1880, and the height of the area affords fine views.

BEAUMARIS, Gwynedd   5 SH67

This name is neither Welsh nor English, but Norman-French. Edward I, after his conquest of Wales, decided that it should be called 'Beau Marais' – meaning fair marsh. Visitors continue to be enchanted by this town on the E corner of Anglesey, and fascinated by its wealth of history. The greatest attraction is undoubtedly Beaumaris Castle (AM), one of a string of fortifications built by Edward I to maintain his hold on the Welsh. Though it lacks the towering majesty of other Edwardian castles such as Harlech or Conwy, or the massive grandeur of Caernarfon, it is regarded as an architectural masterpiece by connoisseurs (see inset opposite).

Plenty of other buildings exist in Beaumaris to interest the visitor. Opposite the castle is the unique court house where the awesome Judge Jeffries of Bloody · Assize fame is said to have presided. It is not true that the judge could lean over and shake hands with the prisoner in the dock, but it is certainly an intimate court, and one of the oldest still in use in Britain. An iron grille separates the public from the court officials, and a branding iron which was used to brand the hands of men and women convicted of theft is displayed on the flagstone floor of the court. Other trappings of medieval cruelty can be seen by arrangement with the court house guides at the County Gaol, which was built 1829. Here is a perfect example of a wooden treadmill, one of the last to be used in Britain, and high on an outer wall is the door through which condemned men stepped for execution in front of the townspeople. The last public execution was of Richard Roland for the murder of his father-in-law.

The parish Church of St Mary and St Nicholas is of 14th-c date and contains many items of interest from Llanfaes Priory, a nearby monastery disbanded by the Dissolution of 1573. These include the 13th-c stone coffin – (rescued from use as a horse watering trough) – of Princess Joan or Siwan, daughter of King John and wife of Llywelyn the Great. Finely-carved misericordes taken from Llanfaes, and a remarkable alabaster altar-tomb to Rowland Bulkeley and his wife Alice are also to be seen. Inside the porch is a watchman's hut, a relic of body-snatching vigils. The name of Bulkeley, once the island's premier family, recurs again and again in this corner of Anglesey. Opposite the Bulkeley Arms in the town's main street is a quaint hostelry called the Bull's Head. Since it was built in 1472 and rebuilt in 1617 it has sheltered many distinguished travellers, including Dr Johnson and Charles Dickens. Present-day visitors will find its collection of antiques remarkable. Farther down the street is the Tudor Rose, a well-preserved 15th-c house.

Beaumaris was one of the main points of entry for travellers who had journeyed across the Lavan Sands from Penmaenmawr, a crossing which they completed by ferry. The pier dates from the time when Beaumaris was a stopping point for pleasure steamers out of Liverpool. Victoria Terrace, a handsome row overlooking the pleasant green and the straits beyond, are attributed to

Hansom of cab fame. Visitors with time to spare will be well rewarded by a visit to Penmon Priory, 4m E.

BEAUPRE, South Glamorgan   25 ST07

Two Renaissance-style porches are features of the remains of this 16th-c Tudor manor house. The secluded ruin (AM, OACT) lies about 1m S of the village of St Hilary, near Cowbridge. One of the porches bears the Bassett arms and the Welsh motto later adopted by the Welch Regiment. The motto in English reads 'Better death than dishonour'. It is thought that buildings with origins in the 13thc occupied the site before the present structure was built. The River Thaw runs past the house through woodland.

BEDDGELERT, Gwynedd   9 SH54

Beddgelert means Gelert's Grave, but latter-day historians have thoroughly debunked the story which gave the village its name. The whole tale was a piece of fantasy woven together by an enterprising inn-keeper who wanted to put the village on the tourist map, but it is solemnly related even today in Welsh schools and rarely leaves children dry-eyed. As someone commented, 'it is too good a story not to be true'. The legend, very briefly, is that Llywelyn the Great returned from hunting to find his dog Gelert covered in blood. Llywelyn assumed that the dog had eaten his baby son, and in a rage slew Gelert. It turned out, in fact, that Gelert had killed a wolf that had attempted to savage the child. The boy was unharmed.

The innkeeper who created the legend was David Pritchard, a S Walian and first landlord of the Goat Inn. Helped by the parish clerk and a Richard Edwards, he built a cairn over the supposed grave c1790. It is still there, a pleasant 20 minutes walk along the riverside, and a point of pilgrimage for wide-eyed susceptible children. It is believed that the name of Beddgelert actually originated from a St Kelert associated with the Augustinian priory which once flourished in the area.

Today Beddgelert needs no fanciful legends to draw visitors. It stands on its own merits as probably the only genuine alpine resort in Snowdonia, completely locked in by mountains. Its solid stone architecture with hardly a discordant feature anywhere reflects the craggy · character of the region. Very little happens to disturb the even tenor of life in Beddgelert, but in September 1949 a meteorite the size of a man's fist plunged through the roof of the Prince Llywelyn Hotel into a bedroom below, only the thirteenth recorded instance of a meteorite in Britain. The parish church which stands near the confluence of the rivers Colwyn and Glaslyn is built on the site of the ancient Augustinian priory, 'The House of the Blessed Mary of Beth Kelert' which in 1286 was described by Bishop Anian as the oldest house of religion in Wales except Bardsey. The church features 13th-c arches and a triple east window.

BEGELLY, Dyfed   19 SN10

Augustus John the painter, who was born 5m S in Tenby, knew this village well. The church tower was used as a look-out point during world war two. The village lies on the A478 Tenby to Cardigan road.

BEGUILDY, Powys   14 SO17

Beguildy is a compact, tidy village which has won an award for being the best kept in old Radnorshire. Some years ago a would-be benefactor offered to donate a large sum of money towards the school if the village would revert to its correct Welsh spelling of *Bugail-dy* – the Shepherd's House – but the offer was declined.

The church has a font and priest's door of the decorated period, a Jacobean pulpit and altar, and a rood screen with fine tracery. Among its treasures are a chalice dated 1688 and a pewter flagon of 1689. The splendid nearby mansion of Bryndraenog is said to be haunted by the ghost of a woman who traditionally lost it on a game of cards. A battle fought in the 12thc beside this village is commemorated by the name 'The Bloody Field'. Uther Pendragon, the legendary father of King Arthur, is believed to have occupied a fortress near this village.

BEGWN MOUNTAINS, Powys

The Begwns are part of the mountain massif which fills the S point of old Radnorshire. They lie between Painscastle and Radnor Forest and are lonely, isolated, and wild.

BENLLECH, Gwynedd   5 SH58

A crescent-shaped bay on the N coast of Anglesey offers 2m of golden sand and safe bathing, making this the most popular seaside resort on the island.

BERRIEW, Powys   11 SJ10

A contraction of the Welsh *Aber Rhiw*, the name Berriew means the mouth of the River Rhiw. This flows into the Severn 1½m E of the village. Down a lane between the two is a large upstanding stone claimed to be a pulpit from which St Beuno, to whom the parish church is dedicated, used to preach. Berriew has more than once won the awards for the best-kept village in Wales and one-time Montgomeryshire, and it is certainly one of the most picturesque. Its many black-and-white timber-framed houses are complemented by trim flower gardens. Pretty falls on the river can be seen a few yards above the stone bridge, and an aqueduct carries the Shropshire Union Canal across the river farther downstream.

BERSHAM, Clwyd   11 SJ34

This quiet village 2m W of Wrexham has been somewhat spoiled by the town's by-pass, which spans the valley. It offers little evidence today of the prominent part it played in the Industrial Revolution. It was at Bersham that John Wilkinson, the great ironmaster, took over the furnace from his father in 1762, and made the village famous throughout the land as a centre for the manufacture of ordnance. The valley of Bersham once teemed with industrial activity, Wilkinson's cannon foundry being followed by two paper mills, but today it is a picture of rural tranquillity. On the outskirts of the village is the pretty little church of St Mary's, originally built as a private chapel to the nearby Plas Power Estate of the Fitzhugh family.

BERWYN MOUNTAINS

This range is the E member of a group of three mountain ranges – the others being Cader Idris and the Arans – which extend across N Wales with such height and dominance that the lowest pass over

cont page 158

THE UNFOUGHT CASTLE

The first glimpse of Beaumaris as one drives along the twisting road from Menai Bridge reveals a flotilla of elegant Victorian houses, giving no indication that the town, like Caernarfon and Conwy, is walled. It is not until one enters the main street that the castle becomes visible. Unlike so many in Wales, it is not perched on a limestone rock or perilously close to a cliff precipice, but stands on a vast area of flat ground, a position which accounts for its grand and spacious lay-out and for its distinction as the finest example of concentric fortification in Britain.

Beaumaris represents the culmination of Edward I's elaborate scheme to impose his own system of authority and government on a people whose proud independence he had finally shattered in 1282, when Llywelyn ap Gruffydd, the last prince of Gwynedd, was killed. Although deprived of their leader and their national status, the Welsh did not lose their morale. Their undiminished spirit expressed itself in a country-wide rebellion in 1294, during which the leader of operations in North Wales was Madog ap Llywelyn, who called himself the Prince of Wales – perhaps because he was a kinsman of Llywelyn ap Gruffydd. Whatever his claims to such a title might have been, he succeeded in taking Caernarfon and destroying the unfinished castle, the greatest symbol of the king's power in North Wales. This was a crushing blow for Edward, whose humiliations were further increased during the uprising when he found himself besieged in his own castle at Conwy. He had been chased into the safety of the building while on his way back to Gwynedd after his plans for an expedition to France had had to be revised. Madog's success however was short-lived, and when Edward regained authority his entire attention was concentrated on Anglesey. A further fortification was needed to strengthen his hold of the North Wales coast; the northern end of the Menai Strait was the answer, at a place which the King called Beaumaris, 'beautiful marsh'.

In 1295 Edward mustered yet another of his enormous labour forces, on this occasion comprising 400 skilled masons, 30 smiths and carpenters, 1,000 unskilled workers, and 200 carters to bring the limestone from Penmon, about 4m away on the easternmost tip of the island. Between them they started to carry out the design and plans of Edward's military architect, James of St George, whose inventive genius and versatility are evident in the castles of Flint, Rhuddlan, Conwy, Caernarfon, and Harlech. Each has its individual style and character, resulting from the inspired application of the principles of military defence.

It was through Edward's cousin Philip, Count of Savoy, that the English king secured the services of James of St George, a name which the architect took from the castle of St George d'Espéranche near Lyons. This was one of many that he built for the count during sixteen years as his household architect. From 1277, when Edward built Flint Castle, until his death in 1309, this architect's energy and initiative as Master of the King's Works in Wales must have been staggering, especially when it is considered that these Edwardian fortresses were not built consecutively. Aberystwyth, Builth, Flint, and Rhuddlan were all started in the same year, during the first phase of warfare between the English crown and the Welsh. Edward's victory after the second phase in 1282 precipitated the colossal programme of building Caernarfon, Conwy, and Harlech, a project which lasted until the end of the decade. 1295 saw the start of operations not only on Beaumaris, but on the rebuilding of Caernarfon. James died before either was completed, for it was not until 1330 that work at Caernarfon had finished. Although building continued at Beaumaris until the 1320's, a number of the architect's intentions were never carried out. In addition to his responsibilities in the design and building of Edward's castles, described as 'the greatest single achievement in the Middle Ages in Britain', it is possible that James supervised works at the castles of Denbigh, Ruthin, Holt, Hawarden, and Chirk.

His importance as a master mason and military engineer is obvious, not only from his considerable salary but from the fact that in 1284 he was granted a pension for life of 3 shillings a day. His wife was promised the then-considerable sum of 1s 6d a day if she survived him.

cont overleaf

Assisting him in the great undertaking were a number of experts and specialists drawn from all over Europe, each with his own responsibility for a particular aspect of the work in hand, while the vast army of quarriers, stone-cutters, masons, smiths, carpenters, plumbers and labourers, came from every county in England. Their services were secured through 'recruitment', and 300 of the 1,845 diggers employed at Flint were accompanied from Lincolnshire by mounted escort 'lest they fled on their way'. The need for such labour forces varied not only according to the intensity of the king's building programme, but to the time of year, for it seems unlikely that any substantial headway was possible in the bleakest months of a North Wales winter. Whatever seasonal working arrangements James of St George had devised, by the time the last of Edward's castles was defensible in 1298 the entire scheme had cost £80,000, of which £7,000 had been spent on Beaumaris – a very large sum in those days.

The castle's defences were linked to those of the town, for near each fortress the king created a borough which, peopled by his own administrative establishment, would further secure his safety and power. Welshmen were prohibited from living here or from having any part in the social and trading life of the 'English' community. A compensatory gesture was made by the provision of a town for those inhabitants deprived of their homes and way of life by another facet of Edward's policy of subjugation. Newborough, a small town on the south-west coast of Anglesey, reminds us to this day of the reason for its existence by its name – 'New Borough'.

Although he had applied the principles of the concentric plan with considerable success at Harlech, James of St George was limited by the demands of its high rocky site. Beaumaris offered no such problems, for it was an expanse of ground larger than that at Caerphilly, where Gilbert de Clare's gigantic fortifications of 1271 had combined with complex

water defences to make one of the most impressive castles in Europe. Taking full advantage of his own previous experience, and possibly that of de Clare's, he perfected the technique of concentric lay-out. He further explored the defensive and offensive potential of the gatehouse-keep which had played a new and important role at Harlech, by providing two such buildings at Beaumaris. Both were identical in external plan, and the Northern Gatehouse balanced the Southern Gatehouse perfectly. Another unique feature in the defenses was achieved by placing the outer gateways not immediately opposite the passages of the inner gatehouse, but on to the blank face of the inner curtain. On his peaceful entry into the castle the modern visitor is immediately struck by the ingenuity of this simple device. He is confronted with the immensity of the projections of the Southern Gatehouse, and the precarious position of the medieval attacker becomes immediately obvious: soldiers succeeding in entering the outer gateway would find themselves in a confined space, having to effect a sudden change of direction while under heavy attack from the archers on the battlements of the inner ward.

Such military and architectural inventiveness was never put to the test, for Beaumaris played a smaller part in hostilities than any of Edward's Welsh castles. Had it been completed and well maintained throughout the centuries, it would have been a show-piece of defensive design at its most sophisticated and coherent. But this was not to be. As early as 1341 a report indicating the serious extent of the rotting timbers of the castle led to a detailed inspection of the fabric. The resulting evidence confirmed that neither the roofs nor the upper storeys of the towers had been completed, and that work on the Southern Gatehouse had not been finished. Despite the fact that Lord Bulkeley of Baron Hill was reputed to have spent the then considerable sum of £3,000 on

renovation in 1660, the condition of the castle continued to deteriorate and decay very soon afterwards. It is the peculiar irony of Beaumaris that even in its present state, not greatly changed since the late 14thc, it is still a showpiece of defensive design, a monument to the extraordinary talent of James of St George.

In plan the inner ward of Beaumaris is a rectangle, with north and south gatehouses similar to the one at Harlech, drum angle-towers, and a centrally placed semi-circular tower in the east and west walls. Surrounding this is the outer ward contained by a 27ft-high octagonal curtain wall (compared with the 43ft of the inner curtain) which is reinforced by no fewer than twelve small towers and two gateways through which the visitor enters after having crossed a modern bridge on the site of the original drawbridge. On the right is the dock, essential in medieval times not only for provisions but for communication with the outside world. This was protected from the threat of the enemy by a projecting wall known as the Gunners' Walk.

The finest part of the castle is the chapel in the central tower of the east curtain. The ribs of the vaulted ceiling spring from capitals of slender columns which divide the chamber into a number of panels, each ending in gothic points and further decorated on the lower part of the wall by trefoil-headed arcading. The five panels on the east side also contain lancet windows, so that the overall design has contrived to give the chapel a feeling of extra height.

As at Conwy, Caernarfon, and Harlech, wall-walks afford excellent opportunities for appreciating the lay-out of the castle and beyond. The moat is full and is the home of swans; chestnut trees cast their shadows on the outer curtain, which in turn shelters the bowling green and the children's playground. To the south are the straits, while north lies the unchanged park of Baron Hill – an appropriately peaceful setting for a castle that knew no war.

---

them rises to over 900ft. The main part of the range lies to the W and SW of Llangollen, extending in the latter direction for about 16m before merging with the 2,000ft foothills of the Aran range N of Lake Vyrnwy.

As in so many other mountain areas, afforestation is changing the character of the range. Extensive forests have been established on the W and NW slopes – the Aberhirnant forest, the plantations above Cwm Pennant, Coed-y-Glyn, and the two sections of the Cynwyd Forest. The NE slopes above Glyndyfrdwy are disappearing beneath the Ceiriog Forest, and probably worst of all is the establishment of a plantation directly beneath the E crags of Cadair Berwyn, reaching almost to the 2,500ft contour.

Views from the two highest summits are superb. On the N side are the Denbigh Moors, partly covered by the vast Clocaenog Forest; the beautiful Vale of Clwyd; and the hills of the Clwyd range rising to 1,820ft on Moel Fammau. In the foreground stretches the Dee Valley from Bala Lake up to Corwen. To the E and SE Shropshire spreads out beyond the foot-hills. Prominent to the SE are the Long Mountain at Welshpool, the Shropshire Hills, Long Mynd, and 1,790ft Brown

Clee Hill. To the S the hills and valleys of central Wales stretch away with few outstanding features. To the SW is 2,469ft Plynlimon. Views W include Bala Lake, the Arennig peaks with Arennig Fawr rising to 2,800ft, 2,408ft Rhobell Fawr, Dduallt, and the distant Rhinog range.

BETHESDA, Gwynedd   5 SH66
Bethesda is a quarryman's village which takes its name from the Nonconformist chapel that was established here. Bethania, Carmel, Salem, and Nebo are other Gwynedd examples of this practice. Several impressive chapels exist apart from the one which gives the town its name, but Bethesda's fame rests firmly with the quarry that has been gouged out of the flanks of towering Elydir Fawr. The largest open-cast slate quarry in the world, it is 1m long, covers an area of 560 acres, and from the top of the workings to the floor is a distance of 1,200ft. The original site had been dotted with small workings, but in 1765 Richard Pennant – son of a Liverpool merchant with sugar plantations in Jamaica – entered upon the scene after marrying the heiress to the estate. When the various leases expired he started operations on a grand scale. In 1790 Abercegin was renamed Port Penrhyn and

converted into 'a commodious harbour', later served by a horse-operated tramway from the quarries 6m away.

Pennant became Lord Penrhyn, and by the time he died in 1808 he had established a substantial industry, opened up the roads, and considerably developed his estate into good agricultural land. This impetus was maintained by the cousin of Lord Penrhyn, George Hay Dawkins, who inherited the estate and added the family name of Pennant to his own. Dawkins Pennant died in 1840 and was succeeded by his son-in-law, who also added the name of Pennant and was created Baron Penrhyn in 1866. In 1873 the quarry employed about 3,500 men, but at the turn of the century the industry went into a sharp decline, faced with competition from other slate-producing countries. Workers' disputes broke out and in 1902 troops were called to Bethesda after violent scenes. Tiled roofs, flat roofs, and cheaper slates from the Continent did nothing to improve the fortunes of the slate industry. Penrhyn is now one of the few quarries still operating.

BETHLEHEM, Dyfed   20 SN62
This hamlet takes its name from its Nonconformist chapel. A Roman villa

has been excavated at Llys Brychan, about 1m E of Bethlehem.

BETTWS CEDEWAIN, Powys 14 SO19
A close-knit village with a stone bridge at its heart spanning the little River Bechan, the most interesting feature of Bettws is its 14th-c church with a typical Montgomeryshire tower of timbers and louvres. This church possesses one of the old barrel organs which were at one time used to provide music for the services. There is also a special treasure in one of the very few and rare survivals of pre-Reformation memorials, a brass depicting a priest vested for Mass and holding a chalice and wafer.

BETTWS NEWYDD, Gwent 22 SO30
The church in this hilltop village has a very good restored screen and loft, and impressive yews grow in the churchyard. Fine views are afforded from the village.

BETWS GARMON, Gwynedd 5 SH55
Betws Garmon is a pleasant village midway between Caernarfon and Beddgelert, overlooked by Mynydd Mawr. Hafodty is a local private garden open every day of the year from dawn to dusk. The walk through this pretty rock and water landscape, noted for the beauty of its azaleas and hydrangeas, passes waterfalls overhung by flowering shrubs and trees.

*BETWS-Y-COED, Gwynedd 5 SH75
Victorian artists and honeymooners found it, coach trippers popularized it, and today tourists threaten to overwhelm Betws-y-coed. The resort suffers from a surfeit of visitors in high summer, but it is still an enchanting spot where it is possible to get away from traffic and people along well-defined riverside and woodland walks. It is also a mountain resort celebrated for its waterfalls – notably the Swallow, Conwy, and Machno. Some people are affronted that access to a natural phenomenon such as the Swallow Falls is barred by a turnstile, but the experience is well worth the small charge – especially after rainfall.

With two rivers, countless roads, and a railway line squeezing themselves into the narrow valley, Betws-y-coed is also celebrated for its bridges; the ancient and well balanced Pont-y-Pair bridge; Telford's beautiful single-span construction with a wrought iron inscription recording that it was built in the year of Waterloo; a picturesque suspension bridge; and a bridge-building novelty – the sloping miner's bridge, which is more like a ship's gang plank. Just outside the town along the Lledr Valley is Gethin's Bridge railway viaduct, castellated, disused, but looking almost indestructible. The 14th-c St Mary's Church contains an effigy of Gruffydd, grandson of Dafydd, the last Welsh prince to resist Edward I. Ty Hwll, or The Ugly House, is a roadside curiosity 2m W of the resort on the A5. It is built of irregular stones and is claimed to be an example of hurried house building to obtain freehold rights on common land. It is open during the summer.

BETWS-Y-CRWYN, Powys 14 SO28
The village's early-English church stands 1,300ft above sea level and houses a notable carved-oak screen, plus a silver chalice dated 1655.

Swallow Falls at Betws-y-coed have been popular tourist attractions since the Victorian era.

BEULAH, Powys 13 SN95
Set on a sharp bend of the A483 Manchester to Milford Haven trunk road between Builth Wells and Llandovery, Beulah stands on a tributary of the Irfon called the Cammarch. It is an open village with a small plain in front and the mountains behind. A straight stretch of Roman road runs S of Beulah for 1½m and comes to an end near the banks of the Irfon. Up the valley of the Cnyffiad brook, 1m away, is the beautiful mansion of Llwyn Madog – a seat of the Bourdillon family set amidst woodlands. On the main road is the Cambrian woollen factory, where ex-service men are employed in the manufacture of tweed and other garments. Beulah has given its name to a breed of sheep (the Beulah speckle-faced) and its famous agricultural show and sheepdog trials which reach their 50th anniversary in 1976.

BISHOPSTON, West Glamorgan 24 SS58
Nearly a suburb of Swansea, Bishopston features an interesting church in the valley. This is dedicated to St Teilo and displays a Norman font. A broken stone cross can be seen in the churchyard.

BISHOPSTON VALLEY, West Glamorgan, 24 SS58
This NT property is a narrow and steep valley leading to Pwlldu Bay. The river that runs through the valley travels for much of its course below ground. Halfway down is an iron-age fort.

BLACKCLIFF AND WYNDCLIFF FOREST RESERVE, Gwent 26 ST59
Situated 2m N of Chepstow, this reserve comprises 200 acres of woodland and limestone scenery. A permit is required to walk away from the paths.

BLACK MOUNTAIN, Dyfed 20
Black Mountain is the name given to the more W of the two Black Mountains of S Wales. The other is a range between the valleys of the Wye and the Usk. Rising to 2,632ft, Carmarthen Van is the highest point of the Dyfed ridge which stretches 10m from the top of the Loughor Valley to the head of the Tawe Valley.

BLACK MOUNTAINS 22
The highest summits of this range are 2,660ft Waun Fach and 2,624ft Pen-y-

Gader-fawr, which can be seen from ridges that overlook Llanthony and Talgarth. To the N of the mountains is Hay-on-Wye, to the S Abergavenny, and to the E the Golden Valley. Llangorse Lake lies to the W.

BLAENAU FFESTINIOG, Gwynedd 9 SH74
There is little need to explain the reason for the existence of this largish town on such an inhospitable hillside – slate abounds everywhere. It has been used to build houses, pave paths, build garden walls, and even in death there is no escape from it; tombstones are often made of slate. Huge waste tips of slate threaten to engulf the town at some points. 'A town of slate and rain' it has been uncharitably called, but if there is not much scenery to enjoy there is plenty to admire in the spirit of human nature which has triumphed over climatic and geological conditions. The slate industry was responsible for the laying of the Festiniog narrow-gauge railway to Porthmadog, which grew rapidly as a slate-port. The trains were initially operated with horses, which rode at the back and hauled the empty train back up the incline. Around the workings are barracks, which housed men who travelled great distances to work the quarries and returned to their families on occasional weekends.

Despite the grim working conditions, Welsh culture flourished in Blaenau Ffestiniog. Huge Nonconformist chapels – 25 at one time and eighteen even today – also testify to the strength of religious belief which has long been a notable characteristic of the town. Slate production went into a decline at the turn of the century with the introduction of new roofing materials, and those mines that remain open operate only on a limited basis. The town's population is 6,000 – about half of what it was at the height of the slate boom. Recently, the defunct slate industry has given birth to an unlikely new industry – the tourist trade. Llechwedd Slate Caverns, an award-winning enterprise, now attracts increasing numbers of visitors who are taken on a tram ride through underground tunnels and into massive chambers where life-size models and period equipment help to recreate the atmosphere of slate mining a century ago. Visitors are also able to inspect the pillaring techniques which allowed tier upon tier of caverns to be mined.

Almost opposite the Llechwedd Slate Caverns is another tourist enterprise – the Gloddfa Canol Mountain Tourist Centre, which has opened in the world's largest slate mine. Here the visitor is invited to split a slate to 1/32in, look down the 350ft quarry hole, inspect the massive machinery, and visit an underground grotto where children will meet their fairy-tale friends. With the promised restoration of the Festiniog narrow-gauge line to its original terminus at Blaenau Ffestiniog (see feature starting page 62), the town looks like being put well and truly on the tourist map.

BLAEN-Y-PANT, Powys 13 SN79
The farmhouses and cottages of Blaen-y-pant preserve a Wales of 200 years ago. Some of the farmhouses were once mansions, and the remote and scattered community itself lies SE of Machynlleth.

BLEDDFA, Powys 14 SO26
Standing at the farthest N tip of Radnor Forest and surrounded on all sides by high mountains, Bleddfa hugs a right-angle bend of the Knighton-Penybont road and has a small village green between the church and the inn. The name means 'the abode of wolves', and these animals continued to exist in and around the forest until Tudor times, the last one being killed at Cregina on the other side of the district.

There is a very curious structure at the back of the 13th-c church, which is built into a large mound at the rear. This is a deep rectangular pit, almost the width of the building itself, lined with thick stone walls. An arch at one corner leads to a stone slipway containing a staircase, also of stone, which ascends to the top of the mound. The purpose of this structure remains a complete mystery. The church was restored earlier this century but still retains its 14th-c font and Jacobean pulpit. The inn on the other side of the triangle is the 'Hundred House', which derives its name from the fact that the manorial Hundred Court was held here. Later the Petty Sessional court sat here until it was removed to Penybont. Small pools 1m along the road towards Penybont are thought to have been fish ponds maintained for the monks of a nearby monastic establishment; 2m in the opposite direction is the imposing stone mansion of Monaughty, to which the Abbot of Abbey Cwm Hir was allowed to retire after the Dissolution.

BODELWYDDAN, Clwyd 6 SJ07
One of the best-known landmarks in N Wales is Bodelwyddan's silvery spire, 202ft high and remarkably intricate. Standing alongside the A55 3m from Rhyl, it is impossible to miss among the flat land of the Clwyd estuary. Its gleaming appearance is due to magnesium limestone which was quarried locally, but the local name 'the marble church' is an allusion to the extraordinary amount of marble – fourteen different varieties – used for the interior. The church, started in 1856, was founded, erected, and endowed by Lady Margaret Willoughby de Broke.

In the churchyard is the grave of Elizabeth Jones, mother of explorer Sir Henry

Morton Stanley. The village, school, and rectory were built at the same time as the church. The high park wall on the opposite side of the road surrounds the estate of what was Bodelwyddan Castle, now Lowther College for Girls. J A Hansom, of cab fame, was responsible for the mid 18th-c alterations which give it its castellated style.

BODFUAN, Gwynedd 8 SH33
This inland village lies in the Lleyn Peninsula halfway between Nefyn and Pwllheli. Well screened by trees is the 18th-c hall of Plas Bodfuan, seat of the Wynn family who were associated with the whole region and Bardsey Island in particular for centuries. Lord Newborough, one of the family, is buried on the island among the reputed 20,000 saints who ended their days there. It is at Plas Bodfuan that the tin crown and regalia used to invest Love Pritchard as the last 'king' of Bardsey are preserved. Bodfuan Church, a neo-Norman building of 1891, was built by the Wynn family on the site of an earlier church dedicated to St Buan. The area's association with the Wynns is very apparent inside the church, and stained glass and tablets exist in memorium to family members. Beyond Bodfuan is Bodfel Hall, a 16th-c mansion which is now a farmhouse.

BODNANT, Gwynedd 5 SH77
Indisputably the finest garden in Wales and one of the finest in Britain, Bodnant occupies a delectable terraced site on the E bank of the Conwy Valley 3m S of Llandudno Junction. Only open on certain days, it is best seen when its celebrated azaleas and rhododendrons are in bloom. The whole garden seems so mature that it is difficult to believe it has been created within the last 100 years. It was laid out by Henry Pochin in 1875, extended by his daughter, and later further extended by his grandson, the 2nd Lord Aberconway. The latter handed it over to the NT in 1949.

Apart from its cedars, cypresses, rhododendrons, azaleas, and magnolias, Bodnant is notable for its laburnum archway, a riot of yellow when in flower. Of the terraces the canal terrace is probably the most impressive, with its yew theatre at one end and the 18th-c Pin Mill at the other. The mill was rescued from Gloucester in 1938 and painstakingly re-constructed at Bodnant. The formality of the terraces gives way to the informality of the Dell, where natural features and an old flour mill have been landscaped into the general scene. The house (not open) is outclassed by this splendid garden.

BODOWYR, Gwynedd 5 SH46
A neolithic burial chamber NW of Bryn-Siencyn, Bodowyr (AM) comprises a polygonal chamber with capstone and low entrance (full OS reference SH 462 681).

BODRHYDDAN HALL, Clwyd 6 SJ07
Situated 4m SE of Rhyl, this hall (OACT) probably has its origins in the late 13thc. A wooden house on the site was rebuilt in stone in the 15thc. Much of the present building dates from the 17th and 18thc, and the hall contains portraits, armour, and a porcelain collection. An ornamental garden is also of interest.

BONTDDU, Gwynedd 9 SH61
Bontddu is a pleasant village on the Dolgellau to Barmouth road, with hospitable-looking hotels. Behind the village in the hills is gold – the same Welsh gold that has traditionally adorned several royal hands, including that of the present queen. The Romans – with their facility for finding precious metals – may have discovered gold in this region, but 1834 is the first recorded date of any find of consequence. Today's visitor would be hard-pressed to find any gold, or indeed any of the 24 mines which sprung up during Merioneth's mini-Klondyke of the last century. The two most successful were Clogau (suppliers of the royal gold) and Gwynfynydd, above Ganllwyd. Clogau in one prosperous year produced ore worth £63,000. Gold mining on any large scale stuttered to a halt in the early 1900's.

BORTH, Dyfed 12 SN68
A quiet family-holiday resort on Cardigan Bay, Borth is little more than one long main street with cottages, small shops, guest-houses, and cafés. To the S towards Aberystwyth are cliffs and reefs of rocks. Bathing here is safe, but the Dyfi estuary needs to be treated with respect as the currents are treacherous. At low tide the remains of a submerged forest can be seen in the shallow water. The parish church is of Victorian design.

BORTH-Y-GEST, Gwynedd 9 SH53
A crescent-shaped village of picture-postcard beauty, Borth-y-gest lies 1m from Porthmadog. It looks its best at high tide, when the sea reflects its neatly-painted villas. Pleasant coves for bathing are situated to the W.

BOSHERSTON, Dyfed 18 SR99
Three streams here are blocked by sandbars and form the interesting Bosherston Pools, marked as 'fishponds' on most maps. A cross dating from the 14thc can be seen in the churchyard, and below Trevallen Downs is the mainly 13th-c St Govan's Chapel. This structure is wedged into the sea cliffs and includes parts which are said to date from the 5thc. Tradition has it that nobody is able to count the chapel's cliff steps on the way up and down and arrive at the same total. A little farther along the coast is Boshersmere, where SW gales cause two blow-holes to shoot water 40ft into the air. To the W of the village is the spectacular Huntsman's Leap, so named because a huntsman made his mount jump the gap and on looking back was so horrified at the drop that he died of heart failure. Access to this, the chapel, and the bird life of Elegug Stack is restricted when a nearby tank range is in use. Firing times are displayed at Bosherston post office. St Govan's Well is said to have healing properties.

BOW STREET, Dyfed 12 SN68
Some 4m out of Aberystwyth on the Machynlleth road, this long straggling village was originally named Brisgaga and today is a clean, tidy collection of chapels, pubs, small shops, and cottages. In the early 19th-c the local squire and magistrate here called his sessions after the famous court in London, and the nick-name stuck.

BRAICH-Y-PWLL, Gwynedd 8 SH12

The farthest W point in Wales, this is popularly known as the 'Welsh Land's End'. Cliffs are backed by Mynydd Mawr, which rises to a height of 524ft, and on a clear day views of the Wicklow Hills in Ireland and the Snowdonia mountains are possible. A footpath from the coastguard lookout post leads down to the beach, where St Mary's Well served as a watering place for pilgrims on their way to Bardsey Island. Although the well is still in existence it is submerged at high tide. The church has vanished, apart from the outline of foundations which are dimly discernible amid the bracken (NT).

BRECHFA, Dyfed 20 SN53

Hidden in the Cothi Valley 9m NE of Carmarthen, this has been described as one of the most secluded villages in S Wales and has a Victorian church which was built by Lingen Baker in 1891. The surrounding landscape is thickly wooded.

*BRECON, Powys 21 SO02

Brecon is a cathedral city of great beauty and interest, set at the confluence of the rivers Usk and Honddu. Its Welsh name is Aberhonddu. The priory church of St John was made a cathedral in 1923, and is a fine structure dating from the 13th and 14thc. It was built over a Norman church that suffered during the wars for Welsh independence. The cathedral is cruciform in plan, with an early-English choir and a decorated nave. Side chapels are dedicated to various trades: tailors; weavers; tuckers; fullers; and corvizors (shoemakers). Domestic buildings of the Benedictine abbey have been restored.

Remains of the castle lie partly in the grounds of the Castle Hotel and partly in the Bishop's garden. The structure is much ruined and consists mostly of fragments from the 12th and 13thc. Brecon's townsfolk deliberately slighted the castle during the civil war to ensure that neither side would feel the need to take it. Remains of the medieval town walls can be seen in several areas, especially along Captain's Walk which was built and used by French prisoners in the Napoleonic wars. Fine Georgian and Jacobean town houses include some which have been the homes of several distinguished people. These include: Mrs Sarah Siddons, the actress; the historian Theophilus Jones; the antiquarian John Aubrey; and Hugh Price, the founder of Jesus College in Oxford. The parish church of St Mary is basically a medieval building on a Norman foundation, but the tower dates from the 16thc.

The other bank of the River Usk, which is spanned by an ancient bridge, is the site of Christ College. This was founded in 1542 and became a public school in 1860. The present building incorporates the 12th- to 14th-c remains of a friary and the early-English style college chapel. In the heart of Brecon is the beautiful Calvinistic Methodist chapel, which seats a congregation of 800. The town is the home of the South Wales Borderers, and their early 19th-c barracks include a military museum. The county museum is in Glamorgan Street. Brecon itself is a market town with a good shopping centre and excellent car-parking facilities. Ample opportunities for the sportsman include a heated swimming pool in Cerrig-cochion Road, a tennis court, bowling greens, two golf courses within easy reach, and pony-trekking and riding centres. Beautiful countryside surrounds Brecon, and the Brecon Beacons are virtually on the doorstep.

BRECON BEACONS NATIONAL PARK

Designated in 1957, this park covers an area of 519sqm and stretches in a wide band from the Black Mountain in the W to the Black Mountains in the E. An arm of the park stretches S from Abergavenny to include 1,833ft Blorenge and its associated uplands. The park is a region of mountains, moorland, and rolling pastoral countryside. Despite its proximity to the S Wales industrial region it has not been disfigured by industrial filth or development. The highest point is 2,907ft Pen-y-fan, one of the Beacons. The Beacons, after which the park was named, are so called because they were used for just that purpose. Most of the park is made up of old red sandstone, but the W and S borders include limestones and millstone grit. The old-red sandstone region includes the Beacons, the Black Mountains, and in the SE the 1,955ft Sugar Loaf and Blorenge. The Carmarthenshire Black Mountain is made up mostly of millstone grit, with limestone and old-red sandstone on its NW flank.

The limestone belt running from W to E in the S half of the park is of great interest. The action of water on this relatively soft rock has created a fantastic series of cave systems. Most of the caves in the area should only be tackled by experts, or under supervision and with the correct equipment; but at Craig-y-nos is another cave system which can be visited by anybody. These are the Dany-yr-ogof caves (see entry). On a limestone cliff at the SW of the park stands Carreg Cennen Castle, overlooking a sheer drop with the river running below and affording superb views of the surrounding countryside and the Black Mountain. It is an ideal place to reflect on the grandeur that nature, and sometimes man, can produce.

There is much evidence of glacial action in the park, including piles of debris called moraines left by melting ice, and cwms or corries gouged out of the living rocks by the glaciers them-selves. These cwms, often filled with water, are among the most distinctive features of the range. The appearance of the Black Mountain and Beacon peaks can be generalized as gently rising S faces and steep N drops, often falling as much as 600ft. Nearly 10,000 acres of the Beacons belong to the NT, including the three highest peaks: Pen-y-fan, 2,868ft Carn Du, and 2,608ft Cribyn. Theophilus Jones, a local 19th-c historian, comments on the views in his *History of Brecknockshire*: 'From the centre beacon we command a view of the Bristol Channel from the Mumble-head to King's road with parts of thirteen or fourteen counties'. Although the park has not been much affected by industry,

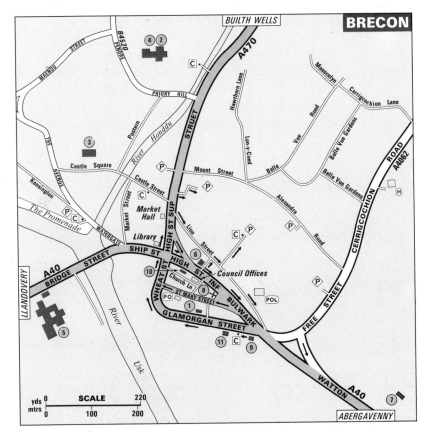

1 Brecknock County Museum
2 Canonry (part of Benedictine abbey)
3 Castle Ruins
4 Cathedral
5 Christ College
6 Guildhall
7 Museum of South Wales Borderers, & Monmouthshire Regiment
8 St Mary's Church
9 Shire Hall
10 Siddons Arms (Sarah Siddons' birthplace)
11 WTB Information Centre

Entries marked * are the starting point of drives included in the Day Drive section of the book (pages 95 to 144).

agriculture has greatly altered its natural appearance. Grazing animals have wrought the biggest changes. Much of the area was once covered in indiginous forests, but these were largely cleared for sheep, who further contributed to the damage by eating seedlings and preventing natural tree renewal. Woodlands were also destroyed for building, industry etc, and the original forests now survive only in small isolated pockets.

The Forestry Commission has eleven forests within, or partly within, the park – a total of 25,000 acres planted mostly with conifers. Many of the large stretches of open water in the park are artificially-created reservoirs serving industrial S Wales. Llangorse Lake, the second largest natural lake in Wales, is of great interest to naturalists and lies E of Brecon. About 200 species of birds have been recorded in the park, and of these about 100 kinds breed in the area.

The highland area is thinly-populated, unenclosed common pasture. Lower down the slopes are the hill farms and hamlets, and in the valleys are arable farms and centres of population. The largest area of common ground is Fforest Fawr (Great Forest), which covered 40,000 acres of land up to 1819. Most of this was used for grazing. In 1819 the forest was enclosed, and some 8,000 acres of the best valley land were sold to pay for the enclosure. It extends from the Black Mountain to the Beacons, and the term forest is here, as elsewhere, deceptive. Although the valley slopes were once densely wooded this area has not been continuous woodland since prehistoric times. The Brecon Beacons national park is one of the best pony-trekking and walking areas in Wales, but much of the scenery is inaccessible by car – which means that only those who truly love natural beauty will take the time and small effort involved to reach the more obscure places. For those who like to enjoy a more leisurely look at the countryside there are boats which can be taken on the Monmouthshire and Brecon Canal, which runs from Brecon to Pontypool.

Many delightful villages and historic places in the park include Llanthony Priory in its beautiful valley; Partrishow church with its priceless rood screen; the city of Brecon – the list is almost endless. A mountain centre is situated at Libanus, off the A470 to the SW of Brecon. All visitors to the park must realize that it does not belong to the public and is a working environment. Because an area is designated a national park does not mean there is unlimited public right of way. Always remember to follow the country code.

BREIDEN HILLS, Powys *11 SJ21*
This series of whaleback hills, with its two tall peaks of the Breidden and Golfa Hill facing the Severn Valley, form the central gateway to Wales and stand as an impressive landmark which can be seen from a considerable distance on the English side of the border. There is the site of a hill fortress here, and some authorities claim that the Breidden was the site of the last stand of Caractacus against the Romans under Ostorius. Several 3rd- and 4th-c potsherds have been discovered here, plus one from the early iron age, and several Constantine coins. A monument on the Briedden commemorates Admiral Rodney, and on the Golfa is a smaller obelisk to a gypsy member of the Burton family.

The Rodney pillar was set up in 1781, ten years before the Admiral died, by subscription of the gentlemen of Montgomeryshire and Shropshire in gratitude for his use of local oak for building naval vessels. It had to be repaired in 1847 and again in 1896. It was in such a bad state that Archdeacon Thomas said it was always his first concern after a bad storm to see whether it was still standing. At one time a local literary society used to hold its meetings on the Breidden. They would elect a Bard Ferniate, who was crowned with a wreath of ferns by an elected Lady of the Hill. The moving spirit of this society was J M Dovaston, who was a remarkable man with a great interest in literary and scientific subjects.

BRIDGEND, Mid Glamorgan *25 SS97*
Situated at the W end of the Vale of Glamorgan, this busy town has four Norman castles and several bays within easy reach. It straddles the Ogmore River, with the mainly-industrial Ogmore, Garw, and Llynfi Valleys to the N and two trading estates on the main road out to Llantrisant. The 12th-c ruins of Coity Castle (AM) are 2m NE off the A4061. Newcastle (AM) gateway and curtain wall are near the square-towered church on a wooded hill above the river. Though called Newcastle its beginnings are obscure. It was certainly in existence in 1262 however, as it is mentioned in a document from that time. The church of Newcastle was here in 1106.

Ogmore Castle (AM) is a 12th-c stone keep 2m S on the B4524 in quiet, pleasant country. Ancient stepping-stones cross a river near by. Candleston Castle, a 15th-c mansion now in ruins, is at the farthest point of the road that runs through Merthyr Mawr 1m SW near sand dunes. This is an excellent place to explore the 200ft wind-blown dunes of Merthyr Mawr Warren, a bronze- and iron-age site. La Tene period brooches are occasionally found when the winds strip off the sand covering. Merthyr Mawr is a thatch-roofed village considered one of the prettiest in S Wales. Ewenny Priory and pottery lies 2m S.

BRITANNIA RAIL BRIDGE, Gwynedd *5 SH57*
In planning the railway bridge linking Anglesey with the mainland, Robert Stephenson the railway pioneer had the same problems experienced by Telford 20 years earlier when spanning the Menai Strait with a road bridge. A 100ft clearance for shipping was again demanded by the Admiralty. Stephenson overcame the problem with cast-iron tubes supported by piers which, like Telford's bridge piers, show an Egyptian influence. The positioning of the tubes provided a great festive spectacle as they were floated into mid stream by barge, and hoisted aloft by hydraulic pumps. The bridge was completed in 1850 at a cost of eighteen lives.

The original tubes are alas no more. In 1970 two boys searching for bats with a lighted flare along the maintenance catwalk accidentally set fire to the roof. The famous structure was soon ablaze from end to end, the leaping flames and cascading sparks providing a gigantic display of pyrotechnics. In the cold light of dawn close inspection showed that the bridge had been destroyed beyond immediate repair. The tubes were hopelessly distorted, and only the stone piers had survived the inferno. Rail traffic was dislocated for three years but is now rolling again, although not through tubes. They were replaced with an open deck supported by steel arches. The Britannia is now being adapted for use by a road 30ft above the railway line.

Stephenson's Britannia Rail Bridge over the Menai Strait was partly destroyed by fire, and is now being used as a base for a new road bridge.

BRITHDIR, Gwynedd *9 SH71*
Brithdir is a pretty village of stone-built cottages 2m E of Dolgellau. St Mark's Church was built in 1896 in memory of Charles Tooth, chaplain of the Anglican Church of St Mark in Florence. The church is constructed of local granite and slate in a cruciform plan. The interior is dimly lit by natural light

which series to emphasize the glow of the beaten copper fronts of the altar, the reredos, and the pulpit. The altar depicts the Annunciation. The leaden font came from the Central School of Design in London. Other features of interest around the village are the celebrated Torrent Walk, the prehistoric camp of Tyddynllwyn Dolysbyty, and the site of a hospice of the Knights of St John. Tyddynygarreg Farm is licensed for Quaker weddings and recalls the strong Quaker influence that once existed in this area.

The Bryn celli ddu passage grave is one of the finest existing in England and Wales.

BROAD HAVEN, Dyfed 18 SM81
Broad Haven and its neighbour Little Haven provide a fine silver strand on St Bride's Bay, bordered by dramatically folded cliffs. This is a remote, beautiful area, with wild flowers, sea birds, and magnificent coastal scenery. The Pembrokeshire Countryside Unit, opened in 1970 in the car park, is the focal point for a range of interesting tours and lectures designed to give a deeper appreciation of the local coast and countryside. Visitors are advised to confirm by telephone that the unit is open at weekends.

BRONANT, Dyfed 12 SN66
Midway between Llanilar and Tregaron on a straight stretch of the A485 which is part of the Sarn Helen Roman road, Bronant stands in a bare and stony district under the Mynydd Bach, with its three chalybeate springs. Nearby Llyn Eidwen is a favourite resort of anglers. This district was noted in the past for its revivalist meetings to which people flocked in multitudes. The enthusiasm is over now, but there are still well-attended anniversary meetings in the local chapels. Bronant church is of Norman origin and has a detached tower. The ruined Norman castle is remarkably small for a fortress.

BRONLLYS, Powys 22 SO13
The local church has a detached tower. In times of trouble women and children were sent to the upper floor, while the cattle were kept safely in the lower part. Entry to 12th-c and later Bronllys Castle (AM) is 1½m S on the A479 Talgarth to Bronllys road. Admission is free.

BRYN BRAS CASTLE, Gwynedd 5 SH56
Situated 4½m E of Caernarfon, this 19th-c castle is more properly called a mansion. The later work was built around a structure dating from pre 1750. It is open from April to October, and is well known for its extensive gardens and fine views of Snowdonia.

BRYN CELLI DDU, Gwynedd 5 SH57
A passage grave situated near Llandanian Fab, this famous tomb (AM) is almost the only example of its type in England and Wales. It basically comprises a long passage leading to a polygonal chamber, and an artificially smoothed pillar stone inside the chamber is thought to be a phallic representation. The covering mound, with its border of kerb stones, probably overlies a henge-type monument. A monolith incised with spirals and wavy lines which now stands at the tomb entrance was found lying prone above a pit containing burnt bones. Now in the care of the Department of the Environment, the tomb has been thoroughly excavated and restored (full OS reference SH 508 702).

BRYNCIR, Gwynedd 9 SH44
This hamlet lies in the Afon Dyfach valley at the beginning of the Lleyn Peninsula. A little to the NE at Llystyngwyn farm is an early-Christian tombstone, probably of the 6thc, bearing inscriptions in Ogham and Latin (full OS reference SH 482 445). A woollen-mill at Bryncir sells good-quality weaving. Various Roman remains have been discovered in the vicinity.

BRYNGWYN, Powys 20 SN14
This village lies on a side road halfway between Newchurch and Painscastle in the Kilvert countryside, 1,160ft above sea level. The church, originally built in the 13thc, has medieval roofs and windows. One of the most interesting features of the area is Rhos Goch (the Red Moor), a peat bog with a 15ft-deep layer of peat overlaying a layer of blue clay and another layer of yellow clay. The latter contains ancient sea shells which crumble when touched, and the whole area is rich in other fossils.

BRYNMAWR, Powys 22 SO11
During the great depression the people of this small Ebbw Vale town formed a committee to ensure that their community survived. They encouraged light industries such as furniture making, weaving, and the construction of boats to preserve and continue employment.

BRYN YR HEN BOBL, Gwynedd 5 SH56
Situated in Llanedwen near the mansion of Plas Newydd, this megalithic tomb comprises a kidney-shaped mound which contains a rectangular chamber. At the entrance to the chamber is a slab with two semicircular depressions carved out of it. Excavations of the tomb have yielded pottery of the new-stone age (full OS reference SH 519 690).

BUCKLEY, Clwyd 7 SJ26
A close-knit community 3m E of Mold, Buckley was once celebrated for coarse pottery which was the basis for a flourishing and localized industry. Today the local clay is used for the production of bricks, particularly for the

nearby Shotton Steelworks. The parish Church of St Matthew is the 19th-c and 20th-c re-building in pink sandstone of a structure originally raised in 1821. Its internal appearance is light and spacious, and the clock is by Lord Grimthorpe – who also designed Big Ben.

BUGEILYN LAKE, Powys 13 SN89
In order to reach this long narrow lake in the N foothills of the Plynlimon range it is necessary to take the mountain road from Dylife to Machynlleth, and then turn left along a track beside the Glaslyn or Blue Lake – which is on private land. Before reaching Bugeilyn the route passes an old farmhouse, the last to be inhabited on these lonely moors which were once the scene of mining operations with 1,000 miners living at Dylife. Not a wall of the mining cottages now remains. This countryside belongs to the grazing sheep, the buzzards, the merlins, and the foxes. Excavations carried out in a burial mound near Bugeilyn Farm just before the last war revealed a bronze-age urn, while a collection of flint arrowheads was discovered under the peat surface near the lake. The peat bogs and several precipitous drops make it imperative for the walker to keep to the tracks.

*BUILTH WELLS, Powys 13 SO05
Builth's main shopping highway changes its name half way along. One part is Broad Street and the other High Street, but they form one thoroughfare which winds and sways through the heart of the town. Between this street and the River Wye is the Groe, a riverside park with games pitches, and at the far end is a picturesque little footbridge which leads out to a side road by the golf course. This pleasant short walk follows the river all the way. Close to the main entrance to the Groe is a very fine grey-stone chapel, with an inscribed and dated scroll painted above the entrance door. This is the Alpha Chapel, and the wording on the scroll reads '1747 Alpha Presbyterian Church of Wales 1903'. In the centre of the scroll is an open book bearing the words 'Ye must be born again'. The parish church was rebuilt in 1793 after a fire had ravaged the town,

and was again reconstructed to a gothic interior design during last century.

The Welsh name for the town is *Llanfair yn Muallt* – St Mary's in Builth – and it originated as a settlement around a Norman castle of which nothing is now left except a mound behind the Lion Hotel. The first reference to the castle relates to the marriage of Maud FitzWalter to Philip de Breos, Lord of Builth, who conquered the local territory. Edward I used the castle to control the Welsh, who made their last stand for independence here in 1282 when Llywelyn the Last passed through the town and was killed at Cilmery on the Llandovery road. Builth rose to popularity in the 18thc when spas became popular. It had two sources – the Park Wells and the Glanau Wells. Neither is now in use.

BULL BAY, Gwynedd 4 SH49
Next door to Amlwch on the north coast of Anglesey, Bull Bay (Porth Llechog) is growing in popularity with holidaymakers. The beach and its sheltered rocky coves are the main attraction. The bay once shared in the ship-building boom, and the resort was also a pilot station with four-oared sailing pilot boats.

BURRY PORT and PEMBREY, Dyfed 20 SN40
These twin towns lie about 6m W of Llanelli on the coast of Carmarthen Bay. Burry Port once exported coal but is now used mainly for yachting. To the W are the Ashburnham golf links and the 5m sand-duned burrows, partly covered by the Tywyn Burrows Forest. In 1928 'Friendship', the first seaplane to cross the Atlantic, landed in the Burry Inlet piloted by Miss Amelia Earhart. A power station has been built at Burry Port. Pembrey has a 13th-c church. In the churchyard is a memorial to the passengers and crew of the French ship 'Jeanne Emma', which was wrecked on the 5m Cefn Sidan sands. This is a good fishing coast.

BWLCH, Powys 22 SO12
A small village affording beautiful views as the A40 climbs up to it from Abergavenny to Brecon, Bwlch lies 4m SE of Llangorse Lake. Views of the Brecon Beacons open up to the S after Bwlch, and the village itself lies in the Brecon Beacons national park. All that remains of Blaen Llyaft Castle, to the NW, are a ditch, parts of the curtain wall, and a ruined tower.

CADER IDRIS, Gwynedd 9 SH71
After Snowdon Cader Idris is probably the best-known mountain in Wales. In fact it is more than just a mountain; like the Berwyns its foothills are far-reaching, and the range is one of the three in the chain which extends across N Wales. The others are the Arans and the Berwyns. The main summit of the Cader Idris range is 2,927ft Penygadair.

There are several versions as to the origin of the mountain's name. As Idris is roughly the equivalent of Arthur in English, it has been suggested that Cader Idris had some connections with King Arthur. Others say that Idris was a descendant of the Celtic chief Cunedda, killed in battle on the banks of the Severn cAD630. To explain the 'chair' part, Idris was popularly held to be a giant, said to have been a poet, philosopher, and astronomer, who used

to sit in the cwm on the N side of the mountain watching the stars. There was also the legend that anyone spending a night on the mountain would wake up blind, mad, or a bard! This did not deter parties of daring young men, who at the beginning of the 19thc climbed the mountain by moonlight in order to see the sun rise the following morning. This was also true of Snowdon, which was climbed by Wordsworth in 1791. Whilst an extremely hazardous occupation, it does not seem to have brought about the results predicted.

The views from the summit of Cader Idris are very fine, possibly even better than those from Snowdon. The distant panorama takes in a vast area but can be affected by climatic conditions – such as valley mist or heat haze – and the direction of sunlight according to the time of day. The clearest conditions are most likely to occur in winter. On fine days it is said to be possible to see the snow-capped top of Snaefell in the Isle of Man, and the mountains along the Irish coast.

CAEO, Dyfed 20 SN63
Sometimes spelt 'Caio', this village is tucked away near Pumsaint in the Cothi Valley. The church carries a 13th-c tower and has been restored. It is thought that there was probably a Roman settlement of some kind here; later on nine archers were sent from Caeo to fight at Agincourt. Some land in the vicinity is NT protected. Four Welsh writers who came from this little village include Joshua Thomas, who wrote *History of the Welsh Baptists* in the 18thc, and a 15th-c poet.

CAER DREWYN, Clwyd 10 SJ04
This major iron-age hillfort is situated about 1m from Corwen, and measures approximately ½m in circumference. It is protected by massive walls, and the foundations of circular dwellings have been discovered in the NE sector. The site was defended by Owain Prince of Gwynedd during a 12th-c battle against Henry II of England.

CAER GAI, Gwynedd 10 SH83
Caer Gai is the site of a Roman fort and settlement situated between the village of Llanuwchllyn and Bala Lake. A manor house of 17th-c origin is now sited within the ditches of the fort. This is a good starting point from which to tour the Arennigs.

CAERGWRLE, Clwyd 7 SJ35
Midway between Wrexham and Mold, Caergwrle enjoyed a short spell of popularity during the railway boom, when Merseyside trippers made it a mecca for day outings. The station was in those days called Caergwrle Castle and Wells. The castle, on a prominent site, is believed to have been of 13th-c origin, but is now nothing more than a heap of masonry. Bryn Yorkin, an attractive 17th-c farmhouse, can be seen on the route to Hope Mountain. A bronze-age bowl found at Caergwrle in 1283 is now displayed at the National Museum in Cardiff.

CAERHUN, Gwynedd 5 SH77
Situated on the W bank of the Conwy Valley, Caerhun is the site of the old Roman Station of *Canovium*. Excavations have brought to light the foundations of a Roman building and a good deal of pottery. Caerhun church, much of which is of 13th-c origin, lies within the remains of the Roman station.

CAERLEON, Gwent 26 ST39
Associations with the Romans and King Arthur make this small town, 4m up the Usk from Newport, one of the most historic in Wales. It was *Isca Silurum*, chief fortress of the Second Augustan Legion, from AD75 to the 4thc BC. The fort measures 540yd by 450yd and held about 6,000 foot soldiers and horsemen. It included barracks, baths, shops, and temples. In AD80 an amphitheatre was added, 267ft long and with a 6,000 seating capacity.

Before excavation the amphitheatre was known as King Arthur's Round Table, a legend perpetuated by Geoffrey of Monmouth, author of *History of the Kings of Britain* in the first half of the 12thc. Tennyson stayed at the Hanbury Arms, which lies on the river bank near an arched bridge over the Usk, while doing research for his *Idylls of the King*. The amphitheatre (AM) can still be seen. In the Prysg field, some 300yd NW of the church, is the excavated foundation work of barrack blocks. The town centre is where the legionary commander's building would have been, and is now occupied by the Legionary Museum – part of the National Museum of Wales. The church is dedicated to a 6th-c Welsh saint Cattwg (Cadoc), and was considerably restored in 1867. Arthur Machen the author was born here in 1863.

*CAERNARFON, Gwynedd 5 SH46
Plan on page 166
Site of the most visited castle (AM) in Wales and one of Britain's leading tourist attractions, Caernarfon receives an attendance boost from every investiture. The last one was in 1969 when Prince Charles was invested Prince of Wales, since when all previous records have been excelled. Even without its royal associations the castle would stand in its own right as a major tourist magnet. It is arguably the finest in Britain (see inset opposite).

There was a settlement probably on Twthill, an earthwork E of the town, long before the Romans established themselves as military overlords of this region with the fortress of Segontium (see inset on page 276). The site on the outskirts of Caernarfon is bisected by the A487 road to Beddgelert. The S area of the fort is occupied by Llanbeblig Vicarage, and there is a small reservoir and some houses on the N part of the site. The remaining 4 acres are in the care of the NT. An excellent museum displays finds made during excavation. The fort was the farthest W outpost of the Roman Empire, and was sited here at the end of the great Roman road, Watling Street, which began in London. Among the remains of buildings which can still be identified are the barrack blocks, the *principia* or chief administrative building with its strongroom below ground, and the commandant's house. It would have housed about 1,000 soldiers, with the usual attendants and families billeted near by. The fort was first established between AD70 and 80, during Agricola's campaign, and was built originally of earth and timber. In about AD150 it was rebuilt in stone. A feature of the castle is the regimental museum of the Royal Welch Fusiliers.

Caernarfon itself is a workaday town overshadowed by its historic past. The town could not possibly live up to the majestic stature of its castle, but it is not as commonplace as it looks and

Entries marked * are the starting point of drives included in the Day Drive section of the book (pages 95 to 144).

repays exploration. The county hall, oddly sited in a narrow street opposite the northern gate of the castle, is a reminder that Caernarfon was the county town of old Caernarfonshire and is indeed administrative centre of the new region of Gwynedd. The county hall, with its figure of Justice perched on the pediment, would have made a more gracious adornment to the town square than some of the nondescript commercial premises which now overlook it. Occupying a prominent site opposite the castle balcony where the newly-invested Prince of Wales is traditionally presented to the people of Wales, is the gesticulating statue of Lloyd George, Prime Minister and Caernarfon MP for more than 50 years. Another statue commemorates the social reformer Sir Hugh Owen (1804–1881). St Mary's Church dates from the 14thc and huddles in an angle of the old town walls.

ROYAL CAERNARFON

Two hundred years ago, when he visited Caernarfon with his Welsh friend Mrs Thrale, Dr Johnson's reaction to the castle was one of astonishment: 'I did not think there had been such buildings. It surpassed my ideas.' It has probably provoked more comment since then than any Welsh castle, and during the last 60 years or so in particular it has played a very public part in the life of the country. There have been only two royal investitures – 1911 and 1969 – and both occasions have granted the two spacious wards and the splendid

*CAERPHILLY, Mid Glamorgan 26 ST18

Caerphilly is renowned for its cheese and its castle. The cheese-making has largely disappeared from the town, but the castle (AM) remains with all grace and dignity as the second largest in Britain after Windsor. The Romans built a fort at Caerphilly cAD75 about 200yd NW of the present castle. Gilbert de Clare, Lord of Glamorgan, started building the castle in 1268. In 1270 the partly-built structure was destroyed by Llywelyn ap Gruffydd, Prince of Wales, but work was started again on it the next year. Over £100,000 has been spent on restoring the castle's Great Hall and repairing the wear of centuries. With its land and water defences, the castle covers 30 acres. The best view of the town itself is from Caerphilly Common, an 800ft ridge which separates the Caerphilly area from the low land on which Cardiff lies 7m S (see inset on page 167).

towers a social dominance and prestige denied to other castles. Yet this is consistent with Edward I's plans and proposals when he embarked on his ambitious and essential building programme in 1283, the year following the death of Llywelyn ap Gruffydd. If its principal function was to subjugate the Welsh, the castle with its walled town was also a chief centre of administrative authority. It symbolized, through its show of splendour as much as by its strength and strategic position, the firmness of the new master's imperial grip.

But Edward miscalculated his strength and misjudged the temper and temperament of the defeated Welsh. In 1294 a revolt led by Madog ap Llywelyn resulted in the destruction of the town walls and the burning down of the wooden castle. Within a year the work

CAERSWS, Powys 13 SO09

Rivers Trannon and Cerist join the Severn in a wide shallow saucer among mountains, and it was here that the large village of Caersws grew up as the successor to a Roman settlement of 1,500 years ago. It derives its name from a legendary Queen Susan, who had her administrative centre here and married the prince who defeated her forces in battle. Caersws is laid out on the gridiron pattern, and although all its streets have names none bears a name plate. It has been a railway centre which employed a large number of railwaymen. A famous bard, John Ceiriog Hughes – whose bardic name was Ceiriog – was manager of the Van Railway which had its terminus here. A memorial plaque has been placed on his house, which lies just beyond the level crossing on the Trefeglwys road. Very little of the Roman station has been discovered, but

of rebuilding had begun, and the next 35 years were spent in securing greater safety and splendour.

Apart from two unsuccessful attempts by Owain Glyndwr to take it in 1403 and 1404, the castle's military history is sparse and the accession of Henry Richmond to the throne in 1485 completely obliterated the need for organized defence. Majestic as Caernarfon had been, it suffered a sustained attack from neglect and decay until orders were given for the demolition of the entire fabric in 1660. These were not carried out and until the last century, when repair and restoration was begun. Both the outline and the setting inspired a range of artistic interpretation of a subject which Thomas Pennant described – with 18th-c detachment – as 'the most magnificent badge of our subjection.' Even if visitors are not convinced that the Eagle Tower was the birthplace of the future Edward II in 1284, they will appreciate why such masonry inspires legend.

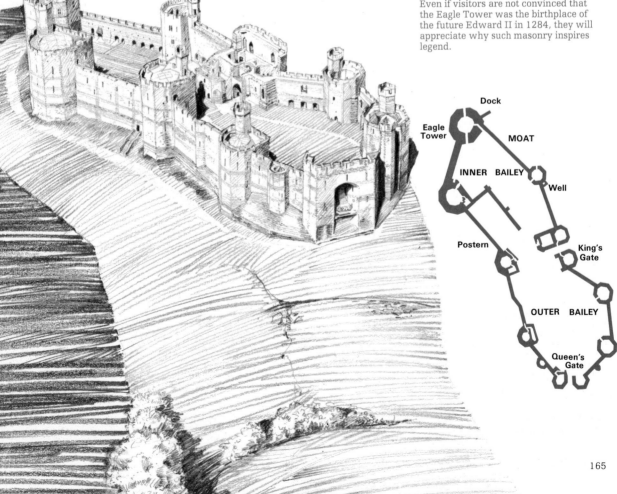

there are traces of an encampment covering 7 acres. Coins from the reigns of Vespasian and Domitian have been found in the area.

CAERWENT, Gwent 26 ST49
Here, under peaceful fields and old cottages, lie the remains of *Venta Silurum*, once a town of some 3,000 people. The Romans built *Venta* to show the natives (the *Silures*) just what the Roman way of life was like. Some of the normally belligerent Silures obviously liked what they saw, for they moved down from their hill-top fort of Llanenellin and settled into life in a Roman city. The wall (AM) surrounding the city still stands for much of its length, and is most impressive in the S where it is over 15ft high in places. This S wall was strengthened with bastions as a defence against raiders coming from the sea in the 4thc. The town of Caerwent stands within the Roman walls, and the main street marks the approximate line of the Roman central avenue. Caerwent church contains several reminders of the Roman past in its porch, and displays an interesting mosaic from the occupation.

A church was founded in Caerwent as early as the 5thc, probably by St Tathan. The present church dates from the 13thc and contains a tomb reputed to hold the bones of St Tathan. Another feature of the church is a finely carved pulpit of 1632.

CAERWYS, Clwyd 6 SJ17
A proud little place, Caerwys is currently trying to substantiate its claim as the smallest town in Britain – local government reorganization in 1974 having restored it to town status with its own mayor. Caerwys was granted its first borough charter in 1290 and remained a municipal borough until 1886. After the disenfranchisement, along with all the other boroughs under the Reform Bill, it had to accept parish status. Caerwys has several other claims to fame. In 1568 it was the site of a memorable eisteddfod when Queen Elizabeth commissioned all those with bardic aspirations to present themselves to be judged, graded, and licensed. It was the means of separating the true bards from the vagrants who were at that time plaguing Wales. This historic eisteddfod

was colourfully re-enacted on the 400th anniversary in 1968, when Princess Margaret opened proceedings.

The Welsh princes had a Court House at Caerwys, and the tomb of the widow of Prince Dafydd (executed in 1282) is incorporated in the chancel wall of the church. Caerwys was an important market town at the time of the Edwardian conquest, which probably explains why – when it was created a borough in 1290 – the freedom was given to the indigenous population. In other Welsh boroughs such as Flint, Conwy, Caernarfon, and Rhuddlan it was limited to Norman settlers. The remains of one wall of what is believed to have been Prince Dafydd's Court still stand in the garden of the Old Court House. A new house was built in front of the old remains c1480, and though altered externally c1800 is probably the oldest lived-in dwelling in Wales. The church is dedicated to St Michael and has some fine features. The remains of an ancient rood screen are incorporated in the panelling. The altar table and font are 17thc, and there

cont page 168

1 Castle
2 Llanbeblig Church
3 Royal Welch Fusiliers Regimental Museum (castle)

4 St Mary's Church
5 Segontium (Roman fort and museum)
6 Town Walls
7 Twthill (prehistoric site)

8 WTB Information Centre

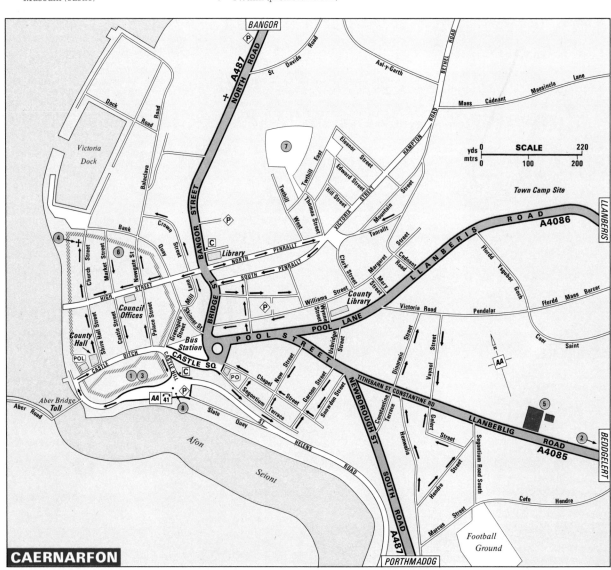

CAERNARFON

CASTLE OF INTRIGUE

Earlier this century the 4th Marquis of Bute ordered the demolition of a street of houses which had previously masked the view of one of the most remarkable features of British military architecture, the Eastern Front of Caerphilly Castle. The 320-yard long curtain is complete with towers and buttresses and includes a centrally-placed gatehouse and a postern gate at each end. It is remarkable, not only because of its impressive size, but because it governs an arrangement of water defences which are as intricate and daunting as the two wards which constitute the concentric plan of this stronghold. The castle stands on an island surrounded by two lakes and an inner and outer moat, the latter spanned by a double drawbridge. This system befits the second largest castle in Britain. but the extent can be more easily appreciated when it is realised that not only is it twice the size of the Tower of London with its outer walls, but that Edward I's castles at Beaumaris, Caernarfon, Conwy, Harlech, and Rhuddlan could all be contained within its 30 acres. Yet it is not an Edwardian fortress, nor even royal, but a great baronial fortification built by Gilbert de Clare, Earl of Gloucester and Lord of Glamorgan – an outstanding example of the concentric plan which predates Edward's by a good 20 years.

In 1268, two years after defeating Gruffydd ap Rhys, the ruler of the district Gilbert de Clare began to work on the castle to consolidate his hold over the Welsh. However, Llywelyn ap Gruffydd's attack on the area resulted in the destruction of the unfinished building. In 1271 work was begun on the existing fortress which, like a number of the great castles of Wales, proved so invulnerable that the little military history attached to it is undistinguished. Nevertheless, Caerphilly played its part in royal intrigue during the reign of Edward II. During a visit to France in

1325 his wife Isabella enlisted the support of a number of exiled nobles, including Roger Mortimer – whose mistress she became – with the idea of ridding the king of the unseemly influence of his favourite, le Despenser. Seeing his safety threatened Edward came to Wales, possibly on his way to Ireland, and spent a few days at Caerphilly before moving on to Neath. The capture of Edward a little later did not deter the queen's army from besieging the castle until the spring of the following year.

What many people regard as the strangest feature of the castle, the leaning tower (which is reputed to be at an angle more precarious than that at Pisa) is the result of parliamentary slighting. The Great Hall of the castle is unique in Wales because it is the only one that has undergone such thorough restoration. Although there are those who prefer to see castles in their ruined or ruinous state, there are many whose imaginations are helped by the replacing of a floor here and the rebuilding of a wall there. The re-roofing of the hall and the re-dressing of the four decorated-style windows, each of which has been recently re-glazed at the expense of either an individual benefactor or a local charitable body, have added considerably to the visitor's appreciation of a castle apartment – normally open to rooks and gulls and the vagaries of the wind. The present hall, with its generous length of 70ft, was probably built by Hugh le Despenser. Hugh had married Gilbert de Clare's daughter, and as favourite of Edward II abused his position and exerted spurious authority on the neighbouring barons to such an extent that in 1321 they united against him and seized the castle. The hall lies alongside other buildings on the southern side of the inner ward, which is of rectangular plan with circular angle-towers. A centrally placed gatehouse allows access through the east and west walls. The Eastern Gatehouse is a

splendid construction worthy of an Edwardian castle, and sports an unusual attacking device above the inner arch of the gate passage. This takes the form of a missile chute.

Going through the Western Gatehouse to the outer ward and thence through the outer gatehouse, the visitor crosses an inner moat to reach the Hornwork, an island adapted to guard the structure's western approach. Although all that may now be seen from this spot are schoolboys fishing and the druidic circle of stones commemorating the visit of the Royal Welsh National Eisteddfod to the town in 1950, the effect of Gilbert de Clare's defence system is still overpoweringly real. The outline of the surrounding hills has remained unchanged throughout the centuries, except for a coal tip or a Forestry Commission growth. Had the visitor stood on this spot a hundred years ago nothing would have come between him and the agricultural land of the treacherous valleys to the north and east. Nowadays the castle is surrounded by development as ugly as it is necessary. Fortunately its acreage and might are able to withstand such a siege.

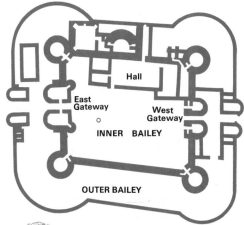

is an interesting bell tower with a small door bearing the old sanctuary ring.

Prior to the building of the church in the 13thc, the site of early Christian worship in this area was St Margaret's Well, secluded in once-beautiful Maesmynan Woods. The 13th-c rectilinear layout of Caerwys' long wide streets was – on the advice of Dr Thomas Wynne, a native of Caerwys – adopted by William Penn for his new town of Philadelphia in Pennsylvania.

CAER-Y-TWR, Gwynedd 4 SH28
Situated at the top of Holyhead mountain and covering some 17 acres, this hill-fort (AM) makes use of precipitous drops as defences. To the N and NE of the site are massive dry-stone walls which protect the enclosure. In some places these still stand to a height of 10ft. A path from the fort leads steeply down to a hut group called Ty Mawr. The remains of about 20 huts dating from the 2nd to 4thc can be seen here. Most are circular but several are oblong; some still have hearths and shelves, and the walls stand at 2ft high in many cases (full OS reference SH 219 829).

CALDICOT, Gwent 26 ST48
The restored castle at Caldicot dates back to the 12thc and was built on the site of a previous structure. The town lies 2m S of the Severn Bridge, and medieval banquets are held at the castle each evening except Sunday. The church is in decorated and perpendicular styles and displays a 15th-c porch. A local inn is curiously named the 'Tippling Philosopher'.

CALDY ISLAND, Dyfed 19 SS19
Also spelt 'Caldey', this island lies 2½m offshore from Tenby and measures 1½ by 1m. Cistercian monks still make a locally-sold perfume from the island's flowers, and have been here since 1929. Benedictines were here before the Cistercians. The church, gatehouse, and refectory were built between the 12th and 15thc, and a stone inscribed in Ogham and Latin can be seen inside the church. Ogham script was not used after c800, but has been found in inscription form in S Wales, Cornwall, and parts of Ireland. Nearer Tenby and only 50yd from the mainland is St Catherine's Island, now a zoo.

CANDLESTON CASTLE, Mid Glamorgan 25 SS87
Ruins of this castle include a 14th-c square tower and courtyard, to which fortified domestic buildings were added during the 15thc. The castle stands between the village of Merthyr Mawr and the sea, and its name is a corruption of Cantelupestown; it was once owned by a branch of the powerful Cantelupe family. Inhabited until Victorian times, the structure is now badly decayed and land to the S has been overwhelmed by the shifting sand dunes. The ruins are freely accessible.

CANTREF-Y-GWAELOD, Powys
Part legend and part fact, the story of Cantref-y-Gwaelod – or the Lowland Hundred – is the story of a land stretching from Barmouth to Aberystwyth below the sea off the Cardigan Bay coast. The submerged forest which can be glimpsed at very low tide off Borth may well be part of it. The earliest mention of this land is made by Leland in the 16thc, but the legend of a sea inundation on this coast has its origins in folk-lore. Stories tell of a woman custodian of a magic well, who fails to keep the cover on it and allows the water to overflow and submerge the land. This story is also found in Welsh, Breton, and Irish lore. But the submergence of Cantref-y-Gwaelod is also attributed to the Governor of the Province, Seithenyn, who through drink or negligence failed to close the sluices and so let in the sea.

Another version attributes the tragedy to a woman who is not named, and Seithenyn is called upon to behold 'the vanguard of the main' and presumably to punish her. Yet another version attributes the tragedy to dissolute princes who failed to attend to the sea defences. There may well have been a genuine incursion of the sea along this bay in prehistoric times, preserved only in the misty realms of folk memory.

CAPEL CURIG, Gwynedd 5 SH75
Travellers along the A5 road get their first introduction to the exciting scenery of Snowdonia here. A scattered village of substantial hotels and guest houses, Capel Curig is a popular resort with climbers, mountain walkers, and anglers. In the early 1800's Telford opened this inland route through the heart of Snowdonia with his A5 road, which a century earlier Pennant had described as 'a dreadful horsepath'. The road is remarkable along its entire length through Wales for its absence of any noticeable gradient, a boon in the days of horse-drawn vehicles. Capel Curig started to develop as a resort with the building of the Royal Hotel by Lord Penrhyn. It is now the Mountain Adventure Centre of Plas-y-Brenin. From this point on the Beddgelert road is one of the best views of Snowdon. Seen in the valley near by are Llynnau Mymbyr, twin lakes joined by a narrow valley.

From Capel Curig the motorist has a choice of two routes, both offering some of the finest mountain scenery in Britain. The A5 continuation to Bangor takes a route past Tryfan, an easily-identified peak on the left-hand side of the road. What looks like two people standing motionless on the summit are in fact two pillars of stone known as Adam and Eve. Climbers can often be seen tackling Tryfan's craggy cliffs from the roadside, and the lucky visitor might spot one of Tryfan's shy goats leaping from boulder to boulder with all the surefootedness of that hardy breed. The next point of interest on this road is Ogwen Cottage, famous as a climbing centre. The motorist can park near by and venture on foot into Cwm Idwal, where a rugged walk leads to the nursery climbing slopes of Idwal Slabs, backed by the Mawr and Fach (Big and Little) Glyders. These actually differ very little in height. To their right is the awesome chasm of Twll Du (Black Hole), or as it is more picturesquely called in English, Devil's Kitchen. It is every bit as sinister as it sounds, and legend has it that no bird ever flies over it or above Llyn Idwal, the sullen lake at its foot.

The A5 road continues from Ogwen and through magnificent Nant Ffrancon, where green-clad flanks look as though they have been moulded from papier mâché. The Carneddau range is to be seen on the right. The first place of any significance on this route is Bethesda, famous for the huge slate quarry which was gouged out of the mountainside of Elidir Fawr on the left-hand side of the road. The other route from Capel Curig runs SW and after a few miles reaches Penygwyryd – an isolated hotel famous for its association with Everest climbers. Here there is a choice of two routes, the savage and scenic Llanberis Pass, and the Nant Gwynant to Beddgelert – gentler, but equally spectacular.

CAPEL GARMON, Gwynedd 6 SH85
Some 2m E of Betws-y-coed is Capel Garmon, a place which can be usefully included in a walking tour of Fairy Glen and the Conwy Falls. The village takes its name from Germanus, the warrior saint, and about 1m S from the village is a burial chamber. The tomb (AM) is of the type called the 'Cotswold-Severn', and comprises a large chamber inside a cairn which has a forecourt and a blind entrance. One immense capstone survives. Partial excavation has revealed part of a neolithic pot, fragments of beakers, flints, and human bones (full OS reference SH 818 544).

CAPEL LLIGWY, Gwynedd 5 SH48
This small, 12th-c chapel (AM) lies about ½m N of Llanallgo. Although the original structure was built c1125, the walls of the building were reconstructed in the 14thc.

CAPEL NEWYDD, Gwynedd 8 SH23
A tiny Nonconformist chapel in the village of Llandegwning, Capel Newydd dates from 1769 and is reputed to be the oldest of its kind in N Wales. The simple, barn-like building has an earthen floor and box pews, and was partly restored in 1958.

CAPEL-Y-FFIN, Powys 22 SO23
The quaint, small church here resembles a cottage rather than an ecclesiastical building. Llanthony Monastery, founded c1870 and partly in ruins, was built by Father Ignatius for the Order of Anglican Benedictines. After the death of the founding father in 1908 the monastic buildings became the property of the Caldey Island Benedictine abbey. Eric Gill, the well-known sculptor, used the abbey buildings as workshops for some years. From here a steep road reaches the 1,778ft Gospel Pass in the Black Mountains on the way to Hay-on-Wye. Llanthony and Llanthony Priory are 3½m SE down the valley of the Honddu.

*CARDIFF, South Glamorgan 26 ST17
Created the capital city of Wales in 1955 by Queen Elizabeth II, Cardiff is a large industrial sea port with a history which can be traced back to at least as far as Roman times. Although always a place of importance, Cardiff began to expand on a large scale only in the 19thc. At the beginning of the 19thc the population was 1,870; by the end of the century this had increased to some 164,000, and today it easily exceeds a quarter of a million. Cardiff had its first written charter between 1122 and 1147, and its most comprehensive early one came in 1340. Elizabeth I granted a royal charter in 1581, and this was confirmed by James I in 1608.

The Romans established a fort here in AD75 to control the Welsh tribesmen. These fortifications were increased in strength and size cAD300 as a defence against possible attack from Irish sea pirates, and the restored walls can be seen within the grounds of Cardiff Castle

(OACT). When the Romans left Cardiff (called in Welsh *Caerdydd*, perhaps recalling a Roman commander named Aulus Didius), it is assumed that the fort was deserted until the arrival of the Normans. Legend connects the site with Lancelot, who is said to have sailed from Cardiff after his treachery to King Arthur. The Normans were called in to quell the kingdom of Morgannwg, of which Cardiff was capital. The leader of the expedition was Robert Fitz Hamon who, after defeating the native Welsh prince,

claimed land for himself at Cardiff, Llantwit Major, and Kenfig. He divided the rest of the captured lands amongst his followers. The castle mound was built in 1090, and a small community sprang up around the castle. By 1100 this had become a borough. As the castle grew and altered to suit changing needs and ideas, so did the town which huddled round its walls. The townsfolk gained more and more independence from their overlords, and in 1421 the burgesses of the town were given the right to elect

two reeves and twelve aldermen, who were responsible for local government. During the reign of Elizabeth I Cardiff was the haunt of pirates, and although enquiries revealed the guilt of many men – some of them important officials – the piracy continued virtually unabated. During the civil war the people of Cardiff sided with the king, who came to the town in 1645 after the Battle of Naseby. Shortly after the king's visit the parliamentary forces captured the town. Throughout the 18thc Cardiff remained a

CARDIFF TOWN
1 Arlington Galleries (craftwork)
2 Blackfriars Priory
3 Cardiff Arms Park International Rugby-Football Ground
4 Castle
5 City Hall
6 County Hall
7 Law Courts
8 Municipal Buildings & City Information Centre
9 National Museum of Wales

10 National Sports Centre
11 New Theatre
12 Public Library
13 St David's Cathedral (RC)
14 St John's Church
15 Sherman Theatre
16 Sophia Gardens Pavilion (conference centre)
17 Temple of Health (& Welsh Office)
18 Temple of Peace
19 University College
20 Wales Empire Pool

21 Welsh Art's Council
22 Welsh National War Memorial
23 WTB Information Centre
CARDIFF ENVIRONS
24 Albany Gallery, Roath
25 Bell Tower, Llandaff
26 Bishop's Palace Gateway, Llandaff
27 Chapter Arts Centre, Llandaff
28 City Cross, Llandaff
29 Llandaff Cathedral
30 Maindy Athletics Stadium
31 Welch Regiment Museum, Maindy

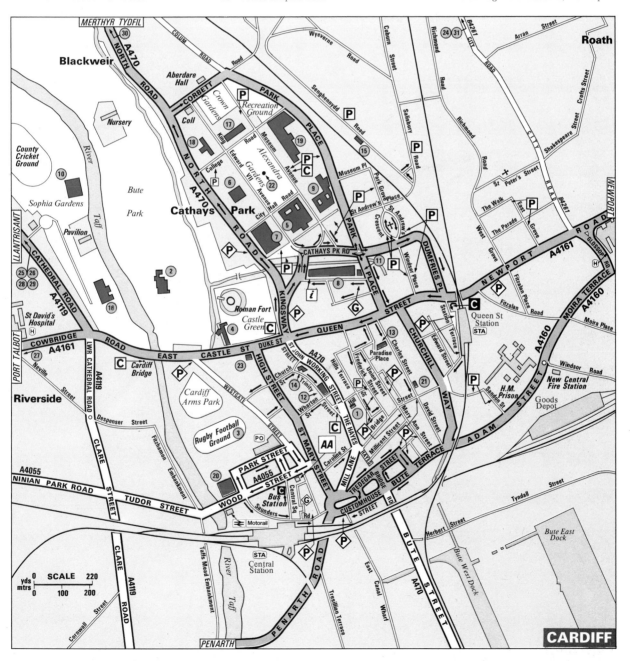

small country community on the medieval pattern. It stayed within its town walls and was surrounded by farmland, with extensive marshland and woods a short distance away. From the end of the 18thc S Wales became the chief iron- and coal-producing region of Britain. It was during this time that the Bute family became connected by marriage with Cardiff and sank huge sums of money into the development of the town. In 1839 the Marquis of Bute constructed a dock to accommodate large ocean-going vessels on the moors of the Taff estuary. Dock construction continued, and by the beginning of the 20thc Cardiff was the most important coal-exporting port in the world.

During the great days of Cardiff's expansion the appearance of the town changed drastically. In the late 18thc the town gates were removed; the High Street was cleared of obstructions in the mid 19thc; the course of the River Taff was altered to reduce the risk of flooding – to which the town had been particularly

prone. In 1905 the town was granted the status of a city by Edward VII, and in 1955 Cardiff was made the capital city of Wales. The only medieval church to survive in Cardiff is St John's. This includes some 13th-c arches, but most of the church dates from a 15th-c rebuilding. The beautiful tower was built in 1473 by the designer John Hart. During the earlier period of Cardiff's expansion building work was carried out in a haphazard and often unpleasant manner, but as the fever died down more thought was given to the design and appearance of buildings – both public and private. Cardiff retains many buildings from this period, and good examples of Victorian architecture can be seen in Cathedral Road (1890), the Great Western Hotel in St Mary's Street (1876), and Park House in Park Place (1874). During the late 19thc several shopping arcades were built off St Mary's Street. These provide excellent 'indoor' shopping facilities and are of architectural interest.

In 1898 the corporation purchased 60 acres of land, called Cathays Park, from the Marquis of Bute. It was intended that this land should be the site for a complex of public buildings befitting a town of the size and importance of Cardiff. The new City Hall and Law Courts were the first buildings to go up and were finished in 1905. These are related in composition and design, and both are built in the extravagant baroque style. The focal point of these two buildings is a magnificent clock tower which crowns the west front of City Hall. In 1910 work was begun on the National Museum of Wales, also in Cathays Park, but this was not completed until 1927 due to the intervention of the first world war. The building is in neo-classical style and houses a rich variety of objects illustrating all aspects of Welsh culture and history. The Fine Art collection includes French Impressionist paintings and is particularly prized. Other buildings in Cathays Park include the Glamorgan County Hall of 1912, the University of Wales Registry dated 1904, the University College of

EXTRAVAGANCE IN CARDIFF

People who pass by Cardiff Castle, dismissing the ornate clock tower as a piece of 19th-c indulgence and reminding themselves that the outer defences are merely examples of early 20th-c masonry, are denying themselves a view of one of the finest Norman motte castles in Britain. They are also depriving their sensibilities of an onslaught which only high-blown Victorian decoration can achieve. However, both the authentic fortress and the apartments containing the 19th-c interpretation of medieval domestic architecture, lie on a site which the Romans first used in AD75 and fortified three centuries later.

Robert Fitz Hamon, the conqueror of Glamorgan, constructed a moated hillock in 1093 which the visitor immediately

sees on entering the spacious grounds of the castle. In place of the original wooden palisade, a masonry keep was built in the late 12thc. This handsome structure is polygonal in plan and today forms a matchless vantage-point from which to see the encroaching city skyline and the occasional glimpse of the channel. Also in view, to the greener and less frenzied north, the Camelot-like towers of Castell Coch rise from the wooded hillside in an unmistakably romantic way. They are as obviously 'modern' as a great deal of Cardiff Castle, since it was the 3rd Marquis of Bute and his architect William Burgess who were responsible for both.

In Norman-occupied Wales there was little time for such exercises in extravagant frivolity. Castles were functional, and however effective their defences there was never complete guarantee of safety and security. The Earl of Gloucester, grandson of Fitz

Hamon, discovered this in 1158 when Ifor ap Meurig of Senghennydd brought his Welsh supporters to Cardiff and captured him and his family. They were not released until both parties had come to full agreement about the rights of Welsh people under the authority of the Anglo-Norman overlords.

During the civil wars the castle served as a prison, and afterwards it became ruinous. It remained in this state until the 1st Marquis of Bute undertook repairs in the late 18thc. It is to the 3rd Marquis that Cardiff owes the castle's excellent state of preservation. Such restoration work required enormous wealth even in the 1870's, when it was begun.

Apartments shown during guided tours of the castle are the extremely Moorish ante-room; the long banqueting hall with its fireplace surmounted by an ornate castellated fortress; a dining room in a relentlessly High-Church style; an octagonal room with balcony, overladen with allusions to fate-stricken ladies and the Canterbury Tales, known as the Chaucer Tower; the chapel, with its bronze door; and the roof garden, with its wall tiles depicting scenes from the life of Elijah. A challenge to the fastidious and endlessly fascinating to everybody else, Cardiff Castle should be seen along with Castell Coch, 5m north of Cardiff.

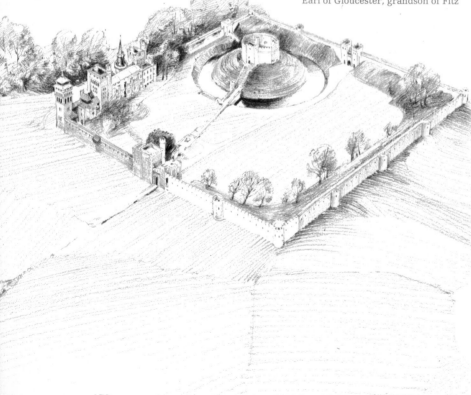

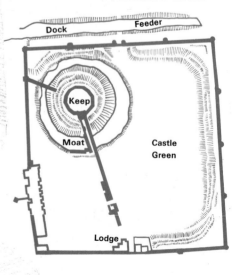

South Wales' buildings and the Welsh Office dated 1938, the Temple of Peace and Health of 1928, and the Welsh National War Memorial of 1928. Cardiff has 440 acres of parks and open spaces, and as one would expect in so large and thriving a city there is a whole host of indoor and outdoor entertainment facilities. The rugby-football ground at Cardiff Arms Park is world famous. Llandaff, now almost one with Cardiff, is described under its own heading elsewhere in this gazetteer. Some 4m from Cardiff city centre is St Fagans Welsh Folk Museum, a superb example of enlightened preservation. This is also listed under its own heading.

*CARDIGAN, Dyfed *17 SN14*
Situated by the side of the River Teifi, Cardigan is a busy market town with some 4,000 inhabitants. There have been two castles which claimed the name Cardigan: Old Cardigan about ½m W of the town was built in 1093 for William Rufus, destroyed in 1165, and rebuilt in stone in 1171. Records after this date are confused, but probably refer to the newer castle which is situated in the town. This castle was called simply Cardigan, and was probably first built in 1160 by Gilbert de Clare. Rhys ap Gruffydd organized the first national eisteddfod here in 1177. Both castles are on private land. Cardigan was once an important seaport, but the Teifi silted up and the trade was lost. The River Teifi is counted as being one of the most beautiful in Wales, and is an excellent fishing and sailing river. Coracle races are held on the river annually, and Cardigan bridge is of Norman origin but was rebuilt in 1640. During the civil war it was broken by the Roundheads and had to be rebuilt for a second time. St Mary's Church was once the priory

church of a Benedictine community. The market is held in the Guildhall of 1859, with the stalls being placed around the pillars of arches which form the ground floor and basement. Like most Welsh towns Cardigan has many chapels. The town's best examples are Bethania of 1847 in William Street, and the Tabernacle of 1760 in High Street. Gwbert-on-Sea, Cardigan's seaside resort, offers good sands and numerous little bays that cry out for exploration.

CARDIGAN ISLAND, Dyfed *17 SN15*
This nature reserve is owned by the West Wales Naturalists' Trust, from whom a permit must be obtained before a landing can be made. The address of the Trust is 4 Victoria Place, Haverfordwest. The island is 40 acres in extent and lies 400yds off the coast N of Gwbert-on-Sea. It is most noted for its prolific bird life.

CAREW, Dyfed *18 SN00*
Carew lies between Tenby and Pembroke and has two treasures – a Celtic cross and a castle. The cross (AM), 14ft high and carved with an intricate series of designs, is thought to date from the 11thc. An inscription in Latin reads: 'Maredudd the King, son of Edwin'. Originally a Norman structure, the castle came to the hands of Gerald de Windsor in 1095 when he married Nest, the daughter of Prince Rhys of Tewdwr. Nest was by all accounts a very beautiful and much sought-after woman, and certainly the unwitting cause of continuing bloodshed between the Normans and Welsh. Extensive changes were made by Sir John Perrott, a reputed son of Henry VIII, who furnished the castle with all manner of luxuries but was thrown in the Tower of London for treason before he could enjoy his possessions (see inset overleaf).

The early-English parish church dates from the 15th and 16thc, and contains the tombs of the Carew family. An interesting tidal mill in the village has been restored and renovated. A ridgeway which runs between Manorbier and Carew was once a burial ground, and was used as a beacon in 1803. Ancient burial mounds can be seen on both sides of Rosemary Lane.

*CARMARTHEN, Dyfed *20 SN42*
Plan on page 173
Carmarthen is a market and county town which forms a centre for some of the best farming land in Wales. Many of the streets are narrow and steep, and modern traffic has been a problem to the town – so much so that its old town bridge has had to be replaced to cater for the vastly-increased influx of motor transport. Excavations have revealed that Carmarthen was a Roman settlement of some importance. It was then known as *Moridunum*, and was the farthest W of the large Roman forts. Next to nothing can be seen of the actual site, which lies in the Priory Street area, though there are many Roman exhibits in the interesting museum in Quay Street. The great Arthurian enchanter Merlin is reputed to have been born in, or very close to, Carmarthen. At the end of Priory Street is the stump of an oak tree, much decayed and supported by iron and concrete. It is very carefully looked after by the townsfolk because Merlin is said to have made the following prophecy:

When Merlin's oak shall tumble down
Then shall fall Carmarthen town.

Above the village of Abergwili, a little to the E of Carmarthen, is Merlin's Hill. This is where tradition says the magician had his retreat from the world, and perhaps here too is the 'crystal cave' in which Merlin sleeps until the day when Britain faces her darkest moment.

The Normans arrived in 1093 and built a wooden castle on a mound above the river. They also established the Augustinian Priory of St John the Evangelist. One of Wales' most priceless treasures was written in Carmarthen. Known as the *Black Book of Carmarthen*, this is the oldest-known manuscript in the Welsh language and is now housed in the National Museum of Wales at Aberystwyth. The castle was at one time the principal residence of the princes of S Wales, and was thus the frequent object of seiges. Much of the site is now taken up by Carmarthen's most imposing building, the County Hall. This was designed by Sir Percy Thomas and displays a high, steep-angled roof. The most venerable of Carmarthen's buildings is St Peter's Church, situated at the top of Priory Street. It dates from the 13th and 14thc and includes some 16th-c work in the south aisle. Many interesting monuments can be seen in the church, but the most notable is the tomb of Sir Rhys ap Thomas and his wife, which lies in the south aisle. This tomb was brought from the Church of the Grey Friars, which stood in Friars Park, after the Dissolution. Sir Rhys did much good service for Henry VII and was instrumental in the victory at Bosworth Field. Also buried in the church is Sir

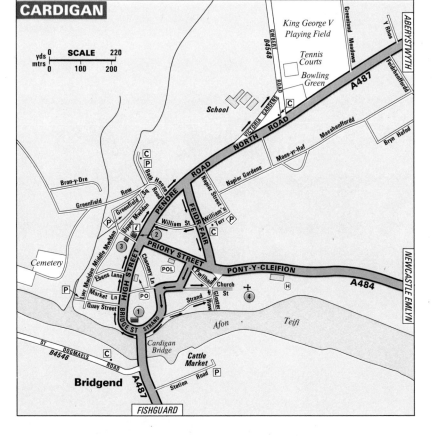

1 Castle
2 Guildhall, Market Hall & WTB Information Centre
3 Quixote (stoneware craft)
4 St Mary's Church

Entries marked * are the starting point of drives included in the Day Drive section of the book (pages 95 to 144). 171

Richard Steele, who became connected with Carmarthen through his marriage to Prudence Scurlock. Steele was an eminent figure in 18th-c life, and was much loved and respected. His wife died in 1716, and he procured a burial in Westminster Abbey for her. Not far from Steele's grave is a monument to Major General Sir William Nott, of whom the historian Edward Foord wrote in 1925 'During the black days of 1841–2, when Afghanistan was in revolt against the British occupation and the British garrisons were being destroyed amid

such circumstances of horror and ignominy as have hardly ever disgraced the warlike annals of our race, General Nott alone upheld the honour of the British name. From him only, when matters appeared most hopeless, came no suggestion that overtures should be made to the savage and treacherous foe'; stirring stuff! General Nott died in Carmarthen in 1845, and Queen Victoria donated £100 to a memorial statue which was erected by public subscription. This monument stands in Nott Square. Also commemorated in the

church are Walter Devereux, the first Earl of Essex; Lady Vaughan; and Bishop Ferrar – who was burned at the stake in Carmarthen during the Marian persecutions of 1555.

During the 18thc Carmarthen was a centre of the Welsh religious and educational revivals, which explains the large number of charity schools and chapels in the town. The Water Street Chapel is the home of the Welsh Calvinistic Methodists. The Lammas Street Chapel is a severe building dating

GALLEON OF MASONRY

This castle is the same distance from both Pembroke and Haverfordwest, and the approach from the north reveals a fine galleon of masonry above the tidal river. There are few castles in Wales which owe their renown to events completely unconnected with warfare, and the appearance of which is still a tribute to the architectural good taste of their owners and builders. One of them is Carew, where the magnificent display of mullioned windows, both bold and elegant, look out fearlessly on to a peaceful and prospering world. Such a

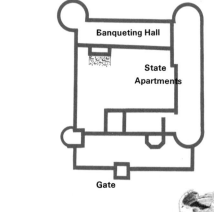

world was Sir John Perrot's, an Elizabethan politician who held posts of considerable importance under the crown, and who wielded more influence in his native region than anybody else. The north façade of Carew is the most frequently featured view. It is unfailingly striking, and forms a fine expression of the intense interest in domestic architecture during the 16thc. With the declining need for defensive building at the end of the 15thc, castles were adapted to a more leisurely and domestic way of life, parading the wealth and ancestry of their owners to the world. Illustrious as his life had been, the owner of Carew received a vicious blow when arrested for high treason; he was imprisoned in the Tower and condemned to death, but he evaded that final ignominy by dying of natural causes in September of 1592.

The one single event connected with Carew which has caught the imagination of most people is the tournament held there in 1507 by Sir Rhys ap Thomas, the most powerful man in south-west Wales at the end of the 15th and beginning of the 16thc. Carew was only one of many castles which he owned in this part of the country. Most of these were granted to him by Henry VII after the victory over Richard III at

Bosworth Field, in which Rhys had played such a decisive part. Rhys was knighted at Bosworth and created Knight of the Garter in 1505; he celebrated his admission into the Order two years later by holding a tournament to which representatives of all the leading Welsh noble families were invited.

The Great Hall is one of the major changes which ap Thomas made to the 13th-c fabric of Carew Castle, which was originally built in the early 12thc by Gerald of Windsor, castellan of Pembroke. When Gerald married the daughter of the Prince of Deheubarth (South Wales) in 1100, he won not only her legendary beauty but a considerable dowry which included Carew. Their son William adopted the surname Carew, a name associated with the castle from then until it was leased by Rhys ap Thomas in 1480, and again from 1607 until the end of the 17thc.

Apart from the 15th- and 16th-c modifications, Carew is very much in the Edwardian tradition of rectangular plan with round angle-towers. Those on the west side are particularly strong and further fortified by semi-pyramidal spurs. The 13th-c gatehouse was replaced by the present structure during Sir Rhys's occupancy. George Carew held the castle for the king in 1644, but it fell to the parliamentarians under Colonel Rowland Laugharne.

from 1726, and the Presbyterian College of 1689 is the oldest of its kind in Wales. The Guildhall dates from 1767 and adjoins the house in which Brinley Richards the composer – noted for *God Bless the Prince of Wales* – was born. At the other end of the long street in which the Guildhall stands is a monument to General Sir Thomas Picton, who died at the battle of Waterloo. Carmarthen is the only town in Wales which has the privilege of having a sword carried before its mayor on occasions of state. This right was granted in 1546 by Henry VIII, and the sword which is carried was presented to the town in about 1564. The Royal National Eisteddfod was held in Carmarthen in 1974, when a stained-glass window designed by John Petts was unveiled at the Ivy Bush Royal Hotel to commemorate the Gorsedd Circle held at a previous eisteddfod here in 1819.

CARMEL HEAD, Gwynedd 4 SH29
Carmel Head is a wild and windy headland in the NE corner of Anglesey, which can be approached on foot from Llanfairynghornwy. It affords the best view of the Skerries, a group of islets named by the Vikings but known in Welsh as *Ynysoedd y Moelrhoniaidd* – island of seals. A lighthouse here throws out a 4 million candle-power beam, a vast improvement on the first light in 1716 which was provided by a coal fire in a conical brazier.

CARNEDDUA HENGWM, Gwynedd 9 SH62
Two chambered long cairns situated E of Tal-y-bont are known by this name. The larger S cairn is nearly 200ft long and is a composite structure comprising two burial chambers. Its W portion consists of a short passage leading to a chamber which is roofed with a single large

capstone. At the E end is a ruined Portal Dolmen, with three uprights and a displaced capstone. The N cairn is badly ruined and comprises a dry-stone walling edge enclosing two chambers, a central depression, and a large displaced capstone. Near these two cairns are the remains of two stone circles, also known as Carneddau Hengwm. These have greatly deteriorated, but the S circle still has a few stones standing (full OS reference SH 614 205).

CARN GOCH, Dyfed SN62
Carn Goch is the largest iron-age hillfort in Wales and stands on a 700ft hill, covering some 30 acres. Remains of massive stone ramparts still rise to 20ft in some places. The rich Vale of Tywi, in which the fortification stands, obviously made it a most desirable 'property' (full OS reference SN 689 243).

CARNO, Powys 20 SN99
A scattered village taking its name from a river which flows parallel with the main road and railway alongside it, Carno was the site of several ancient battles between the rulers of N and S Wales. In AD948 the Voels fought the sons of Hywel Dda – the Welsh lawgiver – and there was another battle here in 1077. Gruffydd ap Cynan won the crown of N Wales and slowed the advance of the Normans into Wales in a later conflict during 1081. A Roman fort known as Caer Noddfa stood on a site alongside the church, which once belonged to the Knights of St John of Jerusalem. The knights are believed to have had a house here, and the church was rebuilt in 1807.

The inn opposite the church has the unusual and romantic name, 'The Aleppo Merchant'. This was conferred

on it by a retired sea captain who had been master of a ship of that name. The house was first licensed as an inn in 1632. Today Carno is famous as the headquarters of the firm of Laura Ashley.

CARREG CENNEN CASTLE, Dyfed 20 SN61
See special gazetteer inset overleaf.

CARROG, Clwyd 10 SJ14
A terraced village on the River Dee near Glyndyfrdwy, Carrog stands in the area where Owain Glyndwr was brought up. A mound here may have been one of his strongholds, and the ruins of a moated grange which is said to have been his palace can be seen near the village. An ancient five-arched bridge here is said to date from 1661, but may be considerably older. St Bride's Church was rebuilt in 1611 above the flood level of the river and restored in 1852. The iron-studded doors and round font are believed to have come from an earlier church, and it is possible that the oak rafters are also older than the rest of the building.

CASCOB, Powys 14 SO26
Less than a village, scarcely even a hamlet, Cascob consists chiefly of a stone church with a half-timbered and louvred tower hidden away in the E edge of Radnor Forest. This building houses a document that may well be unique, displayed on the north wall of the nave. This is a Deed of Exorcism combined with a Talisman, a curious mixture of Christianity and Gnosticism. The deed begins 'In the name of the Father, Son and Holy Ghost Amen, and in the name of the Lord Jesus Christ I will deliver Elizabeth Lloyd from all witchcraft and all evil spirits and from all evil men or women or wizardes or hardness of heart Amen'. After this comes a long prayer and some Biblical quotations, then the phrase *Jal, Jal, Jal* and a series of what appear to be astrological signs. At the head of the deed is the talisman, which takes the form of an *Abracadabra* – that is to say the full word written on the top line and repeated with the dropping of the last letter on each subsequent line until finally only the letter A is left, the whole arranged in the form of a triangle with its apex at the bottom. The Abracadabra talisman is said to have been devised by the Gnostics from secret knowledge which was even more revealing than that of Christianity. But who Elizabeth Lloyd was, or what form her demonic possession took, is not recorded.

CASTELL COCH, South Glamorgan 26 ST18
This beautiful reconstruction of a 13th-c Welsh castle was built in the 1870's by William Burgess for the 3rd Marquis of Bute. Burgess based his work on the remains of a castle constructed between 1260 and 1300 by Gilbert de Clare, Lord of Glamorgan – a structure which was deliberately blown up in the 15thc

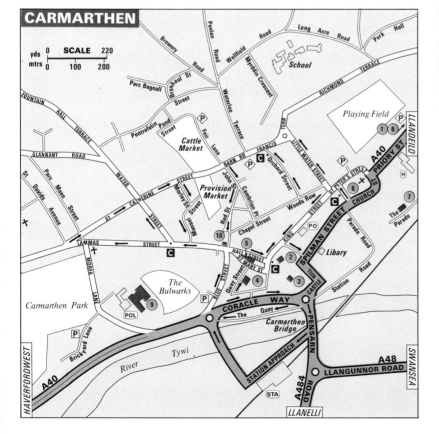

1 Augustinian Priory (site of)
2 Castle Ruins
3 County Hall
4 County Museum
5 Guildhall
6 Merlin's Oak
7 Presbyterian College
8 St Peter's Church
9 The Bulwarks (civil war fortifications)
10 WTB Information Centre

and left to rot for 400 years. In 1871 work was begun on the restoration of the castle, and Burgess' only departure from the appearance of a 13th-c structure was in the conical roofs. These have no parallel in Wales and give the castle (AM) a slightly Continental look.

Its interior is a rich extravaganza of Victorian romantic decoration. The drawing room is two stories high, octagonal in shape, and startlingly decorated throughout with carved and painted scenes from Aesop's Fables. The upper two floors of the keep are occupied by Lady Bute's bedroom, which is decorated in a mixture of medieval and oriental styles. In comparison the Banqueting Hall is fairly restrained, its main features being the tie-beam roof and the carved-stone chimney piece which displays a figure of St Lucius. The shape of the castle is triangular, and three round towers connected by a curving curtain wall form a courtyard which is entered by a wooden drawbridge over a dry moat. A visit to Castell Coch may whet the visitor's appetite for more romantically-restored castles, in which case he should try Cardiff – another joint effort by the Marquis of Bute and William Burgess (see inset on page 170).

KING OF TIME

When the Reverend Eli Jenkins in his daily prayer in Dylan Thomas's *Under Milk Wood* speaks of Carreg Cennen, 'King of Time', he could be referring to the grey stronghold or the formidable limestone crag which it crowns, for the two are inseparable. Just as they were dependent on each other for military defence in medieval Wales, so they were essential to each other in the eyes of 18th- and 19th-c artists and engravers. In a part of south-west Wales particularly well-endowed for its striking combination of lushness and savagery, the area near Llandeilo has no fewer than three castles in situations which have a strong appeal to the romantic spirit. Little now remains of Dryslwyn. Dynevor, the royal seat of South Wales in the Middle Ages, is virtually inaccessible, but Carreg Cennen still stands – a mere fragment of its former self, but still indomitable.

Although the present defences date from the late 13thc, when the area fell into the hands of the English, the castle played a highly important part in the earlier years of the Norman occupation of these parts. This was mainly because of the persistent efforts of 'Lord Rhys' of Dynevor and his son to regain unsurped territories. After the death of Rhys the Welsh cause was substantially weakened due to the jealous wrangling over property between his sons. Attempts at uniting the princes of Deheubarth by Llywelyn the Great proved futile, so that when Edward I started his Welsh campaigns he met little resistance in this region. Carreg Cennen fell in 1277.

The construction of the existing fabric was begun in 1283 when the king granted the castle to John Giffard, in whose family it remained until 1321. Hugh le Despenser the Younger, favourite of Edward II and powerfully placed in Caerphilly as Lord of Glamorgan, provoked a number of marcher lords to rebel against him because of his ruthlessly ambitious plans to annex lands in South Wales. Giffard, a victim of the king's folly and injustice, lost his life for his part in the rebellion and Carreg Cennen was granted to le Despenser.

By the middle of the 14thc the castle was in the possession of the Lancaster family, who also owned Kidwelly. Both became crown property as they passed to John of Gaunt through his wife, a Lancaster co-heiress, and then to his son Henry Bolingbroke, the future Henry IV.

CASTELL COLLEN, Powys *13 SO06*

Surviving traces of this Roman fort include foundation walls, and the site lies 1m N of Llandrindod Wells on the W bank of the Ithon. Castell Collen can be reached by taking a side road off the A4081 at Llanyre, and then a rough track to the right after about ½m. The fort was excavated from 1911 to 1913 and revealed a military headquarters in the centre of the main street, a commandant's residence comprising three ranges of rooms set round a courtyard to the S, and a granary to the N. Further excavations in 1954 resulted in the discovery of pottery, coins, and a gateway of unusual design.

In 1403 Carreg Cennen yielded to Owain Glyndwr, whose attempt at regaining independence for Wales caused so many castles to be brought back into service. In 1455 it saw further activity when Gruffydd ap Nicholas of Dynevor ordered the repair and garrisoning of the fortress, which he then held as a Lancastrian supporter. After the defeat of their cause at Mortimer's Cross in 1461, his sons took refuge at Carreg Cennen until compelled to surrender in the following year at the command of the king's Chief Justice in South Wales.

Henry VII granted the castle, like that at Kidwelly, to Sir Rhys ap Thomas for his allegiance to the Tudor cause before the defeat of Richard III at Bosworth Field in 1485.

The castle stands 300ft above the River Cennen on a rock (the *carreg* in the title), which is unscalable on its south side and a formidable challenge on the west. An intricate barbican leads from the outer ward to the gatehouse, but on entering the inner ward it is immediately obvious that the demolition of 1462 – ordered lest it should become a den of thieves – was as thorough as any parliamentary slighting. Mental reconstruction is essential as the visitor stands in the bailey, with an insistent wind playing a repertoire of eerie tunes. One of the most exciting parts of the castle is the cliffside passage leading to a cave which probably supplied the castle with water, though individual speculation might concoct all sorts of less functional reasons for its existence.

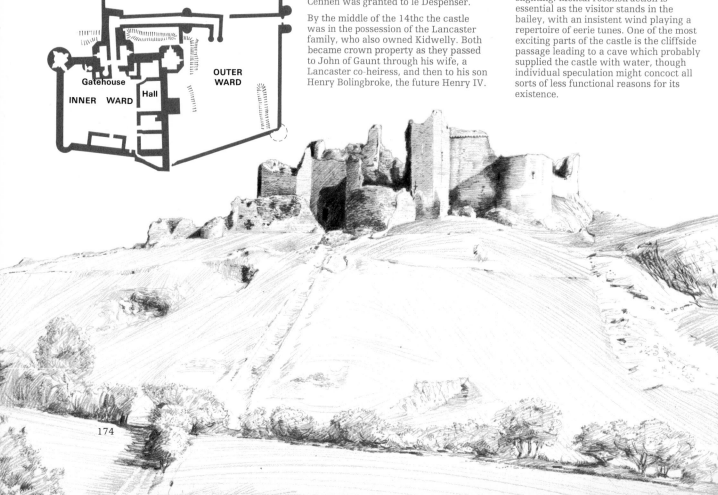

Castell Collen was constructed c85BC and was occupied till AD300. It was one of the Romans' key forts in mid Wales, and a full-strength garrison was maintained there till AD150. An unusually low level of the Ithon in 1929 revealed the stern of a boat resting on the remains of a landing stage. This was raised, floated down to a ford, and on being beached was found to have been made from half a tree. It had a flat bottom like a punt, and the construction timber was oak. It was given preservative treatment and presented to the Llandrindod Wells Museum. There is no reason to think that it was Roman, even though it was discovered near Castell Collen.

CASTELL DINAS, Powys *22 SO13*
Situated off the A479 near the hamlet of Pengenffordd, this hillfort probably dates from the iron age and has massive ramparts which surround a Norman motte. The later castle is now little more than a pile of stones, but when it was built in the 12thc it must have been a large and imposing structure. It is possible to trace the remains of the two wards, the gatehouse, and the oblong keep. Views from this site are impressive and encompass the Black Mountains and Mynydd Epynt.

CASTELL DINAS BRAN, Clwyd *11 SJ24*
Ruins of this castle lie at about 900ft above sea level, and the origin of the castle mound may go back to the 5th or 6thc. Existing remains date from about 1236 and were built by Gruffydd ap Madog. The way this castle has been constructed has posed experts with some difficulties, for in appearance it is neither Norman or Welsh. Near the main entrance is a room with three circular holes in its vaulted roof – a feature with a purpose which remains obscure. The building was in ruins by the time Henry VIII took the throne. A tunnel is reputed to run to a small outbuilding about 1m W of the castle, and views from the site extend over the Dee as far as the Pennines on a clear day.

CASTELL-Y-BERE, Gwynedd *9 SH60*
Set in remote countryside 7m S of Dolgellau and near Abergynolwyn, the dignified remains of Castell-y-Bere (AM) represent a structure which was once the most important fortification in Wales. The last of the Welsh-built castles guarded the spirit of independent Wales and was built and decorated with great care. It was here that Llywelyn the Last's brother Dafydd held out against Edward I and the English. The castle eventually surrendered, and Dafydd fled to Snowdonia where he was eventually captured. He was executed at Shrewsbury. The castle was taken over by Edward I and given borough status like Conwy, Beaumaris, Caernarfon, and Criccieth, but it never developed as a town. Some twelve years after the conquest it lapsed into decay.

CASTLE FLEMISH, Dyfed *16 SN02*
The most important Roman settlement in old Pembrokeshire, Castle Flemish lies N of Ambleston and was probably occupied from the first half of the 2ndc. It forms an irregular rectangular enclosure of bank and ditch straddling the road from Maenclochog to Wolf's Castle. Archaeologists are inclined to the theory that this was a defended farmhouse rather than a fort.

CASTLEMARTIN, Dyfed *18 SR99*
An organ in the local church once belonged to Mendelssohn, and near the church are the remains of a building of unknown date called the Old Rectory. Ermigate Cross, a monument which was re-consecrated in 1963, stands beside the road to Flimston Chapel. The chapel was once used as a barn. Also in the area are the earthwork remains of a rath, but this site is devoid of other surviving fortifications of any size. Prehistoric implements have been found in nearby sand dunes. Well-known Castlemartin Black Cattle originated in the area, and the nearby coast has many good bathing spots – notably Freshwater West Bay. Fine cliff and rock scenery includes Eligug Stack, a limestone rock which forms a nesting ground for guillemots, razorbills, and kittiwakes.

CEFN-COED-Y-CYMMER, Mid Glamorgan *21 SO00*
This is the site of one of the most important early ironworks in the Merthyr area. The operating firm was known as Cyfartha Ironworks and was founded in 1766. A partner in the company was Watkin George, one of the foremost of the early ironworkers. Also here is a fine, fifteen-arch stone viaduct which was constructed in 1866 for the Brecon and Merthyr railway. The chapel of Hen-dy-Cwrdd is an interesting example of its time, and was rebuilt in 1895. To the N of Cefn-Coed-y-Cymmer is the Llwyn-on-Reservoir, and Morlais Castle stands to the E.

CEFN MAWR, Powys *13 SO05*
The largest of a trio of industrial villages – the others being Rhosymedre and Acrefair – Cefn Mawr clings precipitously to a hillside overlooking the vast complex of Monsanto Chemical Works. Chemical manufacture has been carried out here for more than a century, and started with the processing of phenol from the plentiful supply of local shale. A rubbery smell often betrays the factory long before Cefn Mawr is reached.

CEMAES, Gwynedd *4 SH39*
This quaint fishing village on the N coast of Anglesey, more Cornish than Welsh in appearance, is made up of houses clustered tightly around a small harbour and stone quay. Shipbuilding once thrived here, and in the 18th and 19thc Cemaes was one of the most important ports on this coastline. The breakwater

which encloses the harbour was started in the last century, and the second stage was twice damaged by storm before completion this century. Sheltered beaches, romantic coves, and spectacular cliff walks are a feature of Cemaes. About 1m W Wylfa nuclear power station dominates the skyline. Built in 1969 as the biggest nuclear station in the world, it has rapidly established itself as a leading tourist attraction on Anglesey. For the technically-minded there is a public observation tower, a host of diagrams and models, and a bi-lingual commentary which tells the story of Wylfa. Conducted tours can be arranged, but not for children under fourteen.

CEMLYN BAY, Gwynedd *4 SH39*
Situated in the NE corner of Anglesey, this remote bay is almost land-locked by a long causeway which provides a pleasant walk. A privately-owned bird sanctuary exists near by, and the larger Cemlyn nature reserve is owned by the NT. The treacherous coastline led to the establishment of a lifeboat station which operated here from 1828 to 1919. At one period in the last century the lifeboat was in the charge of the Rector of Llanrhyddlad, Canon Owen Williams, who was also a member of the crew.

CENARTH, Dyfed *17 SN24*
Beautifully situated on the River Teifi, this small village has fine waterfalls, a mill, and an old four-arched bridge. The big pool beneath the bridge is popular with anglers, and coracles are still to be seen on the river. In the 12thc the beaver was to be found here, and according to the celebrated cleric and traveller Giraldus Cambrensis, this was the last stronghold of the animal in England and Wales.

CERRIG DUON AND NANT TARW, Powys *21 SN82*
Both these groups of stone circles are in the parish of Traean-glas. Cerrig Duon (OS reference SN 851 206) is a stone circle with a menhir and a stone avenue, and Nant Tarw (OS reference SN 818 258) comprises two stone circles. To the SW of Cerrig Duon on the far side of the River Tawe from Penwyllt station is the fine stone row known as Saeth Maen, or Seven Stones (OS reference SN 833 154).

CERRIG-Y-DRUDION, Clwyd *10 SH94*
Cerrig-y-Drudion marks the beginning of a bleak stretch of moorland which ends

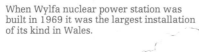
When Wylfa nuclear power station was built in 1969 it was the largest installation of its kind in Wales.

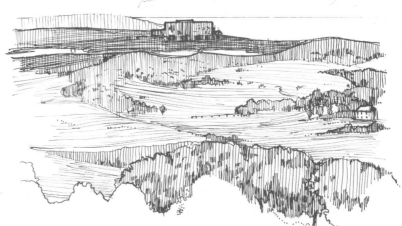

with Pentrefoelas on the W boundary of Clwyd. George Borrow stayed here on his famous tour of *Wild Wales*, and conveys his impressions thus: 'Emerging from the hollow way I found myself on a moor over which the road lay in the direction of the north. Towards the west at an immense distance rose a range of stupendous hills, which I subsequently learned were those of Snowdon – about ten minutes walking brought me to Cerrig-y-Drudion, a small village near a rocky elevation, from which no doubt the place takes its name, which interpreted, is the rock of heroes'. The 'rocky elevation' to which Borrow refers is Pen-y-gaer, which lies SE of the village and is crowned by a hillfort of King Caratacos (or Caractacus). The king was captured by invading legionary forces and taken to Rome in chains. The pretty village church is of interest, as are a group of almshouses dating from 1717. Alwen Reservoir lies N.

CERRIG-Y-GOF, Dyfed   *16 SN03*
This unique example of megalithic-tomb architecture comprises a circular mound with five rectangular cists facing outwards, and is situated near Newport (full OS reference SN 040 390).

*CHEPSTOW, Gwent   *26 ST59*
Situated on the River Wye near its confluence with the Severn, and very close to the M4 and M5 motorways, Chepstow has become considerably better known in recent years. It is a border town, and arguments in the past have never really decided whether it can claim to be the gateway to S Wales, or simply the gateway to one-time

Monmouthshire – Gwent as it now is. There is evidence that the Romans had some sort of settlement here. They certainly built a ford across the river, because some of its stones may be seen upstream from the castle at low tide. The Normans were quick to realize the importance of the river crossing, and the first castle was begun by William Fitz Osbern *c*1067, only one year after the landing at Hastings. Fitz Osbern had been created Earl of Hereford by William, and with the help of his castle at Chepstow soon had most of what is now Gwent in his power. The extensive ruins of the castle (AM), which lies between the River Wye and the town, span 900 years. The oldest surviving part is the base of the Great Tower (see special inset opposite).

Chepstow town is composed of many narrow, steep streets, and a local 18th-c poet summed it up when he wrote:

'Strange to tell, there cannot be found One single inch of horizontal ground'.

Bridge Street leads up from a fine 19th-c iron bridge across the Wye and has several bow-windowed houses. At the top of Bridge Street are the 18th-c Powys almshouses, and the Montague almshouses of 1613 are in nearby Church Street. The town walls (AM) originally ran from the castle ditch in a 1m circuit down to the riverside below the bridge. These are well preserved for much of their length, and are popularly known as the Port Walls. The west gate straddling the main street was rebuilt in 1524. An interesting museum stands in Bridge Street, and sloping Beaufort

Square features a gun presented to Chepstow by King George V to commemorate Charles Williams, who won the Victoria Cross. The stocks came from Portskewett and were set up here in 1947.

The railway bridge over the Wye was originally built by Brunel, but was drastically altered in 1962. Chepstow's partly-Norman parish church stands in Church Street and originally formed part of a Benedictine priory. It has been extensively restored, but the west door and nave were not touched by the repair work. The tower was rebuilt in 1706 and the font dates from the 15thc. Henry the 2nd Earl of Worcester and his wife Elizabeth lie beneath a large canopy in the church; the earl died in 1549. Also in the church is the somewhat eccentric tomb 'In Memory of Thos Shipman and Margaret his wife and their 12 children. Also Richd Clayton Esq who was married to Margaret the Relict of the above mentioned Thos Shipman 1620'. The tomb depicts Margaret lying full length with her two husbands kneeling a little behind her, while at the bottom of the tomb are carved all twelve children.

The town was once an important port and shipbuilding yard, and although trade has now diminished some small boats are still produced. An area of Chepstow called 'The Back' is still evocative of the days of seafaring importance. Tides on this section of coast can rise and fall as much as 40ft. Prehistoric earthworks survive at Bulwark Camp (AM) and Piercefield Park, ½m S of the town. Offa's Dyke, built *c*AD789 and started near the mouth of the Wye, can be traced in several places on the English side of the river near Chepstow. Tintern lies just a little to the N. The town's racecourse is world famous.

CHERITON, West Glamorgan   *24 SS49*
Cheriton is a small village situated on the Burry Pill stream near Llanmadog. Like Llanmadog it is dominated by the heights of 550ft Llanmadog Hill. To the SE is 372ft Ryer's Down, and N is North Hill Tor, with its prominent limestone scar overlooking Landimore Marsh and the Loughor estuary. The early 13th-c church is one of the smallest on the Gower Peninsula and displays many interesting features. These include a good south door, fine arches, a piscina, a rood-loft staircase, and two very old fonts – one Norman and the other possibly Saxon. The older font is not used. The strong battlemented tower has a saddleback roof. A former rector, John David Davis, was well known as a historian on the Gower area and was a skilful wood-carver. His work can be seen in the church's choir stalls, altar rails, altar, and chest.

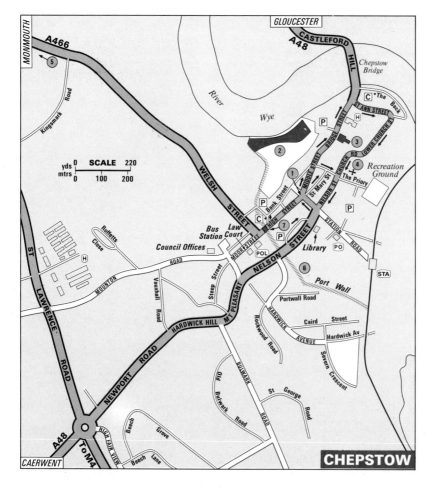

1   Beaufort Square
2   Castle
3   Museum
4   Parish Church
5   Racecourse
6   Town Walls
7   West Gate

CHIRK, Clwyd *11 SJ23*

First in Wales on the A5 approach from Shrewsbury, Chirk is a well-kept village with modern factories discreetly sited on the E side. Several collieries once flourished on the village outskirts. The village is the gateway to the beautiful Ceiriog Valley, but no visitor should pass through without seeing the famous gates to Chirk Castle – considered wrought-iron artistry at its best. The gates (AM) were made by the Davies brothers of Croes Foel near Wrexham and are typical of their work, which adorns many churches and mansions in the border country. They make a splendid introduction to Chirk Castle, an impressive, lived-in structure with plenty of historic interest. It occupies a commanding prospect above the Ceiriog Valley, and was built by one of Edward I's marcher lords – Roger Mortimer – in 1310. The Myddelton family, the present occupants, have lived in it almost continuously since they acquired it in 1595 (see special inset overleaf).

An interesting section of the Shropshire Union Canal is to be seen at Chirk. A long, damp tunnel opens into a wide basin before the canal is carried across the Ceiriog Valley at a dizzy height, and the railway viaduct runs alongside. Chirk is also the family seat of the Trevors of Brynkinallt, one of whose daughters was the mother of the Duke of Wellington.

GRIM GATEWAY

The motorist coming into Wales along the Gloucester road and not across the Severn Bridge is rewarded by a pictorial view of Chepstow Castle on the west bank of the Wye. The outline of its rectangular keep is a compelling feature of what might be called – because of its position – the first castle in Wales. When William Fitz Osbern was created Earl of Hereford and Lord of the Marches after the Norman conquest, his power extended over the border land of Monmouth and Hereford and an area of Gloucester between the Wye and the

CHURCH STOKE, Powys *14 SO29*

This village is the 'capital' of a Welsh promontory which drives into England and is surrounded by English land on three sides, with Corndon Hill rising splendidly in the centre. A castle ring surmounts Todleth Hill behind Old Church Stoke, and the site of a castle lies just off the main road to Craven Arms about ¾m from the village itself. Called Simon's Castle, it is so named because it was said to have been either built or restored by Simon de Montfort. The parish church suffered damage through an attack by a party of parliamentarians from Montgomery castle during the civil war. Most of the building was taken down and rebuilt in 1815. Timber-framed 17th-c farmhouses abound in this district.

CILCAIN, Clwyd *7 SJ16*

Cilcain is a Clwydian-Hills village and a popular starting point for the ascent of Moel Fammau. Its main point of interest is the church, which includes a fine 15th-c hammer-beam roof probably taken from Basingwerk Abbey at the Dissolution. The principals terminate with huge angels bearing shields, and the handsome churchyard gates are of 17th-c vintage. The River Alun runs through the village and has a habit of disappearing into its limestone bed during dry weather. Cilcain is a popular pony-trekking centre, and the surrounding area provides good woodland walks.

Severn. He did not build the usual Norman wooden fortress, but instead created a stone castle on a limestone cliff, with good sea links to Bristol. From here he began to subjugate the people of Gwent. Fitz Osbern's son succeeded him and was found guilty of conspiracy against the king; in 1075 he lost the castle to the crown, in whose possession it remained until Henry I granted the lordship of *Striguil*, the medieval name for Chepstow, to Walter Fitz Richard. Fitz Richard gave land on which the Cistercian abbey at Tintern was established.

In 1189 the castle passed to William Marshall by marriage, whose expert interest in building matched his military skill. A substantial part of the present castle is the result of his occupation and that of his five sons, each of whom succeeded him. It was the family of Bigod which was responsible for what is,

CILCENNIN, Dyfed *12 SN56*

Situated on a tributary of the River Aeron, 5m from Aberaeron and 1m off the A482 road to Lampeter, Cilcennin stands on the site of a castle where rival Welsh princes met in conflict in 1210. The battle resulted in a victory for Rhys and Owain over Maelgwn. Cilçennin's Victorian church was built in 1888 and has some unusual memorial stones in the graveyard. Sion Congregational Chapel of 1859 is a fine example of this type of Nonconformist architecture.

CILGERRAN, Dyfed *17 SN14*

The village is watched over by a mighty 13th-c castle, and coracle races take place in the gorge of the Teifi during August. Local skill with the tiny, ancient vessel is employed in salmon fishing. Perched on its high crag, the castle (AM) has been an inspiration to many poets and painters, including Turner and de Wint. It once belonged to the Norman marcher lord Gerald de Windsor, whose famous wife Nest caused considerable bloodshed and hate between Norman and Welsh simply because she was so beautiful (see special inset on page 179). A stone in the local churchyard commemorates Trenegussus, son of Macutrenus, who died in the 6thc. The inscription is in an ancient form of script called Ogham.

apart from the Norman Keep (or Great Tower), the castle's most splendid structure – Martyn's Tower. This was completed towards the end of the 13thc, but thus named because the regicide Henry Marten was imprisoned here – in some style, it would seem – for 20 years. Jeremy Taylor, the royalist bishop, was one of Chepstow's prisoners in the 17thc.

Through the marriage of Elizabeth Herbert – grand-daughter of the Earl of Pembroke and next owner of Chepstow – to Sir Charles Somerset (who was later the Earl of Worcester) the castle became the property of their descendants the Dukes of Beaufort. In this respect it is similar to Raglan.

The decoration of the tympanum above the entrance to the Great Tower and the finely ornamented window in the chapel are noteworthy. The castle's domestic range, complete with greater and lesser halls, buttery, pantry, servery, and garderobe, is one of the best-preserved units of its kind in any Welsh castle.

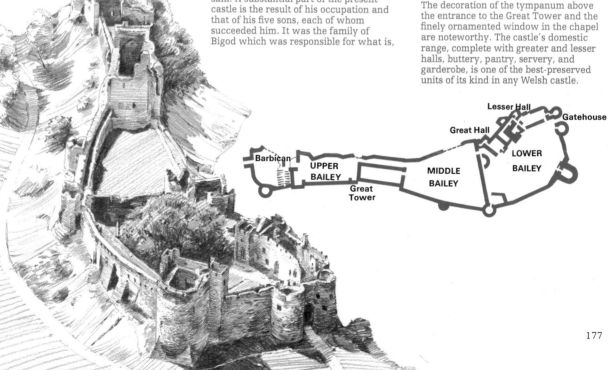

CILMERY, Powys   13 SO05
The main feature of interest in this village, situated 3m from Builth Wells along the A483 Llandovery road, is an obelisk set on a grass bank at the roadside. This commemorates the death of Llywelyn the Last, killed here in 1282 by Adam de Francton. Adam would have preferred to have taken Llywelyn captive, but failed to recognize him in time. Chroniclers have failed to agree on some points of the story, such as whether Builth Castle was held at the time by the Welsh or the English, but all agree that Llywelyn came to the town after his victory at the Menai Strait to confer with his generals about the next move in the campaign. He spent the night at Aberedw, where he had a residence of some kind, though he is reputed to have hidden in a cave above the Aberedw Rocks. This cave can still be found by the patient visitor.

The English got word that Llywelyn was in the district and closed in on him, but he slipped away on a horse shod with its shoes the wrong way round so as to put pursuers off. In this way he came through Builth and had the bridge demolished after him, then continued over the Irfon Bridge. The English were in pursuit and the people of Builth feared

SEAT OF CONQUERORS
Any visitor to Chirk Castle might suppose that the magnificent 18th-c wrought iron gates proclaimed an equally magnificent 18th-c country house. Inside the park, however, is a rare phenomenon – the sturdy symmetry of an Edwardian castle which has been inhabited for over 600 years. This is indeed a border fortress, built from sheer necessity by Edward I to suppress the Welsh whose defeat he had finally achieved in 1282 by the death of Llywelyn, the last native Prince of Wales. If it was Edward's conception, Chirk owes its completion to Roger Mortimer, justice of North Wales, who was given the property by the king and who made use of a former defensive site until he claimed dominance in 1310.
The courtyard and the enormous drum towers at the angles are probably the

to help him. It is believed that it was the blacksmith Madog Goch who finally betrayed him.

CILYCWM, Dyfed   21 SN74
This pretty village of old cottages was an early centre of Welsh Methodism, and its chapel is claimed to be the first Methodist meeting place in Wales. The mainly 15th-c church displays frescoes and family box pews that may date from the same period, and fine yews stand in the churchyard. Near by is a beautiful one-arch bridge over the Tywi, called Dolau-Hirion and built by William Edwards in 1773. Its single span measures 28yds, and is similar to the famous bridge that Williams built at Pontypridd.

Cilycwm is situated in one of the wildest and most romantic parts of S Wales, where the Tywi flows down through its valley and is joined by various tributaries running through rugged and beautiful valleys. The region is the last British stronghold of the kite, which has remained in spite of the creation of the Llyn Brianne Reservoir. A small isolated chapel at Ystradffin was rebuilt by the Earl of Cawdor in the early 19thc and is dedicated to St Peulin. Near by is a tiny cave which is reputed to have been

only features that have remained unchanged since that date. A succession of owners and occupants – among whom were Thomas Seymour the husband of Queen Catherine Parr, and Robert Dudley the Earl of Leicester – each in turn wrought those modifications which go hand in hand with continuous habitation. But it was after 1595 that the greatest changes were made. In that year Thomas Myddelton bought the castle and lordship of Chirk from Lord St John of Bletsloe. A man of considerable business acumen, whose enterprises were as wide as they were productive, Myddelton was one of the original shareholders in the East India Company as well as being a banker and creditor on a large scale. He was knighted in 1603 and made Lord Mayor of London in 1614, with the result that his involvement in the world of commerce confined his activities to the capital city. He did not lose sight altogether of the cultural needs

the hideout of the outlaw Twm Shon Catti, who was made into a folk hero in *The Adventures and Vagaries of Twm Shon Catti* by the 19th-c author Thomas Llewelyn Pritchard.

CLAERWEN RESERVOIR, Powys   13 SN86
Opened by Queen Elizabeth II on 23 October 1952, the dam here holds back a lake of 600 acres. Claerwen and the nearby Elan Valley complex of reservoirs supply Birmingham with water.

CLARACH, Dyfed   12 SN58
The sandy bay of Clarach lies just to the N of Aberystwyth, and is most easily accessible by a path over Constitution Hill. It can also be reached by a side road which turns off the B4572 at Llangorwen. Set between two hills, this was once a notable beauty spot but today is littered with caravans. Llangorwen, in the Clarach Valley, has an 18th-c stone bridge and 19th-c All Saint's Church. The latter carries a tall tower with a spire, and its interior beauty lies in the simplicity of its white walls and clear glass lancet windows. It has associations with the Oxford High Church Movement of the 19thc through the Rev Isaac

of his fellow Welshmen, and was responsible for the publication of the first pocket Bible in Welsh during 1630.

As a result of damage caused to the castle during the civil war, when Sir Thomas's son (also Sir Thomas) had commanded the local parliamentary forces, substantial repair work was undertaken during the first years of Charles II's reign. Just over 100 years later in 1766 a Mr Turner 'surveyor from Hawarden', was made responsible for alterations. However, a sudden dismissal in 1773 left 'unfinished some carving and joiners' work in the drawing room'. This was clearly a temporary condition, for the modern public sees a dignified sequence of rooms, each beautifully proportioned and characteristic of the refined taste of the late 18thc. The most recent major changes were effected in the last century, when Pugin was responsible for gothicizing the east range now used privately by the present owners – the Myddeltons.

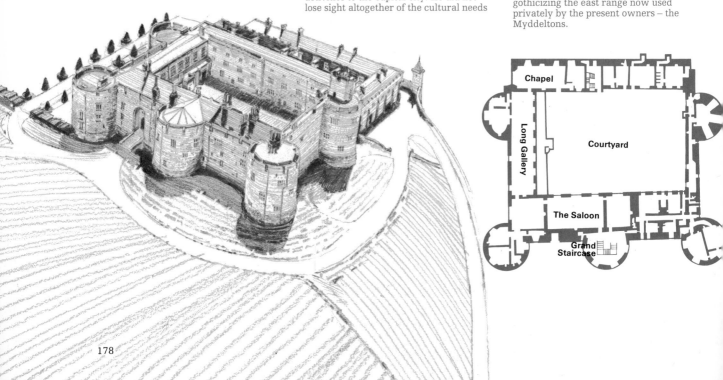

Williams, Dean of Trinity College Oxford, who was one of the movement's leaders. He was born and lived at Cwmcynfelin, an impressive late 18th-c house which is now converted into flats. One of his associates, John Keble, wrote the last part of his *Christian Year* while staying here.

CLWYD HILLS, Clwyd

These attractive rounded hills extend in a 15m range SE from the coast at Prestatyn. Their height is accentuated by the broad, low-lying Vale of Clwyd, which runs below the hills for almost their entire length. As a result of a rift fault long ago, the W face overlooking the vale is one of a steep scarp slope rising in places to 1,500ft, with isolated summits above that. The N end

MEMORABLE RUINS

In the 18th and 19thc, when travellers came up the Afon Teifi from Cardigan to admire the ruined castle of Cilgerran perched high above them, many painted and sketched the scene. But it is the canvases of the artists de Wint, Turner, and Wilson which are renowned for conveying the picturesque quality and atmosphere of this view. Modern visitors to the castle approach it through the quiet and unassuming village of Cilgerran itself, and it is only the coracle men and the leisured angler who see the decayed fortifications very much as those tourists would have 200 years ago.

In order to strengthen his hold on the Norman occupation of south-west Wales, Henry I created two marcher lordships. One of these, Cilgerran, he granted to Gerald de Windsor who already held Pembroke Castle for the king. There are few traces of a fortress dating from that period at Cilgerran, and the ruins that we see today are those of a 13th-c structure. Nevertheless, the early history of the castle is connected with the story of the abduction of Gerald's wife Nest – the 'Helen of Wales' – by Owain, the son of the Prince of Powys. By tradition the castle of Cenarth Bychan, the scene of the outrage, is linked with the present site of Cilgerran.

During the reign of Henry II one of the most illustrious and

near the coast rises steeply to 700ft, but is relatively low and has only two or three points coming close to the 1,000ft contour. The higher part starts at Bodfari, where the River Wheeler has carved a gap through the hills. Moel Fammau rises to 1,820ft and is the highest point in the range. The top is surmounted by the ruins of a tower, and is open to the public as an excellent viewpoint. The name, suitable for the highest of the hills but possibly more fitting in Snowdonia, means 'Mother of Mountains'.

Offa's Dyke path lies some distance to the W of the line of the actual dyke, which crosses Halkyn Mountain to the E and follows the W scarp for some distance, linking most of the hill summits and affording fine views. A TV station on the

relentless leaders of the Welsh cause was 'Lord' Rhys of Dinefwr. A grandson of Rhys ap Tewdwr, ruler of the Welsh kingdom of *Deheubarth* (South Wales) at the time of the conquest, he succeeded in regaining a great deal of power and property, which included Cilgerran. The victory was partial and temporary, for after Rhys's death in 1197 his sons became engaged in so many family rows that any hope of consolidating the success achieved by their father became more and more remote. Within five years Cilgerran was captured by William Marshall, only to be recovered by Llywelyn ap Iorwerth 'the Great', when in his attempt to reunite the princes of Deheubarth and establish his own strength as overlord he also took the castles of Aberystwyth, Carmarthen, and Llanstephan. When William Marshall's son – another William – recaptured Cilgerran in 1223 the building programme showed them to be a family of considerable skill and inventiveness in the field of defensive architecture. The castles of Chepstow and Pembroke offer further evidence of the talent of William Marshall and his five sons, each of whom held Cilgerran in turn until 1245, when it passed to William's daughter Eva and eventually to the Hastings family.

E slopes of 1,304ft Moel-y-Parc is adjacent to a Danger Area.

CLYDACH, West Glamorgan   *20 SN60*

An industrial village 4m NE of Swansea in the Tawe Valley, Clydach is dominated by the Mond nickel refinery. A statue of Dr Ludwig Mond, who invented the process on which the works were founded, stands at the refinery's gates. To the S of Clydach the valley is blocked by remains of a low moraine left by glaciers. The 893ft Mynydd Drumau is to the E behind Glais. A narrow, unspoilt valley cuts back from the W of Clydach into moors, and a road leads to the summit of 1,099ft Mynydd-y-Gwair.

CLYDACH GORGE, Gwent   *22 SO21*

Clydach Gorge runs from Brynmawr to

The castle was reported to be a ruin as early as 1326, but the danger of a French invasion later in the century resulted in Edward III ordering that Cilgerran, along with Pembroke and Tenby, should undergo considerable repairs and be refortified in 1388. Such precautions proved unnecessary, but although there was no attack from the French the castle did play an active part again in 1405 when it was held by the Welsh during the Owain Glyndwr uprising Having been in the possession of the crown during the 15th and most of the 16thc, it was granted by Henry VII – with his customary generosity to his fellow-Welshmen – to the Vaughan family, who built themselves a house in the neighbourhood early in the 17thc. Since Cilgerran played no part in the civil wars its history from then on is one of peaceful decay. The most interesting surviving features of the castle are William Marshall's East and West Towers, which both straddle the curtain wall and supplant the need for a keep. The site is magnificent.

OUTER WARD

INNER WARD

Gatehouse

The otter is one of many wild mammals protected in the Coed Cymerau reserve.

the Usk Valley at Gilwern, and is known as the Fairy Glen. The gorge also links former iron towns at the heads of the coalmining valleys with the Brecon and Newport canal, and with roads along the Usk valley. Several tramroads connected the ironworks and their limestone workings with the canal. The gorge was the route for the Brynmawr to Gilwern tramroad, which was completed in 1804 and is now part of the A465 Heads of the Valleys road. In 1962 the Cwm Clydach nature reserve was set up for preservation and study of the valley's beech woods. Up to 60 years ago many local elopers were married without licences at a 'runaways' chapel' in the valley.

CLYNNOG FAWR, Gwynedd   8 SH44
A remarkable church that has been the recipient of many compliments down the ages is situated in this small Lleyn Peninsula coastal village. It was dedicated to St Beuno and built early in the 16thc. A probable explanation for its size and magnificence is offered by the Rev R D Roberts, vicar of Clynnog from 1950 to 1955, in an informative history: 'The monks probably realized that their tenures would be abolished and began spending all they could in building, running into debt to do so, to evade loss of property'.

St Beuno founded a monastery in Clynnog Fawr in AD616, which was the basis for the monastery which flourished until the Danes ransacked it in the 10thc. It is believed that the church was rebuilt in the same form and on the old foundations. The church was obviously a suitable stopping place for pilgrims making for Bardsey. A well is still visible on the roadside about $\frac{1}{4}$m S, and just inside the main door is *Cyff Beuno*, or St Beuno's Chest, preserved in a glass case. It is an old chest hollowed out of one piece of timber and once used for receiving the offerings of pilgrims on their way to Bardsey. A little over a century ago the custom still prevailed that all lambs and calves born with a notch in the ear – called St Beuno's earmark or *Nod Beuno* – were to be sold and the money put in the chest. Money was also placed in the chest as a sin offering. Hanging on the wall of the south transept are a pair of old dog tongs, viciously-spiked instruments to grip an offending animal around the neck.

This telescopic device was used for ejecting a troublesome dog in the days when it was the practice, from the squire downwards, to bring one's dog to church.

Connected to the church by a passage is St Beuno's Chapel, which was restored from a ruinous condition in 1913. It is commonly believed to be the burial place of St Beuno, and his tomb was said to have great curative value. Anybody lying on the tomb for a night was supposed to be cured of any disease. Another connection with Beuno is a rock called Gored Beuno, which appears from the sea at low tide. St Beuno and his monks are thought to have had a fishing weir here.

CLYRO, Powys   22 SO24
Clyro is a quiet village situated off the A4153 and set under a hill above the widening valley of the Wye. It is 1m NW of Hay-on-Wye and can be reached by road, or across the fields by a footpath. The Romans had a fort and station here between the water-valley and the forests, at a time when their interests were to strike into the W hills for lead, copper, silver, and gold. Some of the original 13th-c church survives, although it was rebuilt by J Nicholson in 1853. The Rev Francis Kilvert was curate here from 1865–1872, and his famous diary – selected and edited by William Plomer – opens with the last two of these years. The diary gives a charming picture of the Radnorshire people and the countryside of his day. A tablet to his memory can be found on Ashbrook house, where he lived. A delightful feature of the churchyard is a fairly modern gravestone fashioned in the shape of a heart.

Near Clyro are the sparse remains of a motte-and-bailey castle. This was built by the direction of the Norman William de Braose and is situated on a natural hillock ideal for defence purposes. The castle was mentioned in 1403 in Henry IV's review, and described as a defensible stronghold. All that remains nowadays is part of the moat, a mound, and numerous traces of masonry which indicate a rather shapeless plan of the vanished structure. Clyro Court was originally a seat of the Baskervilles and later served as a school. Also in the village is Adam Dworski's Pottery, well-known for its fine work.

COED CAMLYN, Gwynedd   9 SH63
This national nature reserve lies $\frac{1}{2}$m S of Maentwrog and is made up of 57 acres of sessile oakwood. A permit is required to visit it, and the area is noted for its rhododendrons. All three British woodpeckers breed here.

COED CYMERAU, Gwynedd   9 SH74
Coed Cymerau is a national nature reserve situated 1m NW of Ffestiniog. It covers 65 acres of sessile oakwood and access other than by public footpath requires a permit. The reserve forms part of the Vale of Ffestiniog, and woods cover both sides of a stream that flows down a deep valley – the haunt of otters and badgers.

COED DOLGARROG, Gwynedd   5 SH76
Situated 7m S of Conwy, this national nature reserve comprises 170 acres of steep oak and alder woodland. A permit is required by anyone wishing to leave the public path.

COED GANLLWYD, Gwynedd   9 SH72
Some 5m N of Dolgellau, this national nature reserve is open without permits and covers 59 acres of woodland. A well-known beauty spot here is the Rhaeadr Du waterfall, and the damp woodland is prolific with ferns and mosses.

COED GORSWEN, Gwynedd   9 SH72
A national nature reserve 4m S of Conwy, Coed Gorswen comprises 33 acres of rich woodland. A permit is required to leave the footpath and venture into the gentle, rolling lowland, which is rich in plant and animal life.

COED MORGANNWG, West & Mid Glamorgan
This is the name given to the largest single area in Wales to be newly afforested. It covers some 15sqm – an area bounded approximately by Neath, Bridgend, Rhondda, and Ystradgynlais – and covers portions of some twelve coal-mining valleys.

COED RHEIDOL, Dyfed   12 SN77
A national nature reserve and forest reserve 10m E of Aberystwyth, this 115-acre area is largely made up of sessile oakwood. A permit is required by anyone wishing to leave the public pathways.

COED TREMADOG, Gwynedd   9 SH53
Cliffs, woodland, and screes are all featured in this national nature reserve, which lies $1\frac{1}{2}$m NE of Porthmadog and covers 49 acres. A permit is required to visit it. Dolerite cliff faces are rich in the minerals which lime-loving plants thrive on, and the types of flowers to be found here include marjoram, hartstongue fern, and shining cranesbill. Pine martens are reputed to live in the reserve, and bird life is prolific.

COED-Y-BRENIN, Gwynedd   9 SH72
The Coed-y-Brenin, or the King's Forest, lies midway between Dolgellau and Trawsfynydd and is the fourth largest forest in Wales, covering an area of some 16,000 acres. The main part of the forest blankets the low hills between the Rhinog Mountains and Rhobell Fawr, through which flow the Afon Mawddach and its tributaries the Gamlan, Eden, Gain, and Wen. Numerous other extensive but isolated areas cover surrounding hills. The main A470 road between Dolgellau and Blaenau Ffestiniog follows the Mawddach and

Eden rivers through the W part of this attractive region. The Forestry Commission have provided extensive facilities for the public to enjoy the woodland, including the Forest Interpretive Centre at Maesgwm, 8m from Dolgellau off the A470. This contains information about the function and value of the forest, and a display of machinery from local gold mines.

The unclassified road from Ty'n-y-Groes hotel crosses the Mawddach, and later the Afon Wen, before climbing towards Llanfachreth and passing an arboretum on the ascent. The area now covered by the coniferous forests has been popular with tourists for over a century because of the attractive waterfalls on some of the streams.

Dolmelynllyn Hall is a tall Victorian building once owned by William Madocks (1774–1828), the famous builder of the Cob at Porthmadog and village of Tremadog. Like Thomas Johnes at Hafod near Devil's Bridge (Dyfed), he made the house into a centre of advanced ideas. The most famous tree in Wales grew in the Mawddach Valley at Ganllwyd. It was a giant oak which, when felled in the late 18thc, produced 609 cubic ft of timber. The bole alone weighed 20 tons. Given the name *Brenhinbren*, or the King Oak, it appeared in a number of Welsh folk songs.

COEDYDD MAENTWROG, Gwynedd 9 SH64
No permit is required to visit the 180 acres of woodland that make up this national nature reserve, which lies about ½m N of Maentwrog.

COED-Y-RHYGEN, Gwynedd 9 SH63
A wild and strange place where lichens and mosses grow on branch and rock, this national nature reserve is situated on the W side of the Trawsfynydd Reservoir. It comprises 52 acres of oak and birch woodland, and visitors require a permit.

COELBREN, Powys 21 SN81
Remains of a Roman fort lie SE of the village of Coelbren. Comparatively little is known about this site, but it is thought to have been occupied until about

AD140. The remains of ramparts and gateways can be traced.

COITY, Mid Glamorgan 25 SS98
Sometimes spelt 'Coety', Coity is noted for its castle and church. The church dates from the early 14thc and is built in the decorated style. It displays attractive rib vaulting, and one of the two fonts is a massive object which now stands in the south transept. Two squints and two piscinas – basins used to wash the sacramental vessels in – are also preserved. Small stone effigies of the Turberville family can be seen in the chancel. An old oak chest carved with the emblems of Christ's Passion may once have been a reliquary or a travelling altar.

Ruins of the castle are the basis for a charming legend. It seems that when Robert Fitz Hamon conquered Glamorgan he gave lands to all his knights except one – Payn de Turberville, who was told to go and find his own land. So off Payn rode with his followers and came to Coity. Before the fight could begin the Welsh prince Morgan came out of the castle, with his sword in one hand and his daughter Sybil held with the other. He is supposed to have said to the Norman: 'You may choose which you will have, my daughter's hand in marriage or war so long as my line and my people shall survive'. It seems that Sybil was beautiful and the sword very sharp, so Payn chose the lady.

By the 14thc there were no more male Turbervilles, and eventually the castle came to the hands of Sir William Gamage. The castle withstood a very long seige during the uprising of Owain Glyndwr. Gamage was in the castle at the time, and it took no less a person than the king to relieve the seige – though even his troops were driven back at least once. In the 16thc the castle passed to Barbara Gamage, who after considerable political argument (she was more than once ordered to the court of Elizabeth I but did not go) married Robert Sidney, brother of famous Sir Philip. The couple lived together very happily at Penshurst in Kent, were praised by Ben Jonson in one of his poems, and seem to have neglected the castle at Coity. The castle

ruins (AM) consist of an inner and outer ward, a keep, gatehouse, and various domestic buildings which include a chapel. Parts of the keep and inner ward date from the 12thc. Building work was conducted in the 13thc, and the 14thc saw extensive alteration and repair. A four-storied building was added to the north-west side of the keep in Tudor times.

COLVA, Powys 14 SO25
This tiny hill parish is situated on a minor road which should be approached with care. The local church stands at 1,260ft and dates from the 13thc. Interesting features include a 13th-c font, doorway, and window, plus a low wooden porch. Pleasant rococo slate tablets inscribed with quaint verses and made by local masons can be found on either side of the altar. Royal Arms of 1753 were altered for Queen Victoria in 1838.

COLWYN BAY, Clwyd 6 SH87
An attractive resort of fine parks, good-looking houses and smart shopping arcades, Colwyn Bay is little more than a century old. The land on which the town stands once had three farms, a few cottages, and the stately home of Pwllycrochan – once the home of the dowager Lady Erskine. Much of the Pwllycrochan Estate was bought by Mr (later Sir) John Pender of Atlantic-Cable fame, who subsequently sold out to a syndicate. By 1900 the population was 8,000, and in 1934 the town became a borough. The population is now 24,000, which makes it one of the biggest towns in N or mid Wales.

The pier pavilion was opened in 1900 by opera singer Madame Adelina Patti, and the promenade stretches 3m around the bay to Rhos-on-Sea, marred only by the proximity of the London to Holyhead railway line. The railway, of course, was there first. One of Colwyn Bay's best features is its parks, Eirias Park in particular, where facilities are continually being improved. Another attractive park is Pwllycrochan Woods, on the hill above the town. The town of Old Colwyn has managed to retain its identity alongside its more sophisticated sister. The two towns are naturally separated by the Nant-y-Groes, a little stream coming down from the hills through a valley known as Nant-y-Glyn.

A 2m walk up the valley leads to Christchurch, known as 'the cathedral on the hill', at Bryn-y-Maen. A post-war enterprise at Colwyn Bay was the establishment of the Welsh Mountain Zoo and Botanic Gardens. Entertainment is offered by two good theatres, and St Trillo's Chapel is of interest.

CONNAH'S QUAY, Clwyd 7 SJ26
Connah's Quay is a Deeside village which lost its maritime usefulness due to the silting sands of the estuary. Today it is an industrial community which leans heavily on the massive Shotton

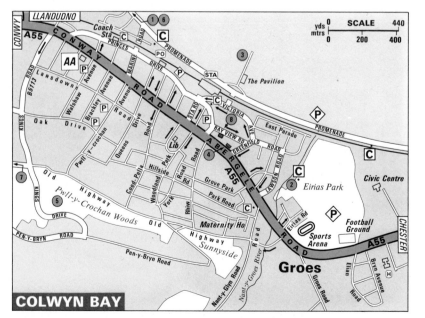

1 Harlequin Theatre
2 Nant-y-Glyn
3 Pier
4 Prince of Wales Theatre
5 Pwllycrochan Woods
6 St Trillo's Chapel
7 Welsh Mountain Zoo & Botanical Gardens
8 WTB Information Centre

Steelworks as a source of employment. The steam power station was the first of its kind to be built in N Wales.

CONWY, Gwynedd 5 SH77

Few towns offer a more exciting prospect to the visitor than Conwy. Three bridges cross the wide estuary, where a veritable armada of small boats bob lazily on the tide, and over the whole scene broods the famous and much fought-over castle. Conwy has always been a place of strategic importance, guarding the estuary of the once-navigable Conwy River and dominating the coastal route into old Caernarfonshire and Anglesey. Its strategic situation may, however, prove its ruination. Few towns in N Wales have suffered more from traffic congestion, and road engineers are now agonising over a new road which some-how must be squeezed between the mountains and the coastline without disturbing the medieval town or disfiguring its estuary. Conwy had to make concessions to traffic needs in the 50's, and a road bridge was constructed masking the famous suspension bridge which Telford built in a style which seemed to be a perfect complement to the historic castle.

Telford's bridge was completed in 1826 – the same year as his Menai Straits bridge – and ended forever the complaints travellers made about the ferry and its apparently surly ferrymen. The ferry crossing was at best a very slow and frustrating journey, passengers often having to wait hours until river conditions and ferrymen's tempers were all in order. At worst it was highly dangerous; on Christmas Day in 1806 thirteen people were drowned when the Irish Mail coach tipped over. This led to increased agitation for a bridge, which Telford started in 1822. The towers and outworks were built in mock 13th-c style in sympathy with the castle, but it was superseded by a new bridge when 20th-c traffic was threatening to pound it to destruction. It now serves merely as a footbridge, but the original chains are

still in position and have resisted corrosion because the metal was apparently dipped in linseed oil while still hot. In 1848 Telford's majestic suspension bridge acquired a neighbour – Stephenson's Tubular Bridge. This employed the same tube principles as the Menai-Straits structure. The new road bridge was completed in 1958.

The magnificent castle (AM) is one of the series that Edward I had built to keep the Welsh in subjection. It was begun in 1283 after Prince Llywelyn, the last of the Welsh native princes, had been killed by Edward's troops. Together with the town walls it is counted as one of the great fortresses of Europe. The castle is now in the care of the DoE, who have done much to repair the damage inflicted by time and man over 700 years (see inset opposite). The town walls (AM, OACT) measure about 1,400yds in length, and with three double gateways and 21 towers make Conwy one of the best surviving examples of a medieval walled town in Britain. There was once a monastery at Conwy, founded by Llywelyn the Great in 1185, but in 1282 Edward I moved it lock, stock, and wine casket to Maenan, which is upriver from the town. Conwy's parish Church of St Mary is built on the site of the monastery and includes some parts of it. It is mainly in the decorated style, has a beautiful and ancient roodscreen, and a 15th-c font. Other features include finely-carved stalls, a stone figure of the daughter of John Williams, Archbishop of York, and a marble bust of the locally-born sculptor John Gibson, who died in 1866.

The name 'Hookes' recurs frequently in the civic history of Conwy, which is not surprising when the inscription on the tomb of one Nicholas Hookes read that he was the 41st child of his father and himself the proud father of 27. Within its medieval walls Conwy is an intimate town of narrow streets, but disappointingly few of its old buildings

have survived. One of the few is Plas Mawr, an Elizabethan town mansion with stepped gables and delightful courtyards, now the home of the Royal Cambrian Academy of Art. The banqueting hall is dated 1580 and is the building's most notable feature. Aberconwy (NT) is an even older house, which possibly dates from 1400 and has a first storey approached by outer stairs – as was the custom before inner staircases were devised. Visitors are inevitably drawn to the picturesque quayside, where sandwiched among a terrace of houses is the 'Smallest House in Great Britain'. The quayside is busy with mussel boats. Open-air facilities include Benarth Wood, Bonlondeb Park, and Bonlondeb Point (viewpoint).

CORRIS, Gwynedd 9 SH70

Corris is actually two villages, with one looking down on the rooftops of the other. Corris Uchaf or Upper Corris is on the top A487 road at the S end of the Peny-Garreg Pass. Corris itself lies in a deep valley of the Afon Dulas, and is almost at the S limits of the Snowdonia Park. It is a slate-quarrying village, a fact reflected by the use to which slate has been put – for fencing fields, bordering roads, and building houses. The slate heaps are an ugly addition to the beautiful surroundings of this village, but Welsh slate was recognized as superior even in Roman times. The local Roman road may have been built partly to cart slate from the outcrops on these hills, although its obvious purpose was to link Dyfi with the Dysynni.

The village has a railway museum dedicated to the narrow-gauge Corris Railway, which once ran alongside the main road to Machynlleth. The village Church of the Holy Trinity was built c1860 and displays a rich Victorian east window.

CORS FOCHNO, Dyfed 12 SN69

Also known as Bog Borth, this expanse of low-lying marsh land is patterned with a multitude of runnels filled with dark water, and stretches along the S side of the Dyfi estuary – all the way from Borth to Glandyfi. Slightly elevated areas of this peaty land form low islands on which hamlets have developed. Such communities include Llancynfelin, which lies between Ynyslas and Tre'r ddol on the only highway to cross the bog. The railway runs almost at the sea's edge beside it. This green and brown expanse of land, with the glint of water present everywhere, forms a forlorn but fascinating landscape.

CORS TREGARON, Dyfed 12 SN66

Entirely filling the angle between the A485 and B4343 roads where they meet just above Tregaron, the Cors Tregaron or Tregaron Bog is also known as *Cors Goch* or the Red Bog. This is because at certain times of the year the seeding
cont page 184

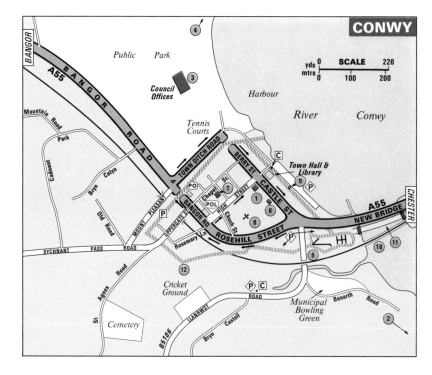

1 Aberconwy House
2 Benarth Wood
3 Bodlondeb Civic Centre and Park
4 Bodlondeb Point (viewpoint)
5 Castle
6 Conwy Pottery
7 Plas Mawr
8 St Mary's Church
9 Smallest house in Great Britain
10 Stephenson's Tubular Railway Bridge
11 Telford's Suspension Bridge
12 Town Walls

THE FORTRESS TOWN

No road can offer a better sight of a medieval town than the eastern approach to Conwy. If the visitor can resist the temptation of giving his entire attention to the castle, and glance at Conwy itself, he will see a great towered and battlemented triangle of wall rising above the tightly-placed buildings – looking like a pre-perspective illumination that might have graced a medieval chronicle. This, the most perfectly preserved of Edward I's walled towns, embraces centuries of building activity and still regards itself very much as an equal neighbour to the castle itself.

Standing on its rocky foundation, Edward's third great fortress has eight battlemented drum towers and seems so compact that it embodies every boy's idea of what a castle should be. This impression is fortified by the presence of Telford's white, 19th-c castellated suspension bridge which appears to lead improbably into the east barbican, while the bulky ends of Stephenson's railway bridge look mockingly on. Closer acquaintance with the castle brings to light the reality of the genius of James of St George, Master of the King's Works in Wales, whose ability as a military architect was unsurpassed in Britain.

As soon as Edward had gained command of the Conwy Valley by the capture of Dolwyddelan in 1283, the enormous operation of building the castle was undertaken at a spot which offered river, sea, and rock defences. The site on a narrow ridge precluded the possiblity of a concentric plan, and as at Caernarfon, the arrangement consisted of an outer and inner ward, with the principal residential part concentrated in the inner and eastern ward. This included the King's Hall, the King's Chamber, the Queen's Chapel, and a Presence Chamber, all with their palatial comforts and refinements. Turrets in the four eastern towers afforded a greater guarantee of protection for the royal occupants. Today they are wonderful vantage points from which to view the lay-out of the rest of the castle, with its evenly-placed towers in the north wall and the protruding south wall, which accounts for the almost segmental shape of the Great Hall. The outer ward is

much larger and once housed the permanent garrison of 30 fencible men. Although only fifteen were professional soldiers they all came under the immediate authority of the constable, who lived there with his family and whose duties included not only the protection of the castle, but the surveillance of prisoners and the supervision of the town. Like other major royal castles Conwy had a permanent chaplain as part of the establishment; also included were a mason, a carpenter, a smith, and an armourer. Until the start of the 20thc access to this outer ward was by a steep ramp of masonry, at the top of which was a gap spanned by a drawbridge. A sloping approach led through an outer and inner doorway to the main gate in the centre of the west curtain, above which were probably the living quarters of the constable.

The most striking apartment in the outer ward – both for its size and state of preservation – is the Great Hall which occupies the entire south wall and which has a handsome window centrally placed in the eastern wall. This vast room was lit by three windows which faced on to the ward, and three each side of the southern fireplace. The best-preserved part of the inner ward is the chapel on the first floor of the north tower. Traditionally this is known as Queen Eleanor's Chapel, but during neither of

her visits to Conwy was the chapel completed. When Edward next visited the castle in 1294 his queen had already been dead four years. It is the most complete and aesthetically pleasing of all the rooms in the castle, with fine arcading and lancet windows.

During Madog ap Llywelyn's revolt in 1294 the king and his company were besieged here for some weeks, but unlike Caernarfon the castle did not fall. Nor was any damage done to the fabric during Owain Glyndwr's revolt in 1401, when the castle was captured by surprise while the garrison were attending Good Friday service in the parish church. By 1590 it had become ruinous, but it underwent considerable structural repair during the civil war, when it was held in the king's name by the Conwy-born John Williams, Archbishop of York. Williams was held responsible for goods deposited there by the local gentry. From the mid 17thc its history was one of dismantling and exploitation, and damage caused by the construction of the two bridges in the last century was considerable. Conwy and the Department of Environment between them have made some highly-successful attempts at restoration.

grasses take on a distinct red tinge. In high summer the colour is white, from the expanse of fluffy tufts of bog cotton which lie like snowflakes over the whole area. This bog is now a national nature reserve covering an area of 1,898 acres, and is claimed to be the largest bog in Britain. A permit is required to explore it off the public footpaths.

CORWEN, Clwyd 10 SJ04
There is no need to remind the visitor to this small Dee Valley town that they are in the heart of Owain Glyndwr country. The hotel overlooking the square takes his name, and according to a picturesque legend, Glyndwr left his mark on the church. A cross on the lintel above the south doorway was supposedly created when he threw his dagger in a fit of pique from a nearby hill. The church is dedicated to Moel and Sulien and has foundations dating back to the 6thc. A 6ft stone which is built into the porch wall was probably once a free-standing monolith. Inside the church is the 14th-c tomb of vicar Iorweth Sulien. Outside are several gravestones with hollows carved out to accommodate those who came to pray over the departed. Near the church is Corwen College, a row of almshouses built by William Eyton of Shropshire for 'the support of six widows of clergymen of the county of Merionedd only'. It was at Corwen in 1789 that the foundations of the present National Eisteddfod were laid, when Thomas Jones of Corwen enlisted the support of the London Welsh Society and prominent Welsh bards for an eisteddfod held at the Owain Glyndwr Hotel – the first event of this nature to which the public at large were admitted.

COWBRIDGE, South Glamorgan 25 SS97
Often called the capital of the Vale of Glamorgan, this old market town lies 12m W of Cardiff and today is by-passed to the N by the main Cardiff to Swansea road. Its original charter dates from the 14thc and a new charter was granted in 1887. The Roman station of *Bovium* may have been sited here. The rectangular lay-out of the town and discovery of Roman coins are thought to give substance to this claim. Remains of the 14th-c town walls survive on the S side, but only the Porte Mellin survives of the three gates that once existed. The 12th-c Church of the Holy Cross is mainly of early-English style and carries a 13th-c embattled tower, an interesting structure of buttresses and stairways. In the last ten years parts of the church have been re-roofed. The original sanctus bell was rehung in 1939 after being used as a fire-bell.

A plaque in the main street recalls 18th-c stonemason and collector of manuscripts Edward Williams, better known by his bardic title of Iolo Morgannwg. He is buried 3m S at Flemingston. The first printing-press used in Glamorgan was established in Cowbridge in 1770, and is now at the National Museum of Wales. In the Town Hall is a painting of the old town hall, given by Charles Jackson Gwyn, who was deputy town clerk from 1900 to 1915. The old hall was demolished in 1830. Stalling Down, E of the town where the by-pass begins, is the traditional site of a victory by Owain Glyndwr over troops of Henry IV in 1405. A monument on the down commemorates men of the Glamorgan Yeomanry. Beaupre Castle and St Quentin's Castle are near by.

COYCHURCH, Mid Glamorgan 25 SS97
Coychurch lies just E of Bridgend, and a large industrial estate links the two. The parish church gives Coychurch a particular claim to fame. It was built in late 13thc and is dedicated to St Crallo. The 15th-c nave roof is beautifully carved, and stonemasons' marks can still be seen on some of the nave arches. The font is probably contemporary with the church's construction. Near the south door is a holy-water stoup, and there are two interesting effigies in the north transept – one of a 14th-c lady, and one of a 16th-c Coychurch parson called Thomas Ivans. There is also a monument to Arthur J Williams, who founded the National Liberal Club. The churchyard contains the grave of Thomas Richards, who compiled an English-Welsh dictionary and was curate of Coychurch for 40 years.

In 1877 the tower fell on the south transept, but both have been carefully rebuilt. Rather battered remains of two stone crosses are also of interest. The tallest is called the Ebisar Cross and was damaged when the tower fell. In its original state it was one of the tallest, if not the tallest, in the country. The smaller cross is inscribed 'Ebisar, the founder of this church, rests here'. A fort known as Gaer lies N of Coychurch, and to the E is the old church of St Mary Hill. Once the property of Neath Abbey, this church contains a Norman font, and the churchyard displays a well-preserved cross.

COYGAN CAVE, Dyfed 19 SN20
Remains of mammoth, woolly rhinoceros, etc have been found in this limestone cave, which was inhabited by men in palaeolithic times. The cave is situated near Llansadurnen (full OS reference SN 285 091).

CRAIG CERRIG GLEISIAD, Powys 21 SN92
A national nature reserve 6m SW of Brecon, this area is made up of 698 acres of sandstone cliff. Visitors require a permit. The reserve lies within the Fforest Fawr region of the Brecon Beacons national park, and has an alpine type of fauna. It is a haunt of dragonflies and a nesting place of ravens.

CRAIG GOCH RESERVOIR, Powys 13 SN87
This is the topmost of the Elan Valley complex of reservoirs and comprises an area of some 200 acres of water. The dam is 390ft long and 120ft high. Birmingham decided that the Elan Valley, once renowned for its isolation and beauty, could supply its water and so built the complex. The poet Shelley lived here for a while. Higher up the valley is still wild and lonely, and hill farmers cut peat turves for fuel.

CRAIG-Y-CILAU, Powys 22 SO11
Some 2m SW of Crickhowell, this national nature reserve covers 157 acres of limestone terrain and includes caves. It is regarded as having the finest limestone vegetation within the Brecon Beacons national park, and includes rare whitebeam trees. The caves may have been used by dissidents in times of religious upheaval. One of them is called *Eglwys Faen*, which means Stone Church, and the cave called Agen Allwedd is well-known to people interested in pot holing. A permit is required to enter the caves.

CRAY, Powys 21 SN82
Cray is a village situated in a beautiful valley to the E of the Carmarthen Van – part of the Black Mountain. Rivers Usk and Tawe rise in the vicinity, and the N flank of Fforest Fawr rises to the S. The local church was built in 1882, and one of the seven forest mills of Fforest Fawr survives here. Fforest Fawr is an area of common land comprising some 40,000 acres. The village was once much bigger and included at least three small Celtic churches. A window in a tractor shed at Tan-y-fedw and a roofless stable are all that remain of these. The Llywel Stone is a famous archaeological mystery which came from Cray. Nobody is sure whether it is of Christian or pagan origin.

CREGENNAN, Gwynedd 9 SH61
This is a NT property which lies 1m E of Arthog, comprising two lakes and 700 acres of rough grazing land. Views to Barmouth, the Mawddach estuary, and Cader Idris can be enjoyed from this wild and mountainous region. Bronze- and iron-age artefacts have been found in the area. A large bungalow which does not belong to the NT was built here in 1897, and was one of the earliest pre-fabricated buildings.

CRICCIETH, Gwynedd 9 SH53
Some 4m W of Porthmadog in an angle made by the arm of the Lleyn Peninsula, Criccieth is a compact Victorian town sloping steeply to the sea. To the E and W of a headland occupied by the ruined castle are sand and pebble beaches backed by short esplanades. The town itself is a mixture of Victorian buildings and older cottages. From April to September the attractive gardens of Cefniwch display an acre of flowering shrubs, a rock garden, and bulbs (OACT). The site of Criccieth Castle has probably had some kind of fortification on it since pre-Roman times. Even in its ruined state the castle displays two distinct styles. It is basically an Edwardian inner ward inside an irregular, early-Welsh outer ward. The present castle was built in 1230 and was extended some 30 years later. Gruffydd, eldest son of Llywelyn the Great, and Llywelyn ap Gruffydd, Llywelyn's grandson who became Prince of Wales, were imprisoned in Criccieth Castle in 1239 for refusing to acknowledge the supremacy of the English crown.

After Llywelyn died in 1282 Edward I captured Criccieth Castle and made it one of the series used to hold down Wales. Many additions were made to the structure, including the building of a complete inner ward with a substantial twin-towered gatehouse. The castle enjoyed a period of relative peace until 1404, when it was captured and burnt by Owain Glyndwr. Although the surrounding countryside was the scene of bitter feuds between the great families, Criccieth Castle was allowed to crumble undisturbed, and it played no part at all in the civil wars. In 1858 it was sold to MP Mr Ormsby Gore by the crown, and repairs were carried out by his family. The castle was opened to the public by Lord Harlech, and in 1933 the site was placed under the guardianship of the government. The Department of the Environment now cares for its conservation. To the NW of Criccieth is Brynawelon, built from 1908 to 1909 by David Lloyd George. There is a lifeboat station on the front, and the parish church is of Church of Wales denomination.

CRICK, Gwent *26 ST49*
King Charles stayed at Crick for a short while during the civil war. He then escaped from Cromwell's soldiers by crossing the River Severn from Black Rock to the Gloucestershire shore.

CRICKADARN, Powys *21 SO04*
Parts of the local church are of Tudor origin. The south porch is especially notable, probably dating from the 15thc.

CRICKHOWELL, Powys *22 SO21*
Nestling beneath 2,302ft Pen Cerrig-Calch mountain, this Usk Valley country town takes its name from Crug Hywel (Howell's Mound). This iron-age camp measures 1,200ft in diameter. Before the counties were created by Henry VIII Crickhowell was a frontier fortress on the E of the great March of Brecheiniog (Brecon). The ruling families of Crickhowell during the Middle Ages were the Pauncefortes and the Turbervilles, who founded the parish church in the 14thc. The building was dedicated to St Edmund the Martyr in 1303 and has a spire roofed with shingles. The church itself contains 19th-c work and was restored with modern aisles.

Crickhowell bridge is a pleasing 17th-c, thirteen-arched, strongly-buttressed bridge spanning the River Usk. It displays segmented arches with double-arch rings built in two orders, with the stones forming the outer ring smaller than those in the inner ring. Two of the arches have been rebuilt. The bridge has been widened on the upstream side, and the total span is 140yds. Only the motte and bailey, parts of the curtain wall, and a small round tower remain of Crickhowell Castle. Built towards the end of the 11thc as a motte-and-bailey structure, it acquired a stone keep in the 13thc. A gatehouse and two towers of the outer ward were added in the 14thc. Owain Glyndwr stormed and destroyed most of the castle in 1403. Some ¾m W of the town is Gwern Vale House, where Sir George Everest was born in 1790. Mount Everest was named after this great military engineer, who did much of his surveying in India. He is buried in the churchyard at Crickhowell. Also W of the town is the 14th-c gatehouse at Porthmawr, which has survived a now-vanished Tudor mansion that belonged to the Herbert family. Fine fishing on the River Usk is mostly hotel or privately controlled, and the Craig-y-Cilau nature reserve lies 2m SW of the

town. The Welsh Brigade Museum is close to Crickhowell at Cwrt-y-Gollen Camp. A Norman castle and Tretower Court can be seen 3m W at Tretower.

CRIGGION, Powys *11 SJ21*
Hiding at the foot of the towering scarp wall of the Breidden, Criggion is no more than a hamlet but has an extremely interesting church. This Renaissance structure has an east end which was rebuilt to the specifications of the Rev Leicester Dowell after his appointment as vicar in 1837. He held the incumbency for 52 years and was one of the stalwarts of the Oxford Movement. His purpose in having the east end of the church altered was to make it more suitable for ritualistic services. He introduced altar lights and vestments, and it was in this church that vestments were first re-introduced after their banishment at the Reformation. The story is set out on a card framed above the pulpit. The cope that the vicar wore was made for him by his wife. He was a cousin of Charlotte Yonge the novelist.

He was succeeded by another remarkable vicar, the Rev Robert Brock, who bankrupted himself through his infatuation for his second wife. He borrowed from moneylenders, pawned his first wife's jewellery, ran up bills, bought jewellery on credit and pawned it immediately for ready cash. His Archdeacon put him straight but failed to keep him solvent, and Brock was ultimately made bankrupt.

CRUMLIN, Gwent *26 ST29*
This small mining town is situated in the Ebbw Vale and has a 200ft-high viaduct which stretches 1,500ft from one mountain to the other, dwarfing the mining works and houses below. The viaduct was designed and erected by the Kennard family, who were responsible for building most of Crumlin. It took four years to complete and was opened in 1857.

CRYMMYCH, Dyfed *17 SN13*
This upland, agricultural area combines the pleasures of the gentle Prescelly hills with the secluded, sandy bays of the coast 8m N. Freni Fawr rises to 1,200ft in the E. Originally only a farmhouse was situated here, but when the railway came to the area a busy agricultural centre developed. Although the railway has now gone Crymmych remains a

thriving agricultural community. The road from Cardigan to Tenby crosses the prehistoric ridgeway near by, above which stands Moel Drygarn and its hill fort of Foelddrygarn to the W. Rivers Nevern and Taf are both near the village, and the area offers good pony trekking.

CWMCARN, Gwent *26 SO29*
Cwmcarn Scenic Forest Drive lies N of Newport in Gwent and E of the A467. It is 7m long and affords fine views of the Bristol Channel and the Brecon Beacons. The drive is in the Ebbw Forest, which comprises 10,000 acres of plantations scattered along 20m of the River Ebbw valley from Ebbw Vale in the N to Newport in the S.

The 1,374ft Twmbarlwm is an iron-age hill fort which can be reached by short steep walks from car parks, or by a longer and gentler mountain walk from another car park. Nearby Nant Gwyddon Valley is approached from Abercarn, and the Wentwood and Tintern Forests are also very attractive areas. The Forest Office is at Graig Wen, Abercarn.

CWM CLYDACH, Powys *22 SO21*
Situated 6m SW of Abergavenny, this national nature reserve comprises 50 acres of beech-grown gorge. No permit is required to visit, and the beech wood with its associated fauna is a rare survivor of a type of environment that has largely been destroyed by man. The Cwm Clydach gorge itself was an important link from the mining valleys to the Brecon and Newport canal. Its slopes are scarred with lines of old tramroads and railways, and the Heads of the Valleys road runs along it.

CWM GLAS CRAFNANT, Gwynedd *5 SH76*
Cwm Glas Crafnant is a national nature reserve 1½m NE of Capel Curig, covering some 38 acres of woodland and rocky slopes. Part of the woodland has been fenced in to allow the vegetation to grow freely, and a permit is required to visit this enclosure. A wide variety of arctic alpine plants grow on the rocks.

CWM IDWAL, Gwynedd *5 SH65*
This national nature reserve lies 5m W of Capel Curig and covers 984 acres. No permit is required to visit. Cwm Idwal was the first nature reserve to be declared in Wales, and is a place of special value, both botanically and geologically. Here the rocks and flowers speak volumes about the Ice Ages and glaciation, and the area has been studied and documented by hosts of geologists and botanists – including Charles Darwin. The reserve comprises the corrie and lake of Cwm Idwal itself, the chasm called Devil's Kitchen, the mountains Y Garn and Glyder Fawr, lakes Llyn Clyd and Llyn-y-Cwm, and the crags Clogwyn Du and the Gribin.

CWM RHEIDOL, Dyfed *12 SN77*
The River Rheidol rises on the slopes of Plynlimon, but the spectacular part of its valley is the Cwm Rheidol reach between Devil's Bridge and the Rheidol Falls.
cont overleaf

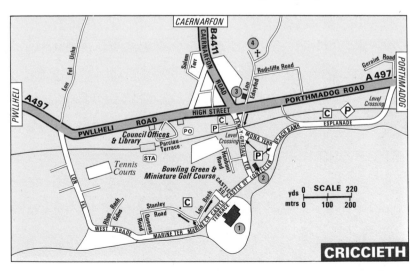

1   Criccieth Castle
2   Lifeboat Station
3   Memorial Hall
4   St Catherine's Parish Church (C of W)

The hydro-electric generating station here has been so cleverly designed and landscaped that it does not constitute a blemish on the lovely surrounding scenery. It won commendation and an award for its design and the way it has been merged with the topography of the valley. Here too is the Coed Rheidol, a national nature and forest reserve comprising 115 acres of oakwood.

CWM YSYWYTH, Dyfed 13 SN77
Both a valley and a village bear this name. The valley is the uppermost reach of the River Ystwyth, extending from a point near its source to Pont-Rhyd-y-Groes; the village is situated just where the mountain road from Rhayader meets the B4574 road at its sharp hairpin bend by Pwll Peiran. This was a mining village, and all around it are derelict workings, mine buildings, and the ruins of miner's cottages. Just past the hairpin is the ruin of Hafod, the ill-fated Johnes mansion which was twice destroyed with all its treasures by fire. Near by is the church, built more than 100 years later and displaying an elaborate memorial to Thomas Johnes' daughter. About 1m beyond the hairpin towards Devil's Bridge is a stone archway across the road. This was set up by Thomas Johnes to commemorate the golden jubilee of George III in 1810.

CWRTYCADNO, Dyfed 9 SH71
Cwrtycadno lies 3m N of Pumsaint in an area of fine woodlands (NT): John Harris, a wizard and astrologer, lived here in the early 19thc and was a well-known herbalist. People came from all over Wales to consult him.

CYFARTHA CASTLE, Mid Glamorgan 21 SO00
Built in 1825 for William Crawshay, one of the great 'Iron Kings' of S Wales, this castle was constructed in 'medieval' style as an escape back to what was thought to have been a more romantic age. It lies 1m N of Merthyr Tydfil, and the living quarters have been turned into a museum and art gallery.

CYMERAU, Gwynedd 12 SN79
Situated in attractive countryside 5m SW of Machynlleth, this garden is noted for its shrubs (OACT).

CYMMER ABBEY, Gwynedd 9 SH71
Ruins of this abbey are situated on a beautiful stretch of the Mawddach Valley near the village of Llanelltyd. Founded in 1199 by Gruffydd ap Cynan, it was the smallest Cistercian monastery in Wales and was populated by monks from Abbey Cwm Hir in old Radnorshire. The sparse remains (AM) date from the 13th and 14thc. They consist only of fragments of the church and some architectural features that have been incorporated into farm buildings.

CYNWYL ELFED, Dyfed 17 SN32
Roman relics found at this village include a small figure of the goddess Diana. The village itself lies 5m NW of Carmarthen in a narrow wooded valley. Welsh hymn writer the Rev D H Elved Lewis was born at Y Gangell, a farmhouse about 1m W.

DALE, Dyfed 18 SM80
This sheltered yachting village lies just inside the entrance to Milford Haven near the sandy beaches of Musselwick Sands; Martins Haven, which is a crossing place to Skomer Island; Marloes Sands; and Westdale Bay. Henry VII landed at nearby Mill Bay in 1485 and marched through Wales to take the crown of England from Richard III on Bosworth Field. Sir Rhys ap Thomas – magnate of S Wales – had sworn to Richard that Henry, who was born at Pembroke Castle, would advance only over his body. According to legend Rhys crouched under a bridge while Henry rode over it. At Dale Point is a 19th-c fort, one of four built to defend the entrance to Pembroke Dock. Here and at Great Castle Head are iron-age promontory forts. Dale Castle stands above the village on a site which was probably occupied by the 13th-c stronghold of Robert de Vale.

DAN-YR-OGOF CAVES, Powys 21 SN81
This popular tourist attraction was first explored in 1912 and is situated in the Brecon Beacons national park. The caves display fine examples of stalactites, caverns, natural bridges, and underground lakes, and are recognized as part of one of Britain's most important caving areas.

DAROWEN, Powys 10 SH80
A S turn at the heart of Commins Coch on the A489 leads to Darowen, where there is an interesting church library. This is one of the Bray libraries, which owe their existence to Dr Bray. He decided to set up parish libraries to enable priests who were too poor to buy books to have access to them. The library at St Tudyr's Church is large and the only one of its kind in Wales. Its facilities were often used by the 19th-c Welsh lexicographer the Rev Silvan Evans, vicar of Llanwrin.

DEFYNNOG, Powys 21 SN92
Defynnog's church was formerly the centre of a large parish. It carries a 15th-c tower and houses a 12th-c font bearing the only Runic inscription in Wales. The village itself lies 9m W of Brecon and used to be important for cattle and sheep marketing in the 19thc.

DEGANWY, Gwynedd 5 SH78
A pleasant suburban face disguises the fact that Deganwy was once an important strategic site, renowned for centuries before Conwy's battlemented towers rose on the opposite bank of the estuary. Behind the village on Vardre Hill stand the ruins of the castle of Deganwy, built on two volcanic outcrops and famous for its position in the struggle between the Welsh and the Anglo-Normans. The original castle was built in the 6thc by King Maelgwn of Gwynedd, but this was partially destroyed by lightning. In 1088 Hugh Lupus, Earl of Chester, built a castle on the same site after taking the coastal plain from the Welsh. King John's army was reduced to eating horseflesh during its encampment here in 1211. Llywelyn the Great destroyed this castle in 1241. It was again rebuilt in 1245 by another Earl of Chester, under the command of Henry III, who during his three-month siege of the castle had also experienced great hardship. The castle was finally destroyed by Llywelyn the Last c1260. Nowadays Deganwy is a small holiday resort, and its S-facing position makes it one of the sunniest places on the N Wales coast.

DENBIGH, Clwyd 6 SJ06
Despite its inland situation, Denbigh (Dinbych in Welsh) somehow contrived to be in the thick of things during the tribal conflicts between England and Wales. The castle (AM) has witnessed the ebb and flow of numerous battles for supremacy, but is now a dignified ruin dominating this walled market town from its hilltop site in the fertile Vale of Clwyd. It was built at the command of Edward I by Hugh de Lacy, Earl of Lincoln, on the site of the hall of Daffydd ap Gruffydd. After an eventful history it was eventually slighted by parliamentary forces in 1660 (see special inset opposite). Beneath the

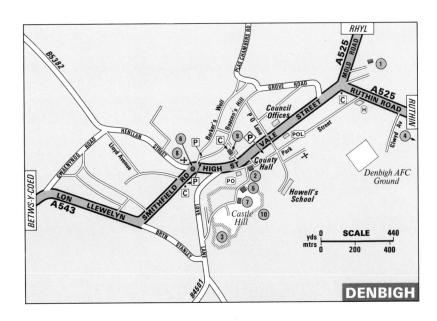

1 Abbey Remains
2 Bull Hotel
3 Castle
4 Frith Pottery
5 Leicester's Folly (ruined cathedral)
6 Market Cross
7 St Hilary's Tower (remains of garrison chapel)
8 St Mary's Church
9 Town Hall
10 Town Walls

castle is a square tower – all that remains of St Hilary's garrison church which existed before 1334. Also inside the town walls are the ruins of 'Leicester's Folly' (AM), a church begun in 1579 by Dudley, Earl of Leicester. This was intended to replace the Cathedral of St Asaph, but was never completed. The Bull Hotel is two adjoining 16th-c houses near Leicester's Folly.

In the lower part of the town are the remains of an abbey (AM) which was largely destroyed by fire in 1898. This was a Carmelite friary founded c1284 by

HOLLOW CROWN

Denbigh itself resembles an Italian hill town, with its castle walls like a hollow crown resting on its summit. Although its Welsh name Dinbych means small fort, and suggests the existence of such a building, the location of this has not been identified. It is certainly not an apt description of the considerable 13th-c stronghold which Henry de Lacy, Earl of Lincoln, built on this high limestone rock when he had been given the lordship of Denbigh by Edward I as recompense for his support during the Welsh campaigns.

Like Chirk, which came into the possession of the Mortimer family for similar reasons, it was a private castle with the primary function – like that of the royal establishments which were being built at the same time – of keeping the recently-defeated Welsh in tight subjection. The first work undertaken soon after 1282 was the building of the town walls. As at Caernarfon and Conwy, so at Denbigh; castle and town were conceived as a single unit of offence and defence, so that the town walls constituted outer defences while the castle itself, in this case, was built inside them on the highest spot in the town.

Within two years of building de Lacy seems to have been sufficiently well established for the king to send him

Sir John Salesbury – who was supposed to have had two thumbs on each hand – and was his family's burial place until 1537, when the friary was suppressed. In the Church of St Mary, built in the late 19thc, are the remains of an ancient altar cloth from the abbey.

A rare 17th-c cockpit could at one time be seen in the yard of the 'Hawk and Buckle' Inn, but this has since been removed to St Fagans museum in Cardiff. Denbigh's market cross stands in Lenton Pool, which traditionally was used in the 18thc for ducking Methodists.

'40 bucks and does . . . to stock his park at Denbigh.' While still in the process of construction Denbigh, like a number of the Edwardian strongholds whether royal or baronial, fell victim to Madog ap Llywelyn's uprising in 1294, with de Lacy defeated under its very walls. Having regained it he set to work on completing the building programme, an achievement which he never saw. Tradition has it that his eldest son Edmund was drowned in the castle well, and that de Lacy left Denbigh, never to return to the spot of the tragedy. On his death in 1311 the castle became the property of his son-in-law, the Duke of Lancaster. After the duke's death by execution eleven years later the castle became crown property which Edward II granted to his favourite Hugh le Despenser. Hugh had accrued vast wealth and property in Wales through this position, but was hanged in 1326.

Having passed through various hands Denbigh became the headquarters of Henry Percy 'Hotspur' in 1399, and he is reputed to have had a garrison of 150 men here. Both Owain Glyndwr's uprising and the Wars of the Roses played a prominent part in the history of town and castle, which in 1563 was granted to Queen Elizabeth's favourite Dudley, the Earl of Leicester. Dudley's unfinished church is still known locally as Leicester's

The town seems to have been carried away by the fleeting visit of Dr Samuel Johnson, but makes little of one of its own illustrious sons, Henry Morton Stanley. Dr Johnson visited Denbigh in 1774 accompanied by Henry and Hester Thrale. Mrs Thrale was one of the Salesburys of Denbigh before marriage. The friends spent eight days as guests of John Myddelton at Gwaenynog. A cottage he used to visit is now called Dr Johnson's Cottage and has taken on the character of a literary shrine bearing an inscription supposedly written by

Cathedral, since it seems that the original intention was to supplant the Cathedral Church at St Asaph.

During the civil wars Charles I spent three days here, but soon after the Restoration a great deal of the fabric was demolished. It was not until the 1920's that the castle underwent considerable repair. The most arresting feature of the structure is the tripartite gatehouse, which even in its ruined state gives a clear notion of the effectiveness of a defensive arrangement where a central octagonal hall is surrounded by three octagonal towers. The sally-port and postern gate are worth inspection, and the view of the Clwyd Valley from here is spectacular.

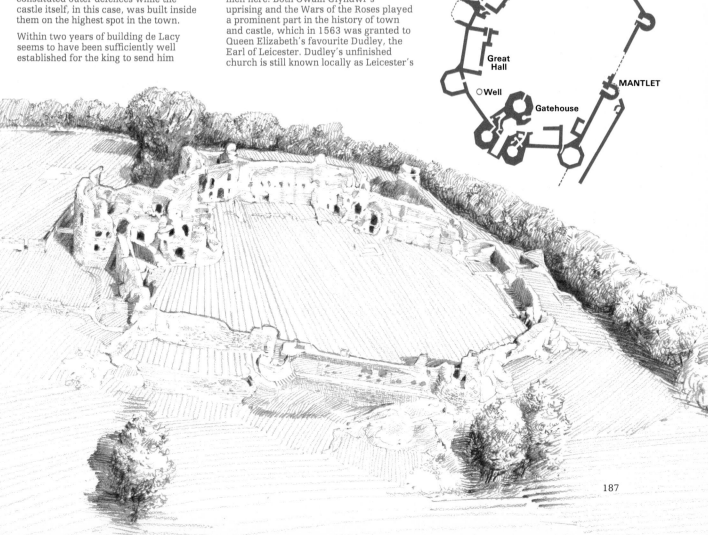

187

him – but dated six years too early. A Grecian urn was set up in the grounds of Gwaenynog and records that 'this spot was often dignified by the presence of Dr Johnson LLD.'

Henry Morton Stanley, a native of Denbigh is best remembered as the author of the most undemonstrative greeting of all time – 'Dr Livingstone, I presume'. A newspaper correspondent with the New York Herald, he led an expedition into darkest Africa in search of explorer Dr Livingstone. Stanley (original name John Rowlands) was a young inmate of the workhouse, and rebelling at the harsh conditions he attacked his cruel master and ran away to sea. He took the name of Stanley from the St Louis trader who befriended him. A model of his demolished birthplace is shown at the castle museum. The Myddeltons were a noted 16th-c Denbigh family who made a considerable impact on London. Sir Hugh Myddelton gave London its first piped water supply at the same time as his brother Sir Thomas was Lord Mayor of the capital.

DENBIGH MOORS (MYNYDD HIRAETHOG), Clwyd
This roughly oval area of moorland lies between the Conwy and Clwyd valleys and extends approximately from Llanrwst to Denbigh, then S to Clocaenog, W to Cerrig-y-drudion, and back to Llanrwst. The E side of the moor finishes among the wooded hills above the Vale of Clwyd, and to the SW it merges with the Migneint and Arennig areas. Geologically composed of Denbigh grits of the Silurian period, it presents a relief of monotonous rounded hills, marshes, streams, reservoirs, and forestry plantations. Very little of the original heather moor remains, as much of this has been ploughed up for grassland or forestry purposes. The average height of the Denbigh Moors area is about 1,400ft, and two hills rise to over 1,700ft – ie 1,703ft Marial Gwyn and 1,742ft Mwdwl-eithin.

DERWEN, Clwyd   6 SJ05
Derwen is a small village surrounded by moorland and situated just off the A494 about 5m N of Corwen. Its 13th-c church has an exceptional 15th-c screen and the only rood loft in the Vale of Clwyd. A perfect 14th-c Celtic cross (AM) stands in the churchyard.

DERWENLAS, Powys   12 SN79
Some 2m down river from Machynlleth, this place was once the town's port and had three quays which could accommodate vessels up to 70 tons. One of the wharves is still visible just past Glandyfi station. A stone stile at the roadside leads down to the railway line, and across it by the river bank are remains of old walls which were part of three shipbuilding yards. Lead ore, timber, and bark were exported from here. A Machynlleth watchmaker called John Rees made a submarine and tested it here. It sank but would not resurface. Luckily some longshoremen who were watching saw that it was in trouble, and hauled it to land manually.

DEVIL'S BRIDGE, Dyfed   12 SN77
Cwm Rheidol closes in to form a spectacular, 500ft-deep wooded gorge here, where the Mynach joins the river and adds its own 300ft of impressive waterfalls to the grandeur of the Gyfarllwyd Falls of the Rheidol. Views into the gorge can be obtained from the road bridge, but the scenic splendour can only be fully appreciated from a descent into the valley bottom. A 91-step descent known as Jacob's Ladder zig-zags down to the river level, where a small bridge and platform affords views of five separate falls. These comprise the 300ft cascade which has carved out cavities known as Punch Bowls at the bottom. Other platforms for viewing the gorge and falls have been provided on the ascent.

There is also a magnificent view across the gorges from the balustraded terrace in front of the Hafod Arms Hotel, which has Swiss snow eaves built by the fourth Duke of Newcastle in the 1830's. The Devil's Bridge is the first of the three bridges which cross the River Mynach. Some authorities say that it was built by the Knights Hospitallers, and others by the Cistercian monks of Strata Florida Abbey 7m to the S. It is at least 12thc, since Gerald the Welshman mentioned that he crossed it in 1188. Legend has it that this pointed-arch bridge was built not by knights or monks, but by the Devil. He is said to have met an old woman named Megan Llandunach – in tears because her cow had somehow got over on to the opposite side of the ravine – and offered to throw a bridge across for her on condition that he should have the first living creature to cross it.

The Devil duly conjured up the bridge and expected Megan to rush across for her cow, but she was too clever for him. She took a crust of bread from her pocket and threw it across the gorge, and a hungry dog dashed across the bridge to get it. Thus the Devil was foiled by a simple old countrywoman. A second bridge, comprising a single, 20yd-span segmental arch and built of stone, was set up above the first in 1753. Finally a third bridge, this time of iron, was built above the other two in 1901. Devil's Bridge is the terminus of the narrow-gauge Vale of Rheidol railway, and the station is a charming miniature complete with all the usual offices and facilities, set amid masses of rhododendron thickets which make a wonderful blaze of colour in summer (see feature on page 62).

DINAS, Dyfed   16 SN03
An attractive little village situated along the A487 about 3m W of Newport, Dinas lies E of an interesting hillfort. The Lady Stone – a standing stone of neolithic or bronze-age date – lies to the SW of the village. Dinas Island, which was separated from the mainland at the end of the Ice Age but is now only separated by an artificial channel, lies to the N. Several pretty coves formed in the shores of the island can be reached from a coastal footpath. The church at Cwmyreglwys was built in 1860 after its predecessor (the ruins of which may still be seen) was destroyed in a violent storm. At the tip of the island is Dinas Head, where impressive cliffs rise to nearly 500ft and strange impressions are displayed by a slab of rock. These are traditionally the Devil's footprints. Grey seals breed in caves around the island.

DINAS DINLLE, Gwynedd   4 SH45
Dinas Dinlle is a small seaside resort situated on a somewhat featureless coastline some 5m S of Caernarfon. It has good sands and offers sea angling, especially for bass. Many angling competitions are held here. On Dinas Hill are the relics of iron-age and Roman encampments, and the ancient Roman road of Watling Street terminated here. The route of the road is still shown by a stony track leading to the coastguard lookout.

DINAS EMRYS, Gwynedd   9 SH64
This iron-age hillfort is situated about 1½m NE of Beddgelert. The original entrance was on the W, but a more gradual ascent is made from the E. Interior iron-age structures were wooden, and most of these were covered by the later stone structures of a Roman building which can be seen near a pool dug during the 1stc AD. Outside the W entrance are three sets of ramparts, and the surrounding hillside displays traces of field terraces and hut circles. A 12th-c medieval tower stands on a cliff above. This fort is connected with the Arthurian legends, and excavation shows that it was occupied during the age of post-Roman occupation.

DINAS GYNFOR, Gwynedd   4 SH39
Probably of Celtic origin, this iron-age hillfort (NT) covers an area measuring 700 by 300yds on top of limestone cliffs. The rocks drop some 200ft to the sea below. To the SE is a defended entrance and two rows of block walling, which during the summer months are covered by vegetation. A marsh on this side must also have helped to keep out intruders. Clay was dug here and exported from a small port at the head of Porth Llanlleiana, which now lies in ruins.

DINAS MAWDDWY, Gwynedd   10 SH81
Pronounced 'Deenass Mouthwe', this village once had a dark reputation as centre for a band of outlaws. During the 16thc the neighbourhood was terrorised by the Gwylliad Cochian (red-haired brigands), and even today there is a noticable prevalence of red-haired inhabitants – although brigandry is not one of their pursuits. The Red Robbers, a kind of Welsh Mafia, were principally cattle and sheep thieves who were not above killing those who stood in their way. As late as the last century instruments such as upturned scythes were found in the broad chimneys of houses, placed there to deter the outlaws from surprising the sleeping household. In 1554 the forces of law and order determined that these outlaws should be dispersed, and more than 80 were caught and subsequently condemned to death.

Lead mining and slate quarrying were once considerable employers of local labour but have long since been abandoned. Old quarry buildings now house the Meirion woollen mills, where visitors are able to purchase Welsh flannels, tweeds, and tapestries in modern and traditional designs. Because of its isolated situation away from the main lines of communication, Dinas Mawddwy has managed to preserve its Welshness better than most places. Three considerable chapels which practically rub shoulders with each other in the village's single street were all built in the 1860's. These testify to the strong Nonconformist belief that flourished here. A robust choral tradition also existed.

The village is an excellent centre for hill walkers in search of solitude. For the motorist in search of wild scenery there are three spectacular passes radiating from Dinas Mawddwy. The Bwlch Oerddrws (Cold Door Pass) leads to Dolgellau along a good road, but Bwlch-y-Groes to Llanuwchllyn is only recommended to drivers with good brakes and a stomach for mountain passes. At 1,790ft it is the highest road in N Wales. Its name 'Pass of the Cross' refers to a medieval cross which was erected at the highest point so that travellers could give thanks for a safe journey. Another route from Dinas is the scenic drive to Lake Vyrnwy.

DINAS POWYS, South Glamorgan 26 ST17
These remains of a Welsh fortress date back to the 5th or 6thc AD and lie about 4m SW of Cardiff on the A4055. A later structure, which was probably built towards the end of the 11thc, incorporated the rampart and ditch of this earlier fortress. The second fortress was constructed of masonry and timber, either by a dark-age prince or a Norman lord, and excavation suggests that a certain amount of wealth and luxury must have prevailed at that time. The castle had two wards, with the inner one enclosing two main buildings which were built roughly at right angles to one another. The larger of the two, about 40ft by 15ft, is the largest post-Roman dwelling yet discovered in Wales. It was probably the hall of the castle's lord, since it had a stone hearth at one end. Documentary evidence suggests that it had quite a stormy past, continually passing between Welsh and English forces during the course of the 13th, 14th, and 15thc.

DIN DRYFOL, Gwynedd 4 SH37
Lying about 1½m NE of a village of the same name, this late-neolithic or early bronze-age burial chamber (AM) is marked by stones. It was probably a passage grave of some 50ft in length. A portal stone stands at its E extremity (full OS reference SH 396 725).

DINGESTOW, Gwent 23 SO41
A small village in the valley of the River Trothy, Dingestow lies about 5m SW of Monmouth. The mound and moat of a former castle may be seen here, and Dingestow Court is a splendid Elizabethan house where the manuscript treasures of Welsh history used to be kept. Ty Mawr is another interesting 17th-c house.

DIN LLIGWY, Gwynedd 5 SH48
One of Anglesey's most remarkable ancient sites, Din Lligwy (AM) comprises a number of enclosed dwellings. A small hut town probably existed here during Roman times, and the community was fortified in the immediate post-Roman period, probably as a stronghold for some chieftain. An area of ½ acre is enclosed by a pentagonal stone wall and includes a group of stone buildings. Two of these were circular, and the other seven rectangular. The walls show a direct Roman influence, originally measured from 4ft to 5ft thick, and include inner and outer facings of large slabs intermingled with smaller stones. Many of these still stand to a height of 6ft. An entrance in the NE wall leads through a rectangular hut or guardhouse, and it is thought that the settlement was

occupied up until the 6thc. Din Lligwy is situated about 5m NNW of Pentraeth, off the A5205 near Penrhoslligwy and Llanallgo (full OS map reference SH 496 826).

DINORBEN, Clwyd 6 SH97
An iron-age hillfort situated on a wooded hill behind the village of St George and S of Abergele, settlement here probably dates from 500 BC to AD 700. The first line of ramparts was built 300 BC. A second line of ramparts built later included stone chambers which guarded the strongly-inturned entrance. The ramparts stretch for some 60ft and incorporate natural scarps. Outside the fort to the N and E are several floors and post holes – remnants of primitive dwellings. Traces of a circular house are also visible. Extensive excavation has uncovered Roman coins of the 3rd and 4thc, along with work in bronze, iron, antler, and pottery.

DOLAUCOTHI, Dyfed 20 SN64
On a hill above Pumsaint are the remains of a gold mine (NT) which was first worked by the ancient Welsh, and later far more extensively by the Romans. They used both opencast and tunnel workings, and the former now look like a disused quarry. Gold was found in veins of quartz, and because these tended to be rather irregular the tunnel workings also varied a great deal in size and shape. The two main adits extended 160ft into the hill and measured about 6ft high by 5ft wide. Heavy iron hammers were used to extract the ore, which was then pounded in mortars cut in the rock, and finally ground down between millstones. The gold dust was then separated from the quartz by washing. Water for this purpose was brought to the mine via two aqueducts, one of which was 7m long and could supply 3,000,000 gallons of water a day.

DOLBADARN, Gwynedd 5 SH56
Forlorn ruins of this castle (AM, OACT) contrast strangely with the huge, moonscape excavations of Dinorwic slate quarry, situated on the opposite shore of Llyn Peris. (See special inset on page 191.)

DOLFOR, Powys 14 SO18
The local inn looks like an ordinary house and is genuinely unspoiled. Dolfor itself stands at over 1,000ft and is reached by 5m of continuously twisting road from Newtown. Magnificent views to the N encompass Snowdon in clear weather. The moorland ridge of the Kerry Hills lies 2m farther S along the Knighton road, and affords views to Snowdon in the N and the Brecon Beacons in the S when conditions permit.

DOLFORWYN, Powys 14 SO19
Neither village nor hamlet but merely the vestigial remnants of an 'ancient castle, Dolforwyn stands on a ridge above Abermule 3½m NE of Newtown. The name means 'Maiden's Meadow' and is supposed to refer to Sabrina and her suicide in the nearby Severn. The castle (AM) was probably built by Llywelyn the Last in the late 13thc, and after his death in 1282 it came into the possession of Roger Mortimer. Its large round tower was recessed into the curtain walls and replaced a slightly earlier square tower. Only faint traces of the masonry remain to-day, and access is by difficult, tortuous back lanes.

DOLGARROG, Gwynedd 5 SH76
Site of a hydro-electricity power station, Dolgarrog is an unattractive village on the W bank of the Conwy. Boulders still to be seen in the village are reminders of the day the dam gave way and claimed sixteen lives. The Eigau Dam was situated 3m above the village in the mountains and burst on 3 November 1923. Boulders of over 200 tons were washed down the valley, water flooding the electric furnaces of the aluminium works caused explosions, and a terrace of houses was demolished. Loss of life would have been greater had not the village cinema, fortunately on higher ground, been packed with local people.

DOLGELLAU, Gwynedd 9 SH71
Plan overleaf
Situated in a wide and fertile valley on the River Wnion under the N slope of Cader Idris, this town's architecture is a simple and restrained contrast between the traditional light grey

Picturesque Eldon Square, Dolgellau.

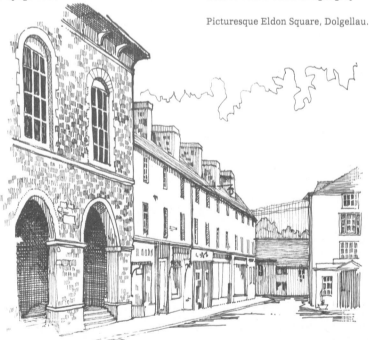

granite and a rough, darker boulder stone. Three Roman roads met here, and some Roman coins bearing the name of Emperor Trajan have been discovered. The name Dolgellau has several interpretations, including, 'Meadow of Hazels' and 'Meadow of Slaves'. Owain Glyndwr assembled the last Welsh parliament here in 1404, and a year later signed his alliance with King Charles VI of France. During the 18thc the town was a centre of the flannel trade. Weaving was a home-industry and many of the farms and cottages had their own looms. Gold has been found in the nearby mountainsides, but a fire at the Gwynfynydd mine in 1935 checked further working of these mines. The Queen's wedding ring is made from Dolgellau gold.

Dolgellau bridge is known as Bont Fawr and was built in the 17thc. Only seven arches remain as three were destroyed when the railway was built; it is probable that the two N arches were rebuilt at the same time. Two arches at the S end show signs of widening, and the only part of the original structure which remains is the downstream portion of the three middle arches. These are built with single-arch rings, indicating that the double-arch ring so commonly seen in Welsh bridges did not come into use until after the middle of the 17thc.

Two toll houses in Dolgellau date from turnpike days and are respectively sited in Arran Road and Cader Road. St Mary's church was built in 1716 against a plain medieval tower. The unusual wooden pillars came from Dinas Mawddwy, the timber being dragged over Bwlch Oerddrws by oxen. The west windows contain 18th-c stained glass. A small alabaster font on a sill on the south side bears the date 1651. The east end of the apse was added in 1864. There is a 14th-c effigy of King Meurig ap Ynyr Fychan, an ancestor of the Vaughans of Nannau, plus a monument which honours Chief Baron Richards – a native of Dolgellau. A monument to the eminent Welsh poet Dafydd Ionawr can be seen in the church yard. The County Hall (or Court House)

was built in 1825 and contains portraits of local 19th-c squires, and the Market Hall was built in 1870. Dolgellau Grammar School for Boys was founded by Dr John Ellis, rector from 1647–1665, and Dolgellau cricket team claims to be the oldest in Wales. It was founded in 1841 by Frederick Temple, then a Balliol undergraduate but later Archbishop of Canterbury.

Some 2m NE of the town is Nannau, the seat of the Vaughan family. Sited at 700ft, this is believed to be one of the highest sites for a mansion in Great Britain. It has been the home of the direct descendants of Cadwgan, son of Bleddyn Prince of Powys, since 1100. The original mansion was the residence of Howel Sele, the cousin and enemy of Owain Glyndwr. Estate houses are recognized by their ornate chimneys and slate verandahs, and the entire property includes 50m of walling. The man largely responsible for the estate was Sir Robert Williams Vaughan (originally Vychan in Welsh), and when he died his funeral was reputedly attended by 3,000 people. A forebear and namesake of Sir Robert, the 17th-c antiquary Robert Vaughan, lived at the nearby mansion of Hengwrt and amassed a fine collection of Welsh manuscripts. A Gorsedd Circle marks an eisteddfod held at Dolgellau.

DOLGOCH, Gwynedd 9 SH60
A stopping place on the picturesque Talyllyn narrow-gauge railway, Dolgoch is noted for its three waterfalls set in superb sylvan surroundings. Access to the first is under the high viaduct of the Talyllyn Line, and the road from Tywyn to Abergynolwyn runs parallel to the railway line at this point. Dolgoch is also a suitable point from which to visit Craig-yr-Aderyn (Bird Rock), a savage looking rock situated 2m N.

DOLMELYNLLYN, Gwynedd 9 SH72
Dolmelynllyn Estate (NT) boundaries encompass the falls of Rhaiadr-du on the Afon Gamlan, which can be reached from a gateway off the main road. Several small falls and cataracts are passed before the main fall is reached.

Carefully-conserved oak woodlands surround the path, and the moist conditions near the falls are favourable to the growth of many rare species of ferns and mosses. An area here is under lease to the Nature Conservancy. The rocky bracken-covered slopes of Y Garn rise to 1,500ft above the estate. Remote Dolmelynllyn Hall was something of an intellectual centre for William Madocks, and his contemporaries during the late 18thc. Thomas Gray's *Ode to the Deity of the Grand Chartreuse* was inscribed in Latin on a rock face above the lower pool of the falls while Madocks was the owner. The hall is now used as a hotel.

DOLWYDDELAN, Gwynedd 5 SH75
This small village SW of Betws-y-coed on the A496 Dolwyddelan was once a centre for a slate-quarrying industry, which has since declined. A fine old church in the village was built by Meredydd ap Ifan in the 16thc, and contains a carved gothic rood screen surmounted by an 18th-c balustrade. Other features include a brass effigy of Meredydd ap Ifan kneeling, some fine pieces of 16th-c glasswork, and a pulpit and benches of the 18thc. The church has a slate floor and limewashed walls, and its roof is constructed of large slates on a thick bed of sphagnum moss – used to keep the draughts out – which was replaced from time to time. This was known as moss-stone roofing. Meredydd ap Ifan was an ancestor of the Wynns of Gwydyr and the Wynns of Wynnstay. He was guarded by a band of tall archers, and had the new church built because the former tree-shrouded building made too good a target for an ambush. There is also a modern church in the village. Dolwyddelan Castle (AM) stands in a prominent position on a broad ledge around the base of 2,860ft Moel Siabod, and is one of the few true pre-Norman Welsh castles (see inset on page 192). Evidence of iron- and bronze-age settlement has been discovered near the castle in the shape of hut-circle groups, and E are cist-burials.

DRUID'S CIRCLE, Gwynedd 5 SH77
This bronze-age stone circle (Welsh name Meini Hirion) is one of the most well-known in Wales and stands on the crest of a hill at 1,200ft above the town of Penmaenmawr. Many of the stones, some of which stand to a height of 6ft, have been removed or destroyed. About a dozen of good size still stand, with many smaller ones in between. The stone-circle can be reached on foot from either Penmaenmawr or Llanfairfechan by equally steep routes. The surrounding moorland yields flints, and large arrow stones – boulders with large grooves cut in them as the result of sharpening tools of some kind – have been found. Such finds point to a well-established stone-weapon industry in neolithic times. Stone axes from here have been found all over Britain (full OS map reference SH 723 747).

DRYSLWYN, Dyfed 20 SN52
Ruins of this 13th-c castle are situated on top of a hill about 5m W of
cont page 192

DOLGELLAU

1 Bridge
2 Court House
3 Gorsedd Circle (eisteddfod site)
4 St Mary's Church
5 WTB Information Centre

LLYWELYN'S STRONGHOLD

When the district of Llanberis was chosen for the location of the film *Inn of the Sixth Happiness*, set mainly in the wild regions of China, the director saw in the area the range and variety of colour and contour that had drawn 18th- and 19th-c travellers and painters to North Wales in search of the 'wild' and the 'grand'. Although the visitor to Dolbadarn Castle today will be assailed by the sound and constant glitter of traffic as he stands on the rocky hill on which the massive round tower is built, he will find little in the view that has changed over the centuries.

The exception is the enormous 19th-c slate quarry of Dinorwic – at one time one of the most important in Europe – which glints and gleams in the sun, with the greens, greys, blues, and purples of its Inca-like steps and platforms changing character with each passing cloud. A pictorial composition at once impressive and forbidding, it in no way intimidates the castle on the other side of Llyn Padarn. The castle was one of the strongholds of the 13th-c princes of Gwynedd, commanding an ancient inland route from Caernarfon to the upper valley of the Conwy and keeping a watchful eye on the entrance to Llanberis Pass. Llanberis is one of the most excitingly austere and brooding stretches in the whole of North Wales, even today, when the only enemies are fellow-motorists. Two of the most fierce and effective leaders of the Welsh cause came from Gwynedd, and their mission and relationship were such that nowadays they often appear as Llywelyn I (1194–1240) and Llywelyn II (1247–82). The more usual form of title – written and verbal – is Llywelyn ab Iorwerth or Llywelyn Fawr 'the Great', and Llywelyn ap Gruffydd 'the Last', a reference to the fact that he was the last of the native princes of Wales. He died in combat in 1282, a disaster which precipitated the Edwardian conquest.

Both were eager to apply contemporary standards of government and jurisdiction, the result of careful consideration of the administrative techniques of their enemies.

Both leaders also profited greatly from the military innovations of their opponents. The resemblance between Dolwyddelan and Dolbadarn is more than the mere geographical situation and the fact that they were both built by the leaders of Gwynedd of their day. They are examples of how a native fortress was built, incorporating the latest devices of fortification, so that Dolwyddelan's rectangular keep of *c*1170 is no mere delayed and badly-interpreted idea of an English defensive system, but an almost direct contemporary of the methods employed by the English themselves. Similarly at Dolbadarn the round keep was a clear indication that this was the prevailing method of aggressive defence in the early part of the 13thc.

Nevertheless when this was built by Llywelyn Fawr 'the Great', it was probably an experiment. The base of the tower on the west defence wall suggests that although contemporary with the principal tower it was rectangular. Llywelyn Fawr died in 1240 and Dafydd, his son and successor by Llywelyn's wife Joan, daughter of King John, lived for only six years afterwards. His death was a severe blow to the spirit of Wales, but his grandson by his illegitimate son Gruffydd showed enough promise and ability to undertake the responsibilities of leadership. By the treaty of Montgomeryshire in 1267 the English crown recognized him as the undisputed Prince of Wales. There was one, however, who had serious misgivings about Llywelyn's claim as successor – namely his brother Owain Goch 'the Red'. During the disputes immediately following Llywelyn's accession he was imprisoned in 1255 and kept at Dolbadarn for 23 years.

The castle was the scene of another incarceration, on this occasion during the Owain Glyndwr uprising at the beginning of the 15thc. This time the prisoner was Owain's personal enemy Lord Grey of Ruthin, the prime instigator of a revolt which achieved enormous dimensions and significance but started as nothing more than a typical border raid. In September of 1400 Owain and his supporters burnt the town of Ruthin, and in the same vengeful spirit attacked the English at Denbigh, Flint, Hawarden, Oswestry, and Rhuddlan – although none of the castles yielded. The campaign was a gesture of retaliation for insults which Owain had already received from Reginald de Grey, but it was also an assault, which though confined to the north-east in the first instance, had wide and protracted repercussions.

It seems unlikely that the castle was engaged in any active combat after the Owain Glyndwr episode, although it appears to have been put to an unexpected use in the 18thc when Hywel Harris, a religious zealot and revivalist, is reputed to have preached a sermon from the red tower. It was through Sir Michael Duff, a descendant of Thomas Assheton Smith who was responsible for the quarries at Dinorwic, that Dolbadarn came under the guardianship of the Department of the Environment. Although the remains are slight, the situation is singularly evocative of internecine warfare.

Llandeilo, off the A40 on the N side of the River Tywi. It played an important part in the 13th-c struggles between the Welsh and the English and was held by Rhys ap Maredudd. The latter, on hearing that Llywelyn the Last was becoming too powerful, joined forces with Edward I against him. When Llywelyn was defeated in 1282 Edward rewarded Rhys ap Maredudd's treachery against his fellow Welsh by taking from him all his territories except Dryslwyn Castle. The king placed him under the jurisdiction of his Justicia Robert Tibetot. Rhys revolted during 1287 in the cause of Welsh independence, and although he managed to gain control of several neighbouring fortifications he was finally driven from the castle at Emlyn after he had laid seige to it. While this was happening his own castle of Dryslwyn was beseiged by the Earl of Cornwall. One of the towers was undermined, but not in a very successful manner. The tower and tunnel – in which Lord Stafford and his men were working – collapsed with a total loss of life. The rest of the force were able to take control of the castle however, and Rhys fled to Ireland. He returned in 1290 at the head of a Welsh peasant force, but was soon defeated, captured, and taken to Edward at York. Here he was dragged behind a horse and finally beheaded. The castle ruins today comprise remains of a chapel and hall.

GUARDIAN OF THE WELSH

Few castles have been less affected by the 20thc than Dolwyddelan – the 'Meadow of Gwyddelan'. On the road between Betwys-y-coed and Blaenau Ffestiniog, along the picturesque Lledr Valley, the battlements of the rectangular keep of this border-like fortress rise from a tree-covered hill. Moel Siabod, which Thomas Pennant the 18th-c traveller and naturalist, called a 'great bending mountain' rises in the background. Like Carreg Cennen and Llanstephan the approach is informal, and even in the castle courtyard the visitor is reminded that he might still be in the farm itself! If any changes have taken place

DYFFRYN ARDUDWY, Gwynedd
9 SH52

Many scattered stone-built houses line the roads of Dyffryn Ardudwy, the main settlement in the parish of Llanendwyn. Sand dunes separate it from the sea and to the landward side, rising to over 2,000ft, are the Rhinog mountains. These hills and mountains are studded with a great many signs of bronze and iron-age settlement cairns, hillforts, and hut circles. A neolithic long barrow (AM) which was excavated during the 1960's can be found not far off the main road alongside the village school playground. In early neolithic times a simple dolmen in a small oval cairn was constructed. To the E of this at a slightly later time a wedge-shaped chamber was built, and finally towards the end of the neolithic period both of these items were enclosed to form a long barrow. Near to the village in a field is Arthur's Quoit (Ceotan Arthur), a large cromlech with marks where King Arthur is said to have held it before he hurled it down from the top of Moelfre.

Llaneinddwyn village touches the N side of Dyffryn Ardudwy. The parish church of St Enddwyn was largely rebuilt in 1883, incorporating a great deal of old stone. It has two short transepts, an open 16th-c roof, benefaction boards in the porch, a finial dated 1558, and a spiral-incised stone in the lychgate.

within the precincts of this stronghold, which tradition observes as the birth-place of Llywelyn ab Iorwerth 'the Great', they can only be for the improvement of the fabric as a result of 15th-c habitation, and the installing of a modern roof and battlements during the last century.

For the last 40 years the Ancient Monuments branch of the Ministry of Works – now called the Department of the Environment – has been responsible for the extremely good condition and evocative atmosphere of the keep. When the visitor enters it at first-floor level the original accommodation is immediately discernible as a central apartment, with a fireplace flanked by a window and integral seats on either side looking down to the valley. One window overlooks the courtyard. A passage built into the thickness of the far wall leads to a latrine, and a stairway to the left of the nearer south-eastern window leads to the upper chamber and the battlements. Views from here of the

Touching on the S end of Dyffryn Ardudwy is the village of Llanddwye. Its church is of perpendicular style and still contains its original east window, medieval roof timbers, a wooden screen dated 1620, and many unusual monuments. The screen separates an adjoining chapel – which is said to have been designed by Inigo Jones – from the rest of the church. The churchyard is circular in shape. Facing the church is the entrance to a long drive leading to the Elizabethan mansion of Cors-y-Gedol, a former home of the Vaughans. This fine old house is also attributed to Inigo Jones, but this seems unlikely as he was only 20 in 1592 – at the time when it was built.

DYFFRYN CASTELL, Dyfed *13 SN78*
Dyffryn Castell is the usual starting point for the ascent of 2,469ft Plynlimon, where both the River Severn and the Wye have their sources. Mountains rise to the NE.

DYFI ESTUARY, Dyfed *12 SN69*
The Dyfi estuary is considered one of the most beautiful in Europe, with whaleback mountains of ever-changing colours sweeping down to the shores, and a road that rivals the Grande Corniche running along the Gwynedd coast. At low tide the expanse of golden sands, with the river winding its way across them, makes an impressive sight. Marshland above the sands is the haunt

awesome vastness of Snowdonia still convey the lethal 13th-c enmity that took advantage of those savage contours. The ruins across the courtyard indicate a parallel structure, and 18th-c engravings suggest the balance achieved by such a building. This might well have been built after the capture of the castle by the English in 1283, soon after the death of Prince Llywelyn. The principal interest of Dolwyddelan is that this castle, erected by a Welsh chieftain in the person of Iorwerth Trwyndwn 'the Flat-nosed' in 1170 and rebuilt in stone in the 13thc, is a Welsh castle with a defensive effectiveness which resulted from military lessons learned at the hands of the Welshmen's very enemies.

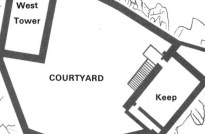

of rare water fowl, and it is an important breeding ground. In the spring families of shellducks – which nest in holes in the ground, often at some distance from the water – can be seen making their way to the estuary. This 3,500 acres of sandbanks and saltings is a national nature reserve.

The curved promontory of Ynys Tachwedd almost closes the estuary at its mouth on the S side, and encloses an expanse of sand known as Traeth Maelgwyn. *Traeth* means a beach or sandbank, and Maelgwyn was a 6th-c king who is said to have floated on the tide seated on a throne made buoyant with feathers and wax. The tides of the estuary make it unsuitable for bathing, though its sheltered aspect makes it safe for sailing. At one time small cargo ships used to venture as far as Derwenlas on the Powys shore. In places the wharfage along this shore can still be seen, and there were even construction shipyards here.

Glandyfi Castle stands high on a ridge but is not a genuine castle. It is a castellated Victorian residence grafted on to an earlier small house. The mound Domen Las at the head of the estuary, standing as it does at the point where the channel narrows, is a more obvious site for a fortress. One of the most fascinating sights of the Dyfi estuary is that of the salmon boats with their sweep nets. Seals are also to be seen here.

DYLIFE, Powys 13 SN89
A tiny group of houses on an isolated mountain road linking Machynlleth with Llanidloes, Dylife affords splendid views of the Plynlimon moors, the gorge of the River Twymyn, and on clear days Cader Idris. The road reaches a height of 1,671ft to the NW of Dylife. In the 18th and 19thc the village was concerned with lead mining, and its inn dates back to these times.

DYNEVOR CASTLE, Dyfed 20 SN62
Ruins of 13th-c Dynevor Castle stand on an isolated hill overlooking the Tywi Valley about 1m W of Llandeilo. The original castle was built AD876 by Rhodri Fawr for his son Cadell. In 1287 the castle was taken by Rhys ap Maredudd, who had been confined to Dryslwyn castle by King Edward I while he was fighting in France. Within three months Rhys and his followers were forced to flee to Ireland. In 1403 Owain Glyndwr tried to take the building, but although he caused a great deal of damage he failed to gain control. Henry VII granted it to Sir Rhys ap Thomas, but it was later confiscated by Henry VIII and Sir Rhys ap Thomas' grandson was executed.

The castle of the first Lord Rhys was dismantled in 1220, but traces of wards constructed in the late 12thc are still visible. In the 13thc a large round keep was built on the side facing the cliffs and river. Following this other towers were built and domestic buildings added during the 14thc. Further alterations were carried out during the 15th and 16thc, and the castle remained occupied until fire damage in the late 18thc. Ruins of a 13th-c keep, a tower, and parts of the irregularly-shaped curtain wall still remain. The present 'castle' is a large mansion which was built in 1856 on the site of a Tudor house about ½m nearer Llandeilo.

Rolling, pastoral countryside near the village of Dyserth.

DYSERTH, Clwyd 6 SJ07
Inland from Rhyl, Dyserth is situated at the N end of the Clwydian range which stretches 20m S to Llandegla. The village is best-known today for its waterfall, which descends 40ft into a limestone gorge and was described by Dr Johnson as 'a very striking cataract' when he visited it in 1774. The local church was restored in 1875 and has a fine 15th-c Jesse window showing the genealogy of Christ. This is reputed to be from the spoils of Basingwerk Abbey. An 8th-c cross known as Croes Einion after Einion ap Ririd Flaidd – who was killed whilst laying siege to the castle – was originally erected in the churchyard and is now located inside the church. An unusual curved pillar, the pedestal of an 11th-c cross, and some fine old yew trees can be seen in the churchyard.

About ½m N a rocky hill forms the site of a vanished castle. It held a good position, with a steep ascent on one side and a sheer rock face on another. It was originally a British stronghold dating back to the new stone age, and was later replaced by a Norman fortress in the early 12thc. In 1241 the castle was rebuilt and garrisoned by Henry III as one of his main strongholds against the Welsh. It was attacked in 1245 and 1263, when Llywelyn ap Gruffydd besieged and took control of it in just five weeks. He then had it demolished. The ruins have now been quarried away except for a few outer ditches. Fine views of the N Wales coastline from Great Orme at Llandudno to Prestatyn can be enjoyed from here.

Siambr Wen is a nearby ruined medieval house which is thought to have been the home of the keepers of the castle. Talagoch lead-mine lies N of the castle and was worked from Roman times until quite recently. Excavation has brought many Roman coins to light.

EBBW VALE, Gwent 22 SO10
Ebbw Vale first emerged as an industrial town in the 18thc, when it was principally concerned with coal mining. The arrival of the steel industry heralded a gradual phasing out of the coal mines, and today only the Marine Colliery at Cwm has survived. The steel industry thrived in Ebbw Vale. Rails for the

Stockton to Darlington railway were rolled here, and in 1856 this was one of the first places to use the Bessemer process of converting molten pig-iron into steel with the impurities removed. Europe's first hot-strip mill was erected here in 1938, and today the town is dominated by the 2½m-long steel sheet and tinplate works of the British Steel Corporation.

One of the most famous names to be associated with Ebbw Vale is that of Aneurin Bevan, who was Labour MP here from 1929 until his death in 1960. A monument consisting of three large stones has been erected to him 1m outside his birthplace at nearby Tredegar. Apart from its considerable industrial heritage, Ebbw Vale boasts a town library at the Ebbw Vale Institute, containing over 15,000 volumes. A local branch of the County Library is sited at Bethcar Street and is open to the public. This is reputed to be one of the largest branch libraries in the country. The large parish church dates from 1858 and has been called the 'Cathedral of the Hills'.

EGLWYSWRW, Dyfed 17 SN13
David Martin, Bishop of St David's, lived at this small picturesque village during the 14thc. His home was a moated manor house known as The Court, and the village itself was one of the 20 knights' fees of the ancient barony of Cemais. A Court Leet still meets here, mainly to allocate sheep earmarks. In Tudor times the body of St Wrw was entombed in a chantry chapel of the local church, and the parishioners would allow nobody else to be buried there. They believed that the saint, a virgin, 'would not have any bedfellows'. St Meugan's Fair is held in the village each year on the Monday after Martinmas in remembrance of St Meugan's Well, which provided three kinds of water – one to remove warts, another to heal sore eyes, and another to cure heart disease.

ELAN VALLEY, Powys 13 SN96
Elan Valley contains a chain of four large reservoirs which were formed between 1892 and 1904 as a water supply for Birmingham. The picturesque hill scenery of this 'Welsh Lake District' is well-known and can be reached most

easily by the B4518 from Rhayader. River Elan rises in the barren peaty upland S of the Plynlimon range, and then descends to the four reservoirs of Craig Goch, Pen-y-Garreg, Garreg Ddu, and Caban Coch. Here it is joined by water from the Claerwen Reservoir, which was constructed in 1952. See individual lake entries. The valley has associations with Shelley, who occupied the house of Cwmlan with his wife between 1811 and 1812. This house, as well as many others, now lies submerged beneath the waters of Caban Coch Reservoir. He was noted for eccentricities such as floating paper boats on the river. One of these curious vessels is said to have contained a cat and had a five pound note for a sail.

ERBISTOCK, Clwyd 11 SJ34
A noted beauty spot 5m SE of Wrexham, Erbistock comprises a quaint riverside inn, a church, and scattered farmsteads. A ferry once used for crossing the River Dee at this point has fallen into disuse. Fishing is good along this stretch of river.

ERWOOD, Powys 21 SO04
Sited 7m S of Builth Wells on one of the most attractive stretches of the River Wye, this village was originally called Y Rhyd, meaning 'The Ford'. The river crossing is now made by a bridge. Erwood is one of the local places associated with Llywelyn the Last, and the men of Edward I probably crossed the river here when they were hunting him. Henry Mayhew is said to have stayed at the inn and devised the idea of the magazine Punch in the parlour. Llangoed Castle lies 2m SE and was rebuilt in 1911. A south porch of 1632 has been preserved in spite of the alterations.

EWENNY, Mid Glamorgan 25 SS97
The priory (AM, OACT) was founded here by Maurice de Londres in 1141, and linked with the Benedictine Abbey of St Peters in Gloucester by deed of gift in 1141. The buildings are mainly ruined, but the 13th-c circuit defensive walls still enclose an area of over 5 acres. The principal gateway has clearly defined portcullis grooves, and the church is still one of the best examples of Norman architecture in Wales, in spite of past alterations. One of its most outstanding external features is a massive fortified tower, and the south wall displays a Mass dial which gave the times of the four principal monastic services. The bowl of the font is thought to be the Norman original, although the stem is definitely a modern one. A solid stone screen divides the nave from the choir, and the transept contains a 12th-c effigy believed to be that of Gilbert de Turberville. The sepulchral slab of the founder provides a fine example of Norman-French inscription in Lombardic capitals. The reredos is situated below the western tower arch, and a very fine 14th-c wooden screen covers the eastern arch.

One of Charles I's cooks and one of Cromwell's smiths, both natives of Ewenny, are said to be buried in the churchyard. An interesting pottery operates in the village, and a chapel on the hill leading to Colwinston is associated with the Victorian preacher and orator Edward Matthews.

EWLOE CASTLE, Clwyd 7 SJ26
Set in woods near Hawarden, this castle (AM, OACT) stands above the junction of two streams near Offa's Dyke and is thought to have been set up by the Welsh Prince Llywelyn the Great as a defence against the English. The D-shaped tower certainly dates from that period. It possibly fell into English hands c1240, but was re-captured when Llywelyn ap Gruffydd reclaimed the border areas. It is known that Gruffydd extended the castle considerably in 1257, adding curtain walls and a steep moat in an imitation of Norman construction. After this it seems that the castle was more or less abandoned in favour of new, much larger fortresses at Flint and Rhuddlan. History has certainly ignored it. There is, however, a record of a Welsh victory over Henry II by Owain Gwynedd in the immediate vicinity during 1157, when the English king was nearly captured. It is likely that the large earth mound S and uphill of the ward was constructed by Edward I's soldiers when they were attempting to besiege Llywelyn. The ruins were cleared c1922 and rescued from an engulfing bramble thicket by the government body now known as the Department of the Environment.

FAIRBOURNE, Gwynedd 9 SH61
Fairbourne has developed over reclaimed land on the S side of the Mawddach estuary. Anti-tank blocks are an unwanted legacy of wartime invasion fears, but Fairbourne can justifiably boast that it has one of the finest beaches in Wales. Miles of golden sand and safe bathing make it a popular spot. Fairbourne's 15in-gauge miniature railway is an added attraction, and runs parallel to the seawall before heading through the sand dunes to Penrhyn Point (see feature starting page 62).

FARMERS, Dyfed 20 SN64
This aptly-named village lies amongst agricultural country in the Twrch Valley near Pumsaint. The church is of 13th-c origin, and the celebrated preacher 'Kilsby' Jones was a schoolmaster for about a year 1m W at the hamlet of Ffaldybrenin. He edited the works of William Williams of Pantycelyn. Ffaldybrenin was the birthplace of Timothy Richards, a Baptist missionary to China who died in 1915.

FERRYSIDE, Dyfed 19 SN31
Ferryside is a small resort on the River Tywi estuary, flanked by 250ft wooded banks. A sandy beach is accessible via a level crossing over the railway line which separates the village from the shore, but bathing is dangerous due to a sharply shelving beach and fast currents. The local fishing trade is devoted to salmon and sea-trout. Cockles may be gathered at low tide, and the village has become a yachting centre. Legend has it that the area was once inundated by the sea. Stories tell of submerged forests, and a town called Halkin which was totally engulfed. The village of Llanstephen can be seen on the other side of the estuary.

FFESTINIOG, Gwynedd 9 SH74
Situated in the beautiful Vale of Ffestiniog amid outstanding mountain and valley scenery, Ffestiniog is only 2½m S of the slate quarrying centre of Blaenau Ffestiniog. It is sometimes known as Llan Ffestiniog to distinguish it from this close neighbour. The local church is dedicated to St Twrog, a 7th-c saint whose memorial stone stands in the churchyard. Archbishop Prys was rector here and is noted for his translation of the Psalter into Welsh. Ffestiniog was the birthplace of Rhys Goch, or Red Rhys of Snowdon, a renowned bard in the era of Owain Glyndwr, who wrote songs exciting the extermination of the English. A small mound near the Pengwen Arms behind the churchyard provides splendid views over the surrounding area, particularly of the Moelwyn and Manod ranges.

There are some exceptionally fine waterfalls in the neighbourhood, and the village is a great centre for mountain walks. In a stream by the nearby Cynfal Falls stands an isolated rock known as Hugh Lloyd's Pulpit. Lloyd was a 17th-c oracle who was reputed to be a magician. Legend has it that he delivered incantations at midnight from the top of this rock. He lived in Cwm Cynfal, 1m outside Ffestiniog. On the other side of the stream is the Goat's Bridge, a slab connecting the bank with a boulder resting in mid stream. Between Ffestiniog and the 200ft Rhaiadr Falls 3m E are Llyn-y-Morwynion (Lake of the Maidens) and Beddau-gwr-Ardudwy (the graves of the men of Ardudwy). Myth relates that the men of Ardudwy raided the Vale of Clwyd in search of brides. Returning with their captives they were overtaken by the wrathful Men of Clwyd at this spot, and every one of the marauders was killed in the ensuing battle. The maidens, who had conveniently fallen in love with their abductors, promptly drowned themselves in the lake rather than be taken home.

Some 3½m from Ffestiniog lies Tomen-y-Mur, the 1st-c site of a Roman garrison and fort. This site has yielded evidence of a bath-house, an amphitheatre which is said to be the only one attached to an auxiliary fort, a parade ground, and a curious artificial platform which may have been the foundation for a catapult. The mound of earth from which the name is derived was thrown up to carry a medieval castle built by William Rufus during his invasion of Wales in 1095. Lonely Migneint Moors lie to the E of Ffestiniog, and the Coed Cymerau nature reserve is situated at nearby Rhyd-y-Sarn.

*FISHGUARD, Dyfed 16 SM93
This small port on Fishguard Bay is backed by fine cliff scenery, and includes a shingle beach with a stone breakwater stretching ½m out to sea. This was erected in 1907 in the hope that Atlantic liners would call here. Its main industries were originally herring fishing and pilchard curing, but these have now dwindled away. The harbour was constructed in 1906 to cope with the Atlantic trade, but this too deteriorated rapidly after the first world war, and nowadays Fishguard is primarily concerned with the ferry service to the Republic of Ireland. During the American War of Independence Paul Jones, a privateer dubbed the 'Father of the American Navy', seized a ship belonging to local Samuel Fenton off Fishguard Bay. He landed and threatened to bombard Fishguard if a sizeable ransom was not forthcoming. He was paid, but even so his warning shots caused not a little damage to the town. Samuel Fenton's brother Richard lived in a charming house known as Glynamel, which still stands at the beginning of the Gwaun Valley. He is remembered for his book Historical Tour Through Pembrokeshire, which was published in 1811.

Entries marked * are the starting point of drives included in the Day Drive section of the book (pages 95 to 144).

Perhaps the most notable event in Fishguard's history occurred in 1797. A French expeditionary force commanded by the Irish-American Tate and consisting mainly of convicts was sent to seize Bristol. Foul weather forced the ships to land NW of Fishguard at Carreg Gwastad, and the so-called soldiers began to pillage the surrounding areas as Welsh forces hurriedly prepared to take defensive action. Legend insists that when the French approached the town they mistook a crowd of women in red shawls and tall hats for Guardsmen, a mistake which led to their total surrender and the signing of a document to that effect at the Royal Oak Inn. Whatever the truth of this story, a memorial tablet exists in the local churchyard commemorating Jemima Nicholas, who is said to have captured a number of Frenchmen single handed armed only with a pitchfork. This was the last time a foreign invading army landed in Britain.

Fishguard has an ideal setting. To the NW runs a delightful stretch of coast terminating in Strumble Head, and SE is the beautifully wooded Gwaun Valley. It is an excellent touring centre, and there are many prehistoric remains in the area. Dylan Thomas' *Under Milk Wood* was filmed here in 1971, and featured the famous Welsh-born actor Richard Burton. To the E of the port is 1,100ft Carn Ingli. Several attractive lanes lead from Dinas and Newport to the Gwaun Valley. The River Gwaun is crossed by interesting old bridges at Llanychaer, Cilrhedyn, and Pont Faen. To the W of Fishguard is the Pencaer Peninsula, which provides good walking country and is rich in standing stones, cromlechs, and iron-age forts. A fort is situated on a headland which juts out from the east side of the bay.

FLAT HOLM and STEEP HOLME, Bristol Channel
These two islands are situated in the Bristol Channel between South Glamorgan and Avon in England. Flat Holm has a lighthouse and fog signal, and there has been a light of some kind here since 1738. The remains of three guns, brought here in 1860 after government recommendation that Severn-estuary defences should be strengthened, can also be seen. Four batteries constructed on the island were dismantled in 1910. A cholera hospital for the Cardiff port was built here in 1883, and has long been out of use.

Steep Holme is the higher of the two islands and has a 400ft summit. It is believed that a priory existed here. The island was recently bought as a bird sanctuary in memory of the late Kenneth Allsop.

FLEMINGSTON, South Glamorgan 25 ST06
A castle is thought to have been sited somewhere in the region of Fleming Court, a local fortified manor house which has now been converted into a farm. The local church is of Norman origin, but most signs of this period were obliterated during its restoration. The register dates back no farther than 1580, but the building does contain the original font and a 14th-c effigy of Joan-le-Fleming. Joan's family gave the village its name, and her memorial bears a Norman-French inscription in Lombardic characters.

The churchyard contains the grave of Iolo Morganwg (Edward Williams), who died in Flemingston in 1826. Morganwg was born in Pennon in 1746, and although a stonemason by trade, became a self-taught poet, historian, and accomplished literary forger. He had a passion for

collecting original Welsh manuscripts and adding to or amending them as he saw fit. While still in London he devised the ritual of *gorsedd*, intended as a revival of the ceremonies of the ancient Druids; this has now been incorporated in the National Eisteddfod.

FLINT, Clwyd 7 SJ27
A workaday town set in the heart of a heavily industrialized region of N Wales, Flint makes little demand on the tourist's time. It is hard to believe that ships could once tie up against the castle walls. The town declined as a port during the last century when the Dee changed its course and its main channel silted up. Flint lies close to the N Wales coalfield and is now an important centre for the rayon industry and the production of chemicals. According to the 12th-c traveller and writer Gerald Cambrensis, the town has also been an important lead and silver-mining community.

Flint Castle (AM) is a sad ruin separated from the town by the main road and a railway, looking out over the Dee estuary with industrial chimneys as neighbours. It was at Flint castle, immortalized by Shakespeare, that Richard II ended his reign in 1399 after having been persuaded to leave the safety of Conwy Castle by the treacherous Earl of Northumberland. The castle saw its last military activity in 1647, when it was slighted by parliamentarians after the civil wars (see inset overleaf).

FORDEN, Powys 11 SJ20
A large scattered village lying under the S end of the Long Mountain, Forden is on a Roman road which runs by the side of Offa's Dyke. A castle mound is situated behind the dyke. The churchyard contains the grave of three brothers, all of whom sang in the church choir. If either one of them could not attend a service the other two would also stay away. An interesting feature of this grave is that there are only two names engraved on the stone; the space for the third brother is blank. Not far from the village is the Roman fortress of Forden Gaer, once *Lauobrinta*. This was probably occupied by a cavalry garrison until the 4thc, and had earth and timber defences which are thought not to have been replaced by stonework. There is, however, evidence that the internal buildings were reconstructed in stone at some time.

FOUR CROSSES, Powys 11 SJ21
The Welsh name for this village is Llandysilio, and a few years ago a quite unauthorized announcement was made that henceforth the Welsh version was to be the official name. This was later ruled to be out of order and Four Crosses it remains – as the roadside boards proclaim. The parish in which it stands is Llandysilio, and the local church is dedicated to St Tisilio. Rebuilt during the Victorian period, the church carries an attractive circular turret at its north-west corner. Its most interesting memorial is a window dedicated to

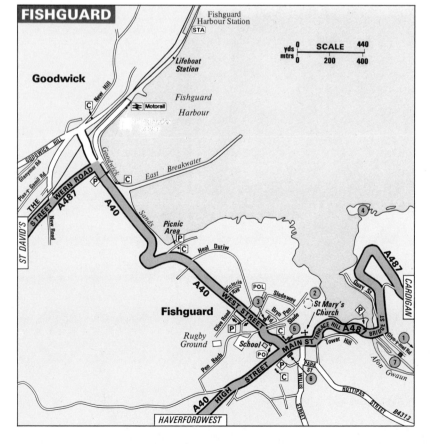

1 Glynamel House
2 Gorsedd Circle (eisteddfod site)
3 Inskin (leather and wood craft)
4 Old Fort
5 Royal Oak Inn
6 Town Hall and WTB Information Centre
7 The Workshop (clay, wood, leather craft)

midshipman Watkin Harold Eingfield of Rhysnant Hall and his two shipmates, who died in the China Sea while trying to rescue a colleague who had fallen overboard. Rhysnant Hall is close to the crossroads in the village and is famous as the place where lawn tennis was devised in 1874 by Walter Clopton Wingfield. The original tennis court still exists beside the house. An aqueduct carries the Shropshire Union Canal across the Vyrnwy beside 18th-c Pentreheylin Bridge.

FRESHWATER EAST, Dyfed *18 SS09*
Freshwater East is a seaside village with a sandy beach backed by low dunes and flanked by red-sandstone cliffs. There is a fine view from Trewent Point at the W corner of the bay, and farther W is an ancient earthwork at Greenale Point.

FRONCYSYLLTE, Clwyd *11 SJ24*
Situated 4m E of Llangollen on the A5, Froncysyllte offers the best approach for close inspection of Telford's masterpiece the Pontcysyllte Aqueduct. This carries the Shropshire Union Canal across the deep ravine of the River Dee. Telford wanted to avoid a stairway of locks at this point, and the result is the 1,007ft aqueduct which ranks alongside the Menai Suspension Bridge as one of his major engineering achievements. It is the longest aqueduct in the United Kingdom. Always the innovator, Telford was the first to use cast iron on a large scale, and the cast-iron trough which carries the water is supported by eighteen stone

piers. The height of the structure from the river is a dizzy 127ft.

Farther downriver is another remarkable structure, the viaduct which carries the Chester to Shrewsbury railway line. Built in 1848 this measures 1,508ft in length and stands at 147ft high. It was designed by a local industrialist and railway pioneer Henry Robertson. Both aqueduct and viaduct are repeated on a minor scale to cross the Ceiriog Valley a few miles S at Chirk. These smaller works can be seen from the A5.

GAERWEN, Gwynedd *5 SH47*
Gaerwen is part of an inland agricultural parish known as Llanfihangel Esceifiog. To the W of the village, on the edge of Malltraeth Marsh, is a remote, secret type of house built under a steeply sloping bank and known as Plas Brew. This was recently restored with the aid of a grant from the Historic Buildings Council of Wales, and consists of a 15th-c hall to which a three-storey tower (now ruined) and a 17th-c wing have been added.

GANLLWYD, Gwynedd *9 SH72*
A small village strung along the beautifully-wooded valley between Dolgellau and Trawsfynydd, Ganllwyd was once in the centre of the Merioneth gold-mining area. Gwynfynydd lies beyond Ganllwyd and was one of the more prosperous mines. It was originally opened for lead working in the 1840's, but in 1864 gold was discovered in a quartz vein. From time to time there were considerable yields, and in 1881

two policemen were posted at the mine entrance because of the value involved. In 1888 some £14,000-worth of gold was extracted and 250 men were employed, most of them lodging in barracks at the mine and returning to their families at weekends. The mine finally closed in 1917, having produced 40,000 ozs of the precious metal. Efforts to secure a government grant to resume gold mining in 1930 were unsuccessful.

GARN BODUAN, Gwynedd *8 SH33*
A dark-age fort with an iron-age rampart, Garn Boduan is set on a 900ft hill 1m S of the village of Nefyn and named after Buan – a 6th-c chieftan. Best approached from the pleasantly wooded road on the S side, it stands amid the skeletal remains of a dead forest and comprises a 28-acre site enclosed by badly preserved iron-age ramparts. Inside these is a post-Roman, stone-walled fort which occupies less than $\frac{1}{2}$ acre and follows the original iron-age pattern. Fine examples of round huts are of interest, and the highest point is a large pile of stones which may be the ruin of a medieval motte.

GARREG DDU RESERVOIR, Powys *13 SN96*
Garreg Ddu is one of the series of artificial lakes built as reservoirs in the Elan Valley in 1904 by Birmingham Corporation. The complex supplies 60-million gallons of water a day to Birmingham, and this particular lake lies between the Pen-y-Garreg and the Caban Coch Reservoirs – separated from the latter by a submerged dam. The

FORTRESS AMONG FACTORIES
During the February tides of 1974, the highest for 300 years, when the Dee estuary rose against the North East tower, the people of Flint were able to see the castle in very much the same setting that Edward I had had in mind when work was begun there in 1277. Less remains of this structure, the first of his line of impregnable defences to keep the Welsh in check, than any of his other, more elaborate, strongholds; but it possesses architectural devices and military features which he did not repeat in his prodigious building programme.

The most notable is the detached round donjon. Like the Norman keep it was the final resort of the garrison in time of siege, but because of its position outside the main curtain it also defended the entrance into the inner bailey. In its second function Edward's architect James of St George might well have seen the great potential for aggressive defence offered by the gatehouse itself, although he did not put such theories to the test until he built Harlech eight years later.

The donjon, in being surrounded not only by a wet moat but also by one linked to the sea, is said to have been the result of Edward's acquaintance with the fortress of Tour de Constance at Aigues-Mortes. This Mediterranean port's deliberately planned town gave the English king the idea of implementing the principle of the *bastide* in Flint – an

arrangement which, until the recent building of two blocks of flats, could still be discerned. The interior of the donjon – which may possibly have been intended as the residence of the royal justice of Chester – comprises a central circular apartment on both floors, surrounded on the lower floor by a circular gallery and on the upper floor by four well-lit rooms and a chapel. In 1399 Richard II heard mass in this chapel on the morning of his surrender to Henry Bolingbroke, soon to be Henry IV.

The castle was built by a vast labour force under the king's supervision at the then considerable cost of £7,000, and is roughly square in shape, consisting of three large angle-towers in addition to the donjon. On a sunny day the sandstone is golden against the Dee, but increasing industrial development in the area guarantees an almost perpetual haze. The ruins of Edward's first castle, so inactive in Welsh history, now cower under the belching towers of a neighbouring factory.

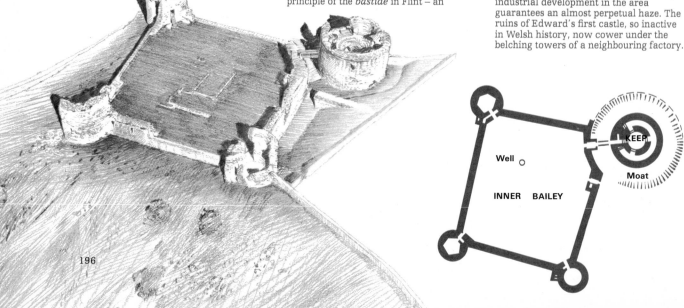

Well

KEEP

Moat

INNER BAILEY

latter structure is regarded as unique, and includes a remarkable device which is used to obtain a sufficient height of water above Frankly Reservoir near Birmingham. A viaduct above this dam supports the road link with Claerwen Reservoir. When the water level is very low the garden walls of submerged Nantgwyllt House can be seen 1m beyond the viaduct. This provided the inspiration for Francis Brett Young's *The House under the Water*, and Shelley lived here during the 19thc.

GARTH, Powys   21 SN94
A number of magnesium springs and a small pump room exist in this small village, which never really developed or flourished as a spa. Outside Garth on the road to Llanwrtyd stands Llanlleonfel church, where Charles Wesley was married to Sarah Gwynne. Inside the building are memorials to Sarah's family and two ancient stones which are thought to be tombstones of Welsh princes.

GELLIGAER, Mid Glamorgan   26 ST19
Gelligaer is sited in a coal-mining district N of Caerphilly on the old Roman road to Brecon, which was built to follow ancient tracks. A Roman garrison camp here held a commanding position on a broad spur of Cefn Gelligaer, and the remains form a fine example of a Roman *castellum* of the smaller variety. Finds here include 1st-c pottery and are housed in the National Museum of Wales.

GILFACH, Gwynedd   5 SH77
Some 3½m S of Conwy, Gilfach village stands off the B5106 and includes the small garden of Roewen. This specialises in shrubs and is open during the summer. Extensive views over the Conwy Valley can be enjoyed from the garden. Cuttings are available and there is a collecting box in aid of the National Gardens Scheme.

GILWERN, Gwent   22 SO21
This pretty village lies 3½m from Abergavenny at the entrance to the Clydach Valley. The Brecon and Newport Canal has made Gilwern one of the most popular boating centres along its length, and the village is full of roads and waterways which seem to proceed at all levels and in all directions. The canal itself was built in 1797 and runs from Brecon to Pontypool. Nowadays it is used exclusively for pleasure cruising, and part of its 33½m length runs through the Brecon Beacons national park.

GLASBURY, Powys   22 SO13
The large village of Glasbury stands at the farthest S tip of the area which once formed the old county of Radnorshire. It occupies both banks of the River Wye, and its most historic feature is a bridge which links the two banks. Two very interesting discoveries were made while the bridge was being repaired in 1965 – a tree which had been preserved in the silt of the river bed for 300 years or more, and the piers of the 17th-c bridge, which had become exposed by flood action some 40ft downstream from the existing structure.

In the 17thc another flood caused the Wye to change its course, separating the church from the vicarage and its

Part of the 33½m Brecon and Newport Canal – now used exclusively for pleasure boating – runs through Gilwern.

15th-c tithe barn. Maesllwch Castle stands in its vast park adjacent to the village and was built in 1829 in a Norman and later-English castellated style. The site was formally occupied by the Wilkins family, who changed their name to de Winton. Just outside Glasbury is Maesyronnen, a very early Nonconformist meeting house. About 1m out of Glasbury on the road to Clyro is Bryn Rhyd bridge, which spans the Cilkenny stream. Built by Walter Wilkins of Maesllwch in 1829 in cast iron, this bears the initials WW and the date. It was bypassed in 1968, but the Radnorshire County Surveyor had it repainted and restored. It is now a showpiece. Roman camps have been found both here and at nearby Clyro, and a Roman road was laid along the valley floor during the occupation.

GLASLYN, Powys   13 SN89
Lying at the base of the cwm or cirque which forms the near-vertical walls of Snowdon, Crib-y-ddysgl, and Crib Goch, Glaslyn is a lake situated at a height of 1,950ft above sea level. This is more than 500ft above the neighbouring Llydaw. Its name is derived from the Welsh word *glas*, which can mean either green or blue, and the water is a bright greenish-blue when seen from above on a bright day. This colouration is due to the presence of washed-out copper salts. Ruins of a 19th-c copper mine can be seen on the shore. A legend states that the lake is bottomless, and that a monster known as *Afanc* lives here. The story tells that the beast once lived in Llyn yr Afanc, a deep pool in the River Conwy near the Fairy Glen, but was captured by the local people and brought to Glaslyn.

The Miner's Track up Snowdon from Llyn Llydaw passes the N shore of Glaslyn before climbing up to join the Pyg Track. From here a long slog up the back of the cwm below Crib-y-ddysgl finally culminates with the saddle between the former and Snowdon's summit (Y Wyddfa).

GLASPWLL, Powys   12 SN79
Interesting old houses, one of which was mentioned by George Borrow in his *Wild Wales*, can be seen in this remote mountain village situated some 2m S of Machynlleth. The village name means

'the blue pool', and it was once a lead mining community. Traces of the old workings are to be found on the surrounding mountains. Waterfalls can be seen in Cwm Rhaeadr, 1m up the River Llyfnant, and fine views are afforded by Rhiw Goch, another mile farther on. Rhiwlwyfan lies 1m NE of the village and is believed to have been a Roman observation post.

GLYN CEIRIOG, Clwyd   11 SJ23
Glyn Ceiriog is the main village in the Ceiriog Valley, where a delightful route follows the River Ceiriog as it tumbles along its rocky bed from the Berwyn foothills. Stone and slate quarrying were once thriving industries here, and were the main reason for the existence of the narrow-gauge Glyn Valley Tramway, which ran as far as Chirk to link up with the main line and the Shropshire Union Canal until 1935. Ceiriog Memorial Institute – a multi-purpose building in the main street – was opened in 1908 and commemorates the Welsh lyric poet Ceiriog (1832–1887), who was born farther along the valley. The building houses remarkable manuscripts, books, bibles, and other mementoes connected with the Ceiriog Valley and beyond (OACT).

Farther along the valley, past Pandy and its pleasantly sited mill and public house, is Pontymeibion – a farmhouse where Huw Morus the Cavalier poet lived. A memorial to Morus stands in the farmyard at Pontymeibion, and the stone chair which he used can be seen in the hedgerow at Erw Gerrig, a nearby farm. George Borrow writes entertainingly of his search for the stone chair and his pilgrimage to Huw's grave at Llansilin in *Wild Wales*.

GLYNDYFRDWY, Clwyd   11 SJ14
Sited on the Dee between Llangollen and Corwen, Glyndyfrdwy has a sentimental niche in Welsh history as the home of Owain Glyndwr – the last Welshman to actively challenge the supremacy of the English in Wales. Glyndwr was a man of noble lineage who studied law at the Inns of Court in London and learnt his soldiering with the army of the English king, Richard II. He fought for Richard at the Battle of Berwick in 1385. His other home was at Sycarth near Llansilin, but

it was a dispute over land at Glyndyfrdwy that caused him to raise a force of 250 men and ransack Ruthin, then held by Earl Reginald Grey, an acolyte of Henry IV. This was the first blow in a revolt against English tyranny that raged intermittently from 1400 to 1412.

After Ruthin was devastated Rhuddlan, Flint, Hawarden, Welshpool, and Oswestry suffered the same fate. Because of the Welsh mood of discontent under English domination Glyndwr gained popular support, was invested by his followers as Prince of Wales, called Welsh parliaments, and even signed a treaty of alliance with France. But when the offer of French troops failed to materialize the tide started to turn against him. He suffered heavy reverses, some of his officers were slain or captured, and he himself went into hiding. No-one knows exactly where he died, but the popular theory was that he ended his days at the home of one of his married daughters in Herefordshire. He was one of the most notable Welshmen of all time, and his memory is cherished. At Glyndyfrdwy the only speculation is about the actual site of his home.

GLYN NEATH, West Glamorgan 21 SN80
Delightful waterfalls and caves hide among thick foliage near Glyn Neath, which lies some 10m up the vale from Neath itself. Near the main road an old church dedicated to St Catwg contains two recumbent effigies believed to have come from Neath Abbey. Craig-y-Llyn rises to 1,969ft in the SE and is the highest point in the country. Some 2m NE is Pontneathvaughan, also situated in an area graced by several fine waterfalls. Glyn Neath can be approached from Hirwaun on the A465 Heads of the Valleys road.

GOGERDDAN, Dyfed 12 SN68
This house lies 3m NE of Aberystwyth on the road to Penrhyncoch, and is occupied to-day as the Welsh Plant Breeding Station. It was formerly the seat of the Pryse family, who for generations held the monopoly of the Aberystwyth or Cardiganshire representation in parliament. This had such general acceptance that in 1714 Lewis Pryce was elected in his absence and without his knowledge or consent. His refusal to take his seat led parliament to order his arrest, but he went into hiding until the seat was declared vacant and a new member elected. The Pryses were one of the last families in Wales to maintain a private harpist, and the last of these musicians was known as Jerry Bach Gogerddan (Little Jerry of Gogerddan). He held the post for 51 years through the first half of the 19thc.

GOLDCLIFF, Gwent 26 ST38
Numerous lanes and footpaths in this scattered little Severn-estuary village lead down to the sea wall which, according to a stone found embedded in it in 1878, is partly of Roman origin. Goldcliff has been mainly concerned with salmon fishing since the 15thc. The method employed then is almost identical to that used today, and utilized 'putches' (wooden buckets) set between poles in two lines – one facing upstream, the other downstream.

The Church of St Mary Magdalene was flooded in 1606, and records show that the water reached a height of 2ft 3in on the chancel floor. A tablet on the sanctuary wall commemorates this event, and a sundial dating from 1729 can be seen in the porch. A Benedictine priory was founded here by the Norman Robert de Chandos in 1113. It was seized by Edward I in 1285 and the lands were given to Tewkesbury Abbey. These lands later passed to Eton College and remained their responsibility until the early 20thc. The priory was inundated by the sea after the Reformation.

GOODWICK, Dyfed 16 SM93
A resort on Fishguard Bay and now almost a suburb of Fishguard, Goodwick has a shingle beach sheltered from the W by the heights of Pen Caer. The town offers sea and river fishing and was only a cluster of fishing cottages until the harbour was built in 1907. It is now the steamer embarkation point for the Republic of Ireland. Irish Quay is $\frac{1}{4}$m long, and a breakwater stretches $\frac{1}{2}$m out to sea. The latter is considered a great engineering feat – 800 tons of rock were required to make up each foot of its length.

GOWER PENINSULA, West Glamorgan 24
The Gower is a peninsula approximately 18m long by 5m wide. During the Ice Age this area was covered by glaciers, and many of its natural features owe their existence to formations which occurred when the ice melted. The peninsula is flanked by the Bristol Channel to the S and W, and by Carmarthen Bay to the N. The coastline is a mixture of limestone and red sandstone, and the 200ft limestone cliffs in the S are considered some of the finest in Britain. Many sandy bays and shingle coves can only be reached on foot and are rarely crowded. The most popular are Langland and Caswell in the S, where the bathing is very safe, and Rhosili in the W – a 3m sweep of golden sands noted for bass fishing. The N landscape is somewhat different, comprising marshlands and saltings which include the silted Burry estuary.

Inland the peninsula has wide commons and tiny hamlets nestling in wooded valleys. Much of the S coast is managed by the NT – notably Thurba Head – and a number of beauty spots include the 180 acres of cliff scenery at Paviland Cliffs and the nature reserve of Whiteford Burrows in the NW. The area is basically agricultural, but today tourism plays a major part in its economy. Nevertheless, considering its proximity to Swansea and industrial S Wales, it has remained amazingly unspoiled and has so far resisted commercial exploitation.

Many ruined castles exist throughout the peninsula, and a number of ancient remains emphasize its former occupation by the Celts and Romans. An impressive iron-age camp survives at Cil Ifor, $\frac{3}{4}$m E of Llanrhidian, and the spectacular burial chamber of Parc Cwm at Penmaen comprises a deep forecourt, a gallery with two pairs of side cells, and an oval cairn. There are also tombs at Sweynes Howes on the Rhosili cliffs, and Arthur's Stone at Reynoldston. A number of prehistoric remains have been discovered at Goat's Cave, Paviland.

GRAIG-LWYD, Gwynedd 5 SH77
Graig-Lwyd is an interesting stone-age site above the village of Penmaenmawr, on the slopes of a hill of the same name. Numerous stone axes, picks, and wasters have been found here, suggesting that it was the site of a large-scale axe factory, similar to those discovered in Westmorland, Antrim, and Cornwall. Its products are believed to have been widely circulated throughout the country. Although there is nothing to be seen above ground, the imagination is fired by the knowledge of past discoveries; it is not difficult to conjure up pictures of the workers each chipping away in his separate hut or shelter. Above the site is one of the best known of the Welsh stone circles – the Druid's Circle or Meini Hirion – a disordered collection of stones which have been greatly disturbed from their original positions (see entry).

GRESFORD, Clwyd 7 SJ35
The name of the village is thought to be derived from the Welsh Y Groesffordd, meaning the cross-road. It is situated 3m N of Wrexham and E of Offa's Dyke. Gresford's most attractive feature is undoubtedly its parish church, which is dedicated to All Saint's and was first built in the 13thc. Only a fragment of the original building remains. The main portion of the church belongs to the 15thc, and its interior is richly adorned with oak panelling, exquisite carvings, sculptured effigies, and stained glass. An ancient screen which separates the nave from the chancel has been preserved in its entirety.

The bells of Gresford church are housed in the handsome perpendicular tower and are noted for their melodious tones. They are listed as one of the seven wonders of Wales. It is said that about 100 years ago one of the bells was dismantled and transported by road to be hung in St Paul's Cathedral, London. Another object of interest associated with the church is a massive yew tree in the churchyard. More than 25ft in girth and 60ft in height, this is reputed to be some 1,500 years old, which makes it one of the oldest and largest yews in Britain.

GROSMONT, Gwent 22 SO42
An old-world town set on a hillside amid beautiful scenery by the River Monnow, Grosmont is small by today's standards but only ceased to be a borough as recently as 1860. It is now mainly a centre for anglers. The Church of St Nicholas carries a massive octagonal tower topped by a spire, and has a large unfinished nave arcade. Inside is a huge flat-faced stone knight which is thought to be an effigy of one of Edmund Crouchback's descendants.

Grosmont was one of three castles erected in the vicinity by the Norman Lords of Abergavenny to protect the Welsh/English border. The others are Skenfrith and White Castle. Records show that a castle existed at Grosmont as early as 1163, and it is quite likely that it was originally set up in some form during the Norman advances c1070. However, the structure was largely rebuilt during the reign of Henry III, who stayed here for a time until Llywelyn the Great stormed the building and forced Henry and his queen to escape in their night attire. In 1410 Owain Glyndwr burned the town and seized the castle, establishing Rhys Gethin there to hold the position. English re-inforcements were hurriedly sent under the command of Harry Monmouth (later to be Henry V), and the Welsh were completely routed. This was Glyndwr's last recorded battle before he lapsed into relative obscurity. The castle is now under the care of the Department of the Environment, and little remains of it except the inner ward gateway, the keep, the containing wall with two drum towers, and a 13th-c octagonal chimney which once served the banqueting hall.

GUILSFIELD, Powys *11 SJ21*

Many half-timbered houses can be seen in this small village, which lies 2m from Welshpool. The 14th-c church of St Aelhaian was built soon after the Black Death and has an early-English style tower, the upper part of which is of the decorated period. The clock face is inscribed with a familiar warning 'Be Diligent. Night Cometh'. A splendid panelled roof is beamed with flowered bosses at the intersection of its ribs, and other features of the church's interior include an old carved font and a Welsh log chest. Near by is a Holy Well, the water from which was mixed with sugar and drunk by the sick.

GUMFRESTON, Dyfed *19 SN10*

Situated between St Florence and Tenby, Gumfreston overlooks Ritee Flats and includes the parish Church of St Lawrence. This originally dates from the 12thc, but the 65ft tower, the main body of the building, and the font are 13th-c additions. On the north wall of the nave are some faint wall pictures which may represent St Lawrence with his gridiron. A bronze sanctus bell and some 16th-c pewter communion vessels are preserved behind a grill, in a recess behind the pulpit. Mineral springs in the churchyard are said to possess the same medicinal qualities as the waters of Tunbridge Wells.

GWALCHMAI, Gwynedd *4 SH37*

This village on the A5 was described in 1833 as being 'on the newly opened line of road, neatly built but small'. It has grown considerably and produced a variety of places of worship since then. The parish church was re-built in 1845 by the rector J Wynne Jones, and contains an ancient east window which came from neighbouring Heneglwys church. The Methodist church dates from 1780 and has an uninspiring exterior, but the impressive interior contains semi-circular seating focused on an elaborately-carved pulpit, and a gallery supported by iron corinthian columns. The RC church dates from the mid 20thc and is built in the new-town style.

GWBERT ON SEA, Dyfed *17 SN14*

Several hotels and a few scattered houses make up this small Cardigan-Bay resort, which is set amid fine cliff scenery. The shingle beach gives way to patches of sand at low tide, and is flanked by low cliffs to the N and sand dunes to the S. Inshore bathing is safe at slack water but dangerous when the ebb tide adds its strength to the pull of the river. There is an active salmon fishery here, and Gwbert is the home of the Cardigan Golf Club.

GWYDDELWERN, Clwyd *10 SJ04*

Gwyddelwern is a village on the main road with a quarrying district to the N

More of a mansion than a castle, Gwydyr has been a refuge for princes and kings for hundreds of years.

and a building material works on the plain below. Fine valley views of the upper reaches of the River Clwyd can be enjoyed beyond here. An old cornmill still functions in the village, though this is now powered by electricity rather than water. The Church of St Beuno was rebuilt in 1830, when an attractive but rather out of place spire was also added. The predominantly late-Victorian interior is embellished with a fine panelled roof over the sanctuary, a 15th-c east window in the chancel, and some pre 17th-c oak panells in the chancel screen. An 18th-c tomb in the churchyard has a row of low kneeling stones beside it.

GWYDYR CASTLE, Gwynedd *5 SH76*

Despite its name this is not a castle but a Tudor mansion dating from the 16thc. It is situated ½m from Llanrwst and was founded by Maredudd ab Ieuan. Ieuan came to the area in the late 15thc and built the tall block opposite the entrance *c*1500. The mansion became the seat of the Wynn family and suffered many structural additions and alterations over the next 100 years. Some of the mediaeval stonework from the dissolved abbey at Maenan was incorporated in these alterations. Legend claims that Queen Elizabeth I stayed here, and that Charles I hid here after his defeat at Chester. The house (OACT) was destroyed by fire between the two world wars but has been carefully reconstructed and contains examples of fine furniture. More than 50 peacocks and many tropical birds inhabit the grounds.

HAFODTY, Gwynedd *5 SH55*

A private garden situated 6m SE of Caernarfon at Betws Garmon, this is open to the public every day of the year from dawn to dusk. A walk through the pretty rock and watergarden – noted for the beauty of its azaleas and hydrangeas – passes the Nant Mill Waterfalls, which are picturesquely overhung by flowering shrubs and trees.

HANMER, Clwyd *11 SJ43*

This attractive village is situated in the corner of an area called English Maelor, or more recently Flintshire Maelor. An extensive mere is connected geographically with the Lake District of N Shropshire and gives the village its name. It was in this unlikely corner of

Wales, one of the farthest E points of the Principality, that the Welsh warrior Owain Glyndwr married Margaret Hanmer. The Hanmer family of nearby Bettisfield is still associated with the region, as are another Welsh family – the Kenyons of Gredington.

HARLECH, Gwynedd *9 SH53*

Granite-built houses and narrow streets clinging to a steep hill which descends to the coastal plain below characterize this town. Extensive views from the summit of the hill extend over Tremadog Bay; to the Lleyn Peninsula; inland to the Snowdon range; and S to the Cader Idris range. The town offers excellent tourist accommodation and has been popular with visitors since 1867, when the Cambrian Railway was opened. The parish church of St Tanwg was built in the 1840's and comprises a single chamber and western gallery. These have been greatly modified to make the building lighter inside. Clear glass has been placed in the gothic windows, and the walls have been whitened. A tall, 15th-c carved font came from the old church of St Tanwg, which stood at the S tip of the parish and now lies amidst the sands of the sea-shore. The flat slate tombstones of its old churchyard date from the early 18thc. Coleg Harlech is a residential adult-education centre founded in 1927 by Dr Thomas Jones. To the N of the town stretches Morfa Harlech, a dune-covered plain which was reclaimed in 1808 and is now a national nature reserve.

Dominating the town from a craggy hill-top are the ruins of the 13th-c castle (AM) (see inset overleaf). This was built on the site of a Celtic fortress known as Twr Branwen, where Branwen of the White Neck – a sister of Bran the Blessed reputed to have been one of the three most lovely women in Wales – was claimed by a king of Ireland as his bride. Evidence of Celtic settlement found here include a looped palstave and a bronze axe-head. The site was later called Caer Collwyn before Edward I erected his great castle between 1283 and 1290. This was constructed on a rectangular plan, with two concentric sets of walls and circular towers at the corners. The two on the western side are turreted. It has seen a great deal

cont page 201

199

A LEGEND IN STONE

In the 12th-c quartet of Welsh legends known as the *Four Branches of the Mabinogion*, the second opens with a description of King Bendigeidfran sitting on the rock of *Harddlech*, in the company of his brother and his retinue, watching the approach of thirteen ships from the direction of Southern Ireland. It is one of the finest stories in the language, both tragic and turbulent, and deals with the fate of Bendigeidfran's sister Branwen at the hands of the Irish king who had come in one of those thirteen ships to seek her hand in marriage and to take her with him to Ireland. Nobody acquainted with the legend·can visit the 13th-c castle at Harlech, a name interpreted as 'high rock', without thinking of that story and imagining those thirteen ships coming across the bay with the wind behind them.

Vivid as the *Mabinogion* account may be, there is no historical evidence that the site was used before Edward I began building another of his mighty fortresses there in 1283. Like those at Flint, Rhuddlan, Conwy, and Caernarfon, the aim of this was to keep the recently-conquered Welsh in the unyielding grip of his power. On the other hand the situation of the rock – majestical above the bay, disdainfully surveying estuary, promontory, and valley – could only but inspire early medieval legend and speculation. In the 18th and 19thc the precipice surmounted by decaying battlements lured artists of wide-ranging ability to give an impression of its rugged grandeur.

To generations of visitors, artists or not, the superiority of Harlech over other Edwardian strongholds, or indeed of any other castle in Britain, will rest in the expansive vista from the western walls. Remarkable at any time, this is unforgettable during sunset. In few places these days can change be so slight that a 20th-c contemporary can see eye-to-eye with the observations of an early 19th-c traveller such as Richard Fenton. He wrote that 'the castle is a most superb building, whether we consider its magnitude, its site, or its masonry and style of Architecture . . . Looked at from every way, it is a most beautiful and magnificent pile, and when you couple it with the grand features of the Snowdonian tract, and the lovely outline of Lleyn, which must come into every view of it, nothing can surpass it.'

Whether or not Edward himself was as sensitive to the aesthetic considerations of the site is debateable, but he was acutely aware of its offensive and defensive potential, and applied those principles of fortification which he had learned rigorously. His own knowledge was strengthened by the expertize of his chief architect Master James of St George, whose salary of £15,000, by today's standards, gives some indication of his professional prestige. He designed at Harlech a castle of the concentric plan –

a form of defence inspired by one of the strongest Crusader castles, Krak des Chevaliers – a 12th-c fortress built by the Hospitallers to guard the vital passes between the East and the Mediterranean coast. This consisted of two rings of walls and bastions, with the inner wall considerably higher than the outer.

However well adapted to its precipice site Harlech may be, Master James achieved his greatest distinction at Beaumaris, where the terrain offered opportunity for a completely symmetrical arrangement of military defences, acknowledged ever since as the perfection of castle design. There are, nevertheless, similarities between Beaumaris and Harlech, some features of which no doubt became a pattern for the later castle which completed Edward's grand design.

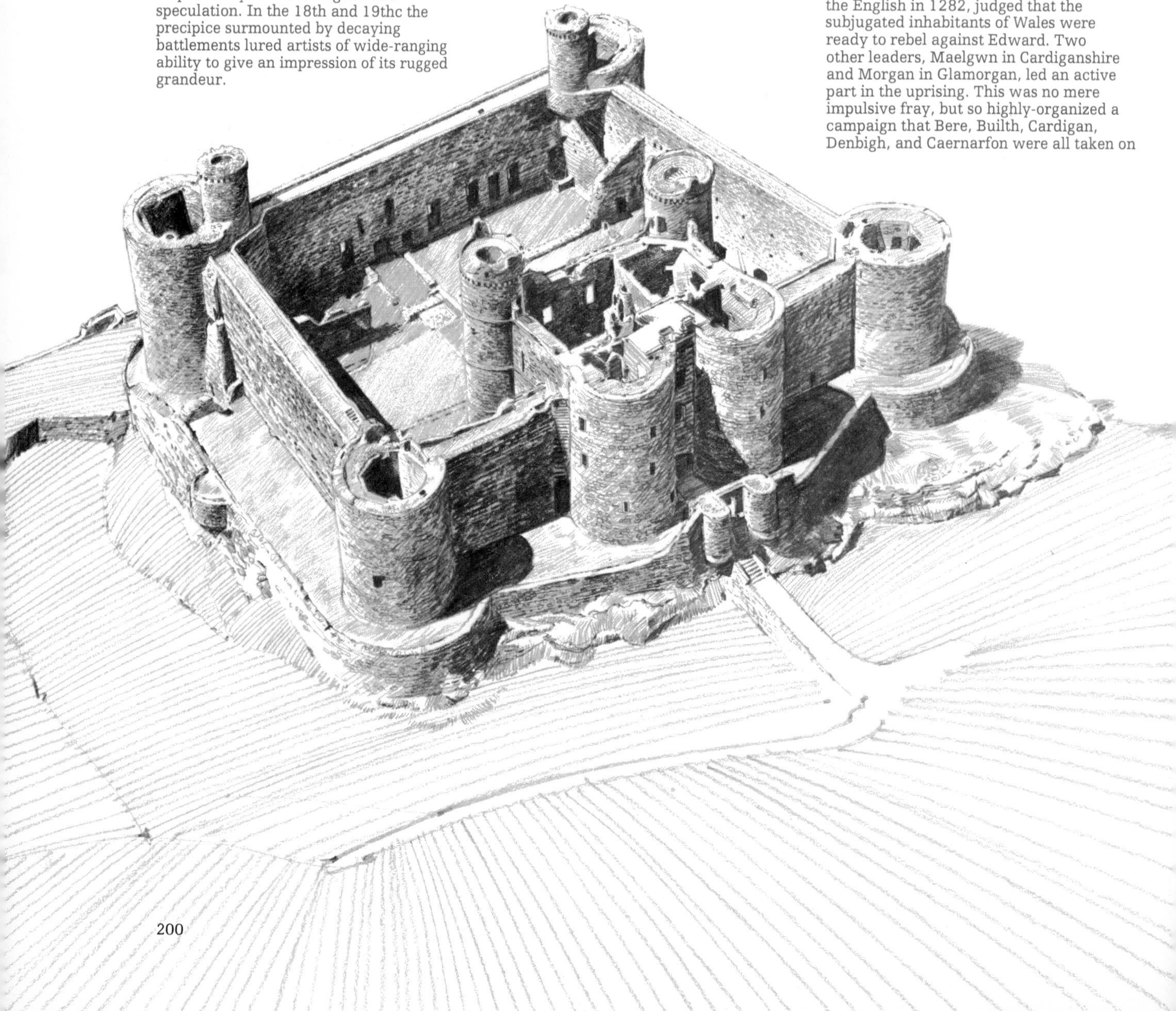

By the time work had finished at Harlech in 1290 the operation had cost between £8,000 and £9,000, a sum which by today's fluctuating monetary values cannot be reliably conveyed in realistic terms. It played a more significant, if not to say spectacular, part in Welsh history than Edward's other castles, and tales of heroism, tenacity, and cunning are linked with skirmishes and sieges spanning three centuries. In 1294 Madog ap Llywelyn, a kinsman of Prince Llywelyn who had died at the hands of the English in 1282, judged that the subjugated inhabitants of Wales were ready to rebel against Edward. Two other leaders, Maelgwn in Cardiganshire and Morgan in Glamorgan, led an active part in the uprising. This was no mere impulsive fray, but so highly-organized a campaign that Bere, Builth, Cardigan, Denbigh, and Caernarfon were all taken on

of action, and fairly recent restoration work has preserved its remains as a still-imposing structure keeping watch over the surrounding area. The battlements can be reached by a staircase in the southern angle of the curtain wall and afford fine views of the surrounding countryside. The large flat plain between the castle and the sea was once covered in water, and the castle's site was a rocky headland at the very brink of the ocean. This one-time sea bed now supports nothing more inspiring than a rash of caravans.

*HAVERFORDWEST, Dyfed *18 SM91*
Plan overleaf
More English than Welsh, this important market town is situated above the Western Cleddau on the slopes of a steep hill which is surmounted by a ruined castle. During the Middle Ages there was quite a large Flemish population in the town, which at one time was a port set at the height of navigation of the Western Cleddau. Its main links were with Bristol and Ireland, but it declined during the 19thc with the development of Milford Haven – which was nearer the sea – and the opening of the S Wales Railway in 1853.

The ruined castle stands in a prominent position above the town and overlooks the river. It was founded prior to 1120 by the first Earl of Pembroke, Gilbert de Clare, and rebuilt in the 13thc by William de Valence, a later Earl of Pembroke. The keep was built into the living rock and commands splendid views. Apart from the keep the only substantial remains are parts of the walls. A legend associated with the castle says that a Welsh robber who was very cruelly treated during his imprisonment here was visited regularly by the son of its Norman lord. The boy came to hear of the prisoner's adventures; to gain revenge over the lord the felon took the young child to the top of the tower, and in spite of pleas and promises from the lord threw the boy and then himself to the ground. The lord erected a monastery called 'Sorrowful' to the memory of his young son.

The castle was captured by Gruffyd ap Rhys in 1136 after the Battle of Cardigan. In 1220 Llywelyn the Great burnt the town, but the stronghold remained undamaged. In 1405 it was besieged by a force of over 2,500 men under the command of Owain Glyndwr, and although he managed to take the town the castle remained impregnable. During the civil war the town was garrisoned by the royalists, but they fled as the parliamentarians advanced victoriously through Wales, and the castle surrendered in 1645. Although the garrison capitulated, Cromwell had the building slighted in 1648 to prevent a recurrence of the revolt at Pembroke. It was used as a jail in the 18th and 19thc until the new county jail was built in 1820, and later became a police station. The castle held this position until well into the present century, and its remains now house the county museum and Pembrokeshire Coast information centre.

The local Church of St Mary is one of the finest in S Wales. It was originally built in the middle of the 13thc, but has been the subject of extensive rebuilding and alteration – particularly in the 15thc. It is mainly perpendicular in style, but the chancel is early English. The nave and north aisle both have curved oak roofs, and that of the former is considered particularly fine. Two stalls remain out of eight which may have come from the priory, and one of these has a 14th-c carved bench end bearing the Royal Arms and a carving of St Michael and the dragon. A mutilated effigy of a pilgrim from the time of Henry VII – thought to represent a traveller from the shrine of St James of Canpostella because of the scallop shells on his satchel – can be seen at the

the same day. Madog, by now claiming for himself the title of Prince of Wales, had no such success at Harlech. The castle resisted his attack and the garrison of 37 men was quickly relieved.

More than 100 years were to pass before it was next besieged. This was the result of an uprising which was infinitely more lacerating and prolonged than the 13th-c episode, but which ultimately failed to secure national independence. The protagonist on this occasion was Owain Glyndwr, whose connection with Harlech eclipses most of the other incidents connected with his bid for freedom. A man of royal pedigree, he was a worthy successor to Prince Llywelyn's title and heritage, and found ready support from members of the Welsh nobility as well as labourers and zealous students at Oxford. Subversive activities of the latter are indicated in a parliamentary report of 1401, which describes how they, 'with many wicked meetings and counsels . . . plotted against our Lord the King and the Realm for the destruction of the Kingdom and the English language.' In 1401 Owain, who has been called the 'father of modern Welsh nationalism', started his attack on the Marcher lords. An attempt to take Harlech in the same year failed, and it was three years later that the garrison surrendered.

Having seized the fortress, Owain made Harlech his capital for the next four years. His family lived in the castle and he called a parliamentary meeting here where he presented his policy of establishing not only an independent Welsh Church, but two universities. Success was short-lived. In 1408 the castle was taken by John and Gilbert Talbot, and Owain's wife, daughter, and four grand-daughters were taken prisoners. The major incidents in the castle's history during the rest of the 15thc were the result of unrest between Yorkists and Lancastrians. After the capture of Henry VI at the Battle of Northampton, his wife Margaret of Anjou fled to Harlech, which held out for the Lancastrian cause for the following eight years under its constable Dafydd ab Ifan ab Einion. His proud though fictional boast was that since he had kept a castle so long in France that all the old women in Wales talked about him, he intended to keep Harlech so long that all the old women in France would talk about him.

What is true is that he was the last commander in England and Wales to yield to the Yorkists. The staunch and heroic defence of the castle appealed greatly to the Welsh poets of the time, but by popular tradition it is the song *The March of the Men of Harlech* that is most closely linked with the event. Harlech achieved a similar distinction in the civil wars, since it was the last castle to hold out for the king. With its eventual surrender to Major-General Mytton in March 1647, the military life of the castle came to an end.

Master James placed great emphasis on the exterior volume of the structure, and by concentrating a great deal on the gatehouse, he made what had been considered the weakest part of the defence the most formidably challenging. Designed as a constable's residence, it has corner turrets facing the inner ward in addition to the twin rounded projections which flank the entrance, and consists of three storeys. The generous traceried windows looking on to the inner court from the upper floors lit the principal living rooms, and the chapel on the first floor also acted as a portcullis chamber. The basement housed offices and store-rooms. The inner ward follows the usual Edwardian rectangular plan and contained the largest apartment. The hall commands a westward view of Cardigan Bay and must have been a particularly pleasant place during the many years of inactivity in the castle's history. Beyond the screens passage, of which there is little evidence, the buttery and pantry lead to the kitchen. At right-angles to the kitchen are the foundation stones on which rested Ystumgwern Hall, the home of Prince Llywelyn once sited about 4m from Harlech. This timber structure was moved bodily to the castle in the earlier part of the 14thc, just as his hall at Conwy was dismantled and shipped to Caernarfon Castle. What motivated such removals is difficult to discern, gratifying as the gesture must have been to Welshmen.

An essential part of a visit to Harlech is a walk along the walls. As at Beaumaris, this is the most immediately effective way of envisaging the layout of the concentric castle as it would have appeared with all its activity in times of siege, and during the more leisurely interludes of castle social life. Looking westward from the wall-walk, or from the healthy sward of the outer ward, it is easy to imagine the further protection offered by that expanse of sea which would have lapped at the base of the high rock in the 13thc.

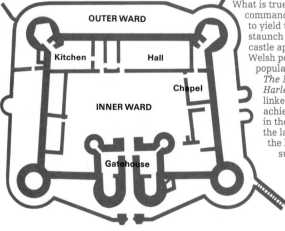

OUTER WARD

Kitchen   Hall

Chapel

INNER WARD

Gatehouse

Entries marked * are the starting point of drives included in the Day Drive section of the book (pages 95 to 144).

western end of the building. The church also contains armorial memorials, a brass of 1651, and an early-English lancet window.

The Church of St Thomas' tall 13th-c tower displays weathered figures on the second storey and is surmounted by a stone crucifix. The grave of a certain Richard the Palmer, who made a pilgrimage to Rome in the 12thc, can be seen here. St Martin's is the oldest church in the town and has been greatly restored. It lies near the castle and carries a high steeple. Prendergast church includes a 14th-c tower. Near the river in a meadow on the S side of the town are sparse ruins of the 13th-c Augustinian Priory of St Mary and St Thomas. Buildings in the town include many fine Regency and Victorian houses, and some of the High Street houses still show their medieval past. Salutation Square contains the County War Memorial. Foley House was designed by John Nash and was once occupied by one of Nelson's

officers, Admiral Sir Thomas Foley. A column of red granite standing on the corner of Dark Street and High Street marks the place where William Nicol was burnt at the stake for his religious beliefs in 1558. Haroldston House now lies in ruins but was the birthplace of Sir John Perrot – reputedly an illegitimate son of Henry VIII – who later became Lord Deputy of Ireland. Other notable buildings in the town include the Shire Hall, Masonic Hall, Temperance Hall, and Market House – where high-quality Welsh weaves may be purchased.

Haverfordwest attracts tourists of all kinds because of its ideal position in relation to the valley of the Western Cleddau, the shores of Milford Haven, and the Pembrokeshire coast. Sir Thomas Picton, killed at the Battle of Waterloo in 1815, was born 3m N at early 18th-c Poyston. To the NE Slebech Hall is surrounded by a fine park extending along the banks of the Eastern

Cleddau, and occupies the site of a former Commandery of the Knights of St John of Jerusalem. Picton Castle lies some 4½m SE, and 13th-c Roch Castle stands on the Haverfordwest to St David's road.

HAWARDEN, Clwyd *7 SJ36*
Hawarden has more affinity with England than with Wales and is only 6m from Chester. Its most famous resident was William Ewart Gladstone, four times prime minister in Victoria's reign, and the 'Grand Old Man' of British politics. He lived at Hawarden Castle after marrying its Welsh heiress Catherine Glynne, daughter of the antiquarian Sir Stephen Glynne. Gladstone, the son of a Scottish merchant who had settled in Liverpool, lived the rest of his life at Hawarden and memorials to him abound in the village. Outstanding among them is St Deiniol's Library and Hall, a national memorial which was opened in 1906 and houses his entire library of 32,000 volumes. Twenty bona-

1	Augustinian Priory (remains)	
2	Castle	
3	County War Memorial	
4	Foley House	
5	Function Centre	
6	Gorsedd Circle (eisteddfod site)	
7	Haverfordwest Pottery	
8	Market Hall	
9	Pembrokeshire County Museum & Art Gallery	
10	Rick Fletcher Pottery	
11	St David's Church, Prendergast	
12	St Mary's Church	
13	St Martin's Church	
14	St Thomas a Becket Church	
15	Shire Hall	
16	Swimming Pool	
17	WTB Information Centre	
18	William Nichol Memorial	

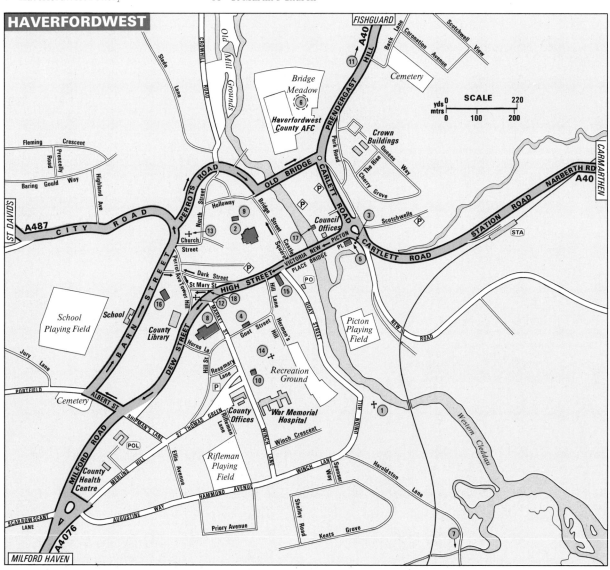

fide research students can be accommodated here. There is also a Gladstone Museum at Broadlane House. Gladstone – among his several Victorian virtues – was a devoutly religious person, so it comes as no surprise to find memorials to him in the parish church. These include a window by Burne-Jones and a marble monument by Henry Neville.

The church is perpendicular in style and has a low central tower. It was rebuilt by Sir Gilbert Scott after the previous church was almost destroyed by fire a year after it had been restored between 1855 and 1856. Damage was estimated at £4,000 and was believed to have been the work of an arsonist. The old church had been ransacked in 1643 by parliamentary soldiers. Hawarden Castle is not of any great antiquity, having been re-named from Broadlane Hall after alterations. The original Hawarden Castle is of 13th-c date and lies in a ruinous pile near by. Remains include a large circular keep containing a chapel, banqueting hall, and parts of the walls. Being a Marcher foundation, the castle suffered many attacks from the Welsh. In 1282 Daffydd, brother of Llywelyn the Last, took the castle on Palm Sunday and had the whole garrison put to death. He was later captured and sentenced to death on four counts, two of which were for committing sacrilege by murdering two knights in the castle on Palm Sunday. In the early 15thc it passed into the hands of the Earls of Derby. During the civil war it was first garrisoned for Charles I, betrayed to the parliamentarians, retaken by the royalists, and finally captured by Major-General Mytton. In 1647 it was slighted at the command of Cromwell. At this time it passed into the hands of the Glynne family.

HAY-ON-WYE, Powys *22 SO24*

Hay-on-Wye is a market town situated at the NE corner of the Brecon Beacons national park on the River Wye. The 2,219ft Hay Bluff and 2,263ft Lord Hereford's Knob rise from the Black Mountains in the S. At one time the town was a centre for the flannel industry, but it is now a local farming focus where Clun and Kerry sheep are sold at the Smithfield, or Market. In the older part of the town the streets contain numerous little shops and are narrow and winding. The parish Church of St Mary dates largely from 1834, when it was rebuilt and enlarged. It still includes the early-English southern entrance and 13th-c lower part of the square tower. A silver chalice inscribed 'Oure Lady Paris of the Haia', dates from 1576, and the church registers date back to 1680. The Steeple Pool is a treacherously deep part of the river which is said to contain the old bells of St Mary's. The chapel of St John was originally founded in 1254 and is now once again used for parish work. Over the years since 1550 it has served a variety of purposes, including Guildhall chapel and Fire Station.

The first castle built here was a motte-and-bailey structure probably erected by a Norman knight called Revell in the 11thc. Traces of this can be found near the church, and the walk past here is known as Bailey Walk. The structure was captured and burnt to the ground by King John in 1216, and a new one built by William de Braose – a notably ruthless Marcher lord. It is the ruins of

the later castle which can still be seen. His wife was imprisoned in Corfe Castle (Dorset) and starved after accusing King John of murdering his nephew Prince Arthur. The castle was finally destroyed by Owain Glyndwr *c*1400. A fine gateway, the keep, and parts of the walls are all that remain. Alongside this ruin is a privately-owned, early 17th-c Jacobean house which replaced the castle. The town itself has been described as a book-buyer's paradise.

HENLLAN, Dyfed *17 SN34*

Picturesquely set on the River Teifi, this hamlet includes a single-span bridge which spans the rapidly-flowing waters of the river and affords excellent views. Near the bridge is an old mill. The village Church of St David's was rebuilt in 1813. Llysnewydd is a house in fine grounds, and farther E the river flows through the Alltcafan gorge.

HIRWAUN, Mid Glamorgan *21 SN90*

Hirwaun is a small industrial town at the NE end of the Aberdare Valley, with the Brecon Beacons rising to the N. Fine views can be enjoyed from the summit of the road leading W to Glyn Neath, and from the mountain road linking Hirwaun with the Rhondda Valley. The latter highway reaches a height of nearly 1,700ft as it crosses Hirwaun Common. Craig-y-Llyn lies W of Hirwaun, and at 1,969ft is the highest point in Glamorgan. Some 30ft below this is the reservoir of Llyn Fawr, originally a natural lake which was drained in 1911 before being converted into a reservoir. Many interesting finds were made at this time, including the roots of felled oak trees still bearing the axe marks, and about 20 metal objects, probably of the 6thc. These were mainly of bronze and included axes, chisels, sickles, two large cauldrons of riveted bronze sheets with cast ring handles, and ornaments. Other finds included iron objects – a spearhead and a wrought-iron sickle – showing evidence of the beginning of the iron age. It has been suggested that there was a lake village here at one time, but the objects could also be the spoils from a raid or offerings to the gods.

Some of the earliest iron works in Wales were located here but closed down early in the last century. Wrought-iron reinforcement bars have been found in the much-ruined furnaces, and also in the narrow tram-road which still preserves several stone sleepers in place. Hirwaun now has a modern industrial estate, and coal is worked in the neighbourhood by the open-cast method.

HODGESTON, Dyfed *18 SS09*

About 5m SE of Pembroke on the A4189, Hodgeston has an old church which carries a narrow tower of local type. The chancel is splendidly decorated, and the remains of a double piscina and a triple sedilia bearing ornaments of the 'ball-flower' type can be seen inside. Also here is an Elizabethan chalice of 1569, one of the oldest in Wales. To the S lie the bays of Swanlake and Freshwater East.

HOLT, Clwyd *7 SJ45*

Holt lies 6m S of Chester, and its eight-arched sandstone bridge across the Dee is one of the gateways to Wales. This bridge is single lane with places of refuge for pedestrians, but it is proving inadequate for 20th-c traffic and plans are afoot to build a new bridge upstream. The village, unpretentious in itself, is steeped in history going back to Roman times. Excavations have revealed that there was intensive Roman activity here, with a tile and pottery factory supplying the 20th Legion garrison at Chester. The depot's Roman name was *Bovium*, and the site was probably chosen for its river connection with Chester.

Upstream on the right of the river are the hardly discernible remains of a castle built by Earl John de Warrene at the time of the Edwardian settlement of the borderlands in the 13thc. Holt was once a medieval borough and returned its own MP long before the neighbouring town of Wrexham had such status. St Chad's Church, of 13th-c origin but since restored, houses many historic links with Holt's past. The village had a fleeting association with HG Wells, who was a young teacher at Holt Academy.

The bridge at Holt spans the Dee and forms one of the gateways to Wales.

HOLYHEAD, Gwynedd *4 SH28*

Britain's third largest passenger port and Anglesey's largest town, Holyhead has a population of 11,000 and has survived as a main sea link with Eire despite attempts by other ports to take over this lucrative trade. The port, which is situated on Holy Island, earned few accolades from early travellers. They were rarely in the mood to be charitable about Holyhead after having experienced the nerve-testing, spine-jarring coach ride through Snowdonia and across Anglesey, not to mention the hazardous ferry crossing of the Menai Strait. There were often frustrating delays in sailing because of bad weather. In 1821 George IV was held up for five days waiting for suitable winds for the royal yacht to sail. Eventually he left in a recently-introduced paddle steamer. The triumphal arch near the car ferry terminal commemorates the royal visit, and marks the end of the A5, which begins with a more famous arch – Marble Arch in London.

Salt Island, approached alongside the car ferry terminal, takes its name from the time when salt was extracted from sea water in the 17thc. A rocky eminence overlooking the inner harbour bears the 1832 monument to the much-loved Captain Skinner, a mailpacket captain and harbour improver who was washed overboard and drowned near the North Stack. Close to the King George IV arch is a formidable-looking chamber for detaining mutinous sailors. Beyond the car ferry terminal entrance is Holyhead's lifeboat station, which has a long and proud record of having saved more than 1,000 lives.

Holyhead's future as a port was assured with the building of the railway in 1845.

Two years later work was started on the great breakwater – a double-jointed affair which, with a length of 1½m, is the longest breakwater in Britain. It took 28 years to complete, cost £1,285,000, and celebrated its centenary in 1973; the limestone of which it is constructed helps to give it a newly-built appearance. Stone was quarried from Holyhead Mountain and brought along a specially-constructed railway to the workshops. Limestone was also brought by sea from Red Wharf Bay, and sandstone from Runcorn. From Soldiers' Point it is possible to walk out to sea along the two-level breakwater to the square, 70ft-high lighthouse. This is now automated, but its brass clockwork machinery of 1873 survives. The breakwater shelters an area of 667 acres and at the turn of the century it was common to see as many as 100 ships seeking refuge here during bad weather. The castellated structure at the start of the breakwater is all that remains of the walled residence which the breakwater contractor built for himself.

A reminder that Holyhead's importance dates back to Roman times is provided by Caer Cybi, a coastal fort just off the town's High Street. The high walls are 6ft thick and enclose the parish Church of St Cybi. The fort (AM) probably dates back to 3rd or 4thc, and was possibly an outpost of the larger Roman fort of *Segontium* in Caernarfon. Its position on a low cliff suggests that it enclosed a small quay. Three of its four walls remain, together with parts of the angle towers. Near the churchyard gate is *Eglwys y Bedd* (Church of the Grave), which is reputed to contain the grave of Sergei Wyddel. Wyddel was leader of the marauding Irish who were driven out of

the island by the Welsh chieftain Caswallon Lawhir. St Cybi obviously chose the protection of the Roman fortress to establish his church here in the 5thc, and the existing church was established on the site of St Cybi's foundation. The present church of St Cybi was much restored, like so many churches in the latter half of the last century, and contains stained glass by Burne-Jones and William Morris – two of the most important influences in the pre-Raphaelite school of thought and art. Also here is a Stanley tomb; this family held the same kind of aristocratic influence in Holyhead as the Bulkeley family had at Beaumaris. Not far from St Cybi's are the Library and Exhibition Room, where attractive displays are exhibited. The 19th-c Church of St Seiriol is also of interest.

HOLY ISLAND, Gwynedd *4 SH27*

The high wall on the railway side of Stanley Embankment disguises the fact that the traveller is crossing on to an island. The main places on Holy Island are Holyhead, Trearddur Bay, and Rhoscolyn. Four Mile Bridge is the only other link with Anglesey, although there were once two or three crossings at low tide. At high tide the sea surges through a central arch to form an inland lake stretching to Four Mile Bridge. When the tide recedes it leaves a muddy expanse which is popular with herons and other water fowl. The present-day approach is dominated by the silhouette of the giant smelter of the Rio Tinto Zinc Corporation, but in the distance 720ft Holyhead Mountain still exercises a magnetic attraction as the highest point on the island.

South Stack is a rocky islet with precipitous cliffs and a famous lighthouse, one of the most-photographed landmarks in Wales. Work on this started in 1808, and within six months Daniel Alexander the architect had the lighthouse in operation. Men and materials were hauled across the stomach-turning chasm by an ingenious pulley system, with the seas raging beneath ready to swallow any unfortunate faller. A rope bridge which was not popular with tourists was followed by a suspension bridge, in turn to be replaced by the present structure. A walk to the now-automatic lighthouse entails the descent of 360 steps to the bridge. An intriguing clifftop tower which overlooks South Stack is known as Ellin's Tower, and is a derelict 18th-c summerhouse which was built by the Stanleys of Penrhos. A nature trail near by gives a magnificent eye-level view of cliffs opposite, alive with many species of sea birds. Holy Island's importance with early settlers is confirmed by Caer-y-Twr, a 17-acre, drystone-wall enclosed site on the summit of the mountain.

Nearby hut circles are called *Cytiau Gwyddelod* (Irishmen's Huts), but there is no evidence to support an Irish connection. More than 50 circular huts were recorded in 1865, and today at least 20 can be seen in two distinct groups. Some of the walls remain to

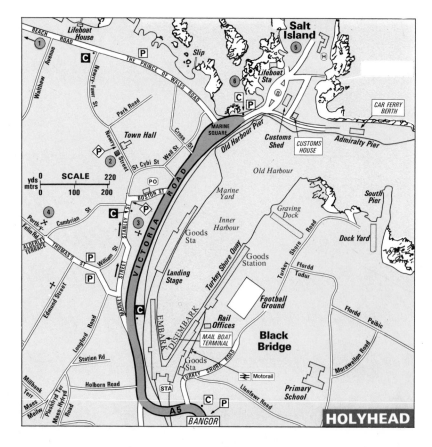

1 Breakwater
2 Library & Exhibition Rooms
3 St Cybi's Church & Remains of
   Roman Fort
4 St Seiriol's Church
5 Salt Island
6 Skinner's Memorial

about 2ft in height and show central hearths and slabs marking the position of beds and benches. Copper slag found in one hut indicates some kind of metal-working activity. One of N Wales' best-known nature reserves is at Penrhos, just off the A5 outside Holyhead. Its 450 acres include part of Penrhos, formerly the home of the Stanleys of Alderley, which was bought by the Anglesey Aluminium Company in 1968. A former pheasant shoot provides an ideal habitat for field and woodland birds. The foreshore along the rocky coastline is the home of sea and wading birds which include curlews, oyster catchers, turnstones, common sandpipers, redshanks, herons, ringed plovers, and widgeon. A nature trail begins near the Stanley Tollhouse, just off the A5, and a specialised sector is limited to bona-fide ornithologists.

HOLYWELL, Clwyd *7 SJ17*

For over 1,300 years pilgrims have flocked to the Holy Well of St Winefride, after which the town is named. St Winefride was a 7th-c virgin who had decided to dedicate her life to God. According to the legend one Caradog, the son of a local chief, declared his love for her. She refused him and as she tried to flee he drew his sword and struck off her head. He was immediately swallowed up by the earth and her head fell near to the church where her uncle, St Bueno, was preaching. At that very spot a spring of water gushed forth, then her uncle came out and reunited the head and body. After he had offered prayers to God she was restored to life. She lived a further fifteen years, bearing a white mark where she had been decapitated, and was Abbess of Gwytherin until she died.

A perpendicular-style chapel was erected at the site of the well by Lady Margaret Beaufort, the mother of Henry VII, towards the end of the 15thc. This replaced an older building which was falling in ruins. The chapel is of quite large proportions, and the arms and unusual figures of Margaret and her family are set around the windows. The spring issues into a basin in the crypt, in front of which is a pool in which people were immersed to be healed. At one time a pile of crutches belonging to those who had been cured lay next to the pool. Near the pool steps is St Bueno's stone, and to the left of the basin is a small altar beneath a statue of St Winefride. A reddish moss growing in the crypt is said to bear the stain of her blood. This well was one of the traditional seven wonders of Wales. The main feast of St Winefride is held on 22 June and commemorates her decapitation; a second is held on 3 November, the anniversary of her natural death.

The parish church stands near the well and is a plain Georgian structure which was rebuilt in 1769, incorporating a 14th-c perpendicular tower. It was restored in 1885. Its interior is rather dark and uninteresting and contains the *Gloch Bach* or little bell, which was rung around the streets until 1857 to call people to church. The church bells could not be heard in the town. A leather knee pad against which it was struck is also preserved. Other notable features include two old dug-out chests, one dated 1679; two small copper collecting pans set in the west wall; and a war memorial window of 1919. The

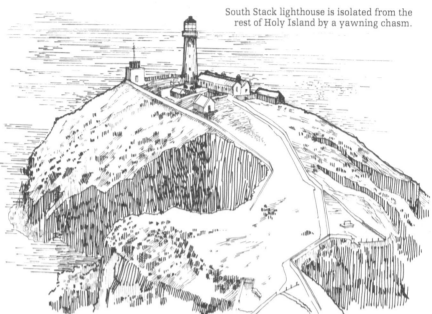

South Stack lighthouse is isolated from the rest of Holy Island by a yawning chasm.

RC Church of St Winefride is a large building with a decorated interior. A marble statue of the saint in contemporary Celtic dress stands in the entrance. Also in the town are St Winefride's Convent, a large hospice for pilgrims run by the Sisters of Charity of St Paul, and an impressive bronze statue of the Sacred Heart in the grounds of St Winefride's Catholic Primary School.

A musical festival catering for all musical tastes is held annually in the first two weeks of June. Halkyn Mountain rises to 900ft to the S and is littered with treacherous mine shafts. It affords fine views of the Dee estuary and Wirral Peninsula. Halkyn Castle was once a seat of the Duke of Westminster and lies 3m to the SE. A pretty church stands near its entrance lodge. Some 2½m W of Holywell is Pantasaph, a village set round an RC community comprising a Franciscan friary founded in 1858, a convent, and an orphanage. The church of St David stands near the friary and contains some fine statues of St David, the Virgin Mary, and St Asaph, plus wood carvings, stained glass, and an effigy of the 19th-c Earl of Denbigh in a canopied tomb. Behind the friary is a winding path with the stations of the cross. This leads up a hill known as Mount Calvary, and ends at the Chapel of the Sepulchre and a huge cross. A disused quarry at the foot of this hill contains a replica of the grotto at Lourdes.

HOPE, Clwyd *7 SJ35*

Hope lies on the Wrexham to Mold road and is invariably linked with its twin village of Caergwrle. 'Live in Hope and die in Caergwrle' say the local wags. Hope has its own little niche in history. During the Edwardian conquest of Wales the king took over the castle at Caergwrle and bestowed it upon Queen Eleanor. On her way to Caernarfon she is reputed to have stayed at Caergwrle Castle and given birth to Edward II, who was shortly to become the first English Prince of Wales. Caernarfon, on the other hand, claimed that their castle was the birthplace of the young Edward. Hope uses the old name of the village, Queen's Hope, to substantiate its rather fragile claim. The community

is physically linked with its neighbour by a 14th-c, five-arched packhorse bridge. A newer bridge at Bridge End stands near a ruined mill and old weir.

The village was mentioned in the *Domesday Book* and granted a charter by the Black Prince in the 14thc. One of the earliest collieries was sited near by, and today Hope is a small centre for local farming and industry. The mainly 15th-c perpendicular church was built by Lady Margaret Beaufort and features a square stone tower and double aisle. The south aisle contains a damaged 15th-c window. Other points of interest include a 15th-c font, an early 17th-c pulpit, a restored 18th-c organ, and 17th-c effigies of Sir John Trevor and his wife – the builders of Jacobean Plas Teg. Plas Teg is a house which was completed in 1610 and stands in the NW corner of the parish. Its staircase was by the famous Grinling Gibbons. Also near by is the pretty, stone-built farmhouse of Bryn Yorkin, which is of 17th-c date.

ILSTON, West Glamorgan *24 SS59*

Ilston lies about ½m SW of Swansea Airport, on the attractively wooded Ilston stream, and has a much-restored church dedicated to St Illtud. St Illtud was founder of the monastery at Llantwit Major and leader of the Celtic Church in the 6thc. The church has a massive tower with a saddleback roof, and one of its bells dates back to the 15thc. A yew-tree in the churchyard is claimed to be even older. John Myles was rector here in the 17thc, and was responsible for founding the first Baptist church in Wales. Remains of this lie beside the stream 1m S of the village near the A4118. An open-air pulpit and a plaque can be seen.

KENFIG, Mid Glamorgan *25 SS88*

To the west of Pyle and the main Cardiff to Swansea railway line lies an area of sand-dunes, said to be the largest in S Wales. Apart from this claim to fame it is better known as the site of one of Britain's lost towns, the ancient borough of Kenfig. The town developed in the 12thc under the protection of a castle built by Robert Earl of Gloucester, and in the following century wall construction completed the defences. However, the greatest threat proved to be that of drifting sand, and by the 14thc many parts of the town were engulfed. The final attack came during a great sand storm in the early 16thc, when the remaining buildings and even the great square keep of the castle were buried almost overnight. Although excavated during this century, the castle ruins have once more been buried by the sand.

The borough continued to exist until 1886, with the records and charters preserved in the present village inn which was used as the Guildhall. Its silver mace is preserved in The National Museum of Wales, Cardiff. To the S of the former town and close to the modern but somewhat scattered village of Kenfig lies Kenfig Pool. This is the largest natural stretch of water in the county and has the distinction of being permanently fresh, in spite of its proximity to the sea. To the W of the Pool are Kenfig Sands, which stretch nearly 3m between the mouth of the Afon Cynffig to the N and Sker Point to the S. To the E of Kenfig Pool Mawdlam Church stands on the edge of the dunes and displays an early-Norman chancel-arch, a Norman font, and the tomb of Elizabeth Francis –who died at the age of 110. Lighting towers of the extensive Margam marshalling yard can be seen to the N, with the massive Abbey Steelworks of Port Talbot and the high slopes of the 1,000ft Mynydd Margam in the background.

KETE, Dyfed *18 SM80*
Kete is situated off the road between Dale and St Ann's Head at the mouth of Milford Haven, and was the site of a former Royal Naval radar station – located on the cliff-tops on the seaward side of the headland. Now completely cleared by the NT, all 168 acres have been returned to agricultural use and a mile of attractive cliff scenery has been re-opened to the public. This stretch of coast is known as Welshman's Bay and extends between Long Point and Little Castle Point. Views encompass Skokholm and Skomer Islands, plus the shore as far as Wooltack Point.

Much of Dylan Thomas's work was created at the Boathouse in Laugharne.

KIDWELLY, Dyfed *20 SN40*
Kidwelly lies at the head of the Gwendraeth inlet off the sandy Tywi estuary, with the vast Towyn Burrows and Pembrey Forest stretching away to the S. This inlet is the confluence and mouth of the two Gwendraeth rivers Fawr and Fach, between which the town is situated and from which it derives its Welsh name of 'Cydweli'. It was the distinction of being the only Welsh place name for which, in the English version, the Welsh pronunciation of double 'L' (LL) does not apply. This was due to a very early spelling error on a map, resulting in the addition of an extra 'L'.

As a borough it is one of the oldest in Wales, the first charter having been granted by Henry I. The older and formerly walled part lies on the W bank of the Gwendraeth Fach below the castle. The newer town has a prominent church and is situated on its E bank. The two are linked by a bridge which, although considerably widened, dates from the 14th or 15thc. An older bridge named Pont Spwdwr (AM) stands beside the B4308 Trimsaran and Llanelli road 2m E of the town, and spans the Gwendraeth Fawr river. It is said to be the oldest bridge in S Wales.

Kidwelly's church was originally the church of a Benedictine priory founded in 1130 by Bishop Roger of Salisbury, who also built the castle. It was constructed as a branch of Sherborne Abbey in Dorset. The priory was dismantled at the Dissolution, but the church survived intact and is now the finest example of early to middle 14th-c style in the diocese of St David's. The chancel, the large span of the nave, and the 13th-c tower with its tall spire are among its more notable features. Unfortunately the town's domestic architecture has not survived so well, and the last of the medieval houses was demolished some time ago.

Kidwelly Castle is the pride of the town, and after careful restoration by the Department of the Environment is now the best preserved of Carmarthenshire's (now part of Dyfed) nine strongholds. It was built by Roger of Salisbury in the

time of Henry I as part of his chain of fortifications to protect territories won during the Norman advance across S Wales (see inset opposite).

KNIGHTON, Powys *14 SO27*
This little tightly-knit, grey-stone town with a clock tower at its heart gives the impression that it is clinging desperately to the sides of the steep hill on which it has grown. Knighton has held on to its hill for a thousand years at least. The Saxons settled here first, then the Welsh arrived in 1052, to be quickly followed by the Normans soon after 1066. The Normans built the first castle, a timber structure on a mound situated behind the Smithfield and still called Bryn-y-Castell. The first stone castle was built on the other side of the town on the top of a hill in the 12thc, and the mound and remnants of a ditch are still visible.

Knighton's situation in the Teme Valley, with the river's heavily-wooded and mountainous left bank near by, is delightful. The Welsh name for Knighton is 'Tref-y-Clawdd' meaning the Town on the Dyke, and Offa's Dyke runs all along its W side. It comes up from the river to the junction of Newtown Road with West Street, and continues along Offa's Road before crossing the Cwm and Ffrydd Road to head through the Great Ffrydd Wood. This is indeed one of the showpieces of the town. It was in the Offa's Dyke Riverside Park, created by the Tref-y-Clawdd '1970' Society as their contribution to the European Conservation Year, that the official opening of the Offa's Dyke Path by Lord Hunt took place on 10 July 1971.

The central Wales railway line through Knighton still operates and is one of only two railway lines left in mid-Wales. Knighton Station is a little gem of Victorian-gothic railway architecture. This is because Sir Richard Green-Price, who released the land for the track, did so only on condition that he should personally approve the design of all stations, bridges, and other structures to be built in the area. The town contains a number of interesting old inns, of which the Swan was once noted for cock fighting. The double-naved, originally Norman church has been twice rebuilt. It is one of the few Welsh churches dedicated to an English saint, and the only one to St Edward.

The most picturesque street in Knighton is The Narrows, which runs uphill from the Clock Tower. Right opposite the tower is the town's prettiest house – a narrow-fronted half-timbered building set back behind a delightfully paved courtyard. Countryside around Knighton is devoted to sheep-rearing, and the Knighton sheep sales are famous. The town is a market centre covering a wide area and holds fairs dating back to 1230. Caer Caradoc is a nearby hill which is one of several locations claimed to be the last stand of Caractacus against the Romans. Ruins of a Roman villa were discovered 2m outside the town in the hamlet of Stow during 1925.

KNUCKLAS, Powys *14 SO27*
A great hill that towers over Knucklas is crowned with the ruins of a castle, and joins Old Oswestry in the claim that it was once the home of the giant Ogyrfan and his daughter Gwynhwyfar (Guinevere), who married King Arthur. The castle remains are 13thc, though an

earlier hillfort may have been established here. Another feature of interest in this village is the beautiful railway viaduct, with its crenellated turrets. Knucklas is famous as the birthplace of Vavasor Powell, the self-appointed parson who forged his letters of ordination. He became one of Cromwell's commissioners – officials who dismissed many Anglican priests from their parishes during the Commonwealth.

LAKE VYRNWY, Powys   10 SJ02

This artificial lake measures $4\frac{3}{4}$m long by about $\frac{1}{2}$m wide and was formed between 1880 and 1890 as a reservoir for Liverpool's water supply. The water is carried to Liverpool by a 75m-long aquaduct. The valley now occupied by the reservoir probably held a natural lake formed by glaciation during the Ice Age. Surrounding landscape comprises woodland and moors leading up to craggy summits. It is possible to drive all round the lake, but it and its environs are best appreciated from the water. The fishing is very good. Llanwyddyn is a new village which replaces one that was submerged when the lake was formed.

*LAMPETER, Dyfed   20 SN54

Lampeter is a market town set in pastoral countryside of neat, hedged fields, and is best known for St David's College. This was founded in 1822 by the Bishop of St David's. The Bishop,

SEAT OF A BISHOP

Native rulers succumbed to the barons more easily in S Wales (*Deheubarth*) than in any other part of the country. Henry I granted the commote of Cydweli – the former property of Hywel ap Gronw – to Roger Bishop of Salisbury in 1106. Building started immediately on a castle which would be one of a network of strongholds to maintain Norman control. On the death of that powerful king the Welsh saw hope for uprising. In 1136, while Gruffydd ap Rhys the tireless rebel was seeking northern aid to free Deheubarth from the foreign yoke, his wife Gwenllian attempted to take Kidwelly. Maurice de Londres, to whom Roger Salisbury had granted the title of Lord of Kidwelly, defeated her at a place near by called to this day Maes Gwenllian, and both she and her young son were killed. Her youngest son and the future 'Lord Rhys', whose name is linked with the first eisteddfod held at Cardigan in 1176, gained Kidwelly in

Thomas Burgess, was the son of a Hampshire grocer, and his intention in founding the college was to enable local men to gain a university education without having to go to either Oxford or Cambridge – the cost of which was prohibitive to most people. The college's main buildings were designed by C R Cockerell in 'gothic' style, and it is definitely an institution founded on English lines. It has the right to confer degrees of BA and BD. The college chapel was rebuilt in 1880 and contains stalls from New College Oxford. The library is housed in modern buildings and has a large collection of early manuscripts and first editions.

The town itself, more properly called 'Llanbedr', is a busy place and focal point for the surrounding community. Its wide main street is lined with small shops intermingled with private houses, the Victorian town hall, and two Georgian hotels. Lampeter no longer holds its once-famous horse fair, but market day is still an occasion of considerable liveliness. The parish church was rebuilt in 1869, but some 17th-c memorials are preserved in the porch. Remains of a Norman motte about which nothing seems to be known lie in the grounds of the college. About $\frac{3}{4}$m N is a castle mound called Castell Olwen.

LAMPHEY, Dyfed   18 SN00

A fast-growing village to the E of Pembroke, Lamphey is the site of one of

1190. For the next 50 years his descendants were active in the defence and recapture of the castle.

Through the marriage of Matilda de Chaworth – heiress of the castle – and Henry of Lancaster, the stronghold passed to the crown during the reign of Henry IV via his father John of Gaunt, whose wife had inherited Kidwelly on the death of her sister Matilda. In the latter part of the 15thc Sir Rhys ap Thomas was granted the castle by Henry VII, in recognition of his support for the Tudor cause. Kidwelly is an excellent example of the way in which Norman foundations have been modified to suit new military needs. The moat and the

the seven palaces of the Bishops of St David's. Most of the building work took place between the 13th and 15thc; the west wing dates from 1250, and the east wing from 1330. The great hall was built by Bishop Gower, often known as the 'building bishop'. It became the property of the Earls of Essex in 1546, who used it as a family mansion. Robert Devereaux, one day to become the favourite of the first Queen Elizabeth, was born and spent his boyhood here. Later the palace was neglected and fell into total ruin. It is now in the care of the DoE, and much restoration work has been carried out.

LAUGHARNE, Dyfed   19 SN31

Whatever else can be said about Laugharne, the first thing that must be recorded is that a little Georgian building called the Boathouse was once the home of the famous and infamous Dylan Thomas. The house stands on a narrow cliff walk near the castle, close to a shed in which he wrote some of his later poetry. He is buried in Laugharne churchyard, and a simple cross marks his grave. This church is cruciform in shape and dates from the 13thc, but it was heavily restored in the 19thc. Stained glass here has come in for a good deal of comment – most of it derisory – and there are several 17th-c memorials of interest. Although Thomas always denied that Laugharne was the inspiration

semi-circular rampart – the two surviving Norman features – formed the outer defences of the castle begun in 1275; the new building, a stone rectangular fortress with circular angle-towers, formed an inner ward. In the early 14thc the stockade on the rampart was replaced with a stone curtain reinforced by three semi-circular towers. The addition of a southern gatehouse and a northern gate, together with the raising of the towers of the inner ward, completed the transformation into a concentric castle.

The building is semi-circular in shape, with the straight side on the east rising high above Gwendraeth Fach, which flows into Carmarthen Bay a few miles away. The state of preservation of a number of its buildings, in particular the early 14th-c chapel and the north-west tower, is remarkable.

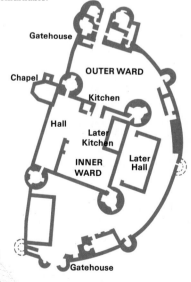

for *Under Milk Wood*, the townsfolk of Laugharne seem more than happy to act the parts, and every three years the play is performed in the town.

Laugharne (pronounced 'Larn') has a long history. It was a border town on the mysterious but very real frontier called the 'Landsker', which separated 'Little England beyond Wales' from Welsh Wales. 'Little England' was settled by Norman and Flemmish peoples very decisively in the 11th and 12thc. The castle was probably first built early in the 12thc, but like most border strongholds it was repeatedly taken and re-taken, destroyed and rebuilt (see inset below).

The town itself is charming, with modest Georgian houses and a white-painted tower that belongs to the town hall in the main street. Built in 1746, the town hall preserves a charter granted by the Normans in 1307. Local government is still conducted under the terms of this charter, and meetings of the Court Leet and Court Baron are presided over by an official known as the Portreeve. Laugharne has attracted other writers beside Dylan Thomas, including Edward Thomas, Ernest Rhys, and Richard Hughes.

The foreshore is muddy and weedy and not very attractive. Romance is lent to it by the fact that once a year General Laugharne, a roundhead who changed sides, became a royalist, and captured the castle during the civil war, sees fit to row himself across the river. The General must have been a man of stamina and more than a little eccentric, for he crosses the river stark naked in a coracle, using a cocked hat as a baler. Perhaps the story has become a trifle amplified during its 300 years of telling. St Johns Hill rises S of the town and affords good views. Remains of Roche Castle lie at its foot.

LAVERNOCK, South Glamorgan *26 ST16*

'Are you ready?' That was the message received here on 11 May 1897 – the first wireless message ever sent across water. It was transmitted by Guglielmo Marconi from Flat Holm (see entry), an island 3m offshore, and was received at Lavernock Point by his partner George Kemp. The message transcript is preserved in the National Museum of Wales at Cardiff.

LAWRENNY, Dyfed *18 SN00*

Situated in the Pembrokeshire Coast national park, this village lies in the section of the park where the Cresswell River meets the Cleddau. This has become a big sailing area and includes a yacht club and yacht station. Stone cottages mark the entrance to the now-demolished Lawrenny Hall, which was built on the site of a home of the Bishops of St David's. Remains of a 13th-c building known as the Palace lie E of Lawrenny at Cresswell. This structure was abandoned in favour of the Lawrenny site.

LEIGHTON, Powys *11 SJ20*

Standing between the Long Mountain and the River Severn 1½m E of Welshpool, Leighton boasts a fantastic folly in the shape of The Hall and its estate. This was the inspiration of the Naylor family a century and more ago. The hall itself is vast, has an extremely high tower, and faces Powis Castle across the valley. An even more intriguing folly is the funicular railway which was constructed up the side of the Moel-y-Mab. The base station is still intact, though somewhat dilapidated, and the track bed is easily distinguishable. There is still something left of the top station, but it is a long time

CASTLE TO MANSION

The battlements of this castle form a compact circle surrounded by trees in the middle of Laugharne (pronounced 'Larne'), 4m from St Clears. Or so it would appear as the visitor descends the hill into the small town. In reality the castle is built on a wide expanse of flat land skirting the mouth of the River Taf. With Llanstephan at the mouth of the River Tywi and Kidwelly on the Gwendraeth, it forms a triumvirate of Norman strongholds commanding Carmarthen Bay and able to take full advantage of its sea communications. Mention is made of Laugharne castle in *Brut y Tywysogion – The Chronicle of the Princes* – in 1189 and 1215, and it was in the possession of Rhys ap Gruffydd for some time. He is better known as 'Lord' Rhys of Dinefwr and leader of *Deheubarth*, and wielded a considerable influence in S Wales during the reign of Henry II.

The early history of the castle, like that of Kidwelly and Llanstephan, consisted of a constant tussle for supremacy between the Anglo-Normans and the Welsh. Llywelyn ab Iorwerth took the castle in 1215, but it was recaptured soon afterwards by Sir Guy de Brian, who held it as a grant from the crown – 'In return for finding two men at arms with horses, all properly equipped, or eight armed soldiers on foot, to be maintained in the field for three days for the king, at his own expense, on receiving due notice from the bailiff of Carmarthen.'

In the 15thc the castle passed to the Percy family, who held it until the time of Henry VII. Queen Elizabeth granted it to Sir John Perrot of Pembrokeshire, a man of considerable influence at court as well as in his native county. His alterations at Laugharne and Carew, his main residence, were symptomatic of the obsessive interest in domestic architecture in the 16thc. At this time vast palaces were built, stately homes erected at enormous and crippling expense, manor houses extended and remodelled,

and medieval defensive buildings transformed into sumptuous displays of wealth – if not comfort. In England Robert Dudley the Earl of Leicester was fully occupied adapting and embellishing Kenilworth Castle in preparation for Queen Elizabeth's visit of 1575. At about the same time William Somerset the Earl of Worcester was 'modernizing' the Grand Hall at Raglan, undoubtedly the best example in Wales of the studied change from stronghold to mansion. Sir John Perrot, as befitted a man of such prestige – and Henry VIII's reputed illegitimate son – was applying similar expressions of fashion at Laugharne. The mullion and transome windows and remains of the great hall looking across the 'heron-priested shore' cohabit in their ruined state with the two drum angle-towers which survive from the 13thc.

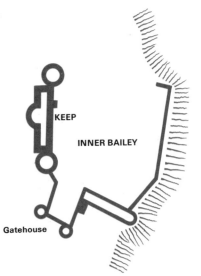

since the railway was operational. It was presumably for the estate workers to attend to the installations on the top of the mountain, which comprised a complicated system of pumps and pipes providing a singularly useless irrigation system. The hall is now owned by a commercial firm who use it to accommodate business visitors.

LETTERSTON, Dyfed 16 SM92
Situated on the A40 between Fishguard and Haverfordwest, this little village includes a 19th-c church which houses some ancient carvings.

LLANABER, Gwynedd 9 SH61
Occupying a commanding clifftop position on the Harlech road 2m N of Barmouth is Llanaber church, a charming building with plenty to interest the antiquarian. Its outstanding feature is the early-English doorway, one of the best examples to be seen anywhere. Other fine early-English features, which firmly date the church to the 13thc, are the clerestory windows on either side of the nave. One of two ancient stones in the north west corner of the church was rescued from use as a footbridge on a nearby farm. Its Latin inscription has been translated as 'Cauxtus, King of Mona' and it has been dated as earlier than the 10thc. The church's proximity to the sea gives rise to many legends associated with smuggling. Table tombs in the graveyard were reputedly convenient repositories for contraband spirits smuggled ashore in the dead of night. A few miles N are the ruins of Egryn Abbey, and E of the abbey is the Carneddau Hengwm site.

LLANAELHAEARN, Gwynedd 8 SH34
Overshadowed by the 1,849ft mass of Yr Eifl on the Lleyn Peninsula, this village has a church founded in the 6thc and dedicated to St Aelhaearn – who is said to have been a servant of St Bueno. When the church was restored inscriptions were found on the walls, and an inscribed stone in the north transept adds weight to the argument that this may once have been a station on the Saint's Road to Bardsey. Also in the church is a 15th-c rood screen and some 18th-c spindle-backed box pews. To the S of the church is St Aelhaearn's Well, which is now roofed over.

The mountains called Yr Eifl are often anglicized to 'The Rivals', although this is not what the name means. The correct translation is 'the two forks'. Views afforded by the summit are praised as being among the finest in Wales. On the E peak is a collection of hut circles and fortifications known as Tre'r Ceiri. Between Yr Eifl and the sea is Nant Gwytheyrn, or Vortigern's Valley. A tumulus in the valley yielded remains of a tall man who was said to be Vortigern himself. Vortigern was a 5th-c leader who is said to have brought Hengist and Horsa to this country. The story tells that he came to this valley to escape the wrath of his countrymen, and built himself a castle which was promptly struck by lightning – killing him and totally destroying the castle.

LLANALLGO, Gwynedd 5 SH58
A mile inland from Moelfre on the N coast of Anglesey, Llanallgo and its church will forever be associated with the wreck of the 'Royal Charter' one stormy night in 1859, when 452 people perished. The tiny church was stripped of its furniture and ornaments to become the mortuary. Charles Dickens, who stayed at Llanallgo Rectory while he was reporting the tragedy, records how the Rev J Rhoose Williams worked tirelessly to identify the dead, bury them, and write more than 1,000 letters to bereaved relatives. So great was the strain that he lived only two years after. About 150 of the victims were buried at Llanallgo, and most of the others at neighbouring churches. An obelisk made from the granite of the cliff where the 'Royal Charter' was wrecked, stands in a corner of the churchyard, and the ship's signal gun is in the rectory grounds.

LLANANNO, Powys 13 SO07
Llananno is a scattered hamlet on the A483 between Newtown and Llandrindod Wells, and as far as maps are concerned the district is known as Castle Vale. Nevertheless, the name is still in official use and the hamlet has its own telephone exchange. It grew up as a parish round the church. The church has now lost that status, but it has retained its most precious treasure – a carved rood screen of the 15thc, believed at one time to have come from nearby Abbey Cwm Hir. This origin has now been disproved by experts. The screen is carved in high relief with the figure of Christ in the centre and the twelve apostles on his left and twelve prophets and patriarchs on his right, along with motifs of foliage and flowers.

About $\frac{1}{2}$m up the road in the Newtown direction – invisible from it apart from a glimpse higher up at Glanithon – is the ruin of Castell Dinboeth. Situated high on the mountainside, this is difficult to reach but worth the effort. This castle was probably built late in the 13thc, and was at one time in the possession of the Mortimers. It was already a ruin in the 16thc, as Leland noted. Across the river is a charming little grey-stone chapel called Maes yr helm, set in a graveyard of evergreen trees. It is one of a trio belonging to the Baptist denomination which serves this district.

LLANARMON DC, Clwyd 11 SJ13
Llanarmon Dyffryn Ceiriog, not to be confused with Llanarmon Dyffryn Clwyd near Ruthin, is where the beautiful Ceiriog Valley ends in a sudden ambush of mountains. On a hillside above the village is Penybryn, birthplace of John Ceiriog Hughes (1832–1887), generally acknowledged as the greatest of Welsh lyrical poets. He left his boyhood home to become a railway clerk in Manchester and later a station master in mid Wales, but it was undoubtedly his boyhood memories of Llanarmon DC which inspired his work.

LLANARMON YN IAL, Clwyd 7 SJ15
This pleasant village is tucked away off the main route between Mold and Ruthin. The church, dedicated to St Germanus, was built in 1736 and restored in 1870 but has retained some old monuments – notably the tomb of Gruffydd ap Llywelyn dated 1350. The 16th-c, three-tier brass chandelier carries a figure of the virgin and was reputedly rescued from Valle Crucis Abbey, Llangollen, at the Dissolution. The cheerfully whitewashed Raven Inn opposite the church completes a harmonious village scene. In 1896 two greenstone axes were found in a cave on the outskirts of the village.

Expert opinion traced them to the stone-age factory at Penmaenmawr.

LLANARTH, Dyfed 12 SN45
On the A487 4m S of Aberaeron and inland from New Quay, the Victorian houses of this village are dominated by the tower of its largely rebuilt church. The church retains an 11th-c font and features a stone with an Ogham inscription which was superimposed by an Irish Celtic inscribed cross in the 9thc. Henry VII is said to have stayed at nearby Wern Newydd on his way to the Battle of Bosworth Field in 1485. John Pugh of Pont-y-gido ran a famous school here in the 18thc, at which several distinguished clergymen received their education.

LLANASA, Clwyd 6 SJ18
Llanasa is a stone-built village sited 2m inland, where it is quietly tucked away from the hectic bustle of the busy coast road between Flint and Prestatyn. The 16th-c church has glass in the east windows reputedly from Basingwerk Abbey, and another eye-catching feature is the twelve-branched, 18th-c chandelier made by a man called Edward Foulkes in 1758. Henblas and Golden Grove are two attractive 17th-c stone-built houses in the vicinity.

LLANBABO, Gwynedd 4 SH38
The isolated church in this agricultural parish of NE Anglesey is dedicated to St Pabo, a 6th-c chieftain who sought refuge in Anglesey. A 14th-c grave slab inside the church represents Pabo, and outside over the door are three crude medieval faces. Near Llanbabo is the new reservoir of Llyn Alaw. Afon Alaw is a stream which flows from it and is associated with the legend of Bedd Branwen, or Branwen's Grave. This is described in the *Mabinogion* – a 12th-c book of Welsh legends. Branwen was a British princess who had married an Irish king, but it was not long before trouble between the two families led to a fight in which her brother was killed. Rescued by the survivors, she returned to Anglesey to die of a broken heart and supposed to have been buried beside the Alaw. When a mound here was opened up in 1813 it revealed a four-sided grave, but this turned out to be a multiple tomb dating from the bronze age.

LLANBADARN FAWR, Dyfed 12 SN68
Today Llanbadarn Fawr is a suburb of Aberystwyth, only 1m from the town centre up the Rheidol Valley, but centuries ago it had Aberystwyth for its own suburb. Aberystwyth was at that time known as Llanbadarn Graerog. The village was an important centre of Christianity, the seat of a bishop, and a place of social and commercial intercourse. It was founded by St Padarn, a contemporary of St David, from whom it derives its name. Tradition has it that he came here from Britanny, but recent research suggests that he was born in S Wales in the 6thc. The Danes destroyed the first church, and the present spacious building dates from the 13thc. It is cruciform in shape, has thick walls and deep window embrasures, and contains an arch which is thought to have been brought from Strata Florida Abbey. The interior is somewhat bare, and the tower is massive. It underwent restoration by J P Seddons in 1870, who raised the roof, added the present

The so-called Roman Steps at Llanbedr
were, in fact, constructed in medieval times.

ceilings, rebuilt the nave, and paved
the floor of the chancel in black marble.
The most important features of interest
are two Celtic stone crosses, one 9ft and
the other 5ft high. The larger is intricately
carved and considered the finest of its
kind in Wales. According to legend St
Samson threw the crosses here from
Pendinas in Aberystwyth – in a temper
because they broke while he was using
them as flails. Lewis Morris, a poet who
lived from 1700 to 1765, is buried in the
chancel and has a memorial stone in the
floor; Dafydd ap Gwilym, referred to by
George Borrow as the greatest of his
country's songsters, was born in the
parish. He admitted that he went to
church to see the pretty girls rather
than to pray. His birthplace lies in ruins
3m NE at Broginin.

LLANBADARN FAWR, Powys   13 SO06
This Llanbadarn Fawr is literally a name
without a village. The community here is
Cross Gates, which stands at the
intersection of the A483 and the A44.
All that remains of the old village is the
church. As with the Dyfed village and
church of the same name, St Padarn was
also the founder of this one. Its most
interesting feature is the tympanum of
the arch over the entrance door, which
contains a curiously-carved stone
almost unique in Wales. The only other
like it is at Penmon in Anglesey. The
carving shows two animal figures each
side of a tree growing out of what
looks like a head, while on the ground is
an object that might be the sun.

A Roman Centurial stone inscribed VAL
FLAVIN, which is believed to
commemorate Valerius Flavinus who
constructed the road from Castell Collen
to Caersws and on into N Wales, can be
seen in the porch. An interesting
memorial inside the church is a plaque
in the chancel to David, Samuel, and
James Jones – father, son and grandson.
They were all rectors of the church during
the 17th and 18thc.

LLANBADARN FYNYDD, Powys   14 SO17
Half way through the present century the
road from Newtown to Llandrindod

Wells was reckoned to contain as many
bends as there are days in the year.
Attention by the old Radnorshire and
Montgomeryshire County Councils
resulted in considerable improvement,
and has greatly reduced the number of
bends. Llanbadarn Fynydd lies 12m S
of Newtown and boasts two plaques
which record a fragment of history
relating to this road. These plaques
were set in the wall of the old smithy,
which was demolished in 1973. The top
one read 'When William Pugh of
Brynllywarch made the road from
Newtown to Builth he fixed a weighing
machine here in 1823, and in 1839
William B Pugh of Dolfor removed it'.
The lower plaque added 'The above
stone was placed in its present position
by Edward Minton-Beddoes, Squire of
Dolfor, in 1930'. Almost the last project
undertaken by the County Surveyor of
Radnorshire, before the county went
out of existence at the end of March
1974, was to have these two plaques
resited in a stone pillar specially
constructed for the purpose and set up
at the roadside on the site of the smithy.

LLANBADRIG, Gwynedd   4 SH39
Situated on the N coast of Anglesey,
Llanbadrig has the only church in Wales
dedicated to St Patrick. Tradition has it
that it was from here that Patrick set
sail to convert the Irish. The church has
been much restored and stands at the
end of a farm road on a cliff. It is
frequently sprayed by the sea in high
winds. To the E of the church is Dinas
Gwynfor, an iron-age hillfort of probable
Celtic origin. It covers an area of 700
by 300 yds on top of limestone cliffs
which drop 200ft to the sea below. A
marsh on the landward side must have
given it additional protection. The island
offshore is quaintly called Middle
Mouse, and sometimes Ynys Badrig.
Nestling snugly on the W side of the
cliff is Porth Llanlleiana, where the
ruined remains of a port date from a
time when clay was dug and exported
from here. Curiously-curved walls
above the high-tide line give it an air of
some abandoned monastery. To the
E of Dinas Gwynfor is the forbiddingly-
named Hell's Mouth, and farther along

is Porth Wen – with its deserted
brickworks and substantial quay. This
is not accessible by road.

LLANBEDR, Gwynedd   9 SH52
Gateway to the grim Rhinogs range,
Llanbedr is a pleasant coastal village
between Barmouth and Harlech, situated
in the heart of an area known as
Ardudwy. The best-known feature of the
locality is Mochras or Shell Island. This
is not actually an island, but a peninsula
which is cut off at high tide. The lagoon
is protected from the open sea by
Mochras, and was artificially formed
when the course of the River Artro was
changed. It now makes a popular
yachting centre. The island is popular
with campers and a paradise for children
who enjoy collecting shells and searching
rocky pools for lobsters and prawns. But
the history and romance of ancient
Merioneth is to be found in the foothills
above Llanbedr.

The valley of the River Artro is liberally
dotted with prehistoric sites, which
suggests this area was one of special
sanctity. To the N of the village are two
standing pillars of great antiquity.
Some 6m NE along the beautiful Cwm
Llyn Bychan are Roman Steps, an
impressive staircase which may not be
Roman in origin, but medieval. They
were used to ease the journey of pack
horses on their way to the coast.
Llanbedr offers excellent walking
country, and the twin valleys of the
Llyn Bychan and Nantcol lead to the
romantic lakes of Bychan, Gloyw, Du,
and Bodlyn. Walking is made easier by
tracks worn by miners of the manganese
deposits that were worked hereabouts.
About 1m E of Llanbedr towards Cwm
Nantcol at Cefn Cymerau is a little
Baptist chapel. Although unpretentious in
itself, this was immortalized by the
English painter Curnow Vosper. His
picture of Salem caught the atmosphere
of a Welsh chapel on some sunlit morning
during the last century. The chapel
remains unchanged – a place of
sentimental pilgrimage for many Welsh
people.

In the lee of the Rhinogs stands one of
the most isolated places in Wales – the
historic house of Maesygarnedd. Col John
Jones, who married Cromwell's sister
Catherine and was later executed for his
part in the death of Charles I, was born
here. To the N of Llanbedr is Llandanwg,
where an ancient church stands amid
the sand dunes. Neglected for many
years, the church dates from the 6thc
and has been rescued and re-roofed. It
was once Harlech's mother church. Out
to sea and visible at low tide is a
remarkable 9m ridge of rocks known as
Sarn Badrig (Patrick's Causeway) or
Sarn Baddwryg (Shipwreck Reef). Legend
connects this with Sarn-y-Bwch, a similar
ridge near Tywyn, and they are both said
to be the defences of a sunken land.
Seafarers give them a wide berth.

LLANBEDROG, Gwynedd   8 SH33
Llanbedrog is a pretty Lleyn resort which
grows annually in popularity. It is split
in half by the Pwllheli to Abersoch road.
The main attraction here is a wide sandy
beach backed by rich woodland, with a
heathery headland to the E. The parish
church of St Pedrog is embowered by
trees and has a fragmentary stained-
glass window – the remains of the former
church window smashed by Cromwell's

men. The fragments were gathered together and stored, and when Lady Jones-Parry of Madryn built the present church in 1865 they were incorporated in an eastern window. Inland is an interesting old mill (NT).

LLANBEDR-Y-CENNIN, Gwynedd
5 SH76
This small village is situated in the hills above the River Conwy, and the church in its yew-filled yard was restored by H Kennedy in 1842. High above the village is the hill fort Pen-y-Gaer, and just to the N is the village of Caerhun – built partly on the site of the Roman fort *Canovium*.

LLANBERIS, Gwynedd   *5 SH56*
Situated some 8m S of Caernarfon, Llanberis makes a double claim on tourist's interest with its mountains and its quarry workings. It is impossible to miss either. The route from here is regarded as the easiest of the three main paths to the summit of Snowdon (Yr Wyddfa), which at 3,650ft is the highest peak in England and Wales. The path provides a long 5m haul which is safe for the properly-equipped walker in good weather. It is pointless searching for solitude on Snowdon's summit in summer, however. Dedicated mountain walkers are just as resentful as the Victorians were at having to share the summit with people who have simply taken a train ride to the top. To add insult to injury, walkers can be showered with hot cinders from the hard-working engine of the Snowdon Mountain Railway if they happen to be walking too near the track (see feature starting page 62).

The vast Dinorwic slate quarry at Llanberis is often described as the world's greatest. Some will find the sight of these disused quarries and their workings romantic and inspiring, others will reflect on the scale of disruption that man can cause. But it is as well to remember the part that these quarries played in roofing houses all over the world, and something that children today are not aware of – the contribution they made to education, providing school slates before exercise books became universal.

Dinorwic quarry employed 3,000 people at its peak but ceased operations in 1969, having lost the battle with manufactured roof tiles. Anyone wishing to take a step back into industrial history will be well-rewarded by a visit to the Dinorwic quarry buildings, nearly opposite the Snowdon Railway Station. A quadrangular construction built like an army fort, the complex was acquired by the old Caernarfonshire County Council and is being developed as an industrial museum. Buildings and machinery have been so well-preserved that it looks as though operations could resume next week if there was a sudden demand for slate. A big attraction of the museum is the impressive water wheel, measuring 50ft in diameter, which was the principal source of power from 1870 to 1925. A six-bed hospital is a reminder that slate quarrying was a hazardous business. Slate was conveyed by rail to Port Dinorwic on the Menai Straits, and as an additional tourist attraction a section of this line has been re-opened to take passengers on a 45-minute return trip along the shore of Lake Padarn (see page 62). Dinorwic Quarry itself is to be used as a site for a

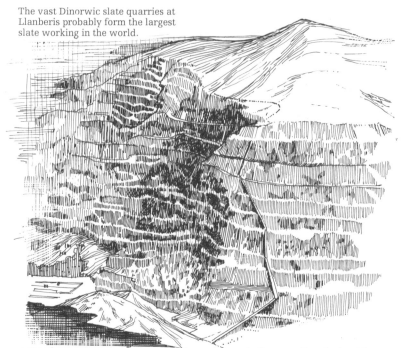

The vast Dinorwic slate quarries at Llanberis probably form the largest slate working in the world.

pumped storage power station, Llyn Peris being the lower reservoir.

The town of Llanberis is typical of a slate-quarrying community. Terraced houses built on sites blasted out of the rock huddle together in narrow side streets. One of the finest waterfalls in N Wales, Ceunant Mawr, is to be seen about $\frac{1}{2}$m from the Snowdon Railway terminus. Alongside the second railway viaduct the River Arddu twists and writhes in a 120ft fall into a spectacular gorge. Care should be taken with children here.

LLANBISTER, Powys   *14 SO17*
This village stands on a steep hill above the Ithon 10m N of Llandrindod Wells, and has a very remarkable 13th-c church. The tower is at the E end instead of the W; it has no chancel, the top bay of the nave being shut off for the choir behind the rood screen; besides a font there is a total immersion baptistry with steps leading down into it. A 15th-c quarrel among members of the Vaughan family of Llymwynt, on the mountains above Llanbadarn Fynydd, had a repercussion at Llanbister. John Vaughan killed David Vaughan in a fight, and David's sister Ellin Gethin revenged herself on him by coming to an archery contest in Llanbister dressed as a man, and instead of aiming at the target when her turn came, shot her arrow at John and killed him. She escaped in the ensuing confusion. The delightful church of Llananno stands N of Llanbister, and to the W is Abbey Cwm Hir.

LLANBLETHIAN, South Glamorgan
25 SS97
Thomas Carlyle described this village, 1m S of Cowbridge, as a 'little sleeping cataract of white houses with trees overshadowing and fringing it'. Carlyle often visited a friend who lived here, John Sterling, a writer on military matters who died in 1844 at the age of 38. The church features a 14th-c memorial slab with a Norman-French inscription, and unusual arches in the south porch. The rare dedication cross and pewter chalice were removed from

a priest's grave. Near by is a 17-acre iron-age fort called the Devil's Foot and Knee. Llanblethian or St Quentin's castle is named after the St Quentin family, who in fact did not own it until long after it had been built. The existing buildings date from the early 14thc and there are indications that there was a much earlier castle on the site. The ruins comprise curtain walls, some towers, and a fine twin-towered gatehouse which is now the most prominent part of the castle.

LLANBOIDY, Dyfed   *17 SN22*
A village set in rolling pastoral countryside NW of St Clears, Llanboidy includes a church which contains the family vault of the Powells. This family's seat was the mansion called Maesgwynne, situated a little outside the village. Maesgwynne once had its own racecourse, and the village hall was built from money won by a Powell backing a horse called Hermit. About 2m N of Llanboidy is Eglwys Fair a Churig, a weed-grown churchyard with the ruins of a church built in 1770. This is not marked on any modern maps.

LLANBORTH FARM, Dyfed   *17 SN25*
This NT property lies NW of the hamlet of Penbryn and E of Aberporth. The trust has done much to protect the sands of Penbryn Beach from over exploitation. The beach runs for over a mile and is reached via a pleasantly-wooded valley.

LLANBRYNMAIR, Powys   *10 SH90*
Interest in Llanbrynmair is almost entirely historical, and the village is connected with important personalities of both the distant and immediate past. Abraham Rees was born here in 1743, while his father was pastor of the Independent Chapel. He began his career as a tutor in mathematics at Hoxton Academy, but switched to the ministry at 23 and attracted such congregations to his chapel in Old Jewry that a larger one had to be built for him. He then turned to literary work, and in 1778 began editing *Chambers Cyclopaedia* – writing about half the material himself. This work appeared in instalments over nine years, and Rees was elected a

Fellow of the Royal Society in recognition of his labours. In 1802 he started his own encyclopaedia, which was issued in half-yearly instalments and ran to 45 volumes. For this he was made a Doctor of Divinity by Edinburgh University.

The year 1773 saw the birth of another celebrated Welshman at Llanbrynmair, Samuel Roberts, the son of a local Nonconformist minister. Like Rees he also became a minister himself, and although he acted first as assistant to his father he eventually had nine chapels under his jurisdiction. He was a great reformist and attacked such evils as slavery and the Corn Laws. He also advocated a penny post before Sir Rowland Hill adopted the idea. Later in life he followed his brother to America, where things went badly for him, and then returned to Britain. He was welcomed home with a national testimonial and a gift of £1,245. Llanbrynmair provided more emigrants to America than any other place in Wales, and one party which set off in 1795 had such a series of misadventures before their ship actually sailed that it is a wonder they ever made the journey. Llanbrynmair's old church has a timber-framed belfry which dates from the 16thc.

LLANCARFAN, South Glamorgan
25 ST07
This largely unspoilt village lies some 4m SE of Cowbridge on the main Cardiff to Bridgend road. A Celtic monastery was founded here in the 6thc by St Cattwg. After the Norman invasion the monastery was given to the Benedictine order and became a parish church. No trace of the early church remains today, but the present 13th-c structure occupies the same site. It is a large building with an embattled tower, and features an interesting 16th-c window in the north wall of the chancel. Parts of the old rood screen can be seen, plus a 12th-c stoup and a hollowed-out oak chest. Iolo Morgannwg was born in the parish at Pennon, and was a self-educated stonemason turned poet, historian, and man of words. He died in 1826 and is buried in Flemingston churchyard. To the E of the village is a hillfort called Castle Ditches.

LLANDAFF, South Glamorgan   *26 ST17*
Although now officially part of Cardiff, Llandaff has managed to keep its identity as a separate community. It is one of the oldest and most long-suffering Christian settlements in Wales. Llandaff Cathedral has been sacked by pagans, burnt by Welshmen, wrecked by gales, threatened by indifference and neglect, and finally bombed. It lies about 2m from the centre of Cardiff on the bank of the River Taff, and is approached through pleasant fields and parks. The first church was founded by St Teilo in the 6thc, and was a small building measuring no more than 28ft long by 15ft wide. Teilo was the first bishop of the cathedral, and after him came 27 others before Urban the Norman became bishop. Urban held this post from 1107 to 1133, and was appointed to the position by the Normans. He was an ambitious man who, as well as building a new cathedral, was determined to extend the bounds of his bishopric. The bones of St Dyfrig were brought here from Bardsey Island and re-interred in the new building to enhance its reputation.

Construction work continued for many years and used nearly every style of medieval architecture. The Chapter House was built by Bishop Henry of Abergavenny in the early-English style, and the Lady Chapel was erected by Bishop William de Braose – who lies buried in it. Bishop William Marshall had much work done on the cathedral, and his tomb lies on the north side of the presbytery. The north-west tower was built by Jasper Tudor, uncle of Henry VII, in perpendicular style. For several centuries the cathedral was virtually neglected, no money was spent on its upkeep, and it was even suggested that the see be removed to Cardiff. Cromwellian soldiers turned part of it into a beer house and the chapter library books were burnt. In the opening decades of the 18thc great storms caused incredible havoc; the south-west tower blew down; parts of the north tower were shattered; the roof of the nave fell in; and the north aisle collapsed.

In 1734 it was decided to rebuild the cathedral, and the architect John Wood was called in. He decided to create a neo-classical temple actually within the walls of the broken church. Fortunately money ran out before Wood's temple completely swamped the old fabric – most people agreed that it was a singularly hideous construction. All that now remains of it are two mock-Grecian urns. The beginning of the 19thc saw an agreement to totally restore the old cathedral. Names especially connected with the faithful rebuilding are Dean Conybeare and Dean Williams, and the architect chosen to undertake the work was a local man named John Pritchard. His work includes the admirable south-east tower and French-style spire, the pepper pot of the 13th-c chapter house, and the carved heads of several British sovereigns on the south wall.

In 1941 a German landmine devastated the cathedral. Once again it was rebuilt, this time by architect Geoffrey Pace of York, and by 1964 the whole work was completed. Next to Coventry, Llandaff was the most war-damaged cathedral in Great Britain. The most impressive new feature is the concrete parabolic arch that separates the nave from the choir, supporting the organ case and Jacob Epstein's *Majestas* – an inspiring figure of Christ cast in aluminium. A chapel dedicated to the men of the Welch Regiment who lost their lives in the two great wars has been built into the north side of the cathedral. St Illtud's chapel features a triptych by the pre-Raphaelite painter Rossetti, and there is a window by John Piper. Fine Norman doorways remain in their original positions, and a 10th-c Celtic cross which was discovered in a well in 1870 stands in the south-west presbytery aisle. Ruins of a detached bell tower can be seen in the cathedral grounds, and at the south end of the building are the ruins of a 13th-c bishop's palace which was wrecked by Owain Glyndwr's forces in 1402. This forms the entrance gate to 18th-c Llandaff Court, now forming part of the cathedral school. The River Taff flows on the E side of the cathedral, and parklands and playing fields extend to the S. Llandaff is the home of the Theological College of St Michael's and all Angels, and the famous Howell's School for girls is also sited here. Just N of the cathedral are the modern headquarters of BBC Wales. See Cardiff town plan on page 169.

LLANDDANIEL FAB, Gwynedd
5 SH47
Bryn Celli Du, a celebrated tomb which is almost the only example of its type in England and Wales, lies 1m E of this Anglesey village. Plas Newydd, home of the Marquis of Anglesey, stands near by on an incomparable site overlooking the finely-wooded banks of the Menai Strait. The gothic harbour and boathouse are the work of James Wyatt and were occupied by HMS 'Conway', a cadet training school for the Merchant Navy. This was moved here from Merseyside during the 1939–45 war but was closed down in 1974, being too expensive to run.

LLANDDERFEL, Gwynedd   *10 SH93*
Sited E of Bala on an attractive route to Corwen, Llandderfel's several fine mansions include the notable Palé – built in 1870 for the railway magnate Henry Robertson, and visited by Queen Victoria. The 15th-c church has an ancient carved screen and rood loft, and there is 16th-c tracery in the east window. The porch contains a wooden statue of a horse (Ceffyl Derfel) which once carried an image of the 6th-c St Derfel. This saint was highly venerated in the Middle Ages, and people would make long journeys to worship the image. It was believed to have magic properties, and attached to it was the prophecy that it would one day catch a forest on fire. The prophecy, according to tradition, came true in a bizarre way. Upon Cromwell's orders the wooden image was taken from Llandderfel to Smithfield, where it was used as part of the pyre when Friar Forest was burnt to death.

LLANDDEUSANT, Gwynedd   *86 SH38*
Wales' best surviving example of a windmill is to be seen at Llynon, in Llanddeusant, in the NW area of Anglesey. Windmills were once a common feature of the Anglesey landscape. Llynon Mill was the last working mill, and the machinery is still intact within the three-storey building. A movable cap enabled the miller to trim the sails to take advantage of the prevailing wind. It was, surprisingly, automated and had three pairs of millstones for grinding, plus hoists for lifting and lowering the grain. A grant was made recently for the restoration of the mill.

LLANDDEW, Powys   *21 SO03*
This quiet place is situated a little way NE of Brecon, and has a cruciform 13th-c church – very unusual for old Breconshire. Its central tower was rebuilt in 1623. Near by are ruins of what was once a palace of the bishops of St David's and a residence of the 12th-c traveller Giraldus Cambrensis. These remains include parts of the wall and an arch.

LLANDDEWI, West Glamorgan   *24 SS48*
Llanddewi is a tiny village on the Gower Peninsula. The local 13th- to 14th-c church has a saddleback tower, and houses an ancient font. A little Norman window is also of interest. Remains of two castles exist here. Scurlage castle was built in the 13thc, and its ruins have been incorporated into farm buildings. Remains of the other castle are minimal, and it was built in the 14thc by Bishop Gower of St David's as a residence. It was demolished in the same century.

LLANDDEWI BREFI, Dyfed   *12 SS65*
St David came to this village, which is set amid beautiful countryside in the

Teifi Valley, in AD519 to refute the Heresy of Pelagius. None of the assembled bishops could make himself heard, but tradition has it that as St David began to speak the ground beneath him rose, forming the mound on which the 13th-c church now stands. This building was formerly larger, but the transepts have been removed. Restoration has not detracted from the pleasing interior, and the modern sculpture depicting St David was executed by Mancini. Other interesting features include five Celtic carved stone crosses, one of which is called St David's Staff. Part of a stone memorial to Idnert, a bishop of Llanbadarn Fawr who died AD720, is set into the outside wall of the church. Bishop Bec of St David's founded a college for a precentor and twelve prebendaries here in 1287.

The village itself is a pleasant huddle of colour-washed cottages and an attractive chapel, and the little stream called Brefi runs through it to join the Teifi. Just to the NE, on the other side of the Teifi, is the site of the Roman station of *Bremia*. A Roman road called Sarn Helen runs N and S from the fort. The road S passes through the village of Llanfair Clydogan, and then continues over the hills to Pumsaint and the ancient Dolaucothi gold mines.

LLANDDOGET, Gwynedd   6 SH86
Good views across the Conwy Valley are afforded from this little village, which lies just above Llanrwst. The pleasant church was rebuilt in 1838 and houses a two-decker pulpit. A sacred well called Ffynnon Ddoget can be seen here.

LLANDDOWROR, Dyfed   19 SN21
The small village of Llanddowror is situated on the main Carmarthen to Pembroke road and stands out in history as the centre of Nonconformist education in Wales. A cause begun in 1730 by the vicar of the parish church, the Rev Griffith Jones, brought about the complete Methodist revival which swept Wales in the 18thc. Although Nonconformity and the Welsh language were outlawed at the time, Griffith Jones and his patron Sir John Phillips of Picton Castle were so concerned at the illiteracy and ignorance of parishioners that they started travelling schools to teach the people how to read their Welsh Bibles. During his lifetime no less than 210 schools were started, and in 24 years 150,000 people are claimed to have been taught to read. The work continued until 1777, after which it began to decline through lack of funds. The parish church, although rebuilt, still retains its tall, battlemented tower and a 15th-c font.

LLANDDULAS, Clwyd   6 SH97
Sandwiched between Abergele and Colwyn Bay, Llanddulas is a popular holiday village with all the usual facilities. The 19th-c church of Llysfaen stands on the hillside above the village. Penmaenrhos, the headland between Llysfaen and Old Colwyn, is traditionally cited as the place where Richard II was captured for Henry Bolingbroke after he had been promised safe conduct from Conwy Castle. Penmaenrhos was a serious obstacle to travellers on the coast route. Pennant in 1773 described it as 'infinitely more terrible and dangerous' than Penmaenmawr, and Mr Windham – a later traveller – wrote 'the path is so narrow and unprotected that few people

dare trust themselves on horses on it'. The hill called Cefn yr Ogof affords good views and is riddled with caves. A little way S is the iron-age hillfort of Pen-y-Corddyn. Ships approach the coast here to load up with limestone from the nearby quarries.

LLANDDWYWE, Gwynedd   9 SH52
The church in this village is of perpendicular style and still contains its original east window and medieval roof timbers. A wooden screen which is dated 1620 and contains many unusual monuments separates an adjoining chapel, said to have been designed by Inigo Jones, from the main body of the church. The churchyard is circular in shape, and facing the church is the entrance to a long drive leading to Cors-y-Gedol Elizabethan mansion – a former home of the Vaughans. This fine old house is surrounded by trees and is also attributed to Inigo Jones. This seems unlikely, as he was only 20 at the time when it was built. Llanddwywe itself stands on the Harlech to Barmouth road.

LLANDEFAELOG-FACH, Powys   21 SO03
Although rebuilt, the church in this pretty little place preserves a Celtic carved stone cross incised with a figure.

LLANDEFALLE, Powys   22 SO13
Llandefalle is a little village situated W of Bronllys. In the S of the parish is a fine group of Tudor farm buildings which belonged with a house called Trebarried, once the property of the Vaughan family. The 15th-c church here is fairly large and has not been greatly restored. It displays a rood screen, waggon roofs, 17th-c communion rails, and very impressive stone monuments on the walls.

LLANDEGAI, Gwynedd   5 SH57
This model village was built by Lord Penrhyn and lies 1m E of Bangor. It makes a refreshing contrast to the staggering pretentiousness of Penrhyn Castle gates, and was founded in the late 1700's to house quarry workers and their families. The architecture is pleasantly varied. A restored church houses a kneeling effigy – complete with

battle helmet – of Archbishop John Williams. The church also has a memorial to the first Lord and Lady Penrhyn. A field near Penrhyn Castle has yielded a pair of henge-type monuments, the size and complexity of which make them comparable in importance with Stonehenge. Interpretation of the monument is difficult, as only the settings of the stones can be traced.

LLANDEGLA, Clwyd   7 SJ15
Situated between Wrexham and Ruthin, this moorland village was once an important point for cattle drovers who herded Welsh cattle along mountainous roads on their way to markets in the English cities. Llandegla was once the site of famous St Tecla's well, associated with an elaborate ritual for the cure of epilepsy. Grouse-shooting takes place on the moors.

LLANDEGLEY, Powys   14 SO16
The church at Llandegley is curiously dedicated to St Tecla, who was converted by St Paul and martyred in the Neronian persecutions. How she came to be associated with this village is not recorded, but the church inherited her reputation for relieving a type of epilepsy known as falling sickness. Sufferers from this malady used to come to this church centuries ago, making an offering of a cockerel from a man and a hen from a woman. The sufferer then spent a night under the altar with a Bible for a pillow, and in the morning left sixpence. A 15th-c screen supported a musician's gallery at one time, but although the screen remains the gallery has gone – presumably discarded when rebuilding was undertaken in 1874. The tower was blown down during a gale in 1947 and the foundation stone of a new one was laid on 28 November 1953 by Dorothy Heywood, who formerly lived at Llwynbarried. The most interesting memorial is to the Rev Benjamin Scott, vicar of Bidford and Priors Salford, who died at the inn here on his way to the coast. A spa is situated down a side road in a field beside the Mithil Brook, and is marked by a small wooden building now fenced with barbed wire.
cont overleaf

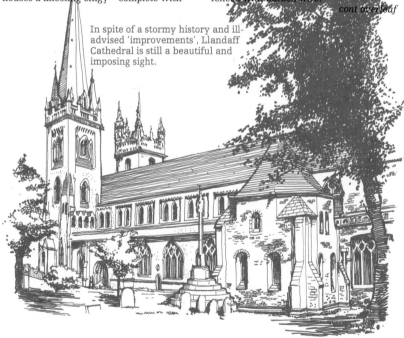
In spite of a stormy history and ill-advised 'improvements', Llandaff Cathedral is still a beautiful and imposing sight.

Farther along the same road under Coed Swydd is a famous Quaker meeting house called The Pales – a delightful little thatched stone building with a deeply-projecting gabled porch built in 1663. The Minister's and Elder's Gallery has a balustrade in front of it and is situated at one end on a raised platform, which is reached by steps at each side. It is simple and dignified. A little graveyard in which each grave is furnished with an identical headstone adjoins the meeting house. Deeds of this burial ground are dated 1673, yet people are still being buried in it. Services are no longer held regularly at The Pales, but an annual meeting is held in June and a harvest meeting in autumn. Llandegley Rocks, a sharp ridge on the moor S of the village, rise to 1,431ft.

*LLANDEILO, Dyfed 20 SN62

A Tywi-side market town standing in rich farming land, Llandeilo is a fine centre for fishing or touring the many castles in the area. The 19th-c stone bridge over the river measures 365ft in length and has a central span of 145ft. Originally of the 13thc, the church is dedicated to St Teilo and was virtually rebuilt in 1840. Inside are two Celtic cross heads dating from the 10th or 11thc. Ruins of Dynevor Castle lie 1m W and overlook the Tywi Valley. These ruins lie near a privately-owned castle which was built in 1856 on the site of a Tudor house. Golden Grove mansion lies SW and has been rebuilt. This was once a residence of the Vaughan family, whose members have played such an important part in Welsh history, and is now the home of the County Agricultural College. The royalist chaplain Jeremy Taylor spent ten years here composing *Holy Living and Holy Dying.*

LLANDINAM, Powys 13 SO08

Half way between Newtown and Llanidloes, the trim tidy village of Llandinam is noted as the home of Lord Davies and his generous, philanthropic family. The family's fortunes were founded by David Davies, the man whose statue stands at the end of the 19th-c iron bridge over the Severn. He was born to a small farmer and his wife in 1818, left school at eleven, and as the oldest of nine became the breadwinner at 20, when his father died. His commercial career began with his purchase of an oak tree for £5, which he sawed into planks and sold for £80. He went on to contract work connected with road and bridge building, and then turned to railways. He built the Newtown and Llanidloes Railway by himself and transported the rolling stock to it by road. From railways he moved on to coal mining, and finally to his greatest achievement – the construction of Barry Docks. When he died in 1890 some 2,000 people attended his funeral in Llandinam. The local church is built on the site of an old hillfort and contains a curious carving and a representation of Adam and Eve.

*LLANDOVERY, Dyfed 21 SN73

Llandovery is a very pleasant little market town with a name which means 'church amidst the water'. The significance of this is immediately apparent, because it is here that the rivers Bran and Gwydderig run into the Tywi. Since Roman times at least Llandovery has been recognized as a place of importance, and the church of Llanfair is built within the ramparts of a Roman fort. The fabric of the church walls includes some Roman tiles. The church itself, more properly called Llanfair-ar-y-Bryn (the Church of St Mary on the hill), is a place of great interest. It was restored in 1915 by W D Caroe – who seems to have been in sympathy with the feeling of antiquity that the church imparts – and he salvaged rather than rebuilt the structure. A fine medieval tie-beam roof covers the nave, and the chancel has a barrel roof. The walls of the building are extremely thick, and the windows appear to have been placed quite haphazardly. There is modern glass in the east window and in the south side of the chancel. Also of interest are hatchments to the Gwynne family, the last of whom died when the stagecoach in which he was riding was driven over a precipice on the Brecon road by a drunken driver. A monument marks the spot and serves as a reminder to 'keep from intoxication'.

A ghastly monument marking the grave of William Williams can be seen in the churchyard. Williams was a local man who lived at a farm called Pantycelyn, which lies about 5m from Llandovery. He is most remembered by Englishmen as being the composer of the hymn *Guide Me O Thou Great Jehovah.* The Williams' Memorial Methodist Chapel was built in 1886 and contains furniture given by Africans who were converted to Christianity partly by the power of Williams' words. In Llandovery there are three other Nonconformist churches of interest: Salem Welsh Methodist Chapel of 1836, Ebenezer Baptist Chapel of 1844, and Tabernacle Congregational Chapel of 1791. All are in Queen Street.

The parish Church of Llandigat dates mostly from the 14th and 15thc and was restored in 1906. It contains a huge and elaborate Victorian font which encases a complete medieval font, and somewhere in the churchyard is the grave of Rhys Pritchard, who wrote a collection of simple verses called *The Welshman's Candle.* This work became as popular in Wales as *Pilgrim's Progress* did in England. Sparse remains of a Norman castle here date mostly from the 13thc and stand on a mound by the river S of the town. Llandovery grew up around the castle and became an important centre for the assembly of cattle prior to their being driven to England. The importance of this trade only died with the coming of the railways.

A building in the main street which was much connected with the cattle drovers now serves as Lloyds Bank, but until 1909 it was the Black Ox Bank of 1799, founded by the drover David Jones. The main street has many attractive Georgian and Victorian houses. The Town Hall is a two-storey building with a tower and a weather vane, and next to it is the Market Hall – a low 19th-c building capped by an extraordinary pepper-pot turret. Llandovery College, a big rival of Christ Church in Brecon on the rugby field, is one of only two public schools in Wales. It is a building in the gothic style and was founded in 1848 by Thomas Philips, who wished the Welsh language to be the basis of the education. To the N of Llandovery a bridge called Dolauhirion spans the Tywi, and the Roman gold mines of Dolaucothi lie NW.

LLANDRILLO, Clwyd 10 SJ03

A small village in the Dee Valley, Llandrillo is situated on the Afon Ceidiog tributary which flows through narrow Cwm Pennant from the slopes of the Berwyn mountains in the S. It is a good starting point for footpaths which lead to the main summits of the range – 2,572ft Cadair Bronwen, 2,712ft Cadair Berwyn, and 2,713ft Moel Sych. Three prehistoric burial sites exist in the area around Llandrillo. At Branas Uchaf on the N side of the River Dee 1½m to the W are three uprights and part of the mound of a neolithic chamber. The same distance to the N, and on the same side of the river as Branas Uchaf, stand fourteen large boulders in a ring outside Tyfos farm. The third site is Rhyd-y-Glafais, on the N side of the B4401 Cynwyd road, 2m NE of Llandrillo.

LLANDRILLO-YN-RHOS, Clwyd 6 SH88

About 1m inland from Rhos-on-Sea is the 13th-c parish church – situated at Llandrillo-yn-Rhos. It is basically perpendicular in style but its northern part and massive tower are more characteristic of early-English and decorated work. The church has obviously served as a place of defence as well as one of worship. Behind the door are large sockets through which a heavy locking bar could be placed. Its battlemented tower also served as a beacon to warn the local people of the approach of enemies by sea. A register of ministers in the church dates back to 1230, and interesting features include a 13th-c font and lych gate dated 1677.

*LLANDRINDOD WELLS, Powys 13 SO06

After the ubiquitous grey stone and slate so characteristic of Welsh towns and villages, Llandrindod Wells comes as a cream and strawberry surprise. From whichever direction this fantastic town is entered, the visitor meets its full impact at first glance with complete amazement. Suddenly he is in the midst of towers, turrets, cupolas, balconies, oriels, colonnades, ornamental ironwork, loggias, balustrades – almost every architectural extravaganza imaginable. The effect is magnificent, and everywhere there are gardens, parks, green banks, and commons.

The town grew up around healing springs that rise here, but it took a long time to do so. The year 1670 is usually accepted as the start of Llandrindod's emergence as a spa, but it did not reach its heyday until the second half of the 19thc. A local resident called Mrs Jenkins rediscovered the saline spring and discovered the sulphur well in 1736. She had some success in curing sick people by administering the waters, then in 1744, after a slow influx of visitors from the beginning of the century, William Grosvenor of Shrewsbury came to test the waters for himself. He was impressed and decided that the spa had a future, in which case hotel accommodation would become a necessity. He took a lease on the farm beside the little church up on the hill and converted it into the Grand Hotel. This soon acquired a bad reputation as a place of gambling and wild parties, although Grosvenor's brother-in-law Ingall – who took over the management – was one of the church wardens. When the lease expired in 1787 the building was demolished.

After 1815 and the end of the Anglo-French wars people began to visit Llandrindod in greater numbers, mostly staying at the Pump Room. The coming of the railway in 1866 took Llandrindod into its golden years. With the passing of a local enclosure act, building land became available, and the streets that now form the town centre were constructed. In 1871 a new church was built and at first called Christ Church, but later renamed Holy Trinity to avoid confusion with the Congregational Christ Church which was an offshoot of Cae Bach Chapel. In 1895 the old church up on the hill was restored and re-opened, and when the Church in Wales became disestablished from the Church of England it was here that the first Archbishop of Wales was elected. Subsequent archbishops were also elected here until Dr Simon's election, when the venue was changed to the new church because the old one was really too cramped for the purpose.

Llandrindod Wells became the ecclesiastical capital of Wales, with the governing body holding its meetings here and other departments also finding the town a convenient half-way point between N and S for committee meetings. When Llandrindod Wells was at the height of its popularity as a spa 80,000 visitors would come to it in a season, with peers, judges, ambassadors, and other celebrities among them. Spa treatment went out of fashion however, and Llandrindod declined. In the 1960's the Pump Room closed and the medicinal centre became a National Health treatment clinic, but new drugs had

already put what was left of medicinal-water treatment in the background. This was by no means the end of Llandrindod, for in 1974 it took on a new lease of life as capital of the newly-formed county of Powys.

It had never really died, for it has enjoyed a vogue as a tourist centre, and the big hotels have continued to exist for holiday visitors instead of spa patients and their society friends. Now, with the establishment of county offices and their departments and a considerable influx of staff, the town has acquired an all-the-year-round activity and vitality. An interesting museum here preserves an ancient boat recovered from the Ithon near Castell Collen, plus a collection of dolls from all over the world donated by Mme Paterson, the French wife of a former Radnor County Surveyor. The Automobile Palace Veteran Cycle Collection displays cycles and tricycles dating from the mid 19thc. About 1m N of the town is Castell Collen, possibly the site of a Roman fort known as *Magos*. Visible remains of the fort are more extensive than is usual.

LLANDRINIO, Powys 11 SJ21

Strung out for almost a mile along one of the minor exit roads into England, Llandrinio's chief claim to distinction today is that it possesses one of only three sets of permanent traffic lights in mid Wales. Only a few yards W of the narrow 18th-c bridge is the church of St Trinio and Saints Peter and Paul. St Trinio was another of the 6th-c Celtic saints, and the church carried his dedication alone until Norman times, when the other saints were added. The carved pulpit and prayer desk were thank-offerings for the return of Parson Griffith to his incumbency at the Restoration, and his appointment as

Bishop of St Asaph. The bell is another Restoration memento, and is inscribed '1661 RE RG CNS God save the King'. Early in the 14thc Llandrinio was granted a charter allowing three fairs a year. Now the village is an agricultural centre.

*LLANDUDNO, Gwynedd 5 SH78
Plan overleaf

Few visitors would begrudge Llandudno its title of 'Queen of the Welsh Resorts', for there is undeniably something regal and gracious about the sweep of the bay enclosed by its headlands of Great Orme and Little Orme. The sea-front façade of hotels and guest-houses, neatly painted and well-kept, is a classic of its kind and surely worthy of preservation. Llandudno is not just a pretty face either. Its spacious boulevards and orderly layout distinguish the town as a notable exercise in Victorian planning. Llandudno was only a cluster of miner's and fishermen's cottages in 1849, when the Hon Edward Mostyn of Gloddaeth (later Lord Mostyn) and a Liverpool surveyor called Owen Williams conceived the idea of a new 'watering place'. As the town took shape people reproved Williams for wasting valuable land by making the promenade and main streets too wide. His retort was that in a hundred years time people would complain that they were too narrow!

Visitors to Llandudno have the choice of two beaches – the N shore, and the W shore, which is not so developed but has the sunnier aspect. A memorial stone on the W promenade features a white rabbit consulting his watch and recalls Llandudno's association with *Alice in Wonderland*. In 1862 Dean Liddell of Christ Church Oxford brought his family to stay at Pen Morfa, and invited a young don named Charles Lutwidge Dodgson to spend a holiday with them. Alice, one of the Liddell children, loved Dodgson's stories and after one outing he resolved to write (under the pen name of Lewis Carroll) the story which has since charmed generations of children. Llandudno's fine pier of 1876 makes a delightful evening walk, but for a spectacular panoramic drive visitors are urged to take the Marine Drive which skirts the noble headland of Great Orme. A short detour halfway around brings the visitor to St Tudno's Church, a small 7th-c building with sheep grazing in its churchyard. Open-air services are held here in summer.

Other ways of reaching the summit of Great Orme are by cable railway or cabin lift. Traces of very early occupation of the Great Orme came to light in the last century when copper miners opened up a large cavern. Evidence that the Romans had used the cave included wooden benches, tools, and remains of a meal left as though the workers had

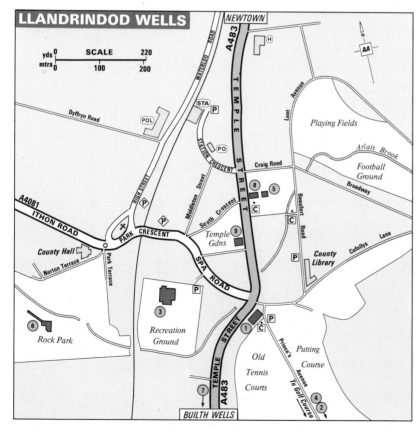

1 Automobile Palace Veteran Cycle
   Collection
2 Boating Lake
3 Grand Pavilion (entertainments)
4 Holy Trinity Old Church
5 Radnorshire County Museum
6 Rock Pump Room
7 Roman Camps
8 Town Hall and WTB Information
   Centre
9 Welsh Craft Centre

departed in a hurry. In 1879 remains of an even earlier occupation was stumbled upon, when a cave nearer the town was opened to reveal bones of the brown bear, boar, short-horned ox, and four human skeletons – possibly of the new stone age. The Rapallo House Museum in Fferm Bach Road has many interesting exhibits and stands near Haulfre gardens. Happy Valley offers outdoor entertainments.

LLANDYBIE, Dyfed 20 SN61
Llandybie is a small town situated on a tributary of the Loughor River to the N of the old Carmarthenshire coalfield at Ammanford. There is a fine waterfall at Glynhir, 1½m along the unclassified road which runs E from the S end of the town. This waterfall is in the grounds of Glynhir, a mansion once owned by the Du Boissons, a Huguenot family said to have been involved in the smuggling of arms to France during the French Revolution.

The church retains a battlemented tower, a medieval barrel-roof, and an unusual interior which gained a row of arches down the centre during enlargement in the 14thc. It also contains a good bust of Sir Henry Vaughan, a descendant of Henry VII's supporter Sir Rhys ap Thomas, who built the partly-Tudor Derwydd House. This stands 2m N of the town, about 1m W of the A483 Llandeilo road. Another house, called the Plas, dates from the 17thc but is now in ruins. It stands in the town off a lane near a bridge over the Marlais stream. Some 4m NE are the ruins of the impressive, 12th-c Carreg Cennen Castle (AM; see inset on page 174).

LLANDYSILIO, Powys 11 SJ21
A hamlet on the main A483 road between Oswestry and Welshpool, Llandysilio has the distinction of being situated right on the line of Offa's Dyke. The church dates from 1868 and carries a circular turret on the north-west corner. To the W runs the now disused Shropshire Union Canal, and 1m W on the B4393 is Pentreheylin Bridge, a pre-1773 structure which spans the Afon Vyrnwy. Alongside this is the canal aqueduct.

LLANDYSSUL, Dyfed 20 SN44
The small and quiet market town of Llandyssul is situated in the Teifi Valley in the remote hill-country of old Cardiganshire (now Dyfed), roughly halfway between Cardigan and Lampeter. Lying just upstream from a junction with a tributary called the Tyweli, it is a noted area for fishing. The Church of St Tyssel is Norman in origin and was restored in the 19thc. It carries a massive battlemented tower which tapers to the top, and an ancient inscribed stone in the churchyard may date from the 6thc. One of Wales' most famous Nonconformist preachers, Christmas Evans, was born in Llandyssul in 1766. Another local man to have reached fame is Caradog Evans, a novelist of contemporary Welsh life who wrote several books in the 1920's attacking the Welsh people for their reluctance to abandon old superstition and folk-lore.

To the E of Llandyssul is Capel Dewi, situated in the pleasant Clettwr Valley. The churchyard here affords views up the valley towards the mansion of

Alltyrodyn, and the church itself dates from 1886. Rock Mill, a woollen mill built in 1890 and still run as a family concern, is one of the last in the area still to use water power. Llandyssul was once an important centre for the whole of the area's woollen industry. Many fortified mounds exist around Llandyssul. Hillforts include Dinascerdin and Carn Wen on opposite sides of the Cerdin Valley 4m NW, Pencoed-y-foel 2m N; Craig Gwrtheyrn (Vortigern's Rock) near by. Castell Pistog is a castle mound 2m W, dating from about the 12thc. Other castle mounds can be seen NE near Rhydowen.

LLANEGRYN, Gwynedd 9 SH60
Well worth the detour off the Dolgellau to Aberdyfi coast road, Llanegryn is situated at the mouth of the Dysynni Valley. Broad and flat for much of its length and entirely unspoilt, this valley leads straight towards the main summits of the Cader Idris range. Some 3m from the village and clearly visible on the right is the famous Bird Rock (Craig-yr-Aderyn), which towers 760ft above the valley floor. About 2m farther on is the historic 13th-c Welsh castle of Castell-y-Bere.

The village of Llanegryn lies in a hollow, with the short main street crossing a narrow stream. Standing on the stream are two chapels linked by their vestries. One of these is Ebenezer Chapel, which contains a monument to Hugh Owen (1637–1699), one of the first Congregational ministers in N Wales. The parish Church of St Mary and St Egryn lies about ½m NW of the village. Although

1	Great Orme Cabin Lift	5	Lewis Carroll Memorial	9	St Tudno's Church
2	Great Orme Railway	6	Marine Drive (entrance to; one-way)	10	Town Hall and WTB Information
3	Happy Valley	7	Pier		Centre
4	Haulfre Gardens	8	Rapallo House Museum & Art Gallery	11	Winter Gardens

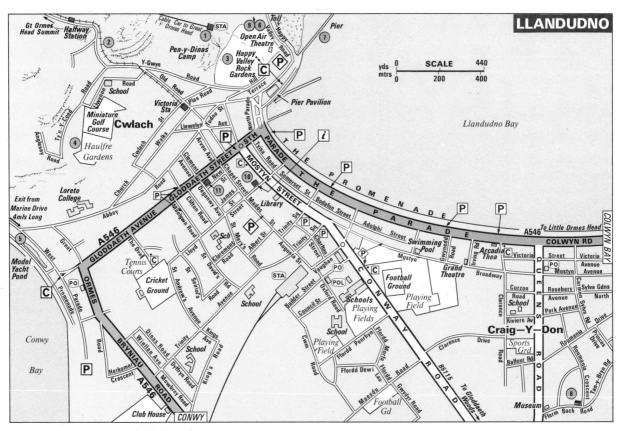

restored in the 19thc this retains its fine timbered cruck roof and contains two 13th-c windows, some good Victorian stained glass, and a medieval font. Its crowning glory is undoubtedly the 15th-c rood loft and screen, a remarkable piece of carving claimed to have come from Cymmer Abbey near Dolgellau. It is accepted as being one of the best carved screens in Wales. There are several monuments to the Owen and Wynne families of Peniarth.

Situated ½m E of Llanegryn and surrounded by trees, Peniarth is a fine mansion rebuilt in the early 18thc on the site of an earlier building. It is remarkable in being brick-faced, the only house of consequence in this part of Gwynedd to make extensive use of that material. Peniarth has been continuously occupied by the descendants of the original owner. The most well known of them was W W E Wynne (1801–1880), who supervised the careful restoration of several churches in the district – including Llanegryn – and owned an unrivalled collection of rare Welsh historical manuscripts which can now be seen in the National Library of Wales at Aberystwyth.

LLANEILIAN, Gwynedd 5 SH49
Llaneilian is a large coastal parish along a rocky coastline on the N coast of Anglesey. Its church is one of the most interesting in the island and stands on the site of the original church, believed to have been built c AD450. The church is embattled, and its tower is surmounted by a spire – an unusual feature in Anglesey churches. Equally unusual for the island is the 15th-c rood screen which stands over a massive screen of richly-carved oak. The church is connected by a passage to St Eilian's Chapel, which occupies the site of the saint's original cell. Inside is the panelled base of a shrine measuring 6ft long, 3ft wide, and 4ft high. Tradition was that if a person could squeeze into this box, turn around three times, and get out with ease, he or she would live the year out. St Eilian's well has a tradition of curative powers which attracted people from all over N Wales.

Antiquities in the church include a pair of dog tongs, complete with a telescopic arrangement and used for catching a noisy or quarrelsome dog during a service. A portrait on the west wall features St Eilian with five fingers – artist's error or an authentic deformity? On the rood screen is a painting with a stark warning, which translated from Welsh says 'Sin is the sting of death'.

LLANELIEU, Powys 22 SO13
High up on the lower slopes of the Black Mountains, 2m E of Talgarth, stands the hamlet of Llanelieu. The local church is dedicated to St Ellyw and stands in a large, almost empty graveyard 1,000ft above sea level, giving excellent views of the 2,200ft-high escarpment of the mountains. Restored in 1905, the building retains many of its oldest features, the best of which is a decorated medieval rood-loft with a tympanium extending up to the roof. Also of interest is the double rood screen. There are Norman clear-glass windows, a wine-glass font, a medieval roof, and several memorial floor stones and wall monuments. The wooden south door shows original ironwork, and there are two incised stones dating from the 7th and 9thc. Stocks, a cross shaft, and a

yew tree which was used as a whipping-post can be seen in the churchyard. The farmhouse below the church incorporates a medieval porch with a monastic pointed arch, which carries a Latin inscription meaning 'God gave us this space of peace' Llanelieu can be reached along a narrow unclassified road which runs past the Mid Wales Hospital.

LLANELLEN, Gwent 22 SO31
A small village on the River Usk, Llanellen is situated beneath the bare rounded mass of 1,833ft Blorenge, which forms the extreme E scarp of the S Wales coalfield. A fine bridge over the river was constructed in 1821 by the county engineer, John Upton of Gloucester. To the SW of Blorenge is the TV station and Foxhunter Memorial and viewpoint, 1,650ft above sea level.

*LLANELLI, Dyfed 20 SN50
Housing a population of about 28,000, Llanelli stands on the River Loughor estuary and became a market centre for the surrounding districts in the late 16thc. The town became industrialized during the early 19thc, when Alexander Raby moved into the district known as the Furnace and established the first ironworks. He was later responsible for building the first modern dock and the Dafen docks, which opened in 1847. The coal industry was also brought to Llanelli, but has since given way to steel. The once flourishing port, which was mainly concerned with the shipment of coal, is now virtually closed.

Trostre Works are the property of the British Steel Corporation and were opened in 1951. This complex covers 270 acres and forms the largest tinplate works in the country. A museum which occupies part of a guest house displays items connected with the early tinplate industry and Llanelli's involvement in it. Llanelli was created a borough in 1913, and much modernization has taken place to transform the original Victorian road structure into one suitable for today's volume of traffic – including the redevelopment of the town centre and the creation of pedestrian shopping

precincts. Parc Howard was presented to the town by Sir Stafford Howard, its first mayor. Within it stands Bryncaerau Castle, which is now a museum containing a collection of Llanelli pottery and a history of the tinplate industry. The castle also houses an art gallery specializing in the work of local painters, the best known being J D Innes, a friend of Augustus John.

The parish church has been rebuilt but the old tower still remains. Inside are some interesting mural monuments commemorating old Llanelli families. Among these are the Stepneys, who settled in the district in 1553, and their Georgian mansion still stands near the church. The neo-Jacobean Town Hall stands among colourful gardens. It is interesting to note that the song *Sospan Fach*, beloved by Welsh Rugby supporters, is particularly connected with the Llanelli club. It is an endearingly-silly little ditty about a saucepan which boils over, and the repercussions suffered by the unfortunate family. 'Good old *Sospan Fach*' was a newspaper headline after the Llanelli side beat the All Blacks in Stradey Park, W of the town centre.

LLANELLTYD, Gwynedd 9 SH71
A friendly little church amid a cluster of cottages bids visitors a welcome, but 'cannot promise thunderous sermons or boisterous singing'. The ancient church is enclosed by a circular churchyard and dedicated to Illtud – the most celebrated of the N Wales saints. An unusual item is a medieval stone with an inscription in Latin denoting that the footprint of Kenyric was imprinted on it before he set out for foreign parts. More contemporary is the picture and story of the silver-gilt chalice and paten found in 1896 by workmen prospecting for gold. These treasures had obviously been hidden at the time of the Dissolution of Cymmer Abbey in 1836. They are now displayed at the National Museum at Cardiff.

LLANENGAN, Gwynedd 8 SH22
Llanengan lies about 1m inland from the great sandy bay known as Porth Neigwl

Famous Bird Rock towers some 760ft above the valley floor about 3m from Llanegryn.

or Hell's Mouth, at the SW end of the Lleyn Peninsula. The church, which may be the oldest in Lleyn, dates from the 15thc and is built on the site of an earlier building constructed by Einion, king of Lleyn, in the 6thc. Einion is buried here, and his shrine and holy well have been the scene of many pilgrimages. The fine tower has a good peal of bells which are said to have come from the abbey on Bardsey Island. The interior has parallel naves and two richly-carved 16th-c rood screens – one with a loft above – which are considered to be amongst the finest in Wales. Other interesting details include a chest carved from solid oak and some of the holy vessels brought over from Bardsey.

Porth Neigwl (Nigel's Beach or landing-place) was so named after the landing there of Nigel de Lorraine, who had been given the towns of Nefyn and Pwllheli by the Black Prince. Set between the headlands of Cilan, it is overshadowed by the 1,000ft mass of Mynydd Rhiw, upon the slopes of which stands Plas-yn-Rhiw (NT). The beach is exposed to the SW winds and offers a spectacular surf, but is dangerous for swimmers. Many ships have been wrecked here, a fact which has probably brought about its other name – Hell's Mouth. Cilan Head is the farthest S point in the Lleyn Peninsula, and is level with Dyffryn Ardudwy between Harlech and Barmouth.

LLANERCHYMEDD, Gwynedd 4 SH48
Centrally located in the N part of Anglesey, Llanerchymedd was once the market town for this region. Apart from its cattle fair it had a flourishing boot- and clog-making industry which employed more than 250 people. Snuffmaking was also one of Llanerchymedd's specialities. The parish church was rebuilt, with the exception of the tower, in the 1850's. The 14th-c font still survives. The Welsh Presbyterian Church makes a good contrast. Some 2m NW is the Llyn Alaw Reservoir, more than 2½m long and ½m wide.

LLANERFYL, Powys 10 SJ00
The churchyard here is interesting for its old yews, one of which is so ancient that its branches are held together by iron bands and chains. A gravestone inscribed 'In Peace' is thought to be one of the earliest to use this phrase. The church has a 15th-c reredos and a reliquary of the same date. Two ancient British camps lie near the village, one on Moel Ddolwen and the other on Gardden. Both have entrances wide enough to admit the passage of chariots with scythes fitted to their wheels. A road only recently macadamized runs from here across the mountains to Talerddig, on the Newtown to Machynlleth road, and forms a spectacular drive.

LLANFACHRETH, Gwynedd 9 SH72
This remote little village lies 550ft above sea level in the hilly area N of Dolgellau. To the NW is Coed-y-Brenin Forest, and NE is 2,408ft Rhobell Fawr. To the SW the two hills Foel Cynwch and Foel Offrwm shelter the historic Welsh mansion of Nannau. At 700ft this is one of the highest-situated country houses in Britain. It was built in 1797 in Georgian style as the seat of the Vaughans, one of the most influential families of mid Wales, but the site has been used for a residence since about 1100. The village church of

St Machreth was rebuilt in 1874 and is approached by steep cobbled steps. Surprisingly it is dedicated to King George III. Many cottages and farmhouses in the area show the influence of the Vaughan Estate in their architecture, having tall ornate chimneys and slate-roofed verandahs.

LLANFAES, Gwynedd 5 SH67
Situated 1m N of Beaumaris, Llanfaes was once the home of a Franciscan friary. Llywelyn the Great granted the friars a site in 1237, but later in the century Edward I removed the people of Llanfaes to establish the new town of Newborough in the opposite corner of Anglesey. Llanfaes was the site of the grave of Llywelyn the Great's wife, Princess Siwan or Joan, daughter of King John. For 200 years her stone coffin was used as a horse trough, but it was recognized and retrieved by one of the Bulkeley family. In 1924 it was placed in Beaumaris Church.

LLANFAETHLU, Gwynedd 4 SH38
Llanfaethlu is a small village on the main road between Holyhead and Amlwch. The church of St Maethlu has been extensively restored and contains an octagonal font of 1640. To the NW of the village lies the attractive 17th- to 18th-c mansion of Carreglwyd (not open), sheltered by one of the very few clumps of trees in this rather windswept part of Anglesey. To the W, along the rocky unspoilt coast, are several attractive sandy coves – Church Bay, Porth Trwyn, and Porth Trefadog. The latter has an attractive farmhouse right on the shore, and a small promontory fort. Set on higher ground than its immediate district, Llanfaethlu affords distant views of Snowdonia, Holyhead Mountain, and the Skerries – a group of rocks off Carmel Head. To the N, overlooking the Head, is the viewpoint summit of 558ft Mynydd-y-Garn.

LLANFAIR CAEREINION, Powys 10 SJ10
This quiet little grey town is built on a hillside above a river which here has two names, Banwy and Einion. The prime attraction here is the narrow-gauge Llanfair and Welshpool Light Railway, which after closure by British Rail was taken over by a preservation society (see feature starting page 62). The church was rebuilt in 1868 and contains a stone figure of a knight in the sanctuary. This is pre-Reformation and possibly dates from the 14thc. The doorway is of 13th-c origin. Gibbet Hill, which rises 1½m outside the town on the Newtown road, is the site of a small Roman fort.

LLANFAIR DC, Clwyd 6 SJ15
Llanfair Dyffryn Clwyd lies 2m S of Ruthin at the S end of the Vale of Clwyd. To the E the summits of 1,531ft Moel Gyw, 1,466ft Moel Llanfair, and 1,400ft Moel-y-Plas rise from the lower end of the Clwydian range of hills. The Church of St Mary dates from the early 15thc and was restored in 1872. It has a plain square tower and retains several monuments and old glass dated 1500. A 17th-c font has been taken to the Jesus Chapel, which is situated on the main road 1m to the S and was built by Rice Williams in 1787. The chapel was rebuilt in 1787. Early 19th-c almshouses and a vestry house of 1831 can be seen in the village. To the SE of Llanfair the A525

Llangollen road climbs round the S end of the Clwyd Hills and through the attractive wooded Nant-y-Garth Pass. Some 3m SW on the Ruthin to Bala road are the beautiful grounds of Nant Clwyd House. This late 17th-c mansion stands beside the River Clwyd.

LLANFAIRFECHAN, Gwynedd 5 SH67
Little Afon Llanfairfechan, which rises on the slopes of 2,000ft-high hills above the coast, descends to the sea halfway between Penmaenmawr and Aber. The lower and flatter part of its valley contains the old town of Llanfairfechan. To the N and along the main road is a newer town with a modern promenade – from which superb views can be enjoyed – catering for holiday season tourists and visitors. The good local beach has extensive low-tide sand, but swimming is only safe inshore. To the W the vast triangular area of Lavan Sands lies at the mouth of the Menai Strait – dangerous because of deep channels and swift incoming tides. Another attraction on the front is the Embankment Walk, which follows the shore W for ½m. This is probably best followed in the evening, when spectacular sunsets can be seen over the water.

Two interesting churches in the town are St Mary's, which is set on a small knoll and has all its services in Welsh; and the English Christ Church. The latter has a prominent spire and is noted for its rood screen and organ, considered to be the best in Wales.

LLANFAIR-MATHAFARN-EITHAF, Gwynedd 5 SH58
It was to this parish with the long name that George Borrow, author of the ever-popular *Wild Wales,* made a special pilgrimage when he visited Anglesey. Llanfair ME was as important to him as Stratford-on-Avon is to students of Shakespeare, for it was the birthplace of Goronwy Owen, the great Welsh poet of the 18thc. Borrow, a garrulous but entertaining writer, was remarkable among English travellers in Wales in that he had learned the Welsh language and studied its culture before ever setting foot in the country. Thus he endeared himself to Welshmen and ensured a popular readership for his book right up until the present day. Borrow described how he visited this village, N of Red Wharf Bay, and how he was depressed by the rockiness and desolation of the region but found a generous welcome from the local people.

He recounts gleefully how he visited the poet's church and then his supposed birthplace, where he met a girl of eight who gave him her autograph which translated from Welsh read 'Ellen Jones, belonging from afar to Gronow Owen'. Other points of interest in this windswept parish include the Pant-y-Saer burial chamber, from which the remains of 36 adults and children were recovered.

LLANFAIR PG, Gwynedd 5 SH57
English visitors get lockjaw trying to pronounce the elongated version of Llanfairpwllgwyngyllgogerychwyrndrobwllllantysiliogogogoch. This is more of a joke than a fact, and it is thought to have been invented as a tourist gimmick by a local businessman anxious to keep the railway station open. The original name was Llanfairpwllgwyngyll – already long enough for most. The railway of that time

entered into the joke, and the station sign was almost as long as the platform. Unaccountably British Rail allowed the sign's removal to a railway museum at Penrhyn Castle a few years ago, but a new sign has now been put up and the station café does a brisk trade in picture postcards and souvenir tickets carrying the name. An obliging lady behind the counter will pronounce the name for the tongue-tied visitor. For easy reference the name is referred to as Llanfair PG. There is plenty to interest the visitor beyond the village's name. It is surprising, for instance, to discover that the most English-sounding of organizations – the Women's Institute – formed its first branch here in 1915, introduced from Canada by a member of an Anglesey family. Next door to the tin building where the WI had its birth is a tollhouse – one of several to be seen along the A5 to Holyhead, all easily identified by their octagonal shape and verandah. The Llanfair list of tolls is displayed and includes a warning that any cart with 'tires fastened with rails projecting and not countersunk' must pay double.

Anyone with a head for heights will be rewarded with fine views of the island by climbing the 116 spiral steps of the Marquis of Anglesey column. One of the most notable landmarks on the island, the column was erected in grateful recognition of the contribution by the gallant marquis (then Earl of Uxbridge) in the battle of Waterloo, where he was second in command to the Duke of Wellington. He lost his right leg, shattered by grape-shot, and his brief exchange with Wellington as he surveyed the dismembered limb is often quoted as an example of the professional soldier's detachment in battle. 'By God Sir' said the Marquis 'I've lost my leg', to which the duke replied 'By God Sir, so you have', and resumed his scrutiny of the retreating French. The Marquis was to earn the nickname of 'One-Leg' and became one of the first wearers of an articulated artificial limb. He continued an active and useful life, held government posts, fathered eighteen children by his two wives, and died at 86. The statue of him is twice life size and was executed by Matthew Noble. It was hoisted atop the column five years after his death. Another fine statue is that of Nelson, a useful landmark for sailors passing up the straits. It was sculpted in 1873 by Clarence Paget, a son of the Marquis of Anglesey. Access is through the churchyard of St Mary's, where there is a monument to the men who lost their lives constructing the Britannia railway bridge between 1846 and 1850. Eight died of injuries, and one from typhus fever.

LLANFAIR TALHAIARN, Clwyd   6 SH97
Situated in the deep valley of the Afon Elwy, this unspoilt village lies in hill-country roughly mid-way between the coast and the Denbighshire Moors. The fishing in the Elwy is very good, and permits are obtainable from the Black Lion Hotel. Llanfair Talhaiarn is well known to Welshmen as the birthplace of the poet and bard John Jones (1810–1869), who took the bardic name of Talhaiarn. He is buried in 15th-c St Mary's Church, which is set high above the level of possible floods. The church has an iron-studded 17th-c door, fine pewter vessels, and a place where baptism by complete immersion can be performed.

LLANFAIRYNGHORNWY, Gwynedd 4 SH39
An exposed, windswept village in the extreme NW corner of Anglesey, Llanfairynghornwy is set amid fine rocky scenery. St Mary's Church dates from the 12thc and stands on the site of early megaliths which are said to have been set up to observe the working of the sun and stars. The Skerries are a group of islands situated 2m out to sea. A lighthouse has been established here since 1717, and the sea around the islands is regarded as good fishing ground.

LLANFECHELL, Gwynedd   4 SH39
Thanks to William Bulkeley, that assiduous diarist of the 18thc, Llanfechell is one of the best-documented areas of Anglesey. The village lies 1m inland from Cemaes in the N corner of the island. Distant relative of the Beaumaris Bulkeley's, William kept a diary from 1734 until he died in 1760. It provides a unique record of a squire's life in the 18thc, and is preserved at the University College of North Wales in Bangor. Bulkeley, early widowed and with a young family to bring up, recorded the everyday happenings concerning the weather, crops, servants, tenants, rich and poor of the parish, and social events. Bulkeley's home Brynddu is near the medieval church, which is easily recognized by its pepperbox tower surmounted by apologetic spire. The latter is in fact a sound suppressor, put there at the insistence of a local squire who was convinced that the pealing bells were upsetting the fermentation of his beer.

LLANFERRES, Clwyd   7 SJ16
The picturesque Druid Inn and the parish church make congenial neighbours in this pleasant village between Ruthin and Mold. Dominating the village are the summits of 1,448ft Fron Hen, 1,676ft Foel Fenlli – which has the remains of an iron-age hillfort – and 1,820ft Moel Fammau, the highest point of the Clwydian range. From Tafarn Gelyn, 1m N of Llanferres, the old Clwydian coaching road offers an interesting diversion through the foothills of Moel Fammau before cresting the ridge and

Tollhouses on the A5 near Llanfair PG are easily identified by their octagonal shape.

descending into the lovely Vale of Clwyd. This ancient route was once the main road between Mold and Ruthin. It skirts the Clwyd Forest and brings the motorist within an easy walk of Moel Fammau, crowned by a Jubilee Tower. This prominent 150ft landmark was erected by public subscription to celebrate the jubilee of George III. In 1862 the column fell during a storm.

LLANFIGAN, Powys   21 SO02
The 13th-c church at Llanfigan stands entirely alone S of the hamlet of Pencelli in the Usk Valley. It is situated nearly 600ft up on the lower slopes of 1,842ft Bryn, a high spur off the main Brecon Beacons ridge, and its parish covers a large area of mountains and reservoirs. Dedicated to St Mengan, it is a large church with a north aisle and carries a medieval tower. There is also part of a screen; unfortunately the rest was removed in the 19thc.

LLANFIHANGEL HELYGEN, Powys 13 SO06
All that this hamlet on the road between Nantmel and Llanyre consists of is two or three cottages and a charming little church. The latter is a plain rectangular stone building with a very low white bellcote that crouches down on the roof just short of its western end. The east window is gothic, but all the rest are square and small paned. The top one on the north side still has old horn panes. Box pews in this church include the squire's, which is four-sided with all-round seating facing inwards. Also of interest are a double-decker pulpit and reading desk in the middle of the north wall, with the choir box below it and a candle beside it. The altar is small and plain, and the sanctuary divided off by a balustraded communion rail. The walls are bare and whitewashed. The vestry floor is perhaps the biggest surprise, being made of cobblestones. On the walls is a plaque inscribed 'To the glory of God. This church was restored with generous help from the Pilgrim Trust and the Welsh Church Fund of the Radnorshire County Council 1956'. There follow the names of three Davieses – the vicar and two wardens.

LLANFIHANGEL RHYDITHON, Powys
14 SO16
Standing on the N edge of Radnor Forest 3m from Penybont, Llanfihangel Rhydithon is little more than a hamlet. The name means the Church of St Michael by the ford over the Ithon, but the Ithon is 2½m away. The river here is the Merwys, which is a tributary of the Aran which does not meet the Ithon until near Penybont. The church stands up on a bank, and in the churchyard is the grave of three Chandler brothers, who all died while searching for sheep in deep snow in the forest during the 17thc. They were found huddled together in a snowdrift with their arms around each other. The original gravestone was replaced earlier this century.

LLANFIHANGEL-Y-PENNANT, Gwynedd
9 SH60
A remote village in beautiful countryside on the S side of Cader Idris, Llanfihangel owes its fame to the incredible journey made by a young girl of the village. Mary Jones was only sixteen when she walked alone to Bala and back to obtain a bible for which she had saved for several years. Mary, daughter of a poor weaver, had relied on visits to a farm 2m away for her knowledge of the bible, but in 1800 she resolved to own her own. She had been told that Thomas Charles, the great Welsh revivalist of Bala, could supply her with one. Clutching a bag containing her money she set out early in the morning on the 25m walk to Bala. Through remote countryside she walked, barefoot for most of the way to save her boots, and reached Bala by nightfall. She stayed overnight at the home of a preacher, who took her early next morning to the home of Thomas Charles. Her journey seemed to have been in vain when Thomas Charles told her that he had sold his stock of bibles, but he was so impressed by her long journey that he gave her one he had put aside for a friend. The bible was Mary Jones' constant companion until her death at the age of 88, and she is commemorated by a memorial in the ruins of her cottage near the bridge ½m beyond the church. Mary's epic walk inspired the formation of the British and Foreign Bible Society.

LLANFILLO, Powys *22 SO13*
Situated above the Afon Dulas 2m W of Talgarth, this tiny village includes an ancient church which has not suffered the mixed blessing of Victorian rebuilding. It contains a very fine and carefully restored 15th-c rood screen and loft, with the original plaster tympanum, box pews, a pre-Norman font, stone-mullioned windows, a pulpit dated 1680, and a barrel roof. The tower and spire are modern.

LLANFOIST, Gwent *22 SO21*
A pleasure-cruising centre situated at the foot of the 1,834ft high sandstone hill of Blorenge, Llanfoist is 1m S of Abergavenny and lies between the Monmouthshire and Brecon Canal and the River Usk. The eighteen-hole course of the Monmouthshire Golf Club is located beside the river on the Llanellen road. There are views of the Black Mountains to the N.

LLANFROTHEN, Gwynedd *9 SH64*
Llanfrothen lies 3m N of Penrhyndeudraeth and represents a significant milestone in the career of David Lloyd George, the small town solicitor who became British prime minister. One night in 1886 some men were discovered burying a child in the churchyard. They were Dissenters – a later description would be Nonconformists – and because Dissenters were not allowed burial in the churchyard a prosecution was pressed by the vicar. No one could be found to defend them until David Lloyd George, a solicitor of only two years experience, came forward. His brilliant and successful defence gained him public notice which helped towards his political career.

LLANFRYNACH, Powys *21 SO02*
This pleasant, compact little village is sited on the Nant Menascin, a tributary of the River Usk. The church is named after the 5th-c Irish missionary St Brynach, and was rebuilt in 1855. It still retains its medieval tower. Situated in a large churchyard and surrounded by many yew trees, it is the centre of attractive groups of cottages. Several interesting old houses exist in and around the village. Ty-Mawr, near the church, is a gothic-revival style house built prior to 1840; Maesderwen is a small Regency villa standing in its own park. Not far from the house is the site of a Roman bath house, and about 1m N of the village stands the interesting Abercynrig. Built in the Tudor period, but late 17th-c in appearance, this building has received a grant from the Historic Buildings Council for Wales.

To the N and E of Llanfrynach there are two interesting aqueducts. The first is adjacent to the four-arch Lock Bridge, which is believed to date from 1773, and carries the B4558 road from Brecon over the River Usk. It lies a little way downstream and takes the Monmouthshire and Brecon Canal over the river. The second is about ½m E on the B4558, and carries the canal over the Nant Menascin tributary.

*LLANFYLLIN, Powys *10 SJ11*
An atmosphere of quiet always seems to pervade this lonely little place on the River Cain, the farthest N of all the towns in the vast new county of Powys. It has an unusual church for a Welsh town, built of red brick in 18th-c Renaissance style to replace an earlier one which had fallen into decay, and contains a chained copy of *The Whole Duty of Man*. Perhaps the most fascinating feature in the town is a grave in the churchyard, just beyond the east end of the church and a little to the right, enclosed in an iron paling. This echoes a most remarkable love story. There are two inscriptions on the stone, one of which reads 'In loving memory of William Augeraud who died December 25th 1917 aged 50, great grandson of the above William Williams, Rector of Llanfyllin and grandson of Captain Augeraud, French Prisoner of War at Llanfyllin 1812'. Captain Augeraud was quartered in the town as a prisoner from the Napoleonic Wars, and while here he fell in love with the rector's daughter. After he was repatriated and given his discharge from the army he returned to Llanfyllin and married her. The William Augeraud in the grave is their grandson. This charming love story has a link with the chemist's shop nearly opposite the church, once called the Council House. A number of French prisoners of war were quartered here, and one room on the first floor has walls covered with frescoes painted by one of them. The colours are mostly grey blue and gold, and are still as fresh as when they were first applied. The Independent Chapel is a lovely example of early Nonconformist architecture before chapels became bare boxes. It was rebuilt in 1715 after an earlier chapel had been destroyed by Jacobites. The old Town Hall, with a market under it at street level, was taken down in 1960 and a new one in contemporary style built on the S edge of the town alongside the road to Welshpool and Oswestry. The site of the old hall is now a pleasant little square at the town centre.

LLANGADOG, Dyfed *20 SN72*
Some 5m SW of Llandovery, this village is situated in the wide Tywi Valley between two tributaries of the river. The church was rebuilt in 1889 but retains its interesting old tower. Once an important town, Llangadog had a native Welsh castle (Castell Meurig) which was probably built in the 12thc. The Normans took no interest in the place, and it was destroyed in 1209 during a local Welsh feud, then rebuilt and destroyed completely by Edward I in 1277. All that remain now are the motte and bailey, situated about ½m S of the village centre. About 3m SE lies the prehistoric camp of Carn Goch.

LLANGADWALADR, Gwynedd *4 SH36*
The Anglesey village of Llangadwaladr is situated S of Llyn Coron. The local church is of 13th- and 14th-c origin and includes a south chapel of 1661, plus some very old glass. It also has the 7th-c Romano-British gravestone of Catamanus, the 7th-c King Cadfan who was ruler of Gwynedd and grandfather of St Cadwaladr – himself a king. A translation of the Latin inscription means 'the wisest and most illustrious of kings'. About 1m S are the wooded grounds of Bodorgan House. This was built c1800 in a sheltered position close to the shore of the Cefni estuary, opposite Malltraeth Sands.

LLANGAMMARCH WELLS, Powys
21 SN94
Situated at the confluence of the Cammarch and Irfon rivers, Llangammarch Wells is the smallest of the central Wales spa towns – although there are smaller medicinal water sources in some of the villages. Its barium-chloride waters were once prescribed for certain heart conditions, and were considered to be of the highest quality in Britain. The Pump Room still exists in the grounds of the Lake Hotel, and the price per glass of the waters and other charges are still faintly visible on old notices in the decaying building. Some 2m SW of the town is the farmhouse Cefn Brith, which was the birthplace of John Henry, who was dubbed the 'Morning Star' of the Reformation in Wales. His protestant reforming zeal got him into trouble with both church and government, and he was arrested, tried, and executed in 1593 at the age of 34.

Scarcely a mile outside Llangammarch on the road to Garth is a short turning to the right, which leads across the railway via a level crossing to a white house with three graceful gables. This is Llwyn Einon, the home of Theophilus Evans (1693–1767), and his more famous

 Entries marked * are the starting point of drives included in the Day Drive section of the book (pages 95 to 144).

grandson Theophilus Jones, the historian of Breconshire. His famous history was brought out in parts. The first volume appeared in 1805 at £2 12s 6d a copy to subscribers only. It was another four years before the second volume was published, and this appeared in two parts, costing £4 to subscribers. Theophilus never gained rightful fame for this work in his lifetime. He died in 1812, and requested that he should be buried with his grandfather, and that the inscription on his gravestone should read 'Here lies Theophilus Jones the grandson of Theophilus Evans'. This stone, which had become dilapidated by the end of last century, was restored through the campaign of Gwenllian Morgan. Morgan wrote a biography to raise funds for this purpose. There is now also a memorial tablet on the south wall of Llangammarch church, which records that 'Here lie the remains of Theophilus Jones, Esq., Deputy Registrar of the Archdeaconry of Brecon and author of the *History of Brecknockshire*. He died January 15th AD 1812 aged 52 years'. The original history ended at 1800, but in 1909 a new and updated edition was brought out by Edwin Davies.

LLANGATHEN, Dyfed *20 SN52*
Llangathen lies 3m W of Llandeilo above the broad Tywi Valley. Its small 13th-c church carries a tall military-style tower and stands on a hillside overlooking the village. The building contains a 16th-c altar and Jacobean altar-rails. A very ornate 17th-c monument to Bishop Rudd of St David's can be seen in the south chapel. On the W side of the village lies the now ruinous Aberglasney House, a mainly-Georgian building incorporating part of a 16th-c bishop's palace which was once the home of Bishop Rudd. The Welsh poet and artist John Dyer (1699–1758) also lived here, and may even have been born in the house. He is well known for the poem *Grongar Hill*. This 410ft hill lies a short distance to the W and may originally have been called Grongaer Hill. It is crowned by a camp or fort believed to have been a Roman legionary marching camp. Near the village are ruins of a castle built by Lord Rhys, probably at the same time that he built Carreg Cennen.

LLANGATTOCK VIBON AVEL, Gwent *23 SO41*
This hamlet lies in hilly country 4m NW of Monmouth. The rebuilt church has a 15th-c tower, and a brass to the Hon Charles Rolls can be seen inside. Of Rolls Royce company fame, this pioneer motorist and airman was killed in a flying accident in 1910. He was born and lived at The Hendre, a gabled mansion in its own grounds situated 1m S.

LLANGEDWYN, Clwyd *11 SJ12*
The church in this small village, situated in the attractive Tanat valley 4m NE of Llanfyllin, was rebuilt in 1869 and contains a 14th-c recumbent effigy of a priest. A memorial in the churchyard records a man who died in 1734, aged 110. The bridge over the river dates from the early 19thc, and much-altered Llangedwyn Hall is of 16th-c origin. This was once the home of Sir Watkin Williams Wynne, friend and patron of the more famous Robert Southey. About 1m W on the summit of an 890ft hill is the ancient earthwork of Llwyn Bryndinas; 1½m NE of Llangedwyn in the valley of the Cynllaith stream is a

Llangeitho lies deep in the upper Aeron Valley and has twice won best-kept village awards.

grass-covered motte and bailey. The latter was the site of Sycharth, one of Owain Glyndwr's two favourite residences, vividly described by his poet Iolo Goch in the poem *Sycharth*. From the descriptions it was an impressive structure, but unfortunately was made of wood and burnt to the ground in 1403 by the English searching for Glyndwr. Led by Prince Henry – later Henry V – the English force went on to find and destroy his other house at Glyndyfrdwy near Corwen.

LLANGEFNI, Gwynedd *5 SH47*
Administrative capital and chief market town of Anglesey, Llangefni is mercifully by-passed by the busy A5. Nevertheless, all roads seem to lead to it – particularly on the market days of Wednesday and Thursday. Livestock from all over the island are brought to Llangefni for the Wednesday market, which at the beginning of the century took place on the High Street. The wide; sloping High Street terminates with a square in front of the solid looking Bull Hotel, and gives the town a central point which is not always evident in Anglesey communities.

The church does not occupy a place in this central scheme, and looks somewhat withdrawn on the edge of the town. It stands beside a pleasant woodland walk called The Dingle. Nonconformist churches are much more noticeable, and the grandest of these is Moriah Calvinistic Methodist – sited alongside the county offices. It commemorates John Elias, a celebrated figure of the Welsh Methodist Revival. Elias (1774–1841) was the greatest pulpit orator of his day, but did not always please his congregations. On one of his preaching tours he had to seek refuge in the Bull's Head from an angry mob in Beaumaris. He spent his last eleven years at Llangefni, and when he died some 10,000 followed him to his grave at Llanfaes. Llangefni's clock tower in the square commemorates a Boer war soldier, and is the most elaborate example of a vogue for clock towers which seems peculiar to Anglesey.

LLANGEITHO, Dyfed *12 SN65*
Deep in the upper valley of the Aeron 7m NE of Lampeter, Llangeitho has twice

won an award for the best-kept village in old Cardiganshire. Its whitewashed cottages are grouped round an ancient yew tree, it has a war memorial at its heart, and a church surrounded by trees in the background. This church is dedicated to St Ceitho and was rebuilt in 1900. Its windows contain early and mid 20th-c stained glass. The church had a remarkable curate – Daniel Rowlands – who lived from 1713 to 1790. He was ordained at 20 as a Church of England curate under his father, and quickly became noted for his powerful preaching. People came from as far as 100m away to hear him, and at times there were 3,000 communicants at his Sunday celebrations. He was eventually suspended and deprived of his office by the bishop in 1763 for preaching in unauthorized places and undertaking itinerant preaching, so he embraced Nonconformity and his followers became known as Rowlandists. A large meeting house was built for him, and his statue has been erected outside a later building. The Roman road Sarn Helen runs near by.

LLANGELYNIN, Gwynedd *9 SH50*
Hardly even a hamlet, Llangelynin is perched on a cliff-ledge SW of Llwyngwril at a point where the main coast road and railway are squeezed right against the shore by the foothills of the Cader Idris range. The medieval Church of St Celynin, almost completely disused but in reasonably good condition, lies below the main road. This barn-like structure has a fine 15th-c roof and a plain, rather primitive interior. The pews date from the early 19thc and retain the names of the original occupiers. Abram Wood, king of the Welsh gypsies – a family of itinerant musicians who were very much part of the rural scene in this area of Wales – is buried near the door. A stone slab is marked AW 1800. He had died at the roadside near the church. Also of interest are two bronze chandeliers of 1845, and an old horse bier with shafts at both ends. This was used for carrying bodies over difficult country.

About 1m S, where the main road turns sharply inland, is Owain Glyndwr's Cave. This overlooks a shingle beach and is said to be where Glyndwr hid while being pursued by the English in the early 15thc. From Rhoslefain, ¾m inland on the A493, an unclassified road leads SW to Tonfanau on the coast. Dry-stone walling is seen at its best in this area, which is the site of a large, disused Royal Artillery camp. A sandy beach can be reached via the level-crossing at the station. The beach may still have dangerous objects on it, and swimming is unsafe near the mouth of the Dysynni River.

LLANGELYNIN, Gwynedd   5 SH77
Llangelynin lies 3m from Conwy and consists of two churches which are widely separated in distance and altitude. The modern one lies in the Vale of Conwy on an unclassified road between the B5106 near Henryd and Roewen. The old church, which is the interesting one, is situated on the slopes of 2,001ft Tal-y-Fan at a height of nearly 950ft. It is one of the highest in Wales, and probably one of the most exposed. The approach from Conwy is via the Upper Gate and along an unclassified road through Hendre and Groesffordd, then up an incline and past a chapel on to the lower slopes of Tal-y-Fan. A track from here leads to Garnedd-wen Farm, opposite the church, from where the keys may be obtained.

The foundation of St Celynin's Church dates back to the 6thc, and the present building is dated c1350. It is typical of the old Welsh type of church, having rectangular-type windows and a very plain, almost primitive interior. The transept has an earth floor and the chancel carries a barrel roof. Part of a solid oak screen, once a feature in early Celtic churches but now very rare, also remains. Another interesting detail is an ancient and crudely-carved font. A corner of the churchyard contains St Celynin's healing well, where sick children were once brought to be cured. They were immersed in the well; if their clothes – once removed – floated on the surface they were said to be on the road to recovery.

LLANGENNITH, West Glamorgan 24 SS49
Llangennith (or in Welsh Llangynydd) owes its origin to St Cenydd, who founded a monastery here in the 6thc. The village lies in a valley between two hills on the landward side of a sandy headland. To the N is 609ft Llanmadog Hill, and to the S the back of 632ft Rhosili Down – the highest point in the Gower. To the SE of Llangennith is 500ft Hardings Down, which has iron-age banks and enclosures on its slopes. To the W beyond a small patch of drained marsh is the N end of Rhosili Bay – a 3m-long arc of golden sand mostly in the care of the NT. At the end of the beach is the small headland of Burry Holms. This grass-covered island is bisected by the remains of an iron-age fort and can be reached 2½ hours either side of low tide. St Cenydd lived on it for several years, and it later became a place of pilgrimage and acquired a medieval chapel. At low tide the remains of the 'City of Bristol', which ran aground off Burry Holms in 1840, can be seen. Behind the headland are the extensive dunes of Llangennith and Broughton Burrows, and the attractive Bluepool Corner.

The monastery founded by St Cenydd appears to have been taken over by monks from Evreux in Normandy and refounded during the reign of Henry I. The remains have been incorporated into the buildings of College Farm near the church. The presence of the monastery may have influenced the builders of Llangennith's 13th-c church. Although the building is relatively small, it is the largest in the Gower Peninsula and has a large, square, saddle-back roofed tower – the best example of its type in the peninsula. The interior contains medieval burial slabs of three priors from the monastery; a damaged effigy of a 14th-c knight holding a sword said to be a member of the De la Mere or Delamere family, who owned Oxwich Castle and the manor of West Town; the decorated base of a Celtic cross; and a square font with a carved base. Modern stained glass depicts St Cenydd, who is supposed to be buried in the church. In the churchyard is the grave of Phil Tanner, a well-known local folksinger who died in 1950.

LLANGERNYW, Clwyd   6 SH86
This small village is situated on the main road between Abergele and Llanrwst, at the junction of the Afon Gallen and Afon Cledwen which together form the Afon Banwy. The 16th-c church has been restored and contains an attractive stained glass window of 1830, some interesting old tombs and wall-tablets, and the original quatrefoiled font. In the churchyard are two pairs of ancient standing stones which must have been placed there many centuries before the church was constructed. A curious feature is that two brothers, Harry and Roger Lloyd, were buried between the stones in 1665. About ½m W on an unclassified road stands Hafodunos, a mansion built by Sir Gilbert Scott. One of his most important country house designs, it is reminiscent of his St Pancras Station style of the 1860's. It now serves as a girls' school and is approached by an avenue of *Araucaria imbricata* – monkey puzzle trees.

LLANGIAN, Gwynedd   8 SH22
A delectable Lleyn village of cosy cottages and flower-filled gardens, Llangian boasts a plaque which proudly tells visitors that it won the best-kept village award for Wales. In the churchyard N of the church is a granite tombstone with a Latin inscription 'Meli Medici fili Martini Iacit' – 'Melus the doctor son of Martin lies here'. The stone dates from the 5th or 6thc and is one of the earliest references to the profession of doctor.

LLANGIBBY, Gwent   26 ST39
Situated in the wide valley of the Usk on the old main road nearly halfway between Usk and Caerleon, this small village lies 1m SE of hilly ground which bears the extensive remains of an unfinished castle. Started in the late 13th or early 14thc, this structure occupied a large hilltop site and was protected by a dry moat on its W side. The site is privately owned. Below the ruins is the site of a motte-and-bailey castle which may have been dismantled so that its masonry could be used in the later structure. Also here was a house known as Llangibby Castle, which was built after the civil war. The church, named after the 6th-c St Cybi, contains memorials to members of the Williams family who owned the house. These

include one to the notorious civil war turncoat Sir Trevor Williams.

LLANGOED, Gwynedd   5 SH67
This village lies about 2m N of Beaumaris, and a similar distance inland from Penmon Priory and Black Point – the SE. headland of Anglesey. Several 19th-c cottages exist in the higher part of the village, and St Cawdraf's Church – severely restored – contains an eight-branch candelabra and a finely carved hexagonal pulpit of 1662. About ½m E on the edge of woodland is Castell Aberlleiniog. Dating from c1088, this was a steep motte constructed by the Earl of Chester. The original wooden castle was replaced by a simple, square masonry structure with a tower at each corner, which was captured and destroyed by the Welsh under Gruffydd ap Cynan in 1094. The ruins were garrisoned during the civil war, and are now privately owned.

*LLANGOLLEN, Clwyd   11 SJ24
This small town has a world-wide reputation, thanks to the International Eisteddfod. For one week in July this transforms the streets into a riot of colourful costumes and a babel of foreign tongues. It is a festival of song and dance which, since its inception in 1947, has drawn people from all over the world to compete in friendly fashion. The surrounding hillsides echo to the sound of great international choirs performing in the huge marquee which seats 10,000 people. Visitors marvel that such a small town can stage a festival of this dimension, but Llangollen's reputation for hospitality was established long before the International Eisteddfod was conceived. Hazlitt, Ruskin, and Browning were among the earlier travellers who sang its praises, and George Borrow made it a base for exploration of the Dee Valley. Llangollen bridge is of interest and the Horseshoe Falls wier feeds water into the Llangollen Canal. The parish church dates from the 12thc.

No-one has brought Llangollen more fame than the 'Ladies of Llangollen', two eccentric spinsters who escaped from the conventions of Irish society in 1779 and set themselves up at Plas Newydd, Llangollen, where they lived out the rest of their lives. Lady Eleanor Butler and Miss Sarah Ponsonby, both of aristocratic stock, attracted interest wherever they went by their eccentric manner of dress – starched neck cloths, powdered hair, masculine-looking coats and black beaver hats. Garrick the actor, peeping through the curtains before a performance at Wynnstay, mistook them for men; another person seeing them for the first time at an Oswestry theatre thought they looked like two respectable, superannuated old clergymen. Many distinguished visitors, including the Duke of Wellington and Sir Walter Scott, were their guests, but Wordsworth incurred their displeasure when writing a poem that was intended to be complimentary. He described Plas Newydd as 'a low-roofed cott'. Visitors who take the trouble to visit Plas Newydd will find it anything but a humble cottage. It is unusually ornamented with wood carvings, and has an overdone black-and-white façade. One section has been demolished, but a wealth of interest remains inside this romantic dwelling.

Another building with romantic associations is Castell Dinas Bran, a stiff climb from the N side of the town.

Sometimes given the English name of Crow Castle, its origins are shrouded in obscurity. Legend has it that it was the eyrie of Myfanwy Fychan, whose beauty inspired generations of Welsh poets. Valle Crucis Abbey, on the road to Ruthin, is an impressive ruin spoilt by the proximity of a caravan site. Cistercian monks established the abbey here in 1199, but their power over this region was destroyed by Henry VIII. Eliseg's Pillar, farther along the road, had stood for nearly 1,000 years before parliamentary soldiers threw it down as some kind of popish idolatry. The truncated monument was re-erected in 1779. The Horseshoe Pass, overcrowded at summer weekends but often impassable in winter, is an exhilarating drive through magnificent scenery. Another renowned beauty spot is World's End, near the Eglwyseg Rocks limestone escarpment. A Tudor manor house in this isolated spot replaces a hunting lodge which stood in the time of Henry I.

LLANGORSE LAKE, Powys   22 SO12

Llangorse Lake (Llyn Syfaddan in Welsh) lies 5m SE of Brecon and is the largest natural lake in S Wales – in fact it is the second largest in the whole country. Although this shallow lake with low, marshy, reeded banks is not visually spectacular, it lies in a very attractive setting with hills or mountains on three sides, and in turn enhances the views from each of them. About 2m long by ½m wide with a shoreline of nearly 4m, the lake is situated in a triangular bowl. On its E side the W flanks of the Black Mountains rise steeply, with the conical summit of 1,997ft Mynydd Troed and the flat-topped, 1,661ft Mynydd Llangorse. To the SE the slopes of Mynydd Llangorse drop down to the 650ft high pass at Bwlch, which leads to the Usk Valley. Buckland Hill rises to 1,038ft W of Bwlch, and is half hidden by 1,250ft Allt yr Esgair – the wooded hill S of the lake. To the W and NW the hills are lower, averaging only 750ft, but the scene to the

SW is dominated by the Brecon Beacons, with the high ridge from 2,504ft Craig Pwllfa leading W to 2,608ft Cribin and the main summits of 2,906ft Pen-y-fan and 2.863ft Corn-dû.

Of the settlements around the lake Llangorse is probably the largest. This pleasant village has a 14th-c church with a small tower. Although heavily restored in the last century, the building retains a good 15th-c wagon roof, a wide south aisle with an arcade of four bays, and an ancient inscribed stone. To the W an unclassified road leads to the shore. Farther W is Llanfihangel Tal-y-llyn. The small church here carries a medieval tower and was restored in 1870. Rev Hugh Bold was rector of the church for 61 years, including the period of restoration, and is buried under the east window. What may have been a Druid altar stone can be seen in the porch, and the good Norman font is of interest. On the S shore almost opposite Llangorse is the church and scattered hamlet of Llangasty Talyllyn. The church, situated right on the water's edge, was built in 1849 for a relative of Robert Raikes. It has many interesting modern interior details, and the tower is considered to be a good viewpoint. To the SW is Treberfedd, a mansion built in the fortified Tudor style for the Raikes family at the same time as the church. This family descended from Robert Raikes, the pioneer of Sunday schools in the late 18thc.

LLANGOWER, Gwynedd   10 SH93

A small hamlet situated on the S shore of Llyn Tegid, or Bala Lake, Llangower lies adjacent to Llangower Point, about 1m from the lake's W end. The Bala Lake Railway (see page 62), running on the trackbed of the former GWR line, has its terminus at Llangower. The local church is dedicated to St Cywair and dates from the 13thc. It is a simple, primitive building which was restored in 1871, and contains a rare horse-bier used where roads or tracks were too

steep or rocky for wheeled transport. Very old flat tombstones can be seen in the large churchyard, plus a yew tree which is said to be the oldest in this part of Gwynedd. Two streams, the Afon Glyn and the Nant Rhyd-wen, drain the high, partly-wooded slopes of the hills behind Llangower – 1,805ft Foel Figenau and 2.054ft Foel-y-Geifr.

LLANGRANOG, Dyfed   17 SN35

Llangranog is an attractive and popular little resort on Cardigan Bay, lying 6m SW of New Quay. The village is approached by the B4334 or B4321, from the main Cardigan to Aberystwyth road 2m away, and lies in a deep narrow valley which reaches the sea at a sheltered, sandy cove between towering cliffs. This, like several smaller coves reached by steep paths, is safe for swimming. Impressive coastal scenery, particularly to the N, comprises small coves, steep cliffs, and isolated rock stacks. About ½m N of the village is 541ft Pen-y-Badell, which affords magnificent views of the coastline in both directions. The summit (NT) is crowned by the prehistoric hillfort of Pendinaslochdyn. Near by is a missile-tracking station connected with the firing range at Aberporth. Below this is the long narrow peninsula of Ynys-Lochtyn (NT).

About 2½m NE of Llangranog is Penmoelciliau, which at 710ft is the highest cliff along the Cardiganshire (Dyfed) coast and provides wide views. Llangranog is also a holiday centre of the *Urdd Gobaith Cymru*, the Welsh League of Youth. Their camp headquarters is at Pigeonsford, a late 18th-c house at the entrance to the village.

LLANGUNNOR, Dyfed   20 SN41

Monuments to the writers Richard Steele and Lewis Morris can be seen in the village church here. The village itself lies near Carmarthen on the B4300 road to Llandeilo. Steele lived at a farmhouse called Ty-gwyn during the latter part of his life, and he died at Carmarthen in 1729. On the other side of the River Tywi is Abergwili, which is situated on the A40.

LLANGURIG, Powys   13 SN97

Small and interesting, Llangurig is beautifully set in the upper valley of the Wye amid high mountain ranges with thickly-wooded flanks.

The base of the historic church's tower is of 12th-c origin, but most of it was built three centuries later. In 1878 it was radically restored by J Y W Lloyd of Llandinam, who began his career as curate here. He left the Anglican church for the RC and served in the Pontifical Zouaves – becoming a Knight of St Gregory – then returned to Anglicanism. He commissioned Sir Gilbert Scott to undertake the restoration work, which cost £11,000. The church was re-roofed to the original design, a new rood screen

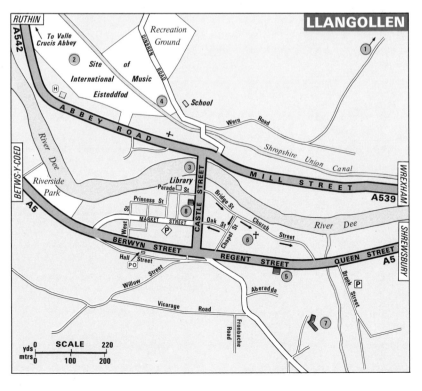

1   Castell Dinas Bran
2   International Eisteddfod Site
3   Llangollen Bridge
4   Llangollen (Shropshire Union) Canal
5   Llangollen Pottery
6   Parish Church of St Collen
7   Plas Newydd
8   Town Hall and WTB Information Centre

was made as a copy of the one destroyed in 1834, and all the stained glass was replaced. The replacement windows depict scenes from the life of St Curig, to whom the church is dedicated, plus incidents relating to the royal families of Wales, and the Lloyds. The tracery of the east and vestry windows is 15thc. Until a few years ago Llangurig was noted for its conjurers – not sleight-of-hand manipulators or magicians, but men with a gift of healing who were constantly in demand for ministering to sick animals and humans. They were famous throughout mid Wales.

LLANGWM, Gwent 22 SO40

Situated 4m E of Usk on the road to Chepstow, this small village has a parish church which lies in a hollow at Llangwm Isaf (Upper), about ¾m to the NE. It dates from the 11thc and is dedicated to St Jerome. The magnificent 15th-c rood-screen and loft form a feature rare to this part of Wales, and it has been suggested that there may be only one other church in Wales where the screenwork is more ornate. This is the one at Llananno in Powys. A connection with ancient pre-Christian religion exists in the carved corbels of the chancel arch. Here there are weird faces with oak leaves sprouting from their mouths – the oak is known to have been a druidical symbol. To the SE of Llangwm an unclassified road climbs up the side of a wooded cwm to reach the 20-acre hillfort of Caer Fawr. Extensive views NW towards the Blorenge above Abergavenny and the Black Mountains can be enjoyed from here.

LLANGYBI, Gwynedd 8 SH44

A hamlet situated in the Lleyn Peninsula 4m NE of Pwllheli, Llangybi lies below the isolated 750ft hill of Carn Pentyrch. The 6th-c Cornish St Cybi founded a church here, and near by is his holy well – Ffynnon Cybi (AM). This was known for centuries for the curing of lameness, rheumatism, warts, scurvy, and blindness. The well is a small roofless rectangular building with wall niches, beehive vaulting, and dry-stone walling found nowhere else in Wales. Close to the church is a group of almshouses dating from 1760.

LLANGYFELACH, West Glamorgan 24 SS69

This village lies on the N outskirts of Swansea and includes a church with a detached tower – the only one in the old county of Glamorgan. This tower belonged to an earlier building on the same site, and the church contains a 17th-c brass, plus memorials to the Dillwyn family – makers of the rare Swansea-ware pottery in the early 19thc. Also of interest are an ancient Celtic wheel-cross with the inscription *Crux Xri* (Cross of Christ), and a stained-glass memorial window by students of Swansea Arts College. A painting by the artist Evan Walters, who was born in Llangyfelach, can also be seen. An intriguing legend about the separated tower says that the devil became jealous of the church and carried the tower off, to drop it some distance away from the rest of the building.

About 1m NW of Llangyfelach is the Velindre tin-plate works of the British Steel Corporation. Like the similar modern works of Trostre (Llanelli) and Margam

(Port Talbot), it was designed to replace the smaller, out-dated units in the Swansea Valley, Neath, and Llanelli areas.

LLANGYNIDR, Powys 22 SO11

Halfway between Abergavenny and Brecon, this small village lies in one of the most attractive stretches of the Usk Valley. To the N of the river are 1,038ft Buckland Hill and the wooded 950ft Myarth, with the lower slopes of 1,661ft Mynydd Llangorse visible between them above the village of Bwlch. On the S side are Mynydd Llangynidr and Mynydd Llangattock, both over 1,700ft high, with the conical peak of 1,806ft Tor-y-Foel overlooking the Dyffryn Crawnan to the W. From Llangynidr the B4560 road to Beaufort makes a winding ascent over Mynydd Llangattock, reaching a summit viewpoint of 1,694ft. The panorama includes the Usk Valley and many of the summits of the Black Mountains. Prominent are 1,661ft Mynydd Llangorse, 2,360ft Pen Allt-mawr, 2,302ft Pen Cerrig-Calch, 1,805ft Crug Mawr, and the 1,955ft Sugar Loaf.

Llangynidr is well-known for its fine old bridge over the River Usk. Dating from c1600, this has six arches and massive cutwaters. Attractive walks along the river extend in both directions from the S side. Between the Usk and the main part of the village lies the Monmouthshire and Brecon Canal, now in use for pleasure craft. Nearly 1m E of the village, on the B4558 Crickhowell road and situated across the canal on an unclassified road, is Aberhoyw – an attractive farmhouse with a coat of arms dated 1726. Near by is the modern house of Worcester Lodge, situated in a fine position by the river almost opposite Gliffaes, an Italianate mansion with a beautiful garden containing rare shrubs and trees. Gliffaes now serves as a hotel.

LLANGYNOG, Powys 10 SJ02

With the high Berwyns towering above it, their sides grey with slate and scree, Llangynog is the last village in this corner of Powys – the final community on the long road that climbs on to the high moors before descending to Bala. Once a railway line served a tiny terminus by the bridge, and the relics of this are still recognizable for what they were, but it went the way of all these mid Wales branch lines. The village lived on its slate quarrying, and in the past the slate was loaded on to a sledge and shot down the steep mountain slopes, manned by a worker. Lead mines here were owned by the Earl of Powis, and at one time assayers were employed to extract silver from the lead ore. The local church is dedicated to St Cynog, from whom the village takes its name. He was the eldest son of Brychan, Prince of Brycheiniog.

LLANGYNWYD, Mid Glamorgan 25 SS88

Known locally as the Old Parish, this village stands 2m S of Maesteg on a ridge above the Llynfi Valley. The Maesteg Rugby Union club is also popularly known as the Old Parish. The village is romantically linked with Wil Hopkin, an 18th-c poet who is said to be buried in the churchyard. The church is dedicated to the 6th-c St Cynwyd, and the font dates from the 15thc. The village is 1m W of the Bridgend to Maesteg road.

LLANHARAN, Mid Glamorgan 25 ST08

A former colliery village on the N edge of the Vale of Glamorgan, Llanharan lies 2½m W of Llantrisant. The modern church contains registers dating back to 1615. To the NE is 880ft Mynydd Garthmaelwg, the slopes of which are covered by the extensive Llantrisant Forest. Llanharan House stands at the foot of the hill and dates from 1757. Its very attractive stable block is situated some distance from the main building.

*LLANIDLOES, Powys 13 SN98

There is no other town in Wales quite like 'Llani' as the locals call it, as it belongs neither to the N nor the S. It has an atmosphere all its own, generated by tree-lined streets; ornate and elaborately-fronted chapels; a half-timbered market house which is the only one of its kind left in Wales; shop fronts surviving from Edwardian and even Victorian days; arches and alleys; and modern buildings cleverly integrated with the old. The Market House is Llani's special treasure. Its arcaded ground floor is open to the streets and was used as a market, and the room above is now a museum. In the course of its history the old building has been used as court house, Quaker meeting house, Wesleyan and Baptist conventicle, public library, and working men's institute. At one corner under the stairs is the old town lock-up, and at the other end of the building is a stone from which John Wesley preached.

Another treasure is the parish church, which is of 13th-c origin with 16th-c additions from Abbey Cwm Hir. These 'extras' include the five-bay north arcade and a hammer-beam roof with carved angels at the ends of the beams – added when the roof was installed. The tower is 14thc and contains the mechanism of a turret clock which could strike the hours but was never given a face. A new RC church in Pen-y-Green road is built in the light pastel-shaded style of today and dedicated to Llanidloes' own martyr, St Richard Gwyn. Gwyn was born in the town and burnt at the stake in Wrexham in 1584 for refusing to recognize the Reformation and to acknowledge Queen Elizabeth I as head of the church. Next to the church is a Franciscan friary.

There are some interesting shop fronts in Llanidloes. Royal Arms are displayed on the fasçia of Hamer's butchers shop in Long Bridge Street. The firm held the royal warrant for three successive reigns, and served eight royal families. A really fierce looking and rather more than life-size red lion lives above the door of an inn of that name, and outside Higgs' shop in Great Oak Street hangs a golden lamb to indicate the sale of woollen goods. This is almost identical to the pendant of the Spanish Order of the Golden Fleece. The Town Hall in Great Oak Street was a gift from the Davies family of Llandinam in 1908, while the Trewythen Hotel opposite has associations with the Chartist riots. Rioters took three policemen prisoner and held them captive there despite the efforts of 50 other constables to rescue them. They also took a former mayor prisoner and sacked the hotel.

The town once had a castle, but only the site – where the Mount Inn now stands – remains. One thing the town is noted for today is its Amateur Operatic Society, which has a multitude of splendid voices – both male and female – and presents an annual opera or operetta of extremely high standard in the new Community Centre every year. The town's two bridges are known, for obvious reasons, as the Long Bridge and the Short Bridge. The Clywedog joins the Severn at the latter.

LLANILAR, Dyfed   *12 SN67*
Some 6m out of Aberystwyth on the road to Tregaron, Llanilar lies in the Ystwyth Valley and has an interesting church which was restored in 1874. Of particular note are its wagon roof, its seven-sided font, and a pre-Norman stone carved with Celtic knots. The church plate includes a silver chalice which was brought from Stockholm by a parishioner called John Parry, a King's Messenger to both George I and II. Two Victorian brass memorials commemorate members of the Williams family of Castle Hill, a three-storey house built in 1777 just S of the village. A motte-and-bailey structure on a nearby hill is known as Penycastell.

LLANLLYFNI, Gwynedd   *5 SH45*
Afon Llyfni flows N of this mid- to late-Victorian quarry village, which lies S of Penygroes on the Caernarfon to Porthmadog road. The river's source is at Llyn Nantlle Uchaf, among derelict slate quarries. In the village there are several old chapels, of which Ebenezer at the N end has an original 19th-c interior with box pews. To the SE of the village a line of mountains runs in a straight line in a NE direction. From the SW end they are 1,996ft Mynydd Craig-goch, 2,301ft Carneddgoch, 2,408ft Craig Cwm Silyn, 2,148ft Mynydd Tal-y-mignedd, 2,329ft Trum-y-Ddysgl and 2,080ft Y Garn.

LLANMADOG, West Glamorgan   *24 SS49*
Llanmadog is situated at the NW corner of the Gower Peninsula under the shadow of 609ft Llanmadog Hill – the second highest point on the peninsula and a fine viewpoint for the Loughor estuary. On the NE side, directly above the village, is the Bulwark. This iron-age fort displays ditches and banks which are still in a good state of preservation. To the N of the village the coastal sands extend out into the Loughor estuary and form a peninsula known as Whitford Burrows (NT). Part of this is leased to the Nature Conservancy as a national nature reserve. Whitford Point, the farthest N point on Gower, has an automatic lighthouse.

The early-English church was restored in 1865 but retains a small tower and saddleback roof with stepped gables. Outside the church is a Celtic cross on the south wall, and an ancient stone known as the Boundary Stone bears incised crosses. Inside are two ancient gravestones, and built into a window-sill is a Celtic, possibly 7th-c gravestone with a Latin inscription. Other features include a square Norman font, traces of early wall paintings, and a curious triangular doorway leading to the tower. The altar front was carved by John Davies, a former rector of nearby Cheriton church.

LLANMARTIN, Gwent   *26 ST38*
The church in this village, which is situated in the Vale of Gwent, 5m E of Newport within sight of the M4 motorway, has a 14th-c tower and contains a fine Morgan tomb of 1510. About 1m E is Pencoed Castle, which dates from obscure origins in the 13thc. One of the towers and part of a wall are incorporated in a ruined Tudor mansion.

LLANON, Dyfed   *20 SN50*
The village that the Aberystwyth to Cardigan coast road passes through, some 12m from the former town is the new Llanon. There is an older village down by the sea. Both have been favoured by Liverpool sea captains for retirement, and in consequence most of the houses are named after the ships they commanded. The church has an unusual dedication to St Non, who was the mother of St David. A dent in one of its walls was made by a shot fired from a parliamentary warship in the civil war. Remains of fish traps which are said to have been constructed by the monks of Strata Florida Abbey can be seen on the beach, and were used until fairly recent times.

LLANNOR, Gwynedd   *8 SH33*
Set inland from Pwllheli, Llannor is dominated by a parish church which was once the centre of religious controversy. In the 18thc William Roberts the bell-ringer inflamed local passions with a scathing interlude mocking the Methodists and championing the Anglican cause. The Rev John Owen, vicar of the parish and chancellor of Bangor Cathedral, was an equally zealous custodian of the establishment and persecutor of Non-conformists. Howell Harris, leader of the new movement, was a particular target for Owen's wrath and once had to flee to escape a physical attack from the enraged vicar. Harris was described by him as worse than the devil, because he was on earth in person!

Local adherents were publicly stripped at Owen's instigation, families were dispossessed, and young men were banished into the army. But the irate chancellor met his match in Dorothy Ellis, a spinster and church member who harried him to an early grave by interrupting his sermons, bursting in on him when he was entertaining visiting gentry, and accusing him of immorality. Ex-communication and being chained to

The half-timbered market house at Llanidloes is the only one of its type left in Wales.

the church railings did not stop 'Dorty Ddu', and she pursued him to the grave – tweaking his nose while his body awaited burial, and allegedly walking all the way to Llanidloes to stamp and spit on his last resting place.

LLANOVER, Gwent   *22 SO30*
This village is situated on the River Usk just below Abergavenny. The riverside church carries a battlemented tower and has a porch dating from 1750. The Usk flows gently through quiet pastoral countryside here, and distant views encompass the heights of Blorenge and the Sugar Loaf. Many of the little cottages in the village have Welsh names. Llanover House was the home of Lady Llanover, a remarkable woman who died in 1896 aged 94. Although English by birth she was a great champion of all things Welsh, and founded the Welsh Manuscript Society. It was she who was responsible for much of the 'Welshness' of Llanover – including the names of the cottages. Lady Llanover was a strict teetotaller and bought up several pubs in the area to convert into coffee houses. The good lady was married to Benjamin Hall, whose most conspicuous monument is Big Ben in London.

LLANPUMPSAINT, Dyfed   *20 SN42*
The name of this little place, which lies N of Carmarthen, means the church of five saints – Ceitho, Celynin, Gwyn, Gwyno, and Gwynoro. It is said that they are all sleeping under a hill waiting for a truly virtuous bishop, but how bishops explain why the saints never awaken during their incumbency is not related. Five pools in the river here are associated with the saints and were once places of pilgrimage and cure.

LLANRHAEADR YM MOCHNANT, Clwyd   *10 SJ12*
Few people after seeing Pystyll Rhaeadr will question the right of these falls to be included among the traditional seven wonders. They are the most spectacular in Wales and comprise a fall of 200ft, preceding a series of leaps for another 100ft. The waters flow under a natural archway of rock and are situated 3m from the market village of Llanrhaeadr

Ym Mochnant. A painting of the falls on public view in Chirk Castle surprisingly shows them with a small fleet of ships at their foot. The falls are 40m inland, but the presence of the ships is explained by a misunderstanding of pronunciation by the French artist. When a local man looking over his shoulder suggested some 'sheeps' the artist, only too anxious to please, added a small armada of ships! The village church has a special significance for Welsh people, for it was here that Dr William Morgan – later to become Bishop of St Asaph – made the first translation of the Bible into Welsh. In those religious days this did much to ensure that the language stayed alive. The book was printed in London during 1588.

LLANRHAEADR-YN-CINMERCH, Clwyd 6 SJ06

A pretty little place comprising a group of cottages, an inn, a blacksmith's shop and a church all hidden in trees, this village lies 2m S of Denbigh in the Vale of Clwyd. The church is of special interest and is a double-naved, 15th-c building which displays some superb woodwork. The porch is of 15th-c carved oak, as is the barrel roof over the chancel. A remarkable Jesse window made in 1533 is considered a very fine piece. The window was purchased with pilgrims' offerings to the holy well near the Church of Ffynnon St Dynog. This well was famous for the cure of skin diseases. During the civil war the parishioners of the village, fearing that the parliamentary forces would destroy the window, carefully dismantled it and placed it in an ancient wooden chest which was then buried. After the war the window was replaced and the chest installed below it, where it can still be seen.

A somewhat bizarre story is related about a Mrs Anne Parry, a devout Methodist who was buried in the churchyard. When, for some unexplained reason, her grave was opened 40 years after her burial, the body was found to be as fresh as the day it was buried. And the flowers that were buried with her were fragrant. It taxes the credulity, but the story relates that

The tiny, refreshingly simple church at Llanrhychwyn is typical of many places of worship in rural Wales.

four years later in 1841 the body was again disinterred, and the parish clerk called on the Mayor of Ruthin to vouch that the condition of the body was unchanged.

LLANRHIDIAN, West Glamorgan 24 SS49

Between this Gower Peninsula village and the estuary of the River Loughor are the extensive salt marshes called Llanrhidian Marsh (part NT). The parish church has been largely rebuilt but retains its strong-looking tower. Its porch contains a large limestone block inscribed with strange worn carvings. This peculiar object, the original function of which can only be guessed at, may date from the 9thc. Not far from the church are two stones, one of which looks as though it was probably the shaft of a Celtic cross. Llanrhidian has a mill which is no longer in use, but the pond remains. Another, much larger pond called Broad Pool is situated about 1m S at Cilibion, and is rich in aquatic flora and fauna.

A hill called Cil Ifor Top stands just E of Llanrhidian and bears the ramparts of a large iron-age fort which covers some 8 acres and is the largest in the peninsula. Remains of Weobley castle lie 1½m W. Farther W is Whitford Burrows national nature reserve, and almost directly S towards Reynoldston is a burial chamber called Arthur's Stone.

LLANRHOS, Gwynedd 5 SH78

This tiny place between Llandudno and Deganwy is noted for its ancient church, which has been very heavily restored. It is said that King Maelgwn Gwynedd died here in AD547. The church contains monuments to the Mostyn family. The Mostyn mansion was the Tudor house of Bodysgallen, which lies a little way SE of Llanrhos. Also in the church are some fragments of very old glass and an inscribed stone dating from 6thc.

LLANRHYCHWYN, Gwynedd 5 SH76

Distinctively simple in the Welsh style, the small local church is difficult to find but well worth the effort. Access is by a lane going W out of Trefriw, which lies

N of Llanrwst. The church stands alone in meadowlands and is surrounded by yew trees. It is of very ancient foundation and it is said that Prince Llywelyn worshipped here. Interesting features include a lych gate of 1762, a 17th-c pulpit and reading desk, and a font possibly of Norman origin.

LLANRHYDD, Clwyd 6 SJ15

Llanrhydd church stands on the site of a former place of worship which is thought to have been founded in the 7thc by St Meugan, a patron saint of travellers. The present building has a 15th-c oak screen and a 17th-c gallery. A sculpture of 1586 depicts John and Jane Thelwall kneeling in prayer, below which are their fourteen children – ten sons facing E and four daughters facing W. Six of them carry skulls in their hands, presumably to indicate that they predeceased their parents. Thelwall was a steward to Francis Bacon and a member of James I's household.

LLANRHYDDLAD, Gwynedd 4 SH38

Llyn Llygeirian and a large number of prehistoric sites are situated N of this NW Anglesey hamlet. The coast offers many popular bays, and Church Bay in particular has a beautiful beach and high cliffs. The church above the bay was rebuilt in 1858 and contains an ancient bronze handbell. Farther N are the remains of a signal station built in 1841 for the Holyhead to Liverpool telegraph. Carmel Head is a wild region of high cliffs and rocky coves made splendid with yellow gorse at the appropriate time of year.

LLANRHYSTYD, Dyfed 12 SN56

Sited just where the hills along the W side of the Aberystwyth to Cardigan road tail off and meadowland appears on the bay side, Llanrhystyd is a village of attractive 19th-c houses set beside the little River Wyre. Close to the village are the remains of Castell Mawr and Castell Bach – the great and the small castle – and Caer Penrhos. At least one of them was built by Cadwaladr, Prince of N Wales. There seems to have been a particularly turbulent period between 1135 and the end of the century, for one of these castles was destroyed in 1135, was rebuilt and changed hands in 1156, was fortified by Roger Earl of Clare in 1158, and was later taken by Maelgwyn ap Rhys. The two beaches at Llanrhystyd are both shingle, but some sand appears at low tide.

LLANRUG, Gwynedd 5 SH56

This quarryman's village lies halfway between Llanberis and Caernarfon. Its church has been restored but retains a 15th-c roof, and Bryn Bras Castle is a piece of pure romanticism which occupies a wooded hillside overlooking the village. Built during 1830 in the Romanesque style on an earlier 18th-c structure, it is very much a lived-in castle. Its numerous interesting internal features include a Louis XV suite. The park is as romantic as the castle itself, with peaceful lawns and tranquil woodland walks.

LLANRWST, Gwynedd 6 SH86

Perhaps the best-known feature of this pleasant market town is the graceful three-arched bridge which spans the River Conwy and was, until the building of the Conwy Suspension Bridge, the lowest crossing. The bridge is dated 1636 and it is attributed without any conclusive evidence to Inigo Jones

(1573–1652). The central arch rises to 60ft, and the whole structure is entirely out of character with other Welsh bridges that were being built at that time. An Italian influence which some people detect tenuously supports the Inigo Jones theory, since he had spent some time on the Continent. It is claimed that he enjoyed the patronage of the Wynne family of nearby Gwydir. The parish church of St Grwst replaces an earlier structure destroyed by fire. Its best feature is its elaborately-carved rood loft and screen of 15th-c origin, removed from Maenan Abbey at the Dissolution. The Wynnes of Gwydir were one of the leading Welsh families, and their local influence is very apparent in the church.

The Gwydir Chapel, built in 1633 for Sir Richard Wynne and also attributed to Inigo Jones, is a tasteful addition to the church, displaying an elaborately-carved wooden ceiling and some less attractive heads decorating the stalls. As the Wynne family mausoleum it houses some notable memorials. Also in the chapel is the large stone coffin of Llywelyn the Great, 12th-c ruler of Gwynedd. The coffin, minus lid, was originally at Aberconwy Abbey (which he founded) and was removed to Maenan Abbey when Edward I transplanted the Cistercian monastery from Conwy. At the Dissolution of Maenan the coffin found a new home in Llanrwst. There is also an effigy of Sir Hywel y Fywaill, who earned the name Sir Howard Poleaxe after capturing the French King at Poitiers by decapitating his horse.

Llanrwst has suffered considerable damage from despoilers over the years. In the early 1400's it suffered so much desecration from Owain Glyndwr's forces that it was said that afterwards grass grew in the deserted streets and deer grazed in the churchyard. In 1648 it was again ransacked. Among the interesting buildings in Llanrwst is Ty Hwnt i'r Bont (NT), on the Caernarfon side of the bridge. It once functioned as a courthouse, but now serves as a café and gift shop. The Jesus Hospital Almshouses at the approach to the church were founded by Sir John Wynne (1553–1627), an oppressive acquisitive landlord but a respected antiquarian and patron of charitable works. Gwydir Castle, former seat of the Wynne family, is across the river and has been painstakingly restored after fire by the present owners. It is open daily. On the opposite side of the road is Gwydir Uchaf (AM), built by Sir John Wynne as an annexe to entertain visitors. It is now used as an exhibition centre by the Forestry Commission. The chapel is noted for its painted ceiling.

LLANSANNAN, Clwyd   6 SH96
This village is situated in the beautiful and unspoilt valley of the Aled. Its double-naved church was rebuilt in 1869 and houses a 17th-c pulpit which came from Liverpool.

LLANSANTFFRAED-JUXTA-USK, Powys   22 SO12
Usually called simply Llansantffraed, this place includes the Church of St Brides and stands on the River Usk and the Monmouthshire and Brecon Canal. Much of the surrounding countryside is part of the Brecon Beacons national park. In the churchyard the grave of Henry Vaughan, 'The Swan of Usk', is marked by a simple stone upon which

the following words are carved: 'Henry Vaughan, Silurist, Doctor of Medicine. He died April 23 in the year of our salvation 1695. What he wished on his tomb. An unprofitable servant, Greatest of Sinners lies here. Glory. Have mercy' The words, which Vaughan himself is said to have composed, do not mention that he was a poet of considerable talent. He was born at the house called Newton in 1622, and educated at Jesus College Oxford, where he studied law and medicine. He was an ardent royalist, a tendency for which he was imprisoned for a number of years. Vaughan loved his native Wales and is called 'The Silurist' after the Welsh tribe which inhabited the area of the country where he was born – the one-time county of Breconshire. He was a Christian man who spent many of his days in contemplation by the banks of his beloved River Usk –

'They are all gone into the world of light
And I alone sit lingring here;
Their very memory is fair and bright,
And my sad thoughts doth clear.'

Upstream are the two houses Newton and Scethrog, once homes of the Vaughan family. Also upstream is the church of Llanhamlech, which contains an odd and very early carved stone. There are several standing stones in the parish, and the Roman road which runs from the nearby fort of Pen-y-Gaer can be traced through the area.

LLANSANTFFRAID YM MECHAIN, Powys   11 SJ22
A long thin village which extends for $\frac{1}{2}$m along the A495 road to Meifod, Llansantffraid is an important centre of agricultural trade. The vast factory-like building beside the former railway line is the headquarters of the Wynnstay and Montgomeryshire Farmers' Association, a big farmers' co-operative. The village has a link with William Morris Hughes, who was prime minister of Australia in 1915 and remained in office until 1923. He was born in Llansantffraid, and there is a memorial window in the chancel to his mother 'Uxoris Carissime Grace', the wife of the Rev R H M Hughes who was vicar in 1847. An elaborate gravestone surmounted by an angel in the churchyard marks the grave of a gypsy queen.

LLANSILIN, Clwyd   11 SJ22
Despite being so near to the English border, Llansilin has historic associations with two notable Welshmen – warrior-hero Owain Glyndwr, and Huw Morus, the Welsh poet. Owain Glyndwr's home Sycarth was sited on a mound S of the village. Nothing remains of Sycarth today, but Welsh bard Iolo Goch described it as a great wooden hall with good chimneys, a tiled roof, and a rarity in those days – windows of glass. According to Iolo Goch 'rarely at that house was there bolt or lock to bar your way'. On New Years Day 1403, at the height of the uprising, Sycarth was attacked and burnt to the ground by English troops. Llansilin churchyard is the burial place of Huw Morus (1622–1709), who was born and spent most of his life not far away in the Ceiriog Valley.

LLANSPYDDYD, Powys   21 SO02
Brychan Brycheiniog, who gave his name to the county of Breconshire, is associated with this tiny village 2m W of Brecon. A ring-cross gravestone in the churchyard is thought to be his. The

14th-c church was restored in 1880, and the north porch includes an unusual barge board. Near here the River Usk flows through a beautiful gorge.

LLANSTEPHAN, Dyfed   19 SN31
This very attractive village is situated on a peninsula formed by the estuaries of the Tywi and the Taf. The village is approached on the B4312 from Carmarthen, which passes the overgrown remains of Green Castle at a sharp bend. Nothing much is known about this structure save that it was built by an English family called Rede. Llanstephan village has many pleasant houses, some of which are Georgian. The church is basically of 13th-c origin and has a good strong tower. Several fine monuments can be seen, and the Norman font is of interest. Tombs of the Lloyd family dating from the 17th and 18thc are housed in the Laques Chapel, and the Meares family of the Plas have hatchment memorials.

The waterfront is called The Green and is a pleasant spot where grass and rushes lead down to the beach. At low tide there is a large expanse of excellent sand. The village is overlooked by a castle perched high on a wooded hill above the estuaries. This can be approached only by foot up a steep footpath past the fine 18th-c house called Plas. Built within the ramparts of an iron-age fort, the castle (see special inset overleaf) has had a long and complex history of intrigue and varied ownership. The first reference to a castle here was in the 12thc. In 1959 the Ministry of Works took over the site and restoration was begun. To the W of the castle is St Anthony's Well, where offerings of pins are still made by those in love. Wharley Point rises to 358ft and offers good views of the Taf, Tywi, Gwendraeth, and surrounding countryside. Farther N are two ruined churches, one at Llanybri and one at Landeilo Abercywyn. This little peninsula has many delightful woody lanes, all of which are worth exploring – not for anything spectacular, but simply for quiet, well-tended farmland.

LLANSTEPHAN, Powys   22 SO14
There is really only one item of interest in this tiny hamlet on the banks of the Wye, and that is the delightful little suspension bridge linking the one-time Radnorshire side of the river with old Breconshire. This single-width bridge has a wood-section floor and is a proper suspension bridge – with uprights of lattice ironwork decorated with finials to match, and latticework sides. It is a little gem of a bridge and it is to be hoped that it will be allowed to remain. It was one of a pair, but the identical twin bridge at Erwood, 2m up river, was recently demolished and replaced by a wide pier bridge. Although a fine structure, this new edifice has none of the historic charm of its predecessor. Llanstephan bridge is now unique. The local church has a 12th-c nave and an early-English doorway. The interior is dark with pitch pine, and the sombre churchyard contains many old yews. Access to the churchyard is via a lych gate which is combined with a stable.

LLANTARNAM, Gwent   26 ST39
Expansion from Newport threatens the S outskirts of this village, which is situated on the edge of Cwmbran. A breath of the old world still remains in the village church and Llantarnam Abbey. Basically

of 15th-c origin, the church houses interesting 18th-c monuments and stands next to Greenhouse Inn. A carved wooden pub sign of 1719 is inscribed in Welsh and translated reads 'The Green House, 1719. Good ale and cider for you. Come in; you shall taste it.' The abbey was founded in the 12thc and bought in 1553 by William Morgan. The present building is a mixture of Norman, Tudor, and Victorian. Although greatly diminished, the abbey grounds are still quite large. A castle mound rises to the E, and the Monmouthshire and Brecon Canal runs SW of the village.

LLANTHONY PRIORY, Gwent   22 SO22

Here the river Honddu runs through the Vale of Ewyas, with the Black Mountains rising directly to the W. To the SE 1,748ft Hatteral Hill rises from the border country, with England just 1m to the E. The national boundary marks the edge of Brecon Beacons national park

BATTLEMENTS ON THE SKYLINE

The site of Llanstephan Castle at the mouth of the Tywi, like that of Kidwelly near the Gwendraeth Fach estuary, proved that the Norman invaders had learned the importance of sea links in defending their newly-acquired domains. Although the view today of Llanstephan from Ferryside, on the other bank of the Tywi, is impressive because of the picturesque quality of the fortification, its strategic importance in times of hostility is obvious because of its high and commanding seaward position. This elevated situation is striking as the visitor drives from Carmarthen to Llanstephan, when an unexpected glimpse of battlements on the skyline suggests a stronghold as impregnable as it is romantic.

Yet its earlier history was one of constant struggle for possession between Normans and Welsh, the first evidence of which appears in 1146 when the castle was taken by Cadell, Maredudd, and Rhys – three brothers of the royal house of South Wales. Rhys, who was only thirteen at the time, was already showing the prowess and stamina which he was

and the route of Offa's Dyke Path. This remote and beautiful valley was where Hugh de Lacy, Marcher lord of Hereford, founded the priory in 1108. The site he chose had been occupied by a chapel dedicated to St David. Hugh de Lacy's decision to quit the world seems to have been quite sudden, and he brought with him Ernisius, chaplain to Henry I, who became the first prior. A community of 40 cannons was created, and Walter de Gloucester, Constable of England, later joined the settlement. Robert de Bethune succeeded Ernisius as prior, and it was he who controlled the building of the structure that stands today.

But even this place, as near to God as anywhere could be, became corrupt. Geraldus Cambrensis visited the priory in 1188 and commented on the beauty of the scenery, but he also noted that material wellbeing was turning the monks from their contemplative life. At the Dissolution only a prior and four

to display as 'Lord Rhys', the tenacious and influential ruler of *Deheubarth*. But the brother who showed most initiative during that episode was Maredudd, who is recorded to have hurled the scaling-ladders of the enemy into the ditch. Lost to the English in 1158, Llanstephan was again successfully attacked by 'Lord Rhys' in 1189 but remained in Welsh hands for only three years.

Again like Kidwelly, the foundations of the early 12th-c castle gave way gradually to masonry defences. The first alterations – reinforcing the upper bailey were made under the supervision of the family of Devon de Camville after they regained possession in 1192. This part of the castle was further fortified by the building of a square inner gatehouse when the family was once again reinstalled after having been ousted by Llywelyn 'the Great', prince of N Wales, Llanstephan had been only one prize during an enormously successful onslaught on *Deheubarth*.

Most of the remaining stages of the transformation were the result of yet another seizure by the Welsh in 1257,

canons remained, the rest having chosen an easier life at Gloucester. The abbey was bought by Walter Savage Landor, a friend of Browning and Swinburne, in 1811. The ruins (AM) are not extensive but have a feeling of strength and an atmosphere of romantic beauty. An inn has been created out of what was the prior's house. The little restored church is contemporary with the priory and displays some Norman features. Llanthony Abbey lies 4m up the valley at Capel-y-ffin, and dates from c1870.

LLANTILIO CROSENNY, Gwent
22 SO31

Set in green fields with a stream bubbling by, this lovely little village includes an early-English and perpendicular church which was founded in the 6thc. No trace of the earliest structure remains, but there is old timbering beneath the tower and the Cil-Llwch Chapel is of note. Three 17th-c stone memorials are of

when an English army mainly comprising garrisons from local castles was completely defeated near the town of Llandeilo. Llanstephan was left defenceless and yielded with little effort. The most remarkable feature of this building phase is the Great Gatehouse, influenced by Gilbert de Clare's impressive Eastern Gateway at Caerphilly. Although another entrance was designed in the more settled 15thc, the Gatehouse remains the culminating defensive unit of a castle which had a fate as chequered as its structural development.

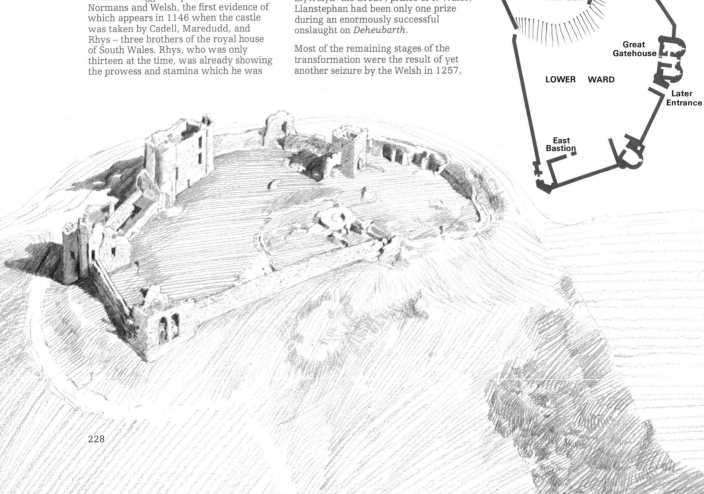

UPPER WARD

Inner Gate

Great Gatehouse

LOWER WARD

Later Entrance

East Bastion

interest, and the entire church is built within the ramparts of an ancient earthwork. Near by are the remains of a moated medieval house called Hen Gwrt.

LLANTILIO PERTHOLEY, Gwent
22 SO31
Just outside Abergavenny, Llantilio Pertholey has a church which displays many different periods. It is distinguished by its beautifully-carved woodwork and includes several small chapels. Two of the latter are separated from the body of the church by carved wooden arches.

LLANTRISANT, Mid Glamorgan
25 ST08
Llantrisant is a splendidly-sited little town overlooking the valley of the river Ely and the Vale of Glamorgan. It is built on a ridge between two hills, and many of the steep streets are graced by attractive houses. The area has appealed to men from very earliest times, and a hill to the E carries well-preserved earthen ramparts of the iron-age hillfort called Caerau. A Norman named Richard de Clare built a castle here *c*1245 after having ousted the native Welsh ruler, but virtually all that remains of this are the ruins of a round keep. Edward II and his friend Despenser were caught here after having left Chepstow in an attempt to escape from Queen Isabella. The king was held in the castle for a while.

Features of the local church, an extensively rebuilt Norman structure which suffered 19th-c restoration, include a very large 13th-c font. An ancient slab inscribed with three crosses survives on the outside of the north wall. One of Wales' most famous eccentrics, Dr William Price (1800–1893), lived here. He was a doctor by profession, and a good one by all accounts, but he hated all things modern. He tried to live his life as he imagined the Druids had done, and worshipped the sun, was a vegetarian, and advocated nudism. He did not believe in marriage and simply set up home with the young lady of his choice. When he was 83 the lady bore him a child which he called Iesu Grist (Jesus Christ). The child died in infancy. Price tried to carry out his religion to the full by cremating the infant in nearby Caerlan Field, but this caused an absolute uproar and he literally had to run for his life. His lady protected him by threatening his pursuers with a shotgun. Price was tried for what was then the crime of cremation, but was acquitted and had only to pay a farthing costs. Cremation became legal in Britain as a result of this.

Dr Price died ten years later and was, according to his wishes, cremated in Caerlan Field. A tablet to his memory has been set up by the Cremation Society and the Federation of British Cremation Authorities. In life Price must have presented an odd figure, for he always wore the most extraordinary clothes – including a fox skin hat with the tail still affixed and dangling down his back. The town was granted its borough charter in 1346, and still retains some of the ancient regalia. The Guildhall was built in 1773. In 1967 the Royal Mint moved to Llantrisant, and this has resulted in the building of what amounted to a new town to the S of the old. Farther S is the mock-gothic Hensol Castle, built in 1835 round an 18th-c mansion.

Ruined Llanthony Priory was originally founded in the 12thc.

LLANTRITHYD, South Glamorgan
25 ST07
The church here contains an amazing 16th-c tomb of the Basset and Mansel families. It looks overwhelmingly huge in the little church and is painted in bright gold, blue, and red. Memorials to the Aubrey family, whose ruined Tudor mansion lies opposite, are also to be seen.

LLANTWIT MAJOR, South Glamorgan
25 SS96
Towards the end of the 5thc St Illtud came to this place, situated near the sea, and founded what was to become one of the most important centres of learning in British Christendom. The most famous people in post-Roman Welsh history came here for instruction: St David, St Samson, Taliesin, and even the 'complaining monk' Gildas – saints, poets, and scholars. After Gildas the history of Llantwit is obscure, as this was the time when wave after wave of invaders streamed into the British Isles. For a while the candle that was the Romano-British sub culture flickered wildly in the gale, and names and faces caught briefly in the candle light are soon lost and confused. Soon the candle was extinguished altogether, and the Dark Ages settled over all the land.

When the Normans came they turned the monastery at Llantwit into a monastic cell of Tewkesbury, and changed the kind of Christianity taught here. They colonized the country here abouts with their own people. Nothing of Illtud's community remains, though the present church is probably built on or very near 6th-c foundations. This Church of St Illtud is extraordinary in being two churches joined together – the 'old' part had a parochial function and the 'new' a monastic function. The old church lies W of the tower and displays some original Norman features, but it was largely rebuilt in the 15thc. The 'new' church E of the tower is basically of 13th-c origin. Interesting features in the old church include a collection of stone crosses and memorials dating from the 8thc. A cross shaft without a head bears Illtud's name and probably dates from the 8thc. St Samson's

has a cross of about the same date, and a cross of King Hywel ap Rhys probably from the latter half of the 9thc. Later monuments include an elaborately-carved effigy of a woman and a 16th-c monument to one Matthew Voss, who was 129 years old when he died.

The 'new' church has a 14th-c stone rood screen, a large and ancient font, and a unique and beautiful carving of Jesse – with the tree that shows Christ's descent from the family of King David. Also in the church are some medieval wall paintings. Near the church is a round dovecote and the remains of the monastery gateway. There is also a tithe barn and a large gabled Tudor house called Ty Mawr. Remains of a very large medieval building, popularly called the Palace, have been excavated in the area. This was probably built at the same time as the 'new' church. The town itself is full of interest and has a 15th-c, two-storied Town Hall. The Old Swan Inn is said to have once been a mint. Llantwit's countryside was settled by men long before St Illtud came. On the coast, where the little stream called Col-huw flows into the sea, are the ramparts of an iron-age camp. A large Roman villa was excavated NW of the town at Caermead in 1888.

LLANTYSILIO, Clwyd *10 SJ14*
Although Llantysilio is the terminal point of the Llangollen branch of the picturesque Shropshire Union Canal, the waterway is not navigable past Llangollen. The Horseshoe Falls – a gentle crescent rather than a raging cascade – feed water from the Dee into the canal, which squeezes itself into this pleasant valley alongside the river, the A5 road, and the now disused Barmouth railway line. There is an interesting suspension footbridge in front of the Chain Bridge. Llantysilio church occupies a delightful site. In full spate the River Dee at this point provides a testing slalom course for experienced canoeists.

LLANUWCHLLYN, Gwynedd *10 SH83*
Two men who did more than most to promote the Welsh language in the past century – Sir O M Edwards, (1858–1920) and his son Sir Ifan ab Owen Edwards –

are commemorated here by a roadside memorial. 'OM' was the first Welsh Inspector of Schools, and through his writing he revived interest in Welsh history and literature. His son pursued the same ideals and founded *Urdd Gobaith Cymru* (Welsh League of Youth) in 1922. Glanllyn, a country mansion overlooking the lake near by, is now used as a centre for *Urdd Gobaith Cymru*. It was formerly a home of the Watkin Williams Wynne family of Ruabon. Llanuwchllyn's village pump commemorates the birth of Sir Watkin Williams Wynne in 1891. The ancient church was rebuilt in 1872 and contains an effigy of a 14th-c mail-clad knight, a portable wooden baptistry of the Victorian period, and communion plate believed to have come from Cymmer Abbey.

Llanuwchllyn is the terminal point for the Bala Lake Railway (see feature starting page 62), and is also the starting point for the precipitous mountain drive to Dinas Mawddwy over Bwlch-y-Groes, the highest pass in N Wales. At Caer Gai there are remains of a Roman fort. Farther up the valley of the Lliw a tiny congregational chapel called Carmel lies in the Coed Wenallt woodland. The River Twrch Valley is beautiful, and N are the Arennig mountain ranges with lakes Colwyn and Arennig Fawr.

LLANVAPLEY, Gwent 22 SO31
A rural crafts museum here displays an extensive collection of farm implements and items of domestic life from days gone by. Exhibits include animal traps, butter-making equipment, and tools used by blacksmiths and coopers. The village lies some 4m E of Abergavenny.

LLANVETHERINE, Gwent 22 SO31
Llanvetherine's 14th-c church was originally founded in the 6thc and contains life-size stone carvings of the Rev David Powell and his wife. These date from the 17thc. An ancient stone slab in the porch is roughly carved with the figure of a priest. This is thought to be a representation of St Gwytherine, the founder of the church. Offa's Dyke Path passes just to the E, and White Castle lies about 1m SE.

LLANVIHANGEL COURT, Gwent 22 SO32
This Tudor mansion (OACT) is situated about 4½m NE of Abergavenny and is 'H'-shaped in plan. The interior was remodelled in 1600 and contains interesting furniture, portraits etc. Attractive gardens which surround the house include several splendid trees.

LLANVIHANGEL CRUCORNEY, Gwent 22 SO32
River Monnow flows past this village of old stone houses, and the ancient Skirrid Inn is of interest. An old carved stone and a rather charming verse commemorating an 18th-c blacksmith can be seen in the church porch.

LLANWDDYN and LAKE VYRNWY, Powys 10 SJ01
The impression that this area resembles the Black Forest of Germany is heightened by the beautiful Lake Vyrnwy, which is complete with a gothic water tower which might have come straight out of the Rhineland. The old village of Llanwddyn now lies under the waters of the lake, and a new village has been built lower down the valley below the dam built by Liverpool Corporation. Old Llanwddyn grew up around a church founded by St Wddyn, a 6th-c Celtic saint who lived a hermit's life in a nearby cell in the rock face. The village became one of Prince Merfyn's possessions when his father, King Rhodri Mawr, divided his lands between his three sons, and so became part of the Principality of Powys. In the 13thc the village came into the possession of the Knights of St John of Jerusalem, who built a stone church dedicated to St John. After the Dissolution of the monasteries the Herbert family acquired the manor, which descended to the earls of Powis who held it until late in the 19thc. In 1865 the idea was first mooted of using the River Vyrnwy for extensive water supplies, and the idea was re-examined in 1867.

Plaques commemorating the work phases and official opening of the lake can be seen on the rock face at the N end of the dam. A road runs right round the lake, and at the reservoir's W end there are mountain roads climbing over the wild terrain to Dinas Mawddwy and Bala. The Lake Vyrnwy Hotel, first built in 1890 and extended in 1905, stands above the lake near the dam and offers wonderful views from its windows and terrace. It controls the lake fishing and holds records of catches from the time of its opening.

LLANWENOG, Dyfed 20 SN44
This small collection of houses lies just off the road from Lampeter to Newcastle Emlyn. The old church is dedicated to St Gwenog and houses an extraordinary font which is decorated with twelve large and identical faces – very crude, but with the direct appeal that primitive art often has. Also of interest are the 18th-c barrel roof and examples of modern woodwork. The 15th-c tower is of decorated style and shows some medieval stonework.

LLANWERN, Gwent 26 ST38
Llanwern is jammed between the E outskirts of Newport, the M4 motorway, and a gigantic steel works. An obelisk in the churchyard commemorates Lord Rhondda, who lived at Llanwern House and died in 1918.

LLANWNDA, Dyfed 16 SM93
Situated about 2m N of Fishguard on the Pen Caer Peninsula, this tiny village has had a church since the 9thc. The church building which now occupies the old site is of simple Welsh design and has a double bellcote. Set into the outside wall are two ancient stones, one inscribed with a face and the other with a cross. The interior has been restored, but there is still some old woodwork in the roof. Window sills are of carved stone and the font is of Norman origin. Asser, King Alfred's friend and biographer, was educated here and is said to have been born at Trefasser – on the other side of the peninsula Giraldus Cambrensis, writer, patriot, cleric, and one of the most famous of all Welshmen, was the rector here in the 13thc.

Pen Caer Peninsula is dotted with many reminders of pre-historic man, including burial chambers, mounds, earthen ramparts, and standing stones – perhaps the most evocative and mysterious of ancient monuments. Carreg Wastad Point is the place where over a thousand French soldiers started an abortive invasion of Britain in February 1797. The whole affair was a joke, and the only shot fired was at a grandfather clock. This was the last invasion of Britain, and a small memorial stone above the bay commemorates the occasion. Between Carreg Wastad and Strumble Head are many small rocky bays, and the Pembrokeshire Coast Path runs round the entire peninsula. A lighthouse at Strumble Head stands on a small islet connected to the mainland by a bridge and can be visited on weekday afternoons. Grey seals are often seen near here. Pwllderi Bay can be reached by those who do not mind a scramble down the steep cliffside. Above the bay is the ancient camp of Garn Fawr, from which there are excellent views of the unspoilt coastline. A monument to the poet Dewi Emrys, who was so enchanted with this countryside that he wrote a poem about it, stands in a nearby lane. The little village of St Nicholas has an interesting church in which there are two inscribed stones.

LLANWNEN, Dyfed 20 SN54
The little Afon Grannell runs through this village, which lies about 3½m W of Lampeter. The local church stands in a circular yard, and although largely rebuilt retains its 15th-c tower.

LLANWNOG, Powys 13 SO09
Llanwnog is a small village which at first sight seems unremarkable, but it was once the site of an episcopal palace. Nothing of this is left now except a few bricks and stones in a corner of a farm field once known as Parc-yr-Esgob – the Bishop's Park. The only bishop known to have had a link with Llanwnog was Robert Morgan, who was appointed vicar of Llanwnog in 1632 and elevated to become bishop of Bangor in 1666. It seems likely that it was he who built the residence at Llanwnog, for use as a conveniently local headquarters. Llanwnog church is dedicated to Gwynog, the son of Gildas the historian, who became bishop of Vannes. This is the only church known to bear his dedication. In the churchyard is the grave of John Ceiriog Hughes, the bard who was manager of the Van Railway at Caersws.

LLANWRIN, Powys 9 SH70
Visitors to Llanwrin have to take the back road from Cemmaes Road across the Dyfi Jubilee Bridge, a nicely-designed and constructed piece of engineering replacing an ugly girder bridge. Llanwrin is the only village on the entire length of this road. It is lonely and isolated, but compact and attractive. A house close by the Jubilee Bridge and named Mathavarn was where the Earl of Richmond, who was to become King Henry VII, spent a night *en route* from Milford to Bosworth.

LLANWRTYD WELLS, Powys 21 SN84
The rise of this trim, tidy little town dates from 1732, when Theophilus Evans – the grandfather of the historian Theophilus Jones – saw a frog disporting itself in the strongly sulphurous waters. Since these waters apparently did not harm the frog he thought that they might be worth trying as a cure for the scurvy, from which he suffered. He began drinking them, found his condition improved, and came to the conclusion

that these were healing waters. So Llanwrtyd became a spa, and the wells at Dol-y-Coed still exist. Nowadays the little town is no longer visited by those in search of health, but by holidaymakers who come for the scenery and pony trekking – which is one of the specialities of the area.

A woollen cloth factory here once provided work for the local people, but that was 150 years ago. Today the Cambrian Factory, a little way outside the town on the main road, provides employment for disabled ex-servicemen and produces a variety of Welsh textiles. The River Irfon makes a sharp rightangle bend here, and up the valley towards the source is the old village of Llanwrtyd. The old church is sparsely windowed and has a bellcote instead of a tower. St David is said to have selected this site for a church after the Synod of Llandewi Brevi in 519; Theophilus Evans was vicar here from 1732 to 1767, and the great hymn writer William Williams Pantycelin was his curate for three years, from 1740 to 1743. His portrait hangs on the west wall.

The famous preacher Kilsby Jones is buried in the churchyard. At fifteen he went to a preparatory school for young preachers at Aberaeron, and then entered the ministry. He was a brilliant preacher, one of the most striking characters in Welsh Nonconformity. He contributed to Welsh publications, was a translator who edited a Welsh edition of the *Pilgrims Progress*, and translated *Brown's Dictionary of the Bible* into Welsh. The name Kilsby was given to him because of his association with the Northamptonshire village of that name, where he was pastor before moving to Llanwrtyd Wells.

LLANYBYDDER, Dyfed 20 SN54
On the last Thursday of each month a large horse fair is held at The Mart in this small River Teifi market town. The Mart is next to the town's restored church, which retains an ancient tower, and the fair is one of the few left in Britain. It attracts dealers and buyers from all over the world. The area was once the centre of a flourishing weaving industry, and some of the mills still produce traditional Welsh designs. A large cross on the Llandysul road commemorates successful negotiations relating to the placing of the country boundary in 1822. Rather scant remains of a hillfort lie S of the town at Pen-y-gaer.

LLANYMAWDDWY, Gwynedd 10 SH91
This remote hamlet lies on the road from Dinas Mawddwy to the narrow mountain pass of Bwlch-y-Groes, and is situated in the mountain-encircled valley of the Afon Dyfi. Its tiny bellcoted church has a plain interior and is dedicated to St Tydecho, who is said to have established a sanctuary here in the Dark Ages. To the N the road follows the Afon Dyfi to its confluence with the Afon Rhiwlech. The road later diverges from the Dyfi, climbing steeply to the pass of Bwlch-y-Groes with gradients up to 1 in $4\frac{1}{2}$. Although well-surfaced, this highway is narrow, with a precipitous drop on its E side to the Afon Rhiwlech, and is the highest in Wales.

LLANYMYNECH, Powys 11 SJ22
Half of Llanymynech is in Wales and the other half in England. The border runs right through the village – actually

Llanvihangel Court stands in splendid grounds, and has an interior which was remodelled in 1600.

through the houses – so that in the days when old Montgomeryshire was 'dry' it was possible to drink in the back bar of the Lion Hotel which was in England, but not in the front, which was in Wales. A frontier demarcation mark can be seen on the wall of a corridor. The most striking feature of Llanymynech is the Rocks, a sheer wall of rock standing up behind the village and spreading right across the horizon for a considerable distance. The Rocks and the country behind have been heavily quarried and include caves where the Romans mined silver, lead, and copper. The Ogof, a big cave on the top by the golf course, allows access to these galleries.

The River Vyrnwy skirts the village and is crossed by a main road via a bridge built by Telford between 1826 and 1828. On the top of the east parapet of this bridge the word 'death' has been cut into the stonework, to commemorate the tragedy of a bolting horse which leapt over the side and drowned its rider, a young local woman.

LLANYNYS, Clwyd 6 SJ16
Lying 2m N of Ruthin on the road to Denbigh, Llanynys boasts one of the most notable churches in the Vale of Clwyd. The name, often literally translated as 'church of the island', mystifies some people. The building is 20m inland, but the name stems from the time when it was frequently marooned in low-lying meadowland. Parishioners have been known to reach it by rowing boat or horseback. The original church was founded in the 6thc, and the present building probably dates from the beginning of the 13thc. Early-English stonework on the west door was recently dated as being of 13th-c origin, and the highly-decorated south door dates from between 1490 and 1500.

Apart from these interesting items, most visitors are drawn to the church by the 15th-c mural paintings of St Christopher, discovered under several layers of whitewash during church renovations in 1968. Much of the painting looked

remarkably fresh, and it is clear that it was the work of an artist of some rank. Renovations also uncovered three wall niches, each containing a skull. Among many other features in this fascinating building are wooden candelabra and a pair of hatchments – coats of arms which were carried before the coffin at funerals of local notabilities, and later hung on the gates or wall of the deceased's home before being placed permanently in the church.

LLANYSTUMDWY, Gwynedd 9 SH43
This village is assured of a permanent place in history because of its association with David Lloyd George, the small-town solicitor who became British prime minister and wartime leader. Posterity will judge him as a great social reformer who was ahead of his time, a campaigner for justice, and an inspired war leader. His progressive social measures alarmed traditionalists, but they were the first steps towards the Welfare State. Lloyd George was prime minister from December 1916 until 1922, and his undoing was the 1921 treaty with Ireland – the effects of which are still felt today. He still managed to cut a lively figure in parliament in spite of his waning power, and his last notable contribution to the nation's affairs was his speech in 1940. This, more than any other, brought about the downfall of Neville Chamberlain and the transfer of the premiership to Winston Churchill.

Lloyd George was of the great Welsh Liberal tradition, and after winning the Caernarfon borough's seat in 1890 by a mere eighteen votes he represented this constituency unbroken for the next 50 years. Throughout his long parliamentary career he never lost his love for Wales and its people, and it was to Llanystumdwy that he returned to spend the latter part of his life. He died at Ty Newydd, a Jacobean mansion just above Llanystumdwy, on 26 March 1945 aged 82. It was at Llanystumdwy, on a high bank overlooking the River Dwyfor, that he was buried by his own wish – although he could have been interred alongside monarchs and

Magnificent Snowdon from Llyn Llydaw.

statesmen at Westminster Abbey. His younger brother William carried on the solicitor's practice which the two brothers had started, and was still working well into his 90's. He died in 1972 aged 101. The two brothers and their sister Mary were brought up in the little roadside cottage at Llanystumdwy. It is open to the public, but the only furniture today are the two desks at which the two boys studied, tutored by their uncle, Richard Lloyd.

Lloyd George's memorial, a simple but effective shrine in Welsh granite, was designed by Clough Williams-Ellis. A curving drive leads to the Lloyd George museum, which is disappointingly bungaloid in appearance but can offer a fascinating hour amongst an impressive collection of caskets, deeds of freedom, documents, scrolls, and mementoes of David, first Earl Lloyd George of Dwyfor – the most celebrated Welshman of recent times. The bridge at Llanystumdwy is most interesting, having two large and two small arches and massive cutwaters. The poet Shelley once lived at Gwynfryn Plas, which now serves as a hotel. Some 2m N, to the E of the roadside community called Rhoslan, are two burial chambers.

LLAWHADEN, Dyfed   19 SN01
Features of this East Cleddau River town, situated NW of Narberth, include an 18th-c river bridge, an 18th-c watermill now used as a store, and a remarkable late 14th-c church built right against the river bank. This church is special in that it has two towers, one of which was left behind when the structure was rebuilt a little farther from the river. Incorporated in the building is an 11th-c wheel cross, and inside are a Norman font and a 14th-c effigy of a priest – possibly a representation of the founder, St Hugo. The castle here was at one time a residence of the Bishops of St David's, and was originally a wooden Norman motte structure. In 1192 it was captured by the Welsh, and it acquired a strong curtain wall after its recapture. It was largely rebuilt in the 14thc by Bishop David Martin. The gatehouse was built in the closing years of the 14thc, and still stands at its original height.

The structure was dismantled in the 16thc and for many years served only as a source of building materials. The ruins have now been restored and are in the care of the DoE. Remains of the Priory of St Mary, a hospice built in 1387 by Bishop Beck, are also of interest. Llawhaden House has a Georgian exterior but a Tudor heart, and St Kennox was the 17th-c house of Pritchard – chancellor of St David's and author of *Cannwyll y Cymry (The Welshman's Candle)*. Ridgeway House has a history going back to the 14thc.

LLECHRYD, Dyfed   17 SN24
A fine old bridge which spans the Teifi here has a total of nine arches. The village itself has many pleasant houses, including the Tudor Glanolmarch and the Carpenter's Arms. A disused church in the area houses box pews. Across the river is 18th-c Castle Maelgwyn Manor, now a hotel.

LLIGWY BURIAL CHAMBER, Gwynedd   5 SH58
This impressive neolithic monument is situated on the road from Llanallgo to Lligwy Bay (full OS reference SH 501 861). Its huge capstone weighs some 25 tons and is supported on low uprights above a rock-cut pit. A large number of human remains were discovered here, and the monument is in the care of the DoE. This part of Anglesey is very rich in ancient remains: to the NW is the wonderful iron-age village of Din Lligwy; SW is Bodafon Mountain and its various prehistoric monuments; farther N, still on the Lligwy Bay road, are the 12th-c ruins of Capel Lligwy (AM).

LLITHFAEN, Gwynedd   8 SH34
In an exposed situation on the S slope of Yr Eifl, this village is the starting point for footpaths to Nant Gwrtheyrn (Vortigern's Valley), and Porth-y-Nant – a weird combination of high cliffs, derelict quarry workings, piers, and buildings. The magnificent prehistoric hut circles of Tre'r Ceiri survive on Yr Eifl.

LLOWES, Powys   22 SO14
This village is situated below Hay in the valley of the Wye. A remarkable stone known locally as Moll Walbee's Stone can

be seen in the church, and for many years stood on The Begwms. Its total height is 11ft, about 3ft of which is buried in the church floor. Inscriptions on the stone comprise two crosses, one from the 7th and one from the 11thc. The stone is now believed to commemorate St Meilig, the 6th-c founder of the church, who is said to be buried here. The church was rebuilt in 1853 but retains a Norman font. Nearby Llowes Court is of interest and dates from the 17thc.

LLWYNLLWYD, Powys   21 SN93
Some 5m NW of Brecon, Llwynllwyd includes the setting of one of the most famous of the Nonconformist academies – The Barn. This was probably founded by Vavasor Griffiths. William Williams the hymnologist taught here.

LLYN ARENNIG FAWR, Gwynedd   10 SH83
This rather gloomy but attractive glacial lake lies 1,326ft above sea level and is overlooked in the W by the 2,800ft mountain from which it takes its name. It can be approached from several directions, the easiest route being via footpath from Llyn Celyn. An alternative but much longer approach can be made from the little village of Parc. To the N across the River Tryweryn is the smaller twin mountain of 2,264ft Arennig Fach. It too has a glacial lake on its E flank and can also be approached from Llyn Celyn.

LLYN BOCHLWYD, Gwynedd   5 SH65
In a sheltered position between 3,010ft Tryfan and the ridge of Y Gribin, Llyn Bochlwyd lies N of 3,262ft Glyder Fach. Access is from the lower end of Llyn Ogwen, and the lake is known for its rare alpine-type flora. The surrounding cliffs are astounding, and the whole of this scenic extravaganza lies at 1,800ft above sea level. The lake and much of the surrounding countryside belongs to the NT.

LLYN BODLYN, Gwynedd   9 SH62
Source of the River Ysgethin, Llyn Bodlyn is situated in mountainous country some 6m NE of Barmouth. It can be approached by track from Dyffryn Ardudwy, or via a footpath from Bontddu on the Mawddach estuary. To the SE is the peak of 2,462ft Diffwys, and 1,932ft Moelfre rises W. Two other small lakes in the vicinity are Dulyn to the E and Irddyn to the SW. Farther W is the prehistoric site of Carneddau Hengwm, considered the best example of many which survive in the area.

LLYN CELYN, Gwynedd   10 SH84
An artificial lake formed by the damming of the Tryweryn Valley, Celyn's N shore carries the main A4212 road from Bala. The W end of the lake is flanked by the twin peaks of 2,800ft Arennig Fawr and 2,264ft Arennig Fach.

LLYN CLYWEDOG, Powys   13 SN88
This beautiful reservoir was formed by the damming of the River Clywedog, and is situated some 3m NW of Llanidloes. It is easily accessible from both Llanidloes and the village of Staylittle. The 237ft dam was opened in 1968 and has the highest wall in Britain. To the W of the dam are the ancient earthworks of Pen-y-gaer, and W beyond the large expanse of Hafren Forest – in the

Plynlimon range – are the sources of the rivers Wye and Severn.

LLYN CONWY, Gwynedd *9 SH74*
High up on the moorland plateau of Migneint, this attractive lake (NT) lies 1,488ft above sea level and is the source of the River Conwy. Excellent views of the Snowdon area can be enjoyed from here, and the trout fishing is good. Access is from a track leading off the B4407 Pentrefoelas to Ffestiniog road.

LLYN COWLYD RESERVOIR, Gwynedd *5 SH76*
Supplier of water to many Welsh towns, this is the deepest lake in N Wales and in places has been measured at 222ft. It is linked to the Llyn Eigiau system, which supplies water to the power station at Dolgarrog. The lake is rather dark and gloomy, being overshadowed by 2,622ft Pen Llithrig-y-Wrach – The Witches' Slide – in the N, and the crags of 2,213ft Creigiau Gleision in the S.

LLYN CRAFNANT RESERVOIR, Gwynedd *5 SH76*
One of the most popular lakes in Wales, Crafnant is easily approached on an unclassified road from the village of Trefriw, which lies in the Vale of the Conwy N of Llanrwst. Crafnant can also be reached on foot over moorland from Capel Curig. The lake is very beautiful, with forest-clad slopes leading up to a horizon of little peaks. At the head of the lake is the Cwm Glas Crafnant national nature reserve. Boats and refreshments are available at the lakeside.

LLYN CWELYN, Gwynedd *5 SH55*
The main A4085 road from Caernarfon to Beddgelert runs along the NE shore of this attractive lake, which is overlooked from the W by 2,290ft Mynydd Mawr. An ascent to the summit of Snowdon, which lies some 3m E, can be made from the Snowdon Ranger Hotel.

LLYN CWM SILIN, Gwynedd *5 SH55*
Actually a pair of lonely and remote lakes, Llyn Cwm Silin can be approached by track from Llanllyfni, which lies just S of Penygroes.

LLYN CWM Y STRADLLYN, Gwynedd *9 SH54*
A gloomy lake with quarry workings at its head, this natural reservoir is over-shadowed by 2,566ft Moel Hebog and 1,811ft Moel Ddu. It is situated at 642ft above sea level and can be approached from either Llanfihangel-y-Pennant, or via an unclassified road which turns right just past Penmorfa on the A487 road from Tremadog.

LLYN DINAS, Gwynedd *9 SH64*
Named after the fort of Dinas Emrys, which is situated at the W end of the lake, beautiful Dinas is set in the valley of the River Glaslyn. Dinas Emrys means Merlin's Fort, and the lake has its own legend connected with the famous magician. It is said that the true throne of Britain was hidden here by the enchanter, and that one day a youth will step on a certain stone and the throne will be revealed. The youth will claim the throne and the true kingdom of Britain will return. Dinas is an enjoyable venue for boating and its situation affords excellent views of mountain scenery. Yr Aran rises to 2,451ft in the NW, and beyond this is the massive, 3,560ft bulk of Snowdon. The main A498 road from Beddgelert to Capel Curig runs along the NW shore of the lake.

LLYN DIWAUNEDD, Gwynedd *5 SH65*
Situated in boggy terrain W of 2,860ft Moel Siabod, this remote lake is overlooked by the crags of 1,938ft Criban and lies 1,208ft above sea level. It can be approached on foot only from Dolwyddelan or Roman Bridge.

LLYN DULYN RESERVOIR, Gwynedd *5 SH76*
The easiest approach to Dulyn is from Dolgarrog, and the region is devoid of roads. It is ideal for the walker who wants beauty and solitude. Very deep and about 1,747ft above sea level, the lake supplies Llandudno's water and is overhung by Craig Dulyn.

LLYN EIGIAU, Gwynedd *5 SH76*
About 1,250ft above sea level and some 4m W of the Conwy Valley at Dolgarrog, Eigiau lies among the mountains and spurs which form the lower slopes of Carnedd Llywelyn. The 3,485ft Carnedd Llywelyn is the third highest mountain in Wales, and the highest in the area between the Nant Ffrancon and the Conwy. Llyn Eigiau is the second largest stretch of water in this area. In 1925 the dam burst and caused a flood which swept down to Dolgarrog and claimed sixteen lives. Water from this reservoir, and from its neighbour Llyn Cowlyd, is used in the large hydro-electric power station at Dolgarrog.

LLYN GWYNANT, Gwynedd *5 SH65*
An attractive lake set partly among trees in the Glaslyn valley, Llyn Gwynant lies 4m NE of Beddgelert and is situated at a height of only 217ft above sea level. It is seen best from the direction of Penygwryd, where the main road from Betws-y-coed to Porthmadog begins a winding 700ft descent to its shores, opposite the steep slopes of 2,032ft Gallt-y-Wenallt. A viewpoint is sited 1m S of Penygwryd on this road.

LLYN HYWEL, Gwynedd *9 SH62*
Situated between 2,333ft Rhinog Fach and 2,475ft Y Llethr at a height of 1,750ft, this lake was described in a Snowdonia national park guide as being 'the most stark and forbidding of all the mountain tarns in the park'. It is surrounded by bare rock, and on its N side the S face of Rhinog Fach rises in an almost sheer, 600ft wall of rock and scree.

LLYN IDWAL, Gwynedd *5 SH65*
Llyn Idwal is a dark and rather sinister lake lying in an impressively wild setting at the back of 3,279ft Glyder Fawr, ½m S of the Ogwen Cottage mountain rescue post at the top of the Nant Ffrancon Pass. According to legend, no bird would fly across the surface of Idwal after the drowning there of Prince Idwal, son of Owain Gwynedd.

At the extreme S end of the lake is a pool overgrown with weeds and plants, known as Llygad Glas (Green Eye). This is a place to be avoided, and has been suggested as the point where Idwal met his death – either by accident or possibly by false advice. High above the shore is a deep, black chasm called Twll Du, almost physically separating Glyder Fawr from Y Garn. Seen at a distance as a V-shaped rift on the skyline, this ravine is sheer-sided, up to 300ft deep, and more popularly known as the Devil's Kitchen. The mountain across the Ogwen Valley from Idwal is 3,211ft Pen-yr-Oleu Wen, or 'the Hill of the White Light'. This explanation can be understood by anyone who has seen it in full moonlight. The lake and much of the surrounding area is owned by the NT, and Cwm Idwal was the first national nature reserve to have been set up in Wales. The reserve's alpine plants are known for their luxuriance and rarity.

LLYN LLYDAW, Gwynedd *5 SH65*
Over 1m long and some 1,400ft above sea level, this lake is magnificently situated in the famous Snowdon horseshoe – the jagged, almost precipitous ridge formed by the notorious knife-edged 3,023ft Crib Goch, 3,493ft Crib-y-ddysgl, 3,560ft Y Wyddfa, (Snowdon's summit), and the equally sharp, 2,947ft Y Lliwedd. On three sides of the lake walls of rock tower up to between 1,500 and 2,000ft. Like many other lakes and reservoirs in the area where a fall of water can be produced, Llydaw is linked to a hydro-electric scheme. In this case the small power station is situated 1,100ft lower down at the bottom of the Glaslyn Valley, above Llyn Gwynant.

LLYN MYMBYR, Gwynedd *5 SH75*
Llyn Mymbyr, or the Capel Curig Lakes, comprises two small lakes linked by a channel on the W side of Capel Curig. The lakes are situated in a broad U-shaped valley between a 2,500ft ridge leading to the 3,262 and 3,279ft Glyders on the N side, and the more rounded shape of 2,860ft Moel Siabod to the S.

LLYN NANTLLE, Gwynedd *5 SH55*
Source of the Afon Nantlle, which flows W to the sea, this lake is situated at the mouth of a V-shaped pass leading to Beddgelert. The main attraction here is the view from the road bridge at its W end across the water to the summit of Snowdon, framed between mountains guarding the pass. To the W and NW the vast, disused slate quarries mark the Cambrian slate-belt. Some of these holes are sheer sided and up to 400ft deep.

LLYN OGWEN, Gwynedd *5 SH66*
Travellers following the A5 through Capel Curig leave behind the narrow wooded valley of the Afon Llugwy, and follow the river up a broad, bleak stretch of open country between craggy mountains. Ahead and to the left is the magnificent triangular peak of 3,010ft Tryfan. Although an excellent viewpoint, its pinnacled and rock-strewn slopes are not for the inexperienced climber. Below Tryfan lies the beautiful Llyn Ogwen, a shallow lake almost 1m long and famous for its eels and trout. To the N of the lake stands a great bastion rising to 3,211ft at the bend in the valley – Pen-yr-Oleu-wen, dubbed 'Hill of the White Light' because it reflects moonlight. At the W end where the valley makes a dramatic 90-degree turn stands Ogwen Cottage. Formerly an inn, this is now a climbing centre and is well known as a Mountain Rescue Post. To the S of the road is the famous Llyn Idwal and The Devil's Kitchen on the precipitous cwm wall below 3,279ft Glyder Fawr.

LLYN PADARN, Gwynedd *5 SH56*
One of two lakes at Llanberis and the gateway to the heart of Snowdon, much painted and photographed Llyn

233

Padarn is seen at its best when approached from the direction of Caernarfon – with the mountains of the Llanberis Pass as a background. There was originally one lake here, dammed by glacial deposits at its NW end, but material from a stream at Llanberis has divided it into two which are joined by a narrow channel. Llyn Padarn, the N one of the pair, is 2m long and the largest of the Snowdon waters.

LLYN PERIS, Gwynedd *5 SH55*
A much smaller and narrower lake than Llyn Padarn, to which it is joined by the channel of the Afon Seiont, Llyn Peris is 1m long and 114ft deep. Its setting is also in complete contrast. Much of its N shore is taken up by the derelict workings of the Dinorwic slate quarries – a solid wall of broken grey slate rising in almost sheer terraces nearly 2,000ft above the water. Above these the mountainside rises another 700ft to the summit of Elidir Fawr. Above the S shore is the almost conical peak of 1,321ft Derlwyn, standing at the lower end of a long sloping ridge which forms the easiest ascent of Snowdon. Behind this is the Snowdon Mountain Railway (see page 62).

LLYN TEIFI, Dyfed *13 SN76*
Llyn Teifi is the source of the Afon Teifi and the largest of six lakes popularly known as the Teifi Pools. The pools are situated in a large hollow among the hills of the 'Great Desert', 3m E of Pontrhyd-fendigaid. The 'desert' is a vast uninhabited area of low rocky hills, rolling moors, and little else but streams, lakes, reservoirs, and occasional extensive areas of afforestation. It covers much of the former E Cardiganshire (Dyfed), W Breconshire, and Radnor (Powys) areas. The lake is said to contain trout of fine quality brought by monks from the former abbey at nearby Strata Florida. It is highly attractive in its wild, peaceful setting. Access is from the Cross Inn at Ffair Rhos – on the B4343 Pontrhydfendigaid to Devil's Bridge road – via an unclassified road which climbs E over hill and moorland slopes to reach a height of 1,510ft directly above the lake.

LLYN TRAWSFYNYDD, Gwynedd *9 SH63*
Occupying part of the valley of the Afon Prysor S of the Vale of Ffestiniog, Llyn Trawsfynydd was formed in the period between the wars as a reservoir for the production of hydro-electric power. The Maentwrog power station which it serves is situated 600ft below in the Vale of Ffestiniog. A 500 megawatt nuclear power station, the first of its kind in Wales, was recently constructed on the N shore to take advantage of the vast quantities of cooling water; the capacity of the lake is 1,200,000,000 cubic feet. This complex is a very prominent and interesting addition to the scenery. Parts of the N, W, and SW shores are thickly wooded, and Coed-y-Rhygen on the W side is a national nature reserve. Llyn Trawsfynydd is 3m long and up to 1m wide, with a surface area of 1,300 acres, or about 2sqm.

LLYN-Y-DYWARCHEN, Gwynedd *5 SH55*
This little lake lies above Rhyd-Ddu and for hundreds of years was a place of pilgrimage for botanists, tourists, and other interested people. In 1188 Giraldus

Cambrensis visited the lake and discovered that it had a floating island which consisted of peat that had broken away from the lake floor. All traces of this natural curiosity have now disappeared, and the only island to be seen today is of the ordinary, non-floating type. Islands of any sort were thought of as being something special in pre- and early-Christian days, and a floating one would have assumed a great sanctity. The lake can be reached via the B4410 road from Rhyd-Ddu. To the S is 2,080ft Y Garn.

LLYSWEN, Powys *22 SO13*
Situated SW of Hay on a horseshoe bend of the River Wye, Llyswen is surrounded by attractive countryside and has a church which was rebuilt in 1863. A large mound in the churchyard contains the remains of John Macnamara. John won Llangoed Castle at gambling, but it only remained his so long as he remained above ground – hence the peculiar grave. Llangoed Castle lies upstream and has been largely rebuilt by Clough Williams Ellis. Llyswen means 'fair palace', and it is said that there was once a palace of the princes of S Wales in the area. To the S of the village are scant remains of a Norman motte, and the hill that overlooks it is surmounted by a prehistoric fortification. Across the river at Boughrood there are a few remains of a 12th-c castle.

LLYS-Y-FRAN, Dyfed *16 SN02*
A little village NE of Haverfordwest, Llys-y-Fran is noted for the large reservoir named after it. This was formed by the damming of the River Syfynwy. The little village church has an ancient font, and Hywel Davies was rector here before he left the established church to become one of the great Nonconformist preachers. To the N of the reservoir is the village of Henrys Moat, a corruption of 'Hendre Motte'. There are two castle mounds in the village.

LLYWEL, Powys *21 SN83*
Llywel is a church just off the main A40 road W of Trecastle. The tower is 15thc, and the church houses a 16th-c screen and cradle roofs. Also in the church is a cast of the 6th-c Ogham-inscribed Llywel stone, discovered on a nearby farm in 1876. The original is in the British Museum. The Taricora Stone, also in the church, dates from about the same time as the Llywel Stone, and the churchyard contains fine yews and old wooden stocks.

LOCHTYN, Dyfed *17 SN35*
This NT property lies N of Llangranog and comprises a magnificent stretch of coastline and a small island. Three lovely beaches can be reached by those who do not mind a scramble down the steep paths. Bird life is abundant and seals are frequently seen. Pendinaslochdyn hillfort (NT) affords excellent views.

LOGGERHEADS, Clwyd *7 SJ26*
Loggerheads was popular with Merseyside day trippers in the days of cycle touring, and coach excursions from Liverpool and Birkenhead came here. Crossville's tea gardens, opposite the celebrated Loggerheads Inn, is a survival of these inter-war days. The inn sign shows two faces with the legend 'We three Loggerheads be'.

Loggerheads is an archaic word for blockhead, and the inquisitive visitor who asks about the missing third face invites an uncomplimentary response. Richard Wilson the landscape artist is reputed to have painted the original sign. He lived out the last years of his life at nearby Colomendy, now a school. He died in 1782 and is buried 3m away in Mold parish churchyard.

LOUGHOR, West Glamorgan *24 SS59*
Romans and Normans recognized the strategic importance of Loughor, situated at the lowest point near the sea where the River Loughor can be bridged. The Romans set up a station here on the road to *Moridunum* (Carmarthen), and the Normans built a castle to guard the river crossing. The Welsh prince Gruffydd ap Rhys destroyed the castle in 1115, but it was rebuilt only to be destroyed again in 1215. The remains (AM) are on a mound near the main road that now crosses a wide bridge. Roman objects, including coins and traces of a bath-house, were found when the railway was being built S of the castle. The local church stands on a mound between the castle remains and the river, and is dedicated to St Michael. It is of perpendicular style.

LYDSTEP, Dyfed *19 SS09*
Situated 5m SW of Tenby in the Pembrokeshire Coast national park, this village includes the ruins of the Palace of Arms, which is said to have been a hunting lodge of Bishop Gower of St David's. The coast views and caves around Lydstep Point (NT) and Proud Giltar are very fine. Skrinkle Haven lies to the W and is attractive. Caves along this coastline can be explored at low tide.

MACHEN, Gwent *26 ST28*
This small town lies in a pleasant stretch of the Rhymney Valley 7m W of Newport, and was once a Roman lead-mining settlement. Fragments of pottery have been found here, and part of an incised portrait of a gorgon's head is now preserved in the tower of the Church of St Michael. This fragment is believed to have come from the base of a pagan shrine dated between AD 75 and 200. First traditions of a Christian community here centre on the religious foundations of Llandanglwys and Llanawst. The former was founded by St Tanglwys, a daughter of King Brychan. No remains of these foundations exist, but some scholars believe the site of the first church was in a field called Cae'r Groes. This is near Llandanglwys Farm, which is at the top of the mountain road that runs N from Lower Machen to Pontymister in the Ebbw Valley.

St Michael's Church dates from the 11thc and is sited nearly at the foot of the mountain road in the rural seclusion of Lower Machen. The church has a 15th-c porch, with a sun-dial and a Tudor door. Eleven hatchments are displayed round the interior walls of the building, many of them in memory of the local Morgan family who had a long connection with the foundation. In 1710 John Morgan bought the lordship of Wentllwg, and with this went the patronage of the church. A number of other monuments to the family can be seen in the Morgan Chapel. The nave is the oldest part; its extraordinary thick walls, and the fact that the tower and chancel are butted on to it, suggest that these were later additions. There has been considerable restoration, but the church retains much of its beauty. The font displays unusual 18th-c work.

The Reformers came to Machen in the 18thc. John Wesley spoke in English and Daniel Rowlands in Welsh on 16 October 1741 at the preaching cross in the churchyard. Next to the church and in extensive grounds is impressive Machen House, a private residence which was once the rectory. The rectory nowadays is next to St John's Church in Machen – or Upper Machen as some describe it to differentiate from Lower Machen. The first stone of this church was laid on 22 June 1854. Features of the building include an ornate clock tower, Victorian enrichments, and light-varnished box pews which lend an air of brightness to the interior. One of the 18th-c 'circulating' schools was established at Machen by Griffith Jones.

Machen, a built-up area which contrasts with the quietness of Lower Machen, lies just off the A468. Mountains and gentle hills rise near by. Lower Machen is also beautifully situated, and in recent years it was three times judged the best-kept village of under 1,000 population in the Magor and St Mellons rural district. The road from Lower Machen to Rudry passes a nature reserve. The small old Church of St James has a saddleback tower and is situated in the attractively-sited village of Rudry.

*MACHYNLLETH, Powys 9 SH70
A little grey low-profile town, just above the Dyfi estuary, Machynlleth has

a history going back to Roman times when it was named *Maglona*. It is a 'T'-shaped town, with a grey stone clock tower at the top of the 'T' and Pentreheydyn Street entering on the left and Penrallt Street going out on the right – the upright of the 'T' is the main thoroughfare, Maengwyn Street. This long, tree-lined road of shops includes the old Maerdy or Court House at the far end. The inscription '1628 Owen Pugh o Uxor' can be read on the timbered front of the Court House. Halfway down the street is the Owain Glyndwr Institute. It was here that Glyndwr held his parliament in 1404, and it is believed that part of the original Parliament House is embedded in the fabric of the present building. It was here too that he just missed being assassinated by his brother-in-law Dafydd Gam. Dafydd, whose life Owain spared, won fame at Agincourt. Owain's seal was adopted by the town as its own official seal.

The centre of municipal government is Plas Machynlleth, the large mansion and estate behind the houses of Maengwyn Street's S side. This 17th-c mansion was presented to the town in 1949 by Lord Londonderry. The Clock Tower was erected by public subscription in 1873 to mark the coming-of-age of Lord Castlereagh, heir to the Marquis of Londonderry. Machynlleth once had a snuff industry. The factory was in Penrallt Street and can be dated back to 1775. Welsh snuff is what is called 'high dried' in contradistinction to the heavy humid variety called Rappee. Machynlleth also had no fewer than seventeen printing houses. The first of the town's presses was started by Titus Evans in 1789. A year later one of his apprentices – Edward Pritchard – started printing, but his press closed down after only eleven years.

Evans' three sons all became printers, and John became the owner of the *Carmarthen Herald.* Then there was Adam Evans, Francis Jones, and several others, the last of them being John Evans. There is still one of the old printing houses left in a court off Maengwyn Street, distinguished by a name plate on one of its walls. In the 19thc Machynlleth had 24 inns, two of which still remain – the White Lion and the Wynnstay, where George Borrow stayed. The National Eisteddfod of Wales was held in Machynlleth in 1937, and there are important sheep dog trials held every summer in the park of Llynlloed Hall, the seat of Mr C D Fenwick – himself a noted handler.

MAENCLOCHOG, Dyfed 17 SN02
One of the largest villages in the area of the Prescelly Hills, this has been called the village where 'stones rang like bells'. Nearby Mynachlog-Ddu once had a stone ring, and some of the original Stonehenge material is thought to have come from the neighbourhood. To the N of the village stands 1,760ft Prescelly Top. The village lies on the B4313 between Narberth and Fishguard.

MAENTWROG, Gwynedd 9 SH64
One of the most picturesque villages in Wales, Maentwrog is situated in the Vale of Ffestiniog at the junction of the Betws-y-coed and Dolgellau roads. Most of the modern village was built in the 19thc by William Oakeley, a pioneer of the slate industry, but the original settlement took its name from Twrog, a 7th-c giant who traditionally threw a stone from the hillside into the churchyard below. Legend claims that this stone still lies embedded in the ground among the gravestones. The church is thought to date from c610, possibly on account of this legend, but it was largely re-built in 1896 when a slate-hung spire was added.

The building contains an Oakeley memorial. The Rev Edmund Prys, a Welsh poet who was rector of Maentwrog and also archdeacon of Merioneth, is buried there. Prys is chiefly remembered for the assistance he gave to Bishop Morgan in translating the Bible into Welsh. The churchyard has a lych gate commemorating the 60 years of Queen Victoria's reign.

MAESTEG, Mid Glamorgan 25 SS89
This important colliery town on the River Llynfi is the largest in the area and is set among high hills. An ironworks operated here until the end of the 19thc, but now coalmining is the most important industry. Agricultural work still takes place on the surrounding hills, with sheep farming forming the main activity.

MAGOR, Gwent 26 ST48
Situated on the edge of Caldicot Level overlooking the Bristol Channel, this village has a large, mainly-Norman

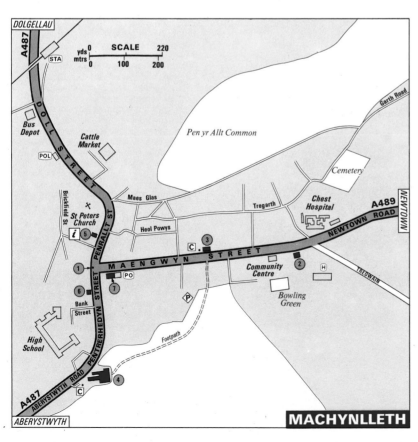

1 Clock Tower
2 Court House or Mayor's House
3 Owain Glyndwr Institute
4 Plas Machynlleth (council offices)
5 WTB Information Centre
6 White Lion Hotel
7 Wynnstay Arms Hotel

MACHYNLLETH

church which was founded in the 7thc by Cadwaladr – the last Welsh prince also to be king of Britain. It is known as the 'Cathedral of the Moors' and carries a 13th-c tower. The chancel is high roofed, and later additions include a two-storey 15th-c porch and an eight-sided font. Ivy-covered remains of an ancient priory can still be seen in the churchyard. A large war memorial in the village square was erected by Lady Rhondda in 1924. The nearby iron-age site of Caerwent is of interest. The neighbouring village of Redwich is closer to the Bristol Channel and boasts an interesting church which features a 15th-c south porch, pinnacled central tower, and a 13th-c rood loft.

MALLTRAETH, Gwynedd *4 SH36*
Malltraeth is a quiet S Anglesey village which saw busier times when boat building and coal mining were local industries. A high embankment was built *c*1800 to stop the incursion of the sea inland, but the result is some very unrewarding farmland. Before this the estuary of the Cefni penetrated almost as far as Llangefni, nearly cutting Anglesey in two. Viking ships were in the habit of roaming up the estuary. There is little trace of the coalmining activity which centred on Malltraeth after coal deposits were found beneath the marshes. Today Malltraeth is best known for its fine beach and salt marshes.

MALLWYD, Gwynedd *10 SH81*
This attractive village lies on the Afon Dyfi between Machynlleth and Dinas Mawddwy, and is the point where slate buildings in the Dyfi Valley give way to stone. The village is much favoured by artists and anglers. The parish church is dedicated to St Tydecho and dates from *c*1641 or even earlier, but it was greatly renovated in 1914. Its slatted belfry is set on a stone foundation, and the huge rib of a prehistoric mammal hangs over the wooden porch. On the south wall is a memorial to Dr John Davies, who produced a Latin/Welsh dictionary and – in defiance of the archbishop – insisted that the altar of

Mallwyd Church should be set in the centre of the building and not at the east end. The name of the Brigands' Inn recalls the escapades of the Red-Headed Men of Mawddwy, who terrorized the area during the 16thc and were responsible for pillaging and multiple murders before a large proportion of them was captured and hanged.

MANORBIER, Dyfed *19 SS09*
A small seaside village overlooking Manorbier Bay, Manorbier offers a sandy beach and safe bathing. The parish church is of Norman origin and carries a 13th-c tower. The north transept is of early-English style, and both the Barri Chapel and the north aisle were added in the 14thc. The chancel, south transept, and south aisle date from the 15thc. About ½m SW on Old Castle Head is King's Quoit, a prehistoric burial chamber capped by a stone 15ft long by 9ft wide. Manorbier Castle (OACT) is a moated Norman structure which dates from *c*12thc and is thought to have been more of a baronial residence than a fortress. It has unusually spacious living quarters, and was originally built by Gerald de Windsor, a constable of Pembrokeshire during the reign of Henry I. Most of the castle today is of 13th-c workmanship (see special inset opposite).

MARCHWIEL, Clwyd *11 SJ34*
Situated close to Wrexham this small village is the location of the town's modern industrial estate. The community formerly belonged to the monastery of Bangor Monachorium, 2m away, and it is claimed that a great eisteddfod was held there during the reign of Edward III. The parish church was entirely rebuilt in 1778, when an armorial window by Francis Eginton and dedicated to the local Yorke family was installed. The transept was added in 1829. Marchwiel Hall was once the seat of the Broughton family, who played a leading part in the civil war.

MARFORD, Clwyd *7 SJ35*
Dormitory village for Wrexham and Chester, Marford lies 5m NE of Wrexham

and occupies a pleasant hillside position overlooking the Cheshire Plain. The quaint gingerbread houses of the old village are somewhat swamped by newer development. These houses, with their iron-latticed windows and ogee arches, were originally thatched and are pleasantly grouped around the Trevor Arms Hotel. Blocked up windows recall the iniquitous window tax. The village dates from the early 19thc and is attributed to the Boscawen family, who lived at Trevalyn Hall alongside Marford Mill at the foot of the hill. It was a unique community in being an island parish of Flintshire, totally surrounded by Denbighshire. Boundary reorganization in 1974 ironed out this oddity and brought it under the administrative roof of Clwyd.

MARGAM, Mid Glamorgan *25 SS78*
On the E outskirts of Port Talbot and ¼m up a side road N of the A48 is Margam's 12th-c Cistercian abbey. The nave now forms the parish church and includes a late-Norman doorway plus effigied tombs and Celtic crosses. There are also slight remains of 16th-c domestic buildings. The old School House now contains the Margam Stones Museum (OACT) and displays early-Christian memorial stones. Both the mountains and the sea are very near, with the Mynydd Margam and Moel Ton-Mawr overlooking sandy Margam Burrows and the giant Margam Abbey steelworks. Prehistoric burial mounds and camps can be seen in the vicinity.

MARLOES, Dyfed *18 SM70*
Leech gathering for the doctors of Harley Street was once a lucrative industry in this fishing village. Nowadays its main concerns are fishing, and the conversion of the brown rubbery seaweed for which the area is renowned into laver bread. The good beach comprises a 1m stretch of flat sand backed by rugged cliffs, and the difficult descent from the village ensures that it is normally uncrowded. Several off-shore islands with Scandinavian-sounding names include Skomer, Skokholm, and Grassholm. All of these bear traces of prehistoric and Roman habitation, although they are now for the most part bird sanctuaries under the care of the Welsh Naturalists' Trust. There is an iron-age promontory fort in the area known as the Deer Park. The parish church is of Norman origin, and has a 19th-c baptistry sunk into the floor. Tradition claims that there was an even earlier church on this site, but it is said to have been destroyed by the sea.

MATHERN, Gwent *26 ST59*
Mathern lies about 3m S of Chepstow and has a parish church dedicated to St Trewdric – a 6th-c Welsh chieftain who was put to death by pagan Saxons. The 13th-c nave has a window which still retains fragments of the original glass, but the stately west tower is a 15th-c addition. Mathern Palace was the official country residence of the Bishops of Llandaff. It is partly of 15th-c origin and carries a low tower. Other features include charming oriel windows. The garden was laid out by H Avray Tipping in 1890. Tipping, a great authority on the 17th-c carver Grinling Griffiths, lived in the palace and undertook its careful restoration. Another beautiful old house in the vicinity is Moynes Court, which was

The intricate Great Cross of Conbelin from Margam.

rebuilt in the 17thc by Francis Godwin, a Bishop of Llandaff. The gatehouse includes two square towers and is much older than the rest of the house. Moynes Court stands to the left of the M4 as the road heads towards Newport.

MATHRY, Dyfed *16 SM83*
A legend attached to this village, situated 2m inland from Abercastle, relates the story of seven children who were born at the same time to a local couple. The father, unable to support them in addition to his already large

family, was about to drown them in the river when they were rescued by St Teilo. They subsequently became known as the Seven Saints of Mathry. Nearby Trefin includes the remains of an old mill that was immortalized by the Welsh bard Crwys.

MEIFOD, Powys *11 SJ11*
Sited on the River Vyrnwy at the head of the Meifod Valley, the village of Meifod has been in the news for some years on account of a proposal from Manchester University to mount a gigantic radio

telescope on the mountain top above the village. The project looks like being abandoned on account of the steep rise in cost. Meifod is a historic village by reason of its association with the princes of Powys, some of whom were buried here – notably Madog, who went over to Henry II of England and was in the end assassinated at the instigation of his English wife. The princes of Powys held their court 2m away at Mathrafal. A mound bowered in trees is all that now remains of their former palace. Dolobran Hall, 1m from Mathrafal off the Pont

A PLACE OF PEACE
Modern historians owe a great deal of their knowledge of Wales in the late 12thc to the lively account written by Giraldus Camrensis, or Gerald of Wales, during his journey through the country in 1188 with Archbishop Baldwin in an attempt to recruit soldiers for the Third Crusade. His remarks were shrewd, often amusingly expressed, and in many cases, still surprisingly relevant. Nowhere is his descriptive style better seen than in the description of his home and birthplace, Maenor Pyrr, 'the pleasantest spot in Wales', as he calls it.

Visitors to the castle will have their own views on the subject, but they will readily agree that Manorbier is unique. It is a place of undisputed peace, where it is difficult to reconstruct the scenes and atmosphere of siege and surrender when the lawn that covers the inner ward is bordered with banks of hypericum and hydrangeas. The reason is that part of the castle is a private residence, and the resultant combination of ruin and garden is rare, refreshing, and singularly appropriate when it is considered that the military history is extremely slight. The building owes its existence to a country that was far from peaceful and under constant threat of attack and retaliation. The Norman conquest of south-west Wales could only be secured by strategically-placed fortresses, some-times of formidable size, such as

Pembroke. Pembroke's castellan at the end of the 11thc was Gerald de Windsor, who had married Nest – daughter of Rhys ap Tewdwr, and a woman of such beauty that she was called the 'Helen of Wales'. Their daughter Angharad married a William de Barri, whose Norman father had held the lordship of Manorbier, and from the union there were several sons of whom Gerald was the only one who did not follow the family tradition by taking to arms. He became a priest instead. His own description of himself as 'sprung from the princes of Wales and from the Barons of the Marches', hints at his strained allegiance. Uncertainty appears at times in his *Description of Wales*, particularly where he advises the Normans how best to conquer Wales and almost simultaneously the Welsh how to resist such an attack.

His struggle with Henry II to establish an Archbishopric of St David's, by which the Welsh Church would become independent, was as ill fated as Owain Glyndwr's attempt in the 15thc. The failure to achieve this prime ambition was a bitter disappointment, and the attempt suggests that Giraldus' true interest was in favour of the Welsh cause.

Most of the structure that can be seen at Manorbier today was built in the 12th and 13thc by the de Barri family, who lived there until the middle of the 14thc. For a short time it was in the possession of Margaret Beaufort, who was born at Pembroke Castle in 1437 and later gave birth to Henry Tudor.

Richard Fenton, the Pembrokeshire traveller and writer of the late 18thc, described Manorbier as 'The most perfect model of an old Norman baron's residence, with all its appendages, church, mill, dovehouse, ponds, park, and grove still to be seen or traced.' There is certainly enough evidence of the domestic as well as the religious aspects of life at Manorbier to help the visitor reconstruct the quality of life in a privileged medieval environment. Models of the incarcerated priests, far from being a plastic intrusion, are an extremely effective reminder of the less civilized aspects of the period.

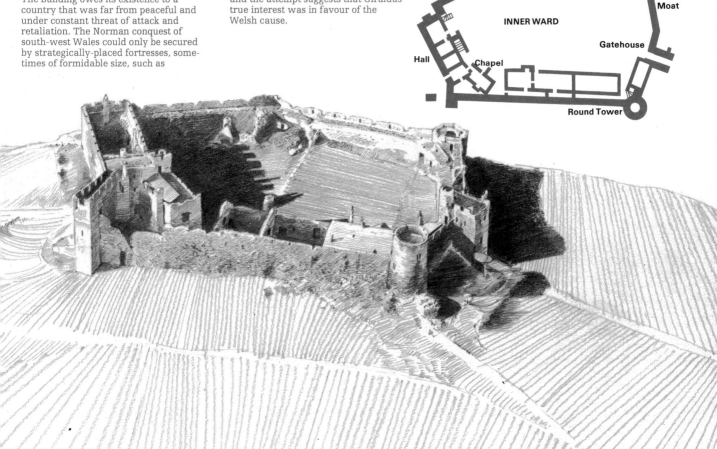

237

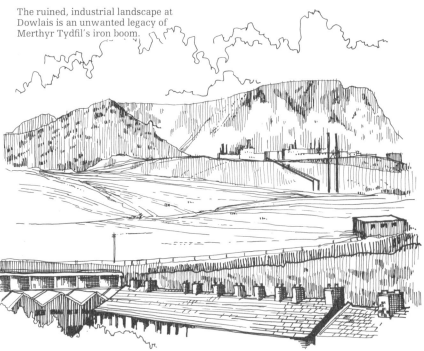

The ruined, industrial landscape at Dowlais is an unwanted legacy of Merthyr Tydfil's iron boom.

Robert road, was the original home of the Lloyds who founded Lloyds Bank. An ineradicable stain on the floor of one of the rooms is said to be blood resulting from the murder of a Lloyd wife's lover by her husband in the 18thc.

*MENAI BRIDGE, Gwynedd   5 SH57
Although it celebrates its 150th birthday in 1976, the bridge which spans the Menai Strait is still as breathtakingly spectacular as it must have been when it opened to a grateful public in 1826. Telford, the son of a Scottish shepherd and a man with little academic training, left no greater monument to his engineering genius than this graceful structure – which still ranks as one of the world's finest. Telford had engineered the A5 road from Shrewsbury to Bangor, a remarkable highway if only for its absence of severe gradients, but met his greatest challenge when it came to crossing the Menai Strait. His assignment was not made easier by Admiralty insistence that the bridge should be 100ft above high-water mark to allow the free passage of tall-masted ships.

Work started in 1819 and the piers, which show a decided Egyptian influence, were built of a local limestone often called Anglesey marble. The first chain went up in 1825 amidst great celebration, with two fifers playing lively tunes to keep the workmen in rhythm as they hoisted the chain. In the following weeks 444 vertical rods were placed in position. The bridge was opened without ceremony on 30 January 1826, and the first vehicle across was the London to Holyhead Royal Mail coach. The bridge was strengthened between 1938 and 1941 to meet modern traffic needs, and will soon be supplemented by the provision of a roadway 1m S above the Britannia Railway Bridge. The bridge cost £120,000 and only four men lost their lives. It was bad business for the people who operated the various ferries across the straits, and £25,557 in compensation was paid out to the owner of the nearest ferry, Miss Jane Silence Williams, later Lady Erskine.

The death of the ferry trade went unlamented by the travelling public. It was a hazardous crossing, particularly with coach horses, which were liable to take fright in stormy weather and fall overboard, putting passengers lives in jeopardy.

The town of Menai Bridge is the gateway to the enchanting island of Anglesey. The visitor will quickly sense the atmosphere of an island, although it is only separated from the mainland by narrow straits, at some points not much wider than a large river. He exchanges the wild craggy heights of Snowdonia for the gentler landscapes of Anglesey, the more languorous climate and the more tolerable pace of life. To gain the best impression of Anglesey he is advised to avoid the busy A5 road, which acts like a tarmacadam ribbon through largely featureless countryside.

Menai Bridge is virtually a one-street town that has developed since the spanning of the straits. It is largely Victorian in character and untypical of Anglesey, but provides some pleasant walks for people wishing to view the bridge from ground level. The most popular is under the bridge and W along the Belgian Promenade, built by Belgian refugees during the 1914 to 1918 war. Here the violent change in tide, which varies by as much as 20ft, can be seen. A causeway allows access to the diminutive Church of St Tysilio. The saint lived a hermit life on this island when it was less accessible. Finely-worked slate headstones exist near the churchyard gate. Two recent innovations in Menai Bridge are the Tegfryn Art Gallery, privately-owned and exhibiting contemporary paintings, and the Museum of Childhood, another privately-owned museum which has made a serious study of toys through the ages.

MERTHYR-CYNOG, Powys   21 SN93
Surrounded by open moors and artillery ranges, this village stands on a site where St Cynog founded a settlement in the

4thc. The parish church is mostly Norman but has a 14th-c screen with a powdering of painted red roses, now only dimly visible. Near by is Yscair-fechan, a former seat of the Vaughan family. This includes an Elizabethan porch. A Tudor farmhouse known as Bailybirth retains its original door, a masterpiece of craftsmanship.

MERTHYR MAWR, Mid Glamorgan
25 SS87
This picturesque village on the River Ogmore lies in a secluded setting and has many thatched cottages. It is mentioned in the 9th-c manuscript *The Book of Llan Dav*, but there is nothing in the village itself which relates to that period. The Church of St Teilo has been recently modernized but retains a few worn medieval effigies and an octagonal font which is said to be many centuries old. A medieval four-arched bridge which spans the Ogmore here has two apertures into which farmers traditionally pushed their sheep to wash them at sheep-dipping time.

Merthyr Mawr House stands farther downstream and has a ruined oratory known as St Roque's Chapel. A collection of stone fragments collected in the area includes two inscribed stones known as the Conbelanus Cross and the Dobilaucus Cross or Goblin Stone, and is kept in the grounds. Woods near the coast contain ruined 15th-c Candleston Castle. Merthyr Mawr Warren lies on the Ogmore estuary and was once inhabited. It has now been engulfed by sand driven by the powerful Atlantic winds. Sand movement has also unearthed a number of prehistoric remains, including La Tene period brooches. Some of these are exhibited in the Museum of the Royal Institute at Swansea. It is thought that a neolithic settlement existed in the area. A tumulus 50ft in diameter and 21ft high marks a spot where six burial chambers were found.

MERTHYR TYDFIL, Mid Glamorgan
21 SO00
Merthyr Tydfil takes its name from St Tydfil, daughter of the Lord of Brycheiniog (Brecon) who was martyred for her Christian faith by pagans in AD 480. Tradition states that heathen Saxons slew her and three of her brothers while the family was praying. Situated in the Taff Valley, this was a market town of some importance in the 12thc and played a considerable part in the wars against the Norman invaders – as ruined Morlais Castle indicates. It later became a coalmining town, and records show local iron workings here as early as the 16thc. However, it was not until the 19thc that the potential of the town's natural iron resources was realized and the community expanded. By 1831 Merthyr Tydfil had become the largest town in Wales, and four large ironworks had been set up by pioneers Josiah Guest, Richard Crawshay, and their contemporaries. In 1804 the first steam locomotive made its journey between Merthyr Tydfil and Abercynon, built by the Cornish engineer Richard Trevithick. Penydarren Works shortly produced the first rails to be made in Wales, for the Liverpool and Manchester railway, and later made cables for the Menai Bridge.

Pay was low in these early days and Merthyr Tydfil was the scene of bitter riots in 1802, when troops were called in to restore order. A man known as Dic Penderyn was accused of murder during these riots, and despite his protests of innocence was found guilty, and hanged at Cardiff. Injustice had, in fact, been done; the real murderer confessed many years later. There were more riots in 1816 and 1831, but the situation gradually resolved itself.

After the first world war heavy industry moved out of the town to areas near the coastal seaports, and Merthyr Tydfil was left in a desperate situation with half the population unemployed. Various parliamentary acts designed to alleviate such eventualities helped to ease the town's economic crisis after the second world war, and the community is now supported by light industries and some coalmining. Cyfartha Castle was built in 1825 as a residence for Richard Crawshay, owner of the Cyfartha Ironworks, and now serves the town as a museum and art gallery. The parish Church of St Tydfil is of 14th-c origin but has undergone a great deal of alteration. It contains three inscribed stones, one of which dates from around the 9thc. An iron bridge over the Taff is believed to be the oldest in existence. Dr Joseph Parry the composer was born in Merthyr Tydfil in 1814, and Kier Hardy the pioneer of socialism was the town's MP during the early years of the 20thc. To the N of the town is the Brecon Beacons national park and the Penmoelallt Forest nature reserve.

MIGNEINT, Gwynedd *9 SH74*
A roughly rectangular area about 5m by 10m, the corners of the Migneint touch Ffestiniog, Trawsfynydd, Llyn Celyn, and the upper Conwy Valley. The region comprises moorland and peat bog at an average height of 1,500ft, with a few isolated summits such as 1,765ft Carnedd Iago relieving the comparative flatness. Numerous bogs and streams drain into four main exits – the Afon Prysor, which flows through Llyn Trawsfynydd; the Tryweryn flowing through Llyn Celyn; the Conwy, the source of which is Llyn Conwy on the edge of the area; the Cynfal, which later enters the Vale of Ffestiniog. An idea of how bleak and inhospitable the whole area is given by its name *Migneint*, meaning 'the swampy place'. Local geology is the same as the Rhinog group – *ie* Cambrian-age grits and sandstones – so there are no quarries or mines. Neither are there any hill farms, except in the deeper, more sheltered valleys. About half of the Migneint belongs to the National Trust as part of the Ysbyty Estate.

MILFORD HAVEN, Dyfed *18 SM90*
Milford Haven is situated on steeply sloping ground on the N shores of a drowned valley also called Milford Haven. The present town dates back to the late 18thc, when it was developed as a naval dockyard and fishing port under the direction of Charles Greville, nephew of Sir William Hamilton. Hamilton owned the land on which it was built and was the husband of Nelson's Emma. In the early 19thc Nelson himself visited the town at the invitation of Greville. He is reputed to have laid a foundation stone in the parish Church of St Katherine, and to have presented it with a Bible and prayer book. The town suffered a setback in its development when the naval dockyard was removed to Pembroke Dock in 1814. This move was in spite of the fact that many fine ships had been built here in a short space of time. The town then developed as a deep-sea fishing port, and was at one time noted as the port with the fourth greatest catch of fish in Britain. To the N of the town are the remains of Pill Priory, built at the beginning of the 13thc by Adam de la Roche. Other features include the Friends' Meeting House, the Town Hall, and attractive gardens.

The Haven itself is a 2m-long – and in some places 2m-wide – valley which was submerged at the end of the Ice Age, forming a natural harbour described by Nelson as being the best in the world. Defoe recorded that '1,000 ships may ride in it, and not the top mast of one may be seen from another'. Right back in prehistoric times it held a place of great strategic importance. In the past it was a place from which to raid the surrounding countryside and for the use of pirates and smugglers. It was often used as a springboard from which to invade England, as Henry Tudor did when he landed on its shores in 1485 to end the Wars of the Roses at the Battle of Bosworth. During the civil wars it sheltered the parliamentary fleet. In more recent times, during the second world war, a total of 170,000 ships sailed from here in convoys. The Haven's main industry today is the refining of oil, with four great oil refineries and one of the largest oil-fired power stations in Britain around its shores.

1 Friend's Meeting House
2 Pill Priory Ruins
3 St Katherine's Church
4 The Rath (gardens)
5 Town Hall

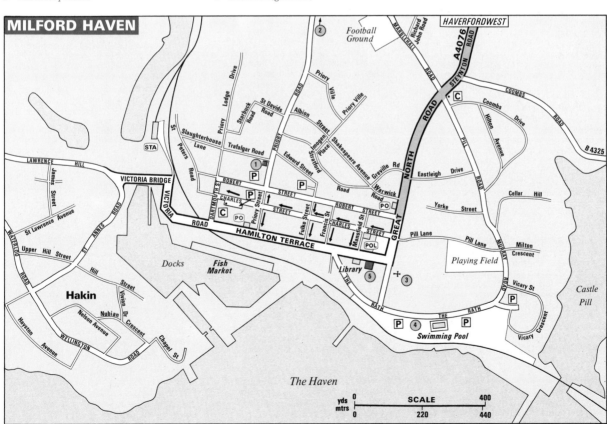

MINERA, Clwyd *7 SJ25*
One of the oldest-established communities in the Wrexham area, Minera has a landscape which still bears witness to centuries of exploitation of its mineral wealth. Its name is of Latin origin, and deposits that have been extracted here include lead, lime, coal, and silica. Lead was extensively worked for many centuries, and more than a hundred shafts still survive. The deepest is 1,380ft. The whole area is fascinating ground for the industrial archaeologist. A nearby public house with the incongruous name of 'City Arms' is a reminder of the time when the lead industry had close associations with the City of Chester. The present church was built in 1864, but the original church – a chapel of ease – dates back to 1597. A picturesque route leads across wild moorland from Minera to World's End, a popular beauty spot, and thence eventually to Llangollen.

MOELFRE, Gwynedd *5 SH58*
Quaint is an overworked adjective in tourist literature, but is the only word to sum up Moelfre – an Anglesey fishing village with its one street winding about the cove. The community has a long and glorious history in lifeboat rescues. In 142 years it has saved more than 600 lives and earned three gold, four silver, and eight bronze awards for outstanding rescues. One of the most remarkable was in October 1959, when the coaster 'Hindlea' with a crew of eight was driven on to the Moelfre rocks in a gale of more than 100mph. This epic rescue was 100 years to the day after one of the greatest sea tragedies of all time, the wrecking of the 'Royal Charter' on the same rocks. It was a disaster of 'Titanic' proportions, 452 passengers and crew losing their lives and only 30 surviving.
'Royal Charter' was within a few hours of the end of the long voyage from Melbourne, Australia. After battling across the Irish Sea in the worst gale of the century, she hove to off Point Lynas and signalled for a pilot to take her into Liverpool. The seas were too heavy for a pilot to board her, so the captain was faced with the dilemma of making his way through the storm to Liverpool or sheltering in Moelfre Bay. He chose to shelter, but the storm separated the ship from the anchor and drove her stern foremost on to the rocks. Moelfre woke up the following morning to a scene of unbelievable destruction. For weeks afterwards bodies were being washed up. A memorial overlooks the spot where the 'Royal Charter' met its end, and in Llanallgo Churchyard is a granite obelisk.

A neighbouring beach, Traeth Bychan, is associated with another sea tragedy – the sinking of the submarine HMS 'Thetis' in 1939. While on engineering trials from Birkenhead the 'Thetis' failed to surface in Liverpool Bay, and only four men escaped before the emergency hatch flooded, trapping the remaining 99 men. The submarine was beached at Traeth Bychan and later served in the war as HMS 'Thunderbolt'.

MOEL HEBOG, Gwynedd *9 SH54*
Moel Hebog, or Hill of the Hawk, lies 2m SW of Beddgelert and consists of both extrusive and intrusive igneous rocks. At 2,566ft it is the highest point in the group of mountains to the W and SW side of Snowdon. From Beddgelert and the Glaslyn valley Moel Hebog appears as a sharp-pointed peak with crags and a very rocky E slope. The W slopes are rounded and grass-covered all the way to the summit. This may offer an easier ascent, although there are no tracks; the recognized approach is via the track from Cwm Cloch Farm on the NE side.

MOEL SIABOD, Gwynedd *5 SH75*
The 'Hill of Siabod' rises to 2,860ft and lies 2m S of Capel Curig. It forms the S side of the Nantygwryd Valley and is situated diagonally opposite the Glyders. Local geology comprises intrusive igneous rocks of the Capel Curig lavas group overlying Ordovician slates. An impressive mountain from any angle, it appears pyramidal from the Llugwy Valley between Betws-y-coed and Capel Curig, but no more than a long high ridge on the road from Capel Curig to Penygwryd. This is partly due to the contrast between the smooth grass-covered NW and W slopes and the craggy, scree-covered E side, where a glacial cwm has cut deeply into the heart of the mountain. This aspect of Moel Siabod can be seen only from the high ground between the Llugwy and Lledr valleys, or from the hills S of the latter. The cwm contains a lake called Llyn-y-Foel, and there are remains of an old quarry near by. The views from Moel Siabod are magnificent, but the mountain is also known for the bronze-age relic found on its slopes – a circular bronze shield which is now to be seen in the British Museum.

MOELWYNS, Gwynedd *9 SH64*
These three peaks overlook the Llyn Stwlan Storage Reservoir SW of Blaenau Ffestiniog. They are 2,527ft Moelwyn Mawr, the highest point between the Snowdon group and Cader Idris; 2,334ft Moelwyn Bach; and 2,124ft Moel-yr-hydd. To the NW is another famous mountain, the 2,265ft Cnicht. Seen from the Moelwyns it is just a long, narrow craggy ridge above Cwm Croesor, but from Porthmadog and the reclaimed Glaslyn Valley it stands out as a pyramidal peak. It has been suggested that the name is a corruption of the English word 'knight', as the shape of the mountain appears to resemble that of a 14th-c knight's basinet helmet.

MOLD, Clwyd *7 SJ26*
Formerly the county town of Flintshire, Mold has emerged as the administrative centre of Clwyd – the re-organized county which constitutes the old counties of Flintshire and Denbighshire. Mold's emergence as the seat of administrative power in the enlarged county can be attributed largely to the building of the Shire Hall in 1967, an interesting piece of civic one-upmanship attractively sited in a rural setting E of the town. The crown courts dispense justice for a wide area of N Wales from an equally modern building alongside.

Mold itself – Yr Wyddgrug in Welsh – is a busy little market town serving the farming area which is sandwiched between the heavily industrialized regions of Deeside to the N, and Wrexham. The town is seen at its liveliest on Wednesdays, when the spacious main street is crowded with market stalls. A dominant feature of the town centre is the parish Church of St Mary, which occupies an elevated site and has been brought more into the scheme of things with the removal of nearby buildings. One of the handsomest churches in the St Asaph Diocese, this was built in 1485 by Lady Margaret Beaufort – of the influential Stanley family. The Manx arms of three legs which appear in a window and on one of the corbels arises from the Stanley's connection with the Isle of Man. Features include excellent carvings, a splendid roof, a Burne-Jones window, and a wealth of interesting memorials. The tower was added in 1773. Richard Wilson, father of the English landscape painters, is buried near the north door, and is commemorated by a window.

Bailey Hill is now a recreation ground with tennis courts and was the site of a Norman motte-and-bailey castle in the 12thc. Nothing now remains of this building. It is thought there may have been a prehistoric fort in this area, but the only notable find in Mold has been a bronze-age ceremonial cape of gold, draped around a male skeleton which was unearthed in 1833 and is now in the British Museum. Mold was the birthplace of the Welsh novelist Daniel Owen (1836 to 1895), who virtually introduced the novel to Wales and was recognized as a craftsman in the Welsh language. He wrote mainly of contemporary Welsh life and has been favourably compared with Thomas Hardy and Charles Dickens. One of his best-known works is *Gwen Tomos*. Clwyd County Council plan to establish a Daniel Owen room in their cultural centre, using fixtures and fittings from his original tailor's shop in Mold.

About 1m W of Mold is the Allelujah Monument, an obelisk erected by Nehemiah Griffith in 1736 to mark the spot where the pagan Saxons and Picts were defeated in AD 430. The war cry of the victorious Christian army is reputed to have been 'Allelujah', uttered with such gusto that the Saxons fled. The Tower lies 1½m S and is a house dating from 1380, but it has been greatly restored. Originally a small fortified border house, it is said to have been the place where a Welsh chieftain hanged the captured Mayor of Chester from a staple in 1450.

MONMOUTH, Gwent *23 SO51*
Monmouth received its charter in 1550, and since then has served as a borough and market town for its neighbourhood. It has many Tudor and Georgian buildings in a network of old streets. Three rivers flow round the town, the Trothy, Monnow, and Wye. The town is sited where the River Monnow flows into the Wye, an important strategic position from which the whole of S Wales could be controlled. The Romans had a station known as *Blestium* near Monmouth, an important link in the chain that ran one way through Caerwent and Caerleon, and another way to Wrexham, Caersws, and Chester. The first lords of Monmouth were Bretons, then the lordship passed to the House of Lancaster in 1256, who built walls, strengthened the castle, and erected Monnow Bridge.

Monnow Bridge is one of Monmouth's prized possessions and the only Norman fortified bridge to survive in Britain. The fortified tower is on the bridge itself and was built in 1260 as one of the four medieval gates into the town. The bridge has three semicircular arches with a total span of 38yds, and each arch has three wide ribs. Originally constructed for pedestrians and horses only, it was licensed for tolls by Edward I. Edward I took Gwent, alone among the territories administered by the Marcher lords, into the kingdom of England after the fall of the last native prince of Wales at the end of the 13thc. This recognized the extreme military importance of the area. More than anywhere else in the Borderlands known as the Marches, Monmouthshire has remained mostly Welsh in the use of language and place-names. In the 20thc the legislation of Westminster has had to refer increasingly to Wales and Monmouthshire together in educational and parliamentary matters, and for recruitment of the Welsh Guards.

Wales has now recovered one of its lost provinces, and the county is once more known by its title of Gwent. The original castle here was probably a simple wooden structure on a motte, but no definite trace of either remains. Monmouth was listed in the *Domesday Book* of 1086 as part of Herefordshire, and was the headquarters of the Marcher Lordship of Monmouth. Henry Somerset,

son of the second Marquis of Worcester, built Great Castle House (AM) on the site of the old castle's Round Tower in 1673. By 1801 the house had become a girls' school, and in 1875 it started its career as the headquarters of the Royal Monmouthshire Engineer Militia. Restoration of the castle's medieval remains was begun by the government in 1913, and both castle and house are open to the public (see inset overleaf).

Shire Hall is situated in Agincourt Square and was built in 1724 on the site of an Elizabethan Market Hall. Until 1939 the Assizes were held here, and in 1839 John Frost and the Chartist leaders were tried here for high treason after the Newport riots. A statue of Henry V was placed in a recess of the wall of Shire Hall in 1792. Alongside this statue is one of Charles S Rolls, founder of Rolls Royce and a pioneer airman who was the first person to fly the Channel both ways without landing. Through the generosity of Charles Rolls' mother, Lady Llangattock, Monmouth's Nelson Museum contains a comprehensive collection of material associated with Lord Nelson – including sextants, Nelson's fighting sword, and models of his ships. To the E of the town a wooded hill known

as Kymin (NT) is surmounted by an 18th-c Round House and Naval Temple. The temple was visited by Nelson in 1802 and commemorates a galaxy of admirals unequalled by any other age or country. Excellent views over the Monnow and Wye valleys are afforded by Kymin.

The Local History Centre provides detailed information about the town's history and houses, including St Brides – a fine house with ceilings contemporary with those in Great Castle House. The parish Church of St Mary retains a decorated-style tower and spire, but the rest of the church was the work of G E Street in 1881, who replaced a Georgian church built by Francis Smith of Warwick. The Baptistry displays 15th-c tiles and a cresset stone from the original medieval building. The Church of St Thomas has a fine Norman chancel arch, an original north door, and a 19th-c pseudo-Norman porch. The interesting font and galleries were made from timber supplied by the Duke of Beaufort. The part of the town where St Thomas's Church is sited is known as Overmonnow, and was once a centre for cap-making. The close-fitting caps from here were the 'Monmouth Caps' mentioned in Shakespeare's *Henry V*. River Monnow has coarse fish and trout for the angler. Monmouth Agricultural Show is held at the end of August each year.

St Peter's Church at Dixton, near Monmouth, is on a site that was an ancient place of worship. The old Celtic name was Llandidwg, meaning the llan or enclosure of Didwg, probably a monk who evangelized this district for the Celtic church. Normans re-dedicated the church to St Peter in the 12thc, but kept the founder's name and referred to St Peter, Tydiuc. By c1250 the 'Ty' had been dropped and it was St Peter's Diuc'ston. The name then evolved through Dukeston, Duxton, to Dixton by the 15thc. The original building was probably destroyed when Gruffydd ap Llywelyn raided the district in 1054, and the herring-bone masonry of c1080 in the north wall of the nave may date from the time of its rebuilding. It was attached to the Benedictine priory in Monmouth until the Dissolution in the 16thc, and was restored twice in the 19thc. This church has been subject to severe flooding, and brass plates on the north side of the chancel arch record heights of three high floods.

*MONTGOMERY, Powys 14 SO29
Once a county capital, modern Montgomery retains its distinctive character and atmosphere. Broad Street is one of the widest streets anywhere – almost a vast square with the red brick Town Hall filling the far end and artistically closing the vista. The town is full of Tudor, Jacobean, and Georgian houses, and has some lovely Regency windows. Part of its charm is the diversity of its buildings, and though Georgian predominates it is full of quaint corners, slopes, and steps.

cont overleaf

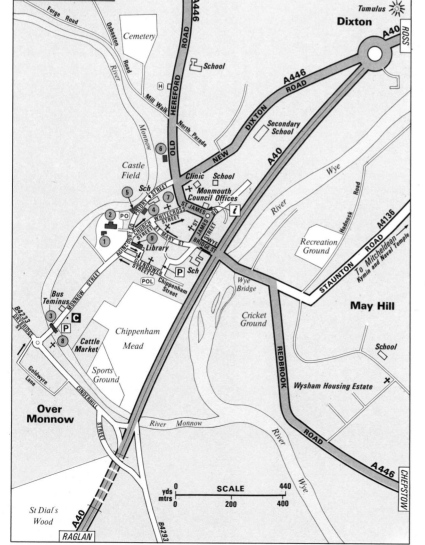

1 Castle Ruins
2 Great Castle House
3 Monnow Bridge & Gatehouse
4 Monmouth Priory Ruins
5 Nelson Museum & Local History
   Centre
6 St Bride's House
7 St Mary's Parish Church
8 St Thomas' Church
9 Shire Hall

Of course the town has its new additions, and one of the most delightful of these is a little parterre garden alongside Arthur Street, recently designed and laid out by the local council and provided with seats. The old jail is still in existence but has now been turned to commercial use. The parish Church of St Nicholas stands high on a bank on the town's E edge, and was built only a few years after Montgomery's Royal Charter was granted by King Henry III in 1227. Like so many other churches it underwent restoration in the 19thc, but its two 15th-c nave roofs, the double screen, the Herbert and Mortimer figures, and the canopied First Elizabethan Herbert tomb have all survived intact. In the churchyard is the well-known Robber's Grave, in which lies John Newton Davies who was hanged for a murder which he claimed he never committed. He declared that his innocence would be proved by the fact that the grass would not grow over his grave for 100 years. That was in

1821, and even now there is a bare cruciform patch on the top of the mound. The 1,000ft Town Hill is crowned by the old county war memorial, a white stone obelisk which can be seen for miles around. The original Norman motte-and-bailey castle built by Roger de Montgomery in 1702 stood at the foot of Castle Hill. It was captured by the Welsh, retaken by the Normans under Baldwyn de Boller, and subsequently held by William Rufus during the border battles. The second castle was erected on the hill top during the reign of Henry III and originally consisted of five wards, possibly all walled, with a strong outer defensive wall encircling a smaller ward with a great round tower. Only fragments of a tower and portions of the walls, dating from c1225, are still standing. The castle was burned and badly damaged by the Welsh under Llywelyn the Great in 1228, but it remained in English hands and later became the home of the Herbert family. During the civil war Lord Herbert garrisoned it

on behalf of Charles I. He was easily ousted, but royalist forces were quick to besiege the parliamentarians who then held it. Their efforts were unsuccessful, and the castle was subsequently destroyed in 1649 by parliamentary order. The old Ministry of Works – now the DoE, has excavated large areas of the interesting site.

MORFA DYFFRYN, Gwynedd *9 SH52*
This Nature Conservancy Reserve lies 4m SW of Harlech and comprises 500 acres of salt marsh and sand dunes. A permit is required to visit the central and N areas.

MORFA HARLECH, Gwynedd *9 SH53*
Situated 2m NW of Harlech, this nature reserve is believed to have been the site of an ancient racecourse. It contains the Royal St David's Golf Course – said to be the first in Wales. A permit is required to visit any part of the reserve.

MORFA NEFYN, Gwynedd *8 SH24*
A village on a small bay with a long

THE TUDOR CRADLE
The most renowned architectural feature of the town of Monmouth is the bridge gate over the Monnow, the only surviving example of such a fortification in Britain, and a reminder of the enmity that existed between the Welsh and English over several centuries. This is a legacy of the Norman conquest and the formation of key points of aggressive defence in Gwent by William Fitz Osbern, who had been created Earl of Hereford by William as early as 1067. Two of his strongholds were Chepstow and Monmouth. Whereas the former underwent an interesting process of evolution and development, the remains of Monmouth are disappointingly slight, especially when it is remembered that this was the birthplace in 1387 of the future King Henry V. Henry's 'romantic hero' image was portrayed by Shakespeare, and Fluellen likens the town to Maçedon – not only because of the great men born in them, but because a river flows through the two 'and there are salmons in both'.

Found guilty of conspiracy against the king, William Fitz Osbern's son and successor forfeited both Chepstow and Monmouth to the crown. In 1256 Henry III gave Monmouth to his son, the future King Edward I, in whose hands it remained for ten years until his younger brother Edmund was created Earl of Lancaster. Edmund was granted not only this castle but the 'Three Castles' of Grosmont, White Castle, and Skenfrith in the neighbourhood. This was just a small porportion of the enormous Welsh property accumulated during the 14thc by the Dukes of Lancaster, one of whom was John of Gaunt. At death his nephew King Richard II confiscated his estates, thereby depriving John of Gaunt's son Henry of Lancaster, who was already exiled by the king, of his inheritance.

Henry returned to this country, and with the support and allegiance of a large number of discontented nobles forced Richard to surrender at Flint Castle. Parliament declared him king, and the Lancaster inheritance was brought into the same line of succession as the crown.

Slighted during the civil wars, Monmouth came into the possession of the future third Marquis of Worcester. His other properties included Chepstow and Raglan, and in 1673 he erected Great Castle House on the site of a demolished tower. This house was sufficiently handsome to culminate the history of so historic a castle, the only remains of which are the hall and Great Tower. The latter is reminiscent in shape and setting of William Fitz Osbern's keep above the Wye at Chepstow.

GREAT CASTLE HOUSE

Site of Castle Gate

Great Tower

Hall

Modern Buildings

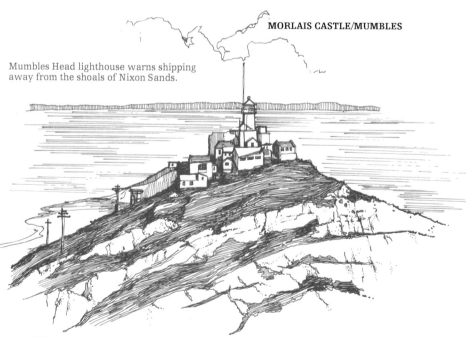

Mumbles Head lighthouse warns shipping away from the shoals of Nixon Sands.

sweep of sand sheltered by rugged headlands, Morfa Nefyn is a fine centre for cliff and shore walks and provides good bathing. The nearby hamlet of Porth Dinllaen, a picturesque cluster of cottages, was a busy coastal trading centre during the 19thc and was once considered as a possible rail terminus point for Ireland. The prehistoric fort of Garn Boduan stands on one of the headlands.

MORLAIS CASTLE, Mid Glamorgan
21 SO00
A 13th-c ruin set on 1,252ft Morlais Hill to the N of Merthyr Tydfil, this castle was set up but never properly finished by Gilbert de Clare. De Clare was one of the Marcher barons who held Wales after its conquest by Edward I, probably c1287. It comprised a large round keep surrounded by four round towers and substantial earthworks on an outer bailey, but only part of the curtain round the inner bailey and two towers have survived. The remains of an old well-shaft can still be seen in the bailey, and one of the towers contains a room with a vaulted roof supported by a central pillar. The only historical mention of the castle relates to a violent legal dispute between de Clare and the Earl of Hereford, de Bohun. Edward I was so angered by their behaviour that he marched to Morlais, fined both participants, and confiscated much of their land.

MOSTYN, Clwyd   7 SJ18
Mostyn is the River Dee's last link with its maritime past. The restless shifting sands of the Dee estuary have made it unnavigable to all but small coasters calling at Mostyn Dock. At one time a regular ferryboat service plied between Liverpool and Mostyn, and it was also a coal trading port with Ireland. Coal was once an important part of the industrial scene in this area, the seam being so shallow that it could be dug on the surface in parts. Nowadays the only coal mined is at Point of Air, which is 3m away in a bleak spot at the mouth of the estuary. Some of the workings go under the sea, and the colliery is one of only two remaining in N Wales. The other is Bersham near Wrexham.

Hidden away in woods above the Dee estuary is Mostyn Hall. This was the home of the Mostyns, who were descended from Welsh chieftains and connected to the royal house of Tudor. The Mostyns helped to change the course of British history by organizing the escape of one of their kinsmen from the troops of Richard III. Henry, Earl of Richmond, was about to take his place at dinner when the king's troops arrived and he had to make a quick escape through a window. When the officer in command questioned the extra place laid at the table he was told that it was the family's practice to keep a place for any unexpected guest. While the officer accepted their hospitality Henry completed his escape from the nearby port, and was later to become King Henry VII – defeating Richard III at Bosworth Field.

Laying an empty place at table became a family tradition, and the window through which Henry escaped was also preserved through subsequent alterations and additions, although it eventually looked into another room. Among the family treasures at Mostyn is a miniature silver harp awarded as a prize at the Caerwys

Eisteddfod in 1568. The Mostyn manuscripts are now in the National Library of Wales. An architectural novelty on the Whitford side of Mostyn Park is a castellated lodge built on the top of a bridge.

MOUNTAIN ASH, Mid Glamorgan
25 ST09
Every New Year's Eve is marked by road-running races through the streets of this Cynon-Valley town, 18m NW of Cardiff, and in neighbouring Penrhiwceiber. These are known as the *Nos Galan* (New Year's Eve) races. Nos Galan races were launched in 1958 with two races in Mountain Ash, and attracted 838 runners in 1966. Many Olympic runners have taken part, and the arrival of the 'Mystery Runner' – coming down a mountainside carrying a torch – is one of the big features. The idea of the Nos Galan races is believed to have arisen from the 'Round the Houses' race in Sao Paulo.

Local organizers decided to link their event with a celebrated Welsh runner of the 18thc. He was Guto Nyth Bran, real name Griffith Morgan, and was born near Porth at Llwyncelyn in 1700. The legend is that he could run from Porth to Llantrisant and back, a distance of 11m, in the time it took his mother to boil a kettle. He died in 1737 and is buried in the churchyard of Llanwonno, which is situated on a mountain top between Mountain Ash and the Rhondda Fach Valley. His grave bears a Welsh inscription and is near the west door of the church of St Gwynno.

The 'Mystery Runner' at each Nos Galan is selected the same evening from a short-list and taken to Llanwonno on a secret route. After a brief visit to Guto's grave, the runner carries a blazing torch 4m down the mountainside to light a beacon outside Mountain Ash Town Hall. The runner's name is not known until he or she leaves Llanwonno at 23.00hrs. The runner has always been a leading British athlete. Mary Rand was the first woman chosen for this event. The Nos Galan programme starts at 13.30hrs, when a runner leaves the City Hall in Cardiff with a message of goodwill from the city's mayor. He carries this 17m to Penrhiwceiber, where it is read to the crowd by a local council official. Mountain Ash itself is a colliery town

sited in the Cynon Valley, which played a most important part in the 19th-c industrial growth of S Wales. During this period its choir became famous throughout the country. The town was badly hit during the depression of the 1930's, and almost a quarter of the population were forced to move elsewhere to obtain work. Since the second world war new industries have been introduced, such as carpet making, the hand-weaving of cloth, and dressmaking, so the unemployment figures are now small. A number of prehistoric graves exist on the surrounding hills.

MOYLGROVE, Dyfed   17 SN14
Moylgrove is a small, well-kept village standing on the River Ceibwr 5m SW of Cardigan and 1m from the sea. To the NE a picturesque stretch of coastal cliffs terminates in Cemmaes Head, which overlooks Cardigan Bay. Ceibwr Harbour is in an attractive bay still used by small cargo ships. To the SW are two fine prehistoric cromlechs – Llech-y-Drybedd and Trellyffan. The latter has been compared to Tintagel in Cornwall. A nearby blowhole is known as the Witches' Cauldron, and a Chalybeate well called Ffynnon Alwm has waters said to be inferior only to those of Tunbridge Wells. Farther up the valley is the quiet little village of Monington.

MUMBLES, West Glamorgan   24 SS68
This fast developing resort encompasses the two Mumbles islets and Oystermouth. A beach of dark brown sand with small patches of rock allows access for safe bathing, and a variety of amusements and entertainments are offered by the 800ft 19th-c pier. Mumbles Head lighthouse, which warns shipping away from the shoals of Nixon Sands near the outer shore to the W, is famous for the exploits of the Ace sisters. These daughters of a lighthousekeeper waded into the surf to rescue a drowning sailor. Beneath the lighthouse is a cavern known as Bob's Cave. Oystermouth parish church is of Norman origin and houses a font dating from 1251. It also contains fragments of Roman pavement and three bells from the Cathedral of Santiago, which was destroyed by fire in 1863. Thomas Bowdler, renowned for his expurgation of Shakespeare and Gibbon, is buried in the churchyard. Some 200yds inland is 12th-c Oystermouth Castle.
cont overleaf

243

A horse-drawn tramway which was introduced to the area first carried passengers in 1807 and subsequently underwent modification. Steam locomotives were brought into use in the 19thc, and electrification followed in 1929. The railway was closed in 1960, and little trace of it now remains. There is some fine scenery to the W at the beginning of the Gower Peninsula, and excellent views extend over the Bristol Channel to the Devon and Somerset coast. Facilities offered by the resort include amenities for fishing, sailing, water ski-ing, and surfing.

MWNT, Dyfed   17 SN15
Under the management of the NT, this coastal area 4m N of Cardigan comprises the Mount of Mwnt and a small sandy beach set deep among the cliffs. This beach is said to have been the scene of a battle between the Welsh and the Flemings in 1155. A caravan and chalet site was destined to be set up there until the region was salvaged by the NT in 1970. At the foot of the hill is a charming, whitewashed, 14th-c church standing on the site of a Dark-Age chapel. The original font survives inside. The mount can be climbed by means of a steep, difficult path and affords fine views from the top.

MYDDFAI, Dyfed   21 SN73
Situated 3m S of Llandovery amid fine scenery on the River Bran, Myddfai has a quaint 14th- to 15th-c church dedicated to St Michael. The double nave, octagonal font, and barrel-vaulted roof are of interest. The hatchment of a local family, the Gwynne Holfords, can be seen on the chancel arch. Their Georgian home Cilgwyn stands 2m W. Myddfai is famous for the long line of physicians who lived here since 1200. According to legend a young farmer who lived 5m N near Llyn-y-Fan Fach Lake fell in love with a beautiful girl who inhabited its waters. He eventually persuaded her to abandon her home in the lake and marry him. She agreed, but stipulated that if he should strike her she would immediately return to her former habitat.

It was not until the five sons that they produced were almost fully grown that he forgot the warning and struck his wife, whereupon she vanished into the lake. Later she appeared to her sons and gave them details of how to cure illness. On the strength of this knowledge they became physicians and set up their homes in Myddfai, passing on their skills to their descendants. The last of these was Rhys ap Williams, who died in 1842. The 13th-c manuscript containing the information their mother is said to have given them is in existence and has been translated into English. It appears to be a manual of herbal lore.

MYNYDD CEFNAMWLCY, Gwynedd 8 SH23
Mynydd Cefnamwlcy is a megalithic burial chamber near the coast E of Pennlech, comprising three widely-spaced orthostats supporting a large capstone (full OS reference SH 227 339).

MYNYDD EPYNT, Powys   21 SN94
This area of moorland rises to a high scarp above the Irfon Valley W of Builth Wells and consists of folded beds of lower old-red sandstones of the Devonian period and older Silurian

shales and sandstones. Away from the ridge bleak undulating moorland extends back for several miles before the SE-facing drainage pattern breaks the slope into a series of spurs. These spurs become progressively more wooded, cultivated, and lower until they merge with the sides of the Usk Valley. The S end of this has an aspect of pleasant wooded hillsides, scattered farms, and peacefully winding river valleys.

Mynydd Epynt forms a roughly triangular area based on Builth Wells, Talgarth, and Llandovery. These boundaries are determined by the major rivers in the area – the Irfon to the N, the Wye to the E, and the Usk to the S. Unfortunately much of the area which is not agricultural is used by the army as a firing range, so it is very necessary to keep to the roads. Danger Areas cover almost the entire moorland, and the B4519 between Upper Chapel and Garth is closed when firing takes place. Remaining areas are forested. To the N of Brecon the slopes and summit – where a radio transmitter is located – of 1,495ft Ysgwydd Hŵch are covered by the small Brycheiniog Forest. In the W corner near Llandovery the slopes of the ridges overlooking the Bran Valley are concealed under the very extensive Crychan Forest.

MYNYDD-Y-CRAIR, RHIW, Gwynedd 8 SH22
Wild moorland of bracken and heather-covered rock overlooking the sea to the W of Porth Neigwl, this area is approachable only on foot. The moor climbs to an imposing pile of ancient dolomite rocks, the site of an iron-age defensive camp, which affords fine views of Porth Neigwl. The latter was known as Hell's Mouth Bay in the days of sail because once a ship had been driven into it by bad weather it had little chance of escape. Both the moor and the 16th-c manor house of Plas-Yn-Rhiw were donated to the NT by the Misses Keating. A romantic little garden containing a cobbled court, box and yew hedges, and falling water, surrounds the house and is glorious with wild roses, fuchsia, and azaleas at the appropriate time of year.

NANHORON, Gwynedd   8 SH23
This Lleyn village lies 4m N of Abersoch and occupies a significant place in the history of Welsh Nonconformism. Capel Newydd was built in 1769 and is the earliest surviving Nonconformist chapel in N Wales. It is to be found along a lane off the Mynytho to Nanhoron road. The signpost describes it as an 18th-c Dissenters' Meeting House, dissenters being the earlier name for Nonconformists. This simple chapel has an earth floor, candle lights, and box pews. At a time when Nonconformism did not enjoy the approval of the landed gentry, Capel Newydd was unusual in having the support of Lady Catherine Edwards of Nanhoron Hall. Special pews were reserved for her and her friends. Lady Catherine's conversion came about after she had been sheltered by Nonconformists at Portsmouth, where she had gone to meet her husband Captain Timothy Edwards, only to learn that he had died at sea.

NANTEOS, Dyfed   12 SN67
Nanteos (OACT) is a Georgian mansion in the Rheidol Valley, 3½m from Aberystwyth. It has been noted for the fact that among the treasures preserved

here was an old olive-wood cup which is believed to be the Cup of the Last Supper – the Holy Grail – brought to Britain by Joseph of Arimathea, and given to the monks of Glastonbury. At the Dissolution it was taken first to Strata Florida and then given into the safe keeping of the Powell family at Nanteos, where it has been ever since. The last of the Powells, Mrs Mirylees, has now taken the cup to her new home. Also at Nanteos there was a delightful little heart-shaped table given to Nelson for his cabin by Lady Hamilton. Dogs' graves, each with a stone and inscription, can be seen in the grounds of the mansion.

NANT FFRANCON, Gwynedd   5 SH66
It was not until the early 19thc that a proper road was built up to the summit of the Nant Ffrancon Pass at Ogwen. Before then walkers and riders had to use a series of rough steps to climb past the falls. Some of these can still be seen, together with a pack-horse bridge underneath the present bridge. Thomas Pennant described the feature as 'The most dreadful horse-path in Wales' in the 18thc. Nant Ffrancon means 'Vale of the Beavers', although beavers are known to have been extinct in this area since the 12th century. A road through the valley takes the E side below the slopes of 3,211ft Pen-yr-Oleu Wen. This is the only summit on the E side, and although the smooth sides of the valley are high there are no higher points above them – only a fairly even slope SE from Bethesda to the top of Carnedd Dafydd. The W side is well visible from the road and very different. Beyond Llyn Idwal and Glyder Fawr there is the craggy summit of 3,104ft Y Garn, followed by a 2,700ft ridge with 2,727ft Foel Goch, 2,665ft Mynydd Perfedd, and 2,695ft Carnedd-y-Filiast – eaten into to a height of 1,300ft by the vast Penrhyn slate quarries of Bethesda.

NANTGARW, Mid Glamorgan 26 ST18
Porcelain was manufactured under the control of William Billingsley at this tiny village in the Taff Valley about 150 years ago. Pieces bearing the name of Nantgarw are eagerly sought after as collectors items today.

NANT GWYNANT, Gwynedd   5 SH65
One of the finest of Snowdonia's valleys, the Nant Gwynant lies between Beddgelert and Penygwryd and features two of the better-known lakes – Llyn Dinas and Llyn Gwynant. From the road there are splendid views of Yr Aran, a peak of the Snowdon horseshoe rising to 2,451ft above Llyn Dinas. The bridge between Llyn Dinas and Llyn Gwynant is the starting point of Watkin Path, named after Sir Edward Watkin who gave the path for public use. Halfway up the cwm is a commemorative slab which marks the spot from where the prime minister, Mr W E Gladstone, addressed a large meeting at the opening of the path in 1892. Watkin Path passes through wooded slopes and beside numerous waterfalls on its way to Snowdon's peak. It is one of the most rewarding routes but it is also one of the most difficult, and climbing experience is necessary to reach the summit. The Nant Gwynant road passes Dinas Emrys, a group of pre-Roman hut circles located 2m N of Beddgelert.

NANT IRFON, Powys 13 SN85

Nant Irfon is a national nature reserve in the valley of the Irfon, some 5m N of Llanwrtyd Wells and just S of Llanerch-yrfa Farm. It covers an area of about 216 acres, comprising fine oak woods and moorland, and forms a sanctuary for birds such as buzzards, redstarts, and pied flycatchers. A permit is necessary to visit the reserve.

NANTLLE, Gwynedd 5 SH55

Largely disfigured by extensive slate quarrying, this area lies 4m E of Penygroes. The biggest and most prosperous quarry in the area was Dorothea, named after the wife of the first proprietor Richard Garnons. It was first worked in 1829 and was largely controlled by the local people. For more than a century it was run by the Williams family, but closed in 1970. It is now being developed as a tourist attraction.

NANT-Y-MOCH RESERVOIR, Dyfed 13 SN78

This is the largest of three reservoirs in the Rheidol hydro-electric project, and has a road along its SW shore which crosses the dam and affords splendid views of Plynlimon. The dam itself is impressive, and a car park overlooks both dam and lake. The surrounding slopes have been afforested, and the lake is well stocked with trout. Fly-fishing only is allowed and a permit is required.

NARBERTH, Dyfed 19 SN11

Centred on the market place, this small town of steep streets lies about 9m N of Tenby. The church was rebuilt in 1879 and incorporates a 13th-c tower. Narberth's Town Hall bears the royal arms. To the S of the town a mound bears the overgrown ruins of 13th-c Narberth Castle. This was probably built by Sir Andrew Perrot, the son of one of the first Norman invaders of Wales, and displays a single ward, impressive gateway, a round keep, and several round towers. It was later held by Roger Mortimer – the favourite of Edward II's wife Isabella – and finally 'slighted' after the civil war. The remains are on private land. About 2m S of Narberth at Templeton is Sentence Castle Mound, again on private land. This existed prior to the structure at Narberth and dates from the end of the 11thc. It was finally demolished in 1215 after capture by Llywelyn the Great.

Pwyll, Prince of Dyfed, is also said to have held court at 'Arberth Castle', and it is hotly disputed as to whether this refers to an earlier castle on the site of 13th-c Narberth Castle or to Sentence Castle. About 3m W over the Eastern Cleddau river is the semi-circular arched bridge of Canaston, with its projecting keystones. The 19th-c Blackpool cornmill lies 1m S of this. Evidence of early settlement in the area is found in round barrows at Redstone Cross to the N of Narberth, and Mollestone Camp to the SE.

*NEATH, West Glamorgan 25 SS79

This industrial town lies 5m NE of Swansea and operates large steel and tin-plate works both here and at Briton Ferry, at the mouth of the River Neath. The surrounding area is spoiled by the presence of collieries and works. Stretching away to the NE of the town, and in contrast to it, are wooded hills

Among the many treasures kept at Nanteos house was a small, olive-wood cup traditionally said to be the Holy Grail.

and narrow gorges which lead off the picturesque Vale of Neath. Many spectacular waterfalls rush down precipitous rock faces to fast flowing streams below. Particularly worthy of note are those of Glyn Neath and Ystrad Fellte, and the 80ft falls near Melin Court at Resolven, 6m NE of Neath. Within the town are the early-English Church of St Thomas and the modern Church of St David. The latter has a 152ft-high spire, known as Vaughan Tower after a local family. The Penscynor Bird Garden lies 2m NW of the A465 and features exotic species flying free and breeding in as natural surroundings as possible. Dogs are not allowed in the gardens.

Both the abbey and castle were founded by Richard de Granville in the early 12thc. Most of the abbey ruins (AM) date from the 14th and 17thc, when additions and alterations were made. At the time of the Dissolution it passed into the hands of the Cranwell family. Of the castle only the 13th-c main gateway, its two towers, and parts of the curtain wall remain. The site of the old Roman fort of *Nidium*, mentioned in the *Twelfth Journey of Antonius*, was discovered in 1949 during the excavation of a building site. It held a strategic position, accessible by both land and sea, and commanded the E-W route and entrance to the Vale of Neath. It is located near the Neath grammar school. The 18th-c Gnoll House was once the home of Sir Humphrey Mackworth, a great industrialist who founded the copper industry in the last century. This mansion is now the town's war memorial, and the 250 acres of Gnoll Woods are public parkland.

NEFYN, Gwynedd 8 SH34

An intimate little town on the N coast of Lleyn, Nefyn (or Nevin in English) now dreams of its celebrated sea-faring past. It was once claimed that there was only one place in Britain that had sent a higher percentage of its male population to sea than Nefyn, and her sturdy little sailing boats ploughed their way through the sea lanes of the oceans. Nefyn was also renowned for its herring

fishing, and the town's coat of arms incorporates three herrings. This fish has since mysteriously deserted Nefyn's waters, although there are plenty of other varieties to interest today's angler. Nefyn has a long history, and it is probably painful for patriotic Welshmen to recall that it was here that Edward I chose to celebrate his conquest of the Welsh.

In 1284 the English king held a Round Table followed by a tournament, and the site of the lists can still be traced. In 1353 the Black Prince, Edward I's great grandson, made it one of the ten royal boroughs of N Wales, and in 1356 he granted it to Nigel de Loryng in appreciation for his assistance at the Battle of Poitiers. Nefyn today rests on its reputation as a quiet resort commanding a wide sweep of golden sand which allows access for safe bathing. At the opposite end of the bay Porth Dinllaen glints invitingly in the sun, and on the clifftop between is the eighteen-hole Nevin Golf Course, which enjoys a reputation for challenging golf. Behind the town rise the wooded slopes of 918ft Garn Boduan and to the N are the triple peaks of Yr Eifl – The Rivals. The village of Boduan lies SE and includes an 18th-c Victorianized house surrounded by well laid-out grounds which are graced by a lake. Bodfel Hall, where Dr Johnson visited Mrs Thrale in 1774, lies near Llanor about 5m SE.

NEVERN, Dyfed 17 SN04

Cottages and a Norman church form this hamlet, which is set in the picturesque Afon Nevern Valley. The church is of late-perpendicular style and carries a battlemented tower as wide as the rest of the building at its W end. It was built on the site of a former structure founded by the Irish St Brynach in the 6thc, and was greatly restored in 1864. This was when the south porch was added. Its nave is of 15th-c origin, and its south transeptal chapel displays a stone-vaulted roof. Near the porch is the Vitialanus stone, inscribed in Latin and 5th-c Ogham script to the memory of Vitialanus – a Welsh chieftain given the title of *emeritus* by the Romans. To the E of the porch stands St Brynach's Cross, which probably dates from the 10thc. This is almost 13ft high and includes panels containing interlaced ribbon and cross carvings. On the E side of the cross are two panels containing inscriptions which have not yet been deciphered. The first cuckoo of spring is supposed to sing on the 7 April – St Brynach's Day – whilst perched on this cross. Another stone inscribed in Latin and Ogham inside the church is known as the Magloconus Stone, and is set into a window-sill. Tegid, the poet who assisted Lady Charlotte Guest in translating the *Mabinogion* into English, is buried in the churchyard. Leading up to the church is a dark avenue of gnarled old yew trees, one of which drops a blood-like sap and is known as The Bleeding Yew. A two-arched medieval bridge spans the river at Nevern.

Robert Fitz Martin de Tours was a Norman invader who made Nevern his capital *c*1087. A motte-and-bailey castle known as Castell Nanhyfer was probably built by his grandson William de Tours, and had a small square keep with an inner ward protected by a rock ditch. Soon after it was started it was captured by a Lord Rhys, who probably built the second motte. It was retaken by William de Tours in 1194, and abandoned after having been demolished in 1195. De Tours later built a new stronghold at nearby Newport. A few earthworks on private land are all that remain of the structure. Near the castle a cross is cut in relief in the rock-face in front of a carved kneeling place, and it is thought that Nevern was probably the last resting and praying place for pilgrims in the 6thc on their way to St David's. Overlooking Nevern is 1,138ft Carn Ingli (Place of Angels), where St Brynach is said to have talked with the angels.

NEVIADD RESERVOIRS, Powys 21 SO01

These form part of a series of Taf Fechan Valley reservoirs, which date from between 1895 and 1927 and supply nearby coalfields. On all sides except to the SE are the main summits of the Brecon Beacons. A Roman road once passed through the area on its way N over the Beacons. A small road allows access to the reservoirs' S limits.

NEWBOROUGH, Gwynedd 4 SH46

One of the few Anglesey villages with an English name, Newborough originated in 1303 when inhabitants of Llanfaes were forced by Edward I to leave their homes and resettle. The original settlement nearer the shore was destroyed by a storm. The area is notable for the national nature reserve of Newborough Warren.

NEWBOROUGH WARREN and YNYS LLANDDWYN, Gwynedd 4 SH46

This national nature reserve covers some 1,566 acres of dune land and rocky coast at the S extremity of Anglesey. Prior to the 14thc this was rich farmland, with ships calling at Abermenai, but violent storms engulfed the land and silted up the harbour with sand from offshore sandbanks. Since 1947 the planting of Newborough Forest to fix the dunes has been taking place in the N part of the reserve. Permits are needed to wander from the public right of way, but a nature trail enables the visitor to see much of the natural beauty of the area.

Llanddwyn Bay lies on the S side of the reserve and has a fine sandy beach which is excellent for bathing. Between this and Maltraeth Sands is the rocky promontory of Llanddwyn Island, with its 19th-c lighthouse. This island is accessible except at times of very high tides. Its rocky shores were once inhabited by a colony of terns. In the centre of the island is the ruined 15th-c Church of St Dwynen, which replaced her oratory built 1,000 years earlier. St Dwynen is said to have come here for peace and quiet after her lover had deceived her. To the N of the church is the place from where she sat to watch her last sunset, and near by is a holy well. A plain Latin cross has been erected to her memory, plus a modern Celtic cross in memory of all those who have died there. On the road to Llanddwyn, just outside Newborough village, is the 14th-c Church of St Peter. This was extended *c*1600 and restored in the 1850's. It's appearance is long and narrow because of the absence of side aisles. Inside is a 12th-c font of gritstone carved with interlaced patterns, and some notable carved 14th-c gravestones.

NEWBRIDGE, Gwent 26 ST39

At one time Newbridge was the head of navigation for barges on the Usk. Iron was transported here by road from the forges at Trostrey, and thence by the Usk to Newport. Tredunnock Bridge spans the river here.

NEWBRIDGE-ON-WYE, Powys 13 SO05

The most significant feature of the village is the Mid-Wales House Gallery, a new art gallery and craft shop started by Mrs Nancy Palmer-Jones in what was once the Mid-Wales Inn. Llysdinam lies across the river and is the seat of the Dillwyn-Venables-Llewelyn's. Memorials to the family are to be found in the church, which is of Victorian-gothic style. A few miles higher up the valley is Doldowlod Hall, the seat of the Gibson-Watt family, descendants of James Watt the famous engineer, who spent his retirement here.

NEWCASTLE EMLYN, Dyfed 17 SN34

A small market town 10m SE of Cardigan on the River Teifi, Newcastle Emlyn consists mainly of one long street running at rightangles to the river at its N end and joining the A484 at its S end. The public buildings form an attractive centre to this small town but are of little individual architectural importance. The church was built in the 1840's, enlarged in the 1920's, and incorporates a great deal of local slate. This material has been used to pave the interior, and the building is approached through an avenue of lime trees. Allen Raine (Mrs A Puddicombe) the famous novelist was born here in 1836, and the town was also the home of Theophilus Evans – vicar of Llangammarch and author of *Drych y Prif Oesoedd*.

Overgrown ruins of a castle are located on a mound almost encircled by a loop of the Teifi and overlooking the town. It was first called 'new' in the 13thc, after Maredudd ap Rhys of Dynevor built a castle here in 1240, probably on the site of a former Welsh fortress. His son Rhys ap Maredudd led an uprising against Edward I after having been confined to Dryslwyn Castle. He besieged Newcastle Emlyn, but after the castle had changed hands three times – all within the year

1288 – the walls were finally battered down and Rhys ap Maredudd was forced to flee. During the succeeding years the English enlarged the castle by adding a gatehouse flanked by two octagonal towers and a small polygonal tower. In 1403 the Welsh under Owain Glyndwr again managed to take it. After this it fell into ruin until it was granted to Sir Rhys ap Thomas by Henry VII, after his help at the Battle of Bosworth in 1485. Ap Thomas carried out extensive rebuilding and made it one of his favourite abodes. After the civil wars, in which it changed hands several times, it was slighted by Cromwell's troops. Today this quiet ruin (AM, OACT), dating mainly from the 15thc, forms a pleasant picnic spot.

Across the river, which is excellent for trout and salmon fishing, lies Adpar – where the first Welsh printing press was built in 1718 by Isaac Carter. The first Welsh-printed book was issued in 1719, and a stone in a house near the bridge commemorates this fact. Cilgwyn Mansion, now a hotel, is also to be found at Adpar. Fine waterfalls can be seen 3m down river at Cenarth.

NEWGALE, Dyfed 16 SM82

Facing the $2\frac{1}{2}$m-long Newgale Sands, this small modern village and seaside resort lies at the NE end of St Brides Bay. Its newest buildings are sited on the slopes of the hill which rises on the N side of the village. The Newgale Sands stretch away to the S and are separated from the road and village by a high ridge of pebbles. Swimming is safest in the centre of the bay, and the surf produced by the W and SW winds is quite impressive. Newgale is a known surfing resort. At exceptionally low tides the drowned stumps of a prehistoric forest are exposed. There are camping sites and an inn at the village.

NEWPORT, Dyfed 17 SN03

Newport is an ancient town on the estuary of the River Nevern, dating back to *c*1195 when William de Tours built a castle here to replace the one at Nevern. From him are descended the Lord (or Lady) Marchers of Cemais, who have been consulted about the appointment of the mayor since the town was first granted its charter in the 13thc. The area was first settled by Flemings, who built up a thriving woollen industry until an epidemic of the plague hit the town in the reign of Queen Elizabeth I, causing a sudden decline of the local industry and a loss of its trade to Fishguard. Today it is a small resort, with the Newport Sands in the mouth of the estuary of the River Nevern to the N and Parrog to the W. To the N of Newport Sands is a nine-hole golf course. The old Welsh name for Newport is *Tref-draeth* or 'the town on the sands'. The Norman Church of St Mary's is in decorated style, but was largely rebuilt in 1879. The rebuilding incorporated the old west tower, and the original square Norman font has a scalloped edge.

Remains of the castle, including a gateway with one of its two towers, some of the outer wall, and another round tower, were incorporated in the construction of a mansion in 1859. This is now a guesthouse and riding centre on the S side of the town. A small stone dungeon was discovered last century. This and a few other remnants of the castle are located in the grounds of the mansion. The castle was taken by Llywelyn the Great in 1215, by Llywelyn the Last in 1257, and was finally destroyed by Owain Glyndwr in 1408.

The surrounding area is richly supplied with prehistoric remains. Newport Cromlech stands in a corner of a field near to the bridge, behind Cromlech farmhouse. The remains of Cerrig-y-Gof and Pentre Ifan, located nearby, are described under their own entries. Overlooking Newport is Carn Ingli (Place of Angels), a 1,138ft outlier of the Prescellys. On its slopes are the remains of an iron-age fort and pre-Christian hut circles.

*NEWPORT, Gwent 26 ST38

Big redevelopment emphasizes that this industrial and historic centre, with a population over 112,000, has its eyes very much on the future. Faster road

communications with London and the Midlands are seen locally as significant factors for the docks – which are at the confluence of the rivers Usk and Ebbw – and for Newport's industries. In 1801 the town had a population of 1,100, which grew to nearly 70,000 by the end of the 19thc as the docks exported the coal and iron products of the Gwent valleys. Today it is one of the major metal-exporting ports in Britain. Access to the docks is gained by one of Britain's largest sea locks, measuring 1,000ft by 100ft. Before the coming of the Normans this was the port or market town of the *Cantref of Gwenllwg*, of the ancient kingdom of *Morgannwg*. A Norman lordship was set up based on Newport Castle (AM, OACT), which was built *c*1126 and is situated on the side of the Usk near Newport Bridge. At first this was a wooden structure, but was later

replaced by a stone-built castle which suffered damage in sieges during the 14th and 15thc. Owain Glyndwr attacked the castle, burnt the town, and destroyed the bridge. In 1536, with the Act of Union between England and Wales, various lordships were formed into the County of Monmouthshire. In 1623 James I gave the town a royal charter.

The Westgate Hotel in Commercial Street was the target for musketmen in the Chartist riots of November 1839. The Museum and Art Gallery in John Frost Square displays details of the riots. The art gallery also has a bust of Newport-born William Henry Davies (1871–1940), the 'tramp poet' who wrote the lines:

What is this life if, full of care,
We have no time to stand and stare? –
No time to stand beneath the boughs
And stare as long as sheep or cows:
                              cont overleaf

1 Castle Ruins	4 Museum and Art Gallery	7 Tredegar Park
2 Civic Centre	5 St Woolos' Cathedral	8 Westgate Hotel
3 Murenger House (Tudor)	6 Transporter Bridge	

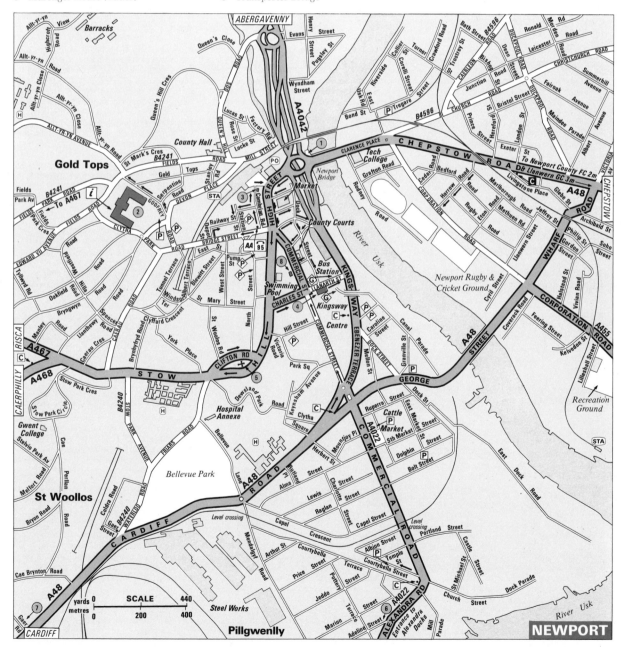

Newtown Parish Church and the grave of social reformer Robert Owen.

in his poem *Leisure*. He was author of *Autobiography of a Super-tramp* in 1908. He went to America at the age of 22 and led a vagrant life both there and after his return to Britain. His collected poems were published in 1943. Murenger House in High Street dates from Elizabeth I and was the home of the officer in charge of the town walls. This was close to the west gate. Outstanding murals are on the four walls of the Central Hall of the impressive Civic Centre, which is on a hill behind the railway station. These were painted by Hans Feibusch between 1961 and 1964, and were commissioned with the assistance of the Edwin Austin Abbey Memorial Trust Fund for mural painting in Great Britain. The panels range from *Celtic Settlement* and *The Roman Settlement at Caerleon* to *The Arrival of the Americans* – on a troop-carrier at the docks in the second world war – and *Building of the New George Street Bridge*, which was opened in 1964 across the Usk, lower down river from Newport Bridge. Stow Hill commands a good view of the town and the Bristol Channel, and is surmounted by St Woolos Cathedral. Built by the Normans, this was originally St Gwynllyw's. Woolos is believed to be a corruption of this name. The 15th-c tower was brought to its present height by Jasper Tudor. The cathedral has stonework of many centuries and a good Norman interior. There is also a modern mural which was added when the east end was considerably extended in the 1960's.

The Transporter Bridge carries the B4237 across the lower reaches of the Usk and was opened on 12 September 1906. It is one of the only two left of its kind in Britain. The other is the Teesside Transporter Bridge at Middlesbrough in Cleveland. A 645ft span stretches between the towers, which are $241\frac{1}{2}$ft high. There is a 177ft clear headway from high water to the underside of the span. A protected cat-walk affords fine views of the town. Over 500 acres of parks and pleasure grounds in Newport include the 58-acre Tredegar Park, which is set in woodlands on the extreme W

boundary by the Cardiff Road and Ebbw River. Rodney Parade lies across the river from the centre and is the home of Newport Athletic Club, founded in 1875.

Inland there are many fine walks from Newport. About 4m across green upland is the 1,374ft Twmbarlwm and an iron-age hillfort. Twmbarlwm lies near the Cwmcarn scenic forest drive, which is part of the Ebbw Forest. Caerleon is situated 3m up the Usk; Caerwent and Chepstow are to the E; Caerphilly Castle lies to the NW.

NEW QUAY, Dyfed   *17 SN35*

This small resort is set on terraces cut into the wooded E-facing slopes of New Quay Head, overlooking the sands of New Quay Bay. Its tiny harbour of fishing boats and pleasure craft attracts fishermen, yachtsmen, and sightseers. The harbour was developed by the New Quay Harbour Company, formed in 1833, soon after a ship-building industry had been set up. A small stone pier, extensively repaired between 1952 and 1953, shelters the harbour. Herring, mackerel, and shell-fish are regularly landed, and at the end of the pier is a navigation light set up in 1964 to commemorate local men who died in the two world wars. The nearby Church of St Llwchaiarn was rebuilt in 1863. Its structure retains a carved beam set over the west doorway, and inside is a Norman font bearing a carved human head at each corner.

New Quay Head rises to 300ft to the W of New Quay, and its rocky cliffs are indented with caves. Among these is Ogof Ddauben – the two-headed cave – so called because it has two entrances. To the W of the Head is Craig-y-Adar, or Bird's Rock, where large numbers of birds congregate at certain times of the year. New Quay Bay extends to Llanina, where the tiny Church of St Ina is perched on the cliff top. This was rebuilt in 1850 as its predecessor was threatened by encroachment of the sea. In its plain interior are preserved a carved beam and font from the old church. The building stands in the private grounds of Llanina House.

NEW RADNOR, Powys   *14 SO26*

It was in 1064 that New Radnor was new, founded by King Harold to replace Old Radnor as the administrative centre of the district and laid out on a grid-iron pattern – anticipating New York by more than half a millenium! Walls and a castle protected it, and traces of the walls can be seen in a field at the end of a rough lane running off the Rhayader road on the left, just beyond the church. A line of wall and one of the angles can be traced. The castle stood behind the church, but nothing is left of it now except the mound. With the high summits of Radnor Forest behind and the Smatcher in front, both closing in on each other to the SW, the town was only vulnerable from the E. The castle was well sited for protection on this side.

Water Street actually has a stream running down it, and small bridges to allow access to the houses. At its lower end is a monument somewhat resembling the Albert Memorial in London. This is a memorial to Sir George Cornwall Lewis, who died in 1863. He was a baronet and MP for the borough from 1855 until his death, and it is thought that he might have become prime minister if he had not died when he did. The church, which was built in the 1840's, is largely devoid of interest but has six heraldic shields on the front of the organ gallery and two 13th-c stones in the porch. Figures carved on these include one with a circular shield, which is said to be rare. In 1188 Archbishop Baldwin preached a rousing recruiting sermon here for the Crusade, but today New Radnor is extremely quiet.

NEWTON, Mid Glamorgan   *25 SS87*

Newton is a small village to the E of Porthcawl, with a 13th-c church designed as a place of defence as well as one of worship. On its massive tower, under the parapet on the eastern side, are parts of the supports of a platform from which missiles were fired. Inside the church are a stone pulpit carved with a crude sculpture of Jesus being scourged, a plain late-Norman octagonal font, and one of the few pre-Reformation altar stones in the country. The Rev John Blackmore, father of R D Blackmore the novelist, is buried in the churchyard. To the S of the church across the neatly-mown village green is St John's Well, notable because at high tide it is full and at low tide empty. The well is now covered in, but steps lead down to its clear waters.

About 1m W is Nottage Court, a Tudor manor house largely rebuilt in 1570 and later restored. It was extended in Victorian times. Inside are some fine panelled rooms, late-Tudor stone fireplaces, a priest's hole, and notable 15th-c tapestries from Tewkesbury Abbey. Sker House is a gabled pre-Reformation building on which is based R D Blackmore's *Maid of Sker*. It is situated some 2m away and is now a farmhouse, but it was originally the grange of Margam Abbey. A number of prehistoric remains are to be found in the area. Of particular interest is one of the few neolithic house foundations yet discovered in Wales, found in a field at Mount Pleasant Farm.

NEWTOWN, Powys   *14 SO19*

If ever a town was appropriately named it is Newtown, for apart from having been designated a New Town and a development area it has been renewed piecemeal over the last few years. The old 16th-c Newtown Hall, which was the seat of the two local councils, has been pulled down and replaced by a new Georgian-style hall. A flood embankment has been constructed alongside the river, and two new bridges have been built. Other new structures include a county library headquarters; a police centre; theatre; car parks; residential and industrial estates. Yet withal Newtown has retained its character and charm, much of which it owes to the diversity of the architecture. No two blocks are alike, and the styles range from Tudor, through Jacobean, Georgian, Regency, Victorian, 19th-c gothic and Byzantine, and Fifth Georgian to contemporary.

There has been considerable clearance of what is called 'substandard property', and much that was characteristic of yesterday's Newtown has been swept away. Across the Long Bridge to the quarter of the town that is properly Llanllwchaiarn the old pattern is better preserved. Here the Newtown Textile Museum has been established in one of the blocks where weavers once worked communally in the top floor factory. Features of this museum include a replica of a house with characteristic portico, old railway exhibits, the history of the wool trade, old tools and machinery – in fact an epitome of Newtown life yesterday. Up-river on this side of the bridge is the smart residential district of Milford Road, with large houses standing in their own grounds. In this quarter is the little stone and half-timbered building called Cwrt yn Dre, which was Owain Glyndwr's parliament house in Dolgellau. It was brought here in 1885.

Over the Midland Bank on the Cross there is a Robert Owen museum. Owen, crusader for social reform, was born in Newtown and returned here at the end of his life. He was buried in the Old Churchyard, where his tomb is one of the showplaces of the town. In the museum is a replica of the room in which he was born. The new Church of St David is a fine example of Victorian gothic architecture. It contains an interesting memorial to the wives of Sir John Pryce, the 5th baronet. Graves in the Old Churchyard include one of Richard Owen and Jane Lewis, a boy and girl who were in love with each other but whose marriage was opposed by both families. Being frustrated over marriage they decided to die together and took poison. Despite the opposition to their marriage they were buried together. The date was 1815, and crowds attended the funeral. For years their grave was visited and tended. Newtown was originally named Llanfair yn Cedewain, or St Mary's Church in Cedewain. As it became more important and expanded it became Drenewydd, the New Town. It was granted a charter in 1280, but no one knows what became of it.

NEYLAND, Dyfed   18 SM90
Neyland is situated on the N shores of Milford Haven opposite Pembroke Dock. It originated in 1856, when Isambard Kingdom Brunel chose it as the terminal of the S Wales railway, and developed as a port for Irish steam packets and deep-sea fishing. Brunel's 'Great Eastern', the largest ship in the world when launched in 1858, had a berthing-place here. The

port later lost its trade to Fishguard in 1906, and is now best known as the car ferry terminal to Hobb's Point for the town of Pembroke Dock. Bathing is safest for two hours either side of high tide. Llanstadwell lies to the W, and has an ancient church which was restored in 1876 but retains some fine Norman work.

NOLTON HAVEN, Dyfed   18 SM81
This small inlet off St Bride's Bay has a sandy beach at low tide and is sheltered by high cliffs. A few cottages, a farm, and a chapel exist here, and during the summer season numerous caravans invade the area. Laver bread is made from seaweed gathered along this part of the Welsh coast. About 1m inland is the village of Nolton, where a bellcoted church includes a barrel-vaulted porch. Inside are the worn effigy of a knight – at one time used as a gate post – and a carved-stone bracket set in the north wall and bearing three carved heads.

NORTHOP, Clwyd   7 SJ26
Northop is a small village situated at a busy road junction midway between Chester and Flint. The 100ft, perpendicular-style fortified tower of the local church is an impressive site, and the building itself is reputed to have been built by Margaret Beaufort, mother of Henry VII. The present pews were added during 19th-c restoration, and three interesting effigies depict a beautiful Welsh lady and two knights respectively. Remains of the 17th-c Old Free School stand in a corner of the churchyard. William Parry, an MP in Elizabeth I's reign, was born here and was later executed in 1584 as a traitor for his Roman Catholic sympathies. The fortified hill-top encampment of Moel-y-Gaer lies to the NW.

OFFA'S DYKE
Developed and controlled by the Countryside Commission, the 168m long-distance path for walkers which follows the historic earthen bank of Offa's Dyke wherever possible, runs through beautiful border country. The dyke extends, with some gaps, from the River Severn near Chepstow to the sea near Prestatyn. It was built by Offa, who was king of an area which roughly encompassed the English W Midlands of today and was called Mercia. He ruled between AD757 and AD796. For centuries the dyke marked the boundary between England and Wales, but only in a few places does it follow the boundary as it is now fixed. This was a demarcation line to mark the frontier rather than a continuously defended barrier against the Welsh, though the ditch facing Wales was 12ft deep and the bank 60ft broad to deter raiders.

OGMORE-BY-SEA, Mid Glamorgan   25 SS87
Situated to the S of the Ogmore estuary, this small village has a sandy beach backed by low cliffs. To the E rise splendid cliffs pitted with caves that can be explored at low tide, and about $1\frac{1}{2}$m offshore from the estuary mouth is notorious Tusker Rock. This rises from the sea at low tide and has been the scene of many a wreck in the past. Near the mouth of the estuary are strong currents, and it is illegal to bathe here. Well-known Sutton stone is quarried at Ogmore.

A little way up the valley of the Ogmore River are the picturesque ruins of 12th-c Ogmore Castle (AM), with stepping stones leading across the river beneath it. This castle has one of the earliest stone keeps to be built in Wales. The base of a 10th-c

Ruined Ogmore Castle was founded in the 12thc as part of a defensive line on the W borders of Glamorgan.

stone cross, now in the National Museum of Wales, was discovered in the ruins. A replica of this now stands here. Also worthy of note are a 12th-c hooded fireplace, and the remains of a 15th-c courthouse located in the outer ward. Probably consisting of only earthworks and ditches at first, the castle was founded in 1116 by William de Londres, who married a Welsh princess. It held a defensive position overlooking a ford of the Ogmore river as one of a series on the W boundary of Glamorgan.

OLD RADNOR, Powys 14 SO25

Today just a village comprising a church, school, inn, a tiny group of council houses and a scatter of cottages, in pre-conquest times Old Radnor was a seat of local government and remained so until 1064. It had a castle which Ordnance Survey maps show as having been on the SW side of the village; but a description of local items of interest which is on display in the church states that it was on the hill behind the school. There is also Castle Nimble, $\frac{1}{4}$m N of the village, which some authorities think may have been Radnor Castle. The consensus of opinion among the experts is that no one really knows where that castle actually stood. The church has a battlemented tower and organ casing dating back to 1500, believed to be the oldest in Britain. The same is believed of the font, a massive circular block of stone with its top surface hollowed out to form a shallow bowl.

The rood screen is of 15th-c origin, and the churchyard contains a huge block of roughly-hewn stone which forms a tombstone at the grave of Sir Herbert Lewis. Sir Herbert was the 4th baronet of Harpton Court, between New Radnor and Walton. The most interesting Lewis memorial is the one to Thomas Lewis, who 'enjoyed a life full of years which on the 5th April 1777 he exchanged for the immortality of Heaven, aged 86 years and 5 months'.

An RAF Sunderland flying boat is a reminder of the part Pembroke Dock played in the second world war.

OVERTON, Clwyd 11 SJ34

This well-kept village has a broad main street and could be called the capital of English Maelor – a region of Wales which is on the other side of the Dee and has more regional affinity with the rich lowland plains of Cheshire to its E than the Welsh uplands. Overton's yews practically obscure the sandstone church and figure in the seven wonders of Wales. The visitor might well wonder what distinguishes them from yews seen in countless other churchyards.

OXWICH, West Glamorgan 24 SS48

In an area of outstanding beauty on the S coast of the Gower, this small seaside village lies on the W side of Oxwich Bay. The fine sandy bay curves round to Three Cliffs Bay and the village of Penmaen, where there is fine rock and cave scenery. To the SE of Oxwich is Oxwich Point, with its green slopes rising to 280ft and commanding fine views across the bay to Pwlldu Head and beyond. A submerged forest is often exposed in the bay at low tide. Behind the dunes of Oxwich Burrows, which extend along the shores of the bay to Nicholaston Wood, is an area of marshland where reeds grow 6ft tall in the mud and water. This is now a national nature reserve covering some 542 acres of marsh and woodland, containing a large variety of unusual species of plant and bird life. The road which runs N of Oxwich passes through the reserve, but a permit is required to venture deeper.

The Church of St Illtud, with its large west tower, stands amidst trees to the SE of the village. Set in a recess in the north wall of the short chancel is the tomb of a 14th-c knight and his wife. These are thought to be the De la Mares, former owners of the castle. The huge font, probably of Norman date, is a rough stone cylinder. The castle was rebuilt in 1541 as a Tudor manor house by Sir Rice Mansell, holder of Penrice Castle.

It incorporates the remnants of the former 14th-c stronghold of a local family of landowners. These remnants included part of the curtain wall, the gatehouse, and part of the great tower. Over the gateway is a square stone on which is carved the Mansell coat of arms. The Oxwich sand trail is an interesting walk which traces the movement of sand and its influence on flora and fauna.

OYSTERMOUTH, West Glamorgan 24 SS68

The first castle on this site was probably erected by an early Norman lord, either in the late 11thc or early 12thc, but all traces were removed during the Welsh uprising of 1287 under Rhys ap Meridith. The present ruins date from late 13th or early 14thc and are of early-English to decorated style. The hall, main apartments, and a chapel exhibiting a fine traceried window are located in the tower. The castle is situated at the top of a hill in a park to the N of Mumbles. The village church has a font dated 1251, and the churchyard contains the grave of Dr Thomas Bowdler (1754 to 1825). His works, which included expurgated editions of Shakespeare and Edward Gibbons' *History*, led to the verb 'bowdlerize'.

PAINSCASTLE, Powys 22 SO14

Clinging to a crossroads, Painscastle is a compact cream and yellow village with one or two unexpected little open spaces among the cottages. It took its name from Henry I's courtier Pain Fitz John, who either built the castle or rebuilt in stone an earlier motte-and-bailey fortress. Later William de Breos enlarged it and renamed it after his wife Maud de St Valerie, but the old name of Pain's Castle persisted nonetheless. It was besieged by Trahaian's cousin Wenwynwyn after de Breos had dragged Trahaian through Brecon at horse tail and beheaded him, but the Normans raised S Wales against the Powysians and defeated them.

Just $1\frac{1}{2}$m W of Painscastle is the hamlet of Llanbedr, famous for its association with the Rev John Price, who was vicar here in Kilvert's time. Instead of living in his vicarage he preferred a shack of dry walling roofed with thin thatch. Just why he had this preference is not clear, for he was a man of means, had two farms in nearby Llandeilo Graban, bought peat for his firing, and could afford domestic help on four days a week. As a young man he had an unhappy love affair and never married, but he treasured his sweetheart's love letters all his life. A thief breaking into his shack and finding nothing of value tore up the letters in disgust, but Price patiently stuck all the pieces together again.

PARKMILL, West Glamorgan 24 SS58

Set in a wooded valley of the Ilston stream, this village lies 7m W of Swansea on the main S road through the Gower Peninsula – an area of outstanding natural beauty. The stream joins the Pennard Pill as it leaves the woods and runs down to the sea at Three Cliffs Bay. Ruined Pennard Castle overlooks the Pill and has little historic significance. From the 13thc sand apparently posed its main invasion problem. Green Cwm, the farthest W of two valleys meeting at Parkmill, passes through the woods of

Parc le Breos, which was the hunting lodge of a 13th-c Gower family. A path leads to Giant's Grave, a megalithic tomb where human remains were found when excavated in the late 19thc. Cathole Cave, one of the Gower bone-caves, is farther up the valley. Llethrid Swallet is a fine cave system near by. The hamlet of Ilston lies at the top of the Ilston Valley.

PARTRISHOW, Powys 22 SO22
Said to have once been called Patricio, this remote little Grwyne-Fawr Valley hamlet is surrounded by the Black Mountains. Amid the trees is a small church which dates mainly from the 15thc, although the font has an 11th-c inscription. The rood loft and screen are beautifully carved, and the faded remains of medieval wall paintings are interesting. Also of interest is a 15th-c cell containing an altar, where a hermit would have passed solitary days. On the road 50yds below the church is a stone with two crosses. This once directed pilgrims to the Holy Well of St Mary, some 200yds away.

PAVILAND CAVES, West Glamorgan 24 SS48
These two caves are just 100yds apart and set in the cliffs under Yellow Top Hill, overlooking the Bristol Channel. They are accessible only at very low water. The most famous of these is Goat's Hole Cave, which was discovered in the 19thc by Dean Buckland. The most notable find was the remains of a Cro-Magnon-type skeleton in 1823. The bones had been dyed red by the ochre from the rocks, and this earned the body the title of the Red Lady – although it was subsequently discovered that the skeleton was male. Other items recovered from the cave included ivory rings, elephants' tusks, and the teeth of a mammoth.

PEMBREY, Dyfed 20 SN40
Pembrey has almost become a subsidiary of its neighbour Burry Port, and lies behind Pembrey Burrows – a 5m stretch of firm sands and dunes on which the Forestry Commission has planted trees.

The parish church dates from the 13thc, and although much restored retains the original timber in the barrel roof. A fine 16th-c window can be seen in the south wall, and the church contains a memorial to the crew and passengers of the French ship 'Jeanne Emma', which foundered on the sands at the mouth of the Tywi estuary in 1828. There are also wall tablets in memory of the Vaughan family, who lived in a 16th-c house called Y Cwrt. This has now been converted into a farm.

PEMBROKE, Dyfed 18 SM90
Small but undoubtedly capital of the arm of land called 'Little England Beyond Wales', Pembroke's name is a corruption of the Welsh *Penfro*, meaning 'lands end'. The Romans did not penetrate far into the Pembrokeshire Peninsula. Why this was is not certain, but it might have been because there were no great reserves of ore to be found. The area was inhabited by natives long before the Romans came, a fact evident from the large numbers of tombs, cairns, standing stones, and hut circles that have been found. In about 1090 the Norman Lord Arnulf de Montgomery founded what was to be one of the most powerful castles in Britain here. The castle at first was only a thing of wood and earth – as were most Norman castles to begin with – but it was built on a spot which had superb natural defences: a butt of rock with steep and treacherous slopes protected on three sides by water. The Normans built a line of castles from Newgale on the N coast down to Laugharne on the S, thus sealing off from the Welsh what was to become 'Little England'. An influx of Englishmen, Normans, and Flemish weavers, caused the development of characteristics that this name implies. The present castle at Pembroke was begun in about 1190 by William Marshall. Underneath the structure is a huge limestone cavern called the Wogan. This was linked to the castle by a winding stair and has an opening to the river (see special inset overleaf). The old town walls can be traced in several places, especially at the

Park and the Mill Bridge. Restoration work was started on the castle in 1880, and has been continued by various people up until the present time. It is now maintained by the local authority.

Arnulf de Montgomery founded a priory here in 1098, and this is separated from the castle by a tidal inlet. The priory was called Monkton and belonged to the Abbey of Sees in Normandy at one time, but in 1441 Henry VI gave it to St Albans Abbey as a cell. At the Dissolution the place fell into ruins, but in 1878 restoration on the church was begun, and today this building is in something like its original condition. St Deniol's has a chapel which displays windows decorated with the symbols of free masonry, and contains monuments to several local families – Meyricks, Corstons, and Owens. Pembroke's main street boasts two more churches, both of 13th-c origin. St Mary the Virgin preserves Norman work of *c*1260, and St Michael's was restored in 1887 but preserves some roof vaulting and 18th-c mural tablets.

PEMBROKE DOCK, Dyfed 18 SM90
Until the 1920's this place was one of the chief Naval dockyards. It is about 2m N of Pembroke town and stands on Milford Haven. It was built on a grid-iron pattern, with grey buildings lining straight streets. An obelisk commemorating the launching of the first two ships made here, the 'Valorius' and the 'Ariadne' *c*1814, stands in Albion Square. In 1834 the dockyard went on to manufacture the first steam ship man-of-war – the 'Tarter' – which was driven by paddles; the first Royal Yacht – the 'Victoria and Albert' in 1834; the first of the iron-clad warship, the 'Warrior' in 1860. The latter is still moored at Pen Ferry. The dockyard was closed in 1926 but re-opened as a flying base during the second world war. An RAF Sunderland flying boat has been preserved in memory of the action the town saw during that period. Pembroke Dock is now used mainly by ship repairers and chandlers, and operates a car ferry from Hobbs Point to Neyland. A motoring museum at the Royal Garrison Theatre displays interesting old cars and mementoes, including a horse-drawn fire engine of 1892.

PEMBROKESHIRE COAST NATIONAL PARK, Dyfed
Pembrokeshire Coast national park extends over an area of 225sqm and comprises the coastal belt from Amroth in the S to Cemaes Head in the N, the Prescellys, and the Daugleddau sector of the upper reaches of Milford Haven. The area is basically low lying, with the landscape dominated by the rounded and grass-covered Prescellys rising gently in the N to the summit of 1,760ft Foel-cwm-cerwyn. Geologically the area is highly complex, with old rocks in the N and the more recent sedimentary rocks of the Devonian and Carboniferous periods in the S. The relative resistance of these rocks has been picked out over the ages by the sea, which has eroded away the softer rocks – such as the coal measures of St Bride's Bay – and exposed the harder rocks as headlands.

cont page 253

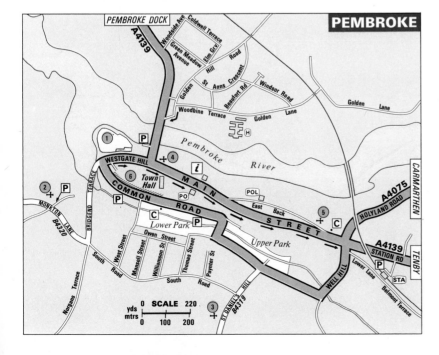

PEMBROKE

1 Castle
2 Monkton Priory
3 St Deiniol's Church
4 St Mary The Virgin Church
5 St Michael's Church
6 Town Walls

DESIGNING FOR DEFENCE

When Arnulph de Montgomery, the Norman conqueror of Dyfed, built his castle at Pembroke in 1090 it was a 'slender fortress of stakes and turfs'. All traces of it have disappeared, but certain episodes in its early history have survived to give a vivid picture of the struggle between the usurpers and the native inhabitants. Arnulph chose for his castellan at Pembroke Gerald de Windsor, whose ingenuity and tenacity were tried to the utmost in 1096 when the castle was besieged by Cadwgan ap Bleddyn. Although food supplies were rapidly dwindling and the morale of the garrison, faced with imminent starvation or surrender, was desperately low, Gerald devised a plan which must have driven his men to the brink of madness. In order to make the enemy believe that their reserves of food and endurance were plentiful, he ordered that the last four hogs in the castle store should be cut up and thrown from the walls in a great display of extravagance. Convinced that the Normans were sufficiently equipped to resist the Welsh siege for a considerable time, Cadwgan ap Bleddyn decided to march away.

The earldom of Pembroke was created in 1138. Gilbert de Clare, the first to hold the title, immediately set to work fortifying the castle. This project was continued by his son Richard 'Strongbow', the conqueror of Ireland who used Pembroke as his military base during his campaign. When William Marshall succeeded to the earldom in 1189 as son-in-law to Richard de Clare, he applied his expertise in the field of military architecture to Pembroke. The most striking legacy of his great talent is the enormous cylindrical keep in the inner ward, built c1200. It is an impressive structure not only because of its size, but because it showed the architect showed an awareness of the latest designs in fortification – in particular the change from a rectangular keep to a round one. An interesting example of this transition can be seen at Henry II's Orford Castle in Suffolk, which was circular with three rectangular towers projecting from the centre. The completely round keep at Pembroke was something new, although it was soon followed by similarly-shaped structures at Skenfrith and Caldicot in Monmouthshire, and Tretower and Bronllys in Breconshire. It is possible that this was the result of rivalry between the Marcher lords at a time when it was imperative to respond to the prevailing fashion. More probably it was due to the increasing sense of unease at the resurgence of power of the native chieftains – notably Llywelyn the Great. Llywelyn was not only building castles of his own in N Wales, but showing a disquieting knowledge of current defensive techniques. Of all the interesting features of medieval military architecture at Pembroke, the 75ft-high round keep or 'donjon', with its massive walls, stone dome, four floors and basement, and fighting platforms, stands out as the most fascinating. It remains to this day the best of the very few examples of a defensive innovation which was soon to disappear completely in favour of a stronger curtain wall and projecting angle towers.

From the Marshalls the castle passed to William de Valence, who was responsible for the outer defences, the six towers, and the extremely fine gatehouse. The latter included an 'architectural freak' in the form of a flying arch complete with battlements, which connected two semi-circular towers facing the outer ward. In 1456, when Jasper Tudor held the castle as earl of Pembroke, he entertained his sister-in-law Margaret Beaufort. She was countess of Richmond and the wife of his brother Edmund, who was away fighting in the Wars of the Roses. Later that year Richmond died, leaving a fifteen-year-old widow who was expecting a child. Early in the new year she gave birth to the future Henry VII in the tower which has been called after him since the 16thc. The

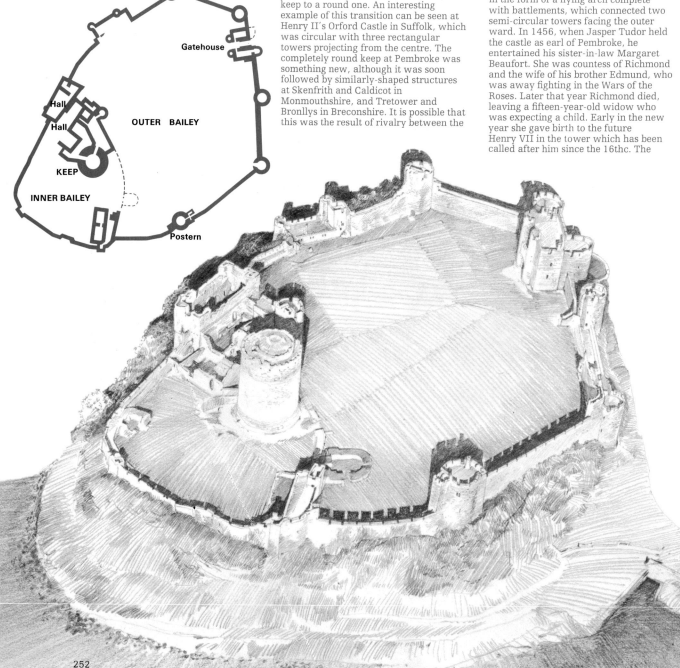

young Richmond was brought up at Pembroke by his uncle Jasper until he was fourteen. The rivalry between Yorkists and Lancastrians became so fierce that his slender claim to the throne greatly endangered his life. He escaped to Brittany, where he stayed in exile for a further fourteen years before returning to the shores of Pembrokeshire in 1485 with a small army and the assurance of support from the gentry of Wales. He then began his campaign against Richard III, whom he met and defeated at Bosworth Field in August of that year.

In a predominantly royalist country Pembroke, like Tenby, declared for parliament during the civil wars. John Poyer the mayor was in command of town and castle, but a shift in allegiance led to a charge of treason and he was executed in Covent Garden. The castle suffered the predictable fate of parliamentary slighting. It is now the responsibility of Pembroke Borough Council.

This complex geology gives rise to contrasting coastal and inland environments, resulting in a wide variety of scenery, vegetation, and animal life. The coastlands – of which most of the park consists – offer quite varied environments within themselves. There are exposed headlands interspersed with sandy bays, dune systems, sheltered inlets, and areas of salt marsh.

Seabird life is particularly notable and there are large colonies around the rugged coasts. One of the largest gannet colonies in the world is to be found on the remote island of Grassholm, and the nature reserves of Skomer and Skokholm are havens for large colonies of Manx shearwaters. There is also a colony of storm petrels on Skokholm. Gulls, particularly herring gulls, guillemots, and razorbills, may also be seen in large numbers. This is particularly so at Eligug Stack off Flimston, where a common marine plant called the tree-mallow grows on the vast quantities of guano deposited by the colonies. Puffins may also be seen strutting up and down the cliff tops during summer.

During spring and early summer the 180m of rocky cliffs, rising to between 400ft and 500ft in places but on average to 100ft, provide a colourful display of wild flowers which have adapted to the salty marine environment. When the SW winds persist beyond April various sailing creatures, among them the deadly Portuguese Man-of-War jelly-fish, are brought to the park's shores. The common porpoise, dolphins, and occasionally pilot and other whales are among the larger creatures found in these waters. This area is also the largest breeding ground of the Atlantic grey seal S of Scotland. The seals' main nurseries are at Ramsey and Skomer islands, and in inaccessible caves in the mainland cliffs. Some 350 pups are produced on average every year. Seals can be observed basking on rocks at low tide, or fishing over the waves at high water. The inland regions of the park include the Prescellys, moorland in the St David's area, and the upper reaches of Milford Haven. The Prescellys are largely moorland interspersed with low-lying areas of bog and marsh, where heather

and gorse mingle their purple and yellow flowers on the lower slopes. Buzzards, kestrels, and sparrow hawks may be seen soaring gracefully above them.

Man first appeared in the park c10,000BC in the last stages of the Pleistocene Ice Age, when tundra and steppe vegetation predominated and herds of reindeer and horses grazed here. Evidence of these animals has been found in bones and implements found in caves in the S, where the paleolithic hunters lived. Neolithic man established cultivation in the area c4,000BC. The main evidence of his settlement lies in tombs found mainly in the N, but with scattered examples around the coast and Milford Haven.

Another type of settlement evidence has been found beneath the later stronghold of Clegyr Boia, where remains of a neolithic hut community have been discovered. Stone axes and pottery in the form of round-bottomed bowls, similar to ones found in Ireland and Cornwall, were among the discoveries. The axes were of two types – one of the famous 'spotted' dolerite and the other of rhyolitic tuff – indicating that they came from axe factories in the Prescellys, at present undiscovered. This spotted dolerite is the bluestone of which the larger stones of the inner ring of Stonehenge are composed, and it is now generally thought that these monoliths came from the Prescellys, regarded as a place of special sanctity in prehistoric times. The so-called sacred centre or altar of Stonehenge is composed of fine-grained micaceous sandstone which comes from Cosherston in Milford Haven. This supports the theory that the stones were brought across land to Milford Haven, then floated downstream and round the S headland before being taken up the Bristol Channel.

By the time the Romans came to Britain the original settlers and their followers had merged into a people called *Demetae* by the Roman geographer Ptolemy. Although it appears that the Romans did not have much interest in this part of Wales, coins and pottery of Roman type are to be found throughout. This suggests that the two peoples traded. The region probably saw little change when the Romans withdrew from Britain towards the end of the 4thc, other than a revival of Celtic culture. The people of this time spoke *Goidelic*, an Irish version of Celtic or early Welsh, and they traded with the Irish and the people of the Mediterranean. Evidence of this is to be found in imported pre 7th-c Mediterranean pottery discovered at some sites.

The Age of Saints is represented largely by inscribed and carved stones to the memory of notable people of that time. The inscriptions were often placed on standing stones, the origins of which lay in prehistoric times. Those of c9th-c origin often bore incised crosses and inscriptions in Latin and Ogham, a 5th-c Gaelic script. Examples of such are to be seen at Nevern. In the 10th and 11thc massive stone crosses with interlaced patterns were erected, examples of which survive at Carew and Nevern. Small churches and cells of the 5th and 6thc are absent from this region, having been generally replaced by medieval churches.

Today agriculture is still the main occupation in the park area, with crops

such as early potatoes and wheat predominating. During the depression of the 1930's milk production was developed, and recently turkey production has become important. As well as the native Welsh black cattle, used as both beef and dairy stock, Fresians have been introduced for milk and Herefords for beef. The park is managed by the Pembrokeshire National Park Committee, whose responsibility is to maintain the natural beauty of the area and to improve the public's enjoyment of it. Nature reserves such as those on the islands of Skomer and Skokholm, and field centres at Dale Fort and Orielton, have been established. Around the coast is a footpath which runs for about 167m and was completed in 1970. It starts at Amroth in the S and finishes at St Dogmaels in the N. Sailing and fishing, popular attractions for people who come to this area, are well catered for. Information Centres are to be found at: the Town Hall, Fishguard; the County Museum, Haverfordwest; the Drill Hall, Main Street, Pembroke; the City Hall, St David's; the Norton, Tenby, and Broad Haven Countryside Unit.

PENALLY, Dyfed 19 SS19
Situated in the Pembrokeshire Coast national park about 2m SW of Tenby, this village stands near Giltar Point and has a shingle beach with sand at low tide. An outstanding Celtic cross can be seen in the churchyard, and the church houses a memorial to people who were drowned when the Caldy Island boat capsized in December 1834. Good views can be enjoyed from this area of the island. Hoyle's Mouth, a cavern associated with Shakespeare's *Cymbeline*, is ¾m N.

PENARTH, South Glamorgan 26 ST17
One of the main water ski-ing and sailing areas of S Wales, Penarth developed from a small fishing village with the shipping trade. Its harbour was in great demand during the coal-export boom, when it became one of the custom's ports of Cardiff. The harbour has now been gradually filled in, although it still provides anchorage for yachts and cruisers, and the town has become mainly tourist orientated. Some 2m of shingle and pebble beach are backed by high cliffs and offer a little sand at low tide. This area is generally considered dangerous for bathing, due to the strong currents. Penarth has been called the 'Garden by the Sea' on account of the beautiful lawns and flowerbeds on the slopes behind the promenade. The town itself lies at the top of these slopes, providing fine views of Penarth Head and the Bristol Channel. There are many pleasant parks and gardens.

Turner House Art Gallery, in Plymouth Road, was founded in 1888 and is part of the National Museum of Wales. It contains both classical and modern exhibits. The 19th-c church was built on the site of one which dated from Norman times and carries a 90ft tower. Fine cliff walks lead to nearby Ranny Bay and St Mary's Well Bay. It has been suggested that Coleridge was inspired to write *The Rime of the Ancient Mariner* after talking to an old seaman in Penarth, but the story has never been confirmed.

PENCADER, Dyfed 20 SN43
Welsh is still fluently spoken in this village – which lies 11m N of Carmarthen

The Celtic cross at Penmon on Anglesey is thought to date from c AD1000.

in the Tyweli Valley – and there is a memorial to a man who forecast that the language and people would survive. Gerald the Welshman, or Giraldus Cambrensis, toured Wales as chaplain to Archbishop Baldwin to preach the Third Crusade in 1188. During his travels he recorded the story of 'an old Welshman at Pencardair'. The man was asked by Henry II, who was marching through S Wales, if he thought the rebels would continue to resist. He replied, 'This nation, O King, may now, as in former times, be harassed and in a great measure weakened and destroyed by you and other powers, and it will often prevail by its laudable exertions. But it can never be totally subdued through the wrath of man, unless the wrath of God shall concur. Nor do I think that any other nation than this of Wales, or any language, whatever may hereafter come to pass, shall in the day of severe examination before the Supreme Judge answer for this corner of the earth.'

The village claimed its place in Welsh history when Gruffydd ap Llywelyn, ruler of Gwynedd, defeated Hywel ap Edwin here in 1041 and carried off Hywel's wife. The village itself is a cluster of red-brick houses which grew up with the opening of the Carmarthen Railway. Some 4m NW is Llandyssul, a centre for traditional Welsh crafts and an angling resort on the Teifi.

PENCLAWDD, West Glamorgan   24 SS59
Cockle gathering has made a name for this straggling village of the Gower Peninsula, situated on the S side of the Burry Inlet. For centuries women drove donkeys over the sands to the cockle beds, and a few still use the old donkey carts. Burrows near here are owned by the NT, who lease them to the Nature Conservancy as a reserve. Penclawdd marks the end of the Gower Peninsula, and thereafter the country gives way to the mines and iron works of industrial S Wales. The area was once an artillery and bombing range, so it is not wise to stray from the main paths.

PENDINE SANDS, Dyfed   19 SN20
This 5m stretch of firm sand is backed by dunes and was once a favourite goal for Sunday-school outings and quiet holidays. In 1920, however, its potential

for use in motor speed trials was realized and since then the beach has periodically echoed to the roar of powerful engines. Sir Malcolm Campbell broke the existing world land-speed record here in 1924, with an average speed of 146.16mph. In 1927 he recorded 174.88mph in 'Bluebird', and during that same year J G Parry-Thomas was killed here when his car 'Babs' crashed and was buried in the dunes. The vehicle remained in the sand until 1969, when it was unearthed for restoration. Motor-cycle races have also been held here. Today all but the W mile of the beach is controlled by the Ministry of Defence, which fires shells and missiles over Carmarthen Bay. The scattered village lies 18m SW of Carmarthen between green, wooded hills and extensive dunes. It is very popular with caravanners.

PENEGOES, Powys   9 SH70
This long, thin village 2m out of Machynlleth on the Newtown road takes its name from Egwert, a Welsh chieftain who was beheaded near where the Church of St Cadfach now stands. His head is said to have been buried beneath a tree in the village. Acceptance of this legend is so strong that moves to dig for the skull were made in 1950. It was to Dolguog, just to the N of the village, that the Cumbrian chief Llywarch Hen retired after the Saxons had invaded his land. He settled here with his harp, became the father of one of the three Holy Families of Wales, and lived to be very old – which resulted in his being called *Hen*. He was born early in the 6thc, and his mother was a daughter of Brychan, the man who gave his name to Brecknock.

Once Penegoes had a tiny curative establishment, a bath 7yds by 3yds and 4ft deep with steps leading down into it, where people bathed in water from a spring that was efficacious for rheumatic complaints. Richard Wilson, the celebrated landscape and portrait painter, was born in Penegoes Rectory in 1714. Although he became famous for his royal portraits, he also enjoyed painting scenes in his native countryside. Works of his are to be found in the National Gallery and National Portrait Gallery. His *Coast Scene near Naples*, and *Caernarfon Castle* are in the National Museum of Wales. Pen Rhos Fach stands

on a hill to the N and is an example of the classic Welsh Long House in which barn, byres, and living accommodation are all under the same roof. There was once internal access to each of these areas, but modernization has divided them off. Until recently the occasional red squirrel and even pine marten have been seen in this district, but they are now extremely rare. A particular habitat of these attractive little animals was the grounds of Gallt-Y-Llan, an 18th- and 19th-c mansion to the left of the main road. An ancient bridge on the Machynlleth road spans a one-time ford which may have been of Roman origin.

PENHOW, Gwent   26 ST49
Remains of a 13th-c castle surmounting a steep hill here are all that survive of a small fortification. The ward and oblong tower were built in the 13thc, and the remainder added in the 15thc or later. The keep is now badly ruined. This castle appears to have no recorded history, and is now part of a farmhouse. Built of the same stone as the castle, the local church has a low conical tower and probably dates from the same period. Of interest is its ancient stone screen and a 13th-c double piscina.

PENLLYN CASTLE, South Glamorgan 25 SS97
Penllyn Castle is believed to date from the 12thc and may have been destroyed by Owain Glyndwr prior to being rebuilt. All that remains of the original fortification is the corner of an early, crudely-constructed rectangular tower, which has been incorporated into a later residential building. There appears to be no recorded history, and the remains stand on private ground. This site is not usually accessible to the public.

PENMACHNO, Gwynedd   5 SH75
Cwm Penmachno, in which this quarryman's village is situated, is virtually a cul-de-sac valley ending in a cluster of disused workings. It is easily reached from the A5 road E of Betws-y-coed. The church has 5th- or 6th-c inscribed stones which are thought to be the oldest inscribed Christian gravestones in Wales. Two painted oak panels are attributed to an unknown 16th-c Flemish painter, and there is a memorial to Bishop Morgan – translator of the Bible into Welsh. His birthplace was Ty Mawr (NT) in the nearby Gwybernant Valley.

PENMAENMAWR, Gwynedd   5 SH77
This name was simply a Welsh word for nightmare to 18th-c English coach travellers along the coast road of N Wales. 'The most heathenish country ever a man travelled' was one description from a writer who had traversed this dangerous route. The great obstacle was the massive buttress of Penmaenmawr, which allowed only a mere shelf of a road beneath its towering flank. Loose rocks from above and a vertiginous drop to the sea below were the twin horrors that travellers faced. There was one particularly rough stretch where the carriages had to be dismantled and carried. At other times the headland was negotiated via the beach if the tide was favourable. With the treacherous ferry at Conwy and the hazardous Lavan Sands crossing to Anglesey, travellers contemplated this coastal route with justifiable dread. It was not until the 19thc that road engineers with explosives

finally tamed the Penmaenmawr headland, but in 1845 it proved as great an obstacle to railway pioneer Stephenson as it had been to road builders.

Stephenson pierced the headland with a short, 235yd tunnel, beyond which the line was carried through a deep cutting covered by avalanche sheds against falling boulders. On either side he took to the shore, where the line was carried by sea walls with great difficulty. In 1846 a strong gale carried the sea over the wall, washing away 500yds of track. Stephenson abandoned the wall and settled for a twelve-arch viaduct. The estimated cost of this stretch of line had been £26,000, but the actual cost was £128,000. Today Penmaenmawr is bisected by the traffic-laden coast road, but away from the main road it is a rewarding place to explore. It has changed little from the last century, when it found much favour with holidaymakers. No-one did more to popularize Penmaenmawr than W E Gladstone, the Victorian prime minister who used it as a summer retreat from the affairs of state, and is now commemorated by a bronze bust in Paradise Road.

Penmaenmawr offers good bathing from its sandy beach, which is backed by a spacious promenade. The mountain from which the town takes its name has lost its original profile through extensive quarrying, and only one huge rock now remains to demonstrate its original height. An interesting iron-age fort was sacrificed in the process, but a bronze-age stone circle – one of the best-known in Wales – exists on the crest of a hill at 1,200ft above the town. Many of the stones, some of which stand to a height of 6ft, have been removed or destroyed, but there are still about a dozen of good size with many smaller ones in between. Archaeologists discovered a vessel and the cremated remains of an infant, which suggested a ritual sacrifice to sanctify the site. The stone circle can be reached on foot from either Penmaenmawr or Llanfairfechan by equally steep routes. Evidence of even earlier occupation came to light in 1919, with the discovery at nearby Graig Llwyd of the site of a neolithic stone-axe factory. Flints and large arrow stones – boulders with large grooves cut in them as the result of sharpening tools of some kind – have been found. Stone axes from Graig Llwyd were found not only on the site itself but as far away as Wiltshire, Gloucestershire, Derbyshire, and Northern Ireland. The tough igneous rock which the neolithic people found so useful is valued today for road construction. From Penmaenmawr it is easy to retreat from the bustle of the coast road into the spectacular scenery of the mountains. The Sychnant Pass provides a breathtaking alternative route to Conwy.

PENMAENPOOL, Gwynedd *9 SH61*
Penmaenpool is an agreeable place to contemplate the beauty of the Mawddach estuary, where sea birds wheel about and Welsh cattle cool themselves in the tidal waters. The last road to cross the point of the Mawddach before the estuary broadens does so here via a clanking toll bridge. In the days of sail ocean-going boats once set out from Penmaenpool, and ships were built in a neighbouring creek.

PENMARK, South Glamorgan *25 ST06*
A small village in the valley of the Kenson stream, Penmark includes a church which carries a plain embattled tower and displays a chancel arch decorated with zig-zag mouldings. Also of interest is the low circular font. Remains of Penmark Castle stand near the churchyard wall. Thought to be of Norman origin, only part of a stone wall and traces of a round tower remain, and the structure appears to have no recorded history. The only real fact to come to light is that it belonged to the Umfraville family until the 14thc. It stands on private land and is not normally accessible to the public. About 1¼ miles SW is Fonmon Castle, the remains of a 13th- and 14th-c fortification consisting of three towers – two round, and a rectangular one which may have been the keep. Some of the remains are incorporated into the structure of a much more modern building. Nothing is known of the castle's history, and it is not normally open for viewing.

PENMOELALLT, Mid Glamorgan *21 SO01*
Rare whitebeams and the more common ash are the predominant tree species found in this 17-acre forest reserve woodland, situated on the W bank of the Taff Fawr 3m N of Merthyr Tydfil. A permit is required away from the marked paths.

PENMON, Gwynedd *5 SH68*
Penmon is a well-preserved priory 4m from Beaumaris. The church of St Seiriol, a Celtic saint, was built in the 6thc and rebuilt in the 12thc. It features some unexpected examples of Norman influence and is surrounded by monastic buildings (AM). The great, 1,000-nest dovecote (AM) was built c1600 and has a beehive dome topped by a hexagonal lantern through which the birds entered. The fishpond where the monks caught their Friday meal, and the well with its ice-cold water, are still to be seen. Farther on from Penmon Priory is Penmon Point, the nearest the visitor is likely to get to Puffin Island, or 'Ynys Seiriol' as it is called in Welsh. The island, to which access is limited, is the site of an early-Christian settlement and, more recently, had a telegraph station. It is now a bird sanctuary, although the number of puffins has declined through the combined depredations of a colony of rats, and local people who once caught and pickled the birds as an English delicacy.

PENMYNYDD, Gwynedd *5 SH57*
One of Penmynydd's main features is the church, the foundations of which date from at least the 7thc, although the structure was much restored in 1840. It contains the fine 14th-c altar tomb of the Tudor family, plus three statues decorated with chevrons, believed to have come from a considerably more ancient building. Outside the village stands Plas Penmynydd, now restored and converted into a farmhouse. This was the birthplace of Owen Tudor. Owen fought at Agincourt with Henry V, and in 1436 secretly married the king's widow Katherine de Valois, daughter of the king of France. It is said that when Henry VI's advisers learnt of the union some years later Katherine was sent to the Abbey of Bermondsey, and Owen was arrested and imprisoned in Newgate. After

Katherine's death Owen was pardoned by Henry VI, but was eventually executed after fighting for the Lancastrians in the Battle of Mortimer Cross. One of his sons by Katherine was Edmund of Richmond, who in turn had a son called Henry. Henry later asserted a claim to the English throne and became Henry VII after his victory at Bosworth Field, thus establishing the House of Tudor.

PENNAL, Powys *9 SH70*
Charmingly set amid fine scenery 6m E of Aberdyfi on the Machynlleth road, this little village mainly comprises low, slate-built cottages grouped around St Peter's Church. The latter was rebuilt during the 19thc in early-classical style, with a hipped roof and a gilded weathercock. It contains some fine 20th-c stained glass and interesting 18th-c medallions. On the outskirts of the village stands Talgarth Hall, an 18th-c house which is now a country hotel and caravan park. Roman coins have been discovered in a tomen, or mound, in the grounds.

To the S of the village on a spur of land projecting into the Dyfi Valley are traces of Cefn Gaer Roman fort. These remains have been almost completely obliterated by later occupation, although it is known that there was an external ditch and probably a bath house. The banks and scarps that now remain are probably more medieval than Roman. Discoveries of Roman coins and pottery in the 17thc have emphasized its true origins.

PENNANT MELANGELL, Powys *10 SJ02*
Hidden away 3m up the Pennant Valley and reached by a road that leads nowhere save to the dale head and a waterfall, Pennant Melangell is a hamlet with a story that goes back to the days of the Princes. St Monacella, daughter of an Irish king, had come here for solitude and to escape a marriage for which she had no liking. After fifteen years she encountered Prince Brochwel Ysgythrog, when a hare he was hunting took shelter under her dress. The hounds found themselves unable to move in for a kill, and the huntsman's horn stuck to his lips when he tried to blow it. Monacella told her story to Prince Brochwel and begged for the life of the hare. The prince was so impressed that he granted her request, and also a piece of land on which to found a religious house. The hare became the emblem of St Monacella and is to be met elsewhere in churches of this area.

PENNARD, West Glamorgan *24 SS58*
An inland village lying to the E of Oxwich Bay, Pennard's church carries a battlemented tower and was constructed after the original building had been engulfed by sand. It contains a Norman font and several beams which came from the earlier church, and is thought to stand on the site of an ancient oratory. Interesting features include a memorial to Major Penrice, who fought in the Peninsular War, and several English Jacobean fitments. The font has a canopy from Sonning in Berkshire, and the pulpit is from Shipton in Oxfordshire. The fine 18th-c barrel organ was kept in the loft and is now on loan to the National Museum of Wales in Cardiff.

A badly-ruined 13th-c castle stands on high ground 1¼m W of the church. This
cont page 257

IMPROBABLE PENRHYN

The A5 approach to Bangor offers a sudden view of Penrhyn's battlements cutting into the skyline. It is a dramatic setting, with heavily wooded parkland and the changing colour of the straits in the background. Penrhyn is nothing if not dramatic and theatrical. If the words *impact, impression* and *improbability* can be applied to certain forms of theatre, they are equally apt in describing this cyclopean edifice. On the A55 approach to Bangor it is the third in a series of impressive piles. Bodelwyddan and Gwrych are the others. They are called castles, though not one of them is a genuine fortification. This is not to deny them their architectural verve and vitality, nor their considerable contribution to the landscape, for they are expressions of the 19th-c fashion for revivalism in a variety of styles. In this respect Penrhyn is no exception, and yet in every other respect it is almost unique.

The keep, immediately recognizable as Norman in style, is said to have been modelled on that of Hedingham Castle in Essex, although it also bears a striking resemblance to that at Rochester. Thomas Hopper, the architect of Penrhyn as we know it today, was born in Rochester. A commission from the Prince Regent early in his career launched Hopper into a wide and fashionable practice, with particular emphasis on country-house designs. Pandering to the whims of his clients gave him ample scope for invention and innovation. Hopper was both versatile and flexible, and although Penrhyn is his major work he fulfilled country house commissions in other parts of Wales in Tudor, Jacobean, and neo-classical styles. By the time he set to work on Penrhyn in 1827 he had already had considerable opportunity to experiment with the Norman style while working on Gosford Castle in Co Armagh. When Penrhyn was completed some fourteen years later it presented what was probably the most impressive example of domestic Norman Revival architecture in Great Britain – at a cost of £500,000.

Although what appears on the skyline today may be a megalomaniac's paradise, the site of Penrhyn can claim a history which dates back at least to the 13thc and which was closely connected with that Anglesey family later called Tudor. Anything recognizable as an estate was not formed until Gwilym ap Gruffydd acquired the property through marriage. The name Gruffydd is connected with Penrhyn until 1628, a year which saw the death of Piers, one of the family's most colourful members. In many ways he was a typical Elizabethan who sought adventure and fortune at sea. In 1600 he succeeded in bringing into Aber Cegin – which was to feature so prominently as a port in the later history of Penrhyn – a Spanish vessel called 'Speranza', with a cargo of oil, silks, and other goods. His name has been connected on more than one occasion with the exploits of Drake and Raleigh, but whatever his other successes at piracy might have been, his attempts to mortgage much of his land to rich Londoners between 1602 and 1612 suggest an inability to handle his own affairs. By 1622 his downfall seems to have been complete, for he is referred to as 'formerly of Penrhyn'. A sequence of intricate dealings resulted in the estate becoming the property of John Williams, Lord Keeper of the Great Seal and later Archbishop of York. Williams' ancestors owned the neighbouring house of Cochwillan. Penrhyn passed from this family to the Warburtons of Winnington in Cheshire, and thence to Richard Pennant in 1765.

Although Pennant already possessed substantial sugar estates in Jamaica, his enormous energy and enterprise spurred him to work the neighbouring slate quarries. Several decades later these brought the village of Bethesda into existence, and have dominated the lives of its inhabitants in one way or another ever since. He also busied himself with a new road between Bangor and Capel Curig, and developed a port at Aber Cegin on the Penrhyn Estate. Both were vital to the expansion of a trade and industry that was to produce phenomenal wealth. Towards the end of the century he set to work on transforming the medieval house into a residence which would display the latest fashion in domestic architecture, the gothic-revival style. He employed Samuel Wyatt, the brother of Benjamin who was agent at Penrhyn, as his designer. The new castellated house incorporated certain parts of the 15th-c building – notably the great hall, which forms the drawing room of the present Penrhyn Castle. Richard Pennant was succeeded on his death in 1808 by his grand-nephew George Hay Dawkins, who assumed the name Pennant. Some 20 years were to elapse before work was begun on Thomas Hopper's gigantic plans, but within half a century two houses representing utterly different revival styles had been completed at Penrhyn – an indication of the profligacy of the age as well as the extravagant gestures of individuals.

While the impressive gateway was being erected in Llandegai, Hopper's plans were being carried out in their final splendid detail. For hundreds of local people the structure must have appeared

former Gower stronghold was rectangular with a square tower at each end, and had a gatehouse on the landward side. It appears to have very little history and is believed to have been disused since the reign of Edward I. The scenery in the vicinity is very fine – especially Three Cliffs Bay – and much of the surrounding cliff country is NT property. To the W of Pwll-du Head is lonely Bacon Hole, containing unique cave paintings.

PENPONT, Powys 21 SN92

Some 5m W of Brecon in the Usk Valley, the area around Penpont was landscaped by the local Williams family in the 18th and 19thc and includes some fine larch plantations. The church was greatly restored in 1865 and contains an organ which was once a fixture in Brighton Pavillion. Penpont Hall dates from 1666 but was modernized in 1815. It was the home of the Williams family, and contains many Tudor relics which include portraits of the Boleyns. At the rear are the original stables and an old granary. The Dower House of 1686 was also owned by a Williams, and displays a carved wooden pediment with swags of fruit and scrolls and the Boleyn arms. Near by stands Abercamlais, a 17th-c

house which was rebuilt during the 18thc and contains many Tudor and Stuart items. An octagonal 17th-c bridge with a cupola spans the Usk at this point.

PENRHOSLLIGWY, Gwynedd 5 SH48

A feature of this coastal village, situated on the S bank of Traeth Dulas on the N coast of Anglesey, is the fascinating Din Lligwy iron-age fort (see entry). The secluded, tree-sheltered site helps the visitor to visualize life as it existed nearly 2,000 years ago. It is well signposted and worth a visit, even to people who are not interested in ancient history. Evidence of an even earlier civilization active in these parts is offered by the Lligwy Burial Chamber, which is dated between 3,000 and 2,500BC (see entry).

PENRHYN CASTLE, Gwynedd 5 SH67

A full description of this Victorian extravaganza, situated 1m E of Bangor on the A5, is contained in the special gazetteer inset opposite.

PENRHYNDEUDRAETH, Gwynedd 9 SH63

A largish quarrying village in the developed area around Porthmadog, the starkness of Penrhyndeudraeth's

immediate location contrasts sharply with the magnificent scenery of Snowdonia to the N. Holy Trinity Church, like most of the village, is of fairly recent date and was built in 1858. It carries a crocketed spire, and the inside is of simple design with clear glass windows. Bertrand Russell the philosopher spent the last years of his life at his country home on the village outskirts. A toll road runs S from here to the Ardudwy region.

PENRICE, West Glamorgan 24 SS48

Penrice is a small village on the Gower Peninsula. It was the local centre for prize fighting and cock fighting, but is now chiefly noted for the castles which were built here during the Norman occupation of Gower. The site of the first castle, a wooden fortress, is near Penrice church. The church was restored during the 19thc but still retains a Norman chancel arch with roll moulding, and an early-English south doorway. The second castle was set up in the 13thc, and the gatehouse and curtain wall are still intact. It was originally the home of the Penres family, but was confiscated by Edward III in 1367 after its owner Robert de Penres had been convicted of

as impregnable as Edward I's castles at Caernarfon and Beaumaris. For this was no mere structural eccentricity, but a symbol of implacable strength. George Dawkins Pennant was succeeded by his son-in-law in 1840. Lord-Lieutenant Edward Douglas MP took the name Pennant on succeeding to the estates, and was created Baron Penrhyn of Llandegai in 1866. On the death of the 4th Lord Penrhyn in 1949 his niece Lady Janet Pelham inherited the property and assumed the name Douglas-Pennant. The castle became the property of the NT in 1951.

Penrhyn is the sort of place where it is easy to pretend that at the end of the long approach lies all the promise of intrigue, secret meetings, ruthless discovery, and dreadful vengeance.

On entering the castle the visitor might be tempted to look for sliding panels, secret passages, and blinking eyes behind the family portraits. Decades of 'gothic' films have given us a rich legacy of fanciful and macabre images. The dimensions of the place are worthy of a Citizen Kane, and a film director would be hard put to find a more evocative location for a chivalric fantasy. Since the vast wealth which made Penrhyn Castle possible depended on slate, it is natural that the material should feature prominently in the building – in decorative devices as well as for structural purposes. The Grand Staircase, the floor of the Great Hall, and several fireplaces are made of slate, but the most remarkable use to which it was put can be seen in the Slate Bedroom. Here, among other items of furniture, is a four-ton bedstead which was shown to Queen Victoria during a visit to the castle with the Prince Consort in 1859. Perhaps half suspecting that she was expected to sleep in it she remarked, 'Very interesting, but uninviting.' Local material other than slate has been used extensively at Penrhyn. The

building itself is constructed of Mona 'marble' from Anglesey, and a considerable amount of the furniture which Hopper designed in 'Norman' style was made from oak grown on the estate. Some of the most notable of these pieces are the bed in the State Bedroom, the couch in the Drawing room, and the octagonal table in the Great Hall.

There are no guided tours at Penrhyn, so visitors can flow freely through the many apartments on display – all with their own individuality and idiosyncrasies, but each contributing to the unity of design which marked Hopper's intentions. The Great Hall, with its slender clustered columns, decorated rib vaulting, balustraded balcony, ornate fireplace, and stained glass leads to the Library which exceeds everybody's notion of Victorian atmosphere: ostentatious, oppressive, and unnerving. The Drawing Room is less cumbersome on the eye, but the Ebony Room is another example of decorative indulgence. The spacious, comparatively unadorned Dining Room houses part of the castle's collection of paintings. On the first floor the Chapel, the King's Room, the Queen's Room, the State Bedroom, and the Slate Bedroom all add to a picture of Dawkins Pennant as a man with little regard for comfort. Although virginia creeper has softened the grey mass of walls and turrets, the general impression is still one of uncompromising sternness. Inside the application of academic thoroughness has produced more varied results. If a large proportion of the decorative motives are of Norman derivation, an equal proportion has found inspiration in what one might call Norman deviation – in the Grand Staircase in particular. Whether the devices are chaste and geometric or profuse and imaginative, the play of light on them gives the construction a surprising mobility and energy. Well worth seeing are the Locomotive Museum, a collection of dolls, a natural-history room, and a splendidly planned walled garden.

Keep

Locomotive Museum

Gardens

murder. His son bought back the estate in 1391, but it returned to the crown soon afterwards as he had no heirs. During the 16thc the castle was finally abandoned when the Mansel family moved into Oxwich Castle. The remains stand on private land and can be viewed by appointment only.

PENSARN, Clwyd *6 SH97*
This seaside resort has 5m of sandy beach and has become a suburb of nearby Abergele. The town became popular in Victorian times and has many boarding houses. There are numerous caravan sites in the surrounding area. Captain Matthew Webb trained here before becoming the first man to swim the English Channel in 1875.

PENTRAETH, Gwynedd *5 SH57*
Maps made in the 17thc show Pentraeth as a small village standing at the head of Red Wharf Bay on Anglesey, but it now lies 1m inland and is backed by high wooded slopes. Anglesey was subjected to continuous attacks by Viking raiding parties from the 8thc onwards, and this area – like Holyhead and Aberffraw – was one of their prime targets. Equally unwelcome visitors were the Llanddonna witches, a collection of smugglers and beggars who arrived in an open boat with neither oars nor rudder and proceeded to terrify the local community. These people were in all probability Irish criminals; one of the punishments in Ireland at that time was to set wrong-doers adrift in a boat with no means of navigation or propulsion.

PENTRE-CWRT, Dyfed *17 SN33*
According to legend this village once incurred the disapproval of the Devil. There is a large mound of earth midway between Pentre-Cwrt and Llandyssul, and the fable maintains that the Devil so disliked the inhabitants of Pentre-Cwrt that he set out with a gigantic spade-full of earth to fill in the River Teifi and drown them. On the way he met a cobbler carrying a sack full of worn out shoes. Realizing what the Evil One had in mind, the cobbler told him that the village was so far away that he had worn out all the shoes getting there. The Devil decided that vengeance was not worth the long walk, abandoned his plan, and deposited his earth where he stood. The mound is still standing for all to see.

PENTREFOELAS, Clwyd *6 SH85*
Points of interest in this 19th-c hamlet, situated alongside the A5 near the River Conwy, include an old watermill which still functions and an 8ft inscribed pillar known as the Levelinus Stone. The latter is a memorial to Llywelyn ap Seisyll, who was killed there in a battle in 1023. Some 2m up the Conwy lies Ysbyty-Ifan, which was once a refuge and sanctuary for travellers and was under the care of the Knights Hospitallers of St John. It later became a haven for thieves and murderers, who pillaged the surrounding countryside until they were finally ejected during the reign of Henry VII. Situated on the old Denbighshire side of Betws-y-coed, the hamlet marks the transition of Snowdon's mountains to gentle moorland. To the NE is the lovely Alwen Reservoir, 3m long and averaging ¼m wide. It is one of the largest in Wales, and its waters are said to be guarded by a monster. This beast is supposed to have killed two oxen who attempted to drink the water.

PENTRE IFAN, Dyfed *17 SN03*
Said to be the finest of its kind in Britain, this 5,000-year-old megalithic long barrow (AM) is situated near Newport and is of prime historical importance. It consists of a 16½ft capstone weighing in the region of 16 tons, and three spindly uprights which seem quite incapable of supporting such a load. The monument was the subject of a painting by Richard Tonge, who emphasized this point by depicting the capstone almost floating in mid air (full OS map reference SN 099 370).

PENYBONT, Powys *14 SO16*
Early last century the postal address of Llandrindod Wells was 'near Penybont', but by the end of the century the positions were reversed. Penybont's importance derived from the fact that it was first a coach stop and later a postal centre. A post master was appointed here in 1818. The question of establishing an agricultural market at Llandrindod Wells was discussed in 1918 and 1919, and was finally disposed of with the decision that it would be inappropriate for sheep and cattle to be driven through the streets of a spa town. So a local auctioneer instituted livestock auctions at Penybont in 1919, and thus the village became a market centre for the spa. It is now one of the best stock markets anywhere around.

Penybont has long been noted for its races, which are still held to this day. Whether they were originally held on Penybont Common is conjectural, but the present riverside course has been in use since early this century. There is a grandstand on the far side of the course, which is reached by a bridge made of railway sleepers constructed in 1963 by the proprietor of the Severn Arms Hotel. The old Victorian atmosphere has been deliberately retained at this hotel, along with modern comfort. It contains the old court room, now divided into two, which was later superseded by a green corrugated-iron building set up alongside the hotel called the Iron Room. Magistrates continued the local administration of justice from here. The hotel is named after the Severn family of Penybont Hall, who acquired it from the Prices through the marriage of J C Severn to John Price's daughter. The Prices originally built the hotel, and J C Severn enlarged and embellished it. The last survivors of the family were the three Misses Severn, who rebuilt Penybontfawr church as a memorial to their parents.

PENYBONTFAWR, Powys *10 SJ02*
A village in a picturesque setting among the Berwyn Mountains, Penybontfawr is near the start of the Cerrig Milltir Pass which climbs over the Berwyns, with 2,713ft Moel Sych rising to the E. The summit of this mountain provides widespread views over the Dee Valley. Some 2m NE is Llanrhaeadr ym Mochnant, where a by-road leads NW to Pistyll Rhaeadr. This 240ft waterfall is one of the traditional seven wonders of Wales.

PEN-Y-CAE, Powys *21 SN81*
Set in the Brecon Beacons national park about 20m SW of Brecon, this Tawe-valley village is located at a point which virtually marks the end of industrial S Wales. To the N lies Craig-y-Nos Castle,

a replica of a Scottish baronial manor which was extended by the Spanish prima donna Adelina Patti, who purchased it in 1878. The house had a large aviary, two lakes, an elaborate winter garden, and the Patti Pavilion – which has now been transported to Victoria Park in Swansea. Following Madam Patti's death in 1919 the property was handed to the Welsh National Memorial Association and now serves as a hospital. Madam Patti's private 200-seat theatre was re-opened in 1963. The surrounding countryside is mountainous, with 2,632ft Carmarthen Van rising among the Black Mountains in the NW, and 2,381ft Fan Gihirych to the NE in the Fforest Fawr.

PEN-Y-CRUG, Powys *21 SO03*
This iron-age hillfort lies N of Brecon and is set on a rounded, 1,088ft hill defended by well-preserved trenches and high embankments. It affords fine views of the Brecon Beacons and Fforest Fawr.

PEN-Y-DARREN, Mid Glamorgan *21 SO00*
Pen-y-Darren is a Roman fort situated in Penydarren Park at Merthyr Tydfil. Its existence first came to light during the building of Penydarren House in 1786, but it was not identified as a fort until more excavations took place between 1902 and 1904. The defences were not discovered until 1957. Most of the remains were removed to make way for a football ground, but evidence suggests that the fort was squarish and set on a spur of land commanding a wide view. It originally covered 5 acres and contained the usual buildings, including a granary and a well. Remains of a cemetery were discovered on the NW side. Dating rests mainly on fragments of pottery found on the site, and it is possible that the fort was set up in AD 74. It is thought that the structure was finally abandoned during the reign of Hadrian.

PEN-Y-GAER, Gwynedd *5 SH76*
Standing on a knoll in the W extremity of the Rhiangoll Valley, the site of this Roman fort is now occupied by Pen-y-Gaer and Greenhill farms. The defences can still be followed however, with the exception of those in the SW corner which have been destroyed by ploughing. The original site covered about 3½ acres, and the fort was probably established between AD 80 and AD 130. It is probable that it was built in three distinct phases.

PEN-Y-GAER, Powys *22 SO12*
This iron-age hillfort overlooks the village of Llanbedr-y-Cennin, and is said to be the only one of its kind in Wales with a slope set with sharp upright stone slabs – apparently arranged to break up attacks. The structure may have been used by the Welsh as a defence against the invading Romans.

PENYGARREG RESERVOIR, Powys *13 SN96*
One of a 9m-long chain of lakes set up in 1904 by Birmingham Corporation to supply the city with 60 million gallons of water per day, this artificial lake forms part of the Elan Valley complex. It lies between Craig Goch Reservoir and Garreg Ddu Reservoir, and has a small, fir-covered island in the centre. The 417½ft-long dam supports a lake surface of 124 acres.

PENYGROES, Gwynedd 5 SH45

Penygroes is a colourful quarryman's town on the W approaches to Snowdonia. To the NE stands Glynlliffon, a 19th-c mansion now converted into a college.

PENYGWRYD, Gwynedd 5 SH65

There is nothing more here than a solitary hotel of the same name, standing at the junction of the Llanberis Pass and the Nant Gwynant. Penygwryd Hotel has played a notable part in the development of Welsh rock climbing and mountaineering. The inn was founded in the 1830's, but it was not until the latter half of the century that interest in climbing as a sport developed. The pioneers were largely Oxford and Cambridge men, and the Climbers' Club was formed at a meeting of 40 frequenters of Penygwryd.

Today the inn could never cope with the numbers who have enthusiastically taken up the sport, but it remains as a veritable museum of climbing history. In 1953 it was the headquarters of the successful Everest team, who did their preparatory training on the neighbouring peaks. One of the ceilings is autographed by the team, and a piece of Everest rock – a gift from Edmund Hillary to the licensees – can be seen behind the bar. One of the best-trodden tracks to Snowdon's summit is the Pyg track, which takes its name from Pen-y-Gwryd. This is more frequently written as 'Pig' track these days.

PENYSARN, Gwynedd 5 SH49

This small town is overlooked by the once coal- and copper-rich Parys Mountain. Mining flourished here during the 18thc, and the mountain now resembles a desolate lunar landscape riddled with disused mine workings and capped by an ancient windmill.

PICTON CASTLE, Dyfed 18 SN01

Situated 4m SE of Haverfordwest off the A40, the original castle on this site was built by William Picton during the reign of William Rufus in the 12thc. This structure has now completely vanished, and the ruins of a castle block, towers and gatehouse which are still standing date from the 13th or 14thc. The castle is the home of the Phillips family, who were in residence when it was garrisoned by royalists during the civil war. A lengthy seige which ensued was terminated when a parliamentary messenger snatched an infant Phillips through an open window and declared the child a hostage. His superiors' disapproval was made apparent by the fact that the garrison was given the full honours of war, and the stronghold was left intact. Today the castle (OACT) has been modernized, and the wooded walks, lawns, azaleas, rhododendrons, and flowering shrubs of the gardens are occasionally available to the public in aid of the National Gardens Scheme.

PIPTON, Powys 22 SO13

This small village is noted for two old farmhouses called respectively the Ddrew and Pipton Farm. Ddrew was a seat of the Morgan family, and 19th-c Pipton Farm is said to stand on the spot where Simon de Montfort signed a treaty with Llywelyn ap Gruffydd. At Three Cocks Junction there is an excavated megalithic long barrow, comprising a blind entrance and forecourt, and two chambers.

19th-c Plas Newydd was built of Moelfre marble by James Wyatt.

PLAS NEWYDD, Gwynedd 5 SH57

About 1½m from Llanfair PG on the A4080, this early 19th-c mansion stands on the site once occupied by a 15th-c structure. The mansion was rebuilt in Moelfre marble by James Wyatt and Joseph Potter in the gothic style, although some of the battlements and towers were removed in the 1930's. A Whistler mural was added to give depth to the long, narrow dining room. The gothic harbour and boathouse below the house are also the work of Wyatt. Opposite the stables is the huge Plas Newydd burial chamber, with an 11ft by 9ft capstone and a small ante-chamber. The house stands in fine parkland which affords excellent views of Snowdonia. Queen Victoria stayed here during the summer of 1832, prior to her accession to the throne.

PLYNLIMON RANGE, THE

Although one of the most important and well-known mountains of Wales, Plynlimon is visually one of the least impressive. It lies about 12m inland from the coast at Aberystwyth and 9m S of the Dyfi Valley at Machynlleth. Much of the surrounding area comprises high moorland hills which rise to 2,000ft in places, and so the full height of 2,469ft Plynlimon is not evident and it cannot be seen from any point near sea level. From almost every direction it appears as a rounded hill a little higher than its neighbours. It is only from the W at the level of the 1,150ft-high Nant-y-Moch Reservoir that the mountain can be properly appreciated. From here it rises another 1,300ft, and the low crags which give it more of a mountain appearance are visible. Climbers will be disappointed; this is walking country which is easy in spite of there being only two recognized paths – in fact only two.

Plynlimon is one of the wettest mountains in Wales, not in terms of rainfall but because of its vast damp and bog-covered slopes. It has been described as 'sodden weariness'. By contrast the summit is dry and heather covered in spite of the high springs which surround it. With so much water available it is not surprising that the area is the source of four rivers, two of which may have been reasons for the mountain's fame. They are the Severn, the Clywedog, the Wye, and the Rheidol.

Views from the top of Plynlimon are famous for the number of mountain ranges which they encompass, and yet depressing for the vast amount of brown, lifeless, moorland which dominates the foreground. On a very good day the panorama takes in most of Wales from Snowdonia to the Prescelly Hills and the Brecon Beacons. The immediate area of Plynlimon has changed in recent years. Much afforestation, mainly to the S and E, has converted useless hill slopes and patches of peat bog into productive and colourful areas of land. To the S of Plynlimon are large scattered plantations of the Rheidol Forest, while to the E around the head waters of the River Severn is the Hafren Forest. Hafren is the seventh largest forest in Wales and covers over 9,000 acres. Stones on the summit are marked WWW, which stands for Watkin Williams Wynne. The Wynne family of Wynnstay Park near Ruabon owned a considerable amount of land between the Ruabon area and Plynlimon, and these stones marked the boundary of one of their properties.

The name of the mountain has varied considerably in spelling over the centuries, with at least eight different versions recorded. The most popular versions now in use are Plynlimon and 'Pumlumon'. The variation of spelling results in different suggestions as to its meaning; *Llumman* is Welsh for a banner, and *llumon* means a beacon. It is known that Foel Fadian was used as a beacon site. The Plym or Plyn part may have some connection with the Latin name for lead and the now abandoned lead mines on its slopes, but this is unlikely. The generally accepted theory is a shortening to *Pum* of *Pump*, Welsh for five. This may refer to five rivers having their source on the mountain – the fifth is taken to be the Ystwyth,

259

although this rises S of the A44 – or to the five prominent lower summits.

PONT ABERGLASLYN, Gwynedd
9 SH54
Picturesquely-wooded Aberglaslyn Pass carries the road from Tremadog Bay to Beddgelert. To the W is 2,566ft Moel Hebog; and E are the twin Moelwyns. The Welsh Highland Railway once traversed the pass by means of tunnels (see feature starting page 62).

PONTARDAWE, West Glamorgan
20 SN70
Hills surround this one-time industrial town, which lies in the Tawe Valley 8m N of Swansea. To the W, along a road that leads on to the mountain side from nearby Rhyd-y-fro, is the megalithic stone circle of Carn Llechart. This features a chambered tomb in the middle. Farther up the road from Rhyd-y-fro is Penlle'r Castell, where there is a pre-Roman earthwork. A large stone circle and several cairns are to be seen on Cefn Gwrhyd to the N of Pontardawe. To the E are 1,350ft Mynydd March Hywel, and Cil-y-bebyll church. The latter carries a 13th-c tower. All Saint's Church is noted for its peal of tubular bells.

PONTARDULAIS, Dyfed 20 SN50
Despite the presence of collieries, foundries, and other heavy industry which developed this Loughor estuary town, Pontardulais still blends pleasantly into its natural setting of wooded hills. The town was at the centre of the bloody Rebecca Riots during the agrarian troubles of the 1840's, and the lane down which the rioters rode can still be pointed out. The Pontardulais Male Voice Choir was one of the finest in the county between the two world wars, and the present choir is held in high esteem.

PONTBLYDDYN, Clwyd 7 SJ26
An enterprising gardener here has cut the village name into his garden hedge, opposite the Druid Inn. Notable houses along this road including Fferm, a 16th-c farmhouse, Pentre Hobyn, Gwysaney, and the eye-catching Plas Teg – a gaunt Jacobean mansion built for the Trevor family on the Wrexham side of the village. It has a reputation for ghost-chasing ghosts, which is probably why it has never been lived in for long. The village itself lies between Mold and Wrexham.

PONT ERWYD, Dyfed 13 SN78
Situated on the A44 highway to Aberystwyth, Pont Erwyd has both an 18th-c and a modern bridge spanning the River Rheidol. The George Borrow Hotel, originally named the Gogerddan Arms, was renamed after the famous author in 1847 to commemorate his stay there. Just in front of the hotel are the Eagle gorge and falls. From here a mountain road leading to Talybont passes the Nant-y-Moch Reservoir and Aber Ceiro Fach, the birthplace of Sir John Rhys. Sir John lived from 1840 to 1915 and became the first Celtic language professor at Oxford University.

PONTRHYDFENDIGAID, Dyfed
12 SN76
About 1m E of this typical Welsh village is the Church of St Mary, which stands in the grounds of Strata Florida Abbey. It was rebuilt in 1815 but still retains the pulpit of 1724 and curved communion rails from an earlier building. Some of its windows were donated by Sir David Jones, who was born in the area and became the owner of Cross and Blackwell. Sir David also provided the village with its huge auditorium, which is a centre for eisteddfodau and Welsh pop festivals. A large yew tree in the churchyard marks the alleged burial place of the 14th-c poet Dafydd ap Gwilym, and a nearby gravestone bears the inscription 'The leg and part of the thigh of Henry Hughs, Cooper, was cut off and interred here June 18 1756'. Hughs had been injured in a stage coach accident, but survived to emigrate to America.

PONTRHYDYGROES, Dyfed 12 SN77
The name means the 'bridge at the ford of the cross', and evidently relates to a ford on the Ystwyth used by monks travelling over the old Monk's Road between Abbey Cwm Hir and Strata Florida. The village named after it stands in a wooded valley surrounded by mountains, and was once a prosperous centre of the lead-mining industry. Nearby is the Hafod estate, once owned by a branch of the Herbert family but now in the possession of the Forestry Commission. Its heyday was the late 18thc, when it was owned by Thomas Johnes (1748–1816). He rebuilt the mansion, landscaped the grounds, and planted more than two million trees. He acquired a priceless library of rare books and manuscripts and kept a private press.

A disastrous fire in 1807 destroyed most of these treasures and did £70,000 worth of damage. But Johnes set to work to build it up all over again. Unfortunately he had not been insured, and he had to sell some of his remaining valuables and realize some of his timber; even then he found his money insufficient. In 1811, when his only daughter Marianne died, his heart went out of the work. He commissioned an elaborate memorial to her, which was placed in the Hafod church, but fire took its toll again in 1922. The church was burnt down and the memorial ruined. The full story of Hafod and its tragedies has been written in the form of the novel *Peacocks in Paradise* by Elizabeth Inglis-Jones.

PONTYPOOL, Gwent 22 SO20
An industrial town in a predominantly coal-mining and tinplate district, Pontypool was the first town in Britain to successfully produce tinplate in 1720. It is claimed that the first forge in America was built by immigrants from Pontypool in 1652, and Japanese-type lacquer ware has been manufactured in the town since the 17thc. Workers from the town played a large part in the Newport Chartist Riots of 1839. Unlike most other industrial centres in S Wales, Pontypool has never abandoned its interests in agriculture. While its urban population level has fallen, the number of inhabitants in rural areas has steadily increased. About 2m E is Llandegfedd Reservoir, which supplies water to Cardiff. Sailing and fishing are allowed here by permit. The Monmouthshire and Brecon Canal runs for 33½m from Pontypool to Brecon, and is used for pleasure cruising.

PONTYPRIDD, Mid Glamorgan 25 ST09
In the S apex of the Rhondda Valley at the confluence of the Taff and the Rhondda, Pontypridd's principal industries are coal and iron. Anchor chains for Nelson's fleet were produced here, and these are still manufactured for large ships. The town suffered considerable unemployment and population loss during the 1930's and although coal and iron are still important, a good proportion of the inhabitants look to the light industries of the nearby Treforest Industrial Estate for employment.

An 18th-c, 140ft single-span bridge over the Taff at Pontypridd was designed by a local self-taught engineer called William Edwards, who completed the project in 1755 after previous efforts had collapsed. The structure is considered a masterpiece of its kind. Ynysangharad Park, in the centre of the town, contains statues by Sir Goscombe John to Evan and James James – the father and son clothmakers who wrote the Welsh national anthem *Hen Wlad Fy Nhadau* (*Land of My Fathers*). A memorial tablet adorns their house in Mill Street. On a common to the E of the town is a 12-ton logan stone which can be rocked by applying very slight pressure.

PORT DINORWIC, Gwynedd 5 SH56
Formerly a busy Menai Strait's port which served the Dinorwic slate quarry at Llanberis, Port Dinorwic has now become primarily a yachting base. It was used as an anchorage by the Vikings during their 8th-c raids and was once a fishing centre. Near by was the mainland point of the Moel-y-Don ferry to Anglesey. To the NW lies the extensive park of the 18th-c Vaynol Hall, once home of the Assheton-Smiths, who owned the Dinorwic quarry.

PORT EYNON, West Glamorgan
24 SS48
Also known as Porteinon, this attractive village preserves a few thatched cottages and lies in a cove at the foot of a steep hill on the S coast of the Gower Peninsula. Named after the 12th-c Welsh prince Einion, it boasts 1m of dune-backed sands which screens a caravan park. The village may well have been a centre for smugglers and pirates, and there is a record of John Lucas of Salt House, a local Robin Hood, being outlawed in the 17thc for 'cozening of pirates and dangerous men'. His house was wrecked by storms in the early 1700's. Culver Hole, a cave just over the headland, may well have featured in these activities. The entrance has been walled up with medieval masonry pierced with slits resembling windows. The true purpose of this structure has never been satisfactorily explained. A corner of the graveyard of the local church contains a carved marble figure of a lifeboatman – a memorial to three members of a local lifeboat who were drowned in January 1916 while answering a distress call. The village lies 16m SW of Swansea on the A4118, and is a noted surfing centre. Outstanding cliff scenery extends E into Oxwich Bay.

*PORTHCAWL, Mid Glamorgan 25 SS87
Ranking as one of the leading resorts on the S coast of Wales, Porthcawl is situated on a low limestone promontory midway between Cardiff and Swansea, overlooking the Bristol Channel. On a clear day the tors of Exmoor can be seen from here. To the E and W of the town stretch sand-dune covered bays from which bathing is generally safe,

Entries marked * are the starting point of drives included in the Day Drive section of the book (pages 95 to 144).

but care should be taken as fast currents flow round the headlands. The town was originally developed during the 19thc as a coal port, but never really became established because of competition from larger ports – particularly Barry, which was constructed soon afterwards. The inner basin has now been filled in to form a car park, but a small harbour for private craft and pleasure steamers still exists between the two piers.

The harbour is the central point of this attractive town, with its numerous hotels, boarding houses, and shops. On the W side is the Esplanade, a marvellous sun-trap which leads past the Grand Pavilion – a venue for first-class entertainment throughout the year. The West Drive leads on from this to Locks Common, Rest Bay, and an eighteen-hole golf course belonging to the Royal Porthcawl Golf Club, considered one of the best in Wales. To the E of the harbour are the fine sandy reaches of Sandy Bay and Trecco Bay, separated by the low rocky headland of Rhych Point. A miniature railway runs alongside the Eastern Promenade. The large funfair of Coney Beach is modelled on and named after Coney Island in New York, and stretches

along Sandy Bay. Near by is a model village and a 3,000 pitch caravan site. The 13th-c church at Newton is of interest.

Porthcawl has a putting course, bowling greens, and tennis courts. Freshwater fishing, particularly for trout and sewin, is possible in the Ogmore, Ewenny, and Kenfig. Pleasure steamers operate cruises along the Bristol Channel from here. All Saint's Church was built before the first world war and is well worth a visit. The handsome Chapel of Ease is situated on Mary Street, and contains two sanctuary chairs which are reputed to have come from a French Monastery. The colours of the Welch Regiment were presented to the church by the late Duke of Windsor when he was Prince of Wales. Beyond Rest Bay are Sker Point and Sker House. R D Blackmore's *The Maid of Sker* features this house and the surrounding area. The resort is a water ski-ing centre.

PORTH DINLLAEN, Gwynedd   8 SH24
The whitewashed cottages of Porth Dinllaen are strung out along the shoreline and present an enchanting prospect viewed from the other side of the bay. The picturesque view inevitably draws the visitor for a closer inspection

of this Lleyn village, which lies 2m from Nefyn on the N coast of the Lleyn Peninsula. Its history is almost exclusively associated with the sea. The remoteness of its situation made it an obvious haunt for smugglers and pirates in the 17thc, and its safe anchorage later helped it to develop into a substantial port in the busy days of sail. Efforts to establish Porth Dinllaen as the main port in the development of communications and trade with Ireland foundered on one vote when parliament came to decide between Holyhead and Porth Dinllaen in the early 1800's. W A Madocks was the promoter of Porth Dinllaen's claims and had the backing of an Irish engineer. Porth Dinllaen once handled as many as 100 ships a month, but declined with the advent of steam.

*PORTHMADOG, Gwynedd   9 SH53
Plan overleaf
The S gateway to the lovely Lleyn Peninsula, Porthmadog developed as a result of the reclamation of land in the Glaslyn estuary by William Alexander Madocks. Travellers have to pay a toll to cross the 1m-long embankment which Madocks built in the early 1800's to reclaim 4,500 acres of sea and sand.
cont overleaf

1   All Saint's Church
2   Coney Beach
3   Grand Pavilion

4   Miniature Railway
5   Model Village
6   Newton Church

7   WTB Information Centre

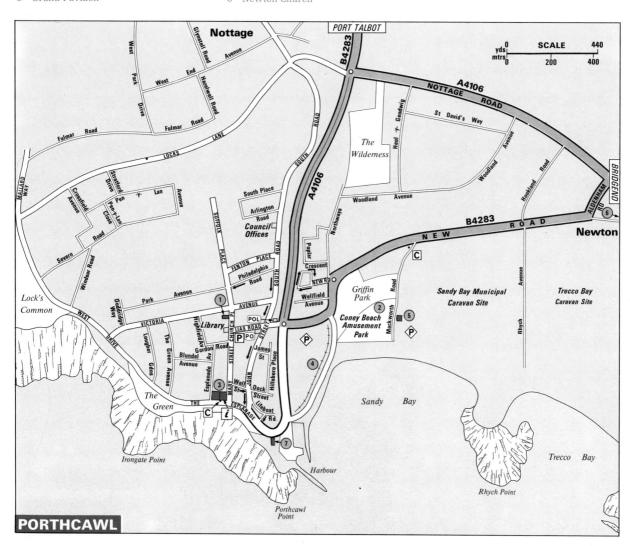

The scheme was first conceived by Sir John Wynne of Gwydir in the 17thc, but he lacked the engineering ability to carry it out. The embankment, or cob as it is called locally, was almost the ruination of Madocks and cost £100,000 – a princely sum for those days. Six months after it was completed the whole scheme was nearly washed away when gales tore a huge hole in it. Some 892 men and 757 horses were engaged in plugging the hole. The rescue scheme almost came to a halt for want of finance, but Lord Bulkeley of Baron Hill in Anglesey called a meeting to raise money. One of the subscribers was the poet Shelley, who contributed £100 and promised to promote the scheme in London.

Although Madocks had ambitious plans for Tremadog and Porth Dinllaen, ironically it was Porthmadog which developed. The building of the embankment created a good harbour and the town became one of the most important ports along the Welsh coast. Its prosperity was assured with the building of the Festiniog narrow-gauge railway in 1836, for it became the point from which the slate quarried at Blaenau Ffestiniog was exported. A station of the revived Welsh Highland line is to be sited in the town (see page 62).

Porthmadog itself attracts thousands of visitors in the summer, and is notable for the extensive beaches near by. Black Rock sands is a popular mecca for motorists because its firm beach allows parking for hundreds of vehicles. Borth-y-Gest is virtually a seaside suburb of Porthmadog. The town provides a fine view of Cnight, a lesser peak of Snowdon, often called the Matterhorn of Wales because of its profile. The flat, marshy country known as Traeth Mawr is backed by the Moelwyns and Snowdon ranges, but there are some people who have never forgiven Madocks for spoiling a delightful estuary by draining it. Among those who lamented this scenic loss was the 18th-c novelist Thomas Love Peacock, who wrote 'The mountain-frame remains unchanged, unchangeable, but the liquid mirror it enclosed is gone'. Holiday cottages, built in 1968 look self-consciously modern on the quayside. Ynys Towyn (NT) is a good viewpoint.

PORTH OER, Gwynedd *8 SH12*
Some 2m from Aberdaron at the tip of the Lleyn Peninsula, Porth Oer is better known to visitors as Whistling Sands. The name is not a piece of tourist gimmickry; the sands actually do whistle underfoot. This effect has something to do with the texture of the sand, and other examples are few and far between. Porth Oer itself is a sheltered sandy bay with good bathing and a beach-side café. A large car park has been provided on the approach to the beach.

PORTH YSGO, Gwynedd *8 SH22*
This delightful bay on the Lleyn Peninsula between Rhiw and Aberdaron is reached from Ysgo Farm by means of a small valley full of ferns, gorse, and foxgloves. This little chine contains a tree-hung stream and a derelict manganese mine half hidden in the undergrowth near the path. The sand and shingle beach is completely submerged at high tide, and backed by an arc of grassy cliffs amid fine coastal scenery. Most of the area is under the management of the NT. Limited parking is available at the head of the valley.

PORTMEIRION, Gwynedd *9 SH53*
Set on a wooded peninsula overlooking Traeth Bay between Porthmadog and Penrhyndeudraeth, Portmeirion is the work of the distinguished Welsh architect Mr Clough Williams-Ellis. He had long been a campaigner against the spoiling of Britain's landscape, and in 1926 he set out to prove that the development of an old estate did not necessarily mean wrecking it. In the heart of the Welsh countryside he erected a 17th-c style Italianate village after the fashion of Portofino or Sorrento. Portmeirion contains a castle, lighthouse, watch tower, campanile, and grottos intermingled with 18th-c English cottages, and each building has been sited to the best advantage of natural slopes and heights. A 19th-c house to the waterfront has been converted into a hotel and contains an 18th-c fireplace and a library removed in its entirety from the Great Exhibition of 1851. Many other items of discarded British architecture have been incorporated in the village.

The estate also encompasses Gwylt Gardens, which is considered one of the finest wild gardens in Wales and contains rhododendrons, hydrangeas, azaleas, a collection of exotic plants introduced by Caton Haigh – one of the foremost authorities on Himalayan flowering trees – palms, cypresses, and eucalyptus. The village has been used as a film set on numerous occasions. and was the setting for the successful television series *The Prisoner*. Noel Coward wrote his comedy *Blithe Spirit* there in one week. Portmeirion has been called 'the last nobleman's folly' and the 'home for fallen buildings', but it remains a triumph of imaginative architecture. The estate is open to visitors on payment of a toll.

PORTSKEWETT, Gwent *26 ST48*
A ferry which crossed the Severn once operated from here, and a legend tells how Charles I used it to escape pursuit by parliamentary troops. When the ferryman had deposited the king on the opposite bank he returned to find a group of Roundheads awaiting him. They forced him to take them across, but he stopped the boat at a reef known as the English Stones and persuaded them that this was the limit to which he was allowed to go. The troopers disembarked and the ferryman quickly sought the safety of deeper waters, from whence he was able to watch them drown as the tide rose. As a result of this incident ferry rights were withdrawn. Today the Severn Tunnel emerges close by the town, which is now the site of factories and a cement works. Nearby Sudbrook Fort has yielded prehistoric finds, and Heston Brake – also in the vicinity – is an unusual chambered tomb where human and ox bones were found in 1888.

PORT TALBOT, West Glamorgan
25 SS79
One of the larger towns of S Wales, Port Talbot is bypassed by the M4 and lies on the shore of the Bristol Channel. It has

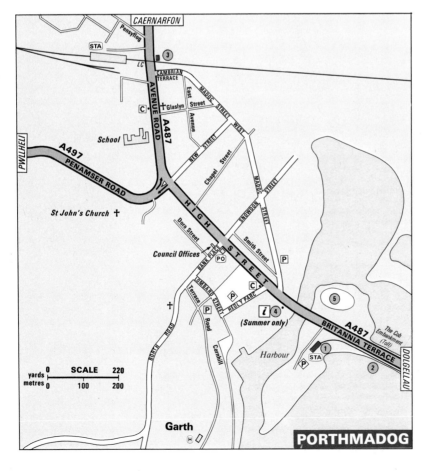

1   Festiniog Railway, Harbour Station, & Museum
2   The Cob
3   Welsh Highland Railway (future site of station)
4   WTB Information Centre
5   Ynys Towyn (NT; viewpoint)

direct road and rail connections with both Swansea and Cardiff, and was originally known as Port Aberavon. Growth of industry around the harbour area developed it into a town in its own right and it was re-named after the Talbot family of Margam Abbey, who were pioneers of its industrial growth. Aberavon, a much older town, has now become Port Talbot's residential suburb and an entertaining coastal resort.

Industry came to Port Talbot in 1770 with the establishment of a copper-smelting works, and its growth continued throughout the 19thc because the port facilities enabled copper ore to be shipped from the nearby Cornish coast. After the opening of the South Wales Railway coal exports grew steadily, and the fact that many coalmining villages of the Rhondda emerged near Port Talbot meant that it now became a major distribution point. New docks were constructed in 1899 to cope with this flow of traffic. In 1946 it was decided to set up a steel works in Port Talbot. The Margam and Abbey steelworks are the largest in Britain and now cover 4½m. BP Chemicals (UK) Ltd have established a petroleum chemicals plant here. Once again harbour facilities proved to be inadequate, and the new tidal harbour which was completed in 1970 is the largest in Great Britain.

Margam Abbey dominated the area during the Middle Ages and was founded in 1147 by Robert, Earl of Gloucester. Under the Cistercian monks it became the local cultural and educational centre until its dissolution in 1537. Remains of the 13th-c Chapter House, the walls of the presbytery, the south transept, and the vast 18th-c Orangery are still visible. The original nave is now part of Margam parish church, which also contains windows by William Morris. A museum on the abbey site contains two 16th-c stones and the great Wheel Cross of Conbelin among many other interesting exhibits.

Inland the narrow Cwm Afan flows between high mountains, with the villages of Cwmavon, Pontrhydyfen, and Cwmmer near its course. Mountain roads from the valley afford excellent views and link with the Rhondda and Maesteg. Actor Richard Burton was born at Pontrhydyfen, and near by is a site once occupied by a grange of Margam Abbey. In Welsh folklore this is celebrated as being the one-time home of a monk whose gift for foretelling the future earned him the nickname 'Tom of the Fair Lies'. The 2m-long Afan-Argoed Country Park lies 3m N of the M4 and can be reached via the A4107. It offers forest walks, picnic sites, and provides a car park.

POWIS CASTLE, Powys   11 SJ20
Full details of this historic castle are given in the special gazetteer inset overleaf.

PRESTATYN, Clwyd   6 SJ08
Like its bigger sister Rhyl, which is 3m W, Prestatyn sets out in a determined way to cater for the family holidaymaker. Few children's amusements are overlooked in its considerable entertainment complex, and the sandy beaches are noted for their safe bathing. At Central Beach is the Royal Lido, containing a large open-air swimming pool, restaurant, ballroom, and children's centre. To the W at Ffrith Beach are boating and canoe lakes, a miniature railway, and a children's playground, among other amusements. Good car parking makes Prestatyn popular with day visitors. A castle was built here in the 12thc at the time when Owain Cyfeiliog, Prince of Powys, was trying to establish a united Wales. Along with Owain Lord of Gwynedd and Rhys Lord of Deheubarth, he fought three victorious battles against Henry II and gained control of Prestatyn castle. The Lords of the N and S, hearing that the Prince of Powys was becoming too strong, united against him and took control of the castle – which they demolished.

Today only the foundations remain of what was once a low motte inside a rectangular bailey. These exist in a field on private land in the lower part of the town. Remains of 8th-c Offa's Dyke, which ended here, are located near the town. The skeleton of a neolithic woman now known as the Prestatyn Lady was found under the High Street. Stone-age graves have also been located in the vicinity of the town. Features of the church at Gwaenysgor, 1m SE of Prestatyn, include a Norman font resembling the one in Lincoln Cathedral, an Elizabethan chalice inscribed 'The Cuppe of Gwaynisker', and registers dating back to 1538.

*PRESTEIGNE, Powys   14 SO36
This charming little town was once the capital of the old county of Radnorshire and is full of period atmosphere. Its streets are an architectural delight. Broad Street is a treasury of Georgian houses, while the Radnorshire Arms is a Jacobean half-timbered building with a priest hole where a member of the clergy lived for two years undiscovered, and kept a diary
cont page 265

1 Cinema & Arts Centre
2 Gwaenysgor Church
3 Miniature Railway
4 Royal Lido
5 WTB Information Centre

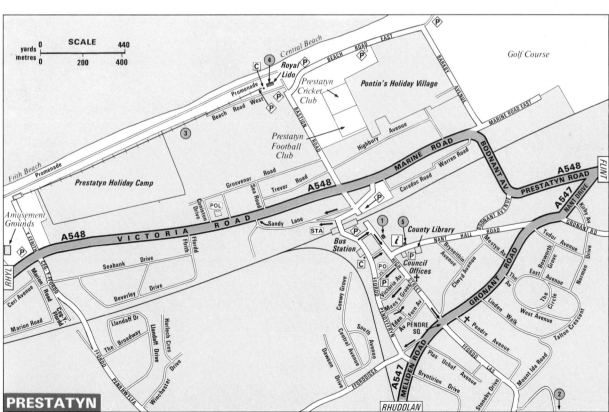

PERMANENT PRESTIGE

The last person to hold the title Prince of Upper Powys was a persistent and tireless fighter in Marcher history. Living in such assailable territory in the 13thc meant constant stress on resources and endurance, but being a staunch supporter of the crown Gruffydd ap Gwenwynwyn found himself reinstated in his domains after several skirmishes and revolts between princedoms. One of these confrontations, however, resulted in the complete destruction of Gruffydd's castle, and it was not until after he had been granted the English barony of de la Pole by Edward I that he set about to build the stronghold which forms the nucleus of what we now recognize as Powis Castle. In Welsh it is appropriately called Castell Coch – the Red Castle – and it is set in rich parkland of giant oaks in the upper reaches of the Severn Valley, just outside Welshpool.

Like Chirk, in essence this is an Edwardian castle; like Chirk it represents a continuity of stylistic modifications suited to the needs and aspirations of successive generations of occupants. Unlike Chirk it dominates a steep hilltop site, and the potential for dramatic use of terrain and terrace made itself evident as soon as the subtleties and ingenuities of garden design had been appreciated in

Great Britain. In the meantime Powis remained in the possession of the de la Pole family until 1551. Soon afterwards it was bought by Sir Edward Herbert, a son of the Earl of Pembroke, and it was during his first years at Powis that he applied Elizabethan tastes and criteria of display and comfort to the property. The most striking result of this awareness of domestic and social prestige was the Long Gallery, and Powis displays the customary attributes of such an apartment – *ie* ample opportunity for showing ancestral portraits and any other object that might effectively enhance the position and importance of the family. Status was confirmed by the bestowing of the Baron Powis title on Sir Edward's son William in 1029. Grander titles were to come the way of the family, for the 3rd Lord Powis was created earl in 1674 and marquis thirteen years later. As in Chirk, the damage caused by the civil war precipitated plans and ideas for renovation. By the 1670's major structural alterations and additions were under way, and resulted in what are now two of the most impressive features which the visitor sees on his tour of the castle – the State Bedroom and the Great Staircase.

The Herbert's allegiance to James II forced them to abandon Powis in 1688 and flee the country. When the exiled marquis died in 1696 William III gave the castle to his nephew, William Van Nassau-Zuylestein, whom he created

Earl of Rochford. Powis' most striking possession – the garden – was due to William's planning. Four terraces, each with its own architectural background, fall dramatically to a vast lawn 100ft below the base of the castle and have inspired admiration and adulation ever since they were created. Thomas Pennant, the 18th-c naturalist and traveller, could arouse no enthusiasm for the place since he found that 'the gardens are to be descended to by terraces below terraces, a laborious flight of steps.'

Although George I permitted the 2nd marquis to return to Powis in 1722, that line of Herberts came to an end 26 years later with the death of the 3rd marquis. In the meantime not only did a great deal of the fabric undergo considerable refinement, but the reinstated owner was faced with the daunting prospect of refurnishing the entire property, since Lord Rochford had 'carried away all that he thought worth taking of the pictures and furniture as well as the family records.' The result is a rich field of study and enjoyment, for in the Blue Drawing Room is a resolute display of 18th-c decorative taste which, seen side by side with the other rooms, offers a remarkably clear idea of the evolution of design and comfort. When the marquisate became extinct in 1748 a distant relative was given the earldom. It was through his daughter, who married the second Lord Clive (son of Clive of India) and who inherited Powis in 1801, that the castle passed through yet another period. If not of renovation and alteration, this was certainly a time of acclaim and acquisition, as much by way of relics and mementoes as by portraits and furniture. In 1804 the second Lord Clive became Earl of Powis and owner of the third creation.

Ironically the most distinctive outward feature of the castle when seen from a distance these days is also the most recent. When G F Bodley was commissioned to undertake major alterations towards the end of the last century, one of his tasks was to enlarge the east tower. A glimpse of an 18th-c engraving of both castle and gardens can only confirm that the innovation is an impressive improvement. Powis was given to the NT by the 4th earl in 1952. Its combination of military history, horticultural distinction, and stately-home opulence forms a prized possession in Wales, where few properties can offer such rich variety.

MOAT

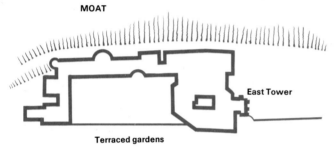

East Tower

Terraced gardens

which has unfortunately vanished. In 1966 a most interesting discovery was made in the parish church – the mechanism of a 17th-c carillon which had remained silent and largely forgotten since it went wrong in 1919. Experts who were called in to advise on its repair had never seen anything like it, although they had inspected 1,500 churches. They knew of two other carillon mechanisms that were beyond repair, and they believe that Presteigne's is the only one of its kind in the whole of Britain.

Presteigne church is unusual in that it has four church wardens instead of the usual two. This is because they represent the four townships which make up the parish. It has a 16th-c tapestry in the north aisle, some medieval glass in the Lady Chapel, and the old jail bell inscribed 'Prosperity to the benefactors, 1725'. The most poignant story connected with Presteigne is that of Mary Morgan, which can be read in brief on her gravestone in the churchyard. She was tried and hanged in 1805 at the age of seventeen for murdering her illegitimate child at the instigation of the father – a well-known local man, who gave her a penknife to do it with. He then sat on the grand jury which returned a true bill against her. She was under-cook in the house of Walter Wilkins at Glasbury, and three of her fellow servants gave evidence against her. Their testimony is preserved in the Public Record Office, in each case signed with a cross since none of them could write.

Mr Justice Hardinge, a man of considerable benevolence and charity in private life, showed neither of these qualities to Mary. He sentenced her to death after reading her a most hypocritical homily, and had her hanged within two days. During this time the junior counsel rode post haste to London to see the king and get her a pardon, but when he returned with it she

was already dead. It was poetic justice that the judge ultimately died in Presteigne, where on every visit he went to read the inscription he had caused to be set on her tombstone. A famous club called The Greycoats was started in Presteigne and used to meet in the Castle Hotel. Its original object was to encourage the wearing of garments made from Welsh wool, but it later became a Whig club which lasted only ten years.

The Judge's drawing room in the old Shire Hall preserves a very unusual article – a jury box. This is not a seat for jurors, but a wooden box into which the names of 24 jurors are placed and twelve drawn out to select those who should sit. The hole in the lid from which the papers are removed is only just large enough to accommodate three fingers, so tampering with the names is impossible. There are drawers in the base of the casket in which the jurors' name papers can be kept. It is believed that only three other jury boxes of this type are in existence. At the lower end of the town is a Carmelite convent. The administration of this convent is extremely democratic. The Mother Superior is not appointed, but elected by the nuns and serves for three years. The grille through which interviews are conducted and which serves to remind the nuns that they are segregated from the world is now more symbolic than actual, being no more than 2ft high. Everyone from the Mother Superior downwards appears to be radiantly happy. The work of the convent is making wafers for Holy Communion, but other work is also undertaken.

PUFFIN ISLAND, Gwynedd *5 SH68*
About ½m off the Anglesey coast, Puffin Island was once the site of an early-Christian monastic settlement founded by St Seiriol in the 5th or 6thc. The island was originally known as Ynys Seiriol.

Danish invaders who overran the settlement in 853 destroyed the monastery buildings and gave the island its second name of Priestholme. It next became a burial place for the monks from Penmon Priory, but today contains little more than a ruined church with a 12th-c tower. Inhabitants of the island are sea birds – in particular an immense number of puffins as the third name implies.

PUMSAINT, Dyfed *20 SN64*
Pumsaint is a hamlet on the banks of the River Cothi and takes its name – meaning Five Saints – from quintuplets born in the vicinity. It is also spelt Pumpsaint, 'pump' being the Welsh for five. According to legend the quins came under the spell of an enchanter, who laid them to rest in a cave where they would sleep until a truely pious bishop was appointed to rule over the diocese. Their subsequent non-appearance has not, however, been taken as a reflection on the local clergy. Their names were Ceitho, Celynin, Gwyn, Gwyno, and Gwynoro. A stone with five indents purported to have been made by the saints' heads stands 1m E, near the site of the ancient Dolaucothi gold mine. The latter was probably first worked in Roman times. Attempts to re-open the mine in the 1930's revealed a fragment of a Roman water wheel. This was recovered from a depth of 160ft. The site is now a picnic area.

*PWLLHELI, Gwynedd *8 SH33*
Unofficial capital of the Lleyn Peninsula, Pwllheli is a mixture of seaside resort and market town. Latterly its role as a seaside place seems to have been eclipsed by its importance as the main town of Lleyn, and its pretentious seafront contrasts sharply with the business-like look of the rest of the town. Pwllheli is also the railhead for Lleyn, having no-doubt managed to preserve its railway connections through the proximity of Butlin's Holiday Camp, which has brought other incidental benefits to the town. The camp, 3m E on a dull stretch of road, was one of the early post-war holiday camps and was established on the site of a former naval base. There is a marina on the sheltered harbour.

Markets and fairs have always been a prominent feature of Pwllheli life. Livestock was sold on the streets, and farm labourers would line up all day waiting to be hired – a practice which persisted up to the outbreak of the last war. Pwllheli was also a considerable port in the days of sail, building some fine ships and rearing exceptional seamen. Colonel Henry Hughes in his booklet *Sailing Ships and Sailors of Wales* records the feat of 'Theda', a three-masted Pwllheli schooner which put up the fastest time for an Atlantic passage by a small ship – Labrador to Gibraltar in twelve days. Pwllheli's harbour was once a forest of masts belonging to coastal and ocean-going vessels, and even now provides a safe haven for pleasure boats. Y Garn is an excellent viewpoint, and 19th-c St Peter's Church is of interest.

Pwllheli's history as a borough stretches back to 1335, when along with Nefyn it was granted the status of a free borough by the Black Prince and given to Nigel

PWLLHELI

1 Marinaland
2 Open-air Market
3 St Peter's Church
4 Y Garn (viewpoint)

Entries marked * are the starting point of drives included in the Day Drive section of the book (pages 95 to 144).

Cormorants are among the many different species of birds to be seen around the RSPB's Ramsey Island reserve.

de Loryng in recognition of his services at the Battle of Poitiers. A more recent piece of history associated with the town was an incident in 1936, when three distinguished Welshmen set fire to a building belonging to an RAF bombing school, causing £3,000 worth of damage. They gave themselves up at Pwllheli police station, protesting that it was a symbolic protest against military incursion into an essentially Welsh region. It cost them nine months in Wormwood Scrubs, but for a time their action fanned the embers of Welsh nationalist feeling.

PYLE, Mid Glamorgan 25 SS88
Pyle is a small town in a colliery district between Bridgend and Port Talbot. The ancient parish church contains a pre-Reformation altar slab.

QUAKERS YARD, Mid Glamorgan 25 ST09
This village lies N of Pontypridd and takes its name from a former burial ground of the Quakers. The English writer George Borrow, who toured Wales in 1854, visited it on his way from Merthyr Tydfil to Caerphilly. He relates in his *Wild Wales* 'The Quakers are no friends to tombstones, and the only visible evidence that this was a place of burial was a single flagstone, with a half-obliterated inscription, which with some difficulty I deciphered.'

RADNOR FOREST, Powys 14 SO16
Radnor is not a true forest. Forest was a medieval term meaning a royal hunting ground, and could therefore be applied to any area. This area is actually a mountain split by numerous streams into a small, compact area of high, rounded hills. Although surrounded by hills of varying height, the Radnor Forest stands out as a distinct region on its own. A roughly triangular area about 6m in each direction, it is enclosed by main roads on all sides, giving the traveller fine views of almost every stream and hillside. Across its N side runs the main road from Knighton to Llandrindod Wells; to the SW is the Kington to Rhayader A44 road; and to the SE is part of the A44 to New Radnor,

then a 'B' class road to Knighton. Afforestation has taken place in various parts, concentrated on the N and E sides.

Crags of Harley Dingle, views from Great Rhos or Black Mixen, Shepherd's Well, Rhiw Pool, and the spectacular Waterfall of 'Water-break-its-neck' are all of interest. 'Water-break-its-neck' lies in the Warren Plantation on the W side of Ffron Hill, and can be easily reached by footpaths to the right of the A44 about 1½m W of New Radnor. The best natural waterfall in the region, it tumbles 70ft into a dark wooded glen. Unfortunately the fall has the habit of drying up completely during very dry weather.

RAGLAN, Gwent 22 SO40
Raglan Castle (AM) was erected on the site of an 11th- or 12th-c motte-and-bailey structure. The present building dates from 1430 to the early 17thc, and the Great Yellow Tower of Gwent is one of its oldest parts (see inset opposite). The 14th- to 15th-c village church has a pinnacled tower and contains a few mutilated effigies of the Somersets, damaged during the siege of the castle by Cromwell's troops. One of two interesting windows displays various coats of arms. Some 3m W is the fine Regency mansion of Clytha House, above which stands Clytha Castle – a castle only by name. It is really a memorial which was built in 1790 to the wife of William Jones, the owner of Clytha House at that time. About 4½m WNW is the notable early 18th-c Pant-y-Gotre bridge over the River Usk.

RAMSEY ISLAND, Dyfed 16 SM72
Surrounded by sheer cliffs indented with caves, and seas made treacherous by underlying rocks, this small island is a nature reserve for the Royal Society for the Protection of Birds. Notorious rocks called the Bitches jut out from the E coast of the island into Ramsey Sound, a deep water strait separating the island from St David's Peninsula. Off the W coast is the group of islands known as Bishops and Clerks. A lighthouse situated on S Bishop warns ships to keep clear of this area.

The island is a breeding ground of fulmars, choughs, shags, kittiwakes, cormorants, razorbills, gulls, and peregrines. Ground-nesting birds are unable to breed here because of the presence of rats. The largest colony of Atlantic grey seals in Wales exists here, producing about 200 young every year. Ramsey island is dominated by two hills which overlook its W shores. On the summit of each is a cairn, probably of bronze-age date. These hills and the S half of the island are composed of igneous rock, which provides a poor soil supporting only rough grassland. The N half is formed of Ordovician sediments, which are rich in fossils and support a fertile soil on which was based the only farm of the island. Trips to and around the island can be made from the lifeboat station at Porth Stinian. The island was the retreat of 2nd-c St Tyfanog, and later St Justinian. It became a religious sanctuary in the 6thc, at which time it is reputed to have been joined to the mainland by a narrow neck of land.

RED WHARF BAY, Gwynedd 5 SH58
Red Wharf Bay is situated on the N coast of Anglesey and boasts 10sqm of sand at low tide, but bathers are warned about the changing tide and quicksands farther out in the bay. Traeth Coch in Welsh, this place was once famous for its cockles. During the last century it had a small shipyard building boats for the Amlwch copper trade, and limestone was quarried extensively near by. To the W of the bay is Cors Goch, a quiet attractive fen which is a reserve of the North Wales Naturalists' Trust.

REDWICK, Gwent 26 ST48
This small village is sited on the low-lying land of Caldicot Level, which was reclaimed in Roman times. The sea has flooded over the land many times, and the worst recorded incident is commemorated by a plaque in the church. This was on 20 January 1606. The church carries a pinnacled tower and displays a 15th-c south porch. Inside is a notable 13th-c rood loft of fifteen traceried arches. Near by is the site of a small Roman settlement.

REYNOLDSTON, West Glamorgan 24 SS48
Situated in the Gower Peninsula about 10m W of Swansea, this pleasant little village is centred on its green and includes a rather uninteresting Victorian church. This was rebuilt on the site of an earlier church and includes a few pieces of Norman work. Inside are some notable monuments, mainly from the 17th and 18thc, including one to the Lucas Bydder families of 1654 to 1684. The latter may be a 19th-c copy. Also of interest are registers dating back to 1560. The village makes an excellent centre for walking, especially along the red sandstone ridge of Cefn-y-Bryn, which stretches 4m to Penmaen and attains a height of 609ft at its E end. This end affords fine views over the shores of the Gower.

About 1m NE of the village on this ridge is a cromlech known as Arthur's Stone, which comprises a massive boulder erected on a pile of smaller stones. Legend states that the capstone, weighing some 25 tons, takes an annual trip down to the sea for a drink on New Year's Eve. To the S of Reynoldston is Stout Hall, a

cont page 268

A CASTLE AT HEART

Since the opening of the new road between Newport and Ross, Raglan Castle has become eminently accessible. Its sturdy outline is impressive from the car but gives little indication of the extent and complexity of defences which, even in their ruined state, are as varied as they are formidable. Raglan came into the possession of William Fitz Osbern soon after he had been created Earl of Hereford by William the Conqueror, and after he had built for himself castles at Chepstow and Monmouth to facilitate his advance on Gwent. Whatever defences might have been raised here at that time have disappeared, and the present ruins – the result of one of the most tortuous sieges in the civil wars – are the eloquent remnants of a 15th-c castle built to display its owner's recently-acquired prestige.

Then a fortified manor house, Raglan had come into the possession of William ap Thomas, a veteran of the French wars and a small-time squire, through his wife Elizabeth Bloet. After her death he married Gwladys, the daughter of Sir Dafydd Gam – a wealthy landowner whose death as 'Davy Gam, Esquire' is simply and touchingly conveyed in Shakespeare's *Henry V*. She was also widow of Sir Roger Vaughan of Bredwardine. Thus connected with two influential families, William's social position was strengthened even more when he was knighted by Henry VI in 1426. Within five years the Blue Knight – as he was called – was given the final accolade when he was made steward of the lordship of Usk and Caerleon. The Great Tower, the 'Yellow Tower of Gwent' and symbol of Sir William's power, was probably built on the site of a former motte and is a five-storey hexagonal structure of enormous strength. It is surrounded by a wet moat and joined to the rest of the castle by a drawbridge. That such an elaborate form of defence was built 100 years after the last of the Edwardian castles had been left uncompleted, and several years after the turbulence of the Owain Glyndwr rebellion had subsided, points to the considerable unrest that still existed in the country. Faction would rise against faction with little provocation, and a man of ap Thomas's position would have to safeguard the security of himself and his family against the fluctuating loyalties – even of his own household – by building a separate stronghold.

The most notable external features of Raglan Castle's main section are the heavy machicolations of the closet tower and the twin towers of the gatehouse – each with its two tiers of gun-ports. The gate-house dates from 1445, when ap Thomas's son William Herbert, later to become the 1st Earl of Pembroke, succeeded him. A man of substantial means, gained through commerce as well as through land, he added the Kitchen Tower and the Fountain Court which even today conveys a great deal of its former splendour. From then onwards each generation added and altered according to changing needs, demands of domestic comfort, convenience, and public show. The visual evidence, though tantalizingly small, is an unusually vivid example of the transition from castle to stately home. Nor is this too grand a title for Raglan Castle. The hall with its great window lighting the dais; the long gallery with its semi-hexagonal end overlooking the countryside; the grand staircase; the remains of ornate fireplaces; the parade of niches that once housed statues of Roman emperors – all celebrated the wealth of William Herbert's descendants, the Earls of Worcester.

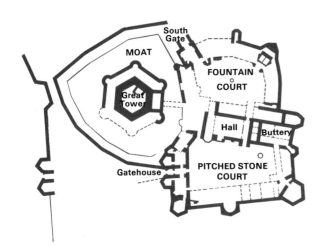

plain Georgian building dating from 1754 which formerly belonged to the Lucas family. It is now a hospital. A Celtic cross standing in a field where the Reynoldston road meets the A4118 was erected by a member of the Lucas family in memory of his horse.

*RHAYADER, Powys   13 SN96

Local people used to call Rhayader *Bwgy*, a contraction of *Bach Gwy* – meaning the Little Wye. This was the name given to a stream which ran down North Street but is now paved over. They had a saying that 'Those who put their feet in the Bwgy always come back' – a saying which time has proved to be remarkably true. This little cruciform market town, with its four main streets named after the chief points of the compass, still retains its atmosphere of the 19thc even though many of its shops have been modernized and given new fronts. Its inns are even older. The oldest of them all is the Triangle, sited across the river in the district of Cwmdeuddwr, and is a partly weather-boarded building which dates from the 14thc. Nearly as old is the Cwmdeuddwr Arms on the Rhayader side of the bridge, which is of similar appearance.

Rhayader once had a castle, but all that is left of this now is a large mound and a few stones in the angle between Church Street and West Street, high above the river. Here the water flows over boulders and rocky platforms, and dashes under the bridge in pretty falls. Upstream behind the castle is Waun Capel Park, from which a bridge leads over to a delightful sylvan riverside walk on the W bank. Extending from here to Llangurig is one of the prettiest reaches of the Wye, an 8m stretch of river with massive steep-sided mountains accompanying it on both banks. The scenery is really spectacular where the Marteg joins the Wye 2½m above Rhayader. The town was one of the centres of the Rebecca Riots last century, when men dressed as women and calling themselves Rebecca's Daughters smashed the turnpike gates as a protest against the heavy tolls. Today it is predominantly a tourist centre for the Elan Valley, which starts only 3m away. It also has its own industries located in a new industrial estate on the E edge of the town, and it is a living, expanding place with new council and private housing estates growing up rapidly. Cwmdeuddwr, although actually part of Rhayader, keeps its own identity and has its own church. In the churchyard is the grave of a soldier who fought at Badajos in the Peninsular War.

RHINOGS, THE, Gwynedd

The Rhinogs form part of the large area known geologically as the Harlech Dome, which has been much eroded to expose the sandstones, shales, and slates of the middle and lower Cambrian period. The dome is part of a huge series of folds and includes the volcanic rocks on the tops of Cader Idris and Snowdon. The 2,362ft mountain known as Rhinog Fawr gives its name to the range, although it is not the highest, and its S slopes fall away to the pass of Bwlch Drws Ardudwy, lying below flat-topped 2,333ft Rhinog Fach. To the S of Rhinog Fach is the highest member of the group, 2,475ft Y Llethr. Between them in the saddle are the lakes of Llyn Hywel and

Llyn Y Bi. The latter forms part of an extensive NT area.

To the W is a deep cwm containing Llyn Bodlyn, with views down the Afon Ysgethin extending to the sea and the isolated hill-spur of 1,932ft Moelfre. A short climb past Llyn Dulyn directly above Llyn Bodlyn leads to 2,462ft Diffwys, the last of the major summits. This faces across the Mawddach estuary to the volcanic crags of Cader Idris. From here the hills and spurs are more rounded and grass-covered, and are rich in minerals such as lead, copper, silver, and gold.

RHIW, Gwynedd   8 SH22

An exposed hamlet on the tip of the Lleyn Peninsula, Rhiw affords magnificent views from the steep descent to the S coastline. The area still carries the scars of manganese mining which was active during the last war. The landscape changes dramatically from a windy hilltop to wooded slopes in the shelter of Mynydd Rhiw, where the NT-owned property Plas yn Rhiw occupies an incomparable site with extensive views over the bay. This 16th-c manor house has 57 acres of woodland and charming gardens, and was handed to the NT with other property by the Misses Keating in 1952. They still live here and open the property on certain days. From Rhiw the visitor can enjoy a good perspective of the forbiddingly-named Hell's Mouth, which looks docile enough on most days but has a bad reputation with sailors when the sea vents its fury on the rocks. Its Welsh name is 'Porth Neigwl' deriving from Nigel de Loryng – the 14th-c overlord who ruled over Pwllheli and Nefyn.

RHOBELL FAWR, Gwynedd   9 SH72

An almost conical hill of Andesitic lavas some 6m NE of Dolgellau, Rhobell Fawr rises to 2,408ft and is the highest point in the wedge of land between the Mawddach and Wnion valleys. Views from the summit encompass the Aran mountains, Cader Idris, the Rhinogs, and the Arennigs. Some 2m NE is the neighbouring peak of 2,155ft Dduallt or the Black Height. Its E side has long precipitous crags which give the impression that almost half of it has been completely sliced off, and overlooks a bog which is the source of both the River Dee and the Afon Mawddach.

RHONDDA, Mid Glamorgan

Quiet green and purple mountains contrast with the bustling industrial life below and hint at what the Rhondda was like before the coal drive of the 19thc and the depression of the 1930's. The Rhondda consists of two densely populated valleys separated by the Cefn Rhondda ridge, which reaches nearly 2,000ft in places. The larger valley of Rhondda Fawr contains Treherbert, Treorcy, Tonypandy, and Porth; the smaller Rhondda Fach includes Maerdy, Ferndale, and Tylorstown. These were green and pleasant valleys with a few isolated farms until the 1850's, when the coal mines were opened up. Rows of terraces set parallel to the road and river and numerous chapels sprang up, and the population increased rapidly from 951 in 1851 to nearly 114,000 in 1901. Steam coal produced here was of excellent quality, but as other sources of power surpassed that of steam during the 1920's the decline of the coalfields began. With the depression of the 1930's the

area soon developed a high level of unemployment, and is now regarded as a special area for re-development. Industrial estates based on light industry have been set up to help alleviate this problem and have had some success.

Although the population declined in the years of depression, it is still a densely populated area with a keen community spirit. Rhondda talks proudly of her boxers, footballers, and professional men. Rhondda Fawr can be approached on the A4061 from Bridgend in the SW, near the Mid Glamorgan coast. This road passes through Ogmore Vale and over the 1,500ft Bwlch-y-Clawdd Pass. From the W the A4107 runs through Abergwynfi and the same pass, and the two roads meet on the mountain top. The A4107 comes up from Port Talbot on the W Glamorgan coast and through the Afan valley. From the N the A4061 approaches Rhondda Fawr over 1,600ft Hirwaun Common Pass. Rhondda Fach is linked in the N to Aberdare, head of the Cynon Valley, by the B4277. This road reaches a summit of 1,300ft. Farther down the Rhondda Fach a road from Blaenllechau climbs a mountain to the E and enters Llanwonno, where the famous Welsh runner Guto Nyth Bran is buried. This road continues across to Mountain Ash, 4m SE of Aberdare in the Cynon Valley. The busy town of Pontypridd, a pivot of the Mid Glamorgan valley system, lies 3m SE of Porth. Inter-valley roads which open up the Brecon Beacons to the N were constructed between the wars.

RHOOSE, South Glamorgan   25 ST06

Rhoose is a small village situated about 4m E of Barry, and has recently become popular as a small resort. A cement works is operated here, and just to the N is the modern airport of Cardiff. Remnants of an old mansion and an ancient chapel survive in the village.

RHOSCOLYN, Gwynedd   4 SH27

This remote and attractive resort has a fine sheltered beach at the farthest S point of Holyhead in Anglesey. It is reached by a narrow winding road from Four Mile Bridge. On both sides of the bay rise rocky headlands, and in the mouth of the bay to the E the coast is littered with rocks. In the rock pools either side of the bay are shellfish which can be netted at low tide. During the summer pollack, bass, and mackerel can be caught off these shores. At one time it had thriving oyster beds and a local fleet of oyster dredgers.

To the E lies Silver Bay and another sandy beach. A splendid clifftop walk to the N leads past a lookout station to Fynnon Gwenfaen, an early holy well named after the nun St Gwenfaen, who also founded the village church in the 6thc. Along the cliffs are two remarkable cliff formations – Bwa Gwyn (White Arch) and Bwa Ddu (Black Arch). Near Bwa Gwyn a stone inscribed 'Tyger September 17, 1819' commemorates a dog who saved the lives of the captain, two men, and a boy when their ketch sank 1m offshore. His barking guided the men ashore in deep fog. Tyger then dragged the boy ashore and swam back to rescue his master, the captain. The dog dropped dead from his rescue efforts.

RHOSCROWTHER, Dyfed   18 SM90

Once a quiet village lying off the B4320 about 5m W of Pembroke, Rhoscrowther is now dominated by the installations of

Entries marked * are the starting point of drives included in the Day Drive section of the book (pages 95 to 144).

two major oil companies. Silvery oil tanks overlook the ancient Church of St Dewmanus, or St Tegan, which was restored at the beginning of this century. The building is cruciform in plan and carries a large pinnacled tower. Above the pointed arch of the north-porch doorway is an unusual stone figure of the risen Christ, seated on his tomb with his hands uplifted to show the nail marks. Inside is a walk-through squint and a square Norman font with a scalloped bowl. The south chancel chapel contains recent stained glass depicting the Holy Family, and in one of four cusped recesses is a medieval figure of a lady with her hands clasped in prayer. Two plain arches join this chapel to the chancel. About ¼m NW, just off the coast of Angle Bay, are the ruins of 'Jestington' manor house. This is now converted into Eastington farm, but some parts of the building are possibly of Norman origin.

RHOSILI, West Glamorgan 24 SS48
Near the SW extremity of the Gower Peninsula, this village is sited on top of cliffs which overlook the sands of Rhosili Bay. St Mary's Church is a plain 13th-c structure with a saddleback tower. The south door displays ornately-carved patterns, and both this and the front are of Norman origin. Also inside is a modern glass of Christ in Glory, set in one of the early-English Lancets of the nave, and a plaque to the memory of Edgar Evans. Evans was born here and died on his return from the Antarctic with Scott's Expedition.

To the S of the bay are the two elongated islands of Worm's Head, accessible with care across the rocks for 2½ hours either side of low tide. This feature extends about 1½m, and the islands are joined by a rocky neck known as Devil's Bridge. At its tip, where the cliffs drop some 200ft sheer into the sea, is a colony of sea birds such as guillemots and kittiwakes. The sands of Rhosili Bay can be reached by a steep walk down the cliffside and extend 3m N to Burry Holms, providing excellent bathing and some surfing when the W and SW winds create ideal conditions. Burry Holms is an island at high tide, and shows a few remains of a medieval religious settlement. Rhosili Downs rise behind the bay and reach their highest point of 632ft at the Beacon, just N of the village. The two neolithic burial chambers of Sweynes Howes are located about ½m N along the downs, and have rounded covering mounds. Scant remains of other ancient remains dating back to iron-age times are found in abundance in the surrounding area. On the other side of Worm's Head is pretty Mewslade Bay, which can be reached from the hamlets of Middleton and Pitton. About 2m SE is Paviland Cave. An attractive walk in the Gower nature reserve starts from the car park in Rhosili and features limestone flora.

RHOSLLANERCHRUGOG, Clwyd 11 SJ24
Rhos – as everyone shortens it to – qualifies for entry in any gazetteer of Wales by virtue of its claim to be the largest village in Wales. It has a population of about 10,000 and sprawls untidily over the hillside off the Wrexham to Llangollen road. It is a veritable warren of narrow streets and a stronghold of Welshness, featuring a host of Nonconformist chapels. Two rival male voice choirs, Rhos Male Voice

Bersham Colliery is the sole survivor of the once-flourishing E Denbighshire coalfield.

and Rhos Orpheus, have spread the fame of Rhos far and wide, including N America and the Continent. A one-time mining village that has seen the coal industry decline, it is now the centre of a diversity of light industry. As a bastion of Welsh culture Rhos has staged two National Eisteddfodau since the war. It can claim many distinguished sons in the field of politics, education, and music.

RHOSNEIGR, Gwynedd 4 SH37
Families seeking simple seaside pleasures, without all the commercialized trappings, are attracted to this cheerful Anglesey resort. Good boating and fishing facilities, and safe bathing from its fine beach are available. Sand dunes farther along offer sunbathing and plane spotting – this is a good vantage point from which to watch aircraft landing and taking off at RAF Valley. Rhosneigr's pleasant countenance hides a seamy past. It once harboured a band of wreckers, who by means of lights on the shore lured passing ships on to rocks, where they could be plundered. Three of the Rhosneigr wreckers tried at Beaumaris in 1741 paid the price by hanging.

RHOS-ON-SEA, Clwyd 6 SH88
Almost indistinguishable from Colwyn Bay, this small resort has a shingly foreshore with sand beyond. The Rhos Fynach Monastery is reputed to date from 1185 and has been converted into an open-air heated swimming pool, hotel, café, and small museum of antiques. The Cistercian monks who formerly inhabited the monastery came from Colwyn and guarded a fish-weir set up here. Fish were trapped behind the weir as the tide ebbed, when the water's only way of escape was by means of a grating. After the Reformation the weir was confiscated, and until it fell into disrepair the fish caught here every tenth day were claimed as tithe by the local vicar of Llandrillo Church. Stakes driven into the foreshore were the only traces of this weir, but even these have now been cut down to lessen the danger to yachting. The rebuilt Chapel of St Trillo stands near the sea and was erected over a well which lies beneath the altar. Its plain stone walls are 2ft thick and enclose an area of

approximately 11ft by 8ft. Services are still held here in spite of its small size.

RHOSTRYFAN, Gwynedd 5 SH45
A hamlet about 3m S of Caernarfon. Rhostryfan is situated in the foothills of the mountains of old Caernarfonshire. Mynydd Mawr rises to 2,290ft in the SE. A local cottage of white-washed boulders and a slate roof was removed in its entirety from here and re-erected in the National Folk Museum of Wales in Cardiff. A cottage shell at Rhosgadfan has been turned into a memorial to Kate Roberts, who wrote Welsh novels.

RHOSTYLLEN, Clwyd 11 SJ34
This largish, red-brick village lies 2m W of Wrexham and has developed around Bersham Colliery – sole survivor of the once-flourishing E Denbighshire coalfield, which once had as many as 39 pits. Bersham is now only one of two operating collieries in N Wales, the other being Point of Ayr on the Dee estuary. On the Llangollen side of the roundabout is a plaque set in a farmyard wall at Croes Foel. This records that the smithy of the Davies brothers, famous 17th-c gatesmiths whose work graces the entrances to many churches, castles, and stately homes in N Wales and the border counties, stood opposite. Robert Davies (1675–1748) was the leading light of this talented family, and his work suggests that he may have been a pupil of the Frenchman Tijou, maker of Hampton Court gates. Examples of Davies' work survive at Eaton Hall near Chester, Cholmondeley Castle in Cheshire, Wrexham parish church, and Leeswood Hall near Wrexham. Chirk Castle gates are generally acknowledged to be his finest creation.

RHOSYGWALIAU, Gwynedd 10 SH93
About 2m SE of Bala, this isolated hamlet lies at the N end of the Hirnant Valley, which leads through wild mountain scenery to Lake Vyrnwy. Holy Trinity Church was founded in 1880 by Henry Richardson, inventor of the tubular lifeboat, a fact which is recorded inside. Near this is the Jacobean manor-house of Plas Rhiwaedog, which displays some fine 17th-c craftsmanship and is now converted into a youth hostel. A small lake in the neighbourhood is called

Pwll-y-Gelanedd – the pool of slaughter – probably a reference to a bloody battle fought here against the Saxons.

RHUDDLAN, Clwyd 6 SJ07

If walls could speak Rhuddlan's ivy-covered ramparts could tell a vivid story. It was here that the Statute of Rhuddlan was passed in 1284, whereby Edward I confirmed his sovereignty over the newly-conquered territory, and established the counties of Flintshire, Caernarfonshire, Anglesey, and Merionethshire – which survived until the 1974 reorganization. Edward I also announced the birth of a son whom he presented to the people as a Prince of Wales here. It was at Rhuddlan too that the hapless Richard II was 'entertained' on his way to Flint Castle, to be forced to concede his throne to Henry Bolingbroke. Today the castle (AM) is a dignified ruin, but the remains indicate that it was once a substantial fortress. It probably owes its historic importance to the strategic value of the site, and to the fact that it was at

the head of the fertile Vale of Clwyd. The vale was doubtless the granary for forces stationed at Rhuddlan.

A diamond-shaped inner ward had double-towered gatehouses at two opposite corners and single round towers at the other two. The domestic buildings are gone but the curtain walls have only their battlements and towers missing. The broad outer ward is encircled by a strong, polygonal wall and moat, except where the castle walls run alongside the river. Gillot's Tower guarded the S corner and the water gate, where ships landed supplies for the castle.

The earliest mention of Rhuddlan is in AD 796, when the Welsh suffered defeat at the hands of the English. It was later a fortress of Gruffydd ap Llywelyn, who plundered nearby English townships from here until 1063, when King Harold burned it down. Robert, nephew of Hugh Lupus Earl of Chester, erected a typical Norman motte-and-bailey of wood over

the ruins of Twt Hill in 1073. During the following two centuries it changed hands several times between the Welsh and the English, but was finally taken from Llywelyn ap Gruffydd by Edward I during his Welsh Campaign of 1277. Construction of the castle began almost immediately on a site to the N of the old castle (AM) on Twt Hill.

Edward I also canalized the Clwyd estuary so that ships could reach the castle, and erected earthworks and timber palisades to defend the town that grew up around the castle. He held a parliament here, and Old Parliament House now occupies the original site in High Street. It contains remnants of the old building which is commemorated by a plaque in the wall. In 1648, after the civil war in which the castle surrendered to the Roundheads under Major General Mytton, the structure was slighted. It's decay continued until 1944, when it passed to the DoE, who have since carried out some restoration.

1   Botanical Gardens
2   Holy Trinity Parish Church
3   Marine Lake Leisure Park

4   Royal Floral Hall
5   St Thomas' Church

6   Town Hall, Library, &
    WTB Information Centre

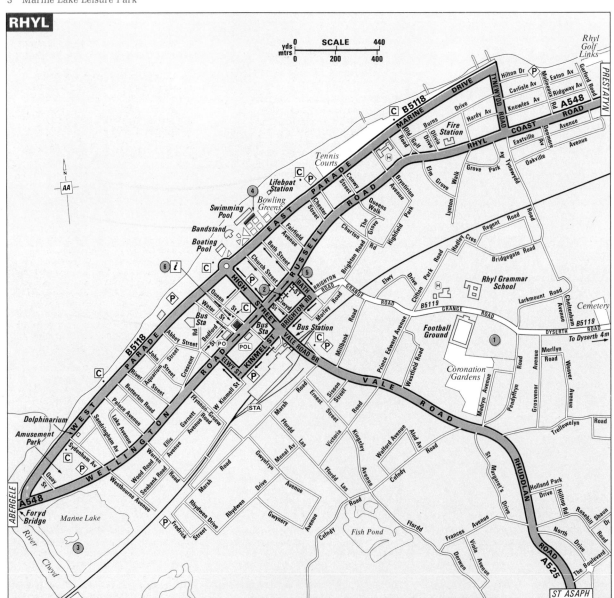

Rhuddlan Church is a much-restored 13th-c building with two aisles separated by an arched arcade. It contains inscribed slabs from a Dominican priory, the ruins of which are incorporated in the outbuildings of nearby Plas Newydd Farm. The bridge which spans the Clwyd here dates partly from a predecessor constructed in 1595. Splendid views across Morfa Rhuddlan are obtained from Bronc or Abbot's Hill.

RHYD, Gwynedd *9 SH64*
Rhyd is situated some 500ft above the Vale of Ffestiniog, a little to the NW of the picturesque, tree-encircled Llyn Mair. The twin Moelwyns and Cnicht dominate the landscape to the N, and the latter is sometimes described as the 'Welsh Matterhorn'.

RHYDD-DDU, Gwynedd *5 SH55*
The small quarrying village of Rhydd-ddu lies in the heart of Snowdonia on the A487, about 4m N of Beddgelert. From here a path some 3½m long ascends the slopes of Snowdon, and on a clear day the W ridge can be seen from the village. Another path crosses moorland and then ascends 2,080ft Y Garn, lying to the SW, before passing along a ridge to 2,329ft Mynydd Drws-y-Coed and 2,301ft Carnedd Goch. It finally descends to Llanllyfni on the A4085. To the N lies Llyn Cwellyn, backed by the crags of Mynydd Mawr. The highest point on the road to Beddgelert is 651ft, about 1m S of Rhydd-ddu. An isolated boulder known as Pitt's Head, after William Pitt the Younger whom it is said to resemble, stands here.

RHYDOWEN, Dyfed *20 SN44*
Situated about 3½m NE of Llandyssul, Rhydowen includes a pleasant Unitarian chapel which was built in 1834. It has unusual slate tombstones incorporated in its front elevation, and on the other side of the road are the chapel stables.

RHYL, Clwyd *6 SJ08*
The most popular resort on the N Wales coast, Rhyl claims 3m of safe, sandy beach and sunshine records which fully entitle it to call itself 'Sunny Rhyl'. The aroma of fish and chips and hot dogs competes with the sea breezes at the season's height, but as far as Rhyl is concerned it is the sweet smell of success. Few resorts in Britain cater better for the family holiday, and Rhyl has been successful since it developed from two fishermen's cottages in 1833. It had a head start on its sister resorts, being a very accessible port of call for steam packets between Liverpool and Voryd. Rhyl was also patronized by the nobility in its early days. As it developed the town was the top of the list for Sunday-school treats and similar outings from all over N Wales and the industrial NW of England. Many thousands of excited youngsters have passed through the portals of its impressively large station, eager to sample the delights of its beach, its promenade amusements, and the entertainment at Marine Lake. The exceptionally wide and well laid-out promenade indicates that Rhyl took the business of catering for the visitor seriously from the start.

Holy Trinity Church and St Thomas Church, both built during the 19thc, lie adjacent to one another in the centre of the town. Holy Trinity is the parish church and was built between 1835 and 1837. Services held here are in Welsh.

St Thomas' Church carries a 203ft spire and overshadows the more humbly-built Holy Trinity. Also of interest are Rhyl's Botanic Gardens and the Royal Floral Hall.

RHYMNEY, Mid Glamorgan *22 SO10*
Sited at the head of the Rhymney Valley, this busy town is important for steel production and other heavy industry. Buildings in its broad main street are mainly constructed of stone. St David's is a rather plain structure, having more in common with Nonconformist chapels than Anglican churches. It was built at the expense of the Rhymney Iron Company between 1839 and 1843. The town bears the same name as the river which rises to the N in the moorland of Llangynidr. A battle fought between the Welsh and Normans at Rhymney Bridge in 1094 resulted in a Welsh withdrawal into the mountains of Brecknock.

RISCA, Gwent *26 ST29*
Twm Barlam stands to the N of Risca and has an iron-age fort at 1,400ft and a medieval castle mound at its E end. From here there are fine views across the valleys to the N and of Newport and the coast to the S.

ROCH CASTLE, Dyfed *16 SM82*
The large pele tower of this 13th-c castle, which is set on an igneous outcrop, dominates the landscape for miles around. It was probably built by Adam de Rupe in the 13thc, who erected it on a rock because a prophecy had been made that he would die of a viper's bite. However, the venemous creature found its way into the castle in a bundle of firewood. The direct line of Roches ended in 1420, and after changing hands several times the castle was purchased by the Walter family in 1601. During the civil war they abandoned it for the safety of London, and the royalists garrisoned it but were eventually beaten by the Roundheads. Lucy Walter was born in the castle in 1630, and later became Charles II's mistress and mother of his son the Duke of Monmouth. Monmouth was later executed for his rebellion against James II. The castle fell into ruin in the following 200 years until it was restored as a private residence by Viscount St David in 1902, when a new wing was added. Restoration was continued by subsequent owners. A small village with a 19th-c church nestles beneath the castle rock about 2m from the coast.

ROCKFIELD, Gwent *23 SO41*
A rebuilt church preserves a partially-timbered tower in this attractive little village, which is situated about 3m NW of Monmouth.

ROEWEN, Gwynedd *5 SH77*
Walks from this pleasant little village, which lies W of the Conwy Valley, include a route to Conwy and one along an old Roman road. The latter was once marked with milestones, and two of these are in the British Museum. The road leads W to Aber and Llanfairfechan. About 1m to the W along this track is the Cromlech of Maen-y-Bardd (The Bard's Stone), and a stone circle can be traced in a nearby field. The Roman road then passes through Bwlch-y-Ddeufaen and past 2,000ft Talyfan, where two ancient monoliths still stand. Gilfach Garden is sited in the village and specializes in shrubs. About 1½m SE is the Roman fort of *Canovium*.

ROSSETT, Clwyd *7 SJ35*
Between Wrexham and Chester, Rossett is a border village which features two water mills facing each other. The black-and-white Rossett Mill was painted by J M W Turner and carries the date 1661 on its façade. Its origins are certainly earlier than that – possibly in the 14thc. Its great undershot wheel survives, but the mill ceased to grind corn in the 1960's. Marford Mill stands on the opposite side of the road and is even older in origin than its black-and-white neighbour. It has recently been tastefully transformed into offices. Near by on the same side of the road as Marford Mill is Trevalyn Hall, an Elizabethan house associated with the Trevor family, and more recently the Boscawens.

RUABON, Clwyd *11 SJ34*
Ruabon is celebrated as the ancestral seat of the Williams Wynne, a family once so powerful as to merit the unofficial title of 'Princes in Wales'. Their land-owning in N and mid Wales was so extensive it was claimed that Sir Watkin Williams Wynne could walk from Ruabon to Aberystwyth without ever stepping off his land. The recurring initials of WWW on farm gates throughout this area seem to confirm that this was once a possibility. Wynnstay, their main residence, was originally approached by a stately avenue of elms from a road opposite St Mary's Church. The park wall extends for miles, and inside the Capability-Brown designed grounds are ruined Nant y Belan Tower, Waterloo Tower, and a bathhouse. The original Wynnstay was destroyed by a disastrous fire in 1858, which also claimed some priceless treasures. The new Wynnstay is a chateau-style residence of 1860, now occupied by the Lindisfarne College public school. Impressive stables dating from the time of the original Wynnstay are a well-preserved feature. David Garrick was one of the more famous visitors to Wynnstay.

St Mary's Church is a squat building containing plenty of links with the Williams Wynne family, including notable memorials by Rhysbrach and Nollekens, and a marble font by Adam. Beneath the church walls on the main road is a quaint little round house, used in its day as a lock-up. Ruabon gives its name to a shiny red brick, a practical if not aesthetically pleasing material which is a feature of so much house building in and around the Wrexham area.

RUTHIN, Clwyd *6 SJ15*
Plan overleaf
Old county town of Denbighshire until reorganization in 1974 robbed it of this status, Ruthin is a place of considerable character. Buildings are pleasantly grouped around a small square, from which narrow streets fall away in a disorderly fashion. One of Ruthin's more endearing features is the variety of architecture which is displayed in its town buildings, most of which have been carefully preserved over the years. The town, once fortified, was garrisoned for the Lancastrians in the Wars of the Roses, and for the royalists in the civil war.

Ruthin Castle was founded by King Edward I in 1281 on the site of an earlier stronghold. It was granted to Reginald de Grey, Justiciar of Chester, and remained with his family until the end of the 15thc. The castle had two wards, the outer being smaller than the inner. Five round towers originally guarded the inner ward, but only the remains of three of them are left, together with the ruined double-towered gatehouse. The uprising of Owain Glyndwr began in Ruthin, when he surprised the town in 1400 and made an unsuccessful attack on the castle. Glyndwr was pursuing an old quarrel with Lord de Grey. In the civil war the castle resisted an attack by parliamentary forces, who returned to besiege it two years later in 1646. The royalist garrison surrendered to Major-General Mytton, and the castle was destroyed by order of parliament. Part of the ruins were incorporated in a large 19th-c castellated mansion, which took the name of the castle and was at one time the seat of Colonel Cornwallis West. A member of the family, George West, married Lady Randolph Churchill – widowed mother of Sir Winston Churchill. In 1910 he married again, this time to the noted contemporary actress Mrs Patrick Campbell. The mansion now serves as a hotel and features banquets based on Tudor recipes. The 15th-c Myddleton Arms is incorporated in the Castle Hotel.

St Peter's Church was once a monastic foundation. Its most interesting feature is the fine oak roof of its north side, presented by King Henry VII in gratitude to the men of Wales who supported him in his successful fight for the English crown against Richard III at Bosworth Field in 1485. Divided into 500 panels, this displays carved devices, pious mottoes, and sacred figures. The gates leading to the church were made in 1727 by Robert and John Davies of Bersham, creators of the magnificent ornamental iron gates at Chirk Castle. The tower contains eight bells. On the W side of the market square is Exmewe Hall, a half-timbered building now housing a bank, built by Sir Thomas Exmewe. He became Lord Mayor of London in 1517. This building was used as a grandstand when bull-baiting was held in the square, and it was restored in 1928. In front of Exmewe Hall is a limestone block known as Maen Huail, on which King Arthur is

said to have had Huail, son of Kaw and Arthur's rival in love, beheaded. Huail was also the brother of Gildas, the 6th-c historian. The old Court House and prison, which now also houses a bank, was built in 1401. Gallows were built into the Court House, and a small part of the gibbet can still be seen. Plas Coch stands in Well Street and is of 13th-c origin. It was restored as a lodging for the castle constable in 1613.

The County Jail in Clwyd Street was built in 1775 and now houses the county library. Conditions were reputedly comparatively humane, and a high wall separated debtors from the hardened criminals. The last execution here was in 1903, and a local resident recalls that the gallows and equipment arrived in no less than eight railway trucks. The prison closed in 1914. Canon A Bukleley Jones, a warden of St Peter's Church in the 19thc, was immortalized by Thomas Hughes in *Tom Brown's Schooldays* in the character of Slogger Williams. The grammar school and Christ's Hospital are Elizabethan foundations. Nantclwyd House is a fine example of a 14th-c town house which has been lovingly restored. It has a magnificent half-timbered front which was only discovered in 1928, and the roof structure is the oldest of its kind in Wales. Other features are the gabled portico, old oak carvings and wainscoting, stained glass with armorial buildings, and a curious gallery. Gabriel Goodman, Dean of Westminster Abbey during the Elizabethan reign, was reputedly born here and became a generous benefactor in his native town. Opposite the 19th-c Town Hall are the County Offices, considered among the finest municipal buildings in N Wales.

SAETH MAEN, Powys 21 SN81
The prehistoric stone row of Saeth Maen, or Seven Stones, is located on the opposite side of the River Tawe from Penwyllt railway station (OS reference SN 883 154).

ST ASAPH, Clwyd 6 SJ07
St Asaph's Cathedral, the smallest in England and Wales, has survived all kinds

of indignities to remain the seat of the diocese. In 1282 the cathedral was destroyed and Edward I attempted to supersede it with a new cathedral at Rhuddlan. Bishop Anian II, with the Pope's backing, persuaded him to rebuild at St Asaph. In 1402 Owain Glyndwr burnt the cathedral during his short-lived uprising, and it remained a shell until it was rebuilt in 1482. During the civil war it was used as a stable. In between times there have been other attempts to subordinate the status of St Asaph. Robert Dudley the Earl of Leicester started to build a church at Denbigh, which was intended to supplant St Asaph, but the money to complete the church was borrowed for war purposes and the church remained unfinished. Wrexham's splendid church entertained similar pretensions about being the diocesan seat, and there was an unsuccessful attempt to merge St Asaph Diocese with Bangor. So St Asaph remains a village that is a city, with a quiet dignity and considerable charm.

Its Welsh name Llanelwy means 'holy place beside the River Elwy'. A monastery was founded here in the 6thc by Kentigern or St Mungo – when he fled from persecution in Scotland – at the invitation of Cadwallon, King of Gwynedd. He later returned to Scotland and appointed Asa or Asaph as his successor, after whom the town and cathedral are named. According to some authorities the Roman settlement of *Varae* was located here, and traces of a Roman road are to be found in the grounds of the Bishop's Palace. The building received thorough restoration at the hand of Sir Gilbert Scott and retains its 13th-c character. Later features include a beautiful reredos of Derbyshire alabaster, and the Bishop's throne and pulpit. Most of the monuments are of recent date, apart from a mutilated effigy of Bishop Anian II on his tomb in the south aisle and the Greyhound stone. The latter bears a coat of arms depicting a hound chasing a hare, and was discovered at the time of the late 19th-c restoration.

Among the more recent monuments is a tablet to the memory of Mrs Hemans, a poetess who wrote new versions of ancient Welsh legends. A small museum located in the cathedral Chapter House exhibits the 16th-c first New Testament in Welsh; the 16th-c first Welsh Bible translated by Dr Morgan at the command of Elizabeth I; earlier 'Breeches' and 'Vinegar' bibles – so-called because of translation errors; a Welsh-Hebrew-Greek dictionary written by Dic Aberdaron, who is buried in the churchyard; and some prehistoric and Roman remains. Outside the cathedral is

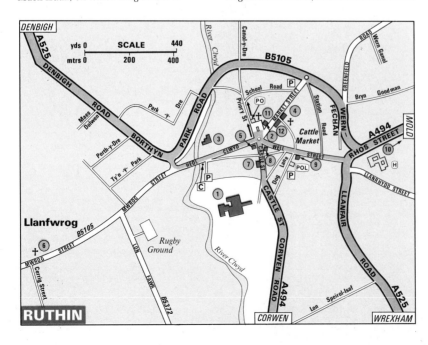

1　Castle
2　Castle Hotel (incorporating 15th-c Myddleton Arms)
3　Clwyd County Library (former County Jail)
4　County Court & County Offices
5　Exmewe Hall & Maen Huail (beheading stone)
6　Llanfwrog Church
7　Nantclwyd House
8　Old Court House (14thc)
9　Plas Coch
10　Ruthin Grammar School
11　St Peter's Church & Christ's Hospital Almshouses
12　Town Hall

an 'Eleanor Cross', erected in 1901 to commemorate the translation of the Bible into Welsh by Dr Morgan, who became Bishop of St Asaph in 1601. It depicts eight figures known for their part in the translation of holy works into Welsh, the most important being Dr Morgan.

The parish Church of St Kentigern is typical of this part of Wales, having two parallel aisles separated by an arcade. It is perpendicular in style, and although mainly of the 15thc has parts dating from the 13thc. The church has a fine hammer-beam roof. The Barrow, still in its original form but now a restaurant, stands near to the cathedral and was founded in 1686 by Bishop Barrow as almshouses for eight widows. About 2½m SW are the Cefn Caves, where implements used by prehistoric man and the bones of animals now extinct in the British Isles were discovered and are thought to date back some 50,000 years. Access to these caves is by a zig-zag path. St Mary's Well, with its tiny ruined chapel, lies about 1m below the caves. Baptisms were once performed here in the holy water, and secret marriages were conducted.

ST ATHAN, South Glamorgan   25 ST06
St Athan's early-English church is cruciform in plan and has two 14th-c altar tombs displaying recumbent effigies of the Berkerolles family. A window commemorates King George VI's coronation. The ruin of East Orchard Castle stands near by. At Eglwys Brewis, a little to the N, is a plain 13th-c church containing a Norman font and a 13th-c tomb slab. There is a large RAF station in the area.

ST BRIDE'S BAY, Dyfed   18 SM71
This is the name given to the broad bay enclosed by the stretch of coastline from Ramsey Island off St David's Head in the N to Skomer Island in the S. It embraces the fine sandy beaches of Newgale, Nolton Haven, and Broad Haven, as well as several stretches of impressive cliff scenery. At low tide the sands reveal traces of a prehistoric forest. Around the bay's coast are many rare species of wild flowers, and numerous seabirds inhabit the area. The NT has endeavoured to fight against development of this coast and to preserve the peaceful and natural qualities of the area.

Porphyra Umbilicalis, an unattractive sea-weed, is gathered along the shores to be stewed and eaten as laver bread. On the S coast of the bay is St Bride's Haven, set in a small cove of red sandstone. A church which stands at its head was restored *c*1860, incorporating an ancient rood loft stairway and door. Remains of stone-lined graves of a former chapel which was engulfed by the sea can be seen near the shore. The hospital was once the mansion of Lord Kensington, who owned St Bride's.

ST BRIDE'S MAJOR, Mid Glamorgan   25 SS87
Situated about 4m S of Bridgend, this village has a church which stands on a small hill and carries a massive battlemented tower. This once held an important defensive position and is largely of decorated style. The north door and chancel arch are of Norman date. A tomb set in a recess of the north wall bears effigies of a knight in armour – possibly John Butler – and his wife, with carvings of their weeping children at the front of the tomb. Several other memorials include monuments to the Butler family of Dunraven and Ogmore.

On the road leading out of the village towards Bridgend is a grove of trees on the right which commemorates General Picton's visit to his brother, the rector of St Bride's. It was from here that the general was called to the Battle of Waterloo and his subsequent death in 1815. The road then passes through a fold in the limestone hills of Ogmore and Old Castle Down. On Old Castle Down are slight remains of an Ogmore Castle outpost. Workmen here in 1818 discovered richly-decorated bronze helmets and daggers of the late Celtic period, but these – fortunately recorded in minute detail – were mysteriously lost on their way to London. Heol-y-Milwr is an ancient military track which crosses the downs to Ogmore Castle.

ST CLEARS, Dyfed   19 SN21
An agricultural town situated about 8m WSW of Carmarthen, St Clears stands at the confluence of the Dewi Fawr and the Afon Cynin where they enter the Taf. It is especially busy with traffic during the summer months because of its situation at an important road junction on the A40. The Church of St Mary

Magdalen was once attached to a Cluniac priory, of which only a few mounds remain. It has thick walls and an impressive defensible west tower. Among the few remnants of Norman work is an unusual elaborately-carved chancel arch. Only the mound of a castle which once belonged to Lord Rhys, and was destroyed by Llywelyn the Great, can now be traced. In 1406 Owain Glyndwr suffered a defeat here. St Clears was a centre of the 19th-c Rebecca Riots, which led to toll-gate reform. The war memorial in the main street commemorates Group Captain Ira Jones, a world war one flying ace. At Llanfihangel Abergwyn, a little to the E, is a modern church containing a Norman font taken from the now roofless remains of a 13th-c church abandoned in 1848. Crudely-carved slabs in the old churchyard traditionally mark the graves of pilgrims to St David's.

ST DAVID'S, Dyfed   16 SM72
To Welshmen this is the most hallowed spot in Great Britain, for it was here in the 6thc that Dewi Sant (St David) was born and grew up to become the special saint of Wales and all Welshmen. The tiny city does not have any buildings of outstanding architectural merit, but the whole effect is harmonious and pleasant. The cathedral and its ancillary buildings are almost hidden in the vale of the little River Alun. It is thought that the building was especially tucked away like this so that pirates and invaders would not see it. None the less, it has been wrecked many times. Opinions differ as to St David's birthdate, but he is said to have died in AD601 at the age of 147. Other estimates given for his birth are AD500 and AD530. He was descended from the ancient kings of Wales, and was perhaps a relative of the historical King Arthur. His mother was Non, to whom a ruined chapel at St Non's Bay is dedicated. St David is said to have been educated at Whitlands Abbey, from where he made many journeys with a small band of followers, including one to Jerusalem. Upon his return from his travels he found Wales embroiled in the bitter controversy of the Pelagian heresy. At the Synod of Brefi in Cardiganshire his eloquent arguments against the Pelagians brought him much honour and respect.

Some little time later Dubricius, Bishop of Caerleon, gave David the see of Menevia (St David's), to where he returned and spent the rest of his life. The early buildings would have been very simple, but after St David's death they were ravaged many times by Scandinavian pirates. The building which survives today was begun in 1180 by Peter de Leia. It was always the ambition of Giraldus Cambrensis to become Bishop of St David's, but despite every effort he never succeeded. Norman builders were skilled, but not skilled enough, for in 1240 the central tower collapsed, causing considerable damage to the choir and the transepts. More damage was done by a severe

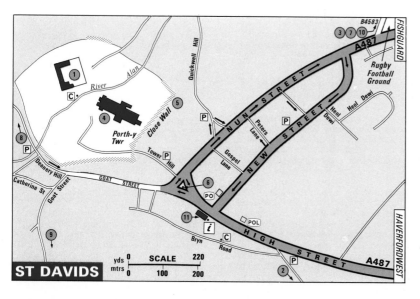

1 Bishop's Palace
2 Caerfai Bay
3 Carn Llidi
4 Cathedral & St Mary's College Ruins
5 Close Walls
6 Old Cross
7 St David's Head (reserve)
8 St Justinian's Chapel
9 St Non's Chapel
10 Whitesand Bay
11 WTB Information Centre

earthquake in 1248. Even today the piers of the nave lean quite considerably from the vertical. The appearance of the nave has altered hardly at all in 800 years.

Bishop Martyn (1296–1328) built the Lady Chapel. His successor Bishop Gower (1328–1347) wrought the greatest changes and improvements to the cathedral, and was evidently a saintly man extremely keen on building things. In fact he was nick-named 'The building Bishop'. He raised the aisles of the cathedral and inserted the decorated windows, built the south porch, the transept chapels, and vaulted the Lady Chapel. Perhaps his greatest monument is the Bishop's Palace (AM). He built this c1340 mainly to accommodate the large numbers of pilgrims that visited the cathedral. It is assumed that Bishop Barlow (in office 1536 to 1548) was responsible for the ruination of the palace, but the remains are impressive – especially the beautiful parapet which runs the whole length of the walls. Also worthy of attention in the palace are the chapel, the great hall, and the lovely rose window. All the palace buildings are carefully preserved. The wooden roof of the cathedral nave was constructed by treasurer Owen Pole between 1472 and 1509. Bishop Vaughan (1509–1523) built the perpendicular chapel which is named after him.

During the reign of Edward VI, at the time of the Protestant Reformation, the cathedral suffered from indifference and neglect. Bishop Barlow tried to move the see to Carmarthen, but only succeeded in moving the Bishop's Palace to Abergwili. During and after Barlow's time the neglect became acute, much damage was done in the civil war, and in 1775 the roof of the Lady Chapel fell in. The first attempts at restoration were made in the 1790's by the famous architect Nash. His solutions were not a success, and the new west front which he built was singularly unfortunate. In 1826 Sir Gilbert Scott was commissioned to examine and begin a thorough restoration of the building. He did a brilliant job, and by the beginning of the 20thc the work was complete. The exterior of the cathedral is not particularly attractive, although in certain qualities of sun and moonlight, the stone, which comes from local quarries, looks quite lovely.

The interior, compared with the exterior, is very rich. One of the first things that is noticed is the rise of the floor from W to E – a slope of almost 3ft which gives the impression of walking up hill towards the altar. Also noticeable is the outward lean of the piers of the nave. Remains of the shrine of St David are situated on the north side of the Presbytery, but this was much damaged during the time of the cathedral's neglect. In a recess between the High Altar and the Holy Trinity Chapel is an iron-bound chest which contains the bones of two men. These were found during Scott's restoration, and are believed to be the bones of St David and his teacher St Justinian. Before the High Altar is the tomb of Edmund Tudor, which was brought here from Grey Friars in Carmarthen at the Dissolution. Edmund was the father of Henry VII and step-brother of Henry VI. The many other tombs in the cathedral include one which is uncertainly attributed to Giraldus

Cambrensis. Of the 28 stalls the first belongs, by tradition, to the reigning monarch. Queen Elizabeth II sat in this stall in 1955. The misereres are extraordinary manifestations of the woodcarver's art. The scenes depicted are all grotesque, and some are very blatant attacks upon the monks of the time. For hundreds of years the Lady Chapel was in ruins, but it has now been fully restored and services are frequently held in it. The Chapel of the Holy Trinity, or Vaughan's Chapel, is one of the greatest treasures in the cathedral. Built in the perpendicular style, it displays beautiful fan tracery in the roof, and the whole is enclosed in delightful screens. A grant from the Pilgrim Trust has enabled the Librarian, with help from the dean and chapter, to make the library a place of interest and distinction.

To the N of the cathedral stands St Mary's College. Parts of the ruins have recently been rebuilt, and it was founded in 1377 by Bishop Houghton and John of Gaunt. It was connected to the cathedral by a cloister. The college was endowed to accommodate a master and seven priests, who lived in strict discipline. All the cathedral buildings are enclosed by the Close Walls, a construction built by Gower, which stand very well preserved in many places. The close is entered through the gatehouse called Porth-y-Twr. Several of the houses in and around St David's City are well worth looking at, and many of them belonged to church dignataries. Farmhouses near St David's have fine Flemish chimneys. Among these are Hendre, Eynon, and Rhosson. The town's old cross is of interest.

St David's Peninsula is a fascinating place to explore. The rock formations are famous, and there is much to enchant and interest the naturalist. This is a windswept and almost treeless land, but it has a rugged beauty that bewitches nearly all who visit it. At Abereiddy there are ruins of a slate quarry where many fossils can be found. A huge man-made pool which was once a quarry is linked to the sea by a narrow channel. The Pembrokeshire Coast Path runs along the magnificent cliff tops from Abereiddy to St David's Head. It passes many remains of prehistoric occupation, the most impressive of which is the Carn Llidi hillfort and hut circles. This stands some 600ft above sea level and affords superb views. At the very end of St David's Head is a small iron-age promontory fort, with a number of ramparts, ditches, and several stone huts. Caerfai Bay is small but very attractive. Seals breed in the area and are frequently seen.

Whitesand Bay is very popular for its fine sand and excellent surfing. Overlooking the bay is the site of St Patrick's Chapel. The bay was a well-used departure and arrival point for Ireland in the early days of Christianity. A site excavated here in 1924 revealed remains of an ancient chapel. The skeleton of a tall man was found under the floor, and subsequent discoveries may herald further large-scale excavations. A little road from St David's passes the ancient site of Clegyr-Boia, where articles from neolithic through to iron-age times have been found. St David's Lifeboat Station is situated at Porthstinian. Near the lifeboat station is St Justinian's Chapel, a small simple building probably built by Bishop

Vaughan on the site of a far earlier structure. Justinian was David's friend and teacher, who founded a small religious community on Ramsey Island. It is said he was murdered on the island. Porthlysgi Bay has a shingle beach and safe bathing. Porth Clais is a narrow, sandy creek where the River Alun flows into the sea. At its end is a very old harbour wall, probably dating from 12thc, and tradition puts the foundation of the first harbour in Roman times.

Above St Non's Bay is St Non's Chapel (AM), reputed to be the oldest Christian monument in Wales. It was on this spot that David is supposed to have been born. A holy well here attracted many people in the Middle Ages, who came in the hope of curing their ailments. The well is said to have sprung forth on the stormy night of David's birth. Caerbweli Bay is overlooked by a promontory fort and is the place from which much of the stone was quarried for the construction of the cathedral. To the E of St David's City is an expanse of wet land called Dowrog Common, which is of interest to naturalists. Remains of the so-called Monk's Dyke, which separated the Dark-Age domain of Menevia from the rest of Wales, can be traced near by. The whole of this uniquely interesting peninsula lies within the Pembrokeshire Coast national park, and there is a park information centre at City Hall. The Pembrokeshire Coast Path follows the whole length of the coast.

ST DOGMAELS, Dyfed *17 SN14*
Light and dark brown-stone houses cluster on the hillsides where the Cardigan road leaves this pretty village. St Dogmaels stands on the W shore of the Teifi estuary, and the local salmon fishing is good. Scant ruins of an abbey (AM) of the Tironian Benedictines, founded by Robert Fitz Martin c1115, are located in the grounds of the vicarage. The church and cloister were rebuilt and the chapter house added in the 14thc. Ruins comprise the early 15th-c north transept, traces of 16th-c vaulting, a 16th-c stone cadaver in a recess, and the north and west walls of the nave. A collection of carved stones is housed on the site of the former abbey infirmary.

Alongside the ruins is the 19th-c parish church, built in early-English style and dedicated to St Thomas the Martyr. A 7ft stone pillar which probably dates from the 6thc and bears both Ogham and Latin inscriptions provided a key to the translation of Ogham script in 1848. A 9th- or 10th-c pillar carved with a cross is placed next to the pulpit and suggests that the site is of 6th-c Celtic foundation. Farther along the W banks of the estuary are Poppit Sands, with a caravan site and excellent bathing. Beyond here rise the magnificent cliffs of Cemaes Head.

ST DONATS, South Glamorgan *25 SS96*
The local castle is of late 13th- or early 14th-c origin and was traditionally founded by Guillaume le Esterling, ancestor of the Stradling family who held it until the 18thc. Now much altered, the castle was originally concentric in plan with a polygonal curtain wall surrounding the main buildings of the inner ward. It looks more like a baronial hall than a place of defence due to subsequent alterations.

From 1925 extensive and thorough restoration work was undertaken by William Randolph Hearst, the American newspaper millionaire. He added masonry details and woodwork from other parts of Britain. It now houses the International Sixth-form United World College.

Memorials to the Stradling family are to be found in the local church, which dates from the 11th-c. The Lady Chapel houses three unusual 16th-c family paintings by Sir Edward Stradling. Also of interest are a Norman font, pre-Reformation altar, and some fine old stained glass. An excellent medieval cross stands in the churchyard. Near by is a 15th-c look-out tower from which the Bristol Channel could be spied on.

ST FAGANS, South Glamorgan 26 ST17
Here, in the grounds of the many-gabled Tudor mansion of St Fagans Castle, is the National Folk Museum of Wales. The 16th-c castle incorporates parts of the 13th-c curtain wall of a former structure, and its 100-acre grounds contain re-erected historic buildings. These were dismantled and brought here from all over Wales, and include an 18th-c cottage of white-washed boulders with a slate roof, from old Caernarfonshire; a timber-framed farmhouse dated c1600 from old Montgomeryshire; a 15th-c farmhouse from old Denbighshire; a long house of 1730 from old Radnorshire; and a 17th-c from old Radnorshire; and a 17th-c stone-built house from the Gower. Each building features examples of furniture and domestic items from the appropriate period. Also located here are a wool mill of 1760, a wooden turner's shop, and a basket-maker's shop where the traditional crafts are still practised – examples of which are on sale. The Gallery of Material Culture has a collection of objects relating to the Welsh way of life.

Within the adjoining village, situated on the banks of the River Ely, are pretty thatched cottages and an old church exhibiting some Norman work. A battle of the second civil war took place here in 1648, when the royalists suffered heavy casualties and 3,000 of them were taken prisoner.

ST FLORENCE, Dyfed 19 SN00
St Florence lies about 4m W of Tenby and is clustered around its old church. The Ritec stream which passes through it to Tenby was an inlet of the sea until the mid 19thc, and St Florence was a harbour in medieval times. Many of the cottages in this village are of Flemish foundation and exhibit the curious round chimneys associated with these people. Old Flemish crafts are still practised here, dating from the 12th-c tradition which Henry II imported along with colonizers from Flanders. The church is of Norman foundation, and has an impressively tall tower. Arches to the chancel and south chapel were probably inserted in the 13thc. Inside are interesting 17th- and 18th-c wall monuments.

ST GEORGE, Clwyd 6 SH97
Some 2m SE of Abergele, St George takes its unusual name from its legendary association with St George and the slaying of a dragon to rescue a damsel in distress. Mysterious hoofmarks on the church wall are pointed out to the credulous as substantiation of the legend.

The village largely developed as a result of nearby Kinmel Hall, one of the finest country houses in N Wales and now Clarendon Girls' School. Through the impressive wrought-iron gates alongside a richly-carved lodge house are glimpses of the pink brick mansion – the third house on this site. The first was established by Baron de Lacey in 1311.

Notable occupants have included the Dukes of Exeter and the Earl of Essex, and early in the 19thc the estate was bought by the son of the Rev Edward Hughes, who made a considerable fortune out of his copper find at Amlwch. The son became Lord Dinorben. In 1841 the second house, by Samuel Wyatt, was destroyed by fire. The existing house is reputedly styled on the Palace of Versailles. In the old churchyard is a grandiose mausoleum of Victorian gothic, containing six coffins of Lord Dinorben and his family. Plas Kinmel is a nearby farmhouse by W E Neasfield, the architect of the hall. Local amateur archeologists are restoring an ancient holy well in the hall grounds, which is remarkable for having two chambers – an inner shrine presumably for human use and the larger outer one where – according to local documents – sick horses were brought from a wide area to be splashed with the curative water.

ST HARMON, Powys 13 SN97
This small village is situated in the valley of the Afon Marteg about 3m NNE of Rhayader. The church was rebuilt in 1908 and stands in a circular churchyard on a site dating back to the 5thc. Inside is a Norman font with a large bowl carved with four human heads, and a handsome two-tiered brass chandelier with six branches. Francis Kilvert, vicar here from 1876 to 1877, wrote a daily journal describing life in this part of Wales at that time.

ST HILARY, South Glamorgan 25 ST07
Typical of the secluded villages to be found in the Vale of Glamorgan, St Hilary looks out over the vale from less than 1m S of the A48, E of Cowbridge. The church has a Norman chancel arch and two interesting family monuments.

ST LYTHANS, South Glamorgan 26 ST17
St Lythans (AM) is an isolated megalithic long barrow at OS reference ST 101 723, about 1¼m S of St Nicholas. The cairn is almost gone, leaving the capstone and three upright stones of the chamber exposed. This ancient structure dates from c6200BC.

ST MELLONS, South Glamorgan 26 ST28
The interesting church here is of decorated and perpendicular style, and includes a chancel arch column of the same approximate period as the nave. Fine views are afforded from the churchyard. Cefn Mably, a fine old mansion which is of partly 16th-c origin, lies 2½m N.

ST NICHOLAS, South Glamorgan 25 ST07
Although of ancient foundation, the church in this neat little village has been rebuilt and restored on many occasions. In the churchyard is a tombstone bearing the opening bar of Chopin's 20th Prelude. About 1¼m S 19th-c Dyffryn House stands in beautiful grounds which are open to the public. Over 100 acres of

splendid gardens contain rare trees and shrubs, and of special interest are some Chinese plants. Near by are Tinkinswood Cairn and St Lythan's burial chamber.

ST TUDWAL'S ISLANDS, Gwynedd 8 SH32
These two small grass-covered islands lie in the bay of St Tudwal just offshore from Abersoch. St Tudwal was a Breton who set up a cell here in the 6thc after he had fled from fear of persecution at the fall of the Roman Empire. During the Middle Ages an Augustinian priory occupied the cell, and after the Reformation a pirate band took control of it. Today all that remains are the ruins of a 12th-c chapel. On the W isle is an automatic lighthouse. Now privately owned, the islands form a seabird sanctuary and can be viewed from boats available from Abersoch.

SARN, Powys 14 SO29
This small scattered village on the N edge of Clun Forest is a mere 2m from the English border along the A489 road from Newtown to Craven Arms. A further 2m brings the motorist back into Wales to cross the Church Stoke promontory. The village name means a causeway, indicating that at one time the road here traversed marsh land. Mary Webb used the name for her character Prue Sarn, and for Sarn Mere in Precious Bane. About ½m S of the village is a hamlet intriguingly named 'The City'.

SAUNDERSFOOT, Dyfed 19 SN10
One of the most popular yachting and fishing holiday villages in S Wales, this pleasant resort is situated about 3m N of Tenby and has a good size harbour for small pleasure craft. Either side are pleasant sandy beaches which afford safe bathing. Behind these the much folded and faulted cliffs are topped by trees. An anticline at the back of the beach is of particular geological interest. The harbour was constructed in 1829 for the purpose of exporting locally mined anthracite coal, but this trade has now died out.

SEGONTIUM (Caernarfon), Gwynedd 5 SH46
This fascinating and extensive Roman fort near Caernarfon Castle is fully described in the special inset overleaf.

SENGHENYDD, Mid Glamorgan 26 ST19
At the top of the Aber Valley coal-mining area NW of Caerphilly, Senghenydd can vouch for the price of coal. In October 1913 an explosion at the Universal Colliery – now closed – killed 439 miners and left hundreds widowed and fatherless. King George V and Queen Mary contributed to a fund which raised £10,000. About eight days later there was an explosion at a colliery in the Merthyr Vale, over the mountains farther NW, and the fund was shared between nearly 900 dependants of those who died in the two catastrophes.

Senghenydd lies in the valley just above Abertridwr and figures in Welsh history. Gilbert de Clare, the Lord of Glamorgan who started building Caerphilly Castle in 1268, claimed overlordship over the cantref of Senghenydd which extended between the Rivers Rhymney and Taff from the S Wales coast to their sources in Brecknock. Welsh rulers of Senghenydd were often involved in maintaining their peoples' rights against Anglo-Norman encroachment. In 1266 the then Welsh ruler of Senghenydd, Gruffydd ap Rhys, was captured and sent to Ireland. In 1314 the descendant of the ruling Welsh family in Senghenydd was Llywelyn Bren, who lived at Gelligaer.

A road leads over 1,169ft Mynydd Eglwysilan to Nelson in the N, and the mountain to the W of the Aber Valley and 3m from Caerphilly bears the oldest church in the Caerphilly district. Situated at Eglwysilan, this building was dedicated to St Ilan and was restored in 1873. It was once the parish church of the whole Caerphilly area. Sion Cent, a 14th-c priest and poet, is believed to have been born at Abertridwr. According to tradition the nearby Groeswen (White Cross), situated on the S slopes of Mynydd Meio overlooking the A468 Caerphilly to Nantgarw road, was connected with a religious order centuries ago. William Edwards built the single-span bridge over the Taff at Pontypridd in 1755, and was a pastor at the Groeswen Chapel. He is buried in Eglwysilan churchyard.

SENNYBRIDGE, Powys 21 SN92
Situated where the Senni flows into the River Usk about 8m W of Brecon, Sennybridge lies on the N edge of the Brecon Beacons national park. It developed as an important centre for the marketing of sheep and cattle for the surrounding area after the opening of the A40 in 1819, and the Neath-Brecon Railway in 1872. Castell Du, now a ruin, stands on the W bank of the Senni and was probably constructed during the 13thc. It comprised a small round keep with a smaller building attached, and at one time was used as a prison by the keepers of Fforest Fawr.

SHIRENEWTON, Gwent 26 ST49
Fine views of the Severn Valley are afforded by this village, which lies about 4m W of Chepstow on the summit of a hill. Its 13th-c church has a battlemented tower and houses a fine brass commemorating Joseph Lowe, a famous botanist who died at Shirenewton Hall in 1900. A paper mill producing fine white paper was once located here because of the clearness of the water. Two women were imprisoned for holding a Quaker meeting in a local house in 1658, during the period of Nonconformist persecution.

SKENFRITH, Gwent 23 SO42
Close to the English border, this village stands beside the River Monnow about 8m NW of Monmouth. The river is excellent for trout fishing. Skenfrith's castle (AM) is one of three forming a triangle of defence, the others being Grosmont and White Castle. Ruins include a round tower enclosed by a four-sided curtain wall and a moat. The wall probably had five towers, but only four remain. This 13th-c structure, possibly built by Hubert de Burgh, the Justiciar of Henry III, replaced an earlier motte-and-bailey castle. At one time other stone buildings stood in the courtyard, but now only traces of foundations can be seen among the apple trees. It ceased to be of importance after the end of Welsh uprisings, and was probably in ruins by the 16thc. The local church also dates back to the 13thc and has an impressive, partially-timbered tower. Inside is the tomb of the last governor of the castle, John Morgan, who died in 1357. His family pew is set apart from the rest, which are of a more recent date.

BEFORE THE BARONS
A mile or so from Edward I's Caernarfon castle, lying astride the road to Beddgelert, is Segontium. This is considered the most important Roman auxiliary fort in North Wales. Excavations were carried out on the northern half of the site in the early 1920's by Mortimer Wheeler, and many of the finds are on display in the museum. It was Agricola who was responsible for the first stages of the fort in AD78, but the structure was considerably extended c150 when stone rather than wood, was used as building material. Occupation was sporadic until c383, when the Emperor Maximus scoured these islands for troops for his campaign in Gaul.

The fame of Maximus was perpetuated in the 12th-c Welsh legends known collectively as the *Mabinogion*, where he appears as Macsen Wledig. While sleeping he was supposed to have seen the most beautiful woman, and the vision disturbed him so much that he sought the counsel of wise men, to whom he described the minutest details of his dream. Thirteen men were then sent from Rome as messengers from the emperor in search of the enigma, following closely the clues provided by Maximus, until they came to a vast castle at the mouth of a river and saw the beautiful woman. When Maximus eventually arrived there himself he claimed Elen of the Hosts, as she was called, as his wife. The description of the splendid legendary castle of Caer Aber Seint is, ironically enough, more appropriately applied to the position of the 13th-c castle than to Segontium itself.

There were at least two sons from the union of the Roman emperor and his Welsh wife: Constantine and Publicius, who has given his name to the local parish Church of St Peblig. According to tradition the tomb of his brother Constantine was moved here by Edward I. The building which accommodated the headquarters was divided into three parts comprising an enclosed court and an assembly hall, behind which were five rooms and the regimental chapel. Next to this was the commandant's house, which followed the usual Roman villa plan of a number of rooms arranged around a central courtyard or garden, and adjoining this was a workshop used by the soldiers. On the opposite side of the headquarters stood the granaries, essential parts of the establishment when it is remembered that the diet of the occupants was substantially bread. The neatly-arranged museum should be seen before and after inspecting the site.

Modern Ground Level

SKOKHOLM ISLAND, Dyfed 18 SM70
The first bird-migration observatory in
Britain was established here by R M
Lockley in 1933. Lockley farmed the
island from 1927 to 1939, and described
it in his books *Dream Island* and *Island
Days*. The island is composed of old-
red sandstone and lies a few miles off the
SW coast of Dyfed. It provides a home for
many types of seabirds, particularly for
a colony of approximately 1,000 pairs of
storm petrels. A permit is required to visit
the reserve, which is now controlled by
the W Wales Naturalists' Trust.

SKOMER ISLAND, Dyfed 18 SM70
A national nature reserve covering some
700 acres, this island lies about 1½m off
the W tip of St Bride's Bay. It is
surrounded by cliffs of dark igneous rock,
where Atlantic grey seals breed in caves,
and forms the home of numerous species
of seabirds – particularly Manx
shearwaters, puffins, guillemots,
razorbills, and various types of gulls.
Wheatears, meadow pippits, linnets, other
smaller breeds, and the short-eared owl
also nest here. Thrift covers vast areas
of the island and blooms profusely in the
early summer months. Bluebells,
primroses, and celandines can also be
found. Traces of iron-age field patterns
and hut groups can be seen on the island,
and a simple promontory fort is located
on the Neck. No permit is necessary to
visit, and boat trips can be arranged
from Martin's Haven.

SNOWDONIA NATIONAL PARK, Gwynedd
The Snowdonia national park covers
845 sqm in the new administrative
county of Gwynedd, and comprises large
blocks of mountain and moorland divided
from each other by deep valleys along
which most of the main roads have been
made. Each mountain is intersected by
deep radiating valleys. The great beauty
and variety of the park is due mainly to
the presence of so many valleys so close
to each other. Most of the land is
privately owned, and rights of access are
the same as in other parts of the
countryside. Permission must be obtained
before visiting many of the nature
reserves. Local planning authorities are
responsible for the administration of the
park, with the Park Planning Committee
responsible for preserving and enhancing
the natural beauty. This committee
operates a warden service and provides
facilities.

There are approximately 22m of coastline
on Cardigan Bay. This is mostly sand and
dunes, but several miles of small cliffs
can be seen N of Tywyn. Most of the
mountains belong to the Palaeozoic
period, and the ranges can be divided
into distinct groups. The farthest N is the
Carneddau and the extreme S Cader
Idris. The Glyderau range runs from
NW to SE between Carneddau and
Snowdon, and the Snowdon range is star
shaped, with Snowdon at the centre.
The summit of Snowdon has two peaks,
3,493ft Crib-y-Ddisgl to the N and the
3,560ft main peak Yr Wyddfa – which is
the highest point in the British Isles S
of the Scottish Highlands. The Hebog
range is in the NW of the park, with
the Moelwyn and Siabod ranges to the
NE. In the centre of the park, S of the
Moelwyn range, are the Migneint,
Arennig Fawr, and Rhobell Fawr
mountains. To the SW is the Rhinog
range, and on the SE borders are the
Gylchedd, Arennig, and Aran ranges.
The park offers ample opportunity for

mountain walking, and many areas are
suitable for rock-climbing – both for the
beginner and the expert. Lliwedd in Cwm
Dyli is one of the largest and most
imposing of the Welsh crags, criss-crossed
with routes of all standards of difficulty.
Most climbers stay in one of the popular
centres for climbing, such as the Nant
Ffrancon Pass or the Llanberis Pass. The
valleys show pronounced effects of the
Ice Age, many are U-shaped, and the
Nant Ffrancon Pass and Llanberis Pass
have splendid examples of hanging
valleys. The lakes were also formed
during the Ice Age, some having been
scooped out by glaciers and others
dammed behind moraines left by the
melting ice. Excellent examples include
Llyn-y-Gadair under Cader Idris,
Glaslyn under Snowdon, and Llyn
Dulyn under Foel Fras. Rivers have cut
through hard and soft rock alike, and the
principal waters flow along courses that
are unrelated to the fundamental
geological structure. Major rivers found
in the area are the Conwy, Dyfi, and
Mawddach.

Gwydyr, Lledr, Machno, and Beddgelert
forests combine to form the Snowdonia
forest park. This covers 23,463 acres, of
which 17,750 are planted. The Forestry
Commission found it necessary to try
many species before establishing which
were most suitable for the Snowdonia
area, and the Sitka spruce has proved the
most successful and useful. Also to be
seen are Douglas fir, western red cedar,
lodge-pole pine, western hemlock, and
various silver firs. Snowdonia is the
farthest S known British limit for many
mountain plants. On the mountain
summits there is a scarcity of plant
species, the most luxuriant being woolly-
haired moss. Least willow can be found
on some summits, plus a variety of
grasses. The mountain sides are covered
with the turfy grasslands which
contribute much to the beauty of the
area. Where drainage is impeded the
slopes are marshy, and a bog is
recognizable from miles away by the
blackness of its bare peat, the dark
mantle of its heather, and beautiful
white sheets of cotton grass. Some plant
species survive on mountain crags, where
sheep are unable to reach them, while
others adapt to become specialized
mountain forms. The rare Snowdon lily
is found only in Cwm Idwal, a lake valley
which is protected as a national nature
reserve.

Some fifteen reserves exist in Snowdonia,
and it is sometimes necessary to obtain
a permit before visiting them. Permits
and further information are available
from The Nature Conservancy, Penrhos
Road, Bangor, Gwynedd. A great deal of
research is carried out at the Bangor
Research Station, particularly into
different types of grasslands. A team of
wardens protects the reserves, and
keepers are available to conduct parties
and give lectures. The rarest mammals
to be found in Snowdonia are the pine-
marten and polecat. Large herds of wild
goats are evident on the mountains. Now
almost extinct is a local variety of
mountain hare which turns white in
winter, but the red squirrel is still fairly
common in wooded areas – although the
grey squirrel has infiltrated extensively.

Several types of bat live in the valleys,
and colonies of grey seals are found
around the coast. Various species of
whale – especially the black whale –
can also be seen at times. Salmon, sea

trout, and brown trout are fairly
common in the rivers, and char is to be
found in Llyn Padarn and a few other
lakes. Perch and pike are numerous,
and the deep, cold-water gwyniad is
found in Bala Lake. Coarse species are
not fished for. An enormous variety
of birdlife includes peregrine falcons,
buzzards, and kestrels. Eagles are extinct
in Snowdonia. The ring ouzel is common
above the 1,000ft contour in summer,
and the pied flycatcher is found in valley
woodlands. Snowdonia is one of the
latter species' major breeding grounds.
Wild geese come to the coastal salt
marshes in winter, and both whooper
and Berwick swans settle on the lowland
lakes in winter.

Disused quarries disfigure mountain faces
in many parts of the park, and include
the Dinorwic Slate Quarry opposite
Llanberis. Two slate mines at Blaenau
Ffestiniog are open to the public.
Many of the narrow-gauge railways which
were built for the transportation of slate
have been preserved (see feature starting
page 62). The first inland nuclear
power station to be built in Britain
lies on the shores of Trawsfynydd
Lake, and the first pumped-storage power
station lies below the Stwlan Dam at
Tanygrisiau. Visits to these can be
arranged. The Roman Steps, which are
situated E of Harlech and begin near
Llyn Cwm Bychan, climb up the N side
of Rhinog Fawr and were built during
the Middle Ages. Many remains of the
late stone, bronze, and iron ages can be
found. At Carneddau Hengwm near
Barmouth there is the great capstone of
a late stone-age cromlech. Fine examples
of medieval castles can be found at
Conwy, Harlech, and Caernarfon.

SOLVA, Dyfed 16 SM82
Solva comprises a group of white,
typically Welsh cottages clustering on
hillsides surrounding a small inlet in the
N shore of St Bride's Bay. The village is
best viewed from Gribyn Cove, where
there are many rare wild flowers.
Ancient earthworks lie at each end of the
head, and in the vicinity are two dolmens.
Once a place for smugglers, this was
later a port for coal and lime. A row of
disused 19th-c lime kilns still stands
near the road bridge. Now it is a haven
for small boats, pleasure craft, and
yachts, with a sailing club providing the
best facilities on St Bride's Bay. The cliff
scenery on either side of Solva is
magnificent, and the sheltered sandy
cove affords excellent bathing. About
1m N at Middle Mill is a watermill, open
to visitors, where woollen weaves are
manufactured. Hand-carved furniture is
also sold here. The village is a good
centre for walks in the Pembrokeshire
Coast national park. The first Small
Rocks lighthouse was assembled here in
1773, and finally erected after a great
deal of difficulty.

**SOUTHERNDOWN, Mid Glamorgan
25 SS87**
This small resort is set on the cliff tops
above Dunraven Bay, where fine golden
sands are exposed at low tide. Rock
formations in the cliffs, which reach over
200ft in places and are pitted with caves
and blow holes, are of special interest to
the geologist. Trwyn-y-Witch (Witch's
Nose) is a massive headland at the
S extremity of the bay, rising from
waters torn by fierce currents. Behind
this are a tumulus and traces of the
embankments of an iron-age fort.
cont overleaf

The last Castle of Dunraven was a 19th-c mansion dismantled after the second world war. A stronghold had existed here since the time of the pre-Roman leader Caradog, or Caractacus. In Norman times it passed to Arnold le Boteler, an ancestor of the Butlers, and eventually by marriage to a line of the Vaughan family in the 16thc. A legend connected with Ogmore Castle near Bridgend is said to point to how Southerndown came by its name. Maurice de Londres, holder of the castle and estate in 1130, caught a Welshman killing a deer. As the prisoner was about to be tortured the daughter of de Londres pleaded for his life, and asked that some of the land at least should be restored to the Welsh. She was told her wish would be granted, and he would restore to the Welsh as much land as she could walk barefooted between sunrise and sunset. She accepted the challenge, and with torn and bleeding feet she walked all day. At sunset she reached King's Wood 1m N of St Bride's Major near a quarry, where in great pain she: 'sat down. Thus it is that Satterdown, or Southerndown Common, is common land won for the people by the heroism of a Norman girl,' concludes the legend. A fine cliff walk runs 1m W near the road from Southerndown to Ogmore-by-Sea.

STACKPOLE, Dyfed 18 SR99

Stackpole Court – now demolished – was the centre of this small village and the home of the Earls of Cawdor. Stackpole village lies 3m S of Pembroke, a little off the coast, and is surrounded by golden fields of corn in the summer. About ½m away on the coast is Stackpole Quay, with a disused limestone quarry and a stone jetty from which limestone was exported. The beach here is rocky, but a short walk over the cliffs to the S leads to the quiet, sandy beach of Barafundle Bay, behind which lie the dunes of Stackpole Warren. There is a standing stone in the warren at OS reference SR 983 951. To the S of the bay is the rocky promontory of Stackpole Head, where a natural arch has been carved out by the sea.

Strata Florida Abbey was founded on the 'Road of Flowers' in the 12thc.

A little to the N of Stackpole is Cheriton, or Stackpole Elidyr, where a 14th-c church was restored in the 19th-c by Sir Gilbert Scott. Its tall thin tower is unusually placed at the northern end of the north transept, and the church contains many interesting monuments. Among these are 14th-c effigies of Richard de Stackpole and his wife, and a 7th-c inscribed altar slab. The Lort chapel behind the pews houses a 17th-c monument of Roger Lort and his wife, surrounded by their twelve weeping children. A restored preaching cross can be seen near the south porch.

STAYLITTLE, Powys 13 SN89

Staylittle lies low in the Clywedog Valley, exactly half way between Llanidloes and Llanbrynmair on the B4518 mountain road. The road falls steeply into it and climbs as steeply out again. Perhaps the main feature of interest in the village is the Quaker burial ground up on the hillside. The village is reputed to have been named from the speed with which two local blacksmiths would shoe horses – customers needed only to 'stay a little'.

STRATA FLORIDA, Dyfed 13 SN76

A Cistercian community was founded here on the 'Road of Flowers' in the upper valley of the Teifi by Robert Fitz Stephen in 1164, but the building of the abbey (AM) did not begin until two years later, when Rhys ap Gruffydd conquered the district and took over the foundation. He and his descendants are buried in the abbey, some of them in the Chapter House. In 1238 a great assembly of Welsh princes took place in the abbey for the purpose of swearing allegiance to Dafydd, the son of Llywelyn the Great; here part of the *Chronicles of the Princes,* which recorded a century and a quarter of Welsh history, were written.

Lightning struck the abbey in 1285, and it was badly burned; later it was damaged in the Glyndwr wars, when it was taken over by the military; finally, after the Dissolution, it was acquired by the Stedman family and later passed from them to the Powells of Nanteos. It was to

this mansion that the few remaining monks of Strata Florida retired in 1539 when it was closed down, taking with them the olive-wood cup believed to be the Holy Grail. The Cistercians were sheep breeders who established the wool industry in this part of Wales, and they held a licence granted by King John which enabled them to export to France and Flanders free of duty.

Of the splendid buildings which once stood on this site only the great west entrance door with its Norman arch remains. Apart from this there are lines of walls which have been excavated to reveal the positions of the various rooms. In 1951 a memorial to Dafydd ap Gwilym was placed in the north transept. He was a 14th-c poet who was noted for his love poems, especially those to two of his sweethearts, Morfudd and Dyddgu.

STRATA MARCELLA, Powys 11 SJ20

All that is left of this 12th-c abbey on the banks of the Severn outside Welshpool is the site. This is on the right of the Oswestry road 1m beyond the turn for Shrewsbury at the end of the straight mile. It was founded in 1170 by Owain Cyfeiliog, Prince of Powys, and was enriched by his son Wenwynwyn. Edward III had the Welsh monks transferred to monasteries in England and replaced them with English monks from English monasteries, but the reason for this is obscure. The monks of Strata Marcella are credited with having been the first inhabitants of the district to construct dykes and embankments to contain the Severn in times of flood. They also built a weir in the river, the remains of which can still be seen. Relics of the abbey found from time to time have been presented to the Powysland Museum at Welshpool.

SUGAR LOAF, Gwent 22 SO21

An outlier of the Black Mountains, the cone of this extinct volcano rises to 1,955ft about 3m NW of Abergavenny and was presented to the NT in 1936 by Viscountess Rhondda as a memorial to her late husband. It dominates the landscape for miles around and affords fine views over the Bristol Channel and round to the Malvern Hills. It can be ascended via a walk of some 3½m from Abergavenny, or from Llangenny Bridge near Crickhowell.

*SWANSEA, West Glamorgan 24 SS69

Second largest city and centre of the biggest industrial complex in Wales, Swansea is a product of the Industrial Revolution. Ironworks, steelworks, chemical factories, mills – factories, and works of every variety, shape, size and description – are all sited here. Iron and coal were the keywords to the growth of Swansea's population from some 6,000 at the beginning of the 19thc to its present 170,000. But Swansea's beginning goes back a great deal farther than the 19thc. The name is derived from *Sweyn's Ea – Ea* means island, and Sweyn was a Viking pirate who chose this spot as his base from which to plunder the coast. In 1099 the Normans arrived, and Henry Beaumont captured the region called Gower before building the inevitable castle. No traces of this first castle survive. The fortified ruins that exist today are those of a large manor house built by Henry Gower, Bishop of St David's, c1340. These ruins (AM exterior

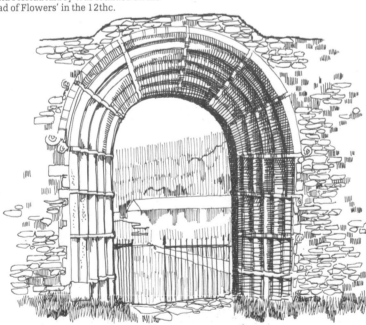

Entries marked * are the starting point of drives included in the Day Drive section of the book (pages 95 to 144).

only) consist of a large quadrilateral tower and various domestic buildings. Owain Glyndwr damaged the castle very badly in the 15thc, and in 1306 the town was given a charter which conferred the right to build and equip ships – the beginning of the huge docks and dock installation that Swansea now boasts.

When the Industrial Revolution came Swansea could not fail. Near by were anthracite coalfields and iron ore, and the docks were waiting, but the town did not keep its eggs all in one basket. Other industries included the manufacture of Swansea-ware pottery, even now a much sought-after type. This was called Cambrian Ware in the 18thc, and the company was taken over by one Lewis Weston Dillwyn in 1802. It was he who was largely responsible for the fine porcelain which the firm subsequently produced. Dillwyn's son John was a noted Swansea figure. An amateur scientist with a great breadth of interest, he partook in some of the early experiments in photography.

Swansea was extensively damaged by bombing in the second world war, and its old town centre was demolished. St Mary's Church is a 15th-c building which was bombed in 1941 and rebuilt in 1955. Among the treasures lost was the tomb of Sir Matthew and Catherine Craddock. Catherine had once been the wife of Perkin Warbeck, the Pretender who claimed to be one of the young princes whom Richard III had disposed of. Swansea Market, the biggest in Wales, lost all its windows during the bombing. Two local delicacies, cockles and laver bread, can be purchased here. Laver bread is made from seaweed and has a

taste which requires perseverance to be appreciated. The Guildhall was built in 1934, and sixteen panels in its Brangwyn Hall were painted for the House of Lords by Frank Brangwyn. The Fine Art's Commission decided that the panels were too flamboyant for the Lords and rejected them.

In Alexandra Road the Glynn Vivian Art Gallery displays a collection which includes examples of Swansea and Nantgarw Porcelain. The Royal Institution of South Wales in Victoria Street houses the museum and a library, and the Patti Pavilion near the Guildhall stages a wide variety of entertainments throughout the summer months. Among Swansea's famous sons are Beau Nash, who was born in 1674 and dictated the lifestyle of the fashionable people of Bath, and Dylan Thomas – poet and drinker extraordinary. Swansea is a city and a university town with its feet firmly in the 20thc. Coal is no longer the principal energy source that it once was, but Swansea has oil refineries and the factories still produce tin plate, iron, steel, flour, etc. Situated on the beautiful Gower Peninsula, which is designated an area of outstanding natural beauty, the city is within easy reach of many sandy bays with good, safe bathing. There are opportunities for sailing, golf, canoeing, fishing, and general touring. Extensive hotel accommodation is available, and the city provides more than amply for leisure pursuits. There are 700 acres of parks; Brynmill Park has a small zoo and lake, and Clyne Gardens has splendid displays of flowers. The Swansea Music Festival is held in October.

TAF FAWR RESERVOIRS, Powys
21 SN91
The river Taff rises on the S slopes of the Brecon Beacons and flows SE to reach the outskirts of Merthyr Tydfil, where it is joined by the Taf Fechan River. Between 1892 and 1927 three reservoirs were constructed in the Cwm Taff for Cardiff Corporation – The Beacons, Cantref, and Llwyn-on reservoirs. All lie on the W side of the main A470 Brecon to Cardiff and Merthyr road, partly in Powys and partly in Mid Glamorgan.

TAF-FECHAN RESERVOIR, Powys
21 SO01
Largest and farthest S of a four-reservoir system built in the Taf Fechan Valley between 1895 and 1927 to supply the nearby coalfields, Taf Fechan lies a little to the N of Merthyr Tydfil in the Brecon Beacons national park. The slopes on either side are wooded – partly planted by the Forestry Commission – and a road runs along the reservoir's more gently sloping W side.

TAFF'S WELL, Mid Glamorgan   26 ST18
Sited in the Vale of Taff about 5m NW of Cardiff, this village was once a health spa. The cool waters of the well, which lies near the river, are locally reputed to provide a cure for muscular rheumatism. People visited the well in its brick bath house, and bottled spa water was sent all over the world, but those days have gone. A railway viaduct once spanned the valley just S of the village, but this too has vanished. Garth Mountain towers NW, and Castell Coch lies $\frac{3}{4}$m SE.

TALGARTH, Powys   22 SO13
A small market town in a setting of rural

1 Castle
2 Civic Centre & Guildhall
3 Glynn Vivian Art Gallery

4 Grand Theatre
5 Patti Pavilion
6 Royal Institution of South Wales

7 St Mary's Church
8 Swansea Market
9 University College (part of)

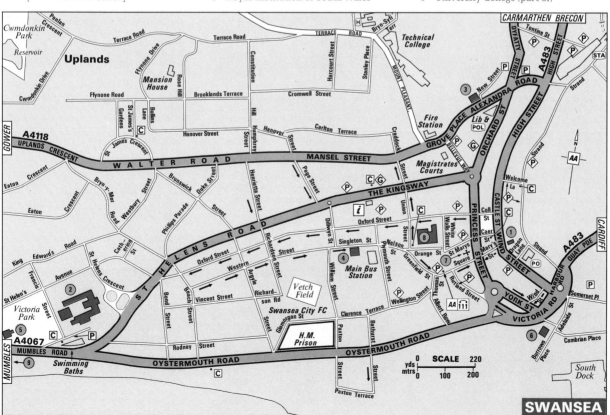

SWANSEA

beauty at the foot of the Black Mountains, Talgarth lies in the Brecon Beacons national park. To the SE rise the lofty peaks of 2,660ft Waun Fach and 2,624ft Pen-y-Gader, and eight cattle markets were once held here annually. The church is dedicated to St Gwendoline and dates from the 13th to 15thc. It was restored in 1873, is cruciform in plan, and carries a 14th-c tower. The south aisle displays an excellent 14th-c sepulchral slab. A square 14th-c pele tower standing at the E end of a local bridge was once used as a lookout post, but has since been converted into a house.

Hywel Harris, a founder of Methodism in Wales, came from here. He intended to enter the Church of England, but after he was refused ordination on three occasions by the bishop of St David's he became a wandering preacher. Later in life he set up a communal farming centre at nearby Trefecca, where the inhabitants lived an almost monastic life. As well as farming they worked at over 60 different country crafts. He was supported in this venture by the Countess of Huntingdon. After his death in 1773 and subsequent burial in Talgarth churchyard, a chapel was erected at Trefecca to his memory.

TALIESIN, Dyfed   12 SN69
This village on the Aberystwyth to Machynlleth road lies 1½m N of Talybont, and is more correctly called *Tre'r Taliesin – ie* the place of Taliesin. Taliesin was a 6th-c bard of great distinction, who is said to be buried on the mountainside at Bedd Taliesin, 1m E of the village. Whether Bedd Taliesin is the authentic burial place cannot be stated with certainty. A human skull was found here 150 years ago, but it was that of a prehistoric man and not a 6th-c poet.

TALLEY, Dyfed   20 SN63
Two lakes encircled by a road gave this pretty little village its Welsh name of Talyllychau. An abbey (AM) of the Premonstratensian order was founded here, probably by Rhys ap Gruffydd, towards the end of the 12thc. Rhys was a lord of the S who passed considerable estates into the care of the abbey. In 1277 it came under the control of Edward I, who placed it in the hands of English houses of the same order. It suffered during the Glyndwr rising, and when dissolved at the time of Henry VIII only eight of its White Canons were left.

Much of the abbey's fabric has been dismantled for use as building stone. The most impressive remains are those of the eastern and northern walls of the central tower of the church, which displays a tall pointed arch and a smaller archway. The outline of the rest of the church and the cloisters can still be traced. Between the abbey and the lakes lies the 13th-c parish church. Its unusual western entrance has two pointed doorways set below three lancet windows. A plain interior contains a set of box pews, of which the one for the squire's family is slightly larger. Near the abbey is an 18th-c Georgian farmhouse, pleasantly set amid trees, and the 17th-c manor house of Edwinsford.

TALSARNAU, Gwynedd   9 SH63
Talsarnau is a comparatively recently built village on the A496, set behind a turf embankment constructed in 1810 across a marsh S of the sandy Traeth Bach estuary. Portmeirion and its sandy beach lie just across the estuary. About 1m SW is Llanfihangel-y-Traethau, with the parish church of St Michael. Before reclamation took place this church occupied an island outcrop, and even today it is still rather isolated. Rebuilt in 1871, it contains a 17th-c stone inscribed in both Latin and Welsh, and its churchyard features a 12th-c inscribed stone pillar. The Jacobean houses of Glyn Clywarch and Maes-y-Neudd stand near by and have both been greatly restored.

TALYBONT, Dyfed   12 SN68
In the past Talybont had two thriving industries – lead mining and woollen-cloth manufacture. Today a family firm which was weaving wool in 1809 is still operating. This is the Lerry Tweed Mills, now run by the Hughes family and visited by as many as 2,000 people a day in the summer holiday months. Up until 1914 they were still using hand looms installed in 1809, but these became so worn that they had to be replaced. The new ones, however, were specially made as exact copies of the originals, and are still in use today. The mills derive their name from the River Leri, which flows through the village and activates two water wheels. One of these drives a power loom which has had to supplement the hand looms, while the other drives carding and spinning machinery. A mountain road from here runs up the Leri valley to Nant-y-Moch Reservoir, and thence across the mountains to Pont Erwyd on the Aberystwyth to Llangurig road.

TALYBONT RESERVOIR, Powys   21 SO01
This is one of many reservoirs set in the Brecon Beacons built to serve industrial S Wales. This particular one takes its name from Talybont-on-Usk – which lies to the N – and serves Newport. It is situated in a wooded valley and provides a refuge for wild fowl.

TAL-Y-LLYN, Gwynedd   9 SH70
Picturesquely situated above a lake of the same name, this hamlet is overshadowed by the rugged Cader Idris range which can be seen from here. St Mary's Church dates from *c*1600 and was restored in 1876. The wood panels of its chancel roof are painted with red and white roses, and at the east end of the church is a painting of the Twelve Apostles.

TAL-Y-LLYN, Gwynedd   9 SH70
One of the most beautiful lakes in Wales, Tal-y-llyn lies in completely unspoilt surroundings below the S flanks of Cader Idris. It is situated at the end of a broad, deep, and almost straight valley which is nearly 10m long and was caused by a geological feature known as the Bala Fault. Running NE from Tywyn to Bala, this tear-fault caused rock strata on one side to slip sideways. About 1m long, shallow, and surrounded by reeded banks, the lake is the source of the Dysynni River, which flows down to Abergynolwyn and produces a remarkable feature known as river capture – *ie* turning to the NW it passes through the hills to reach a parallel valley which was the proper Dysynni route. The original outlet from Tal-y-llyn flowed beyond Abergynolwyn to the sea, but was captured by the tributary streams of the river in the next valley. Its remains, the Afon Fathew, is now no more than a stream draining the sides of its valley.

TANYGRISIAU, Gwynedd   9 SH64
Tanygrisiau is an industrial village with the same slatey appearance as its neighbour Blaenau Ffestiniog, but offers several points of interest to the visitor. A special bus runs regularly along a corkscrew road to the 1,500ft-high Cwm Stwlan dam and offers an exhilarating mountain drive. This reservoir, high in the flanks of the Moelwyn, was created by the enlargement of Llyn Stwlan. The dam wall is visible for miles, and is the longest in England and Wales. Water from the reservoir supplies Ffestiniog Power Station, which was opened in 1963 and was the first pumped-storage power station in Britain.

The lower level reservoir has been created by damming the Afon Ystradau. Water is pumped from the lower reservoir overnight, when demand for electricity is low, and stored in the upper reservoir to drive water turbines during the day, when demand is high. Within a minute of operations beginning the station can produce 360,000 Kw of electricity. Visits can be arranged with advance notice to the station superintendant, Ffestiniog Power Station, Tanygrisiau. A slate mine at Manod Mawr near Tanygrisiau was the repository for many national treasures during the war. The mine provided the even temperature necessary for safe storage. Tanygrisiau is the best point from which to climb 2,527ft Moelwyn.

Construction of the power station and the lower reservoir had a considerable effect upon the Festiniog Railway and efforts to re-open the line to its terminus at Blaenau Ffestiniog. The original line of the railway ran through the ½m-long Moelwyn Tunnel before reaching Tanygrisiau. When the reservoir was constructed the trackbed on this section was flooded, and the tunnel mouth blocked. After much negotiation and legal proceedings a new line of route along the W shore, passing behind the power station to rejoin the original line, was agreed. As this was at a higher level, a spiral which is unique in Britain had to be constructed to bring the line up to the required height. This can be seen at the present terminus of Dduallt. Remains of the original line through Tanygrisiau and up to Blaenau Ffestiniog can still be seen, and there may be old waggons, signals, and sections of track to mark the route.

TAN-Y-MURIAU, Gwynedd   8 SH22
To the N of Rhiw in the Lleyn Peninsula at OS reference SH 227 280, this megalithic long cairn has a portalled chamber with a subsidiary lateral chamber.

*TENBY, Dyfed   19 SN10
Narrow streets with houses and shops built against the ruins of the 13th-c town walls impart a distinctive charm to this pleasant resort. From medieval times the sheltered harbour to the N served as an important link with Bristol and Ireland, and the town is ideally situated on a narrow, rocky promontory on the W side of Carmarthen Bay. The sides of the peninsula are formed of limestone cliffs scored by paths leading to the Esplanade and sands. It is thought that Tenby may have been a Norse settlement,

but by the 9thc it was a Welsh stronghold. It takes it name from *Dinbych-y-Pysgod* – the little fort of fishes – and it appears in one of the earliest recorded Welsh poems. In the late 11th and early 12thc Norman invaders and their followers provided the non-Welsh elements in the area, which Elizabethan William Camden was to call *Anglia Transwalliana* – England beyond Wales.

Under successive Earls of Pembroke from 1139 onwards, the little port grew as part of their estates. Defences were built to resist periodic Welsh raids and to protect the harbour. Charters were granted by the earls, and later by the crown, providing trading and marketing privileges. Especially important were the Mayoral Charter of Henry IV in 1402, and the Charter of Incorporations of Elizabeth I in 1581. During the civil wars Tenby was garrisoned and besieged by both sides. Parliamentary ships engaged land batteries in 1643, and some of their cannons still serve as bollards around the harbour. The town became popular as a health resort in the 18thc, and with the coming of the railway

in 1853 it developed into a major holiday resort. Present-day attractions include two cinemas, a dance hall, amusement arcades, and facilities for golf, angling, bowls, and water ski-ing. There is a regular motor launch service to Caldy Island from the harbour, and St Catherine's Island features a zoo and a 19th-c fort. The lifeboat station and North Beach Gallery are of interest.

Ruins of the 13th-c keep and walls of Tenby Castle can be seen on Castle Hill. The keep now contains a museum with displays relating to Pembrokeshire's archeology, geology, natural history, and medieval history. Also on show are the Smith Collection of animal remains from local caves, and the Lyons Collection of shells. A statue of Prince Albert stands among the ruined walls. Extensive remains of the 13th-c town walls survive. Originally there were probably 20 towers and five gateways, and the walls ran from a small watchtower on the cliffs above South Sands to a similar tower that stood above North Bay. The walls were strengthened in 1457, and again during the Armada scare in 1588. They have been partly rebuilt and the

barbican, in front of the S gate, has five arches. The watchtower above South Sands is still standing.

On Quay Hill is the Tudor Merchants' House (NT, OACT), a good example of 15th-c architecture displaying a gabled front and corbelled chimney breast. The ground floor is now a NT information centre which includes an exhibition of the Tudor period. Adjacent Plantagenet House (NT) is of the same date and has a Flemish-type chimney. St Mary's is the largest parish church in Wales and dates from the 13thc. It contains the tomb of Robert Recorde the mathematician, and the tower and steeple are situated between the south aisle and chapel. Bosses decorate the 15th-c chancel roof. Beside the harbour is St Julian's Chapel, a largely reconstructed building where the last special fishermen's services were held in Wales. Augustus John the painter was born at Tenby in 1878. The meadows near Tenby are the only home of the Tenby daffodil, a Welsh speciality. St Margaret's Fair is held in July under the charter granted by Queen Elizabeth I.

1	Five Arches (SW tower of town walls)	5	St Catherine's Island & Zoo	9 Tenby Pottery
2	Lifeboat House	6	St Julian's Chapel	10 Town Walls
3	North Beach Art Gallery	7	St Mary's Church	
4	Plantagenet & Tudor Merchants' Houses	8	Tenby Castle & Museum	

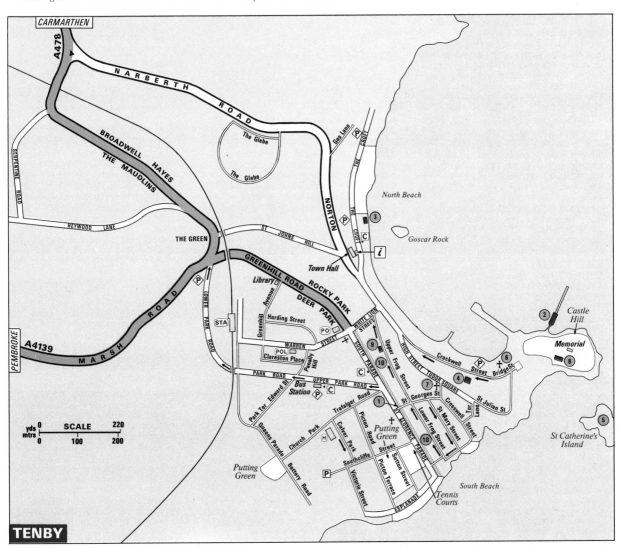

THORN ISLAND, Dyfed *18 SM80*
Thorn Island is situated in Milford
Haven off West Angle Bay. A fort was
built here in the 19thc as part of a
defence system for Pembroke Dock,
although it had first been suggested as a
site for a battery in the late 16thc. This
has now been converted into a hotel.

TINKINSWOOD, South Glamorgan
25 ST07
An impressive neolithic burial chamber
(AM) of the 'Cotswold-Severn' type,
Tinkinswood is situated a little to the S of
St Nicholas. Large and rectangular, it is
approached through a horned forecourt
and slab-lined entrance in the drystone
walling which encloses the long wedge-
shaped mound. The massive capstone
measures some 7½yds by 3yds and
weighs about 40 tons (OS reference
ST 092 733).

TINTERN, Gwent *23 SO50*
Ruins of a famous Cistercian abbey (AM)
form the main attraction offered by this
picturesque village, which is situated in
a loop of the River Wye. Tintern Abbey
was founded in 1131 by a member of the
de Clare family, and enlarged in the
13th and 14thc. The walls of its roofless
church, which was consecrated in 1288,
stand almost intact and appear to
reach upwards to heaven. Four great
arches are preserved in the centre, and
a fine traceried rose window over 60ft
high is set in the east wall. In decorated
style, the church measures some 228ft
long by 150ft wide. Ruins of many
monastic buildings also survive,
including the sacristy, Chapter House,
refectory, and kitchen. Edward II spent
two nights here in 1326 on his way from
Gloucester to Chepstow, and the
chronicler and traveller William of
Worcester visited the abbey in 1478.

Important brass and iron foundries have
been sited in the village, but today it is
mainly a tourist centre for visitors to
the Wye Valley. Good accommodation
facilities are available. The Anchor Inn
is connected to a slipway by a 13th-c
arch, and was probably once the abbey's
water gate. Wyndcliff is a notable
viewpoint which lies 2m S. Walkers can
enjoy fine views of the Wye Valley from
the Tintern Forest, Chapel Hill, and
Barbadoes Forest trails – all controlled
by the Forestry Commission.

TOMEN-Y-MUR, Gwynedd *9 SH73*
About 2m N of Trawsfynydd at OS
reference SH 707 387 is the site of a 1st-c
Roman fort. This probably had earth
defences constructed on a foundation of
turf and surmounted by timber palisades,
but during the 2ndc the size of the fort
was considerably reduced and it was
rebuilt in stone. The fort had an
amphitheatre – probably the only one
attached to an auxiliary fort, a parade
ground, and an artificial platform of
unknown purpose. Of the two Roman
roads which meet near by, one leads
down from the fort to the stream, where
remains of various other buildings
include a bath house. On the other side
of the stream are several little square
burial mounds. Inside the walls are the
remains of a Norman motte, possibly
built by William Rufus in 1095. This
stands over the west wall of the second
Roman fort and may enclose a gateway.
It is to this early medieval motte that
the name Tomen-y-Mur, meaning Mound
of the Wall, refers.

TONYPANDY, Mid Glamorgan *25 SS99*
Unlike other towns in the Rhondda
Valley, the origins of this community lie
not in coal but in the woollen industry.
Its name means 'The Untilled Land
Where the Fulling Mills are', but today
it is a typical example of the large towns
in the S Wales mining area. It is one of
the four main shopping towns in the
Rhondda.

TOWYN, Clwyd *6 SH97*
Caravan and chalet developments which
were allowed to disfigure this coastline
during the inter-war years have
submerged this small coastal resort,
which lies between Rhyl and Abergele. A
redeeming feature is the pleasant
grouping of the 19th-c church, vicarage,
and school by architect G E Street. This
community used to be confused with
Towyn in mid Wales, but the latter town
has recently been changed to Tywyn.

TRAETH DULAS, Gwynedd *5 SH48*
Derelict quays recall busier times when
coastal tramps called into this remote
and almost landlocked estuary on the
N coast of Anglesey, carrying fuel for the
brickworks. A reef which is 3m away
and which makes the coastline
treacherous is known as Ynys Dulas, or
Seal Island. It carries a round tower of
refuge for sailors whose boats fell foul
of the rocks. A local lady used to
provision the tower with food and drink.

TRAWSFYNYDD, Gwynedd *9 SH73*
Modern technology has transformed the
local landscape with a huge nuclear
power station, which dominates the
skyline like a great concrete cathedral.
Landscaping architects were brought in
on its design, but opinions vary on
whether it blends with the scenery.
Nevertheless it fulfils an important
function in keeping the wheels of modern
industry turning. Its siting was dictated
by the vast quantities of cooling water
available from the man-made reservoir
now called Llyn Trawsfynydd. The lake
was created in 1926 to supply hydro-
electric power to the Maentwrog Power
Station, which is situated 600ft below
in the Vale of Ffestiniog. Measuring 3m
long and up to 1m wide, the lake covers
an area of 1,300 acres and has a
reputation for good fishing. The power
station can be visited by arrangement.

Trawsfynydd village is a compact little
community by-passed by the main road,
and is associated with one of the most
dramatic moments in the history of the
National Eisteddfod. At Birkenhead in
1917 – one of the rare occasions when
the National Eisteddfod was held outside
Wales – the archdruid announced the
winner of the poetry competition. This
was Hedd Wyn, a gifted shepherd boy
who had joined the war. The ritual of
sounding trumpets and asking the winner
to stand up and be escorted to the stage
followed, but no-one stirred. It was then
announced that Hedd Wyn had been
killed in action on the Somme on 31 July.
A telegram had been received that
morning. Hedd Wyn's real name was
Ellis Humphrey Evans, and he has often
been compared with the similarly
sensitive English poet Rupert Brooke,
who died in the same war. Hedd Wyn's
bronze statue, showing him shirt-sleeved
and gaitered, stands in the village main
street. The black chair of Birkenhead
stands in the farmhouse where Hedd
Wyn was born.

TREARDDUR BAY, Gwynedd *4 SH27*
This fashionable Anglesey resort has
developed tremendously during the last
few decades. Fine sandy beaches broken
up by rocky outcrops make it ideal for
bathers and sunbathers. Porthdafarch
is another sandy bay within 2m NW
of Trearddur on the road to South
Stack. On the W side of the Porthdafarch
Bay are the remains of a quay built
during the days of sail as an alternative
to Holyhead, when contrary winds
prevailed. Four Mile Bridge, an ancient
bridge between Trearddur Bay and
Valley, was the main route for coaches
before Telford firmly linked Holy
Island to Anglesey with his A5 Stanley
Embankment. Three alternative routes
across the sands once existed at low tide.

TRECASTLE, Powys *21 SN82*
This quiet village on the main Brecon to
Llandovery road takes its name from the
motte-and-bailey castle which once stood
near by. The Norman castle mound is
covered in fine beech trees and is the
tallest motte in the Brecon Beacons
national park. It forms an impressive
landmark and was founded in the early
12thc as an outpost by the Lord of
Brecon. In the main village street are two
former mail-coach inns with coachyard
entrances, and some good early 19th-c
houses. About 6m S Carmarthen Van
rises to 2,632ft, and enclosed in hollows
on its sides are the two small lakes of
Llyn-y-Fan Fach and Llyn-y-Fan Fawr.
Both are well known for their trout. Also
near by is a circle of thirteen stones. An
interesting church can be seen 1m W at
Llywel.

TREFECCA, Powys *22 SO13*
One of the fathers of Welsh Methodism,
Hywel Harris (1714–1773), founded a
communal farming centre here. Exhibits
from the community are displayed at
Trefecca Museum, which is housed in the
Chapel Block at Coleg Trefeca (Trefecca
College). Harris is buried N at nearby
Talgarth.

TREFFGARNE, Dyfed *16 SM92*
Treffgarne lies about 6m N of
Haverfordwest in the rocky gorge of
the Western Cleddau River, where a
gold mine is reputed to have once
existed. Many earthworks exist in the
area, and the massive igneous outcrop
of Great Treffgarne Mountain rises up
on the W side of the gorge. On its side, at
OS reference SM 956 250, are the remains
of bank and ditch defences which
protected Great Treffgarne Rocks Camp.
Slightly to the W of this are traces of hut
circles and early field patterns, and
Great Treffgarne Wood Camp can be
seen at OS reference SM 960 233. Owain
Glyndwr was born at Treffgarne manor
house, which was owned by his mother's
family in the 14thc. About 4m N is Wolf's
Castle, set between the Western Cleddau
and a tributary.

TREFIGNATH, Gwynedd *4 SH28*
Trefignath Farm lies a little to the SE of
Holyhead and features an elaborate
megalithic communal burial chamber
(AM). At first sight this appears to be
three separate tombs set end to end, but
on closer inspection it has been found
that it was more probably one long grave
divided into three chambers – similar to
ones found in Ulster and SW Scotland.
The farthest E chamber is the most
complete. Large angular stones near the
entrance of the latter appear to be part
of a portal and forecourt. (The full OS
reference for this is SH 259 805.)

TREFLYS, Gwynedd *9 SH53*
On a small hill behind the shore to the E of Criccieth stands the church of Treflys. A 6th-c stone inscribed with the Chi Rho monogram of Christ – one of only seven such stones in Great Britain – is preserved here. Craig Ddu, or the Black Rock, and the extensive sands of Tremadog Bay are near by.

TREFNANT, Clwyd *6 SJ07*
Of Victorian origin and situated about 2½m N of Denbigh, this small village has a 19th-c decorated-style church which was designed by Gilbert Scott. The font and columns – with capitals carved with elaborate leaf designs – are of grey Anglesey marble.

TREFRIW, Gwynedd *5 SH76*
Situated on the W bank of the Conwy, this village enjoyed a fleeting popularity as the only spa in N Wales. Trefriw's wells are rich in iron and sulphur and lie 1m N of the village, with accompanying pump rooms and baths. The spa was established in 1833, and in 1865 it was being visited by 100 people a day. Today it is the woollen mill in the centre of the village which attracts visitors. This is the largest of the N Wales mills, and visitors are able to see all the various stages from the fleece to the finished product. They are also able to see what happens to the wool of black sheep.

The Conwy is tidal almost as far as Trefriw, and during the last century steamers carried passengers and merchandise between Trefriw and Conwy town. A climb through woods out of the village leads to Llanrhychwyn Church, known locally as Prince Llywelyn's old church. Llywelyn, one of the best-known native Welsh princes, had a residence at Trefriw. Llanrhychwyn Church is double-aisled and delightfully primitive, with ancient roof timbers, slate-slabbed floors, and whitewashed walls. The font is a square tub on stone steps and must be one of the oldest survivors in Britain. Trefriw is also one of the points from which to reach Llyn Crafnant. Boating can be enjoyed and refreshments are available at a lakeside farmhouse. Llyn Geirionydd is another attractive lake in a neighbouring valley.

TREGARON, Dyfed *12 SN65*
Another of the little mid Wales towns which still wears an air of yesterday, Tregaron is full of atmosphere and derives its name from Caron – a shepherd boy who became king of Ceredigion and was buried here early in the 3rdc. Twm Shon Catti, whose real name was Thomas Jones, was born at Porth Fynnon House. He was a strange character who acquired a literary reputation, but who lived by plundering his neighbours. He amassed a fortune through marrying an heiress by means of a trick, and was later appointed High Sheriff of the county. The statue in the square at the town centre is that of Henry Richard, who lived from 1812 to 1888. This Congregational minister became secretary of the Peace Society in 1848 and MP for Merthyr from 1868 until his death. He was known as the MP for Wales. The church is dedicated to St Caron, and features an unusual wrought-iron rood screen and a modern stained-glass window depicting the Adoration of the Magi. In the mid-19thc it was used as a school during the

winter; in summer the children had to work on the farms.

TRELAWNYD, Clwyd *6 SJ07*
Situated some 3m SE of Prestatyn, for three centuries Trelawnyd was known as Newmarket. It acquired its English name when a local squire named John Wynn established several trades here, including silk weaving, tanning, tobacco manufacture, and hop cultivation. It had a town hall and a considerable market, which gave the village its name. In the late 1950's the village assumed its original Welsh name of Trelawnyd. The churchyard of St Michael and All Angels contains a tall stone cross of 13th-c workmanship. A church charity set up by Squire Wynn in 1712 left the interest of £5 for the purchase of flannel for four old men and women, the applicants to draw lots or throw dice in the church porch!

A little to the N of the village is Gop Hill, on the summit of which is a massive cairn which was constructed of white limestone pebbles and probably dates from the bronze age. Bones of prehistoric animals, notably the woolly rhinoceros and hyena which have been found in caves on the hillside probably date from 4,000 to 3,000 BC. A cave on the S facing slope of the hill has yielded a communal neolithic burial ground. The hill has also been known as Bryn-y-Saethau, a pointer to the number of flint arrowheads found on it. Views from here extend across the Dee estuary.

TRELLECK, Gwent *23 SO50*
To the W of the Wye Valley and S of Monmouth on the B4293, this village takes its name from three prehistoric stones standing near each other in a field. Locally they are known as Harold's stones. The church is of early-decorated style and displays good 16th- and 17th-c woodwork, plus a sundial dated 1689. The sundial has the stones depicted in relief at its base, with a Latin inscription said to reflect an old belief that they were a monument to a victory here by King Harold in the 11thc. For the record, they are considerably older than that. The ancient preaching cross in the churchyard may date back to the 5thc, and nearby St Anne's Well was a place of pilgrimage in the 17thc.

TRELOGAN, Clwyd *6 SJ18*
Sited between Holywell and Prestatyn, this off-the-beaten-track village has nurtured two distinguished Welsh figures of recent memory. At the village school, of which he writes nostalgically and fondly in his autobiography, actor and playwright Emlyn Williams received his early schooling. A later pupil was David Lloyd, possessor of one of the finest tenor voices Wales has ever heard, but who unfortunately died at an early age.

TREMADOG, Gwynedd *9 SH54*
A town nucleus that never really developed, Tremadog was conceived by William Alexander Madocks – MP for Boston, local landowner, and an energetic innovator. He intended Tremadog as the last staging post on the mail-packet route for Ireland. He was proposing Porth Dinllaen on the N coast of the Lleyn Peninsula as a rival port to Holyhead, but when the two routes were put forward the government chose Holyhead. Tremadog remained a village – but one with a town hall. Madocks built the model town on reclaimed land

and boasted that he had founded a town 9ft under high-water mark. It consisted of the town hall, an inn, market hall, church, chapel, and 68 houses. Most of the houses are nicely grouped around the square. The town hall is now a craft centre, and the five-storey woollen mill which Madocks built on the N outskirts of the village is now part of a laundry.

The gothic-spired church of 1806 stands on a hill to the S of the town, and Peniel Chapel of 1811 is a pastel-coloured and porticoed structure which stands somewhat aloof from the town on the Porthmadog road. Two streets – Dublin Street and London Street – are reminders of an ambitious scheme that did not come off. Madocks lived at Tan yr Allt, a mansion on a wooded hillside which provides a pleasant backcloth to the village. The house was rented to the poet Shelly and his wife from 1812 to 1813, and it was here that Shelley wrote part of *Queen Mab*. He was an active supporter of Madock's schemes, but left suddenly after an unidentified man broke into Tan yr Allt and fired shots. Shelley is supposed to have incurred the wrath of local people by his habit of despatching sick sheep without first finding out if they could be cured.

Peacock and other biographers dismissed the episode as a figment of Shelley's imagination but a new book called *Shelley – The Pursuit*, written by Richard Holmes, claims that the attack was real enough. Holmes says that it arose through the poet's support of agitation for workers on the Porthmadog embankment scheme, for which he had originally been an active fund-raiser. Another famous figure associated with Tremadog was Lawrence of Arabia, who was born in 1888 at the Woodlands on the Porthmadog road – now a mountaineering centre. A plaque on the wall commemorates this fact. Coed Tremadog is a national nature reserve embracing the nearby wooded cliffs.

*TREORCHY, Mid Glamorgan *25 SS99*
Treorchy is a Rhondda Fawr Valley mining town from which several of the S Wales inter-valley mountain roads radiate, giving wide views from heights between 1,500ft and 2,000ft in places. The Chapel of Capel Noddfa is a well-proportioned stone building preserving an interesting plant-stencil decoration.

TRE'R CEIRI, Gwynedd *8 SH34*
The best preserved iron-age hillfort in N Wales, Tre'r Ceiri stands at 1,591ft on the E peak of Yr Eifl. Within its walls are numerous circular and rectangular dwellings, some very small, others up to 16ft in diameter. In all it covers some 5 acres, an area originally enclosed by three walls. Parts of these still stand 15ft tall. The main entrance was on the NW side and penetrated a rampart of loosely piled stones some 200ft from the main wall, guarded by a parapet with a small postern gate. On the SW side, beside a walled roadway which extends from the SW entrance, are enclosures with dry stone walls – probably for cattle – and more circular huts. The fort was later occupied by the Romans, who probably abandoned it *c*400AD.

TRE'R DDOL, Dyfed *12 SN69*
This village came into the news a few years ago when the late Elma Williams established her Valley of Animals home and sanctuary up in the hills near by. Since her death there has been difficulty

over maintaining it as she desired, and it has now closed. A Wesleyan chapel of 1845, where the Rev Humphrey R Jones started a religious revival in 1859, has become a local history museum. As well as exhibits of general local interest, the museum has a collection of books and documents relating to Methodism. Tre'r Ddol stands on the Aberystwyth to Machynlleth road, almost exactly half way between the two towns, at the junction of the B4353 road to Ynys-las and Borth.

TRETOWER, Powys   22 SO12
Lying beside the Rhiangoll stream about 2½m NW of Crickhowell are the remains of a 13th-c Norman castle (AM) and a fortified mansion (AM) of the 14th and 15thc. The land was granted to the Norman knight Picard by the Lord of Brecon, and he constructed a motte surrounded by a polygonal stone wall. After the Welsh had managed to capture it for a short while in 1233, the English strengthened it by building a tall circular keep inside the wall. To this they added three round towers, and the castle was defended against Owain Glyndwr in 1404. Although it suffered great damage at Glyndwr's hands he was unable to take it. Before this attack the owners had built the 14th-c manor house of Tretower Court near by. This later passed into the hands of the Vaughan family, who rebuilt much of it and turned it into one of the finest early fortified mansions in Wales. It is built round a courtyard and has an impressive gateway which still looks as if it could withstand an attack. The main room is a large 15th-c banqueting hall, and overlooking the courtyard is a gallery dating from the 14thc. The mystic poet Henry Vaughan lived here during the 17thc, and sixteen generations of the family inhabited the court until the late 18thc.

TREVINE, Dyfed   16 SM83
Set between the headlands of Ynys Daulyn and Pen Clegyr about 7m NE of St David's, this pretty village lies a little N of rocky cove with a shingle beach crossed by a small stream. Here on the shore are the remains of an old mill, complete with a pair of millstones. Bishop Martin of St David's built a palace at Trevine, but no trace of this remains today. The farm of Ty Hir – or Long House – lies a little to the NE and includes a magnificent megalithic dolmen measuring some 15ft by 9ft (full OS reference SM 847 335).

TUDWEILIOG, Gwynedd   8 SH23
Tudweiliog is situated on a hill about 1m inland from the NW coast of the Lleyn Peninsula. To the S lies Cefnamwlch, a former home of the Griffith family which retains its fine gateway of 1629 and is surrounded by trees. At Llandudwen to the E lies a tiny medieval church containing an octagonal font which may date from the 10thc. Carn Fadryn lies to the S of this and rises to 1,217ft. The nearby coast is indented by many small sandy coves, backed by formidable cliffs pocked with caves.

TY ILLTYD, Powys   21 SO02
This well-preserved megalithic long barrow is situated on Manest Farm in the Usk Valley about 4m E of Brecon. The upright stones support a chambered capstone and have been inscribed with crosses at some later date. A slab-lined forecourt is a traceable (full OS reference SO 098 263).

TY ISAF, Powys   22 SO12
Situated just off the A479 between Crickhowell and Talgarth, Ty Isaf is a megalithic long barrow with a blind entrance at its N end and various side chambers (OS reference SO 182 290).

TY MAWR, Gwynedd   4 SH28
Near Ty Mawr is a hut group (AM) – or Cytiau'r Gwyddelod – sited on the SW facing slopes of Holyhead Mountain. Of the 20 surviving huts most are circular in plan, but some are oval or rectangular. Overgrown walls stand 2ft in some places. Excavation has revealed grinding stones and mortars, and fireplaces can still be seen in some of the huts. Traces of an enclosure wall and cultivation terraces are also visible (full OS reference SH 212 820).

TY MAWR, Gwynedd   5 SH75
Bishop William Morgan (1541–1604), the first translator of the Bible into Welsh, was born at Ty Mawr. The village lies 2m E of Dolwyddelan.

TY NEWYDD, Gwynedd   4 SH37
Ty Newydd, a neolithic burial chamber (AM) near Llanfaelog in Anglesey, is a passage grave comprising a large capstone on three supports. Fragments of white quartz and a tanged flint arrowhead were found here during excavation (full OS reference SH 344 738).

TYWYN, Gwynedd   9 SH50
A recent name change for this mid Wales coastal resort has ended the confusion with Towyn on the N Wales coast. Tywyn stands in the plain of the lower reaches of the Dysynni River, surrounded by foothills of the Cader Idris range. The older part of the town lies about 1m inland, but it has developed towards the sea. Safe bathing is available from the sandy beach. The esplanade was the work of John Corbett, a salt magnate who bought the Ynysmaengwyn Estate in 1884. Walks along the sand may be taken to Aberdyfi, but it is not just sand and sea which attract people to Tywyn – the Talyllyn narrow-gauge railway has its terminus here (see page 62).

Tywyn's foundations lie in the 6thc, when St Cadfan of Brittany established a church here on his way to Bardsey Island. The present Church of St Cadfan is of 12th-c foundation and still retains the Norman nave, aisles, clerestory, and north transept. The latter displays roughly-plastered and uncapitalled pillars. During the 1880's the building was extensively restored, but although the central tower was rebuilt it retains its original character. Inside are two 14th-c effigies, one of a priest with his amice or hood covering his head, and the other of Grufydd ap Adda – a knight of Dolgoch and Ynysmaengwyn. An old bass viol from the pre-organ days and a finely-carved organ case are remnants from the Victorian era. The town's Market Hall is of interest.

St Cadfan's stone is a 7ft relic of the 7thc. Preserved at the church it bears the earliest Welsh inscription extant and two incised crosses. The inscription was originally translated as: 'The body of Cyngen is on the side between where the marks will be. In the retreat beneath the mound is extended Cadfan, sad that it should enclose the praise of the earth. May he rest without blemish'. Other translations put forward replace the name Cadfan, and it does seem unlikely that he was actually buried here. The

Dolgoch hills, Talyllyn, and Cader Idris can all be visited from Tywyn. Castell-y-Bere stands some 7½m away, and the notable viewpoint of Escuan Hill rises to the S.

UPTON, Dyfed   18 SN00
Remains of a 13th-c castle, now incorporated in a private house, are situated 2m NW of Upton. Only the gatehouse and three towers are original.

USK, Gwent   22 SO30
Particularly noted as an angling centre, this old market town is situated on the river of the same name. Beneath the town are the remains of an old Roman settlement called *Burrium*. Overlooking Usk are the ruins of a castle which was founded by the de Clare family as a Marcher lord's stronghold in the 12thc. The de Clares built a small square keep with earthworks, then in the 13thc the outer bailey and gatehouse were added, and later that century the large round tower was constructed. During the 15thc other buildings were added to the outer ward. The castle supported the royalists in the civil war and was subsequently dismantled.

The Church of St Mary's was once attached to a Benedictine priory of nuns and dates back to the 13thc. Inside is a notable Tudor screen, which was restored in 1899, and a 17th-c pulpit. The nave is of decorated style, and the porches perpendicular. A 13th-c gabled priory gateway stands near the churchyard. Cefntilla Court, built in 1616 and restored in 1856, lies 2½m NE of Usk and contains fine pictures and pieces of porcelain. Relics from the Crimea and the Peninsular Campaign are also preserved here. The Roman remains of Caerleon lie 8m S. The town is a good touring centre; Brecon Beacons national park lies NW, and to the E above Chepstow is the Wye Valley. Raglan Castle lies 5m NE.

USK RESERVOIR, Dyfed   21 SN82
About 6m SE of Llandovery beneath the gentle SW facing slope of 1,443ft Mynydd Myddfai, this reservoir is surrounded by woods planted by the Forestry Commission. The Usk flows into it from the S and runs E from the dam. The lake was formed to serve Swansea, and is the most recent of the six reservoirs in the Brecon Beacons national park. Part of the reservoir is in Dyfed and part in Powys.

VALLE CRUCIS ABBEY, Clwyd   11 SJ24
Founded c1200 by Madog ap Gruffydd Maelor the Prince of Powys, this Cistercian abbey (AM) is situated about 2m NW of Llangollen. Much of its church still survives, including a fine western front which was restored by Sir Gilbert Scott, and an elaborately-carved doorway. Above are three early-English windows and a rose window. The nave aisles, its two transepts, and the choir end containing five lancet windows, also remain. Attached to the south transept is the eastern range of the cloister. To the S of the church lie the remains of monastic buildings which were at one time used as a farmhouse. These include a Chapter House with fine vaulting.

The abbey takes its name – meaning Vale of the Cross – from Eliseg's Pillar

(AM), which stands to the N. This was set up by Concenn to commemorate a battle fought in AD603 by his great grandfather Eliseg against the Saxons. An inscription on the pillar shows the line of descent from Eliseg to Concenn. Originally it stood 12ft high, but was knocked down and broken during the civil war, and is now only just above 7ft tall. Before the monument was replaced in 1779, the tumulus on which it stands was excavated and revealed a grave and skeleton – possibly of Eliseg himself. Overlooking the abbey is the famous 3,000ft Horseshoe Pass.

VALLEY, Gwynedd 4 SH27
Valley is best-known for the airfield which the RAF uses for pilot training. Plane spotters will be able to identify Gnats, Hunters, Phantoms, Lightnings, and Chipmunks practising low level and formation flying. Occasionally they will be able to see yellow Whirlwind helicopters taking off on search and rescue missions. RAF Mona lies alongside the A5 as a satellite airfield of Valley. It was the construction of Valley airfield in 1943 which uncovered an exciting collection of iron-age treasures scooped up by a mechanical digger at Llyn Cerrig Bach – 'Lake of the Little Stone'. These shed considerable light on the Celtic period. Dating from the 2ndcBC to the 1stcAD, they included swords, spears, chariot fittings, horse harness, a battle trumpet – and more grisly, a chain of neck irons, presumably for a slave-gang or prisoners of war. All were exceptionally preserved and showed intricate workmanship. One chain recovered was actually used for towing a stranded vehicle out of the mud. The objects are now displayed at the National Museum of Wales in Cardiff. The village of Valley is situated on the A5 some distance from the airfield.

VELINDRE FARCHOG, Dyfed 17 SN13
Until recently the mill after which this pretty little village was named still stood. The name means 'Knights Milton'. A small house bearing the date 1559–1620 is known as The College, and was built as a school by George Owen, Lord of Cemais.

WALTON, Powys 14 SO25
Walton is a small village beside Hindwell Brook, 3m E of New Radnor and close to the English border. Walton Court is an old timber-framed house which stands by Hindwell Pool, and Womaston is another interesting old country house in the area. The neolithic Four Stones can be seen near by.

*WELSHPOOL, Powys 11 SJ20
Plan overleaf
The Welsh name of this town is *Y Trallwng*. Translated literally this means 'the very marshy or sinking land'. From marsh to a waterlogged countryside is an easy transition, and this in turn is readily referred to as a land of pools – or one vast Welsh pool. So the town that grew up here on this low-lying Severnside land became known as Pool and ultimately as Welsh Pool to distinguish it from Poole in Dorset. The older form survives in Pool Quay, the next village on the road to Oswestry, and in Newtown's Pool Road, which is the main highway to Welshpool. This cramped, tightly-packed little town can only expand in one direction – upward along the steep hillsides of its NW edge. It is squeezed in between Powis Castle Park and the triple barrier of canal, railway line, and river. It has, however, developed an industrial estate segregated from the residential districts and town centre.

Welshpool is of a cruciform pattern, and the cross is the centre of everything. The bulk of NS and EW traffic passes over it, and it is impossible to walk between the E and W sectors without traversing it. This is because there are so few side roads, though until recently the entire heart of the town was a warren of narrow streets, a few of which still survive despite extensive demolitions. One at the lower end of Broad Street works round to Church Street, passing on its way a piece of now derelict land on which an ancient maypole is still standing. The estate agent's offices on the Cross were once the residence of Gilbert and Ann Jones who, as the wall plaque explains, claimed to be descendants of the 'original Jones' and later of Robert Owen's grandfather and father. At the

other end of Church Street is the parish church, which has the unusual dedication of St Mary of the Salutation. It stands high on a bank and has been several times rebuilt and restored since its foundation in the 13thc. Inside it is seen to be lopsided, the central aisle between the west end and the high altar having two shifts of direction. Its greatest treasure is a gold chalice of 1662, which was used until comparatively recently on great festivals. It is now kept in the bank vaults. A boulder in the churchyard was once regarded as a Wishing Stone.

The pretty black-and-white cottage next to the church is known as Grace Evans' Cottage. It was given to her by Lady Nithsdale for the part she played in getting the Earl of Nithsdale out of the Tower of London, disguised as a woman, while he was awaiting execution for his part in the 1715 Jacobite rising. Behind the National Westminster Bank is an ancient cockpit house where cock fights used to take place. It stands on land once known as the Field of Blood, thus named as a result of a fight contestant murdering one of Lord Herbert's servants for his refusal to substitute the peer's best bird for his own. Once the narrow-gauge Welshpool and Llanfair Railway ran through the streets of the town and a new terminus will be set up at Raven Square when the final section of the line is re-opened (see page 62).

By the garage next to the old Seven Stars Station is a plaque which records that the bridge over the Sylfaen Brook, which was built in 1817, was a memorial to the marriage of two of the most important local families. This was when the third Sir Watkin Williams Wynne married Lady Henrietta Antonia Clive. On the slope leading up to the church a few steps farther along St Mary's Street there is some interesting cobblestone work, with the initials 'EM' and the date 1846 worked into it. Another relic of the past exists in the handles of the lock gates of the canal off Severn Street, which were made from the barrels of guns captured at Sebastopol in the Crimean War. Welshpool has always been an important agricultural centre. It has held a weekly market on Mondays ever since 1406, and is only suspended when Christmas Day falls on a Monday. The town is now one of the most important market centres in Wales.

At the bottom of Severn Road is the railway station, a very fine structure with many gables, end towers, and complicated wrought-iron arcading to the platform canopy on the main platform. It was built in the expectation of its becoming the headquarters of the Cambrian Railways, but in the end Oswestry had the honour. It is still in use. Just past the railway sidings and opposite the Smithfield is a large mound. It was near here that the first settlement sprang up from a Celtic monastery, and the mound was designed as a strong point from which to guard a ford which had made the site desirable for occupation. The present Welshpool received its first charter in 1263 from Gruffydd ap Wenwynwyn, but it was

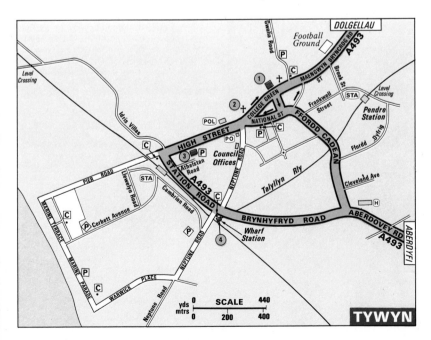

1 Market Hall
2 St Cadfan's Church
3 Swimming Pool
4 Talyllyn Railway, Tywyn Wharf Station, & Narrow-gauge Railway Museum

TYWYN

SCALE yds 0 200 440 mtrs 0 200 400

always a highly-anglicized town on account of its proximity to the border. When Owain Glyndwr sought the support of its people for his wars against the English they rejected him. For this fidelity to the English king they were given additional lands and a new charter. Finally James I gave the town yet another charter, and this lasted until 1835 when a new corporation was established. This was when Pool became Welsh Pool. In 1843 the Smithfield was first established; in 1848 a cholera outbreak obliged the authorities to adopt the Public Health Act, giving them power to lay down sewers and provide a pure water supply; in 1874 Morris Jones of Gungrog, who had founded the Powysland Club, the oldest archaeological society in Wales, started the Powysland Museum; also in 1874, the Town Hall was built. Among the modern features of interest in Welshpool are a charming little war memorial garden down by the swimming pool at the bottom of Severn Road; a delightful row of modern almshouses opposite the railway station; the new RC church on the site of the Packhorse Inn at the top of Mount Street; the trees alongside the canal where it accompanies the Newtown road. Powis Castle lies to the SW of the town.

WEOBLEY, West Glamorgan 24 SS49

Weobley Castle (AM OACT) is set on a 150ft grassy hill about 1¼m W of Llanrhidian, overlooking Llanrhidian Marsh and the Loughor estuary. Most of its construction dates from the late 13thc when the hall and kitchen wing were built. The west tower and adjoining wall and gatehouse were constructed during the early 14thc. The tower was never completed, and other buildings that had been planned were never built – probably due to a lack of financial resources. The buildings enclose a courtyard, giving the appearance of a fortified mansion rather than a castle, and provide an insight into life of the Middle Ages.

Probably built by Henry Beaufort, the Earl of Warwick, the castle led a comparatively quiet life apart from some damage during the Glyndwr revolt. In Henry VII's reign it fell into the hands of

Sir Rhys ap Thomas, but reverted to the crown under Henry VIII when Sir Rhys's grandson was executed for treason. Later owners rented it out, and the porch rooms added in the 15thc were converted into a farmhouse by a tenant in the 16thc.

WHITCHURCH, Clwyd 6 SJ06

Situated here about 1m E of Denbigh is St Marcella's, the mother church of Denbigh. Perpendicular in style and largely of the 15thc, this church carries a plain 13th-c tower and preserves a hammer-beam roof plus some 14th-c glass. Several notable monuments also exist, including a rare brass which depicts Richard Myddleton and his wife kneeling before an altar with their sixteen children behind them. These were the parents of Sir Hugh Myddleton, who gave London its water supply. The tomb of Sir John Salisbury and his wife bears recumbent effigies carved in alabaster. Humphrey Llwyd the 16th-c historian, and Thomas Edwards (Twm O'r Nant) – a local 18th- and 19th-c writer of witty interludes or morality plays – are also buried here.

WHITE CASTLE, Gwent 22 SO31

This well-preserved example of a ring castle (AM) is considered the finest of a group of three comprising Grosmont, Skenfrith, and White Castle itself. It lies about 6m SW of Skenfrith, just off the Abergavenny road. Around the middle of the 12thc a small rectangular keep was constructed in a low, oval-shaped inner ward surrounded by a substantial moat and with a small crescent-shaped bailey at its S end. At this time the structure was known as Llantilio Castle. During the 13thc the keep was demolished, and a gatehouse with two flanking towers was built at the N end. Four round towers were added to the wall of the inner ward, and the old gateway at the S end was replaced by a simple arched opening. A larger and irregularly shaped bailey with four flanking towers was also added at the N end for use as an encampment. The light-coloured plaster covering from which it derives its present name was probably added at this stage.

In its early days it was held by Hubert de Burgh, William de Braose, and Peter

Rivaux, but each lost it as he fell from favour with the king. Waleran, a German, held it from 1234 and it was probably under his direction that the structural changes were made. In 1254 it was granted to Henry III's eldest son Lord Edward, and in 1267 he transferred it to his younger brother Edmund Crouchback, Earl of Lancaster. During the uprising of Llywelyn ap Gruffydd it held a strategic position, for if Abergavenny Castle had fallen it would have been in the front line of the English defence. After the Edwardian conquest of Wales it lost its strategic importance, but remained for a time an important administrative and financial centre. By the 16thc it was in ruin, and in 1922 it passed into the care of the government.

WHITEFORD BURROWS, West Glamorgan 24 SS49

Whiteford Burrows is a narrow spit of land bought by the NT in 1965, which now forms a national nature reserve covering some 1,933 acres. It comprises shore, dunes, salt marsh, and some woodland, and extends to the extreme N point of the Gower at Whiteford Point, where there is a mechanized lighthouse. The shore has pleasant sands and rock pools at low tide, but local waters are unsafe for bathing because of strong currents. The plant and birdlife of the reserve is of great interest. Permits are required away from the shore.

WHITFORD, Clwyd 6 SJ17

Celebrated birthplace of Thomas Pennant the writer, antiquary, and naturalist, Whitford is an attractive hilltop hamlet 2m inland from the Dee estuary. Pennant (1726–1798) – with his well-informed *Tours of Wales* – was the first of a new genre of traveller-writers. Instead of regarding the Welsh mountains with horror and foreboding, he recognized them as the majestic creations of nature that they are. Pennant was a naturalist of European repute, and his interests took him away from the well-trodden routes of travellers before him. He was always accompanied by Moses Griffiths, an untrained but naturally-gifted artist who provided the illustrations for Pennant's volumes.

Downing Hall, a 16th-c house where Pennant was born, lived, and died, was unfortunately damaged beyond repair by fire in the 1920's. Pennant is buried at the parish church, and there is a memorial to him by Flaxman inside the building. A 14th-c sarcophagus, 17th-c font, and dug-out chest are also to be found in the church. W of Whitford is Garreg Hill, on the summit of which is Garreg Tower – almost lost in woodland. Historians have argued endlessly about its origin. Some, including Pennant, believed it to be a Roman pharos; others dismissed it as a 16th-c construction. It was restored in 1897 to commemorate the 60th jubilee of Queen Victoria. Another notable antiquity in the Whitford vicinity is Maen Achwyfan, at 11ft the tallest surviving Celtic cross in Wales or England. It stands 1½m W near the turning to Trelogan, and is inscribed on

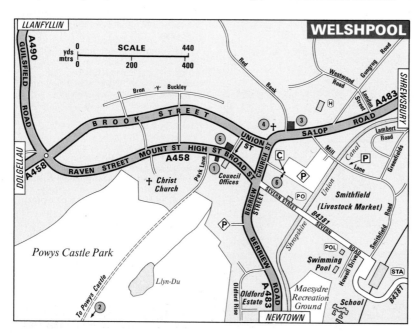

1	Anderson's Antique Shop
2	Powis Castle
3	Powysland Museum
4	St Mary's Parish Church
5	Town Hall
6	WTB Information Centre

all sides with elaborately carved Celtic patterns. It is probably an early-Christian monument of the 10thc.

WHITLAND, Dyfed *19 SN11*
A small market town on the Taf River, Whitland takes its name from the ruined abbey which lies about 1m to the NE. Founded in 1143, this was the first abbey of the Cistercian order in Wales and therefore was also the mother house of both Strata Florida and Strata Marcella. A few overgrown fragments remain today in a picturesque rural setting. It was probably founded on the site of a 5th-c abbey known as 'Ty Gwyn ar Daf' or 'The White House on the River Taf', where the 10th-c Prince of Wales Hywel Dda (Howell the Good) established a united system of laws for the whole of Wales. This system lasted until the time of Edward I.

WISTON, Dyfed *18 SN01*
Overgrown ruins of a 12th-c round keep lie in a field opposite the church of this tiny hamlet. The structure was probably founded by Wizo the Fleming *c*1130, and comprised a thick-walled keep on a low motte with an unwalled bailey and earthworks. The doorway of the keep still shows a socket for the drawbar. It was captured by the Welsh in 1147 and 1193, and finally destroyed by Llywelyn ap Iorwerth in 1220 during his campaign to free Dyfed from Norman rule. Plans to rebuild it were never executed. In its time it had been the home of the Wogan family and a centre of the barony of Daugleddau. Royalists were defeated at nearby Colby Moor in a battle which took place in August of 1645.

WONASTOW, Gwent *23 SO41*
The Court here is a modernized 16th-c house with civil war associations. About 1m W is Tre Owen, a partly 16th-c building which is now a farmhouse.

WORTHENBURY, Clwyd *11 SJ44*
Situated in the English Maelor on the Afon Dyfrdwy (River Dee) as it meanders towards Chester, Worthenbury's notable church retains box pews which include one for the Puleston family who came from the nearby hall of Emral. The hall was demolished in the inter-war years, but a celebrated ceiling depicting the Labours of Hercules was rescued by Clough Williams Ellis and is now the *pièce de resistance* of his town hall at the model village of Portmeirion.

WREXHAM, Clwyd *7 SJ35*
Largest town in N or mid Wales, Wrexham has changed in character over the years from a border market town to the administrative, commercial, and shopping centre for a concentrated industrial area. Wrexham's population is approximately 38,000, and the immediate rural area has a population of 60,000 with several large industrial villages on the W side. It is also one of the fastest growing towns in N Wales, and town-centre developments within the next decade threaten to change the town beyond all recognition. One feature which remains inviolate amidst all this change, however, is the parish Church of St Giles, which was built in 1472 on the site of an earlier church.

Towering 136ft high and making the surrounding buildings look rather squat, Wrexham's church qualifies for inclusion among any list of notable churches of England and Wales. The tower figures in the Seven Wonders of Wales as a steeple – poetic licence – and is said to have inspired the designer of the Houses of Parliament in his conception of the Victoria Tower. A full scale copy of the tower is to be seen among the university buildings of Yale at Newhaven, Connecticut, USA. Wrexham's link with Yale University arises from a generous benefaction to the founders by Elihu Yale, a Massachusets-born, East India merchant and Governor of Madras, who chose to retire to Wrexham near his family's ancestral home. A timely consignment of silks, books, and furniture in the early 18thc enabled the building of the university to go ahead, and the grateful foundation adopted the name of Yale. His tomb, near the W door of the church, is a constant place of pilgrimage for American visitors.

The church tower is ornamented by 29 sculptured figures, the most prominent of them being St Giles, to whom the church is dedicated. Inside is a fine Roubillac sculpture to the memory of Margaret Myddelton, and the soldiers' chapel commemorates the town's long association with the Royal Welch Fusiliers, who had their depot at Wrexham. One of the stained-glass windows commemorates Bishop Heber, who wrote the missionary hymn *From Greenland's Icy Mountains* while staying at the vicarage in 1819. This was first sung at Wrexham parish church. The fine wrought-iron gates are by Robert Davies of nearby Croes Foel. Yale retired to live in Wrexham at Plas Gronow, a romantic farmhouse which is now demolished but used to stand on the outskirts of the town. It was

1 Acton Park
2 Guildhall

3 Market Hall
4 St Giles' Church

5 Wrexham Crest Hotel (18th-c frontage)

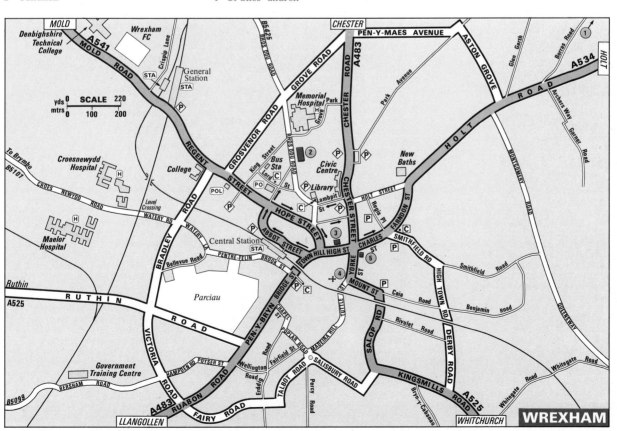

287

subsequently the home of C J Apperley, better known by his pen name of Nimrod. His articles and books give an interesting insight into the social and sporting life of 19th-c gentry. An infamous resident of Wrexham was Judge Jeffreys, whose notorious conduct of trials after the Monmouth Rebellion resulted in the sending of hundreds to the gallows or at best to slavery in the colonies. This earned him the name of Bloody Judge Jeffreys. He died unlamented in the Tower of London, and no trace of his home at Acton remains.

Wrexham's three covered markets are a reminder of the town's former importance as a market town, and today it is the shopping centre for a wide area. Being only 6m from the Cheshire border the town is more English than Welsh in character. Coalmining, brewing, steelmaking, and leather tanning were once basic industries, but with the post-war development of an ordnance factory site into an industrial estate, a diversity of industries now produces tyres, toys, plastics, man-made fibres, cables, cereals, and clothing. Two breweries in the town maintain Wrexham's tradition as a brewing centre, and one of them still produces a lager which was first brewed in Britain at Wrexham. This was introduced by a naturalized German family in the 1880's. Apart from its splendid parish church, Wrexham also has a cathedral – Regent Street's RC Cathedral of St Mary. In the town's High Street is the Wrexham Crest Hotel, a notable exercise in town conservation. After a public outcry plans for a completely new building on the site were changed in favour of a hotel which preserved the Georgian façade of the Wynnstay Arms, the town's main hotel. Behind the front wall the hotel is new. The Guildhall stands in Rhos Ddu Street.

Another building of architectural interest is the town's new swimming baths, which features a hyperbolic paraboloid roof, one of the few such roofs in Europe. Erddig Hall, a venerable Jacobean mansion set in beautiful parkland on the S outskirts of Wrexham, was recently acquired by the NT from the Yorke family, who have occupied it for centuries. It is being restored after considerable damage through mining subsidence. When open the house, with its exquisite treasures accumulated over centuries, should prove a major tourist attraction in this part of N Wales.

Y GAER, Powys 21 SO02
Once occupied by the Roman fort of *Cicutio*, this site (AM OACT) is on a slight hill overlooking the point where the Afon Yscir joins the River Usk just 3m W of Brecon. It was one of the largest auxiliary forts in Wales, and enclosed an area of some 5 acres. The strategic position which it held allowed it to guard several Roman roads which passed near by. The original earthworks were constructed to a rectangular plan, and in the 2ndcAD most of the buildings – including the gates and commandant's quarters – were rebuilt in stone. A stone wall was placed in front of the earth bank at the same time. Some 500 Spanish Cavalrymen of the *Vetonian* Regiment were housed in the fort, as indicated by a gravestone found here. Its number of occupants was later reduced, and the fort was finally abandoned cAD200. Extensive excavations between 1924

and 1925 exposed the foundations of the W, E, and S gates, plus parts of the walls and ramparts on the NE side. Access is restricted when the hay crop is standing – around May, June, and July.

Y PIGWN, Powys 21 SN83
Situated on the summit of Trecastle Mountain at OS reference SN 823 312, this temporary Roman camp overlooked a Roman road and the River Usk. Low grassy embankments indicate a line of defences which once protected about 10,000 troops. The camp was probably erected towards the end of 1stcAD, during the Roman invasion of Wales. Two stone circles near by on the SE slopes at OS reference SN 382 291 belong to a group of seven situated around the Upper Usk and Tawe.

YSBYTY CYNFYN, Dyfed 13 SN77
This hamlet lies exactly halfway between Devil's Bridge and Pont Erwyd, and has a church which stands in a stone circle from which most of the stones have been removed to new positions. This may well be an example of how the church, in its early days, would take over and Christianize pagan temples and festivals. Up until the middle of last century it was customary to read out from one of these pillars a list of missing sheep on Sunday. Gravestones in the churchyard bear many names which are not Welsh. Several are Cornish, originating from the days when Cornish miners came to Wales in search of better opportunities. Inside the church is an unusual wooden font in the form of an octagonal bowl held up by eight figures. Beside the church is a path leading to a wooded gorge with a waterfall and the Parson's Bridge, so named because the parson from Llanbadarn Fawr who came to take the services needed a bridge to cross the river.

YSBYTY-IFAN, Clwyd 10 SH84
Some 2m S of Pentrefoelas, this remote village has a chequered history. Its name means Hospice of St John and derives from the days when it was a refuge and sanctuary for travellers, under the care of the Knights Hospitallers of St John. It later became a centre for thieves and murderers, who pillaged the surrounding countryside until they were finally ejected during the reign of Henry VII. One of the area's more notable inhabitants was Elis Prys of Plas Iolyn. Called the Red Doctor because he habitually wore the red gown of a Doctor of Law, he was given the job of dissolving the Welsh monasteries by Cromwell. He became both rich and powerful in the process. In 1561 he was made chancellor of Bangor, and there was an attempt to make him bishop, until archbishop Parker opposed it on the grounds that Elis Prys was not in holy orders – nor was he fit to be.

A poor judge and an oppressive landlord, he was nevertheless well thought of as a patron of Welsh poets and literature. When Queen Elizabeth granted a commission to hold an eisteddfod at Caerwys to sort out the genuine poets from the charlatans in 1568, Elis Prys was one of the leading figures to attend. The Red Doctor died in 1595. A more attractive person was his son, Tomos Prys, who successfully combined poetry and piracy. He was a privateer – *ie* a pirate officially recognized by the

government – and it was his piracy that led to a dubious claim to fame. He and a friend were the first to smoke in the streets of London; they had just captured a ship full of tobacco.

YSBYTY YSTWYTH, Dyfed 12 SN77
The word *Ysbyty* signifies a hospice, and at one time there was a house of the Knights Hospitallers here. Despite the second part of the name the village is a little way from the Ystwyth River; it is Pontrhydygroes, 1m farther N, which is actually upon its banks. An ancient benefaction provided free education for poor children of the parish at the Ystrad Meurig Free Grammar School, 2½m SW of the village.

YSTALYFERA, West Glamorgan 21 SN70
An industrial town in the Tawe Valley, Ystalyfera dates back only as far as the coalmining era. Dr Vaughan Thomas the Welsh musician was born here.

YSTRADFELLTE, Powys 21 SN91
Wooded slopes of the Fforest Fawr provide the site of this Mellte Valley hamlet, and the river flows through a rocky gorge. A 16th-c church here was restored in the late 19thc and stands amidst ancient yews claimed to be 800-years old. About ¾m downstream the river disappears beneath a wide arch known as Porth-yr-Ogof, and then flows through underground caverns for about ⅛m. It emerges from a small hole to the S. These limestone caverns can be explored by artificial light for almost half of their extent. Farther downstream, and also on a tributary called Afon Hepste are many picturesque waterfalls. It is possible to walk behind the fall of Sgwd yr Eira on the Hepste by means of a rocky ledge. The Roman road Sarn Helen passes to the W of Ystradfellte, and along its course are the standing stones of Maen Madoc at OS reference SN 918 158. These are inscribed with Latin, and 8ft-high Maen Llia is a similar monument situated at OS reference SN 924 192.

YSTRADFELLTE RESERVOIR, Powys 21 SN91
One of several reservoirs in the Brecon Beacons national park, this lies in the steep-sided valley of the Afon Dringarth between 2,409ft Fan Fawr to the E and 2,071ft Fan Llia in the W. It is well-stocked with trout. Farther downstream the Afon Dringarth joins the Afon Llia to form the Mellte River; the ruin of Castell Coch stands at the confluence.

YSTRADGYNLAIS, Powys 21 SN71
Ystradgynlais is a Tawe Valley town lying on the border of the Brecon Beacons to the N and the industrial towns to the S. A little to the SW is the well-preserved mansion of Ynyscedwyn, which has been converted into a watch factory. St Mary's Church dates from 1648. Farther up the valley are fine examples of limestone scenery, and the upper reaches of the Afon Giedd are swallowed up at Sinc-y-Giedd to emerge 2½-m SW at Dan-yr-Ogof cave. Here the caverns are partially open to the public and reveal fine stalactites, stalagmites, chambers, and underground lakes. On the other side of the valley the Ffynon Ddu (Black Spring) issues forth from a gloomy cavern, carrying water that has sunk in the pot hole of Pwll Byfre to the NE.

Wales at Leisure

The vast open spaces of Wales act as a magnet to people who are tired of the crowds and hustle of everyday life. Wild moors break around the bases of ancient mountains like frozen purple seas, offering acre upon acre of undulating wilderness to the seeker after solitude who does not mind leaving his car and walking. Dramatic ridges edged with tumbled scree form spectacular if precarious paths for the intrepid hill walker, primeval peaks challenge the mountaineer, and lush green valleys musical with the sound of falling water beckon the pony trekker. Three enormous national parks provide habitats for some of the rarest wildlife in Great Britain, while two long-distance footpaths lead the walker through amazing scenic contrasts and past remnants of ancient history. And the water-sports enthusiast need not look far for diversion. Drowned valleys which provide water for teeming English cities offer excellent sailing, boating, and water ski-ing; reservoirs and

rivers alike are thick with fish of all types; the Welsh coast is ragged with sweeping bays and tiny coves, golden with fine sands, and loud with the pounding of rollers large enough to gladden the heart of any surfer.

The following gazetteer of towns able to offer comprehensive leisure facilities is not exhaustive, but should be used to select bases from which to tour areas offering particular activities. All places listed here are described in the main gazetteer and appear on the touring atlas in red type. Each is also referenced to the five special location maps at the end of this article. Keys to symbols used in the text appear on the relevant maps.

Visitors to Wales should remember that most land and water belongs to somebody and should not be used without prior permission. Anglers should take particular

care to ensure that they have all the requisite permits and licences, as well as information concerning restrictions over the weight and number of fish that may be taken. These details are usually available from tourist information centres or local post offices. The walker and hill climber should determine restricted areas during the shooting season, and should always communicate plans to somebody before setting out on an expedition. The Welsh mountains can be killers, and warm, waterproof clothing is essential. Sea anglers should seek local information regarding boat hire, beach-fishing restrictions, pier tariffs, etc.

Nature reserves, walks, trails, and national parks are set aside and preserved to protect wildlife, so visitors should stay on the paths unless they hold permits to do otherwise. In many cases it may be against local by-laws to pick or uproot plants and flowers, and dogs and children must be kept under control. Observe the country code and help to preserve a valuable legacy for future generations.

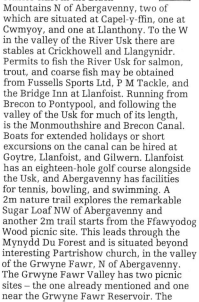

ABERAERON AND NEW QUAY, Dyfed *A2*

The harbour of this pleasant Cardigan Bay resort is a haven for yachts and small craft, and the town has its own sailing club. Farther down the coast is New Quay, also a popular yachting base with a sailing club, where power-boat enthusiasts have made use of excellent facilities in recent years. The shingle and stone beach at Aberaeron is washed by clear water and has some sand. New Quay has its own sandy beach, and beyond New Quay is superb cliff scenery at Cwm Tudu and Llangrannog. Sea fishing is popular at New Quay, particularly for bass, and the River Aeron holds salmon, sewin, and trout. The valley of the Aeron affords enjoyable walks inland to unspoiled upland landscapes. Tourist information may be obtained at 26 Alban Square, Aberaeron, and from the Wales Tourist Board Information Centre on the Promenade at New Quay.

ABERDYFI, Gwynedd *A2*

This excellent sailing centre has both a yachting and water ski-ing club, and is a major water ski-ing centre. Facilities for boat launchings exist here and various small craft may be hired from Mike Bendall, Glandovery Terrace. The boat fishing in Cardigan Bay yields turbot, black bream, rays, and sharks, while bass can be caught from the shore. At the mouth of Dyfi estuary are flatfish of all sorts, whilst farther up the river it is possible to catch sea trout. The Dyfi is famous for salmon. Aberdyfi has a sandy beach which stretches 3m N to Tywyn, but some of the currents in the Dyfi estuary are extremely dangerous to swimmers. Overlooking the beach is an excellent eighteen-hole golf course; the

town also has tennis courts and bowling greens. The Outward Bound Sea School has its HQ here. Hills overlooking the town command fine views, particularly in delightful Cwm Dyffryn – or Happy Valley. Tourist information offices are situated at both The Wharfe and Cliff Side.

*ABERGAVENNY, Gwent *B3*

This town is a centre for pony trekking in the Brecon Beacons national park. Four pony-trekking stables exist in the Black Mountains N of Abergavenny, two of which are situated at Capel-y-ffin, one at Cwmyoy, and one at Llanthony. To the W in the valley of the River Usk there are stables at Crickhowell and Llangynidr. Permits to fish the River Usk for salmon, trout, and coarse fish may be obtained from Fussells Sports Ltd, P M Tackle, and the Bridge Inn at Llanfoist. Running from Brecon to Pontypool, and following the valley of the Usk for much of its length, is the Monmouthshire and Brecon Canal. Boats for extended holidays or short excursions on the canal can be hired at Goytre, Llanfoist, and Gilwern. Llanfoist has an eighteen-hole golf course alongside the Usk, and Abergavenny has facilities for tennis, bowling, and swimming. A 2m nature trail explores the remarkable Sugar Loaf NW of Abergavenny and another 2m trail starts from the Ffawyodog Wood picnic site. This leads through the Mynydd Du Forest and is situated beyond interesting Partrishow church, in the valley of the Grwyne Fawr, N of Abergavenny. The Grwyne Fawr Valley has two picnic sites – the one already mentioned and one near the Grwyne Fawr Reservoir. The

valley can be approached from either Abergavenny or Crickhowell. Superb hill-walking country in the area includes the 1,955ft Sugar Loaf, 1,833ft Blorenge to the S of Abergavenny, and 1,601ft Skirrid Fawr to the N. A superb ridge walk for the energetic leads across the Black Mountains from Crickhowell to Capel-y-ffin, taking in the peaks of Pencerrig-calch, Pen-twyn-mawr, Pen-y-gader-fawr, and Waun Fach – all of which top 2,000ft. A less energetic walk leads through the lovely wooded gorge of the Clydach, situated W of Abergavenny on the A465. Walks up the valleys of the Grwyne Fawr and Honddu wend through beautiful scenery and, in the latter area around the romantic ruins of Llanthony Priory. Tourist information may be obtained from the information centre in Monk Street, Abergavenny.

*ABERYSTWYTH, Dyfed *A2*

One of Wales's oldest and most well established seaside resorts, Aberystwyth has all the usual amenities connected with a holiday town – donkey rides on the beach, paddling pools, trampolines, etc. Other facilities include an eighteen-hole golf course, tennis courts, plus bowling and putting greens. Pony trekking centres in the area can be found at Penrhyncoch, Capel Bangor, and Llanilar. Welsh Romany horse-drawn caravans are hired to tour the beautiful scenery of the Ystwyth and Rheidol valleys from the Llanilar stable.

cont overleaf

The Capel Bangor centre caters for people who wish to take part in more advanced riding pursuits such as jumping, dressage, menage, and cross-country riding. The resort has a yacht club and a sub-aqua school, and sailing is facilitated by the excellent tidal harbour. Local sea fishing yields bass, mullet, flounders, pollack, tope, thornbacks, conger, codling, and whiting. Boats may be hired for fishing in Cardigan Bay.

The shingle beach has some sand and a scattering of rock pools. Just N of Aberystwyth is a sandy beach at Clarach, and even farther N a large expanse of firm sand stretches from Borth to the Dyfi estuary. A nature trail which starts at Ynyslas on the Dyfi estuary leads through extensive sand dunes, and 3m N of Aberystwyth is the ¾m-long Rheidol Forest Walk. Some 10m SE of Aberystwyth, on the road from Llanilar to Pontrhydygroes, a picnic site marks the start of the 2½m Ystwyth forest walk. Devil's Bridge lies about 12m E of Aberystwyth and has a nature trail which leads down into the gorge below the remarkable bridges and affords excellent views of 300ft Mynach Falls. Some 2m beyond Devil's Bridge the Forestry Commission's 1½m-long Arch forest trail starts from the Cwm Ystwyth road.

The angler can fish Dinas and Nant-y-moch reservoirs for trout by permission from the post office at Ponterwyd. Overlooking Aberystwyth is the 485ft viewpoint of Constitution Hill. Cwm Woods run alongside the golf links and offer excellent walks. Other superb walks may be enjoyed in the Devil's Bridge area – which can be approached from Aberystwyth on the Vale of Rheidol narrow-gauge railway – and in the wooded valley of the River Rheidol. One of the most important peaks in Wales, 2,468ft Pen Plynlimon Fawr, can be approached from the A44 about 15m E of Aberystwyth at Dyffryn Castell. The mountain is rather bare and featureless and affords views of extensive moorland; the very emptiness of this landscape is exhilarating to many people. The Plynlimon range is the source of the rivers Severn and Wye. Aberystwyth has tourist information offices in the Town Hall and on the Promenade.

ANGLESEY, ISLE OF, Gwynedd A1

The Island of Anglesey has much to offer both the active and the peace-seeking holiday maker. For the active there are eighteen-hole golf courses at Beaumaris, Amlwch, and Rhosneigr. Riding, hacking, and jumping are offered by the well-appointed riding centres at Rhosneigr and Trefor. The Menai Strait is a major sailing area which has yacht clubs at Menai Bridge and Beaumaris. The latter is also a power-boat centre. Good sailing may also be enjoyed at Benllech Bay, where there is a sailing club, and the opportunities for sea fishing are numerous. Menai Strait is one of the richest fishing grounds in Britain,

and typical catches from Beaumaris include flounders, bass, mullet, and codling. Sea fishing may also prove productive in Benllech Bay, Dulas Bay, Point Lynas, Bull Bay, Cemlyn Bay, and Caernarfon Bay. Sandy beaches, secluded bays, and rocky coves abound and there are extensive sands at Benllech, Dulas Bay, Llanfaethlu, Rhosneigr, and Newborough.

Permits for brown and rainbow trout fishing in Alaw Reservoir are obtainable from the Shire Hall at Llangefni, or from the fishing office at the reservoir. A nature reserve and two nature trails exist at Newborough on the S tip of the island; the 1m Hendai forest trail starts at the Newborough Forest carpark, and the Newborough Forest trail is ¾m long. Windswept rock alternates with gently rolling farmland and extremely varied coastal scenery on the island, which is ideal for the wanderer who likes to be constantly reminded of the ancient past. Everywhere there are stones, houses, and burial places of the peoples for whom this was *Mona*, 'The Mother of Wales'.

*BALA, Gwynedd B1

Situated at the N end of the 4½m-long Bala Lake – more properly called 'Llyn Tegid' – the town of Bala is most decidedly Welsh. The lake provides excellent sailing and has its own sailing club. Anglers can pursue game fish, perch, and pike, and the lake also has its very own species of fish – the gwyniad. It is highly unlikely that gwyniad will be taken on a rod, but day tickets for the more usual species are obtainable from local tackle shops or the information centre. Another local fishing water is Llyn Celyn, which is stocked with trout; the angler must obtain a Dee and Clwyd River Authority licence before fishing this water, and permits are available from the Water Division, Steers House, Canning Place, Liverpool. Lake Vyrnwy lies SE and is stocked with brown and rainbow trout. Permits can be obtained from the Lake Vyrnwy Hotel. Permits for fishing the River Dee are obtainable from 74 High Street, Bradford House, and the post office at Frangoch.

Pony trekking can be enjoyed from the Tytandderwen Riding and Trekking Centre, which is situated just E of the town. Bala has a new eighteen-hole golf course, and an established nine-hole course with motel accommodation. The YHA offer sailing tuition from their base at Plas Rhiwaedog. Further details can be obtained from YHA Travel, Trevelyan House, St Albans, Herts. An official picnic site is located by the lake 1m from Bala on the B4391. Walkers have a vast number of excursions to choose from among the many important peaks and places of interest that can be reached on foot from Bala. A short journey by car or public transport will vastly increase the range of possibilities. The

circuit of Llyn Tegid itself is a very pleasant exercise. This route passes through the village of Llanycil – with Bala's mother church – and 17th-c Caer Gai, built on the site of a Roman fort and connected by legend with Sir Kay of King Arthur's round table. It is perhaps here that young Arthur spent his boyhood. At the S end of the lake is the village of Llanuwchllyn, which makes an excellent starting point from which to explore the Aran mountains and the source of the Dee.

Dduallt rises to 2,155ft and can be reached from the A484 Llanuwchllyn to Dolgellau road with reasonable ease. The Dee rises at the foot of this 'Black Height', from a wide flat marsh which may hide the remains of a Roman temple with a dedication to a river which they regarded as sacred. The easily accessible summit of Dduallt affords views of 2,408ft Rhobell Fawr to the SW. The two major peaks of the Aran range – 2,901ft Aran Benllyn and 2,970ft Aran Fawddwy – can be reached via a track which starts at the far end of Llanuwchllyn village. Aran Benllyn is reached first and allows access to an exhilarating ridge walk to Aran Fawddwy, where superb views extend to the Pembrokeshire coast. The impressive 2,800ft peak of Arennig Fawr rises W of Bala and may be approached without difficulty from a minor road which links Bala with Ffestiniog. Views from its summit encompass the heather covered slopes of 2,259ft Arennig Fach to the N, sometimes known as the Little Arennig. These two peaks differ in appearance, but both have lakes at their feet. To the SE of Bala are the Berwyn mountains, a very attractive range with many streams and valleys. Perhaps the most spectacular features of this range are the Pistyll Rhaeadr Falls, which can be reached 15m SE of Bala off the B4391 from the village of Llanrhaeadr ym Mochnant. Bala has a tourist information centre in the High Street.

*BANGOR, Gwynedd A1

Bangor and Beaumaris share the important fishing and sailing waters of the E Menai Strait. Yacht clubs exist at Bangor and 2m W at Menai Bridge, and the straits themselves provide some of the best and most exciting fishing in Britain. Local pier fishing can yield bass, flounders, plaice, and eels, whilst boat-based anglers can expect plaice, pollack, tope, and thornback rays. The freshwater angler can try the River Ogwen, Llyn Ogwen, and Llyn Idwal. Some 4m E on the A55 the village of Aber offers beautiful walking country and provides access to the splendid Aber Falls. Beyond the slate mining town of Bethesda, to the S of Bangor on the A5, is the dramatic Nant Ffrancon gorge. This was formed by the passage of a mighty glacier during the Ice Age and is overlooked by two important mountain ranges – the Glyders to the W and S, and the Carnedds to the N. The Carnedds can be explored from various starting points, including the hamlet of Gerlan on the outskirts of Bethesda, Llyn Ogwen in the S, Aber in the N, and Llanbedr-y-Cennin on the A5110 Conwy road in the E.

A 13m walk from Llyn Ogwen to Llanfairfechan in the N will take in all the important peaks. The first climb is up the steep slopes of Pen-yr-Oleu-Wen to the 3,427ft summit of Carnedd Dafydd, then the route leads on to the prince of this range – 3,485ft Carnedd Llywelyn. Between Dafydd and Llywelyn is the stunning precipice called the Black Ladders. From Llywelyn the trek heads to 2,876ft Yr Aryg, with dark Llyn Dulyn down to the E, then continues to 3,092ft Foel Fras and descends to Llyn Anafon. A clear track leads to Llanfairfechan. Bangor has an eighteen-hole golf course.

*BARMOUTH, Gwynedd   A2

Built on the slopes of the last outposts of the Rhinog mountain range, this seaside resort has beaches which form part of a sandy strip which stretches almost without a break from Aberdyfi in the S to Porthmadog in the N. To the N of Barmouth on the coast at Llanbedr is Mochras, the remarkable Shell Island where hundreds of different sorts of shells may be found. A small fee is charged to visit the island. Barmouth's many amenities include funfairs, donkey rides on the sand, pedal cars, etc, for children, and the Memorial Park has swings, slides, tennis courts, and well-kept bowling and putting greens. Two nature trails exist N of Barmouth at Llanbedr. The Cefn Isaf farm trail is 2m long and starts near Salem Chapel, and the ½m Nantcol nature trail starts from the car park in the valley of the Artro. There is a riding stable at Aber Artro Hall.

A minor road follows the valley of the Artro and leads to some fine mountain walks. Beautiful Llyn Cwm Bychan provides a good starting point for expeditions along the fascinating Roman Steps, which allow access to the 2,362ft summit of Rhinog Fawr. Between Rhinog Fawr and 2,333ft Rhinog Fach is the wild pass of Bwlch Drws Ardudwy. Other notable peaks in this range are 2,462ft Diffwys, 2,475ft Y Llethr, and 1,932ft Moelfre. All these peaks can be reached either via the Roman Steps route, or from the A496 Barmouth to Llanbedr at Dyffyn. The region is rich in prehistoric remains. Nearer to Barmouth is the less arduous Panorama Walk above the Mawddach estuary, which affords splendid views and can be approached from a point just beyond Porkington Terrace on the Barmouth-Dolgellau road. Tourist information can be obtained from Barmouth's town hall, or from a kiosk on the Promenade.

BARRY, South Glamorgan   B3

A major holiday resort liberally supplied with all those amenities without which many people regard their holiday as being incomplete, Barry includes amusement parks, gardens, a zoo, the Porthkerry Country Park (between Barry and Rhoose), tennis courts, bowling greens, an eighteen-hole golf course, boating lakes, etc – the list is virtually endless. The Knap Lido is a superb swimming pool measuring some 350ft long and 90ft wide. Whitmore Bay's well-known expanse of sand is frequented by children and pony carts; to the W is a quieter, pebbly beach at the Knap; E are the sandy beaches of Jacksons Bay, Sully, and Lavernock. Beyond Lavernock Point lie pebbly Ranny Bay and the less resort of Penarth, with its beach of sand and shingle. Both Barry and Penarth have yacht clubs. Penarth is a centre for water ski-ing and has a slipway launch and ski club. Sea angling produces bass, whiting, and cod along this coast. Tourist information may be obtained from 1 Woodlands House, Woodlands Road.

BEDDGELERT, Gwynedd   A1

Beddgelert has a real feeling of mountains and climbing about it and is in the heart of Snowdonia. The Beddgelert forest trail runs for 1m and begins 2m NW of Beddgelert on the A4085 Caernarfon road. The 4m Cwm-y-Llan

nature trail begins at Bethania Bridge, 3m E of Beddgelert, and follows part of the Watkin Path – one of the Snowdon ascents. This region is renowned for its spectacular mountain scenery and offers scope for an endless number of delightful expeditions from Beddgelert. An essential destination for many people will be the grave of Llywelyn the Great's faithful dog Gelert. A well-signposted path leads ½m to the grave and can be continued to take in the romantic Pass of Aberglaslyn. More energetic walkers might care to continue along the main road to Nantmor, where a small lane leads E into wooded countryside alongside tumbling streams. This path affords superb views of Snowdon and eventually leads down to Nant Gwynant, opposite the Watkin Path.

Snowdon itself can be ascended from Beddgelert via the Watkin Path, which begins in Nant Gwynant on the A498 and is well trodden. This is probably the most enchanting way to climb the king of Welsh mountains, beginning as it does amidst dense foliage and tumbling water. Another ascent can be made via the Beddgelert Path, which starts in the Pass of Llyn Cwellyn on the A4085. To the W of Beddgelert is the 2,566ft peak of Moel Hebog, which can be reached after a two-hour walk from a track on the N side of the Goat Hotel.

The 2,265ft climb to the summit of Cnicht starts at Beddgelert, and a long 14m walk from Beddgelert to Ffestiniog might include Cnicht, 2,527ft Moelwyn Mawr, and 2,334ft Moelwyn Bach. This gruelling expedition will take about six hours and should not be undertaken lightly. The Gift Shop in Beddgelert issues permits for game fishing on the River Glaslyn, Llyn Dinas, and Llyn Gwynant.

*BETWS-Y-COED, Gwynedd   B1

Perhaps the best known of Snowdonia's resorts, Betws-y-coed lies SW of the grassy Carneddau mountain range – the largest group of hills in Snowdonia. Lovely Llyn Crafnant can be approached from Capel Curig, which lies W on the A5 road. Nearer to Betws-y-coed there are some lovely beauty spots. The Fairy Glen lies about 1m from the village centre and can be approached via a path from the Fairy Glen Hotel. This walk can be continued to include the Conwy Falls. A walk from Pont-y-Pair – on the W side of the village – leads alongside the river to the Miners Bridge and Swallow Falls, and can be continued on the A5 to Ty Hyll, or The Ugly House. Some 3m W above Ty Hyll is the 3m Gwydir forest trail, one of ten walks which penetrate Gwydir Forest and vary from ¾ to 5½m in length.

cont overleaf

Salmon, sea trout, and brown trout can be fished for in the Conwy River on receipt of a permit from Betws-y-coed Angling Club or the Gwydir Hotel. To the S of Betws-y-coed at Penmachno are the Gwybernant Stables, which provide facilities for hacking and riding. Tourist information can be obtained from the Waterloo Hotel complex in Betws-y-coed.

*BRECON, Powys B3

Brecon is an excellent centre from which to explore the Brecon Beacons national park. The town has a nine-hole golf course, and the Penoyre Golf and Country Club has an excellent eighteen-hole course superbly laid out against a setting of green mountains. Hotel accommodation on the course provides 26 rooms and additional sporting amenities which include a tennis court and an outdoor heated swimming pool. Brecon town has its own indoor heated swimming pool, plus facilities for tennis, bowling, and putting.

Pony trekking and riding are exceptionally popular pastimes in the Beacons, and numerous stables in the area cater for all pockets and tastes. The Cantref Pony Trekking Centre at Llanfrynach offers trekking, hacking, and riding, and there are two stables E of Brecon at Llangorse Lake. These are the Ellesmere Pony Trekking and Riding Centre, which has trekking, hacking, and riding, and the Llangorse Riding and Trekking Centre. Pony trekking, sailing, and canoeing holidays are run by PGL Limited from their base at the Tan Troed Adventure Centre, Llangorse Lake. Further information is available from PGL Adventure Ltd, Station Street, Ross-on-Wye. The Mountain Hotel and Riding Club at Crickhowell runs the Black Mountains trail ride, and the Blaenau Pony-Trekking and Trail-Riding Centre at Llanddeusant runs both the Usk Valley and Towy Mountains Trail Rides. Hay-on-Wye lies NE of Brecon and is also a major trekking centre. Other stables exist in Llandefalle, and at Penycae in the Beacons.

Llangorse Lake lies E of Brecon and is a major leisure area offering the aforementioned adventure holiday, a sailing club, a sailing school which gives courses in dinghy handling, and water ski-ing and canoeing centre facilities. The Monmouthshire and Brecon Canal runs for $33\frac{1}{2}$m from Brecon to Pontypool, and for much of its length flows through attractive national park scenery. Boats for holidays or excursions may be hired on the canal.

Angling prospects in the area are very good. The Canal Office at Govilon in Abergavenny will issue permits enabling visitors to fish the canal for bream, carp, and other coarse species. The River Usk may be fished for salmon and trout on receipt of a permit from W Hutchingson at the Watergate, Brecon. Trecastle lies W of Brecon on the A40 and offers trout fishing on both the Cray and Usk Reservoirs – on application to the respective reservoir keepers. Talybont Reservoir also holds trout but cannot be fished without an Usk River Authority rod licence. Permits are obtainable from Gwent Water Board, 191 Dock Street, Newport. Brown and rainbow trout can be taken from Cwm Taff Fawr by holders of a Glamorgan River Authority rod licence, available from the Municipal Offices, Greyfriars Road, Cardiff.

Priory Groves nature trail can be approached either through the cathedral churchyard or from Struet car park and runs for $1\frac{1}{2}$m. The Brecon Beacons Mountain Centre supplies information concerning all aspects of the national park and lies just S of Brecon on the A470 at Libanus. There is a picnic site at the centre. The Beacons are best approached either from Cantref along the old drovers track to Merthyr, or from Storey Arms on the A470. On clear days the view from 2,907ft Pen-y-fan is breathtaking, and the Beacons themselves are an extraordinary sight – long grass covered S slopes, breaking at their apex like frozen waves and falling away to the N in stunning precipices. One of the most enchanting walks in the Beacons follows the little Cwm Llwch stream up to Llyn Cwm Llwch beneath towering waves of rock. Tourist information can be obtained from the Cattle Market Car Park or from 6 Glamorgan Street, Brecon.

*CAERNARFON, Gwynedd A1

Undoubtedly the most important tourist centre in Snowdonia, Caernarfon is situated just outside the park but in easy reach of it. Menai Strait offers fine sailing, and Caernarfon has two yacht clubs. Farther up the Strait at Port Dinorwic there is a major yachting marina and sailing club, and the waters here are said to provide the finest tope fishing to be had anywhere in Britain. Local jetty and pier fishing yields bass and mullet, Dinas Dinlle Beach

produces good catches of tope, bass, and flatfish, and boat-based anglers can expect codling, whiting, and flatfish from the Strait. Caernarfon Bay is renowned for its tope and bass, but also offers thornback rays, bull huss, dogfish, and sometimes sharks. Opportunities for salmon and trout fishing are available on the Afon Seiont. A nine-hole golf course is situated at Llanfaglan, and other local facilities include tennis courts, bowling greens, and a swimming pool. A pony trekking and riding centre is situated SE on the A4085 at Betws. Pleasant walks can be enjoyed by the Afon Seiont and along the shores of the strait. Tourist information can be obtained from the Wales Tourist Board Office at Slate Quay.

*CARDIFF, South Glamorgan B3

The Welsh capital has five eighteen-hole and eight other golf courses within a 10m radius. Other sporting facilities are of a very high standard and include the National Sports Centre for Wales in Llandaff Park, plus the nearby Glamorgan county cricket ground. Llandaff Fields is equipped with a 200yd-long golf range which is open to non-members, but members have the added facilities of two sauna baths, two squash courts, and a discotheque. Cardiff's famous rugby club is situated at the new Cardiff Arms Park Rugby Stadium below Castle Bridge. The Olympic-standard Wales Empire swimming pool adjoins Wood Street, and squash enthusiasts can play to their hearts content at Maindy Stadium. Fishing, boating, and leisurely walking can be enjoyed in $1\frac{1}{4}$m-long Roath Park.

Cardiff has a riding and equitation centre at Pontcanna Fields, and there is a riding centre offering hacking, riding, and menage at St Fagans. Marshfield Reen Fishery is stocked with coarse fish and permits are obtainable from 172 Penarth Road, Cardiff. Rainbow and brown trout may be fished for in Llanishen and Lisvane waters by holders of Glamorgan River Authority rod licences, and permits are obtainable from the Municipal Offices. The sea fisherman has good prospects along the foreshore, which can be reached via the docks, and can expect to catch cod, bass, flatfish, whiting, codling, pouting, dogfish, conger, and rays. The pier and foreshore S of Cardiff at Penarth also offer good fishing opportunities.

The city's 2,700 acres of parks and recreation grounds contain eight nature walks. The Bute Park walk starts at the North Lodge in the castle grounds, a walk on Caerphilly Common is approached from the A469 Cardiff to Caerphilly road, the Wenalt trail in Rhiwbina is approached from Wenalt Road, and the $1\frac{1}{4}$m-long Cefn On walk is situated half way between Cardiff and Caerphilly. The 3m Nant Fawr walk is entered from a point just N of

St Margarets Church, and the 5m Taff Valley walk starts in the castle grounds. A walk from Canton to Llandaff, 3m long and divided into four sections, begins at Victoria Park from Cowbridge Road. Some 5m N of Cardiff is the 42-acre Cefn On country park. Tourist information can be obtained from 3 Castle Street and from the Municipal Offices in Greyfriars Road.

*CARDIGAN, Dyfed A2

Cardigan is situated just outside the Pembrokeshire Coast national park at the mouth of the Teifi. This river can be fished for salmon and sea trout, and the Afons Nevern and Cych also offer good angling opportunities. Permits are obtainable from Squibbs in the High Street. The estuary of the Teifi holds bass, mullet, and flatfish. The riding centre S of Cardigan at Bridell offers opportunities for pony trekking, hacking, riding, and jumping. Other stables exist at Eglwyswrw and Crymych, which both lie S of Cardigan in the Prescelly Hills. Sands and bathing can be enjoyed in the sheltered bays and beaches at Gwbert-on-Sea, and there is an eighteen-hole golf course on the dunes. Cliff walks afford views of Cardigan Island bird sanctuary. The annual coracle regatta held at Cilgerran on the Teifi each August is a reminder of a different time and culture. Tourist information can be obtained from the Market Hall, Cardigan.

*CHEPSTOW, Gwent B3

The largest racecourse in Wales is situated on the outskirts of Chepstow, and the town is known for the superb and luxurious St Pierre Golf and Country Club. This eighteen-hole course has everything to satisfy the golfing addict, but is open only to members of bona fide golf clubs. Accommodation, tennis, and squash are offered by the club. The Wyndcliff nature trail begins at a car park in a lane ½m N of St Arvans, while the Tintern Forest, Chapel Hill, and Barbadoes forest trails begin at the car park near old sawmills close to the Royal George Hotel at Tintern. The walks vary from 1½ to 2m in length and afford views of the Wye Valley. Several picnic sites exist between Chepstow and Usk – Cadira Beeches is 10m from Chepstow and 5m from Usk on an unclassified road; Nine Wells is 9m from Chepstow and 6m from Usk on an unclassified road; the two picnic sites in the Wentwood area are situated off the road from Chepstow to Llantrisant. Tourist information may be obtained from the Wales Tourist Board Office, Severn Bridge, Aust.

COLWYN BAY, Clwyd B1

One of N Wales' most popular coastal resorts, Colwyn Bay has a beach and promenade crowded with seaside attractions. Facilities for enjoyment include donkey rides, boating, a paddling pool, and a miniature railway. Eirias Park includes tennis, bowling, and novelty golf, and golfers are catered for with a nine-hole and two eighteen-hole courses at nearby Rhos on Sea and Abergele. The beach is part of a stretch of sand which extends virtually without a break from Llandudno in the W to Prestatyn in the E. Sailing and water ski-ing are very popular here and the resort has a sailing club. Pier, beach, and boat fishing yields cod, bass, mackerel, whiting, tope, flatfish, and rays. The Valley Riding Stable in Nant-y-Glyn Road offers pony trekking and hacking

facilities. Pwllycrochan Woods lie behind the town and provide a 1m nature trail as well as pleasant unguided walks. Eirias Park has a 20-acre picnic site, and another site overlooks the bay ¼m N of the A55. Enjoyable walks commanding fine views penetrate the Nant-y-Glyn Valley to the hamlet of Bryn-y-Maen. Tourist information can be obtained from the Wales Tourist Board's mobile centre on the Promenade, or from the Prince of Wales Theatre.

CONWY, Gwynedd B1

An eighteen-hole championship golf course is situated at Morfa Conwy, where there is also a sandy beach, and the Conwy River and estuary provide a safe yachting anchorage. The town has a yacht club and there are other sailing clubs along the coast at Penmaenmawr and Llanfairfechan. Penmaenmawr is a water ski-ing centre. Deganwy is a centre for those who prefer engines to sails, and boat trips lasting about 3½ hours can be made up the River Conwy. Sea anglers can expect to catch bass, mullet, flounders, plaice, codling, whiting, tope, thornback rays, and congers. The estuary is especially well known for its flounders and mullet, and the tidal waters of the Conwy River may be fished for bass, mullet, flatfish, and occasionally sea trout. Salmon are not common. Inquiries for fishing the Conwy should be made at the Red Lion Hotel, Tyn-y-groes. The Pinewood Riding Stables in Sychnant Pass Road offer riding and hacking. Good walks in the area include a route to Sychnant Pass and Penmaenmawr via 800ft Conwy Mountain. The marine walk to Bodlondeb Park affords good views of Conwy Castle. A pleasant walk to Benarth Wood, which can be reached via a footpath off the Trefriw road, can be continued to Baclaw Farm. Outings to Llangelynin old church and Ro-wen should also be considered. The NT has an information centre at the Telford Suspension Bridge.

CRICCIETH, Gwynedd A1

This pleasant resort is popular with swimmers and canoeists, and fishermen can expect to catch bass, mullet, whiting, and flatfish here. Afons Dwyfawr and Dwyfach hold

salmon, sewin, and trout and are controlled by the local angling association. Other facilities in the town include a nine-hole golf course, tennis courts, and a bowling green. Hacking, riding, and showjumping facilities are provided by the Dwyfor Welsh Cob Stud Riding Centre at Llanystumdwy, about 1½m W of Criccieth. From Dolbenmaen, N of the town, the Penant Valley can be followed into secluded countryside dotted with deserted copper workings. Another walk leads E of Criccieth to the 861ft viewpoint of Moel-y-gest, via Black Rock and Treflys. Little 443ft Ednyfed Hill lies 1m N of the town and commands extensive views. Tourist information can be obtained from the Publicity Association, Llwynderw, Radcliffe Road.

DOLGELLAU, Gwynedd B2

Leisure facilities in Dolgellau include a nine-hole golf course, tennis courts, and bowling and putting greens. Many local lakes and streams offer game fishing, and 3m W of the town the Abergwynant Farm Trekking Centre at Pen-maenpool offers pony trekking and riding amid superb mountain scenery. The 2m Ganllwyd to Ty'n-y-groes forest walk starts at a forest picnic site opposite the Ty'n-y-groes Hotel on the A487, 6m N of Dolgellau. Ganllwyd to Dolgefeiliau forest trails start at the Dolgefeiliau Bridge picnic site, where the A487 crosses the river 8m N of Dolgellau. These walks vary from 1 to 1½m in length. The famous 7m Precipice Walk has been turned into a nature trail which is well signposted and can be joined from the Llanfachreth road, off the A494 Dolgellau to Bala road.

The Torrent Walk is approached from the A487 Aran Road about 1m out of the town and leads along the Clwedog stream, with the water often far below. Tal-y-llyn pass can be reached via the A470 for about ¼m then by a turn for Cross Foxes. Aran Glen is approached from Aran Road, and a 10m-round walk can be made from Dolgellau to the waterfalls and glens at Ty'n-y-groes. To the NW and easily

accessible from Dolgellau are the peaks of 2,462ft Diffwys, 2,475ft Y Lethr, and 2,063ft Y Garn. A walk from the A496 Barmouth road to the summit of Diffwys runs via Llyn Mynach and can be continued to Y Lethr, Rhinog Fach, and Y Garn.

The magnificent range of hills known collectively as Cader Idris is easily climbed from all sides, making it the most popular clamber in Wales after Snowdon. Views from 2,927ft Pen-y-gader, the highest point, rival those from Snowdon. Eight possible ascents of Cader Idris are the Foxes Path, approached via footpath from Gwernan Lake Hotel; the Bridle Path, approached from the national park car park beyond the Gwernan Lake Hotel; the Aran Path, approached from Aran Road and up the Aran Stream; Llyn Cau Path, approached from the iron gate at Minffordd on the A487; Oerddrws Pass, approached from Tabor off the A470; Rhaiadr Ddu, approached from the NT car park at Ganllwyd; Cregennen Lakes, approached from Arthog village; Tal-y-llyn Route, approached from the lake of that name. This last is considered to be the best route. General tourist information can be obtained from the Rural Community Council in Eldon Square, Dolgellau. Information on Snowdonia national park can be obtained from the Countryside Centre, The Bridge, Dolgellau.

*FISHGUARD, Dyfed A2

This boisterous ferry port makes a lively base from which to explore the NW arm of Dyfed. The sheltered waters of Fishguard Bay provide a good anchorage and the town has a yacht club. Fishing from the harbour and breakwater produces conger, whiting, mullet, bass, pollack, and flounders; boat angling from Strumble Head is productive. The North Pembrokeshire Adventure Riding and Trekking Centre at Pontfaen offers pony trekking, riding, and hacking facilities. Goodwick Bay has a safe, sandy beach with a childrens' play area, and a number of isolated and little frequented coves await the diligent searcher between Strumble Head and St David's. Excellent walks in the area open up the Prescelly Hills to the SW, the Pen Caer Peninsula to the NW, and parts of the Pembrokeshire Coast Path. The most delightful walk in the area follows the wooded Gwaun Valley into the Prescelly Hills, full of an old and powerful magic and remnants of prehistoric cultures. Tourist information can be obtained from the Town Hall at Fishguard.

HAY ON WYE, Powys B2

The Hay Pony Trekking Centre offers trail riding, pony trekking, hacking, and riding and is based at the town's Swan Hotel. Pen-y-Beacon Trekking Centre at Llanigon offers pony trekking. The Tregoyd Riding and Trekking Centre is situated at Tregoyd Farm near Three Cocks, and riding, hacking, show jumping, dressage, and menage are offered by the Upper Dan-y-Parc Hacking and Hunting Stables situated at Llandefalle. Excellent fishing can be enjoyed on the Wye, and a stretch upstream at the Warren is safe for bathing. Beautiful walks are offered by the Vale of Ewyas, where the Afon Honddu flows below 2,220ft Hay Bluff, 2,263ft Lord Herefords Knob, and past the priory ruins at Llanthony.

HOLYHEAD, Gwynedd A1

Holyhead is situated on Holy Island, a rocky outcrop dominated by 720ft Holyhead Mountain, and has a sailing club. Another club is sited S at Trearddur Bay, and the Scimitar School of Sailing and Seamanship gives courses in coastal cruising and dinghy handling. Sea fishermen can expect to catch congers, and bass from the breakwater; bass from Penrhos beach; pollack and wrasse from the headlands; thornbacks, plaice, tope, congers, and dogfish from the Lilypond. Boat fishing may yield bass, mullet, tope, flatfish, and shark. Trefor Riding Stables offer riding, hacking, jumping, dressage, and menage facilities, and there is an eighteen-hole golf course at Trearddur Bay.

There are beaches at Llanfawr, Trearddur Bay, and Rhoscolyn, and the 2½m Penrhos nature trail starts where the Stanley Embankment joins Holy Island. A nature trail has been created on the 350 steps which lead down to South Stack Lighthouse. Holyhead Mountain is an obvious goal for walkers; the ascent presents no problems, and the views obtained from the summit are extensive. North Stack and South Stack are renowned for their sea bird colonies, and there is some very fine cliff scenery between South Stack and Rhoscolyn.

LLANBERIS, Gwynedd A1

A centre for climbers, fishermen and tourists, Llanberis is the base from which the easiest ascent of Snowdon may be made. Llyns Padarn and Peris may be fished for salmon, trout, and char, and pony trekking can be enjoyed SW of Llanberis from Betws Garmon. Canoeing is popular on Llyn Padarn. The path from Llanberis to the summit of Snowdon is 5m long and follows the famous rack-and-pinion railway. Views from this handsome mountain are grand indeed and are not to be rivalled anywhere else in Wales. Other ascents of Snowdon include the Crib Goch Trail, the Pyg Track, and the Miners Path from Pen-y-pass, they demand fitness and should not be tackled by those without decent footwear, good lungs, and strong legs. The mountain may also be climbed from the Nant Gwynant Pass or from Llyn Cwelyn. Also accessible from Llanberis are 3,104ft Y Garn and the 3,029ft Elidirs. The spectacular scenery above Nant Ffrancon is best approached from Ogwen Cottage in the pass, also the start of a walk to the 3,000ft plus Glyders. Tourist information may be obtained from the Snowdonia national park and Wales Tourist Board countryside centre at Llanberis.

*LLANDOVERY, Dyfed B2

Afons Bran and Gwydderig meet the Tywi here, and the angling opportunities are excellent. There is a picnic site on the main A40 6m S of Llandovery, and the Dinas nature trail begins at a warden's hut about 11m from Llandovery on the Rhandirmwyn to Ystradffin road. Carmarthen Van lies S and may be approached either from the hamlet of Myddfai or from Llangadog. The highest points of this range are 2,366ft Fan Hir and 2,630ft Fan Brycheiniog, both of which shadow many small lakes. On the other side of the hills at Craig-y-Nos are the wonderful Dan-yr-ogof caves. Pumsaint offers nature trails based on Roman goldmines and lies W of the town. There are some beautiful and unspoilt walks to be enjoyed around Llyn Brianne, which lies on the Rhandirmwyn to Ystradffin road. Information about Brecon Beacons national park can be obtained at 8 Broad Street, Llandovery.

*LLANDRINDOD WELLS, Powys B2

This spa town is especially proud of its bowling greens, on which the Welsh national championships are held in August. Other amenities include tennis courts, a swimming pool, recreation grounds, and a really excellent eighteen-hole golf course. Llandrindod Lake has paddle boats and is stocked with large carp, tench, bream, and roach. Day tickets can be obtained from the boat house. Afon Ithon also offers good fishing. Enchanting strolls in the town's extensive parks and longer treks along the Ithon above Cefrillys (2m E) will satisfy most walkers. A ridge of hills known as Carneddau and Gilwern Hill rise to 1,430ft S and E of the town. Tourist information can be obtained from the Town Hall.

*LLANDUDNO, Gwynedd B1

Everything in the way of amusements to keep the children happy exists in this major seaside town, plus two eighteen-hole golf courses – one of which is of championship quality. Rhos on Sea lies E and has an eighteen-hole course which offers hotel accommodation. Sea anglers can expect bass, plaice, codling, dabs, eels, mullet, conger, whiting, tope, flatfish, gurnard, dogfish, and thornback rays. Both the N and S shores are sandy, and the resort has a yacht club. Nearby 679ft Great Orme has a 5m nature trail which begins at Happy Valley Cafè, and the views from here and from 463ft Little Orme are extensive. Other walks available in the immediate vicinity of Llandudno are across fields to Gloddaeth; a scramble to Bodysgallen, on a hill above Llanrhos; to the viewpoint of Quarry hill and through Bodysgallen wood. Tourist information can be obtained either from the Town Hall, or from the kiosk on North Beach promenade.

*LLANGOLLEN, Clwyd B1

Majestic scenery, the salmon-filled Dee, and the international musical eisteddfod are the main attractions of Llangollen. The Dee is controlled by the Liverpool and District Angling Association and may be fished for salmon, trout, grayling, and coarse fish. Boats for touring the Llangollen Canal can be hired in the town, and pleasure boats travel up the canal to the Horseshoe Falls. A canoeing slalom course of world class has been laid out on the Dee. An eighteen-hole golf course is situated on the E outskirts of the town just off the A5. Pony trekking, hacking, riding, and showjumping facilities are offered by the Ddolhir Pony-Trekking Farm and Stud at Glynceiriog, to the S of Llangollen; the Pontymebion Pony-Trekking Centre at Glynceriog; the Ty'n Dwr Trekking Centre at Llangollen; the Riding Centre at the Golden Pheasant Hotel, Llwynmawr. About ¼m E of Froncysyllte and off the A5 at the canal tunnel is the start of the Tan-y-cut Wood nature trail. A 1m trail begins 5m N of Llangollen at the World's End, and the area is ideal for attractive walks and excursions. Castell Dinas Bran affords excellent views from its 1,062ft situation, and the towpath of the Llangollen Canal leads to the elegant Horseshoe Fall. Valle Crucis Abbey lies away from the canal towpath at Pentre-felin, and is the start of the climb to the top of 1,897ft Moel-y-Gamelin. Excellent views are afforded by 1,068ft Moel-y-Geraint on the W outskirts of the town, and N are the astonishing limestone cliffs of Eglwyseg Rocks. A walk along their base can lead

to World's End, over Ruabon Mountain, and even to the village of Rhosllannerchrugog. Another delightful walk leads over the hills to Glynceiriog, up the Vale of Ceiriog, and thence to the spectacular Pistyll Rhaeadr Falls. Between the Vale of Ceiriog and the Vale of Edeyrnion are the Berwyn Mountains. Tourist information may be obtained from Smithfield Car Park.

*LLANIDLOES, Powys B2

Some 2m NW of this attractive town the new Clywedog Lake and Dam offers brown and rainbow-trout fishing to holders of a Severn River Authority rod licence. Permits are available from Llanidloes and District Angling Association, Foundry House, Llanidloes. The reservoir also has a sailing club. A nature trail begins from the viewing area at the reservoir, and several trails start from the car park at Rhyd-y-Bennwch. Llanidloes itself has a nine-hole golf course, and to the W the Plynlimon range culminates with 2,468ft Pen Plynlimon-fawr. This range may be approached from Dyffryn Castell on the A44, or from Nant-y-moch Reservoir on the Aberystwyth side of the hills. Tourist information can be obtained from 3 China Street, Llanidloes.

LLANRWST, Gwynedd B1

Set by the side of the Afon Conwy, Llanrwst is surrounded by hills, woods, and rich meadows to delight the visitor. Enquiries about fishing the Afon Conwy for salmon and sea trout should be made to the library. Llyn Crafnant is stocked with brown trout, and permits are available from the lakeside café. Gwydir Park has bowling greens, a putting course, and a play area, and the Penrallt Riding Stables at Trefriw offer hacking and riding. Lady Mary's Walk is a 1m nature trail which begins near Gwydir Castle, and there are picnic sites at Llyn Bodgynedd and Llyn Geirionydd – both of which are reached from the B5106. Walks from Llanrwst to Betws-y-coed are pleasant, delightful Llanrhychwyn church may be approached on foot either from Llanrwst or Trefriw, and Llyns Crafnant and Geirionydd are set in beautiful mountain scenery most easily approached from Trefriw. Information on Snowdonia national park may be obtained from the centre at Glan-y-borth, Llanrwst.

LLANWRTYD WELLS, Powys B2

Llanwrtyd Wells was one of the founder centres of the Pony Trekking Society of Wales. Pony trekking and riding facilities are offered by Llanwrtyd Wells Pony Trekking Association; and hacking, riding, and jumping are offered by the Mid Wales Riding Centre from the Neuadd Arms Hotel. The Afon Irfon may be fished for salmon and trout by day ticket, and rod licences are issued at the post office. Delightful scenery accompanies the walker up the Irfon, and much more rugged countryside is encountered beyond Abergwesyn along the road to Tregaron. It is possible to approach Llyn Brianne from the Tregaron Road.

MERTHYR TYDFIL, Mid Glamorgan B3

Brown and rainbow trout may be fished for in the Taf Fechan Reservoirs, which lie to the N of Merthyr, and details concerning rod licences are obtainable from Taf Fechan Water Board, Pentwyn Road, Nelson, Treharris. The town has nine-hole golf. The reservoirs also offer sailing, and walking. Owl Grove picnic site lies ½m N of Taf Fechan Reservoir and is the start of the Torpantau to Taf Fechan forest trail. Many picnic sites exist in the Brecon Beacons, which lie immediately to the N of Merthyr, and fine walking country abounds.

MILFORD HAVEN, Dyfed A3

This major water-sports centre has several yacht clubs, a cruiser racing club, and a superbly-equipped yachting station at Lawrenny, E of Milford on the Cresswell River. Local pier and jetty fishing produces codling, whiting, conger, and thornback rays; bass may be caught from most of the bays in the area; cod, whiting, mackerel, pollack, tope, pouting, and dogfish may be taken by boat-based anglers beyond the harbour. Hamilton Terrace has pleasant

walks and gardens, the Rath has an open-air swimming pool and commands good views over the haven, and the town itself boasts an interesting nine-hole golf course. Nature trails include the 6m Dale Peninsula which begins at the Griffin Inn, and the 2½m Marloes Sands trail. Both lie to the W. Good beaches can be found E at Neyland and Hazelbeach, and W at Sandy Haven, St Ishmaels, and all around the Dale Peninsula. Tourist information can be obtained from the Town Hall, in Hamilton Terrace.

*NEWPORT, Gwent   B3

This large industrial town boasts over 500 acres of parks and recreation grounds, several swimming baths, and three eighteen-hole golf courses – including the outstanding Rogerstone. Pony trekking facilities are available from the Blaengwrne Farm Pony Trekking Centre at Crumlin, and Northernhay Equestrian Centre at Groesllanfro Farm, Rogerstone. The Usk offers excellent sport with salmon, trout, roach, and dace; applications for permits should be made to the local angling associations. Tench, carp, perch, pike, roach, and eels may be fished for in the Monmouthshire and Brecon canal, and permits are available from 19 Park Avenue, Newport. Permits for tench, carp, and roach fishing in Liswerry Pond are also available from here. Wentwood, Ynysfro, Pantyraes, and Llandegfedd reservoirs hold trout, and the necessary Usk River Authority rod licences are available from Gwent Water Board, 191 Dock Street, Newport. Day tickets and permits may be issued by the relevant reservoir keepers. Llandegfedd Reservoir lies N of Newport and offers sailing. The town has a sailing club.

The 1½m Grey Hill countryside trail begins at Wentwood Reserve car park and picnic site, about 6m NE of Newport off the A449. The 2m Ebbw forest trail begins E of Abercarn off the A467 Newport to Brymawr Road. A popular viewpoint about 4m from Newport is 1,373ft Twm Barlwm, and a walk along the course of canal leads to unspoilt hills and valleys. Tourist information can be obtained from the Civic Centre.

OFFA'S DYKE PATH

The 168m Offa's Dyke Path was formally opened in 1971 and in places closely follows the route of the ancient dyke. The latter runs from the Dee estuary in the N to the Severn estuary in the S.

Two or three weeks must be allowed to walk the entire route, and stout boots and a stout heart are essential requirements. Shorter stretches of the path are accessible from roads in several places. Features of the path include mountains, moorlands, picturesque wooded countryside in the valleys of the Dee and the Wye, castles, hillforts, and ecclesiastical sites, etc.

PEMBROKE, Dyfed   A3

The Hobbs Point yacht station 1m N at Pembroke Dock offers a complete range of sailing services, and Pembroke Haven Yacht Club has its base at the dockyard. Neyland boatyard hires out self-drive boats, Burton is a water ski-ing centre, and the superbly-equipped Lawrenny yacht station lies NE on the Cresswell River. The waters of the Haven hold mullet, pollack, whiting, and bass. Several of the local ponds may be fished by day ticket, and 5m S are the attractive Bosherston Pools. These hold various coarse species and can be fished by day ticket. Good beaches on the Pembroke Peninsula exist at Angle Bay, Freshwater West, Broadhaven, Barafundle Bay, and Freshwater East. Information about the Pembrokeshire Coast national park may be obtained from Castle Terrace, Pembroke.

PEMBROKESHIRE COAST PATH

Completed in 1970, the 167m Pembrokeshire Coast Path runs along the whole length of the coast from Amroth in the S to St Dogmaels in the N. It can be tackled as a whole or can be joined and left at any point along its route. The cliff and sea scenery is magnificent along the entire course of the path, and inland there are many verdant little stream valleys. The S coast is gentle in comparison to the windswept harshness of the N cliffs and bracken-clad slopes. There are information centres at Fishguard, Haverfordwest, Pembroke, St Davids, and Tenby.

*PORTHCAWL, Mid Glamorgan   B3

Porthcawl's large beach offers a wide range of holiday entertainment facilities and is part of a sandy stretch which extends almost unbroken from Margam Sands in the N to Southerndown in the E. Facilities for yachting, water ski-ing, surfing, and power-boat sailing are provided by a boat club, marine club, and

a power-boat and water ski-ing club. Sea fishing from boats, piers, and shores yields tope, bass, cod, whiting, dogfish, skate, rays, and pouting. The Royal Porthcawl eighteen-hole golf course is reputed to be the best in Wales, and there is another a little to the N at Kenfig. Other facilities offered by Porthcawl include tennis courts, bowling and putting greens, and a swimming pool. Tourist information may be obtained from the Grand Pavilion on the Esplanade.

*PWLLHELI, Gwynedd   A1

Pwllheli is the most important place on the Lleyn Peninsula, where beaches of sand or shingle stretch away for miles in both directions. Good sea fishing produces bass and flatfish, and several little streams hold game fish. Pwllheli is a sailing, water ski-ing, and power boat centre with two sailing and water ski-ing clubs. Marinaland offers boating lessons and trips. Pony trekking and hacking facilities are offered by the Llwynffynnon Pony Trekking Centre, and the town has an eighteen-hole golf course. Fine views of the peninsula and Snowdonia are afforded by Pen-y-Garn, a hill behind the town. To the SW of Pwllheli is the richly wooded Nanthorn Valley, which can be followed to 1,217ft Carn Fadryn. The N coast of the peninsula has many coves, bays, superb cliff scenery, and 1,849ft Yr Eifl.

*RHAYADER, Powys   B2

High hills and rolling moorland around Rhayader are ideal for pony trekking, and there are three stables in the town – the Lion Royal Hotel Pony Trekking Centre, Trevors Treks in Church Street, and the Rhayader Pony Trekking Association in Church Street.

Waun Capel Park is situated by the Wye and is reputed to be one of the most beautiful of its kind in Wales. It includes the town's sporting facilities. Some 3½m W the huge Elan and Claerwen reservoir complexes are stocked with trout and may be fished by day ticket, but a Wye River Authority rod licence is also necessary. The reservoirs make good starting points from which to explore the wild regions of the Great Desert, a huge area of hills, streams, moors, and peat.

*RHYL, Clwyd B1

Sandy beaches, golf, tennis, bowls, a tropical fish garden, children's zoo, paddling pools, swimming pool, and a cycle track are some of the leisure facilities available in Rhyl – one of the most popular resorts in Wales. The resort has a yacht club and a water ski-ing club. Offshore fishing yields tope, skate, whiting, pouting, gurnard, and flatfish. Enjoyable inland walks can be taken up the Vale of Clwyd to Rhuddlan and St Asaph. Tourist information may be obtained either from the Town Hall, or from the information centre on the Promenade.

ST DAVID'S, Dyfed A3

Whitesands Bay lies 2m N of this tiny city and is the local resort. A stretch of firm sand here is popular with surfers. Facilities include a picnic site and nine-hole golf. This is good, though sometimes bleak, walking country, and the coastal scenery is unfailingly fine. One route negotiates pretty sunken lanes to Porthstinian, where there is a ruined chapel and a lifeboat station. Boats leave the bay frequently for trips round Ramsey Island. A walk S from St David's to ruined St Non's Chapel allows access to the Pembrokeshire Coast Path. Information about the Pembrokeshire Coast national park may be obtained from the City Hall in St David's.

*SWANSEA, West Glamorgan B3

Combined with the Gower Peninsula Swansea forms an extremely comprehensive holiday area. The city has 48 parks containing paddling pools, boating lakes, play areas, etc, and there is an indoor heated swimming pool near the Guildhall as well as an outdoor pool in Morriston Park. Golfers are catered for by six eighteen-hole golf courses, and the 135-acre Fairwood Park Golf and Country Club offers limited hotel accommodation.

The Mumbles, S of Swansea on the Gower, is a major water-sports centre with two yacht clubs, a motor boat and fishing club, a water ski-ing club, and a surfer's shop. Surfing is popular all round the Gower, especially at The Mumbles, Langland Bay, Caswell Bay, Rhosili Bay, and Broughton Bay. The Sports Council for Wales runs sailing courses at The Mumbles, and E of Swansea Port Talbot is also a major sea-sports centre. The National Coastal Rescue Training Centre is based at Afan Lido, Port Talbot and runs courses in everything to do with the sea and sea sports. Sandy beaches can be enjoyed at Port Talbot. The Mumbles, and all round the Gower. Fishing from beaches, piers, and jetties produces flatfish, eels, and bass, while offshore boat fishing yields tope, conger, eels, thornback rays, monkfish, dogfish, codling, mackerel, whiting, flounders, plaice, and sometimes shark. Burry Holm and Worm's Head on the Gower are particularly noted for their bass. Brown and rainbow trout may be fished for in the Eglwys Nunydd water at Port Talbot by Glamorgan River Authority rod-licence holders. Permits can be obtained from the Steel Co of Wales Sports Club, Groes Margam, Port Talbot. Pony trekking is offered by the Park le Breos Trekking Centre at Parkmill, on the Gower; riding, hacking, showjumping, dressage, and menage facilities are available from the Caswell Riding School at Caswell, on the Gower; pony trekking, hacking, and riding are offered by the L and A Pony Trekking Centre at Goytre, Port Talbot.

Oxwich Sand nature trail starts from the beach car park at Oxwich and highlights the interaction of differing life forms. A 3m nature trail leads through the Gower Coast national nature reserve from Rhosili car park, on the W tip of the Gower. Some 14m E of Swansea off the A4107 road out of Port Talbot is the 11-acre Afan Argoed Country Park – a joint Glamorgan County Council and Forestry Commission project. The Gower Peninsula has been designated an area of outstanding natural beauty, and is ideal country for the walker. The scenery includes spectacular cliffs on the S coast and many attractive little valleys inland. Tourist information is obtainable from the Parks Department, Publicity House, 64/65 The Kingsway, Swansea; the Welsh Tourist Board Centre in Upper Killay, Swansea; the Afan Lido at Port Talbot; the Countryside Centre at Oxwich.

*TENBY, Dyfed A3

An ideal centre from which to explore SW Pembrokeshire, Tenby has an excellent eighteen-hole golf course, bowling greens, a putting green, and a large indoor heated pool. The town is also an important yachting centre which boasts a sailing club, a sub-aqua school, and special areas set aside for water ski-ing. Saundersfoot lies 2m N and offers a sailing club, facilities for power boats, dinghy-handling courses at the West Wales Sailing Centre, and water ski-ing facilities.

Beach fishing produces mackerel, skate, monkfish, and flatfish, and tope and bass are fairly common off Caldy Island. Boats for sea angling may be hired. Tenby has the North Sands and South Sands beaches. Saundersfoot has sands and a harbour, and farther round the coast are the 5m-long Pendine Sands. Pony trekking, riding, hacking, and jumping are offered by East Tarr Riding Stables. 1½m Lydstep Head nature trail lies 2m W of Tenby and can be joined either from the village of Lydstep or the car park at the Haven. The whole area is excellent for walkers and includes the magnificent cliff scenery of the Pembroke Coast Path. Tourist information can be obtained from the Guildhall, the Norton, Tenby.

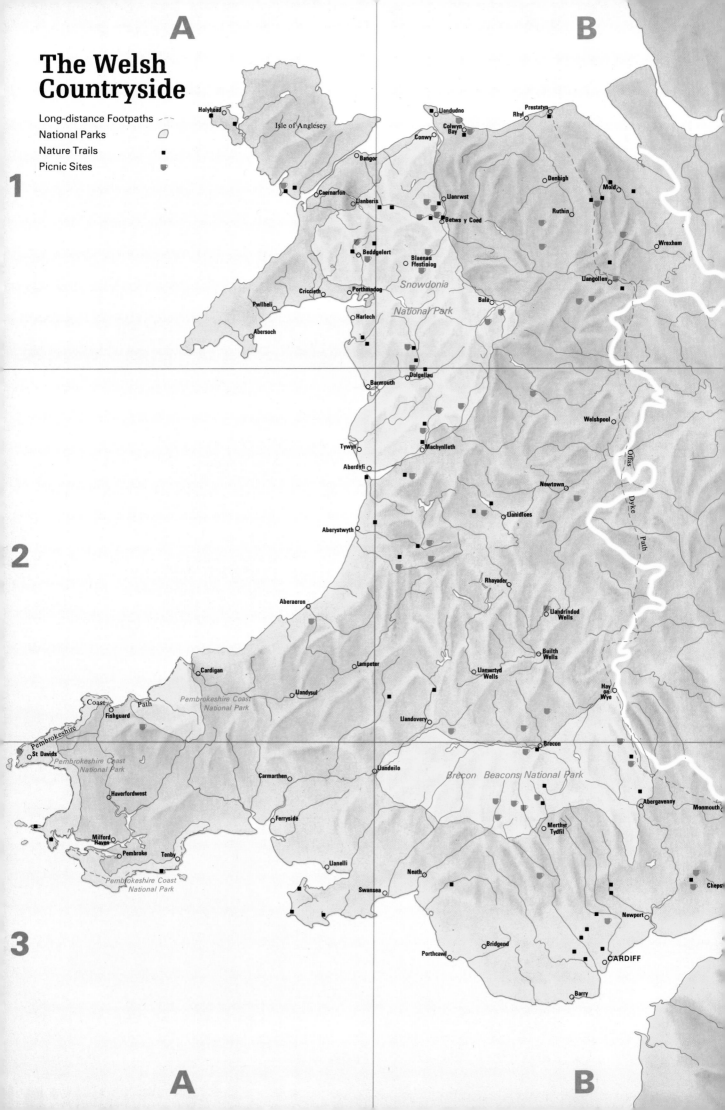

The Welsh Countryside

Long-distance Footpaths
National Parks
Nature Trails
Picnic Sites

A   **B**

1

Holyhead
Isle of Anglesey
Llandudno
Prestatyn
Rhyl
Colwyn Bay
Conwy
Bangor
Denbigh
Mold
Ruthin
Wrexham
Caernarfon
Llanberis
Llanrwst
Betws y Coed
Beddgelert
Blaenau Ffestiniog
Llangollen
Criccieth
Porthmadog
Snowdonia
National Park
Bala
Pwllheli
Harlech
Abersoch
Dolgellau
Barmouth
Welshpool

2

Tywyn
Machynlleth
Aberdyfi
Newtown
Llanidloes
Aberystwyth
Rhayader
Offa's Dyke Path
Aberaeron
Llandrindod Wells
Builth Wells
Cardigan
Lampeter
Llanwrtyd Wells
Hay on Wye
Pembrokeshire Coast National Park
Llandysul
Coast Path
Fishguard
Llandovery
Pembrokeshire
Brecon
St Davids
Pembrokeshire Coast National Park
Carmarthen
Llandeilo
Brecon Beacons National Park
Abergavenny
Haverfordwest
Monmouth
Ferryside
Merthyr Tydfil

3

Milford Haven
Pembroke
Tenby
Llanelli
Neath
Chepstow
Pembrokeshire Coast National Park
Swansea
Newport
Porthcawl
Bridgend
CARDIFF
Barry

A   **B**

Discovering the Hills

Hill Walking

Pony Trekking and Riding

Holyhead

Isle of Anglesey

Bangor

Caernarfon

Llanberis

Beddgelert

Criccieth

Porthmadog

Pwllheli

Abersoch

Harlech

Barmouth

Dolgellau

Blaenau Ffestiniog

Llandudno

Colwyn Bay

Conwy

Rhyl

Prestatyn

Denbigh

Ruthin

Mold

Wrexham

Llangollen

Bala

Llanrwst

Betws y Coed

Welshpool

Tywyn

Aberdyfi

Machynlleth

Newtown

Llanidloes

Aberystwyth

Rhayader

Aberaeron

Llandrindod Wells

Builth Wells

Cardigan

Lampeter

Llanwrtyd Wells

Hay on Wye

Llandysul

Fishguard

Llandovery

Brecon

St Davids

Carmarthen

Llandeilo

Abergavenny

Monmouth

Haverfordwest

Ferryside

Merthyr Tydfil

Milford Haven

Pembroke

Tenby

Llanelli

Neath

Chepstow

Swansea

Newport

Porthcawl

Bridgend

CARDIFF

Barry

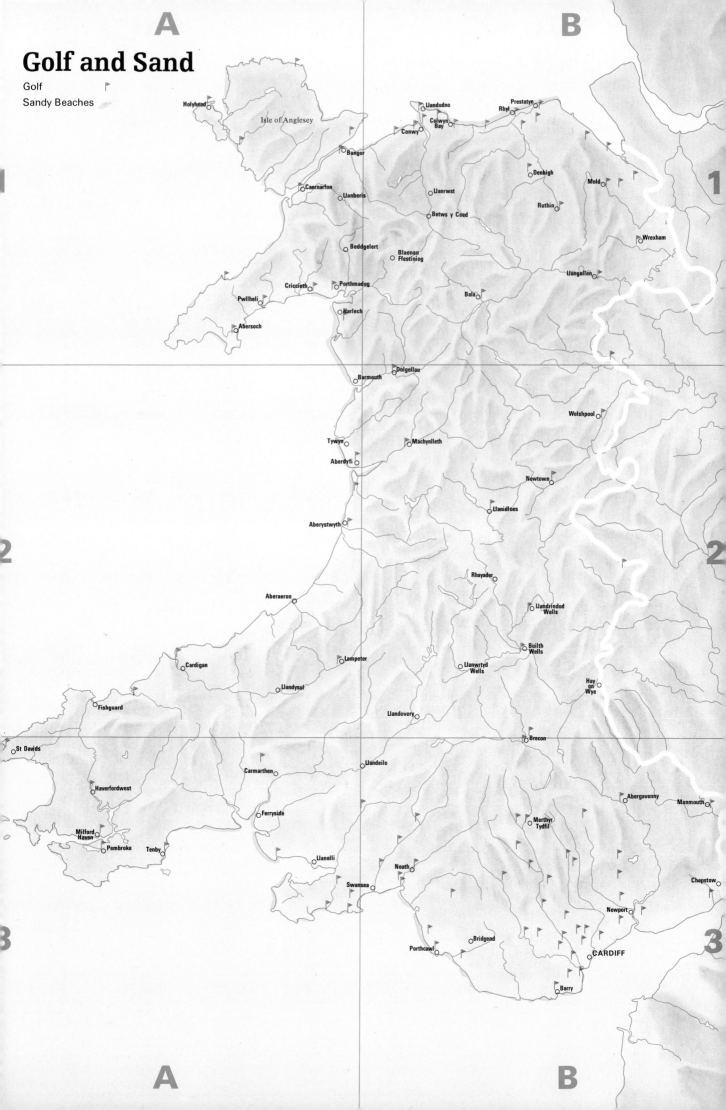

Golf and Sand

Golf
Sandy Beaches

A **B**

1 **1**

2 **2**

3 **3**

A **B**

Isle of Anglesey

Holyhead
Bangor
Caernarfon
Llanberis
Beddgelert
Criccieth
Porthmadog
Pwllheli
Harlech
Abersoch
Barmouth
Dolgellau
Tywyn
Aberdyfi
Machynlleth
Aberystwyth
Rhayader
Aberaeron
Cardigan
Lampeter
Llandysul
Llandrindod Wells
Builth Wells
Llanwrtyd Wells
Fishguard
St Davids
Llandovery
Brecon
Hay on Wye
Haverfordwest
Carmarthen
Llandeilo
Abergavenny
Monmouth
Milford Haven
Pembroke
Tenby
Ferryside
Merthyr Tydfil
Llanelli
Neath
Swansea
Chepstow
Newport
Bridgend
Porthcawl
CARDIFF
Barry

Llandudno
Colwyn Bay
Conwy
Rhyl
Prestatyn
Denbigh
Mold
Llanrwst
Ruthin
Betws y Coed
Wrexham
Blaenau Ffestiniog
Llangollen
Bala
Welshpool
Newtown
Llanidloes

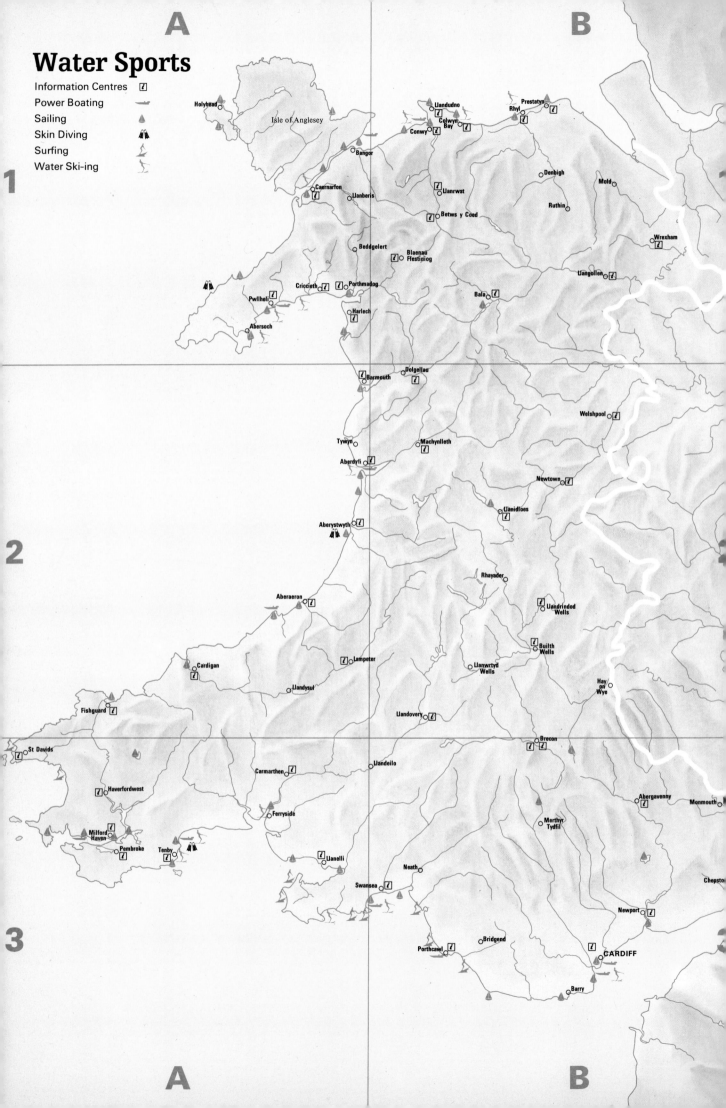

The National Grid

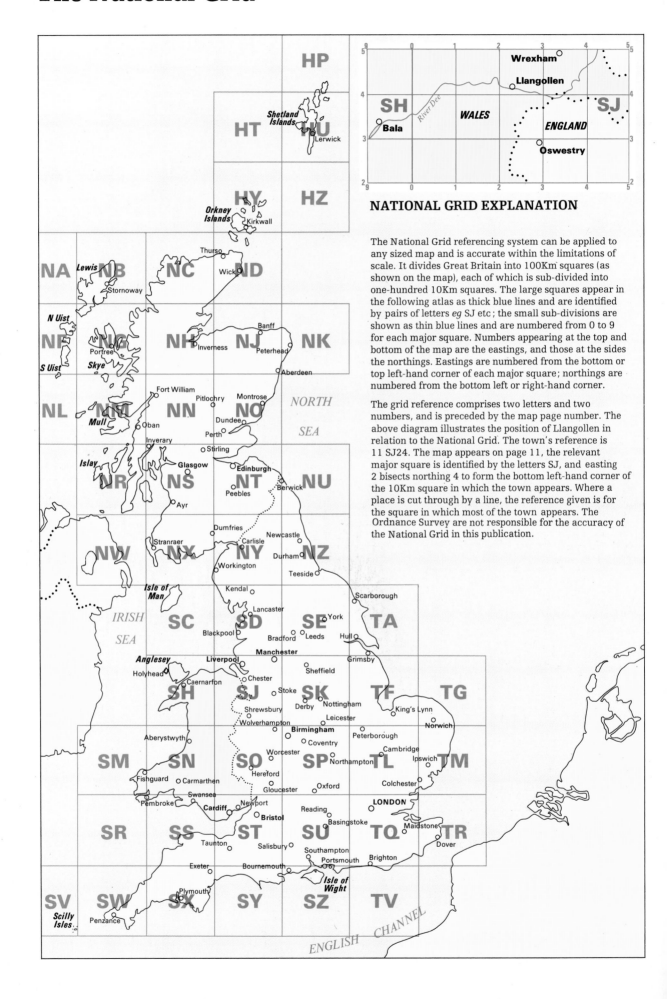

NATIONAL GRID EXPLANATION

The National Grid referencing system can be applied to any sized map and is accurate within the limitations of scale. It divides Great Britain into 100Km squares (as shown on the map), each of which is sub-divided into one-hundred 10Km squares. The large squares appear in the following atlas as thick blue lines and are identified by pairs of letters eg SJ etc; the small sub-divisions are shown as thin blue lines and are numbered from 0 to 9 for each major square. Numbers appearing at the top and bottom of the map are the eastings, and those at the sides the northings. Eastings are numbered from the bottom or top left-hand corner of each major square; northings are numbered from the bottom left or right-hand corner.

The grid reference comprises two letters and two numbers, and is preceded by the map page number. The above diagram illustrates the position of Llangollen in relation to the National Grid. The town's reference is 11 SJ24. The map appears on page 11, the relevant major square is identified by the letters SJ, and easting 2 bisects northing 4 to form the bottom left-hand corner of the 10Km square in which the town appears. Where a place is cut through by a line, the reference given is for the square in which most of the town appears. The Ordnance Survey are not responsible for the accuracy of the National Grid in this publication.

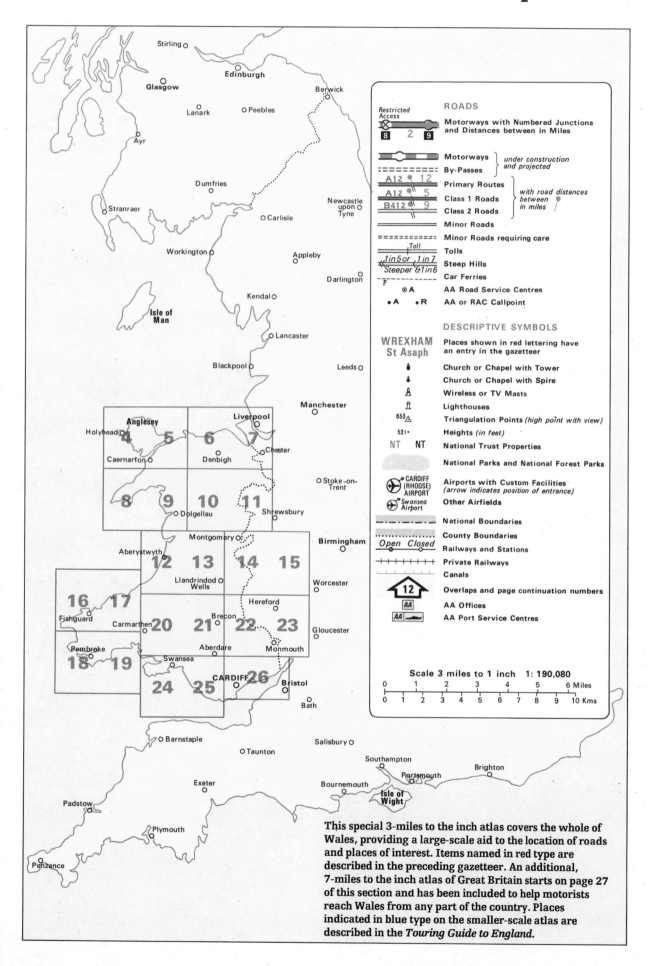

ROADS

Restricted Access ⊗ **8** 2 **9**	Motorways with Numbered Junctions and Distances between in Miles
	Motorways } *under construction and projected*
=========	By-Passes
A12 ● 12	Primary Routes }
A12 ● 5	Class 1 Roads } *with road distances between in miles* ●
B412 ● 9	Class 2 Roads }
	Minor Roads
=============	Minor Roads requiring care
Toll	Tolls
1 in 5 or 1 in 7 Steeper &1in6	Steep Hills
F -------	Car Ferries
⊚ A	AA Road Service Centres
● A ● R	AA or RAC Callpoint

DESCRIPTIVE SYMBOLS

WREXHAM St Asaph	Places shown in red lettering have an entry in the gazetteer
♠	Church or Chapel with Tower
♠	Church or Chapel with Spire
Ã	Wireless or TV Masts
�A̋	Lighthouses
653 △	Triangulation Points *(high point with view)*
521 ●	Heights *(in feet)*
NT NT	National Trust Properties
	National Parks and National Forest Parks
✈ CARDIFF (RHOOSE) AIRPORT	Airports with Custom Facilities *(arrow indicates position of entrance)*
✈ Swansea Airport	Other Airfields
	National Boundaries
....	County Boundaries
Open Closed	Railways and Stations
+++++++	Private Railways
	Canals
◁12▷	Overlaps and page continuation numbers
AA	AA Offices
AA ⎯	AA Port Service Centres

Scale 3 miles to 1 inch   1: 190,080

0	1	2	3	4	5	6 Miles
0 1	2	3 4	5	6 7	8	9 10 Kms

This special 3-miles to the inch atlas covers the whole of Wales, providing a large-scale aid to the location of roads and places of interest. Items named in red type are described in the preceding gazetteer. An additional, 7-miles to the inch atlas of Great Britain starts on page 27 of this section and has been included to help motorists reach Wales from any part of the country. Places indicated in blue type on the smaller-scale atlas are described in the *Touring Guide to England.*

0
1 2 3 4

The Skerries
West Mouse
Dinas Gynfor
Llanbadrig
Cemaes Bay
Bull Bay
Roman Baths
Bull B
Carmel Head
Mynaendy
Plas Cemlyn
Wylfa
Penrhyn
Pentrergof
Betws
Burwen
A5025
AMLWCH
Ty Wion
Tregele
Rhyd-y-groes
Hafodllin
Pentrefelin
Llanfairynghornwy
Llanfechell
Rhosbeirio
Bodewryd
B5111
Mynydd-y-Garn
Church Bay
Llanfaethlu
Llanfflewyn
Carreglefn
Rhosgoch
Rhydwen
A5025
Rhosybol
Pen-y-
Carreglwyd
20½
Llanbabo
Tyn-y-
HOLYHEAD BAY
Trefadog
Pant-Ednyfed
Llwyn Ohn
Llanddeusant
Treffynnon
Gwredog
Ceidio
Llanerchyn
North Stack
Breakwater
Gogarth Bay
Holyhead
Caer-y-Twr
720
Salt I.
AA
Llanfwrog
Tan-yr-allt
Llantrisant
Alaw Res.
Bachau
Lighthouse
South Stack
Holyhead Mountain
Tor
Llaingoch
Kingsland
HOLYHEAD
A5
Penrhos
Llanfachraeth
Stryd y Facsen
Chwaen-hen
Llanfigael
Carmel
Coede
Erw-goch
Llanynghenedl
Pen-llyn
Llyn Llywenan
Llechcynfarwy
Ty Mawr
90
Trefignath
Penrhyn Mawr
Bodedern
B5112
Trefor
Valley
A5025
Rhosydd
B5109
Llangwyllog
8
HOLY ISLAND
Treaddur Bay
Caergeiliog
Bryngwran
Llynfaes
A5
Tywyn
Four Mile Bridge
A N G L
Llanfihangel yn Nhowyn
Bodfforde
Heneglwys
A5
Llanfair-yn-Neubwll
Bodior
Tywyn
Llechylched
Gwalchmai
Rhoscolyn
Cymyran
Capel-gwyn
A4080
Valley Airfield
Groeslon
Cerrigceinwen
Llang
SH
Rhoscolyn Head
Ddrydwy
Cymyran Bay
Ty Newydd
Din Dryfol
Llanfaelog
Pencarnising
Rhosneigr
Bryn-y-Croes Sta.
Tynrhos
Soar
Capel Mawr
Bryn Du
Ty-calch
Glanrafon
B4422
Barclodiad-y-Gawres
Bethel
Trecastell
Bodorgan Sta.
Trefdraeth
Afon
Llangadwaladr
A4080
Llangwyfan-isaf
Aberffraw
Hermon
Malltraeth Yard
24½
Llangwyfan Church & Bay
Bodorgan
Hen-dy
7
Aberffraw Bay
Malltraeth Sands
Cwr
Newborough
Pen-lôn
Malltraeth Bay
Newborough Forest
Newborough Warren
Llanddwyn Island
Llanddwyn Bay
The Bo
6
M D
Dinas Dinlle
Llc
C A E R N A R V O N

B A Y

Pontllyfni
Caen-y-morfa
Aberdesach
Bachwen
Church of the Grave
Tai'r-le
Clynnog-fawr
Ca
A4
20½
5
1 2 8 3 4
Gyrn gôch Gurn Gôch
1670
1607
Bwlch Mawr

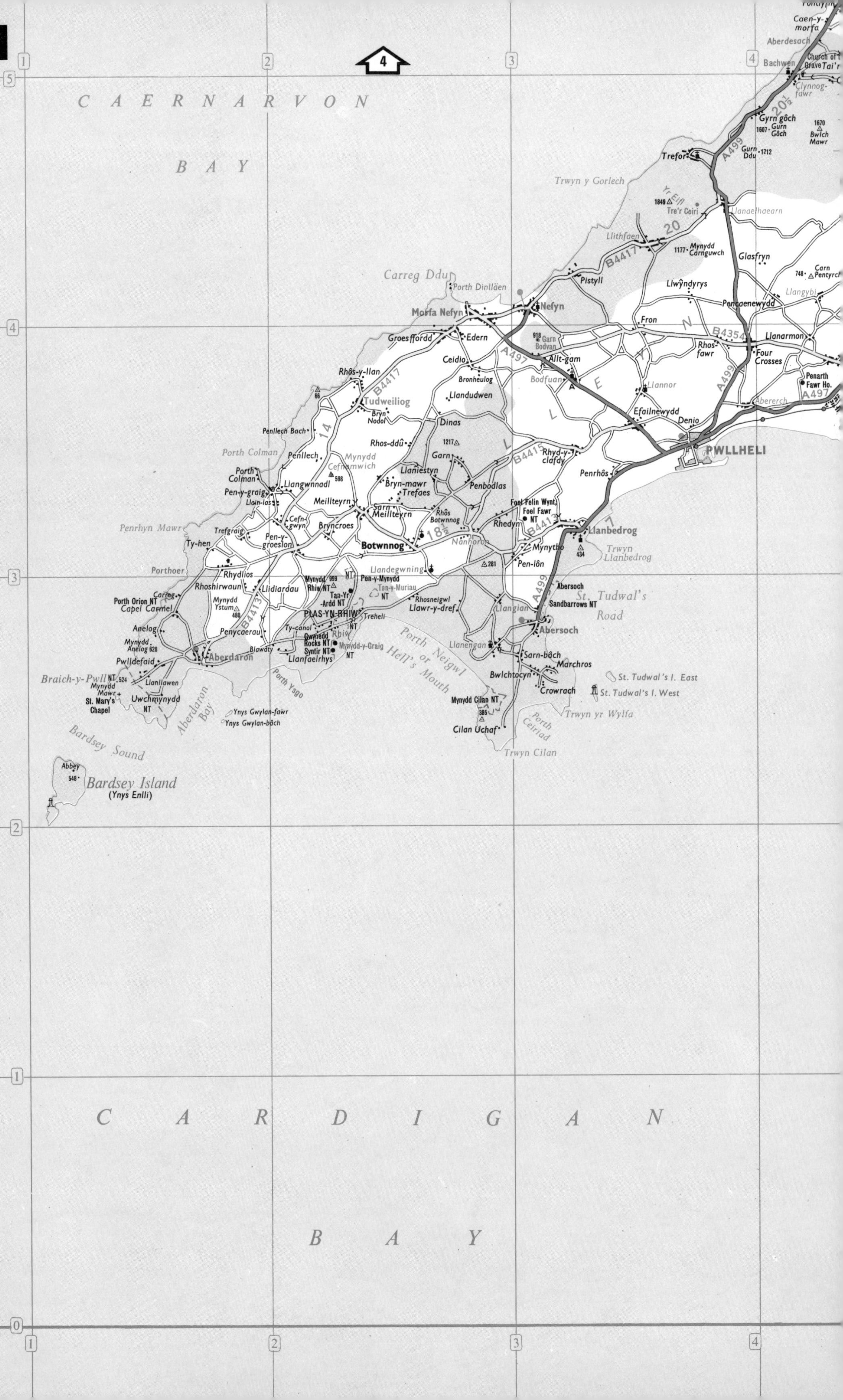
4
CAERNARVON
BAY
CARDIGAN
BAY
Caen-y-morfa
Aberdesach
Bachwen
Church of Grave Tai'r
Clynnog-fawr
Gyrn gôch
1607 Gurn Gôch
1670 Bwlch Mawr
Trefor
Gurn Ddu 1712
Trwyn y Gorlech
Yr Eifl
1849 Tre'r Ceiri
Llanaelhaearn
Llithfaen
1177 Mynydd Carnguwch
Glasfryn
Carn Pentyrch 748
Carreg Ddu
Porth Dinlläen
Pistyll
Llwyndyrys
Llangybi
Morfa Nefyn
Nefyn
Pencaenewydd
Fron
Groesffordd
Edern
918 Garn Bodvan
Allt-gam
Rhos-fawr
Llanarmon
Four Crosses
Ceidio
Bronheulog
Bodfuan
Llannor
Penarth Fawr Ho.
Abererch
Rhôs-y-llan
Tudweiliog
Bryn Nodol
Llandudwen
Efailnewydd
Denio
PWLLHELI
Penllech Bach
Dinas
Rhos-ddû
1217
Porth Colman
Penllech
Mynydd Cefnamwich
598
Garn
Rhyd-y-clafdy
Porth Colman
Llangwnnadl
Pen-y-graig
Llainiestyn
Bryn-mawr
Trefaes
Penrhôs
Penbodlas
Lloin-las
Meillteyrn
Foel Felin Wynt
Foel Fawr NT
Penrhyn Mawr
Cefn-gwyn
Sarn Meillteyrn
Rhôs Botwnnog
Rhedyn
Llanbedrog
Trefgraig
Bryncroes
Ty-hen
Pen-y-groeslon
Botwnnog
Nanhoron
Mynytho
434
Trwyn Llanbedrog
Porthoer
Rhydlios
Llandegwning
281
Pen-lôn
Rhoshirwaun
Llidiardau
Mynydd Rhiw NT
999
Pen-y-Mynydd
Tan-y-Muriau NT
Abersoch
Sandbarrows NT
St. Tudwal's Road
Carreg
Porth Orion NT
Capel Carmel
Mynydd Ystum 480
Tan-Yr-Ardd NT
Rhosneigwl
Llawr-y-dref
Anelog
PLAS-YN-RHIW
Treheli
Llangian
Mynydd Anelog 628
Penycaerau
Ty-canol
Gwynedd Rocks NT
Syntir NT
Rhiw
Mynydd-y-Graig NT
Porth Neigwl or Hell's Mouth
Llanengan
Abersoch
Pwlldefaid
Aberdaron
Blawdty
Llanfaelrhys
Sarn-bâch
Marchros
Braich-y-Pwll NT 524
Llanllawen
Mynydd Mawr
St. Mary's Chapel
Uwchmynydd NT
Aberdaron Bay
Porth Ysgo
Bwlchtocyn
St. Tudwal's I. East
Crowrach
St. Tudwal's I. West
Ynys Gwylan-fawr
Ynys Gwylan-bâch
Mynydd Cilan NT
385
Cilan Uchaf
Porth Ceiriad
Trwyn yr Wylfa
Trwyn Cilan
Bardsey Sound
Abbey
548
Bardsey Island
(Ynys Enlli)
LLEYN
A499
A497
B4417
B4354
B4415
B4413
20½
20
14
18½
7
1
2
3
4
5
0

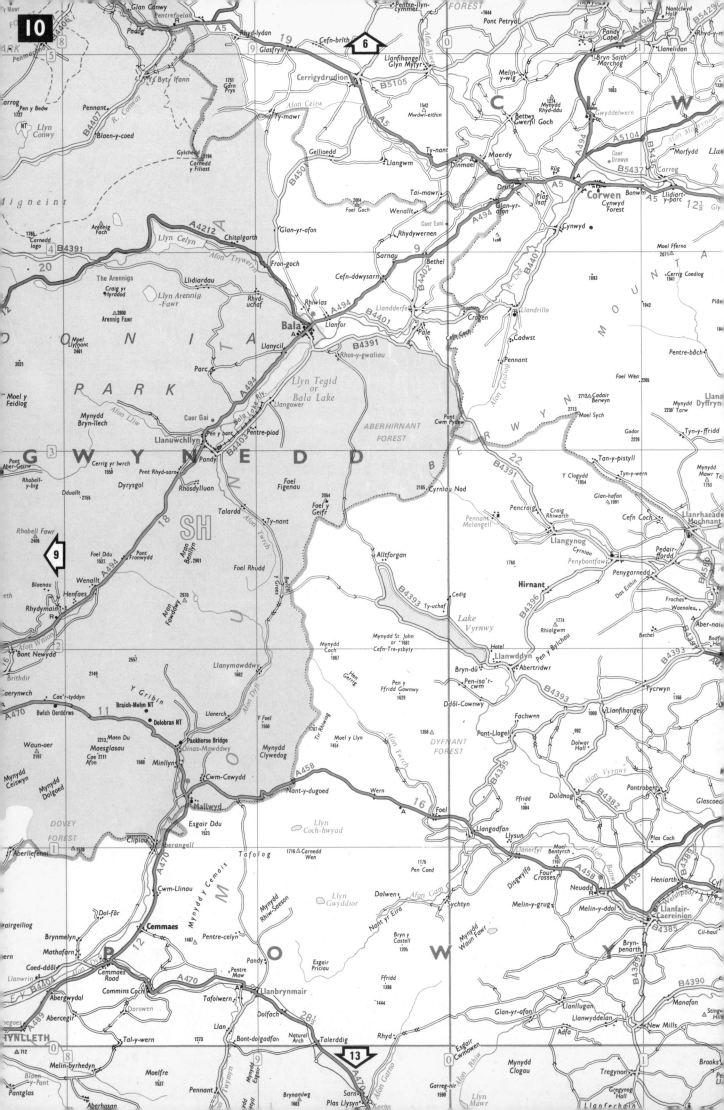

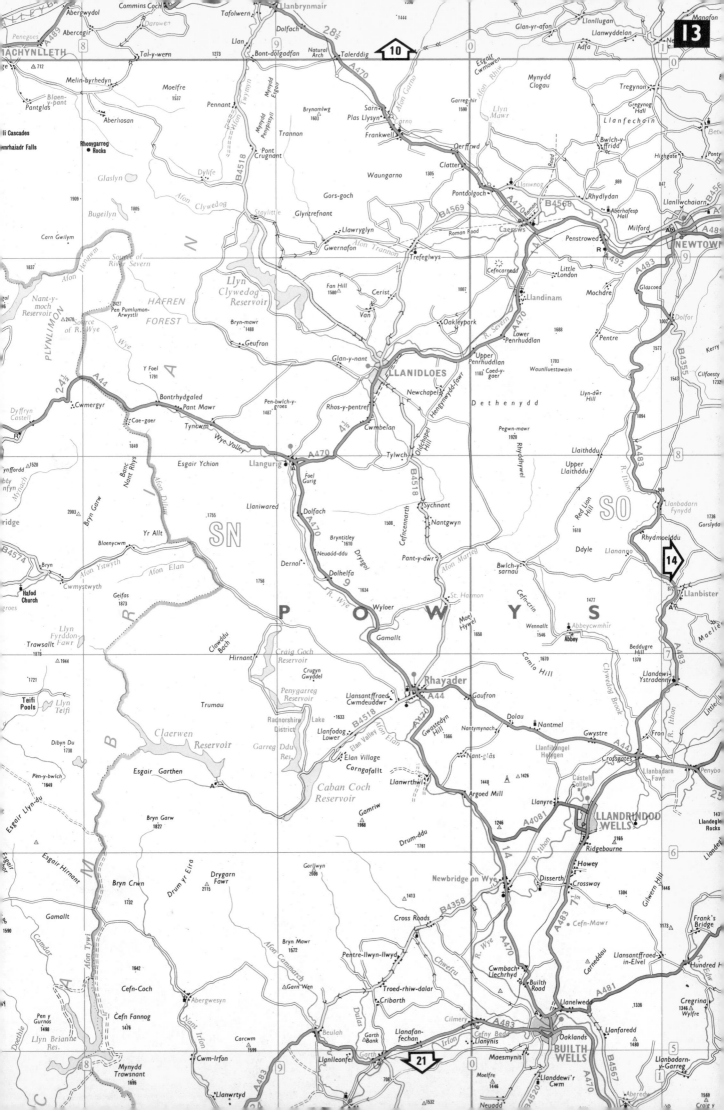

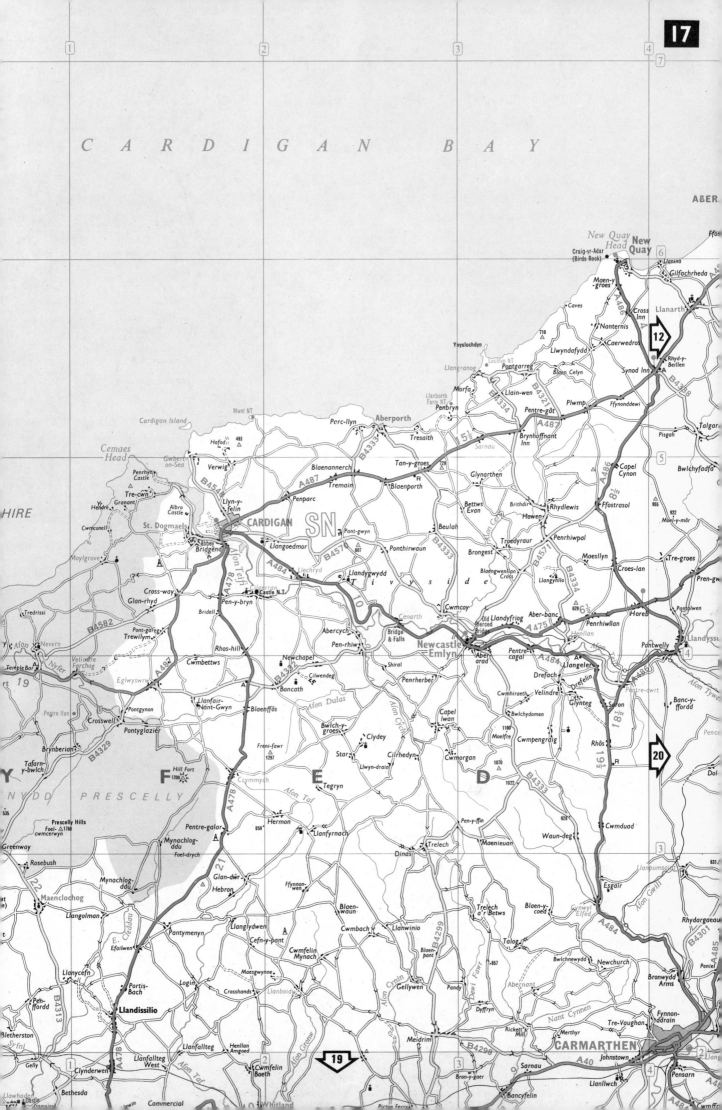

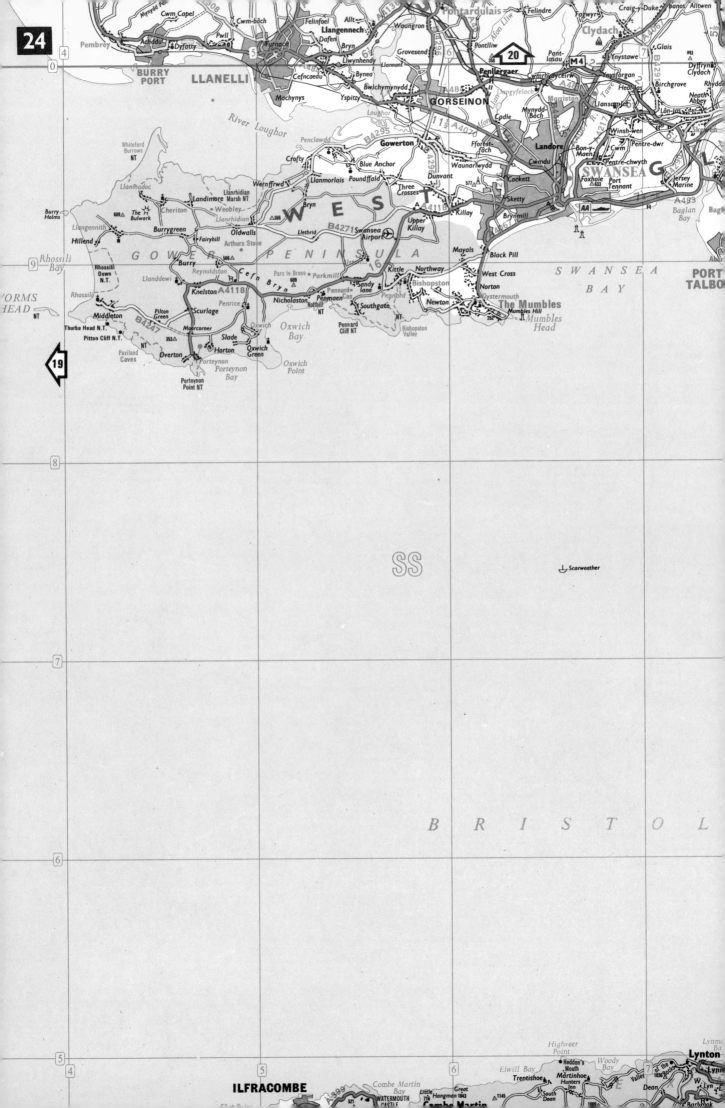

Touring Atlas of Great Britain

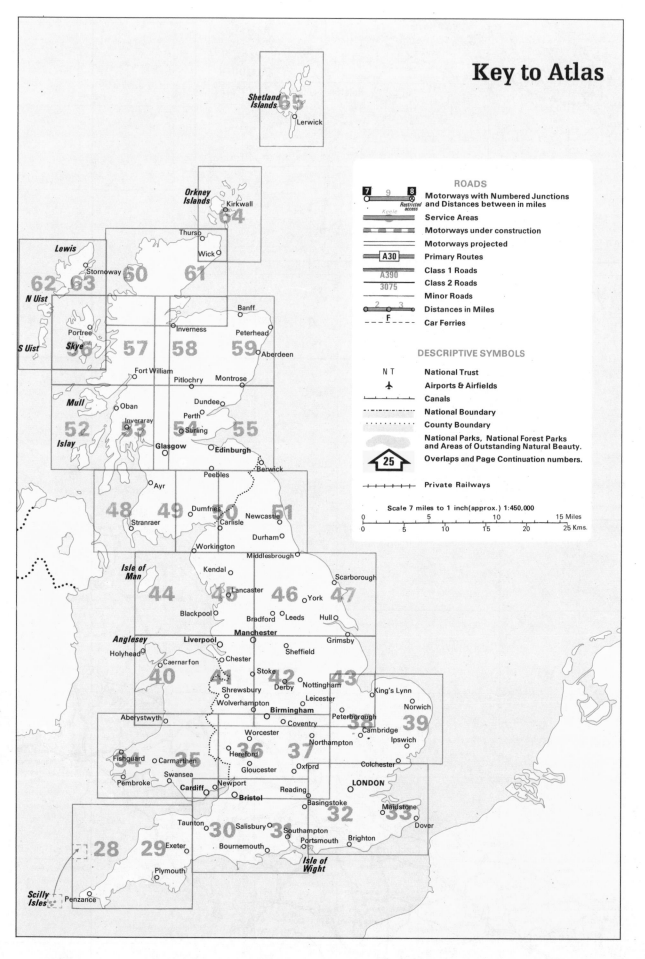

Key to Atlas

ROADS

7 9 **8** Restricted access	Motorways with Numbered Junctions and Distances between in miles
Keele	Service Areas
	Motorways under construction
	Motorways projected
A30	Primary Routes
A390	Class 1 Roads
3075	Class 2 Roads
	Minor Roads
2 3	Distances in Miles
F	Car Ferries

DESCRIPTIVE SYMBOLS

N T	National Trust
✈	Airports & Airfields
	Canals
	National Boundary
	County Boundary
	National Parks, National Forest Parks and Areas of Outstanding Natural Beauty.
25	Overlaps and Page Continuation numbers.
	Private Railways

Scale 7 miles to 1 inch(approx.) 1:450,000

0   5   10   15 Miles
0   5   10   15   20   25 Kms.

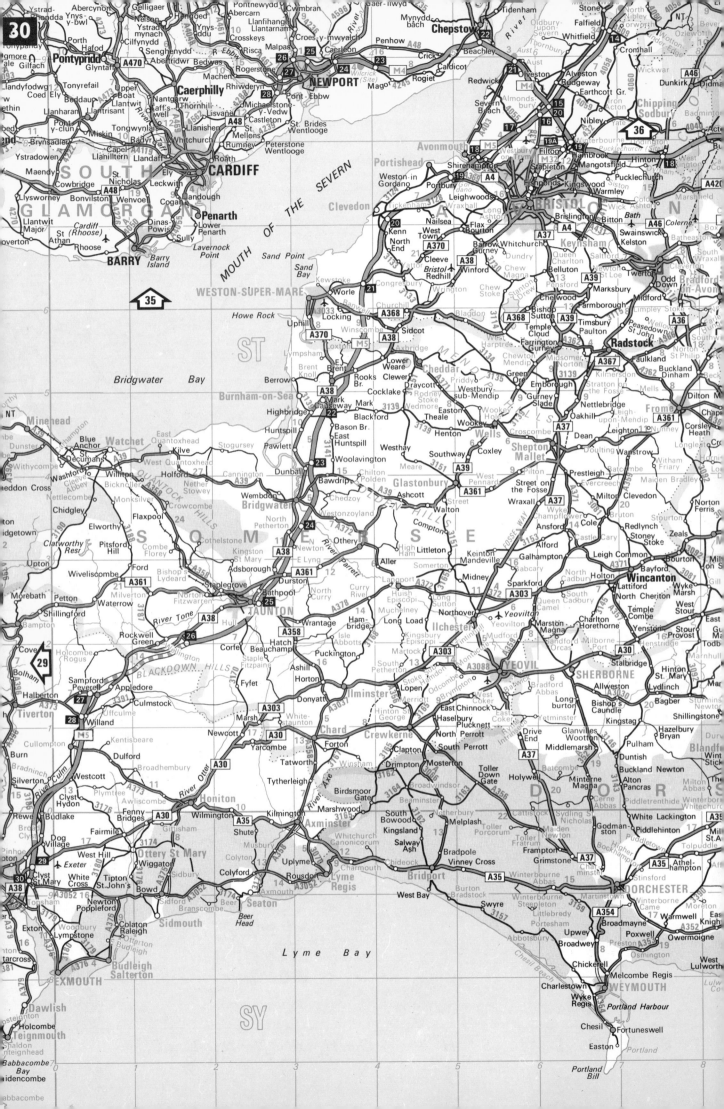

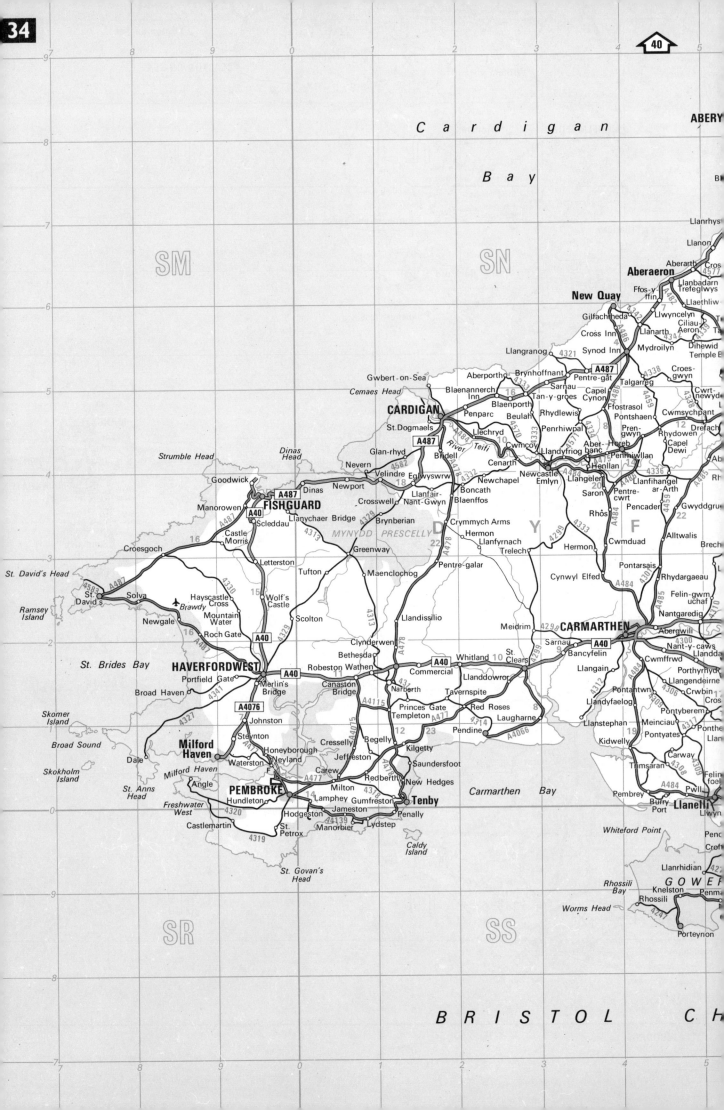

C a r d i g a n

ABERY

B a y

SM

SN

Llanrhys

Llanon

Aberarth   Cros
Aberaeron   4577
Ffos-y-   Llanbadarn
ffin   Trefeglwys
New Quay   7   Llaethliw
Gilfach-rheda   Llwyncelyn
Cross Inn   Synod Inn   Llanarth   Ciliau-
Gwbert-on-Sea   Llangranog   4321   Mydroilyn   Aeron
Cemaes Head   Blaenannerch   Pentre-gât   Dihewid
Inn   Sarnau   A487   Croes-   Temple
Aberporth   Brynhoffnant   Talgarreg   gwyn
16   4333   Capel   4338   Cwrt-
Blaenporth   Tan-y-groes   Cynon   Ffostrasol   newydd
CARDIGAN   Penparc   Beulah   Rhydlewis   Pontshaen   Cwmsychpant
St.Dogmaels   Llechryd   Penrhiwpal   Pren-   Rhydowen   Drefach
Strumble Head   Dinas   River   Penrhiwllan   Cenarth   Cwmcoy   Llandyfriog   Aber-   Horeb   gwyn   Capel
Head   Glan-rhyd   Teifi   banc   A475   Dewi
A487   Bridell   10   4336
Goodwick   Nevern   4582   Cenarth   Newcastle   Henllan   4485
Velindre   Eglwyswrw   Emlyn   Llangeler
Manorowen   Dinas   Newport   18   Newchapel   Llanfihangel
FISHGUARD   Llanfair-   Saron   Pentre-   ar-Arth
A40   Crosswell   Nant-Gwyn   Boncath   20   cwt
Llanychaer Bridge   4329   Blaenffos   Rhôs   Pencader   4459   22
Scleddau   Brynberian   Gwyddgrug
Croesgoch   A487   Castle   MYNYDD PRESCELLY   Crymmych Arms   Cwmduad   Alltwalis   Brech
16   Morris   Hermon   F
Letterston   Greenway   4478   Llanfyrnach
St.David's Head   Tufton   Maenclochog   Pentre-galar   Trelech   Hermon   Cwmbach   Pontarsais
St.   A487   15   Wolf's   4313   Cynwyl Elfed   A484   Rhydargaeau
David's   Solva   Hayscastle   Castle   Llandissilio   Felin-gwm   4485
Ramsey   Brawdy   Cross   Scolton   4299   4333   uchaf
Island   Mountain   4478   Meidrim   4295   CARMARTHEN   Nantgaredig
Newgale   Water   Clynderwen   Sarnau   A40   Abergwili
16   Roch Gate   Bethesda   Whitland   10   St.   9   Bancyfelin   A40   Nant-y-caws   Llandda
A40   Robeston Wathen   Clears   Llangain   Cwmffrwd   Porthyrhyd
St. Brides Bay   HAVERFORDWEST   A40   Commercial   Pontantwn   Llangendeirne
Portfield Gate   Canaston   Narberth   Llanddowror   Llandyfaelog   4306   Crwbin   Cros
Broad Haven   Merlin's   Bridge   4115   Tavernspite   Red Roses   Llanstephan   Meinciau   Pontyberem
Bridge   Princes Gate   8   4914   Pontyates   Llan
A4076   Templeton   A477   Laugharne   Kidwelly   Carway
Skomer   Johnston   12   23   Pendine   A4066   Trimsaran   4308   Felin
Island   Steynton   Begelly   Pembrey   4484   foel
Broad Sound   Cresselly   Kilgetty   Carmarthen Bay   Burry   Llanelli
Milford   Honeyborough   Jeffreston   Saundersfoot   Port
Haven   Dale   Neyland   Carew   Redberth   New Hedges   Llwyn
Skokholm   Milford Haven   Waterston   Milton   4378   Tenby   Whiteford Point   Penc
Island   Angle   Carew   Lamphey   Gumfreston   Penally   Croft
St. Anns   PEMBROKE   14   Jameston   Llanrhidian
Head   Hundleton   Hodgeston   Manorbier   Lydstep   Rhossili   GOWER
Freshwater   4320   St.   44139   Caldy   Bay   Knelston   Penma
West   Castlemartin   Petrox   4319   Island   Worms Head   Rhossili   4247
St. Govan's   Porteynon
Head

SR   SS

B R I S T O L   C H

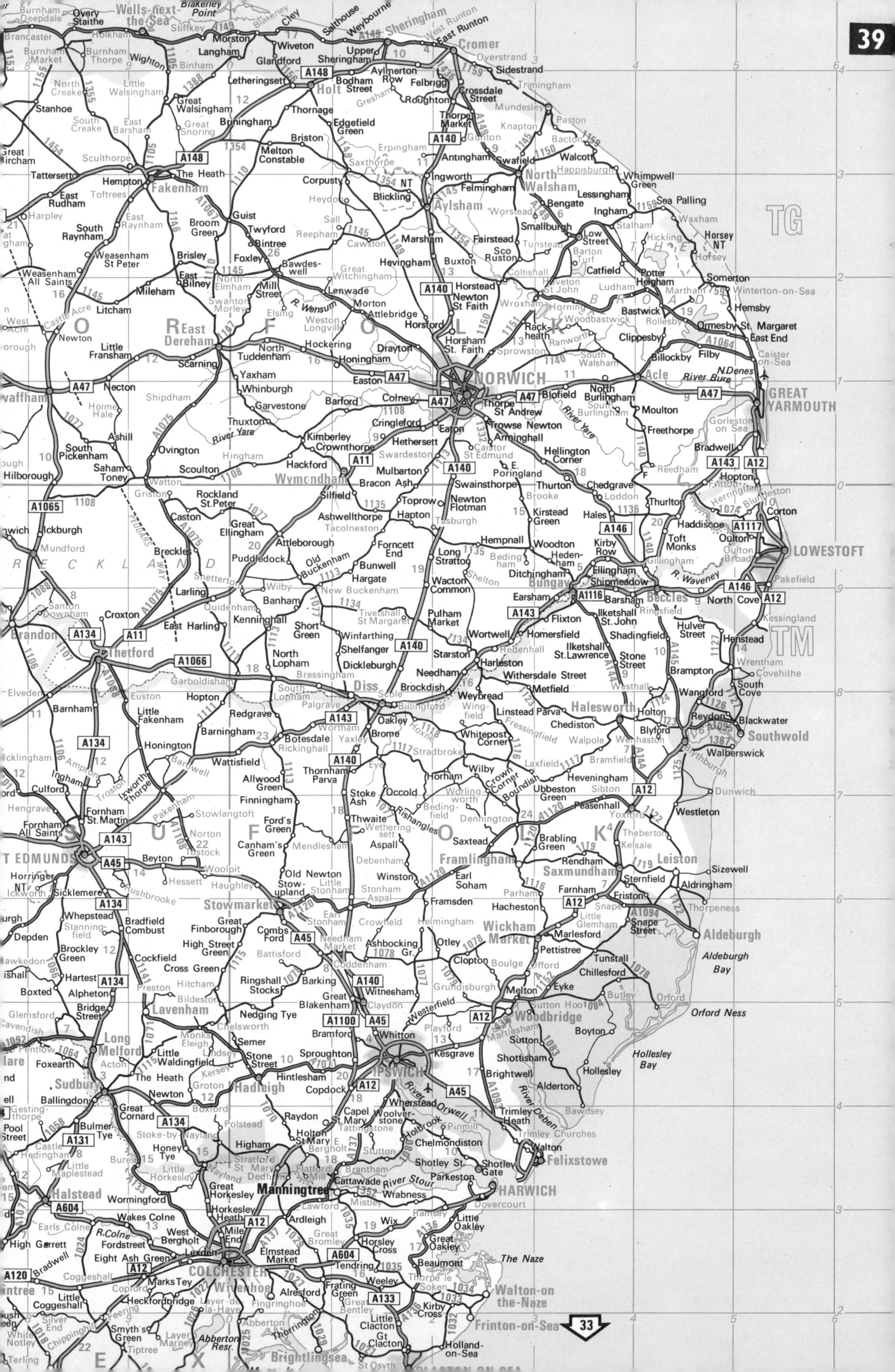

Wells-next-the-Sea
Sheringham
Cromer
Holt
Fakenham
Aylsham
North Walsham
East Dereham
NORWICH
GREAT YARMOUTH
LOWESTOFT
Wymondham
Attleborough
Thetford
Diss
Bungay
Beccles
Halesworth
Southwold
Framlingham
Saxmundham
Leiston
Aldeburgh
Wickham Market
Woodbridge
IPSWICH
Felixstowe
HARWICH
Stowmarket
Hadleigh
Lavenham
Long Melford
Sudbury
Halstead
COLCHESTER
Manningtree
Wivenhoe
Brightlingsea
Walton-on the-Naze
Frinton-on-Sea
Clacton
Brandon
Swaffham
Acle
Harleston
Eye
T EDMUNDS
NORFOLK
SUFFOLK
BRECKLAND
THE BROADS
TG
TM
River Yare
R. Waveney
River Orwell
River Deben
River Stour
R. Colne
R. Wensum
River Bure
Aldeburgh Bay
Orford Ness
Hollesley Bay
The Naze
Abberton Resr.
A11
A12
A47
A134
A140
A143
A146
A148
A1065
A1066
A1117
A1100
A604
A45
A133
A120
A131

33

44

2 3 4 5 6 7 8 9 0

Carmel Head
Cemaes
Bay
Tregele
Burwen
Bull Bay
Amlwch
Penysarn
Llanrhyddlad
Holyhead
Bay
Rhosybol
City
Dulas
Llanfaethlu
Moelfre
Llanfachraeth
Alaw
Resr.
Llanerchymedd
Llanallgo
Marianglas
Red Wharf
Bay
Puffin
Island
Great Ormes
Head
HOLYHEAD
Carmel
Coedana
Benllech
LLANDUDNO
Penrhyn Bay
Rhos-on-Sea
RHYL
Holy
Island
Bodedern
Trefor
Rhosfawr
Llangoed
Conway
Bay
Llanrhos
Deganwy
Rhos-on-Sea
COLWYN BAY
Kinmel Bay
Towyn
Pentraeth
Penmaenmawr
Conwy
(Conway)
Llandudno
Junc.
Old
Colwyn
Abergele
Pensarn
A55
Bodelw
Valley
Treaddur
Bay
Four
Mile
Bridge
Caergeiliog
Bryngwran
Valley
Anglesey
Rhos-meirch
Llangefni
Beaumaris
Gyffin
Llanfairfechan
Bryn-
y-maen
Betws yn Rhos
Llanddulas
Dolwyd
Llanfair
Talhaiarn
Plasisaf
Henllan
Der
Rhosneigr
Llanfaelog
Gwalchmai
Cerrigceinwen
Gaerwen
Menai
Br.
BANGOR
Aber
Ty'n-y-groes
Tal-y-cafn
Pentre
Isaf
Llangernyw
Glascoed
Dolwen
Llansannan
Groes
Bylchau
Penie
Aberffraw
Hermon
Newborough
Llanfairisgaer
Bryn-
Siencyn
Pentre
Berw
Bethel
Bethel
Llanddeiniolen
Saron
Llandegai
Tregarth
Bethesda
Dolgarrog
Pont Dolgarrog
Carnedd Llywelyn
3485
Trefriw
Pandy
Tudur
Nantglyn
Caernarfon
Caeathraw
Llanrug
Cwm-y-glo
Llanberis
Llyn Padarn
Llyn Peris
Capel
Curig
Llanrwst
Pentre-
tafarn-y-
fedw
Gwytherin
Sportsman's
Arms Inn
Alwen
Resr.
Bont-
newydd
Waunfawr
Betws-
Garmon
Nant Peris
Glyder Fawr
3279
Glyn
Pont
Cyfyng
Betws-
y-coed
Nebo
Rhyd-
lanfair
Hafod
Dinbych
Groeslon
Salem
Snowdon
3560
Pen-y-pass
Pont-y-pant
A5
Pentrefoelas
Rhyd-lydan
Penygroes
Nantlle
Rhyd-
Ddu
Llyn
Gwynant
Dolwyddelan
Pont-y-pant
Pádog
Glasfryn
Llanfihangel
Glyn Myf
Talysarn
Llanllyfni
Glanaber
A470
Penmachno
Cerrigydrudion
A5
Ty-nant
Clynnog-
fawr
Gyrn-gôch
Pant-glas
Beddgelert
Aber Glaslyn
Ysbyty-Ifan
Llyn
Celyn
Gellioedd
Glan-
yr-afon
Glan-yr-afon
A494
Bethel
Llithfaen
Llanaelhaearn
Bryncir
Glan
Dwyfach
Dolbenmaen
Prenteg
Penmorfa
Garreg
Rhyd-
y-sarn
Festiniog
BLAENAU
FFESTINIOG
Congl-
y-wal
Chitalgarth
Cefn-ddwy
Llanderfel
Morfa-Nefyn
Nefyn
Fron
Four Crosses
Rhoslan
Pentrefelin
Tremadog
Maentwrog
Pont Islyn
Pont
A4212
Bala
Edern
Allt-gam
Rhos-
fawr
Chwilog
Llanystumdwy
Criccieth
PORTHMADOG
Minffordd
Talsarnau
Trawsfynydd
Llanfor
Tudweiliog
Efailnewydd
Rhyd-
y-clafdy
Penrhôs
PWLLHELI
Llanfihangel-y-
traethau
Glyn
Cywarch
Llyn
Trawsfynydd
Bronaber
Llangower
Bala
Lake
Pale
Pen-y-groeslon
Meillteyrn
Nanhoron
Sarn
Mynytho
Llanbedrog
Tremadoc
Bay
Harlech
Llanfair
Glyn
Cywarch
2800
Arennig Fawr
Llanuwchllyn
Pentre-piod
Bardsey Island
Llidiardau
Abersoch
Trwyn Cilan
Llanbedr
Y Llethr
2475
Bryn-Eden
A470
A494
Talardd
Ty-nant
Alltforgan
Aberdaron
Ystrumgwern
Dyffryn Ardudwy
Ganllwyd
Wenallt
2970
Aran Fawddwy
Henfaes
Llanymawddwy
Lake
Vyrnwy
Llanwddyn
Tal-y-bont
Llanelltyd
Bont
Newydd
Brithdir
Llanaber
Caerdeon
Bontddu
Penmaenpool
Cae'r-tyddyn
Cross Foxes
Inn
A470
BARMOUTH
Cutiau
Aber-
gwynant
Dolgellau
Dinas
Mawddwy
Cwm-
Cewydd
A458
Pont-Llog
Barmouth
Bay
Arthog
2927
Cader Idris
Mallwyd
Foel
Fairbourne
A470
Afon Banwy
Friog
Upper Corris
Cwm-Llinan
Llwyngwril
Tal-y-llyn
A487
Cemmaes
Llanbrynmair
Talerddig
Llangelynin
Abergynolwyn
Esgairgeiliog
Mathafarn
Llanwrin
Cemmaes Rd.
Rhoslefain
Dolgoch
Pantperthog
A489
Commins
Coch
Llan
Bryncrug
Pennal
A493
Penegoes
Machynlleth
Plas Llysyn
Carno
A470
TYWYN
(Towyn)
Cwrt
Derwen-lâs
Pennant
Frankwell
Clatter
Trefri
Pont
Crugnant
A470
Trefeglwys
Aberdovey
Glandyfi
River Dovey
Ysgubor-
y-coed
Dylife
Staylittle
A487
Llancynfelyn
Tre'r-ddôl
Taliesin
35
Van
Llanidloes
Talybont
Nant-y-
moch Resr.
Llangurig
A470
Upper
Borth
Borth
Llandre
Rhyd-y-pennau
Eisteddfa-Gurig
Pant
Mawr
Llangorwen
Bow Street
Capel Dewi
Pont-erwyd
Duffryn
Castell
Cwmbelan
ABERYSTWYTH
Llanbadarn Fawr
A44
Penparcau
Moriah
Capel
Bangor
Goginan
Llanfyfford
Ponterwyd
Ysbyty Cynfyn
Rhyd-y-felin
New Cross
Devil's Bridge
Nantgw
Chancery
Blaenplwyf
Dolfach

Caernarvon Bay

Cardigan Bay

SNOWDONIA

GWYNEDD

POWYS

DYFED

SH

SN

CLWYD

Maxholme Scawby Brigg Grasby Irby upon Humber Scarthor Humberston
Messingham Howsham Hibaldstow Waltham Brigsley New Waltham
Scotter Sturton Moortown Caistor Cabourne Swallow Holton le Clay Tetney Marsh Chapel Eskham North Somercotes
A159 Kirton in Lindsey Redbourne Brandy Wharf South Kelsey Usselby Kirmond le Mire Binbrook Utterby Fotherby Conisholme Saltfleet
Craiselound Blyton Waddingham Bishop Bridge Walesby Tealby Ludford Magna South Elkington Manby Saltfleetby St. Peter Saltfleetby All Saints
Corringham Hemswell Harpswell Caenby Corner Glentham W. Rasen Middle Rasen North Willingham Louth Grimoldby Saltfleetby St. Clements
Saundby Lea Kexby Glentworth Fillingham Faldingworth Lissington Hainton Burgh on Bain Legbourne South Reston Mablethorpe Trusthorpe
Marton Willingham Stow Brattleby Scampton Holton East Barkwith West Barkwith Wragby Cawkwell Scamblesby Withern Maltby le Marsh Beesby Sutton on Sea Sutton le Marsh
Saxilby Burton Dunholme Langworth Bullington Baumber West Ashby White Pit Saleby Bilsby Huttoft Mumby
Dunham Newton on Trent Swallow Beck Bracebridge Heath Bardney Bucknall Horncastle High Toynton Winceby Sausthorpe Ulceby Willoughby Hogsthorpe
Harby Doddington Hykeham Branston Potterhanworth Horsington Thornton Dalderby Old Bolingbroke Hundleby Scremby Candlesby Skegness Ingoldmells
Weston Collingham Waddington Nocton Metheringham Scrivelby Haltham Moorby East Kirkby East Keal Spilsby Burgh le Marsh SKEGNESS
Langford Boothby Graffoe Blankney Martin Woodhall Spa Tumby Mareham le Fen Revesby Keal Cotes Great Steeping Thorpe St Peter Wainfleet
Winthorpe Navenby Scopwick Kirkby Green Walcot Tattershall Coningsby New Bolingbroke Stickford Irby in the Marsh
Wellingore Brant Broughton Ashby de la Launde Billinghay Tattershall Bridge New York Carrington Stickney Wrangle Lowgate
Beckingham Welbourn Dorrington North Kyme Thornton le Fen Cowbridge Sibsey Leverton
Caythorpe Leadenham Cranwell Ruskington South Kyme Langrick Frithville Benington
Hough-on-the-Hill Normanton Leasingham Ewerby Kirkby la Thorpe East Heckington Brothertoft Hubbert's Bridge Halltoft End Freiston
Long Bennington Carlton Scroop Honington Ancaster Wilsford Sleaford Silk Willoughby Heckington Hale Swineshead Bridge Kirton BOSTON Skirbeck
Allington Syston Barkston Belton Scott Willoughby Osbournby Swaton Bicker Drayton Kirton End Skirbeck Quarter
Muston Great Gonerby Manthorpe Threekingham Bridge End Wigtoft Sutterton Algarkirk
Sedgebrook Woolsthorpe GRANTHAM Horbling Billingborough Donington Fosdyke Gedney Drove End
Belvoir Castle Harlaxton Old Somerby Boothby Pagnell Folkingham Pointon Dowsby Risegate Quadring Gosberton Three Bridges
Denton Great Ponton Aslackby Surfleet Moulton Seas End Saracen's Head Fleet Hargate Gedney Dyke Wolferton
Croxton Kerrial Skillington Bitchfield Dunsby Pinchbeck Spalding Fulney Moulton Holbeach Long Sutton KING'S LYNN
Waltham on the Wolds Colsterworth Corby Glen Morton Pinchbeck Bars Weston Little London Sutton St James Clenchwarton
Stainby Grimsthorpe Edenham Twenty Pode Hole Holbeach St Johns Sutton St Mary Tydd Gote Terrington St Clement Tilney All Saints West Winch
Buckminster Swinstead Bourne Deeping St Nicholas Cowbit Moulton Chapel Holbeach St Matthew Tydd St Giles Walpole St Peter St Johns Highway
Garthorpe Creeton Castle Bytham Thurlby Deeping St Nicholas Holbeach Drove Gedney Hill Newton Walpole Highway Wiggenhall
Sewstern South Witham Witham-on-the-Hill Baston Langtoft Shepeau Stow Clough's Cross Leverington WISBECH South Runcton
Thistleton Stretton Careby Carlby Market Deeping Crowland Walsoken
Wymondham Greetham Cottesmore Essendine Ryhall Deeping Gate Deeping St James St Vincent's Cross Parson Drove Wisbech St Mary Elm Emneth Stow Bardolph Wimbotsham
Langham Exton Tickencote Great Casterton Newborough Murrow Guyhirn Friday Bridge Upwell Downham Market
Barleythorpe Burley Empingham STAMFORD Uffington Northborough Eye Ring's End Three Holes Nordelph Fordham
Oakham Whitwell Tinwell Burghley House Helpston Peakirk Glinton Thorney North Side Ryston Crimplesham
Manton Edith Weston Ketton Barnack Werrington Walton Wansford Newark Castor PETERBOROUGH Whittlesey Eastrea Coates Westry MARCH Lakes End Southery
Preston Allexton South Luffenham Collyweston Easton-on-the-Hill Longthorpe Fletton Orton Farcet Angle Bridge Town End Wimblington Welney Brandon Creek
Glaston Uppingham Morcott Duddington Stibbington Kings Cliffe Water Newton Alwalton Chesterton Yaxley Pondersbridge Benwick Doddington Manea Littleport
Stockerston Harringworth Apethorpe Bulwick Fotheringhay Elton Warmington Norman Cross Stilton Holme Ramsey St Mary's Forty Feet Br. Primrose Hill Pymore
Medbourne Caldecott Gretton Deene Upper Benefield Polebrook Conington CHATTERIS Shippea
Middleton Cottingham Weldon Benefield Oundle Stoke Doyle Glatton Welches Dam Mepal ELY Chettisham Prickwillow
CORBY Wilbarston Stanion Brigstock Barnwell Great Gidding Little Gidding Sawtry Bury Ferry Hill Downham Queen Adelaide Kennyhill
Stoke Albany Desborough Geddington Sudborough Lowick Thorpe Waterville Clopton Winwick Alconbury Hill Old Hurst Pidley Somersham Witchford Stuntney
Rothwell Weekley Twywell Islip Titchmarsh Old Weston Leighton Bromswold Lit Stukeley Haddenham Thetford Mepal
KETTERING Barton Seagrave Cranford St John Thrapston Bythorn Gt Stukeley Bluntisham Corner
Broughton Burton Latimer Denford Aldwincle Alconbury Bluntisham

THE WASH
Old Hunstanton
Hunstanton
Ingoldsthorpe
Castle Rising
Wolferton

LINCOLN KESTEVEN HOLLAND THE FENS CAMBRIDGE

2

48

49

High Harrington

A595

Morest

Parton

WHITEHAVEN

Hensingh

NX

Cleator Moor

Woodend

Cle

St Bees

Egr

1

Thornhill

Sellafield

Seasca

0

Point of Ayre

The Lhen Smeale Cranstal

A10 A16

14 A17 Bride

Jurby East Andreas

Jurby West

Ballasalla Sandygate Regaby

Jurby Dhoor *Ramsey*

The Cronk St. Judes *Bay*

A10 Sulby **Ramsey**

Ballaugh 4 A3

A3

Kirk Michael Port e Vullen

9 A14 *Maughold*

14 15 Corrany

I s l e *o f* Ballajora

Shaughlaige- Barregarrow Glen Mona

e-Quiggin *Snaefell* A2

Knocksharry 7 10 2034 Dhoon

A31 Cronk-y-Voddy

Peel *M a n* 18

St 3 Lambfell Laxey

Patrick Johns Moar 12 Old Laxey

A27 Ballacraine Baldrine

Glenmaye A1 Greeba Baldwin Baldrine

8 Crosby Hillberry *Clay Head*

Dalby Foxdale Glen Vine Union *Onchan*

A3 Eairy Garth Mills

12 St. Braaid Kirk

NT Mark's Braddan **DOUGLAS**

Ballamodha Newtown Quine's Hill

Lingague Silverburn A25

Bradda Colby Ballabeg

West A7 Ballasalla

Port Erin A3 Ronaldsway

regneish Derbyhaven

NT Port St **Castletown**

Spanish Mary

Calf of Head

Man

SC

6

5

I R I S H S E A

4

3

2

1

40

51
45
42
STOCKTON-ON-TEES
MIDDLESBROUGH
Redcar
Guisborough
Barnard Castle
DARLINGTON
Teesside
Richmond
Northallerton
Thirsk
Helmsley
Ripon
Knaresborough
HARROGATE
Wetherby
YORK
Skipton
Ilkley
Otley
Keighley
Bingley
Shipley
Nelson
BURNLEY
BRADFORD
LEEDS
HALIFAX
Brighouse
Dewsbury
Batley
Morley
WAKEFIELD
Castleford
Pontefract
Selby
Tadcaster
HUDDERSFIELD
ROCHDALE
OLDHAM
Holmfirth
BARNSLEY
DONCASTER
Stocksbridge
Ashton-under-Lyne
MANCHESTER
Hyde
NORTH YORKSHIRE
WEST YORKSHIRE
SOUTH YORKSHIRE
CLEVELAND
YORKSHIRE DALES
NORTH YORK MOORS NATIONAL
HOWARDIAN HILLS
HAMBLETON HILLS
STAINMORE FOREST
NY
NZ
SD
SE

NZ

NORTH SEA

TA

Staithes
Hinderwell
Runswick Bay
erby
Lythe
Sandsend
A174
Whitby
A171
Briggswath
Ruswarp
Sleights
High Hawsker
Sheaton
Egton
B1416
Grosmont
A171
Robin Hoods Bay
Goathland
Ravenscar

MOORS PARK
FYLINGDALES MOOR
A169
21
20
Staintondale
Saltergate
Bridestones Moor NT
Cloughton Newlands
Langdale End
Cloughton
Burniston
Hackness
Scalby
A165
elton
Middleton
Everley
Newby
Wilton
Ebberston
A170
Falsgrave
SCARBOROUGH
West Ayton
East Ayton
Osgodby
A64
Irton
Cayton
Thornton Dale
Allerston
Brompton
Seamer
A165
Yedingham
Wykeham
Willerby
Flixton
A1039
Filey
R. Derwent
East Heslerton
Staxton
Muston
Filey Bay
A64
West Heslerton
Sherburn
Ganton
1249
Rillington
Foxholes
Reighton
Scagglethorpe
Wold Newton
Buckton
Bempton
Norton
Weaverthorpe
Burton Fleming
A165
Flamborough Head
1248
Octon Cross Roads
1253
Flamborough
North Grimston
1229
1255
Duggleby
Rudston
Boynton
BRIDLINGTON
Langtoft
Carnaby
Bridlington Bay
Wharram le-Street
1253
Sledmere
Haisthorpe
Hilderthorpe
1251
1252
Thornholme
12
Fimber
Garton-on-the-Wolds
Great Kendale
A166
Burton Agnes
Fraisthorpe
Fridaythorpe
1249
Great Driffield
A165
A166
Wetwang
Little Driffield
Lissett
by
29
Bishop Wilton
1248
Wansford
Ulrome
North Dalton
A164
Eastburn
Beeford
Skipsea
A163
1246
Bainton
Hutton Cranswick
1249
Skipsea Brough
Warter
16
Watton
North Frodingham
1242
armby
Pocklington
13
Beswick
Atwick
oor
Kipling Cotes
Middleton-on-the-Wolds
Scorborough
Hayton
Thorpe le Street
Leconfield
Brandesburton
Hornsea
Shiptonthorpe
1248
Leconfield
A165
1244
Seaton
Rolston
Seaton Ross
A163
Market Weighton
Leven
Catwick
Mappleton
upon Moor
A1079
Molescroft
Routh
Long Riston
Sancton
Bishop Burton
Tickton
South Skirlaugh
North Skirlaugh
gathorpe
8
A1034
Beverley
A164
Aldbrough
A614
Walkington
Woodmansey
14
High Hunsley
Dunswell
Coniston
Garton
UMBERSIDE
North Newbald
1230
Skidby
Flinton
12
North Cave
Ganstead
Wyton
Sproatley
HOLDERNESS
avil
Scalby
1230
South Cave
Cottingham
Bilton
North End
den
Newport
A63
Willerby
A164
Sutton on Hull
A165
Preston
Roos
Gilberdyke
Swanland
Anlaby
1233
Marfleet
A1033
Burstwick
1242
Withernsea
Elloughton
Welton
13
A1105
KINGSTON UPON HULL
Hedon
Thorngumbald
1362
Brough
North Ferriby
Hessle
F
Paull
Keyingham
20
Ottringham
Hollym
New Holland
River Humber
A1033
vinefleet
A161
Alkborough
Barton-upon-Humber
Patrington
Welwick
14
Barrow upon Humber
1445
Easington
toft
Burton upon Stather
20
South Ferriby
Horkstow
Thornton Abbey
Luddington
Winterton
7
Thornton Curtis
Normanby
Saxby All Saints
Wootton
A160
Amcotts
Roxby
Bonby
Immingham
1207
A160
Ulceby
Habrough
Keadby
Appleby
Worlaby
1271
Stallingborough
Spurn Head
A18
Crosby
SCUNTHORPE
Melton Ross
Croxton
A1136
GRIMSBY
Ealand
Brumby
A18
Brockesby
10
Gt. Coates
Cleethorpes
Althorpe
Ashby
Broughton
Keelby
Healing
A18
Humberston
A161
8
Wrawby
16
Riby
Laceby
Scartho
AXHOLME
Scawby
Bigby
Irby upon Humber
Waltham
New Waltham
Messingham
Brigg
Howsham
Grasby
Brigsley
Holton le Clay
Sturton
A1084
Scotter
Hibaldstow
Caistor
A46
Swallow
Cabourne
Tetney
Marsh Chapel
A159
A15
Redbourne
Moortown
43
Eskham
Blyton
Kirton in Lindsey
Brandy Wharf
South Kelsey
Holton le Moor
East Ravendale
A16
North Thoresby
aiselound
1205
Waddingham
A46
Binbrook
Ludborough
Conisholme
North Somercotes

62
63
52

Rodel
Renish
Point
Ensay
egray
Hermetray
ochportain
addy

Rubha Hunish
Duntulm
Kilmaluag
Flodigarry
Kilvaxter
Kilmuir
Digg
Staffin Island
Balgown
Quiraing
Stenscoll
Linicro
Brogaig
Staffin
Totscore
Valtos
Culnaknock
Loch Mealt
Uig Bay
Uig
Earlish
2006
Beinn Edra
35

Vaternish Point
Ascrib Islands
Geary
Loch
Trumpan
Snizort
Hallin
Lusta
VATERNISH
A855
Dunvegan
Head
Flashader
Edinbain
Bernisdale
15
Eyre
Kensaleyre
Blackhill
Snizort
Lwr.
Milovaig
Colbost
Dunvegan
Skeabost
Borve
Bridge
Upr.
Milovaig
Lephin
Carbost
Skinidin
Kilmuir
Lonmore
Glengrasco
Roskhill
Seafield
Portree
Island
NG
Ose
Healaval Bheag
1601
Bracadale
Glenvarragill
of
Coillore
Struan
Ollach
Gedintailor
Loch
Bracadale
Port
na Long
Skye
Loch
Sligachan
Peinchorran
Wiay
Fiskavaig
Fernilea
42
Drynoch
Sconser
Idrigill Point
Carbost
Sligachan
Merkadale
2537
Glamaig
Talisker
Beinn Bhreac
1468
MINGINISH
Loch Eynort
CUILLIN HILLS
Loch
Glenbrittle
3309 Coruisk
Sgùrr Alasdair
L. Brittle
Blà Bheinn
3044
15
Torrin
Soay Sound
Loch
Scavaig
Soay
Kilmarie
Elgol

TROTTERNISH
The Storr
2358
Loch
Leathan
Loch Fada

Rona

Sound of Raasay

Rona

Brochel
Raasay
Glame
1455
Dùn Caan

Loch
Torridon
Lower
Diabaig
W
Longa Island
Smithstown
Port Henderson
Badachre
Opinan
Shieldaig Lodge
Redpoint
Loch
Shieldaig
Shieldaig
Loch
Lundie
Beinn Bhàn
2938
Applecross
Camasterach
Culduie
Toscaig
Crowlin
Islands
Inner Sound
Drumbuie
Plock
Kyle of
Lochalsh
Kyleakin
Sgùrr na Coinnich
2424
Kylerhea
Glenelg
Scalpay
Pabay
Dunan
L. Ainort
Luib
Corry
Broadford
Harrapool
Heast
L. Eishort
Ord
Duisdalemore
Isleornsay
Tokavaig
Tarskavaig
Teangue
Achnacloich
Kilmore
Armadale
Castle
Armadale
Ardvasar
Aird of Sleat

North Erradale
Peterburn
Naust
Pool
Gairloch
Cha
Loch Gairloch

Fass of
the Cattle
Kishor
Tornapress
Stro
Duirinis
Balma
Auchte
Berr
Ga
Eila
Upper S
Ber
KNOYD
Inverie
Mallaig
NORTH MORAR
Loch Nevis

Canna
Sound of Canna
Kilmory
Oryal
1872
Kinloch Castle
Rhum
Harris
2663
Askival

Cleadale
Eigg
1291
Galmisdale

Muck

Glasnacardoch
Beoraidbeg
Morar
Bracora
Camusdarrach
A830
Portnaluchaig
Bunacaimb
ARISAIG
Loch nan Ceall
Arisaig 19
Loch Morar
SOUTH
MORAR

Loch nan
Uamh
Lochailort
Inverailort
Sound of Arisaig
L. Ailort
Rois-Bheinn
2895
Roshven
19
Loch Eilt
Loch Eilt

MOIDART
Kinlochmoidart
Ardmolich
Loch
Moidart
Ardtoe
Dalilea
Branault
Ockle
Kentra
Dalnabreck
Polloch
Sanna
Bay
Kentra
Bay
Acharacle
Ardshealach
SUNA
Ardnamurchan Point
ARDNAMURCHAN
Achosnich
NM
Kilchoan
Glenbeg Ben Laga
1679
Salen
A861
Anaheilt
Ardnastang
Camasine
Camasinas
Bousd
Sorisdale
Ardslignish
Glen Borrodale
Liddesdale
A8
Gallanach
Arnabost
Auliston
Point
Oronsay
Ballyhaugh
Arinagour
Tobermory
Lochu
Coll
MORVERN
INNER
HEBRIDES

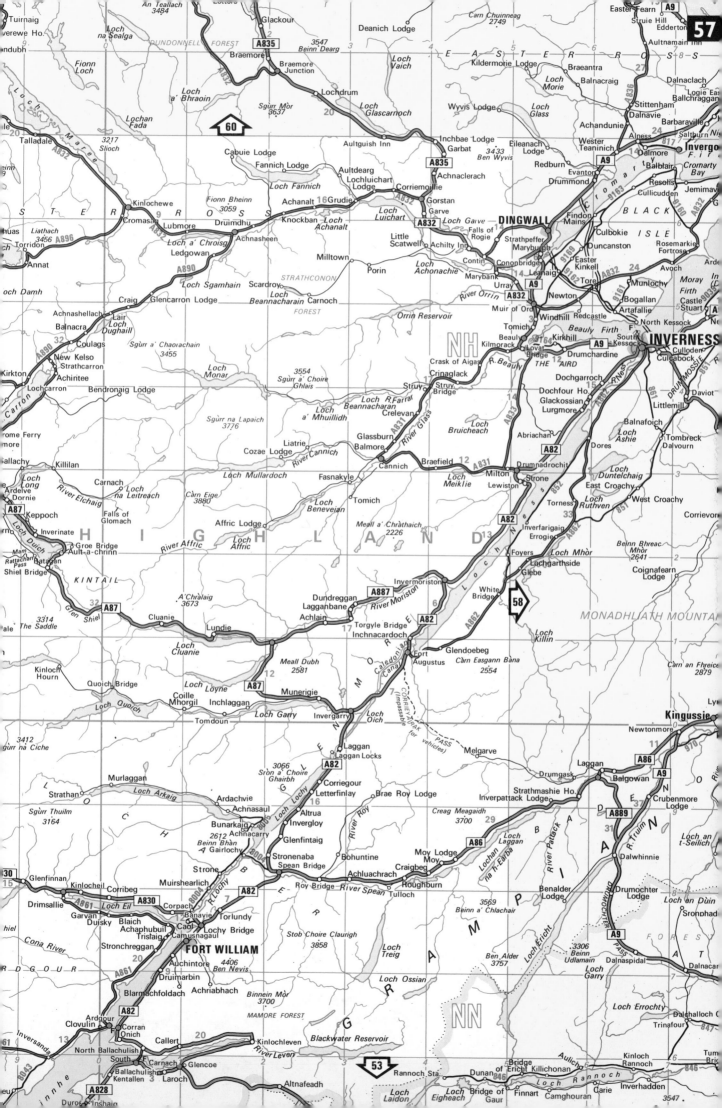

Spey Bay, Kingston, Spey Bay, Garmouth, Scots, Lhanbryde, Mosstodloch, Fochabers, Inchberry, Orton, Lowlands, Crofts, Craigellachie, Aberlour, Dufftown, Glenrinnes, Aultbeg, Bridgend

Portknockie, Findochty, Portessie, Buckie, Portgordon, Bogmuir, Slackhead, Tynet Bridge, Berryhillock, Aultmore, Newmill, Forgie, Mulben, Blackhillock, Keith, Towiemore, Maggieknockater, Newtack, Newton, Drummuir, Milltown of Auchindown, Mains of Cairnborrow, Haugh of Glass, Auchindown Laggan Castle, Dumeath, Huntly, STRATHBOGIE

Cullen Bay, Cullen, Portsoy, Whitehills, Lintmill, Fordyce, Deskford, Ordens, Gordonstown, Cornhill, Peatknowe, Finnygaud, Drumnagorrach, Farmtown, Marnoch, Aberchirder, Rothiemay, Milltown, Bogniebrae, Parkdargue, Forgue, Fortrie, Westerton, Aucharnie, Ythan Wells, Badenscoth, Newtongarry Croft, Bainshole, Fisherford, Culdrain, Skares, Culsalmond, Colpy, Cairnhill

Macduff, BANFF, Silverford, Longmanhill, Kirktown of Alvah, Keilhill, Greenlaw, Brigend of Mountblairy, Plaidy, Fintry, Turriff, Darra, Birkenhills, Mains of Idoch, Mains of Towie, Auchterless, Fyvie, Rothienorman, St. Katherines, Woodhead

Crovie, Gardenstown, Pennan, Protstonhill, Dubford, New Aberdour, King Edward, Cauldwells, New Byth, Cuminestown, Cot-town, Brownhill, Cairnorrie, Methlick, Michael Muir, Hilton, Wedderlairs, Tarves

Rosehearty, Percyhorner, Coburty, Sandhaven, Pitsligo, Ladysford, Craigmaud, New Pitsligo, Strichen, New Leeds, Denhead, New Deer, Maud, Old Deer, Drymuir, Stuartfield, Backhill, Auchnagatt, Clola, Millbreck

Fraserburgh, Fraserburgh Bay, Memsie, Mid Ardlaw, Inverallochy, St. Combs, Lonmay, Old Rattray, Crimond, Blackhill, St. Fergus, PETERHEAD, Burnhaven, Boddam, Stirling, Coldwells, Auchiries, Hatton, Cruden Bay, Port Erroll, Chapel Hill, Bogbrae

BUCHAN, NJ, Dunshillock, Mintlaw, Longside, Flushing

FORMARTINE, Cairnhill, Pitmachie, Insch, Oldmeldrum, Inveramsay, Whiterashes, Ellon, Collieston, Udny, Kingoodie, Pitmedden, Bridgend, Housieside, Newburgh, Pettymuck, Rashiereive, Foveran

Millton of Noth, Kennethmont, Rhynie, Clatt, Hardgate, Leslie, Auchleven, Oyne, Kirkton of Oyne, Chapel of Garioch, Pitcaple, Burgh Muir, Inverurie, Keig, Port Elphinstone, Kintore, Newmachar, North Kinmundy, Whitecairns, Balmedie

Cabrach, Belhinnie, Craig Castle, Newton, The Buck 2368, Lumsden, Correen Hills 1588, GRAMPIAN, Badenyon, Mossat, Invermossat, Tullynessle, Kildrummy, Milltown, Bridge of Alford, Alford, Whitehouse, PITFICHIE FOREST, Kenmay, Kintore, Leylodge, Hatton of Fintray, Little Fintray, R. Don, Blackburn, Reisque

CLASHINDARROCH FOREST, Easterton, Bridgend, Badenyon, Belnacraig, Mains of Glenbuchat, Bellabeg, Strathdon, Boultenstone, Glenkindie, Muir of Fowlis, Tillyfourie, Monymusk, Ordhead, Lyne of Skene, Dunecht, Echt, Loch of Skene, Kirkton of Skene, Elrick, Kingsford

Garchory, Colnabaichin, Cairn Mona Gowan 2456, Newkirk, Tarland, Craskins, Lumphanan, Midmar Castle, South Kirkton, Hill of Fare 1545, Garlogie, Cairnie, Cullerlie, Bieldside, Craighton, Cults, Aberdeen (Dyce), Stoneywood, Bridge of Don, Bucksburn, Jessiefield, ABERDEEN, Girdle Ness, Nigg

Gairnshiel Bridge, Torbeg, Cambus o' May, Ordie, Dinnet, Aboyne, Kincardine O'Neil, Mid Beltie, Milltown of Campfield, Torphins, Craiglug, Milltimber, Culter, Blairs, Peterculter, Findon, Cove, Charlestown, Hillside, Cammachmore, Newtonhill, Muchalls

Bridge of Gairn, Pannanich Wells, Deecastle, Birsemore, Bridge of Ess, Marywell, Ballogie, Feughside Inn, Whitestone, Strachan, Bridge of Canny, Crathes Castle, Bridge of Feugh, Blairydryne, Craiggiecat, Durris, Netherley

Littlemill, BALLATER, Aucholzie, Ballochan, Rickarton, Mowtie, New Mains of Ury, Cowie, STONEHAVEN, Dunnottar Castle, NO

Mount Keen 3077, Kerloch 1747, Spitalburn, Hill of Trusta 1051, Invermark Lodge, Mount Battock 2555, Cairn O'Mount, Auchenblae, Glenbervie, Fiddes, Mill of Uras, Tarfside, Lochlee, Loch Lee, Mid Cairncross, Millden Lodge, Clattering Bridge, Fordoun Church, Drumlithie, Parkneuk, Roadside of Kinneff

Ben Tirran 2939, Braedownie, Clova, Newbigging, Wheen, Hunthill Lodge, Haughend, HOWE OF THE MEARNS, Woodhead, Redmyre, Scotston, Arbuthnott, Kinneff, Inverbervie, Gourdon, Rottal, Clachnabrain, Bridgend, Dunlappie, Inchbare, Edzell, Sauchieburn, Laurencekirk, Marykirk, N. Craigo, St. Cyrus, Johnshaven, Pathhead

Ben Tirran, Lednathie, Cat Law 2196, Pearsie, Cortachy, Tannadice, Finhaven, West Muir, Fern, Trinity, BRECHIN, Mains of Dun, Montrose Basin, MONTROSE, Ferryden, Maryton, Usan, Aberlemno, Netherton, Northmuir, Kirkton of, KIRRIEMUIR

ORKNEY ISLANDS

Mull Head
Papa Westray
Noup Head
Rackwick
Papa Sound
Gayfield
Dennis Head
Holland
North Ronaldsay
North Ronaldsay Firth
Pierowall
Westray
9067
Midbea
The North Sound
Scar
Otters Wick
Sandquoy
Start Point
Sanday
Rapness
9068
9069
Roadside
9070
Kettletoft
Tres Ness
HY
Calf of Eday
Braeswick
Els Ness
Sanday Sound

Westray Firth
Faray
Carrick
Sacquoy Head
Saviskaill Bay
Millbounds
Spur Ness
Papa Stronsay
9065
Wasbister
Rousay
9064
Skail
Egilsay
Eday
Eday Sound
Samsonslane
Whitehall
Stronsay
Eynhallow
Banks
Westness
Brinyan
Muckle Green Holm
Backaland
9063
Millgrip
9061
9066
Holland
9060
Brough Head
Birsay
Wyre
Bay of Holland
Boardhouse
Loch of Swanney
Georth
Gairsay
Ness
Stronsay Firth
9056
9057
A966
Veantrow Bay
Scarwell
13
Dounby
Milldoe 735
24
Auskerry Sound
Skara Brae
9055
L. of Harray
A986
19
Balfour
9058
9059
Shapinsay
Auskerry
Neban Point
A967
L. of Stenness
Finstown
Sandgarth
A965
15
Mainland
Shapinsay Sound
Stromness
Stenness
KIRKWALL
Rerwick Head
Hoy Sound
Loch of Kirbister
Kirkwall
Deer Sound
Mull Head
Graemsay
A964
18
Swanbister
6
10
A960
9051
9050
Quoyburray
Orgill
Deerness
9047
Scapa Flow
9052
A961
Rackwick
Cava
St Marys
Lamb Holm
Copinsay
Rora Head
Fara
Hunda
Rose Ness
Hoy
Flotta
Burray
8
9045
Uppertown
9049
Lyness
Bow
9043
St Margarets Hope
Longhope
Wing
Herston
9042
Saltness
9047
Switha
A961
South Ronaldsay
Tor Ness
South Walls
Swona
Halcro Head
Burwick
Cleat
9041

Pentland Firth
Island of Stroma
ND

Dunnet Head
61
St. John's Loch
Scarfskerry
Gills Bay
John o'Groats
Duncansby Head
855
Brough
East Mey
Gills
Duncansby
Hunspow
Mey
Huna
Canisbay
Scrabster
Dunnet Bay
Dunnet
Brabstermire
Freswick
16
874
20
Loch Heilen
Murkle
Thurso
Castletown
Slickly
Auckingill
Westfield
876
Durran
Lyth
Nybster
A882
knockglass
Sordale
Hastigrow
Keiss
Aimster
Roadside
874
Kirk
17
Loch Calder
Halkirk
Loch Scarmclate
Gillock
876
Killimster
Brawlbin
21
Sinclair's Bay
Reiss
M9Thurso
Old Hall
Loch Watten
Mains of Watten
Noss Head
Olgrinmore
Spital
870
Watten
Bilbster
874
Sibster
Ackergill
Westerdale
Mybster
Strath
A882
Janetstown
Staxigoe
28
Badlibster
Wick
HIGHLAND
WICK
Strathmore Lodge
A895
Thrumster
A9
Loch More
Achavanich
18
Sarclet
Loch Rangag
Ulbster
Roster
Braehungie
West Clyth
Bruan
Lybster
Mid Clyth
142
Alisky
Occumster

SHETLAND ISLANDS

HP

HU

Herma Ness
Lamba Ness
Norwick
Loch of Cliff
Haroldswick
Baltasound
9086
9087
3
Unst
6
A968
Balta
Uyeasound
Castleton
Muness Castle
Gloup
Cullivoe
Bluemull Sound
Uyea
Gossa Water
Gutcher
North Sandwick
Nev of Stuis
Strandburgh Ness
Fetlar
Grimister
Camb
9088
Hascosay
Tresta
Funzie
Yell
Wick of Tresta
8
10
Hillend
A968
Colgrave Sound
West Sandwick
9081
Otterswick
Uyea
Roer Water
Houll
Housetter
Setter
Hamnavoe
Ronas Hill 1475
Collafirth
A970
9071
Oilaberry
Burravoe
Esha Ness
9078
11
Urafirth
A970
17
Ulsta
Copister
Hillswick
Brough
Mossbank
Sullom
Sullom Voe
Graven
Hamnavoe
Housay
Bruray
Mangaster
9076
Trondavoe
A968
Out Skerries
St Magnus Bay
Brae
10
Lunna
Ve Skerries
9705
Hillside
Laxo
Vidlin
Brough
Skaw
Muckle Roe
Minn
Dury Voe
Symbister
Whalsay
Swarbacks
Vementry
9071
Dury
Huxter
Papa Stour
Mid Setter
Sound of Papa
Sandness
A971
Aith
18
9075
Skellister
Mainland
Weisdale Voe
Weisdale
Bixter
Tresta
9071
17
12
Effirth
Girlsta
Wats Ness
Walls
Braens
Whiteness
Hawks Ness
Vaila
Culswick
9071
A9
12
Logat Head
Ham
Foula
South Ness
The Deeps
Scalloway
Veensgarth
9074
10
A970
Heogan
Hoversta
LERWICK
Bressay
Isle of Noss
Hildasay
Oxna
Tronda
A970
Kirkabister
Hamnavoe
Easter Quarff
West Burra
East Burra
A970
Bremire-houll
South Havra
17
9122
Stove
Mousa
St Ninians Isle
Levenwick
Scousburgh
Loch of Spiggie
8
A970
Fitful Head
Sumburgh
9122
Grutness
Jarlshof
Sumburgh Head

Ancient Monuments in Wales

One of the most fascinating aspects of Wales is its history – not the dust-dry dogmatism of words on a page, but a living past caught in hundreds of monuments, monoliths, and ancient ruins. Circles of stones that have been standing for thousands of years add a depth of mystery to lonely hillsides, and ruins from the Age of Saints echo with the harsh praises of jackdaw choirs. And then there are the hillforts, passage graves, crosses, and inscriptions; each is

an exciting relic of another world, and most are entwined with the tendrils of myth and legend. This map does not attempt to show all the ancient monuments that exist in Wales, but picks out a few of the finest and most famous. The visitor who finds these awesome should think of Stonehenge, and the incredible journey of the inner-ring bluestones from prehistoric quarries in West Wales to the rolling uplands of Salisbury Plain.

LEGEND

Before 54 BC

- Burial ground
- Earthworks
- Hill fort
- Inhabited site
- Probable route of the bluestones to Stonehenge
- Standing stones

54BC–1066 AD

- Fort
- Inscribed pillar
- Linear earthworks
- Settlement

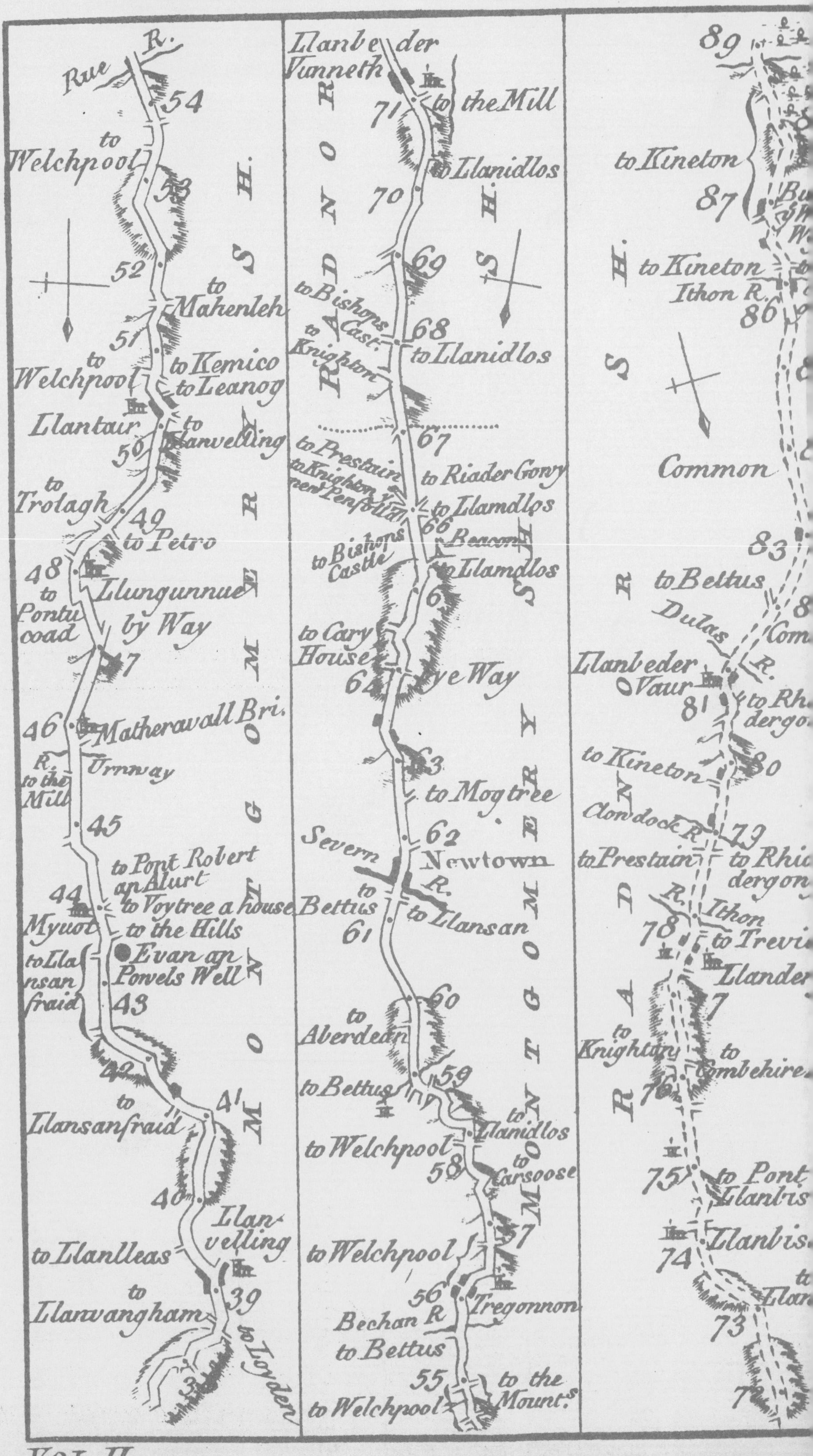

Rue R.
54
to
Welchpool
53
52
to
Mahenleh
51
to   to Kemico
Welchpool   to Leanog
Llantair   to
50   Llanvelling
to
Trolagh
49
to Petro
48
to   Llungunnue
Pontu   by Way
coad
47
46   Matheravall Bri.
R.   Urmway
to the
Mill
45
to Pont Robert
ap Alurt
44   to Voytree a house
Myuot   to the Hills
to Lla   Evan ap
nsan   Povels Well
fraid   43
42
to
41
Llansanfraid
40
Llan
velling
to Llanlleas
to
Llanvangham   39

MONTGOMRY SH.

38
to Zoylen

Llanbeder
Vunneth
71
to the Mill
70   to Llanidlos
69
68
to Bishons   to Llanidlos
Cast.
to
Knighton
67
to Prestain   to Riader Gony
to Knighton   to Llamdlos
near Pensotun 66
Beacon
to Bishons   to Llamdlos
Castle
65
to Cary
House   64   ye Way
63
to Mogtree
62
Severn Newtown
R.
to
Bettus   to Llansan
61
60
to
Aberdean
59
to Bettus
to Welchpool   to Llanidlos
58   to Carsoose
to Welchpool   57
56   Tregonnon
Bechan R.
to Bettus
55   to the
to Welchpool   Mount.

RADNOR SH.

89
to Kineton
87
86
to Kineton
Ithon R.
83
Common
to Bettus
Dulas
Llanbeder   R.
Vaur
81   to Rh
dergo
80
to Kineton
Clondock R.   79
to Prestain   to Rhi
dergon
R. Ithon
78   to Trevi
Llander
77
to
Knightan   to
76   Combehire
75   to Pont
Llanbis
Llanbis
74
73
7

RADNOR SH.